INSURANCE

AND

RISK MANAGEMENT

DR. P.K. GUPTA

M.Com, Ph.D. (Finance), FICWA, FCS, CFA, FIII

Associate Professor (Finance & Risk Management)
Centre for Management Studies
Jamia Millia Islamia, New Delhi.

Himalaya Publishing House

ISO 9001:2015 CERTIFIED

First Edition : 2004
Edition : 2008, 2009
Second Edition : 2010
Edition : 2011, 2012, 2014, 2015, 2016, 2017, 2018, 2019
Edition : 2021

Published by : Mrs. Meena Pandey for **Himalaya Publishing House Pvt. Ltd.,**
"Ramdoot", Dr. Bhalerao Marg, Girgaon, **Mumbai - 400 004.**
Phone: 022-23860170/23863863, Fax: 022-23877178
E-mail: himpub@bharatmail.co.in; **Website:** www.himpub.com

Branch Offices :

New Delhi : "Pooja Apartments", 4-B, Murari Lal Street, Ansari Road, Darya Ganj, New Delhi - 110 002. Phone: 011-23270392, 23278631; Fax: 011-23256286

Nagpur : Kundanlal Chandak Industrial Estate, Ghat Road, Nagpur - 440 018. Phone: 0712-2738731, 3296733; Telefax: 0712-2721216

Bengaluru : Plot No. 91-33, 2nd Main Road Seshadripuram, Behind Nataraja Theatre, Bengaluru - 560020. Phone: 08041138821, Mobile: 09379847017, 09379847005

Hyderabad : No. 3-4-184, Lingampally, Besides Raghavendra Swamy Matham, Kachiguda, Hyderabad - 500 027. Phone: 040-27560041, 27550139

Chennai : New No. 48/2, Old No. 28/2, Ground Floor, Sarangapani Street, T. Nagar, Chennai - 600 012. Mobile: 09380460419

Pune : First Floor, "Laksha" Apartment, No. 527, Mehunpura, Shaniwarpeth (Near Prabhat Theatre), Pune - 411 030. Phone: 020-24496323/24496333; Mobile: 09370579333

Lucknow : House No 731, Shekhupura Colony, Near B.D. Convent School, Aliganj, Lucknow - 226 022. Phone: 0522-4012353; Mobile: 09307501549

Ahmedabad : 114, "SHAIL", 1st Floor, Opp. Madhu Sudan House, C.G. Road, Navrang Pura, Ahmedabad - 380 009. Phone: 079-26560126; Mobile: 09377088847

Ernakulam : 39/176 (New No: 60/251) 1st Floor, Karikkamuri Road, Ernakulam, Kochi - 682011, Phone: 0484-2378012, 2378016; Mobile: 09344199799

Cuttack : New LIC Colony, Behind Kamala Mandap, Badambadi, Cuttack - 753 012, Odisha. Mobile: 9338746007

Kolkata : 108/4, Beliaghata Main Road, Near ID Hospital, Opp. SBI Bank, Kolkata - 700 010, Phone: 033-32449649, Mobile: 09883055590, 07439040301

DTP by : Twinkle Graphics, Delhi-110088

Printed at : Geetanjali Press Pvt. Ltd., Nagpur. On behalf of HPH.

Dedicated to the

Sacred memory of my father

Preface

Insurance is now fast growing area of academic study or profession. The recent financial crisis has witnessed the indispensable need of professionals in the area of risk management. Due to the complexity of the dynamic environment, new insurance products are evolving as well as the existing business models of insurance companies are undergoing significant change. After liberalisation of the economy, large number of alternative products and financial services have evolved that paved the way for the potential and unconventional entrants to penetrate the financial market through innovative higher product profile and portfolios, resulting into a sudden spurt in the demand of insurance professionals. The study of insurance as an academic discipline *in new form* is an obvious outcome. More and more academic institutions all over the countries are offering highly specialised insurance programmes to cater to this demand.

Since my first edition in 2004, many universities and institutions in India and abroad have introduced insurance as a specialised formal area of study both at graduate and postgraduate level. My first edition - *Insurance and Risk Management, Himalaya Publishing 2004* has been quite successful and the basis of feedback from the readers and the mentors.

Changes from the First Edition

The second edition is an attempt to a give a more in-depth view of the insurance business and risk concepts. This edition gives more elaborate view of the legal environment in insurance context. This section introduces four new chapters on insurance laws, which I believe would give the reader a relatively comprehensive framework within which the insurance industry in India operates. The chapter on accounting and taxation is now wider covering the accounting methodologies of insurance companies. Chapter 14 compares the Indian insurance industry with global situation and highlights the new developments. Part IV elaborates the life insurance business into 7 comprehensive chapters.

Part VI contains a new chapter on risk management in insurance companies, which is highly emphasised these days. All the tables, graphs have been amended with new statistics available till 2009.

I hope that the new edition of the book shall be useful to the students and as well as the trainers. I expect and would be highly obliged, if I receive comments and criticism from the readers. This would further help me in improving the book.

Organisation of the Book

The book is organised from a combination of three perspectives – (a) insurance and risk management (b) insurance classes and products and (c) managerial aspects in insurance business.

Part I introduces the concept of risk management to the readers. Chapter 1 conceptualises the risk definitions, classes of risk and the methods of handling risk. Chapter 2 attempts to provide an overall view of the risk management and control systems. Chapter 3 has been deliberately included to apprise the readers about the distinct approaches to risk management i.e. individual approach and the organisational approach popularly titled as Enterprise Wide Risk Management.

Part II introduces insurance as a risk-mitigating device. Chapter 4, 5 and 6 respectively deal with the insurance terminologies and concepts and how risk is mitigated via insurance markets principles underlying insurance contracts and the mathematical theory.

Part III explores the insurance business environment in India. It has been divided into two sections Section I deals with legal environment covering the various insurance laws and enactments concerning insurance business. Section II deals with economic and financial environment covering the historical evolution of insurance, the privatisation of the insurance sector and insurance industry facts, accounting and taxation aspects and global picture of insurance.

Part IV deals with the life insurance business covering the life insurance players and products, claim settlement and procedural aspects, group insurance and life assurance management.

Part V focuses on non-life category. It covers the history of general insurance, the players and their performance, product wise the various non-life insurance categories. Attempt has been made to provide the statistics to the maximum possible extent.

Part VI of the book is an attempt to explore the functional areas of insurance business more specifically the organisation structures of insurance companies, design and development of products, management of claims, pricing and marketing of products and the financial operations of insurance companies. Chapter 40 is elaborated to include the ALM aspects. It also includes the emerging areas like reinsurance business, automation of insurers operations and risk management for insurance companies.

Acknowledgements

I am inspired by my wife Rachna Gupta who strongly suggested me write a book on the subject from a pure student's perspective. I am indebted to my brother who has provided valuable suggestions to the organisation of text and its contents. I am indebted to my mother, sisters and family members especially my beloved Tinku, Chinki, Pintoo and Minkoo who have made sacrifices at all levels in various forms and contexts for timely completions of this book.

I also thank my Ph.D. supervisor, Dr. B.L. Surolia, who has provided me presentation skills, which, I feel is the most important tool in any literary work.

I am thankful to Prof. D.K. Agarwal, Dean (Academics), IIM Shillong for building motivation to update and revise the text of the book.

I specifically thank Prof. Shiba P. Padhi, IMIS, Bhubaneswar and Prof. Chandan Parhi, HDF School of Management Bhubaneswar for providing necessary inputs for the second edition which indeed in valuable.

I thank from my heart Mr. Vijay Rawat at Delhi office who provided me immense support and motivation for timely completion of this edition.

I am thankful to my colleagues and staff members at Centre for Management Studies, JMI. I would be failing in my duty if do not thank my colleagues and staff of various libraries who have helped at various stages in provision of statistics and other information required for the book.

The last but not the least, my thanks are due to the academicians at various institutions and insurance companies who provided me an idea as to contents and other valuable suggestions.

New Delhi

July 2010 **P.K. GUPTA**

Contents

Understanding Risk

Chapter 1

CHAPTER OBJECTIVES

After reading this chapter you will be able to understand :

- *The Concept of Risk*
- *Risk vs. Uncertainty*
- *Types of Risk*
- *Pure Risk and its Management*
- *Financial Risk and its Management*

Human beings are considered the most intelligent creatures on this earth. The thinking power available to human beings is enormous and this has led human beings to define their style of living and distinguish between good and bad situations. The criteria for deciding whether the situation is good or bad depend upon *individual's perception*. However, one thing is sure — *that human beings always prefer and strive for happy situations and wants to avoid the adverse ones.* Actually, the zeal to be happy always has given birth to the jargon **risk!**

1.1 The Concept of Risk

People express risk in different ways. To some, it is the chance or possibility of loss, to others, its may be uncertain situations or deviations or what statisticians call dispersions from the expectations. Different authors on the subject have defined risk differently. However, in most of the terminology the term risk includes exposure to adverse situations. The indeterminateness of outcome is one of the basic criteria to define a risk situation. Also, when the outcome is indeterminate, there is a possibility that some of them may be adverse and therefore need special emphasis. Let us have a look at the popular definitions of risk.

According to the Dictionary, risk refers to the possibility that something unpleasant or dangerous might happen.[1]

"Risk is a condition in which there is a possibility of an adverse deviation from a desired outcome that is expected or hoped for."[2]

"At its most general level, risk is used to describe any situation where there is uncertainty about what outcome will occur. Life is obviously risky."[3]

Risk may be objective or subjective. *Objective Risk* is defined as the relative variation of actual loss from expected loss. For example, assume that a property insure has 10,000 houses insured over a long period and, on average 1% or 100 houses, burn each year. However, it would be rare for exactly 100 houses to burn. In some years, 90 houses may burn, in other years 110 houses may burn. Thus there is a variation of 10 houses or 10%, from the expected number of 100. This relative variation of actual loss from expected loss is known as objective risk.

Subjective Risk is defined as uncertainly based on a person's mental condition or state of mind. For example, a customer who was drinking heavily in a bar may foolishly attempt to drive home. The driver may be uncertain

1. *Macmillan English Dictionary,* Macmillan Publishers Ltd. 2002, p. 1227.
2. Emmett J. Vaughan, *Risk Management*, John Wiley & Sons, Inc., 1997, p. 8.
3. S.E. Harrinton and G.R. Michaus, *Risk Management and Insurance,* McGraw-Hill, 1999, p. 3.

whether he will arrive home safely without being arrested by the police for drunk driving. This mental uncertainty is called subjective risk.

There is no single definition of risk. Economists, risk theorists, statisticians and actuaries each have there own concept of risk.

"At its most general level, risk is used to describe any situation where there is uncertainty about what outcome will occur life is obviously risky".

- *S.E Herrinton*

"Risk is measurable uncertainty" - *Frank Knight*

"Risk is an objectified uncertainly regarding the occurrence of an undesirable event". - *A.M. Willet*

"Risk may be defined as combination of hazards measured by probability". - *Lrving Fisher*

According to federation of insurance institute, "Risk can be thought of as the degree of variation in the possible outcome from an uncertain event or as the variable in the possible outcomes".

According life Insurance Corporation(LIC) of India, risk may be defined as" a condition where there is a possibility of an adverse deviation from a desired outcome that is expected or hoped for, there is no requirement that the possibility be unmeasurable, only that it must exist".

In business risks include changing demand, price falls, change in desire and taste of consumers, change in market conditions, high competitions, new inventions, and heir development, fire, flood, accident and etc.

In insurance practice, risk is used for perils or loss producing events. Any risk bearing object needs to be insured so as to cover its unexpected losses caused by uncertain events.

The degree of risk refers to the likelihood of occurrence of an event. It is a measure of accuracy with which the outcome of a chance event can be predicted.

In most of the risky situations, two elements are commonly found:

1. The outcome is uncertain i.e. there is a possibility that one or other(s) may occur. Therefore, logically, there are at least two possible outcomes for a given situation.
2. Out of the possible outcomes, one is unfavorable or not liked by the individual or the analyst.

1.2 RISK VS. UNCERTAINTY

Uncertainty is often confused with the risk. Uncertainty refers to a situation where the outcome is not certain or unknown. Uncertainty refers to a state of mind characterised by doubt, based on the lack of knowledge about what will or what will not happen in the future.[4]

Uncertainty can be perceived as opposite of certainty where you are assure of outcome or what will happen. Accordingly, some weights or probabilities can be assigned into risky situations but uncertainty; the psychological reaction to the absence of knowledge lacks this privilege.

Decision under uncertain situations is very difficult for the decision-maker. It all depends upon the skill, the judgement and of course luck.

Uncertainty being a perceptual phenomenon implies different degrees to different person. Assume a situation where an individual has to appear for the first in the newly introduced insurance examination.

(a) an individual student undergone a training in insurance.

(b) an individual with training or experience in insurance.

A's perception towards uncertainty (of performance in examination) is different from that of B. Nonetheless, in both situations, the outcome that is the questions which will be asked in the examination are different.

4. Vaughan, *op. cit.*, p. 7.

1.2.1 Loss and Chance of Loss

A risk refers to a situation where there is the possibility of a loss. What is a loss?

Loss has been defined in many ways. *Loss in accounting sense means that portion of the expired cost for which no compensating value has been received.*[5]

Loss refers to the Act or instance of losing the detriment or a disadvantage resulting from losing.[6]

Loss means being without something previously possessed.[7]

The chance of loss refers to a fraction or the relative frequency of loss. The chance of loss in insurance sense is the probability of loss. For example, assume there are 10,000 factories in the insurance pool which may be affected due to earthquake and on the basis of past experience, 5 have been affected, then the probability of loss is 0.0005. The whole game of insurance business is based on the probability of loss. If the insurer estimates correctly, he wins else loses or is forced to close the business.

From the insurer's perspective, it is the probability of loss that essentiates the need for insurances. The probabilities of losses may be ex-post or ex-ante. In practice, the ex-ante probabilities are widely used for undertaking risk in insurance business. The chance or probabilities of loss estimation requires accounting for causes of losses popularly characterised as *perils* and *hazards.*[8]

1.2.2 Perils

A peril refers to the cause of loss or the contingency that may cause a loss.8 In literary sense, it means the serious and immediate danger.[9] Perils refer to the immediate causes of loss. Perils may be general or specific e.g. fire may affect assets like building, automobile, machinery, equipment and also, humans. Collusion may cause damage to the automobile resulting in a financial loss.

1.2.3 Hazards

Hazards are the conditions that increase the severity of loss or the conditions affecting perils. These are the conditions that create or increase the severity of losses. Economic slow down is a peril that may cause a loss to the business, but it is also a hazard that may cause a heart attack or mental shock to the proprietor of the business. Hazards can be classified as follows:

1. **Physical Hazards :** Property Conditions — consists of those physical properties that increase the chance of loss from the various perils. E.g. stocking crackers in a packed commercial complex increases the peril of fire.
2. **Intangible Hazards :** Attitudes and Culture — Intangible hazards are more or less psychological in nature. These can be further classified as follows:
   (*a*) *Moral Hazard* : Fraud — These refer to the increase in the possibility or severity of loss emanating from the intention to deceive or cheat. For example — putting fire to a factory running in losses. With an intention to make benefit out of exaggerated claims, deliberately indulging into automobile

5. M.N. Arora, *Cost Accounting,* Vikas Publishing House, 2000, p. 122.
6. *Oxford Advance Learner's Dictionary,* Oxford University Press, 1984, p. 504.
7. M.S. Dorfman, *Introduction to Risk Management and Insurance,* Prentice-Hall, 2002, pp. 4-5.
8. Dorfrman, *op.cit,* p. 5.
9. *Oxford Advance Learner's Dictionary, op.cit.* p. 622.

collusion or damaging it or tendency on part of the doctor to go for unnecessary checks when they are not required, since the loss will be reimbursed by the insurance company.

(*b*) *Morale Hazard* : Indifference – It is the attitude of indifference to take care of the property on the premise that the loss will be indemnified by the insurance company. So, it is the carelessness or indifference to a loss because of the existence of insurance contract. For example – smoking in an oil refinery, careless driving etc.

(c) *Societal Hazards* : Legal and Cultural – these refer to the increase in the frequency and severity of loss arising from legal doctrines or societal customs and structure. For example, the construction or the possibility of demolition of buildings in unauthorised colonies.

1.3 TYPES OF RISKS

Risk can be classified into several distinct categories. The following are the major categories:

1. Financial and non-financial risk
2. Static and dynamic risk
3. Fundamental And particular risk (or) group individual risk
4. Pure and speculative risk.
5. Quantifiable and Non-quantifiable Risks

Financial and Non-Financial Risks

If any risk is concerned with financial loss, it is termed as financial risk, financial risk involves the simultaneous existence of three important elements of a risky situation.

1. Some one is adversely affected by the happening of an event.
2. The assets or income is likely to be exposed to a financial loss from the occurrence of the event.
3. Paril can cause the loss. For example, loss accuned in case of damage of property, theft of property, loss of business any financial losses. This is financial risk, out put can be measured in monetary terms.

When the possibility of a financial loss does not exist, the situation can be referred to as non-financial in nature. For example, risk in the selection of career, Risk in the in the choice of course of study etc. they may or may not have any financial implications. These types of risk are difficult to measure.

As per the insurance is concerned, risk is involved with financial loss.

Individual and Group Risks

A risk is said to be a *group* risk or *fundamental* risk if it affects the economy or its participants on a macro basis. These are impersonal in origin and consequence. They affect most of the social segments or the entire population. These risk factors may be socio-economic or political or natural calamities e.g. earthquakes, floods, wars, unemployment or situations like 11th September attack on U.S. etc.

Individual/particular risks are confined to individual identities or small groups. Thefts, robbery, fire etc. are risks that are particular in nature. Some of these are insurable. The methods of handling fundamental and particular risks differ by their very nature e.g. Social insurance programmes may be undertaken by the government to handle fundamental risks. Similarly, fire insurance policy may be bought by an individual to prevent against the adverse consequences of fire.

Pure and Speculative Risks

Pure risk situations are those where there is a possibility of loss or no loss. There is no gain to the individual or the organisation. For example, a car can meet with an accident or it may not meet with an accident. If an insurance policy is bought for the purpose, then if accident does not occur, there is no gain to the insured. Contrarily, if the accident occurs, the insurance company will indemnify the loss.

Speculative risk is defined as a situation in which either a profit or loss is possible. For example, investing in share market as I situation of speculation risk. If the prices of the shares increase, the person who bought the shares will gain. If the prices decreases, he will definitely loose. Horse racing, investing money in others are some examples of speculative risk.

The distinguishing characteristics of the pure and speculative risks are:

1. The pure risks are generally insurable while speculative ones are not.
2. The law of large number can be applied more easily to pure risk than to speculative risk. It is more difficult to apply the law of large number to speculative risk to predict the future loss.
3. The society may benefit from a speculative risk, even though a loss occurs but it is harmful if a pure risk is present and a loss occurs. For example, a firm may develop now technology for producing inexpensive computers. As a result, the competitors may be forced to produce computers at a lower price. Consequently, the society benefit. However, society normally does not benefit when a loss from a pure risk occurs, such as a flood, or earthquake that devastates an area.

Static and Dynamic Risks

Dynamic risks are those resulting from the changes in the economy or the environment. Economic variables like inflation, income level, price level, technology changes and etc. since the dynamic risk emanates from the economic environment, these are very difficult to anticipate and quantify. Dynamic risk involves losses mainly concerned with financial losses. These risks affect the public and society. These risks are the best indicators of progress of society, because they are the results of adjustment is misallocation of resources.

On the other hand, static risks are more or loss predictable and are not affected by the economic conditions. Static risk involves losses resulting from the destruction of an asset or changes in its possession as a result of dishonesty or human failure. Such financial losses arise, even if there are no changes in the economic environment. There losses are not useful for the society. There arise with a degree of regularity overtime and as a result, are generally predictable. Example for static risk includes possibility of loss is a business: unemployment after undergoing a professional qualification, loss due to act of others and ect.

Dynamic Risk	*vs.*	Static Risks
1. Losses are not easily predictable.		1. Losses can be predicted.
2. There results from the changes in economic environment.		2. There occur even if there is no change in economic environment.
3. There are not caused by insurance		3. There can be covered by insurance.
4. There risks benefit the society		4. There risks don't benefit the society.

Quantifiable and Non-quantifiable Risks

The risk which can be measured using numerical scales are known to be quantifiable while the situations which may result in repercussions like tension or loss of peace are called as non-quantifiable.

The newer classification of risk adopted by financial institutions and also insurance companies is : (*a*) credit, (*b*) market, (*c*) operational and (*d*) other. These are discussed in detail in next section.

1.4 Pure Risks and Its Management

Since pure risks are generally *insurable*, the discussion on risk in various chapters of this book is skewed towards pure risks only.

1.4.1 Classification of Pure Risk

On the presumption that insurable pure risks being *static* can be classified as follows:

Exhibit 1-A

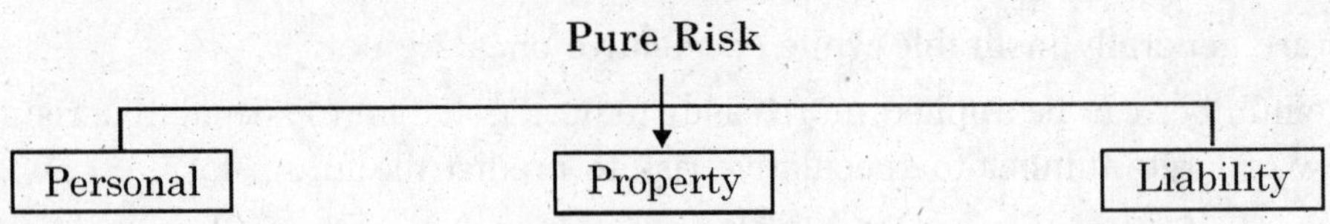

Personal Risks

Personal risks are risks that directly affect an individual. They involve the possibility of the complete loss or reduction of earned income. There are four major personal risks.

Risk of Premature Death : premature death is defined as the death of the household head with unfulfilled financial obligations. If the surviving family members receive an insufficient amount of replacement income from other sources or have insufficient financial assets to replace the lost income, they may be financial insecure. Premature death can cause financial problems only if the deceased has dependents to support or does with unsatisfied financial obligations. Thus the death of a child aged 5 is not premature in the economic sense.

Risk of Insufficient Income During Retirement : It refers to the risk of not having sufficient income at the age of retirement or the age becoming so that there is a possibility that individual may not be able to earn the livelihood. When one retires, he looses his earned income. Unless he has sufficient financial assets from which to draw or has access to other sources of retirement income such as social security or a private pension, he will be exposed to financial insecurity during retirement.

Risk of Poor Health : It refers to the risk of poor health or disability of a person to earn the means of survival, For example, losing the legs due to accident, heart surgery, which will cost lakhs, etc. Unless the person has adequate health insurance, private savings or other sources of income to meet these loss, he will be financially insecure. The loss of insecurity, if the disability is severe. In case of long term disability, things will become worst and some one must take care of the disabled person. The loss of earned income can be financially vary painful.

Risk of Unemployment : The risk of unemployment is another major threat to financial security. Unemployment can result from business cycle downswings, technological and structural changes in the economy, seasonal factors and etc. Employers are increasingly hiring temporary or part time workers to reduce labor costs. Being temporary employees, workers lose their employee benefits. Unless there is adequate replacement income or past savings on which to draw, the workers (unemployed, part time, temporary) will be financially insecure. If the period, past savings and unemployment benefits may be exhausted.

Property Risks

It refers to the risk of having property damaged or lost because of fire, windstorm, earthquake and numerous other causes. There are two major types of loss associated with the destruction or theft of property.

Direct Loss : A direct loss is defined as a financial loss that results from the physical damage destruction, or theft of the property. For example, physical damage to a factory due to fire is known as direct loss.

Indirect or Consequential Loss : An indirect loss is a financial loss that results indirectly from the occurrence of a direct physical damage or theft loss. For example, Apart from the financial loss resulted from the profit for several months while the factory as rebuilt. Extra expenses are also indirect loss. To aperate regardless of cost. Otherwise they will lose their customers. Therefore it is necessary setup a temporary operation at some alternative location and extra expenses would occur. There are the indirect expenses resulted from the damage of the factory.

Liability Risks

These are the risks arising out of the intentional or unintentional injury to the persons or damages to their properties through negligence or carelessness. Liability risks generally arise from the law. For example, liability of the employer under the workmen's compensation law or other labour laws in India.

In addition to the above categories, risks may also arise *due to the failure of others*. For example, the financial loss arising from the non-performance or standard performance in a contract — in engineering/construction contracts.

1.4.2 Methods of Handling Pure Risk

Risk is burden not only to the individuals but to society as well. Thus it is important to examine some techniques for meeting the problem of risk. There are five major methods of handling risk.

1. Avoidance of risk.
2. Loss control.
   (a) Loss prevention.
   (b) Loss reduction.
3. Risk Retention.
4. Non-insurance Transfers
   (a) Transfer of risk by contracts.
   (b) Hedging price risks
   (c) Incorporation of a business firm.
5. Insurance

1. Avoidance of Risk

Avoiding the risk or the circumstances which may lead to losses is one method of handling risk. For example, one can avoid the risk of death or disability in a plane crash by refusing to fly. It is not possible to find a formula to avoid risk completely, but to a great extent the risk can be reduced. For example, if you avoid plane, you have to drive yourself or take train/bus which are also not appealing losses from fire can be completely avoided by constructing a fire proof building for stocking products. Avoiding the visit to the border area at the time of war tensions is another example.

2. Loss Control

It is another important method of handling risk. Loss control consists of certain activities that reduce the frequencies and severely of losses. Thus loss control has two major objectives: loss prevention and loss reduction.

(a) Loss Prevention : Loss prevention aims at reducing the probability of loss so that the frequency minimized/ prevented by using safely lockers, number of heart attacks can be reduced, if individuals reduce their weight, diet, etc. accidents can be reduced is also important for business firms. Machine breakdown can be reduced by periodic inspections by engineers. Strict security measures in airports can reduce hijacking of aircrafts by terrorists.

(b) Loss Reduction : Even though strict loss prevention can reduce the frequency of losses, some losses will inevitably occur. Thus the second objective of loss control is to reduce the severity or a loss offer it occurred. For example, keeping fire-fighting equipments will reduce the severity of loss from fire. Keeping first-aid box will reduce the severity of injury.

3. Risk Retention

An individual or a business firm retains all or part of a given risk, is retains the obligations to pay for part or all of the losses. For example, a transport company may decide to retain the risk that cash flows will drop due to increases in the price of oil. Retention is done with a formal plan to fund losses can be paid by the firm. It is the easiest and cheapest way of dealing with relatively small losses by paying out of one's own resources whenever they occur or by creating some fund to meet such losses if their magnitude is somewhat large.

In general, Risk retention is appropriate for low severity risks where potential losses are relatively small. For example, A House owner may retain the small, part of the risk of damage to the house (small repairs). The motorist may wish to retain the risk of low severely accidents. Even if a person has purchased a mediclaim policy, he can pay for small medical expenses and he does not need to claim from the insurance company.

4. Non-insurance Transfers

Some type of risks involving loss can be shifted or transferred to other's shoulders. Risk is transferred to a party other than a insured company. A risk can be transferred by several methods. Following are some major methods of risk transfer.

(a) Transfer of Risk by Contract : Unwanted risk can be transferred by contracts. For example, the risk of defective computers can be transferred to a service provider through annual maintenance contract. The contractor is responsible for all repairs and maintenance. The risk of price increase in the construction material can be transferred to the builder by having a fixed price in the contract

(b) Hedging Price Risk : This is a technique for transferring the risk of unfavorable price fluctuations to a speculator by purchasing and selling forward contracts on an organized exchange. These contracts can be used to hedge risk,ie, they may be used to offset losses that can occur from changes in interest rates, commodity prices, foreign exchange rates, etc.. Firms that use oil in the production process are subject to losses from unexpected increase in oil prices. Similarly, oil producers are subject to loss from unexpected decrease in oil prices. Both firms can hedge their risk by entering into a forward contract that requires the oil producer to provide the oil user with a specified future delivery date at a predetermined price (known as forward price), regardless of the market price of oil . Oil price may be increasing or decreasing, but the supplier sells the oil at the agreed price.

(c) Incorporation of Business Firm : If a firm is a sole proprietorship, owners personal assets can be attached by creditors for satisfaction of debts. If a firm incorporates, personal assets cannot be attached by creditors for payment of the firm's debts. In essence, by incorporation, the liability of the stockholders is limited, and the risk of the firm having insufficient assets to pay business debts is shifted to the creditors.

5. Insurance

Even if we try to avoid, control and prevent, still the risk will exist. Therefore insurance is the most practical method for handling a major risk. The risk is transferred to the insurer. The basic objective of insurance is to transfer the risk of a person to the insurance company which has easily similar risks. As such for handling risks which involve large financial losses or which are dangerous and uncontrollable by any single person, insurance is a mean of shifting such risks to insure in consideration of a nominal cost called premium. In fact, among the various methods of handling risks, insurance is the only widely used method.

1.5 Financial Risk and its Management

Financial Risk is the risk arising from the change sin the values of measurable financial variables. For example- Financial risk is that a company will not have adequate cash flow to meet financial obligations. In a corporate financing context, financial risk is the additional risk a shareholder bears when a company uses debt in addition to equity financing. Companies that issue more debt instruments would have higher financial risk than companies financed mostly or entirely by equity. Finance theory prescribes that a firm undertakes activities that maximize shareholder value. A firm cannot create value for shareholders by taking on project that shareholders could do for themselves at the same return. This implies that firm managers should not hedge risks that investors can hedge for themselves. Since financial markets are not perfect, firm managers likely have many opportunities to create value for shareholders using financial risk management.

Sources of Financial Risk

An organization may be faced with the following financial risks :

1. Risk arising from organization's exposure to changes in market prices viz. interest rates, exchange rates, commodity prices.
2. Risk arising from actions of, and transactions with, other organizations such as vendors, customers, and counter parties in derivative transactions.
3. Risk arising from the internal actions or failures of the organization, particularly people, processes and systems.

Financial risk in business organizations arises from transactions of financial nature including sales purchases, investments and loans and various other business activities. It can arise as a result of legal transactions, new projects, mergers and acquisitions, debt financing, the energy component of cists, or through the activities of management and other stakeholders. Fluctuations the value of financial variable comprised in these activities reduces value giving risk to financial risk.

Classification of Financial Risk

On the basis of above, James Lam (2001) has suggested the following classification of risk :

(a) Credit : Credit risk is the risk that a customer, counter party, or supplier will fail to meet its obligations. It includes every thing from a borrower default to suppliers missing deadlines because of credit problems. Credit Risk is the change in value of a debt due to changes in the perceived ability of counter parties to meet their contractual obligations (or credit rating). Also known as default risk or counter party risk, credit risk is faced by lending institutions like banks, investors in debt instruments of corporate houses, and by parties involved in contractual agreements like forward contracts. There are independent agencies that assess the credit risk in form of credit ratings.

Credit rating is an opinion (of the credit rating agency) on the ability of the organization to perform its contractual obligations (pay the principle and/or interest of the loan) on a timely basis. Each level of rating indicates a probability of default. International credit rating agencies (like Moody's, Fitch, and S&P) use quantitative models along with their experience to predict the credit ratings. Credit scoring models of banks and lending institutions use stock prices (if available), financial performance and sector specific data, and macroeconomic forecasts to predict the credit rating.

Credit risk can be transferred using credit derivatives, and also by securitization. For business organizations swaps and structured notes are useful financial products to hedge.

(b) Market **:** Market risk is the risk that process will move in a way that has negative consequences for a company. Market Risk is the change in value of assets due to changes in the underlying economic factors such as interest rates, foreign exchange rates, macroeconomic variables, stock prices, and commodity prices. All economic entities that own assets face market risk. For example, bills receivable of software exporters that are denominated in foreign currencies are exposed to exchange rate fluctuations; while value of bonds/government securities owned by investors depend on prevailing interest rates. Organizations with huge exposures, either have a dedicated treasury department, or outsource market risk management to banks.

Modeling market risk requires forecasting the changes in the economic factors, and assess their impact on the asset value. Amost popular measure for expressing market risk is Value-at-Risk, which is 'the maximum loss' from an unfavorable event, within a given level of confidence, for a given holding period. Various financial instruments like options, futures, forwards, swaps etc. can be used effectively to hedge the market risk. Availability of huge data on various markets has facilitated the development of many sophisticated models.

(c) Operational **:** Operational risk the risk that people, processes, or systems will fail or that an external event will negatively affect the company. Practically speaking, all organizations face operational risk. For a financial institution/bank, operational risk can be defined as the possibility of loss due to mistakes made in carrying out transactions such as settlement failures, failures to meet regulatory requirements, and untimely collections. No concrete model of managing credit risk available till today. Still lot of research is being done in this direction.

(d) Other **:** Other risks are extensions of the above mentioned categories viz. Business risk is the risk that future operating results may not meet expectations and also, organizational risk is the risk that arises from a badly designed organizational structure or lack of sufficient human resources.

Financial Risk Management Process

The financial risk management process in every organization involves the following logical steps (Gupta, June 2004) :

- *Defining Objectives/Establishing Context* : Drawing a structure of the operating environment, both external and internal, overview of the organization mission, objectives, stakeholders interests and the developing the risk management context activities and their relationships across business segments.
- *Identifying the Risk Exposures* : Documenting the conditions and events that represent material threats to the organization's achievement of its objectives or represent areas to exploit for competitive advantage.
- *Evaluating the Risk Exposures* : Analyzing/Quantifying Risks the risks - probability distributions, computing Value at Risk (VaR)[10] etc. (Linda, 2004).
- *Analysing Solutions* : Aggregating all risk distributions, reflecting correlation and portfolio effects, and expressing results in terms of impact on the organisation's key performance indicators, prioritising risks and determining the feasibility of various risk management alternatives. It includes feasibility analysis of the various alternatives and developing strategies for controlling or exploiting the various risks.
- *Implementation and Review* : Implementing the solutions and continuous appraisal of the performance of the risk management strategies.

The assessment of financial risk hinges around the probability of adverse events. There are events that have a low probability of occurring but result in a high loss. Risk is not always possible to eliminate, it is better to hedge to transfer to reduce its severity.

10. VaR is the maximum possible loss that can occur in a situation at a given confidence level.

Financial Risk Modeling

Financial risk modeling is the practice of measuring risks in various domains of finance viz. financial markets, banking, insurance etc. It is the most important part of pricing financial instruments and also helps in regulation of financial activities like investment banking, and lending. The following matrix gives an illustration of the various risk measurement models (detailed description is out of the preview of this book).

Risk Type	Measurement Models	Manage/Hedge/Transfer
Market Risk	Nelson-Seigel Svennson Model, Cubic B-Spline, Cox, Ingersoll & Ross Model, Vasicek Model, Black Kara, Riskmetrics	Derivatives (Options, Futures, Swaps etc.)
Credit Risk	*Structural Models* - Black & Scholes, Merton Model, Black & Cox, Geske, Delianedis & Geske*Reduced form Models* - Litterman & Iben, Jarrow & Turnbull, Duffie & Singleton*Products* - KMV, Creditmetrics, Credit Portfolio View, Credit Risk+, Loan Analysis System etc.	Credit Derivatives, Securitization
Operational Risk	Score card, Simulation, Causal Modeling etc.	Insurance

Source : www.decisioncraft.com/dmdirect/financial.htm

The risk management strategies highlighted above keeps on changing in view of the market conditions, business environment changes or changes in the political conditions.

1.6 Rationale for Risk Management

The rationales for risk aversion can usefully be segmented into four categories:

(a) Managerial Self Interest

(b) The Non-Linearity of Taxes

(c) The Cost of Financial Distress

(d) The Existence of Capital Market Imperfections

A. Managerial Self Interest

Managers have limited ability to diversify their own personal wealth position, associated with stock holdings and the capitalization of their career earnings associated with their own employment position. Therefore, they prefer stability to volatility because, other things equal, such stability improves their own utility, at little or no expense to other stakeholders.

B. The Non-Linearity of Taxes

Beyond managerial motives, firm level performance and market value may be directly associated with volatility for a number of other reasons. The first is the nature of the tax code, which both historically and internationally is highly non-linear. By reducing the effective long term average tax rate, activities which reduce the volatility in reported earnings will enhance shareholder value.

C. The Cost of Financial Distress

Firms may also be concerned about volatility of earnings because of the consequences of severely negative deviations from expected value and their implications for corporate viability.

D. Capital Market Imperfections

Conventionally, external financing is more costly than internally generated funds due to any number of capital market imperfections. These may include discrete transaction costs to obtain external financing, imperfect information as to the riskiness of the investment opportunities present in the firm, or the high cost of the potential future bankruptcy state. In the case of mutual insurers, who have little access to the capital market, this line of argument is particularly compelling. At the same time, the firm has an investment opportunity set which can be ordered in terms of net present value.

The volatility of profitability causes the firm to seek external finance to exploit investment opportunities when profits are low. The cost of such external finance is higher than the internal funds due to the market's higher cost structure.

Key Terms

- ❒ Financial Risk
- ❒ Market Risk
- ❒ Risk Modeling
- ❒ Value Maximization
- ❒ Static Risk
- ❒ Speculative Risk
- ❒ Peril
- ❒ Credit Risk
- ❒ Operational Risk
- ❒ Value at Risk
- ❒ Risk
- ❒ Dynamic Risk
- ❒ Event
- ❒ Hazard

Questions for Review

1. Discuss the various types of financial risk and how they can be managed.
2. Explain the logical steps in financial risk management.
3. Define risk. List some ways in which risk creates an economic burden for society.
4. Differentiate between the following type of risk:
   (a) Pure versus speculative
   (b) Static versus dynamic and
   (c) Subjective versus objective.
5. Give an example of a risk that is both pure and static.
6. An insurable loss is :
   (a) An event that has not been predicted.
   (b) An exposure that cannot be easily measured before the event has occurred.
   (c) An unexpected reduction of economic value.
   (d) Being without something one has previously possessed.
7. Differentiate between a peril and a hazard and give an example of each.
8. For each of the following hazards, state the peril to which the hazard relates.
   (a) A drunken driver of a truck
   (b) A person with damaged kidneys
   (c) A house with poor quality of electricity cable fittings.

(d) An unlocked car in no-parking area.

9. "Pure Risks are always insurable." Comment.

Suggested Readings

1. Dun and Bradstreet, Financial Risk management, 2007, Tata Mc Graw Hill, Delhi.
2. Gupta, P.K., Insurance & Risk Management, 2004, Himalaya Publishing House, Mumbai.
3. Emmett Vaughan and Therese Vaughan, *Essentials of Risk Management and Insurance,* John Wiley and Sons Inc. 2002.
4. M.W. Jones - Lee, *The Economics of Safety and Physical Risk,* Basic Blackwell Ltd., 1989.
5. M.W. Jones - Lee, *The Value of Life,* The University of Chicago University Press, Chicago, 1976
6. Margot Naylor, *The Truth about Life,* George Allen and Unwin Ltd., London, 1971.
7. Mark S. Dorfman, *Fundamentals of Insurance*, Prentice-Hall, 2002.
8. Scott E. Harrington and Gregory R, Niehaus, *Insurance and Risk Management*, IRWIN/McGraw-Hill, 1999.

Web Resources

- www.erisks.com
- www.bimaonline.com

Risk Management and Control

Chapter 2

Chapter Objectives

After reading this chapter you will be able to understand :

- *Risk Management – Conceptual Framework*
- *Risk Management Objectives*
- *Risk Management Information Systems*

2.1 Risk Management

The Role of Risk Management

The future is largely unknown. Most business decision-making takes place on the basic of expectations about the future. Making a decision on the basis of assumptions, expectations, estimates and forecasts of future events involves taking risks. Risk has been described as the *"sugar and salt of life"*. This implies that risk can have an upside as well downside. People take risk in order to achieve some goal they would otherwise not have reached without taking that risk. On the other hand, risk can mean that some danger or loss may be involved in carrying out an activity and therefore, care has to be taken to avoid that loss. This is where Risk Management is important, in that it can be used to protect against loss or danger arising from a risky activity.

Definition

Risk management is an integrated process of delineating specific areas or risk, developing a comprehensive plan, integrating the plan, and conducting ongoing evaluation.

The Process

The risk management process involves the following logical steps :

1. Defining the objectives of the risk management exercise
2. Identifying the risk exposures
3. Evaluating the exposures
4. Critical analysis of risk management alternatives and selecting one of them
5. Implementation and review.

The job of risk management can, therefore, be broken down into three elements, which follow each other in a logical sequence:

- Risk analysis
- Risk control
- Risk financing

Because the conditions under which firms operate change, the risk management process has a necessity to be dynamic. All three elements of the process have therefore to be continuing reassessment and monitoring of the results.

RISK MANAGMENT PROCESS

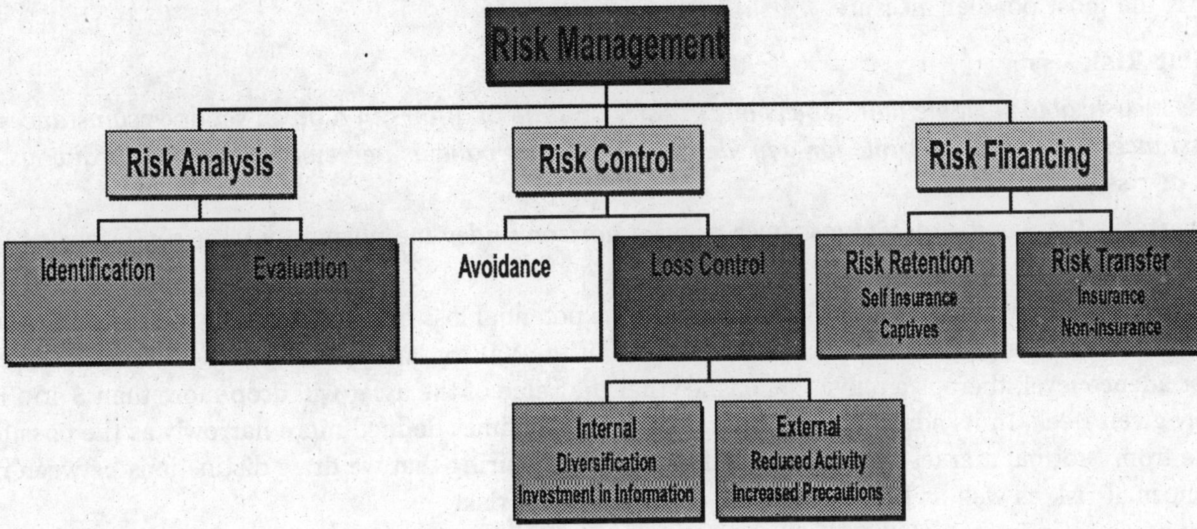

All Risk Manger's believe that *"prevention is better than cure"*. It is better not to have suffered a loss than to suffer and collect under an insurance policy. Insurance will not compensate for all losses; for example, time spent dealing with the claim loss of client base and reputation. There is also a growing body of evidence to suggest that a significant proportion of firms never fully recover from the effects of a major loss and have to be wound-up within a short time even if fully insured.

Risk Identification

The first step in the process is to anlalyse the risk to which an organisation may be exposed. Risk analysis has to prime elements — the identification of risk and its evaluation.

Risk Identification requires knowledge of the organisation, the market in which it operates, the legal, social, economic, political, and climatic environment in which it does it's business, it's financial strengths and weakness, its vulnerability to unplanned losses, the manufacturing processes, and the management systems and business mechanism by which it operates. Any failure at this stage to identify risk may cause a major loss for the organisation. Risk identification provides the foundation for risk management. The various methods of risk identification are:

- Checklist Method
- Financial Statement Method
- Flowchart Method
- On-site Inspections
- Interactions with Others
- Contract Analysis
- Statistical Records of Losses

Risk Evaluation

Risk Evaluation breaks down into two parts, the assessment of:

- The probability of loss occurring, and
- Its severity

The underlying logic of risk management is that "Risk Reduces Value". Therefore, in order to quantify risk, value at risk is the most popular measure.

Value at Risk

Value is measurable variable that depicts one's desire or state of affairs in a given set of circumstances. Since circumstances never remain same for any identity, what ever value is perceived or created is always at risk (Value-at-risk).

VaR measures the worst expected loss over a given horizon under the normal market conditions at a given confidence level.

In its most general form, the Value at Risk measures the potential loss in value of a risky asset or portfolio over a defined period for a given confidence interval. Thus, if the VaR on an asset is \$ 100 million at a one-week, 95% confidence level, there is a only a 5% chance that the value of the asset will drop more than \$ 100 million over any given week. In its adapted form, the measure is sometimes defined more narrowly as the possible loss in value from "normal market risk" as opposed to all risk, requiring that we draw distinctions between normal and abnormal risk as well as between market and nonmarket risk.

While Value at Risk can be used by any entity to measure its risk exposure, it is used most often by commercial and investment banks to capture the potential loss in value of their traded portfolios from adverse market movements over a specified period; this can then be compared to their available capital and cash reserves to ensure that the losses can be covered without putting the firms at risk.

To estimate the probability of the loss, with a confidence interval, we need to define the probability distributions of individual risks, the correlation across these risks and the effect of such risks on value. Simulations are widely used to measure the VaR for asset portfolio.

There are three key elements of VaR – a specified level of loss in value, a fixed time period over which risk is assessed and a confidence interval. The VaR can be specified for an individual asset, a portfolio of assets or for an entire firm.

A one day VAR of \$10mm using a probability of 5% means that there is a 5% chance that the portfolio could lose more than \$10mm in the next trading day.

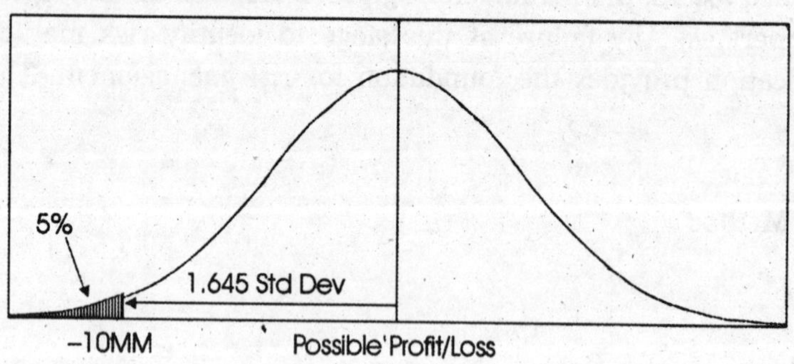

VaR Methodologies

- Historical Simulations Approach
- Variance-Covariance Approach
- Monte-Carlo Simulation

Supplementing VaR

VaR estimation can be made more robust by the techniques like (a) *Stress Testing :* Hypothetical estimation of various market scenarios, valuation of the impact, development of contingency plans, or (b) *Sensitivity Analysis :*

Hypothetical changes in the value of the individual market factor, use of pricing models to compute the overall value, formulating strategies for the combined impact.

2.2 RISK CONTROL

Risk control covers all those measures aimed at avoiding, eliminating or reducing the chances of loss-producing events occurring, or limiting the severity of the losses that do happen. Here, one is seeking to change the conditions that bring about loss-producing events or increase their severity. Though some measures call for little more than common sense, often-considerable technical knowledge is required, for which the risk manager will need to turn to experts in the particular field.

Risk can be controlled either by avoidance or by controlling losses. Avoidance implies that either a certain loss exposure is not acquired or an existing one is abandoned.

Loss control can be exercised in two ways :

(*a*) One way is to enhance and monitor the level of precautions taken to minimise the losses due to exposures.

(*b*) Another is to control and minimise the risk operations, internal risk control techniques include diversification and/or investments in getting information of loss exposures so as to control them.

Risk management objectives differs from individual to individual and organisation to organisation. However, as a concept these can be segregated into two:

(*a*) Before occurrence of losses — these can be of following types:

  (*i*) Reduction in worry and fear

  (*ii*) Economical ways of handing risk

  (*iii*) Overcome legal obligations

(*b*) After occurrence of losses:-

  (*i*) Survival

  (*ii*) Congruence with mission and objectives

  (*iii*) Optimising social effects

2.2.1 Risk Financing

When the risk exposure for an organisation exceeds the maximum limit that the organisation can bear, it becomes necessary to either transfer or reduce risk. However, there is cost involved in both of these exercises. If the method adopted is insurance, the consequential impact on taxes and profits also becomes important. Risk Financing, therefore, refers *to the manner in which the risk control measures that have been implemented shall be financed.*

It has to be recognised that in the long run an organisation will have to pay for its own losses. The primary objective of risk financing is *to spread more evenly over time cost of risk in order to reduce the financial strain* and possible insolvency which random concurrency of large losses may cause. The secondary objective is *to minimise risk costs.*

Essentially an organisation can finance its risk cost in three ways:

- Losses may be charged as they occur to current operating costs; or
- Ex-ante provision may be made for losses, either through the purchase of insurance or by building up a contingency found to which losses can be charged; or

- When losses occur they may be financed with loans, which are repaid over the next few months or years.

Risk financing includes the following alternatives:

2.2.2 Risk Retention

Risk retention implies that the losses arising due to a risk exposure shall be *retained* or *assumed* by the party or the organisation. Risk retention is generally a deliberate decision for business organisations inherited with the following characteristics:

(*a*) The consequential losses are small;

(*b*) Losses are shown as operating expenses or can be funded with retained profits.

Self-Insurance

Self-insurance is one of the forms of planned retention by which the part or full of the exposure arising due to a risk factor is retained by the firm. Self-insurance programmes differ from the other programmes in the sense of the formal arrangements made. It acts as an alternative to buying insurance in the market or when a part of the claim is not insured in the commercial market. It may be done by keeping aside funds to meet insurable losses. The main reason for self insurance is that the organisation believes it has large funds to finance losses and the opportunity cost of transfer is less than the cost of insurance.

Benefits of Self-insurance

(*a*) *Saves transaction costs* — it helps to save cost in the form of amount payable to insurer for overheads and profits, commissions and taxes and the social loading (arising from the statutory requirements) inherent in the premium.

(*b*) *Accuracy of predictions* — the risk managers in the organisation think that they are better judges of the adverse exposures and can estimate better than the insurers.

(c) *Investment of funds* — since insurance companies invest large chunk of funds in various securities and the returns arising therefrom is not reflected in the rates charged by the insurers, the cost reduction becomes obvious for the insured.

(*d*) *Minimisation of disputes* — self-managed funds enhances satisfaction to the insured and reduces the conflicts in claims settlement. Also, there is a direct incentive to reduce and control the risk of loss.

Captive Insurance

Captive insurance companies represent a special case of risk retention. *A captive insurance company* is an entity created and controlled by a parent, whose main purpose is to provide insurance to its corporate owner. The ideology behind this method is that the parent company may save in terms of overhead costs and profits which would otherwise be charged by the insurance company. Also, the insured companies claim premiums as expenses, which may lead to advantages in terms of differential cash flows. These captives may either be pure *captives or group captives.*

A pure captive is an insurance company established by the parent (generally into non-insurance business) organisation to provide insurance cover to itself or its subsidiary or affiliated organisations.

Group captives are those formed by a group of companies for providing insurance cover to control their respective and collective risks. In U.S. terminology these are also known as "trade association insurance companies."

Motives Behind Captives

(*a*) *Optimised loss prevention benefits:* The benefits enduring from loss prevention are available directly to the insured.

(*b*) *Economies of scale:* Groups with several subsidiaries can enjoy the benefit of perfectly tailored insurance products made available to cover risks.

(*c*) *Non-availability of insurance:* Captives provide to cover risk exposures for which covers are otherwise not available in the market.

(*d*) *Stability of earnings:* The captives reduce the chances of adverse impact of sudden fluctuations in profits on the firm.

(*e*) *Cost and tax advantages:* Obviously, as said earlier, captives reduce cost of risk financing and provide gains in the regime of differential taxes.

2.2.3 Risk Transfer

Risk transfer implies that the exposed party transfers whole or part of the losses consequential to risk exposure to another party for a cost. The insurance contracts fundamentally involve risk transfers. Apart from the insurance device, there are certain other techniques by which the risk may be transferred. Some of the these have been discussed in detail in chapter 7.

(*a*) *Insurance:* Insurance is a contractual transfer of risk. The insurance company agrees to indemnify the losses arising out an occurrence pre-determined and charges some cost for this act, called as premium. The insurance method of risk transfer is most appropriate when the severity of losses is very high.[1] Since the important constraint. i.e. the cost of transfer prevails, the suitability of this method depends upon the *size* of the organisation and *affordability*.

(*b*) *Non-insurance transfers:* Out of the various methods of non-insurance risk transfers, the most common are:

(*i*) Hold-harmless agreements or indemnity agreements are the contractual relationships specifying that all losses shall be borne by the designated party e.g. a landlord contracting that all losses shall be borne by the tenant. These agreements by themselves do not reduce original risk.[2] The form and jurisdiction of hold harmless agreements varies from contract to contract.

(*ii*) Incorporation is another method by which, for example, the sole proprietorship firm or partnership firm can convert themselves into companies and reduce the liability on them. To quote, the liability of a proprietorship firm is unlimited compared to that of a company limited by shares — the liability of the members is limited to the extent of capital contributed by them.

(*iii*) Hedging can be used to transfer speculative risk. The popular of the instruments used in hedging are derivative contracts.

(*iv*) Diversification across business or geographic locations justified or coupled with synergies or economies of scale can also significantly reduce risk in aggregate.

2.3 Risk Management Information Systems (RMIS)

In view of the growing competition in the insurance sector, risk managers are now feeling a dire need of computer information systems that will help them hold down their costs.

"They also (Risk Managers) want computer applications that are customized to meet their unique needs, and they are seeking true Web-based systems that facilitate the sharing of loss information and reports with managers in remote locations. In the current market, risk managers are demanding the ability to pluck credible data from their information systems."

1. Dorfman M.S., *Introduction to Risk Management and Insurance,* Prentice-Hall 2002, P. 58.
2. J.S. Trieshman *et. al.*, *Risk Management and Insurance,* South-Western College Publishing, 2001, pp. 84-85.

"Risk management information systems are software tools designed to assist risk managers in their functions. Traditional RMIS software emphasizes claim management, safety monitoring, and financing losses. Other tools available in a RMIS are management of insurance policies, exposure data and insurance certificates.

An enterprisewide RMIS system can help managers with a wide array of functions. At the outset, once connected to an organization's existing information systems, the RMIS gathers information from all these various systems into one database. There, the data can be analyzed from various angles to get different perspectives on the risks the organization faces.

With this rich database and analysis tool, various custom reports can be produced not just for a risk manager, but also for managers throughout the organization, giving them a detailed look at their exposures.

Initially, in the late 1960s and early 1970s, risk management information technology was limited to systems utilizing mainframe computers that allowed insurers to print out summaries of claim losses as a courtesy to their larger policyholders. These primitive loss run were often months behind real time, contained numerous errors, and were difficult to read. Moreover, they contained little useful information, the only exception being the total incurred loss figures for any particular claim.

Nevertheless, these computer print-out loss runs were the precursor of client reports that risk managers, or "insurance managers" as they were called then, were beginning to request with greater frequency. As their superiors demanded more and more financial information about the nature of losses driving their premium costs, obtaining such information was vital."

RMIS can be used for the following :

1. Reporting

Creation of reports that summarize loss payments and estimates of future losses. Accounting and finance departments use these reports in preparing the organization's financial statements.

2. Examination of Causes of Accidents

By identifying the reasons for accidents, risk managers can determine where safety and loss prevention expenditures would be most helpful. A large number of employees or customers slipping and falling in a certain area may warrant a review of cleanup procedures or a study of the costs for installing special carpet.

3. Review of Claims Adjustment Process

Risk managers use RMIS to evaluate the performance of claims adjusters by comparing actual results to standards. Typical evaluation areas are promptness of initial contact, case settlement time, amount paid for type of injury, and accuracy of the adjuster's case value estimate.

The emergence of internet as a critical tool for business communication and services has rapidly impacted RMIS, as many vendors have "Web-Enabled" new and existing products to take advantage of the Internet's broad availability and low end user maintenance costs. The internet has also permitted older legacy systems to remain viable in the marketplace because end-users work with a newer, standard interface even though processing may be occurring on a mainframe or other older computer system.

Software products have also been introduced to serve special application needs, such as catastrophe simulation software to assist in examining the effects of disasters on a group of exposed properties, and hazardous material tracking programmes to record the uses and locations of potentially hazardous items.

2.3.1 Risk Manager Tasks and Responsibilities

Risk manager is a person who performs the risk management function in an organisation by whatever name called. He is responsible for overall risk management activities including risk control and financing. They are also sometimes responsible for employee benefit plans. The responsibilities of risk manager vary with the organisation size.

In most of the professional organisations, RMIS are computerised, in such cases risk manager has to force relatively new problems.

- data impurity
- lacks of service
- software incompatibility
- mapping errors (when changing vendors)
- poor system documentation
- obsolescence
- bugs
- hardware incompatibility
- system inflexibility
- proprietary problems (only the creator knows how the system is put together)

The possible remedies are:

- solid assessment of needs
- comprehensive and clear specifications
- good contract negotiation
- reference checks, including on-site inspection
- financial check (especially important if relying solely on the vendor for support)
- source code (the actual programming code for the system, especially useful should the vendor go out of business)
- standard software configuration, such as DOS or Windows
- internal access to systems expert
- solid vendor account team

2.3.2 Some RMIS Vendors

Independent, claims administration-oriented RMIS vendors.

CARE System Corp.

GenSource Corp. (formerly CIC).

Nichols Engineering (formerly Conway).

These three vendors offer solid property/causality claims administration software for large self-insureds and TPAs on a global basis.

Broker and TPA-based RMIS Vendors

Crawford RSG.

Envision/Near North Risk Technologies Inc.

J&H Marsh & McLennan Inc.'s STARS

Sedgwick Information Systems

Insurer/TPA-based Vendors

IG.

Chubb.

CIGNA (ESIS Inc.)

RISKTRAC Inc. (Liberty Mutual Group).

2.3.3 Organisation of Risk Management Department

The organisation structure of a large risk management department in a corporate form or organisation may be as follows on next page. (Exhibit 2C)

In small organisations, the risk management job is confined to the president or the owner. In medium type organisations, the risk handling job is entrusted to the chief financial officer or someone at middle level management position.

In large business organisation, the risk management department is headed by a top official generally director, who is also a member of the board of directors. He is duly supported by an analyst, generally a professional who is entrusted with all risk research responsibilities. Below the chain are middle level managers designated by the respective risk management methods. viz., prevention and loss control, insurance etc.

Exhibit 2-C

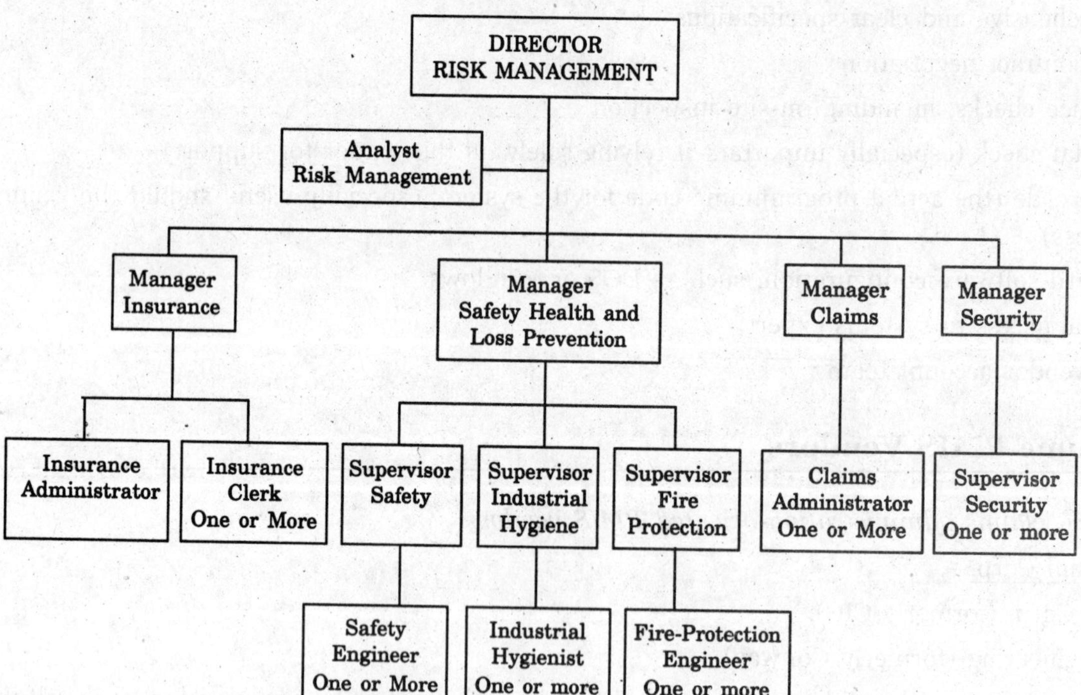

2.4 Risk Management by Individuals

Risk Management is an indispensable tool since it is considered as a complex task that requires a lot of analytical skills. For its effectiveness risk management program should be reviewed periodically to analyses whether the objectives are been attained.

Individual risk management refers to the identification of pure risk faced by an individual or family and to the selection of most appropriate technique for treating such risk. In order to reduce risk element certain basic steps have been allowed under individual risk management process:

- ❑ Potential losses must be identified.
- ❑ Potential losses should be evaluated in terms of loss frequency and loss severity.
- ❑ Appropriate methods for treating loss exposures must be selected.
- ❑ The risk management program must be implemented and properly administered.

(A) Identification of Potential Losses

The process of risk management for individuals begins with identifying of potential losses which can arise due to the following risks:

Personal Risk

- ❑ Risk arising due to loss of earned income to the family because of premature death of family head.
- ❑ Insufficient income and financial assets during retirement.
- ❑ Loss of earned income from unemployment.

Property Risk

- ❑ Direct physical damage to a home and personal property because of fire, lightning, flood, earthquake, or other causes.
- ❑ Theft of valuable personal property including money, securities and antiques.
- ❑ Theft of car, motor cycle etc., or direct physical damage.

Liability Risk

- ❑ Legal liabilities arising out of defamation of character and similar exposures.
- ❑ Legal liability arising out of the negligent operation of a car, motorcycle, boat or recreational vehicle.
- ❑ Legal liability arising of business or professional activities.
- ❑ Payment of attorney fees and other legal defense cost.

(B) Evaluation of Potential Losses

Estimating the frequency and severity of potential losses is the most appropriate technique which is used to deal with the risk.

For example: The chance that your home will be totally destroyed by certain natural clamity – thunder, storm, flood, earthquake etc. is relatively small, but the severity of the loss can be catastrophic. Such losses should be insured because of their catastrophic potentials. Certain techniques such as retention are more appropriate for handling situations where loss frequency is high and loss severity is low, such losses should not be insured.

(C) Selecting the Appropriate Techniques for Handling Losses

Losses are managed by selecting the most appropriate method for handling potential losses. Some of the methods are discussed below:

(1) Loss Control: Is a method by which frequency and security of losses are controlled.

For example: Car theft can be prevented by locking the car, removing the key from the ignition and installing anti theft device. Wearing a helmet reduces the severity of a head injury in a two-wheeler accidents. Having a fire extinguisher on the premises reduces the severity of a fire.

Thus occurrence of any loss could be controlled by having loss control devices properly installed.

(2) Avoidance: Apart from controlling losses the other substitute for preventing losses to occur is avoidance a method for handling potential losses.

Example : You can avoid risk by not travelling on a lonely road in the night and not to drive a vehicle with poor brakes.

(3) Retention: Retention means the amount of loss that you bear it at all some loss occurs. Risk Retention can also be further classified into:

Active Risk Retention: Which is you are aware of the risk and plan to retain part or all of it.

Example: You can retain 'losses of your car by buying Motor Insurance of your car in case the car meets with an accident or eventually if it gets stolen.

Passive Risk Retention: Risk on the other hand could also be retained passively because of ignorance, indifference, or laziners. This could be dangerous if the retained risk could result in catastropic loss.

(4) Non Insurance Transfers: Non Insurance transfer is an instrument by which a pure risk is transferred to a party other than an insurer.

For example: Risk associated with a defective music system is transferred to a retailer by purchasing an extended–warranty contract that makes the retailer responsible for repairs after warranty expires.

(5) Insurance: It is one of the cheapest mode generally used by individuals for risk management. Individual use life and non-life coverages for personal, property and liability risks.

(D) Review the Program Periodically

The risk management program must be reviewed periodically to find out deviations, if these deviations are significant, it requires a modification or complete renewal of the whole model.

2.5 Factors Affecting Individual's Demand for Insurance

Individuals demand for insurance depends on various factors, sometimes particular to an individual. However, following factors are generally common:

(1) Price for risk transformation — the cost of insurance vis-a-vis other products.

(2) Perception towards losses – if the individual feels that insurer's calculation of risk and expected losses is better than his own, he will opt for insurance cover.

(3) Income and wealth states – Insurance demand, logically, is positively correlated with the income and wealth of the potential insured.

(4) Social Insurance programs – if as per individual's satisfaction good social program by government or other public agencies are available, demand for private insurance will be lower.

(5) Nature of losses — insurance covers for non-monetary losses like mental tension and pain, psychological suffering are generally not very common and also legal structure takes care of these partially e.g., Specific Relief Act.

2.6 Corporate Risk Management

Risk management by business firm differs substantially from risk aversion by individuals. Diversification is one of the strategy pursued by the business firms to tackle risk by spread into number of businesses. Individual shareholders diversify risk by spreading their investments in various stocks. However, for a given firm the perception is different. What is important is the variability of cash flows for the firm being a separate entity. Though "corporate insurance contracts and shareholder's diversification are alternative mechanisms for diversifying pure risk for shareholders." Yet, "any corporate activities that reduce the variability of corporate cash flows will not necessarily reduce the shareholders risk, because shareholders already may have diversified away the risk."

"Business insurance purchases can (1) provide an efficient method of purchasing claims processing and loss control services; (2) reduce the expected cost of financing losses; (3) reduce the likelihood that the firm will have to raise costly external capital for new investment projects and thereby increase the likelihood that it will adopt good investment projects; (4) reduce the likelihood of financial distress and thereby improve the terms at which the firm will be able to contract with other claimants, such as employees suppliers, lenders and customers; and (5) reduce expected tax payments."

Doubts are sometimes raised whether the diversification by shareholders is cheaper or the insurance mechanism. Since, the cost of buying a mutual fund is lower than an individual stock it look a cheaper option compared to insurance were the prices include margin and administrative costs. But, even if the shareholders are diversified, insurance can enhance value by restricting losses.

2.6.1 Corporate Risk Management Models

Corporate Risk Management, in a classical sense, has been viewed in terms of cost management primarily focusing on financial risks. However, in present scenario, the focus has changed to holistic view rather than as a narrow approach. "Risk management can be viewed as a means to improve efficiency of other activities of the firm. Or, a firm may extend its internal risk management process for providing risk management products demanded by its customer."

Corporate Risk Management as a Control Exercise

Risk controlling firms use risk management or internal management and control. In these firms, the focus is on cost/loss aspects, popularly known as negative effects of risk, rather than as a business opportunity. The main areas of concern in these firms are:

(*a*) Maintenance of risk tolerance levels as per expectations of stockholders;

(*b*) Using risk control tools enhances efficiency of their business operations;

(*c*) Maintenance of sound governance process which should provide support required for the design, implementation and evaluation and fine tuning of the risk management process.

2.6.2 The Process

In case of business organisation, following process of risk management modelling is generally followed:

(1) To analyse the risk profile of the firm and the changes brought by fluctuations in the factors that influence the cash flows relating to assets and liabilities.

(2) To restructure the factors depending on the nature of the risk and organisational strategies to manage them.

(3) To develop a model, dynamic in nature which keeps a continuous watch on actual risk undertaken, relative to that targeted.

(4) Comparison of actuals with targets calls for corrective action and application of suitable risk transformation products.

The process of risk management need to be aimed not only to meet the requirements of internal policies and guidelines but also to improve the efficiency at other activities of the firm.

Thus, the process of 'risk management' is dynamic in nature, however it gives managers an opportunity to realign goals and ensure that the needs of the firm and design of the risk management system fits together.

2.6.3 Types of Risk Managing Firms

Business firms, on the basis of risk perception can be classified as follows:

(*a*) *Risk controllers* are the firms which use risk management for purely internal control purposes.

(*b*) "*Efficient enhancers* are firms that use their risk control tools to operate their business more efficiently. They focus more on the strategic issues relating to risk management rather than tactical or implementation issues, which are the main issues of concern of the risk controllers."[3] Generally, these firms use customised software solutions.

(*c*) *Risk transformers* are optimistic and view the risk management as a business opportunity and the main focus area is on design of new financial products for risk management.

2.7 Process of Risk Management by Individuals

Risk Management is an indispensable tool since it is considered as a complex task that requires a lot of analytical skills. For its effectiveness risk management program should be reviewed periodically to analyses whether the objectives are been attained.

The personal risk management process applied to the loss exposures of the individuals and families. They are general least expected to implement a plan, and expect insurance to take care of all possible exposures.

Individual risk management refers to the identification of pure risk faced by an individual or family and to the selection of most appropriate technique for treating such risk. In order to reduce risk element certain basic steps have been allowed under individual risk management process:

- Potential losses must be identified.
- Potential losses should be evaluated in terms of loss frequency and loss severity.
- Appropriate methods for treating loss exposures must be selected.
- The risk management program must be implemented and properly administered.

(i) Identifying Potential Losses : The first step is to identity all potential losses that can cause serious financial problems. Financial losses can result from the following:

- Loss of earned income to the family became of the premature death of the family head.
- Insufficient income and financial assets during retirement.
- Medical bills and the loss of earnings during an extended period of disability.
- Loss of earned income from unemployment.

(ii) Evaluating Potential Losses : The second step is to evaluate the potential losses, it is estimate the frequency and severity of potential losses so that the most appropriate technique can be used to deal with the personal risk. Loss frequency refers to the probable number of losses that may occur during some given time period. Loss severity refers is the probable size of losses that may occur. If these two are not evaluated accurately, then it will be very difficult to adopt the appropriate technique to handle the risk.

(iii) Selecting the Appropriate Technique : The third step is to select the most appropriate technique for handling each potential loss. The major methods for potential losses are:

(a) Avoidance

(b) Risk control

(c) Risk retention

(d) Non-insurance transfers

(e) Insurance

(a) Avoidance : Avoidance is one method for handling a potential loss. It means a certain loss exposure is never acquired or an existing loss exposure is abandoned. For example, one can avoid being mugged in a high crime rate area by staying out of the area. The major advantage of avoidance is that the chance of loss is slightly reduced. However, one cannot be able to avoid all losses. For example, a company may not be able to avoid the premature death of a key executive

(b) Risk Control : Risk control refers to the activities that reduce both the frequently and severity of losses. For example, one can reduce the risk of an auto accident by driving within the speed limits, taking a safe driving course, and driving defensively. Risk control also aims at reducing the severity of a loss. For example, weaving a helmet reduces the severity of a head injury is a motorcycle accident. Wearing a seal bell reduces the severity of an injury in a car accident.

(c) Retention : Retention means that one retains part or all of a loss if it occurs. For example, one can retain the small expenses; say medical expenses like normal check-ups, blood - test and etc. He or she can set aside a certain amount from their income to meet these. Retention can be done if the possible is not serious. Retention can be either active or passive. Active risk retention means that one is aware of the loss exposure and plans to retain all or part of it. Passive retention is the failure to identity a loss exposure, failure to act, no forgetting to out. Retention can be effectively used when not other method is available.

(d) Non-insurance Transfers : Non-insurance transfers are methods other than insurance by which a pure risk is transferred to a party other than an insurer. For example, periodic (say, half-yearly) medical check-ups for the workers the owner of the plant. This can be done through an agreement between the employer and employees. Non-insurance transfers often cost less than insurance. In Non-insurance transfers, the potential loss may be shifted to someone who is a better position to exercise loss control.

(e) Insurance : In a personal risk management program, must people rely heavily on insurance as the major method for dealing with risk. Insurance is appropriate for loss exposures that have a low probability of loss but for which the severity of loss is high. Insurance policies fulfill the needs of the public.

(iv) Peridic Review : The last step is to implement and review the programe periodically. At least every two or three years, one should determine all major risks are adequately covered one should also review the program at major events in his/her life such as divorce, birth of a child, purchase of a her life, such as divorce, birth of a child, purchase of a house, change of jobs or death of spouse or family member.

2.8 Personal Risk Management Strategies

A personal risk management strategy should ensure that assets are protected and debts are cleared in the event of the unforeseen death, major accident or major illness of a key financial member(s) of a family or partnership. This entails personal protection insurance. In much the same way as one would insure a home or car, one should insure for the protection of income, accumulated wealth and lifestyle.

There are four key forms of personal protection insurances :

Life Term Insurance

Life Term Insurance (often called Term Insurance) pays a lump sum benefit to the policy owner upon the death of the life insured, where this occurs during the term of the insurance cover (this can be up to age 99).

Term insurance is usually taken out in order to repay liabilities, such as mortgage, credit cards, etc., cover funeral costs, pay off credit cards and, in the event of the death of the main breadwinner, provide a substitute income stream for the spouse so that the current standard of living may be maintained. This is especially important where dependent children are involved.

Total & Permanent Disability (TPD) Insurance

TPD insurance provides a lump sum upon medical confirmation that the insured person is totally and permanently disabled based on the definition provided in the policy document. This type of policy is generally sold as an additional benefit to term life insurance.

It is important to be clear about how the life company defines the total and permanent disability in the context of you being able to continue to work in your current capacity. This definition will assist in the selection of particular products for recommendation. Generally, in order to claim on TPD, you must be off work for at least six months and, in the opinion of the medical practitioners, unlikely to ever work again; or have irrecoverably lost the use of both eyes, legs, arms or one of each.

Trauma (Critical Illness) Insurance

Modern medicine can keep more people alive following major traumas. Trauma insurance pays you a lump sum in the event of a major trauma such as a major heart attack, cancer or stroke. Most life offices also pay the benefit under trauma in the event of death. Statistics show that we will suffer some major illness or trauma during our lifetime and that we are three times more likely to suffer a condition such as heart attack, cancer, stroke or bypass surgery than to die.

Most of us will survive the trauma but many are not able to continue working. In that case their income stream, upon which they rely for their livelihood, ceases.

Trauma insurance is designed to ensure that lifestyle suffers as little as possible by paying at and when the need is highest, therefore aiding recovery.

Income Protection Insurance

Most people state that their greatest physical asset is their home. They see the importance of insuring their home building and contents but most overlook their most valuable asset, their income. Your ability to earn an income between now and retirement determines what you and your family are able to do day-to-day.

Income Protection cover is designed to provide you with a regular monthly income whilst you cannot work due to sickness or accident. You are able to protect up to 75% of your gross income, inclusive of any packaged benefits such as car and superannuation.

2.9 Risk Management Process

Risk management is the process of identification, analysis and control of those risks. Risk management involves the following steps.

1. Defining the Objective of Risk Management : The First step in the risk management is to define the objective. Risk management is widely used by corporations, small employers, farmers, government bodies and even by individuals. Different risky situations result in deferent kind of losses. Loss from accident is significantly differ from loss from firm when risk managers deal with there risks, they must have certain objectives, produce and post loss.

2. Identifying Potential Losses : The next step is to identify the potential loss exposures. Risk managers must have the knowledge about the firm, the market in which it operates, the legal, social, economical and political environment in which it operates the firm's financial background and also the business mechanism. Then the risk may cause a major loss for the organization. Property loss, liability loss, business income lose, death or disability, retirement or unemployment, robbery and etc are some of the major loss exposures using some sources of flowcharts, financial statements, on-site physical inspection and interaction with exports.

3. Evaluating the Potential Losses : Next step as to evaluate and measure the impact of the losses. This step involves an estimation of the potential frequency and security of losses. Loss frequency refers to the probable number of losses that may occur during some given time period. Loss servile refers to the probable size of the losses.

Once the frequency and security of each type of loss exposures are estimated, various loss exposures can be ranked according to their relative importance. Because a loss exposure with high potential is much more important than an exposure with small loss potential. Also the estimation of frequency and security of loss will help the risk manager to select most appropriate each exposure. For example, if certain losses occur regularly and are fairly predictable, they can be budgeted out of the firms income and treated as normal operating expenses.

So the loss severity is more important than the loss frequency. Because a single catastrophic loss will wipe out the entire firm. There fore it is important to consider the maximum possible loss that can result from a single event. For example, if a plant is totally destroyed in a earthquake, the total loss may be 20 lakhs. But occur more than in 50 years. So the risk manager ignores the event which occurs so infrequently. Thus the potential losses should be evaluated, even if they occur frequently or infrequently.

4. Selecting Appropriate Techniques for Losses : The next step in the risk management process is to select the most appropriate technique for treating loss exposures. These techniques can be broadly classified as risk control and risk financing.

***(a) Risk Control* :** Risk control is a technique in which no monetary compensation is involved. Loss controls are those actions which reduce the expected cost of losses by reducing the frequency and severity of losses major risk control techniques involve the following:-

(i) Avoidance

(ii) Loss prevention

(iii) Loss reduction

***(b)* Risk Financing :** Risk financing refers to the manner in which the risk control measures that have been implemented shall be financed. It refers to techniques that provide for the funding of losses offer they occur. Major risk-financing techniques include the following:

(i) Risk retention

(ii) Non-insurance transfers

(iii) Commercial insurance

5. Implementing and Reviewing the Programme : To have an effective risk management programme, a risk management policy statement is necessary. This statement outlines the risk management objectives of the firm as well as the company policy with respect to the treatment of loss exposures. In addition to this, a risk treatment manual can be developed. This manual describes the details of the program. It is a very useful tool for training new employees of the firm. This manual also includes important information's such as procedures to follow in an emergency. The risk manager should have cooperation with other financial departments like marketing, production, finance, hr, ect.

Finally, the risk management programme must be periodically reviewed and evaluated to determine whether the objectives are being attained. Risk management costs, safety programs must be carefully monitored. Loss records must be periodically examined to detect any changes in frequency and severity.

2.10 Risk Management Objectives

As discussed earlier, risk management is an integrated process of describing specific areas of risk, developing a comprehensive plan, integrating the plan and conducting ongoing evaluation. It is a process that identifies loss exposures faced by an organization and selects the most appropriate techniques including insurance for treating such exposures.

Risk management should not be confused with insurance management. Risk management is broader concept and includes all techniques for treating loss exposures, in addition to insurance. Risk management has important objectives. These objectives can be classified follows:-

(a) Preloss Objective : Following are the objectives before the loss.

(i) *Reduction in worry and fear :* The risk management should be able to reduce anxiety and fear in the mind of the likely exposed unit and should be able to enhance value without constraints on operating activities.

(ii) *Economy* : This means that the firm should prepare for potential losses in the most economical way. This preparation involves an analysis of the cost safety programs, insurance premium paid and the costs assonated with the deferent techniques for handling losses.

(iii) *Meeting legal obligations :* The next objective is to meet any legal obligations. Risk managers must see that all these obligations are met or not. For example, government regulation may require a firm to install safely devices to protect workers from harm, to dispose hazardous waste materials property ect.

(b) Post Loss Objective : Following are the objective of risk management after a loss occurs.

(i) *Survival :* The most important post loss objective is survival of the firm. If a loss occurs, the firm can not be totally shut down. The firm should be able to resume the operations or at least partial operations within some reasonable time period so that the firm will survive in the market.

(ii) *Continued operation :* Even if a loss occurs, the firms mainly service provider should be able to continue their operations,. For example, public utility firms such as airlines, banks, bakeries and dories must continued to operate even after a loss. Otherwise business will be lost to competitors.

(iii) *Stability of earning :* The next post loss objective is stability in earning. If the firm continues to operate, then there will be a stability in the earning of the firm. The firm will have to face substantial additional expenses to achieve this goal. The firm can shift their operation to another location.

(iv) *Continued Growth :* After the stability is earning the company can show a continuous growth. It can develop new products and enter into new markets. They can acquire or merge with another company. The risk manager must consider the effect that a loss will have on the firm's ability to grow.

(v) *Optimizing Social Effects :* The objective of social responsibility of risk management is to minimize the effects that a loss will have on other person and on socially. A severe loss can adversely affect employees, suppliers, creditors and the community in general. For example, a severe loss that shut down a plant in a small town for an extended period can cause considerable economic distress in the town.

2.11 Risk Management : Guidelines and Responsibilities

General Risk Management Guidelines

- ❑ All human activity involving technical devices or complex processes entails some element of risk.
- ❑ Hazards can be controlled; they are not a cause for panic.
- ❑ Problems should be kept in perspective.
- ❑ Judgments should be based upon knowledge, experience and mission requirements.
- ❑ Encouraging all participants in an operation to adopt risk management principles both reduces risk and makes the task of reducing it easier.
- ❑ Good analysis tilts the odds in favor of safe and successful operation.
- ❑ Hazard analysis and risk assessment do not replace good judgment: they improve it.
- ❑ Establishing clear objectives and parameters in risk management works better than using a cookbook approach.
- ❑ No one best solution may exist. Normally, there are a variety of alternatives, each of which may produce a different degree of risk reduction.
- ❑ Tact is essential. It is more productive to show a mission planner how he can better manage risk than to condemn his approach as unworkable, risky, unsafe or unsound.
- ❑ Seldom can complete safety be achieved.
- ❑ There are no "safety problems" in planning or design, only management problems that may cause accidents, if left unresolved.

Risk Management Responsibilities

Managers

- ❑ Are responsible for effective management of risk.
- ❑ Select from risk reduction options recommended by staff.
- ❑ Accept or reject risk based upon the benefit to be derived.
- ❑ Train and motivate personnel to use risk management techniques.
- ❑ Elevate decisions to a higher level when it is appropriate.

Staff

- ❑ Assess risks and develop risk reduction alternatives.
- ❑ Integrate risk controls into plans and orders.
- ❑ Identify unnecessary risk controls.

Supervisors

- ❑ Apply the risk management process
- ❑ Consistently apply effective risk management concepts and methods to operations and tasks.
- ❑ Elevate risk issues beyond their control or authority to superiors for resolution.

Individuals

- ❑ Understand, accept and implement risk management processes.

- ❑ Maintain a constant awareness of the changing risks associated with the operation or task.
- ❑ Make supervisors immediately aware of any unrealistic risk reduction measures or high-risk procedures.

2.12 Levels of Risk Management

The risk management process operates on three levels. Although it would be preferable to perform an in-depth application of risk management for every operation or task, the time and resources may not always be available. The three levels are as follow:

Time-Critical

Time-critical risk management is an "on the run" mental or verbal review of the situation using the basic risk management process without necessarily recording the information. This time-critical process of risk management is employed by personnel to consider risk while making decisions in a time-compressed situation. This level of risk management is used during the execution phase of training or operations as well as in planning and execution during crisis responses. It is also the most easily applied level of risk management in off-duty situations. It is particularly helpful for choosing the appropriate course of action when an unplanned event occurs during execution of a planned operation or daily routine.

Deliberate

Deliberate Risk Management is the application of the complete process. It primarily uses experience and brainstorming to identify risks, hazards and develops controls and is therefore most effective when done in a group. Examples of deliberate applications include the planning of upcoming operations, review of standard operating, maintenance, or training procedures, and damage control or disaster response planning.

Strategic

This is the deliberate process with more thorough hazard identification and risk assessment involving research of available data, use of diagram and analysis tools, formal testing, or long term tracking of the risks associated with the system or operation (normally with assistance from technical experts). It is used to study the hazards and their associated risks in a complex operation or system, or one in which the hazards are not well understood. Examples of strategic applications include the long-term planning of complex operations, introduction of new equipment, materials and operational, development of tactics and training curricula, high risk facility construction, and major system overhaul or repair. Strategic risk management should be used on high priority or high visibility risks.

2.12.1 Areas of Personal Risk Management

In our personal lives we will face risk in :

- ❑ investments we make
- ❑ the impact of death or disability on our lives and those of our immediate family
- ❑ health risks and the costs associated with health care
- ❑ the business environment (more so for some of us than others).

2.13 Risk Management and Derivatives

The Derivatives are the most modern financial instruments in hedging risk. All over the world derivatives is the key part of the financial system. The term "Derivative" indicates that it has no independent value, i.e. its value is entirely "derived" from the value of the underlying asset. The underlying asset can be securities, commodities, bullion, currency, live stock or anything else. In other words, Derivative means a forward, future, option or any other hybrid contract of pre determined fixed duration, linked for the purpose of contract fulfillment to the value of a specified real or financial asset or to an index of securities. With Securities Laws (Second Amendment) Act, 1999, Derivatives has been included in the definition of Securities. The term Derivative has been defined in Securities Contracts (Regulations) Act, as :

A Derivative includes :

- a security derived from a debt instrument, share, loan, whether secured or unsecured, risk instrument or contract for differences or any other form of security;
- a contract which derives its value from the prices, or index of prices, of underlying securities.

Derivative markets can be broadly classified into two types :

- Commodity derivative markets
- Financial derivative markets

In commodity derivative markets the trade contract for the underlying asset is a commodity. It can be agricultural commodity like wheat, soybean, cotton, rapeseed, pepper, chana, mustard seed etc or precious metals like gold, silver, mega silver etc. Due to the bulky nature of the underlying assets, physical settlement in commodity derivative creates the need for warehousing. In case of commodities the quality of the underlying asset can vary largely. In financial derivative markets the trade contracts for the underlying asset is a financial asset. It can be equity, interest rates and exchange rates. Financial derivatives are used to hedge the exposure to market risk.

2.13.1 Types/Classification of Derivatives

Derivatives can be classified into four types :

- Forwards
- Futures
- Options
- Swaps

Forward Contract

In a forward contract, two parties agree to do a trade at some future date, at a price and quantity agreed today. No money changes hands at the time the deal is signed. The agreed upon price is called the forward price with a forward market the transfer of ownership occurs on the spot, but the delivery of the commodity or instrument does not occur until some future date.

Example: a wheat farmer may wish to contract their harvest at a future date to eliminate the risk of a change in prices by that date.

Features of forward contracts :

- They are bilateral contracts and hence exposed to counter-party risk.
- Each contract is custom designed, and hence is unique in terms of contract size, expiration date and the asset type and quality.
- The contract price is generally not available in public domain.
- The contract has to be settled by delivery of the asset on expiration date.
- In case, the party wishes to reverse the contract, it has to compulsorily go to the same counter party.

Futures Contract

Futures contract means a legally binding agreement to buy or sell the underlying security on a future date. Future contracts are the organized/standardized contracts in terms of quantity, quality (in case of commodities), delivery time and place for settlement on any date in future. The contract expires on a pre-specified date which is called the expiry date of the contract. On expiry, futures can be settled by delivery of the underlying asset or cash. Cash settlement enables the settlement of obligations arising out of the future/option contract in cash. The agreed upon price is called the future price.

Important features of a futures contract :

Originally future trading was exclusively concentrated in agricultural commodities due to the seasonal nature of its supply. But now a days future trading has extended to financial instruments with greater intensity.

- *Use of standard contracts :* The important feature of future contract is the standardization of contract. The standardization of the contract fetches the potential buyers and sellers and increases the marketability and liquidity of the contracts.
- *Clearing House :* An organization called Futures exchange will act as a clearing house. In futures contract the obligation of the buyer and seller is not to each other but to the clearing house in fulfilling the contract which ensures the elimination of the default risk on any transaction.
- *Margin Requirements :* The clearing house requires the participants to keep margin money, normally ranging between 5% to 10% of the face value of the contract.
- *Time spreads :* There is a relationship between the spot price and future price of the contract. The relationship also exists between prices of future contracts which are on the same commodity or instrument but which have different expiry dates. The difference between the prices of two contracts is known as the time spread.
- *Simple pay–off positions in Futures :* In futures market the pay-off can be either positive or negative.

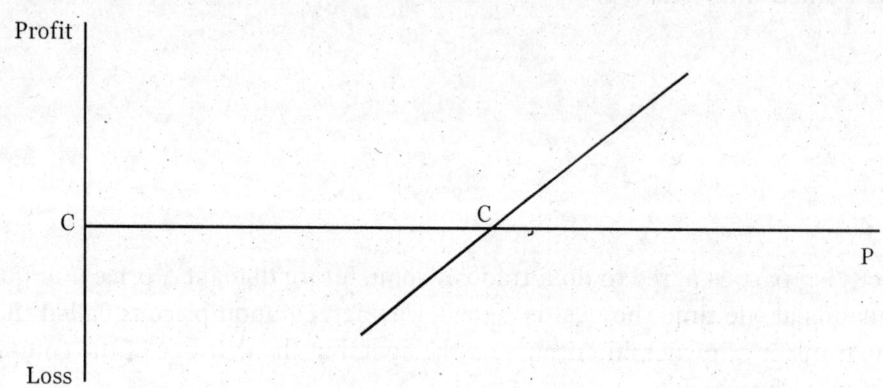

Figure 1 : Buyer's Pay Off

where C = contract price and P= price of security

The buyer of the contract has an obligation to purchase the underlying instrument at a price of C.When the spot price is above the contract price the buyer will buy the instrument for the price C and sell the instrument for higher spot price, thus making a profit. When the spot price is below the contract price, a loss is made by the buyer of the contract.

The seller of the contract makes a profit when the contract price is above the spot price (the seller will purchase the instrument at the spot price and sell at the contract price) and makes a loss when the spot price is above the contract price.

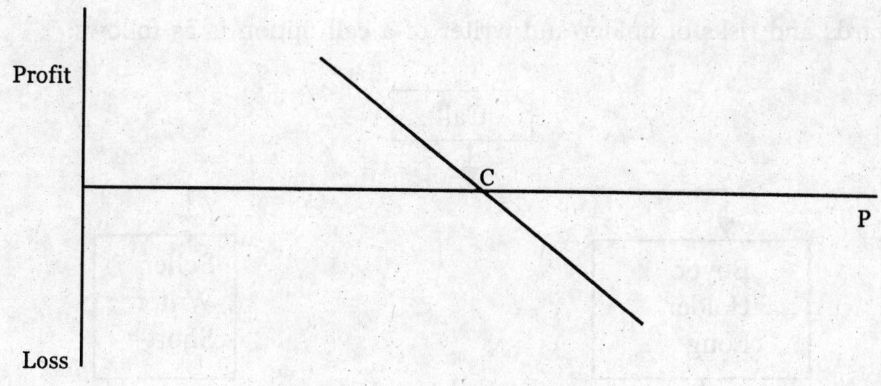

Figure 2 : Seller's Pay Off

Options Contract : option contract is a type of Derivatives Contract which gives the buyer/holder of the contract the right (but not the obligation) to buy/sell the underlying asset at a predetermined price within or at end of a specified period. The buyer/holder of the option purchase the right from the seller/writer for a consideration which is called the premium. The seller/writer of an option is obligated to settle the option as per the terms of the contract when the buyer/holder exercises his right. The underlying asset could include securities, an index of prices of securities etc.

European and American Options

If an option that is exercisable on or before the expiry date is called *American option* .the holder can exercise the right anytime between purchase date and expiration date. An option that is exercisable only on expiry date is called *European option.* In this case the holder of the option can only exercise his right on the expiration date. The price at which the option is to be exercised is called *Strike price or Exercise price*.

Call and Put Options

Call Option: A call option is the right (not the obligation) to buy the commodity or security at a specific price called the exercise price.

Rights and obligations of the holder and writer of a call options is given in the figure.

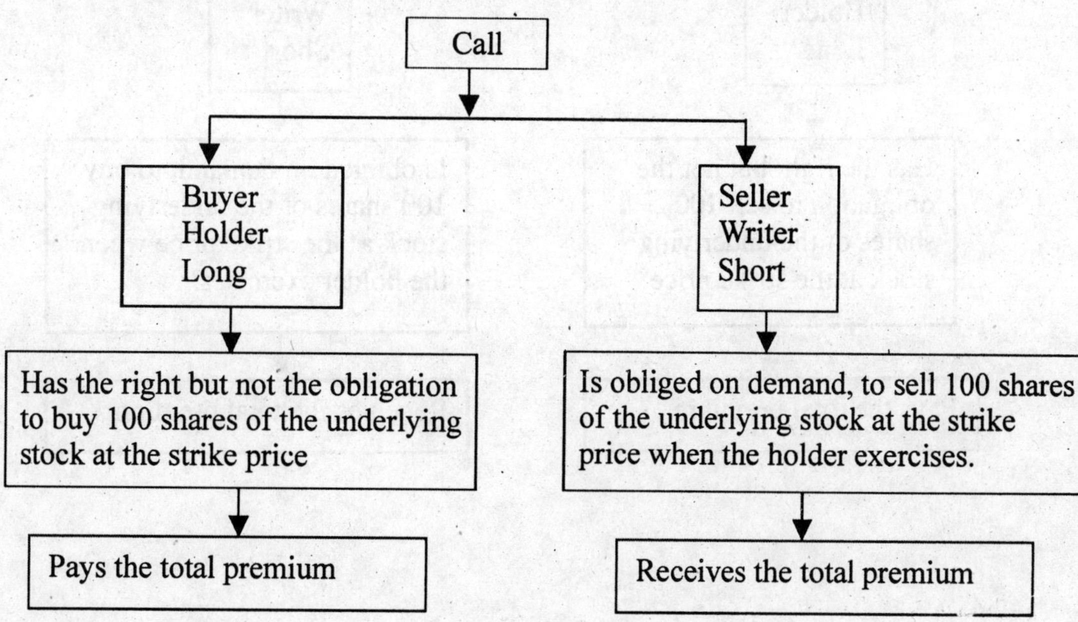

Expectations, rewards and risks of holder and writer of a call option is as follows:

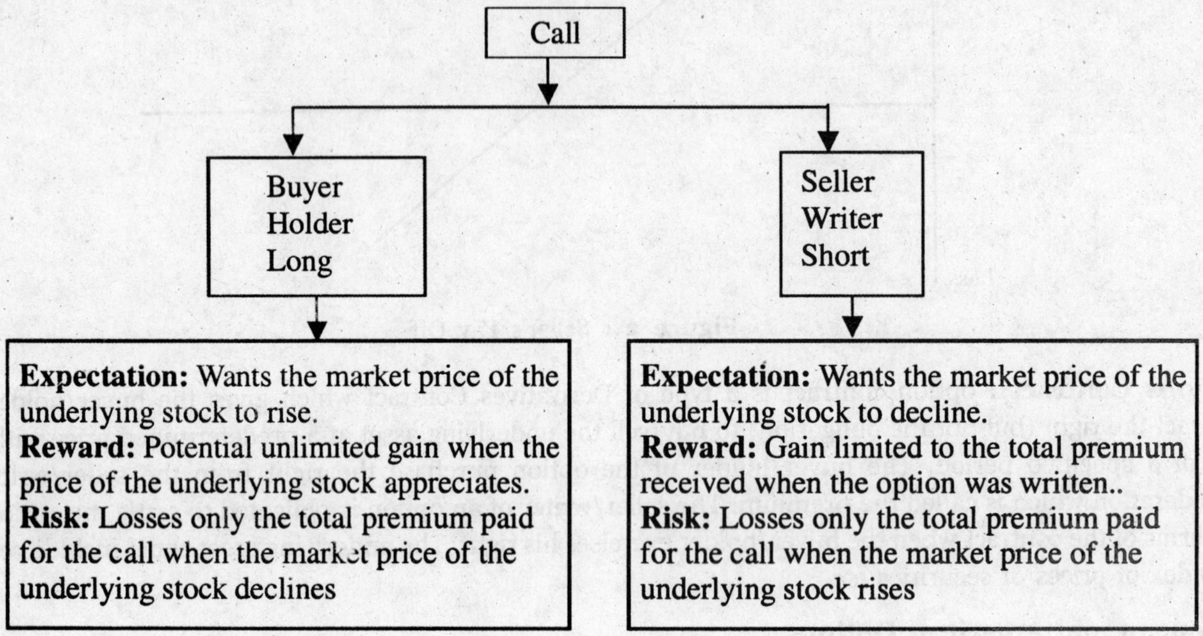

Put Option : option to sell is called *Put option.*

Rights and obligations of the holder and writer of a put options is given in the figure

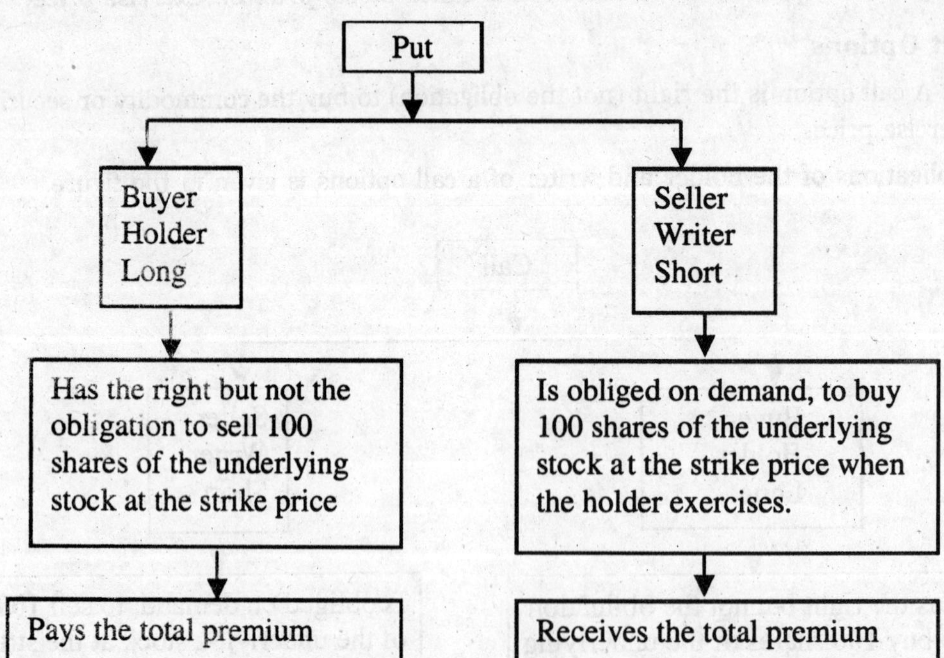

Expectations, rewards and risks of holder and writer of a put option is as follows:

Put

Buyer / Holder / Long	Seller / Writer / Short
Expectation: Wants the market price of the underlying stock to decline. **Reward:** Maximum profit when the price of the underlying stock declines to Zero **Risk:** Losses only the total premium paid for the call when the market price of the underlying stock rises.	**Expectation:** Wants the market price of the underlying stock stay flat or rise. **Reward:** Gain limited to the total premium received when the option was written. **Risk:** Losses more and more as the stock price declines lower and lower.

Difference Between Futures and Options

FUTURES	*OPTIONS*
Future contract involve obligations.	Option contracts involve rights
Future contracts have symmetric risk.	Options have asymmetric risk

The prices are affected by the prices of the underlying asset.Prices are affected by the prices of the underlying asset, time, interest rate, volatility etc.

Swap Contract: A swap is a derivative, where two counterparties exchange one stream of cash flows against another stream. These streams are called the legs of the swap. The cash flows are calculated over a notional principal amount. Swaps are often used to hedge certain risks, for instance interest rate risk. Swaps are over-the-counter (OTC) derivatives. This means that they are negotiated outside exchanges and they cannot be bought and sold like securities or **futures contracts.**

The two commonly used swaps are:

- **Interest rate swaps**: These entail swapping only the interest related cash flows between the parties in the same currency.
- **Currency swaps:** These entail swapping both principal and interest between the parties, with the cash flows in one direction being in a different currency than those in the opposite direction.
- **Swaption:** Swaption are options to buy or sell a swap that will become operative at the expiry of the options. Thus a swaption is an option on a forward swap.

2.13.2 Need for derivative markets

- The derivative market helps to transfer risks from those who have them but may not like them to those who have an appetite for them.
- Prices of an organized derivative market reflect the perception of market participants about the future and lead the prices of underlying to the perceived future level.

- Derivative markets helps in discovering the future as well as current prices.

With the introduction of derivatives, the underlying market witnesses higher trading volumes because of participation by more players who would not otherwise participate for lack of arrangement to transfer risk.

- Derivatives facilitate investment and arbitrage strategies that straddle market segments.
- It helps to increase asset substitutability, both domestically and internationally.
- It helps to improve liquidity
- It helps to facilitate the creation of pay off characteristics at a lower cost that would result from the acquisition of underlying assets.
- Derivative markets help increase savings and investment in the long run. The transfer of risk enables market participants to expand their volume of activity.
- Derivative trading act as a catalyst for new entrepreneurial activity. Derivatives have a history of attracting many bright, creative and well educated people with an entrepreneurial attitude.

2.13.3 Risks involved in derivatives market

There are several risks inherent in financial transactions. Derivatives are used to separate risks from traditional instruments and transfer these risks to parties willing to bear these risks. The fundamental risks involved in derivative business include:

Credit Risk

This is the risk of failure of counterparty to perform its obligation as per the contract. Also known as default or counterparty risk, it differs with different instruments.

Market Risk

Market risk is a risk of financial loss as a result of adverse movements of prices of the underlying asset/ instrument.

Liquidity Risk

The inability of a firm to arrange a transaction at prevailing market prices is termed as liquidity risk. A firm faces two types of liquidity risks

- Related to liquidity of separate products
- Related to the funding of activities of the firm including derivatives.

Legal Risk

Derivatives cut across judicial boundaries, therefore the legal aspects associated with the deal should be looked into carefully.

Operating Risk : it involves errors, omissions, loss of important documents, frauds, forgeries, delays in settlement, loss of dividends and other corporate actions etc.

2.13.4 Participants in the Derivative Markets

- **Hedgers** : Operators, who want to transfer a risk component of their portfolio. Hedgers face risk associated with the price of an asset. They use the futures or options markets to reduce or eliminate this risk. example: farmers.

- **Speculators** : Operators, who intentionally take the risk from hedgers in pursuit of profit. Speculators are participants who wish to bet on future movements in the price of an asset. Futures and option contracts can give them leverage, by putting in small amounts of money upfront, they can take large positions on the market. As a result of this leveraged speculative position, they increase the potential for large gains as well as losses.
- **Arbitrageurs :** Operators who operate in the different markets simultaneously, in pursuit of profit and eliminate mis-pricing. If for example, they see the futures price of an asset getting out of line with the cash price, they would take offsetting positions in the two markets to lock in the profit.
- **Day traders :** Day traders are speculators who take positions in futures or options contracts and liquidate them prior to the close of the same trading day.
- **Floor trader :** A floor trader is an exchange member or employee, who executes trade by being personally present in the trading ring or pit and they have no place in electronic trading system.
- **Market maker :** A market maker is a trader, who simultaneously quotes both bid and offer price for a same commodity throughout the trading session.

There are two distinct groups of derivative contracts, which are distinguished by the way they are traded in market:

Over-the-counter (OTC) derivatives are contracts that are traded (and privately negotiated) directly between two parties, without going through an exchange or other intermediary. Products such as swaps, forward rate agreements, and exotic options are almost always traded in OTC from Exchange-traded derivatives are those derivatives products that are traded via specialized Derivatives exchanges or other exchanges. A derivatives exchange acts as an intermediary to all related transactions, and takes Initial margin from both sides of the trade to act as a guarantee. Products like futures, options etc. are traded on exchanges.

2.13.5 Risk Management via Derivatives

Derivatives can be used to transfer risk by taking the opposite position in the derivative (futures) market against the underlying assets. Derivatives are used both by speculators and hedgers. Speculators may trade with other speculators as well as with hedgers. In most financial derivatives markets, the value of speculative trading is far higher than the value of true hedge trading. As well as outright speculation, derivatives traders may also look for arbitrage opportunities between different derivatives on identical or closely related underlying securities. Other uses of derivatives are to gain an economic exposure to an underlying security in situations where direct ownership of the underlying security is too costly or is prohibited by legal or regulatory restrictions, or to create a synthetic short position. In addition to directional plays (i.e. simply betting on the direction of the underlying security), speculators can use derivatives to place bets on the volatility of the underlying security. This technique is commonly used when speculating with traded options.

Let us look at some examples of risk management using financial derivatives.

Short Hedge Using Options

A short hedge in the options market is referred to as the purchasing of a put option. Entering into (short) hedge in the options market can reduce the price risk associated with selling an output/asset that will arise in future. For example, a producer knows he will be selling the output three months from now but is afraid of prices. He can enter the options market and partially off-set any loss in value (decrease in price) with a gain in option value.

Short Hedge Example with Futures

One can enter the futures market and off-set any loss in value (decrease in price) with a gain in the futures market. So the price can be locked in advance.

Long Hedge Example with Options

A long hedge in the options market is accomplished by purchasing a call option. For example, a manufacturer needs to buy raw material two months from now. It can enter the options market and partially off-set any loss in value (increase in price) with a gain in the options value.

Hedging via Options vs. Futures

Options provide market players with a powerful strategy to protect themselves from the potential negative affects of market fluctuations. Despite being expensive or risky, options serve as a cost effective and economical practice to hedge against market exposures. In contrast, the buying or selling futures or forwards is bit inflexible way of dealing with a dynamic and ever-changing market because they lock the price. Options offer flexibility and can be tailored to provide payoffs that match end users' exposures more closely, and also suit their tolerance to risk, mirror corporate policy as well as satisfy their accounting and compliance requirements. Additionally, options can reflect users' general outlook on the market. They can enable users to benefit from a favorable market move while being fully hedged against an undesired market fluctuation. All this can be done cost effectively and, frequently, at a lower final cost than using forwards.

Managing Interest Rate Risk with Derivatives

An important business risks for corporations is unexpected fluctuation in the cost of funding the company's operations through debt financing - borrowing from bank or corporate bonds. The company may want to benefit falling interest rates and likely to hedge against higher interest rates. This can be done through an interest rate swap whereby the company can swap fixed to floating or floating top fixed rate.

Another popular interest rate derivative used by companies to manage the cost of their debt capital is the interest rate cap option. In buying an interest rate cap, the corporation limits its debt service cost while retaining some of the benefit of potential falling interest rates.

2.13.6 Derivatives as Tools of Risk Management

Relation between the values of derivatives and their underlying assets.

When the values of underlying assets change, so do the values of derivatives based on them. For some derivative instruments such as swaps and futures, the relation between the underlying assets and the instrument is straight forward i.e. if the product price changes the instrument price also changes. In a currency future contract, the price to be paid when the currency delivered will be fixed by the future contract, the value of the currency delivered will fluctuate depending on the movements of the underling currency. Thus, the value of the future contract depends on the value of the underlying currency. The relation between values of the underlying asset and option are more complicated, but the values of the option and underlying assets are still be related. Due to this unique quality the derivatives appear similar to real commodities for many traders.

It is easier to take short position in derivatives than in other assets : As all transactions in derivatives take place in future specific dates it is easy for the investor to sell the underlying assets i.e. in an asset if he is obligated to deliver the asset in future. The short position means taking stand for selling the underlying asset, with or without possessing the asset he can take view of the market or product which is not possible in any other asset.

Exchange traded derivatives are liquid and have low transaction cost : Exchange traded derivatives are more liquid and have lower transaction costs than other assets. They are more liquid because they have standardized terms and low credit risk. Furthermore, their transaction costs are low due to high volume in trade and due to high competition. In addition, margin requirement in the exchange traded derivatives is relatively low, which reflects that the risk associated with this instrument is low.

It is possible to construct portfolio, which is exactly needed, without having the underlying assets: Derivatives can be constructed or combined to closely match specific portfolio requirement. For example, suppose a firm with a floating-rate loan needs to limit its exposure to sharp increases in the interest rate. The firm can purchase a derivative called an interest rate cap. This derivative pays the firm the difference between the floating rate of interest and a predetermined maximum called the cap rate whenever the floating rate exceeds the cap. Similarly, the lender can protect the decrease in the interest rate by buying the floor.

The derivative product seller pays the lender the difference between a predetermined maximum rate called the floor rate whenever the floating rate falls below the floor rate.

Key Terms

- Risk Analysis
- Risk Transfer
- Self-insurance
- Risk Retention
- Risk Identification
- Forwards
- Swaps
- Short and Long Positions
- Hedging
- Demand Based Pricing
- Idea Generation
- Classification of Products
- Concept testing
- Risk Control
- Pure Risk
- Risk Financing
- RMIS
- Diversification
- Futures
- Hedging
- Speculation
- Product Design
- Product Development
- Market Analysis
- Intermediaries
- Competition based pricing

Questions for Review

1. A risk manager stated "If a risk is to be properly controlled, it must be perceived, and it must be appreciated in terms of probable frequency and possible severity." The writers went on to give two examples as follows:
   (*a*) A company brings together in two airplane flights nearly all of its dealers and distributors from a certain country.
   (*b*) Another company makes a special contract with the government of a foreign country to set up a factory in that country. Special machinery is to be sent by ship and customs duty is to be waived if the machinery arrives by a certain date.

   For each of these situations, indicate the potential loss exposure for the company.
2. What data would be most helpful to include in a risk management information system designed particularly for an automobile manufacturers? How might the RMIS requirement for such a firm differ from those of an amusement theme park? Explain.
3. List and explain three desirable risk management goals likely to be found in risk management and control process.
4. What are the steps in developing a risk management plan? Why is the order of the steps important? Which step is the most difficult to accomplish.

5. Explain how does enterprise risk management process differs from traditional form of risk management.
6. Define a captive insurer and explain why captive insurers are formed.
7. Explain the basic factor that a risk manager must consider if commercial insurance is used in a risk management programme? List and explain the three main category of loss control activities.
8. Distinguish between (a) forwards and futures and (b) options and futures.
9. Briefly explain the various types of derivatives. How derivatives can be used as effective tools of risk management.
10. Briefly explain the new product development process. Do you think that pricing is an integral part of product development?
11. List the major areas of concern for insurers in India with reference to product development and customisation.

Suggested Readings

1. Emett Vaughan and Therese Vaughan, *Essentials of Risk Management and Insurance*, John Wiley and Sons Inc., 2002.
2. G.E. Rejda, *Principles of Risk Management and Insurance*, Pearson Education Inc. 2002.
3. Kenneth A. Froot, *The Financing of Catastrophic Risk*, The University of Chicago Press, 1999.
4. Robert I. Mehr, *Fundamentals of Insurance*, Irwin, 1986.
5. Scott E. Harrington and Gregory R. Niehaus, *Insurance and Risk Management*, IRWIN/McGraw-Hill, 1999.
6. Kolb Robert W.(2000), *Futures, Options, and Swaps*, Blackwell Publishers.
7. Hull John C. (2003), *Options, Futures, and Other Derivatives*, Pearson Education.
8. D.C. Srivastava, *et. al. Indian Insurance Industry — Transition and Prospects*, New Century Publication.

Web Resources

- www.erisks.com
- www.insure-magic.com
- www.sra.org
- www.rmis.org
- www.aria.org

Enterprise Risk Management

Chapter **3**

CHAPTER OBJECTIVES

After reading this chapter you will be able to understand :

- *ERM Basics*
- *Identifying Risk Exposures*
- *Emerging Role of CRO*
- *ERM in Insurance*

3.1 ERM BASICS

The recent development in technologies and growing need for globalisation has made an imperative for corporations to come out from labelled boxes of "bit-by-bit" risk management. The journey of corporate risk management has witnessed significant improvements in the last few decades viz., credit risk management in 1970s, financial risk management in 1980s and a primitive form of ERM in 1990s. In the last couple of years, enterprise-wide-risk management has acquired a wholistic view of the total risk management exercise in corporations focused on core business processes with more sophisticated analytical tools and risk management technologies. ERM is a step towards a more defined and formalised risk management.

"ERM, as its name suggests, can be a daunty undertaking requiring a significant commitment of resources, resulting in inevitable managerial conflict within an organisation, at times, introducing new uncertainties and risk leading to the ultimate transformation of a firm's entire business decision-making process."[1]

ERM is differentiated from "Hazard Risk Management" by addressing the strategic, operational and financial risks.

Most of the authors on the subject believe that managerial decision making based on 'integrated approach' is bound to be better than the piecemeal style/approach.

More and more companies are now creating position in a global marketplace. A few internet symposia suggests that a major chunk of the CRO on a global basis are concentrated to financial institutions followed by energy and utility companies while implements ERM some of the key issues which may merge are:

(a) What is the present perception and understanding of the risk management by corporate executives?

(b) Has the organisation practicing traditional models and to what extent they have been successful?

(c) What is the state of relationships rivalry/co-operation between the organisational risk managers?

(d) What solution ERM can offer?

(e) Can ERM seriously affect the business and organisational style?

(f) What infrastructure may be required to implement ERM and its affordability to the organisation?

An important thing to be kept in mind about ERM is that it intensifies the risk management activities through corn relationships risk evaluation but it is not exhaustive and ERM, too, may be risky.

1. David R. Koenig, *An Introduction to ERM – Beyond the Black marble,* Global CEO, ICFAI Press, 2003, p. 7.

3.2 COSO FRAMEWORK FOR ERM

Enterprise risk management is a process, effected by an entity's board of directors, management and other personnel, applied in strategy setting and across the enterprise, designed to identify potential events that may affect the entity, and manage risk to be within its risk appetite, to provide reasonable assurance regarding the *achievement of entity objectives.*

The underlying premise of enterprise risk management is that every entity exists to provide value for its stakeholders. All entities face uncertainty, and the challenge for management is to determine how much uncertainty to accept as it strives to grow stakeholder value. Uncertainty presents both risk and opportunity, with the potential to erode or enhance value. Enterprise risk management enables management to effectively deal with uncertainty and associated risk and opportunity, enhancing the capacity to build value. Value is maximized when management sets strategy and objectives to strike an optimal balance between growth and return goals and related risks, and efficiently and effectively deploys resources in pursuit of the entity's objectives. Enterprise risk management encompasses:

- *Aligning risk appetite and strategy* – Management considers the entity's risk appetite in evaluating strategic alternatives, setting related objectives, and developing mechanisms to manage related risks.
- *Enhancing risk response decisions* – Enterprise risk management provides the rigor to identify and select among alternative risk responses – risk avoidance, reduction, sharing, and acceptance.
- *Reducing operational surprises and losses* – Entities gain enhanced capability to identify potential events and establish responses, reducing surprises and associated costs or losses.
- *Identifying and managing multiple and cross-enterprise risks* – Every enterprise faces a myriad of risks affecting different parts of the organization, and enterprise risk management facilitates effective response to the interrelated impacts, and integrated responses to multiple risks.
- *Seizing opportunities* – By considering a full range of potential events, management is positioned to identify and proactively realize opportunities.
- *Improving deployment of capital* – Obtaining robust risk information allows management to effectively assess overall capital needs and enhance capital allocation.

These capabilities inherent in enterprise risk management help management achieve the entity's performance and profitability targets and prevent loss of resources. Enterprise risk management helps ensure effective reporting and compliance with laws and regulations, and helps avoid damage to the entity's reputation and associated consequences. In sum, enterprise risk management helps an entity get to where it wants to go and avoid pitfalls and surprises along the way.

Components of Enterprise Risk Management

Enterprise risk management consists of eight interrelated components. These are derived from the way management runs an enterprise and are integrated with the management process. These components are:

- *Internal Environment* – The internal environment encompasses the tone of an organization, and sets the basis for how risk is viewed and addressed by an entity's people, including risk management philosophy and risk appetite, integrity and ethical values, and the environment in which they operate.
- *Objective Setting* – Objectives must exist before management can identify potential events affecting their achievement. Enterprise risk management ensures that Executive Summary management has in place a process to set objectives and that the chosen objectives support and align with the entity's mission and are consistent with its risk appetite.

- *Event Identification* – Internal and external events affecting achievement of an entity's objectives must be identified, distinguishing between risks and opportunities.

Opportunities are channeled back to management's strategy or objective-setting processes.

- *Risk Assessment* – Risks are analyzed, considering likelihood and impact, as a basis for determining how they should be managed. Risks are assessed on an inherent and a residual basis.
- *Risk Response* – Management selects risk responses – avoiding, accepting, reducing, or sharing risk – developing a set of actions to align risks with the entity's risk tolerances and risk appetite.
- *Control Activities* – Policies and procedures are established and implemented to help ensure the risk responses are effectively carried out.
- *Information and Communication* – Relevant information is identified, captured, and communicated in a form and timeframe that enable people to carry out their responsibilities. Effective communication also occurs in a broader sense, flowing down, across, and up the entity.
- *Monitoring* – The entirety of enterprise risk management is monitored and modifications made as necessary. Monitoring is accomplished through ongoing management activities, separate evaluations, or both.

Enterprise risk management deals with risks and opportunities affecting value creation or preservation, defined as follows:

3.3 Identifying Risk Exposures

A corporation may be exposed to various types of risks depending upon the nature of business (Exhibit 3-A). However, popular identifiable categories of these risks are:

Exhibit 3-A
RISK EXPOSURES

Market place risk	♦ Changing markets ♦ Evolving product lines ♦ New operations ♦ Increasing customer expectations ♦ De-regulations ♦ Effects of globalization
Operational risks	♦ Technology ♦ Human Resources ♦ Property ♦ Legal and Liability
Financial risks	♦ Capital management ♦ Asset-Liability management related ♦ Tax related
International risks	♦ Economic ♦ Political ♦ Cultural ♦ Demographic
M & A risks	♦ Strategic failures ♦ Integration issues ♦ Operational exposures

Source: Global CEO, ICFAI Press Special Issue, 2003, p. 20.

Identification of risk can be carried out by using the following methods:

(a) *Environmental Assessment :* Using the knowledge of the organisations operation, considering the probable changes in the environment to identify possible consequences.

(b) *Exposure Assessment :* Using the knowledge of the organisation's resources, considering the possible consequences to the assets based on: size or value, Type (Financial, Physical, Human, Intangible/Information Assets), Portability/Accessibility and location.

(c) *Threat Scenarios :* Defining the difficult-to-measure low-probability and high consequence events such as natural disasters, sabotage, terrorism and fraud.

Exhibit 3-B

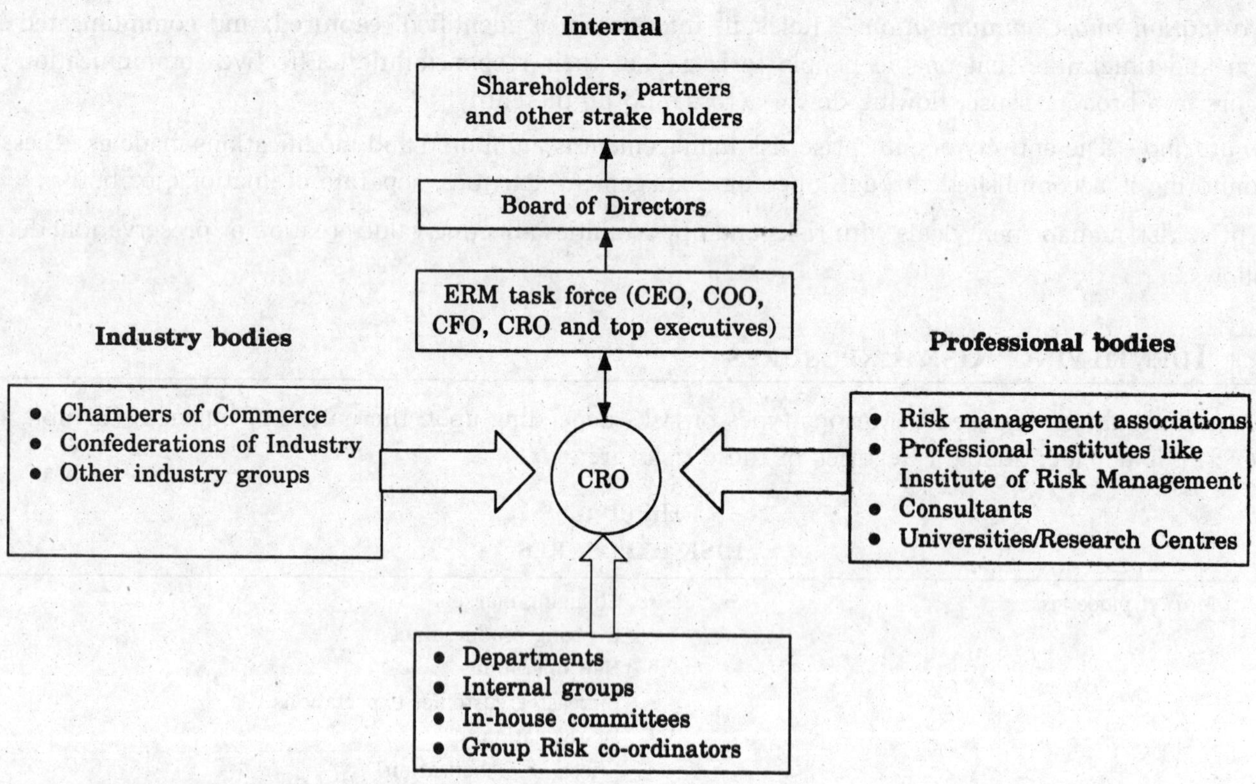

Source: Global CEO, February 2003, ICFAI Press.

3.4 EMERGING ROLE OF CRO

Traditionally, the financial managers in the Indian companies assumed the role of "Risk Officer" whose main attention was polarized towards financial risks. Alternatively, the general management bosses were too focused on operational risks. The approach was therefore component-wise risk management. This has resulted in mass failures of substantial number of organisation. It is only that in last few couple of years, the need has felt in most of the business organisations to more towards an "integrated approach" to risk management. This has forced companies to assign specific tasks to the so called "Chief Risk Officer" to play a critical role in the management of strategic and operations risks of enterprises. The role of CRO is multiface including the following:

(1) Establishment of Risk Management Information Systems (RMIS)

(2) Building up of Risk Information database.

(3) Communication of Risk Management Strategy to various levels of management.

(4) Training of the key participants in the ERM.

(5) Continuous evaluation of ERM philosophy.

The following exhibit depicts the position of a CRO with various interaction at different levels with internal and external bodies/organisation (Exhibit 3-B). CRO must strive to provide a unification of the viewpoints of the various people in different departments of the organisation. "He acts as a facilitator, administrator, of the risk management program, an educator, owner of the risk management manual and a one point contact for everyone in the organization from the board to the lowest decision maker on matters pertaining to risk. He reviews risk documentation and reports prepared by different groups in the organisation and ensures uniformity in documentation and reporting." He should try to balance the risk attitudes of the various concerned parties. None the less, he should continuously review the RMIS and communicate to the various stakeholders.

3·5 ERM in Insurance

The recent catastrophes including September 11 have seriously affected the insurance industry. Though the industry survived, the fate of various insurers is in doldrums. These catastrophes have raised concerns whether the insurance industry full prepared to face disasters. The issue is that what type of approach is needed? Suggestively, ERM is one of the best approach to tackle the catastrophic affects. ERM can be effective tool for insurance companies in the following areas:

(a) *Management of Exposures* : ERM can help insures in identifying the "cross silo" effects in advance and mitigate them. e.g., a catastrophe or a natural disaster may affect several times of insurance, the primary and reinsurance sectors, the underwriting operations and also the investment operations, because of declining security prices. These interdependencies can be beautifully identified and managed through EWRM.

(b) *Scenario Analysis* : ERM can effectively be utilized to manage extreme events through sophisticated modelling techniques. It may effectively ensure solution to catastrophic problems through worst-case analysis.

(c) *Disaster Response* : "On the financial side, ERM based structural simulation modelling allows insurers to quickly evaluate alternative financial responses to a disaster, whether the event creates a short-term emergency that requires an immediate infusion of capital or whether it creates a short-term opportunity, such as capital restructuring.[2] Accordingly the insurers can assess the capital needs and modelling can suggest the investment strategies so as to save the company from being ruined.

(d) *ALM* : ERM models can help insures companies to optimize Asset Liability Management (ALM) and achieve their twin objectives of solvency and profitability.

(e) *Relationship Management* : ERM lies at the heart of the core business processes and essentially involves communication/continuous interaction with various stakeholders – the regulators, the owners and the analysts.

Key Terms

- ❒ ERM
- ❒ Risk Exposures
- ❒ Integrated Risk Management
- ❒ CRO
- ❒ EWRM

2. Jarry Miccolis, ERM and September 11, *Treasury Management,* ICFAI Press, January 2002, pp. 55-58.

Questions

1. Define ERM. Explain the rationale for implantation of ERM in the current scenario.
2. Write short notes on:
   (a) Integrated Risk Management
   (b) Role of Chief Risk Officer
   (c) ERM in Insurance

Suggested Readings

1. *Treasury Management,* ICAI Press, January 2002.
2. *Global CEO,* ICFAI Press, Special Issue, 2003.
3. A.V. Vedapuriswar, *Enterprise Risk Management. A Strategic Approach to Derisking an Enterprise,* Vision Books, 2003.
4. James Lam, *Enterprise Risk Management: From Incentives to Controls,* Wiley, 2003.

Web Resources

- www.erm.com
- www.erisk.com
- www.rmis.com
- www.gartner.com

Introduction to Insurance

Chapter 4

CHAPTER OBJECTIVES

After reading this chapter you will be able to understand :

- *Definition of Insurance*
- *Costs and Benefits of Insurance*
- *Elements of an Insurable Risk*
- *Principles of Insurance*
- *Kinds of Insurance*

4.1 DEFINITION OF INSURANCE

The term "insurance" can be defined in both financial and legal terms. The financial definition focuses on an arrangement that redistributes the cost of unexpected losses. That is, the collection of a small premium payment from all exposed and distributed to those suffering loss. The legal definition focuses on a contractual arrangement whereby one party agrees to compensate another party for losses. The financial definition provides for the funding of the losses whereas the legal definition provides for the legally enforceable contract that spells out the legal rights, duties and obligations of all the parties to the contract. Let us have a look at these definitions.

In Financial Sense

Insurance is a social device in which a group of individuals (insureds) transfer risk to another party (insurer) in order to combine loss experience, which permits statistical prediction of losses and provides for payment of losses from funds contributed (premiums) by all members who transferred risk.

In Legal Sense

A contract of insurance is a contract by which one party in consideration of the price paid to him proportionate to the risk provides security to the other party that he shall not suffer loss, damage or prejudice by the happening of certain specified events. Insurance is meant to protect the insured against uncertain events which may cause disadvantage to him. Life insurance however is a distinctive type of insurance where there is certainty of the payment of a specified amount either on the death of the insured or on the maturity of the policy whichever is earlier.[1]

4.2 COSTS AND BENEFITS OF INSURANCE

The purpose of insurance mode of risk transfer is to provide economic protection against the losses that may be incurred but to chance events such as — (a) death, (b) disability, (c) economic losses. One party (the insurer) for a set amount of money, (premium) agrees to pay the other party (insured or beneficiary), a sum of money (benefit) upon the occurrence of an event which may or may not occur. Insurance provides economic protection against losses that may be incurred due to chance events that may or may not occur during the effective time of the contract called a policy. The insurance of business organisations is essential in the sense that adverse

1. *Insurance Laws and Practice,* Vidhi Publications, 2002, p. 2.1.

events, if not guarded, may affect — the business itself, the business owner or owner's personal property and may also threaten the continued operation of the business and threaten the owner's financial well-being.

Insurance Device

The fundamental characteristics of insurance are:

(a) It involves transfer of risk from the individual to the group, and

(b) There is a sharing (pooling) of losses on some equitable basis such that fortuitous losses will be indemnified (paid).

More specifically, the cost and benefits of insurance are:

Benefits

- Reimbursement for losses
- Reduction in tension and fear
- Avenue for investment — life insurance investment officer attractive return.
- Prevention of losses
- Credit multiplication
- Costs of Insurance to Society
- Cost of Business operations — Social wastage of resources
- Fraudulent and exaggerated claims — Malacious and undesirable transfer of wealth.

4.3 ELEMENTS OF AN INSURABLE RISK

For pure risk to be insurable, it should posess the following characteristics :

Large Numbers of Exposure Units

The theory of insurance is based on law of large numbers. Therefore the prime necessity for a rise to be insurable is that there must be a sufficiently large number of homogenous exposure in order that losses are reasonable predictable. Also, the probabilistic estimates used by the insurance company, by logic, assume large number of units in a distribution and insurance products are priced accordingly.

Define and Measurable (Calculable) Loss

The losses are fairly predictable and can be measured in money terms. Loss of peace of mind, tension etc. or loss of life cannot be indemnified.

Determinable Probability Distribution

The probability distribution of the happening of adverse event is determinable. This condition is necessary to establish the free premium according to the theory of equivalence. If there is not determinable distribution, there is no question of issuing a cover by an insurance company.

Random (Fortuitous) Loss

The adverse event may or may not occur in future and once which the insurance company has not control. Naturally, if the event is non-random or the loss has occurred in the past, there is no question of insurance.

Also, it is important to note that randomness is ensured by underwriters who guard against adverse selection—the tendency of the poorer than average insured to seek or continue insurance coverage.

Non-catastrophic Loss

The losses should be non-catastrophic. Not all the units in a homogenous group will be subject to an adverse event. Recall that if all the units meet losses, the company will be ruined only few out of a large group will be exposed.

Premium should be Economically Feasible

Since, the insurance pool is structured to be sufficiently large, the price charged by the insurer for buying the risk is generally low. It should be sufficient to cause the rich for the insurer as well as viable for the insured.

Insurance Versus Gambling

If gambling events were insurable, the gambler would be put in the enviable position of being unable to lose because if it is head, he wins else if fails, he collects the money from insurance company. Since, the insurance premium must include the charge for the losses and the expenses of operating the insurance pool, the resulting premium must be more than the mathematically fair value of the potential loss. Moreover, the gambler presumably enjoys the risk of gambling and therefore would be unlikely to pay the premium needed for transferring the risk being enjoyed. Law prohibits the use of insurance for gambling purposes because fraud and murder would increase thus making a social device prohibitively expensive and therefore making the system fail. In summary, the gambling can be distinguished from an insurance contract in the following ways:

(a) Gambling creates risk while insurance transfers an existing risk.

(b) Gambling deals with speculative risk — there might be gains or losses, while Insurance deals with pure risk.

4.4 Insurance as a Macro-economic Issue

Insurers can promote efficiency in the financial system as follows:

(1) Mobilisation of Scattered Resources : The money collected from the scattered and distant policyholders by way of premium is pooled and invested in projects which would otherwise have not been possible. This reduces the transaction cost of financing and eases the pressure on other financial intermediaries.

(2) Creation of Liquidity : Instead of policyholders directly landing their money to entrepreneurs and projects, the money is lent on their behalf by the insurance company. This creates liquidity in the system and in case the adverse event occurs, money is immediately paid to the insured without time lags.

(3) Economies of Scale : The bulk funds invested in large and infrastructure projects promote economies of scale, promoter economic development and growth and other technological innovation.

Insurance and GDP

The relationship between the insurance density and GDP is direct. Insurance density varies directly with GDP.

Insurance and Income Redistribution

Life insurance essential serves to transfer funds from currently employed persons via. premium payments to unemployed persons, and thereby helps alleviate the problem of economic distress. Insurance proceeds on an important element in the economic well-being of dependents Government-sponsored insurance programmes strive to comprehensive achieve social goals while private programme provide attractive alternative to public welfare system.

Inflation, Business Cycles and Insurance

Inflation and business recessions directly reduces the real purchasing power and network of the people respectively. Insurance can provide a cover to these, yet the negative side is the adverse impact on the financial performance of companies.

Population Changes and Insurance

Population changes materially affects the insurance industry because of the economic consequences of changing rates of birth, death, marriage and family formation. The shifting age distribution affects the kinds and amount of insurance the people will buy.

Fiscal Policy

Fiscal Policy affects in Insurance sector in the following form:

(1) Government spending
(2) Taxation
(3) Direct Controls on the business systems
(4) Moral Suasion (assistance).

4.5 Kinds of Insurance

The commonly known insurance covers can be categorised as follows:

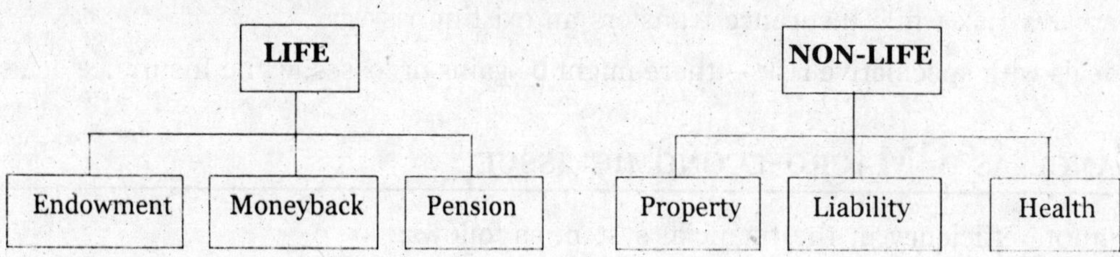

NON-LIFE INSURANCE

Property

Personal and business property insurance that covers risks against fire, marine, theft and burglary. The types of insurance under this category are:

- Home Insurance/Domestic cover
- Business insurance
- Commercial Insurance

Liability

This protects the insured against injury or damage claims made by a third party. The types of insurance under this category are:

- Automobile insurance
- Workers compensation
- Liability insurance
- Aviation insurance

Health

In case of an illness or injury suffered by the insured or his/her dependents, health insurance covers their medical expenses incurred. The types of insurance under this category are: (a) Hospital Insurance and (b) Medical cover.

Few examples of general (Non Life) insurance policies are:

Health

- Medi claim policy
- Personal accident-individual
- Personal accident-family
- Group accident insurance
- Jan arogya bima policy
- Bhavishya arogya policy
- Traffic accident policy

Business

- Burglary insurance for Business premises
- Shopkeepers' Insurance Policy
- Key-man Insurance
- Partnership Insurance
- Workmen's Compensation Insurance
- Fidelity Guarantee Insurance
- Professional Indemnity Insurance
- Machinery Breakdown Policy
- Boiler Explosion Insurance Policy
- Contractor's Plant & Machinery Insurance Policy
- Contractor's All Risks Policy
- Industrial All Risks Policy
- Air Transit Insurance Policy
- Inland Transit Insurance Policy
- Loss of Stock in Cold Storage Insurance Policy
- Product's Liability Insurance

Fire Insurance

- Fire Insurance policy
- Fire consequential loss policy

Travel

- Overseas Mediclaim Policy
- Videsh Yatra Mitra
- Baggage Insurance Policy
- Executive Travel Insurance
- Suhana Safar

General Insurance

- Money insurance
- Television Insurance Policy
- Pager Insurance Policy
- Mobile Phone Insurance

LIFE-INSURANCE

Life Insurance products can be broadly divided into 9 categories, which include disabled, money back, pension women, girl-child, couple, endowments, whole life and child insurance.

Money Back

- Jeevan Sanchay
- Money back with profits policy
- Jeevan surabhi

Pension

- New Jeevan Dhara
- Jeevan Suraksha with life-cover
- Jeevan Suraksha without life-cover plan
- Jeevan Suraksha Endowment plan

Women, Girl child and Couple

- Jeevan Saathi-for married couples
- Jeevan Saritha-for married couples
- Jeevan Sneha-for woman only
- Jeevan Sukanya-for the girl child

Endowment

- Jeevan Shree
- Endowment Policy without profits
- Endowment Policy with profits
- Limited payment endowments with profit
- Jeevan Mitra
- Jeevan Mitra-triple cover
- Bima Kiran
- Jeevan Ariha

Whole Life

- Whole life policy with profits
- Limited payment whole life
- Convertible whole life

Child Insurance Policy

- Jeevan Kishore
- Children's deferred Assurance Plan
- New children's deferred Assurance Plans
- Bal Vidya

Key Terms

❒ Contribution	❒ Subrogation
❒ Indemnity	❒ Fortuitous
❒ Catastrophic	❒ Insurable Risk
❒ Gambling	❒ Assurance

Questions for Review

1. Define insurance. Briefly explain the costs and benefits of insurance.
2. List the various life and non-life insurance covers available in India.
3. Write short notes on:
   (1) Principle of Subrogation
   (2) Principle of Contribution
4. Distinguish between assurance and insurance in view of principle of indemnity.

Suggested Readings

1. Douglas Caddy, *Legislative Trends in Insurance Regulation*, Texas A&M University Press, 1986.
2. Fredricke G.Crane, *Insurance Principles and Practice,* John Wiley, 1980.
3. H.L. Muller-Lutz, *Basic Principles of Insurance Management*, International Insurance Mnitor, N.Y. 1966.
4. H.S. Dennenberg, R.D. Elers, J.J. Melone and R.A. Zetten, *Insurance Concepts — Basic and Legal,* Prentice-Hall, Englewood Cliffs, 1974.
5. Jorg Finsinger and Mark V. Pauly, *The Economics of Insurance Regulation,* Macmillan Press Ltd., 1986.
6. R.A. Blanchard, *Risk and Insurance and other Papers,* 1965.
7. G.E. Rejda, *Insurance and Risk Management,* Pearson Education, 2002.

Web Resources

- www.insure.com
- www.fool.com
- insurance.yahoo.com
- www.montana.edu
- www.bimaonline.com

Principles of Insurance

Chapter 5

Chapter Objectives

After reading this chapter you will be able to understand :

- *Principles of Insurance and their applications Related concepts and corollaries.*

5.1 Principles of Insurance

Principle of Indemnity

The principle of indemnity implies that *on the happening of an event insured against, the Insured will be placed by the insurer in the same pecuniary (monetary) position that he/she occupied immediately before the event. Indemnity means that the insured person is placed, financially, in the same position, as he was before the loss.*

Indemnity does not imply that the insured will be indemnified to the full falue of his loss e.g. a person whose factory is destroyed by fire cannot recover for loss of profits or against any liability that may arise from the fire unless he has appropriate policies in place specifically designed to deal with these losses.

Indemnity can be achieved through the following methods :

1. Cash
2. Reinstatement e.g. where a building is destroyed, insurers may reinstate it.
3. Repair e.g. where a motor vehicle is partially damaged.
4. Replacement-instead of paying cash a replacement item may be tendered.
5. New for old-used for household contents. This is not a violation of the principle of indemnity as there is no principle of law aht requires indemnity to be determined in terms of the market value of the asset.
6. Valued policies-in terms of which the insurer and the insured agree before hand on the value to be paid sentimental rather than a commercial value e.g. jewellery works of art etc.

The non-life insurance covers viz. Property and Liability are basically contracts of indemnity. However, the indemnity must not be construed as an instrument to profit. The indemnity goes along with two checks :

(*a*) to prevent the insured from benefiting under the contract

(*b*) to reduce the impact of moral hazards

The exceptions to the application of indemnity are found in Personal Accident Policies, Agreed Value policies in Marine Insurance and valuables and reinstatement policies like in Engineering policies. These are also contracts of indemnity but by a special application of the principle, the measure of indemnity is decided at the time of entering into the contract itself in the event of a claim the insured must :

- prove that he/she has sustained a monetary loss
- prove the extent and value of his/her loss
- prove the extent and value of his/her loss
- transfer any rights which he/she may have for recovery from another source to the Insurer, if he/she has been fully indemnified.

Example

In a valued (marine) policy, if there is damage/loss to the cargo, the claim is limited to the value expressed in the policy cover irrespective of the actual value of the cargo lost or damaged. The settlement of the loss will be subject to (*a*) Sum insured and (*b*) Average (*c*) Excess/Deductible.1

It is important to note that the contract of life insurance is not as such insurance, but it is in the nature of assurance. This is logical in the sense that life can not be indemnified, instead if a person dies, then under the contract of life insurance the sum assured will be paid by the insured.

Utmost Good Faith (Ubrrima Fides)

- Insurance contracts are characterized by information asymmetries between the parties. Generally the insured knows more about the risk to be insured than the insurer. To rectify this imbalance the law compels disclosure of information between the parties.
- To act in good faith entails that parties must deal openly and honestly with each other withoug suppressing material facts that may influence the judgment of the other party.

Under the contract of insurance, the insured is duty bound to disclose all material facts relating to the risk to be covered.

Utmost good faith is a positive duty voluntarily to disclose, accurately and fully, all facts material to the risk being proposed, whether requested or not.

The duly to act in good faith applies to all types of insurance contracts. In contracts of sale the maxim *caveat vendito* applies meaning let the buyer beware. This maxim places an obligation on the boyer to take all reasonable steps to verify that the item he intends to buy meets his expectations. In insurance this maxim does not apply.

A material fact is a fact, which would influence the mind of a prudent underwriter in deciding whether to accept a risk for insurance and on what terms. Both the parties to a contract are expected to observe good faith. However, the good faith assumes utmost importance when Material Facts are concerned and therefore utmost good faith should be observed on matters relating to Material facts. Examples of material facts in various classes of insurance are :

(1) *Motor* : Details of any young drivers

(2) *Household* : Details of any commercial use of private dwelling house

(3) *Commercial :* Previous losses/hazards

(4) *Life :* Details of Heart Diseases

Some facts though material need not be disclosed. Thus the insured has no obligation to disclose the following facts :

1. Any circumstance that diminishes the risk.
2. Any fact known or presumed to be known by the insurer.
3. Facts on which insurers have waived information.

Duty of disclosure applies to both the *Proposer* and the *Insurer.* Duty of disclosure operates at : inception–until the date cover is confirmed by the Insurers renewal–up to the renewal date mid term alterations–until the Insurers confirm cover in respect of the alterations.

The duty of disclosure lasts for the duration of the negotiations and terminates when the contract is concluded. Material facts that come to light after the contract has been concluded are deemed to be part of the risk that the insurer would have assumed.

To avoid liability on grounds of non-disclosure the onus is on the insurer to prove that :

1. The undisclosed facts were material.
2. That the facts were within the actual or presumed knowledge of the insured.
3. That the facts were not communicated to the insurer.

Upon discovering the non-disclosure the insurer must exercise the right to repudiate the contract within a reasonable time.

Breach of utmost good faith is essentially a violation of "Consensus ad idem", a prerequisite for a valid contract. The breach may relate to (*a*) misrepresentation or (*b*) non-representation. Intentional misrepresentation may be termed as fraudulent and the intentional non-disclosure may be termed as concealment of facts. When misrepresentation or non-representation is unintentional, it may be termed as breach of general duty. The utmost good faith is vital from an insurer's perspective. It is important for the insurer to decide about :

(*a*) Acceptance or rejection of a proposal
(*b*) Pricing of the insurance cover
(*c*) Contribution to indemnity
(*d*) Powers of subrogation under the contract
(*e*) Imposition of conditions and warranties.

Subrogation

Subrogation in general, means the legal right of one person, having indemnified the other in a contractual obligation to do so, to stand in the place of another and avail of all the rights and remedies of the another, whether enforced or not.

It entitles the Insurer who has granted an indemnity to receive after payment of a loss the advantage of every right of the Insured. Subrogation condition is a corollary to the principle of Indemnity. A loss may occur accidentally or by the action or negligence of third party (not workmen). The property owners have a right to proceed against the offending third party to recover the loss/damage and also under their insurance policy but not under both. If the insured opts to recover the loss under the insurance policy which is faster and does not involve litigation, he will surrender his rights against the third parties in favour of the insurers signing a 'Letter of subrogation' on an appropriate stamp paper.

An exception to this are life insurance policies wherein insured/beneficiaries can claim under an insurance policy and also proceed against the offending third party.

The insurer must exercise the right of recovery in the name of the Insured (prevents the Insured from obtaining more than one indemnity).

Example

The Insurer of an importer of electrical goods receives a claim in respect of a faulty toaster. The Insurer pays the claim but takes over the insured's rights to claim back against the manufacturer. The insurance company can proceed with this claim in the Insured's name.

Subrogation rights only apply where there is a legal liability under the policy *i.e.,* where policy cover existed and the claims are paid. However, the policy conditions customarily provide for such subrogation rights before the claim payment. However, recovery from third parties can be made only if claim is paid.

Subrogation has a number of sub-principles namely :

- The insurer cannot be subrogated to the insured's right of action until it has paid the insured the made good the loss.

- The insurer can be subrogated only to actions which the insured would have brought himself.
- The insurer must not prejudice the insurer's right of subrogation. Thus the insured may not compromise or renounce any right of action he has against the 3rd party if by doing so he could diminish his loss.
- Subrogation against the insurer. Just as insured cannot profit from his loss the insurer may nto make a profit from the subrogation rights. The insurer is only entitled to recover the exact amount they paid as indemnity nothing more. If they recover more the balance should be given to the insured.
- Subrogatioon gives hte insurer the right of salvage.

Insurable Interest

The Insured must have an insurable interest in the subject matter of insurance, *i.e.*, he/she must benefit by its safety or be prejudiced by its loss.

It is the legal right to insure arising out of financial relationship recognised under law, between the insured and the subject matter of insurance.

Insurable interest distinguishes contracts of insurance from gambling in order to define the legitimate area of insurance business.

Insurance interest is required for all types of insurance and its absence renders the contract void and hence unenforceable.

Insurance contracts without insurable interests have no sanction of the law as they amount to speculation The owner of a property has absolute insurance interest When a person insures a property, what is insured therein, is his interest in that property. By this principle, insurance interest exists to other parties like lessor, lessee, financiers, etc., but their interest is limited to the extent of their financial commitment only. The leading Roman-Dutch law case on insurable interest is *Littlejohn v. Norwich Union Fire Insurance Society 1905 TH 374* where it was held that if the insured can show that he stands to lose something of an appreciable commercial value by the destruction of the thing insured then his interest will be an insurable one. The Court went further to state that as a general rule insurable interest should exist at the time of taking the policy and at the time the loss is incurred.

If a person has insurable interest in an asset at the time of taking the policy but loses the interest thereafter e.g. if he sells the car, the policy ceases to have any validity. The insurable interest must exist both at the time of the proposal and at the time of claims. However, in the case of marine insurance contracts, which are assignable without the consent of the insurers, insurable interest must exist at the time of loss only (Marine insurance contracts are governed by Marine Insurance Act of 1963). Insurable Interest may be created either by :

Obligation to Insure

(*a*) By Statute

(*b*) By Contract

(*c*) By Custom

Option to Insure

(*a*) Owners

(*b*) Mortgagors

(*c*) Lessors

(*d*) Trustees

(*e*) Tenants

Example

Everybody would have an insurable interest in their own personal possessions *e.g.* car, watch. An employee would have no insurable interest in their desk at work but the employer has. A husband has insurable interest in his wife.

Insurable interest can be acquired in various ways notably :

1. Ownership
2. Legal possession
3. Custody of property belonging to others e.g. bailees.
4. Marriage-spouses have an insurable interest in each other's life.
5. A lien-holder has insurable interest in the property subject to the lien.
6. A debt creates insurable interest between debtor and creditor.
7. An employer has an insurable interest in the life of an employee.

In life insurance the general rule is that insurable interest need only exist at the time of taking the policy. Thus if A who is married to B takes a life policy on his life and they later divorce the policy will pay on B's death even if technically insurable interest no longer exists because the parties divorced.

Proximate Cause

It is defined as the active efficient cause that sets into motion a train of events, which bring about a result, without the intervention of any force started and working actively from a new and independent source. Therefore there must be an efficient cause, which brings about a loss with no other intervening cause, which breaks the chain of events. A loss could be due to a cause of causes. In the chain reaction, it is the dominant cause, which would be the proximate cause to be considered for the purpose of a claim. It is always the duty of the insured to prove that the loss arose out of the insured peril, which is proximate.

Example

Firemen remove undamaged stock from a burning building to avoid its involvement in the fire. It is stacked in the open yard and subsequently damaged by rain. Was the proximate cause of the damage the fire or the rain? If the rain damage occurred before the Insured had an opportunity to protect it then the proximate cause of the damage would be the fire. However, if the stock were left unprotected for an unreasonably long period, the rain would be a new and independent cause of damage.

If there are more than one cause operating together and one of the cause is excepted peril, the claim shall not be payable under the policy. However, if the results of the operation of an insured peril can be separated from the excluded peril, the claim shall be payable in respect of insured peril.

Example

During the war period, a bomb was dropped on a factory, which caused fire to the factory. The proximate cause of loss in this case is enemy action and not fire.

In *Etherington v. Lancashire and Yorkshire Accidental Insurance Co. (1909)* a man fell from a horse and sustained injuries that prevented him from moving. As a result he contracted pneumonia due to lying in the wet and died.

The proximate cause of his death was held to be the fall not pneumonia.

Similarly if furniture is thrown out of a burning house to arrest the spread of the fire and its damaged in the process the proximate cause of the damage would be the fire.

If the insured makes a prima-facie case that the loss was proximately caused by an insured peril the insurer is obliged to indemnify unless they can prove that an exception applies.

Contribution

Contribution condition is a corollary to the Principle of indemnity. If an insured obtains more than one policy covering the same risk, he cannot recover the same loss from more than one source so that more than 'Indemnity' does not benefit him. Although the Insured may affect more than one policy to cover the same property or interest, he/she cannot recover in total more than a full indemnity. Contribution condition checks that each policy pays only a rateable portion under each separate policy. Application of contribution principle can arise only when the policies :

- Cover the same peril
- Cover the same subject matter
- Are effected by or on behalf of the same Insured

Example

An insured loses his/her watch on holidays. He/She has holiday insurance and All Risks Cover on his/her household policy. The cost of the claim should be shared under both policies

Example

If an insured has taken three policies from insurers X, Y and Z for Rs. 5,00,000, Rs. 5,00,000 and Rs. 2,00,000 respectively, an the loss to the property due to the operation of the insured peril is Rs. 1,20,000, then the ratio of contribution will be 5 :5 :2 Hence the claim payable by X, Y and Z will be Rs. 50,000, Rs. 50,000 and Rs. 20,000 respectively.

In the same example if the value of the property at the time of loss was Rs. 15,00,000 then the indemnity in respect of X, Y and Z shall be reduced proportionately by the factor {Sum Insured/Actual Value}. Such cases shall be deemed to be cases of under insurance and the under cover shall be construed to *self insured* by the insured. Hence, the losses shall be borne by the parties X, Y, Z and insured as Rs. 16,667, Rs. 16,667, Rs. 6,667 and Rs. 10,000 respectively.

5.2 Related Concepts

Arbitration

When liability under the policy is admitted but the quantum is disputed, the insured cannot rush to a Court of law without first referring the dispute to Arbitration as per 'Indian Arbitration and reconciliation Act–1996'. In keeping with the provisions of the Act, the insured may appoint an arbitrator to be followed by appointment of another arbitrator by the insurers They can also appoint a single arbitrator, to represent both of them. If the two separate arbitrators cannot reach an agreement, both the arbitrators can appoint a third arbitrator called umpire. The award of the Arbitrators is binding on both the parties to the dispute and cannot be challenged unless a point of law is involved. The jurisdiction of Arbitration proceedings is within Indian territory. However, when foreign funding is involved, the financiers who are also joined in the policy as co-insured, may insist upon conducting the Arbitration proceedings in their own country. In such a case, the insurers may agree to modify the arbitration condition suitably.

Average

Average is a concept used by insurers to deal with under-insurance occurs when an item is insured for less than its market value.

In terms of the common law the general rule is that a person who under-insurers his property is entitled to the full amount of his loss whether total or partial subject to the limits of the policy in the absence of any provision in the policy to the contrary *e.g.*, if a house worth Rs. 5000000 is insured for Rs. 300000 and a loss of Rs. 100000 occurs the insured in the absence of an average clause in the policy would be entitled to Rs. 100000. By implication therefore average is an alien concept to the common law.

Reduced to its logical conclusion average entails that if there is under-insurance the insured shall be his own insurer to the extent of the under-insurance. This means the insured will bear part of the loss as a penalty for underinsurance.

Because average is not recognized by the common law its application in insurance is not automatic. Insurer would have to include the average condition in the policy for average to apply.

In marine insurance the term average has a meaning to that ascribed to it in property. Insurance in marine average may mean one of two things :

1. General average sacrifice
2. General average expenditure.

* The formula for average is : Sum insured/Market value × loss sustained.

Average only applies to contracts of indemnity hence since life insurance contracts are not contracts of indemnity all concepts derived from indemnity like subrogation, contribution and average do not apply to life policies.

The rationale behind average is that the insured should pay a premium that is commensurate with the risk he introduces to the pool to avoid prejudicing other contributors.

Key Terms

- ❒ Contribution
- ❒ Indemnity
- ❒ Catastrophic
- ❒ Gambling
- ❒ Subrogation
- ❒ Fortuitous
- ❒ Insurable Risk
- ❒ Assurance

Questions for Review

1. Define insurance. Briefly explain the costs and benefits of insurance.
2. List the various life and non-life insurance covers available in India.
3. Write short notes on:
   (1) Principle of Subrogation
   (2) Principle of Contribution
4. Distinguish between assurance and insurance in view of principle of indemnity.

Suggested Readings

1. Douglas Caddy, *Legislative Trends in Insurance Regulation*, Texas A&M University Press, 1986.
2. Fredricke G.Crane, *Insurance Principles and Practice*, John Wiley, 1980.
3. H.L. Muller-Lutz, *Basic Principles of Insurance Management*, International Insurance Mnitor, N.Y. 1966.
4. H.S. Dennenberg, R.D. Elers, J.J. Melone and R.A. Zetten, *Insurance Concepts — Basic and Legal*, Prentice-Hall, Englewood Cliffs, 1974.
5. Jorg Finsinger and Mark V. Pauly, *The Economics of Insurance Regulation*, Macmillan Press Ltd., 1986.

6. R.A. Blanchard, *Risk and Insurance and other Papers,* 1965.

7. G.E. Rejda, *Insurance and Risk Management,* Pearson Education, 2002.

Web Resources

- www.insure.com
- www.fool.com
- insurance.yahoo.com
- www.montana.edu
- www.bimaonline.com

Mathematical Basis of Insurance

Chapter 6

Chapter Objectives

After reading this chapter you will be able to understand :

- *Probability and its use in Insurance*
- *Dual Application of Law of Large Numbers*
- *Pooling in Insurance*
- *Theories of Risk Management*
- *Mortality Table*
- *Calculation of Life Premium*

The bread and butter of the insurance industry is based on the probability and statistics. Actually speaking, the insurance game is a game of probability. One, who correctly estimates wins, otherwise loses. The Insurance actuaries constantly face a trade off when determining the premium to charge for coverage: the premium must be high enough to cover expected losses and expenses, but low enough to remain competitive with premiums charged by other insurers. Actuaries apply statistical analysis to determine expected loss levels and expected deviations from these loss levels. Through the application of the law of large numbers, insurers reduce their risk of adverse outcomes.

6.1 Probability and its Use in Insurance

The probability of an event refers to the chances of its occurrence of the total set of possible occurrences. For a given pool of automobile covers sold by an insurance company, it is important to find out for the underwriter, what is the chance of occurrence of an automobile accident? If he correctly estimates the probability, the correct cost of bearing the risk i.e. the premium will be charged from the clients, otherwise, if adverse happens the claims may *ruin* the company.

Probability is mathematically defined as follows :

"If an event A can happen in 'm' ways out of 'n' equally likely mutually exclusive and exhaustive ways then the probability that the event will happen is $\frac{m}{n}$." That is, probability is the ratio of the number of favourable outcomes to the total number of possible outcomes.

$$P(A) = \frac{\text{Number of outcome favourable to the event } A}{\text{Total number of possible outcomes}}$$

i.e., $$P = \frac{m}{n}$$

The probability of non-occurrence of the event A is given by

$$q = p\ (\text{not } A)$$

i.e., $$q = \frac{n - m}{n}$$

i.e., $q = 1 - \frac{m}{n}$

i.e., $q = 1 - p.$

In practical life the probabilit lies between the two extremes 0 and 1. When $p = 0$, it denotes impossibility of the event taking place, *i.e.*, the event cannot take place. On the other hand, when $p = 1$, it denotes certainty, *i.e.*, the event is bound to take place. Consider a well-shuffled deck of s_2 cards. When a card is drawn at random any one can come out. Thus there are s_2 possible ways. Out of s_2 cards, 13 cards are of diamond suit. Thus, there are 13 ways favourable for getting a diamond card when a card is drawn. The probability that the card drawn is a diamond is $\frac{13}{52}$ *i.e.*, $\frac{1}{4}$. This means that we have a 25% chance of drawing a diamond card.

A *probability distribution* or a *theoretical frequency distribution* is the distribution of all possible outcomes of a random variable (A random variable is a variable whose outcome is uncertain). For example, suppose a coin is tossed, either there can be head or a tail. The coin was tossed 50 times and the following observations *cumulatively* were noted for 10, 20, 30, 40 and 50 experiments:

No. of Experiments	10	20	30	40	50
Heads	4	9	13	18	24
Tails	6	11	17	22	26
Probability of a head	40%	45%	43.33%	45%	48%

We all know that if we increase the number of trials such that it approaches infinity (¥), the probability of getting a head will be 50%. The logical conclusion which flows from this illustration is that by increasing the number of experiments for a given random variable, *the probability of the occurrence for a given outcome can be accurately estimated and used for decision making.* Risk management decisions need to be made prior to knowing what the actual (realized) outcomes of key variables will be. A manager does not know beforehand which outcomes of random variable affecting the firm's profits will occur. Nevertheless, he or she must make decisions. Once the outcomes are observed, it usual is easy to say what would have been the best decision. However, we cannot evaluate decisions from this perspective, which is why probability distribution are so important. Probability distribution tell us all the possible outcomes and the possible outcomes and the probability of those outcomes. Information about probability distribution is needed to make a good risk management decision.

6.1.1 Probability Distributions

Probability distributions can either be discrete or continuous. A discrete distribution can take limited values which can be listed, however a continuous can take any value within a given range. In insurance we use the three popular variable distributions- the Binomial, the Normal and the Poisson. In each of these distributions, it is assumed that events occur in a random fashion, meaning that the probability that any one event will occur is equal to the probability that any other event will occur. It is also assumed that events are independent of each other, in other words, when one event occurs; the probability that a second event will occur is not changed.

6.1.2 The Binomial Distribution

Assuming the probability of occurrence of an event is p. Then the probability q that the event will not occur can be stated by the equation q = 1 – *p*. Using the following formula, we can calculate how often an event will happen *i.e.* the probability of *r* events in n possible times is

$$\frac{n!}{r!(n-r)!} \times p^{r} q^{n-r}$$

Note that the expression n! is read "n factorial" and refers to a successive multiplication of the numbers n, $n - 1$, $n - 2$ ....1. The means and variance of binomial distribution are np and npq respectively.

6.1.3 The Normal Distribution

As the number of observations increases, the binomial distribution may be used to approximate what is called the normal distribution, which is a very useful type of mathematical distribution. If shown graphically in figure it is perfectly bell shaped. If its mean and standard deviation are known the distribution is said to be completely defined.

It should be noted that the binomial distribution requires variables to be discrete (*i.e.* there is either a loss or no loss). With the normal distribution the variables may be continuous having a value of any number from O to infinity. As a result normal distribution can be applied in more situations and is more versatile and often more realistic than the binomial distribution.

6.1.4 The Poisson Distribution

The poisson distribution is another theoretical distribution that is useful in risk management applications. For example, auto accident, fires, and other losses tend to occur in a way that can be approximated with the Poisson distribution. The probability of an event under the Poisson distribution can be estimated using the following formula:

Where p = the probability that an event n occurs

r = the number of events for which the probability estimate is needed

m = mean = expected loss frequency

e = a constant, the base of the natural logarithms, equal to 2.71828

The mean *'m'* of a poisson distribution is also its variance. Consequently its standard deviation s is equal to m.

Poisson distribution is best to be used when the probability of occurrence of an event is small and the population size is very large. Now let us take an example to illustrate the use of probability. Assume that for a given life insurance group of 5 members, the premium charged is Rs. 3,000 and the coverage (sum assured) is Rs.90,000. If one of those five persons is likely to die in a given period, we are interested in finding whether there will be profit or loss to the insurance company.

Total Premiums collected $= \text{Rs. } 3000 \times 5$

$= \text{Rs. } 15000$

Expected value of losses $= \sum_{i=1}^{n} \times ipi$

$= 90{,}000 \times \frac{1}{5}$

$= \text{Rs. } 18{,}000$

Since Expected values of losses > total premiums collected, the pricing was improper.

6.2 Dual Application of Law of Large Numbers

It implies from the above discussion that a large sample will improve our estimates of the underlying probability.

Even in the case of priori probabilities where the probability is known, it must be applied to large number of trials if we expect actual results to approximate in true probability. Therefore, in the case of empirical probabilities, the requirements of a large number has dual application:

- To estimate the underlying probability accurately, the insurance company must have a sufficiently large sample, the more accurate will be the estimate of the probability.
- Once the estimate of the probability has been made, it must be applied to a sufficiently large number of exposure units to permit the underlying probability to work itself out.

In this sense, to the insurance company, the law of large numbers means that the larger the number of cases examined in the sampling process, the better the chance of that actual experience will approximate a good estimate of the probability.

In making predictions on the basis of historical data, the insurance company assumes that things will happen in the future as they have happened in the past. But it may not be true. It is likely that the probability involved is constantly changing. Since the insurance company bases its rates on the expectation of future losses, it must be concerned with the extent to which actual experience is likely to deviate from the predicted results. For the insurance risk is measured by potential deviation of actual from predicted results.

It should be noted that although probability theory plays an important role in the operation of insurance, insurance does not always depend on probabilities and predictions. It is only when insurance is to be operated on an advance premium basis, with the participants paying their share of losses in advance, the probability theory and predictions become important.

Insurance is about spreading the risks. From the perspective of an insurance company, represents the probability of compensation payouts being greater than the premium revenue, resulting in a net loss to the company. In general, the insurers risk is reduced if there are many individuals or business taking up insurance. A large pool of policyholders would reduce the administration cost of processing a policy. A large pool would also reduce average insurance premiums because the revenue required to meet the claims is spread over a large number of policyholders. The general assumption is that claims do not increase proportionately with the number of policyholders.

Therefore it is the probability that must be correctly estimated otherwise, the insurance company may default or go into liquidation. The various theories associated with risk management are given in Section 6.4.

6.3 POOLING IN INSURANCE

Pooling of risks is the underlying feature of insurance. Insurance companies try to make a group or pool of homogenous exposures with a view to reduce the losses arising from that exposure. It is most advantageous when the losses are uncorrelated. When the group agrees to bear the losses in some proportion, the burden on a given member is reduced. This has the effect of loss distribution for the group flater and flater.

The application of large numbers and pooling suggests that normal curve becomes flater any flater when the members are added to a group – logically, because of reduction in the variance and likely concentration towards mean (μ).

6.3.1 Forms of Pooling

Bulk Buying

One form of pooling is known as "bulk buying" which enables a group of individuals or businesses to collectively purchase insurance. The group collectively obtains the services of an insurance broker to find an appropriate underwriter to provide the insurance cover.

Self-Insurance

Another form of pooling is self-insurance. This is where individuals or businesses group together to provide their own insurance through the establishment of mutual funds. Members contribute to the mutual fund, which is used to pay for any compensation payouts.

The funds may also reinsure part of the liability against the probability of big compensation payouts. This form of reinsurance policy is used in high cost and high-risk areas such as aviation and marine insurance.

Mutual funds are often established by an industry body for the benefits of its members. For example, the legal profession and local governments in states of USA have their own mutual funds, which provide insurance cover for their members.

Expertise is required in the establishment of a mutual fund. It is important to consult an expert in this area before deciding if it is appropriate for the business or group. Insurance brokers will be able to provide advice on such matters.

6.3.2 Cost and Benefits of Pooling

Insurance pooling enables small companies or community groups to gain access to insurance, otherwise which is not available to them individually.

Pooling to facilitate bulk buying can increase the ability of individuals and business to negotiate better terms and conditions, including premiums, from the insurer. This is because risk is spread across all policyholders in the pool and loss expectancies are reduced. This could lead to lower premiums or containment of future premium increases. As pool size increases, loss expectancies become more predictable, and insurers would be more comfortable in allowing premiums to stabilize. Pooling can also provide an opportunity to attract insurers back to the market.

Advantages of Pooling

In cases where the community or group gets together and pools their funds the following advantages are obtained:

- Coverages are specialized for and geared to exposures faced by the individuals pooling in their money for insurance purposes.
- Stability Pooling is not subject to the market whims of the standard insurance market.
- No taxes or fees are required to be paid (in some cases).
- Profits belong to members of the Pool, and they are distributed as per the policy document or consensus as the case may be.
- Members are able to participate in claims handling.
- Flexibility of coverage forms, more customization leads to flexibility.
- Emphasis on Loss Control, including on-site surveys. Safety Committee Set-up.
- Funds are invested in the focused area or location and are less susceptible to market fluctuations.

Besides the above there are other advantages that come by way of pooling:

- Pools offer favourable coverages, terms conditions, and limits tailored to the needs of the public entity participants.
- Pooling spreads the risk of a severe financial loss over a group, rather than being borne by one entity.
- The combined purchasing power of pool members gives each member group more clout when negotiating terms and conditions for excess insurance.

- Pool premiums are generally more stable, since the pool is somewhat insulated from the regular fluctuations of the insurance market.
- Pool participants have ownership in any equity that the pool accumulates.
- Pool members have a significant voice in how the pool is operated, since the policy-making board is composed of representatives of its members.
- Data regarding losses are provided to members on a regular basis.
- Claims handling is dictated by the pool's claim philosophy, and members have a voice in how claims are resolved.
- Services, especially risk control, are tailored to the needs of its members.

Administrating the Pool

A group representative (industry association, a lobby or a person or organization which is willing and able to represent the group) could perform the role of coordinating the insurance requirements of the pool. An industry association or lobby group would also provide the focal point for attracting members to participate in the pool.

Effective Pool

A pool to facilitate bulk buying has to be sufficiently big to increase the ability to negotiate premiums and to spread the risks. An adequate pool size depends on the type of activities and the levels or risk being insured. In general, high risk and high cost activities would require a bigger pool relative to low risk activities.

A pool cannot cater to a wide range of risks. The spread of risks for the group should ideally be small so that subsidization of the high-risk policyholder by the low risk policyholder is minimized. In addition the insurers should know that they are in for a long haul.

A small "bulk buying" pool has less bargaining power and the ability to negotiate lower premiums. A small group wishing to form a pool insurance purpose may have to consider joining other groups of similar activities and risk levels, to increase the size of the pool. For example, a state industry association may join up with another state or with the national industry association to increase the size of the pool.

Intergovernmental pooling is a risk financing mechanism based on cooperative agreements among public entities to provide for many of their risk financing needs through a jointly owned program. This program while very successful abroad (mainly USA and Europe) is yet to catch up stem in India. Pooling involves group self-insurance and/or group insurance purchasing. (Now public entity pools account for almost 40 percent of the insurance marketing for the countries specified above).

The financial viability of a private insurance pool depends on the balance between **premium income and losses.** If losses are consistently greater than premium income, a private insurer may default on the contract, leaving the insured worse off than if no insurance had been available. Financial balance is also important to most government insurance programs, the ones mentioned above and all of the largest ones because they are intended to protect the insured from losses without simply shifting those losses to others.

Multinational Pooling – is another Concept that has been Gaining Importance

Multinational pooling is a technique that allows organizations with multiple operations around the world to consolidate their employee benefit insurance contracts in these countries with a local insurer of an international insurance network. Principal among the merits multinational pooling can offer are:

- Economies of scale and purchasing power
- Global experience rating
- Financial cost savings

- Improved underwriting terms and conditions
- Annual reporting
- A management tool and information base.

But in case of insurance pooling by multinationals of MNC's there are more complexities involved and regular check on management is vital.

Pooling is appropriate in situations when individuals or business are unable to obtain insurance on their own or when insurance is expensive. In the majority of the cases these would be areas, which the insurance industry at large are not targeting.

6.4 THEORIES OF RISK MANAGEMENT

Classical Theory of Risk

The basis concept in insurance is the insurance contract. In its simplest form, insurance contract gives right to the insured to claim an amount of money (say S), from the insurance company, if certain events should occur. In order to be entitled for this right, the inured pays the company a premium P. Now, if the probability of events leading to a claim is p, the premium is determined so that

$$P = pS$$

This equation illustrated the *principle of equivalence*, which is the basic foundation of the insurance theory. The implicit principle thereby is that expected value of claims payments under a contract should be equal to the expected value of premiums received.

Since, *prima-facie*, this premium is net premium, the administrative costs in the form of loading must be added to the net premium to arrive at the premium which should be charged by the insurance company.

If F(x) is defined as the probability distribution that claim payments will not exceed x, then

$$P = \int_0^\infty x d F(x)$$

Illustration

Assume that a person buys a life insurance policy on which he has to pay premium P at the Karl Borch, the Mathematical Theory of Insurance, Lexington Book, 1974 start of every year till he lives and will get a claim of S, if he dies.

If q_t is the probability that he will die in year t, the probability distribution will have outcomes as follows:

$$q_1, q_2, q_3, q_4 \ldots q_t \ldots$$

and logically, $q_1, + q_2 + q_3 + \ldots q_t + \ldots = 1$

The premiums expected in the contract will be

$$P (q_1 + 2 q_2 + \ldots + t q_t + \ldots)$$

If $v = (1 + i)^{-1}$; i is the rate of interest, then the expected present value of premiums will be

$$P\{q_1 + (1 + r)q_2 + (1 + r + r^2) q_3 + \ldots\} \qquad \ldots(1)$$

Also, the expected claim payments will be

$$S \{rq_1 + r^2 q_2 + r^3 q_3 + \ldots\} \qquad \ldots(2)$$

According to the principle of equivalence (1) and (2) must be equal.

The above presentation of classical actuarial mathematics are not easy to draw up always for complicated insurance contracts.

Now consider two insurance contracts

First, $S_1 = 100$, $P_1 = 0.1$

Second, $S_2 = 1{,}000$, $P_2 = 0.01$

According to principle of equivalence,

$$P = S_1 P_1 = 100 \times 0.1 = 10 \text{ and } P = S_2 P_2$$
$$= 1000 \times 0.01 = 10$$

So, P = 10 in both the cases but second contract is more riskier than the first one and the premium on this contract should be greater than the first.

Question is why?

Assume that the risk function is defined as

$$R = \int_0^\infty (x - P)\, dF(x)$$

$$= \frac{1}{2}\int_0^\infty |x - P|\, dF(x) \qquad \text{...(3)}$$

$$\Rightarrow \quad R_1 = \frac{1}{2}[0.9 \times 10 + 0.1 \times 90] = 9$$

$$R_2 = \frac{1}{2}[0.99 \times 10 + 990] = 9.9$$

$$R_2 > R_1$$

If M is defined as the risk function based on standard deviation,

$$M^2 = \int_0^\infty (x - P)^2\, dF(x)$$

Accordingly for the above case $M_1 = 30$ and $M_2 = 99$.

Bernoulli presented a more relevant version of the expectations theory – moral expectations, replacing mathematical expectation. This theory is popularly known as expected utility. According to this theory, the insurance company has a preference ordering over the set of all insurance contracts. This ordering can be represented by utility function m(x) such that the expected utility

$$\int_0^\infty \mu(P - x)\, dF(x) \qquad \text{...(4)}$$

Higher the expected utility, the higher the contract is placed in the preference ordering. The company will logically accept an insurance contract if and only if it is preferred to a degenerate contract, which is certain to give neither loss of gain.

∴ Premium Q must be determined so that

$$\mu(o) \leq \int_{0}^{\infty} \mu(Q - x)\, dF(x) \qquad ...(5)$$

Barrios further developed this idea to evolve the modern theory of fire insurance.

Illustration

If a person possesses wealth S and he may suffer a loss from fire as *x*. If the utility function for money of this person is $w(x)$, he is willing to pay a premium Q to be insured against the loss, provided that

$$\int_{0}^{\infty} w(s - x)\, dF(x) \leq w(S - Q) \qquad ...(5)$$

All premiums which satisfy the inequalities in (5) and (6) should be acceptable to the insurance company and the insured. The undertaking of insurance contract will reduce the expected utility of both parties.

The economic theory of insurance illustrates that the insurance cover must be viewed as a commodity and the premium be viewed as a price determined by the interaction of demand and supply forces.

Ruin Theory

Assume that an insurance company has a portfolio of n independent contracts with premiums $P_1, P_2 P_n$ ... In and risks $M_1 M_2 ... M_n$. The risk of the portfolio will be

$$M^2 = M_1^2 + M_2^2 + ... + M_n^2$$

Further assume that the gain on this portfolio is denoted by *z*. If premiums are determined by principle of equivalence

$$E\{z\} = O$$

If n is large, *z* will be normally distributed with standard deviation M.

If Reserve Fund for this company is S, in addition to premiums collected for contracts in force, the probability that the company will not be able to fulfill its commitments under the contracts in the portfolio is denoted by

$$\text{Probability } \{z < -S\} = \phi\left(\frac{-S}{M}\right) \qquad ... (7)$$

If S is large such that the Pr (Probability of Ruin) is smaller than this maximum, the company may choose to give dividends, else it should invoke additional capital fund. If this additional funds is raised by loading the premiums so that premium actually paid = (1 + l) P_i then

$$P_r\{z < -S\} = \phi\left(\frac{-S + \lambda P}{M}\right)$$

Collective Risk Theory

This theory was created by Lundberg primarily. He considered an insurance company as a container or as a dam. Into this dam follows a continuous stream of premiums, and out of the dam goes a sequence of claim payments. Accordingly,

P(*t*) = the total value of premiums received in the period (o, t).

Q(*n*,*t*) = the probability that n claims occur in the period (o, t).

G(*x*) = the probability that if a claim should occur, the amount payable will not exceed *x*. G(*x*) is independent of *t* and *n*.

The probability that claim payments in the period (*o*, *t*) shall not exceed *x* is given by the formula

$$F(x,t) = \sum_{n=o}^{\infty} q(n,t)\, G^{(n)}(x)$$

Where $G^{(n)}(x)$ for $n > o$ is the nth convolution of G(x) with itself, ad $G^{(o)}(x) = H(x)$, where H(x) is the Heaviside function defined by

$$H(x) = \begin{cases} 1 & \text{for } x \geq o \\ o & \text{for } x < o \end{cases}$$

Using Poisson process

$$F(x,t) = \sum_{n=o}^{\infty} \frac{(\alpha t)}{n!} G^{(n)}(x)$$

The expected value of claim payments will be

$$E\{x_t\} = \int_{o}^{\infty} x d\, G(x)$$

However, collective risk theory found virtually no application in practice. Assume that an insurance company has to make a decision in regard to loading and reinsurance. The collective risk theory suggests that one should compute the probability that the company will never be ruined, provided that the decision, once it is made, can never be changed. Accordingly, the operational decision is the one which gives the highest value to this "probability of survival". However, it is unlikely that companies will be making decision in this fashion.

The Modern Risk Theory

The model suggested by de Finetti on modern theory describes as follows:

(*i*) The insurance company has initial capital S.

(*ii*) In each operating period, the company underwrites a portfolio of insurance contracts with a claim distribution F(x). Assume $F(x) = O$ for $x \leq O$.

(*iii*) In each operating period, the company collects an amount of premium P.

(*iv*) If at the end of an operating period, the companys capital exceeds z, the excess is paid out as dividends or taxes, as the case may be.

(*v*) If at the end of an operating period, the capital is negative, the company is ruined, and has to go out of business.

The company's capital performs a random walk, and there is an absorbing barrier at S = O, and a reflecting barrier at S = Z.

Case 1

Let as denote the expected life of the company as

$$D(S, Z) = O \text{ for } S < O$$

$$D(S, Z) = D(Z, Z) \text{ for } S > Z$$

Where the initial capital is S and upper limit is Z.

$$D(S, Z) = 1 + \int_{o}^{S+P} D(S+P-x, z)\, dF(x)$$

Where for D (S, Z), $O \leq S \leq Z$

He considers a special case where P = 1, and where x can take only the values O and 2.

$\therefore$ D (S, Z) + 1 + pD (S + 1, Z) + qD(S − 1, Z)

Where Pr {x = o} = p

Pr {x = z} = q = 1 − p

If $p > q$

$$D(S, Z) = \frac{p}{(p-q)^2}\left\{\left(\frac{p}{q}\right)^{Z+1} - \left(\frac{p}{q}\right)^{Z-S}\right\} - \frac{S+1}{p-q}$$

Hence, D (S, Z) will go to infinity with Z and the probability of ruin will be smaller than one. The probability of ruin in this limit would be

$$1 - R(S) = \left(\frac{q}{p}\right)^S$$

$$\therefore \quad D(S+1, Z) - D(S, Z) = \frac{1}{p-q}\left\{\left(\frac{p}{q}\right)^{Z-S} - 1\right\}$$

$\Rightarrow$ D(S, Z) increases with S.

Case 2

If excess capital is paid out as dividends and V (S, Z) be the expected discounted value of the dividend payment, which the company will make during its lifetime.

V(S, Z) = O for S > O

V(S, Z) = S − Z + V (Z, z) for S > Z

For $O \leq S \leq Z$, $V(S, Z)$ must satisfy the integral equation

$$V(S, Z) = r\int_{0}^{S+P} V(S+P-x, Z)\, dF(x)$$

Where V is a discount factor

$$\Rightarrow \quad V(S, Z) = rp\, V(S+1, Z) + rq\, V(S-1, Z)$$

$$V(S, Z) = \frac{r_1^{S+1} - r_2^{S+1}}{r_1^{Z+2} - r_2^{Z+2} - r_1^{Z+1} + r_2^{Z+2}}$$

Where r_1 and r_2 are the roots of the characteristic equation

$$r = rpr^2 + rq$$

$\therefore$ V(S, Z) will increase with S, and will go to zero as Z goes to infinity *i.e.* dividends payments are postponed indefinitely. However, for one value of $Z > O$, which maximise $V(S, Z)$ implying optimal reserve capital for the company.

6.5 MORTALITY TABLE

In life insurance, certain asssumptions have to be made by the insurer about the interest rates, mortality rates and the expenses which will be incurved in the year to come for the purpose of fixing the premium rates or assessing the liabilities under the insurance contracts. It is important to have a correct estimate of these factors as otherwise the results deducted from the assumptions made may not be reasonably close to the actual experience of the insuner. He depends upon the mortality experience of the insuned lives observed inb the recent past as a basis for estimating the probabilities of survival and deaths.

If it is observed that out of 1000 lives all aged 35, 20 die within one year *i.e.,* before attaining the age 36, the observed mortality rate at age 35 works out to $\frac{20}{10000} = 0.002$ and is denoted by q_{35}. The mortality rates at various ages are determined in the same manner.

A mortality table represents a record of mortality observed in the past and is arranged so as to show the probabilities of death and survival at each separate age. A large number of persons are selected at a particular age and number of deaths are observed each and every year. Each years number of living is the previous year's number of living minus previous year's number of dying. As the persons go on dying year after year the number of living goes on shrinking. When the last person dies it is reduced to zero and the mortality table ends there.

The following are the two major mortality tables :

(*a*) LIC (1970-73) ultimate Table

(*b*) H^M Table (Makehan Graduation)

6.5.1 Construction of Mortality Table

The main objective for having a mortality table for an insuner is to work out the probabilities of deaths and survivors to enable him to make a reasonably accurate estimate of his liabilities under the insurance contracts and also to calculate premium to be charged. The past experience from which the table is constructed will never be exactly reproduced in future. There will be fluctuations in different directions at different ages but on the whole the estimates in respect of mortality rates may be close to the actual experience. So the mortality table should be constructed to represent the past experience as accurately as possible. The following are the two methods of construction of mortality table.

(i) On Generation Basis : In this method, we select a large number of persons at an attained age. The attained age means the age nearer to the birth date. For example, persons of age 14 years 6 months to 15 years 6 months will be treated as the age of 15 years. The selected persons of this attained age will be observed each and every year and the number of deaths will be recorded during the year. The observation will be continuing till all the persons selected are dead. Preparation of such table is very difficult, because it requires a long-period to construct the table and constant watch on the selected persons is practically impossible. A lot of money and manpower will be required to record number of deaths every time. To avoid these difficulties death rate is calculated on yearly basis.

Mortality Table (on generation basis)

AgeNumber	*Number of Living*	*Mortality Rate of Deaths*	*Survival Rate*	
25	987095	1263	0.00128	0.00872
26	985832	1252	0.00127	0.99873
27	984580	1250	0.00127	0.99873
28	983330	1268	0.00129	0.99871
29	982062	1286	0.00131	0.99869

(ii) On Yearly Basis : In this method the death rate is calculated for every age. Separate sample is taken for each age. The number of death during the age is recorded and the mortality rate is calculated. By this method we can construct the mortality table within the duration of one year. For example, 5000 persons are taken at age 25, 4000 persons at age 26, 6000 persons at age 27, 10000 persons at age 28 and 3000 persons at age 29. The number of deaths observed at these ages are 10, 16, 18, 60 and 15 respectively. The following table summarizes the mortality rates at the above ages.

Age	*Number of Living*	*Number of Deaths*	*Mortality Rate*	*Survival Rate*
25	5000	10	0.002	0.998
26	4000	16	0.004	0.996
27	6000	18	0.003	0.997
28	10000	60	0.006	0.994
29	3000	15	0.005	0.995

6.5.2 Components of a Complete Mortality Table

Apart from the ordinary mortality table, the insurers use complete mortality table. Generally the H^m Makeham graduation mortalkity table is used. All the components of this complete mortality table is discussed below :

(i) Column (*x*) : It denotes the age of prospects. The mortality table can start from any age (5, 8, 10 etc.) depending upon the requirement of the insurer and continue to 100-120 years and required by the insurers. LIC (1970-73) ultimate table starts from the age 15 and ends at the age 103. The H^m table starts from the age 0 and ends at the age 102.

(ii) Column (l_x) : It indicates the number of living persons at the beginning of each year (*x*). If the table starts from age 0, then the number in l_x column against this age, say l_0 is any convenient number like 10,00,000 or even an arbitrary number like 2714321 and represents the numbers of persons of age 0 *i.e.*, the number of persons just born having fixed the starting number l_0 any other number l_x in the column appearing against age *x* gives the number of persons living out of the l_0 persons born who reach the age *x*. Thus, l_{30} is the number of persons who reach age 30. In case of LIC (1970-73) ultimate table, l_{30} is 980776.

(iii) Column (d_x) : It indicates the number of persons dying b/w the age *x* and *x* + 1. The number of survivors at the age *x* + 1 is given by $l_{x+1} = l_x - d_x$.

$$\boxed{d_x = l_x - l_{x+1}}$$

For example the number of deaths at the age of 30 is given by :

$$d_{30} = l_{30} - l_{31}$$

Similarly, we can calculate the number of death between two particular years.

The number of death between age 40 and 45 is given by :

$$\sum_{x=40}^{44} dx = d_{40} + d_{41} + d_{42} + d_{43} + d_{44}$$

$$= (l_{40} - l_{41}) + (l_{41} - l_{42}) + (l_{42} - l_{43}) + (l_{43} - l_{44}) + (l_{44} - l_{45})$$

$$= l_{40} - l_{45}$$

$$= 963206 - 946656$$
$$= 16550$$

$$\sum_{x=a}^{b} dx = l_a - l_{b+1} .$$

(iv) Column (q_x) : It indicates the probability that a person aged x dies within 1 year *i.e.*, before reaching the age $x + 1$.

$$\therefore \quad q_x = \frac{\text{number of death between age } x \text{ and } x+1}{\text{total number of livings at age } x}$$

i.e., $$q_x = \frac{d_x}{l_x}$$

i.e., $$q_x = \frac{l_x - l_{x+1}}{l_x}.$$

q_x is called the rate of mortality at age x. For e.g., from the LIC (1970-73) table the rate of mortality at age 30.

i.e., $$q_{30} = \frac{d_{30}}{l_{30}}$$
$$= \frac{1314}{980776}$$
$$= 0.00134.$$

(v) Column (p_x) : It indicates the survival rate. It gives for successive ages the probability that a life survive to age $x + 1$.

$$p_x = \frac{\text{number of survivors to age } x+1}{\text{total number living at age } x}$$

$$p_x = \frac{l_{x+1}}{l_x}.$$

For example from the H^m table.

$$p_{30} = \frac{l_{31}}{l_{30}}$$
$$= \frac{88994}{89685}$$
$$= .99229.$$

Clearly, the probability that a person aged x will die within 1 years and the probability that he will survive for 1 year or the complementary probabilities.

i.e., $$p_x + q_x = 1.$$

We know that, $$q_x = \frac{d_x}{l_x}$$

$$\Rightarrow \quad q_x = \frac{l_x - l_{x+1}}{l_x}$$

$$\Rightarrow \quad q_x = 1 - \frac{l_{x+1}}{l_x}$$

$$\Rightarrow \quad q_x = 1 - p_x$$

$$\Rightarrow \quad p_x + q_x = 1$$

(vi) Column (U_x) : It represents the force of mortality at age x is defined as the limiting value of the normal yearly rate of mortality at age x over a small interval dt. In practice, the smallest interval be considered is 1 day

$$\delta t = \frac{1}{365} \text{ year.}$$

The deaths between age x and $x + \frac{1}{365}$ are $l_x - l_x + \frac{1}{365}$ and the rate of mortality at age x per day is $\frac{l_x - l_{x+1/365}}{l_x}$ and the corresponding yearly rate is $365 \times \left(\frac{l_x - l_{x+1/365}}{l_x}\right)$.

(vii) Column (L_x) : It represents the number of persons in the population between x and $x + 1$ *i.e.*, the number of survivals at the middle of age x and $x + 1$. It is also denoted by (l_x + ½).

$$L_x = \frac{1}{2}(l_x + l_{x+1})$$

Now $\quad l_{x+1} = l_x - d_x$

$$L_x = \frac{1}{2}(l_x + l_x - d_x)$$

$$= \frac{1}{2}(2l_x - d_x)$$

$$\boxed{L_x = l_x - \frac{1}{2}d_x.}$$

In H^m table, at age x = 50, l_x = 72795, d_x = 1144.

$$L_x = l_x - \frac{1}{2}d_x$$

$$= 72795 - \frac{1}{2} \times 1144$$

$$= 72795 - 572$$

$$= 72223.$$

(viii) Column (T_x) : It denotes the total number of persons living at any time who are aged x or more. Total number of survivors at any age is equal to the summation of number of persons living between mid of age x and at the end of the table *i.e.*,

T_x = number of persons living between x and $x + 1$ +
number of persons living between $x + 1$ and $x + 2$ +
number of persons living between $x + 2$ and $x + 3$ + ...

i.e., $\quad T_x = L_x + L_{x+1} + L_{x+2} + \ldots\ldots$

$$= \frac{1}{2}(l_x + l_{x+1}) + \frac{1}{2}(l_{x+1} + l_{x+2}) + \frac{1}{2}(l_{x+2} + l_{x+3}) + \ldots\ldots$$

$$= \frac{1}{2} l_x + l_{x+1} + l_{x+2} + l_{x+3} + \ldots\ldots$$

$$\therefore \quad T_x = \frac{1}{2} l_x + N'_{x+1}$$

where, $\quad N'_{x+1} = l_{x+1} + l_{x+2} + l_{x+3} + \ldots.$

For *e.g.*, from the H^m table, at age 89.

$$N_{89+1} = l_{89+1(90)} + l_{91} + l_{92} \ldots . l_{101}$$

$$= 1273 + 871 + 575 + 366 + 222 + 129 + 71 + 37 + 19 + 9 + 4 + 1.$$

$$= 3577$$

$$T_{89} = \frac{1}{2} l_{89} + N_{90}$$

$$= \frac{1}{2} 1800 + 3577$$

$$= 900 + 3577$$

$$= 4477.$$

(*ix*) *Column* (*lx*) : This symbol is known as the complete expectation of life. *lx* represents the expectation of life.

The expectation of life at age *x* is the average no. of complete yrs. of life lived by each person age *x* after reaching age *x*. Out of l_x lives, l_{x+1} reach age $x + 1$ *i.e.*, each of l_{x+1} lives completes 1 yr. after age *x*. Similarly, each of l_{x+2} completes 2 yrs. after reaching age *x* and so on.

The total no. of completed yrs. lived by l_x persons is given by :

$$l_{x+1} + l_{x+2} + l_{x+3} + \ldots$$

The average no. of complete yrs. that each peron aged *x* will live is given by

$$l_x = \frac{l_{x+1} + l_{x+2} + l_{x+3}}{l_x}$$

$$l_x = \frac{N'_{x+1}}{l_x}.$$

This expectation of life is called the curtate expectation of life as it takes into account only complete yrs. of lives and ignores fraction of the year lived in the yr. of death.

If the fractions are taken into account, we get the complete expectation of life denoted by l^o_x.

∴ the additional no. of years of life to be included in respect of the fractional yrs. is given by

$$= \frac{1}{2} d_x + \frac{1}{2} d_{x+1} + \frac{1}{2} d_{x+2} + \ldots$$

$$= \frac{1}{2} (d_x + d_{x+1} + \ldots.)$$

$$= \frac{1}{2} l_x.$$

$$\therefore \quad l_x = \frac{N_{x+1} + \frac{1}{2} l_x}{l_x}$$

$$l_x = \frac{T_x}{l_x}.$$

$$\Rightarrow \quad e_x^0 = \frac{N_{x+1}}{l_x} + \frac{1}{2}\frac{l_x}{l_x}$$

$$\Rightarrow \quad e_x^0 = l_x + 1/2.$$

For eq. in H^m table

$$e_{20}^0 = \frac{T_{20}}{l_{20}}$$

$$= \frac{4044238}{96061}$$

$$= 42.101.$$

6.5.3 Probabilities of Survival and Death

The mortality table can be used for calculating the various probabilities of survival and death.

(a) np_x : It indicates the probability that the person aged x survives n yrs. When n it l, it is denoted by p_x.

$$\therefore \quad np_x = \frac{\text{no. of persons living at age } x + n}{\text{no. of persons living at age } x}.$$

$$np_x = \frac{l_{x+n}}{l_x}.$$

(b) mq_x : This symbol denotes the probability that a person aged x dies within the next 'm' yrs.

$$\therefore \quad mq_x = \frac{\text{total no. of persons dying b/w age } x \text{ and } x + m}{\text{total no. of persons living at age } x}.$$

$$mq_x = \frac{l_x - l_{x+m}}{l_x}.$$

$$mq_x = \frac{l_x}{l_x} - \frac{l_{x+m}}{l_x}.$$

$$\therefore \quad mq_x = 1 - mp_x.$$

(c) m/q_x : This symbol denotes the probability that a person aged x will die : b/w the age. $x + m$ and $x + m + 1$

$$\therefore \quad m/q_x = \frac{\text{total no. of persons dying b/w } x + m \text{ \& } x + m + 1}{\text{total no. of living at age } x}.$$

$$m/q_x = \frac{l_{x+m} - l_{x+m+1}}{l_x}$$

$$\Rightarrow \quad m/q_x = \frac{d_{x+m}}{l_x}.$$

(d) m/nq_x : This symbol represents the probability that a person aged x dies within 'n' yrs. following 'm' yrs. from now, *i.e.*, b/w the yrs. of age $x + m$ and age $x + m + n$.

$$\therefore \quad m/nq_x = \frac{\text{total no. of deaths in b/w age } x + m \;\&\; x + m + n}{\text{no. of living at age } x}.$$

$$\therefore \quad m/nq_x = \frac{l_{x+m} - l_{x+m+n}}{l_x}.$$

The probability that a person ased x will survive between the age $x + m$ and age $x + m + n$ is given by

$1 - m/nq_x$

Illustration 1: Find the following probabilities that

(*a*) a life aged 30 survives 10 yrs.

(*b*) a life aged 30 dies within next 10 yrs.

(*c*) a life aged 30 dies after 10 yrs.

(Use LIC mortablity table).

Solution. (*a*) the probability that a life aged 30 survives 10 yrs. *i.e.*, $= {}^{10}P_{30}$.

$$= \frac{l_{30+10}}{l_{30}} \qquad \left[\because np_x = \frac{l_{x+n}}{l_x}.\right]$$

$$= \frac{l_{40}}{l_{30}} = \frac{963206}{980776}$$

$= 0.9821.$

(*b*) the prob. that a person aged 30 dies within next 10 yrs.

i.e., $10q_{30}$

$= 1 - 10p_{30}$

$= 1 - 0.9821$

$= 0.0179$

alternatively $\quad 10q_{30} = \dfrac{l_{30} - l_{30+10}}{l_{30}}$

$$= \frac{980776 - 963206}{980776}$$

$= 0.0179.$

(*c*) the prob. that the person aged 30 dies after 10 yrs. *i.e.*,

$= 1 -$ the prob. that the person died within 10 yrs.

$= 1 - 0.0179$

$= 0.9821.$

Illustration 2. Using the LIC (1970–73) ultimate table, find the following probabilities that —

(*a*) a life aged 35 dies within 12 yrs.

(*b*) a life aged 40 dies not earlier than 12 yrs. and not later than 15 yrs.

(*c*) a life aged 52 survives 12 yrs.

(*d*) a life aged 52 will not dies b/w 65 and 70.

Solution. (*a*) Prob. that a life aged 35 dies within 12 yrs.

$$= {}_{12}q_{35}$$

$$= \frac{l_{35} - l_{35+12}}{l_{35}} \qquad \left[\because \ {}_nq_x = \frac{l_x - l_{x+n}}{l_x}\right]$$

$$= \frac{l_{35} - l_{47}}{l_{35}}$$

$$= \frac{983550 - 937401}{973550}$$

$$= 0.0371.$$

(*b*) prob. that life aged 40 dies not earlier than 12 yrs. and not later than 15 yrs. *i.e.,*

$$\left[\begin{aligned} n &= 40; \\ m &= 12; \\ m + n &= 15; \\ n &= 3; \end{aligned}\right]$$

$$= {}_{12/3}q_{40}$$

$$= \frac{l_{40+12} - l_{40+12+3}}{l_{40}} \qquad \left[\because \ {}_{m/n}q_x = \frac{l_{x+m} - l_{x+m+n}}{l_x}\right]$$

$$= \frac{l_{52} - l_{55}}{l_{40}} = \frac{904837 - 876889}{963206}.$$

$$= 0.029.$$

(*c*) the prob. that a life aged 52 survives 12 yrs.

$$= {}_{12}p_{52}$$

$$= \frac{l_{52+12}}{l_{52}} \qquad \left[{}_np_x = \frac{l_{x+n}}{l_n}\right]$$

$$= \frac{l_{64}}{l_{52}} = \frac{738825}{904837} = 0.8165.$$

(*d*) the prob. that a life aged 52 will not dies b/w age 65 and 70 *i.e.,*

= 1 – prob. that a life aged 52 will dies b/w 65 and 70.

$$\left[\begin{aligned} x &= 52 \\ x + m &= 65 \Rightarrow m = 13 \\ x + m + n &= 70 \\ &\Rightarrow n = 5 \end{aligned}\right]$$

$$= 1 - {}_{13/5}q_{52}$$

$$= 1 - \frac{l_{52+3} - l_{52+13+5}}{l_{52}}$$

$$= 1 - \frac{l_{65} - l_{70}}{l_{52}}$$

$$= 1 - \frac{904837 - 591285}{904837}$$

$$= 1 - \frac{126151}{904837}.$$

$$= 1 - 0.1394$$

$$= 0.08606.$$

Illustration 3. Fill up the blanks in the following portion of a life table

x	l_x	d_x	q_x	p_x
10	1000000	...	0.00409	...
11	...	...	0.00370	...
12	...	...	...	0.99653
13	...	...	...	0.99658
14	...	...	0.00342	...

Solution. We know that

$$q_x = \frac{d_x}{l_x} \quad \Rightarrow \quad d_x = q_x \times l_x$$

$$p_x = 1 - d_x$$

$$l_{x+1} = l_x - d_x$$

For age 10 :

$$d_{10} = q_{10} \times l_{10} = 0.00409 \times 1000000 = 4090$$

$$P_{10} = 1 - q_{10} = 1 - 0.00409 = 0.99591$$

For age 11 :

$$l_{11} = l_{10} - d_{10} = 1000000 - 4090 = 995910$$

$$d_{11} = q_{11} \times l_4 = 0.00370 \times 995910 = 3685$$

$$P_{11} = 1 - q_{11} = 1 - 0.00370 = 0.99630$$

For age 12 :

$$l_{12} = l_{11} - d_{11} = 995910 - 3685 = 992225$$

$$q_{12} = 1 - P_{12} = 1 - 0.99653 = 0.00347$$

$$d_{12} = q_{12} \times l_{12} = 0.00347 \times 992225 = 3443$$

Similarly

$$l_{13} = 988782 \ ; \quad q_{13} = 0.00342 \ ; \quad d_{13} = 3382$$

$$l_{14} = 985400 \ ; \quad d_{14} = 3370 \ ; \quad P_{14} = 0.99658$$

The complete table is

x	l_x	d_x	q_x	p_x
10	1000000	4090	0.00409	0.99591
11	995910	3685	0.00370	0.99630
12	992225	3443	0.00347	0.99653
13	988782	3382	0.00342	0.99658
14	985400	3370	0.00342	0.99658

Illustration 4. Find the probability that of 2 persons A and B aged 30 and 35 respectively :

(*a*) both died before attaining age 55

(*b*) both die after attaining age 60.

(*c*) A dies before 65 while B dies after 60.

(*d*) atleast one of them survives to age 70.

Solution. (*a*) prob. of both A and B dies before attaining age 50 and 55.

$$= P\ (A \text{ dies}) \times P(B \text{ dies})$$

$$= {}_{25}q_{30} \times {}_{20}q_{35}$$

$$= \left(\frac{l_{30} - l_{30+25}}{l_{30}}\right) \times \left(\frac{l_{35} - l_{35+20}}{l_{35}}\right)$$

$$= \left(\frac{l_{30} - l_{55}}{l_{30}}\right) \times \left(\frac{l_{35} - l_{55}}{l_{35}}\right)$$

$$= \left(\frac{980776 - 876889}{980776}\right) \times \left(\frac{973550 - 876889}{973550}\right)$$

$$= \frac{103887}{980776} \times \frac{96661}{973550}$$

$$= 0.1059 \times 0.0993$$

$$= 0.0105$$

(*b*) prob. that both died after attaining 60 yrs. *i.e.*,

$$= P(A \text{ died after } 60) \times P(B \text{ dies after } 60)$$

$$= (1 - {}_{30}q_{30})\ (1 - {}_{25}q_{35})$$

$$= \left(1 - \frac{l_{30} - l_{60}}{l_{30}}\right)\left(1 - \frac{l_{35} - l_{60}}{l_{35}}\right)$$

$$= \left(1 - \frac{980776 - 811640}{980776}\right)\left(1 - \frac{973550 - 811640}{973550}\right)$$

$$= (1 - 0.17245)\ (1 - 0.16631)$$

$$= 0.8276 \times 0.8337$$

$$= 0.68897$$

(*c*) *P*(*A* dies after 65 yrs and *B* dies after 60 yrs)

$$= P(A \text{ dies before } 65)\ ' \ P(B \text{ dies after } 60)$$

$$= 1 \times 2,\ (say)$$

$$P\ (A \text{ dies after } 65)$$

$$= {}_{35}q_{30}$$

$$= \frac{l_{30} - l_{30+35}}{l_{30}} = \frac{l_{30} - l_{65}}{l_{30}}$$

$$= \frac{980776 - 717436}{980776}$$

$= 0.2685$ /–

2. $P(B \text{ dies after } 60)$

$= 0.8337$ (before (6))

Required prob.= 1 × 2

$= 0.2685 \times 0.8337$

$= 0.2238$

(d) P (atleast one of them survive to 70)

$= 1 - P(\text{Both dies before } 70)$

$= 1 - [P(A \text{ dies before } 70) \text{ ´ } P(B \text{ dies before } 70)]$

$P(A \text{ dies before } 70) = {}_{40}q_{30}$

$$= \frac{l_{30} - l_{70}}{l_{30}}$$

$$= \frac{980776 - 591285}{980776}$$

$$= \frac{389491}{980776} = 0.3971$$

$P(B \text{ dies before } 70) = {}_{35}q_{35}$

$$= \frac{l_{35} - l_{70}}{l_{35}}$$

$$= \frac{973550 - 591285}{973550}$$

$$= \frac{382265}{973550} = 0.3927$$

Required prob.= 1 – (0.3971 × 0.3927

$= 1 - 0.1559$

$= 0.8441$

6.6 CALCULATION OF LIFE PREMIUM

Life assurance is a guarantee or a promise to pay a particular benefit designed by a living person. The insurei who offers assurance and the life assured who seeks protection, are the two parties entering into a contrast of life assurance. The insurer experts to review the premiums from the life assured. The life assured, in return, experts the payment of promised benefits. The values of there two expertations at the commencement of the contract should be identical, if no party is to loose in the transaction. Appropriate premium for any particular benefit is arrived at on the basis of the equation of present values of both life insurance benefit and premium payable.

The premium is of two types :

Premium

- Net Premium
  - Single premium
  - Level premium
- Gross Premium
  - Single premium
  - Level premium

New premium is based in the mortality and interest rates. The gross premium includes the net premium and loading. Loading is the process of adding the expenses to net premium. These expenses include the expenses that vary with the amount of policy such as stamp fee and medical examiner's fee business such as salaries and establishment charges. Single premium is paid in one Lump sum while the level premium is paid periodically in instalments, *i.e.*, yearly, half-yearly, quarterly or monthly. Firstly, net single premium (NSP) is calculated and other premium are based on this calculations.

This is the simplest type of contract where by payment is made only when the life assured dies within the term specified. Nothing will be paid if the death does not occur darring the designated term. This is called term assurance or temporary assurance. The premium is received in advance and will not be return if the life insured survives. The death claims will be paid at the end of the yr. in which the death occurs and not at the end of the term.

In case of 1 yrs.

We know $\quad d_x = l_x \times q_x$

Total amount of claim payable = no. of deaths × amount of policy

$$= d_x \cdot S$$

$$\text{Premium} = S \frac{d_x}{l_x}$$

If the insurer earns interest at '*i*' % then the premium will be the present values of $S \cdot \frac{d_x}{l_x}$.

$$\therefore \quad \text{Premium} = S \frac{d_x}{l_x} (1 + i)^{-1}$$

i.e., $\quad PNSP = S \cdot V \cdot \frac{d_x}{l_x} \quad$ where $\upsilon = (1 + i)^{-1}$

In case the term is more than 1 yrs.

Consider a temporary assurance of person aged *x* at entry for the term of '*n*' yrs.

The present value of claims of death at a particular age = no of death × amt. of claims × Present value of Re. 1.

PV of Re. 1 is called discounting factor.

Let *S* be the amt. of policy or sum assured and let *i* be the discounting rate.

The present value of claims on death occurring in 1st yrs. = $d_x \times S \times V$

Present value of claims on death occurring in 2nd yr. = $d_{x+1} \times S \times V^2$

Present value of claims on death occurring in '*n*' yrs. = $d_{x+n-1} \times S \times V^2$

$$\text{Total P.V. of claim} = d_x S V + d_{x+1} S V^2 + d_{x+2} S V^3 + \dots + d_{x+n-1}$$
$$= S [Vd_x + V^2 d_{x+1} + V^3 d_{x+2} + \dots V^n . d_{x+n-1}]$$

$$\text{Premium} = \frac{\text{Total P.V. of claim}}{\text{Total no. of livings at age } x}$$

i.e.,
$$NSP = S \left[\frac{Vd_x + V^2 d_{x+1} + V^3 d_{x+2} + \dots V^n d_{x+n-1}}{l_x} \right]$$

i.e.,
$$\boxed{NSP = S A_{x.\overline{n}1}}$$

If the insurer does not earn interest then.

$$NSP = S \left[\frac{d_x + d_{x+1} + \dots . d_{x+n-1}}{l_x} \right].$$

Illustration 4. 2000 persons all age 50 yrs. are insured from Rs. 1,00,000 for 1 yr. If the rate of mortality (q_{50}) is 0.004. Calculate the *NSP* of this term assurance.

(*i*) if the insurer earns no interest.

(*ii*) if the insurer earns interest at 6%.

Solution. $l_{50} = 2000$

$$q_{50} = 0.004$$
$$\therefore \quad d_{50} = l_{50} \times q_{50}$$
$$= 2000 \times 0.004$$
$$= 8$$

$$\text{Total amt. of claim} = 8 \times 100{,}000$$
$$= 8{,}00{,}000$$

$$\text{Premium} = \frac{8,00,000}{2000} = 400.$$

$$\text{Present value of total claims} = 8 \times 1{,}00{,}000 \times (1.06)^{-1}$$
$$= 8{,}00{,}000 \times (1.06)^{-1}$$
$$= 754717.$$

$$\therefore \quad \text{Premium} = \frac{754717}{2000}$$
$$= 377{\cdot}35.$$

Illustrations 5. Consider a group of 10,000 persons all aged 35 seeking an amt. of Rs. 1,00,000 to their families in case of death during the next 10 yrs.

x	35	36	37	38	39	40	40	42	43	44	45
l_x	10,000	9972	9941	9907	9869	9827	9780	9728	9671	9608	9538
d_x	28	31	34	38	42	47	52	57	63	70	75

Calculate the Net Single premium for their term assurance, if (*i*) the insurer earns interest @ 6% p.a.

(*ii*) the insurer earns no interest.

Solution. (*i*) In case of 6% p.a. rate of interest :

no. of livings at age 35, l_{35} = 10,000

Policy amount 5 = Rs. 1,00,000

interest rate, i = 6% = 0.06

no. of years, n = 10 yrs.

Year	Age x	l_x	d_x	$V^n = (1.06)^{-n}$	P.V. of Claim $d_x \times V^n \times S$
1	35	10,000	28	0.94340	26,41520
2	36	9972	31	0389000	27,59,000
3	37	9941	34	0.83962	28,54,710
4	38	9907	38	0.79209	30,09940
5	39	9869	42	0.74726	31,38,490
6	40	9827	47	0.70496	33,13,310
7	41	9780	52	0.66506	34,58,310
8	42	9728	57	0.62741	35,76,240
9	43	9671	63	0.59190	37,28,970
10	44	9608	70	0.55839	39,08,730
				Total	**3,23,89,220**

Present value of total claims = 32389220

No. of insured (l_x) = 10,000

$$\therefore \quad NSP = \frac{32389220}{10,000}$$

$$= 3238.92$$

(*ii*) In case of no. interest.

$$NSP = S\left(\frac{d_x + d_{x+1} + \ldots d_{x+n+1}}{l_x}\right)$$

$$= 1,00,000\,[28 + 31 + 34 + 38 + 42 + 47 + 52 + 57 + 63 + 70]$$

$$= \frac{1,00,00 \times 462}{10,000}$$

$$= \text{Rs. } 4620.$$

6.6.2 Whole Life Assurance

It continues for whole of life and promises to pay the sum assured upon the death of tie insurer. This policy is like the term assurance. The only difference is that instead of being limited to a definite no. of yrs. it continues for largest possible length of life and will certainly be paid at the time of the death. According to LIC (1970–73), mortality table, a life will continue upto 102 yrs.

∴ the calculation of premium will start from the date of commencement upto 102 yrs. The no. of death in each separate yrs. will be multiplied by the face value of the policy and this amt is discounted by the present value factor for the period. Net single premium (NSP) is given by

$$NSP = S\left(\frac{Vd_x + V^2 d_{x+1} + V^3 d_{x+n+2} + \ldots.}{l_x}\right)$$

Simply, $NSP = S\, A_x$

where, $$A_x = S\left(\frac{Vd_x + V^2 d_{x+1} + V^3 d_{x+n+2} \ldots.}{l_x}\right)$$

6.6.3 Pure Endowment Assurance

In this policy, the assured sum is payable in case the policy holders survives a certain definite period. The person can get the policy amt. at the end of the endowment period. If the insured dies during the period no claim should be made. Thus, the policy holder of the 2 yr pure endowment policy will be paid the assured sum only when he survives at the end of the 2nr yr. The present value of claims of the pure endowment policy of a person aged x on his survival to the term of n yrs. is given by

$$PV \text{ of claims} = S \times l_{x+n} \times V^n$$

$$NSP = \frac{S\,.\,V^n\,.\,l_{x+n}}{l_x}$$

$$NSP = S\,.\,A_x;\ \frac{1}{n}$$

where, $$A_x : \frac{1}{n!} = \frac{V^n\ l_{x+n}}{l_x}.$$

In case, the insurer does not earn interest, then

$$NSP = \frac{S\,.\,l_{x+n}}{l_x}.$$

6.6.4 (Ordinary) Endowment Assurance

It is the combination of temporary assurance and pure endowment assurance, simply it is called endowment assurance. Under this policy, payment of claim amt. is made at the survival upto the end of the term or at the death of the life, assumed whichever is earlier.

Anyhow, payment is certain in this case. Since payment is based on survival and death, the NSP is calculated on both death and survival rates.

$$NSP = S\left(\frac{Vd_x + V^2 d_{x+1} + \ldots.\ V^n d_{x+n-1}}{l_x}\right) + \frac{S\,.V^n\ l_{x+n}}{l_x}.$$

i.e., $$NSP = S\,A^{1}_{x:\overline{n}\,!} + S\,A_x : \frac{1}{n!}$$

$$NSP = S\left[A^{1}_{x:\overline{n}\,!} + S\,A_x : \frac{1}{n!}\right]$$

$$NSP = S\,.\,A_{x\,:\,n}$$

where $A_{x:n} = S\left[A^{1}_{x:\overline{n}|} + S\, A_{x:\frac{1}{\overline{n}|}}\right]$

In case the insurer does not earn interest

$$NSP = S\left[\frac{d_x + d_{x+1} + \ldots d_{x+n-1}}{l_x}\right] + \frac{S.l_{x+n}}{l_x}.$$

6.6.5 Double Endowment Assurance

Under this policy, double of the amt. is paid if the life assured survives at the end of the term of the policy and only single amt. will be paid if the death occurs within the term.
Thus, it is just like ordinary endowment policy with only difference that double amt. is paid if the life insured survives upto the term. Since the double of the policy amt. is paid at the survival, one more premium on the basis of pure endowment is added to the premium of ordinary endowment policy.
Therefore, *NSP* under this policy is calculated as follows :

$$NSP = S\left[\frac{Vd_x + V^2 d_{x+1} + \ldots V^n d_{x+n-1}}{l_x}\right] + 2\frac{S.V^n\, l_{x+n}}{l_x}$$

$$NSP = S.A'_{x:\overline{n}|} + 2S.A''_{x:\overline{n}|}$$

$$NSP = S\left[A'_{x:\overline{n}|} + 2A''_{x:\overline{n}|}\right]$$

$$NSP = S\left[A'_{x:\overline{n}|} + 2A'_{x:\frac{1}{\overline{n}|}} + A'_{x:\frac{1}{\overline{n}|}}\right]$$

In case, the insurer does not each interest then,

$$NSP = S\left[\frac{d_x + d_{x+1} + \ldots d_{x+n-1}}{l_x}\right] + \frac{2S.l_{x+n}}{l_x}.$$

Illustration 6 : Calculate the value of an anticipated endowment assurance for a person aged 25 with the following benefits :

(*i*) a sum of Rs. 1000 payable on survival at the end of 2nd yr.

(*ii*) a sum of Rs. 2000 payable on survival at the end of 3rd yr.

(*iii*) a sum of Rs. 3000 payable on survival at the end of 5th yrs.

(*iv*) a sum of Rs. 6000 whereever he dies during the 5yrs. period.

(Use LIC (1970–73) mortality table and int. rate 6%).

Solution. In the policy 4 different benefits are given.

∴ first we calculate them separately.

(*i*) In case sum of Rs. 1000 payable on survival at the end of 2nd yr.

It is a pure endowment case

$$\therefore \quad NSP = \frac{S \cdot V^n \, l_{x+n}}{l_x}$$

$$l_x = l_{25} = 987095$$

$$l_{x+n} = l_{25+2} = l_{27} = 984580$$

$$i = 0.06$$

$$S = \text{Rs. } 1000$$

$$NSP = 1000 \left[\frac{(1.06)^{-2} \, 984580}{987095} \right]$$

$$= 1000 \times 0.8877286$$

$$= 887.73/-$$

(*ii*) In case of sum of Rs. 2000 payable on survival at the end of 3rd yr.

It is the case of pure endowment.

$$n = 3$$

$$l_x = l_{25} = 987095$$

$$l_{x+n} = l_{25+3} = l_{28} = 983330$$

$$i = 0.06$$

$$S = \text{Rs. } 2000/-.$$

$$NSP = S \cdot \frac{V^3 \, l_{28}}{l_{25}}$$

$$= 2000 \left[\frac{(1.06)^{-3} \, 983330}{987095} \right]$$

$$= 2000 \times 0.833364167$$

$$= 1672.83/-$$

(*iii*) In case of sum of Rs. 3000 payable on survival at the end of 5th yr.

$$n = 5$$

$$l_x = l_{25} = 987095$$

$$l_{x+n} = l_{25+5} = l_{30} = 980776$$

$$i = 0.06$$

$$S = \text{Rs. } 3000/-$$

$$NSP = S \, \frac{V^5 \, l_{30}}{l_{25}}$$

$$= 3000 \left[\frac{(1.06)^{-5} \, 980776}{987095} \right]$$

$$= 3000 \times 0.7424744$$

$$= 2227.42/-$$

(*iv*) In case a sum of Rs. 6000 wherever he dies during the 5 yrs. period.

It is the case of term assurance.

$$NSP = S\left[\frac{Vd_x + V^2 d_{x+1} + ... V^n d_{x+n-1}}{l_x}\right]$$

$$n = 5$$

$$NSP = S\left[\frac{Vd_{25} + V^2 d_{26} + V^3 d_{27} + V^4 d_{28} + V^5 d_{29}}{l_{25}}\right]$$

$$= \frac{6000}{987095}\left[\begin{matrix}(1.06)^{-1}1263 + (1.06)^{-2}1252 + (1.06)^{-3}1250 \\ +(1.06)^{-4}1268 + (1.06)^{-5}1286\end{matrix}\right]$$

$$= \frac{6000}{987095}\left[\begin{matrix}1191.5094 + 1114.2754 + 1049.5239 \\ +1004.3746 + 960.9738\end{matrix}\right]$$

$$= \frac{6000}{987095} \times 5320.6571$$

$$= \text{Rs. } 3234/-$$

Therefore the NSP of anticipated endowment assurance

$$= \text{Rs. } (887.73 + 1672.83 + 2227.42 + 3234)$$

$$= \text{Rs. } 4820.32/-.$$

6.6.6 Net Level Premium

It may not be possible for all the persons desirous of having ins. protection to pay single premium *i.e.*, their lump-sum contribution to secure benefits under an insurance plan. If the period of ins. is more than 1 yr. it is possible to pay the premium every year at the beg. of each year instead of single lump-sum payment. The first premium is paid at the commencement of policy. They may be periodically, half yearly, quarterly or any other premium.

***Illustration** 7* **:** Consider the illustration 5. Calculate net level premium for the term assurance if

(*i*) the insurers earns no interest.

(*ii*) he earns interest at 6%.

Solution. (*i*) In case of no interest

Let P be the level annual premium.

1st year – 10,000 persons pay premium.

∴ Total premium rec. in 1st yr = 10,000 P.

2nd yr. – 9972 persons pay premium.

∴ Total prem. rec. in 2nd yr. = 9972 P

Thus, in 10 yrs, total premium rec.

$$= 10{,}000P + 9972\,P + ...\,9608\,P$$

$= 98303\ P$ ...(1)

Total claim amt. $= 462 ´ 10{,}000$ (refer illustration 5.)

$= 46200000$ $(462 = d_{35} + d_{36} + d + d_{44})$

Total premium = Total claim ...(2)

$\therefore$ $98303P = 46200000.$

$P = 470/-$

(ii) In case 6% interest

Present value of total claims paid during 10 yrs.

$= 32389220$ ...(1)

(refer illustration 2)

To find present value of premiums :

Yr.	*Age*	l_x	*Pr. of Premium*
1	35	10,000	10,000 *P*
2	36	9972	$9972\ P\ (1.06)^{-1} = 9{,}408\ P$
3	37	9941	$9941\ P\ (1.06)^{-2} = 8{,}847\ P$
4	38	9907	$9907\ P\ (1.06)^{-3} = 8{,}318\ P$
5	39	9869	$9869\ P\ (1.06)^{-4} = 7{,}817\ P$
6	40	9827	$9827\ P\ (1.06)^{-5} = 7{,}343\ P$
7	41	9780	$9870\ P\ (1.06)^{-6} = 6{,}895\ P$
8	42	9828	$9728\ P\ (1.06)^{-7} = 6{,}470\ P$
9	43	9671	$9671\ P\ (1.06)^{8} = 6{,}068\ P$
10	44	9603	$9603\ P\ (1.06)^{-9} = 5{,}687\ P$
			Total = 76,853 *P*

PV of total premiums collected $= 76853\ P$

PV of total premiums = *PV* of total claims

$\therefore$ $76853P = 32389220$

$$P = \frac{32389220}{76853}$$

$P =$ Rs. 421.44/–

Illustration 8 : The following particulars are given below :

x	25	26	27	28	29	30
l_x	97380	97088	96794	96496	94194	95887
d_x	292	294	298	302	307	313

Calculate the *NLP* for the assurances given below considering the interest rate 6%.

(*a*) a temporary assurance of Rs. 1000 for 2 yrs.

(*b*) a pure endowment policy of Rs. 600 for the person aged 27 at the end of 3 yrs.

Solution. (*a*) Let *P* be the Level Annual Premium.

PV of total premium $= 97380\ P + 97088\ P\ (1.06)^{-1}$

$= 98380\ P + 91592\ P$

$= 188972\ P$ ...(1)

Policy amt. = Rs. 1000.

PV of total claim $= 292 \times 1000\ (1.06)^{-1} + 294 \times 1000\ (1.06)^{-1}$

$= 275471.69 + 261688.95$

$= 537130.64$ ...(2)

PV of total premium = PV of total claim

$\therefore$ $188972\ P = 537130.64$

$P = 2.84/-$

(*b*) Pure endowment of Rs. 600 for a person aged 27 at the end of 3 yrs.

The no. of persons who reach age 30 *i.e.*, completes age 29 $= l_{30}$

$= 95887$

Total amt. of claim $= 95887 \times 600$

PV of total claims $= 95887 \times 600\ (1.06)^{-3}$

$= 48305143$ ...(1)

PV of total premium $= 96794\ P + 96496\ P\ (1.06)^{-1} + 96194\ P\ (1.06)^{-2}$

$= 96794\ P + 91034\ P + 85612\ P$

$= 273440\ P$

PV of total claim = PV of total premium

$48305143 = 273440\ P$

$\therefore$ $P = 176.66/-$

6.6.7 Calculation of Gross Premium

The GP is that premium which is charged by the insurer to meet the amt. of both claim and expenses. Thus the GP includes the net premium and Loading. Loading is the process to add expenses to net premium. This is also called office premium. The GP (P') is calculated as follows :

$$P' = P + \frac{I}{a} + r\%\text{ of } P' + C$$

where $P' \rightarrow$ Gross Premium

$P \rightarrow$ Single Premium

$I \rightarrow$ Initial expenses

$a \rightarrow$ present value of annuity due to Re. 1.

$r \rightarrow$ renewal expenses at a% of office premium

$c \rightarrow$ constant expenditure.

Illustration 9 **:** If the annual premium for an endowment assurance of Rs. 1000 for person age 40 yrs. for a term of 20 yrs is Rs. 30. Calculate of office premium having the following provisions :

(*a*) initial expenses Rs. 40 per 1000 sum assurance

(*b*) renewal expenses at 10% office premium

(c) a constant exp. of Rs. 2.50 per 1000 sum assured $\left(\text{Given, } a_{40:\overline{19|}} = 16\right)$.

Solution. $P' = P + \frac{I}{a} + r\%$ of $P' + C.$

Given, p = Rs. 30

I = Rs. 40

Renewal exp. $r\%$ = 10%

$$P' = 30 + \frac{40}{16} + 10\% \text{ of } P' + 2.5.$$

$$P' = 30 + 2.5 + 0.1\,P' + 2.5$$

$$0.9\,P' = 35$$

$$P' = \frac{35}{0.9}$$

$$P' = 38.90.$$

Key Terms

- ❒ Pool
- ❒ Probability
- ❒ Probability
- ❒ Binomial Distribution
- ❒ Poisson Distribution
- ❒ Mortality rate
- ❒ Mortality Table
- ❒ Components of Mortality Table
- ❒ Probability of Survival
- ❒ Premium
- ❒ Loading
- ❒ Term Assurance
- ❒ Pure Endowment Assurance
- ❒ Double Endowment Assurance
- ❒ Law of Large Numbers
- ❒ Bulk Buyer
- ❒ Self-insurance
- ❒ Ruin Theory
- ❒ Collective Risk Theory
- ❒ Survival rate
- ❒ Construction of Morality Table
- ❒ Expectation of Life
- ❒ Probability of Death
- ❒ Net Premium
- ❒ Gross Premium
- ❒ Whole Life Assurance
- ❒ Endowment Assurance

Questions for Review

1. "Insurance is a dual application of law of large numbers." Discuss.
2. Define Pooling. Briefly explain the advantages of pooling to insurance institutions.
3. What is mortality Table? Explain how it is used in Calculation of premium.
4. Explain how mortality table is constructed.
5. What are the components of a complete mortality table?
6. Derive the relation : $P_x' + q_x = 1.$
7. What is net premium? How does it differ from Gross premium?
8. Write a short note on Endowment Assurance.

9. How does term assurance differ from whole life assurance?

10. Find the probability that

(*i*) a life aged 35 will die between the age 45 and 50;

(*ii*) a life aged 35 will not die between 45 and 50;

(*iii*) a life aged 35 will die in the 10th year from now;

(*iv*) a life aged 35 will not die in the 10th year from now.

Ans. : (*i*) 0.0277; (*ii*) 0.9723; (*iii*) 0.0041; (*iv*) 0.9959

11. Given the following rates of mortality, what is the probability that a person aged 65 will die between ages 69 and 70?

Age	*Rate of Mortality*
65	0.035
66	0.040
67	0.045
68	0.050
69	0.055

Ans. : 0.04623

12. Using the LIC (1970–73) ultimate table, compute the following probabilities.

(*i*) Probability that a life aged 40 survives 10 years;

(*ii*) Probability that a life aged 40 dies within the next 10 years.

(*iii*) Probability that a life aged 40 dies after 10 years.

Ans. : (*i*) 0.9548; (*ii*) 0.0452; (*iii*) 0.9548

13. Of two persons *A* aged 35 and *B* aged 42, find the probability that

(*i*) *A* and *B* both survive 10 years

(*ii*) *A* and *B* both die within 10 years

(*iii*) One of the two lives survives 10 years while the other dies within that period.

(*iv*) Atleast one survives 10 years.

Ans. : (*i*) 0.9189; (*ii*) 0.0015; (*iii*) 0.0796; (*iv*) 0.9985

14. Fill up the blanks in the following portion of a life table :

x	l_x	d_x	q_x	P_x
20	1000000	—	0.0050	—
21	—	—	0.0045	—
22	—	—	—	0.9960
23	—	—	—	0.9965
24	—	—	—	0.9970
25	—	—	0.0025	—

Ans. : d_{20} = 5000 l_{22} = 990522 l_{24} =983107

$P_{20} = 0.9950$	$d_{22} = 3962$	$d_{24} = 2949$
$P_{21} = 995000$	$q_{22} = 0.0040$	$q_{24} = 0.0030$
$d_{21} = 4478$	$l_{23} = 986560$	$l_{25} = 980158$
$P_{21} = 0.9955$	$d_{23} = 3453$	$d_{25} = 2450$
$q_{23} = 0.0035$	$P_{25} = 0.9975$	

15. From the following data, find the number of livings at age 43.

x	l_x	d_x	q_x
40	–	400	0.006
41	–	–	0.007
42	–	–	0.008
43	–	–	–

Ans. : 65277

16. Calculate the value of an assurance of Rs. 1000 for a person aged 25 under which the sum assured is payable in case of death between ages 28 and 30 or on survival to age 30 years from the following data with 6% interest

x :	35	36	37	38	39	40	41	42	43	44	45
l_x :	10000	9972	9941	9907	9869	9827	9780	9728	9671	9608	9538
d_x :	28	31	34	38	42	47	52	57	63	70	75

Ans. : Rs. 740.62

17. Consider the following data :

x :	25	26	27	28	29	30
l_x :	97380	97088	96794	96496	96194	95887
d_x :	292	294	298	302	307	313

(*i*) Ignoring interest and expenses

(*ii*) allowing a rate of 6% per annum

(*a*) The value of temporary assurance of Rs. 10,000 for 2 years for a person aged 26.

(*b*) The value of endowment assurance of Rs. 10,000 for 4 years 15to a person aged 26.

(*c*) The value of pure endowment assurance of Rs. 500 for a person aged 28 receivable on attaining age 0.

Ans. : (*i a*) Rs. 60.98; (*i b*) Rs. 10,000; (*i c*) 496.84
(*ii a*) Rs. 55.87; (*ii b*) 7929.04 (*ii c*) 442.19

18. Calculate the net annual level premium for a double endowment assurance of Rs. 100 for a person aged 60 years, the assured benefit being Rs. 100 in the case of his death before attaining age 63 and Rs. 200 if he survives to age 63. Use the following mortality table and 5% rate of interest.

x :	60	61	62	63	64	65
l_x :	1000	980	958	933	900	860
d_x :	20	22	25	33	40	45

Ans. : 59.69

19. The ent premium of an endowment assurance of Rs. 1000 for a person aged 30 for a term of 25 years is Rs. 30.97. Calculate the office premium making the following provisions

(*a*) Initial expenses at Rs. 40 per Rs. 1000 sum assured

(*b*) Renewal expenses at 8% of Office premium

(*c*) Constrant expenses of Rs. 2.50 per Rs. 1000 sum assured

(Given $a_{40\,:\,\overline{24}|}$ = 15.64) ***Ans. :*** Rs. 39.16

Suggested Readings

1. Hanes U. Garber, *Life Insurance Mathematics,* Springer, 1997.
2. *Mathematical Basis of Life Insurance,* IC 61, Insurance Institute of India, Mumbai, 1999.
3. Hillary S. Seal, *Survival Probabilities — The Goal of Risk Theory,* John Wiley and Sons Ltd., 1978.
4. Karl Borch, *Research Papers in Insurance Models,* Lexington Books, 1974.
5. Statistics, IC 62, *Insurance Institute of India*, Mumbai, 1999.
6. G.H. Monney, *The Valuation of Human Life,* The MacMillan Press Ltd., 1977.
7. S.M. Ross, *Stochastic Processes,* Wiley, 1967.
8. Harrington and Niehaus, *Insurance and Risk Management*, McGraw-Hill, 1999.

Web Resources

- www.math.ethz.ch
- www.probability.net
- www.statsoftinc.com
- www.socstats.saton.ac.uk

Insurance Contracts and Provisions

Chapter 7

Chapter Objectives

After reading this chapter you will be able to understand :

- *Regulation of Insurance Business in India*
- *Nature and element of Insurance Contracts*
- *Various enactments affecting insurance business in India*

7.1 Regulation of Insurance Business in India

Insurance is a federal subject in India. The insurance business is primarily regulated by two statutes:

(*a*) Insurance Act 1938

(*b*) Insurance and Regulatory Development Authority Act, 1999.

The Insurance business is classified into four classes :

(1) Life Insurance business

(2) Fire Insurance Business

(3) Marine

(4) Miscellaneous insurance

Life Insurers transact life insurance business and the rate is transacted by General Insurers. Apart from this, GIC and its subsidiaries are regulated by General Insurance Business (Nationalization) Act, 1972 and LIC of India being regulated by The Life Insurance Corporation Act, 1956. The text of IRDA Act, 1999, General Insurance Business (Nationalisation) Act, 1972 and Life Insurance Corporation Act, 1956 is given in Annexure 9A, 9B and 9C respectively. Regulation of Insurance business provides the insurance market with direction, management control and correction. Insurance, generally, all over the world is widely regulated. This is because of the following reasons:

(*a*) Widespread severe impact of insurer solvency. Since solvency ensures that insurance transactions are certain ad predictable, promotion and maintenance of insurer solvency are at the heart of all regulatory activity. Insureds are generally incapable of self protection and if the insurance company becomes insolvent, the results may be disastrous. Insurance generally mobilise savings, and therefore they bear a kind of fiduciary relationship as that of a banker and customer, and therefore, it requires public regulation.

(*b*) Unequal knowledge and bargaining power of the buyers and seller – insurance contacts are complex and the insurance itself is an intangible product.

(*c*) Insurance pricing is — typical and unique and requires estimation before the costs are fully known.

(*d*) Social welfare – insurance by definition is a sound device and optimally should be made available to public at large without discrimination.

7.2 Legal Framework of Insurance Business

Insurance is made available to the public through the medium of contracts that detail the rights and duties of the parties to the insurance agreement. These contracts may range from implied or oral agreements, as in the binders given by fire and casualty insurance agents, to formal written contracts issued by companies.

Most of the insurance contracts are expressed in writing even when an oral binder initiates the transaction.

Insurance contracts are complicated because of the technical nature of the subject matter, the statutory requirement that certain language be employed, and the need to avoid terms that may be construed as ambiguous. However, the need for legal clarity may lead to a contract that is beyond the comprehension of the typical insurance consumer. Furthermore, the technical nature of many contracts often distracts from the mutual understanding of its terms by the parties to the contract.

Insurance contract can broadly be classified into two categories (a) life and (b) non-life insurance. The subject matter of life insurance is life of the assured. In a life policy the life is covered for a certain amount which is payable on the maturity of the policy or on the death of policyholder which is earlier. The amount is payable on death to the nominee/legal heir of the deceased.

Non-life insurance can again be categorised according to the uncertainties and events covered by the respective policies. Some examples of non-life insurance policies are householders insurance and fire insurance. Personal accident insurance is linked to human life hence would not strictly fall in the category of non-life insurance though the characteristic of uncertainty which attracts to non life insurance is manifested even in personal accident and medical insurance policies respectively.

The primary law governing contracts of insurance is the Indian Contract Act, 1872. However, there many issues not covered by the said Act. This may relate to torts, consumer rights, transfer of property, agency issues etc.

Torts and Crimes

Torts

A tort is a private wrong. It occurs whenever someone acts or fails to act in such a manner that an individual's peace of mind or right are jeopardized. It refers to any individual's action that effectively deprives another of his right to security of person, reputation, or property. Technically, each tort is defined in terms of specific statutory or common law requirements, and these vary substantially in different jurisdictions. Negligence, assault, battery, libel, slander, trespass, fraud, and false imprisonment are examples of torts. Torts differ from crimes in that the latter are public wrongs. A crime is any act that the legislature determines to be punishable by law. The same act may include all of the elements of a particular tort and a particular crime, in which case there exists a public remedy in the form of punishment prescribed by law and a private remedy that is often in the form of monetary damages.

Torts are important in insurance because they are a major source of loss covered by liability insurance. The automobile insurance policy is essential because it provides for payment of judgments awarded by the courts in negligence cases as well as the costs of litigation or claims settlement. The comprehensive personal liability insurance policy covers losses arising from negligent conduct unrelated to the care, custody, or control of the automobile or to business pursuits. The comprehensive general liability insurance policy covers losses occurring as a direct result of negligence in many business situations.

Crimes

Some crimes that are recognized by statute are specific to insurance, while others are relevant to insurance law because they are crimes committed to obtain funds illegally from insurance companies. A few example of crimes are:

(*a*) *Rebating* : passing of commission/incentives by agents to prospective insureds to purchase on insurance policy.

(b) *Twisting* : inducing an individual to terminate are life insurance policy in order to buy another to the disadvantage of the insured.

(c) *Filing of false claims* : attempt to collect money from an insurance company when there is no loss or the padding or inflation of claims by procuring excessive and fraudulent estimates of damages.

(d) *Unlicensed insurance activity* : Unlicensed person engaging in any insurance transaction that requires licensing (guilty of a misdemeanor).

(e) *Defamation* : publication of material that might tend to lessen public confidence in the institution of insurance.

(f) *Asson* : felonious burning of property of another to defraud an insurance company.

(g) *Homicide* : when the beneficiary of a life insurance policy swindles the insured for the purpose of obtaining the proceeds of the policy or otherwise.

(h) *Breach of trust* : agents using or mingling the client's insurance premiums with their own funds.

(i) *Unfair discrimination* : charging of different rates by a single insurance company to similar risk class.

(j) *Conspiracy* : dishonest agent conspires with his client to defraud the insurance company by misrepresentation, by filing false claims or falsifying documents.

7.3 Indian Contract Act, 1872

Insurance contracts are agreements between insurance companies and insured for the purpose of transferring from insured to the insurer a part of the risk of loss arising out of contingent event. Therefore all the provisions of Indian Contract Act, 1872, in general are applicable to insurance contracts. Under Section 10 of the Indian Contract Act, following conditions are necessary to form a valid contract:

(a) Agreement between two parties

(b) Lawful object

(c) Capacity to contract

(d) Consideration

(e) Possibility of performance etc.

Offer and Acceptance

The offer for entering into insurance contract generally come from the insured (proposer). The insurance company may also propose to make the contract. In order to constitute a valid acceptance, offer and its acceptance must fulfil the requirements as prescribed by the Indian Contract Act, 1872. Whether the offer is made by the insurer or insured, the moot point is acceptance.

Any act that precedes it is an offer or a counter-offer. All that precede the offer or counter-offer is an invitation to offer. In insurance, the publication of prospectus, the canvassing of the agents are invitations to offer. When the proposer proposes to enter the contract it is an offer and if there is any alteration in the offer that would be a counter-offer. If this alteration or change (counter-offer) is accepted by the proposer, it would be an acceptance. In absence of counter-offer, the acceptance of offer will be an acceptance by the insurer. At the moment, the notice of acceptance is given to other party, it would be a valid acceptance.

On acceptance of the proposal by the insurer, a valid and binding contract comes into existence. If the insurer indicates a higher premium than the normal as per proposal or conditions of acceptance are different from the standards ones, such indication tantamounts to a counter-offer which the proposer may or may not accept. It is necessary that in order to make a binding contract of insurance, the parties must agree upon every material term affecting the agreement.

In case of Life insurance a valid and binding contract comes into existence upon payment of first premium. When a proposal form duly filled in by the proposer is accepted by the insurer, the acceptance communicated to the proposer is in reality a counter-offer indicating that the proposal will be accepted on payment of the premium and communication of the assent of the proposer to special terms, if any. Unless the proposer assents to or complies with the terms of insurer no contract would come into existence.

Every contract of insurance must be in writing and must comply with the provisions of the Indian Stamp Act. An oral or informal contract gives the insured a right to call for a stamped policy, even after the loss insured against has occurred in view of the Indian Stamp Act, 1899.

An issuance of a policy may some time takes time after acceptance of risk in view of underwriting and administrative procedures. The issuers may issue a cover note for a stipulated period which is also a valid evidence of contract.

Legal Object

For a valid contract, the object of the agreement should be lawful and must not be prohibited by any law. Any subject matter of contract that is (*i*) not forbidden by law, or (*ii*) is not immoral, or (*iii*) opposed to public policy, or (*iv*) which does not defeat the provisions of any law, is lawful. The subject matter of insurance in the proposal form and also the consideration should be legal. If there is any contract to defraud the insurer rather than based on round principles of indemnity, the contract is void.

Mistake and Misrepresentation

A contract of insurance is a contract uberrimae fidei, *i.e.*, is based on the principle of utmost good faith. If utmost good faith is not observed by either party insurer or insured the contract may be avoided by the other.

Capacity to Contract

The rules laid down under the Indian Contract Act, 1872, defining the contractual capacity of the parties apply generally to insurance contracts in the same manner as they apply to other types of contracts.

Every person is competent to contract (*a*) who is of the age of majority according to the law, (*b*) who is of sound mind, and (*c*) who is not disqualified from contracting by any law to which he is subject.

The capacity of an insurer to enter into contracts of insurance depends upon its constitution.

A minor is, therefore, incompetent to contract, and a contract with a minor is a nullity; but under certain circumstances, an insurer may issue a policy on the life of a minor. Under the system of deferred assurance policies, the insurance contract is with a parent or legal guardian, who is competent to contract.

Consideration

For insurance contracts, consideration is in the form of premium to be paid by the insured and a promise to pay, compensate or indemnify in accordance with the terms and conditions incorporated in the policy, on the part of the insurer. A premium is the price for the risk undertaken by the insurers. It is the consideration receivable by the insurers from the insured in exchange for their undertaking to pay the sum insured in case the event insured against takes place.

Amount of premium is not the criteria, but a contract without payment of premium is void.

Free Consent

Parties entering into the contract should enter into the contract by their free and genuine consent. The consent shall be free with it is not caused by : (1) coercion, (2) undue influence, (3) fraud, or (4) misrepresentation,or (5) mistake. When there is no free consent except fraud the contract becomes voidable at the option of the party whose consent was so obtained. In case of fraud, the contract would be void. The proposal for free consent, must sign a declaration to this effect, the person explaining the subject-matter of the proposal to the proposer must also accordingly make a written declaration on the proposal.

The proposer must full disclose all material information and sign a declaration in the proposal. Also, the insurer must full disclose the product details to the proposer.

Examples of Material Circumstances in Marine Insurance

1. Concealing the nationality of the insured when such nationality is of importance [*Associated Oil Carriers Ltd. v. Union Ins. Society of Canton* (1917) 2 K.B. 184].
2. The fact that the ship had developed a leak before the insurance was effected [*Russel v. Thorton* 1859 20 L.R. Ex. 9].
3. The fact that the goods carried on the ship are grossly over-valued when the ship is insured. [*Ionidies* v. *Pender* (1874) L.R. 7. Q.B. 531].

Discharge of Contract

A contract terminates in the following situations :

1. **Performance :** *When all the terms of the contract* in terms of performance have been carried out. Payment of premium and payment of claim by respective parties.
2. **Release :** *When one party to the contract* agrees to excuse performance by the other party after breach of the contract by the latters. Denial of a claim by insured on account of fraud.
3. **Discharge :** (*a*) ***Discharge by implied consent or impossibility of performance:*** *The law does not compel a man to do the impossible thing. Contract* is discharged when performance becomes impossible:
   (*i*) Due to destruction of the subject-matter;
   (*ii*) Due to death or incapacity of the promisor in a contract for personal services;
   (*iii*) Due to subsequent change of legislation;
   (*iv*) Due to non-existence or cessation of a state of affairs, the existence or continuance of which formed the basis of the contract; and
   (*v*) Due to such an alternation of circumstances as to bring about complete frustration of the commercial object.

   (*b*) **Discharge by tender :** *Where on party is ready and willing to perform his promise and has offered to do so at the right time and place, but the other party does not accept performance, the contract* is discharged by tender or 'attempted performance'.
4. **Void Contracts :** *When an agreement is discovered to be void.*
5. **Breach of Contract :** *When a contract has been broken.* Where the insured has committed such a breach the insurer can terminate the contract of insurance.
6. **Novation :** *If the parties to a contract* for it or rescind or later it, the original contract need not be performed.

Agency

The law relating to agency is part of the Indian Contract Act. An agent is defined as "a person employed to do any act for another, or to represent in dealings with third persons."

The person for whom such an act is done or who is so represented is called the Principal. Section 226 of the Contract Act states that "Contracts entered into through an agent, an obligation arising from acts done by an agent, may be enforced in the same manner, and will have the same legal consequences as if the contracts has been entered into and the acts done by the principal in person". A contract of agency may be made in writing or verbally. When it is in writing, it is in the form of power of attorney. Following provision's are worthnoting:

- An agent cannot lawfully employ another to perform acts, which he has expressly or implied undertaken to perform personally, unless by ordinary custom of trade or from the nature of the agency, a sub-agent must be employed. This involves the general maxim of law that a delegatee cannot further sub-delegate. A "sub-agent" is a person employed by, and acting under the control of, the original agent in the business of the agency.
- Where a sub agent is properly appointed, the principal is, represented by the sub-agent and is bound by and responsible for his acts as if he were an agent originally appointed by the principal.
- The agent is responsible to the principal for the acts of the sub-agent.
- The sub-agent is responsible for his acts to the agent, but not to the principal, except in cases of fraud of wilful wrong.
- If an agent does something on behalf of the principal but without his knowledge or authority, the principal may elect to ratify the action or to disown it. A principal ratifying any unauthorized act done on his behalf ratifies the whole of the transaction of which such act formed part.

In an agent deals on his own account in the business of the agency, without first obtaining the consent of his principal and acquainting him with all material circumstances which have come on his own knowledge on the subject, the principal may repudiate the transaction, if the case shows either that any material fact has been dishonestly concealed from him by the agent or that the dealings of the agent have been disadvantageous to him.

If an agent does a criminal act, the principal is not liable to the agent, either upon an express or an implied promise, to indemnify him against the consequence of that act.

Where an agent does more than he is authorized to do, and what he does beyond the scope of his authority cannot be separated from what is within it, the principal is not bound to recognise the transaction.

In the absence of any contract to that effect, an agent cannot personally enforce contracts entered into by him on behalf of his principal nor is he personally bound by them.

Termination of Agency : An agency is terminated by the principal revoking his authority; or by the agent renouncing the business of the agency; or by the business of the agency being completed; or on the death of either the principal or the agent.

Agent's Duty : An agent is bound to conduct the business of his principal according to the directions given by the principal, or in the absence of any such directions, according to the custom which prevails in doing business of the same kind at the place where the agent conducts such business. When the agent acts otherwise and any loss is caused, he must make it good to his principal, and if any profit accrues, he must account for it.

Misrepresentations made or frauds committed by agents acting in the course of their business for their principals have the same effect on agreement made by such agents as if such misrepresentations or frauds has been made or committed by the principals; but misrepresentations made or frauds committed by agents in matters which do not fall within their authority, do not affect their principals.

7.4 LAWS CONCERNING INSURANCE

Insurance Act, 1938

Insurance Act, 1938 is the primary law that governs the insurance business in India. It provides for the registration and licensing of insurers, payment of premiums, alteration and other policy matters, powers of governments, accounts, audit and other reporting requirements, mode of deposits and investments, constitution of claim settlement authorities.

Insurance Regulatory and Development Authority Act, 1999

The Insurance Regulatory and Development Authority Act, 1999 provides for the establishment of an Authority to protect the interests of holders of insurance policies, to regulate, promote and ensure orderly growth of the insurance industry and for matters connected therewith or incidental thereto and further to amend the Insurance Act, 1938, the Life Insurance Corporation Act, 1956 and the General Insurance Business (Nationalisation) Act, 1972.

Life Insurance Corporation Act, 1956

Life Insurance Corporation Act, 1956 and the regulations made thereunder deals with the formation of Life Insurance Corporation–its functions, powers, capital, transfer of business, conduct of business and other related matters.

General Insurance Business (Nationalisation) Act, 1972

It deals with the formation of GIC and amalgamation of insurers existing prior to the promulation of the Act. It describes the powers and functions of GIC, powers of Central Government and other related issues.

Motor Vehicles Act, 1988

Motor Vehicles Act, 1988 provides for compulsory insurance of motor vehicles. The Act provides that no motor vehicle can be used in a public place unless there is in force in relation to vehicle a policy issued by an authorised insurer. This policy covers the insured person's liability in the event of death, bodily injury of certain persons or damage to property of third persons.

The Inland Steam Vessels Act, 1917 and the Amended Act, 1977

The Act provides that the provisions of chapter VII of the Motors Vehicles Act, 1955 regarding insurance of mechanically propell vessels against third party risks are applicable to steam vessels. The Act maker it compulsory for the owners of operators of inland vessels to insure against legal liability of death, bodily injury or damage caused to the property of third persons and passengers.

Marine Insurance Act, 1963

Marine Insurance Act, 1963 (based on Marine Insurance Act 1906) codifies the law relating the conduct of marine insurance business in India. The provisions of the Act *inter-alia* includes provisions relating to basic insurance principles (Indemnification, insurable interest, utmost goodfaith, subrogation and contribution, valuation, losses, warranties, return of premiums etc.

The Carriage of Goods by Sea Act, 1925

The Act defines the minimum rights, liabilities and immunities of a shipowner on loss or damage to cargo. The act deals with three aspects of a shipowners liabilities towards cargo owner:

(*i*) the circumstances when the shipowner is deemed to be liable for loss or damage to cargo unless he proves otherwise;

(*ii*) the circumstance when the shipowner is exempted from liability, *i.e.*, when loss or damage is caused by events outside his control, *e.g.*, perils of the seas;

(*iii*) the limits of liability of a shipowner for loss of or damage to cargo calculated in monetary terms per package or unit of cargo.

The Merchant Shipping Act, 1958

This Act also provides a certain protection to shipowners. For example, the liability of a shipowner can be limited to certain maximum sum for certain losses, provided the incident giving rise to such claim has arisen without the actual fault or privy of the shipowner.

These claims may relate to loss of life, personal injury or loss of or damage to property on land or water. The Act also confers the obligation on the shipowner to send his ship to sea in a seaworthy and safe condition.

The Bill of Lading Act, 1855

This Act defines the character of the Bill of Lading as an evidence of the contract of carriage of goods between the shipowner and the shipper, as an acknowledgement of the receipt of the goods on board the vessel and, as a document of title. The bill of lading is one of the various documents required in connection with settlement of marine cargo claims.

The Indian Ports (Major Ports) Act, 1963

This Act defines the liability of Port Trust Authorities for loss of or damage to goods whilst in their custody and prescribes time limits for filing monetary claim on, or suit against, the Port Trust Authorities.

The Indian Railways Act, 1890

The Indian Railways Act, passed in 1890 was amended in 1961 and the amendment came into force from 1st January, 1962. The Act deals with various aspects of Railway Administration. However, Chapter VII is relevant to Marine Insurance practice as it deals with the responsibility of Railway Administration as carriers.

This Chapter makes provision, *inter alia,* for the following:

(*a*) rights and liabilities of railways as carriers of goods:

(*b*) procedure for notification of claims for compensation for losses.

The Railways Claims Tribunal Act, 1987 provides for formation of tribunals to deal with claims for cargo loss, personal injuries, excess freight, etc. and prescribes procedures thereunder.

The Carriers Act, 1865

The Act defines the rights and liabilities of truck owners or operators who carry goods for public hire in respect of loss or damage to goods carried by them.

The Act also prescribes the time limit within which notice of loss or damage must be filed with the road carriers.

The Indian Post Office Act, 1898

This Act defines the liability of the Government for loss, misdelivery, delay of or damage to any postal articles in course of transmission by post.

The Carriage by Air Act, 1972

This Act gives effect to the provisions of the Warsaw Convention, 1929 and the Hague Protocol, 1955 relating to international carriage of passengers and goods by air.

The Act defines the liability of the air carrier for death of or injury to passengers and loss of or damage to registered luggage and cargo.

The Act also prescribes the maximum limits of liability for death, injury, damage etc. and also prescribes the time limits within which claims have to be filed on the air carrier.

The provisions of the Act also apply with some changes, to domestic carriage, that is, carriage within India.

Multi Modal Transportation Act, 1993

The Act provides for registration of multi-modal transport operators engaged in transportation of goods under more than one mode of transport, i.e., by rail/road and sea. The Act prescribes limits of liability of the operator, contents of documents to be issued by them, notice of loss, etc.

Workmen's Compensation Act, 1923

The Act provides for the payment by employers to their workmen of compensation for injury by accident, arising out of and in the course of employment. The object of this legislation has been stated as follows:

The growing complexity of industry in this country, with the increasing use of machinery and consequent danger to workmen, along with the comparative poverty of the workmen themselves render it advisable that they should be protected as far as possible, from hardship out of accidents.

It provides certain benefits to employees in case of accidents during employment, sickness, maternity etc.

Employees State Insurance Act, 1948

The Employees' State Insurance Act, 1948, has been described as an Act "to provide for certain benefits to employees in cases of sickness, maternity and employment injury and to make provision for certain other matters in relation thereof "Under the Act, the Employees' State Insurance Corporation has been set up to administer the Insurance Scheme.

The Scheme is applicable to industrial employees as defined in the Act. The Act operated in certain industrial areas as notified by the Government from time to time. It is intended that the Act will be eventually extended to all industrial areas in the country. Under the scheme a fund is maintained consisting of contributions from the employees, employers and the Government. From this fund the following expenses are met:

(*i*) Sickness benefit, maternity benefit, disablement benefit, dependants' benefit (death) and medical treatment

(*ii*) Establishment and maintenance of hospital, dispensaries, etc. for the benefit of the insured persons and their families.

(*iii*) Administration of the Scheme.

The Indian Stamp Act, 1899

The Indian Stamp Act requires that a policy of insurance be stamped in accordance with the schedule of rate prescribed.

The Consumer Protection Act, 1986

The Act applies to all goods and services unless specifically exempted by Central Government. The provisions of the Act are compensatory in nature.

It enshrines the following rights of the consumers:

(*i*) The right to be protected against the marketing of goods which are hazardous of life and property;

(*ii*) The right to be informed about the quality, quantity, potency, purity, standard and price of goods so as to protect the consumer against unfair trade practices;

(*iii*) The right to be heard and to be assured that consumers interest will receive due consideration at appropriate forum;

(*iv*) The right to seek redressal against unfair trade practices or unscrupulous exploitation of consumers;

(*v*) The right to consumer education.

Under Section 2(e) of the Act, the insurance is recognised as services. Chapter 32 of the Act elaborates various consumer rights.

Arbitration and Conciliation Act, 1996

Arbitration means the reference of a matter in dispute to the judgment of a person selected by the parties to the dispute. Arbitration thus is a private process of resolution of disputes and it is commonly resorted to because it is less formal, less expensive and less time consuming than proceedings in a court of law.

An arbitration condition is incorporated in a majority of "Non-marine general insurance policies."

The main objectives of the Act, *inter alia*, are:

(*i*) To comprehensively cover international and commercial arbitration and conciliation as also domestic arbitration and conciliation;

(*ii*) To make provision for an arbitral procedure which is fair, efficient and capable of meeting the needs of the specific arbitration;

(*iii*) To provide that the arbitral tribunal gives reasons for its arbitral award;

(*iv*) To minimise the supervisory role of courts in the arbitral process;

(*v*) To permit an arbitral tribunal to use mediation, conciliation or other procedures during the arbitral proceedings to encourage settlement of disputes;

(*vi*) To provide that every final arbitral award is enforced in the same manner as if it were a decree of the court.

7·5 INSURANCE CONTRACTS – IMPORTANT FEATURES

The principle functions of an insurance contract are :

(1) to define the risk that is to be transferred

(2) to state the conditions under which the contract applies and

(3) to explain the procedure for settling losses.

Nature of Contract

An insurance contract as four attributes:

(*a*) *Entirety* : all the terms and conditions are to be found in the policy document. If the terms and conditions are oral or not stated explicitly they are difficult for parties to prove.

(*b*) *Personal* : the contact follows the person, the insured, rather than property.

(*c*) *Unilateral* : After the insured pays the premiums the performance is obligatory on one party, i.e. the insurer.

(*d*) *Aleatory* : performance is conditioned upon an event that may or may not happen

7·5·1 Elements of Insurance Contract

The four basic elements to every insurance contract are:

(*a*) **Application :** An application is required for every contract of insurance. In the application, which is an offer to enter into a contract, the prospective insured sets forth the facts and figures required by the insurance carrier's underwriting department. The application may be brief and oral, or of any length and in written form. In life insurance, the application itself becomes a part of the contract.

(*b*) **Binders :** A binder is a memorandum specifying some of the details of the property or liability policy to be issued by the company. It is memorandum of insurance issued pending delivery of the formal policy. The binder may be oral or written and may be given either by an agent or a company. A broker, not being an agent of an insurance company, cannot issue binders. The binder is usually a temporary document and ordinarily would remain in force no more than ten days. For example, in automobile insurance a car buyer wants immediate coverage. By binding the insurance company to the risk, the agent need not wait for the insurance to become effective.

Binders are not used in life insurance. Given the long term nature of the contract and the insurer's inability to cancel a life insurance policy, the life insurer requires an opportunity to examine the application (and possible the applicant) before being bound to a lifetime contract. However, in place of binders the life insurance agent can provide the applicant with a receipt (assuming the first premium installment is paid) that will provide varying insurance benefits depending on the nature of the receipt.

(c) **Policy Forms :** are formal written contract of insurance that sets forth all of the terms of the agreement. The policy had two parts:

(*i*) *Heading :* It is the declaration page and identifies the risk by specifying the name of the issued, the address location of the risk, period covered by the policy, description of the subject being insured, the amount of insurance the amount of the premium, and any warranties of representations made by the insured.

(*ii*) *Body :* It is the contract itself containing the various clauses pertaining to agreements exclusion and condition.

(*iii*) *Back :* It specifies the rights of the insured and the duties of the insurer. The condition, and stipulations define the rights and duties of the parties aside from injury agreement.

Standardization of policy forms is an ongoing process, and most insurance contracts have uniform language for the greater part of their terms. Such standardisation makes possible economies of operation, statistical uniformity, and better communication between the insured, his agent, and the insurance company. Where language has been standardised, determination of the meaning of the words and phrases by the courts reduces the chance a misunderstanding.

(*iv*) *Endorsement :* An endorsement is a form that is used to modify the policy contract Endorsements may extend or restrict coverage, permit transfers of interest in property, transfer coverage, transfer coverage from one place to another, increases or decreases limits of coverage, provide for assignment of policies or changes in beneficiary designations, provide for changes in settlement options elected, or in any other legal manner permit amendments to the contract.

Endorsement are usually done by party forms or by embossing through rubber stamps of the desired alteration.

7.5.2 Maxims Applicable to Insurance Contracts

The following maxims are elemental to insurance contracts and their interpretation:

(*a*) *Uberrimac fiddi :* Utmost good faith

(*b*) *Spes successions :* hope of succession — direct and not hope of insurable interest

(c) *Cause proxima :* the proximate and immediate cause of loss is important

(*d*) *Pari Delicto :* parties to be equally blamed — in case of illegal policies, the premium cannot be recovered/ returned.

(*e*) *Salus Populist supermen :* the regard for pubic interest and welfare is the highest in law

(f) *Rao ipsa loquitor :* the thing speaks for itself for example in case of accidents, the circumstances of the case and not more occurrence of the events has to be seen.

7.6 AGENCY

The law relating to agency is part of the Indian Contract Act. An agent is defined as "a person employed to do any act for another, or to represent in dealings with third persons."

The person for whom such an act is done or who is so represented is called the Principal. Section 226 of the Contract Act states that "Contracts entered into through an agent, an obligation arising from acts done by an agent, may be enforced in the same manner, and will have the same legal consequences as if the contracts has been entered into and the acts done by the principal in person". A contract of agency may be made in writing or verbally. When it is in writing, it is in the form of power of attorney. Following provision]s are worthnoting:

- An agent cannot lawfully employ another to perform acts, which he has expressly or implied undertaken to perform personally, unless by ordinary custom of trade or from the nature of the agency, a sub-agent must be employed. This involves the general maxim of law that a delegatee cannot further sub-delegate. A "sub-agent" is a person employed by, and acting under the control of, the original agent in the business of the agency.
- Where a sub agent is properly appointed, the principal is, represented by the sub-agent and is bound by and responsible for his acts as if he were an agent originally appointed by the principal.
- The agent is responsible to the principal for the acts of the sub-agent.
- The sub-agent is responsible for his acts to the agent, but not to the principal, except in cases of fraud of wilful wrong.
- If an agent does something on behalf of the principal but without his knowledge or authority, the principal may elect to ratify the action or to disown it. A principal ratifying any unauthorized act done on his behalf ratifies the whole of the transaction of which such act formed part.

In an agent deals on his own account in the business of the agency, without first obtaining the consent of his principal and acquainting him with all material circumstances which have come on his own knowledge on the subject, the principal may repudiate the transaction, if the case shows either that any material fact has been dishonestly concealed from him by the agent or that the dealings of the agent have been disadvantageous to him.

If an agent does a criminal act, the principal is not liable to the agent, either upon an express or an implied promise, to indemnify him against the consequence of that act.

Where an agent does more than he is authorized to do, and what he does beyond the scope of his authority cannot be separated from what is within it, the principal is not bound to recognise the transaction.

In the absence of any contract to that effect, an agent cannot personally enforce contracts entered into by him on behalf of his principal nor is he personally bound by them.

Termination of Agency : An agency is terminated by the principal revoking his authority; or by the agent renouncing the business of the agency; or by the business of the agency being completed; or on the death of either the principal or the agent.

Agent's Duty : An agent is bound to conduct the business of his principal according to the directions given by the principal, or in the absence of any such directions, according to the custom which prevails in doing business of the same kind at the place where the agent conducts such business. When the agent acts otherwise and any loss is caused, he must make it good to his principal, and if any profit accrues, he must account for it.

Misrepresentations made or frauds committed by agents acting in the course of their business for their principals have the same effect on agreement made by such agents as if such misrepresentations or frauds has been made or committed by the principals; but misrepresentations made or frauds committed by agents in matters which do not fall within their authority, do not affect their principals.

Key Terms

- ❒ Contract
- ❒ Indemnity
- ❒ Subrogation
- ❒ Exempted Insurers
- ❒ Crime
- ❒ Binders
- ❒ Cause Proxima
- ❒ Void Contracts

Questions for Review

1. Briefly summarise the various legal provisions applicable to insurance business in India.
2. Write short notes on :
   (a) Licensing of insurance companies
   (b) Elements of insurance contracts
   (c) Maxims applicable to insurance contracts.
3. "Insurance business is partially regulated in India." Do you agree? Give reasons for your answer.

Suggested Readings

1. Anoop K. Kaushal and S.K. Mohanty, *Insurance Law Manual,* Universal Law Publishing Co. Pvt. Ltd. 2002.
2. Kenneth S. Abraham, *Distributing Risk — Insurance, Legal Theory and Public Policy,* Yate University Press, 1986.
3. J.E. Grieder and W.T. Breadles, *Law and the Life Insurance Contract,* Richard D. Irwin, 1968.
4. *Practice of General Insurance,* Insurance Institute of India, Mumbai, 1999.
5. M.N. Srinivasan, Principles of Insurance Law, Wadwa & Company, Nagpur, 2006.

Web Resources

- www.irdaindia.org
- www.bimaonline.com
- www.indiacore.com
- www.insuranceinstituteindia.com

Primary Insurance Laws

Chapter 8

Chapter Objectives

After reading this chapter you will be able to understand :

- *Structure of various laws govering insurance business in India.*
- *Regulation of Insurance Business by IRDA.*
- *Conduct of Life and Non-Life Insurance Business in India.*

The building blocs of the insurance law are Insurance Act 1938, IRDA Act 1999, LIC Insurance Corporation Act 1956 and General Insurance Business (Nationalisation) Act, 1972.

8.1 Insurance Act, 1938

Insurance Act, 1938 and Insurance Rule, 1939 primarily govern the conduct of insurance business in India. As per the preamble of the Act, Insurance Act, 1938 is an act to consolidate and amend the law relating to the business of insurance. Most of the provisions of the Act are applicable to all classes of insurance business.

8.1.1 Definitions

(*i*) Life insurance business is defined in the Section 2(11) and includes the contracts of insurance upon human life, which include the granting of disability, allowances, accident benefits, annuities and superannuation allowances. This business may be linked or non-linked business or both.

(*ii*) General insurance business is defined under Section 2(6-B) that includes the marine fire and miscellaneous insurance business whether carried on singly or in combination with one or more of them, *i.e.,* may be linked insurance business.

(*iii*) Marine insurance business includes the business effecting the contract of insurance upon vessels of any description, including the cargo of freights and other interests. (Section 2.13A)

(*iv*) Fire insurance is the insurance, which includes the risks insured against the fire and incidental to fire. (Section 2(6A))

(*v*) Miscellaneous insurance includes the business of effecting contracts of insurance, which are not principally, or wholly of the kind or kinds included above. (Section 2.13B)

The insurer, as defined by Section 2(9) as amended by the IRDA Act, 1999 means and includes

- An individual
- Body of individuals unincorporated
- Body corporate but not incorporated under the law of country
- Anybody corporate (not being a person specified above) standing as subsidiary company within the meaning of Indian Companies Act, 1956
- Any person who has standing contract with the underwriter who is a member of the society of Lloyds and authorized to issue cover notes and other documents to others on their behalf in conducting the insurance business, provided they carryon business of insurance in India, or their principal place of business is

domiciled in India, or established with the object of obtaining insurance business, employs a representative or maintains a place of business in India.

8.1.2 Prohibition on Conduct of Insurance Business

Section 2c of the Act prohibits persons to carry on insurance business until he is:

(*a*) A public company.

(*b*) A registered society under.

(*c*) A body corporate incorporated under the law of any country outside India not being in the nature of a private company. However, the central government is empowered to exempt any insurer or any person for the purpose of carrying on the business of granting superannuation allowances and annuities as per Section 211(c) or for the purpose of carrying general insurance business. Exempted insurer after the promulgation of IRDA Act, 1999 only Indian Insurance company can carry insurance business.

8.1.3 Licencing

Section 3 of the Act, as ammended by IRDA Act, 1999 read together with Section 3A and 3B deals with the registration, sanctioning of license and its renewal and issuance of certificate of soundness for life insurers.

Licensing Conditions

Only Indian Insurance companies to be granted licenses : Under the Act, it is mandatory that only an Indian insurance company can carry on an insurance business in India. An Indian insurance company is a company registered under the Companies Act 1956 where the aggregate foreign equity shareholding does not exceed 26 per cent and whose sole purpose is to carry on a life, general or reinsurance business.

Two-stage Licensing Process

Stage 1 – Requisition for Registration

An application has to be made to the Authority with all the prescribed disclosure norms. Some of the important items cover :

1. Promoter's background, financial strength, share-holders' agreement and reasons for entering the sector.
2. Director's background.
3. Capital structure, initial and future.
4. Financial projections for 5 years.
5. Scenario Building and Sensitivity analyses.
6. Rural and social sector strategy.

There is no provision for appeal in the event of a second rejection. A revised application is permissible by the applicant company only after 2 years with an additional condition that this will be with a new set of promoters or for a different class of insurance business.

Stage 2 – Application for Registration

After the requisition is granted by the Authority, the applicant is required to make an application for registration. Information to be disclosed includes :

- Proof of paid-up capital of Rs. 100 crore.
- Proof of deposit.

- Marketing and distribution information. This should include information on Market Research. Product information, Distribution Strategy and Details, Sales promotion, Customer service.
- *Operations :* Information should cover underwriting, information technology, Internal controls, Personnel.
- *Investment :* Information on investment Philosophy, Strategy and ground level arrangements.
- *Reinsurance :* Information on Approach and Terms.
- *Expenditure :* This should include a description of the manner in which the expenses of administration have been estimated. These expenses will have to be distinguished between first year and renewal, fixed and variable. The proposed expenses as a percent of premium at levels of operational offices, supervisory offices and head office.

Licensing Criteria

Some of the important parameters include :

- Promoter and directors' background
- Promoter financial strength
- Volume of business and earning prospects
- Rural and social sector focus
- Product profit
- Capital structure
- Actuarial and professional expertise
- Infrastructure
- Public interest

Other Licensing Issues

An appeal can be made to the Central Government against the decision of Authority, which shall be final. The applicant company can submit a new application only after two years with the additional condition that it has to be with a new set of promoters or for a different class of insurance business. The Authority will grant more licenses to applicants for life and health insurance than general insurance. Licenses expire on the 31st day of March each year and have to be renewed each year.

Capital Requirement and Foreign Stake

Section 6 of the Act requires that minimum paid-up equity capital required for a life insurance is Rs. 100 crore and for a reinsurer Rs. 200 crore. The capital contributed can only be in the form of equity shares as preference shares cannot be issued. The incumbent, LIC, would be required to increase its equity share capital from the existing Rs. 5 crore to Rs. 100 crore within a period of six months from the date of commencement of the IRDA Act. Also, the four GIC subsidiaries would have to increase the equity share capital to Rs. 100 crore from Rs. 40 crore are resent. The GIC will not be required to bring in additional capital since its present capital base is Rs. 215 crore.

The certificate of registration of insurance business is for a period of one year only. The certificate is renewal every year. The insurance company has to apply for renewal of license by paying the requisite fee of Rs. 50,000 and along with one percent of total gross premium written directly by insurer in India during the last financial year. This application for renewal has to be made in the month of December every year.

8.1.4 Policies – Premiums, Claims and Related Issues

Advance Payment of Premium

No insurer shall assume any risk unless and until the premium is received in advance or is guaranteed to be paid or a deposit is made in advance in the prescribed manner. This rule of advance payment of premium may be relaxed in circumstances specified in the rules framed under the Act.

Section 38 of Insurance Act, 1938 explains the procedure by which the insurance policy can be transferred to the transferee, and insurer being the transferee.

Assignment and Transfer of Insurance Policies

Section 38 : (1) A transfer or assignment of a policy of life insurance, whether with or without consideration, may be made only by an endorsement upon the policy itself or by a separate instrument, signed in either case by the transferor or by the assignor or his duly authorised agent and attested by at least one witness, specifically setting forth the fact of transfer or assignment.

(2) The transfer or assignment shall be complete and effectual upon the execution of such endorsement or instrument duly attested but except where the transfer or assignment is in favour of the insurer shall not be operative as against an Insurer and shall not confer upon the transferee or assignee, or his legal representative, any right to sue for the amount of such policy or the moneys secured thereby until a notice in writing of the transfer or assignment if and either the said endorsement or instrument itself or a copy thereof certified to be correct by both transferor and transferee or their duly authorised agents have been delivered to the insurer:

Provided that where the insurer maintains one or more places of business in India, such notice shall be delivered only at the place in India mentioned in the policy for the purpose or at his principal place of business in India.

(3) The date on which the notice referred to in sub section (2) is delivered to the insurer shall regulate the priority of all claims under a transfer or assignment as between persons interested in the policy: and where there is more then one instrument of transfer or assignment, the priority of the claims under such instruments shall be governed by the order in which the notices referred to in sub section (2) are delivered.

(4) Upon the receipt of the notice referred to in sub section (2), the insurer shall record the fact of such transfer or assignment together with the date thereof and the name of the transferee or the assignee and shall, on the request of the person by whom the notice was given, or of the transferee or assignee, on payment of a fee not exceeding one rupee, grant a written acknowledgment of the receipt of such notice; and any such acknowledgment shall be conclusive evidence against the insurer that he has duly received the notice to which such acknowledgment relates.

(5) Subject to the terms and conditions of the transfer or assignment, the insurer shall, from the date of the receipt of the notice referred to in subsection (2), recognise the transferee or assignee named in the notice as the only person entitled to benefit under the policy, and such person shall subject to all liabilities and equities to which the transferor or assignor was subject at the date of the transfer or assignment and may institute any proceedings in relation to the policy without obtaining the consent of the transferor or assignor or making him a party to such proceedings.

(6) Any rights and remedies of an assignee or transferee of a policy of life insurance under an assignment or transfer affected prior to the commencement of this Act shall not be affected by the provisions of this section.

(7) Notwithstanding any law or custom having the force of law to the contrary, and assignment in favour of a person made with the condition that it shall be inoperative or that the interest shall pass to some other person on the happening of a specified event during the lifetime of the person whose life is insured, and an assignment in favour of the survivor or survivors of a number of persons shall be valid.

The *Section 39* of the Insurance Act, 1938 and amendments made thereafter deals with the provisions of nomination of a policy by the policyholder.

The holder of a policy of life insurance on his own life may nominate the person or persons to whom he wants the policy money to be paid in the event of his death. He may do so either at the time of effecting the policy or at any time before the policy matures for payment. Where the nominee is a minor, the policy-holder may indicate in the prescribed manner any person to receive the money during the minority of the nominee.

Nomination by Policy Holder

Section 39 : (1) The holder of a policy of life insurance on his own life, may, when effecting the policy or at any time before the policy matures for payment, nominate the person or persons to whom the money secured by the policy shall be paid in the event of his death:

Provided that, where any nominee is a minor, it shall be lawful for the policy holder to appoint in the prescribed manner any person to receive the money secured by the policy in the event of his death during the minority of the nominee.

(2) Any such nomination in order to be effectual shall, unless it is incorporated in the text of the policy itself, be made by an endorsement on the policy communicated to the insurer and registered by him in the records relating to the policy and any such nomination may at any time before the policy matures for payment be cancelled or changed by an endorsement or a further endorsement or a will, as the case may be, but unless notice in writing of any such cancellation or change has been delivered to the insurer, the insurer shall not be liable for any payment under the policy made *bona fide* by him to a nominee mentioned in the text of the policy or registered in records of the insurer.

(3) The insurer shall furnish to the policy holder a written acknowledgment of having registered a nomination or a cancellation change thereof, and may charge a fee not exceeding one rupee for registering such cancellation or change.

(4) A transfer or assignment of a policy made in accordance with section 38 shall automatically cancel a nomination:

Provided that the assignment of a policy to the insurer who bears the rats on the policy at the time of the assignment, in consideration of a loan granted by that insurer on the security of the policy within its surrender value, or its re-assignment on repayment of the loan shall not cancel a nomination, but shall affect the rights of the nominee only to the extent of the insurer's interest in the policy.

(5) Where the policy matures for payment during the lifetime of the person whose life is insured or where the nominee or, if there are more nominees than one, all the nominees die before the policy-holder or his heirs or legal representatives or the holder of a succession certificate, as the case may be.

(6) Where the nominee or, if there are more nominees than one, a nominee or nominees survive the person whose life is insured, the amount secured by the policy shall be payable to such survivor or survivors.

(7) The provisions of this section shall not apply to any policy of life insurance to which section 6 of the Married Women's Property Act, 1874 (3 of 1874), applies or has at any time applied:

Provided that where a nomination made whether before or after the commencement of the Insurance (Amendment) Act, 1946 (VII of 1946), in favour of the wife of the person who has insured his life or of his wife and children or any of them is expressed, whether or not on the face of the policy as being made under this section, the said section 6 shall be deemed not to apply or not to have applied to the policy.

Misstatement or Concealment [S. 45]

Section 45 provides that after the expiry of two years from the date on which a policy is effected, the policy shall not be called in question by the insurer on the ground that a statement made in the proposal, or medical officer's report, or by a referee or friend of the assured, or in any other document relating to the issue of the policy, was inaccurate or false. Thus a policy can be avoided by the insurer on the ground of a misrepresentation or suppression only within two years of the date of the policy.

Payment of Money into Court

Section 47 of the Act explains the method of payment of claim by the insurer into the court and settlement of claim by the interference of the Court. Section 47A explains the method of payment of small amounts of claims under life insurance policy.

Section 47 : (1) Where in respect of any policy of life insurance maturing for payment an insurer is of opinion that by reason of conflicting claims to or insufficiency of proof of title to the amount secured thereby or for any other adequate reason it is impossible otherwise for the insurer to obtain a satisfactory discharge for the payment of such amount, the insurer may, apply to pay the amount into the Court within the jurisdiction of which is situated the place at which such amount is payable under the terms of the policy or otherwise.

(2) A receipt granted by the Court for any such payment shall be a satisfactory discharge to the insurer for the payment of such amount.

(3) An application for permission to make a payment into Court under this section, shall be made by a petition verified by an affidavit signed by a principal officer of the insurer setting forth the following particulars, namely:

(*a*) the name of the insured person and his address;

(*b*) if the insured person is deceased, the date and place of his death;

(*c*) the nature of the policy and the amount secured by it;

(*d*) the name and address of each claimant so far as is known to the insurer with details of every notice of claim received;

(*e*) the reasons why in the opinion of the insurer satisfactory discharge cannot be obtained for the payment of the amount; and

(*f*) the address at which the insurer may be served with notice of any proceeding relating to disposal of the amount paid into Court.

(4) An application under this section shall not be entertained by the Court if the application is made before the expiry of six months from the maturing of the policy by survival, or from the date of receipt of notice by the insurer of the death of the insured, as the case may be.

(5) If it appears to the Court that a satisfactory discharge for the payment of the amount cannot otherwise be obtained by the insurer it shall allow the amount to be paid into Court and shall invest the amount in Government securities pending its disposal.

(6) The insurer shall transmit to the Court every notice of claim received after the making of the application under sub section (3), and any payment required by the Court as costs of the proceedings or otherwise in connection with the disposal of the amount paid into Court shall as to the cost of the application under sub section (3) be borne by the insurer and as to any other costs be in the discretion of the Court.

(7) The Court shall cause notice to be given to every ascertained claimant of the fact that the amount has been paid into Court, and shall cause notice at the cost of any claimant applying to withdraw the amount to be given to every other ascertained claimant.

(8) The Court shall decide all questions relating to the disposal of claims to the amount paid into Court.

Claims on Small Life Insurance Policies

Section 47A : (1) In the event of any dispute relating to the settlement of a claim on a policy of life insurance assuring a sum not exceeding two thousand rupees (exclusive of any profit or bonus not being a guaranteed profit or bonus) issued by an insurer in respect of insurance business transacted in India, arising between a claimant under the policy and the insurer who issued the policy or has otherwise assumed liability in respect thereof, the dispute may at the option of the claimant be referred to the Authority for decision and the Authority may, after giving an opportunity to the parties to be heard and after making such further inquires as he may think fit, decide the matter.

(2) The decision of the Authority under this sub section shall be final and shall not be called in question in any Court, and may be executed by the Court which would have been competent to decide the dispute if it had not been referred to the Authority as if it wore a decree passed by that Court.

(3) There shall be charged and collected in respect of the duties of the Authority under this section such fees whether by way of percentage or otherwise as may be prescribed.

8.1.5 Appointment of Agents

Prohibition of Payment by Way of Commission or Otherwise for Procuring Business

Section 40 : (1) No person shall after the expiry of six months from the commencement of this Act, pay or contract to pay any remuneration or reward whether by way of commission or otherwise for soliciting or procuring insurance business in India to any person except an insurance agent or an intermediary or insurance intermediary.

(1A) In this section and section 40A, 41 and 43 references to an insurance agent shell be construed as including references to an individual soliciting or procuring insurance business exclusively in the territories which Immediately before the 1st November, 1956 were comprised in a Part B State notified in this behalf by the Central Government in the Official Gazette and holding a valid licence as an insurance agent under the law of that Part B State.

(2) No insurance agent shall be paid or contract to be paid by way of commission or as remuneration in any form an amount exceeding, in the case of life insurance business, forty per cent of the first year's premium payable on any policy or policies effected through him and five per cent of a renewal premium, payable on such a policy, or, in the case of business of any other class, fifteen per cent of the premium:

Provided that insurers in respect of life insurance business only may pay during the first ten years of their business to their insurance agents fifty five per cent of the first years premium payable on any policy or policies effected through them and six per cent of the renewal premiums payable on such policies:

Provided further that nothing in this sub section shall apply in respect of any policy of life insurance issued after the 31st day of December, 1950, or in respect of any policy of general insurance issued after the commencement of the Insurance (Amendment) Act, 1950 (47 of 1950).

(2A) Save as hereinafter provided, no insurance agent or intermediary or insurance intermediary shall be paid or contract to be paid by way of commission or as remuneration in any form any amount in respect of any policy not effected through him:

Provided that where a policy of life insurance has lapsed and it cannot under the terms and conditions applicable to it be revived without further medical examination of the person whose life was insured thereby, an insurer, after giving by notice in writing to the insurance agent through whom the policy was effected if such agent continues to be an agent of the insist an opportunity to effect the revival of the policy within a time specified in the notice, being not less than one month from the date of the receipt by him of the notice, may pay to another insurance agent who effects the revival of the policy an amount calculated at a rate not exceeding half the rate of commission at which the agent through whom the policy was effected would have been paid had the policy not lapsed, on the sum payable on revival of the policy on account of arrear premiums (excluding any interest on such arrear premiums) and also on the subsequent renewal premiums payable on the policy.

(3) Nothing in this section shall prevent the payment under any contract existing prior to the 27th day of January, 1937, of gratuities or renewal commission to many person, whether an insurance agent within the meaning of this Act or not, or to his representatives after his decease in respect of insurance business effected through him before the said date.

Limitation of Expenditure on Commission

Section 40A : (l) No person shall pay or contract to pay to an insurance agent, and no insurance agent shall receive or contract to receive by way of commission or remuneration in any form in respect of any policy of life insurance issued in India by an insurer after the 31st day of December, 1950, and effected through an insurance agent, an amount exceeding:

(*a*) where the policy grants an *immediate annuity or a deferred* annuity in consideration of a single premium, or where only one premium is payable on the policy, two per cent of that premium,

(*b*) where the policy grants a deferred annuity in consideration or more than one premium, seven and a half per cent of the first year's premium, and two per cent of each renewal premium payable on the policy, and

(c) in any other case, thirty five per cent of the first year's premium, seven and a half per cent of the second and third year's renewal premium, and thereafter five per cent of each renewal premium payable on the policy.

Provided that in a case referred to in clause (c), an insurer, during the first ten years of his business may pay to an insurance agent and an insurance agent may receive from such an insurer, forty per cent of the first year's premium payable on the policy:

Provided further that in case referred to in clause (c) where the rate of commission payable on the first year's premium is equal to or less than twenty-one per cent thereof, and the rate on the fourth and fifth year's premiums does not exceeds is per cent thereof, the Life Insurance Corporation of India may pay to an insurance agent, and the insurance agent may receive from it, commission on the sixth and subsequent year's renewal premiums payable on the policy at a rate not exceeding six per cent of each renewal premium.

(2) No person shall pay or contract to pay to a special agent, and no special agent, shall receive or contract to receive, by way of commission or as remuneration in any form, in respect of any policy of life insurance issued in India by an insurer after the 31st day of December, 1950, and effected through a special agent, an amount exceeding—

(*a*) in a case referred to in clause (a) of sub section (1), one half per cent of the premium,

(*b*) in a case referred to in clause (b) of sub section (1), two per cent of the first year's premium payable on the policy and

(c) in a case referred to in clause (c) of sub section (1), fifteen per cent of the first year's premium payable on the policy:

Provided that in a case referred to in clause (c), an insurer, during the first ten years of his business, may pay to a special agent, and a special agent may receive from such an insurer, seventeen and a half per cent of the first year's premium payable on the policy:

Provided further that in a case referred to in clause (c), where the rate of commission payable on the first year's premium is equal to or less than twenty-one per cent thereof, and the rate on the fourth and fifty year's premiums does not exceed six per cent thereof, the Life Insurance Corporation of India may pay to an insurance agent, and the insurance agent may receive from it, commission on the sixth and subsequent year's renewal premiums payable on the policy at a rate not exceeding six per cent of each renewal premium.

(3) No person shall pay or contract to pay to a special agent, and no special agent, shall receive or contract to receive, by way of commission or remuneration in any form in respect of any policy of general insurance issued in India by an insurer after the commencement of Insurance (Amendment Act), 1968, and effected through an insurance agent, an amount not exceeding fifteen per cent of the premium payable on the policy where the policy relates to fire or marine insurance or miscellaneous insurance.

(4) No person shall pay or contract to pay to a principal agent, and no principal agent shall receive or contract to receive, by way of commission or remuneration in any form, in respect of any policy of general insurance

issued in India by an insurer after the commencement of the Insurance (Amendment) Act, 1950, and effected through a principal agent, an amount exceeding-

(*a*) in the case referred to in clause (*a*) of sub section (3), twenty per cent of the premium payable on the policy, and

(*b*) in the case referred to in clause (*b*) of that sub section, fifteen per cent of the policy, less any commission payable to any insurance agent in respect of the said policy:

Provided that the Authority may, in such circumstances and to such extent and for such period as may be specified, authorise the payment of commission or remuneration exceeding the limits specified in this sub section to a principal agent of an insurer incorporated or domiciled elsewhere than in India, if such agent carries out and has continuously carried out in his own office duties on behalf of the insurer which would otherwise have been performed by the insurer.

(5) Without prejudice to the provisions of section 102 in respect of a contravention of any of the provisions of the preceding sub sections by an insurer, any insurance agent who contravenes the provisions of sub section (1) or sub-section (3) shall be punishable with fine which may extend to one hundred rupees.

Limitation of Expenses of Management in Life Insurance Business

Section 40B : (l) Every insurer transacting life insurance business in India shall furnish to the Controller, within such time as may be prescribed, statements in the prescribed form certified by an actuary on the basis of premiums currently used by him in regard to new business in respect of mortality, rate of interest, expenses and bonus loading.

(2) After the 31st day of December, 1950, no insurer shall, in respect of life insurance business transacted by him in India, spend as expenses of management in any calendar year an amount in excess of the prescribed limits and in prescribing any such limits regard shall be had to the size and age of the insurer and the provision generally Made for expenses of management in the premium rates of insurers:

Provided that where an insurer has spent as such expenses in any year an amount in excess of the amount permissible under this sub section, he shall not be deemed to have contravened the provisions of this section, if the excess amount so spent is within such limits as may be fixed in respect of the year by the Authority after consultation with the Executive Committee of the Life Insurance Council constituted under section 64 F, by which the actual expenses incurred may exceed the expenses permissible under this sub-section.

(3) In respect of any statement mentioned in subsection (1), the Authority may require that it shall be submitted to another actuary, appointed by the insurer for the purpose and approved by the Authority, for certification by him, whether with or without modifications.

(4) Every insurer transacting life insurance business in India shall incorporate in the revenue account:

(*a*) a certificate signed by the chairman and two directors and by the principal officer of the insurer, and an auditor's certificate, certifying that all expenses of management in respect of life insurance business transacted by the insurer in India have been fully debited in the revenue account as expenses, and

(*b*) if the insurer in carrying on any other class of insurance business in addition to life insurance business an auditor's certificate certifying that all charges incurred in respect of his life insurance business and in respect of his business other than life insurance business have been fully debited in the respective revenue accounts.

Explanation : in this section.

(*a*) "calendar year" or "year" means, in relation to an insurer who is required to furnish returns in accordance with sub section (2) of section 16, the period covered by the revenue account furnished by such insurer under clause (b) of that sub section;

(*b*) "expenses of management" means all charges wherever incurred whether directly or indirectly, and includes:

(*i*) commission payments of all kinds,

(*ii*) any amount of expenses capitalized,

(*iii*) in the case of an insurer having his principal place of business outside India, a proper share of head office expenses which shall not be less than such percentage as may be prescribed of the total premiums (less re insurance) received during the year in respect of life insurance business transacted by him in India, but does not include in the case of an insurer having his principal place of business in India any share of head office expenses in respect of life insurance business transacted by him outside India.

Limitation of Expenses of Management in General Insurance Business

Section 40C : (1) After the 31st day of December, 1949, no insurer shall, in respect of any class of general insurance business transacted by him in India, spend in any calendar year as expenses of management including commission or remuneration for procuring business an amount in excess of the prescribed limits arid in prescribing any such limits regard shall be had to the size and age of the insurer:

Provided that where an insurer has spend as such expenses in any year an amount in excess of the amount permissible under this subsection, he shall not be deemed to have contravened the provisions of this section, if the excess amount so spent is within such limits as may be fixed in respect of the year by the Authority after consultation with the Executive Committee of the General Insurance. Council constituted under section 64F, by which the actual expenses incurred may exceed the expenses permissible under this sub-section.

(2) Every insurer as aforesaid shall incorporate in the revenue account a certificate signed by the chairman and two directors and by the principal officer of the insurer, and by an auditor certifying that all expenses of management wherever incurred, whether directly or indirectly, in respect of the business referred to in this section have been fully debited in the revenue account as expenses.

Explanation : In this section.

(*a*) "calendar year" shall have the meaning assigned to it in section 40B;

(*b*) "expenses of management" means all charges, wherever insured whether directly or indirectly, including commission payments of all kinds and, in the case of an insurer having his principal place of business outside India, a proper share of head office expenses, which shall not be less than such percentage as may be prescribed, of his gross premium income (that is to say, the premium income without taking into account premiums or re-insurance ceded or accepted) written direct in India during the year, but in computing the expenses of management in India the following, and only the following expenses may be excluded, namely :

(*i*) in the case of an insurer having his principal place of business in India, a share of head office expenses in respect of general insurance business transacted by him outside India not exceeding such percentage of his gross direct premium written outside India as may be prescribed;

(*ii*) in the case of an insurer having his principal place of business outside India, a share of the expenses of his office in India in respect of general insurance business transacted by him outside India through his office in India, not exceeding such percentage of his gross direct premium written outside India through his office in India, as may be prescribed;

(*iii*) any expenses debited to profit and loss account relating exclusively to the management of capital, and dealings with share holders and a proper share of managerial expenses calculated in such manner as may be prescribed; and

(iv) any expenses debited to claims in the revenue account in Form F of Part II of the Third Schedule;

(c) "insurance business transacted in India" includes insurance business, wherever effected relating to any property situate in India or to any vessel or aircraft registered in India.

Prohibition of Rebates

Section 41 : (1) No person shall allow or offer to allow, either directly or indirectly, as an inducement to any person to take or renew or continue an insurance in respect of any kind of risk relating to lives or property in India, any rebate of the whole or part of the commission payable or any rebate of the premium shown on the policy, nor shall any person taking out or renewing or continuing a policy accept any rebate, except such rebate as may be allowed in accordance with the published prospectuses or tables of the insurer:

Provided that acceptance by an insurance agent of commission in connection with a policy of life insurance taken out by himself on his own life shall not be deemed to be acceptance of a rebate of premium within the meaning of this sub section if at the time of such acceptance the insurance agent satisfies the prescribed conditions establishing that he is a *bona fide* insurance agent employed by the insurer.

(2) Any person making default in complying with the provisions of this section shall be punishable with fine which may extend to five hundred rupees.

Licensing of Insurance Agents

Section 42 : (1) The Authority or an officer authorised by him in this behalf shall, in the manner determined by the regulations made by it and on payment of the fee which shall not be determined by the regulations, which shall not be more than two hundred and fifty rupees, issue to any person making any application in the manner determined by the regulations, a licence to act as an insurance agent for the purpose of soliciting or procuring insurance business:

Provided that–

(i) in the case of an individual, he does not suffer from any of the disqualification mentioned in sub section (4); and

(ii) in the case of a company or firm, any of its directors or partners does not suffer from any of the said disqualifications:

Provided further that any licence issued immediately before the commencement of the Insurance Regulatory and Development Authority Act, 1999, shall be deemed to have been issued in accordance with the regulations which provide for such licence.

(2) A licence issued under this section shall entitle the holder to act as an insurance agent for any insurer.

(3) A licence issued under this section, after the commencement of the Insurance Regulatory and Development Authority Act, 1999, shall remain in force for a period of three years only from the date of issue, but shall, if the applicant being an individual does not, or being a company or firm any of its directors or partners, does not suffer from any of the disqualification mentioned in clauses (b), (c), (d), (e), (ea) and (f) of sub section (4) and the application for renewal of the licence reaches the issuing authority at least thirty days before the date on which the licence ceases to remain in force, be renewed for a period of three years at any one time on payment of the fee determined by the regulations made by the Authority which shall not be more than rupees two hundred and fifty, and an additional fee of an amount determined by the regulations not exceeding rupees one hundred by way of penalty, if the application for renewal of the licence does not reach the issuing authority at least thirty days before the date on which the licence ceases to remain in force.

(3A) No application for the renewal of a licence under this section shall be entertained if the application does not reach the issuing authority before the licence ceases to remain in force:

Provided that the Authority may, if satisfied that undue hardship would be caused otherwise, accept any application in contravention of this subsection on payment by the applicant of a penalty of seven hundred and fifty rupees.

(4) The disqualifications above referred to shall be the following:

(*a*) that the person is a minor;

(*b*) that he is found to be of unsound mind by a Court of competent jurisdiction;

(*c*) that he has been found guilty of criminal misappropriation or criminal breach of trust or cheating or forgery or an abetment of or attempt to commit any such offence by a Court of competent jurisdiction:

Provided that where at least five years have elapsed since the completion of the sentence imposed on any person in respect of any such offence, the Authority shall ordinarily declare in respect of such person that his conviction shall cease to operate as a disqualification under this clause;

(*d*) that in the course of any judicial proceeding relating to any policy of insurance of the winding up of an insurance company or in the course of an investigation of the affairs of all insurer it has then found that he has been guilty off or has knowingly participated in or connived at any fraud, dishonestly fir misrepresentation against an insurer or an insured.

(*e*) that in the case of an individual, he does not possess the requisite qualifications and practical training for a period not exceeding twelve months, as may be specified by the regulations made by the Authority in this behalf;

(*f*) that in the case of a company or firm making an application under sub-section (1) or sub-section (3), a director or a partner or one or more of its officers or other employees so designated by it and in the case of any other person, the chief executive, by whatever name called, or one or more of his employees designated by him, do not possess the requisite qualifications and practical training and have not passed such an examination as required under clauses (e) and (f);

(*g*) that he violates the code of conduct as may be specified by the regulations made by the Authority.

(5) if it be found that an insurance agent being an individual is, or being a company or firm contains a director or partner who is suffering from any of the disqualifications mentioned in sub section (4), then, without prejudice to any other penalty to which he may be liable, the Authority shall, and if the insurance agent has knowingly contravened any of the provisions of this Act may, cancel the licence issued to the agent under this section.

(6) The Authority may issue a duplicate licence to replace a licence lost, destroyed or mutilated on payment of such fee not exceeding rupees fifty as may be determined by the regulations.

(7) Any person who acts as an insurance agent without holding a licence issued under this section to act as such shall be punishable with fine which may extend to five hundred rupees., and any insurer or any person acting on behalf of an insurer, who appoints as an insurance agent any person not licensed to act as such or transacts any insurance business in India through any such person shall be punishable with fine which may extend to one thousand rupees.

(8) Where the person contravening sub section (7) is a company or a firm, then, without prejudice to any other proceedings which may be taken against the company, or firm, every director, manager, secretary or other officer of the company, and every partner of the firm who is knowingly a party to such contravention shall be punishable with fine which may extend to five thousand rupees.

Registration of Principal Agents, Chief Agents and Special Agents

Section 42A : (1) The Authority or an officer authorised by it in this behalf shall in the prescribed manner and on payment of the prescribed fee, which shall not be more than twenty five rupees for a principal agent or a chief agent and ten rupees for a special agent, register any person who makes an application to him in the prescribed manner if,—

(*a*) in the case of an individual, he does not suffer from any of the disqualifications mentioned in sub section (4) of Section 42, or

(*b*) in the case of a company or firm, any of its directors or partners does not suffer from any of the said disqualifications,

and a certificate to Act as a principal agent, chief agent or special agent, as the case may be, for the purpose of procuring insurance business shall be issued to him.

(2) A certificate issued under this section shall entitle the holder thereof to act as a principal agent, chief agent, or special agent, as the case may be, for any insurer.

(3) A certificate issued under this section shall remain in force for a period of twelve months only from the date of issue, but shall, on application made on this behalf, be renewed from year to year on production of a certificate from the insurer concerned that the provisions of clauses (2) and (3) of Part A of the Sixth Schedule in the case of a principal agent, the provisions of clauses (2) and (4) of Part B of the said Schedule in the case of a chief agent, and the provisions of clauses (2) and (3) of Part C of the said Schedule in the case of a special agent, have been complied with, and on payment of the prescribed fee, which shall not be more than twenty five rupees, in the case of a principal agent or a chief agent, and ten rupees in the case of a special agent, and an additional fee of the prescribed amount not exceeding five rupees by way of penalty, in cases where the application for renewal of the certificate does not reach the issuing authority before the date on which the certificate ceases to remain in force:

Provided that, where the applicant is an individual, he does not suffer from any of the disqualifications mentioned in clauses (b) to (d) of sub section (4) of section 42 and where the applicant is a company or a firm, any of its directors or partners does not suffer from any of the said disqualifications.

(4) Where it is found that the principal agent, chief agent or special agent being an individual is, or being a company or firm contains a director or partner who is suffering from any of the disqualifications mentioned in sub-section (4) of section 42, without prejudice to any other penalty to which he may be liable, the Authority shall, and where a principal agent, chief agent or special agent has contravened any of the provisions of this Act may cancel the certificate issued under this section to such principal agent, chief agent or special agent.

(5) The authority which issued any certificate under this section may issue a duplicate certificate to replace a certificate lost, destroyed or mutilated on payment of the prescribed fee, which shall not be more than two rupees.

(6) Any person who acts as a principal agent, chief agent or special agent, without holding a certificate issued under this section to act as such, shall be punishable with fine which may extend to five hundred rupees, and any insurer or any person acting on behalf of an insurer, who appoints as a principal agent, chief agent or special agent any person not entitled to act as such or transacts any insurance business in India through any such person, shall be punishable with fine which may extend to one thousand rupees.

(7) Where the person contravening sub section (6) is a company or a firm, then, without prejudice to any other proceedings which may be taken against the company or firm, every director, manager, secretary or any other officer of the company, and every partner of the firm who is knowingly a party to such contravention shall be punishable with fine which may extend to five hundred rupees.

(8) The provisions of sub sections (6) and (7) shall not take effect until the expiry of six months from the commencement of the Insurance (Amendment) Act, 1950.

(9) No insurer shall, on or after the commencement of the Insurance (Amendment) Act, 2002, appointment or transact any insurance business in India through any principal agent, chief agent or special agent.

Regulation of Employment of Principal Agents

Section 42B : (1) No insurer shall, after the expiration of seven years from the commencement of the Insurance (Amendment) Act, 1950, appoint, or transact any insurance business in India, through a principal agent.

(2) Every contract between an insurer and a principal agent shall be in writing and the terms contained in Part A of the Sixth Schedule shall be deemed to be incorporated in, and form part of, every such contract.

(3) No insurer shall, after the commencement of the Insurance (Amendment) Act, 1950 (47 of 1950), appoint any person as a principal agent except in a presidency town unless the appointment is by way of renewal of any contract subsisting at such commencement.

(4) Within sixty days of the commencement of the Insurance (Amendment) Act, 1950 (47 of 1950), every principal agent shall file with the insurer concerned a full list of insurance agents employed by him indicating the terms of the contract between the principal agent and each of such insurance agents, and, if any principal agent fails to file such a list within the period specified, any commission payable to such principal agent on premiums received from the date of expiry of the said period of sixty days until the date of the filing of the said list shall, notwithstanding anything in any contract to the contrary, cease to be so payable.

(5) A certified copy of every contract as is referred to in sub section (2) shall be furnished by the insurer to the Authority within thirty days of his entering into such contract, and intimation of any change in any such contract shall be furnished by the insurer with full particulars thereof to the Authority within thirty days of the making of any such change.

(6) If the commission due to any insurance agent in respect of any general insurance business procured by such agent is not paid by the principal agent for any reason, the insurer may pay the insurance agent the commission so due and recover the amount so paid from the principal agent concerned.

(7) Every contract as is referred to in sub section (2), subsisting at the commencement of the Insurance (Amendment) Act, 1950 (47 of 1950), shall, with respect to terms regarding remuneration, be deemed to have been so altered as to be in accordance with the provisions of sub section (4) of section 40A.

(8) If any dispute arises as to whether a person is or was a principal agent the matter shall be referred to the Authority, whose decision shall be final.

(9) Every insurer shall maintain a register in which the name and address of every principal agent appointed by him, the date of such appointment and the date, if any, on which the appointment ceased shall be entered.

Regulation of Employment of Chief and Special Agents

Section 42C : (1) Every contract between art insurer carrying on life insurance business and a chief agent shall be in writing, and shall specify the area (not being less in extent than a district or the equivalent thereof) for which the chief agent is appointed, and the terms contained in Part B of the Sixth Schedule shall be deemed to be incorporated in, and form part of, every such contract.

(2) No chief agent shall, either directly or through insurance agents or special agents employed by or through him procure life insurance business for the insurer or any area outside the area for which he has been appointed or In any area for which another chief agent has been appointed or in any area in which the head office or any branch office of the insurer is operating, and neither the head office nor any branch office of the insurer shall operate in any area for which a chief agent has been appointed:

Provided that nothing in this sub section shall be deemed to prohibit the head office of an insurer which had been operating at the commencement of the Insurance (Amendment) Act, 1950; for a period of not less than ten years before such commencement within the municipal limits of any town where the head office is situate, and a chief agent who, in pursuance of an agreement in writing, had been operating for a similar period within such limits, from continuing to operate within the said limits:

Provided further that nothing in this sub section shall be deemed to prohibit an insurance agent from procuring life insurance business in or from any area and submitting the proposals direct to the principal office of the insurer in India.

(3) Within sixty days of the commencement of the Insurance (Amendment) Act, 1950, every chief agent shall file with the insurer concerned a full list of the insurance agents employed by him, indicating the terms of the contract between the chief agent and each of such insurance agents and the business secured by each of such agents, and if any chief agent fails to file such a list within the period specified, any commission payable to such chief agent on premiums received from the date of the expiry of the said period of sixty days until the date of the filing of the said list shall, notwithstanding anything in any contract to the contrary, cease to be so payable.

(4) Every contract between an insurer carrying on life insurance business and a special agent, or between a chief agent of such insurer and a special agent, shall be in writing and the terms contained in Part C of the Sixth Schedule shall be deemed to be incorporated in, and form part of, every such contract:

Provided that the Authority may, in the case of a contract between a co-operative life insurance society as defined in clause (b) of sub section (1) of section 95 and a co-operative society registered under the Indian Co-operative Societies Act, 1912 (2 of 1912), or under any other law for the time being in force and acting as a special agent, alter, to such extent as he thinks fit, all or any of the said terms.

(5) A certified copy of every contract as is referred to in sub section (1) or sub section (4) shall be furnished by the insurer or the chief agent to the Authority within thirty days of his entering into such contract, and intimation of any change in any such contract shall be furnished by the insurer or the chief agent with full particulars thereof to the Authority within thirty days of the making of any such change.

(6) No such contract as is referred to in sub section (1) or sub section (4) shall be entered into or renewed for a period exceeding ten years at any one time and notwithstanding the terms of any contract to the contrary, no option to renew any such contract given to any of the parties shall be enforceable without the consent of the other.

(7) Every contract between an insurer and a person acting on behalf of such insurer who, before the commencement of the Insurance (Amendment) Act, 1950), has been employing insurance agents for the purpose of life insurance business, which is subsisting on such commencement, shall terminate after the expiration of ten years from such commencement, if it does not terminate earlier:

Provided that every such contract shall be modified by the parties before the 1st day of January, 1951, to bring it into conformity with this act, and ant, such modification shall :

(*i*) as respects remuneration, whether in respect of business already procured or in respect of business to be procured thereafter, be such as may be mutually agreed upon between the parties, subject in the case of remuneration payable on business procured before such commencement, to a maximum of an overriding commission of two and a half per cent plus a further commission not exceeding three and three quarter per cent on premiums in respect of which no commission is payable to any insurance agent;

(*ii*) be deemed to include all the terms specified in Part B or Part C of the Sixth Schedule, as the case may be:

Provided further that, in the event of any dispute as to the terms of any fresh contract, the matter shall be referred to arbitration

(8) Any such contract as is referred to in sub section (7) which was subsisting on the 1st day of January, 1949, but has terminated or has been terminated before the commencement of the Insurance (Amendment) Act, 1950, shall be subject to the maximum limits specified in clause (i) of the proviso to sub-section (7) as respects remuneration, if any, payable on business procured before the termination of the contract.

(9) Nothing in this section shall be deemed to prevent any special agent from receiving any renewal commission on policies effected through him as an insurance agent at any time before his appointment as such special agent.

(10) If any dispute arises as to whether a person is or was a chief agent or a special agent for the purposes of this Act, the matter shall be referred to the Authority whose decision shall be final.

(11) Every insurer shall maintain a register in which the name and address of every chief agent appointed by him, the date on which the appointment was made and the date, if any, on which the appointment ceased shall be entered, and a separate register in which similar particulars relating to every special agent shall be entered, and every chief agent shall maintain a register in which similar particulars relating to every special agent appointed by him shall be entered.

Issue of Licence to Intermediary or Insurance Intermediary

Section 42D : (1) The Authority or an officer authorized by it in this behalf shall, in the manner determined by the regulations made by the Authority and on payment of the fees determined by the regulations made by the Authority, issue to any person making an application in the manner determined by the regulations, and not suffering from any of the disqualifications herein mentioned, a licence to act as an intermediary or an insurance intermediary under this Act:

Provided that, :

(*a*) in the case of an individual, he does not suffer from any of the disqualifications mentioned in sub-section (4) of section 42, or

(*b*) in the case of a company or firm, any of its directors or partners does not suffer from any of the said disqualifications.

(2) A licence issued under this section shall entitle the holder thereof to act as an intermediary or insurance intermediary.

(3) A licence issued under this section shall remain in force for a period of three years only from the date of issue, but shall, if the applicant, being an individual does not, or being a company or firm any of its directors or partners does not suffer from any of the disqualifications mentioned in clauses (*b*), (*c*), (*d*), (*e*) and (*f*) of sub-section (4) of section 42 and the application for renewal of licence reaches the issuing authority at least thirty days before the date on which the licence ceases to remain in force, be renewed for a period of three years at any one time on payment of the fee, determined by the regulations made by the Authority and additional fee for an amount determined by the regulations, not exceeding one hundred rupees by way of penalty, if the application for renewal of the licence does not reach the issuing authority at least thirty days before the date on which the licence ceases to remain in force.

(4) No application for the renewal of a licence under this section shall be entertained if the application does not reach the issuing authority before the licence ceases to remain in force:

Provided that the Authority may, if satisfied that undue hardship would be caused otherwise, accept any application in contravention of this sub-section on payment by the application of the penalty of seven hundred and fifty rupees.

(5) The disqualifications above referred to shall be the following :

(*a*) that the person is a minor;

(*b*) that he is found to be a unsound mind by a court of competent jurisdiction;

(*c*) that he has been found guilty of criminal misappropriation or criminal breach of trust or cheating or forgery or an abetment of or attempt to commit any such offence by a court of competent jurisdiction:

Provided that, where at least five years have elapsed since the completion of the sentence imposed on any person in respect of any such offence, the Authority shall ordinarily declare in respect of such person that his conviction shall cease to operate as a disqualification under this clause;

(*d*) that in the course of any judicial proceedings relating to any policy of insurance of the winding up of an insurance company or in the course of an investigation of the affairs of an insurer it has been found that he has been guilty of or has knowingly participated in or connived at any fraud dishonestly or misrepresentation against an insurer or an insured;

(*e*) that he does not possess the requisite qualifications and practical training for a period not exceeding twelve months, as may be specified by the regulations made by the Authority in this behalf;

(*f*) that he has not passed such examinations as may be specified by the regulations made by the Authority in this behalf;

(*g*) that he violates the code of conduct as may be specified by the regulations made by the Authority.

(6) If it be found that an intermediary or an insurance intermediary suffers from any of the foregoing disqualifications, without prejudice to any other penalty to which he may be liable, the Authority shall, and if the intermediary or an insurance intermediary has knowingly contravened any provisions of this Act may cancel the licence issued to the intermediary or insurance intermediary under this section.

(7) The Authority may issue a duplicate licence to replace a licence lost, destroyed or mutilated, on payment of such fee, as may be determined by the regulations made by the Authority.

(8) Any person who acts as an intermediary or an insurance intermediary without holding a licence issued under this section to act as such, shall be punishable with fine, and any insurer or any person who appoints as an intermediary or an insurance intermediary or any person not licensed to act as such or transacts any insurance business in India through any such person, shall be punishable with fine.

(9) Where the person contravening sub-section (8) is a company or a firm, then, without prejudice to any other proceedings which may be taken against the company or firm, every director, manager, secretary or other officer of the company, and every partner of the firm who is knowingly a party to such contravention shall be punishable with fine.

Commission, Brokerage or Fee Payable to Intermediary or Insurance Intermediary

Section 42E : (1) No intermediary or insurance intermediary shall be paid or contract to be paid by way of commission, fee or as remuneration in any form, an amount exceeding thirty per cent of the premium payable as may be specified by the regulations made by the Authority, in respect of any policy or policies effected through him:

Provided that the Authority may specify different amounts payable by way of commission, fee or as remuneration to an intermediary or insurance intermediary or different classes of business of insurance.

(2) Without prejudice to the provisions contained in this Act, the Authority may, by the regulations made in this behalf, specify the requirements of capital, form of business and other conditions to act as an intermediary or insurance intermediary.

Register of Insurance Agents

Section 43 : (l) Every insurer and every person who acting on behalf of an insurer employs insurance agents shall maintain a register showing the name and address of every insurance agent appointed by him and the date on which his appointment began and the date, if any, on which his appointment ceased.

8.1.6 Deposits and Investments

Section 7, 8 and 9 of the Insurance Act, 1938 deals with the deposits which are required to be made by the insurer for obtaining the license to undertake the insurance and registration of the insurer with IRD Authority.

Deposits

Section 7 : (1) Every insurer shall, in respect of the insurance business carried on by him in India, deposit and keep deposited with the Reserve Bank of India in one of the offices in India of the Bank for and on behalf of the Central Government the amount hereafter specified, either in cash or in approved securities estimated at the market value of the securities on the day of deposit, or partly in cash and partly in approved securities so estimated :

(*a*) in the case of life insurance business, a sum equivalent to one per cent of his total gross premium written direct in India in any financial year commencing after the 31st day of March, 2000, not exceeding rupees ten crores;

(*b*) in the case of general insurance business, a sum equivalent to three per cent of his total gross premium written in India, in any financial year commencing after the 31st day of March, 2000, not exceeding rupees ten crores;

(*c*) in the case of re-insurance business, a sum of rupees twenty crores

Provided that, where the business done or to be done is marine insurance only and relates exclusively to country craft or its cargo or both, the amount to be deposited under this sub-section shall be one hundred thousand rupees only:

Provided further that in respect of an insurer not having a share capital and carrying on only such insurance business as in the opinion of the Central Government is not carried on ordinarily by insurers under separate policies, the Central Government may, by notification under Official Gazette, order that the provisions of this sub section shall apply to such insurer with the modification that instead of sum of rupees twenty lakhs or rupees ten lakhs, as the case may be, the deposit to be made by such insurer shall be such amount, being not less than one hundred and fifty thousand rupees, as may be specified in the said order.

(2) Where the insurer is an insurer specified in sub clause (*c*) of clause (9) of Section 2, he shall be deemed to have complied with the provisions of this section as to deposits, if in respect of insurance business carried on by him in India under a standing contract of the nature referred to in sub-clause (*c*) of clause (9) of section 2 a deposit of an amount one-and-a half times that specified in sub-section (1) has been made in the Reserve Bank of India in one of the offices in India of the Bank for and on behalf of the Central Government in cash or approved securities estimated at the market value of the securities on the day of deposit by or on behalf of the underwriters who are members of the Society of Lloyd's with whom he has his standing contract.

(3) Where the deposit to be made by an insurer not carrying on insurance business in India immediately before the commencement of the Insurance (Amendment) Act, 1968, a deposit of rupees ten lakhs shall be made before the application for registration is made, and the provision of clause (*ii*) of sub section (1A) shall apply to such insurer after his registration as they apply to an insurer specified in clause (a) of sub-section (1).

(4) An insurer shall not be registered for any class of insurance business in addition to the class or classes for which is already registered until the full deposit required under sub-section (1) has been made.

(5) Where an insurer who intends to become a member of a group, does not carry on all the classes of insurance business carried on by the other insurers in such group, or, where out of the several insurers who desire to form themselves into a group, any insurer does not carry on all the classes of insurance business carried on by the other insurers who desire to form themselves into the group, such insurer may be registered for that class or

those classes of insurance business which is or are carried on by the other insurers of the group or the proposed group, as the case may be, and where any application for registration is made by any such insurer, the Authority may, notwithstanding anything contained in sub section (2A) of Section 3 or sub section (4), register such insurer for one or more additional classes of insurance, if the following conditions are fulfilled, namely:

(*a*) the Authority is satisfied that registration for the proposed one or more additional classes of insurance business would qualify the insurer to become number of a group;

(*b*) agreements have been executed by all the insurers in the group or proposed group, as the case may be, and such agreements in the opinion of the Authority, satisfy the requirements of the *Explanation* to sub-section (1B); and

(*c*) the insurer has, after the commencement of the Insurance (Amendment) Act, 1968, made deposit of a sum not less than the total of all the instalments of deposit which he would have been required to make after such commencement till the date of his becoming a member of the group, had he been a member of the group from such commencement.

(6) The Authority shall cancel the registration made in pursuance of the provisions of sub section (5), if the insurer referred to therein fails to become, within a period of three months from the date of such registration' a member of the group or proposed group, as the case may be, and, where such registration has been cancelled, the provisions of this Act shall apply to the insurer as if he had not been registered for the class or classes of insurance business in relation to which his registration has been cancelled.

(7) Securities already deposited with the Controller of Currency in compliance with the Indian Life Assurance Companies Act, 1912 (6 of 1912), shall be transferred by him to the Reserve Bank of India and shall, to the extent of their market value as at the date of the commencement of this Act, be deemed to be deposited under this Act, as the instalment or as part of this instalment to be made under the foregoing provisions of this section before the application for registration is made whether any such application is or is not in fact made.

(8) A deposit made in cash shall be held by the Reserve Bank of India to the credit of the insurer and shall except to the extent, if any, to which the cash has been invested in securities under sub section (9A), be returnable to the insurer in cash in any case in which under the provisions of this Act a deposit is to be returned; and any interest accruing due and collected on securities deposited under sub section (1) or sub section (2) shall be paid to the insurer, subject only to deduction of the normal commission chargeable for the realization of interest.

(9) The insurer may at any time replace any securities deposited by him under this section with the Reserve Bank of India either by cash or by other approved securities or partly by cash and partly by other approved securities, provided that such cash, or the value of such other approved securities estimated at the market rates prevailing at the time of replacement, or such cash together with such value, as the case may be, is not less than the value of the securities replaced estimated at the market rates prevailing when they were deposited.

(9A) The Reserve Bank of India shall, if so requested by the insurer,—

(*a*) sell any securities deposited by him with the Bank under this section and hold the cash realized by such sale as deposit, or

(*b*) invest in approved securities specified by the insurer the whole or any part of a deposit held by it in cash or the whole or any part of cash received by it on the sale of or on the maturing of securities deposited by the insurer, and hold the securities in which investment is so made as deposit.

and may charge the normal commission on such sale or on such investment.

(9B) where sub-section (9A) applies

(*a*) if the cash realized by the sale of or on the maturing of the securities (excluding in the former case the interest accrued) falls short of the market value of the securities at the date on which they were deposited with the Bank, the insurer shall make good the deficiency by a further deposit either in cash or in approved securities estimated at the market value of the securities, on the day on which they are deposited, or partly in cash and partly in approved securities so estimated, within a period of two months from the date on which the securities matured or were sold or where the securities matured or were sold before the 21st day of March, 1940, within a period of four months from the commencement of the Insurance (Amendment) Act, 1940 (20 of 1940); and unless he does so the insurer shall be deemed to have failed to comply with the requirements of this section as to deposits; and

(*b*) if the cash realized by the sale of or on the maturing of the securities (excluding in the former case the interest accrued) exceeds the market value of the securities at the date on which they were deposited with the Bank, the Central Government may, if satisfied that the full amount required to be deposited under sub section (1) is in deposit, direct the Reserve Bank to return the excess.

(10) If any part of a deposit made under this section is used in the discharge of any liability of the insurer, the insurer shall deposit such additional sum in cash or approved securities estimated at the market value of the securities on the day of deposit, or partly in cash and partly in such securities, as will make up the amount so used. The insurer shall be deemed to have failed to comply with the requirements of sub section (1), unless the deficiency is supplied within a period of two months from the date when the deposit or any part thereof is so used for discharge of liabilities.

Reservation of Deposits

Section 8 : (1) Any deposit made under section 7 or section 98 shall be deemed to be part of the assets of the insurer but shall not be susceptible of any assignment or charge; nor shall it be available for the discharge of any liability of the insurer other than liabilities arising out of policies of insurance issued by the insurer so long as any such liabilities remain undischarged; nor shall it be liable to attachment in execution of any decree except a decree obtained by a policy holder of the insurer in respect of a debt due upon a policy which debt the policy holder has failed to realise in any other way.

(2) Where a deposit is made in respect of life insurance business the deposit made in respect thereof shall not be available for discharge of any liability of the insurer other than liabilities arising out of policies of life insurance issued by the insurer.

Refund of Deposit

Section 9 : Where an insurer has ceased to carry on in India all classes of insurance business, and his liabilities in India in respect of all classes of insurance business have been satisfied or are otherwise provided for, the court may, on the application of the insurer, order the return to the insurer of the deposit made by him under this Act.

Section 27 and 28 deals with investments by insurance companies. Following provisions have been made :

For Life Insurance

(*a*) 25% of the sum stated above in the Government Securities.

(*b*) Not less than 25% of the sum in the Government securities or other Approved securities.

[(*a*) and (*b*) put together should not be more than 50%.]

(*c*) Not less than 15% of the sum in infrastructure and social sector

(*d*) Not less than 20% in other securities as stated in Schedule I of IRDA Regulations 2000.

(*e*) Not less than 15% in other approved investments to be governed by the prudential norms specified in the above referred Regulation.

[(*d*) and (*e*) put together should not be more than 25%.]

For Pension

(*a*) Not less than 20% in Government securities.

(*b*) And annuity business not less than 20% in Government securities or in approved Securities.

(*c*) Balance 60% in the approved investments specified in the Schedule I of IRDA Regulations 2000.

General Insurance Business

(*a*) 20% in the Central Government Securities.

(*b*) Not less than 10% State Government Securities.

[(*a*) and (*b*) class should not be more than 30%].

(*c*) 5% housing and loans to the state Government.

(*d*) Not less than 10% in infrastructure and social sector.

(*e*) Not exceeding 55% in other approved investments governed by the prudential norms including the securities specified by IRDA.

8.1.7 Management and Administration

Power to Appoint Staff

Section 33A : The Authority may appoint such staff, and at such places as it or he may consider necessary, for the scrutiny of the returns, statements and information furnished by insurers under this Act and generally to ensure the efficient performance of the functions of the Authority under this Act.

Power of Authority to Issue Directions

Section 34 : (1) where the Authority is satisfied that-

(*a*) in the public interest; or

(*b*) to prevent the affairs of any insurer being conducted in a marina detrimental to the interests of the policy holders or in a manner prejudicial to the interests of the insurer; or

(*c*) generally to secure the proper management of any insurer, it is necessary to issue directions to insurers generally or to any insurer In particular, he may, from time to time, issue such directions as he deems fit, and the insurers or the insurer, as the case may be, shall be bound to comply with such directions:

Provided that no such directions shall be issued to any insurer in particular unless such insurer has been given a reasonable opportunity of being heard

(2) The Authority may, on representation made to him or on his own motion, modify or cancel any direction issued under sub section (1), and in so modifying or canceling any directions, may impose such conditions as he thinks fit, subject to which the modification or cancellation shall have effect.

Appointing of Managing Directors etc.

Section 34A to 34D provides the IRDA to appoint, reappoint remove the managerial and other staff and decide the renumeration payable to them.

Amendment of provisions relating to appointments of managing directors, etc., to be subject to previous approval of the Authority

Section 34A : (1) In the case of an insurer,—

(*a*) no amendment made, after the commencement of the Insurance (Amendment) Act, 1968, of any provision relating to the appointment, re appointment, termination of appointment or remuneration of a managing or whole time director, or of a manager or a chief executive officer, by whatever name called, whether that provision be contained in the insurers memorandum or articles of associations, or in an agreement entered into by him, or in any resolution passed by the insurer in general meeting or by his Board of Directors shall have effect unless approved by the Authority;

(*b*) no appointment, re appointment or termination of appointment made after the commencement of the Insurance (Amendment) Act, 1968, of a managing or whole time director, or a manager or a chief executive officer, by whatever name called, shall have effect unless such appointment, re-appointment or termination of appointment is made with the previous approval of the Authority.

Explanation : For the purposes of this sub section, any provision conferring any benefit or providing any amenity or perquisite, in whatever form, whether during or after the termination of the term of office of the manager or the chief executive officer, by whatever name called or a managing or whole time director, shall be deemed to be a provision relating to his remuneration.

(2) Nothing contained in Sections 268 and 269, the proviso to sub section (3) of Section 309, Sections 310 and 311, the proviso to Section 387 and Section 388 (in so far as Section 388 makes the provisions of Sections 310 and 311 apply in relation to the manager of a company) of the Companies Act, 1956 (1 of 1956), shall apply to any matter in respect of which the approval of the Authority has to be obtained under sum section (1).

(3) No act done by a person as a managing or whole time director or a director not liable to retire by rotation or a manager or a chief executive officer, by whatever name called, shall be deemed to be invalid on the ground that it is subsequently discovered that his appointment or re appointment had not taken effect by reason of any of the provisions of this Act; but nothing in this subsection shall be construed as rendering valid any act done by such person after his appointment or re appointment has been shown to the insurer not to have had effect.

Power of Authority to Remove Managerial Persons from Office

Section 34B : (1) Where the Authority is satisfied that in the public interest or for preventing the affairs of an insurer being conducted in a manner detrimental to the interests of the policy holders or for securing the proper management of any insurer it is necessary so to do, he may, for reasons to be recorded in writing, by order, remove from office, with effect from such date as may be specified in the order, any director or the chief executive officer, by whatever name called, of the insurer.

(2) No order under sub section (1) shall be made unless the director or chief executive officer concerned has been given a reasonable opportunity of making a representation to the Authority against the proposed order:

Provided that if, in the opinion of the Controller, any delay would be detrimental to the interests of the insurer or his policy holders, he may, at the time of giving the opportunity aforesaid or at any time thereafter, by order direct that, pending the consideration of the representation aforesaid, if any, the director or, as the case may be, chief executive officer, shall not, with effect from the date of such order, :

(*a*) act as such director or chief executive officer of the insurer;

(*b*) in any way, whether directly, indirectly, be concerned with, or take part in the management of the insurer.

(3) Where any order is made in respect of a director or chief executive officer of an insurer under sub section (1), he shall cease to be a director or as the case may be chief executive officer of the insurer and shall not, in any way, whether directly or indirectly, be concerned with, or take part in, the management of any insurer for such period not exceeding five years as may be specified in the order.

(4) If any person in respect of whom an order is made by the Authority under sub section (1) or under the proviso to sub section (2) contravenes the provisions of this section, he shall be punishable with fine which may extend to two hundred and fifty rupees for each day during which such contravention continues.

(5) Where an order under sub section (1) has been made, the Authority may, by order in writing, appoint a suitable person in place of the director or chief executive officer who has been removed from his office under that sub-section, with effect from such date as may be specified in the order.

(6) Any person appointed as director or chief executive officer under this section shall :

(*a*) hold office during the pleasure of the Controller and subject thereto for a period not exceeding three years or such further periods not exceeding three years at a time as the Authority may specify;

(*b*) not incur any obligation or liability by reason only of his being a director or chief executive officer or for anything done or omitted to be done in good faith in the execution of the duties of his office or in relation thereto.

(7) Notwithstanding anything contained in any law or in any contract, memorandum or articles of association, on the removal of a person from office under this section, that person shall not be entitled to claim any compensation for the loss or termination of office.

Power of Controller to Appoint Additional Directors

Section 34C : (1) If the Authority is of opinion that in the public interest or in the interests of an insurer or his policy holders it is necessary so to do, he may, from time to time, by order in writing, appoint, with effect from such date as may be specified in the order, one or more persons to hold office as additional directors of the insurer:

Provided that the number of additional directors so appointed shall not, at any time, exceed five or one third of the maximum strength fixed for the Board by the articles of association of the insurer, whichever is less.

(2) Any person appointed as additional director in pursuance of this section,—

(*a*) shall hold office during the pleasure of the Authority, and subject thereto for a period not exceeding three years or such further periods not exceeding three years at a time as the Authority may specify;

(*b*) shall not incur any obligation or liability by reason only of his being a director or for anything done or omitted to be done in good faith in the execution of the duties of his office or in relation thereto; and

(*c*) shall not be required to hold qualification shares of the insurer.

(3) For the purpose of reckoning any preparation of the total number of directors of the insurer, any additional director appointed under this section shall not be taken into account.

Sections 34B and 34C to Override Other Laws

Section 34 D : Any appointment or removal of a director or chief executive officer in pursuance of Section 34B or Section 34C shall have effect notwithstanding anything to the contrary contained in the Companies Act, 1956 (1 of 1956), or any other law for the time being in force or in any contract or any other instrument.

Powers of Tariff Advisory Committee (TAC)

Section 64UC read together with the Insurance Rules 1939 defines the role and powers of TAC.

Power of the Advisory Committee to Regulate Rates, Advantages, etc.

Section 64UC : (1) The Advisory Committee may, from time to time and to the extent it deems expedient, control and regulate the rates, advantages, terms and conditions that may be offered by insurers in respect of any risk or any class or category of risks, the rates, advantages, terms and conditions of which, in its opinion, it is proper to control and regulate, and any such rate, advantages, terms and conditions shall be binding on all insurers: *Provided* that the Authority may, permit any insurer to offer, during such period (being not more than two years but which may be extended by periods of not more than two years at a time) and subject to such conditions as may be specified by him, rates, advantages, terms or conditions different from those fixed by the Advisory Committee in respect of any particular category of risks, if he is satisfied that such insurer generally issues policies only to a restricted class of the public or under a restricted category of risks.

(2) In fixing, amending or modifying any rates, advantages, terms or conditions, relating to any risk, the Advisory Committee shall try to ensure, as far as possible, that there is no unfair discrimination between risk of essentially the same hazard, and also that consideration is given to past and prospective loss experience:

Provided that the Advisory Committee may, at its discretion, make suitable allowances for the degree of credibility to be assigned to the past experience including allowances for random fluctuations and may also, at its discretion, make suitable allowances for future fluctuations and unforeseen future contingencies including hazards of conflagration or catastrophe or both.

(3) Every decision of the Advisory Committee shall be valid only after and to the extent it is ratified by the Authority, and every such decision shall take effect from the date on which it is so ratified by the Authority, or if the Authority so orders in any case, from such earlier date as he may specify in the order.

(4) The decisions of the Advisory Committee in pursuance of the provisions of this section shall be final.

(5) Where an insurer is guilty of breach of any rate, advantage, term or condition fixed by the Advisory Committee, he shall be deemed to have contravened the provisions of this Act.

Provided that instead of proceeding against the insurer for such contravention, the Authority may, if the insurer removes the contravention by recovering the deficiency in the premium, or where it is not practicable to do so, modifies suitably or cancels the contract of insurance, compound the offence on payment to the Advisory Committee of such fine, not exceeding rupees one thousand, as he may decide in consultation with the Advisory Committee.

Transitional Provisions

Section 64UD : (1) Notwithstanding anything contained in this Part, until the names of the members of the Advisory Committee elected for the first time after the commencement of the Insurance (Amendment) Act, 1968, are notified, the Tariff Committee of the General Insurance Council appointed under regulations made under sub section (2) of Section 64-o as it was in force immediately before the commencement of the Insurance (Amendment) Act, 1968, and in existence on such commencement (hereafter in this Part referred to as the Tariff Committee) shall continue to function and shall be deemed to be the Advisory Committee duly elected under this Part and the Authority of Insurance shall become the Chairman of that Committee with effect from the commencement of the Insurance (Amendment) Act, 1968, and function as such, and any chairman of the Tariff Committee holding office immediately before such commencement shall cease to be the Chairman thereof from the date of such commencement but shall continue to be an ordinary member of the Advisory Committee.

Provided that the Chairperson of the Authority shall become the Chairman of the Advisory committee with effect from the commencement of the Insurance Regulatory and Development Authority Act, 1999 and function as such, and any chairman of the Tariff Committee holding office immediately before such commencement shall cease to be the Chairman.

(2) Notwithstanding anything contained in this Part, the constitution of the Regional Councils established under Section 64 P, as in force immediately before the commencement of the Insurance (Amendment) Act, 1968 (hereafter referred to as the Regional Councils), and of the Sectional Committees formed there under, existing immediately before such commencement, shall continue to be in full force and be of full effect until the regulations made by the Advisory Committee for the first time under Section 64UB come into effect and as soon as such regulations have come into effect such constitutions shall cease to have effect.

(3) Notwithstanding anything contained in this Part, until the Secretary to the Advisory Committee is nominated

under sub section (2) of Section 64UA, the Secretary to the Tariff Committee holding office immediately before the commencement of the Insurance (Amendment) Act, 1968, shall function as the Secretary and shall be deemed to have been duly nominated under this Part.

(4) All rates, advantages, terms and conditions fixed by the Tariff Committee or the Regional Councils prior to the commencement of the Insurance (Amendment) Act, 1968, and in force immediately before such commencement shall continue, except to such extent as they may be altered, replaced or abolished by the Advisory Committee, to be valid and fully in force as if they were rates, advantages, terms and conditions fixed by the Advisory Committee.

Power of the Advisory Committee to Require Information, etc.

Section 64UE : (1) The Advisory Committee may require, by notice in writing, any insurer to supply to it such information or statements, periodical or *ad hoc, as* it may consider necessary to enable it to discharge its functions under this Part and every insurer shall comply with such requirements within such period as may be specified by the Advisory Committee in this behalf, failing which the insurer shall be deemed to have contravened the provisions of this Act.

(2) Any information supplied under this section shall be certified by a principal officer of the insurer or where the Advisory Committee has agreed in advance, by such other officer or officers of the insurer as the principal officer of the insurer may nominate for the purpose and if the notice so requires, also by an auditor.

(3) The Authority may, at any time, in writing, depute any subordinate of his, to make a personal inspection of the books of account, ledgers, policy registers and other books or documents of any insurer to verify the accuracy of any return or statement furnished by him under sub section (1), or to verify that full particulars have been supplied by him in respect of all policies issued by him and the insurer shall provide all facilities for such inspection, and make available to such person all the books of account, ledgers, policy registers and other books or documents of the insurer which might be needed by him for such verification and the person deputed may himself extract from out of the books and records of the insurer such information as may be needed to fill up or complete the returns required to be submitted to the Advisory Committee under this section.

(4) The Advisory Committee may, at any time, on the application of an insurer, make arrangements for the inspection of an organization which is concerned with the inspection of risks, adjustment of losses or fire fighting appliances, and may, whenever necessary, advise insurers about the adequacy of the arrangements for the inspection of risks and adjustment of losses or the suitability of such appliances:

Provided that no such inspection shall be made without the written permission of the concerned organization

Insurance Association of India

All the existing insurers, provident societies and also new entrants to join the Insurance Association of India and the Central Government, by an official notification in the Gazette will declare that all the existing insurers and provident societies are the members of the Insurance Association of India. This association is a separate entity with a common seal and perpetual succession and will have the power to acquire, hold, to sell the movable and immovable property of the association. The Insurance Association shall maintain a register of the membership and register of associate members of the Insurance Association of India. And, the names of the insurer or provident society will be removed from the register on ceasing its business of insurance. The Insurance Association of India is having two councils – Life Insurance Council and General Insurance Council.

8.1.8 Accounts and Returns (Section 10-26)

An insurer is required to keep a separate account of all receipts and payments in respect of each class of insurance viz., Fire, Marine and miscellaneous Insurance. Every insurer is required to prepare, at the expiration of each financial year, in the prescribed forms, (*a*) a balance sheet

(*b*) a profit and loss account

(*c*) a revenue account for each class of insurance business

These accounts are required to be audited annually by an auditor and printed and four copies to be furnished as returns to the IRDA within 6 months from the close of the financial year. Every Insurer is required to furnish to the authority a certified copy of the minutes of the proceedings of every General Meeting, within 30 days from the holding of the meeting. The Insurance Rules framed under the Act provide that the following items of information shall be maintained in respect of each class of business :

- A record of cover notes specifying the identification number, name of party, dates of commencement and expiry, type of cover granted, the amount of premium and cross- reference to the policy.
- A record of policies, which should be serially numbered, listing all policies issued, entered in chronological order, stating the number of policy, date of commencement and expiry of risk, name/s of the insured, premium received, cross reference to the relevant bank Guarantee or deposit and the nature of risk granted, cross reference to any cover-note issued prior to the issue to the policy and cross-reference to any endorsement passed subsequent to the issue of the policy.
- A record of premiums showing, according to chronological order or receipt of premiums, date of receipt, the amount, and name of party from whom received and with cross- reference to policy number.
- A record of endorsements mentioning the policy number to which attached, dates of commencement and expiry of the endorsement, the type of endorsement and the additional premium charged or refund due and cross reference to the premium register.
- A record of bank guarantees and deposits giving particulars of the party, amount and conditions of guarantee or deposits and cross-reference to the relevant policy or policies.
- A record of claims intimate mentioning name of claimant, giving reference to policy number, date of intimation of claim, interest covered, nature and cause of the loss or damage, provisional estimate of loss, amount at which settled, date of settlement of claim, recoveries from salvage or otherwise and whether surveyed. Two separate records, one relating to claims intimated and the other relating to claims paid, may be maintained if there is adequate cross referring of information between them and if the information required under this clause is readily available from them taken together.

The rules framed under the Insurance Act, 1938 also provide that the following items of information shall be maintained for the business of the insurer as a whole.

(*i*) A register of agents.

(*ii*) A record of business procured by each agent and the amount of commission paid thereon.

(*iii*) Records of employees including field workers.

(*iv*) Cash book and disbursement book.

(*v*) A record of investments and assets.

(*vi*) Records of insurance companies with which common and facultative reinsurance arrangements of reinsurance treaties are entered into.

(*vii*) Record of facultative reinsurance ceded and accepted.

Further, the Rules provide that receipts for payments received shall be maintained in a systematic manner and documents used for assuming risk are serially numbered and field accordingly. The documents relating to claims settled, including copies of any survey of loss assessment reports, shall be maintained as follows :

(*i*) in respect of every loss or damage on which a claim of less than Rs. 5,000 has been made, for a period of three years;

(*ii*) in respect of every loss or damage on which a claim of Rs. 5,000 or more but less than rupees Rs. 20,000 has been made, for a period of five years;

(*iii*) in respect of every loss or damage on which a claim of Rs. 20,000 or more but less than rupees one lakh has been made, for a period of seven years;

(*iv*) in respect of every loss or damage on which a claim of rupees one lakh or more has been made, for a period of twelve years;

such period being counted from the date on which the claim is settled.

8.1.9 Winding up of Insurance Companies

All the existing insurers, provident societies and also new entrants to join the Insurance Association of India and the Central Government, by an official notification in the Gazette will declare that all the existing insurers and provident societies are the members of the Insúrance Association of India. This association is a separate entity with a common seal and perpetual succession and will have the power to acquire, hold, to sell the movable and immovable property of the association. The Insurance Association shall maintain a register of the membership and register of associate members of the Insurance Association of India. And, the names of the insurer of provident society will be removed from the register on ceasing its business of insurance. The Insurance Association of India is having two councils – Life Insurance Council and General Insurance Council.

Power of Central Government to Acquire Undertakings of Insurers in Certain Cases

Section 52H : (1) If, upon receipt of a report from the Authority, the Central Government is satisfied that an insurer,-

(*a*) has persistently failed to comply with—

(*i*) any direction given to him under Section 34, Section 34 F or Section 34G, or

(*ii*) any order made under Sec. 34 E; or

(*b*) is being managed in a manner detrimental to the public interest or to the interests of his policy holders, or share holders,

and that-

I. in the public interest, or

II. in the interest of the policy holders or share holders of such insurer,

it is necessary to acquire the undertaking of such insurer, the Central Government may, by notified order, acquire the undertaking of such insurer (hereafter in this section and in Sections 52 I, 52 J and 52 N and in the Eighth Schedule referred to as the acquired insurer) with effect from such date as maybe specified in the order (hereinafter in this section and in Sections 52 1 and 52J and in the Eighth Schedule referred to as the appointed day):

Provided that no undertaking off an insurer shall be so acquired unless such insurer has been given a reasonable opportunity of showing cause against the proposed action.

Explanation : For the purposes of this section and of Sections 52 I to 52N—

(*a*) "notified order" means an order published in the official Gazette;

(*b*) "undertaking", in relation to an insurer incorporated outside India, means the undertaking of the insurer in India,

(2) Subject to the other provisions contained in this section and in Sections 52-I to 52M, on the appointed day, all the assets and liabilities of the undertaking of the acquired insurer shall stand transferred to, and vest in, the Central Government.

(3) The assets and liabilities of the undertaking of the acquired insurer shall be deemed to include all rights, powers, authorities and privileges and all property, whether movable or immovable, including, in particular, cash balances, reserve funds, investments, deposits and all other interests and rights in, or arising out of, such property' as may be in the possession of or held by, the acquired insurer immediately before the appointed day and all books, accounts and documents relating thereto, and shall also be deemed to include all debts, liabilities and obligations of whatever kind, then existing of the acquired insurer.

(4) Notwithstanding anything contained in sub section (2), the Central Government may, if it is satisfied that all the assets and liabilities of the undertaking of the acquired insurer should, instead of vesting in the Central Government, or continuing to so vest, vest in a corporation or company, whether established under the scheme made under Sec. 52 I or not (hereafter In this section and in Section 52 1 to 52 N and in the Eighth Schedule referred to as the acquired insurer), by order, direct that the assets and liabilities of the said undertaking, shall vest in the acquiring insurer, either on the publication of the notified order or no such other date as may be specified in this behalf in the direction.

(5) Where the undertaking of the acquired insurer vests in an acquiring insurer under sub section (4), the acquiring insurer shall, on and from the date of such vesting, be deemed to have become the transferee of the acquired insurer and all the rights and liabilities in relation to the acquired insurer shall, on and from the date of such vesting, be deemed to have been the rights and liabilities of such acquiring insurer.

(6) Unless otherwise expressly provided by or under this section or Sections 52 I to 52M, all contracts, deeds, bonds, agreements, powers of attorney, grants of legal representation and other instruments of whatever nature subsisting, having effect immediately before the appointed day and to which the acquired insurer is a party or which are in favour of the acquired insurer shall be of as full force and effect against or in favour, of the Central Government or, as the case may be, the acquiring insurer, and may be enforced or acted upon as fully and effectually as of in the place of the acquired insurer the Central Government or the acquiring insurer had been a party thereto or as if they had been issued in favour of the Central Government or the acquiring insurer, as the case may be.

(7) If, on the appointed day, any suit, appeal or other proceeding, of whatever nature, is pending by or against the acquired insurer the same shall not abate, be discontinued or be, in any way, prejudicially affected by reason of the transfer of the undertaking of the acquired insurer or of anything contained in this section or in Sections 52 I to 52M, but the suit, appeal or other proceeding may be continued, prosecuted and enforced by or against the Central Government or the acquiring insurer, as the case may be.

Winding up by the Court

Section 53 : (1) The Court may order the winding up in accordance with the Indian Companies Act, 1913 (7 of 1913), of any insurance company and the provisions of that Act shall, subject to the provisions of this Act apply accordingly.

(2) In additional to the grounds on which such an order may be based, the Court may order the winding up of an insurance company

(*a*) if with the sanction of the Court previously obtained a petition in this behalf is presented by shareholders not less in number than one tenth of the whole body of shareholders and holding not less than one tenth of the whole share capital or by not less than fifty policy holders holding policies of life insurance that have been in force for not less than three years and are of the total value of not less than fifty thousand rupees; or (*b*) if the Authority, who is hereby authorised to do so, applies in this behalf to the Court on any of the following grounds, namely-

(*i*) that the company has failed to deposit or to keep deposited with the Reserve Bank of India the amounts required by Section 7 or Section 98;

(*ii*) that the company having failed to comply with any requirement of this Act has continued such failure Nor having contravened any provision of this Act has continued such contravention for a period of three months after notice of such failure Nor contravention has been conveyed to the company by the Authority.

(*iii*) that it appears from Many returns or statements furnished under the provisions of this Act or from the results of any investigation made there under that the company is, or is deemed to be, insolvent, or

(*iv*) that the continuance of the company is prejudicial to the interest if the policy holders or to the public interest generally

Voluntary Winding Up

Section 54 : Notwithstanding anything contained in the Indian Companies Act, 1913 (7 of 1913), an insurance company shall not be wound up voluntarily except for the purpose of effecting an amalgamation or a re construction of the company, or on the ground that by reason of its liabilities it cannot continue its business.

Valuation of Liabilities

Section 55 : (1) In the winding up of an insurance company or in the insolvency of any other insurer the value of the assets and the liabilities of the insurer shall be ascertained in such manner and upon such basis as the liquidator or receiver in insolvency thinks fit, subject, so far as applicable, to the rule contained in the Seventh Schedule and to any directions which may be given by the Court.

(2) For the purposes of any reduction by the Court of the amount of the contracts of any insurance company the value of the assets and liabilities of the company and all claims in respect of policies issued by it shall be ascertained in such manner and upon such basis as the Court thinks proper having regard to the rule aforesaid.

(3) The rule in the Seventh Schedule shall be of the same force and may be repealed, altered or amended as if it were a rule made in pursuance of section 246 of the Indian Companies Act, 1913 (7 of 1913) and rules may be made under that section for the purpose of carrying into effect the provisions of this Act with respect to the winding up of insurance companies.

Application of Surplus Assets of Life Insurance Fund in Liquidation or Insolvency

Section 56 : (1) In the winding up of an insurance company and in the insolvency of any other insurer the value of the assets and the liabilities of the insurer in respect of life insurance business shall be ascertained separately from the value of any other assets or any other liabilities of the insurer and no such assets shall be applied to the discharge of any liabilities other than those in respect of life insurance business except in so far as those assets exceed the liabilities in respect of life insurance business.

(2) In the winding up of an insurance company carrying on the business of life insurance or in the insolvency of any other insurer carrying on such business where any proportion of the profits of the insurer was before the commencement of the winding up or insolvency allocated to policy holders, if, when the assets and liabilities of the insurer have been ascertained, there is found to be a surplus of assets over liabilities (hereinafter referred to as a *prima facie* surplus) there shall be added to the liabilities of the insurer in respect of the life insurance business an amount equal to such proportion of the *prima facie* surplus as is equivalent to such proportion of the profits allocated to share-holders and policy holders as was allocated to policy holders during the ten years

immediately preceding the commencement of the winding up and the assets of the insurer shall be deemed to exceed his liabilities only in so far as those assets exceed those liabilities after such addition:

Provided that :

(*a*) if in any case there has been no such allocation or if it appears to the Court that by reason of special circumstances it would be inequitable that the amount to be added to the liabilities of the insurer in respect of the life insurance business should be an amount equal to such proportion as aforesaid, the amount to be so added shall be such amount as the Court may direct, and

(*b*) for the purpose of the application of this sub section to any case where before the commencement of the winding up or insolvency a proportion of such profits as aforesaid of a branch only of the life insurance business in question has been allocated to policy holders, the value of the assets and liabilities of the insurer in respect of that branch shall be separately ascertained in like manner as the value of his assets and liabilities in respect to the life insurance business was ascertained, and the surplus so found, if any, of assets over liabilities shall, for the purpose of determining the amount to be added to :the liabilities of the insurer in respect of the life insurance business be deemed to be the *prima facie surplus*.

Winding up of Secondary Companies

Section 57 : (l) Where the insurance business or any part of the insurance business of an insurance company has been transferred to another insurance company under an arrangement in pursuance of which the first mentioned company (in this section referred to as the secondary company) or the creditors thereof has or have claims against the company to which such transfer was made (in this section referred to as the principal company) then, if the principal company is being wound up by or under the supervision of the Court, the Court shall (subject as hereinafter mentioned) order the secondary company to be wound up in conjunction with the principal company and may, by the same or any subsequent order appoint the same person to be liquidator for the two companies and make provision for such other matters as may seem to the Court necessary with a view to the companies being wound up as if they were one company.

(2) The commencement of the winding up of the principal company shall, save as otherwise ordered by the Court, be the commencement of the winding up of the secondary company.

(3) In adjusting the rights and liabilities of the members of the several companies among themselves the Court shall have regard to the constitution of the companies and to the arrangements entered into between the companies in the same manner as the Court has regard to the rights and liabilities of different classes of contributories in the case of the winding up of a single company or as near thereto as circumstances admit.

(4) Where any company alleged to be secondary is not in process of being wound up at the same time as the principal company to which it is alleged to be secondary, the Court shall not direct the secondary company to be wound up, unless, after hearing all objections (if any) that may be urged by or on behalf of the company against its being wound up, the Court is of opinion that the company is secondary to the principal company and that the winding up of the company in conjunction with the principal company is just and equitable.

(5) An application may be made in relation to the winding up of any secondary company in conjunction with the principal company by any creditor of, or person interested in, the principal or secondary company.

(6) Where a company stands in the relation of a principal company to one insurance company and in the relation of a secondary company to some other insurance company or where there are several insurance companies standing in the relation of secondary companies to one principal company, the court may deal with any number of such companies together or in separate groups as it thinks most expedient upon the principles laid down in this section.

Schemes for Partial Winding up of Insurance Companies

Section 58 : (1) If at any time it appears expedient that the affairs of an insurance company in respect of any class of business comprised in the undertaking of the Company should be wound up but that any other class of business comprised in the undertaking should continue to be carried on by the company or be transferred to another insurer, a scheme for such purposes may be prepared and submitted for confirmation of the Court in accordance with the provisions of this Act.

(2) Any scheme prepared under this section shall provide for the allocation and distribution of the assets and liabilities of the company between any classes of business affected (including the allocation of any surplus assets which may arise on the proposed winding up) for any future rights of every class of policy holders in respect of their policies and for the manner of winding up any of the affairs of the company which are proposed to be wound up and may contain provisions for altering the memorandum of the company with respect to its objects and such further provisions as may be expedient for giving effect to the scheme.

(3) The provisions of this Act relating to the valuation of liabilities of insurers in liquidation and insolvency and to the application of surplus assets of the life insurance fund in liquidation or insolvency shall apply to the winding up of any part of the affairs of a company in accordance with the scheme under this section in like manner as they apply in the winding up of an insurance company, and any scheme under this section may apply with the necessary modifications any of the provisions of the Indian Companies Act, 1913 (7 of 1913), relating to the winding up of companies.

(4) An order of the Court confirming a scheme under this section whereby the memorandum of a company is altered with respect to its objects shall as respects the alteration have effect as if it where an order confirmed under Sec. 12 of the Indian Companies Act, 1913 (7 of 1913), and the provisions of Sections 15 and 16 of that Act shall apply accordingly.

Notice of Policy Values

Section 60 : In the winding up of an insurance company for the purposes of a cash distribution of the assets and in the insolvency of any other insurer the liquidator or assignee, as the case may be, in the case of all persons appearing by the books of the company or other insurer to be entitled to or interested in the policies granted by the company or other insurer shall ascertain the value of the liability of the company or other insurer to each such person and shall give notice of such value to those persons in such manner as the Court may direct and any person to whom notice is so given shall be bound by the value so ascertained unless he gives notice of his intention to dispute such value in such manner and within such time as may be specified by a rule or order of the Court.

Power of Court to Reduce Amount of Contracts of Insurance

Section 61 : (1) where an insurance company is in liquidation or any other insurer is insolvent, the Court may make an order reducing the amount of the insurance contracts of the company or other insurer upon such terms and subject to such conditions as the Court thinks Just.

(2) Where a company carrying on the business of life insurance has been proved to be insolvent, the Court may if it thinks fit in place of making a winding up order reduce the amount of the insurance contracts of the company upon such terms and subject to such conditions as the Court thinks fit.

(3) Application for an order under this section may be made either by the liquidator or by or on behalf of the company or by a policy holder, or by the Authority and the Authority and any person whom the Court thinks likely to be affected shall be entitled to be heard on any such application.

8.1.10 Miscellaneous Provisions

Prohibition of Rebates

No person shall allow or offer to allow as an inducement to any person to take out insurance any rebate of the whole or part of commission payable or any rebate of the premium shown in the policy. Any person making default in complying with these provisions shall be punishable with fine which may extend to five hundred rupees.

Licensing of Surveyor or Loss Assessor

A surveyor or a loss assessor must hold a valid licence, which is subject to renewal after a period of 5 years. Before admitting a claim exceeding Rs. 20,000 a general insurance company needs to obtain a report on the loss that has occurred from the surveyor or loss assessor.

Penalties

The Act has laid down penalties for contravention of the following provisions :

- Failure to maintain solvency margins.
- Failure to comply with investment norms.
- Failure to carry out rural and social sector obligations.
- Making a false statement or furnishing a false document.
- Failure to comply with the directions of the Authority.
- Failure to furnish documents, statements and returns required by the Act.

8.2 Life Insurance Corporation Act, 1956

Life insurance business in India is regulated by the provisions of the Insurance Act, 1938, Insurance Rule, 1939 and the Life Insurance Corporation Act, 1956 and rules and regulation made thereunder.

Life Insurance Corporation of India (LIC) was formed in September, 1956 by an Act of Parliament, *viz.*, Life Insurance Corporation Act, 1956, with Capital contribution of Rs. 5 crore from the Government of India. Its main duty was to spread the message of Life Insurance in the country and mobilise peoples saving for nation-building activities. Life Insurance Corporation has also framed regulations *viz.*, Life Insurance Corporation (Staff) Regulation, 1960 and Life Insurance Corporation (Agents) Rules, 1972.

Section 2 (11) of the Insurance Act, 1938 defines the life insurance business as 'the business effecting contract of insurance upon human life, including any contract where by the payment of money is assured on death (except death by accident) or the happening of any contingency dependent on human life, and any contract which is subject to payment of premiums for a term dependent on human life and shall deemed to include (1) the granting of disability and double and triple indemnity accident benefits, if so, provided in the contract of insurance; (ii) the granting of annuities upon human life and granting of superannuation allowances and annuities payable out of any fund applicable solely to the relief and maintenance of persons engaged or who have been engaged in any particular profession, trade or employment or of the dependents of such persons.

8.2.1 Other Definitions

(1) *"appointed day"* means the date on which the Corporation is established under section 3;

(2) *"composite insurer"* means an insurer carrying on in addition to controlled business any other kind of insurance business;

(3) *"controlled business"* means :

(*i*) in the case of any insurer specified in sub-clause (*a*) (*ii*) or sub-clause (*b*) of clause (9) of section 2 of the Insurance Act and carrying on life insurance business :

(*a*) all his business, if he carries on no other class of insurance business;

(*b*) all the business appertaining to his life insurance business, if he carries on any other class of insurance business also;

(c) all his business if his certificate of registration under the Insurance Act in respect of general insurance business stands wholly cancelled for a period of more than six months on the 19th day of January, 1956.

(*ii*) in the case of any other insurer specified in clause (9) of section 2 of the Insurance Act and carrying on life insurance business :

(*a*) all his business in India, if he carries on no other class of insurance business in India;

(*b*) all the business appertaining to his life insurance business in India, if he carries on any other class of insurance business also in India;

(c) all his business in India if he certificate of registration under the Insurance Act in respect of general insurance business in India stands wholly cancelled for a period of more than six months on the 19th day of January, 1956.

Explanation : An insurer is said to carry on no class of insurance business other than life insurance business, if in addition to life insurance business, he carries on only capital redemption business or annuity certain business or both; and the expression "business appertaining to his life insurance business" in sub-clause (*i*) and (*ii*) shall be construed accordingly;

(*iii*) in the case of a provident society, as defined in section 65 of the Insurance Act, all its business;

(*iv*) in the case of the Central Government or a State Government, all life insurance business carried on by it, subject to the exceptions specified in section 44;

(4) *"Corporation"* means the Life Insurance Corporation of India established under section 3;

(5) *"Insurance Act"* means the Insurance Act, 1938 (4 of 1938);

(6) *"insurer"* means an insurer as defined in the Insurance Act who carries on life insurance business in India and includes the Government and a provident society as defined in section 65 of the Insurance Act;

(7) *"member"* means a member of the Corporation;

(8) *"prescribed"* means prescribed by rules made under this Act;

(9) *"Tribunal"* means a Tribunal constituted under section 17 and having jurisdiction in respect of any matter under the rules made under this Act;

(10) all other words and expressions used herein but not defined and defined in the Insurance Act shall have the meanings respectively assigned to them in that Act.

8.2.2 Establishment of Life Insurance Corporation of India

Establishment and Incorporation of Life Insurance Corporation of India *Section 3:* (1) With effect from such date {1st September, 1956, vide Notification No. S.R.O. 1937, dated 30-8-1956, Gazette of India, Extraordinary, Pt. II, Sec.3, p. 1799.} as the Central Government may, by notification in the Official Gazette, appoint, there shall be established a Corporation called the Life Insurance Corporation of India.

(2) The Corporation shall be a body corporate having perpetual succession and a common seal with power subject to the provisions of this Act, to acquire, hold and dispose of property, and may by its name sue and be sued.

Constitution of the Corporation

Section 4 : (1) The Corporation shall consist of such number of persons not exceeding fifteen as the Central Government may think fit to appoint thereto and one of them shall be appointed by the Central Government to be the Chairman thereof.

(2) Before appointing a person to be a member, the Central Government shall satisfy itself that person will have no such financial or other interest as is likely to affect prejudicially the exercise or performance by him of his functions as a member, and the Central Government shall also satisfy itself from time to time with respect to every member that he has no such interest; and any person who is, or whom the Central Government proposes to appoint and who has consented to be, a member shall, whenever required by the Central Government so to do, furnish to it such information as the Central Government considers necessary for the performance of its duties under this sub-section.

(3) A member who is in any way directly or indirectly interested in a contract made or proposed to be made by the Corporation shall as soon as possible after the relevant circumstances have come to his knowledge, disclose the nature of his interest to the Corporation and the member shall not take part in any deliberation or discussion of the Corporation with respect to that contact.

Capital of the Corporation

Section 5 : (1) The original capital of the Corporation shall be five crores of rupees provided by the Central Government after due appropriation made by Parliament by law for the purpose, and the terms and conditions relating to the provision of such capital shall be such as may be determined by the Central Government.

(2) The Central Government may, on the recommendation of the Corporation, reduce the capital of the Corporation to such extent and in such manner as the Central Government may determine.

8.2.3 Functions of the Corporation

Section 6 : (1) Subject, to the rules, if any, made by the Central Government in this behalf, it shall be the general duty of the Corporation to carry on life insurance business, whether in or outside India, and the Corporation shall so exercise its powers under this Act as to secure that life insurance business is developed to the best advantage of the community.

(2) Without prejudice to the generality of the provisions contained in sub-section (1) but subject to the other provisions contained in this Act, the Corporation shall have power :

(*a*) to carry on capital redemption business, annuity certain business or reinsurance business in so far as such re insurance business appertains to life insurance business;

(*b*) subject to the rules, if any, made by the Central Government in this behalf, to invest the funds of the Corporation in such manner as the Corporation may think fit and to take all such steps as may be necessary or expedient for the protection or realization of any investment; including the taking over of and administering any property offered as security for the investment until a suitable opportunity arises for its disposal;

(*c*) to acquire, hold and dispose of any property for the purpose of its business;

(*d*) to transfer the whole or any part of the life insurance business carried on outside India to any other person or persons, if in the interest of the Corporation it is expedient so to do;

(*e*) to advance or lend money upon the security of any movable property or otherwise;

(*f*) to borrow or raise any money in such manner and upon such security as the Corporation may think fit;

(*g*) to carry on either by itself or through any subsidiary any other business in any case where such other business was being carried on by a subsidiary of an insurer whose controlled business has been transferred to an vested in the Corporation under this Act;

(*h*) to carry on any other business which may seen to the Corporation to be capable of being conveniently carried on in connection with its business and calculated directly or indirectly to render profitable the business of the Corporation;

(*i*) to do all such things as may be incidental or conducive to the proper exercise of any of the powers of the Corporation.

(3) In the discharge of any of its functions the Corporation shall act so far as may be on business principles.

8.2.4 Transfer of Existing Life Insurance Business to the Corporation

Assets and Liabilities of Existing Insurers Carrying on Controlled Business

Section 7 : (1) On the appointed day there shall be transferred to and vested in the Corporation all the assets and liabilities appertaining to the controlled business of all insurers.

(2) The assets appertaining to the controlled business of an insurer shall be deemed to include all rights and powers, and all property, whether movable or immovable, appertaining to his controlled business, including, in particular, cash balances, reserve funds, investments, deposits and all other interests and rights in or arising out of such property as may be in the possession of the insurer and all books of account or documents relating to the controlled business of the insurer; and liabilities shall be deemed to include all debts, liabilities and obligations of whatever kind then existing and appertaining to the controlled business of the insurer.

Explanation : The expression "assets appertaining" to the controlled business of an insurer" :

(*a*) in relation to a composite insurer, includes that part of the paid-up capital of the insurer or assets representing such part which has or have been allocated to the controlled business of the insurer in accordance with the rules made in this behalf;

(*b*) in relation to a Government, means the amount lying to the credit of that business on the appointed day.

(3) Where any such assets are subject to any trust referred to in sub-section (6) of section 27 of the Insurance Act or to any other trust for the benefit of policy-holders, the assets shall be deemed to have vested in the Corporation free from any such trust.

On 01-09-1956, all the assets and liabilities of the existing insurers were transferred to the corporation.

8.2.5 Conduct of Business

Provident, Superannuation and Other Like Funds

Section 8 : (1) Where an insurer whose controlled business is to be transferred to and vested in the Corporation under section 7, has established a provident or superannuation fund or any other like fund for the benefit of his employees and constituted a trust in respect thereof (hereinafter in this section referred to as an existing trust), the moneys standing to the credit of any such fund on the appointed day, together with any other assets belonging to such fund, shall, subject to the provisions of sub-section (2) stand transferred to and vest in the Corporation on the appointed day free from any such trust.

(2) Where all the employees of any such insurer do not become employees of the Corporation under section 11, the moneys and other assets belonging to any such fund as it referred to in sub-section (1), shall be apportioned between the trustees of the fund and the Corporation in the prescribed manner; and in case of any dispute regarding such apportionment, the decision of the Central Government thereon shall be final.

(3) The Corporation shall, as soon as may be after the appointed day, constitute in respect of the moneys and other assets which are transferred to and vested in it under this section, one or more trusts having objects as similar to the objects of the existing trusts as in the circumstances may be practicable.

(4) Where all the moneys and other assets belonging to an existing trust are transferred to and vested in the Corporation under this section, the trustees of such trust, except as respects things done or omitted to be done before the appointed day.

General Effect of Vesting of Controlled Business

Section 9 : (1) Unless otherwise expressly provided by or under this Act, all contracts, agreements and other instruments of whatever nature subsisting or having effect immediately before the appointed day and to which an insurer whose controlled business has been transferred to and vested in the Corporation is a party or which are in favour of such insurer shall in so far as they relate to the controlled business of the insurer be of as full force and affect against or in favour of the Corporation, as the case may be, and may be enforced or acted upon as fully and effectually as if, instead of the insurer, the Corporation had been a party thereto or as if they had been entered into or issued in favour of the Corporation.

(2) If on the appointed day any suit, appeal or other legal proceeding of whatever nature is pending by or against an insurer, then, in so far as it relates to his controlled business, it shall not abate, be discontinued or be in any way prejudicially affected by reason of the transfer to the Corporation of the business of the insurer or anything done under this Act, but the suit, appeal or other proceeding may be continued prosecuted and enforced by or against the Corporation.

Provisions as to Composite Insurers

Section 10 : (1) For the removal of doubts it is hereby declared that in any case where an insurer whose controlled business has been transferred to an vested in the corporation under this Act is a composite insurer, the provisions of the preceding sections shall only apply to the extent to which any property appertains to his controlled business and to rights and powers acquired, and to debts, liabilities and obligations incurred, and to contracts, agreements and other instruments made by the insurer for the purposes of his controlled business and to legal proceedings relating to those purposes, and the provisions of those sections shall be construed accordingly.

(2) The Central Government may, by rules made in this behalf provide :

(*a*) for the determination of the question whether any property appertains to his controlled business or whether any rights, powers, debts, liabilities or obligations were acquired or incurred or any contract, agreement or other instrument was made by the insurer for the purposes of his controlled business or whether any documents relate to those purposes;

(*b*) doe the allocation of the paid-up capital or assets representing such paid-up capital, as the case may be, between the controlled business of the insurer and any other business;

(*c*) for substituting for any agreements entered into by any insurer partly for the purposes of his controlled business and partly for other purposes separate agreements in the requisite terms and for any apportionments and indemnities consequent thereon;

(*d*) for the severance of leases comprising property of which part only is transferred to And vested in the Corporation by virtue of this Act and for apportionment consequent on such severance;

(*e*) for the apportionment and the making of financial adjustments with respects to any debts, liabilities of obligations incurred by any such insurer partly for the purposes of his controlled business and partly for other purposes and for any necessary variation of mortgages and encumbrances relating to such debts, liabilities or obligations;

(*f*) for the apportionment of the moneys and other assets belonging to any provident or superannuation fund or any other like fund to which the provisions of section 8 do not apply between persons employed in connection with the controlled business of an insurer and other persons;

(*g*) for any other matters supplementary to or consequential on the matters aforesaid for which provision appears to be necessary or expedient.

(3) All rules made under this section shall be laid for not less than thirty days before both Houses of Parliament as soon as possible after they are made and shall be subject to such modifications as Parliament may make during the session in which they are so laid or the session immediately following.

(4) Where at any time before the expiration of six months from the appointed day a question has arisen under this section or under any rules made thereunder as to whether any property is or was held or used by the insurer for the purposes of his controlled business, the question shall be referred to the Tribunal for decision.

Power of Corporation to Modify Contracts of Life Insurance in Certain Cases

Section 14 : The corporation may, having regard to the financial condition on the appointed day of any insurer whose controlled business has been transferred to an vested in the Corporation, reduce the amounts of insurance under contracts of life insurance entered into by such insurer before the 19th day of January 1956, in such manner and subject to such conditions as it thinks fit:

Provided that no such reduction shall be made except in accordance with a scheme prepared by the Corporation in this behalf and approved by the Central Government.

Right of Corporation to Seek Relief in Respect of Certain Transactions of the Insurer

Section 15 : (1) Where an insurer whose controlled business has been transferred to and vested in the Corporation under this Act has, at any time within five years before the 19th day of January, 1956 :

(*a*) made any payment to any person without consideration;

(*b*) sold or disposed of any property of the insurer without consideration or for an inadequate consideration;

(*c*) acquired any property or rights for an excessive consideration:

(*d*) entered into or varied any agreement so as to require an excessive consideration to be paid or given by the insurer;

(*e*) entered into any other transaction of such an onerous nature as to cause a loss to, or impose a liability on, the insurer exceeding any benefit accruing to the insurer;

(*f*) if a composite insurer, transferred any property from his life department to his general department without consideration or for an inadequate consideration.

and the payment, sale, disposal, acquisition, agreement or variation thereof or other transaction or transfer was not reasonably necessary for the purpose of the controlled business of the insurer or was made with an unreasonable lack of prudence on the part of the insurer, regard being had in either case to the circumstances at the time, the Corporation may apply for relief to the Tribunal in respect of such transaction, and all parties to the transaction shall, unless the Tribunal otherwise directs, be made parties to the application.

(2) The Tribunal may make such order against any of the parties to the application as it thinks just having regard to the extent to which those parties were respectively responsible for the transaction or benefited from it and all the circumstances of the case.

(3) Where an application is made to the Tribunal under this section is respect of any transaction and the application is determined in favour of the Corporation, the Tribunal shall have exclusive jurisdiction to determine any claims outstanding in respect of the transaction.

Compensation for Acquisition of Controlled Business

Section 16 : (1) Where the controlled business of an insurer has been transferred to and vested in the Corporation under this Act, compensation shall be given by the Corporation to that insurer in accordance with the principles contained in the First Schedule.

(2) The amount of the compensation to be given in accordance with the aforesaid principles shall be determined by the Corporation in the first instance, and if the amount so determined is approved by the Central Government it shall be offered to the insurer in full satisfaction of the compensation payable to him under this Act, and if, on the other hand, the amount so offered is not acceptable to the insurer he may within such time as may be prescribed for the purpose have the matter referred to the Tribunal for decision.

Constitution of Tribunals

Section 17 : (1) The Central Government may for the purposes of this Act constitute one or more Tribunals and each of the Tribunals shall consist of three members appointed by the Central Government one of whom shall be a person who is, or has been, a Judge of a High Court or has been a Judge of the Supreme Court, and he shall be the Chairman thereof.

(2) A Tribunal may choose one or more persons possessing special knowledge of any matter relating to any case under inquiry to assist the Tribunal in determining any question which has to be decided by it under this Act.

(3) Every Tribunal shall have the powers of a civil court while trying a suit under the Code of Civil Procedure, 1908 (5 of 1908), in respect of the following matters:

(*a*) summoning and enforcing the attendance of any person and examining him on oath;

(*b*) requiring the discovery and production of documents;

(*c*) receiving evidence on affidavits;

(*d*) issuing commissions for the examination of witnesses or documents.

(4) Every Tribunal shall have power to regulate its own procedure and decide all matters within its competence, and may review any of its decisions in the event of there being a mistake on the face of the record or correct any arithmetic or clerical error therein.

8.2.6 Organisational Structure

Offices, Branches and Agencies

Section 18 : (1) The central office of the Corporation shall be at such place as the Central Government may, by notification in the Official Gazette, specify.

(2) The Corporation shall establish a zonal office at each of the following places, namely, Bombay, Calcutta, Delhi, Kanpur and Madras, and, subject to the previous approval of the Central Government, may establish such other zonal offices as it thinks fit.

(3) The territorial limits of each zone shall be such as may be specified by the Corporation.

(4) There may be established as many divisional offices and branches in each zone as the Zonal Manager thinks fit.

Committees of the Corporation

Section 19 : (1) The Corporation may entrust the general superintendence and direction of its affairs and business to an Executive Committee consisting of not more than five of its members and the Executive Committee may exercise all powers and do all such acts and things as may be delegated to it by the Corporation.

(2) The Corporation may also constitute an investment Committed for the purpose of advising it in matters relating to the investment of its funds, and the Investment Committee shall consist of not more than seven members of whom not less than three shall be members of the Corporation and the remaining members shall be persons (whether members of the Corporation or not) who have special knowledge and experience in financial matters, particularly, matters relating to investment of funds.

(3) The Corporation may constitute such other Committees as it may think fir for the purpose of discharging such of its functions as may be delegated to them.

Managing Directors

Section 20 : The Corporation may appoint one or more persons to be the Managing Director or Directors of the Corporation, and every Managing Director shall be a whole-time officer of the Corporation and shall exercise such powers and perform such duties as may be entrusted or delegated to him by the Executive Committee or the Corporation.

Corporation to be Guided by the Directions of Central Government

Section 21 : In the discharge of its functions under this Act, the Corporation shall be guided by such directions in matters of policy involving public interest as the Central Government may give to it in writing; and if any question arises whether a direction relates to a matter of policy involving public interest the decision of the Central Government thereon shall be final.

8.2.7 Other Important Provisions

Exclusive privilege of carrying on life insurance in India : Section 30 of the Act gives the Corporation the exclusive privilege of carrying on life insurance business in India on and from the appointed day.

Policies guaranteed by Central Government : By virtue of Section 37, the sums assured by all policies issued by the Corporation or by any insurer the liabilities under which have vested in the Corporation and all bonuses declared in respect thereof are guaranteed as to payment in cash by the Central Government.

Rule making powers of the Central Government : Section 48 empowers the Central Government to make rules to carry out the purposes of the Act. The rules may provide, *interalia*, for :

(*i*) the terms of office and conditions of service of members;

(*ii*) the manner in which and the conditions subject to which investment may be made by the Corporation;

(*iii*) the form in which the report giving an account of the activities of the Corporation shall be prepared;

(*iv*) the conditions subject to which the Corporation may appoint employees.

Powers of the Corporation to make Regulations : Section 49 empowers the Corporation, with the previous approval of the Central Government, by notification in the Gazette of India, to make regulations for the purpose of giving effect to the provisions of the Act.

The Schedules to the Act deal with principles for determining, compensation, principles for determining the value of liabilities in certain cases and principles for determining compensation payable to chief agents.

8.2.8 Life Insurance Corporation Regulations, 1959

These regulation have been made by the Life Insurance Corporation of India in accordance with the powers vested u/s 49 of the Act subject to previous approval of Central Government. A brief summary of these regulations is given below :

Corporation shall meet atleast once in three months at a place which the Chairman may determine. Five members personally present shall be a quorum for a meeting and in the absence of quorum at a meeting, the meeting shall be adjourned to another date within a week of such meeting. If at the adjourned meeting also, the quorum is not present within half an hour from the time appointed for the meeting, the members present shall be the quorum. These provisions are similar to those given in the companies Act, 1956. Three high powered (management) committees have been prescribed :

1. The Executive Committee
2. Investment Committee
3. Building Advisory Committee

Chairman shall be the Chief Executive of the Corporation. The Managing Directors may, with the approval of the Chairman and with prior sanction of the Corporation or any Committee of the Corporation, delegate to officers or employees the powers, authorities and discretions necessary for efficient conduct of the business of the Corporation.

The Regulations also provide that :

(*a*) all amount received on behalf of the Corporation by any officer or employee shall be credited to the appropriate Bank account of the Corporation;

(*b*) payments on behalf of the Corporation shall be made only by duly authorised officers;

(*c*) the accounts of all the offices of the Corporation shall be regularly audited by Internal Auditors;

(*d*) every office of the Corporation shall be inspected by Inspecting Officers.

8.3 General Insurance Business (Nationalisation) Act, 1972

General Insurance Business was nationalised in 1972 and company by name of General Insurance Corporation of India (GIC) was formed under Companies Act, 1956 and was entrusted with the task of supervising, controlling and carrying on the business of general insurance. On the formation of the Corporation, the shares of Indian Insurance Companies vested in the Central Government stood automatically transferred to the Corporation and all the Indian Insurance Companies became subsidiaries of the Corporation. Amalgamation schemes were also framed whereby the Indian Insurance Companies were merged in one another so that ultimately there would be only four Indian companies to promote competition and also consolidate general insurance business in India.

8.3.1 Formation of GIC

GIC, under *Section 9* of the Act has an authorised capital of Rs. 75 crores into Rs. 75 lakhs fully paid up shares of Rs. 100/- each. Of which, Rs. 5 crores is the initial subscribed capital of the Corporation. The Central Government could frame one or more schemes under Section 16 of the Act for merger of the companies. A copy of every scheme framed under Section 16 shall be laid before each House of Parliament.

By virtue of the provisions of Section 4 to 8 the Central Government is authorised to acquire the assets and liabilities including the share holdings of the existing Indian Insurers on an appointed day *i.e.* 01-01-73. Section 7 of the Act authorised the central government to acquire the services of existing employees on the service conditions formulated by the newly established company *viz.*, GIC.

Section 3 of the Act defines an "acquiring company" as any Indian Insurance Company and where a scheme has been framed involving the merger of one Indian Insurance Company in another or the amalgamation of two more such companies, it shall mean the Indian Insurance Company in which any other company has been merged or the company which has been formed as a result of the amalgamation.

Chapter VA of the Act contains the terms and conditions of service of officers and other employees. The company is authorized to make amendments or make rules, amend or add to the schemes which are already in existence or make new provisions or schemes for the staff of the company. All the schemes, which are newly framed or the existing schemes with amendments made thereto are to be placed before the houses of Parliament for their approval. These schemes will be operative notwithstanding anything contrary contained in any other law or any agreement, award or other instrument for the time being in force.

8.3.2 Functions of the Corporation

Section 18 of the Act describes the various functions of the GIC as follows :

"18. Functions of Corporation : (1) The functions of the Corporation shall include:

(*a*) the carrying on of any part of the general insurance business, if it thinks it desirable to do so;

(*b*) aiding, assisting and advising the acquiring companies in the matter of setting up of standards of conduct and sound practice in general insurance business and in the matter of rendering efficient service to holders of policies of general insurance;

(*c*) advising the acquiring companies in the matter of the controlling their expenses including the payment of commission and other expenses.

(*d*) advising the acquiring companies in the matter of the investment of their funds;

(*e*) issuing directions to acquiring companies in relation to the conduct of general insurance business.

(2) In issuing any directions under sub-section (1), the Corporation shall keep in mind the desirability of encouraging competition amongst the acquiring companies as far as possible in order to render their services more efficient."

Section 19 defines the functions of acquiring companies :

"19. Functions of acquiring companies :

1. Subject to the rules, if any, made by the Central Government in this behalf and to its memorandum and articles of association, it shall be the duty of every acquiring company to carry on general insurance business.
2. Each acquiring company shall so function under this Act as to secure that general insurance business is developed to the best advantage of the community.
3. In the discharge of any of its functions, each acquiring company shall act so far as may be on business principles and where any directions have been issued by the Corporation shall be guided by such directions.
4. For the removal of doubts it is hereby declared that the Corporation and any acquiring company may, subject to the rules, if any, made by the Central Government in this behalf, enter into such contracts of reinsurance of reinsurance treaties as it may think fit for the protection of its interests."

8.3.3 Powers of Central Government

Section 23 of the Act empowers the Central Government is vested with the power to issue directions to the General Insurance Corporation of India and every acquiring company in the discharge of its functions and they shall be guided by such directions in regard to matters of policy involving public interest. No provision of law relating to winding up of a company shall apply to the Corporation or to an acquiring company and neither the Corporation nor any such company shall be placed in liquidation save by order of the Central Government and in such manner as it may direct.

Section 24, provides the acquiring companies, the exclusive privilege of carrying on general insurance business in India. No person shall take out or renew any policy of insurance in respect of any property in India or in shipping or vessel or aircraft registered in India with an insurer whose principal place of business is outside India save with the prior permission of the Central Government.

Under *Section 35,* the Central Government may be notification specify the application of the provisions of the Insurance Act, 1958 with such modifications as is deemed necessary to the Corporation and the acquiring companies. The Central Government is also empowered to make rules to carry out the provisions of the Act and such rules may provide for :

(*a*) manner in which the profits and other moneys received by the Corporation may be dealt with;

(*b*) the conditions subject to which the Corporation and the acquiring companies shall carry on general insurance business;

(*c*) the terms and conditions subject to which any re-insurance contract or treaties may be entered into;

(*d*) form and manner in which any notice or application may be made to the Central Government;

(*e*) the reports which may be called for by the Central Government from the Corporation and acquiring companies; and

(*f*) any other matter which is required to be or may be prescribed.

8.4 INSURANCE REGULATORY AND DEVELOPMENT AUTHORITY ACT, 1999

The Insurance Regulatory and Development Authority Act, 1999 provides for the establishment of an Authority to protect the interests of holders of insurance policies, to regulate, promote and ensure orderly growth of the insurance industry and for matters connected therewith or incidental thereto and further to amend the Insurance Act, 1938, the Life Insurance Corporation Act, 1956 and the General Insurance Business (Nationalisation) Act, 1972.

The Statement of Objects and Reasons of the Act provides that the insurance industry requires a high degree of regulation. The Insurance Act, 1938 provided for the institution of the Controller of Insurance to act as a strong and powerful supervisory and regulatory authority with powers to direct, advise, caution, prohibit, investigate, inspect, prosecute, search, seize, amalgamate, authorise, register and liquidate insurance companies. However, after the nationalisation of Life Insurance in 1956 and the General Insurance in 1972, the role of Controller of Insurance diminished in significance over a period of time.

8.4.1 Constitution of the Authority

Section 2(b) of the IRDA Act, 1999 defines the Authority as the Insurance Regulatory and Development Authority established under Section 3 of the Act. The Section 3 lays down the procedure for establishing the Authority. It is established by a notification by the Central Government in the Official Gazettee. The date of operation of the Authority is also notified by the Central Government by a notification. The other important characteristics of the Authority are as follows:

- It is a body corporate with perpetual succession and common seal.
- It has the powers to acquire, hold and dispose the property in its name. The property may be a movable or immovable.
- It has the powers to enter into contract in its name.
- It can sue the parties and it can be sued by the parties.

- The Central Government by notification decides the principal place of office of the Authority and the Authority has the powers to open branches or other offices as required by it.
- It consists of a Chairperson, not more than five wholetime members, and not more than four part-time members. (S. 4).
- All the members are appointed by the Central Government by a notification.
- The Chairperson and members are appointed from the person of ability, integrity having the standing and experience or knowledge in life insurance or general insurance, actuarial science, finance, economics, law, accountancy, administration or any other discipline which is useful for the Authority. And preferably, the Chairperson and one of the whole time members should be experienced persons or have the knowledge in the life insurance or the general insurance or actuarial science. (S. 4).
- The term of the office of the Chairperson and the wholetime members of five years and the part-time members will hold office for a period not more than the five years from the date of joining the office.
- The Chairperson will be in the office till the attains the age of sixty five years and the wholetime member will be in the office till he attains the age of sixty two years (S. 5).
- The Chairperson or the whole time member or part-time member can relinquish the office by giving a notice of three months to the Central Government.
- The Central Government can remove the Chairperson, wholetime member or the part-time member for the reasons of they become insolvent, physically or mentally incapable of performing duties, convicted for the moral turpitude, has acquired the financial or other interest in the insurance business, or the position of the member or the Chairperson is detrimental to the interest of the insurance or public or the policyholders. (S. 6)
- The Central Government, before removing a person from the office, has to give opportunity to the member to explain the reasons and after hearing him, if not satisfied can remove a member from service giving causes of removal.
- Any defect found in the process of appointment or any irregularity of procedures or appointment of members cannot vitiate the appointment of the member. The existence of vacancy in the body of the Authority does not affect the proceedings of the meeting of the Authority.
- The Chairperson or the members should not take any employment at least for a period of two years after they leave their positions. Under special circumstances, they can hold any office with the previous approval of the Central Government (S. 8).
- The salaries, allowance and other remunerations will be paid to the Chairperson and members as per the provisions laid down by the Central Government. The allowances and other service conditions will be prescribed by a notification.

8.4.2 Duties, Powers and Functions of the Authority

Duties

- The primary duty of the IRDA is to regulate, promote and ensure orderly growth and conduct of the insurance business and reinsurance business (S.14).
- It has to maintain proper accounts and other relevant records, prepare annual statements of accounts in such form as may be prescribed by the Central Government in consultation with the CAG.
- It has to comply with the directions of the Central Government and CAG will arrange the audit of the accounts and rectify any defects pointed by the audit conducted by it.

- The Authority has to submit the audited balance sheet and other financial statements to the Central Government and the Government will lay the reports before the houses of the Parliament.
- The Authority has to submit all the financial statements to the Central Government within nine months from the completion of the relevant financial year.
- It has the duty to scrutinise all existing and new insurance products, rates charged, terms and conditions offered and act in best interest of consumers.
- The authority is duty bound to follow the directions issued by the Central Government and report the outcome of the directions.
- Authority has the general duty to protect the interest of policyholders in matters concerning assignment, nomination, settlement of insurance claim, surrenders etc. and other terms and conditions of contract of insurance.

Powers

- The Authority has the general supervisory power of insurance industry and it has the administrative powers.
- Powers to appoint the staff and officers required to conduct the business of the Authority smoothly.
- Authority can even delegate some general or special powers by an order in writing to the Chairperson or the Members of the Authority along with conditions if it feels as necessity.
- Power to constitute committees of the members and delegate the powers to the committee.
- Power to hold and acquire movable or immovable property.
- Power to issue a certificate of registration, renew, modify, withdraw, suspend or cancel such registration to the insurer.
- Power to prepare a code of conduct to the agents, surveyors and loss assessors and other intermediaries associated with insurance business.
- Power to levy fees and other charges for carrying out the purposes of this Act.
- Power to call information from insurers' inspect accounts and other documents conduct enquiries and investigate including the audit of the insurers, intermediaries' and other organizations connected with the insurance business.
- It has the power to regulate the margin of solvency and investment of funds by insurance companies.
- Power to exercise the powers sanctioned by other insurance laws of the country or by other notifications issued by the Central Government from time to time.
- It has the powers to make regulations with the consultancy of Insurance Advisory Committee in the field of finalizing the service conditions of the members regarding the meeting and transactions to be carried out by the Advisory committee in promoting the insurance business.

Functions

- Promoting and regulating the professional organizations connected with the insurance and reinsurance business.
- Promoting efficiency in the conduct of insurance business in India.
- To act as adjudicator in the settlement of disputes between the insurers, intermediaries of the insurers.
- To act as supervisory authority and regulate the functioning of Tariff Advisory Committee and various insurance companies.

- To control and regulate the rates, advantages, terms and conditions that may be offered by insurers in respect of general insurances, which are not controlled by the Tariff Advisory Committee (Non-Tariff Products).
- To formulate the regulations concerning insurance in rural and social sectors.

8.4.3 Other Provisions

The Central Government has the powers under the Act to direct the Authority and grant funds under the head with sanction of the Parliament. The fund so constituted is called the Insurance Regulatory and Development Fund. This fund can be used to meet the expenses of the salaries, allowances and other remuneration of the members, officers and other employees of the Authority and to meet all other expenses required to discharge the duties and functions of the Authority. Registration fees, application frees from insurers and other intermediaries are also credited to the fund. A credit is also received u/s 7 of the Insurance Act, 1938.

The Central Government under the Act has the power to give directions to the Authority on the questions of policy of insurance business. If the central government finds that the Authority is not able to discharge the functions or perform the duties prescribed under the provisions of this Act or the Authority has defaulted in complying with the directions of the Central Government or the provisions of the Act, the financial position of the Authority is under deterrent conditions and if the Central Government feels that the Authority is working against the interest of public, can supercede the Authority and exercise its powers. This it may do by giving a notice with reasons and the authority may continue to act accordingly for a period not exceeding six months. Authority has to submit report of action taken to the Parliament. The Central Government has the power to make following rules in relations the authority :

1. The format of annual statement of accounts of the authority form and manner of submission of returns and statements and particulars are to be furnished.
2. Rules concerning the fixation of remunerations and service conditions of the staff, officers, members of the Authority.
3. To fix the allowances payable to part-time members of the Authority.
4. Any matter as may be required for by Insurance Advisory Committee.

The Act empowers the IRDA to appoint a committee by notification, to provide the advice on various insurance matters to the Authority called as Insurance Advisory Committee (IAC). This committee is established by a notification by the Authority. IAC contains not more than 25 members excluding ex-officio members to represent the various interests of commerce, industry, transport, agriculture, consumer forums, surveyors, agents, intermediaries, organizations engaged in safety and loss prevention, research bodies and employees association of insurance companies and intermediaries. The chairperson and the members of the authority are the ex-officio members the Insurance Advisory Committee. The objects of the automatically IAC shall be to advise the Authority on matters relating to the framing the regulations in relation to service conditions of the staff, conducting the transactions of various meetings and deciding the powers to be delegated etc. and any other matters required by the Authority.

The Regulatory Authority is under a duty to submit all the rules framed by it for the approval of Parliament. The provisions of other insurance laws are also applicable for the Authority, which are not in contradiction with the policy of public interest. IRDA is also generally subject to various insurance and other laws in best interest of the public.

8.4.4 IRDA Regulations

Various regulations have been framed by IRDA since its inception. These relate to licencing of insurers, regulation of intermediaries, reporting requirements, business practices, etc.

Regulations Framed under Insurance Regulatory and Development Authority Act, 1999 and the Insurance (Amendment) Act, 2002.

1. Insurance Regulatory and Development Authority (Actuarial Report and Abstract) Regulations, 2000.
2. Insurance Regulatory and Development Authority (Obligation of insure of Rural or Social Sectors) Regulation, 2000.
3. Insurance Regulatory and Development Authority (Insurance Advertisements and Disclosure) Regulations, 2000.
4. Insurance Regulatory and Development Authority (Licensing of Insurance Agents) Regulations, 2000.
5. Insurance Regulatory and Development Authority (General Insurance – Reinsurance) Regulations, 2000.
6. Insurance Regulatory and Development Authority (Appointed Actuary) Regulations, 2000.
7. Insurance Regulatory and Development Authority (Assets, Liabilities and Solvency Margin of Insurers) Regulations, 2000.
8. Insurance Regulatory and Development Authority (Meetings) Regulations, 2000.
9. Insurance Regulatory and Development Authority (Registration of Indian Insurance Companies) Regulations, 2000.
10. Insurance Advisory Committee (Meetings) Regulations, 2000.
11. Insurance Regulatory and Development Authority (Investment) Regulations, 2000.
12. Insurance Regulatory and Development Authority (Preparation of Financial Statements and Auditor's Report of Insurance Companies) Regulations, 2002.
13. Insurance Regulatory and Development Authority (Licensing, Professional Requirements and Code of Conduct) Regulations, 2000.
14. Insurance Regulatory and Development Authority (Conditions of Service of Officers and Other Employees) Regulations, 2000.
15. Insurance Regulatory and Development Authority (Life Insurance — Reinsurance) Regulations, 2000.
16. Insurance Regulatory and Development Authority (Investment) (Amendment) Regulations, 2001.
17. Insurance Regulatory and Development Authority (Third Party Administrators – Health Services) Regulations, 2001.
18. Insurance Regulatory and Development Authority (Re-insurance Advisory Committee) Regulations, 2001.
19. Insurance Regulatory and Development Authority (Protection of Policy Holders' Interest) Regulations, 2002.
20. Insurance Regulatory and Development Authority (Investment) (Amendment) Regulations, 2002.
21. Insurance Regulatory and Development Authority (Assets, Liabilities and Solvency Margin of Insurers) (Amendment) Regulations, 2002.
22. Insurance Regulatory and Development Authority (Licensing of Corporate Agents) Regulations, 2002.
23. Insurance Regulatory and Development Authority (Licensing of Insurance Agents) (Amendment) Regulations, 2002.

24. Insurance Regulatory and Development Authority (Insurance Bookers) Regulations, 2002.
25. Insurance Regulatory and Development Authority (Manner of Payment of Premium) Regulations, 2002.
26. Insurance Regulatory and Development Authority (Obligations of Insurers to Rural or Social Sectors) (Amendment) Regulations, 2002 and 2008.
27. Insurance Regulatory and Development Authority (Protection of Policyholders Interest) (Amendment) Regulations, 2002.
28. Insurance Regulatory and Development Authority (Qualification of Actuary) Regulations, 2004.

8.5 SCHEDULES TO THE IRDA ACT

AMENDMENTS TO THE INSURANCE ACT, 1938 (*4 of 1938*)

1. In the Act, except in clause (5B) of section 2 and section 2B, for "Controller" wherever it occurs, substitute "Authority" and such consequential changes as the rules of grammar may require shall also be made.

2. In sections 27, 27A, 27B, 31, 32A, 40A, 48B, 64F, 64G, 64-I, 64J, 64L, 64R, 64UC, 64UM, 113 and 115, for "Central Government" wherever they occur, substitute "Authority".

3. Section 2, :

(*a*) after clause (1), insert the following :

'(IA) "Authority" means the Insurance Regulatory and Development Authority established under sub-section (1) of section 3 of the Insurance Regulatory and Development Authority Act, 1999;';

(*b*) for clause (5B), substitute the following :

'(5B) "Controller of Insurance" means the officer appointed by the Central Government under section 2B to exercise all the powers, discharge the functions and perform the duties of the Authority under this Act or the Life Insurance Corporation Act, 1956 (31 of 1956) or the General Insurance Business (Nationalisation) Act, 1972 (57 of 1972) or the Insurance Regulatory and Development Authority Act, 1999;

(*c*) After clause (7), insert the following :

'(7A) "Indian insurance company" means any insurer being a company :

(*a*) which is formed and registered under the Companies Act, 1956 (1 of 1956);

(*b*) in which the aggregate holdings of equity shares by a foreign company, either by itself or through its subsidiary companies or its nominees, do not exceed twenty-six per cent paid-up equity capital of such Indian insurance company;

(*c*) whose sole purpose is to carry on life insurance business or general insurance business or re-insurance business.

Explanation : For the purposes of this clause, the expression "foreign company" shall have the meaning assigned to it under clause (23A) of section 2 of the Income-tax Act, 1961 (43 of 1961).';

(*d*) in clause (14), for "section 114", substitute "this Act".

4. After section 2, insert the following :

"2A. Interpretation of certain words and expressions : Words and expressions used and not defined in the Life Insurance Corporation Act, 1956 (31 of 1965), the General Insurance Business (Nationalisation) Act, 1972 (57 of 1972) and the Insurance Regulatory and Development Authority Act, 1999 shall have the meanings respectively assigned to them in those Acts."

5. Section 2B, for sub-section (1), substitute the following :

"(1) If at any time, the Authority is superseded under sub-section (1) of section 19 of the Insurance Regulatory and Development Authority Act, 1999, the Central Government may, by notification in the Official Gazette, appoint a person to be the Controller of Insurance till such time the Authority is reconstituted under sub-section (3) of section 19 of that Act."

6. Section 2C, in sub-section (1), after the second proviso, insert the following :

'Provided also that no insurer other than an Indian insurance company shall begin to carry on any class of insurance business in India under this Act on or after the commencement of the Insurance Regulatory and Development Authority Act, 1999.".

7. Section 3,

(*a*) In sub-section (1), after the first proviso, insert the following :

"Provided further that a person or insurer, as the case may be, carrying on any class of insurance business in India, on or before the commencement of the Insurance Regulatory and Development Authority Act, 1999, for which no registration certificate was necessary prior to such commencement, may continue to do so for a period of three months from such commencement or, if he had made an application for such registration within the said period of three months, till the disposal of such application :

Provided also that any certificate of registration, obtained immediately before the commencement of the Insurance Regulatory and Development Authority Act, 1999, shall be deemed to have been obtained from the Authority in accordance with the provisions of this Act,";

(*b*) in sub-section (2), :

(*i*) in the opening portion, for "Every application for registration shall be accompanied by-", substitute the following :

"Every application for registration shall be made in such manner as may be determined by the regulations made by the Authority and shall be accompanied by-";

(*ii*) in clause (d), for "working capital", substitute "paid-up equity capital or working capital";

(*iii*) in clause (f), in the proviso, omit "and" occurring and the end;

(*iv*) for clause (g), substitute the following :

"(*g*) the receipt showing payment of fee as may be determined by the regulations which shall not exceed fifty thousand rupees for each class of business as may be specified by the regulations made by the Authority;

(*h*) such other documents as may be specified by the regulations made by the Authority."

(c) after sub-section (2A), insert :

"(2AA) The Authority shall give preference to register the applicant and grant him a certificate of registration if such applicant agrees, in the form and manner as may be specified by the regulations made by the Authority, to carry on the life insurance business or general insurance business for providing health cover to individuals or group of individuals."

(*d*) in sub-section (4), :

(*i*) in clause (f), for "of any rule or order made thereunder, or", substitute the following :

"of any rule or any regulation or order made or, any direction issued thereunder, or";

(*ii*) in clause (h), insert "or" at the end;

(*iii*) after clause (h), insert the following :

"(*i*) if the insurer makes a default in complying with any direction issued or order made, as the case may be, by the Authority under the Insurance Regulatory and Development Authority Act, 1999, or

"(*j*) if the insurer makes a default in complying with, or acts in contravention of, any requirement of the Companies Act, 1956 (1 of 1956) or the Life Insurance Corporation Act, 1956 (31 of 1956) or the General Insurance Business (Nationalisation) Act, 1972 (57 of 1972) or the Foreign Exchange Regulation Act, 1973 (46 of 1973)."

(*e*) in sub-section (5C), :

(*i*) for "clause (h)", substitute "clause(h) or clause (i) or clause (j)";

(*ii*) for "any requirement of this Act or of any rule or order made thereunder", substitute the following :

"any requirement of this Act or the Insurance Regulatory and Development Authority Act, 1999 or of any rule or any regulation, or any order made thereunder or any direction issued under those Acts";

(*f*) after sub-section (5D), insert the following :

"(5E) The Authority may, by order, suspend or cancel any registration in such manner as may be determined by the regulations made by it :

Provided that no order under this sub-section shall be made unless the person concerned has been given a reasonable opportunity of being heard."

(*g*) for sub-section (7), substitute the following :

"(7) The Authority may, on payment of such fee, not exceeding five thousand rupees, as may be determined by the regulations, issue a duplicate certificate of registration to replace a certificate lost, destroyed or mutilated, or in any other case where the Authority is of opinion that the issue of duplicate certificate is necessary."

8. Section 3A, :

(*a*) in sub-section(1), for "the 31st day of December, 1941.", substitute the following :

"the 31st day of March, after the commencement of the Insurance Regulatory and Development Authority Act, 1999."

(*b*) in sub-section(2), :

(*i*) for "prescribed fee", substitute "fee as determined by the regulations made by the Authority";

(*ii*) for clause (i), substitute the following :

"(i) exceed one-fourth of one per cent of such premium income or rupees five crores, whichever is less,";

(*iii*) for clause (ii), substitute the following :

"(ii) be less, in any case, than fifty thousand rupees for each class of insurance business:";

(*c*) in sub-section (3), for "prescribed fee", substitute "fee as determined by the regulations made by the Authority";

(*d*) in sub-section (4), for "prescribed fee", substitute "fee as determined by the regulations made by the Authority, and"

9. For section 6, substitute the following :

"6. Requirement as to capital : No insurer carrying on the business of life insurance, general insurance or re-insurance in India on or after the commencement of the Insurance Regulatory and Development Authority Act, 1999, shall be registered unless he has, :

(*i*) a paid-up equity capital of rupees one hundred crores, in case of a person carrying on the business of life insurance or general insurance; or

(*ii*) a paid-up equity capital of rupees two hundred crores, in case of a person carrying on exclusively the business as a re-insurer :

Provided that in determining the paid-up equity capital specified under clause (I) or clause (ii), the deposit to be made under section 7 and any preliminary expenses incurred in the formation and registration of the company shall be excluded :

Provided further that an insurer carrying on business of life insurance, general insurance or re-insurance in India before the commencement of the Insurance Regulatory and Development Authority Act, 1999 and who is required to be registered under this Act, shall have a paid-up equity capital in accordance with clause (I) and clause (ii), as the case may be, within six months of the commencement of that Act."

10. Section 6A, :

(*a*) in sub-section (4), in clause (b), :

(*i*) in sub-clause (i), omit "and" occurring at the end;

(*ii*) in sub-clause (ii), for "sanction of the Central Government has been obtained to the transfer.", substitute "approval of the Authority has been obtained to the transfer;"

(*iii*) after sub-clause (ii), insert the following :

'(*iii*) where, the nominal value of the shares intended to be transferred by any individual, firm, group, constituents of a group, or body corporate under the same management, jointly or severally exceeds one per cent of the paid-up equity capital of the insurer, unless the previous approval of the Authority has been obtained for the transfer.

Explanation : For the purposes of this sub-clause, the expressions "group" and "same management" shall have the same meanings respectively assigned to them in the Monopolies and Restrictive Trade Practices Act, 1969 (54 of 1969).'

(*b*) in sub-section (11),

(*i*) for "Explanation 1.", substitute "Explanation";

(*ii*) omit Explanation 2.

11. After section 6A, insert the following :

"6AA. Manner of divesting excess shareholding by promoter in certain cases. : (1) No promoter shall at any time hold more than twenty-six per cent or such other percentage as may be prescribed, of the paid-up equity capital in an Indian insurance company.

Provided that in a case where an Indian insurance company begins the business of life insurance, general insurance or re-insurance in which the promoters hold more than twenty-six per cent of the paid-up equity capital or such other excess percentage as may be prescribed, the promoters shall divest in a phased manner the share capital in excess of the twenty-six per cent of the paid-up equity capital or such excess paid-up equity capital as may be prescribed, after a period of ten years from the date of the commencement of the said business by such Indian insurance company or within such period as may be prescribed by the Central Government.

Explanation : For the removal of doubts, it is hereby declared that nothing contained in the proviso shall apply to the promoters being foreign company, referred to in sub-clause (b) of clause (7A) of section 2.

(2) The manner and procedure for divesting the excess share capital under sub-section (1) shall be specified by the regulations made by the Authority."

12. Section 7, :

(*a*) in sub-section (1),-

(*i*) omit "not being an insurer specified in sub-clause (c) of clause (9) of section 2";

(*ii*) for clauses (a) and (b), substitute the following :

"(*a*) in the case of life insurance business, a sum equivalent to one per cent of his total gross premium written in India in any financial year commencing after the 31st day of March, 2000, not exceeding rupees ten crores;

(*b*) in the case of general insurance business, a sum equivalent to three per cent of his total gross premium written in India, in any financial year commencing after the 31st day of March, 2000, not exceeding rupees ten crores;

(c) in the case of re-insurance business, a sum of rupees twenty crores;";

(*d*) omit sub-sections (1A), (1B), (1C), (1D) and (1E).

13. Section 11, :

(*a*) in sub-section (1), for "calendar year", substitute "financial year";

(*b*) after sub-section (1), insert the following :

"(1A) Notwithstanding anything contained in sub-section (1), every insurer, on or after the commencement of the Insurance Regulatory and Development Authority Act, 1999, in respect of insurance business transacted by him and in respect of his shareholders' funds, shall at the expiration of each financial year, prepare with reference to that year, a balance-sheet, a profit and loss account, a separate account of receipts and payments, a revenue account in accordance with the regulations made by the Authority.

(1B) Every insurer shall keep separate accounts relating to funds of shareholders and policy-holders."

14. Section 13, :

(*a*) in sub-section (1), :

(*i*) for "once at least in every three years", substitute "every year";

(*ii*) in the first proviso, for "not later than four years" substitute "not later than two years";

(*iii*) after the second proviso, insert the following :

"Provided also that for an insurer carrying on life insurance business in India immediately before the commencement of the Insurance Regulatory and Development Authority Act, 1999, the last date as at which the first investigation after such commencement should be caused by an actuary, shall be the 31st day of March, 2001";

(*iv*) after the third proviso, insert the following :

"Provided also that every insurer on or after the commencement of the Insurance Regulatory and Development Authority Act, 1999, shall cause an abstract of the report of actuary to be made in the manner specified by the regulations made by the Authority.";

(*b*) in sub-section (4), after the proviso, insert the following :

"Provided further that the statement referred to in sub-section (4) shall be appended in the form and in the manner specified by the regulations made by the Authority."

15. After section 27B, insert the following :

"27C. *Prohibition of investment of funds outside India* : No insurer shall directly or indirectly invest outside India the funds of the policy-holders.

27D. *Manner and conditions of investment* : (1) Without prejudice to anything contained in sections 27, 27A and 27B, the Authority may, in the interests of the policy-holders, specify by the regulations made by it, the time, manner and other conditions of investment of assets to be held by an insurer for the purposes of this Act.

(2) The Authority may give specific directions for the time, manner and other conditions subject to which the funds of policy holders shall be invested in the infrastructure and social sector as may be specified by regulations made by the Authority and such regulations shall apply uniformly to all the insurers carrying on the business of life insurance, general insurance, or re-insurance in India on or after the commencement of the Insurance Regulatory and Development Authority Act, 1999.

(3) The Authority may, after taking into account the nature of business and to protect the interests of the policy-holders, issue to an insurer the directions relating to the time, manner and other conditions of investment of assets to be held by him:

Provided that no direction under this sub-section shall be issued unless the insurer concerned has been given a reasonable opportunity of being heard."

16. Section 28A, in sub-section (1), for "31st day of December", substitute "31st day of March".

17. Section 28B, in sub-section (1), for "31st day of December", substitute "31st day of March".

18. Section 31B, :

(*a*) in sub-section (1), for "Central Government" at both the places where they occur, substitute "Authority";

(*b*) in sub-section (2), for "a statement in the prescribed from", substitute "a statement, in the form specified by the regulations made by the Authority,";

(*c*) after sub-section (3), insert the following :

"(4) Every direction under this section shall be issued by an order made by the Authority:

Provided that no order under this section shall be made unless the person concerned has been given an opportunity of being heard."

19. After section 32A, insert the following :

"32B. Insurance business in rural or social sector : Every insurer shall, after the commencement of the Insurance Regulatory and Development Authority Act, 1999, undertake such percentages of life insurance business and general insurance business in the rural or social sector, as may be specified, in the Official Gazette by the Authority, in this behalf.

32C. Obligations of insurer in respect of rural or unorganised sector and backward classes. : Every insurer shall, after the commencement of the Insurance Regulatory and Development Authority Act, 1999 discharge the obligations specified under section 32B to provided life insurance or general insurance policies to the persons residing in the rural sector, workers in the unorganised or informal sector or for economically vulnerable or backward classes of the society and other categories of persons as may specified by regulations made by the Authority and such insurance policies shall include insurance for crops."

20. For section 33, substitute the following :

Investigation : 33. Power of investigation and inspection by Authority : (1) The Authority may, at any time, by order in writing, direct any person (hereafter in this section referred to as "Investigating Authority") specified in the order to investigate the affairs of any insurer and to report to the Authority on any investigation made by such Investigating Authority :

Provided that the Investigating Authority may, wherever necessary, employ any auditor or actuary or both for the purpose of assisting him in any investigation under this section.

(2) Notwithstanding anything to the contrary contained in section 235 of the time, and shall, on being directed so to do by the Authority, cause an inspection to be made by one or more of his officers of any insurer and his books and account; and the Investigating Authority shall supply to the insurer a copy of this report on such inspection.

(3) It shall be the duty of every manager, managing director or other officer of the insurer to produce before the Investigating Authority directed to make the investigation under sub-section (1), or inspection under sub-section (2), all such books of account, registers and other documents in his custody or power and to furnish him with any statement and information relating to the affairs of the insurer as the said Investigating Authority may require of him within such time as the said Investigating Authority may specify.

(4) Any Investigating Authority, directed to make an investigation under sub-section (1), or inspection under sub-section (2), may examine on oath, any manager, managing director or other officer of the insurer in relation to his business and may administer oaths accordingly.

(5) The Investigating Authority shall, if he has been directed by the Authority to cause an inspection to be made, and may, in any other case, report to the Authority on any inspection made under this section.

(6) On receipt of any report under sub-section (1) or sub-section (5), the Authority may, after giving such opportunity to the insurer to make a representation in connection with the report as, in the opinion of the Authority, seems reasonable, by order in writing :

(*a*) require the insurer, to take such action in respect of any matter arising out of the report as the Authority may think fit; or

(*b*) cancel the registration of the insurer; or

(*c*) direct any person to apply to the court for the winding up of the insurer,

if a company, whether the registration of the insurer has been cancelled under clause (b) or not.

(7) The Authority may, after giving reasonable notice to the insurer, publish the report submitted by the Investigating Authority under sub-section (5) or such portion thereof as may appear to it to be necessary.

(8) The Authority may by the regulations made by it specify the minimum information to be maintained by insurers in their books, the manner in which such information shall be maintained, the checks and other verifications to be adopted by insurers in that connection

and all other matters incidental thereto as are, in its opinion, necessary to enable the Investigating Authority to discharge satisfactorily his functions under this section.

Explanation : For the purposes of this section, the expression "insurer" shall include in the case of an insurer incorporated in India :

(*a*) all its subsidiaries formed for the purpose of carrying on the business of insurance exclusively outside India; and

(*b*) all its branches whether situated in India or outside India.

(9) No order made under this section other than an order made under clause (b) of sub-section (6) shall be capable of being called in question in any court.

(10) All expenses of, and incidental to, any investigation made under this section shall be defrayed by the insurer, shall have priority over that debts due from the insurer and shall be recoverable as an arrear of land revenue.'

21. Section 33A, omit "Central Government or the" :

22. Section 34H, :

(*a*) in sub-section (1), :

(*i*) for "Controller", substitute "Chairperson of the Authority";

(*ii*) for "an Assistant Controller of Insurance", substitute "an officer authorised by the Authority";

(*b*) in sub-sections (5) and (7) for "Controller" wherever it occurs, substitute "Chairperson of the Authority".

23. Section 35 :

(*a*) in sub-section (1), for "sanctioned by the Controller", substitute "approved by the Authority";

(*b*) in sub-section (3), :

(*i*) in the first paragraph, for "to sanction any such scheme substitute "to approve any such scheme";

(*ii*) in the second paragraph for "the amalgamation or transfer if sanctioned", substitute "the amalgamation or transfer if approved".

24. Section 36,

(*a*) in sub-section (1) for "may sanction the arrangement", substitute "may approve the arrangement";

(*b*) in sub-section (2), :

(*i*) for "the insurers concerned in the amalgamation, the Controller may sanction", substitute "the insurers concerned in the amalgamation, the Authority may approve";

(*ii*) for "contracts as sanctioned by the Controller", substitute "contracts as approved by the Authority".

25. Section 37, in clause (c) for "scheme sanctioned", substitute "scheme approved".

26. In section 40A, in sub-section (3), for the portion beginning with the words "an amount exceeding" and ending with the words "ten per cent of the premium payable on the policy", substitute "an amount not exceeding fifteen per cent of the premium payable on the policy where the policy relates to fire or marine insurance or miscellaneous insurance."

27. Section 42, :

(*a*) for sub-section (1), substitute the following :

"(1) The Authority or an officer authorised by it in this behalf shall, in the manner determined by the regulations made by it and on payment of the fee determined by the regulations, which shall not be more than two hundred and fifty rupees, issue to any person making an application in the manner determined by the regulations, a licence to act as an insurance agent for the purpose of soliciting or procuring insurance business :

Provided that, :

(*i*) in the case of an individual, he does not suffer from any of the disqualifications mentioned in sub-section (4); and

(*ii*) in the case of a company or firm, any of its directors or partners does not suffer from any of the said disqualifications :

Provided further that any licence issued immediately before the commencement of the Insurance Regulatory and Development Authority Act, 1999 shall be deemed to have been issued in accordance with the regulations which provide for such licence."

(*b*) for sub-section (3) substitute the following :

"(3) A licence issued under this section, after the date of the commencement of the Insurance Regulatory and Development Authority

Act, 1999, shall remain in force for a period of three years only from the date of issue, but shall, if the applicant, being an individual does not, or being a company or firm any of its directors or partners does not, suffer from any of the disqualifications mentioned in clauses (b), (c), (d), (e) and (f) of sub-section (4) and the application for renewal of licence reaches the issuing authority at least thirty days before the date in which the licence ceases to remain in force, be renewed for a period of three years at any one time on payment of the fee determined by the regulations made by the Authority which shall not be more than rupees two hundred and fifty, and additional fee of an amount determined by the regulations not exceeding rupees one hundred by way of penalty, if the application for renewal of the licence does not reach the issued authority at least thirty days before the date on which the licence ceases to remain in force.";

(*c*) in sub-section (3A), for the proviso, substitute the following :

"Provided that the Authority may, if satisfied that undue hardship would be caused otherwise, accept any application in contravention of this sub-section of payment by the applicant of a penalty of seven hundred and fifty rupees.";

(*d*) in sub-section (4), after clause (*d*) insert the following :

"(*e*) that he does not possess the requisite qualifications and practical training for a period not exceeding twelve months, as may be specified by the regulations made by the Authority in this behalf;

(*f*) that he has not passed such examination as may be specified by the regulations made by the Authority in this behalf:

Provided that a person who had been issued a licence under sub-section (1) of this section or sub-section (1) of section 64UM shall not be required to possess the requisite qualifications, practical training and pass such examination as required by clauses (*e*) and (*f*);

(*g*) that he violates the code of conduct as may be specified by the regulations made by the Authority.";

(*e*) for sub-section (6), substitute the following :

"(6) The Authority may issue a duplicate licence to replace a licence lost, destroyed or mutilated, on payment of such fee not exceeding rupees fifty as may be determined by the regulations.";

(*f*) in sub-section (7),-

(*i*) for "fifty rupees", substitute "five hundred rupees";

(*ii*) for "one hundred rupees", substitute "one thousand rupees";

(*g*) in sub-section (8), for "fifty rupees", substitute "five thousand rupees".

28. Section 42A, in sub-section (1), :

(*a*) for "Controller or an officer authorised by him" substitute" Authority or an officer authorised by it";

(*b*) for "an application to him", substitute "an application to it".

29. After section 42C, insert the following :

"42D. Issue of licence to intermediary or insurance intermediary.

(1) The Authority or an officer authorised by it in this behalf shall, in the manner determined by the regulations made by the Authority and on payment of the fees determined by the regulations made by the Authority, issue to any person making an application in the manner determined by the regulations, and not suffering from any of the disqualifications herein mentioned, a licence to act as an intermediary or an insurance intermediary under this Act :

Provided that, :

(*a*) in the case of an individual, he does not suffer from any of the disqualifications mentioned in sub-section (4) of section 42, or

(*b*) in the case of a company or firm, any of its directors or partners does not suffer from any of the said disqualifications.

(2) A licence issued under this section shall entitle the holder thereof to act as an intermediary or insurance intermediary.

(3) A licence issued under this section shall remain in force for a period of three years only from the date of issue, but shall, if the applicant, being an individual does not, or being a company or firm any of its directors or partners does not suffer from any of the disqualifications mentioned in clauses (b), (c), (d), (e) and (f) of sub-section (4) of section 42, and the application for renewal of licence reaches the issuing authority at least thirty days before the date on which the licence ceases to remain in force, be renewed for a period of three years at any one time on payment of the fee, determined by the regulations made by the Authority and additional fee for an amount determined by the regulations, not exceeding one hundred rupees by way of penalty, if the application for renewal of the licence does not reach the issuing authority at least thirty days before the date on which the licence ceases to remain in force.

(4) no application for the renewal of a licence under this section shall be entertained if the application does not reach the issuing authority before the licence ceases to remain in force:

Provided that the Authority may, if satisfied that undue hardship would be caused otherwise, accept any application in contravention of this sub-section on payment by the applicant of a penalty of seven hundred and fifty rupees.

(5) The disqualifications above referred to shall be the following :

(*a*) that the person is a minor;

(*b*) that he is found to be of unsound mind by a court of competent jurisdiction;

(*c*) that he has been found guilty of criminal misappropriation or criminal breach of trust or cheating or forgery or an abetment of or attempt to commit any such office by a court of competent jurisdiction:

Provided that, where at least five years have elapsed since the completion of the sentence imposed on any person in respect of any such offence, the Authority shall ordinarily declare in respect of such person that his conviction shall cease to operate as a disqualification under this clause;

(*d*) that in the course of any judicial proceedings relating to any policy of insurance of the winding up of an insurance company or in the course of an investigation of the affairs of an insurer it has been found that he has been guilty of or has knowingly participated in or connived at any fraud dishonestly or misrepresentation against an insurer or an insured;

(*e*) that he does not possess the requisite qualifications and practical training for a period not exceeding twelve months, as may be specified by the regulations made by the Authority in this behalf;

(*f*) that he has not passed such examinations as may be specified by the regulations made by the Authority in this behalf;

(*g*) that he violates the code of conduct as may be specified by the regulations made by the Authority.

(6) If it be found that an intermediary or an insurance intermediary suffers from any of the foregoing disqualifications, without prejudice to any other penalty to which he may be liable, the Authority shall, and if the intermediary or an insurance intermediary has knowingly contravened any provision of this Act may cancel the licence issued to the intermediary or insurance intermediary under this section.

(7) The Authority may issue a duplicate licence to replace a licence lost, destroyed or mutilated, on payment of such fee, as may be determined by the regulations made by the Authority.

(8) Any person who acts as an intermediary or an insurance intermediary without holding a licence issued under this section to act as such, shall be punishable with fine, and any insurer or any person who appoints as an intermediary or an insurance intermediary or any person not licensed to act as such or transacts any insurance business in India through any such person, shall be punishable with fine.

(9) Where the person contravening sub-section (8) is a company or a firm, then, without prejudice to any other proceedings which may be taken against the company or firm, every director, manager, secretary or other officer of the company, and every partner of the firm who is knowingly a party to such contravention shall be punishable with fine.".

30. Section 64UA, in sub-section (1), in sub-clause(a), for "Controller or Insurance", substitute "Chairperson of the Authority".

31. Section 64UB,:

(*a*) for sub-section (1), substitute the following :

"(1) The Authority may, by notification in the Official Gazette, make regulations to carry out the purposes of this Part.";

(*b*) in sub-section (2), for "rules", substitute "regulations";

(c) in sub-section (3) for "Central Government" at both the places where it occur, substitute "Authority";

(*d*) in sub-section (5), for "Controller of Insurance", substitute "Chairperson of the Authority".

32. Section 64UC in sub-section (1), in proviso, for "the controller may, with the previous approval of the Central Government", substitute "the Authority may."

33. Section 64UD, after sub-section (1), insert the following :

"Provided that the Chairperson of the Authority shall become the Chairman of the Advisory Committee with effect from the commencement of the Insurance Regulatory and Development Authority Act, 1999 and function as such, and any Chairman of the Tariff Committee holding office immediately before such commencement shall cease to be the Chairman.".

34. Section 64UJ, in sub-section (5), for "Central Government", wherever it occurs, substitute "Authority".

35. Section 64UM, :

(*a*) in sub-section (1), :

(*i*) in paragraph (B), after "the Insurance (Amendment) Act, 1968", insert "but before the commencement of the Insurance Regulatory and Development Authority Act, 1999";

(*ii*) after paragraph (B), insert the following :

"(BA) Every person who intends to act as a surveyor or loss assessor after the expiry of a period of one year from the commencement of the Insurance Regulatory and Development Authority Act, 1999, shall make an application to the Authority within such time, in such manner and on payment of such fee as may be determined by the regulations made by the Authority:

Provided that any licence issued immediately before the commencement of the Insurance Regulatory and Development Authority Act, 1999 shall be deemed to have been issued in accordance with the regulations providing for such licence.";

(*iii*) in paragraph (C), for "as may be prescribed", substitute "as may be determined by the regulations";

(*iv*) in paragraph (D), in clause (*i*) :

(A) for item (*a*), substitute the following :

"(*a*) has been in practice as a surveyor or loss assessor on the date of commencement of the Insurance Regulatory and Development Authority Act, 1999, or";

(B) in item (*f*), for "prescribed ", substitute, "specified by the regulations made by the Authority";

(*b*) after sub-section (1), insert :

"(1A) Every surveyor and loss assessor shall comply with the code of conduct in respect of their duties, responsibilities and other professional requirements as may be specified by the regulations made by the Authority.".

36. Section 64V, :

(*a*) in sub-section (1), :

(*i*) in clause (i), after sub-clause (g), insert the following :

"(h) such other asset or assets as may be specified by the regulations made in this behalf;";

(*ii*) in clause (ii) :

(A) in sub-clause (b), in items (i) and (ii), for "40 per cent", substitute "50 per cent.";

(B) after sub-clause (f), insert the following :

"(g) such other liability which may be made in this behalf to be included for the purpose of clause (ii).";

(*b*) for sub-section (2), substitute the following :

"(2) Every insurer shall furnish to the Authority with his returns under section 15 or section 16, as the case may be, a statement certified by an auditor approved by the Authority in respect of general insurance business, or an actuary approved by the Authority in respect of life insurance business, as the case may be, of his assets and liabilities assessed in the manner required by this section as on the 31st day of March of the preceding year.

(3) Every insurer shall value his assets and liabilities in the manner required by this section and in accordance with the regulations which may be made by the Authority in this behalf.".

37. Section 64VA, :

(*a*) in sub-section (1), for "at all times", substitute "at all times before the commencement of the Insurance Regulatory and Development Authority Act, 1999";

(*b*) after sub-section (1), insert the following :

'(1A) Every insurer shall, at all times, on or after the commencement of the Insurance Regulatory and Development Authority Act, 1999, maintain an excess of the value of his assets over the amount of his liabilities of not less than the amount arrived at as follows (hereinafter referred to in this section referred to as the "required solvency margin"), namely :

(*i*) in the case of an insurer carrying on life insurance business, the required solvency margin shall be the higher of the following amounts :

(*a*) fifty crores of rupees (one hundred crores of rupees in case of re-insurers); or

(*b*) the aggregate sums of the results arrived at in items (I) and (II) stated below :

(I) the aggregate of the results arrived at by applying the calculation described in item (A) below (Step - I) and the calculation described in item (B) below (Step II) :

(A) for Step I :

(A.1) there shall be taken, a sum equal to a percentage determined by the regulations not exceeding five per cent of the mathematical reserves for direct business and re-insurance acceptances without any deduction for re-insurance cessions.

(A.2) the amount of mathematical reserves at the end of the preceding financial year after the deduction of re-insurance cessions shall be expressed as a percentage of the amount of those mathematical reserves before any such deduction; and

(A.3) the sum mentioned in item (A.1) above shall be multiplied :

(A.3.1) where the percentage arrived at under item (A.2) above is greater than eighty-five per cent (or in the case of a re-insurer carrying on exclusive re-insurance business, fifty per cent), by that greater percentage; and

(A.3.2) in any other case, by eighty-five per cent (or in the case of re-insurer carrying on exclusive re-insurance business, by fifty per cent);

(B) for Step II :

(B.1) there shall be taken, a sum equal to a percentage determined by the regulations made by the Authority not exceeding one per cent of the sum at risk for the policies on which the sum at risk is not a negative figure, and

(B.2) the amount of sum at risk at the end of the preceding financial year for policies on which the sum at risk is not a negative figure after the deduction of re-insurance cession shall be expressed as a percentage of the amount of that sum at risk before any such deduction, and

(B.3) the sum arrived at under item (B.1) above shall be multiplied:

(B.3.1) where the percentage arrived at under item (B.3.2) above is greater than fifty per cent, by that greater percentage; and

(B.3.2) in any other case, by fifty per cent,

(II) a percentage determined by the regulations made by the Authority of the value of assets determined in accordance with the provisions of section 64V;

(ii) in the case of an insurer carrying on general insurance business, the required solvency margin, shall be the highest of the following amounts:

(*a*) fifty crores of rupees (one hundred crores of rupees in case of re-insurer); or

(*b*) a sum equivalent to twenty per cent of net premium income; or

(*c*) a sum equivalent to thirty per cent of net incurred claims,

subject to credit for re-insurance in computing net premiums and net incurred claims being actual but a percentage, determined by the regulations not exceeding fifty per cent:

Provided that if in respect of any insurer, the Authority is satisfied that either by reason of an unfavourable claim experience or because of sharp increase in the volume of the business, or for any other reason, compliance with the provisions of this sub-section would cause undue hardship to the insurer, the Authority may direct, for such period and subject to such conditions, such solvency margin not being less than the lower of the amount mentioned in sub-clause (i) or sub-clause (ii) above, as the case may be.

Explanation : For the purposes of this sub-section, the expressions :

(i) "mathematical reserves" means the provision made by an insurer to cover liabilities (excluding liabilities which have fallen due and liabilities arising from the deposit back arrangement in relation to any policy whereby an amount is deposited by re-insurer with the cedant) arising under or in connection with policies or contracts for life insurance business. Mathematical reserves also include specific provision for adverse deviations of the bases, such as mortality and morbidity rates, interest rates, and expense rates, and any explicit provisions made, in the valuation of liabilities, in accordance with the regulations made by the Authority for this purpose;

(ii) "net incurred claims". means the average of the net incurred claims during the specified period of not exceeding three preceding financial years;

(iii) "sum at risk" in relation to a life insurance policy, means a sum which is :

(*a*) in any case in which an amount is payable inconsequence of death other than a case falling within sub-clause (b) below, the amount payable on death, and

(*b*) in any case in which the benefit under the policy in question consist of the making, in consequence of death, of the payments of annuity, payment of sum by instalments or any other kind of periodic payments, the present value of that benefit, less in either case the mathematical reserves in respect of the relevant policies."

(c) after sub-section (2), insert the following :

"(2A) If, at any time an insurer does not maintain the required solvency margin in accordance with the provisions of this section, he shall, in accordance with the provisions of this section, he shall, in accordance with the directions issued by the Authority, submit a financial plan, indicating a plan of action to correct the deficiency to the Authority within a specified period not exceeding three months.

(2B) An insurer who has submitted a plan under sub-section (2A) to the Authority shall propose modifications to the plan if the Authority considers it inadequate, and shall give effect to any plan accepted by the Authority as adequate.

(2C) An insurer who does not comply with the provisions of sub-section (2A) shall be deemed to be insolvent and may be wound up by the Court.";

(d) after sub-section (6); insert the following :

"(7) Every insurer shall furnish to the Authority his returns under section 15 or section 16, as the case may be, in case of life insurance business a statement certified by an actuary approved by the authority, and in case of general insurance business a statement certified by an auditor approved by the Authority, of the required solvency margin maintained by the insurer in the manner required by sub-section (1A).".

38. Section 70 in sub-section (1), for "the Controller a certificate of registration", substitute "the Authority, before the date of commencement of the Insurance Regulatory and Development Authority Act, 1999, a certificate of registration."

39. Section 95, in sub-section (1), for "In this Part -", substitute "In this part, before the date of commencement of the Insurance Regulatory and Development Act, 1999, -".

40. Section 101A, :

(a) in sub-section (1), for "the Central Government" substitute "the Authority, with the previous approval of the Central Government,";

(b) in sub-section (2), for "the Central Government" substitute "the Authority."

41. Section 101B, :

(a) in sub-section (1), for "the Central Government", substitute "the Authority with the previous approval of the Central Government.";

(b) in sub-section (2), for "prescribed", substitute determined by the regulations made by the Authority".

42. For sections 102 to 105, substitute the following :

"102. *Penalty for default in complying with, or Act in contravention of, this Act:* If any person who is required under this Act, or rules or regulations made thereunder,:

(a) to furnish any document, statement, account, return or report to the Authority, fails to furnish the same; or

(b) to comply with the directions, fails to comply with such directions;

(c) to maintain solvency margin, fails to maintain such solvency margin;

(d) to comply with the directions on the insurance treaties, fails to comply with such directions on the insurance treaties,

he shall be liable to a penalty not exceeding five lakh rupees for each such failure and punishable with fine.

103. *Penalty for carrying on insurance business in contravention of section 3,7. and 98:* If a person makes a statement, or furnishes any document, statement, account, return or report which is false and which he either knows or believes to be false or does not believe to be true,

(a) he shall be liable to a penalty not exceeding five lakh rupees for each such failure; and

(b) he shall be punishable with imprisonment which may extend to three years or with fine for each such failure.

104. *Penalty for false statement in document :* If a person fails to comply with the provisions of section 27 or section 27A or section 27B or section 27C or section 27D, he shall be liable to a penalty not exceeding five lakh rupees for each such failure.

105. *Wrongfully obtaining or withholding property :* If any director, managing director, manager or other officer or employees of an insurer wrongfully obtains possession of any property or wrongfully applies to any purpose of the Act, he shall be liable to a penalty not exceeding two lakh rupees for each such failure.

105A. *Offences by companies :* (1) Where any offence under this Act has been committed by a company, every person who, at the time the offence was committed, was in charge of, and was responsible to, the company for the conduct of the business of the company as well as the company shall be deemed to be guilty of the offence and shall be liable to be proceeded against and punished accordingly;

Provided that nothing contained in this sub-section shall render any such person liable to any punishment, if he proves that the offence was committed without his knowledge or that he had exercised all due diligence to prevent the commission of such offence.

(2) Notwithstanding anything contained in sub-section (1), where any offence under this Act has been committed by a company and it is proved that the offence has been committed with the consent or connivance of, or is attributable to any neglect on the part of, any director, manager, secretary or other officer of the company, such director, manager, secretary or other officer shall be deemed to be guilty of that offence and shall be liable to be proceeded against and punished accordingly.

Explanation : For the purposes of this section, :

(*a*) "company" means any body corporate, and includes :

(*i*) a firm; and

(*ii*) an association of persons or a body of individuals whether incorporated or not; and

(*b*) "director", in relation to :

(*i*) a firm, means a partner in the firm;

(*ii*) an association of persons or a body of individuals, means any member controlling the affairs thereof.

105B. Penalty for failure to comply with section 32B. : If an insurer fails to comply with the provisions of section 32B, he shall be liable to a penalty not exceeding five lakh rupees for each such failure and shall be punishable with imprisonment which may extend to three years or with fine for each such failure.

105C. Penalty for failure to comply with section 32C. : If an insurer fails to comply with the provisions of section 32C, he shall be liable to a penalty not exceeding twenty-five lakh rupees for each such failure and in the case of subsequent and continuing failure, the registration granted to such insurer under section 3 shall be cancelled by the Authority.".

43. In sections 110A, 110B and 110C, for "Controller" wherever it occurs, substitute "Chairperson of the Authority".

44. Section 110G, for "Controller" at both the places where it occurs, substitute "Chairperson of the Authority".

45. Section 110H, in sub-section (1), for "under sections", substitute "under section 27D,".

46. Section 114, in sub-section (2), :

(*a*) after clause (a), insert the following :

"(*aa*) such other percentage of paid-up equity capital in excess twenty-six per cent of the paid-up equity capital and the period within which such excess paid-up equity capital shall be divested under sub-section (1) of section 6AA.";

(*b*) omit clauses (g) and (ll),

47. After section 114, insert the following :

"114A. *Power of Authority to make regulations* : (1) The Authority may, by notification in the Official Gazette, make regulations consistent with this Act and the rules made thereunder, to carryout the purposes of this Act.

(2) In particular, and without prejudice to the generality of the foregoing power, such regulation may provide for all or any of the following matters, namely :

(*a*) the matters including fee relating to the registration of insurers under section 3;

(*b*) the manner of suspension or cancellation of registration under sub-section (5E) of section 3;

(*c*) such fee, not exceeding five thousand rupees, as may be determined by the regulations for issue of a duplicate certificate of registration under sub-section (7) of section 3;

(*d*) the matters relating to the renewal of registration and fee therefore under section 3A;

(*e*) the manner and procedure for divesting excess share capital under sub-section (2) of section 6AA;

(*f*) the preparation of balance-sheet, profit and loss account and a separate account of receipts and payments and revenue account under section (1A) of section 11;

(*g*) the manner in which an abstract of the report of the actuary to be specified under the fourth proviso to sub-section (1) of section 13;

(*h*) the form and manner in which the statement referred to in sub-section(4) of section 13 shall be appended;

(*i*) the time, manner and other conditions of investment of assets held by an insurer under sub-sections (1), (1A) and (2) of section 27D;

(*j*) the minimum information to be maintained by insurer in their books, the manner in which such information should be maintained, the checks and other verifications to be adopted by insurers in that connection and all other matters incidental thereto under sub-section (8) of section 33;

(k) the manner for making an application, the manner and the fee for issue of a licence to act as an insurance agent under sub-section (1) of section 42;

(l) the fee and the additional fee to be determined for renewal of licence of insurance agent under sub-section (3) of section 42;

(m) the requisite qualifications and practical training to act as an insurance agent under clause (e) of sub-section (4) of section 42;

(n) the passing of examination to act as an insurance agent under clause (f) of sub-section (4) of section 42;

(o) the code of conduct under clause (g) of sub-section (4) of section 42;

(p) the fee not exceeding rupees fifty for issue of duplicate licence under sub-section (6) of section 42;

(q) the manner and the fees for issue of a licence to an intermediary or an insurance intermediary under sub-section (1) of section 42D;

(r) the fee and the additional fee to be determined for renewal of licence of intermediaries or insurance intermediaries under sub-section (3) of section 42D;

(s) the requisite qualifications and practical training of intermediaries or insurance intermediaries under clause (e) of sub-section (5) of section 42D;

(t) the examination to be passed to acts as an intermediary or insurance intermediary under clause (f) of sub-section (5) of section 42D;

(u) the code of conduct under clause (g) of sub-section (5) of section 42D;

(v) the fee for issue of duplicate licence under sub-section (7) of section 42D;

(w) such matters as specified under sub-section (2) of section 64UB relating to the Tariff Advisory Committee;

(x) the matters relating to licensing of surveyors and loss assessors, their duties, responsibilities and other professional requirements under section 64UM;

(y) such other asset or assets as may be specified under clause (h) of sub-section (1) of section 64V for the purposes of ascertaining sufficiency of assets under section 64VA;

(z) the valuation of assets and liabilities under sub-section (3) of section 64V;

(za) the matters specified under sub-section (1A) of section 64VA relating to sufficiency of assets;

(zb) the matters relating to re-insurance under sections 101A and 101B;

(zc) the matters relating to redressal of grievances of policy-holders to protect their interest and to regulate, promote and ensure orderly growth of insurance industry; and

(zd) any other matter which is to be, or may be, specified by the regulation made by the Authority or in respect of which provision is to be made or may be made by the regulations.

(3) Every regulation made under this Act shall be laid, as soon as may be after it is made, before each House of Parliament, while it is in session, for a total period of thirty days which may be comprised in one session or in two or more successive sessions, and if, before the expiry of the session immediately following the session or the successive sessions aforesaid, both Houses agree in making any modification in the regulation or both Houses agree that the regulation should not be made, the regulation shall thereafter have effect only in such modified form or be of no effect, as the case may be; so, however, that any such modification or annulment shall be without prejudice to the validity of anything previously done under that regulation.".

48. Section 116 A, for "Central Government", at both places where they occur, substitute "Central Government, before the date of commencement of the Insurance Regulatory and Development Authority Act, 1999,".

THE SECOND SCHEDULE
(See Section 31)

AMENDMENTS TO THE LIFE INSURANCE CORPORATION ACT, 1956 (31 of 1956)

1. In the Act, for "Controller" wherever it occurs, substitute "Authority".
2. After section 30, insert the following :

"30A. *Exclusive privilege of Corporation to cease* : Notwithstanding anything contained in this Act, the exclusive privilege of carrying on life insurance business in India by the Corporation shall cease on and from commencement of the Insurance Regulatory and Development Authority Act, 1999 and the Corporation shall, thereafter, carry on life insurance business in India in accordance with the provisions of the Insurance Act, 1938 (4 of 1938).".

THE THIRD SCHEDULE
(See Section 32)

AMENDMENT TO THE GENERAL INSURANCE BUSINESS (NATIONALISATION) ACT, 1972 (57 of 1972)

After section 24, insert the following :

"24A. *Exclusive privilege of Corporation and acquiring companies to cease.* : Notwithstanding anything contained in this Act, the exclusive privilege of the Corporation and the acquiring companies of carrying on general insurance business in India shall cease on an from the commencement of the Insurance Regulatory and Development Authority Act, 1999 and the Corporation and the acquiring companies shall, thereafter, carry on general insurance business in India in accordance with the provisions of the Insurance Act, 1938 (4 of 1938)."

Key Terms

- Licensing
- Rebate
- Registration
- Refund
- Investment
- Tariff Advisory Committee
- Assignment
- Commission
- Tribunal
- Committees
- Quorum
- Adjudicator
- Tariff Advisory Committee
- Authorised Capital
- General Insurance Corporation of India
- Reinsurance
- Winding up
- Insurance Association of India
- Deposits
- Paid-up Capital
- Remuneration
- Controller
- Nomination
- Appointed Day
- Composite Insurer
- Controlled Business
- Insurance Regulatory and Development Authority
- Insurance Advisory Committee
- Acquiring Companies
- Memorandum and Articles of Association

Questions for Review

1. Briefly explain the licensing procedure for insurers under the Insurance Act, 1938.
2. Write short notes on :
   (*a*) Accounts and Return
   (*b*) Advance Premium
   (*c*) Appointment of Agents / in light of the Insurance Act, 1938.
3. Enumerate the manner of investments by insurer as prescribed by the Insurance Act, 1938.
4. Discuss the various modes of winding up of insurance companies.
5. Briefly describe the functions of Life Insurance Corporation as enumerated in Life Insurance Corporation Act, 1956.

6. Write short notes on :
   (*a*) Controlled Business
   (*b*) LIC Regulations, 1959
7. Briefly describe the functions of GIC as per the provisions of General Insurance Business (Nationalisation) Act, 1972.
8. Write short notes on :
   (*a*) Powers of Central Government
   (*b*) Formation of GIC
9. Briefly explain the constitution of IRDA.
10. Explain the duties, powers and functions of the IRDA under the IRDA Act, 1999.
11. Summarise the various ammendments made to different laws by the promulgation of the IRDA Act, 1999.

Suggested Readings

- *Bare Act – Insurance Act, 1938*
    - *Bare Act* – Life Insurance Corporation Act, 1956
    - *Bare Act* – Life Insurance Corporation Regulations, 1959.
- *Avtar Singh,* Law of Insurance, Eastern Book Company, 2004.
- *Law and Economics of Insurance,* IC87, Insurance Institute of India, Mumbai, 2003.
- *Bare Act* : General Insurance Business (Nationalisation) Act, 1972.
- *P.K. Gupta,* Insurance & Risk Management, Himalaya Publishing House, Mumbai, 2004.
- Avtar Singh, Law of Insurance, Eastern Book Company, 2005.
- *Bare Act* – IRDA Act, 1999.
- M.N. Srinivasan, Principles of Insurance Law, Wadwa & Company, Nagpur, 2006.

Web Resources

- *www.irdaindia*
- *www.licindia.com*
- *www.irdaonline.com*
- *www.bimaonline.com*
- *www.licindia.com*

Special Purpose Insurance Laws

Chapter 9

Chapter Objectives

After reading this chapter you will be able to understand :

- *Motor Insurance Laws and Regulation*
- *Marine Insurance Law and Policy Provision.*
- *Workmen Compennsation Act, Public Liabilies Insurance and Employees State Insurance Clause*

9.1 Motor Vehicles Act 1938 & 1988

Motor Vehicles Act, 1939 was the principle act that regulated the practice of motor insurance in India. The act was amended many times thereafter. The most important act is that of 1988 that replaced the 1939 act. Insurance under the Act is insurance of person and property. If from the use of vehicle, a person sustains injuries or the other parties (third party) suffers injuries or damages, the driver of the vehicle is liable and for his personal loss/ damages, he can claim from the insurance company. The following paragraphs discuss the important provisions of the Act and simultaneously refer to the erstwhile provisions of the act of 1939, (given in brackets).

9.1.1 Definitions - Sec. 2

Definitions. – In this Act, unless the context otherwise requires,

(1) "area", in relation to any provision of this Act, means such area as the State Government may, having regard to the requirements of that provision, specify by notification in the Official Gazette;

(2) "articulated vehicle" means a motor vehicle to which a semi-trailer is attached; [2(2)]

(3) "axle weight" means in relation to an axle of a vehicle the total weight transmitted by the several wheels attached to that axle to the surface on which the vehicle rests; [2(1-B)]

(4) "certificate of registration" means the certificate issued by a competent authority to the effect that a motor vehicle has been duly registered in accordance with the provisions of Chapter IV; [2(2)].

(5) "conductor", in relation to a stage carriage, means a person engaged in collecting fares from passengers, regulating their entrance into, or exit from, the stage carriage and performing such other functions as may be prescribed; [2(2-B)].

(6) "conductor's licence" means the licence issued by a competent authority under Chapter III authorising the person specified therein to act as a conductor; [2(2-C)].

(7) "contract carriage" means a motor vehicle which carries a passenger or passengers for hire or reward and is engaged under a contract, whether expressed or implied, for the use of such vehicle as a whole for the carriage of passengers mentioned therein and entered into by a person with a holder of a permit in relation to such vehicle or any person authorised by him in this behalf on a fixed or an agreed rate or sum –

(*a*) on a time basis, whether or not with reference to any route or distance; or

(*b*) from one point to another, and in either case, without stopping to pick up or set down passengers not included in the contract anywhere during the journey, and includes –

(*i*) a maxicab; and

(*ii*) a motorcab notwithstanding that separate fares are charged for its passengers; [2(3)].

(9) "driver" includes, in relation to a motor vehicle which is drawn by another motor vehicle, the person who acts as a steersman of the drawn vehicle; [2(5)].

(10) "driving licence" means the licence issued by a competent authority under Chapter II authorising the person specified therein to drive, otherwise than as a learner, a motor vehicle or a motor vehicle of any specified class or description; [2(5-A)].

(13) "goods" includes livestock, and anything (other than equipment ordinarily used with the vehicle) carried by a vehicle except living persons, but does not include luggage or personal effects carried in a motor car or in a trailer attached to a motor car or the personal luggage of passengers travelling in the vehicle; [2(7)].

(14) "goods carriage" means any motor vehicle constructed or adapted for use solely for the carriage of goods, or any motor vehicle not so constructed or adapted when used for the carriage of goods; [2(8)].

(15) "gross vehicle weight" means in respect of any vehicle the total weight of the vehicle and load certified and registered by the registering authority as permissible for that vehicle; [Newly Inserted].

(16) "heavy goods vehicle" means any goods carriage the gross vehicle weight of which, or a tractor or a road-roller the unladen weight of either of which, exceeds 12,000 kilograms; [2(9)].

(17) "heavy passenger motor vehicle" means any public service vehicle or private service vehicle or educational institution bus or omnibus the gross vehicle weight of any of which, or a motor car the unladen weight of which, exceeds 12,000 kilograms. [2(9-A)].

(18) "invalid carriage" means a motor vehicle specially designed and constructed, and not merely adapted, for the use of a person suffering from some physical defect or disability, and used solely by or for such a person; [2(10)].

(20) "licensing authority" means an authority empowered to issue licence under Chapter II or, as the case may be, chapter III; [2(12)].

(21) "light motor vehicle" means a transport vehicle or omnibus the gross vehicle weight of either of which or a motor car or tractor or road-roller the unladen weight of any of which, does not exceed 7500 kilograms; [2(13)].

(21-A) "manufacturer" means a person who is engaged in the manufacture of motor vehicles ; [Newly Inserted].

(22) "maxicab" means any motor vehicle constructed or adapted to carry more than six passengers, but not more than twelve passengers, excluding the driver, for hire or reward; [Newly Inserted].

(23) "medium goods vehicle" means any goods carriage other than a light motor vehicle or a heavy goods vehicle; [2(14)].

(24) "medium passenger motor vehicle" means any public service vehicle or private service vehicle, or educational institution bus other than a motor cycle, invalid carriage, light motor vehicle or heavy passenger motor vehicle; [2(14-A)].

3. "motorcab" means any motor vehicle constructed or adapted to carry not more than six passengers excluding the driver for hire or reward; [2(15)].

(25) "motor car" means any motor vehicle other than a transport vehicle, omnibus, road-roller, tractor, motor cycle or invalid carriage; [2(16)].

(26) "motor cycle" means a two-wheeled motor vehicle, inclusive of any detachable side-car having an extra wheel, attached to the motor vehicle; [2(17)].

(28) "motor vehicle" or "vehicle" means any mechanically propelled vehicle adapted for use upon roads whether the power of propulsion is transmitted thereto from an external or internal source and includes a chassis to which a body has not been attached and a trailer ; but does not include a vehicle running upon fixed rails or a vehicle of a special type adapted for use only in a factory or in any other enclosed premises or a vehicle having less than four wheels fitted with engine capacity of not exceeding 25 C.C. [2(18)]

(29) "omnibus" means any motor vehicle constructed or adapted to carry more than six persons excluding the driver ; [2(18-A)]

(30) "owner" means a person in whose name a motor vehicle stands registered and where such person is a minor, the guardian of such minor, and in relation to a motor vehicle which is the subject of a hire-purchase, agreement, or an agreement of lease or an agreement of hypothecation, the person in possession of the vehicle under that agreement ; [2(19)]

(31) "permit" means a permit issued by a State or Regional Transport Authority or an authority prescribed in this behalf under this Act authorising the use of motor vehicle as a transport vehicle; [2(20)]

(32) "prescribed" means prescribed by rules made under this Act; [2(21)]

(33) "private service vehicle" means a motor vehicle constructed or adapted to carry more than six persons excluding the driver and ordinarily used by or on behalf of the owner of such vehicle for the purpose of carrying persons for, or in connection with, his trade or business otherwise than for hire or reward but does not include a motor vehicle used for public purposes ; [2(22)]

Corresponding Law. - Section 2 (33) corresponds to section 2 (22) of the Motor Vehicles Act, 1939.

(34) "public place" means a road, street, way or other place, whether a thoroughfare or not, to which the public have a right of access, and includes any place or stand at which passengers are picked up or set down by a stage carriage ; [2(24)]

(35) "public service vehicle" means any motor vehicle used or adapted to be used for the carriage of passengers for hire or reward, and includes a maxicab, a motorcab, contract carriage, and stage carriage ; [2(25)]

(36) "registered axle weight" means in respect of the axle of any vehicle, the axle weight certified and registered by the registering authority as permissible for that axle ; [2(26)]

(37) "registering authority" means an authority empowered to register motor vehicles under Chapter IV; [2(28)]

(38) "route" means a line of travel which specifies the highway which may be traversed by a motor vehicle between one terminus and another ; [2(28-A)]

(39) "semi-trailer" means a vehicle not mechanically propelled (other than a trailer), which is intended to be connected to motor vehicle and which is so constructed that a portion of it is super-imposed on, and a part of whose weight is borne by, that motor vehicle ; [Newly Inserted]

(40) "stage carriage" means a motor vehicle constructed or adapted to carry more than six passengers excluding the driver for hire or reward at separate fares paid by or for individual passengers, either for the whole journey or for stages of the journey ; [2(29)]

(41) "State Government" in relation to a Union territory, means the Administrator thereof appointed under article 239 of the Constitution ; [Newly Inserted]

(42) "State transport undertaking" means any undertaking providing road transport service, where such undertaking is carried on by –

(*i*) the Central Government or a State Government ;

(*ii*) any Road Transport Corporation established under section 3 of the Road Transport Corporations Act, 1950 ;

(*iii*) any municipality or any corporation or company owned or controlled by the Central Government or one or more State Governments, or by the Central Government and one or more State Government ;

(*iv*) Zilla Parishad or any other similar local authority. [2(42)]

Explanation : For the purposes of this clause, "road transport service" means a service of motor vehicles carrying passengers or goods or both by road for hire or reward;

(43) "tourist vehicle" means a contract carriage constructed or adapted and equipped and maintained in accordance with such specifications as may be prescribed in this behalf; [2(29-A)]

(44) "tractor" means a motor vehicle which is not itself constructed to carry any load (other than equipment used for the purpose of propulsion); but excludes a road-roller ; [2(30)]

(45) "traffic signs" includes all signals, warning sign posts, direction posts, markings on the road or other devices for the information, guidance or direction of drivers of motor vehicles ; [2(31)]

(46) "trailer" means any vehicle, other than a semi-trailer and a sidecar, drawn or intended to be drawn by a motor vehicle ; [2(32)]

(47) "transport vehicle" means a public service vehicle, a goods carriage, an educational institution bus or a private service vehicle ; [2(33)]

(48) "unladen weight" means the weight of a vehicle or trailer including all equipment ordinarily used with the vehicle or trailer when working, but excluding the weight of a driver or attendant; and where alternative parts or bodies are used the unladen weight of the vehicle means the weight of the vehicle with the heaviest such alternative part or body ; [2(34)]

(49) "weight" means the total weight transmitted for the time being by the wheels of a vehicle to the surface on which the vehicle rests. [Newly Inserted]

9.1.2 Necessity for Third Party Insurance

Compulsory Insurance for Third Party Risks

Section 146 provides that : (1) No person shall use, except as a passenger, or cause or allow any other person to use, a motor vehicle in a public place, unless there is in force in relation to the use of the vehicle by that person or that other person, as the case may be, a policy of insurance complying with the requirements of this Chapter:

Provided that in the case of a vehicle carrying, or meant to carry, dangerous or hazardous goods, there shall also be a policy of insurance under the Public Liability Insurance Act, 1991 (6 of 1991).

Explanation : A person driving a motor vehicle merely as a paid employee, while there is in force in relation to the use of the vehicle no such policy as is required by this sub-section, shall not be deemed to act in contravention of the sub-section unless he knows or has reason to believe that there is no such policy in force.

(2) Sub-section (1) shall not apply to any vehicle owned by the Central Government or a State Government and used for Government purposes unconnected with any commercial enterprise.

(3) The appropriate Government may, by order, exempt from the operation of sub-section (1) any vehicle owned by any of the following authorities, namely :

(*a*) the Central Government or a State Government, if the vehicle is used for Government purposes connected with any commercial enterprise;

(*b*) any local authority;

(*c*) any State transport undertaking :

Provided that no such order shall be made in relation to any such authority unless a fund has been established and is maintained by that authority in accordance with the rules made in that behalf under this Act for meeting any liability arising out of the use of any vehicle of that authority which that authority or any person in its employment may incur to third parties.

Explanation : For the purposes of this sub-section, "appropriate Government" means the Central Government or a State Government, as the case may be, and–

(*i*) in relation to any corporation or company owned by the Central Government or any State Government, means the Central Government or that State Government;

(*ii*) in relation to any corporation or company owned by the Central Government & one or more State Governments, means the Central Government;

(*iii*) in relation to any other State transport undertaking or any local authority, means that Government which has control over that undertaking or authority. [94]

9.1.3 Insurance Policies

Policy of Insurance and Limits of Liability

Section 147 lays down the requirements of the policies and the limit of liability in respect of passengers and persons other than passengers in relation to passenger vehicles and goods carriages.

Section 147 : Requirement of policies and limits of liability : (1) In order to comply with the requirements of this Chapter, a policy of insurance must be a policy which:

(*a*) is issued by a person who is an authorised insurer; and

(*b*) insurers the person or classes of persons specified in the policy to the extent specified in sub-section (2):

(*i*) against any liability which may be incurred by him in respect of the death of or bodily 90[injury to any person, including owner of the goods or his authorised representative carried in the vehicle] or damage to any property of a third party caused by or arising out of the use of the vehicle in a public place;

(*ii*) against the death of or bodily injury to any passenger of a public service vehicle caused by or arising out of the use of the vehicle in a public place;

Provided that a policy shall not be required –

(*i*) to cover liability in respect of the death, arising out of and in the course of this employment, of the employee of a person insured by the policy or in respect of bodily injury sustained by such an employee arising out of and in the course of his employment other than a liability arising under the Workmen's Compensation Act, 1923 (8 of 1923), in respect of the death of, or bodily injury to, any such employee :

(*a*) engaged in driving the vehicle, or

(*b*) if it is a public service vehicle, engaged as a conductor of the vehicle or in examining tickets on the vehicle, or

(*c*) if it is a goods carriage, being carried in the vehicle, or

(*ii*) to cover any contractual liability.

Explanation : For the removal of doubts, it is hereby declared that the death of or bodily injury to any person or damage to any property of a third party shall be deemed to have been caused by or to have arisen out of, the use of a vehicle in a public place notwithstanding that the person who is dead or injured or the property which is damaged was not in a public place at the time of the accident, if the act or omission which led to the accident occurred in a public place.

(2) Subject to the proviso to sub-section (1), a policy of insurance referred to in sub-section (1), shall cover any liability incurred in respect of any accident, up to the following limits, namely :

(*a*) save as provided in clause (b), the amount of liability incurred.

(*b*) in respect of damage to any property of a third party, a limit of rupees six thousand :

Provided that any policy of insurance issued with any limited liability and in force, immediately before the commencement of this Act, shall continue to be effective for a period of four months after such commencement or till the date of expiry of such policy whichever is earlier.

(3) A policy shall be of no effect for the purposes of this Chapter unless and until there is issued by the insurer in favour of the person by whom the policy is effected a certificate of insurance in the prescribed form and containing the prescribed particulars of any condition subject to which the policy is issued and of any other prescribed matters; and different forms, particulars and matters may be prescribed in different cases.

(4) where a cover note issued by the insurer under the provisions of this Chapter or the rules made thereunder is not followed by a policy of insurance within the prescribed time, the insurer shall, within seven days of the expiry of the period of the validity of the cover note, notify the fact to the registering authority in whose records the vehicle to which the cover note relates has been registered or to such other authority as the State Government may prescribe.

(5) Notwithstanding anything contained in any law for the time being in force, an insurer issuing a policy of insurance under this section shall be liable to indemnify the person or classes of persons specified in the policy in respect of any liability which the policy purports to cover in the case of that person or those classes of persons.

Validity of Policies in Reciprocating Countries

Section 148 provides for the validity of policies of insurance issued in a reciprocating country in respect of motor vehicle of the reciprocating country operating on any route common to the two countries.

Section 148 : Validity of polices of insurance issued in reciprocating countries. – Where, in pursuance of an arrangement between India and any reciprocating country, the motor vehicle registered in the reciprocating country operates on any route or within any area common to the two countries and there is in force in relation to the use of the vehicle in the reciprocating country, a policy of insurance complying with the requirements of the law of insurance in force in that country, then, notwithstanding anything contained in section 147 but subject to any rules which may be made under section 164, such policy of insurance shall be effective throughout the route or area in respect of which, the arrangement has been made, as if the policy of insurance had complied with the requirements of this Chapter. [95-A]

Transfer of Certificate of Insurance

Section 156 provides that where the insurer has issued a certificate of insurance, and the policy of insurance has not been issued, then the policy to be issued be deemed to be in terms conforming in all respects to the particulars mentioned in the certificate of insurance.

Section 156 : Effect of certificate of insurance : When an insurer has issued a certificate of insurance in respect of a contract of insurance between the insurer and the insured person, then :

(*a*) if and so long as the policy described in the certificate has not been issued by the insurer to the insured, the insurer shall, as between himself and any other person except the insured, be deemed to have issued to the insured person a policy of insurance conforming in all respects with the description and particulars stated in such certificate; and (*b*) if the insurer has issued to the insured the policy described in the certificate, but the actual terms of the policy are less favourable to persons claiming under or by virtue of the policy against the insurer either directly or through the insured than the particulars of the policy as stated in the certificate, the policy shall, as between the insurer and any other person except the insured, be deemed to be in terms conforming in all respects with the particulars stated in the said certificate. [103]

Section 157 lays down that when the certificate of registration is transferred from one person to another, then the policy of insurance in respect of that vehicle is also deemed to have been transferred to that other person from the date on which the ownership of the motor vehicle stands transferred.

It provides that (1) Where a person in whose favour the certificate of insurance has been issued in accordance with the provisions of this Chapter transfer to another person the ownership of the another vehicle in respect of which such insurance was taken together with the policy of insurance relating thereto, the certificate of insurance and the policy described in the certificate shall be deemed to have been transferred in favour of the person to whom the motor vehicle is transferred with effect from the date of its transfer.

Explanation. – For the removal of doubts, it is hereby declared that such deemed transfer shall include transfer of rights and liabilities of the said certificate of insurance and policy of insurance.

(2) The transferee shall apply within fourteen days from the date of transfer in the prescribed form to the insurer for making necessary changes in regard to the fact of transfer in the certificate of insurance and the policy described in the certificate in his favour and the insurer shall make the necessary changes in the certificate and the policy of insurance in regard to the transfer of insurance. [103-A]

In many decided cases the Supreme Court has held that such deemed transfer is only in respect of third party risks.

Under *Section 103-A of the 1939 Act,* Insurance companies had choice of refusal to transfer the Certificate of Insurance and issuing new policy in the name of the new owner, if the driving history and other features of the risk become undersirable and adverse. *Section 157* shall be automatically deemed to be transferred in favour of the new owner from the date of transfer of ownership of the vehicle.

Section 157 (1), which states that such deemed transfer, shall include transfer of rights and liabilities of the said Certificate of Insurance and Policy of Insurance. That such deemed transfer of Certificate of Insurance can only be in respect of third party risks.

9.1.4 Claims Tribunal

Award of the Claim Tribunal

Section 168 states the duty and obligation of the Claims Tribunal to give prior notice of the third party's application for compensation to the Insurer as also giving opportunity to the insurer of being heard.

Procedures and Powers of the Claims Tribunal

Section 169 provides that where any Claims Tribunal has been constituted Civil Courts have no jurisdiction to entertain any question relating to claims for compensation.

Section 171 empowers the Claim Tribunal to order that simple interest at such rates as it thinks fit shall also be paid along with the award of compensation.

Appeal Against the Orders of the Tribunal

Within 90 days of an award by the Tribunal, any person who is aggrieved or not satisfied mya appeal to the High Court in the appropriate jurisdiction. However, the insurers cannot challenge the decision of Tribunal on grounds of Negligence. [Rohatgi S.C., National Insurance Co *vs.* MicoMeta 2002]

9.1.5 Miscellaneous Provisions

Duty of Insurers

Section 149 lays down that it is the duty of the insurers to satisfy judgements against persons insured in respect of third party risk.

Section 149 : Duty of insurers to satisfy judgments and awards against persons insured in respect of third party risks :

(1) if, after a certificate of insurance has been issued under sub-section (3) of section 147 in favour of the person by whom a policy has been effected, judgement or award in respect of any such liability as is requirement to be covered by a policy under clause (b) of sub-section (1) of section 147 (being a liability covered by the terms of the policy) or under the provisions of section 163 – A is obtained against any person insured by the policy, then, notwithstanding that the insurer may be entitled to avoid of cancel or may have avoided or cancelled the policy, the insurer shall, subject to the provisions of this section, pay to the person entitled to the benefit of the decree any sum not exceeding the sum assured payable thereunder, as if he were the judgement debtor, in respect of the liability, together with any amount payable in respect of costs and any sum payable in respect of interest on that sum by virtue of any enactment relating to interest on judgements.

(2) No sum shall be payable by an insurer under sub-section (1) in respect of any judgement or award unless, before the commencement of the proceedings in which the judgement or award is given the insurer had notice through the Court or, as the case may be, the Claims Tribunal of the bringing of the proceedings, or in respect of such judgement or award so long as execution is stayed thereon pending an appeal; and an insurer to whom notice of the bringing of any such proceedings is so given shall be entitled to be made a party thereto and to defend the action on any of the following grounds, namely :

(*a*) that there has been a breach of a specified condition of the policy, being one of the following conditions, namely :

(*i*) a condition excluding the use of the vehicle :

(*a*) for hire or reward, where the vehicle is on the date of the contract of insurance a vehicle not covered by a permit to ply for hire or reward, or

(*b*) for organised racing and speed testing, or

(*c*) for a purpose not allowed by the permit under which the vehicle is used, where the vehicle is a transport vehicle, or

(*d*) without side-car being attached where the vehicle is a motor cycle; or

(*ii*) a condition excluding driving by a named person or persons or by any person who is not duly licenced, or by any person who has been disqualified for holding or obtaining a driving licence during the period of disqualification; or

(*iii*) a condition excluding liability for injury caused or contributed to by conditions of war, civil war, riot or civil commotion; or

(*b*) that the policy is void on the ground that it was obtained by the non-disclosure of a material fact or by a representation of fact which was false in some material particular.

(3) Where any such judgement as is referred to in sub-section (1) is obtained from a Court in a reciprocating country and in the case of a foreign judgement is, by virtue of the provisions of section 13 of the Code of Civil Procedure, 1908 (5 of 1908) conclusive as to any matter adjudicated upon by it, the insurer (being an insurer registered under the Insurance Act, 1938 (4 of 1938) and whether or not he is registered under the corresponding law of the reciprocating country) shall be liable to the person entitled to the benefit of the decree in the manner and to the extent specified in sub-section (1), as if the judgement were given by a Court in India :

Provided that no sum shall be payable by the insurer in respect of any such judgement unless, before the commencement of the proceedings in which the judgement is given, the insurer had notice through the Court concerned of the bringing of the proceedings and the insurer to whom notice is so given is entitled under the corresponding law of the reciprocating country, to be made a party to the proceedings and to defend the action on grounds similar to those specified in sub-section (2).

(4) Where a certificate of insurance has been issued under sub-section (3) of section 147 to the person by whom a policy has been effected, so much of the policy as purports to restrict the insurance of the persons insured thereby by reference to any conditions other than those in clause (b) of subsection (2) shall, as respects such liabilities as are required to be covered by a policy under clause (b) of sub-section (1) of section 147, be of no effect :

Provided that any sum paid by the insurer in or towards the discharge of any liability of any person which is covered by the policy by virtue only of this sub-section shall be recoverable by the insurer from that person.

(5) If the amount which an insurer becomes liable under this section to pay in respect of a liability incurred by a person insured by a policy exceeds the amount for which the insurer would apart from the provisions of this section be liable under the policy in respect of that liability, the insurer shall be entitled to recover the excess from that person.

(6) In this section the expression "material fact" and "material particular" means, respectively, a fact or particular of such a nature as to influence the judgement of a prudent insurer in determining whether he will take the risk and, if so, at what premium and on what conditions, and the expression "liability covered by the terms of the policy" means liability which is covered by the policy or which would be so covered but for the fact that the insurer is entitled to avoid or cancel or has avoided or cancelled the policy.

(7) No insurer to whom the notice referred to in sub-section (2) or sub-section (3) has been given shall be entitled to avoid his liability to any person entitled to the benefit of any such judgement or award as is referred to in sub-section (1) or in such judgement as is referred to in sub-section (3) otherwise than in the manner provided for in sub-section (2) or in the corresponding law of the reciprocating country, as the case may be. [96]

Explanation : For the purposes of this section, "Claims Tribunal" means a Claims Tribunal constituted under section 165 and "award" means an award made by that Tribunal under section 168.

Impleading Insurer in Certain Cases

Section 170 : Where in the course of any inquiry, the Claims Tribunal is satisfied that :

(*a*) there is collusion between the person making the claim and the person against whom the claim is made, or

(*b*) the persons against whom the claim is made has failed to contest the claim, it may, for reasons to be recorded in writing, direct that the insurer who may be liable in respect of such claim, shall be impleaded as a party to the proceeding and the insurer so impleaded shall thereupon have, without prejudice to the provisions contained in sub-section (2) of section 149, the right to contest the claim on all or any of the grounds that are available to the person against whom the claim has been made. [110-C(2-A)]

Rights of Third Parties

Section 150 provides that in the event of the insured becoming insolvent any liability incurred by the insured person and his rights against the insurer will be transferred to and vest in the third party to whom the liability was so incurred.

Section 150 : Rights of third parties against insurers on insolvency of the insured.– (1) Where under any contract of insurance effected in accordance with the provisions of this Chapter, a person is insured against liabilities which he may incur to third parties, then :

(*a*) in the event of the person becoming insolvent or making a composition or arrangement with his creditors, or

(*b*) where the insured person is a company, in the event of a winding-up order being made or a resolution for a voluntary winding-up being passed with respect to the company or of a receiver or manager of the company's business or undertaking being duly appointed, or of possession being taken by or on behalf of the holders of any debentures secured by a floating charge of any property comprised in or subject to the charge, if, either before or after that event, any such liability is incurred by the insured person, his rights against the insurer under the contract in respect of the liability shall, notwithstanding anything to the contrary in any provision of law, be transferred to and vest in the third party to whom the liability was so incurred.

(2) Where an order for the administration of the estate of a deceased debtor is made according to the law of insolvency, then, if any debt provable in insolvency is owing by the deceased in respect of a liability to a third party against which he was insured under a contract of insurance in accordance with the provisions of this Chapter, the deceased debtor's rights against the insurer in respect of that liability shall, notwithstanding anything to the contrary is any provision of law, be transferred to and vest in the person to whom the debt is owing.

(3) Any condition in a policy issued for the purposes of this Chapter purporting either directly or indirectly to avoid the policy or to alter the rights of the parties thereunder upon the happening to the insured person of any of the events specified in clause (a) or clause (b) of sub-section (1) or upon the making of an order for the administration of the estate of a deceased debtor according to the law of insolvency shall be of no effect.

(4) Upon a transfer under sub-section (1) or sub-section (2), the insurer shall be under the same liability to the third party as he would have been to the insured person, but :

(*a*) if the liability of the insurer to the insured person exceeds the liability of the insured person to the third party, nothing in this Chapter shall affect the rights of the insured person against the insurer in respect of the excess, and

(*b*) if the liability of the insurer to the insured person is less than the liability of the insured person to the third party, nothing in this Chapter shall affect the rights of the third party against the insured person in respect of the balance. [97]

Duty to Give Information as to Insurance

Section 151 prescribes that it is the duty of the insured to give information relating to the insurance on demand by or on behalf of the person making the claim for compensation.

Section 151 : (1) No person against whom a claim is made in respect of any liability referred to in clause (b) of sub-section (1) of section 147 shall on demand by or on behalf of the person making the claim refuse to state whether or not he was insured in respect of that liability by any policy issued under the provisions of this Chapter, or would have been so insured if the insurer had not avoided or cancelled the policy, nor shall he refuse, if he was or would have been so insured, to give such particulars with respect to that policy as were specified in the certificate of insurance issued in respect hereof.

(2) In the event of any person becoming insolvent or making a composition or arrangement with his creditors or in the event of an order being made for the administration of the estate of a deceased person according to the law of insolvency,

or in the event of a winding-up order being made or a resolution for a voluntary winding-up being passed with respect to any company or of a receiver or manager of the company's business or undertaking being duly appointed

or of possession being taken by or on behalf of the holders of any debentures secured by a floating charge on any property comprised in or subject to the charge, it shall be the duty of the insolvent debtor, personal representative of the deceased debtor or company, as the case may be, or the official assignee or receiver in insolvency, trustee, liquidator, receiver or manager, or person in possession of the property to give at the request of any person claiming that the insolvent debtor, deceased debtor or company is under such liability to him as is covered by the provision of this Chapter, such information as may reasonably be required by him for the purpose of ascertaining whether any rights have been transferred to an vested in him by section 150,

and for the purpose of enforcing such rights, if any; and any such contract of insurance as purports whether directly or indirectly to avoid the contract or to alter the rights of the parties thereunder upon the giving of such information in the events aforesaid, or otherwise to prohibit or prevent the giving thereof in the said events, shall be of no effect.

(3) If, from the information given to any person in pursuance of subsection (2) or otherwise, he has reasonable ground for supporting that there have or may have been transferred to him under this Chapter rights against any particular insurer, that insurer shall be subject to the same duty as is imposed by the said sub-section on the persons therein mentioned.

(4) The duty to give the information imposed by this section shall include a duty to allow all contracts of insurance, receipts for premiums, and other relevant documents in the possession or power of the person on whom the duty so imposed to be inspected and copies thereof to be taken.

Settlement Between Insurers and Insured Persons

Section 152 lays down that any settlement made by the insurer in respect of any claim which may be made by the third party will not be valid unless the third party is a party to the claim.

Section 152 : (1) No settlement made by an insurer in respect of any claim which might be made by a third party in respect of any liability of the nature referred to in clause (b) of sub-section (1) of section 147 shall be valid unless such third party is a party to the settlement.

(2) Where a person who is insured under a policy issued for the purpose of this Chapter has become insolvent, or where, if such insured person is a company, a winding-up order has been made or a resolution for a voluntary winding-up has been passed with respect to the company, no agreement made between the insurer and the insured person after the liability has been incurred to a third party and after the commencement of the insolvency or winding-up, as the case may be, nor any waiver, assignment or other disposition made by or payment made to the insured person after the commencement aforesaid shall be effective to defeat the rights transferred to the third party under this Chapter, but those rights shall be the same as if no such agreement, waiver, assignment or disposition or payment has been made.

Production of Documents on Demand

Section 158 : This Section makes it compulsory on the part of the driver of the vehicle involved in accident, to produce the certificate of registration and insurance, the certificate of fitness and permit and driving licence without delay. It also provides that the police officer that makes a report of accident shall send a copy of the report to the Accident Claims Tribunal.

(1) Any person driving a motor vehicle in any public place shall, on being so required by a police officer in uniform authorised in this behalf by the State Government, produce :

(*a*) the certificate of insurance;

(*b*) the certificate of registration;

(*c*) the driving licence; and

(*d*) in the case of a transport vehicle also the certificate of fitness referred to in section 56 and the permit, relating to the use of the vehicle.

(2) If, where owing to the presence of a motor vehicle in a public place an accident occurs involving death or bodily injury to another person, the driver of the vehicle does not at the time produce the certificate, driving licence and permit referred to in sub-section (1) to a police officer, he shall produce the said certificates, licence and permit at the police station at which he makes the report required by section 134.

(3) No person shall be liable to conviction under sub-section (1) or sub-section (2) by reason only of the failure to produce the certificate of insurance if, within seven days from the date on which its production was required under sub-section (1), or as the case may be, from the date of occurrence of the accident, he produces the certificate at such police station as may have been specified by him to the police officer who required its production or, as the case may be, to the police officer at the site of the accident or to the officer-in-charge of the police station at which he reported the accident :

Provided that except to such extent and with such modifications as may be prescribed, the provisions of this sub-section shall not apply to the driver of a transport vehicle.

(4) The owner of a motor vehicle shall give such information as he may be required by or on behalf of a police officer empowered in this behalf by the State Government to give for the purpose of determining whether the vehicle was or was not being driven in contravention of section 146 and on any occasion when the driver was required under this section to produce his certificate of insurance.

(5) In this section, the expression "produce his certificate of insurance" means produce for examination the relevant certificate of insurance or such other evidence as may be prescribed that the vehicle was not being driven in contravention of section 146.

(6) As soon as any information regarding any accident involving death or bodily injury to any person is recorded or report under this section is completed by a police officer, the officer-in-charge of the police station shall forward a copy of the same within thirty days from the date of recording of information or, as the case may be, on completion of such report to the Claims Tribunal having jurisdiction and a copy thereof to the concerned insurer, and where a copy is made available to the owner, he shall also within thirty days of receipt of such report, forward the same to such Claims Tribunal and insurer]. [106]

Production of Certificate of Insurance on Application for Authority to use Vehicle [*Section 159*]

Section 159 empowers the State Government to make rules to require production of certificate of insurance of a motor vehicle at the time of payment of taxes and in the case of transport vehicle to have a valid certificate of insurance before the vehicle is put on public road after obtaining a permit.

It provides that – A State Government may make rules requiring the owner of any motor vehicle when applying whether by payment of a tax or otherwise for authority to use the vehicle in a public place to produce such evidence as may be prescribed by those rules to the effect that either :

(*a*) on the date when the authority to use the vehicle comes into operation there will be in force the necessary policy of insurance in relation to the use of the vehicle by the applicant or by other persons on his order or with his permission, or

(*b*) the vehicle is a vehicle to which section 146 does not apply. [107]

Effect of Death of Insured Person

Section 155 provides that if the insured person dies after incurring third party liability, then the cause of action survives against the insured's estate, or legal heirs or against the insurer. If this provision is not made, then the third party's right of action against the negligent owner of the vehicle would die with the death of the owner.

Liability Without Fault

Section 140 : *Liability to pay compensaiton in certain cases on the principle of no fault*

1. Where death or permanent disablement of any person has resulted from an accident arising out of the use of motor vehicle or motor vehicles, the owner of the vehicle shall, or, as the case may be, the owners of the vehicles shall, jointly and severally, be liable to pay compensation in respect of such death or disablement in accordance with the provisions of this section.
2. The amount of compensation which shall be payable under sub-section (1) in respect of the death of any person shall be a fixed sum of [fifty thousand rupees] and the amount of compensation payable under that sub-section in respect of the permanent disablement of any person shall be a fixed sum of twenty-five thousand rupees.
3. In any claim for compensation under sub-section (1), the claimant shall not be required to plead and establish that the death or permanent diablement in respect of which the claim has been made was due to any wrongful act, neglect or default of the owner or owners of the vehicles concerned or of any other person.
4. A claim for compensation under sub-section (1) shall not be defeated by reason of any wrongful act, neglect or default of the person in respect of whose death or permanent disablement the claim has been made nor shall the quantum of compensation recoverable in respect of such death or permanent disablement be reduced on the basis of the share of such person in the responsibility for such death or permanent disablement.
5. Notwithstanding anyting contained in sub-section (2) regarding death or bodily injury to any person, for which the owner of the vehicle is liable to give compensation for relief, he is also liable to pay compensation under any other law for the time being in force.

Provided that the amount of compensation payable under this section or under section 163.

***Section 141** : Provisions as to other right to claim compensaiton for death or permanent disablement*

1. The right to claim compensation under section 140 in respect of death or permanent disablement of any person shall be in addition to [any other right, except the right to claim under the scheme referred to section 163A (such other right thereafter) in this section referred to as the right on the principle of fault) to claim compensation in respect thereof under any other provision of this Act or of any other law for the time being in force.
2. A claim for compensation under section 140 in respect of death or permanent disablement of any person shall be disposed of as expeditiously as possible and where compensation is claimed in respect of such death of permanent disablement under section 140 and also in pursuance of any right on the principle of fault, the claim for compensation under section 140 shall be disposed of as aforesaid in the first place.
3. Notwithstanding anything contained in sub-section (1), where in respect of the death, or permanent disablement of any person, the person liable to pay compensation under section 140 is also liable to pay compensaiton in accordance with the right on the principle of fault, the person so liable shall pay the first mentioned compensation and :
   (*a*) if the amount of the first-mentioned compensation is less than the amount of the second-mentioned compensation, he shall be liable to pay (in addition to the first-mentioned compensation) only so much which it exceeds the first-mentioned compensaiton,
   (*b*) if the amount of the first-mentioned compensation is equal to or more than the amount of the second-mentioned compensaiton, he shall not be liable to pay the second-mentioned compensation.

***Section 142** : Permanent disablement*

For the purpose of this Chapter, permanent disablement of a person shall be deemed to have resulted from an accident of the nature referred to in sub-section (1) of section 140 if such person has suffered by reason of the accident, any injury or injuries involving :

(a) permanent privation of the either eye or the hearing of either ear, or privation of any member of joint; or

(b) destruction or permanent impairing of the powers of any member or joint; or

(c) permanent disfiguration of the head or face.

Section 143 : *Applicability of Chapter to certain claims under Act 8 of 1923*

The provisions of this Chapter shall also apply in relation to any claim for compensation in respect of death or permanent disablement of any person under the Workmen's Compensation Act, 1923 resulting from an accident of the nature referred to in sub-section (1) of section 140 and for this purpose, the said provisions shall, will necessary modifications, be deemed to form part of that Act.

Section 144 : *Overriding effect*

The provisions of this Chapter shall have effect notwithstanding anything contained in any other provisions of this Act or of any other law for the time being in force.

The following therefore follows :

(a) In a claim for compensation, the claimant is not required to prove any wrongful act, neglect, or default/negligence on the part of the owner of the vehicle concerned or by any other person.

(b) The claim shall not be defeated in any way by any wrongful act, neglect or default on the part of the claimant; nor can the quantum of compensation be reduced on the basis of the claimant's share of responsibility for the accident. This implies that the legal defense of 'contributory negligence' is not available to the motorist and insurer of the vehicle.

(c) The compensation is available if and only if where the claimant suffers death or permanent disablement, as defined in the Act.

(d) The amount of compensation is Death, Rs. 50,000; Permanent Disablement, Rs. 25,000.

The theme of this section is to provide minimum statutory relief on grounds of social justice.

Hit and Run Accident

Section 161 : (1) The payment of compensation in respect of the death of, or grievous hurt to, any person under section 161 shall be subject to the condition that if any compensation (hereafter in this sub-section referred to as the other compensation) or other amount in lieu of or by way of satisfaction of a claim for compensation is awarded or paid in respect of such death or grievous hurt under any other provision of this Act or any other law or otherwise so much of the other compensation or other amount aforesaid as is equal to the compensation paid under section 161 shall be refunded to the insurer.

(2) Before awarding compensation in respect of an accident involving the death of, or bodily injury to, any person arising out of the use of a motor vehicle or motor vehicles under any provision of this Act (other than section 161) or any other law, the Tribunal Court or other authority awarding such compensation shall verify as to whether in respect of such death or bodily injury compensation has already been paid under section 161 or an application for payment of compensation is pending under that section, and such Tribunal, Court or other authority shall, :

(a) if compensation has already been paid under section 161, direct the person liable to pay the compensation awarded by it to refund to the insurer, so much thereof as is required to be refunded in accordance with the provisions of sub-section (1);

(b) if an application for payment of compensation is pending under section 161 forward the particulars as to the compensation awarded by it to the insurer.

Explanation : For the purpose of this sub-section, an application for compensation under section 161 shall be deemed to be pending :

(*i*) if such application has been rejected, till the date of the rejection of the application, and

(*ii*) in any other case, till the date of payment of compensation in pursuance of the application. [109-B]

Section 162 seeks to provide that when compensation is awarded in a case where compensation under clause 161 has already been paid then so much of the compensation paid as per clause 161 shall be refunded to the insurer.

Scheme for payment of compensation in case of hit and run motor accidents.

Section 163 : (1) The Central Government may, by notification in the Official Gazette, make a scheme specifying, the manner in which the scheme shall be administered by the General Insurance Corporation, the form, manner and the time within which applications for compensation may be made, the officers or authorities to whom such applications may be made, the procedure to be followed by such officers or authorities for considering and passing orders on such applications, and all other matters connected with, or incidental to, the administration of the scheme and the payment of compensation.

(2) A scheme made under sub-section (1) may provide that :

(*a*) a contravention of any provision thereof shall be punishable with imprisonment for such term as may be specified but in no case exceeding three months, or with fine which may extend to such amount as may be specified but in no case exceeding five hundred rupees or with both;

(*b*) the powers, functions or duties conferred or imposed on any officer or authority by such scheme may be delegated with the prior approval in writing of the Central Government, by such officer or authority to any other officer or authority;

(*c*) any provision of such scheme may operate with retrospective effect from a date not earlier than the date of establishment of the Solatium Fund under the Motor Vehicles Act, 1939 (4 of 1939) as it stood immediately before the commencement of this Act.

Provided that no such retrospective effect shall be given so as to prejudicially affect the interests of any person who may be governed by such provision. [109-C]

Section 163 empowers the Central Government to makes scheme for payment of compensation in "hit and run" accident cases detailing the procedure for making claim, the authorities to whom the claim should be made, etc.

Section 163 : A. Special provisions as to payment of compensation on structured formulae basis. – (1) Notwithstanding anything contained in this Act or in any other law for the time being in force or instrument having the force of law, the owner of the motor vehicle of the authorised insurer shall be liable to pay in the case of death or permanent disablement due to accident arising out of the use of motor vehicle compensation, as indicated in the Second Schedule, to the legal heirs or the victim, as the case may be.

Explanation. – For the purposes of this sub-section, "permanent disability" shall have the same meaning and extent as in the Workmen's Compensation Act, 1923.

(2) In any claim for compensation under sub-section (1), the claimant shall not be required to plead or establish that the death or permanent disablement in respect of which the claim has been made was due to any wrongful act or neglect or default of the owner of the vehicle or vehicles concerned or of any other person.

(3) The Central Government may, keeping in view the cost of living by notification in the Official Gazette, from time to time amend the Second Schedule. [Newly Inserted]

Section 163-B : Option to file claim in certain cases. – Where a person is entitled to claim compensation under section 140 and section 163-A, he shall file the claim under either of the said sections and not under both. [Newly Inserted]

Application for Compensation

Section 166 provides for the form of application for compensation, the person who may claim compensation, the time within which the application should be filed, etc. It also provides that if the Claims Tribunal, think so, may treat the accident report filed by the Police Officer as per Section 158 as an application under this Act.

Section 166 : Application for compensation. – (1) An application for compensation arising out of an accident of the nature specified in sub-section (1) of section 165 may be made :

(*a*) by the person who has sustained the injury; or

(*b*) by the owner of the property; or

(c) where death has resulted from the accident, by all or any of the legal representatives of the deceased; or

(*d*) by any agent duly authorised by the person injured or all or any of the legal representatives of the deceased, as the case may be :

Provided that where all the legal representatives of the deceased have not joined in any such application for compensation, the application shall be made on behalf of or for the benefit of all the legal representatives of the deceased and the legal representatives who have not so joined, shall be impleaded as respondents to the application.

(2) Every application under sub - section (1) shall be made, at the option of the claimant, either to the Claims Tribunal having jurisdiction over the area in which the accident occurred or to the Claims Tribunal within the local limits of whose jurisdiction the claimant resides, or carries on business or within the local limits of whose jurisdiction the defendant resides and shall be in such form and contain such particulars as may be prescribed:

Provided that where no claim for compensation under section 140 is made in such application, the application shall contain a separate statement to that effect immediately before the signature of the applicant.

(4) The Claims Tribunal shall treat any report of accidents forwarded to it under sub-section (6) of section 158 as an application for compensation under this Act.

Marine Insurance Act was passed in 1963 and is largely based on the English Marine Insurance Act, 1906. The Insurance Act, 1938 defines the marine insurance business as the business of effecting contracts of insurance upon vessels of any description, including cargos, freights and other interest, which may be legally assured, in relation to such vessels, cargoes and freights, goods, wares, merchandize and property of whatever description assured for any transit by land or water or by both, and whether or not including warehouse risks or similar risks in addition or as incidental to, such transit, and includes any other risks customarily including among the risks assured against in marine insurance policies (Section 13A).

9.2 Marine Insurance Act, 1963

Maritime insurance business includes the following :

- Insurance of vessels of any description (Hull).
- Insurance of cargo in the vessel (Cargo).
- Freight paid or received by the assured (Freight).
- Other merchandize and other property assured, which is in the transit either in water or on the land to water or both.
- Insurance of third party liability (TPL).
- Insurance of the transactions which are incidental to the marine adventure of marine transport or transport of cargo from place of godown to the vessel or *vis-a-vis*.

- Insurance also includes all perils and risks incidental to money, documents, securities, other valuable goods in the ship.
- Freight, insurance premium paid by the assured, packaging and forwarding expenses.
- Any other incidental activities concerned to building, launching of ship or transport of stores concerned.

9.2.1 Contract of Marine Insurance and Policy

Section 3 defines marine insurance as :

"A contract of marine insurance is an agreement whereby the insurer undertakes to indemnify the assured, in the manner and to the extent thereby agreed, against marine losses, that is to say, the losses incidental to marine adventure."

A defeasible interest is insurable, as also is a contingent interest. For example, liability for salvage expenses is insurable and also the liability for carriage of passengers.

A partial interest of any nature is insurable. (Section 10)

Reinsurance [S. 11]

The insurer under a contract of marine insurance has an insurable interest in his risk, and may reinsure in respect of it. The original assured will have no right in respect of such reinsurance, unless the policy so provides. This is so for the obvious reason that a reinsurance is taken out by an insurer for his own protection.

Bottomry and Respondentia [S. 12]

The lender of money on bottomry or respondentia has an insurable interest in respect of the loan. He can effect a policy on the ship to the extent of his interest.

Master's and Seamen's Wages [S. 13]

The master or any member of the crew of a ship has an insurable interest in respect of wages.

Advance Freight [S. 14]

The shipowner has an interest in the freight which he will earn on the successful completion of the voyage. He can insure the risk of his being not able to earn the freight by any accident. This interest arises out of ownership of the ship.

Section 24 of the Act provides the marine insurance policy may be issued as a token of a conclusion of the contract and can be executed and issued either at the time when the contract is conducted or afterwards. Also, the marine insurance policy must fulfil the requirements as to description as specified by the Act. The marine insurance policy should contain following particulars :

- Name of the assured or group of the assured.
- The subject matter of insurance and risk assured.
- Voyage details.
- Sum assured.
- The name or names of insurers.
- The signatures of authorized person of the insurer.
- Where the marine policy designates the subject matter assured in general terms, it shall be construed to apply to the interest intended by the assured to be covered. (Section 28).
- Schedule forming part of policy.

Insurable Interest

A contract of marine insurance made without insurable interest has been expressly declared by Section 6 to be by way of wagering and void. The section says that a contract of marine insurance shall be deemed to be a wager:

1. where the insured does not have an insurable interest in the subject-matter of insurance and the contract is entered into with no expectation of acquiring such an interest; or
2. where the policy is made "interest or no interest", or "without further proof of interest than the policy itself", or "without benefit of salvage to the insurer" or subject to any other like term.

Also, where there is no possibility of salvage, a policy may be effected without benefit of salvage to the insurer. A policy of insurance which declares that the policy itself is a proof of interest is called a policy with a "PPI clause" (policy proof of interest). Such a policy becomes void by virtue of the above declaration stating that a policy shall be valid without further proof of interest.

Section 7 of the Act says that every person who is interested in a marine adventure is deemed to have insurable interest in it. In particular a person is interested in a marine adventure where he stands in any legal or equitable relation to the adventure or to any insurable property at risk in consequence of which he may be benefited by the safety or due arrival of insurable property or may be prejudiced by its loss, damage or detention or may incur liability in respect thereof.

The insurable interest should exist at the time of the loss. It is not necessary that it should exit at the time when the policy is effected. When the parties are not aware about the existence or loss of the goods, they are permitted to insure them under a clause "loss or not lost".

A defeasible interest is insurable, as also is a contingent interest. For example, liability for salvage expenses is insurable and also the liability for carriage of passengers. (Section 9).

A partial interest of any nature is insurable. (Section 10).

Principle of Indemnity and Evaluation of Loss

The marine insurance contract is a contract of indemnity where the insurer(s) are under obligation to compensate the loss suffered by the assured due to happening of risk covering the asset. If there are more than one insurers, they are liable to contribute such proportion of the measure of indemnity as the amount of the subscription bears to the value fixed by the policy in the case of a valued policy or to the insurable value in the case of an unvalued policy. (Section 67).

Subject to the terms of the policy, where there is a total loss of the subject-matter insured, in the case of valued policy, the measure of indemnity is the sum fixed by the policy and, in the case of an unvalued policy, the insurable value of the subject-matter insured. (S. 68).

Section 69(3) requires the measure of indemnity to be qualified on the basis of what it would have cost to repair if the repairs has been carried out.

In the case of partial loss of freight, the measure of indemnity is such proportion of the sum fixed by the policy in the case of a valued policy or of the insurable value in the case of an unvalued policy, as the proportion of the freight loss by the assured bears to the whole freight at the risk of the assured under the policy.

Insurable Value

If there is no express valuation of the subject-matter insured in the policy, Section 18 lays down as to how this value be ascertained :

1. In an insurance *on ship* – the insurable value is the value of the ship at the commencement of the risk, including her outfit, provisions and stores for the officers and crew, money advanced for seamen's wages,

and other disbursements, if any, made to make the ship seaworthy for the voyage, plus the insurance charges on the whole. In case of steamships, the value of boilers, machinery, coal, etc., and other special requisites, if any, must also be included.

2. In an insurance *on freight,* the insurable value is the gross amount of the freight plus the charges of insurance.
3. In an insurance on goods, the insurable value in the prime cost of the goods incurred plus the expenses of shipping and insurance charges.
4. In an insurance on nay other subject matter – the insurable value includes the amount at risk plus insurance charges.

Disclosure and Representation : A contract of marine insurance, like any other contract of insurance, is a contract *uberrimae fidei, i.e.,* a contract requiring utmost good faith. If the utmost good faith is not observed by either party, the contract may be avoided by the other (Section 19).

Duty of Disclosure : Section 20 provides that the assured must disclose to insurer every material circumstances which is known to him. He is deemed to know everything which he ought to know in the ordinary course of the business. A circumstance is material if it would influence the judgement of a prudent insurer in fixing of determining whether to take the risk.

Every circumstance is material which would influence the judgement of a prudent insurer in fixing the premium, or determining whether he will take the risk. In the absence of an inquiry the following circumstances need not be disclosed :

(*a*) any circumstance which diminishes the risk;

(*b*) any circumstance which is known or presumed to be known to the insurer. The insurer is presumed to know matters of common notoriety or knowledge, and matters which an insurer in the ordinary course of business as such, ought to know;

(*c*) any circumstance as to which information is waived by the insurer;

(*d*) any circumstance which is superfluous to disclose by reason of any express or implied warranty; [S. 20(3)].

Whether any particular circumstance, which is not disclosed, be material or not is, in each case, a question of fact. [S. 20(4)]

The term "circumstances" includes any communication made to, or information received, by the assured. [S. 20(5)].

When the policy is effected through an agent, the extent of his duty of disclosure is the same as that of the assured. He is also bound to disclose every material circumstance which the assured ought to disclose, unless it comes to his knowledge too late to communicate to his agent. (S. 21)

Representations Pending Negotiations [*S.* 22]

Representations made during the course of negotiations must be true otherwise the insurer may avoid the contract, whether the representation is as to a matter of fact or expectation or belief.

A representation will be regarded as true if it is substantially correct, that is, if the difference between the truth and the representation would not be considered material by a prudent insurer.

A representation as to expectation or belief is true if it is made in good faith.

A representation may be withdrawn or corrected before the contract is concluded.

A contract is deemed to be concluded when the proposal is accepted, whether the policy be then issued or not, and to know whether a proposal has been accepted or not reference may be made to any customary method of acceptance, although it be unstamped. (S. 23)

Double Insurance [S. 34]

Where more than one policies are effected by or on behalf of the assured on the same adventure or interest, and the sums insured exceed the indemnity allowed by the Act, the insured is said to be overinsured by double insurance. The consequences of such double insurance are as follows :

1. The assured can claim payment from any of the insurers in such order as he may think fit. But in no case he would be allowed to recover more than the indemnity allowed by the Act.
2. When he claims under a policy which is a valued policy, he will have to give credit as against the valuation, for any sum received by him under any other policy, without regard to the actual value of the subject-matter assured.
3. Whether the policy under which a claim is made is an unvalued policy, he must give credit, as against the full insurable value, for any sum received by him under any other policy.
4. Where the assured receives any sum in excess of the indemnity allowed by the Act, he shall hold such sum in trust for the insurers, according to their right of contribution among themselves.

Right of Contribution [S. 80]

Where the assured is over-assured by double insurance, each insurer is bound, as between himself and other insurers, to contribute rateably to the loss in proportion to the amount for which he is liable under the contract. If any insurer pays more than his proportion of the loss, he is entitled to maintain a suit for contribution against the other insurers, and is entitled to the like remedies as a surety who has paid more than his proportion of the debt.

Effect of Under Insurance [S. 81]

Where the assured is insured for an amount less than the insurable value, or, in the case of a valued policy, for an amount less than the policy valuation, he is deemed to be his own insurer in respect of the uninsured balance.

If the goods are damaged/loss value, the insurer may dispose the goods at immediate port and indemnify the difference between the sale value and insured value to the insured.

Assignment of Policy

The assignment of the policy can be made either by on endorsement or by other method which is approved and established by the law in force. The assignee acquires all rights of the assignor upon assignment and can file suits or defend suits, file claims and receive the claims and settle any dispute concerned to the policy unless otherwise stated in the policy and assignment clause.

When and How Assignable [S. 52]

A marine policy is assignable, that is, transferable to any other person unless there is some provision in the policy itself prohibiting the transfer. Assignment may be made either before or after loss. The assignee will be entitled to sue in his own name. The insurer will be entitled to raise against the assignee any defence that would have been available to him against the insured. In other words, an assignment is subject to all the equities.

The assignee must have insurable interest in the subject-matter of the policy.

Where an assured has already lost or parted with his interest in the subject-matter insured, and this without any assignment at the time, any subsequent assignment will be inoperative.

The Premium [S. 54]

Unless otherwise agreed, payment of the premium and issue of the policy are concurrent conditions. The insurer is not bound to issue the policy until payment or tender of the premium.

The Voyage and Insurance

In a voyage policy it is not necessary that the ship shall be at the place mentioned in the contract as the place of sailing, but there is an implied condition that the adventure shall be commenced within a reasonable time. If the adventure is not so commenced, the insurer can avoid the contract. This implied condition of reasonable dispatch may, however, be negatived by showing that the delay was caused by circumstances known to the insurer before the contract was concluded or by showing that he waived the condition. If the ship sails to different destinations than which are mentioned in the policy the insurance contract is invalid and the risk is not covered.

The deviation of the voyage in voyage policy can be excused in the following events cases :

1. when it is authorised by the special terms of the policy;
2. where caused by circumstances beyond the control of the master, and his employer;
3. where reasonably necessary in order to comply with an express or implied warranty;
4. where reasonably necessary for the safety of the ship or subject-matter insured;
5. for the purpose of saving human life or aiding a ship in distress where human life may be in danger;
6. where reasonably necessary for the purpose of obtaining medical or surgical aid for any person on board the ship;
7. where caused by the barratrous conduct of the master or crew, if barratry be one of the perils insured against.

Sub-section (2) provides that once the cause excusing the deviation or delay ceases to operate, the ship must resume her course, and prosecute her voyage, with reasonable dispatch.

9.2.2 Warranties and Disclosures

Warranties and Disclosures

A warranty, as defined in the Act, means a promissory warranty. A warranty becomes a condition logically in a marine insurance contract.

- A warranty stated in the marine insurance is promissory warranty. The promissory warranty is the undertaking of the assured stating the intention to do or not to do some work in a particular way.
- An insurer may waive the compliance of warranty as per the provisionary of Section 36.
- Warranty of neutrality implies that the goods or ship which is insured is of neutral character at the commencement of risk and will continue to be a neutral during the coverage of risk (Section 38).
- In a time policy there is no implied warranty that the ship shall be seaworthy at any stage of the adventure and insurer is not liable for any loss attributable to unseaworthiness.
- In a policy on goods or other movables there is no implied warranty that the goods or movables are seaworthy (Section 42).
- There is an implied warranty that the adventure is lawful and is carried on in a lawful manner.

Non-compliance with a warranty is excused in the following cases :

1. When, on account of change of circumstances, the warranty ceases to be applicable to the circumstances of the contract.

2. When compliance with the warranty is rendered unlawful by any subsequent law.
3. A breach of warranty may be waived by the insurer.
4. Express warranty must be written upon the policy or upon some document incorporated by reference into the policy and an express warranty will not exclude an implied warranty unless it is inconsistent therewith.

No Implied Warranty of Nationality [S. 39]

There is no implied warranty as to the nationality of a ship or that her nationality shall not be changed during the risk.

Warranty of Good Safety [S. 40]

When the subject-matter insured is warranted "well" or "in good safety" on a particular day, it is sufficient if it is safe at any time during that day.

Warranty of Seaworthiness [S. 41]

In a voyage policy there is an implied warranty that at the commencement of the voyage the ship shall be seaworthy for the purpose of the particular venture insured. There is also the implied warranty that, at the commencement of the risk, the ship shall be reasonably fit to encounter the ordinary perils of the sea.

In a voyage policy it is not necessary that the ship shall be at the place mentioned in the contract as the place of sailing, but there is an implied condition that the adventure shall be commenced within a reasonable time. If the adventure is not so commenced, the insurer can avoid the contract. This implied condition of reasonable dispatch may, however, be negatived by showing that the delay was caused by circumstances known to the insurer before the contract was concluded or by showing that he waived the condition.

Examples of Material Circumstances

(1) Concealing the nationality of the insured when such nationality is of importance [*Associated Oil Carriers Ltd.* v. *Union Ins. Society of Canton* (1917) 2 K.B. 184].

(2) The fact that the ship had developed a leak before the insurance was effected [*Russel* v. *Thorton* 1859 20 L.R. Ex. 9].

(3) The fact that the goods carried on the ship are grossly over-valued when the ship is insured. [*Ionidies* v. *Pender* (1874) L.R. 7. Q.B. 531].

9.2.3 Premiums

Refund of Premiums

Enforcement of Refund [S. 82]

If the premium has become refundable, it can be recovered back, and if it has not been paid, it shall cease to be payable. The policy itself may provide that in the happening of an event, the premium, or any part of it, shall become refundable. This will be known as return by agreement.

Return on Failure of Consideration [S. 84]

Where the consideration for the payment of the premium totally fails, and there has been no illegality or fraud on the part of the assured, the premium becomes refundable.

When the goods are insured for damage during the transit and the goods become useless by the time the vessel arrives at the destination then the insurer faces total loss. This makes the insurer to take prudent decision of disposing the goods at an immediate port for best value before they are totally damaged. The insurer has to pay the difference of amount received by selling the goods and the amount payable to the assured. As such the insurer is saved from indemnifying the assured from the total loss.

If the goods are damaged/loss value, the insurer may dispose the goods at immediate port and indemnify the difference between the sale value and insured value to be insured.

9.2.4 Marine Losses and Damages

Loss and Abandonment

Included and Excluded Losses : Proximate Cause [S. 55]

Unless the policy otherwise provides, the insurer is liable for any loss proximately caused by a peril insured against and is not liable for a loss not proximately caused.

This statement has been further particularised in terms of the following principles:

1. The insurer is not liable for any loss attributable to the wilful misconduct of the assured. But he is liable for a loss proximately caused by a peril insured against, even though the loss would not have happened but for the misconduct or negligence of the master or crew.
2. Unless the policy otherwise provides that insurer is not liable for the consequences of delay even if the delay is caused by a peril insured against.
3. Unless the policy otherwise provides the insurer is not liable for ordinary wear and tear, ordinary leakage and breakage, inherent vice or nature of the subject-matter insured, for any loss proximately caused by rats or vermin or for any injury to machinery not proximately caused by maritime perils.

Partial and Total Loss [S. 56]

A loss may be either total or partial. While there is no definition given of "partial loss", the section defines total loss and then says that any loss which is not total as thus defined is a partial loss. Total loss may be actual or constructive.

Actual Total Loss

1. Where the subject-matter insured is destroyed, or so damaged as to cease to be a thing of the kind insured, or where the assured is irretrievably deprived of the subject-matter, there is an actual total loss. (S. 57)
2. Where the ship concerned in the adventure is missing, and after the lapse of a reasonable time no news of her has been received, an actual total loss may be presumed. (S. 58)

Thus, there is actual total loss in three cases : (1) where the subject-matter is totally destroyed or annihilated; (2) where the subject-matter ceases to remain in its original condition; (3) though the thing is not destroyed, but the assured cannot get it, it being irretrievably lost to him.

Constructive Total Loss [S. 60]

There is constructive total loss when the cargo is abandoned on account of its actual total loss appearing to be unavoidable or when it could be saved from actual total loss only at an expense which would exceed the value of the subject-matter insured.

Sub-section (2) says that in particular there is constructive total loss in the following cases :

1. Where the assured is deprived of the possession of his ship or goods by a peril insured against and (*a*) it is unlikely that he can recover the ship or the goods; (*b*) the cost of recovering the ship or goods would exceed there value;

2. In the case of damage to a ship, where she is so damaged by a peril insured against that the cost of repairing the damage would exceed the value of the ship.

In estimating the cost of repair, general average contributions payable by others to the repair are not to be taken into account. But the cost of salvage operations and the liability of the ship to make general average contributions are to be included.

Option of the Assured [S. 61]

Section 61 which deals with the effect of constructive total loss gives this option to the assured that he may treat the constructive total loss as a partial loss or abandon the subject-matter insured to the insurer and treat the loss as if it were an actual total loss.

Notice of Abandonment [S. 62]

If he elects to treat the loss as an actual total loss he must give notice of abandonment to the insurer. If he fails to do so the loss can only be treated as a partial loss.

Notice may be in any form, *viz.*, written, oral or partily written and partly oral. All that is necessary is that is should indicate to the insurer the intention to surrender unconditionally the subject-matter of insurance.

Notice should be given with reasonable diligence after the assured reliably learns of the loss. But if the information as to loss is of doubtful nature, he is entitled to reasonable time to make an inquiry.

Where proper notice has been given but the insurer refuses to accept it, that will not prejudice the rights of the assured. The acceptance of abandonment on the part of the insurer may be express or implied, but mere silence of the insurer after notice is not an acceptance.

An unaccepted notice of abandonment can be withdrawn by the assured.

Once the notice is accepted, the abandonment becomes irrevocable. The acceptance of the notice is a conclusive admission of the liability for the loss and of the sufficiency of the notice.

When Notice not Necessary

No notice is necessary in the following cases :

1. Where at the time when the assured receives information of the loss, there would be no possibility of benefit to the insurer if notice were given to him.
2. Notice of abandonment may be waived by the insurer.
3. Where an insurer has re-insured his risk, no notice of abandonment need be given by him.

Effect of Abandonment [S. 63]

When a valid abandonment has taken place, the assured is entitled to take over the whole of the interest of the assured in the subject-matter of insurance including proprietary rights over it.

Where a ship is abandoned, the insurer will be entitled to freight which is in the course of being earned and which is earned subsequent to the casualty causing the loss, less the expenses insurred in earning it after the casualty. If the ship is carrying the owner's goods, the insurer will be entitled to a reasonable remuneration for the carriage of them subsequent to the casualty causing the loss.

Partial Losses : Salvage, General Average and Particular Charges

Particular Average Loss [S. 64]

A particular average loss is a partial loss of the subject-matter insured, and which is not a general average loss. Expenses incurred by the assured for the safety or preservation of the subject-matter insured, other than general average and salvage charges, are called particular charges. Particular charges are not included in particular average.

Salvage Charges [S. 65]

Subject to the terms of the policy, salvage charges incurred in preventing a loss by perils insured against may be recovered as a loss by those perils. "Salvage charges" means charges recoverable under maritime law by a salvor independently of contract. They do not include the expenses of services in the nature of salvage rendered by the assured or his agent, or any person employed for hire by them, for the purpose of averting a peril insured against. Such expenses where properly incurred, may be recovered as particular charges or as a general average loss, according to the circumstances under which they were incurred.

General Average Loss [S. 66]

A general average loss is a loss caused by or directly consequential on a general average act. It includes a general average expenditure as well as a general average sacrifice. Explaining the meaning of the expression "general average act", sub-section (2) says that there is a general average act where any extraordinary sacrifice or expenditure is voluntarily and reasonably made or incurred in time of peril for the purpose of preserving the property imperilled in the common adventure. It has been pointed out in *Watson (Joseph) & Son Ltd. v. Fireman's Fund Insurance Co. of San Francisco* that the peril sought to be averted should be a real one.

Where there is a general average loss, the party on whom it falls is entitled to a rateable contribution from the other parties interested, and such contribution is called a general average contribution.

Where an assured has incurred a general average of expenditure, he may recover from the insurer in respect of the proportion of the loss which falls upon him. In the case of a general average sacrifice, he may recover from the insurer in respect of the whole loss without having enforced his right of contribution from the other parties liable to contribute.

Where an assured has paid or is liable to pay, a general average contribution in respect of the interest insured, he may recover the same from the insurer.

There is no liability on the part of the insurer where the loss was not incurred for the purpose of avoiding or in connection with the avoidance of a peril against.

Where ship, freight and cargo, or any two of those interests, are owned by the same assured, the liability of the insurer in respect of general average losses or contributions is to be determined as if these interest were owned by different persons.

The right to sue for general average loss commences from the date of the loss and the period of limitation begins to run from the date and not from the date when the average adjusters publish their statements as to the liability of the parties.

Partial Loss of Goods, Merchandise, etc. [S. 71]

In the case of partial loss of goods, merchandise or other movables, the measure of indemnity, subject to the provisions of policy, is as follows :

1. In the case of a valued policy, the measure of indemnity is such proportion of the sum fixed by the policy as the insurable value of the part loss bears to the insurable value of the whole, ascertained as in the case of an unvalued policy.
2. In the case of an unvalued policy, the measure of indemnity is the insurable value of the part lost, ascertained as in the case of total loss.
3. Where the goods have been delivered damaged at their destination, the measure of indemnity is such proportion of the sum fixed by the policy in the case of a valued policy, or of the insurable value in the case of an unvalued policy, as the difference between the gross sound and damaged values at the place of arrival bears to the gross sound value.

4. "Gross value" means the whole sale price, or, if there be no such price, the estimated value, with, in either case, freight, landing charges, and duty paid before hand; provided that, in the case of goods or merchandise customarily sold in bond, the bonded price is deemed to be the gross value. "Gross proceeds" means the actual price obtained at a sale where all charges on sale are paid by the sellers.

Where the assured has paid or is liable for any general average contribution, the measure of indemnity is the full amount of such contribution if the subject-matter liable to contribution is insured for its full contributory value. But if it is not insured for its full contributory value, or if only part if it be assured, the indemnity payable by the insurer must be reduced in proportion to the underinsurance. Where there has been a particular average loss which constitutes a deduction from the contributory value, and for which the insurer is liable, that amount must be deducted from the insured value in order to ascertain what the insurer is liable to contribute.

9.2.5 Decided Cases

Conditions in a Contract; Gartsman et al. *vs.* Elite Insurance *et. al.,* 2004 ONSC 11157

The Plaintiff in this matter purchased a vessel from the Defendant marina and asked the marina about insurance. She was told that the marina could not provide insurance but was given the name of a broker who arranged insurance with the Defendant insurer. A temporary binder was issued for 30 days that was conditional on the vessel being laid up at the dock pending receipt of a completed application and survey. It was also conditional on the vessel not being used except for instructional purposes by the marina.

Although the Plaintiff alleged she was not advised of these conditions the Court did not believe her. In breach of the conditions the Plaintiff took the vessel on a cruise during which it was damaged. Predictably, the insurer denied coverage and the Court upheld the insurer's denial.

Right of Insurer on Payment; Yorkshire Insurance Co. Ltd. *vs.* Nisbet Shipping Company Ltd. (1961) 2 All ER 487

A ship became a total loss on account of a collision caused by the negligence of a Canadian government ship. The insurer paid the total loss of £ 72,000. The assured also claimed the damages from the Canadian Government and recovered £1,27,000. The insurer claimed that they were entitled to the whole amount. It was held that they are entitled only to the amount they have paid. Had there been a clause of assignment into the policy, they could have recovered whole of the amount even if it exceeds the amount indemnified.

{*Source:* Avtar Singh, Law of Insurance, Eastern Book Company, 2004}

Sue and Labour – Proportion payable when insured and uninsured property involved; North Coast Sea Products Ltd. v. ING Insurance Company of Canada, 2004 BCCA 95 affirming 2003 BCSC 592

The insured Plaintiffs incurred expenses in recovering trays and the oysters in them from the seabed when the lines of their oyster farm were vandalized. The Plaintiffs were insured for the loss of the trays but not for the oysters themselves. They claimed under the sue and labour provisions of their marine insurance policy for all the expenses incurred in recovering the trays and oysters.

Underwriters claimed that only a portion of the expenses could be claimed and that the claim should be in ratable proportion to the value of the insured trays to the uninsured oysters. The policy wording included provisions for reducing recoverable sue and labour expenses where the property was underinsured but was silent with respect to cases where there was both insured and uninsured property.

The matter was disposed of by Special Case. The underwriters relied on English case law from 1902 (Cunard Steamship Co. Ltd. v. Marten) that appeared to state that sue and labour expenses should be recoverable ratably where expenses are incurred for both insured and uninsured property. However, the trial Judge found for the insureds because the terms of the policy did not specify what would happen when expenses were incurred in respect of insured and uninsured property.

On appeal, the Court of Appeal upheld the trial Judge holding that the sue and labour clause of the policy only limited the insurer's obligation in the specific circumstances identified in that clause, none of which applied.

Insurance – Direct Action against Insurers – Interpretation of Policies – Limits of Coverage; Solway v. Lloyd's Underwriters, 2005 ONSC 13407

In this case, the Plaintiffs arranged for a motor carrier to move and store their personal belongings. The truck was stolen and the Plaintiffs' belongings were never recovered. The Plaintiffs obtained a judgment against the carrier, which was not satisfied. The Plaintiffs then commenced this direct action against the carrier's primary and excess liability underwriters.

Both underwriters agreed that the Plaintiffs' loss was covered but disagreed as to how the loss should be apportioned between them. The primary underwriter argued that the limit of its policy was $500,000 as provided for in the transportation section of its policy. The excess underwriter argued that the applicable limit was that in the warehouse and storage section of the primary policy of $1,000,000. The issue was then one of interpretation of the primary policy.

The Court noted that the normal rule for construction of insurance contracts requires a search for an interpretation, which, from the whole of the contract, advances the true intent of the parties at the time the contract was entered into.

The Court further noted that the general principles of interpretation of insurance contracts include the expected performance of parties, provisions to be interpreted broadly and exclusion clauses narrowly and the desirability, at least where the policy is ambiguous, of giving effect to the reasonable expectations of the parties.

The Court finally concluded that the applicable limit depended on the proper characterization of the claim against the carrier either as breach of a transportation contract or breach of a storage contract. The Court held that since liability was imposed on the carrier at the trial for breach of a term relating to storage of the Plaintiffs' goods, the limitation of $1,000,000 for warehousing or storage was applicable.

Charters – Bailment – Waiver of Subrogation; North King Lodge Ltd. *v* Gowlland Towing Ltd. et. al., 2004 BCSC 460.

This matter concerned was liability for the sinking of the barge "Sea Lion VI". The owner had hired the barge to the first Defendant for use as an accommodation barge at a remote logging camp. One of the terms of the agreement was that the owner would provide a watchman. When the logging operations had ceased, the second Defendant, the towing company was retained to remove the log booms. In doing so "Sea Lion VI" went aground and sank.

The court found as a fact that the removal of the port lines caused the sinking. The Plaintiff, the owner of the barge, commenced proceedings against both the hirer and the towing company. The Plaintiff contended that the hire contract was a charter party by demise or, alternatively a bailment and that the hirer was responsible for the safekeeping of the barge. The hirer, on the other hand, argued that it did not have possession of the barge and that the contract was a time charter. The court held that it was not possible to fit the agreement between the parties into one of the traditional forms of charter party since the barge was not chartered for a voyage and had no master or crew. Also, the agreement was one of bailment but declined to imply all of the usual obligations that a contract of bailment entails.

Moreover, the owner's obligation to provide a watchman made the owner primarily responsible for the safe moorage of the barge. At the time of the sinking and for some time previous there had been no watchman on the barge and this was known to the hirer. The fact that the hirer failed to complain about the removal of the watchman by the owner was held not to be a waiver of the owner's obligation to provide a watchman.

It was also found that the hirer owed an obligation to take reasonable care of the vessel and that it breached this duty by failing to promptly advise the owner when it became apparent that the barge was in danger.

With respect to the liability of the towing company, the trial Judge found that owner of the "Sea Lion VI" committed an act of trespass in tying the barge to the log booms and that the duty owed by the towing company to a trespasser is to not intentionally harm the Plaintiff, act recklessly or without common humanity. He held that although the towing company did not act with reasonable care it did not breach the duties it in fact owed to the trespasser.

In the result, liability for the sinking was apportioned 80% to the owner and 20% to the hirer. One final issue considered in the case was whether the hirer was immune from suit by reason of clauses in the hull insurance policy including charterers as additional assured and waiving subrogation against charterers.

The court held that these clauses were not effective since the policy also contained an express clause which provided that the benefits of the insurance policy would not automatically extend to third parties but would only be extended if the option was exercised by the owner. The trial Judge found that the owner did not exercise this option.

Bad Faith – Punitive Damages – Whiten *v.* Pilot Insurance Co., 2002 SCC 18{Canada}

In this case, the Supreme Court of Canada awarded $1 Million damages to the plaintiff. The facts were that the Plaintiff's home was destroyed in a fire and the insurer (defendant) denied the claim made under the insurance policy on the grounds that the fire had been deliberately set even though the local fire chief, the Defendant's own fire investigator and the Defendant's initial expert all agreed that there was no evidence of arson. The court awarded punitive damages against the Defendant for bad faith denial of coverage and failure to act in good faith.

Liability insurance laws have been framed to provide indemnity to the insured against the financial consequences of legal liabilities including third party risks. These liabilities may be :

(*a*) *Contractual* : which arise out of a contractual relationship.

(*b*) *Statutory* : prescribed in the various enactments.

In this chapter the employers' liability and the public liability for industrial and non-industrial risks are discussed in light of respective enactments.

9.3 Workmen Compensation Act, 1923

The employer in any organisation is liable under the common law of the land to his employees for negligence or injuries or diseases arising out of and in course of employment. The Workmen Compensation Act, 1923 has been promulgated for the following object and reasons:

The Act provides for the payment by employers to their workmen of compensation for injury by accident, arising out of and in the course of employment. The object of this legislation has been stated as follows:

The growing complexity of industry in this country, with the increasing use of machinery and consequent danger to workmen, along with the comparative poverty of the workmen themselves render it advisable that they should be protected as far as possible, from hardship out of accidents. The act provides certain benefits to employees in case of accidents during employment, sickness, maternity etc.

9.3.1 Employer's Liability for Compensation

Section 3 : (1) If personal injury is caused to a workman by accident arising out of and in the course of his employment, his employer shall be liable to pay compensation in accordance with the provisions of this Chapter mean Provided that the employer shall not be so liable :

(*a*) in respect of any injury which does not result in the total or partial disablement of the workman for a period exceeding three days;

(*b*) in respect of any injury, not resulting in death, caused by] an accident which is directly attributable to :

(i) the workman having been at the time thereof under the influence of drink or drugs, or

(ii) the wilful disobedience of the workman to an order expressly given, or to a rule expressly framed, for the purpose of securing the safety of workmen, or

(iii) the wilful removal or disregard by the workman of any safety guard or other device which he knew to have been provided for the purpose of securing the safety of workmen.

(2) The words 'in the course of employment' indicate the time when injury is caused, whereas the words 'out of employment' establishes the causal connection between the injury and the employment.

(3) If the workman dies a natural death while on duty, no liability attaches to the employer unless it is proved that the death was caused by strains and stresses peculiar to the particular employment. When the death of the workman is caused by aggravation of a pre-existing disease due to an accident it has been held that the death is deemed to have resulted from the accident.

In *Laxmibai Atmaram v. Bombay Port Trust, 1954, the Bombay High Court* held, where a workman suffers from a heart aliment dies on account of excessive strain associated with the work, the accident occurred out of employment.

In *Divisional Personnel Officer, Southern Railway v. Karthiayani (1987)* the facts were: Drinking water was provided by the railway for the workmen. The death of the workman was caused by gastro-enteritis which itself was caused by the contaminated water which the deceased had drunk a few hours before his death. Death arose out of and in the course of employment. The High Court found that the railway was liable in terms of Section 3 of the Act to pay compensation.

In *Koduri Alchayamma v. Palangi Alchamma* (High Court at Hyderabad) it was held that the act which resulted in the injury should not be foreign to the employment. The facts of the case were : Palangi was engaged to load the quarry material in the lorry and travel alongwith the lorry and to unload it at the work site. The deceased who was in the lorry saw a wild rabbit passing on the road and he attempted to hit it and in this attempt he fell down from the lorry and met with a fatal accident.

The High Court observed, it was not part of the duties of a workman to hit a wild rabbit running across the road. His act does not arise out of the employment. The principle is that if the workman was responsible for an act unconnected with his duties and that resulted in the injury, the employer is not liable.

9.3.2 Amount of Compensation

Section 4 : (1) Subject to the provisions of this Act, the amount of compensation shall be as follows, namely :

(a) Where death results an amount equal to forty per from the injury cent of the monthly wages of the deceased workman multiplied by the relevant factor; or an amount of twenty thousand rupees, whichever is more;

(b) Where permanent total an amount equal to fifty per disablement results from cent. of the monthly wages the injury of the injured workman multiplied by the relevant factor; or an amount of twenty-four thousand rupees, whichever is more;

Explanation I : For the purposes of clause (a) and clause (b), "relevant factor", in relation to a workman means the factor specified in the second column of Schedule IV against the entry in the first column of that Schedule specifying the number of years which are the same as the completed years of the age of the workman on his last birthday immediately preceding the date on which the compensation fell due;

Explanation II : Where the monthly wages of a workman exceed one thousand rupees, his monthly wages for the purposes of clause (a) and clause (b) shall be deemed to be one thousand rupees only,

(c) Where permanent partial disablement result from injury

(*i*) in the case of an injury disablement results from specified in Part II of Schedule the injury I, such percentage of the compensation which would have been payable in the case of permanent total disablement as is specified therein as being the percentage of the loss of earning capacity caused by that injury, and

(*ii*) in the case of an injury not specified in Schedule I, such percentage of the compensation payable in the case of permanent total disablement as is proportionate to the loss of earning capacity (as assessed by the qualified medical practitioner) permanently caused by the injury;

Explanation I : Where more injuries than one are caused by the same accident, the amount of compensation payable under this head shall be aggregated but not so in any case as to exceed the amount which would have been payable if permanent total disablement had resulted from the injuries;

Explanation II : In assessing the loss of earning capacity for the purposes of sub-clause (ii), the qualified medical practitioner shall have due regard to the percentages of loss of earning capacity in relation to different injuries specified in Schedule I;

(*d*) Where temporary disablement whether total or partial result from injury - a half-monthly payment of the sum equivalent to twenty-five the per cent. of monthly wages of the workman, to be paid in accordance with the provisions of sub- section 2.

(2) The half-monthly payment referred to in clause (d) of sub- section (1) shall be payable on the sixteenth day:

(*i*) from the date of disablement where such disablement lasts for a period of twenty-eight days or more, or

(*ii*) after the expiry of a waiting period of three days from the date of disablement where such disablement lasts for a period of less than twenty-eight days; and thereafter half-monthly during the disablement or during a period of five years, whichever period is shorter: Provided that—(*a*) there shall be deducted from any lump sum or half- monthly payments to which the workman is entitled the amount of any payment or allowance which the workman has received from the employer by way of compensation during the period of disablement prior to the receipt of such lump sum or of the first half- monthly payment, as the case may be; and (*b*) no half-monthly payment shall in any case exceed the amount, if any, by which half the amount of the monthly wages of the workman before the accident exceeds half the amount of such wages which he is earning after the accident. *Explanation :* Any payment or allowance which the workman has received from the employer towards his medical treatment shall not be deemed to be a payment or allowance received by him by way of compensation within the meaning of clause (a) of the proviso. (3) On the ceasing of the disablement before the date on which any half-monthly payment falls due, there shall be payable in respect of that half-month a sum proportionate to the duration of the disablement in that half-month.

Section 4A : Compensation to be paid when due and penalty for default:

(1) Compensation under section 4 shall be paid as soon as it falls due.

(2) In cases where the employer does not accept the liability for compensation to the extent claimed, he shall be bound to make provisional payment based on the extent of liability which he accepts, and, such payment shall be deposited with the Commissioner or made to the workman, as the case may be, without prejudice to the right of the workman to make any further claim.

(3) Where any employer is in default in paying the compensation due under this Act within one month from the date it fell due, the Commissioner may direct that, in addition to the amount of the arrears, simple interest at the rate of six per cent per annum on the amount due together with, if in the opinion of the Commissioner there is no justification for the delay, a further sum not exceeding fifty per cent of such amount, shall be recovered from the employer by way of penalty.

The amount of compensation payable for death is 50% of monthly wages multiplied by the relevant factor (minimum Rs. 50,000/-) and for permanent total disablement 60% of monthly wages multiplied by the relevant factor (minimum Rs. 60,000/-).

9.3.3 Notice and Claim

Section 10 : Notice and Claim : (1) [No claim for compensation shall be entertained by a Commissioner unless notice of the accident has been given in the manner hereinafter provided as soon as practicable after the happening thereof and unless the claim is preferred before him within two years of the occurrence of the accident or, in case of death, within two years from the date of death;

Provided that, where the accident is the contracting of a disease in respect of which the provisions of sub-section (2) of section 3 are applicable, the accident shall be deemed to have occurred on the first of the days during which the workman was continuously absent from work in consequence of the disablement caused by the disease;

Provided further that in case of partial disablement due to the contracting of any such disease and which does not force the workman to absent himself from work, the period of two years shall be counted from the day the workman gives notice of the disablement to his employer: Provided further that if a workman who, having been employed in an employment for a continuous period, specified under sub-section (2) of section 3 in respect of that employment, ceases to be so employed and develops symptoms of an occupational disease peculiar to that employment within two years of the cessation of employment, the accident shall be deemed to have occurred on the day on which the symptoms were first detected;

Provided further that the want of or any defect or irregularity in a notice shall not be a bar to the entertainment of a claim—

(*a*) if the claim is preferred in respect of the death of a workman resulting from an accident which occurred on the premises of the employer, or at any place where the workman at the time of the accident was working under the control of the employer or of any person employed by him, and the workman died on such premises or at such place, or on any premises belonging to the employer, or died without having left the vicinity of the premises or place where the accident occurred, or

(*b*) if the employer or any one of several employers or any person responsible to the employer for the management of any branch of the trade or business in which the injured workman was employed] had knowledge of the accident from any other source at or about the time when it occurred;

Provided further, that the Commissioner may entertain and decide any claim to compensation in any case notwithstanding that the notice has not been given, or the claim has not been preferred, in due time as provided in this sub-section, if he is satisfied that the failure so to give the notice or prefer the claim, as the case may be, was due to sufficient cause.

(2) Every such notice shall give the name and address of the person injured and shall state in ordinary language the cause of the injury and the date on which the accident happened, and shall be served on the employer or upon any one of several employers, or upon any person responsible to the employer for the management of any branch of the trade or business in which the injured workman was employed.

(3) The State Government may require that any prescribed class of employers shall maintain at their premises at which workmen are employed a notice-book, in the prescribed form, which shall be readily accessible at all reasonable times to any injured workman employed on the premises and to any person acting bona fide on his behalf. (4) A notice under this section may be served by delivering it at, or sending it by registered post addressed to, the residence or any office or place of business of the person on whom it is to be served, or, where a notice-book is maintained, by entry in the notice-book.

Payment of compensation for death has to be deposited by the employer with the Commissioner whose receipt shall be a sufficient discharge.

Where the amount of any lumpsum as compensation has been agreed, whether by way or redemption of a half-monthly payment or otherwise, a memorandum has to be sent by the employer to the Commissioner for registration.

If payment is not made within one month from the date it fell due the employer would be liable to pay interest and in case the delay is unjustified pay further amount by way of penalty subject to a maximum of 50% of the amount payable as ordered by the Commissioner.

9.3.4 Contracting

Section 12 : (1) Where any person (hereinafter in this section referred to as the principal) in the course of or for the purposes of his trade or business contracts with any other person (hereinafter in this section referred to as the contractor) for the execution by or under the contractor of the whole or any part of any work which is ordinarily part of the trade or business of the principal, the principal shall be liable to pay to any workman employed in the execution of the work any compensation which he would have been liable to pay if that workman had been immediately employed by him; and where compensation is claimed from the principal, this Act shall apply as if references to the principal were substituted for references to the employer except that the amount of compensation shall be calculated with reference to the wages of the workman under the employer by whom he is immediately employed.

(2) Where the principal is liable to pay compensation under this section, he shall be entitled to be indemnified by the contractor, or any other person from whom the workman could have recovered compensation and where a contractor who is himself a principal is liable to pay compensation or to indemnify a principal under this section he shall be entitled to be indemnified by any person standing to him in the relation of a contractor from whom the workman could have recovered compensation,] and all questions as to the right to and the amount of any such indemnity shall, in default of agreement, be settled by the Commissioner.

(3) Nothing in this section shall be construed as preventing a workman from recovering compensation from the contractor instead of the principal.

(4) This section shall not apply in any case where the accident occurred elsewhere than on, in or about the premises on which the principal has undertaken or usually undertakes, as the case may be, to execute the work or which are otherwise under his control or management.

Where the employer (referred to in the Section as Principal) contracts with any other person (referred to as Contractor) for the execution of the whole or part of any work which is ordinarily part of the business of the principal, the employer shall be liable to pay compensation to workmen employed by the contractor.

If the insured employer becomes insolvent his rights under the insurance policy are transferred to and vest in the workman who can recover the claim subject to the terms and conditions of the policy.

9.4 Public Liability Insurance Act, 1991

The Public Liability Insurance Act, 1991 imposes "no fault" liability in respect of use of hazardous substances as specified by the Act. The object of this Act is to provide through insurance immediate relief to persons affected due to "accident" while "handling" "hazardous substance" by the owners on "no fault liability basis". This has also been brought under Tariff. The definition of "Owner" is so comprehensive as to cover any person who owns or has control over any hazardous substance at the time of accident. This includes any Firm or its partners. Association or its members, Company or its Directors and all other persons associated and responsible to that Company in the conduct of their business.

9.4.1 Definitions

The various terms like "Accident", "Hazardous substances" as defined in Section 2 of the Act are given below:

"Accident" means an accident involving a fortuitous, sudden or unintentional occurrence while handling any hazardous substance resulting in continuous, intermittent or repeated exposure to death of, or injury to any person or damage to any property but does not include an accident by reason only of war or radioactivity.

"Handling" in relation to any hazardous substance, means the manufacture, processing, treatment, package, storage, transportation by vehicle, use, collection, destruction, conversion, offering for sale, transfer or the like of such hazardous substance.

"Hazardous Substance" means any substance or preparation which is defined as hazardous substance under the Environment (Protection) Act, 1986 and exceeding such quantity as may be specified by notification by the Central Government.

"Hazardous Substance" means any substance or preparation which, by reason of its chemical properties or handling is liable to cause harm to human beings, other living creatures, plants, micro-organism, property or the environment (as per the Environment (Protection) Act, 1986).

Maximum Liability

Any one accident : Minimum equal to Paid up Capital upto a maximum of Rs. 5 crores.

Any one year : Three times of 'Any one accident' limit subject to a maximum of Rs. 15 crores.

In case of claim/s exceeding the above statutory limit/s, it is to be met by the Environmental Relief Fund to be set up under Section 7A of the Act and managed by the Authority appointed by the Central Government.

The liability beyond the total of the insurance and the Relief/Fund is to be borne by the "Owner". Every owner , in addition to premium, has to pay to the insurer and equivalent amount to be credited to the said fund. However, the central government has powers to exempt any establishment from compulsory insurance, if a fund has been established and maintained for an amount not less than Rs. 5.0 crores or equal to the paid up capital of the establishment, in any nationalized bank for meeting liability under the act.

Schedule of Compensation

1. Reimbursement of medical expenses incurred upto a maximum of Rs. 12,500/- in each case.
2. For a fatal accident the relief will be Rs. 25,000/- per person in addition to reimbursement of medical expenses, if any incurred on the victim upto a maximum of Rs. 12,500/-.
3. For permanent total or permanent partial disability or other injury or sickness, the relief will be :
   (*a*) Reimbursement of medical expenses incurred, if any, upto a maximum of Rs. 12,500/- in each case and,
   (*b*) Cash relief on the basis of percentage of disablement as certified by an authorized physician. The relief for total permanent disability will be Rs. 25,000/-.
4. For loss of wages due to temporary partial disability which reduce the earning capacity of the victim, there will be a fixed monthly relief not exceeding Rs. 1,000/- per month upto a maximum of 3 months provided the victim has been hospitalized for a period exceeding 3 days and above 16 years of age.
5. In respect of damage to private property, upto Rs. 6,000/- per claim.
6. Apart from Public liability insurance Act policy, policies are also available to cover the legal liability of the insured against third parties for claims arising due to industrial accidents. Two different types of policies are available to cover accidents in industries like factories etc. and non industries like hotels, schools, exhibitions and storage tanks etc.

9.4.2 Claim Procedure

- The Insured has to give written notice to the company as soon as possible of any claim made against him (or any specific event or circumstance that may give rise to a claim being made against the Insured) which forms the subject of indemnity under the policy and shall give all such additional information as the company may require.
- Every claim, writ, summons or process and all documents relating to the event shall be forwarded to the Company immediately after they are received by the Insured, alongwith the claim form duly filled up.
- No admission, offer, promise or payment shall be made or given by or on behalf of the insured without the written consent of the company.
- The insured will have the right to take over and conduct in the name of the Insured in defense of any claim in case of voluntary public liability policies.
- In the event of liability rising under the policy or payment of a claim under the policy, the limit of indemnity per anyone year under the policy shall get reduced to the extent of quantum of liability to be paid or actual payment of such claim.
- No claim is payable under the policy unless the cause of action arises in India and the liability to pay claim is established against the Insured in an Indian Court. It is also to be understood that only Indian Law shall be applicable in such action.

9.5 EMPLOYEE STATE INSURANCE ACT, 1948

The Employees' State Insurance Act, 1948, has been described as an Act "to provide for certain benefits to employees in cases of sickness, maternity and employment injury and to make provision for certain other matters in relation thereof "Under the Act, the Employees' State Insurance Corporation has been set up to administer the Insurance Scheme.

The Scheme is applicable to industrial employees as defined in the Act. The Act operated in certain industrial areas as notified by the Government from time to time. It is intended that the Act will be eventually extended to all industrial areas in the country. Under the scheme a fund is maintained consisting of contributions from the employees, employers and the Government.

From this fund the following expenses are met:

(*i*) Sickness benefit, maternity benefit, disablement benefit, dependants' benefit (death) and medical treatment

(*ii*) Establishment and maintenance of hospital, dispensaries, etc. for the benefit of the insured persons and their families.

(*iii*) Administration of the Scheme.

9.5.1 Some Important Definitions

In this Act, unless there is anything repugnant in the subject or context,:

(1) *"appropriate government"* means, in respect of establishments under the control of the Central Government or a railway administration or a major port or a mine or oil field, the Central Government, and in all other cases, the State Government;

(2) *"confinement"* means labour resulting in the issue of a living child or labour after twenty-six weeks of pregnancy resulting in the issue of a child whether alive or dead;

(3) *"contribution"* means the sum of money payable to the Corporation by the principal employer in respect of an employee and includes any amount payable by or on behalf of the employee in accordance with the provisions of this Act;

(6) *"Corporation"* means the Employees' State Insurance Corporation set up under this Act;

[(6A) *"dependant"* means any of the following relatives of a deceased insured person, namely, :

(*i*) a widow, a minor legitimate or adopted son, an unmarried legitimate or adopted daughter;

(*ia*) a widowed mother;

(*ii*) if wholly dependent on the earnings of the insured person at the time of his death, a legitimate or adopted son or daughter who has attained the age of eighteen years and is infirm;

(*iii*) if wholly or in part dependent on the earnings of the insured person at the time of his death,:

(*a*) a parent other than a widowed mother,

(*b*) a minor illegitimate son, an unmarried illegitimate daughter or a daughter legitimate or adopted or illegitimate if married and a minor or if widowed and a minor,

(*c*) a minor brother or an unmarried sister or a widowed sister if a minor,

(*d*) a widowed daughter-in-law,

(*e*) a minor child of a pre-deceased son,

(*f*) a minor child of a pre-deceased daughter where no parent of the child is alive, or

(*g*) a paternal grand-parent if no parent of the insured person is alive,

(8) *"employment injury"* means a personal injury to an employee caused by accident or an occupational disease arising out of and in the course of his employment, being an insurable employment, whether the accident occurs or the occupational disease is contracted within or outside the territorial limits of India;]

(9) *"employee"* means any person employed for wages in or in connection with the work of a factory or establishment to which this Act applies and :

(*i*) who is directly employed by the principal employer on any work of, or incidental or preliminary to or connected with the work of, the factory or establishment whether such work is done by the employee in the factory or establishment or elsewhere; or

(*ii*) who is employed by or through an immediate employer on the premises of the factory or establishment or under the supervision of the principal employer or his agent on work which is ordinarily part of the work of the factory or establishment or which is preliminary to the work carried on in or incidental to the purpose of the factory or establishment; or

(*iii*) whose services are temporarily lent or let on hire to the principal employer by the person with whom the person whose services are so lent or let on hire has entered into a contract of service;

and includes any person employed for wages on any work connected with the administration of the factory or establishment or any part, department or branch thereof or with the purchase of raw materials for, or the distribution or sale of the products of, the factory or establishment or any person engaged as an apprentice, not being an apprentice engaged under the Apprentices Act, 1961, or under the standing orders of the establishment; but does not include :

(*a*) any member of the Indian naval, military or air forces; or

(*b*) any person so employed whose wages excluding remuneration for overtime work exceed such wages as may be prescribed by the Central Government:

PROVIDED that an employee whose wages excluding remuneration for overtime work exceed such wages as may be prescribed by the Central Government at any time after and not before the beginning of the contribution period, shall continue to be an employee until the end of that period;]

(10) *"exempted employee"* means an employee who is not liable under this Act to pay the employee's contribution;

(11) *"family"* means all or any of the following relatives of an insured person, namely, :

(*i*) a spouse;

(*ii*) a minor legitimate or adopted child dependent upon the insured person;

(*iii*) a child who is wholly dependent on the earnings of the insured person and who is :

(*a*) receiving education, till he or she attains the age of twenty-one years,

(*b*) an unmarried daughter;

(*iv*) a child who is infirm by reason of any physical or mental abnormality or injury and is wholly dependent on the earnings of the insured person, so long as the infirmity continues;

(*v*) dependent parents;

(12) *"factory"* means any premises including the precincts thereof :

(*a*) whereon ten or more persons are employed or were employed for wages on any day of the preceding twelve months, and in any part of which a manufacturing process is being carried on with the aid of power or is ordinarily so carried on, or

(*b*) whereon twenty or more persons are employed or were employed for wages on any day of the preceding twelve months, and in any part of which a manufacturing process is being carried on without the aid of power or is ordinarily so carried on.

but does not include a mine subject to the operation of the Mines Act, 1952 or a railway running shed;]

(13) *"immediate employer"*, in relation to employees employed by or through him, means a person who has undertaken the execution, on the premises of a factory, or an establishment to which this Act applies or under the supervision of the principal employer or his agent, of the whole or any part of any work which is ordinarily part of the work of the factory or establishment of the principal employer or is preliminary to the work carried on in, or incidental to the purpose of, any such factory or establishment, and includes a person by whom the services of an employee who has entered into a contract of service with him are temporarily lent or let on hire to the principal employer [4][and includes a contractor];

(13A) *"insurable employment"* means an employment in a factory or establishment to which this Act applies;]

(14) *"insured person"* means a person who is or was an employee in respect of whom contributions are or were payable under this Act and who is, by reason thereof, entitled to any of the benefits provided by this Act;

(14A) *"managing agent"* means any person appointed or acting as the representative of another person for the purpose of carrying on such other person's trade or business, but does not include an individual manager subordinate to an employer;]

(14AA) *"manufacturing process"* shall have the meaning assigned to it in the Factories Act, 1948;

(14B) *"mis-carriage"* means expulsion of the contents of a pregnant uterus at any period prior to or during the twenty-sixth week of pregnancy but does not include any mis-carriage, the causing of which is punishable under the Indian Penal Code;

(15) *"occupier"* of the factory shall have the meaning assigned to it in the Factories Act, 1948;

(15A) *"permanent partial disablement"* means such disablement of a permanent nature, as reduces the earning capacity of an employee in every employment which he was capable of undertaking at the time of the accident resulting in the disablement:

PROVIDED that every injury specified in Part II of the Second Schedule shall be deemed to result in permanent partial disablement;

(15B) *"permanent total disablement"* means such disablement of a permanent nature as incapacitates an employee for all work which he was capable of performing at the time of the accident resulting in such disablement:

PROVIDED that permanent total disablement shall be deemed to result from every injury specified in Part I of the Second Schedule or from any combination of injuries specified in Part II thereof where the aggregate percentage of the loss of earning capacity, as specified in the said Part II against those injuries, amounts to one hundred per cent or more;

(17) *"principal employer"* means :

(*i*) in a factory, the owner or occupier of the factory, and includes the managing agent of such owner or occupier, the legal representative of a deceased owner or occupier, and where a person has been named as the manager of the factory under the Factories Act, 1948; the person so named;

(*ii*) in any establishment under the control of any department of any government in India, the authority appointed by such government in this behalf or where no authority is so appointed, the head of the department;

(*iii*) in any other establishment, any person responsible for the supervision and control of the establishment;

(19A) *"seasonal factory"* means a factory which is exclusively engaged in one or more of the following manufacturing processes, namely, cotton ginning, cotton or jute pressing, decortication of groundnuts, the manufacture of coffee, indigo, lac, rubber, sugar including gur or tea or any manufacturing process which is incidental to or connected with any of the aforesaid processes and includes a factory which is engaged for a period not exceeding seven months in a year :

(*a*) in any process of blending, packing or repacking of tea or coffee; or

(*b*) in such other manufacturing process as the Central Government may, by notification in the Official Gazette, specify;

(20) *"sickness"* means a condition which requires medical treatment and attendance and necessitates abstention from work on medical grounds;

(21) *"temporary disablement"* means a condition resulting from an employment injury which requires medical treatment and renders an employee, as a result of such injury, temporarily incapable of doing the work which he was doing prior to or at the time of the injury;

(22) *"wages"* means all remuneration paid or payable, in cash to an employee, if the terms of the contract of employment, express or implied, were fulfilled and includes any payment to an employee in respect of any period of authorised leave, lock-out, strike which is not illegal or lay-off and other additional remuneration, if any, paid at intervals not exceeding two months], but does not include :

(*a*) any contribution paid by the employer to any pension fund or provident fund, or under this Act;

(*b*) any travelling allowance or the value of any travelling concession;

(*c*) any sum paid to the person employed to defray special expenses entailed on him by the nature of his employment; or

(*d*) any gratuity payable on discharge.

(23) *"wage period"* in relation to an employee means the period in respect of which wages are ordinarily payable to him whether in terms of the contract of employment, express or implied or otherwise.

Registration of Factories and Establishments

Section 2A : Every factory or establishment to which this Act applies shall be registered within such time and in such manner as may be specified in the regulations made in this behalf.

Applicability

1. All factories excluding seasonal factories employing 10 or more persons and working with electric power.
2. All factories excluding seasonal factories employing 20 or more persons and working without electric power.
3. Any establishment which the Government may specifically notify as being covered.
4. Shop employing 20 or more persons.

Eligibility

1. Any person employed for wages (upto Rs. 6,500) in or in connection with the work of a factory or establishment end.
2. Any person who is directly employed by the employer in a factory or through his agent on work which is ordinarily part of the work of the factory or incidental to purpose of the factory.

All Employees to be Insured

Section 38 : Subject to the provisions of this Act, all employees in factories or establishments to which this Act applies shall be insured in the manner provided by this Act.

Establishment of Employees' State insurance Corporation

Section 3 of the Act provides that :

(1) With effect from such date as the Central Government may, by notification in the Official Gazette, appoint in this behalf, there shall be established for the administration of the scheme of employees' state insurance in accordance with the provisions of this Act a Corporation to be known as the Employees' State Insurance Corporation.

(2) The Corporation shall be a body corporate by the name of Employees' State Insurance Corporation having perpetual succession and a common seal and shall by the said name sue and be sued.

Employees' State Insurance Fund

Section 26 deals with the establishment of Employees' State Insurance Fund (ESIF):

(1) All contributions paid under this Act and all other moneys received on behalf of the Corporation shall be paid into a fund called the Employees' State Insurance Fund which shall be held and administered by the Corporation for the purposes of this Act.

(2) The Corporation may accept grants, donations and gifts from the Central or any State Government, local authority, or any individual or body whether incorporated or not, for all or any of the purposes of this Act.

(3) Subject to the other provisions contained in this Act and to any rules or regulations made in this behalf, all moneys accruing or payable to the said Fund shall be paid into the Reserve Bank of India or such other bank as may be approved by the Central Government to the credit on an account styled the account of the Employees' State Insurance Fund.

(4) Such account shall be operated on by such officers as may be authorised by the Standing Committee with the approval of the Corporation.

Purposes for which the Fund may be Expended

Section 28 : Subject to the provisions of this Act and of any rules made by the Central Government in that behalf, the Employees' State Insurance Fund shall be expended only for the following purposes, namely:

(*i*) payment of benefits and provision of medical treatment and attendance to insured persons and, where the medical benefit is extended to their families, the provision of such medical benefit to their families, in accordance with the provisions of this Act and defraying the charges and costs in connection therewith;

(*ii*) payment of fees and allowances to members of the Corporation, the Standing Committee and the Medical Benefit Council, the regional boards, local committees and regional and local Medical Benefit Councils;

(*iii*) payment of salaries, leave and joining time allowances, travelling and compensatory allowances, gratuities and compassionate allowances, pensions, contributions to provident or other benefit fund of officers and servants of the Corporation and meeting the expenditure in respect of offices and other services set up for the purpose of giving effect to the provisions of this Act;

(*iv*) establishment and maintenance of hospitals, dispensaries and other institutions and the provisions of medical and other ancillary services for the benefit of insured persons and, where the medical benefit is extended to their families, their families;

(*v*) payment of contributions to any State Government, local authority or any private body or individual, towards the cost of medical treatment and attendance provided to insured persons and, where the medical benefit is extended to their families, their families including the cost of any building and equipment in accordance with any agreement entered into by the Corporation;

(*vi*) defraying the cost including all expenses of auditing the accounts of the Corporation and of the valuation of its assets and liabilities;

(*vii*) defraying the cost including all expenses of the Employees' State Insurance Courts set up under this Act;

(*viii*) payment of any sums under any contract entered into for the purposes of this Act by the Corporation or the Standing Committee or by any officer duly authorised by the Corporation or the Standing Committee in that behalf;

(*ix*) payment of sums under any decree, order or award of any Court or Tribunal against the Corporation or any of its officers or servants for any act done in the execution of his duty or under a compromise or settlement of any suit or other legal proceeding or claim instituted or made against the Corporation;

(*x*) defraying the cost and other charges of instituting or defending any civil or criminal proceedings arising out of any action taken under this Act;

(*xi*) defraying expenditure, within the limits prescribed, on measures for the improvement of the health and welfare of insured persons and for the rehabilitation and re-employment of insured persons who have been disabled or injured; and

(*xii*) such other purposes as may be authorised by the Corporation with the previous approval of the Central Government.

9.5.2 Contributions

Section 39

(1) The contribution payable under this Act in respect of an employee shall comprise contribution payable by the employer (hereinafter referred to as the employer's contribution) and contribution payable by the employee (hereinafter referred to as the employee's contribution) and shall be paid to the Corporation.

(2) The contributions shall be paid at such rates as may be prescribed by the Central Government:

PROVIDED that the rates so prescribed shall not be more than the rates which were in force immediately before the commencement of the Employees' State Insurance (Amendment) Act, 1989.

(3) The wage period in relation to an employee shall be the unit in respect of which all contributions shall be payable under this Act.

(4) The contributions payable in respect of each wage period shall ordinarily fall due on the last day of the wage period, and where an employee is employed for part of the wage period, or is employed under two or more employers during the same wage period, the contributions shall fall due on such days as may be specified in the regulations.

(5)(*a*) If any contribution payable under this Act is not paid by the principal employer on the date on which such contribution has become due, he shall be liable to pay simple interest at the rate of twelve per cent per annum or at such higher rate as may be specified in the regulations till the date of its actual payment:

PROVIDED that higher interest specified in the regulations shall not exceed the lending rate of interest charged by any scheduled bank.

(*b*) Any interest recoverable under clause (a) may be recovered as an arrear of land revenue or under sections 45C to 45-1.

Explanation : In this sub-section, "scheduled bank" means a bank for the time being included in the Second Schedule to the Reserve Bank of India Act, 1934 (2 of 1934).]

9.5.3 Benefits

Section 46 : (1) Subject to the provisions of this Act, the insured persons, their dependants or the persons hereinafter mentioned, as the case may be, shall be entitled to the following benefits, namely:

(*a*) periodical payments to any insured person in case of his sickness certified by a duly appointed medical practitioner or by any other person possessing such qualifications and experience as the Corporation may, by regulations, specify in this behalf (hereinafter referred to as sickness benefit;

(*b*) periodical payments to an insured woman in case of confinement or miscarriage or sickness arising out of pregnancy, confinement, premature birth of child or miscarriage, such woman being certified to be eligible for such payments by an authority specified in this behalf by the regulations (hereinafter referred to as maternity benefit);

(*c*) periodical payments to an insured person suffering from disablement as a result of an employment injury sustained as an employee under this Act and certified to be eligible for such payments by an authority specified in this behalf by the regulations (hereinafter referred to as disablement benefit;

(*d*) periodical payments to such dependants of an insured person who dies as a result of an employment injury sustained as an employee under this Act, as are entitled to compensation under this Act (hereinafter referred to as dependants' benefit;

(*e*) medical treatment for and attendance on insured persons (hereinafter referred to as medical benefit; and

(*f*) payment to the eldest surviving member of the family of an insured person who has died, towards the expenditure on the funeral of the deceased insured person or, where the insured person did not have a family or was not living with his family at the time of his death, to the person who actually incurs the expenditure on the funeral of the deceased insured person (to be known as funeral expenses):

PROVIDED that the amount of such payment shall not exceed such amount as may be prescribed by the Central Government] and the claim for such payment shall be made within three months of the death of the insured person or within such extended period as the Corporation or any officer or authority authorised by it in this behalf may allow.

(2) The Corporation may, at the request of the appropriate government, and subject to such conditions as may be laid down in the regulations, extend the medical benefit to the family of an insured person.

Benefits Illustrated

1. Free medical treatment is offered to covered employees at hospital and dispensaries run by the ESI Corporation.
2. About 7/12th of employees normal wage will be payable to him by ESI during sickness.
3. Maternity benefit for 12 weeks of which not more than 6 weeks should be preceding confinement.
4. Injury during/in course of employment resulting in temporary/permanent disablement entities the covered employee to a regular payment to substitute his lost wages.
5. Death during course of employment entities specified dependents to a regular payment.
6. One time payment of Rs. 1,500 to help meet furneral expenses.

Other Benefits

Supply of special aids : Insured persons and members of their families are provided artificial limbs, hearing aids, artificial dentures, spectacles (for insured person only) and artificial appliances like spinal supports, cervical collars, walking callopers, crutches, wheel chairs and cardiac pace makers, dialysis/dialysis with kidney transplant etc. as part of medical care under the ESI Scheme.

9.5.4 Punishment for False Statements

Section 84 : Whoever, for the purpose of causing any increase in payment or benefit under this Act, or for the purpose of causing any payment or benefit to be made where no payment or benefit is authorised by or under this Act, or for the purpose of avoiding any payment to be made by himself under this Act or enabling any other person to avoid any such payment, knowingly makes or causes to be made any false statement or false representation, shall be punishable with imprisonment for a term which may extend to [six months], or with fine not exceeding [two thousand] rupees, or with both.

PROVIDED that where an insured person is convicted under this section, he shall not be entitled for any cash benefit under this Act for such period as may be prescribed by the Central Government.

Punishment for failure to pay contributions, etc.

Section 85 : If any person :

(*a*) fails to pay any contribution which under this Act he is liable to pay, or

(*b*) deducts or attempts to deduct from the wages of an employee the whole or any part of the employer's contribution, or

(*c*) in contravention of section 72 reduces the wages or any privileges or benefits admissible to an employee, or

(*d*) in contravention of section 73 or any regulation dismisses, discharges, reduces or otherwise punishes an employee, or

(*e*) fails or refuses to submit any return required by the regulations, or makes a false return, or

(*f*) obstructs any Inspector or other official of the Corporation in the discharge of his duties, or

(*g*) is guilty of any contravention of or non-compliance with any of the requirements of this Act or the rules or the regulations in respect of which no special penalty is provided, [he shall be punishable :

[(*i*) where he commits an offence under clause (*a*), with imprisonment for a term which may extend to three years but

(*a*) which shall not be less than one year, in case of failure to pay the employee's contribution which has been deducted by him from the employee's wages and shall also be liable to fine of ten thousand rupees;

(*b*) which shall not be less than six months, in any other case and shall also be liable to fine of five thousand rupees:

PROVIDED that the Court may, for any adequate and special reasons to be recorded in the judgement, impose a sentence of imprisonment for a lesser term;

(*ii*) where he commits an offence under any of the clauses (b) to (g) (both inclusive), with imprisonment for a term which may extend to one year or with fine which may extend to four thousand rupees, or with both.]

Enhanced Punishment in certain cases after previous conviction

Section 185A : Whoever, having been convicted by a court of an offence punishable under this Act, commits the same offence shall, for every such subsequent offence, be punishable with imprisonment for a term which may extend to two years and with fine of five thousand rupees:

PROVIDED that where such subsequent offence is for failure by the employer to pay any contribution which under this Act he is liable to pay, he shall, for every such subsequent offence, be punishable with imprisonment for a term which may extend to five years but which shall not be less than two years and shall also be liable to fine of twenty-five thousand rupees.

The penal provisions may be summarised as follows:

Penal Provisions

1. *For employees' contribution* : Imprisonment for minimum 2 years to maximum 5 years and/or fine of Rs. 25,000/-.
2. *For employer's contribution* : Imprisonment for minimum 6 months to maximum 3 years and/or fine of Rs. 10,000/-.

Every employer has to the following documents as per the Act which shall at all time are ready for inspection.

9.5.5 Records to be kept Ready for Inspection

1. Attendance Register/Muster Roll.
2. Salary/Wage Register/Payroll.
3. EC (Employee's & Employer's Contribution) Statement.
4. Employees' Register U/R 32 (Form 7).
5. Accident Register U/R 66.
6. Return of Contribution (RC-Form 6).
7. Return of Declaration Forms (RDF-Form 3).
8. Receipted Copies of Challans.
9. Books of Account *viz.*, Cash/Bank, Expense Register, Sales/Purchase, Petty Cash Book, Ledger, Supporting Bills and Vouchers, a/w Delivery Challans (if any).

Key Terms

- Negligence
- Compensation
- Temporary Disablement
- Accident
- Motor Accident Claims Tribunal
- No Fault
- Certificate of Insurance
- Abandonment
- Sue and Labour Charges
- Contribution
- Subrogation
- Under Insurance
- Dependant
- Employee
- Family
- Permanent Partial Disablement
- Temporary Disablement
- Employees' State Insurance Fund
- In the Course of Employment
- Permanent Partial Disablement
- No Fault
- Hazardous Substance
- Hits and Run Accident
- Motor Vehicle
- Driving Licence
- Double Insurance
- General Average
- Particular Average
- Advance Freight
- Bottomry and Respondentia
- Employment Injury
- Exempted Employee
- Immediate Employer
- Permanent Total Disablement
- Wages

Questions for Review

1. Write short notes on :

   (*a*) in course of employment (*b*) disablement

   within the meaning of Workman Compensation Act, 1923.
2. Explain the liability of the employer under the Workman Compensation Act, 1923. How compensation is arrived at under the Act.
3. Explain the liability of the "owner" under the Public Liability Insurance Act, 1991. What procedure is followed for claiming relief and the compensation under the Act.
4. Discuss the powers and functions of Motor Accident Claims Tribunal (MACT).
5. Write short notes on :

   (*a*) Hit and Run Accident (*b*) No Fault Liability

   (*c*) Certificate of Insurance.
6. Briefly describe the compensation available to third parties for loss or damages under the Motor Vehicles Act, 1939 and 1988.
7. Define Insurable Interest. When insurable interest should exist? Distinguish between contingent and defeasible interest with reference to Marine Insurance Act, 1963.
8. Briefly explain the various maritime losses and their computation as per the provisions of Marine Insurance, Act, 1963.

9. Write short notes on :
   (a) Warranties
   (b) Voyage Policy
10. Define the following terms as per Employees State Insurance Act, 1948.
   (a) Dependent
   (b) Contribution
   (c) Family
   (d) Permanent Partial Disablement
   (e) Permanent Total Disablement
   (f) Principal Employer
11. Write short notes on :
   (a) Registration of Factories and Establishment
   (b) Employees State Insurance Fund
12. List the various benefits to employees under the Employees State Insurance Act, 1948.

Sugested Readings

1. *Bare Acts*
2. *Liability and Engineering Insurance,* IC79, Insurance Institute of India, Mumbai, 2000.
3. *Motor Insurance,* IC72, Insurance Institute of India, Mumbai, 2003.
4. *Bare Acts*
5. Avtar Singh, *Law of Insurance,* Eastern Book Company, 2004.
6. *Marine Clauses,* IC-63, Insurance Institute of India, Mumbai, 2000.
7. *Marine Insurance Claims,* IC-66, Insurance Institute of India, Mumbai, 2005.
8. N.D. Kapoor & Rajni Abbi, *General Law,* Sultan Chand & Sons, 1991.
9. Avtar Singh, *Law of Insurance,* Eastern Book Company, 2005.

Web Resources

- *www.ndc-nihfw.org*
- *www.irdaindia.org*
- *www.bimaonline.com*
- *www.bimaonline.com*
- *orientalinsurance.nic.in*
- *on-lyne.com*
- *invert.economictimes.indiatimes.com*
- *www.bimaonline.com*
- *www.indiainfoline.com*

Miscellaneous Laws Concerning Insurance

Chapter **10**

Chapter Objectives

After reading this chapter you will be able to understand :

- *Miscellaneous Laws affects Insurance Contracts*
- *Documents and Procedures in such statutes.*

The goods and passengers may be transported by land, air and sea routes. In India, various statutes have been promulgated from time to time with respect to these modes. These laws have a reference to the various *aspects* of insurance business which *inter-alia* include the subject matter of insurance, insurable interest, liability of the insurer towards insured and third parties, settlement of claims, powers of the central government etc. The said laws include:

(*a*) The Marine Insurance Act, 1963
(*b*) The Motor Vehicles Act 1939 & 1988
(*c*) The Inland Steam Vessels Act, 1917 & Amended Act of 1977
(*d*) The Carriage of Goods by Sea Act, 1925
(*e*) The Merchant Shipping Act, 1958
(*f*) The Indian Railways Act, 1890
(*g*) The Carriers Act, 1865
(*h*) The Carriage by Air Act, 1972
(*i*) The Indian Ports (Major Ports) Act, 1963
(*j*) The Bill of Lading Act, 1855
(*k*) The Indian Post Office Act, 1898
(*l*) Multi Modal Transportation Act, 1993
(*m*) Indian State Act, 1990
(*n*) Consumer Protection Act, 1986
(*o*) Arbitration Act, Lok Adalat and Ombodsment.

The act referred to in (*a*) & (*b*) above have been discussed in detail in the earlier chapters. The others are briefly discussed in the following sections.

10.1 The Inland Steam Vessels Act, 1917 & Ammended Act of 1977

Inland Steam Vessels Act, 1917 was promulgated in 1917 and was amended several times. A major amendment was in 1977 and afterwards it was amended in 2005 recently. The act provides that the provisions of Chapter VII of the Motor Vehicles Act regarding insurance of mechanically propelled vehicles against third party risks are applicable to steam vessels. The act makes compulsory for the owners of operator of inland vessels to insure against legal liability of death, bodily injury or damage cause to third parties and passengers.

10.1.1 Definitions

Section 2 of the Act defines an inland mechanically propelled vessel :

In this Act, unless there is anything repugnant in the subject or context,

(*a*) "inland vessel" or "inland mechanically propelled vessel" means a mechanically propelled vessel, which ordinarily plies on inland water, but does not include fishing vessel and a ship registered under the Merchant Shipping Act, 1958;

(*b*) "inland water" means any canal, river, lake or other navigable water;

(*c*) "mechanically propelled vessel" means every description of vessel propelled wholly or in part by electricity, steam or other mechanical power including dumb vessel towed by the mechanically propelled vessel and vessel propelled by outboard motor

A "goods service vessel" means any mechanically propelled vessel used or adapted to be used for carriage of cargo for hire or reward (Section 145);

A "public service vessel" means any mechanically propelled vessel used or adapted to be used for the carriage of passengers for hire or reward;

Chapter VI A of the Act deals with insurance of *mechanically propelled vehicles* against third party risks. Section 54C of the Act was amended in 2005 so as to make section 134 and Chapters X, XI and XII of the Motor Vehicles Act, 1988, applicable in relation to mechanically propelled vessels with certain modifications and also to provide insurance of vessels against third party risks, compensation for accidents and Claims Tribunal, etc.

10.1.2 Application of the Act

Section 54C : The provisions of Chapter VIII of the Motor Vehicles Act, 1939, shall *mutatis mutandis* apply, in relation to the insurance of mechanically propelled vessels against third party risks as they apply in relation to motor vehicles, subject to the following modifications, namely :

(*a*) in section 134 and throughout in Chapters X, XI and XII, :

(*i*) references to "motor" or "motor vehicle" or "vehicle" shall be construed as references to "mechanically propelled vessel";

(*ii*) references to "public place" shall be construed as references to "inland water", and such other consequential amendments as the rules of grammar may require shall also be made;

(*iii*) references to "public service vehicle" shall be construed as references to "public service vessel";

(*iv*) references to "goods vehicle" shall be construed as references to "goods service vessel";

(*v*) references to "State Transport" shall be construed as references to "State Water Transport";

(*vi*) references to "driver" or "driver of a vehicle" shall be construed as references to "master of a vessel";

(*vii*) references to "driving licence" shall be construed as references to "a certificate granted under Chapter III of the Inland Vessels Act, 1917";

A driving licence under the act means "a certificate granted under Chapter III.

It therefore follows that an inland vessel is a mechanically propelled vessel for the purposes of Motor Vehicles Act, 1988 and all provisions of third party risks apply accordingly.

Duty of Driver in Case of Accident or Injury to a Person

Section 105A : When any person is injured or any property of third party is damaged as a result of an accident in which an inland mechanically propelled vessel is involved, the master or the driver of the vessel or other person in charge of the vessel shall :

(*a*) take all reasonable steps to secure medical attention for the injured person, and, if necessary, convey him to the nearest hospital, unless the injured person or his guardian in case he is a minor, desires otherwise;

(*b*) give on demand by a police officer any information required by him, or, if no police officer is present, report the circumstances of the occurrence at the nearest police station as soon as possible, and in any case within twenty-four hours of the occurrence."

10.1.3 Claims Tribunal

State government is empowered to constitute tribunals in respective areas. Section 110 also defines the constitution of the tribunal.

Section 110. (1) The State Government may, by notification in the Official Gazette, constitute one or more Inland Vessels Accidents Claims Tribunals (hereinafter referred to as the Claims Tribunals) for such areas as may be specified in the notification for the purpose of adjudicating upon claims for compensation in respect of accidents involving the death of, or bodily injury to, persons arising out of the use of mechanically propelled vessels or damage to any property of a third party so arising, or both :

Provided that where such claim includes a claim for compensation in respect of damage to property exceeding rupees ten thousand the claimant may, at his option, refer the claim to a civil court for adjudication and where a reference is so made, the Claims Tribunal shall have no jurisdiction to entertain any question relating to such claim.

(2) A Claims Tribunal shall consist of such number of members, as the State Government may think fit to appoint and where it consists of two or more members, one of them shall be appointed as the Chairman thereof.

(3) A person shall not be qualified for appointment as a member of a Claims Tribunal unless he :

(*a*) is, or has been, a Judge of a High Court, or

(*b*) is, or has been, a District Judge, or

(c) is qualified for appointment as a Judge of the High Court.

(4) Where two or more Claims Tribunals are constituted for any area, the State Government may, by general or special order, regulate the distribution of business among them.

Application for Compensation

Section 110A : (1) An application for compensation arising out of an accident of the nature specified in sub-section (1) of section 110 may be made :

(*a*) by the person who has sustained the injury, or

(*b*) where death has resulted from the accident, by all or any of the legal representatives of the deceased, or

(c) by any agent duly authorised by the person injured or all or any of the legal representatives of the deceased, as the case may be :

Provided that where all the legal representatives of the deceased have not joined in any such application for compensation, the application shall be made on behalf of or for the benefit of all the legal representatives of the deceased and the legal representatives who have not so joined, shall be impleaded as respondents to the application.

(2) Every application under sub-section (1) shall be made to the Claims Tribunal having jurisdiction over the area in which the accident occurred, and shall be in such form and shall contain such particulars as may be prescribed.

(3) No application for compensation under this section shall be entertained unless it is made within six months of the occurrence of the accident:

Provided that the Claims Tribunal may entertain the application after the expiry of the said period of six months if it is satisfied that the applicant was prevented by sufficient cause from making the application in time.

Option Regarding Claim for Compensation in Certain Cases

Section 110AA : Notwithstanding anything contained in the Workmen's Compensation Act, 1923, where the death or bodily injury to any person gives rise to a claim for compensation under this Act and also under the Workmen's Compensation Act, 1923, the person entitled to compensation may claim such compensation under either of those Acts but not under both.

Award of Claim Tribunal

Section 110B : On receipt of an application for compensation made under Section 110A, the Claims Tribunal shall, after giving the parties an opportunity of being heard, hold an inquiry into the claim and may make an award determining the amount of compensation which appears to it to be just and specifying the person or persons to whom compensation shall be paid; and in making the award the Claims Tribunal shall specify the amount which shall be paid by the insurer or owner or master or driver of the vessel involved in the accident or by all or any of them, as the case may be."

Persons who carry goods or passengers, for hire or gratuitously, by land, water or air, are the carriers. In India, among the land carriers, the railways are governed under Indian Railways Act, 1890, and the road transport vehicles under the Carriers Act, 1865. The sea carriers are governed under the Carriage of Goods by Sea Act, 1925, and the international air carriers by the Carriage by Air Act, 1934. The inland air carriers are governed by the common law.

10.2 The Carriage of Goods by Sea Act, 1925

The law relating to carriage of goods by sea is contained in the Bill of Lading Act, 1856 and the Carriage of Goods by Sea Act, 1925. The contract involved in the carriage of goods by Sea Act, 1925 is popularly known as contract of affreightment. A contract of affreightment[1] may be of two forms:

(*a*) *Charter party* : where an entire ship, or a principal part of a ship is placed at the disposal of merchant (known as a charterer)

(*b*) *Bill of lading* : where the goods are to be carried in a general ship and the person consigning the goods is known as a shipper.

10.2.1 Definitions

The Act *inter-alia* defines the various terms as follows :

(*a*) *"carrier"* includes the owner or the charterer who enters into a contract of carriage with a shipper;

(*b*) *"contract of carriage"* applies only to contracts of carriage covered by a bill of lading or any similar document of title, in so far as such, document relates to the carriage of goods by sea including any bill of lading or any similar document as aforesaid issued under or pursuant to a charter party from the moment at which such bill of lading or similar document of title regulates the relations between a carrier and a holder of the same;

(*c*) *"goods"* includes goods, wares, merchandises, and articles of every kind whatsoever, except live animals and cargo which by the contract of carriage is stated as being carried on deck and is so carried;

(*d*) *"ship"* means any vessel used for the carriage of goods by sea;

(*e*) *"carriage of goods"* covers the period from the time when the goods are loaded on to the time when they are discharged from the ship.

Nature of Contract

The carrier (ship owner) undertakes the responsibility of carrying the goods of a consignor (charterer/shipper) safely and securely to the destination. In a contract of Carriage by Sea following conditions are implied:

(*a*) Warranty of seaworthiness.

(*b*) Warranty of commencement of voyage : that the ship shall be ready to commence the voyage and shall carry out the same with all reasonable dispatch and diligence.

(*c*) Non-deviation of voyage.

(*d*) Shipper not to ship dangerous goods.

Schedule to the Act contains the various rules and regulations.

Article III : Responsibilities and Liabilities

The carrier shall be bound, before and at the beginning of the voyage, to exercise due diligence to :

(*a*) make the ship seaworthy;

(*b*) properly man, equip, and supply the ship;

(*c*) make the holds, refrigerating and cool chambers, and all other parts of the ship in which goods are carried, fit and safe for their reception, carriage and preservation.

The act deals with three aspects of a shipowners liabilities towards cargo owner:

(*i*) the circumstances when the shipowner is deemed to be liable for loss or damage to cargo unless he proves otherwise;

(*ii*) the circumstance when the shipowner is exempted from liability, i.e., when loss or damage is caused by events outside his control, e.g., perils of the seas;

(*iii*) the limits of liability of a shipowner for loss of or damage to cargo calculated in monetary terms per package or unit of cargo.

Article IV : Rights and Immunities

It provides that :

1. Neither the carrier nor the ship shall be liable for loss or damage arising or resulting from unseaworthiness unless caused by want of due diligence on the part of the carrier to make the ship seaworthy, and to secure that the ship is properly manned, equipped and supplied, and to make the holds, refrigerating and cool chambers and all other parts of the ship in which goods are carried fit and safe for their reception, carriage and preservation in accordance with the provisions of paragraph 1 of Article III.

   Whenever loss or damage has resulted from unseaworthiness the burden of proving the exercise of due diligence shall be on the carrier or other person claiming exemption under this section.

2. Neither the carrier nor the ship shall be responsible for loss or damage arising or resulting from:

   (*a*) act, neglect, or default of the master, mariner, pilot, or the servants of the carrier in the navigation or in the management of the ship;

   (*b*) fire, unless caused by the actual fault or privity of the carrier;

   (*c*) perils, dangers and accidents of the sea or other navigable waters;

   (*d*) act of God;

   (*e*) act of war;

   (*f*) act of public enemies;

(*g*) arrest or restraint of princes, rulers of people, or seizure under legal process;
(*h*) quarantine restriction;
(*i*) act or omission of the shipper or owner of the goods, his agent, or representative;
(*j*) strikes or lock-outs or stoppage or restraint of labour from whatever cause, whether partial or general;
(*k*) riots and civil commotions;
(*l*) saving or attempting to save life or property at sea;
(*m*) wastage in bulk or weight or any other loss or damage arising from inherent defect, quality, or vice of the goods;
(*n*) insufficiency of packing;
(*o*) insufficiency or inadequacy of marks;
(*p*) latent defects not discoverable by due diligence;
(*q*) any other cause arising without the actual fault or privity of the carrier, or without the fault or neglect of the agents or servants of the carrier, but the burden of proof shall be on the person claiming the benefit of this exception to show that neither the actual fault or privity of the carrier nor the fault or neglect of the agents or servants of the carrier contributed to the loss or damage.

3. The shipper shall not be responsible for loss or damage sustained by the carrier or the ship arising or resulting from any cause without the act, fault or neglect of the shipper, his agents or his servants.

4. Any deviation in saving or attempting to save life or property at sea, or any reasonable deviation shall not be deemed to be infringement or breach of these Rules or of the contract of carriage, and the carrier shall not be liable for any loss or damage resulting therefrom.

5. Neither the carrier nor the ship shall in any event be or become liable for any loss or damage to or in connection with goods in an amount exceeding £ 100 per package or unit, or the equivalent of that sum in other currency, unless the nature and value of such goods have been declared by the shipper before shipment and inserted in the bill of lading.

This declaration is embodied in the bill of lading shall be *prima facie* evidence, but shall not be binding or conclusive on the carrier.

By agreement between the carrier, master or agent of the carrier and the shipper another maximum amount than that mentioned in this paragraph may be fixed, provided that such maximum shall not be less than the figure above named.

Neither the carrier nor the ship shall be responsible in any event for loss or damage to or in connection with goods if the nature or value thereof has been knowingly mis-stated by the shipper in the bill of lading.

6. Goods of an inflammable, explosive or dangerous nature to the shipment whereof the carrier, master or agent of the carrier, has not consented, with knowledge of their nature and character, may at any time before discharge be landed at any place or destroyed or rendered innocuous by the carrier without compensation, and the shipper of such goods shall be liable for all damages and expenses directly or indirectly arising out of or resulting from such shipment.

If any such goods shipped with such knowledge and consent shall become a danger to the ship or cargo, they may in like manner be landed at any place or destroyed or rendered innocuous by the carrier without liability on the part of the carrier except to general average, if any.

It therefore implies that :

1. A carrier of goods by sea, that is, a shipowner is liable only for loss or damage arising or resulting from his negligence, fault or failure in the duties and obligations provided in the Act, and not otherwise.

2. A shipowner cannot limit his liability arising from his negligence or failure in the duties and any clause in the contract to that effect shall be null and void and inoperative.
3. The carrier is not responsible for any loss or damage to goods exceeding £ 100 per package or unit or its equivalent unless the nature and value of such goods have been declared by the shipper and inserted in the bill of lading.

Article V : Surrender of Rights and Immunities Increase of Responsibilities and Liabilities

A carrier shall be at liberty to surrender in whole or in part all or any of his rights and immunities or to increase any of his responsibilities and liabilities under the Rules contained in any of these Articles, provided such surrender or increase shall be embodied in the bill of lading issued to the shipper.

The provisions of these Rules shall not be applicable to charter-parties, but if bills of lading are issued in the case of a ship under a charter-party, they shall comply with the terms of these Rules. Nothing in these Rules shall be held, to prevent the insertion in a bill of lading of any lawful provision regarding general average.

Average VI : Special Conditions

Notwithstanding the provisions of the preceding Articles, a carrier, master or agent of the carrier, and a shipper shall, in regard to any particular goods, be at liberty to enter into any agreement in any terms as to the responsibility and liability of the carrier for such goods, and as to the rights and immunities of the carrier in respect of such goods, or his obligation as to seaworthiness so far as the stipulation is not contrary to public policy, or the care of diligence of his servants or agents in regard to the loading, handling, stowage, carriage, custody, care, and discharge of the goods carried by sea, provided that in this case no bill of lading has been or shall be issued and that the terms agreed shall be embodied in a receipt which shall be a non-negotiable document and shall be marked as such.

Any agreement so entered into shall have full legal effect :

Provided that this Article shall not apply to ordinary commercial shipment made in the ordinary course of trade, but only to other shipments where the character or condition of the property to be carried or the circumstances, terms and conditions under which the carriage is to be performed, as such are reasonably to justify a special agreement.

Average VII : Limitations on the Application of the Rules

Nothing herein contained shall prevent a carrier or a shipper from entering into any agreement, stipulation, condition, reservation or exemption as to the responsibility and liability of the carrier or the ship for the loss or damage to or in connection with the custody and care and handling of goods prior to the loading on and subsequent to the discharge from the ship on which the goods are carried by sea.

The carrier can enter into agreements etc. relating to the responsibility and liability for loss/damage before loading of goods and also after discharge of goods.

Average VIII : Limitation of Liability

The provisions of these Rules shall not affect the right and obligation of the carrier under any Statute for the time being in force relating to the limitation of the liability of owners of sea-going vessels.

Bill of Lading : *A bill of lading is a document acknowledging the shipment of goods, signed by or on behalf of the carrier and containing the terms and conditions on which it has been agreed to carry the goods. It is a quasi-negotiable instrument. It is a document of title and can be transferred by endorsement and delivery. It is generally used for the carriage of goods on a general ship, i.e., a ship which is used for the carriage of the goods of several merchants who wish to have them conveyed by her and which is not employed for the carriage of a charterer's goods only.*

A bill of lading may be issued even where the ship is chartered. In such a case charter party will be the document evidencing the contract of affreightment, while the bill of lading would only operate as a mere acknowledgement of the receipt of the goods.

{*Source:* Website of the Indian Institute of Materials Management}

10.3 THE MERCHANT SHIPPING ACT, 1958

The Merchant Shipping Act, 1958 provides a certain protection to shipowners against carriage losses. For example- the liability of the shipowner can be limited to certain maximum sum of certain losses, provided the incident- giving rise to such claim has arisen without the actual fault or privy of the shipowner. These claims may relate to loss of life personal injury or loss or damage to property on land or water. The act also confers the obligation on the shipowner to send his ship to sea in a seaworthy and safe condition. A gist of some important sections from an insurance perspective is given below :

10.3.1 Liability of Owners

Section 71 : Where any person is beneficially interested otherwise than by way of mortgage in any ship or share in a ship registered in the name of some other person as owner, the person so interested shall, as well as the registered owner, be subject to all the pecuniary penalties imposed by this or any other Act on the owners of ships or shares therein, so nevertheless that proceedings for the enforcement of any such penalties may be taken against both or either of the said parties with or without joining the other of them.

This section provides that if any beneficial interest is attached in name of any person other than mortgage, that person shall be liable for all pecuniary penalties which may arise under the act.

Engagements Between Seamen and Masters of Ships other than Indian Ships

Section 114 : (1) When the master of a ship other than an Indian ship engages a seaman at any port in India to proceed to any port outside India, he shall enter into an agreement with such seaman, and the agreement shall be made before a shipping master in the manner provided by this Act for the making of agreements in the case of foreign-going Indian ships.

(2) All the provisions of this Act respecting the form of such agreements and the stipulations to be contained in them and the making and signing of the same, shall be applicable to the engagement of such seaman.

(3) The master of a ship other than an Indian ship hall give to the shipping master a bond with the security of some approved person resident in India for such amount as may be fixed by the Central Government in respect of each seaman engaged by him at any port in India and conditioned for the due performance of such agreement and stipulations, and for the repayment to the Central Government of all expenses which may be incurred by it in respect of any such seaman who is discharged or left behind at any port out of India and becomes distressed and is relieved under the provisions of this Act:

Provided that the shipping master may waive the execution of a bond under this section where the owner of the ship has an agent at any port in India and such agent accepts liability in respect of all matters for which the master of the ship would be liable if he were to execute a bond under this section or may accept from the agent such security as may be approved by the Central Governmental.

(4) The fees fixed under section 90 shall be payable in respect of weary such engagement, and deductions from the wages of seamen so engaged may be made to the extent and in the manner allowed under the said section 90.

Payment Over of Property of Deceased Seamen by Shipping Master

Section 159 : Where any property of a deceased seaman or apprentice is paid or delivered to a shipping master, the shipping master, after deducting for expenses incurred in respect of that seaman or apprentice or of his property such sums as he thinks proper to allow, may :

(*a*) pay and deliver the residue to any claimants who can prove themselves to the satisfaction of the said shipping master to be entitled thereto, and the said shipping master shall discharged from all further liability in respect of the residue so paid or delivered; or

(*b*) if he thinks fit so to do, require probate or letters of administration or a certificate under the Indian Succession Act, 1925 (39 of 1925), to be taken out, and thereupon-pay and deliver the residue to the legal representatives of the deceased.

Liability of Central Government for Costs and Damage when Ship Wrongly Detained

Section 337 : If it appears that there was not reasonable and probable cause, by reason of the condition of the ship or the at or default of the owner or the master, for the provisional detention of a ship, the Central Government shall be liable to pay to the owner of the ship his costs of and incidental to the detention and survey of the ship, and also compensation for any loss or damage sustained by him by reason of the detention or survey.

When the central government wrongly detains any ship, it shall be liable for compensation for loss or damages.

Liability of Ship Owner for Costs when Ship Rightly Detained

Section 338 : If a ship is finally detained under this Part, or if it appears that a ship provisionally detained was at the time of such detention unsafe, or if a ship is detained was at the time of such detention unsafe, or if a ship is detained in pursuance of any provision of this Part which provides for the detention of a ship until a certain event occurs, the owner of the ship shall be liable to pay to the Central Government it costs of and incidental to the detention and survey of the ship; and the ship shall not be released until such costs are paid.

10.3.2 Procedures and Claims

Division of Loss in Case of Collision

Section 345 : (1) Whenever by the fault of two or more ships damage or loss is caused to one or more of them or to the cargo of one or more of them or to any property on board one or more of them, the liability to make good the damage or loss shall be in proportion to the degree in which each ship was at fault:

Provided that :

(*a*) if, having regard to all the circumstances of the case, it is not possible to establish different degrees of fault, the liability shall be apportioned equally;

(*b*) nothing in this section shall operate so as to render any ship liable for any loss or damage to which her fault has not contributed;

(c) nothing in this section shall operate so as to render any person under any contract, or shall be construed as imposing any liability upon any person from which he is exempted by any contract or by any provision of law, or as affecting the right of any person to limit his liability in the manner provided by law.

(2) For the purposes of this Part, references to damage or loss caused by the fault of a ship shall be construed as including references to any salvage or other expenses, consequent upon that fault, recoverable in law by way of damages.

Damages for Personal Injury

Section 346 : (1) Whenever loss of life or personal injuries are suffered by any person on board a ship owing to the fault of that ship and of any other ship or ships, the liability of the owners of the ships concerned shall be joint and several.

(2) Nothing in this section shall be construed as depriving any person of any right of defence on which, independently of this section, he might have relied in an action brought against him by the person injured, or any person entitled to sue in respect of such loss of life, or shall affect the right of any person to limit his liability in cases to which this section relates in the manner provided by law.

Right of Contribution

Section 347 : (1) Whenever loss of life or personal injuries are suffered by a person on board a ship owing to the fault of that ship and of any other ship or ships, and a proportion of the damages is recovered from the owner of one of the ships which exceeds the proportion in which she was in fault, the said owner may recover by way of contribution the amount of the excess from the owners of the other ship or ships to the extent to which those ships were respectively in fault:

Provided that no amount shall be so recovered which could not, by reason of any statutory or contractual limitation of, or exemption from, liability, or which could not for any the reason, have been recovered in the first instance as damages by the persons entitled to sue therefor.

(2) In addition to any other remedy provided by law, the person entitled to any contribution under sub-section (1) shall, for the purpose of recovering the contribution, have, subject to the provisions of this Act, the same rights and powers as the persons entitled to sue for damages in the first instance.

Duty of Master of Ship to Assist in Case of Collision

Section 348 : In every case of collision between two ships it shall be the duty of the master or person in charge of each ship, if and so far as be can do so without danger to his own ship, crew and passengers, if any :

(*a*) to render to the other ship, her master, crew and passengers, if any, such assistance as may be practicable and may be necessary to save them from any danger caused by the collision and to stay by the other ship until he has ascertained that she has no need of further assistance, and

(*b*) to give to the masters or persons in charge of the other ships the name of his own ship and of the port to which she belongs and also the names of the ports from which she comes and to which she is bound.

Collision to be Entered in Official Log

Section 349 : In every case of collision in which it is practicable so to do, the master of every ship concerned shall, immediately after the occurrence, cause a statement thereof and of the circumstances under which the same occurred to be entered in the official log book, if any, and the entry shall be signed by the master and also by the matte or one of the crew.

Report to Central Government of Accidents to Ships

Section 350 : When a ship has sustained or caused any accident occasioning loss of life or any serious injury to any person or has received any material damage affecting her seaworthiness or her efficiency either in her hull or is so altered in any part of her machinery as not to correspond with the particulars contained in any of the certificates issued under this Act in respect of the ship, the owner or master shall, within twenty-four hours after the happening of the accident or damage or as soon thereafter as possible, transmit to the Central Government or the nearest principal officer a report of the accident or damage and of the probable cause thereof stating the name of the ship, her official number, if any, her port of registry and the place where she is.

Notice of Loss of Indian Ship to be given to Central Government

Section 351 : If the owner or agent of any Indian ship has reason, owing to the non-appearance of the ship or to any other circumstance, to apprehend that the ship has been wholly lost, he shall, as soon as conveniently may be, send to the Central Government notice in writing of the loss and of the probable cause thereof stating the name of the ship, her official number, if any, and her port of registry.

Limitation of Liability of Owner for Damage

Section 352 : (1) The owner of a ship, whether an Indian ship or not, shall not, if any loss of life or personal injury to any person, or any loss of or damage to any property or rights of any kind, whether movable or immovable is caused without his actual fault or privity, :

(*a*) if no claim for damages in respect of loss of or damage to property or rights arises, be liable for damages in respect of loss of life or personal injury to an aggregate amount exceeding two hundred rupees for each ton of the ship's tonnage; or

(*b*) if no claim for damages in respect of loss of life or personal injury arises, be liable for damages in respect of loss of or damage to property or rights to an aggregate amount exceeding one hundred rupees for each ton of the ships tonnage; or

(*c*) if claims for damages in respect of loss of life or personal injury and also claims for damages in respect of loss of or damage to property or rights arise, be liable for damages to an aggregate amount exceeding two hundred rupees for each ton of the ship's tonnage:

Provided that in such a case claims for damages in respect of loss of life or personal injury shall, to the extent of an aggregate amount of one hundred rupees for each ton of the ship's tonnage, have priority over claims for damages in respect of loss of or damage to property or rights, and, as regards the balance or the aggregate amount of two hundred rupees for each ton of the ship's tonnage, the unsatisfied portion of the first mentioned claims shall rank pari pasu with the last-mentioned claims.

(2) The provisions of this section shall extend and apply to the owners, builders or other persons interested in any ship built at any port or place in India, from and including the launching of such ship until the registration thereof under the provisions of this Act.

(3) The provisions of this section shall apply in respect of claims for damages in respect of loss of life, personal injury and loss of or damage to property or rights arising on any single occasion, and in the application of the said provisions, claims for damages in respect of loss, injury or damage arising out of two or more distinct occasions shall not be combined.

(4) For the purposes of this section a ship's tonnage shall be determined in such manner as the Central Government may by general or special order, specify.

No Ship to Carry Passengers Without a Certificate of Survey

Section 220 : (1) No ship shall carry more than twelve passengers between ports or places in India or to or from any port or place in India from or to any port or place outside India, unless she has a certificate or survey under this Part in force and applicable to the voyage on which she is about to proceed or the service on which she is about to be employed:

Provided that nothing in this section shall apply to any ship which has been granted a certificate under section 235, unless it appears from the certificate that it is inapplicable to the voyage on which the ship is about to unless there is reason to believe that the ship has, since the grant of the certificate, sustained injury or damage or been found seaworthy or otherwise inefficient.

Survey of Ship

Section 244 : After receiving the notice required by section 238, the certifying officer may, if he thinks fit, cause the ship to be surveyed at the expense of the master or owner by a surveyor, who shall report to him whether the ship is, in his opinion, seaworthy and properly equipped, fitted and ventilated for the service on which she is to be employed:

Provided that he shall not cause a ship holding a certificate of survey or a safety certificate to be surveyed unless, by reason of the ship having met with damage or having undergone alterations, or on other reasonable grounds, he considers it likely that she may be found unseaworthy or not properly equipped fitted or ventilated for the service on which she is to be employed.

Unseaworthy Ship not to be Sent to Sea

Section 334 : (1) Every person who sends or attempts to send an Indian ship to sea from any port in India in such an unseaworthy state that the life of any person is likely to be thereby endangered shall, unless he proves that he used all reasonable means to insure her being sent to sea in a seaworthy state or that her going to sea in such unseaworthy state was under the circumstances reasonable and justifiable, be guilty of an offence under this sub-section.

(2) Every master of an Indian ship who knowingly takes such ship to sea in such unseaworthy state that the life of any person is likely to be thereby endangered shall, unless he proves that her going to sea in such unseaworthy state was, under the circumstances, reasonable and justifiable , be guilty of an offence under this sub-section.

(3) For the purpose of giving such proof, every person charged under this section may give evidence in the same manner as any other witness.

(4) No prosecution under this section shall be instituted except by, or with the consent of, the Central Government.

(5) A ship is "unseaworthy" within the meaning of this Act where the materials of which she is made, her construction, the qualifications of the master, the number, description and qualifications of the crew including officers, the weight, description and stowage of the cargo and ballast, the condition f her hull and equipment, boilers and machinery are not such as to render her in every respect fit for the proposed voyage or service.

Obligation of Owner to Crew with Respect to Seaworthiness

Section 335 : (1) In every contract of service, express or implied between the owner of an Indian ship and the master or any seaman thereof, and in every contract of apprenticeship whereby any person is bound to serve as an apprentice on board any such ship, there shall be implied, notwithstanding any agreement to the contrary, an obligation on the owner that such owner and the master, and every agent charged with the loading of such ship or the preparing thereof for sea, or the sending thereof to sea, shall use all reasonable means to ensure the seaworthiness of such ship for the voyage at the time when such voyage commences, and to keep her in a unseaworthy state during the voyage.

(2) For the purpose of seeing that the provisions of this section have been complied with the Central Government may, either at the request of the owner or otherwise, arrange for a survey of the hull, equipment or machinery of any sea-going ship by a surveyor.

No Ship to Carry Passengers Without a Certificate of Survey

Section 220 : (1) No ship shall carry more than twelve passengers between ports or places in India or to or from any port or place in India from or to any port or place outside India, unless she has a certificate or survey under this Part in force and applicable to the voyage on which she is about to proceed or the service on which she is about to be employed:

Provided that nothing in this section shall apply to any ship which has been granted a certificate under section 235, unless it appears from the certificate that it is inapplicable to the voyage on which the ship is about to unless there is reason to believe that the ship has, since the grant of the certificate, sustained injury or damage or been found seaworthy or otherwise inefficient.

(2) No customs collector shall granted a port clearance, nor shall any pilot be assigned, to any ship for which a certificate of survey is required by this Part until after the production by the owner, agent or master thereof of a certificate under this Part in force and applicable to the voyage on which she is about to proceed or the service on which she is about to be employed.

(3) If any ship for which a certificate of survey is required by this Part leaves or attempts to leave any port of survey without a certificate, any customs collector or any pilot on board the ship may detain her until she obtains a certificate.

10.4 The Indian Railways Act, 1890

The Indian Railways Act was passed in 1890 and was amended in 1961. Further it was substituted by the act of 1989. The Act was further amended in 2003. The Act deals with the various aspects of Railway Administration. Chapter IX and Chapter XI of the Act deals with "Carriage of Goods" and "Responsibilities of Railway Administration as Carriers".

10.4.1 Carriage of Goods

Maintenance of rate-books, etc., for carriage of goods : *Section 1* : Every railway administration shall maintain, at each station and at such other places where goods are received for carriage, the rate-books or other documents which shall contain the rate authorised for the carriage of goods from one section to another and make them available for the reference of any person during all reasonable hours without payment of any fee.

Railway administration is required to maintain the rate-books or other documents containing the rate for carrying goods from one station to another,–

(*i*) at each station; and

(*ii*) at such other places where goods are received for carriage. Any person can refer to them free during all reasonable hours.

Conditions for receiving, etc., of goods : *Section 2 :* (1) A railway administration may impose conditions, not inconsistent with this Act or any rules made thereunder, with respect to the receiving, forwarding, carrying or delivering of any goods.

(2) A railway administration shall maintain, at each station and at such other places where goods are received for carriage, a copy of the conditions for the time being in force under sub-section (1) and make them available for the reference of any person during all reasonable hours without payment of any fee.

A railway administration may impose conditions with respect to the receiving, forwarding, carrying or delivering of any goods. (Section 62).

A forwarding note is a necessary condition precedent to the entrusting of any goods to a railway administration for carriage.

The consignor is responsible for the correctness of the particulars furnished in the forwarding note.

The railway administration has to be indemnified by the consignor against any damage suffered by it due to any defective particular furnished in the forwarding note. (Section 64)

Railway Receipt

Section 3 : (1) A railway administration shall, :

(*a*) in a case where the goods are to be loaded by a person entrusting such goods, on the completion of such leading; or

(*b*) in any other case, on the acceptance of the goods by it,

issue a railway receipt in such form as may be specified by the Central Government.

(2) A railway receipt shall be *prima facie* evidence of the weight and the number of packages stated therein:

Provided that in the case of a consignment in wagon-load or train-load and the weight or the number of packages is not checked by a railway servant authorised in this behalf, and a statement to that effect is recorded in such railway receipt by him, the burden of proving the weight or, as the case may be, the number of packages stated therein, shall lie on the consignor, the consignee or the endorsee.

A railway administration is bound to issue a railway receipt (RR) to the person who has entrusted any goods to it for carriage.

Carriage of Animal Suffering from Infectious or Contagious Diseases

Section 4: A railway administration shall not be bound to carry any animal suffering from such infectious or contagious disease as may be prescribed.

Passing of Property in the Goods Covered by Railway Receipt

Section 5 : The property in the consignment covered by a railway receipt shall pass to the consignee or the endorsee, as the case may be, on the delivery of such railway receipt to him and he shall have all the rights and liabilities of the consignor.

The property in the consignment covered by a railway receipt (RR) passes to the consignee or, as the case may be, to the endorse, including the consignor's rights and liabilities.

Section 74 not to Affect Right of Stoppage in Transit or Claims for Freight

Section 6 : Nothing contained in section 74 shall prejudice or affect :

(*a*) any right of the consignor for stoppage of goods in transit as an unpaid vendor [as defined under the Sale of Goods Act, 1930 (3 of 1930)] on his written request to the railway administration;

(*b*) any right of the railway to claim freight from the consignor; or

(*c*) any liability of the consignee or the endorsee, referred to in that section by reason of his being such consignee or endorsee.

Liability of Railway Administration for Wrong Delivery

Section 7 : Where a railway administration delivers the consignment to the person who produces the railway receipt, it shall not be responsible for any wrong delivery on the ground that such person is not entitled thereto or that the endorsement on the railway receipt is forged or otherwise defective.

When the consignor, or the consignee, or the endorsee, has failed to pay on demand any freight or other charges due from him in respect of any consignment, the railway administration shall have a lien on any consignment which is in, or thereafter comes into, its possession.

In order to realising a sum equal to the freight or other charges, the railway administration can sell the consignment or part thereof :

(*i*) at once, or

(*ii*) by public auction. (Section 83)

The railway administration has two rights :

(*i*) of sale under sections 83 to 85 and

(*ii*) of recovery by suit, any freight, charge, amount or other expenses due to it. (Section 86)

When the person concerned fails to remove goods within 7 days after the termination of transit thereof, the railway administration is free to sell the unremoved goods by public auction.

If the person entitled to remove the goods pays the freight and other charges, before the sale thereof, to the railway administration, then he can remove such goods. (Section 90)

10.4.2 Responsibilities of Railway Administration as Carriers

The liability of a railway administration is the same as that of a common carrier. In other words, even where any loss, destruction, damage, deterioration or non-delivery is proved to have arisen from any one or more of the aforesaid nine cases, a railway administration shall not be relieved of its responsibility unless it further proves that it has used reasonable foresight and care in the carriage of the goods [Union of India *v.* Orissa Textile Mills, AIR (1979) Ori. 165]. A railway administration, like a common carrier, is bound to carry the goods of every person who is willing to pay the freight and comply with other requirements.

General Responsibility of a Railway Administration as Carrier of Goods

Section 93 : Save as otherwise provided in this Act, a railway administration shall be responsible for the loss, destruction, damage or deterioration in transit, or non-delivery of any consignment, arising from any cause except the following namely:

(*a*) act of God

(*b*) act of war

(*c*) act of public enemies

(*d*) arrest, restraint or seizure under legal process

(*e*) orders or restrictions imposed by the Central Government or a State Government or by an officer or authority subordinate to the Central Government or a State Government authorised by it in this behalf

(*f*) act or omission or negligence of the consignor or the consignee or the endorsee or the agent or servant of the consignor or the consignee or the endorsee

(*g*) natural deterioration or wastage in bulk or weight due to inherent defect, quality ore vice of the goods

(*h*) latent defects

(*i*) fire, explosion or any unforeseen risk.

Provided that even where such loss, destruction, damage, deterioration or non-delivery is proved to have arisen from any one or more of the aforesaid causes, the railway administration shall not be relieved of its responsibility for the loss, destruction, damage, deterioration or non-delivery unless the railway administration further proves that it has used reasonable foresight and care in the carriage of the goods.

A railway administration is responsible not only for the loss, destruction, damage or deterioration in transit but also for the non-delivery of any consignment unless it proves that it has used reasonable foresight and care in the carriage of the goods.

Delay or Detention in Transit

Section 95 : A railway administration shall not be responsible for the loss, destruction, damage or deterioration of any consignment proved by the owner to have been caused by the delay or detention in their carriage if the railway administration proves that the delay or detention arose for reasons beyond its control or without negligence or misconduct on its part or on the part of any of its servants.

A railway administration cannot be held responsible for the loss, destruction, damage or deterioration of any consignment due to delay or detention in their carriage.

However, the railway administration has to prove that the delay or detention arose:

(*i*) for reasons beyond its control, or

(*ii*) without negligence on its part or on the part of any its servants, or

(*iii*) without misconduct on its part or on the part of any its servants.

Traffic Passing Over Railway in India and Railways in Foreign Countries

Section 96 : Where in the course of carriage of any consignment from a place in India to a place outside India or from a place outside India to a place in India or from one place outside India to another place outside India or from one place in India to another place in India over any territory outside India, it is carried over the railways of any railway administration in India, the railway administration shall not be responsible under any of the provisions of this chapter for the loss, destruction, damage or deterioration of the goods, from whatever cause arising, unless it is proved by the owner of the goods that such loss, destruction, damage or deterioration arose over the railway of the railway administration.

The owner of goods, while claiming damages, is required to prove that the loss, destruction, damage or deterioration of goods arose over the railway of the railway administration.

Owner's Risk Rate or Railway Risk Rate

Section 97 : A consignment may be carried by a railway administration either at owner's risk rate or railway risk rate. Owner's risk rate is a special reduced rate whereas railway risk rate is an ordinary tariff rate. Owner's risk rate is lower than the railway risk rate for the simple reason that the goods in this case are carried at the owner's risk. In case of owner's risk rate, the railway administration is not responsible unless it is proved that any loss, destruction, damage or deterioration or non-delivery of goods arose from negligence or misconduct on the part of the railway administration or its servants.

Liability for Damage to Goods in Defective Condition or Defectively Packed

Section 98 : Goods tendered to a railway administration to be carried by railway may be (a) in a defective condition or (b) defectively packed. As a result of these, goods are liable to damage, deterioration, leakage or wastage. If the fact of such condition or defective or improper packing has been recorded by the sender or his agent in the forwarding note, the railway administration is not responsible for any damage, deterioration, leakage or wastage unless negligence or misconduct on the part of the railway administration or of its servants is proved.

Liability After Termination of Transit

Section 99 : Whether the goods are carried at owner's risk rate or railway risk rate, the liability of the railway administration for any loss of goods within a period of seven days after the termination of transit is that of a bailee under Sections 151, 152 and 161 of the Indian Contract Act, 1872. But where the goods are carried at owner's risk rate the railway administration is not liable for such loss, destruction, damage, deterioration or non-delivery of goods except on proof of negligence or misconduct on the part of the railway administration or any of its servants.

After seven days from the date of termination of transit the railway administration is not liable in any case for any loss of such goods. Notwithstanding this provision, the railway administration is not responsible after the termination of transit for the loss, destruction, damage, deterioration or non-delivery of articles of perishable goods, animals, explosives and other dangerous goods.

Responsibility as Carrier of Luggage

Section 100 : A railway administration shall not be responsible for the loss, destruction, damage, deterioration or non-delivery of any luggage unless a railway servant has booked the luggage and given a receipt therefor. Also it is to be proved that the loss, etc., was due to the negligence or misconduct on the part of the railway administration or on the part of any of its servants.

In the case of luggage which is carried by the passenger in his own charge, the railway administration shall not be responsible for the loss, etc., unless it is proved that the loss, etc., was due to the negligence or misconduct on the part of the railway administration or on the part of any of its servants.

Responsibility as a carrier of animals (*Section 101*). A railway administration shall not be responsible for any loss or destruction of, or injuries to, any animal carried by railway arising from fright or restiveness of the animal or from overloading of wagons by the consignor.

Exoneration from liability in certain cases (*Section 102*). A railway administration shall not be responsible for the loss, destruction, damage or deterioration or nondelivery of any consignment :

(*i*) when such loss, etc., is due to the fact that a materially false description of the consignment is given; or

(*ii*) where a fraud has been practised by the consignor or the endorsee, or by an agent of the consignor, consignee or the endorsee; or

(*iii*) where it is proved by the railway administration to have been caused by, or to have arisen from:

(*a*) improper loading or unloading by the consignor, or the consignee or the endorsee, or by an agent of the consignor, consignee or the endorsee;

(*b*) riot, civil commotion, strike, lock-out, stoppage or restraint of labour from whatever cause arising whether partial or general; or

(*iv*) for any indirect or consequential loss or damage or for loss of particular market.

The liability of the railway administration for the loss, destruction, damage, deterioration or non-delivery of the consignment cannot exceed

(*a*) the amount calculated with reference to the weight of the consignment as may be prescribed, or

(*b*) the amount as may be prescribed when the consignment consists of an animal, or

(*c*) the value of the consigned declared at the time of entrustment. Sub-section (3) overrides the provisions of sub-sections (1) and (2).

The Central Government can notify goods for which the value must be declared and percentage charge has to be. (*Section 103*)

The responsibility of railway administration for the destruction, damage or deterioration of any goods, with the consignor's consent, carried in open wagon, shall be ½ of the amount of liability to be determined under this Chapter. (Section 104).

A person who claims compensation against a railway administer for the loss, destruction, damage, deterioration or non-delivery of goods, must served a notice thereof, :

(*a*) to the railway administration to which the goods were entrusted for carriage; or

(*b*) to the railway administration on whose railway the destination station lies, or the loss, destruction, damage or deterioration occurred.

Such notice is required to be served upon either of the railway administration within a period of 6 months (not 180 days) from the date of entrustment of the goods.

A complaint, or any communication, in writing regarding the non-delivery or delayed delivery of the goods is deemed to be a notice of claim for compensation.

Similarly, a person who claims refund of an overcharge, should also serve a notice in the manner aforesaid. (*Section 106*)

Applications for Compensation for Loss, etc., of Goods

Section 107 : An application for compensation for loss, destruction, damage, deterioration or non-delivery of goods shall be filed against the railway administration on whom a notice under section 106 has been served.

Person Entitled to Claim Compensation

Section 108 : (1) If a railway administration pays compensation for loss, destruction, damage, deterioration or non-delivery of goods entrusted to it for carriage, to the consignee or the endorsee producing the railway receipt, the railway administration shall be deemed to have discharged its liability and no application before the Claims Tribunal or any other legal proceeding shall lie against the railway administration on the ground that the consigned or the endorsee was not legally entitled to receive such compensation.

(2) Nothing in sub-section (1) shall affect the right of any person having any interest in the goods to enforce the same against the consignee or the endorsee receiving compensation under that sub-section.

An application before the Claims Tribunal for compensation for the loss of life or personal injury to a passenger lies against the railway administration, :

(*i*) from which the passenger obtained his pass or purchased his ticket; or

(*ii*) on whose railway the destination lies or the loss or personal injury occurred. (Section 102)

Burden of Proof

Section 110 : In an application before the Claims Tribunal for compensation for loss, destruction, damage, deterioration or non-delivery of any goods, the burden of proving :

(*a*) the monetary loss actually sustained; or

(*b*) where the value has been declared under sub-section (2) of section 103 in respect of any consignment that the value so declared is its true value,

shall lie on the person claiming compensation, but subject to the other provisions contained in this Act, it shall not be necessary for him to prove how the loss, destruction, damage, deterioration or non-delivery was caused.

Where a railway administration contracts to carry passengers or goods partly by railway and partly by sea, it is liable to pay compensation for any loss of life, personal injury, or loss of or damage to goods which has happened during the carriage by sea. (Section 111)

10.4.3 Railway Claims Tribunal Act, 1987

The Railway Claims Tribunal Act, 1987 provides for the formation of tribunal to deal with claims for cargo losses, personal injuries, excess freight etc. and prescribes the procedure thereunder.

Chapter III of deals with the jurisdiction, powers and authority of claims tribunal. Section 13 of the Act provides that :

Application to Claims Tribunal : (1) A person seeking any relief in respect of the matters referred to in sub-section (1) [or sub-section (1A)] of Section 13 may make an application to the Claims Tribunal.

(2) Every application under sub-section (1) shall be in such form and be accompanied by such documents or other evidence and by such fee in respect of the filing of such application and by such other fees for the service or execution of processes as may be prescribed :

Provided that no such fee shall be payable in respect of an application under sub-clause (*ii*) of clause (*a*) of sub-section (1) [or, as the case may be, sub-section (1A)] of section 13.

An application seeking relief in respect of the matters referred to in section 13(1) or (1A) is to be made in the prescribed form and manner to the Claims Tribunal.

No fee is payable to an application, if made, under section 13(1)(a)(ii) or section 13(1A) of the Act.

Limitation : (1) The Claims Tribunal shall not admit an application for any claim:

(*a*) under sub-section (*i*) of clause (*a*) of sub-section (1) of section 13 unless the application is made within three years from the date on which the goods in question were entrusted to the railway administration for carriage by railway;

(*b*) under sub-section (*ii*) of clause (*a*) of sub-section (1) [or, as the case may be, sub-section (1A)] of section 13 unless the application is made within one year of occurrence of the accident;

(*c*) under clause (*b*) of sub-section (1) of section 13 unless the application is made within three years from the date on which the fare or freight is paid to the railway administration:

Provided that no application for any claim referred to in sub-clause (1) of clause (*a*) of sub-section (1) of section 13 shall be preferred to the Claims Tribunal until the expiration of three months next after the date on which the intimation of the claim has been preferred under section 78B of the Railway Act.

(2) Notwithstanding anything contained in sub-section (1), an application may be entertained after the period specified in sub-section (1) if the applicant satisfies the Claims Tribunal that he had sufficient cause for not making the application within such period.

Procedure and Powers of Claims Tribunal : (1) The Claims Tribunal shall not be bound by the procedure laid down by the Code of Civil Procedure, 1908 (5 of 1908), but shall be guided by the principles of natural justice and, subject to the other provisions of this Act and of any rules, the Claims Tribunal shall have powers to regulate its own procedure including the fixing of places and times of its enquiry.

(2) The Claims Tribunal shall decide every application as expeditiously as possible and ordinarily every application shall be decided on a perusal of documents, written representations and affidavits and after hearing such oral arguments as may be advanced.

(3) The Claims Tribunal shall have, for the purposes of discharging its functions under this Act, the same powers as are vested in a civil court under the Code of Civil Procedure, 1908 (5 of 1908), while trying a suit, in respect of the following matters, namely :

(*a*) summoning and enforcing the attendance of any person and examining him on oath;

(*b*) requiring the discovery and production of documents;

(*c*) receiving evidence on affidavits;

(*d*) subject to the provisions of sections 123 and 124 of the Indian Evidence Act, 1872 (1 of 1872), requisitioning any public record or document or copy of such record or document from any office;

(*e*) issuing commissions for the examination of witnesses or documents;

(*f*) reviewing its decisions;

(*g*) dismissing an application for default or deciding it *ex parte*;

(*h*) setting aside any order of dismissal of any application for default or any order passed by it *ex parte;*

(*i*) any other matter which may be prescribed.

It therefore implies that the claims tribunal,

(*i*) shall not be bound by the procedure laid down in the Code of Civil Procedure, 1908;

(*ii*) shall be guided by the principles of natural justice;

(*iii*) shall have powers to regulate its own procedure.

It shall decide every application as expeditiously as possible and the powers as vested in a civil court under the 1908 Code, while trying a suit, have been conferred on the Claims Tribunal in respect of the matters referred to in sub-section (3)(*a*) to (*i*).

10.5 THE CARRIERS ACT, 1865

The Carriers Act, 1865, is framed by the legislature on the lines of the English Carriers Act, 1930.

The carriers are generally classified into common carriers and private carriers. The distinction between a common carrier and private carrier is important for the purpose of attaching liability against the loss or damage of the goods in transit.

Common Carrier vs. Private Carrier

A common carrier is insurer of the goods and he is liable to the consignor or consignee in all events save and except where the loss is occurred on account of an Act of God, State's enemies or inherent vice in the goods itself. Thus a common carrier may not be liable in respect of perishable goods if the goods are delivered in time or where the loss or damage arises on account of some supernatural act. A private carrier does not hold himself out as exercising the public employment of common carrier. He reserves the right to accept the goods or rejects it and one who carries goods casually or occasionally. Private carriers select the goods of his choice and also looks to the attractiveness of the freight he is getting. He does not accept the goods indiscriminately and when he accept the goods by entering into a regular contract his liability is governed by the terms of the contract and not under the Act.

A private carrier is not an insurer of the goods but merely a *bailee* and in case of loss or damage, the consignor or consignee must prove negligence on the part of the private to recover damages (R.R.N. Ramalinga Nadar *v.* V. Narayan Reddiar, AIR 1971 Ker. 197).

Liability under the Indian Contract Act, 1972

In Kuverji Tulsidas *v.* G. I. P. Rly. Company (ILR 3 Bom., 109), the Bombay High Court has decided that the rights and liabilities of the common carrier in India were governed under Section 151 and 152 of the Indian Contract Act, 1872. The Court had taken the view that the effect of the Indian Contract Act, 1872, was to relieve common carriers from the liability of insurers answerable for the goods entrusted to them 'at all events', except in the case of loss or damage by the act of God or the Queen's enemies, and to make them responsible only for that amount care which the Contract Act requires of all bailees a like in the absence of special contract. However, after some years, the Calcutta High Court came to the conclusion that the liability of the common carriers were not affected by the Contract Act, 1872.

A carrier of passengers in law is neither an insurer nor precluded from making a special contract with his passengers, which may either enlarge, diminish or exclude his general duty to exercise care. In Indian Airlines corporation *v.* Jothaji Maniram, AIR 1959 Mad 285, it was held that the rights and liabilities of the inland Air Carriers are not governed either by the Carriers Act, 1965 or the Carriage by Air Act, 1934, though the Airlines Corporation was a common Carrier. Its rights and liabilities were governed by the common law. At the common law, the Airlines Corporation was entitled to enter into a contract absolving its liabilities even against negligence.

A common carrier of animals is expected provide vehicle reasonably and sufficient for such animals as the professes to carry and his rights and liabilities are within the Act. He is insurer of animal's safety and he is not liable for accident if the same happens on account of inherent vice.

Carrier not Liable for Losses

Section 3 : Where the consignor has declared the value and contents of the goods to be carried, the carrier accept the same under his full common law liability as an insurer, unless such loss or damage results from an act of God, an act of the state's enemies, the fault of the consignor or inherent vice in the goods themselves. The carrier is liable in all events save and except as mentioned above even cases where he was robbed by highway men Forward v. Pittard (1785) 1 Term Re. 27(34); Goggs v. Bernard (1703) 2 Ld. Raym 909.

Section 10 : If the loss or injury occurs to the goods intended for carriage and such loss or injury may arise where the goods are not delivered to the consignee in the same condition in which it was delivered to him by the consignor for carriage , the notice of loss or injury to be given within six months. No suit shall be instituted against a common carrier for the loss of, or injury to, goods entrusted to him for carriage, unless notice in writing of the loss or injury has been given to him before the institution of the suit and within six months of the time when the loss or injury first came to the knowledge of the plaintiff.

Notice in Writing

To enable the common carrier to locate the exact location of the goods entrusted to him for carriage, the consignor or consignee is required to give notice in writing before filing of the suit. It is only if the notice is given within a period of six months from the date of knowledge that the plaintiff can file a suit within three years from the date of loss or damage of the goods. It is not necessary for the plaintiff to state the issue of notice in the plaint.

Loss of or Injury to the Goods

The notice is required to be given where there is a loss of or injury to the goods occurred. It has been held that the provisions of this section will not be applicable If the goods are not delivered to the consignee or the owner of the goods intended to be delivered for whatsoever reasons other than for loss of or injury to the goods (Union of India v. Jatmall Sukaurai (1971) 2 M.L.J. 257(262)).

Institution of the Suit

The suit against the common carrier for loss of or injury to the goods or for compensation for non-delivery of, or delay in delivering the goods to be instituted within a period of three years as per Article 11 of the Limitation Act, 1963. The limitation period commences from the date when the goods ought to have been delivered which means the reasonable time from the date of despatch of the goods to the consignee.

10.6 THE CARRIAGE BY AIR ACT, 1972

This act gives effects to the provisions of the Warsaw Convention, 1929 and the Hague Protocol, 1955 relating to the international carriage of passengers and goods by air.

The Warsaw convention was given effect to in India by the enactment of the Indian Carriage by Air Act, 1934 in regard to the international carriage and the provisions of the Act have been extended to the domestic carriage, by means of notification issued in 1964.

A diplomatic conference under the auspices of International Civil Aviation Organisation was held in Hague in September 1955 which adopted a protocol to amend the provisions of Warsaw Convention. The act of 1934 was repealed to apply the provisions based on Warsaw Convention and on 15th May 1973 the act came into force as the Carriage by Air Act, 1972. The act defines the liability of the air carrier for death of, injury, or injury to passengers and damage/loss to registered luggage and cargo.

Liability in Case of Death

(1) Notwithstanding anything contained in the Fatal Accidents Act, 1855 or any other enactment or rule of law in force in any part of India, the rules contained in the First Schedule and in the Second Schedule shall, in all cases to which those rules apply, determine the liability of a carrier in respect of the death of a passenger.

(2) The liability shall be enforceable for the benefit of such of the members of the passenger's family as sustained damage by reason on his death.

Explanation : In this sub-section, the expression "member of a family" means wife or husband, parent, step-parent, grand parent, brother, sister, half-brother, half-sister, child, step-child and grand child:

Provided that indeducing any such relationship as aforesaid any illegitimate person and any adopted person shall be treated as being or as having been, the legitimate child of his mother and reputed father or, as the case may be, of his adopters.

(3) An action to enforce the liability may be brought by the personal representative of the passenger or by any person for whose benefit the liability is under sub-section (2) enforceable, but only one action shall be brought in India in respect of the death of any one passenger, and every such action by whomsoever brought shall be for the benefit of all such persons so entitled as aforesaid as either are domiciled in India or not being domiciled there express a desire of take the benefit of the action.

(4) Subject to the provisions of sub-section (5), the amount recovered in any such action after deducing any costs not recovered from the defendant, shall be divided between the persons entitled in such proportion as the Court may direct.

(5) The Court before which any such action is brought may, at any stage of the proceedings make any such order as appears to the Court to be just and equitable in view of the provisions, the First Schedule or of the Second Schedule, as the case may be, limiting the liability of a carrier and of any proceedings which have been or are likely to be commenced outside India in respect of the death of the passenger in question.

The liability of a carrier in respect of death of a passenger is determined by the rules contained in the first schedule and the second schedule of the Act.

The act also provides for the maximum limits of liability for death, injury damage etc. and also prescribes the time limits within which the claims have to be filed on the air carrier.

First Schedule to The Act (Rules – Chapter III]

1. The carrier is liable for damage sustained in the event of the death or wounding of a passenger or any other bodily injury suffered by a passenger, if the accident which caused the damage so sustained took place on board the aircraft or in the course of any of the operations of embarking or disembarking.

2. (1) The carrier is liable for damage sustained in the event of the destruction or loss of, or of damage to, any registered luggage or any goods, if the occurrence which caused the damage so sustained took place during the carriage by air.

(2) The carriage by air within the meaning of sub-rule (1) comprises the period during which the luggage or goods are in charge of the carrier, whether in an aerodrome or on board an aircraft, or, in the case of a landing outside an aerodrome in any place whatsoever.

(3) The period of the carriage by air does not extend to any carriage by land, by sea or by river performed outside an aerodrome. If, however, such a carriage takes place in the performance of a contract for carriage by air, for the purpose of loading, delivery or transhipment, any damage is presumed, subject to proof to the contrary, to have been the result of an event which took place during the carriage by air.

3. The carrier is liable for damage occasioned by delay in the carriage by air of passengers, luggage or goods.

4. (1) The carrier is not liable if he proves that he and his agents have taken all necessary measures to avoid the damage or that it was impossible for him or them to take such measures.

(2) In the carriage of goods and luggage the carrier is not liable if he proves that the damage was occasioned by negligent pilotage or negligence in the handling of the aircraft or in navigation and that, in all other respects, he and his agents have taken all necessary measures to avoid the damage.

5. If the carrier proves that the damage was caused by or contributed to by the negligence of the injured person the Court may exonerate the carrier wholly or partly from his liability.

6. (1) In the carriage of passengers the liability of the carrier for each passenger is limited to the sum of 1,25,000 francs. Where damages may be awarded in form of periodical payments, the equivalent capital value of the said payments shall not exceed 1,25,000 francs. Nevertheless, by special contract the carrier and the passenger may agree to a higher limit of liability.

(2) In the carriage of registered luggage and of goods, the liability of the carrier is limited to a sum of 250 fracs per kilogramme, unless the consignor has made, at the time when the package was handed over to the carrier, a special declaration of the value at delivery and has paid a supplementary sum if the case so requires. In that case the carrier will be liable to pay a sum not exceeding the declared sum, unless he proves that sum is greater than the actual value to the consignor at delivery.

(3) As regards objects of which the passenger takes charge himself the liability of the carrier is limited to 5,000 francs per passenger.

(4) The sums mentioned in this rule shall be deemed to refer to the French franc consisting of sixty-five and a half miligrammes gold of millesimal fineness nine hundred.

7. Any provision tending to relieve the carrier of liability or to fix a lower limit than that which is laid down in these rules shall be null and void, but the nullity of any such provision does not involve the nullity of the whole contract which shall remain subject to the provisions of this Schedule.

8. (1) In the cases covered by rules 18 to 19 any action for damage, however founded, can only be brought subject to the conditions and limits set out in this Schedule.

(2) In the cases covered by rule 17, the provisions of sub-rule (1) also apply, without prejudice to the questions as to who are the person who have the right to bring suit and what are their respective rights.

9. (1) The carrier shall not be entitled to avail himself of the provisions of this Schedule which exclude or limit his liability, if the damage is caused by his wilful misconduct or by such default on his part as is in the opinion of the Court equivalent to wilful misconduct.

(2) Similarly the carrier shall not be entitled to avail himself of the said provisions, if the damage is caused as aforesaid by any agent of the carrier acting within the scope of his employment.

10. (1) Receipt by the person entitled to delivery of luggage or goods without complaint is *prima facie* evidence that the same have been delivered in good condition and in accordance with the document of carriage.

(2) In the case of damage, the person entitled to delivery must complain to the carrier forthwith after the discovery of the damage, and, at the latest, within three days from the date of receipt in the case of luggage and seven days from the date of receipt in the case of goods. In the case of delay the complaint must be made at the latest within fourteen days from the date on which the luggage or goods have been placed at his disposal.

(3) Every complaint must be made in writing upon the document of carriage or by separate notice in writing despatched within the times aforesaid.

(4) Failing complaint within the times aforesaid, no action shall be against the carrier, save in the case of fraud on his part.

11. In the case of the death of the person liable, an action for damages lies in accordance with these rules against those legally representing his estate.

12. An action for damages must be brought at the option of the plaintiff either before the Court having jurisdiction whether the carrier is ordinarily resident, or has his principal place for business, or has an establishment by which the contract has been made of before the Court having jurisdiction at the place of destination.

13. The right of damages shall be extinguished if an action is not brought within two years reckoned from the date of arrival at the destination, or from the date on which the aircraft ought to have arrived, or from the date on which the carriage stopped.

14. (1) In the case of carriage to be performed by various successive carriers and falling within and definition set out in sub-rule (4) of rule 1, each carrier who accepts passenger's luggage or goods is subjected to the rules set out in this Schedule, and is deemed to be one of the contracting parties to the contract of carriage in so far as the contract deals with that part of the carriage which is performed under his supervision.

(2) In the case of carriage of this nature, the passenger or his representative can take action only against the carrier who performed the carriage during which the accident of the delay occurred, save in the case where, by express agreement, the first carrier has assumed liability for the whole journey.

(3) As regards luggage or goods, the passenger or consignor will have a right of action against the first carrier, and the passenger or consignee who is entitled to delivery will have a right of action against the last carrier, and further, each may take action against the carrier who performed the carriage during which the destruction, loss, damage or delay took place. These carriers will be jointly and severally liable to the passenger or to the consignor or consignee.

10.7 The Indian Ports(Major Ports) Act, 1963

This Act defines the liability of Port Trust Authorities for loss of or damage to goods whilst in their custody and prescribes time limits for filing monetary claim on, or suit against, the Port Trust Authorities.

10.8 The Bill of Lading Act, 1855

This Act defines the character of the Bill of Lading as an evidence of the contract of carriage of goods between the shipowner and the shipper, as an acknowledgement of the receipt of the goods on board the vessel and, as a document of title. The bill of lading is one of the various documents required in connection with settlement of marine cargo claims.

10.9 The Indian Post Office Act, 1898

This Act defines the liability of the Government for loss, misdelivery, delay of or damage to any postal articles in course of transmission by post.

10.10 Multi Modal Transportation Act, 1993

The Act provides for registration of multi-modal transport operators engaged in transportation of goods under more than one mode of transport, i.e., by rail/road and sea. The Act prescribes limits of liability of the operator, contents of documents to be issued by them, notice of loss, etc.

As per Section 2 of the Act, "multimodal transportation" means carriage of goods, by atleast two different modes of transport under a multimodal transport contract, from the place of acceptance of goods in India to a place of delivery of the goods outside India;

Section 3 of the act prohibits any person from carrying on or even commencing the business of multi-modal transportation without registration under the act.

Basis of Liability of Multimodal Transport Operator

Section 13 : Section 13 of the Act provides that if any loss of, or damage to, the consignment, delay in delivery of the consignment and any consequential loss or damage arising out of such delay happens to take place then the multimodal transport operator shall be liable for such loss or damage. (1) The multimodal transport operator shall be liable for loss resulting from :

(*a*) any loss of, or damage to, the consignment;

(*b*) delay in delivery of the consignment and any consequential loss or damage arising from such delay, where such loss, damage or delay in delivery took place which the consignment was in his charge :

Provided that the multimodal transport operator shall mot be liable if he proves that no fault or neglect on his part or that of his servants or agents had caused or contributed to such loss, damage or delay in delivery:

Provided further that the multimodal transport operator shall not be liable for loss or damage arising out of delay in delivery unless the consignor had made a declaration of interest in timely delivery which has been accepted by the multimodal transport operator.

Explanation : For the purposes of this sub-section," delay in delivery" shall be deemed to occur when the consignment has not been delivered within the time expressly agreed upon or , in the absence of such agreement, within a reasonable time required by a diligent multimodal transport operator, having regard to the circumstances of the case, to effect the delivery of the consignment.

(2) If the consignment has not been delivered within ninety consecutive days following the date of delivery expressly agreed upon or the reasonable time referred to in the *Explanation* to sub-section (1), the claimant may treat the consignment as lost.

Limits of liability when the nature and value of the consignment have not been declared and stage of transport where loss or damage occurred is not known

Section 14 : When the nature and value of consignment have not been declared and the stage of transport where loss or damage occurred is unknown, then liability of the operator to pay compensation is limited as per section 14. (1) Where a multimodal transport operator becomes liable for any loss of, or damage to, any consignment, the nature and value where of have not been declared by the consignor before such consignment has been taken in charge by the multimodal transport operator and the stage of transport at which such loss or damage occurred is not known, then the liability of the multimodal transport operator to pay compensation shall not exceed two Special Drawing Rights per kilogram of the gross weight of the consignment lost or damage or 666.67 Special Drawing Rights per package or unit lost or damaged, whichever is higher.

Explanation : For the purposes of this sub-section, where a container, pallet or similar article of transport is loaded with more than one package or unit, the package or units enumerated in the multimodal transport document, as packed in such container, pallet or similar article of transport shall be deemed as packages or units.

(2) Notwithstanding anything contained in sub-section (1), if the multimodal transportation does not, according to the multimodal transport contract , include carriage of goods by sea or by inland waterways, the liability of the multimodal transport operator shall be limited to an amount not exceeding 8.33 Special Drawing Rights per kilogram of the gross weight of the goods lost or damaged.

Limits of liability when the nature and value of the consignment have not been declared and stage of transport where loss or damage occurred is known

Section 15 : Where a multimodal transport operator becomes liable for any loss of ,or damage to, any consignment, the nature and value whereof have not been declared by the consignor before such consignment has been taken in charge by the multimodal transport operator and the stage of transport at which such loss or damage occurred is known, then the limit of the liability of the multimodal transport operator for such loss or damage shall be determined in accordance with the provisions of the relevant law applicable in relation to the mode of transport during the course of which the loss or damage occurred and any stipulation in the multimodal transport contract to the contrary shall be void and unenforceable.

Liability of the multimodal transport operator in case of delay in delivery of goods under certain circumstances

Section 16 : In case of delay in delivery, the liability of the operator is limited to freight payable for the consignment so delayed. Where delay in delivery of the consignment occurs under any of the circumstances mentioned in the

Explanation to sub-section (1) of section 13, or any consequential loss or damage arises from such delay, then the liability of the multimodal transport operator shall be limited to the freight payable for the consignment so delayed.

Assessment of Compensation

Section 17 : (1) Assessment of compensation for loss of ,or damage to, the consignment shall be made with reference to the value of such consignment at the place where, and the time at which, such consignment is delivered to the consignee or at the place and time when, in accordance with the multimodal transport contract, it should have been delivered.

(2) The value of the consignment shall be determined according to the current commodity exchange price, or if there is no such price, according to the current market price, or if the current market price is not ascertainable, with reference to the normal value of a consignment of the same king and quantity.

Loss of Right of Multimodal Transport Operator to Limit Liability

Section 18 : The multimodal transport operator shall not be entitled to the benefit of limitation of liability under any of the provisions of the Chapter if it is proved that the loss, damage of delay in delivery of consignment resulted from an act or omission of the multimodal transport operator with intent to cause such loss damage or delay or recklessly and with knowledge that such loss, damage or delay would probably result.

Limit of Liability of Multimodal Transport Operator for Total Loss of Goods

Section 19 : The operator shall not, in any case, be liable for an amount greater than the liability for total loss of goods for which a person will be entitled to make a claim against him under the provision of this Act. The multimodal transport operator shall not, in any case, be liable for an amount greater than the liability for total loss of goods for which a person will be entitled to make a claim against him under the provisions of this Act.

Notice of Loss of or Damage to Goods

Section 20 : The responsibility of the multimodal transport operator starts from the time when the goods are put under his charge and ends when the delivery thereof has been made. (1) The delivery of the consignment to the consignee by the multimodal transport operator shall be treated as *prima facie* evidence of delivery of the goods as described in the multimodal transport document unless notice of the general nature of loss of, or damage to, the goods is given, in writing, by the consignee to the multimodal transport operator at the time of handing over of the goods to the consignee.

(2) Where the loss or damage is not apparent, the provisions of sub-section (1) shall apply unless notice in writing is given by the consignee of the loss of, or damage to, the goods within six consecutive days after the day when the goods were handed over to the consignee.

10.11 INDIAN STAMP ACT, 1899

Definition

Section 2 of the act defines policy of insurance, policy of group insurance and policy of sea insurance.

(19) "*Policy of insurance*" includes :

(*a*) any instrument by which one person, in consideration of a premium, engages to indemnify another against loss, damage or liability arising from an unknown or contingent event;

(*b*) a life-policy, and any policy insuring any person against accident or sickness, and any other personal insurance;

(19A) *"Policy of group insurance"* means any instrument covering not less than fifty or such smaller number as the Central Government may approve, either generally or with reference to any particular case, by which an insurer, in consideration of a premium paid by an employer or by an employer and his employees, jointly, engages to cover, with or without medical examination and for the sole benefit of persons other than the employer, the lives of all the employees or of any class of them, determined by conditions pertaining to the employment, for amounts of insurance based upon a plan which precludes individual selection;]

(20) *"Policy of sea-insurance"* or *"sea-policy"* :

(*a*) means any insurance made upon any ship or vessel (whether for marine or inland navigation), or upon the machinery, tackle or furniture of any ship or vessel, or upon any goods, merchandise or property of any description whatever on board of any ship or vessel, or upon the freight of, or any other interest which may be lawfully insured in, or relating to, any ship or vessel, and

(*b*) includes any insurance of goods, merchandise or property for any transit which includes, not a sea risk within the meaning of clause (a), but also any other risk incidental to the transit insured from the commencement of the transit to the ultimate destination covered by the insurance.

Where any person, in consideration of any sum of money paid or to be paid for additional freight or otherwise, agrees to take upon himself any risk attending goods, merchandise or property of any description whatever while on board of any ship or vessel, or engages to indemnify the owner of any such goods, merchandise or property from any risk, loss or damage, such agreement or engagement shall be deemed to be a contract for sea-insurance;

Instruments Chargeable with Duty

According to *Section 3*, an instrument is to be chargeable with duty of the amount indicated in Schedule I to the Act which gives a list of instruments liable to stamp duty. The liability of an instrument to stamp duty is determined by the Act in force at the time the instrument was executed. Instruments not mentioned in this Schedule are not subject to duty.

Section 17 provides that all instruments chargeable with duty and executed by any person in India shall be stamped before or at the time of execution.

Section 3 : Subject to the provisions of this Act and the exemptions contained in Schedule I, the following instruments shall be chargeable with duty of the amount indicated in that Schedule as the proper duty therefor, respectively, that is to say-

(*a*) every instrument mentioned in that Schedule which, not having been previously executed by any person, is executed in India on or after the first day of July, 1899;

(*b*) every bill of exchange payable otherwise than on demand or promissory note drawn or made out of India on or after that day and accepted or paid, or presented for acceptance or payment, or endorsed, transferred or otherwise negotiated, in India; and

(*c*) every instrument other than a bill of exchange or promissory note mentioned in that Schedule, which, not having been previously executed by any person, is executed out of India on or after that day relates to any property situate, or to any matter or thing done or to be done, in India and is received in India:

PROVIDED that no duty shall be chargeable in respect of–(1) any instrument executed by, or on behalf of, or in favour of, the government in cases where, but for this exemption, the government would be liable to pay the duty chargeable in respect of such instrument;

(2) any instrument for the sale, transfer or other disposition, either absolutely or by way of mortgage or otherwise, of any ship or vessel, or any part, interest, share or property of or in any ship or vessel registered under the

Merchant Shipping Act, 1894, or under Act 19 of 1938, or the Indian Registration of Ships Act, 1841, as amended by subsequent Acts.

Every instrument chargeable with duty executed out of India and not being a bill of exchange or promissory note, may be stamped within *three months* after it has been fist received in India [Sec. 18(1)]. Sec. 18 does not make an instrument which is not stamped within the time prescribed by this Section, inadmissible in evidence. Such an instrument is impoundable and can be admitted in evidence on payment of stamp duty and penalty.

Policies of Sea-insurance

Section 7(4) : Where any sea-insurance is made for or upon a voyage and also for time, or to extend to or cover any time beyond thirty days after the ship shall have arrived at her destination and been there moored at anchor, the policy shall be charged with duty as a policy for or upon a voyage, and also with duty as a policy for time.

The object of Section 7 is to prevent loss of revenue which would occur if the business of sea-insurance were to be done on ships and not on formal stamped policies. Omission to issue stamped policies is made punishable under Sec. 66.

A contract of sea-insurance, which is expressed in the form of cover notes or slips, bearing date and insured against damages for 'all risks' is invalid and unenforceable as it is not expressed in a sea-policy.

Power to Reduce, Remit or Compound Duties

Sec. 9 deals with the power of the Government to remit, reduce, or compound duties in case of particular instruments or any particular class of instruments or groups of instruments.

Section 9(1) : The government may, by rule or order published in Official Gazette :

(*a*) reduce or remit, whether prospectively or retrospectively, in the whole or any part of the territories under its administration, the duties with which any instruments or any particular class or instruments, or any of the instruments belonging to such class, or any instruments when executed by or in favour of any particular class of persons, by or in favour or any members of such class, are chargeable, and

(*b*) provide for the composition or consolidation of duties in the case of issues by any incorporated company or other body corporate 30[or of transfers (where there is a single transferee, whether incorporated or not).

Section 9(2) In this section, the expression "the government" means,:

(*a*) in relation to stamp-duty in respect of bills of exchange, cheques, promissory notes, bills of lading, letters of credit, policies of insurance, transfer of shares, debentures, proxies and receipts, and in relation to any other stamp-duty chargeable under this Act and failing within entry 96 of List I in Schedule VII to the Constitution, the Central Government;

(*b*) save as aforesaid, the State Government.

Cancellation of Adhesive Stamps

Section 12 deals with the cancellation of adhesive stamps. The object of cancellation is to prevent the same stamps from being used more than once.

Instruments Stamped with Impressed Stamps – How to be Written

Section 13 : Every instrument written upon paper stamped with an impressed stamp shall be written in such manner that the stamp may appear on the face of the instrument and cannot be used for or applied to any other instrument.

Instruments Executed in India

According to *Section 17*, all instruments chargeable with duty and executed by any person in India must be stamped before or at the time of execution.

It is sufficient if stamping and execution are part of the same transaction, so that it is permissible to stamp immediately after the execution of the document.

Instruments Executed out of India (Sec. 18)

Section 18 deals with the time of stamping of instruments other than bills of exchange and promissory notes executed out of India, [*i.e.,* instruments chargeable under Sec. 3(*c*)]. When any such instrument is received in India, it must be stamped within three months of its receipt in India [Sec. 18(1)].

Duties by Whom Payable

Section 29 names the persons by whom stamp duty is payable. It lays down that, in the absence of any agreement to the contrary, the expense of providing the proper stamp shall be borne–

(*a*) in the case of any instrument described in any of the following Articles of Schedule I, namely :

.........,No. 16. (Bottomry Bond),........ No. 56. (Respondentia Bond),..........No. 62(c). (Transfer of any interest secured by a bond, mortgage-deed or policy of insurance), by the person drawing, making or executing such instrument:

(*b*) in the case of a policy of insurance other than fire-insurance- by the person effecting the insurance:

(*bb*) in the case of a policy of fire-insurance- by the person issuing the policy:

Obligation to Give Receipt in Certain Cases

Section 30 : Any person receiving any money, exceeding five thousand in amount, or any bill of exchange, Cheque or promissory note for an amount exceeding five thousand, or receiving in satisfaction or part satisfaction of a debt any movable property exceeding twenty rupees in value, shall, on demand by the person paying or delivering such money, bill, Cheque, note or property, give a duly stamped receipt for the same.

Any person receiving or taking credit for any premium or consideration for any renewal of any contract of fire-insurance, shall, within one month after receiving or taking credit for such premium or consideration, give a duly stamped receipt for the same.

Section 33 casts a duty upon Courts, arbitrators and public officers (except officers of police) to examine every instrument which is chargeable with duty, and is produced or comes before them in the performance of their functions, in order to ascertain whether it is duly stamped. If they are satisfied that the instrument is not duly stamped, they shall impound it.

Instruments not duly stamped in admissible in evidence, etc. (Sec. 35)

Section 35 contains a rule of procedure. According to it no instrument chargeable with duty shall be :

(*i*) admitted in evidence for any purpose by any person having by law or consent of parties authority to receive evidence, or

(*ii*) acted upon, or

(*iii*) registered, or

(*iv*) authenticated, by any such person or by any public officer, unless such instrument is duly stamped.

Collector's Power to Stamp Impounded Instruments (Sec. 40)

Section 40 deals with Collector's power to stamp any instrument impounded by him under Sec. 33 or an instrument sent to him under Sec. 38 (2), not being an instrument chargeable with a duty not exceeding ten paise only or a bill of exchange or promissory note. In such a case, he *shall* adopt the following procedure:

(*a*) If he is of opinion that the instrument is duly stamped, or is not chargeable with duty, he shall certify by endorsement thereon that it is duly stamped, or that it is not so chargeable, as the case may be [Sec. 40(1) (*a*)];

(*b*) If the is of opinion that the instrument is chargeable with duty and is not duly stamped, he shall require the payment of the proper duty, or the amount required to make up the same, together with a penalty of five rupees; or, if he thinks fit, an amount not exceeding ten times the amount of the proper duty or of the deficient portion thereof, whether such amount exceeds or falls short of five rupees [Sec. 40(1) (*b*)].

10.12 CONSUMER PROTECTION ACT, 1986

Insurance is a *service* and therefore it is covered by Section 2(e) of the Consumer Protection Act, 1986.

The Consumer Protection Act was passed in 1986 with a view to provide for better protection of the interests of the consumers. The Act makes provisions for the establishment of Consumer Protection Councils and other authorities such as Consumer Disputes Redressal Forums at the National, State and District levels for speedy and simple settlement of consumer disputes.

Aggrieved consumers can seek the following relief under Sec. 14 of the Act depending on the nature of relief sought by the consumer and the facts of case.

(*a*) removal of defects from the goods,

(*b*) replacement of the goods;

(*c*) refund of the price paid;

(*d*) award of compensation for the loss or injury suffered;

(*e*) removal of defects or deficiencies in the services;

(*f*) discontinuance of unfair trade practices or restrictive trade practices or direction not to repeat them;

(*g*) withdrawal of the hazardous goods from being offered to sale; or

(*h*) award for adequate costs to parties.

The Act recognises the right of the user other than the buyer also to sue the manufacturer by defining the word consumer to include user also. A summary of the provisions is given below :

- It empowers an individual consumer or a recognised consumer. Association whether the consumer is a member of such association or not to file a complaint in respect of affective goods or deficient services.
- It covers not only goods as defined under the Sale of Goods Act, 1930 but also services including services provided by public sector undertakings and government departments such as banking, financing, insurance, transport, processing, supply of electrical or other energy etc.
- It defines the rights of consumers.
- It provides for the establishment of advisory bodies at the Central and State levels to be known as Central Consumer Protection Council and the State Consumer Protection Councils with the object of promoting and protecting the rights of consumers.
- It provides for the establishment of quasi-judicial bodies for the redressel of the grievances of consumers at the District, State and Central levels known as District Forum, State Commission and National Consumer Disputes Redressal Commission
- It lays down the procedure to be followed in redressing consumer grievances and provides a time limit for the disposal of their complaints.
- It empowers the District Forum to issue orders to the opposite party to remove the defect from 'the goods or to replace the goods or to return the price or charges paid and or to pay compensation for any loss or injury suffered by the consumer due to the negligence of the opposite party, in respect of defective goods or deficient services.

- It empowers the District Forum, the State or the National Commission to enforce its order in the same manner as if it were a decree or order made by the Court, and in the event of its inability to execute it, to send such order to a court of competent jurisdiction for its execution.
- It empowers the forum or commission to impose a sentence of imprisonment of not less than one month extending to 3 years or with a minimum fine of Rs. 2,000/- extending upto Rs. 10,000/- or with both, for failure to comply with any order made by it.

The 1993 amendment has empowered the forum or commission to order payment of compensation by the complainant to the opposite party if the petition appears to be frivolous or vexatious in nature. The amount shall not be more than Rs. 10,000/-.

Consumer Defined

It defines *"Consumer"* as a person who :

(*i*) buys any goods for a consideration which has been paid or promised or partly paid and partly promised, or under any system of deferred payment and includes any user of such goods other than the person who buys such goods for consideration paid or promised or partly paid or partly promised, or under any system of deferred payment when such use is made with the approval of such person, but does not include a person who obtains such goods for resale or any other commercial purpose; or

(*ii*) hires or avails of any services for a consideration which has been paid or promised or partly paid and partly promised, or under any system of deferred payment and includes any beneficiary of such services goods other than the person who hires or avails of the services for consideration paid or promised or partly paid or partly promised , or under any system of deferred payment when such services are availed of with the approval of the first mentioned person.

Other Definitions

"Deficiency" means any fault, imperfection, shortcoming or inadequacy in the quality, nature and manner of performance which is required to be maintained by or under any law for the time being in force or has been undertaken to be performed by a person in pursuance of a contract or otherwise in relation to any service.

A *"service"* means service of service of any description which is made available to potential users and includes a provision of facilities in connection with banking, financing, insurance, transport, processing, supply of electrical or other energy, board or lodging or both, housing construction entertainment, amusement or the previewing of news or other information but does not include the rendering of any service free of charge or under a contract of personal service.

"Unfair trade practice" means a trade practice which, for the purpose of promoting the sale, use or supply of any goods or for the provision of any service, adopts any unfair method or unfair or deceptive practice including any of following practices, namely :

(*a*) false or misleading representation,

(*b*) bargain price

(*c*) offering of gifts, prize, contest etc.

(*d*) non compliance of product safety standard.

(*e*) hoarding or destruction of goods.

Complaint Under the Act

Under the Act, *a complaint* means any allegation in writing made by a complainant in regard to one or more of the following :

- Any unfair trade practice as defined in the Act or restrictive trade practices like tie-up sales adopted by any trader.
- One or more defects in goods. The goods hazardous to life and safety, when used are being offered for sale to public in contravention of provisions of any law for the time being in force.
- Deficiencies in services.
- A trader charging excess of price.

Who can file a complaint?

The following can file a complaint under Sec. 12 of the Act :

- A consumer.
- Any voluntary consumer organisation registered under the Societies Registration Act, 1860 or under the Companies Act, 1956 or under any other law for the time being in force.
- The Central Government.
- The State Government or Union Territory Administrations.
- One or more consumers on behalf of numerous consumers who are having the same interest (Class action complaints).

It has been held that the wife of a deceased husband is a beneficiary and can claim compensation under the Consumer Protection Act, 1986 (Sushilaban Bupatrai Soni *vs.* New India Assurance Co. Ltd., 1996, 3 CPJ, Gujrat 404.

Where to file a complaint?

In the district forum if the value of services and compensation claimed is less than one lakh of rupees; before the state commission, if the value of the goods or services and the compensation claimed does of the goods or services and the state commission, the compensation does not exceed more than twenty lakhs of rupees. In the national commission, if the value of the goods or services and the compensation exceeds more than twenty lakhs of rupees.

Procedure under the Act

Procedures for filing complaints and seeking redressel are simple enough.

- There is no fee for filing a complaint before the District Forum, the State Commission, or the National Commission. (A stamp paper is also not required) There should be 3 to 5 copies of the complaint on plain paper.
- The complainant or his authorised agent can present the complaint in person.
- The complaint can be sent by post to the appropriate Forum / Commission.
- A complaint should contain the following information:

(*a*) The name, description and the address of the complainant.

(*b*) The name , description and address of the opposite party or parties, as the case may be, as far as they can be ascertained;

(*c*) The facts relating to complaint and when and where it arose;

(*d*) Documents, if any, in support of the allegations contained in the complaint.

(*e*) The relief which the complainant is seeking.

(*f*) The complainant or his authorised agent should sign the complaint.

(*g*) The complaint is to be filed within two years from the date on which cause of action has arisen.

On the receipt of the complaint, the District Forum has to refer a copy of the complaint to the opposite party mentioned in the complaint directing him to give his version of the case within a period of 30 days or such extended period not exceeding 15 days as may be granted by the Forum. In case the opposite party, on the receipt of the complaint referred to him denies or disputes the allegations contained in the complain, or omits or fails to take may action to represent his case within the time given by the District Forum, the District Forum has to proceed to settle the dispute in the manner provided in the Act.

To sum up, on the receipt of the complaint, the District Forum should:

- Give notice to the opposite party
- The notice should be accompanied with the copy of the complaint
- The opposite party should be given a minimum of 30 days to give his version
- The period of 30 days may be extended by the District Forum for the further period, but not exceeding 15 days.
- The District Forum should wait for a statutory period of 30 days from the date of notice for the version of the opposite party and should not order ex parte proceedings before the expiry of the minimum period of 30 days from the notice and
- Even if the opposite party fails to give his version within 30 days of the notice or the extended time, the complaint should be decided by the District Forum, after recording the evidence of the complainant on merits.

In case the complaint pertains to deficiency in service, the District Forum, as per the mandate of the Act should refer a copy of such complaint to the opposite party directing him to give his version of the cause within a period of 30 days or such extended period, not exceeding 15 days, as may be granted by the District Forum.

After the notice of the complaint to the opposite party, if the opposite party admits the claim of the complainant, the District Forum may pass the consent order in favour of the complainant provided the claim is justified on the basis of the documents and affidavits filed before the Forum. However, before passing such a consent order, the Commission has to satisfy itself, that there is no collusion and that the admissions have been made under no influence.

Section 13(2)(b) of the Consumer Protection Act lays down that if the opposite party does not respond to the notice sent to him by the Commission or denies or disputes the allegations made by the Complainant, the Commission shall have the power to decide the dispute on the basis of the evidence brought to its notice by the complainant and the opposite party, where the opposite party denies or disputes the allegation of the complainant or on the basis of the evidence supplied to it by the complainant, if the opposite party does not respond to the notice of the Commission.

On the other hand, if the complainant fails to appear on the day of hearing the District Forum has the power to either dismiss the complaint for default of decide it on merits. This is provided for in the Rules and not in the Act itself. The Commission also has the power to restore the complaint if sufficient reasons for non-appearance are given.

With regard to setting aside of ex parte orders, it has been held that if sufficient cause is shown for non-appearance of the parties, the Consumer Forum has the power to set aside the order passed ex parte.

Powers of District Forum

The Consumer Protection Act vests the District forum with the powers given to a Civil Court by the Code of Civil Procedure, 1908. These are:

- The power to summon and enforce the attendance of any defendant or witness and examining the witness on oath.

- The authority to order for discovery and production of any document or other material object producible as evidence;
- The power to receive evidence on affidavits;
- The power to requisition the report of the concerned analysis or test from the appropriate laboratory or from any other relevant source;
- The power to issue any commission for the examination of any witness.

Moreover, the Act says that the proceedings before the District Forum shall be deemed to be a judicial proceeding within the meaning of Section 193 and 228 of the Indian Penal Code. Hence, a person giving false evidence can be punished under the Penal Code. The power to proceed against a person for contempt of court is also provided for.

The proceedings of the District forum as per the Act has to be conducted by the President of the Forum and at least one member sitting together. The decision of the Forum has to be signed by the President and the other member or members sitting with him for the proceeding. If there is a split decision between the President and a member, the matter has to be referred to a third member for his opinion. The opinion of the majority then becomes the order of the Forum.

State Commission and Appeals

In case any person is aggrieved by the order of the District Forum, he may prefer an appeal against such order to the State Commission within a period of thirty days from the date of the order. The State Commission however has the power to entertain the appeal after the said period of thirty days if it is satisfied that there was sufficient reason not to file the appeal within the stipulated time.

The Consumer Protection Act, as mentioned earlier, provides for the setting up of a State Commission. This State Commission, as per the Act shall consist of a President, who shall be or has been a Judge of a High Court. There is a provision for two other members, one of whom has to be a woman. The State Commission has the jurisdiction to entertain complaints where the value of the goods or services and compensation, if any, claimed exceeds rupees five lakhs, but does not exceed rupees twenty lakhs. It also has the power to entertain appeals against the orders of any District Forum, within the State. It further has the authority to summon the records and pass appropriate orders in any consumer dispute pending before any District Forum in the State or which has been decided by any District Forum if it has failed to exercise a jurisdiction so vested or has acted in exercise of its jurisdiction illegally or with material irregularity. The same procedure that applies to District forums applies to the State Commissions also.

Any person aggrieved by an order made by the State Commission under its original jurisdiction has the right to prefer an appeal to the National Consumer Disputes Redressal Forum. The appeal has to be filed within a period of thirty days from the date of the order. It is however provided that the National Commission may allow the appeal after thirty days if it is satisfied that there was sufficient cause for not filing within that said period.

National Commission

The Consumer Protection Act provides for a National Consumer Disputes Redressal Forum. The forum consists of a President and four other members. The President has to be either a sitting or retired Judge of the Supreme Court.

The National Commission has the jurisdiction to entertain complaints where the value of the goods or services and the compensation, if any, claimed exceeds rupees twenty lakhs. It also has the jurisdiction to entertain appeals any orders of any State Commission. Further, it has the power to call for the records and pass appropriate orders in any consumer dispute pending or decided by any State Commission, where the State Commission has acted in excess of its jurisdiction or has failed to exercise the jurisdiction vested in it or has exercised jurisdiction illegally. The National Commission also has the powers that are vested in the Civil Court, as prescribed in Section 13, Consumer Protection Act.

A person aggrieved by the order of the National Commission has the right to appeal to the Supreme Court. The appeal has to be filed in the Supreme Court within thirty days of the order of the National Commission. The Supreme Court, however has the power to accept the appeal after thirty days if sufficient reasons are given for the delay. Moreover, the Act stipulates that if either of the parties do not appeal to the Appellate body, within the stipulated time, the order of the Forum shall be final.

Limitation Period

Limitation means a legally specified period beyond which an action cannot be brought, or a property right is not to continue. The Limitation Act provides for the period within which the suit has to be filed. In addition to this, some statutes prescribe a period of limitation for certain procedures.

Before the amendment in 1993, the limitation period for filing complaints before the various forums was governed by the Indian Limitation Act. However, in 1993, Section 24A was introduced, which specifies the Limitation period.

As per Section 24 A, the limitation period for filing a complaint before the District, State or National Commission is two years from the date on which the cause of action arises. However, as mentioned earlier the forums have the power to condone the delay if they feel that there was sufficient cause for the same. The reasons for condoning the delay has to be mentioned in the records.

It has been held that where the complainant claimed that he was busy in negotiating the claim with the insurance company and could not explain the delay, the claim is time barred (Tehri Hydro Development Corporation Ltd. *vs.* New India Assurance Co. Ltd., 2003, ICLD 318.

In a civil court, the suit is not maintainable unless and until the requisite court fee as per the Court Fees and Suit Valuation Act is affixed on the same. The Consumer Protection Act has done away with the requirement of a court fee. Hence, a complaint can be filed in any of the forums without paying any court fees, which is very advantageous, unlike in the case of civil courts, where if the compensation being claimed is high, proportionate amount has to be paid as Court Fees.

However, to check that the bona fide complainant is not dragged into an appeal, vide rule 5 of the Supreme Court (First Amendment) Rules, 1990, for an appeal under Section 23 of the Consumer Protection Act before the Supreme Court, a fixed court fee of Rs. 250/- is payable. There is no court fee for an appeal to the State Commission against the order of the District Forum and to the National Commission against the order of the State Commission.

The District Forum, State Commission and the National Commission have the power to execute the orders passed by them in the same manner in which a Civil Court executes a decree. If they are not able to enforce the order, it can be sent to the court within the local limits of whose jurisdiction, in the case of a company, the registered office of the company is situated or in the case of an order against any other person, the place where the person concerned ordinarily resides or carries on business or personally works for gain is situated. On receipt of such order, the Court to which the order is sent has to execute it as if it is a decree or order sent to it for execution.

Remedy for Frivolous or Vexatious Complaints

If the District Forum, State Commission or the National Commission finds that a complaint is frivolous, they have the power to dismiss the complaint, but they have to give valid reasons for the same. Further, the complainant may be ordered to pay the costs, not exceeding Rupees Ten Thousand.

Penalties Imposed by the Act

Where a person against whom a complaint is made or the complainant fails to comply with the order of the District Forum, State Commission or the National Commission, such person may be imprisoned for a term which shall not be less than one month, but which may be extend to three years, or with fine which shall not be less than two thousand rupees, but which may extend to ten thousand rupees or both.

10.13 ARBITRATION ACT, 1940

Arbitration is a method whereby parties can resolve their disputes privately. It is known as an *alternative dispute resolution mechanism.* Instead of filing a case in a court, parties can refer their case to an arbitral tribunal, which is the forum where arbitration proceedings are conducted. The arbitral tribunal will consider the questions over which the parties are in conflict and will arrive at a decision. This decision is known as an 'award'.

In India, till the promulgation of the Arbitration and Conciliation Ordinance, 1996, which is now repealed and replaced by the Arbitration and Conciliation Act, 1996, with effect from 25th January 1996, the law relating to arbitration was governed principally by the Arbitration (Protocol and Convention) Act, 1937; the Arbitration Act, 1940 and the Foreign Awards (Recognition and Enforcement) Act, 1961.

Now these statutes stand repealed (Section 85) by the enactment of the 1996 Act. The object of the Act is to consolidate and amend the law relating to domestic arbitration, international commercial arbitration and the enforcement of foreign arbitral awards and for related matters.

Arbitration Agreement

Section 7 : (1) In this part "arbitration agreement" means an agreement by the parties to submit to arbitration all or certain disputes which have arisen or which may arise between them in respect of a defined legal relationship, whether contractual or not.

(2) An arbitration agreement may be in the form of an arbitration clause in a contract or in the form of a separate agreement.

(3) An arbitration agreement shall be in writing.

(4) An arbitration agreement is in writing if it is contained in :

- (*a*) a document signed by the parties;
- (*b*) an exchange of letters, telex, telegrams or other means of telecommunication which provide a record of the agreement; or
- (*c*) an exchange of statements of claim and defence in which the existence of the agreement is alleged by one party and not denied by the other.

(5) The reference in a contract to a document containing an arbitration clause constitutes an arbitration agreement if the contract is in writing and the reference is such as to make that arbitration clause part of the contract.

Essentials of Arbitration Agreement

1. It must be in writing. [Section 7(3)].
2. It must have all the essential elements of a valid contract.
3. The agreement must be to refer a dispute, present or future, between the parties to arbitration.
4. An arbitration agreement may be in the form of an arbitration.

Power of the Judicial Authority to Refer to Arbitration

Section 8 : Power to refer parties to arbitration where there is an arbitration agreement :

1. A judicial authority before which an action is brought in a matter which is the subject of an arbitration agreement shall, if a party so applies not later than when submitting his first statement on the substance of the dispute, refer the parties to arbitration.

2. The application referred to in sub-section (1) shall not be entertained unless it is accompanied by the original arbitration agreement or duly certified copy thereof.
3. Notwithstanding that an application has been made under sub-section (1) and that the issue is pending before the judicial authority, an arbitration may be a commenced or continued and an arbitral award made.
4. There must be a valid and subsisting agreement between the parties.
5. The matter about which a suit has been filed should be within the scope of the arbitration agreement.
6. The party asking for the stay must have applied at the earliest opportunity, *i.e.*, before submitting his first statement on the substance of the dispute.
7. The application must be made to the judicial authority before which the proceedings are pending.
8. The application must be accompanied by the original arbitration agreement or by a duly certified copy thereof.
9. The judicial authority must be satisfied that there is no sufficient reason why the matter should not be referred.

Composition of Arbitration Tribunal

An arbitrator is a person selected by mutual consent of the parties to settle the matters in controversy between them. A person appointed to adjudicate the difference between two or more parties is called an arbitrator. An arbitrator is a tribunal chosen by the consent of the parties. The person who is so appointed must also give his consent to act as an arbitrator.

Number of Arbitrators

The parties are free to determine the number of arbitrators provided that such number shall not be an even number. If the parties fail to make the determination the arbitral tribunal shall consist of a sole arbitrator. (Section 10).

Appointment of Arbitrators

A person of any nationality may be an arbitrator, unless otherwise agreed by the parties. The parties are free to agree on a procedure for appointing the arbitrator or arbitrators. (*Section 11*).

Challenge Procedure

The parties are free to agree on a procedure for challenging an arbitrator. [*Section 13(1)*]

Replacement of Arbitrator

Where the mandate of an arbitrator terminates, a substitute arbitrator shall be appointed according to the rules that were applicable to the appointment of the arbitrator being replaced. [*Section 15(2)*]

Death or Insolvency of a Party to the Arbitration Agreement

Death of a party (*Section 40*)

An arbitration agreement shall not be discharged by the death of any party thereto either as respects the deceased or as respects any other party, but shall in such event be enforceable by or against the legal representative of the deceased. [*Section 40(1)*]

The mandate of an arbitrator shall not be terminated by the death of any party by whom he was appointed. [*Section 40(2)*]

Insolvency (Section 41) : A contract entered into by a person who is declared insolvent might contain an arbitration clause. If the Official Receiver or Assignee adopts the contract, then such clause is enforceable by or against him.

Equal Treatment of Parties

The parties shall be treated with equality and each party shall be given a full opportunity to present his case. (Section 18)

Place of Arbitration

Section 20(1) provides that parties are free to agree on the place of arbitration.

Court Assistance in taking Evidence

Application : The arbitral tribunal, or a party with the approval of the arbitral tribunal, may apply to the Court for assistance in taking evidence. [*Section 27(1)*].

Particulars of Application : The application shall specify :

(*a*) the names and addresses of the parties and the arbitrators;

(*b*) the general nature of the claim and the relief sought;

(*c*) the evidence to be obtained, in particular :

- (*i*) the name and address of any person to be heard as witness or expert witness and a statement of the subject-matter of the testimony required;
- (*ii*) the description of any document to be produced or property to be inspected. [*Section 27(2)*].

Settlement

Section 30 provides that :

(1) It is not incompatible with an arbitration agreement for an arbitral tribunal to encourage settlement of the dispute and, with the agreement of the parties, the arbitral tribunal may use mediation, conciliation or other procedures at any time during the arbitral proceedings to encourage settlement.

(2) If, during arbitral proceedings, the parties settle the dispute, the arbitral tribunal shall terminate the proceedings and, if requested by the parties and not objected to by the arbitral tribunal, record the settlement in the form of an arbitral award on agreed terms.

(3) An arbitral award on agreed terms shall be made in accordance with section 31 and shall state that it is an arbitral award.

(4) An arbitral award on agreed terms shall have the same status and effect as any other arbitral award on the substance of the dispute.

Form and Contents of Arbitral Award

Section 31 deals with Arbitral Award. It provides that :

(1) An arbitral award shall be made in writing and shall be signed by the members of the arbitral tribunal.

(2) For the purposes of sub-section (1), in arbitral proceedings with more than one arbitrator, the signatures of the majority of all the members of the arbitral tribunal shall be sufficient so long as the reason for any omitted signature is stated.

(3) The arbitral award shall state the reasons upon which it is based, unless,:

- (*a*) the parties have agreed that no reasons are to be given, or
- (*b*) the award is an arbitral award on agreed terms under section 30.

(4) The arbitral award shall state its date and the place of arbitration as determined in accordance with section 20 and the award shall be deemed to have been made at that place.

(5) After the arbitral award is made, a signed copy shall be delivered to each party.

(6) The arbitral tribunal may, at any time during the arbitral proceedings, make an interim arbitral award on any matter with respect to which it may make a final arbitral award.

(7) (*a*) Unless otherwise agreed by the parties, where and in so far as an arbitral award is for the payment of money, the arbitral tribunal may include in the sum for which the award is made interest, at such rate as it deems reasonable, on the whole or any part of the money, for the whole or any part of the period between the date on which the cause of action arose and the date on which the award is made.

(*b*) A sum directed to be paid by an arbitral award shall, unless the award otherwise directs, carry interest at the rate of eighteen per centum per annum from the date of the award to the date of payment.

(8) Unless otherwise agreed by the parties, :

(*a*) the costs of an arbitration shall be fixed by the arbitral tribunal;

(*b*) the arbitral tribunal shall specify, :

(*i*) the party entitled to costs,

(*ii*) the party who shall pay the costs,

(*iii*) the amount of costs or method of determining that amount, and

(*iv*) the manner in which the costs shall be paid.

Explanation : For the purpose of clause (a), "costs" means reasonable costs relating to, :

(*i*) the fees and expenses of the arbitrators and witnesses,

(*ii*) legal fees and expenses,

(*iii*) any administration fees of the institution supervising the arbitration, and

(*iv*) any other expenses incurred in connection with the arbitral proceedings and the arbitral award.

Termination of Proceedings

Section 32 : (1) The arbitral proceedings shall be terminated by the final arbitral award or by an order of the arbitral tribunal under sub-section (2).

(2) The arbitral tribunal shall issue an order for the termination of the arbitral proceedings where, :

(*a*) the claimant withdraws his claim, unless the respondent objects to the order and the arbitral tribunal recognises a legitimate interest on his part in obtaining a final settlement of the dispute,

(*b*) the parties agree on the termination of the proceedings, or

(*c*) the arbitral tribunal finds that the continuation of the proceedings has for any other reason become unnecessary or impossible.

(3) Subject to section 33 and sub-section (4) of section 34, the mandate of the arbitral tribunal shall terminate with the termination of the arbitral proceedings.

Arbitration Clause in Insurance Policies

Arbitration clause is generally found in insurance policies. It is a time saving and cost saving method of claims settlement. The arbitration condition in fire and motor insurance policies currently in use in India reads :

"If any difference shall arise as to the quantum to be paid under this policy, (liability being otherwise admitted) such difference shall independently of all other questions be referred to the decision of an arbitrator, to be appointed in writing by the parties in difference, or if they cannot agree upon a single arbitrator to the decision of two disinterested persons as arbitrators of whom one shall be appointed in writing by each of the parties within two calendar months after having been required so to do in writing by the other party in accordance with the provisions of the Arbitration Act, 1940, as amended from time to time and for the time being in force. In case either party shall refuse or fail to appoint arbitrator within two calender months after receipt of notice in writing requiring an appointment the other party shall be at liberty to appoint sole arbitrator; and in case of disagreement between the arbitrators, the difference shall be referred to the decision of an umpire who shall have been appointed by them in writing before entering on the reference and who shall sit with the arbitrators and, preside at their meetings.

It is clearly agreed and understood that no difference or dispute shall be referable to arbitration as hereinbefore provided, if the Company has disputed or not accepted liability under or in respect of this Policy.

It is hereby expressly stipulated and declared that it shall be a condition precedent to any right of action or suit upon this policy that the award by such arbitrator, arbitrators or umpire of the amount of the loss or damage shall be first obtained."

10.14 LOK ADALATS

The enactments or legal aid boards of state governments establish Lok Adalat (Lok Nyayalaya). It settles dispute through conciliation and compromise. Lok Adalat accepts the cases which could be settled by conciliation and compromise, and pending in the regular courts within their jurisdiction. As per Chapter XI of the Lok Nyayalaya Rules, 1986, special provisions are made to settle amicably the cases pending before MACT.

Since April 1985, Lok Adalats have been exclusively organised for settlement of motor third party claims. Although the concept of Lok Adalat was very much vogue since early years. This form was made available for settlement of Motor Third Party claims under the initiative of former Chief Justice of India, Shri. P.N. Bhagwati.

The First Lok Adalat was held in Chennai in 1986. The Lok Adalat is presided over by a sitting or retired judicial officer as the chairman, with two other members, usually a lawyer and a social worker. There is no court fee. If the case is already filed in the regular court, the fee paid will be refunded if the dispute is settled at the Lok Adalat. The procedural laws, and the Evidence Act are not strictly followed while assessing the merits of the claim by the Lok Adalat.

The primary requisite for seeking relief in Lok Adalat is that both parties in dispute should agree for settlement and its decision is binding on the parties to the dispute and its order is capable of execution through legal process. No appeal lies against the order of the Lok Adalat.

Lok Adalats have been successful in settling huge number of Third Party claims referred by Motor Accident Claim Tribunal (MACT). Except matters relating to offences, which are not compoundable, a Lok Adalat has jurisdiction to deal with all matters. Matters pending or at pre-trial stage, provided a reference is made to it by a court or by the concerned authority or committee, when the dispute is at a pre-trial stage and not before a Court of Law it can be referred to Lok Adalat.

Legal Services Authorities Act was promulgated in 1987, which aimed to organise Lok Adalat to secure that the operation of legal system promotes justice on the basis of an equal opportunity. The Act gives statutory recognition to the resolution of disputes by compromise and settlement by the Lok Adalats.

According to Legal Services Authorities (Amendment) Act 1994, Lok Adalat settlement is no longer a voluntary concept. By this Act, Lok Adalat has got statutory character and has been legally recognised.

Constitution of Lok Adalats

Section 18 : **Organisation of Lok Adalats :** (1) Every State Authority or District Authority or the Supreme Court Legal Services Committee or every High Court Legal Services Committee or, as the case may be, Taluk Legal Services Committee may organise Lok Adalats at such intervals and places and for exercising such jurisdiction and for such areas as it thinks fit.

(2) Every Lok Adalat organised for an area shall consist of such number of :

(*a*) serving or retired judicial officers; and

(*b*) other persons, of the area as may be specified by the State Authority or the District Authority or the Supreme Court Legal Services Committee or the High Court Legal Services Committee, or as the case may be, the Taluk Legal Services Committee, organising such Lok Adalats.

(3) The experience and qualifications of other persons referred to in clause (b) of sub-section (2) for Lok Adalats organised by the Supreme Court Legal Services Committee shall be such as may be prescribed by the Central Government in consultation with the Chief Justice of India.

(4) The experience and qualifications of other persons referred to in clause (b) of sub-section (2) for Lok Adalats other than referred to in sub-section (3) shall be such as may be prescribed by the State Government in consultation with the Chief Justice of the High Court.

(5) A Lok Adalat shall have jurisdiction to determine and to arrive at a compromise or settlement between the parties to a dispute in respect of :

(*i*) any case pending before; or

(*ii*) any matter which is falling within the jurisdiction of, and is not brought before, any court for which the Lok Adalat is organised:

Provided that the Lok Adalat shall have no jurisdiction in respect of any case or matter relating to an offence not compoundable under any law.

Section 19 : 1. Central, State, District and Taluk Legal Services Authority has been created who are responsible for organising Lok Adalats at such intervals and place.

2. Conciliators for Lok Adalat comprise the following :

A. A sitting or retired judicial officer.

B. Other persons of repute as may be prescribed by the State Government in consultation with the Chief Justice of High Court.

Reference of Cases

Section 20 : Cases can be referred for consideration of Lok Adalat as under:

1. By consent of both the parties to the disputes.
2. One of the parties makes an application for reference.
3. Where the Court is satisfied that the matter is an appropriate one to be taken cognisance of by the Lok Adalat.
4. The principles of justice, equity, fair play and other legal principles shall guide compromise settlement.
5. Where no compromise has been arrived at through conciliation, the matter shall be returned to the concerned court for disposal in accordance with Law.

Effect of the Orders

Section 21 : After the agreement is arrived by the consent of the parties, award is passed by the conciliators. The matter need not be referred to the concerned Court for consent decree.

1. ***Award of Lok Adalat :*** (1) Every award of the Lok Adalat shall be deemed to be a decree of a civil court or, as the case may be, an order of any other court and where a compromise or settlement has been arrived at, by a Lok Adalat in a case referred to it under sub-section (1) of Section 20, the court-fee paid in such case shall be refunded in the manner provided under the Court Fees Act, 1870 (7 of 1870).

(2) Every award made by a Lok Adalat shall be final and binding on all the parties to the dispute, and no appeal shall lie to any court against the award.

Proceedings to be Recognised as Judicial

Every proceedings of the Lok Adalat shall be deemed to be judicial proceedings for the purpose of summoning of witnesses, discovery of documents, reception of evidences, requisitioning of Public record etc.

Powers of Lok Adalats

Section 22 : (1) The Lok Adalat shall, for the purposes of holding any determination under this Act, have the same powers as are vested in a civil court under the Code of Civil Procedure, 1908 (5 of 1908), while trying a suit in respect of the following matters, namely :

(*a*) the summoning and enforcing the attendance of any witness and examining him on oath;

(*b*) the discovery and production of any document;

(*c*) the reception of evidence on affidavits;

(*d*) the requisitioning of any public record or document or copy of such record or document from any court or office; and

(*e*) such other matters as may be prescribed.

(2) Without prejudice to the generality of the powers contained in sub-section(1), every Lok Adalat shall have the requisite powers to specify its own procedure for the determination of any dispute coming before it.

(3) All proceedings before a Lok Adalat shall be deemed to be judicial proceedings within the meaning of Sections 193, 219 and 228 of the Indian Penal Code (45 of 1860) and every Lok Adalat shall be deemed to be a civil court for the purpose of Section 195 and Chapter XXVI of the Code of Criminal Procedure, 1973(2 of 1974).

Ombudsman

Ombudsman traces its history to Sweden way back in 19th century and it literally means an authority that is empowered to investigate individual complaints against public authorities, departments etc. Later it has been adopted in many countries including UK, Australia etc.

In India the idea of insurance ombudsman was first mooted in the year 1998. Central government by the powers conferred on it by sub section (1) section 114 of insurance act 1938 has set up an ombudsman specifically for Insurance sector. Main objective of insurance ombudsman is redressal and settlement of disputes arising between insured and insurer. Insurance ombudsman is a quasi-judicial body established for speedy settlement of disputes in fair, impartial and judicial manner.

Any individual policyholder (including a sole proprietor but not partnerships or companies) or his legal heir can approach the Insurance Ombudsman for complaints in respect of policies on personal lines of business.

Personal lines of business include coverage under Personal Accident policies, Mediclaim, insurance of property of the individual such as motor vehicles, household articles etc. There is no fee or charge required to be paid and there is no requirement to approach the Ombudsman through a lawyer. However, before approaching Ombudsman, a representation should be made to the insurance Company. If no reply is received within one month or the reply is not satisfactory, the Ombudsman can be approached. The maximum limit for the amount under dispute for which the Ombudsman can entertain is Rs. 20 lakhs and Complaints can be made to Ombudsman within one year of the rejection by insurer of the representation of the complainant or the insurer's final reply to the Complainant's representation.

Types of Complaints

The insurance ombudsman may consider or receives the complaints regarding:

- Partial or total repudiation of claims
- Delay in settlement of claims
- Legal construction of policy (policy wordings)
- Premium paid or payable
- Non-issue of insurance documents to customers after receipt of premium.

An insurance ombudsman cannot act on :

- Any complaint which falls outside the territorial limits of the ombudsman
- Any complaint where the claims amount is more than 20 lakhs.
- Any dispute/issue/complaint which is under trial in any other judicial or quasi-judicial body.
- Where the complaint is not regarding personal lines of business.
- Where the complaint is filed by any artificial judicial person
- Any complaint which is lodged after one year from the date of issue of first reply by the insurer.

Procedure for Redressel

1. The insured has to apply in writing to the Insurance Ombudsman under whose jurisdiction the insurer falls. A complaint may be filed either by the insured or his legal heirs and should clearly state the name and address of the insurer against whom the complaint is made, nature and circumstances giving rise to dispute, nature of loss sustained by the complainant and relief sought from Insurance Ombudsman.
2. The complainant has to substantiate his claim with all the documentary evidences.
3. The Insurance Ombudsman would first act as a mediator to settle the grievance on a mutually agreeable basis. This mediation process would be for a maximum of one month. After hearing both the parties Insurance Ombudsman may pass an award, which if acceptable to the complainant, is sent to insurer for final execution. Insurer has to comply with the award within 15 days and it has to be informed to the Insurance Ombudsman.
4. If the grievance is not settled on a mutually agreeable basis, Insurance Ombudsman gives a speaking award within a period not exceeding three months. If the complainant is not satisfied with the award, he can appeal in any other forum or court, however such facility is not available to the insurer.
5. An award passed by the Insurance Ombudsman has to be complied with, by the insurer within the 15 days. However, no action lies if the insurer opts for non-compliance of the award because he no judicial powers for the execution of award compared to other judicial systems like consumer forums, civil courts etc.

No advocates are allowed to represent insurer/ complainant to argue their respective cases. Further Insurance Ombudsman being a non-judicial authority, does not have the powers of summoning particular persons/witness and examining them on oath. Another specific feature of Insurance Ombudsman is that it can pass award for *ex-gratia* settlement of disputes, while such powers of exgratia settlement are not vested with other redressal mechanisms such as consumer courts etc.

Key Terms

- Bill of Lading
- Charter Party
- Mechanically Propelled Vehicle
- Multimodal Transportation

- ❒ Private Carrier
- ❒ Public Carrier
- ❒ Railway Claim Tribunal
- ❒ Third Party Risks
- ❒ Warranties
- ❒ Inland Vessels Accident Claims Tribunal
- ❒ Policy of Insurance
- ❒ Policy of Group Insurance
- ❒ Policy of Sea-Insurance
- ❒ Adhesive Stamps
- ❒ Impressed Stamps
- ❒ Impounded Instruments
- ❒ Deficiency
- ❒ Service
- ❒ Unfair Trade Practice
- ❒ Complaint
- ❒ District Forum
- ❒ State Commission
- ❒ National Commission
- ❒ Dependant
- ❒ Employment Injury
- ❒ Employee
- ❒ Exempted Employee
- ❒ Family
- ❒ Immediate Employer
- ❒ Permanent Partial Disablement
- ❒ Permanent Total Disablement
- ❒ Temporary Disablement
- ❒ Wages
- ❒ Employees' State Insurance Fund
- ❒ Arbitration
- ❒ Arbitration Tribunal
- ❒ Award
- ❒ Lok Adalas
- ❒ Insurance Ombudsman

Questions for Review

1. Define "a mechanically propelled vessel" under the Inland Steam Vessels Act, 1977 & Amended Act of 1977. Briefly explain the liability of the owners of inland mechanically propelled vessel towards third parties.
2. List the various steps involved in claiming compensation via Claims Tribunal under the Inland Steam, 1977.
3. Distinguish Between :
   (*a*) Public Carrier and Private Carrier
   (*b*) Charter Party and Bill of Lading
   in view of the provisions of Carriage of Goods by Sea Act, 1925.
4. Write short notes on :
   (*a*) Implied Condition and Warranties
   (*b*) Rights and Immunities of Carrier
   in view of the provisions of Carriage of Goods by Sea Act, 1925.
5. List the various provisions relating to the liability of shipowners against carriage losses as per the provisions of Merchant Shipping Act, 1958.
6. Discuss the various provisions contained in Chapter IX and XI of the Indian Railway Act, 1890 relating to "Carriage of Goods" and "Responsibilities of Railway Administration as Carrier".
7. Briefly describe the jurisdiction, powers and authority of claims tribunal as per the provisions of the Railway Claims Tribunal Act, 1987.
8. List the various liabilities of common carrier under the Carriers Act, 1965.

9. Explain the liability of air carrier towards :
   (*a*) death of injury to passengers
   (*b*) damage/loss registered luggage and cargo
   under the carriage by Air Act, 1972.
10. Write short notes on :
    (*a*) Multimodel Transportation
    (*b*) Basis of Liability of Multi-model Transport Operator
    (*c*) Assessment of Compensation under the Provisions of Multi-Model Transportation Act, 1993.
11. What is the consequence of an instrument requiring to be stamped under the Indian Stamp Act, 1899 not being duly stamped?
12. Define the various types of policies as per Section 2 of Indian Stamp Act, 1899.
13. Define "Consumer" and "Deficiency in Services" as per the provisions of Consumer Protection Act, 1986. What is the redressal mechanism available to the insured (consumer) under the Act.
14. Write short notes on :
    (1) False Complaints
    (2) Limitation Period
    under the Consumer Protection Act, 1986.
15. What is an arbitration agreement? What matters may be referred for arbitration?
16. What are the powers and duties of arbitrator? When may the Cowet remove an arbitrator?
17. Write short notes on :
    (*a*) Arbitration Clause in Insurance Policies
    (*b*) Lok Adalats
    (*c*) Insurance Ombudsman

Suggested Readings

1. Bare Acts
2. Gulshan & Kapoor, Business Law Including Company Law, New Age, Delhi, 2004.
3. Motor Insurance, IC72, Insurance Institute of India, Mumbai, 2003.
4. R.C. Chawla & K.C. Garg, Commercial Law, Kalyani Publishers, 1998.
5. N.D. Kapoor & Rajni Abbi, General Law, Sultan Chand & Sons, 1991.
6. Avtar Singh, Law of Insurance, Eastern Book Company, 2005.

References

- www.indianlawinfor.com
- www.indialawinfo.com
- www.bimaonline.com
- on-lyne.com
- http:\\shipping.inc.in
- www.indiainfoline.com
- orientalinsurance.nic.in
- *invert.economictimes.indiatimes.com*

Insurance and Economy

Chapter 11

CHAPTER OBJECTIVES

After reading this chapter you will be able to understand :

- *The economic importance of insurance*
- *Contribution to Indian Economy*
- *Libralisation of Insurance Markets*

The primary purpose of insurance is to provide risk coverage, when the contract period extends over a long time, as in the case of life insurance, premium payments comprise of two components – one for buying risk coverage and the other towards savings. This bundling together of risk coverage and savings is peculiar to life insurance and is more common in developing countries like India. In the industrially advanced countries, this is not necessarily so and short duration life insurance contracts without a savings component are equally popular. In the developing economies because of the savings component and the long nature of the contract, life insurance has become an important instrument of mobilising long-term funds. The savings component puts the life insurance in direct competition with other financial institutions and savings instruments.

Insurance and economic growth mutually influence each other. As the economy grows, the living standards of people increase. As a consequence, the demand for life insurance increases. As the assets of people and of business enterprises increase in the growth process, the demand for general insurance also increases. In fact, as the economy widens the demand for new types of insurance products emerges. Insurance is no longer confined to product markets; they also cover service industries. It is equally true that growth itself is facilitated by insurance. A well-developed insurance sector promotes economic growth by encouraging risk-taking.

Also insurance and more particularly life insurance is a mobilizer of long term savings and life insurance companies are thus able to support infrastructure projects which require long term funds. There is thus a mutually beneficial interaction between insurance and economic growth. The low income levels of the vast majority of population has been one of the factors inhibiting a faster growth of insurance in India.

As in the case of all financial institutions, insurance is an activity that needs to be regulated. This is so because the smooth functioning of business depends on the trust and confidence reposed by the customers in the solvency of the financial institutions. Insurance products are of little value to customers, if they cannot trust the company to keep its promise. The regulatory framework in relation to the insurance companies seeks to take care of three major concerns – (a) protection of consumers' interest, (b) to ensure the financial soundness of the insurance industry, and (c) to help the healthy growth of the insurance market.

11.1 THE ECONOMIC IMPORTANCE OF INSURANCE

11.1.1 Risk Transfer

One of insurance's key roles is safeguarding the financial health of small and medium-sized enterprises. In addition to the protection provided by social security systems, private insurance cover is crucial for people to insure themselves against inability to work, set aside money for retirement or protect themselves against the loss of their assets. This is where insurance comes in as a key component in ensuring the healthy development of small and medium-sized enterprises - a fact which is of paramount importance to a country's political stability.

A sophisticated insurance sector is also important in encouraging domestic production, innovation and trade. Insurance reduces the investment risk faced by companies and the state. Many companies find it far more expensive, if not impossible, to take out a loan without purchasing the requisite insurance protection. Insured, thereby reduces the costs of raising the capital they need. This is especially important in emerging markets, as a shortage of capital is one of the major disincentives to investment. By reducing investment risk, insurance can also encourage companies to think more long term and increase their risk tolerance. A lot of investments in new production facilities and newly founded companies would never happen if every company was required to have the necessary financial means to make good every conceivable loss. While arguable, it is no exaggeration that the availability of insurance is sometimes being heralded as a factor of production in itself.

The same applies to infrastructure investments: if it weren't for insurance, a lot of infrastructure projects - such as power plants, railways or airports - would never be realised; because in the absence of sufficient financial funds to enable them to resume operations in the wake of a loss event, and without insurance, these projects would be reduced to nothing more than white elephants.

11.1.2 Information Role

Insurance plays an additional role in the economy: that of providing information. The level of insurance premiums provides an indication of existing risks and of how probable it is that a loss will occur. This helps companies make a comparison of the risk/return profiles of projects, thereby ensuring that the available resources are put to the best possible use. Insurance companies also offer consultancy services, advising on how to improve safety standards and a product's quality.

11.1.3 Capital Market Role

As well as stabilising the financial circumstances of private individuals, companies and the state, in their role as institutional investors, insurance companies contribute to the development of a well-functioning capital market thanks to the huge amount of assets they have to invest. Insurance companies receive premiums and set them aside as provisions for the payment of future claims. They proceed to invest them in the capital market, which gives them the status of major investors. From a macro-economic point of view, the insurance market could help to mobilise national savings and narrow the investment gap of emerging economies. In emerging markets, domestic savings have not been fully mobilised despite huge funding needs arising from infrastructure projects, for example. Insurance companies as important long-term institutional investors, therefore functioning as financial intermediaries, contribute to bringing together savers and borrowers. Life insurance, in particular, can make savings available – although life insurers are themselves dependent on a functioning capital market if they are to measure up to their role in the area of risk transfer.

11.2 Contribution to Indian Economy

Insurance Companies receive, without much default, a steady cash stream of premium or contributions to pension plans. Various actuary studies and models enable them to predict, relatively accurately, their expected cash outflows.

Liabilities of Insurance companies being long-germ or contingent in nature, liquidity is excellent and their investments are also long-term in nature.

As a combined result of all this, investments of insurance companies have been largely in bonds floated by GOI, PSUs, state governments, local bodies, corporate bodies and mortgages of long term nature.

The insurance industry also provides crucial financial intermediary services, transferring funds from the insured to capital investment, critical for continued economic expansion and growth, simultaneously generating long-term funds for infrastructure development.

In fact infrastructure investments are ideal for asset-liability matching for life insurance companies given their long term liability profile. According to preliminary estimates published by the Reserve Bank of India, contribution of insurance funds to financial savings was 14.2 per cent in 2005-06, *viz.*, 2.4 per cent of the GDP at current market prices. Development of the insurance sector is thus necessary to support continued economic transformation. Social security and pension reforms too benefit from a mature insurance industry.

Employment Generation

Life insurance industry provides increased employment opportunities. Employees in insurance sector as on 31st March, 2005 is around 2 lakhs. Many agents depend on insurance for their livelihood. No. of agents on 31st March 2004 – 15.59 lakhs. Brokers, corporate agents, training establishments provide extra employment opportunities. Many of these openings are in rural sectors. Let us have a look at global figures (Exhibit 11-A).

Exhibit – 11A

Employment in Insurance, 1999-2008

(Annual averages, 000)

2004	764.4	604.4	29.8	1,398.6	643.3	216.8	860.1	2,258.6	47.0
2005	761.9	595.0	28.8	1,385.7	650.1	223.5	873.6	2,259.3	46.4
2006	787.4	597.4	28.0	1,412.8	659.9	230.9	890.8	2,303.7	47.8
2007	784.0	586.1	27.0	1,397.1	675.3	234.5	909.8	2,306.8	48.6
2008	804.2	569.2	28.4	1,401.8	670.1	236.9	907.0	2,308.8	49.2

1. Establishments primarily engaged in initially underwriting insurance policies.
2. Includes claims adjusters, third-party administrators of insurance funds and other service personnel such as advisory and insurance ratemaking services.
3. Includes employees of legal entities organized to provide insurance and employee benefits exclusively for the sponsor, or its employees or members. These employees are not included in the total for the insurance industry.

Source : U.S. Department of Labor, Bureau of Labor Statistics.

11.3 ROLE OF INSURANCE IN THE ECONOMIC SYSTEM

In a modern economic and financial system the insurance sector plays three main roles. First, it provides individuals, corporations and other organisations with a mechanism for transferring some of the non-entrepreneurial risks that they face. Second, it provides a means for mobilising long-term savings and investing them profitably in the capital market, thus indirectly stimulating the growth of the capital market itself. Third, it complements state social insurance programmes, especially in the areas of pensions, disability and health care financing.

Insurance companies provide an effective risk-transfer mechanism. They can bring together a large portfolio of insurable risks where the incidence of these losses are reasonably independent of each other, and thus reduce the overall risk through portfolio diversification *i.e.*, the law of large numbers. In order to underwrite these risks insurance companies must be able to price them. This means collecting credible information to allow them to estimate the frequency and severity of figure losses. In addition, the risk absorption capacity of individual insurance companies is increased dramatically through reinsurance. Reinsurance is a well-established network of risk sharing between insurance companies allowing large risk exposures to be spread not just within a national market but globally. Hence the collective capital and risk assessment resource of the world insurance market can be drawn on to finance catastrophic losses.

Insurance companies plays a major role in mobilising small-scale savings from across the economy, which can collectively appreciate substantially if well invested in the capital market. Insurance companies generate private sector saving in a variety of ways. First, all insurance contracts, whether life or non-life (property and casualty) insurance, give rise to some form of private saving. This arises primarily from insurance premiums being paid in advance by customers, while claims and policy settlements paid back to consumers at a later date, after convering operating and marketing costs. This time lag between the receipt of premiums and return payments to consumers varies between different classes of insurance. Clearly, the time lag is longer for life insurance contracts than for non-life insurance contracts, hence the accumulation of investable funds is higher. In addition, the plough back of investment returns earned on the accumulation of these invested funds by insurance companies also contributes to the total level of saving. Second, life insurance contracts, especially endowment and linked-life policies and those concerned with pension provision, have a more significant saving element.

An important aspect of the insurance risk transfer mechanism is that not only do insurance companies have access through reinsurance to a network of other insurers but also that large potential losses can be spread across domestic and international markets. Essentially, the mechanism of reinsurance is one of accessing the capital of other insurance companies. When an insurance company buys reinsurance, the premium paid is effectively a payment for the use of the capital of the reinsurer. Due to reinsurance, therefore, the capital of a national insurance market is extended internationally since it allows domestic insurance companies access to the combined capital base of the global reinsurance market.

Economic Benefits of an Efficient Risk Transfer Mechanism

Transferring insurable risks onto efficient insurance markets has potential benefits in the following ways. When operating in competitive markets, Industrial, commercial and trading enterprises have to take business risks in order to make profits. By being able to transfer some of the risks associated with these commercial and investment decisions, the decision-taking process is made less risky. Hence, decision-makers faced with less uncertainty will be more prepared to undertake more adventurous and potentially more profitable activities. Insurance markets also provide protection against some of the risks associated with international trade, *e.g.*, damage or loss of goods in transit and credit risks associated with non-payment by foreign customers. Cargo marine insurance and international credit insurance thus helps to lubricate the flow of international trade.

The risks transfer facility provided by insurance companies can be viewed in terms of the efficient use of capital. Industrial, commercial and trading enterprises would have to hold more precautionary capital to run their enterprises if there were no insurance markets. In effect, insurance companies supply contingent equity capital to industrial and commercial enterprises. This means that across the economy as a whole less equity capital is needed to support for banks in their role as financial intermediaries. One area of companies also provide some risk support for banks in their role as financial intermediaries. One area of support is the risk transfer facilities provided by credit insurance. Credit insurance is input into the supply of banking lending products. In addition, when commercial and mortgage banks have sought to increase the liquidity within their asset portfolios through the securitisation of their loans, the bonds issued from this process have often been purchased by life insurance companies. Long-term liabilities, and strong cash flow positions, mean that life insurance companies are "natural" investors in the capital market. This transfer of long term interest rate risk through loan securitisations into life insurance companies indirectly stimulates the development of the capital market.

Life insurance has historically been an important method through which individuals with relatively low incomes have been able to save and invest effectively for the longer term. By designing relatively simple life insurance and savings contracts, which can be purchased in small amounts on a regular basis, insurance companies have been able to accumulate large amounts to money from across a large proportion of population. By pooling these savings from many small investors into large accumulations of funds, insurance companies are able to invest these in a wider range of financial assets than individuals would be able to do so themselves, as well as in larger scale and more uncertain investment opportunities. This pooling benefit to individuals is not unique to life insurance. It is provided by other saving instruments, especially collective investments (CIS). In addition, because in life insurance there is a regular or contractual payment by consumers, the level and stability of personal saving may be increased, compared to what would be the case if the saving arrangement were more discretionary in nature. Life insurance companies often have active marketing strategies that encourage myopic individuals to save rather than consume. However, aggressive marketing strategies are sometimes used and this can lead to consumers purchasing inappropriate saving products. This is a negative aspect of active marketing, but these adverse effects can be minimised by a combination of statutory regulation, market self-regulation and sound corporate governance system for insurance companies and other institutional investors. Evidence exists that an active life insurance sector increases the level of long-term saving in emerging economies, not least because it provides an alternative to bank deposits for smaller investors, but also because the CIS sector does not develop until the capital market itself is relatively well developed (see chapter 15 on Capital Markets).

Economic Benefits of the Saving and Investment Role

What are the wider economic benefits derived from the stimulation of private sector saving and its subsequent investment in the capital market? Firstly, these savings can be made available, either in the form of equity or debt capital, to manufacturing, agricultural, energy, trading or service enterprises. New companies can be set up and finance is available for existing companies to increase their level of capital expenditure in new plant, equipment etc. Moreover, particularly for life insurance, since the time horizons for investment are long-term, these savings can be tied up for a long period of time and hence can be made available for capital expenditure decisions that will only produce profits in the future. Since banks can frequently only provide short-term finance to manufacturing and other enterprises, this investment activity of life insurance complements the lending practices of the banking system because of the short-term nature of their deposits.

The long-term savings generated by life insurance companies can also be made available to help fund large-scale projects to strengthen economic infrastructure. Such infrastructure investment is especially important in emerging economies not only to underpin the growth of domestic enterprises but also to encourage foreign companies to enter the market and invest further. Other possible financial assets for insurance companies are government bonds and mortgage or mortgage-backed securities. The latter stimulate the development of the housing market.

In many OECD and emerging market economies (EMEs), governments are seeking to reform their social security or social insurance systems to reduce the current and future burden of these systems on government finances. Pressures for reform arise from a combination of factors: demographic changes, rising standards of living, and increasing public expectations. Retirement provision, health care and disability support feature as a major component of social security budgets. Through these reforms, the insurance sector and other parts of the financial services industry are increasingly being seen as potential government partners. Pension and annuity schemes, private heath insurance and accident and disability insurances are core business of insurance companies.

Insurance is of primordial importance in domestic economies and internationally. The role of insurance in the development process is difficult to access but there is some evidence that the promotion of insurance programmes might have a particularly significant impact on the level of personal saving in many developing countries.

Exhibit – 11B

Insurance as a %age of GDP

	Premiums (in USDmn) 2007	*Premiums in % of GDP 2007*
America	1,417,463	7.58
North America	1,330,066	8.71
Latin America and Caribbean	87,397	2.54
Europe	1,680,693	8.03
Western Europe	1,606,324	8.85
Central and Eastern Europe	74,369	2.78
Asia	840,601	6.20
Japan and newly industrialised Asian economies	640,754	10.38
South and East Asia	176,654	3.05
Middle East and Central Asia	23,193	1.45
Africa	68,818	6.58
Oceania	53,294	4.31
World	4,060,870	7.49
Industrialised countries	3,646,523	9.05
Emerging markets	414,347	2.75
OECD	3,586,703	8.65
G7	2,852,637	9.22
EU, 15 countries	1,527,535	9.16
NAFTA	1,347,482	8.34
ASEAN	41,358	3.17

Source: Swiss Re, Economic Research & Consulting, Sigma No. 4/2007.

The economic significance of the insurance industry in a country is commonly evaluated by means of the ratio of premiums to the gross domestic products (GDP). Although this measure of insurance penetration does not give a complete picture of the insurance output because of the considerable variation in premiums rates between different countries, it has the advantage of not being influenced by currency factors. (Exhibit 11B)

Grace and Skipper (1991) found that the income elasticity for developing countries was lower than the income elasticity for developed countries suggesting that as countries progress economically, non-life insurance becomes relatively more important.

In fact, individual country experiences are too heterogeneous to accord neatly with any very simple generalization and very little is known about the demand and supply relationship in these countries (Grace and Skipper, 1991). Some societies have achieved high levels of human development at modest levels of per capita income.

Insurance and GDP

The relationship between the insurance density and GDP is direct. Insurance density varies directly with GDP. Have a look at Exhibit 11C.

Exhibit 11C

International Comparison (Insurance Penetration)

Countries	Insurance penetration (Premiums as % of GDP-1999)			Insurance Penetration (Premiums as % of GDP 2000)		
	Total	Non-life	Life	Total	Non-life	Life
United States	8.55	4.32	4.23	8.76	4.28	4.48
Canada	6.49	3.31	3.19	6.56	3.28	3.27
Brazil	2.01	1.66	0.35	2.11	1.75	0.36
Mexico	1.68	0.86	0.82	1.72	0.85	0.86
Chile	3.78	1.13	2.65	4.07	1.15	2.92
United Kingdom	13.35	3.05	10.30	15.78	3.07	12.71
Germany	6.52	3.55	2.96	6.54	3.55	3.00
France	8.52	2.82	5.70	9.40	2.81	6.59
Russia	2.13	1.34	0.78	2.42	1.29	1.13
Japan	11.17	2.30	8.87	10.92	2.22	8.70
South Korea	11.18	2.89	8.39	13.05	3.16	9.89
PR China	1.63	0.61	1.02	1.79	0.67	1.12
India	1.93	0.54	1.39	2.32	0.55	1.77
Malaysia	3.88	1.72	2.16	3.72	1.59	2.13
Indonesia	1.42	0.76	0.66	1.18	0.64	0.54
South Africa	16.54	2.62	13.92	16.86	2.83	14.04
Nigeria	0.95	0.88	0.07	0.66	0.53	0.13
Kenya	3.26	2.48	0.78	2.63	1.91	0.72
Australia	9.82	3.39	6.43	9.41	3.37	6.04

Source: Swiss Re, SIGMA volumes 9/2000 and 6/2001.

The statistics shows that the penetration is extremely low in India compared to our Asian partners like Japan and South Korea. This indicates a huge potential for Indian Insurance Market.

Insurance and Income Redistribution

Life insurance essential serves to transfer funds from currently employed persons via. premium payments to unemployed persons, and thereby helps alleviate the problem of economic distress. Insurance proceeds on an important element in the economic well-being of dependents Government-sponsored insurance programmes strive to comprehensive achieve social goals while private programme provide attractive alternative to public welfare system.

Inflation, Business Cycles and Insurance

Inflation and business recessions directly reduces the real purchasing power and network of the people respectively. Insurance can provide a cover to these, yet the negative side is the adverse impact on the financial performance of companies.

Population Changes and Insurance

Population changes materially affects the insurance industry because of the economic consequences of changing rates of birth, death, marriage and family formation. The shifting age distribution affects the kinds and amount of insurance the people will buy.

Exhibit 11D

International Comparison (Insurance Density)

Countries	*Insurance Density (Premiums per capita in USD-1999)*			*Insurance Density (Premiums per capita in USD-2000)*		
	Total	*Non-life*	*Life*	*Total*	*Non-life*	*Life*
United States	2921.1	1474.4	1446.6	3152.1	1540.7	1611.4
Canada	1375.3	700.6	674.6	1516.8	759.6	757.2
Brazil	68.6	56.7	11.8	75.6	62.7	12.9
Mexico	84.6	43.3	41.3	101.2	50.4	50.8
Chile	163.0	48.7	114.3	175.8	49.7	126.0
United Kingdom	3244.3	741.5	2502.8	3759.2	730.7	3028.5
Germany	1675.7	913.5	762.2	1491.4	808.5	683.0
France	2080.9	688.6	1392.3	2051.1	613.7	1437.4
Russia	26.8	17.0	9.9	41.8	22.3	19.5
Japan	3908.9	805.5	3103.4	3973.3	808.2	3165.1
South Korea	1022.8	262.3	760.5	1234.1	298.5	935.6
PR China	13.3	5.0	8.3	15.2	5.7	9.5
India	8.5	2.4	6.1	9.9	2.3	7.6
Malaysia	140.4	62.3	78.1	150.9	64.6	86.4
Indonesia	9.5	5.1	4.4	8.6	4.6	4.0
South Africa	490.9	77.9	413.0	472.1	79.1	393.9
Nigeria	2.6	2.4	0.2	2.0	1.6	0.4
Kenya	9.9	7.5	2.4	8.9	6.5	2.4
Australia	2037.4	703.8	1333.6	1859.3	665.8	1193.5

Source: Swiss Re, SIGMA volumes 9/2000 & 6/2001.

Fiscal Policy

Fiscal Policy affects in Insurance sector in the following form:

(1) Government spending

(2) Taxation

(3) Direct Controls on the business systems

(4) Moral Suasion (assistance).

11.4 LIBERALISATION OF INSURANCE MARKETS — ISSUES AND CONCERNS

Opening of the insurance sector pose certain issues before every government and of course for India. Let us have a look at liberalisation – its meaning, and implications.

Meaning

A liberal insurance market is one in which the market, subject only to economically justifiable government restrictions, determines; who should be allowed to sell insurance, what products should be sold, how product should be sold, and the prices at which products should be sold. The first item, therefore, deals with issues such as market access and equality of competitive opportunity, including national treatment. In turn, market access issues encompass prudential regulation. Second and fourth items commonly deal with issues such as product, price, and market conduct regulation. All four items subsume competition regulation.

Pre-conditions for Liberalisation

(*a*) Sound competition law
(*b*) Efficient and reliable regulation
(*c*) Phased-liberalisation
(*d*) Consistency and impartiability between competitors.
(*e*) Optimum quantum of regulation.
(*f*) Efficient disclose and dissemination of information to the society.

For developing countries, the regulation of insurance business in liberalisation era poses following concerns and special interests.

(*a*) restrictions on entry, especially foreign players;
(*b*) suppression of price and product competition; and
(*c*) control of inter-industry competition from those selling similar or complementary products."

Insurance markets in countries like India inherently possess certain imperfections justifying the need for competition as well as regulation. This is attributable of the following reasons:

(*a*) Lack of knowledge on part of insureds
(*b*) Insurance is a technical, complicated subject
(*c*) Intensity of price discrimination is high when there is a competition
(*d*) Externalities is cause of concern
(*e*) Government sponsored free insurance hurts private insurance markets and thus causes imperfection.

Key Terms

- Insurance Density
- Liberalisation
- Bottomry Contracts
- Inflation
- Insurance Density
- Liberalisation
- Malhotra Committee
- Population
- GDP
- Fiscal Policy
- IRDA Act, 1999
- Insurance Reforms
- Macroeconomic Issues
- Respondentia

Questions for Review

1. Explain the importance of insurance sector to the economy.
2. What are the necessary condition for liberalisation?
3. Trace the history of Indian Insurance industry for the period 1818-1999. What are your comments on the present state of Insurance Market.
4. Write short notes on.
   (1) Insurance Sector Reforms
   (2) Insurance Player in India
5. "From a global perspective insurance has emerged as a business risk management device to a highly sophisticated risk transfer mechanism for both individuals and corporations." Discuss.

Suggested Readings

- D.C. Srivastava and S. Srivastava, *Indian Insurance Industry — Transition and Prospects*, New Century Publications, 2001.
- *IRDA Annual Report,* 2001-02.
- Spencer L. Kimbell and Herbert S. Demenberg, *Insurance, Government and Social Policy: Studies in Insurance Regulation,* The S.S. Haubner Foundation for Insurance Education, 1969.
- Irving Pfeffer and David R. Klock, *Perspective on Insurance,* Prentice-Hall, Englewood Cliffs, 1994.

Web Resources

- www.bimaonline.com
- www.bajajallianz.com
- www.tata-aig.com
- www.hdfc.com

Insurance Industry in India

Chapter 12

CHAPTER OBJECTIVES

After reading this chapter you will be able to understand :

- *Historical Framework of Insurance*
- *Insurance Sector Reforms*
- *Insurance Players in India*

12.1 HISTORICAL FRAMEWORK OF INSURANCE

Historical framework of insurance can be discussed in two perspectives — (a) Global; (b) Indian

12.1.1 Global Perspective

Insurance in the Pre-Greek Period

The history of western civilisation focuses on Babylon (500 B.C.) as the centre of early economy linking China, India and Persia with Phoenicia, Egypt and Aromania. The principal imports of Babylonia included gold, silver, copper, tin precious and semiprecious stones, ivory, woods such as ebony and oil, essences, wine and slaves. During trade routes, Bandits, pirates, fire storms and death were common occurrings. The loss chances were very high and the Babylon Merchants who extended credit on such vulnerable collateral as cargo in transit charged risk premiums above the interest charges on capital. The borrower usually pledged all of his property and his family in order to secure the loan. If the misfortune befell him, the borrower lost everything and he and his family might be sold into slavery.

Under the pressures of high risk, trade declined, and by 2250 B.C. there was little commercial activity along the trade routes of the Near East. The *Code of Hammurabi,* which formalized the concepts of *civic responsibility, bottomry,* and *respondentia,* improved trade conditions and established doctrines that were to play significant roles in the evolution of insurance. *Bottomry* and *respondentia* loans were maritime contracts on vessels (bottoms) or on cargoes (*res*). There were three basic elements in such agreements: (1) a loan on the vessel, cargo, or freight, (2) an interest rate on the loan, and (3) a risk premium for the chance of loss of the venture and the consequent cancellation of the debt. Under the provsions of a bottomry bond, the borrower was freed of his obligation on the event that the collateral was lost through no wilful act of his own. Modern credit life and disability insurance is used in the same manner as the bottomry loan. In the event of death or total disability of the borrower the debt is cancelled. The insurance premium, which is separate from the interest on the loan, corresponds to the risk premium of ancient times.

Ancient Greece Period

The Greek era of modern history witnessed (750 B.C.), the two most significant developments of early times, brought to a high degree of refinement (a) well-establishment of bottomry contract (b) concept of averages evolved. Risk premiums were differentially charged based on various factors, mostly contemporary in the manner the insurance rates are set. The first insurance exchange is believed to have been established in Athens in this early period similar to the later developed at Lloyd's of London.

Insurance in Roman Empire

The Greek tradition in insurance was conveyed to the Romans, who adopted the practices of bottomry and its related contracts. The laws of warranty and general average were further refined. The Romans even had an insurance exchange, although it is not believed to have been formalized as was the one in Athens. The major contribution of the Romans to the insurance heritage was the organized burial society, a rudimentary form of life and health insurance.

Burial societies, known as *Eranoi* and *Thiasoi*, existed in Greece for the purpose of providing prepaid bunals for members, but the Romans provided more elaborate burial and benevolent services through their *collegia*. Authorized by special Senate decree, the *collegia* were the true counterparts of the fraternal insurance organisations of modern times. Members prepare their contributions, a fund was maintained, and benefits were paid in terms of decent burial and last expenses incurred by the family of the deceased member.

The annuity concept appeals to have been comprehended by the Romans, because they apparently solved the problem of valuation.

The *collegia* represented the distinctive contribution of the Romans to the history of insurance. By formal organisation, the promise of definite benefits, and the collection of regular prepaid assessments, they are direct antecedents of the guilds of the Middle Ages and of fraternal insurance in modern times. While there is little evidence of actuarial skill, adequacy of dues collections must surely have been a criterion of membership fee setting.

Dark Ages

The decay and disintegration of Roman Expire in the fifth century A.D. bought in its wake an era of negligible international commerce and the development of small isolated self sufficient, and self contained communities. The *collegia* of Rome evolved into the guilds of the Middle Ages. The early Anglo-Saxon Guild was a family association loosely knit for the purpose of providing mutual aid. When a youth attained the age of fourteen years, the Norman conquerors of England required him to find sureties to guarantee his keeping the peace. To meet this contingency, the early guilds were formed.

In time, the guilds enlarged their functions to include benefits to craftsmen, artisans, and professional persons. The full-fledged development led to religious, economic, political, and defensive organizations. About the eighth century, trade guilds in Flanders and West Germany offered mutual protection against loss arising from fire damage to livestock and against other misfortune.

Insurance became an instrumentality of a commercial society, and until the revival of trade in Europe and Asia, thee can be found few examples. Of the existence of insurance institution in the modern sense.

Revival of International Commerce

Bottomry agreements were common in Venice, Geneva, Florence, Naples, Tarentum, and Bari before the year A.D. 1000, as evidenced by the Amalfitan Sea Codes.

Marine insurance made progress during the twelfth through fourteenth centuries and there appears to have been a Chamber of Assurance at Bruges, about 1310, at which merchants could insure their goods upon payment of a stipulated percentage.

The antecedents of fire insurance are found in the custom, recorded as early as 1240 in the village of Verambacht which held that a person whose house burned down was to be indemnified without delay by the whole village. By 1227, outside merchants wishing to sell their wares at local fairs could be insured against loss by fire or theft for a duty of four deniers.

By 1400, Europe's trade pattern was well-developed, considering the relatively low state of transportation technology. Small ships hugging the coastlines of Europe, caravans of small wagons travelling overland, and countless peddlers carrying their inventories on their backs supplied a network that moved goods in high demand to and from all parts of the civilized world.

Bottomry bonds were used extensively throughout the renaissance of commerce, and insurance was a basic consideration in all shipping along major routes. A cargo of armor shipped from Hamburg to London in 1560 was insured by the Hanse underwriters at a rate of 6 per cent. This rate is similar to contemporary levels.

Insurance Business in 1600

Toward the end of the Elizabeth reign, the insurance business in England was a flourishing trade with well established centers of activity, respected contracts, competitive rates, and an adequate market for most of the needs of the time. Insurance was conducted by sole proprietors on an individual basis, but it was customary for the insured to obtain joint participation of as many underwriters as were required to provide full coverage.

Afterwards, the insurance market developed very fast with a variety of product offering witnessing huge competition throughout the globe.

12.1.2 Indian Perspective

The Insurance Sector in India dates back to 1818 when the first insurance company was established– the Oriental Life Insurance Company at Calcutta. This was followed in quick succession with the establishment of Bombay Life Assurance Company (1823) and Madras Equitable Life Assurance Society (1829). In the general insurance business Triton Insurance Company (1850) was the first to be established.

Prior to 1871, Indians were charged about 15 percent more premium as compared to Europeans. Bombay Mutual Life Assurance Society (1871) was the first company not to differentiate between Indians and Europeans in the matter of fixation of premiums.

The first attempt at regulation of the insurance business in India was through the Indian Life Assurance Companies Act in 1912. This was later broad-based and the Insurance Act came into existence from the year 1928 onwards. The Insurance Act was subsequently reviewed and a comprehensive legislation was enacted called the Insurance Act, 1938.

The nationalization of life insurance business took place in 1956 when 245 Indian and foreign insurance and provident societies were first amalgamated and then nationalized. The Life Insurance Corporation of India (LIC) came into existence and has since enjoyed a monopoly over the life insurance business in India.

The milestones in the Insurance sector 1912 onwards can be summarised as under. The life insurance sector witnessed the following development.

- 1912: The Indian Life Assurance Companies Act enacted as the first statute to regulate the life insurance business.
- 1928: The Indian Insurance Companies Act enacted to enable the government to collect statistical information about both life and non-life insurance businesses.
- 1938: Earlier legislation consolidated and amended to by the Insurance Act with the objective of protecting the interests of the insuring public.
- 1956: 245 Indian and foreign insurers and provident societies taken over by the central government and nationalised. LIC formed by an Act of Parliament, viz. LIC Act, 1956, with a capital contribution of Rs. 5 crore from the Government of India.

The General insurance business in India, on the other hand, can trace its roots to the Triton Insurance Company Ltd., the first general insurance company established in the year 1850 in Calcutta by the British.

Some of the important milestones in the general insurance business in India are:

1907: The Indian Mercantile Insurance Ltd. set up, the first company to transact all classes of general insurance business.

1957: General Insurance Council, a wing of the Insurance Association of India, frames a code of conduct for ensuring fair conduct and sound business practices.

1968: The Insurance Act amended to regulate investments and set minimum solvency margins and the Tariff Advisory Committee set up.

1972: The General Insurance Business (Nationalisation) Act, 1972 nationalised the general insurance business in India with effect from 1st January 1973. 107 insurers amalgamated and grouped into four companies viz., the National Insurance Company Ltd., the New India Assurance Company Ltd., the Oriental Insurance Company Ltd. and the United India Insurance Company Ltd. GIC incorporated as a company.

12.2 Insurance Sector Reforms

In 1993, Malhotra Committee, headed by former Finance Secretary and RBI Governor, R.N. Malhotra was formed to evaluate the Indian Insurance Industry and recommend its future direction.

The committee was set up with an objective of complementing the reforms in the Indian Financial sector. The reforms were aimed at "creating a more efficient and competitive financial system suitable for the requirements of the economy keeping in mind the structural changes currently underway and recognising that insurance is an important part of the overall financial system where it was necessary to address the need for similar reforms."

Malhotra Committee – Purpose and Recommendations

Purpose

(*a*) To suggest the structure of the insurance industry, to assess its strengths and weaknesses of insurance companies in terms of the objectives of creating an efficient and viable insurance industry, which will have a wide reach of insurance services, a variety of insurance products with a high quality of services to the public and servicing as an effective instrument for mobilization of financial resources for development.

(*b*) To make recommendations for changing structure of insurance industry, for changing general policy frame work etc.

(*c*) To take specific suggestions regarding LIC and GIC with a view to improve functioning of LIC and GIC.

(*d*) To make recommendations on regulation and supervision of the insurance sector in India.

(*e*) To make recommendations on role and functioning of surveyors, intermediaries like agents etc. in the insurance sector.

(*f*) To make recommendations on any other matter which are relevant for development of the insurance industry in India.

Recommendations

In 1994, the committee submitted the report and gave the following recommendations now in the point form:

Structure

- Government stake in the insurance Companies to be brought down to 50%
- Government should take over the holdings of GIC and its subsidiaries so that these subsidiaries can act as independent corporations
- All the insurance companies should be given greater freedom to operate.

Competition

- Private Companies with a minimum paid up capital of Rs. 1 billion should be allowed to enter the industry
- No Company should deal in both Life and General Insurance through a single entity
- Foreign companies may be allowed to enter the industry in collaboration with the domestic companies
- Postal Life Insurance should be allowed to operate in the rural market
- Only one State Level Life Insurance Company should be allowed to operate in each state
- The Insurance Act should be changed
- An Insurance Regulatory body should be set up
- Controller of Insurance (Currently a part from the Finance Ministry) should be made independent.

Investments

- Mandatory Investments of LIC Life Fund in government securities to be reduced from 75% to 50%
- GIC and its subsidiaries are not to hold more than 5% in any company (There current holdings to be brought down to this level over a period of time).

Customer Service

- LIC should pay interest on delays in payments beyond 30 days
- Insurance companies must be encouraged to set up unit linked pension plans
- Computerization of operations and updating of technology to be carried out in the insurance industry.

Overall, the committee strongly felt that in order to improve the customer services and increase the coverage of the insurance industry should be opened up to competition.

But at the same time, the committee felt the need to exercise caution as any failure on the part of new players could ruin the public confidence in the industry.

Hence, it was decided to allow competition in a limited way by stipulating the minimum capital requirement of Rs. 1 bn. This amount is not very high for foreign firms, as it translates to only about US$25 million. Further, to date it is unclear whether equity should be payable in one go or should be brought in as installments. Also, the foreign equity participation was to be restricted to only 40%.

The committee felt the need to provide greater autonomy to insurance companies in order to improve their performance and enable them to act as independent companies with economic motives. For this purpose, it had proposed setting up an independent regulatory body.

The industry and analysts find that there is lack of clarity in the following areas:

- Though coverage of rural areas was to be made compulsory, it raises the question as to who would subsidize the rural policies as they would be difficult to service and hence costs will go up.
- There is some confusion with respect to investments. Where should the funds be invested? Currently 70% of the funds with LIC & GIC are invested in Government securities. Would new entrants be allowed to invest in GOI securities?
- The report also does not enumerate exit options available to the new entrants. In the event of failure, there should be an arrangement made whereby the other companies pool in to bail the customers, who in all probability would be middle class individuals.

It was on the basis of this report, that the then Finance Minister P. Chidambaram proposed the opening up of insurance to the private sector, including multinational companies.

IRDA Bill

The IRDA Bill was drafted keeping the Malhotra Committee recommendations in view and hence the government has ruled out privatization of public sector insurance companies, LIC and GIC. The bill did not provide for any dilution of 100 per cent government equity in the two premier companies.

The 71-page IRDA bill sought to give a statutory status to the interim Insurance Regulatory Authority and amend the 1938 Insurance Act, the 1956 Life Insurance Corporation Act and the 1972 General Insurance Business (Nationalization) Act to open up the sector. It provides for a nine-member regulatory body with statutory powers.

The IRDA Bill also fixed minimum capital requirement for life and general insurance at Rs 100 crore and for reinsurance firms at Rs 200 crore. The minimum solvency margin for private insurers is Rs 500 million for life insurance companies, Rs 500 million or a sum equivalent to 20 per cent of net premium income for general insurance and Rs. 1 billion for reinsurance companies. The Malhotra Committee Report justified the entry of foreign insurance companies by arguing that if it is permitted, it should be done on selective basis preferably through joint venture with Indian partner.

When the bill was first introduced in the parliament, the reactions were mixed. The Vajpayee government reintroduced the bill with some changes. In 1999, the bill was finally passed and IRDA was formed to regulate and promote insurance business in India.

12.3 Insurance Players in India

NON-LIFE INSURERS

Bajaj Allianz General Insurance Company Limited

Bajaj Allianz General Insurance Company Limited is a joint venture between Bajaj Auto Limited and Allianz AG of Germany. Incorporated on 19th September 2000. Bajaj Allianz General Insurance Company received the Insurance Regulatory and Development Authority (IRDA) Certificate of Registration (R3) on May 2nd, 2001 to conduct General Insurance business (including Health Insurance business) in India. The Company has an authorized and paid up capital of Rs 110 crores and has a network of 31 offices across the length and breadth of the country. The business focus of the company is to position itself as a leading corporate & retail insurance company catering to the needs of our customers. The company is headquartered in Pune, with branch offices in Mumbai, Chennai, Bangalore, New Delhi, Baroda, Kolkata and Hyderabad. The company has following categories of product offerings.

Tariff Products

- Fire Insurance
- Consequential Loss (Fire) Insurance
- Industrial All Risk
- Workmen's Compensation
- Engineering (includes Contractors Plant and Machinery, Electronic equipment, Machinery Loss of Profits, Machinery, Boiler Explosion, Machinery Breakdown, Deterioration of stock)

Non-Tariff Products

- Motor (includes private cars, two wheelers and commercial vehicles)
  - Critical Illness
  - Health Guard

- Personal Accident Burglary
- Plate Glass
- House Holders
- Hospital Cash
- Money
- Public Liability
- Overseas Travel
- Office Package

ICICI Lombard General Insurance Company Ltd.

The ICICI Lombard General Insurance Company Limited ("ICICI Lombard") is a joint venture between ICICI Bank Limited India's second largest bank and Lombard Canada Limited, one of the oldest property and casualty insurance companies in Canada. ICICI Lombard leverages the ICICI Bank Group's strong brand equity, extensive distribution networks and sound technological infrastructure to service customer needs. ICICI Lombard has the guidance of Lombard, Canada, on domain knowledge, product innovation, business processes based on cutting-edge technology and international best practice in the insurance business. ICICI Lombard offers a wide range of retail and corporate general insurance customised products. The company claims to have over 100 relationship managers and 850 Insurance Advisors working from 20 locations across the country. This is proposed to be expanded to 33 locations, covering the length & breadth of the country.

Personal Needs

- Home Insurance
- Personal Care

Business Needs

- Fire and Special Perils Policy
- Inland Transit Insurance
- Machinery Policy
- All Risks Insurance
- Money Insurance
- Industrial All Risks
- Tea Crop Insurance
- Consequential Loss (Fire) Insurance
- Electronic Equipment Insurance
- Burglary Insurance
- Boiler Explosion Policy
- Fidelity Guarantee Policy
- Marine (Export-Import) Insurance Policy

Health and Disability

- Group Health Insurance Policy
- Group Personal Accident Policy

Project Insurance

- Erection All Risk Policy
- Contractor's Plant & Machinery Policy
- Contractor's All Risk Policy

Liability Products

- Public Liability (Industrial Risks) Policy
- Public Liability Insurance Act Policy
- Public Liability (Non-Industrial Risks) Policy
- Workmen's Compensation Insurance

For Small & Medium Enterprise

- Corporate Cover
- Merchants Cover

IFFCO-TOKIO General Insurance Co. Ltd.

IFFCO-Tokio General Insurance Co. Ltd. (ITGI) is a joint venture between IFFCO and The Tokio Marine and Fire Insurance Co. Ltd, Japan Krishak Bharathi Cooperative Ltd. (KRIBHCO), and Indian Potash contributing 49 percent, 26 percent, 20 percent and 5 percent respectively to its Rs. 100 crore capital.

After getting the licence on 4th December 2000, the company started operations and is one the leading private General Insurance Company in India in few segments. ITGI is also the pioneer in launching a very innovative insurance cover for farmers called the "Sankat Haran Policy". With the Corporate Office in Gurgaon and operating Offices in about 20 cities, ITGI is looking at expanding the market base of general insurance in India by opening Offices in most major cities in India. The company operates on a mission of — "To win the TRUST of Individuals, Trade, Industry and Commerce and protect Citizens, Corporates, Cooperatives and International Investors in India." The major products are:

- Standard Fire and Special Perils
- Fire Loss of Profit
- Industrial All Risk
- Erection All Risk
- Contractor's All Risk
- Contractor's Plant and Machinery
- Electronic Equipment Insurances
- Machinery Breakdown
- Machinery Loss of Profit
- Boiler and Pressure Plant
- Public Liability (Act)
- Public Liability (Industrial/Non-Industrial)
- Product Liability
- Professional Indemnity
- Bankers Indemnity
- Marine (Cargo)
- Workmen's Compensation
- Burglary
- Motor (Private/Personal Car)
- Motor (Motor Cycle, Scooter)
- Motor (Commercial Vehicles)
- Cash Insurance
- All Risk
- Group Medshield
- Group/Individual Personal Accident
- Agricultural Pump set
- Sankath Haran
- Critical Illness
- Overseas Travel Insurance
- Trader's Package
- Householder's Package

National Insurance Company Ltd.

National Insurance Company was incorporated in 1906 and has been carrying out general insurance business under private management till its nationalisation in 1972. In the same year, 22 foreign and 11 Indian Insurance Companies were amalgamated with National Insurance Company Limited, as a subsidiary company of General Insurance Corporation of India. Later on in 2002, with the passage of Insurance amendment Bill (2002), National Insurance Company has been delinked from GIC and has been functioning as an independent company. Apart from readymade product offerings, the company has designed products to cater to the average insurance requirements of all sections of the country through customised and innovative insurance solutions. Apart from domestic insurance business the company also undertakes reinsurance and foreign operations.

New India Assurance Company Ltd.

The New India Assurance Company was incorporated on 23rd July, 1919 and commenced business from 14th October, 1919. In 1972, the year of its nationalisation, Government of India took over the management of the company along with all other non-life insurers in the country. New India Assurance (NIA) was subsequently reconstituted taking over 23 companies under the Scheme of Merger, following the nationalization of General Insurance Business in 1973. Later on in 2002, with the passage of Insurance amendment Bill (2002), New India Assurance Co. Ltd. has been delinked from GIC and has been functioning as an independent company.

Oriental Insurance Company Ltd.

The Oriental Insurance Company Ltd. is a public sector company and is one of the four subsidiary companies of the General Insurance Corporation of India. The Oriental Fire & General Insurance Co. Ltd., was incorporated in the year 1947 as a subsidiary of Oriental Government Security Life Assurance Co. Ltd. In 1956, Oriental became a subsidiary of the Life Insurance Corporation of India. On 13th May 1971, Government of India (GOI) took over the management of all general insurance companies in India.

This was followed by the nationalisation of general insurance business with effect from 1st January 1973 and the Oriental Fire and General insurance company came under the General Insurance Corporation of India as one of the four subsidiaries. It commenced its operations from 1st January 1975. Later on in 2002, with the passage of Insurance amendment Bill (2002), The Oriental Insurance Company Ltd. has been delinked from GIC and has been functioning as an independent company.

The company has its Head Office in New Delhi. The Company has 21 Regional Offices, 311 Divisional Offices and 635 Branch offices in various cities of the country. The Company has overseas operations in Nepal, Kuwait and Dubai.

United India Insurance Company Ltd.

United India Insurance is one of the four subsidiaries of the General Insurance Company carrying on general insurance business with its head office at Chennai. Later on in 2002, with the passage of Insurance amendment Bill (2002), United India Insurance has been delinked from GIC and has been functioning as an independent company. Ul spans the country with a network of 1123 offices and manpower of over 21,000 employees. The organisational structure comprises 22 regional offices, 313 divisional offices, and 789 branch offices.

The insurance covers offered by all these public sector insurance companies *inter-alia* included the following:

- Risks
- Bhagyashree Insurance
- Directors Liability Insurance
- Domestic Appliances
- Employer's Liability
- Fire Policy
- Gun Insurance
- Janta Personal Accident
- Motor Car Insurance
- Pedal Cycle
- Plate glass Insurance
- Public Liability Policy
- Retired Persons
- Suhana Safar
- Transit Policy
- Two Wheelers Insurance
- Advance Loss of Profits
- Boiler and Pressure Plans
- Commercial Vehicles
- Baggage Insurance
- Burglary Insurance
- Dogs Insurance
- Electric Equipment Insurance
- Fidelity Guarantee
- Guarantee Policy
- Household Insurance
- Mediclaim
- Overseas Mediclaim
- Personal Accident
- Professional Liability
- Rajrajeshwari Mahila
- Sports Insurance
- Traffic Accident
- T.V. Policy
- Sampoorna Suraksha Bima
- Banker's Indemnity
- Civil Engineering Completed Rest
- Contractor's All Risk's

- Contractor's Plant and Machinery
- Electronic Equipment Policy
- Fire Consequential Loss
- LPG Dealers
- Machinery Loss of Profit
- Office Umbrella
- Shopkeeper's Policy
- Aquaculture Insurance
- Cattle Insurance
- Farmer's Package
- Floriculture Insurance
- Plantation/Horticultural
- Deterioration of Sticks
- Erection All Risks
- Jeweller's Block
- Machinery Insurance Policy
- Marine Insurance
- Product Liability
- Agricultural Pumpsets
- Agriculture Insurance
- Failed Well Insurance
- Fire Insurance
- Lift Irrigation/Sprinkler
- Paultry Insurance

Tata AIG General Insurance Company Limited

Tata AIG General Insurance Company Ltd, and Tata AIG Life Insurance Company Ltd., (collectively "Tata AIG") are joint venture companies between the Tata group India's most trusted industrial house and American International Group, Inc. (AIG), the leading U.S. based international insurance and financial services organisation. Tata AIG General Insurance Co. Ltd. has (start-up capital of Rs. 125 crores of which 74 percent has been brought in by Tata Sons and the American partner brings in this balance 26 per cent. Both promoters have a deep and abiding interest in India's insurance sector. Prior to nationalisation, the Tatas pioneered private insurance in India when Sir Dorab Tata set up New India Assurance in 1919. By 1973, when General Insurance was nationalised the Tata company had a global presence with 56 overseas offices. AIG too, has always considered the Indian insurance sector to be of significance. The AIG companies entered India in 1945 and had offices in several Indian cities prior to nationalisation.

AIG is the leading U.S.-based international insurance and financial services organisation and the largest underwriter of commercial and industrial insurance in the United States. Its member companies write a wide range of commercial, personal and life insurance products through a variety of distribution channels in approximately 130 countries and jurisdiction throughout the world. Tata AIG General Insurance Company Ltd. Claims to be the first Indian insurance company to offers a comprehensive policy to cover various risks in the IT sector; risk arising out of virus, cyber crime, negligent acts, errors and omissions and third party liability from a security failure. Other products on offer are property, casualty, marine, directors and officers liability, accident and health, homeowners and automobile insurance. A list of its non-life products are:

- Executive Guard
- Travel Guard
- Group Personal Accident Plan
- Crime against Policy
- Business Guard Jyothi
- Various Marine Covers
- Family Guard
- Home Secure
- Property
- Business Guard Sanjeevini
- Comprehensive accident and own damages policy
- Various engineering and project insurance covers

Royal Sundaram General Insurance Company Limited

The joint venture bringing together Royal & Sun Alliance Insurance and Sundaram Finance Limited, started its operations from March 2001. The company is Head Quartered at Chennai, and has two Regional Offices, one at Mumbai and another one at New Delhi. The venture is aiming at Rs.120 Crores in revenue during first year of its operations and is confident of breaking even by fifth year. Royal & Sun Alliance is one of the world's leading international insurance companies. The Sun was established in 1710 and is the oldest insurance company in existence still trading under its original name. The Alliance was founded in 1824 and the Royal in 1845. The products offered by the company are:

- Travel Shield
- Health Shield
- Accident Shield
- Home Shield

Cholamandalam General Insurance Company Limited

Cholamandalam General Insurance Company Limited is promoted by Chennai based Murugappa Group. The company is capitalised at Rs. 105 crore with 75% being held by Tube investment, a Murugappa group company. While Cholamandalam Investment and Finance Company Ltd holds 15 per cent equity, the rest is held by other privately held Murugappa companies with 5 per cent stake each. The company is planning to garner a premium income of Rs. 100 crore in the first year of its operation, and expects to break even by the fourth year of its operation with a premium income of Rs. 500 crore. The general insurer plans to be in 30 cities in 18 months and would offer its customers about 50 products.

- Motor Insurance
- 2-Wheeler
- Home Insurance
- Travel Health Insurance
- Baggage Insurance
- Electronic Equipment
- Property & Crime
- Engineering Insurance
- Burglary Insurance
- Contractors All Risk
- Erection All Risk
- Machinery Breakdown
- Neon Sign Insurance
- Casualty & Financial Lines
- Fidelity Insurance
- Professional Indemnity
- Workmen's Policy
- Private Car
- Health Insurance
- Personal Accident
- Pet Insurance
- Burglary Insurance
- Pedal Cycle Insurance
- All Risks Insurance
- Baggage Insurance
- Contractors Plant
- Electronic Equipment
- Fire Insurance
- Money Insurance
- Plate Glass Insurance
- Directors & Officers
- Product Liability
- Public Liability
- Marine Insurance

Reliance General Insurance Company Limited

Reliance group has announced its plans to enter the Indian insurance sector — both in the life and general insurance businesses. Reliance Industries plans to bring in around Rs. 300 Crores into its insurance venture through its financial arm Reliance Capital Ltd. Reliance group will be the lead investor for this initiative. The two companies will have an initial authorised capital of Rs. 200 crores (US$ 43.62 million) each. This is the first application from an Indian company without a foreign insurance tie-up. However, Reliance will associate with international insurance consultants to bring the best practices in the business to India.

Export Credit Guarantee Corporation of India Ltd.

Export Credit Guarantee Corporation of India Limited, was established in the year 1957 by the Government of India to strengthen the export promotion drive by covering the risk of exporting on credit. Being essentially an export promotion organisation, it functions under the administrative control of the Ministry of Commerce, Government of India. It is managed by a Board of Directors comprising representatives of the Government, Reserve Bank of India, banking, insurance and exporting community. ECGC is the fifth largest credit insurer of the world in terms of coverage of national exports. The present paid-up capital of the company is Rs.390 crores, which is expected to be enhanced to Rs.500 crores by the year 2002.

The insurance products offered by ECGC are broadly classified as under:

- Standard Policy
- Small Exporters Policy
- Buyerwise Policy
- Insurance cover for Buyer's Credit and Line of Credit
- Services Policy
- Turnover Policy
- Specific Shipment Policy (Short term)
- Specific Policy for Supply Contract
- Construction Works Policy

HDFC Chubb General Insurance Ltd.

HDFC, India's premier financial services company and Chubb Corporation, leading global non-life insurer, entered in to a joint venture agreement for non-life insurance in 2002. HDFC holds 74 percent and Chubb 26 percent in the joint venture company, HDFC Chubb General Insurance Ltd., initially capitalised at Rs 100 crore.

Over the years HDFC has grown into a very strong brand, promoting various companies to offer financial services like banking, mutual fund, life insurance, stock market related services, real estate services.

The Chubb Corporation is one of the world's financially strongest insurance companies and has more than $25 billion in assets. Chubb and its affiliates are known around the world for introducing leading edge insurance products and services to meet the changing needs of consumers in diverse markets. Chubb's global network includes over 130 offices in 33 countries across North America, Europe, Latin America, Asia and Australia.

LIFE INSURERS

Allianz Bajaj Life Insurance Co. Ltd.

Allianz Bajaj Life Insurance Co. Ltd. is a joint venture between Allianz AG and Bajaj Auto Limited. Characterised by global presence with a local focus and driven by customer orientation to establish high earnings potential and financial strength, Allianz Bajaj Life Insurance Co. Ltd. was incorporated on 12th March 2001. The company received the Insurance Regulatory and Development Authority (IRDA) Certificate of Registration (R3) No 116 on 3rd August 2001 to conduct Life Insurance business in India. The key to Allianz's success world wide, has been its ability to use its global presence and experience while adapting to local market conditions and develop customer-focused solutions. In India, Allianz AG with Bajaj Auto, is confident of replicating this. The various products offered by the company are:

- ***Individuals***
  - Risk Care
  - Save Care
  - Life Time
  - Term Care
  - Cash Care
- ***Group***
  - Group Risk Care Plan Employer-Employee
  - Group Risk Care Plan Non-Employer-Employee

- Group Credit Care Plan Employer-Employee
- Invest Gain Plan
- Group Risk Credit Plan Non-Employer-Employee

Birla Sun Life Insurance Company Ltd.

Birla Sun Life (BSLI) is a joint venture between Birla Group and Sun Life Corporation of U.S. The products of BSLI are distributed through a fully owned subsidiary — BSDL Insurance Advisory Services Ltd (BSDL IAS) BSDL. The company claims to have unique products, presenting a powerful combination of returns, liquidity, safety, tax benefits, transparency and convenience. The products of Birla Sun Life Insurance are:

- Flexi Save Plus Endowment Plan
- Flexi Cash Flow Moneyback Plan
- Flexi Secure Life Retirement Plan (Pension)
- Flexi Life Line Whole Life Plan
- Single Premium Bond
- Birla Sun Life Term Plan

HDFC Standard Life Insurance Company Ltd.

HDFC and Standard Life was the first joint venture to enter the life Insurance market, in January 1995. In October 1998, the joint venture agreement was renewed and Standard Life purchased 2% of Infrastructure Development Finance Company Ltd. (IDFC). Standard Life also started to use the services of the HDFC Treasury department to advise them upon their investments in India. The company as such, was incorporated on 14th August 2000 under the name of HDFC Standard Life Insurance Company Limited. HDFC are the main shareholders in HDFC Standard Life, with 81.4%, while Standard Life owns 18.6%. HDFC and Standard Life have a long and close relationship built upon shared values and trust. The ambition of HDFC Standard Life is to mirror the success of the parent companies and be the yardstick by which all other insurance company's in India are measured.

Individual Products

- With Profits Endowment Assurance
- Single Premium Whole of Life
- Loan Cover Term Assurance
- Children's Plan
- With Profits Money Back
- Term Assurance Plan
- Personal Pension Plan

Group Products

- Group Term Insurance
- Development Insurance Plan

ICICI Prudential Life Insurance Company Ltd.

The company was incorporated on 20th July 2000, with an authorised capital of Rs. 230 crores. (Paid up Rs. 190 crores). It is a joint venture of ICICI (74%) and Prudential plc UK. (26%). The company is on the top of the list of competitors to LIC in life segment. The company was granted certificate of incorporation on 26-11-2000 and it started its operations on 19-12-2000. The company has its offices in Mumbai, New Delhi and other 8 major cities. The products offered by it are:

- Individuals
- Cash back
- Forever Life
- Life Time Pension
- *Investment Products*
- Assure Invest
- Group Gratuity
- Save & Protect
- Life Guard
- Life Link Pension
- ReAssure
- Life Link
- *Group Plans*
- Group Term Assurance

Life Insurance Corporation of India Ltd.

LIC was established in 1956 and is the dominant leader in life insurance in India. It has 7 zonal offices, over 100 divisional offices and 204 branches in India with over 6.50 lakh agents. It also has offices in London, Fiji and Mauritius. The products range of the company includes the following:

Whole Life

- Whole Life with Profits
- Limited Payment Whole Life Plan
- Single Premium Whole Life Plan
- Convertible Whole Life Plan

Endowment Schemes

- Endowment Plan with Profit
- Limited Payment Endowment Plan With Profit
- Jeevan Mitra (Double Cover)
- Jeevan Mitra (Triple Cover)
- Bhavishya Jeevan
- Jeevan Anand
- Double Endowment Plan
- New Janaraksha
- Anmol Jeevan Plan
- Two Year Temp. Assurance Plan
- Convertible Term Assurance Plan
- New Bima Kiran

Plans for needs of Children

- Komal Jeevan
- Jeevan Sukanya
- Jeevan Kishore
- Jeevan Balya
- Jeevan Chhaya
- Marriage/educational Annuity
- Deferred Endowment

Periodic Money Back Plans

- Jeevan Samruddhi
- Jeevan Rekha Plan
- Money Back Plan
- Jeevan Surbhi
- Jeevan Bharati
- Marriage/educational annuity
- Deferred Endowment Assurance for Children
- New Janaraksha

Medical Benefits Linked Insurance

- Asha Deep II
- Jeevan Asha II

For Benefit of Handicapped

- Jeevan Aadhar
- Jeevan Vishwas

Plans To Cover Housing-loans

- Mortgage Redemption — Plan No. 52

Joint Life Plans

- Jeevan Sathi

Investment Plans

- Bima Nivesh Triple Cover
- Capital Market Linked Plan
- Bima Plus

Group Term Insurance Schemes

- Group Insurance Scheme in lieu of EDLI
- Group Gratuity Scheme
- Group Superannuation Scheme
- Group Savings Link Insurance Scheme
- New Jeevan Akshay I
- New Jeevan Dhara I
- New Jeevan Suraksha I

Tata AIG Life Insurance Company Limited

Tata AIG Life Insurance Co. Ltd. is capitalised at Rs. 185 crores of which 74 percent has been brought in by Tata Sons and the American partner brings in the balance 26 per cent. Mr. George Oommen has been named managing director of Tata AIG Life. Tata-AIG plans to provide broad array of life insurance plans to cover to both individuals and groups. American Insurance Group (AIG) is the leading U.S. based international insurance and financial services organization and the largest underwriter of commercial and industrial insurance in the United States. Its member companies write a wide range of commercial and personal insurance products through a variety of distribution channels in over 130 countries and jurisdictions throughout the world. AIG's Life Insurance operations comprise of the most extensive worldwide network of any life insurer. AIG's global businesses also include financial services and asset management, including aircraft leasing, financial products, trading and market making, consumer finance, institutional, retail and direct investment fund asset management, real estate investment management, and retirement savings products. Tata AIG Life Insurance Company products are:

- Assure Lifeline Plans
- 15 Year Lifeline (with Return of Premiums) Plan
- Money Saver Plan
- Security and Growth Plans
- Mahalife

SBI Life Insurance Company Ltd.

India's largest bank SBI and Cardiff S.A a leading insurer in France have formed SBI Life. It is a 74:26 venture; with Cardiff the foreign partner contributing 26% in the paid capital of Rs. 250 crore. SBI plans to market the insurance products through select branches of SBI and its seven associate banks. SBI is the largest bank in the country with more than 9000 branches. It has BNP Paribas, which is one among the three largest banks in Europe, is the holding company of Cardiff. BNP's presence in India dates as far back as 1860 and has 9 branches here. Cardiff, the insurance arm of BNP Paribas was set up in 1973 that specializes in long-term savings, protection products and creditor insurance. In 1999 its premium income stood at US$ 4 billion, with assets worth over US $ 23 billion under its management Cardiff based in France, has the expertise for selling insurance products through banks and has operations in over 20 countries. The company products are:

- Sanjeevan
- Sudarshan
- Young Sanjeevan
- SBI Scholar
- Super Suraksha
- Suvarna Ganga
- Life Long Pensions

OM Kotak Mahindra Insurance Company Ltd.

The joint venture OM Kotak Mahindra Life Insurance started off with an initial net worth of Rs. 150 crore, with 74:26 stake between KMFL and OM. The Life Insurance business offers Kotak Mahindra with an opportunity to leverage its core strengths of Wealth Management and Retail Distribution. Kotak Mahindra is one of India's premier financial services groups, with a range of over two dozen highly-specialised products and services spread over a number of companies and with a client list that spans more than 500 Indian and international firms. Starting as a one-product company in the mid-80s, they've evolved into a full-service financial conglomerate employing over 550 people across 30 centres in India and in Dubai, London, New York and Mauritius. Kotak Mahindra Finance Limited(KMFL) is a diversified financial services company covering auto and consumer finance, asset management, investment banking, securities trading and equity research. Old Mutual pic. is a leading financial services provider in the world, providing a broad range of financial services in the area of insurance, asset management and banking. It is a leading life insurer in South Africa, with more than 30% market share. The partnership with Old Mutual plc., provides the Kotak Mahindra group with an international perspective and expertise in the life insurance business. The various products offered are:

- Endowment
- Moneyback
- Group Term
- Credit Term Group
- Gramin Bima Yojana
- Capital Multiplier
- Insurance Bond
- Term Assurance
- Preferred Term
- Child Advantage
- Retirement Plan
- Gratuity Plan

Max New York Life Insurance Co. Ltd.

Max New York Life is a partnership between Max India Limited, one of India's leading multi-business corporations and New York Life, a Fortune 100 company. The paid-up capital of the Joint Venture is Rs. 250 crores. Max India Ltd. is building businesses in the emerging knowledge-based areas of Healthcare, Financial Services and Information Technology. It has grown independently on its own and by joining hands in partnerships with major international companies where specific business opportunities are best addressed through joint ventures. Max India has a significant presence in the most vital & fast growing sectors of the Indian Economy, Telecommunication services, Electronic components distribution, Speciality Plastic Films and Bulk Pharmaceuticals. These diversified businesses are organised as Max India's 100% owned Business Units (BU) and equity sharing Joint Ventures (JV). Each of the BUs & JVs, fully empowered to lead their operations, have grown and obtained leadership position in their respective industries by providing high quality products and services, working closely with their customers.

- Whole Life Plan
- 5 Year term and Convertible Insurance
- Endowment to Age 60 Policy
- Single Premium Insurance Bond
- Level Term
- Endowment Plan
- Children's Endowment Policy
- Easy Life Retirement (Participating) Plan.

ING Vysya Life Insurance Company Ltd.

ING Vysya Life Insurance Company Ltd. Is a joint venture between ING , Vysya Bank, one of India's leading private sector banks and GMR group. As per the JV agreement, Vysya Bank holds 49 per cent stake, ING 26 percent, and the GMR Group would hold 25 per cent. The paid up capital of the joint venture is Rs. 110 crore. The company which is headquartered at Bangalore has commenced its operations at Mumbai and Delhi. Vysya Bank is one of the most aggressive of the older-generation private-sector banks. With the investment from a foreign partner, Bank Brussels Lamberts, in the equity of the bank, it is expected to gear up to effectively fight competition in the new liberalised era. Vysya Bank is a big player given its significant branch penetration. It has a very high degree of retail focus with good customer service. The Vysya Bank is one of the largest private banks in India with around 2 million customers and 480 retail outlets. ING Group, with an asset base of over Rs. 28,42,000 crore is a global financial institution of Dutch origin, which is active in the field of banking, insurance and asset management in more than 60 countries, with nearly 90,000 employees. ING comprises a broad spectrum of prominent companies working close to the customer, many of them operating under their own brand names. The product offered by INGV are:

- Reassuring Life Endowment Assurance Plan
- Maximising Life Money Back Plan
- Conquering Life
- Fulfilling Life Anticipated Whole Life Plan
- Rewarding Life

Aviva Life Insurance Company Ltd.

Aviva Life Insurance Company, a joint venture between Dabur India and CGU, a wholly owned subsidiary of Aviva Pic, is capitalised at Rs. 110 crore. Aviva Pic is the largest life and general insurance group of UK and the world's seventh largest insurer with world wide premium income and retail investment sales of £28 billion and more than £200 billion in assets under management. Aviva Pic is the holding company of Aviva group of companies which is in to life assurance business, long term savings, all classes of general insurance business and fund management. The group has 64,000 employees serving 25 million customers. Aviva Life has tied up with ABN Amro, Canara Bank, Laxmi Vilas Bank and American Express for distribution of its products. The company is headquartered in Gurgaon, with branch offices in Mumbai, Chennai, New Delhi, Hyderabad, Bangalore and Kolkata. Its products are:

- Life Long
- Life Bond
- Secure Life
- Pension Plus
- Life Saver
- Easy Life plus
- Credit Plus
- Corporate Life

AMP Sanmar Assurance Company Limited

AMP Sanmar Assurance Company Limited is a joint venture between AMP having a stake of 26 percent and the Sanmar Group holding 74 percent. The company expects to break even by the end of seventh year of its operations. AMP Sanmar is targeting to sell 30,000 policies in the first year of its operations in India and hoping to collect Rs. 26 crore in premiums in this period. The Sanmar group is one of the largest industrial groups in South India, with a turnover for 1998-99 of close to Rs. 10 billion. The group's businesses are professionally managed by its over 650 highly qualified managers. It has a significant presence in the businesses that have been identified as its 'core' areas: PVC/ Chlorochemicals, Speciality Chemicals, Shipping and Engineering. AMP Limited is one of the world's leading financial services businesses providing around nine million customers worldwide with wealth creation and asset protection products and services. AMP has been the largest life insurer in Australia, and one of the largest in NZ, for most of the last century and is a major provider of superannuation and asset management products and services. AMP has a significant presence in the UK through Pearl, London Life, Virgin Direct and Henderson.

- Dhana Shree
- Nitya Shree
- Yuva Shree
- Subha Shree
- Raksha Shree
- Bhagya Shree

MetLife India Insurance Company Private Limited

MetLife India Insurance Company Private Limited was incorporated in India on April 11, 2001 as a joint venture between MetLife International Holdings Inc., The Jammu and Kashmir Bank, M. Pallonji and Co. Private Limited and other private investors. The Metropolitan Life Insurance Company (MetLife) is the number one insurer in the U.S. based on over US $2.1 trillion of life insurance in force. With 44 million policyholders on roll, MetLife serves approximately 10 million individual households in the US as well as 88 of the top Fortune 100 companies that include 33 million employees and members. Headquartered in New York, MetLife through its affiliates, subsidiaries and representative offices operate in 13 countries throughout the Americas, Europe and

Asia. MetLife India seeks to derive benefits greatly from the MetLife Group's visit global experience in the field of insurance along with its track record of successfully establishing businesses in emerging markets and other unique strengths of each of it promoters to address the specific needs of the Indian customer. The various products offered by metlife are:

- Met Mortgage Protector
- Met Suph (NP-Money Back)
- Met 100 Platinum (P-Limited Pay Whole Life)
- Met Platinum (P-EA)
- Met Platinum (NP-EA)
- Met Junior (P-EA)
- Met Junior MB
- Met 100 Gold (P-Limited Pay Whole Life)
- Met 100 (NP-Pay Whole Life)
- Met Gold (P-EA)
- Met Gold (NP-EA)
- Met Junior (NP-Juvenile EA)

(P - Participating, NP - Non-Participating)

Apart from above mentioned companies many new Life and Non Life Companies have also started business in India (Annexure 10A and 10B).

Annexure 10A

LIFE INSURANCE COMPANIES

Sl. No.	*Insurers*	*Foreign Partners*	*Regn. No*	*Date of Registration*	*Year of Operation*
1.	HDFC Standard Life Insurance Co. Ltd.	Standard Life Assurance, UK	101	23.10.2000	2000-01
2.	Max New York Life Insurance Co. Ltd.	New York Life, USA	104	15.11.2000	2000-01
3.	ICICI-Prudential Life Insurance Co. Ltd.	Prudential , UK	105	24.11.2000	2000-01
4.	Om Kotak Life Insurance Co. Ltd.	Old Mutual, South Africa	107	10.01.2001	2001-02
5.	Birla Sun Life Insurance Co. Ltd.	Sun Life, Canada	109	31.01.2001	2000-01
6.	Tata-AIG Life Insurance Co. Ltd.	American International Assurance Co., USA	110	12.02.2001	2000-01
7.	SBI Life Insurance Co. Ltd.	BNP Paribas Assurance SA, France	111	29.03.2001	2001-02
8.	ING Vysya Life Insurance Co. Ltd.	ING Insurance International B.V., Netherlands	114	02.08.2001	2001-02
9.	Allianz Bajaj Life Insurance Co. Ltd.	Allianz, Germany	116	03.08.2001	2001-02
10.	Metlife India Insurance Co. Ltd.	Metlife International Holdings Ltd., USA	117	06.08.2001	2001-02
11.	Reliance Life Insurance Co. Ltd. (Earlier AMP Sanmar Life Insurance Company from 3.1.02 to 29.9.05)	—	121	03.01.2002	2001-02
12.	AVIVA	Aviva International Holdings Ltd., UK	122	14.05.2002	2002-03
13.	Sahara Life Insurance Co. Ltd.	—	127	06.02.2004	2004-05
14.	Shriram Life Insurance Co. Ltd.	Sanlam, South Africa	128	17.11.2005	2005-06
15.	Bharti AXA Life Insurance Co. Ltd.	AXA Holdings, France	130	14.07.2006	2006-07
16.	Future Generali India Life Insurance Company Ltd.	Pantaloon Retail Ltd.; Sain Marketing Network Pvt. Ltd. (SMNPL), Generali, Italy	133	04.09.2007	2007-08
17.	IDBI Fortis Life Insurance Company Ltd.	Fortis, Netherlands	135	19.12.2007	2007-08
18.	Canara HSBC OBC Life Insurance Company Ltd.	HSBC, UK	136	08.05.2008	2008-09
19.	Aegon Religare Life Insurance Company Ltd.	Religare, Netherlands	138	27.06.2008	2008-09
20.	DLF Pramerica Life Insurance Co. Ltd.	Prudential of America, USA	140	27.06.2008	2008-09
21.	Life Insurance Corporation of India		512		

TOTAL LIFE INSURANCE PREMIUM

(RS. CRORE)

INSURER	2007-08	2006-07	2005-06	2004-05	2003-04	2002-03	2001-02
LIC	149789.99	127822.84	90792.22	75127.29	63533.43	54628.49	49821.91
	(17.19)	(40.79)	(20.85)	(18.25)	(16.30)	(9.65)	(42.79)
Aviva	1891.88	1147.23	600.27	253.42	81.50	13.47	
Bajaj Allianz	9725.31	5345.24	3133.58	1001.68	220.80	69.17	7.14
Bharti Axa	118.41	7.78					
Birla Sunlife	3272.19	1776.71	1259.68	915.47	537.54	143.92	28.26
Future Generali	2.49						
HDFC Std	4858.56	2855.87	1569.91	686.63	297.76	148.83	33.46
ICICI Pru	13561.06	7912.99	4261.05	2363.82	989.28	417.62	116.38
IDBI Fortis	11.90						
ING Vysya	1158.87	707.20	425.38	338.86	88.51	21.16	4.19
Kotak Mahindra	1691.14	971.51	621.85	466.16	150.72	40.32	7.58
Met Life	1159.54	492.71	205.99	81.53	28.73	7.91	0.48
Max New York	2714.60	1500.28	788.13	413.43	215.25	96.59	38.95
Reliance Life	3225.44	1004.66	224.21	106.55	31.06	6.47	0.28
Sahara	143.49	51.00	27.66	1.74			
SBI Life	5622.14	2928.49	1075.32	601.18	225.67	72.39	14.69
Shriram	358.05	184.17	10.33				
Tata AIG	2046.35	1367.18	880.19	497.04	253.53	81.21	21.14
Private Total	51561.42	28253.00	15083.54	7727.51	3120.33	1119.06	272.55
	(82.50)	(87.31)	(95.19)	(147.65)	(178.83)	(310.59)	(4124.31)
Total (LIC+Private)	201351.41	156075.84	105875.76	82854.80	66653.75	55747.55	50094.46
	(29.01)	(47.38)	(27.78)	(24.31)	(19.56)	(11.28)	(43.54)

Note : Figure in bracket indicates the growth over the previous year in percent.

Annexure 10B

NON-LIFE INSURANCE COMPANIES IN INDIA

Sl. No.	*Insurers*	*Foreign Partners*	*Regn. No*	*Date of Registration*	*Year of Operation*
1.	Royal Sundaram Alliance Insurance	Royal Sun Alliance, UK	102	23.10.2000	2000-01
2.	Reliance General Insurance Co.	—	103	23.10.200	2000-01
3.	IFFCO-TOKIO General Insurance Co.	Millea Asia Pte. Ltd., Japan	106	04.12.2000	2000-01
4.	TATA AIG General Insurance Co. Ltd.	American International Assurance Co., USA	108	22.01.200	2000-01
5.	Bajaj Allianz General Insurance Co.	Allianz, Germany	113	02.05.2001	2001-02
6.	Cholamandalam MS General Insurance Co.	Mitsui Sumitomo, Japan	123	15.07.2002	2002-03
7.	ICICI Lombard General Insurance Co.	Fairfax through its affiliates, Canada	115	03.08.2001	2001-02
8.	HDFC ERGO General Insurance Co. (Earlier HDFC General Insurance Co. from 27.9.2000 to 5.4.2008)	ERGO, Germany	125	27.09.2000	2002-03
9.	Star Health & Allied Insurance Company Limited	Individual Promoters, UAE	129	16.03.2006	2006-07
10.	Apollo DKV Insurance Company Ltd.	Apollo Hospital Enterprises Ltd.; Apollo Energy Company Ltd.; PCR Investments Ltd. & DKV, Germany (August 3, 2007)	131	03.08.2007	2007-08
11.	Future Generali India Assurance Company Ltd.	Pantaloon Retail Ltd.; Shendra Infrastructure Development Ltd. (SIDL); Participatie Maatschapij Graafsschap Holland NV, Netherlands ("Generali")	132	04.09.2007	2007-08
12.	Universal Sompo General Insurance Company Ltd.	Sompo, Japan	134	16.11.2007	2007-08
13.	Shriram General Insurance Company Ltd.	Santam, South Africa	137	08.05.2008	2008-09
14.	Bharti AXA General Insurance Company Ltd.	AXA Holdings, France	139	27.06.2008	2008-09
15.	Raheja QBE General Insurance Company Ltd.	QBE, Australia	141	11.12.2008	2008-09
16.	New India Assurance Co. Ltd.				
17.	National Insurance Co. Ltd.				
18.	The Oriental Insurance Co. Ltd.				
19.	United India Insurance Co. Ltd.				
20.	Export Credit Guarantee Co. Ltd.				
21.	Agriculture Insurance Co. of India Ltd.				

GROSS DIRECT PREMIUM OF NON-LIFE INSURANCE (WITHIN & OUTSIDE INDIA)

INSURER	*2007-08*	*2006-07*	*2005-06*	*2004-05*	*2003-04*	*2002-03*	*2001-02*
National	4021.97	3827.12	3536.34	3810.65	3399.97	2869.87	2439.41
New India	6151.97	5936.78	5675.54	5103.16	4921.47	4812.79	4198.06
Oriental	3900.22	4020.78	3609.77	3090.55	2899.74	2868.15	2498.64
United	3739.56	3498.77	3154.78	2944.46	3063.47	2969.63	2781.48
Public Sector	17813.71	17283.45	15976.44	14948.82	14284.65	13520.44	11917.59
	(3.07)	(8.18)	(6.87)	(4.65)	(5.65)	(13.45)	(13.59)
Bajaj Allianx	2379.92	1786.34	1272.29	851.62	476.53	296.48	141.96
Cholamandalam	522.34	311.73	220.18	169.25	97.05	14.79	
Future Generali	9.81						
HDFC Ergo	220.60	194.00	200.94	175.63	112.95	9.49	
ICICI Lombard	3307.12	2989.07	1582.86	873.86	486.73	211.66	28.13
Iffco-Tokio	1128.15	1144.47	892.72	496.64	322.24	213.33	70.51
Reliance	1946.42	912.23	162.33	161.68	161.06	185.68	77.46
Royal Sundaram	694.41	598.20	458.64	330.70	257.76	184.44	71.13
Tata AIG	782.64	710.55	572.70	448.24	343.52	233.93	78.46
Universal Sompo	0.48						
Private Sector	10991.89	8646.57	5362.66	3507.62	2257.83	1349.80	467.65
	(27.12)	(61.24)	(52.89)	(55.35)	(67.27)	(188.64)	(6453.98)
Total	28805.60	25930.02	21339.10	18456.45	16542.49	14870.25	12385.24
	(11.09)	(21.51)	(15.62)	(11.57)	(11.25)	(20.06)	(17.97)
Specialised Insurers							
AIC	835.11	564.67	555.83	549.72	369.21		
ECGC	668.37	617.66	577.33	515.55	445.48	374.78	338.52
Stand-alone Health Insurers							
Star Health	168.19	22.51					
Apollo DKV	2.97						

Figure in the bracket represent the growth over the previous year in percent.

EQUITY SHARE CAPITAL OF INSURANCE COMPANIES
(As on 31st March) (Rs. Crore)

Name of the insurer	*2007*	*Infusion During the year*	*2008*	*Indian Promoter*	*Foreign Promoter*	*FDI (%)*
Life Insurers						
AVIVA India Life Insurance Co. Pvt. Ltd.	758.20	246.30	1004.50	743.33	261.17	26.00%
Bajaj Allianz Life Insurance Co. Ltd.	150.37	0.34	150.71	111.52	39.18	26.00%
Bharti AXA Life Insurance Co.Ltd.	150.00	216.11	366.11	284.75	81.36	22.22%
Birla Sun Life Insurance Co. Ltd.	671.50	603.00	1274.50	943.13	331.37	26.00%
Future Generali Life Insurance Co.Ltd.*		•	185.00	137.83	47.18	25.50%
HDFC Standard Life Insurance Co. Ltd.	801.26	469.74	1271.00	940.54	330.46	26.00%
ICICI-Prudential Life Insurance Co. Ltd.	1312.30	88.81	1401.11	1037.48	363.63	25.95%
IDBI Fortis Life Insurance Co.Ltd.*			200.00	148.00	52.00	26.00%
ING Vysya Life Insurance Co. Ltd.	690.00	100.00	790.00	584.60	205.40	26.00%
Kotak Mahindra Old Mutual Life Insurance Co. Ltd.	330.35	149.93	480.27	355.40	124.87	26.00%
Max New York Life Insurance Co. Ltd.	732.43	300.00	1032.43	764.00	268.43	26.00%
Metlife India Insurance Co. Pvt. Ltd.	530.00	231.08	761.08	563.20	197.88	26.00%
Reliance Life Insurance Co. Ltd.	664.00	483.70	1147.70	1147.70	-	0.00%
Sahara India Life Insurance Co. Ltd.	157.00	75.00	232.00	232.00	-	0.00%
SBI Life Insurance Co. Ltd.	500.00	500.00	1000.00	740.00	260.00	26.00%
Shriram Life Insurance Co.Ltd.	125.00	0.00	125.00	92.50	32.50	26.00%
TATA-AIG Life Insurance Co. Ltd.	547.00	323.00	870.00	643.80	226.20	26.00%
Sub Total (Private Sector)	**8119.41**	**3787.01**	**12291.42**	**9469.78**	**2821.63**	22.96%
Life Insurance Corporation of India	5.00	0.00	5.00	5.0		
Total (Life)	**8124.41**	**3787.01**	**12296.42**	**9474.78**	**2821.63**	22.95%
Non-Life Insurers						
Bajaj Allianz General Insurance Co.	110.13	0.09	110.23	81.57	28.66	26.00%
Cholamandalam MS General Insurance Co. Ltd.	141.96	0.00	141.96	105.05	36.91	26.00%
Future Generlai Insurance Co.Ltd.*	150.00	111.75	38.25	25.50%		
HDFC Chubb General Insurance Co.	125.00	25.00	150.00	111.00	39.00	26.00%
ICICI Lombard General Insurance Co.	335.71	41.65	377.36	279.47	97.89	25.94%
IFFCO-TOKIO General Insurance Co.	220.00	0.00	220.00	162.80	57.20	26.00%
Reliance General Insurance Co. Ltd.	103.07	4.08	107.15	107.15	-	0.00%
Royal Sundaram Alliance Insurance Co. Ltd.	140.00	30.00	170.00	125.80	44.20	26.00%
TATA AIG General Insurance Co. Ltd.	225.00	0.00	225.00	166.50	58.50	26.00%
Universal Sompo Insurance Co.Ltd.*	150.00	111.00	39.00	26.00%		
Sub Total (Private Sector)	1400.87	100.83	1801.70	1362.09	439.61	24.40%
National Insurance Co. Ltd.	100.00	0.00	100.00	100.00	-	0.00%
The New India Assurance Co. Ltd.	200.00	0.00	200.00	200.00	-	0.00%
The Oriental Insurance Co.Ltd.	100.00	0.00	100.00	100.00	-	0.00%
United India Insurance Co. Ltd.	150.00	0.00	150.00	150.00	-	0.00%
Sub Total (Public Sector)	**550.00**	**0.00**	**550.00**	**550.00**	-	0.00%
Total (Non Life)	**1950.87**	**100.83**	**2351.70**	**1912.09**	**439.61**	18.69%
Agriculture Insurance Company of India.	200.00	0.00	200.00	200.00	-	0.00%
Apollo DKV Insurance Co.Ltd.*	100.55	74.54	26.01	25.87%		
Export Credit Guarantee Corporation.	800.00	100.00	900.00	900.00	-	0.00%
General Insurance Corporation of India	430.00	0.00	430.00	430.00	-	0.00%
Star Health & Allied Insurance Co.Ltd.	105.00	3.60	108.60	80.97	27.63	25.44%
GRAND TOTAL	**116101.28**	**3991.43**	**16387.27**	**13072.38**	**3314.89**	20.23%

*Note : * Insurers have commenced operations in 2007-08.*

Key terms

- ❒ Respondentia
- ❒ Bottomry Contracts
- ❒ Insurance Reforms
- ❒ Malhotra Committee
- ❒ Inflation
- ❒ IRDA Act, 1999
- ❒ Macroeconomic Issues
- ❒ Liberalisation
- ❒ Insurance Density
- ❒ Fiscal Policy

Questions for Review

1. Trace the history of Indian Insurance industry for the period 1818-1999. What are your comments on the present state of Insurance Market.
2. Write short notes on.
   (1) Insurance Sector Reforms
   (2) Insurance Player in India
3. "From a global perspective insurance has emerged as a business risk management device to a highly sophisticated risk transfer mechanism for both individuals and corporations." Discuss.

Suggested Readings

- D.C. Srivastava and S. Srivastava, *Indian Insurance Industry – Transition and Prospects,* New Century Publications, 2001.
- *IRDA Annual Report,* 2001-02.
- Spencer L. Kimbell and Herbert S. Demenberg, *Insurance, Government and Social Policy: Studies in Insurance Regulation,* the S.S. Haubner Foundation for Insurance Education, 1969.
- Irving Pfeffer and David R. Klock, *Perspective on Insurance,* Prentice-Hall, Englewood Cliffs, 1994.

Web Resources

- www.bimaonline.com
- www.tata-aig.com
- www.bajajallianz.com
- www.hdfc.com

Accounting and Taxation for Insurance

Chapter 13

CHAPTER OBJECTIVES

After reading this chapter you will be able to understand :

- *Accounting Principles for Preparation of Financial Statements*
- *Accounts for Life Insurance Companies*
- *International Financial Reporting Standards*
- *Taxation Aspects of Insurance*

Accounting for insurance companies is different from other businesses because of uncertainity of cash outflows and in case of life insurance companies a long time period between receipt of premiums and the payment of claims. The financial statements of insurance companies differ from conventional financila statements and should follow the IRDA guidelines in India.

13.1 ACCOUNTING PRINCIPLES FOR PREPARATION OF FINANCIAL STATEMENTS

Every insurance company is required to prepare the financial statements and make disclosures from 30th March 2002 onwards in accordance with the guidelines of IRDA titled The Insurance Regulatory And Development Authority (Preparation of Financial Statements And Auditors Report of Insurance Companies) Regulations, 2002.[1]

The formats of the financial statements applicable as per the said guidelines are:

1. For Life Insurance Business {Schedule A Part V}
   - (a) Revenue Account [Policyholder's Account] — Form No. A-RA
   - (b) Profit and Loss Account [Shareholders' Account] — Form No. A-PL
   - (c) Balance Sheet — Form No. A-BS
2. For General Insurance Business [Schedule B Part V]
   - (a) Revenue Account — Form No. B-RA
   - (b) Profit and Loss Account [Shareholders' Account] — Form No. B-PL
   - (c) Balance Sheet — Form No. B-BS

In addition, as per the guidelines, every life insurance company has to comply with the requirements of Schedule A and every general insurance company has to comply with the requirements of Schedule B. Also, the auditor's report has to be prepared in accordance with Schedule C of the guidelines.A summary of guidelines contained in various scheduled above referred is as under:

Schedule A & B

Part 1

Applicability of Accounting Standards

In exercise of the powers conferred by section 114A of the Insurance Act, 1938 (4 of 1938), and in supersession

1. www.irdaindia.org

of the Insurance Regulatory and Development Authority (Preparation of Financial Statements and Auditors Report of Insurance Companies) Regulations, 2000, Authority, in consultation with the Insurance Advisory Committee, has made the Insurance Regulatory and Development Authority (Preparation of Financial Statements and Auditors Report of Insurance Companies) Regulations, 2002. Thus the Regulations made in the year 2000 were modified and superceded by the Regulations made in the year 2002. As per these Regulations, an insurer carrying on general insurance business has to comply with the requirements of Schedule B and Life Companies Schedule A.

Every Balance Sheet, Receipts and Payments Account [Cash Flow Statement] and Profit and Loss Account [Shareholders' Account] of the insurer shall be in conformity with the Accounting Standards (AS) issued by the ICAI, to the extent applicable to the insurers carrying on general insurance business, except that:

(a) Accounting Standard 3 (AS 3) — Cash Flow Statements — Cash Flow Statement shall be prepared only under the Direct Method.

(b) Accounting Standard 13 (AS 13) — Accounting for Investments, shall not be applicable.

(c) Accounting Standard 17 (AS 17) — Segment Reporting — shall apply irrespective of whether the securities of the insurer are traded publicly or not.

Treatment of Premium

- Premium received in advance shall not be included in the unearned premium and shall be shown separately.
- Premium revenue recognition is based on the pattern of risk to which the insurer is exposed. An insurer, based on past experience can reliably estimate the pattern of risk for a particular type of insurance business. Most insurers bring premium revenue to account on the basis of the passage of time. This is generally appropriate where the risk of events occurring that give rise to claims is more or less uniform throughout the policy period subject to any regulatory prescription in this regard.
- For some classes of insurance, it is usual for the premium to be adjusted as a result of events and information that becomes known during or after the policy period, e.g. marine cargo. Further, in some cases, risk pattern may not be evenly spread over the period of insurance because of the very nature of the risk covered e.g. some infrastructure projects involving varying degrees of risk factors.
- A deposit premium is paid in such cases at the beginning of the policy period and subsequently adjusted.
- The basis of determination of premium earned shall be adequately justified, preferably supported by external evidence such as by certification from an actuary and/or other technical experts. Adequate disclosure of such basis shall be made.

General Insurance

- Premium shall be recognised as income over the contract period or the period of risk, whichever is appropriate. Unearned premium as well as premium received in advance, both of which represent premium income not relating to the current accounting period, shall be disclosed separately in the financial statements. A reserve for Unearned Premium may be created as the amount representing that part of the premium written which is attributable and to be allocated to the succeeding accounting periods.
- Premium Received in Advance, which represents premium received prior to the commencement of the risk, shall be shown separately under the head *"Current Liabilities'* in the financial statements.
- Unearned premium shall be shown separately under the head *'Current Liabilities'* and appropriate disclosures regarding management's basis of assessment shall be made in the financial statements.
- Premium deficiency shall be recognised if the sum of expected claim costs, related expenses and maintenance costs exceeds related unearned premiums.

- For contracts exceeding four years, one a premium deficiency has occurred, future changes to the liability shall be based on actuarial/technical evaluation.

Life Insurance

Premium shall be recognised as income on due basis. For linked businesses, the due date for payment may be taken as the date when the associated units are created.

Acquisition Costs

Acquisition costs, if any, shall be expensed in the period in which they are incurred. Acquisition costs are those costs that vary with, and are primarily related to, the acquisition of new and renewal insurance contracts. The most essential test is the obligatory relationship between costs and the execution of insurance contracts (i.e. commencement of risk).

Claims

The components of the ultimate cost of claims to an insurer comprise the claims under policies and claims settlement costs. Claims under policies comprise the claims made for losses incurred, and those estimated or anticipated under the policies. A liability for outstanding claims shall be brought to account in respect of both direct business and inward reinsurance business. The liability shall include:

(a) Future payments in relation to unpaid reported claims;

(b) Claims Incurred But Not Reported (IBNR) including inadequate reserves (sometimes referred to as Claims Incurred But Not Enough Reported (IBNER) which will result in future cash/asset outgo for settling liabilities against those claims. Change in estimated liability represents the difference between the estimated liability for outstanding claims in respect of claims under policies whether due or intimated at the beginning and at the end of the financial period. The accounting estimate shall also include claims cost adjusted for estimated salvage value if there is sufficient degree of certainty of its realisation.

  - Estimate of claims made in respect of contracts exceeding four years shall be recognised on an actuarial basis, subject to regulations that may be prescribed by the Authority. In such cases, certificate from a recognised actuary as to the fairness of liability assessment must be obtained. Actuarial assumptions shall be suitably disclosed by way of notes to the account. Necessary provision for unexpired risk shall be made subject to any minimum, statutorily required.

Procedure to determine the value of investments

An insurer shall determine the values of investments in the following manner:

Real Estate

- Investment Property- Investment Property shall be measured at historical cost less accumulated depreciation and impairment loss, residual value being considered zero and no revaluation being permissible.
- The Insurer shall asses at each balance sheet date whether any impairment of the investment property has occurred.
- An impairment loss shall be recognised as an expense in the Revenue/Profit and Loss Account immediately.
- Fair value as at the balance sheet date and the basis of its determination shall be disclosed in the financial statements as additional information.

Debt Securities

- Debt securities including government securities and redeemable preference shares shall be considered as "held to maturity" securities and shall be measured at historical cost subject to amortisation.

Equity Securities and Derivative Instruments that are Traded in Active Markets

- Listed equity securities and derivative instruments that are traded in active markets shall be measured at fair value as at the balance sheet date. For the purpose of calculation of fair value, the lowest of the last quoted closing price of the stock exchanges where the securities are listed shall be taken.
- The insurer shall assess on each balance sheet date whether any impairment of listed equity security(ies)/ derivative(s) instruments has occurred.
- An active market shall mean a market, where the securities traded are homogenous, availability of willing buyers and willing sellers is normal and the prices are publicly available.
- Unrealised gains/losses arising due to changes in the fair value of listed equity shares and derivative instruments shall be taken to equity under the head 'Fair Value Change Account' and on realisation reported in Profit and Loss Account. The 'Profit on sale of investments' or 'Loss on sale of investments', as the case may be, shall include accumulated changes in the fair value previously recognised in equity under the heading Fair Value Change Account in respect of a particular security and being recycled to Profit and Loss Account on actual sale of that listed security.
- For the removal of doubt it is clarified that balance or any part thereof shall not be available for distribution as dividends. Also, any debit balance in the said Fair Value Change Account shall be reduced from the profit/free reserves while declaring dividends.
- The insurer shall assess, at each balance sheet date, whether any impairment has occurred. An impairment loss shall be recognised as an expense in Revenue/Profit and Loss Account to the extent of the difference between the remeasured fair value of the security/ investment and its acquisition cost as reduced by any previous impairment loss recognised as expense in Revenue/Profit and Loss Account. Any reversal of impairment loss, earlier recognised in Revenue/Profit and Loss Account shall be recognised in Revenue/ Profit and Loss Account.

Unlisted and other than actively traded Equity Securities and Derivative Instruments

- Unlisted equity securities and derivative instruments and listed equity securities and derivative instruments that are not regularly traded in active market will be measured at historical costs. Provision shall be made for diminution in value of such investments. The provision so made shall be reversed in subsequent periods if estimates based on external evidence show and increase in the value of the investment over its carrying amount. The increased carrying amount of the investment due to the reversal of the provision shall not exceed the historical cost.
- For the purposes of this regulation, a security shall be considered as being not actively traded, if its trading volume does not exceed ten thousand units in any trading session during the last twelve months.

Loans

- Loans shall be measured at historical cost subject to impairment provisions.
- The insurer shall assess the quality of its loan assets and shall provide for impairment. The impairment provision shall not be less than the aggregate amount of loans which are subject to defaults of the nature mentioned below:
  (i) interest remaining unpaid for over a period of six months; and
  (ii) installment(s) of loan falling due and remaining unpaid during the last six months.

Catastrophe Reserve

Catastrophe reserve shall be created in accordance with norms, if any, prescribed by the Authority. Investment of funds out of catastrophe reserve shall be made in accordance with prescription of Authority.

It is clarified that this reserve is towards meeting losses which might arise due to an entirely unexpected set of event and not for any specific known purpose. This reserve is in the nature of an amount set aside for the potential future liability against the insurance policies in force.

Part II

Disclosures Forming Part of Financial Statements

The following shall be disclosed by way of notes to the Balance Sheet:

- Contingent Liabilities:
  - Partly-paid up investments
  - Underwriting commitments outstanding
  - Claims, other than those under policies, not acknowledged as debts
  - Guarantees given by or on behalf of the company
  - Statutory demands/liabilities in dispute, not provided for
  - Reinsurance obligations
  - Others (to be specified)
- Encumbrances to assets of the company in and outside India.
- Commitments made and outstanding for Loans, Investment and Fixed Assets.
- Claims, less reinsurance, paid to claimants in/outside India.
- Actuarial assumptions for claim liabilities in the case of policies exceeding four years.
- Ageing of claims – distinguishing between claims outstanding for more than six months and other claims.
- Premiums, less reinsurance, written from business in/outside India.
- Extent of premium income recognised, based on varying risk pattern, category wise with basis and justification therefor, including whether reliance has been placed on external evidence.
- Value of contracts in relation to investments, for:
- Purchases where deliveries are pending.
- Sales where payments are overdue.
- Operating expenses relating to insurance business: basis of allocation of expenditure to various classes of business.
- Historical costs of those investments valued on fair value basis.
- Computation of managerial remuneration.
- Basis of amortisation of debt securities.
- Unrealised gains/losses arising due to changes in the fair value of listed equity shares and derivative instruments are to be taken to equity under the head 'Fair Value Change Account' and on realisation reported in profit and loss Account.
- Pending realisation, the credit balance in the 'Fair Value Change Account' is not available for distribution.
- Fair value of investment property and the basis therefor.
- Claims settled and remaining outstanding for a period of more than six months on the balance sheet date.

The following accounting policies shall form an integral part of the financial statements:

- All significant accounting policies in terms of the accounting standards issued by the ICAI, and significant principles and policies given in Part 1 of Accounting Principles. Any other accounting policies followed by the insurer shall be stated in the manner required under Accounting Standard AS 1 issued by ICAI.

- Any departure from the accounting policies as aforesaid shall be separately disclosed with reason for such departure.

The following information shall also be disclosed:

- Investments made in accordance with any statutory requirement should be disclosed separately together with its amount, nature, security and any special rights in and outside India.
- Segregation into performing/ non-performing investments for purpose of income recognition as per the directions, if any, issued by the Authority.
- Percentage of business sector-wise.
- A summary of financial statements for the last five years, in the manner as may be prescribed by the Authority.
- Accounting Ratios as may be prescribed by the Authority.
- Basis of allocation of Interest, Dividends and Rent between Revenue Account and Profit and Loss Account.

Part III

- All the financial statements for a given year must show the corresponding figures for the previous year.
- Interest, dividends and rentals receivable should be grossed and TDS be included under the head 'Advance Tax Paid'
- Risks retained and reinsured must be shown separately.
- Provisions for possible losses under lawsuits must be made.
- Excess provision, based on management's perception shall be treated as reserves.

Part IV

A management report is required to be attached to the financial statements which inter-alia certifies the following:

- Validity of registration certificate
- Payment of statutory dues
- Confirmation of shareholding pattern and share transfer in accordance with the prescribed norms
- Maintenance of solvency margin
- Certificate as to proper valuation of assets
- Opinions and disclosures for various risk exposures and strategies followed
- Ageing of claims
- Certificate as to observance of various norms and applicable guidelines
- Review of asset quality and performance
- Schedule of payments in connections where directors are interested.

Part V

- Every insurer shall prepare the financial statements in the prescribed form.
- Separate disclosures are required for Participating policies and Non-participating policies; Linked business and Non-linked business separately for Ordinary Life, General Annuity, Pensions and Health Insurance; Business within India and business outside India. (in case of life insurance).

- In case of general insurance business, revenue accounts for fire, marine and miscellaneous insurances shall be prepared separately.
- An insurer shall prepare separate Receipts and Payments Account in accordance with the Direct Method prescribed in AS 3 – "Cash Flow Statement" issued by the ICAI.

13.2 ACCOUNTING FOR NON-LIFE INSURANCE COMPANIES

Organizational Structure

A large general insurance company having operations through out India and abroad usually has three tier organization structure. At level one, there are operating offices transacting general insurance business. These are called branch/divisional offices. Basic general insurance functions like acceptance of general insurance business, issuance of policies, development and training of agency force, payment of commission/brokerage to various insurance intermediaries, settlement of insurance claims under policies and payment of management expenses and other statutory payments. At level two, there are Regional Offices which are controling 20-25 operating offices depending on the geographical area and the requirements and policies of each company. The main function of the regional office would be to supervise the operating offices under their jurisdiction and to give them support and guidance for expanding the business and settlement of large claims. At the top there is a Head Office or a Corporate Office whose main function is to guide, supervise and control the various activities carried on by the operating offices and regional offices. Head office also superwises the operations of overseas offices.

Further two specialised functions *viz.*, re-insurance and investments are traditionaly handled only by head office.

Premium Accounting : In case of Tariff business such as fire insurance, motor insurance etc., the premium is charged as per tariff. In case of non-tariff business the premium is charged as per the guideline rates fixed by the respective technical departments of Head Office of the insurer with certain discretion to the operating offices while underwriting such business. According to section 64VB of the Insurance Act, 1938; no risk can be assumed by an insurer unless premium is received in advance.

Recently, in addition to collection of premium by cash/cheque/DD/BG/CD, IRDA has permitted to collect the premium by other manner of receipt of premium such as credit card/Debit card/E transfer etc. However, the same has to be collected before assumption of the risk. Applicable service tax (at present 8%) has to be collected on taxable premium and deposited with the respective excise authorities within prescribed time limit. Sometimes, same business is shared by more than one insurer as desired by the insured. The lead insurer has to collect the full premium alongwith service tax on tax on the full premium. However, only own share of premium is accounted as premium and the balance is shown as amount due to other co-insurers. A policy stamp is required to be affixed as per the provisions of the Stamp Act and has to be accounted properly by debiting policy stamp expenses. A premium register is generated in the system on daily basis.

As seen earlier, as per IRDA Regulation, the premium has to be recognised as income over the contract period or the period of risk, whichever is appropriate. Most of the general insurance policies are annual contracts and hence the earned premium is worked out by 1/365 method. Where the same is not practicable, the same is worked out either 1/24 or 1/12 method. At the end of the financial year, the unearned premium is compared with the reserve for unexpired risks as required under section 64V(1)(ii)(b) of the Insurance Act, 1938 and the shortfall if any is accounted as unearned premium.

Accounting of Commission/Brokerage : Commission/brokerage is paid at different rates on different classes of insurance business. No commission/brokerage is paid on certain classes of business. Commission/

brokerage becomes payable as soon as business is underwritten. However, the same is paid on monthly basis. The applicable service tax on commission is bourne by the insurer and paid to the excise authorities. TDS is deducted as per provisions of IT Act and deposited in Govt. account within prescribed time limit. In case of cancellation of a policy due to cheque dishonour or any other reason, commission/brokerage payable is reversed or recovered if already paid to the agent/broker.

Claims Accounting : Claims outgo is the major outgo of an insurance company. A claim processing is done by the respective technical department and approved by the competent authority. The payment and accounting of the claims is done by the accounts department. In case of claims on policies involving co-insurance arrangements, the full amount of claim is paid by the lead insurer, but only own share of claim is accounted as claims cost and the balance is shown as amount recoverable from the co-insurers, where a claim is reported but not settled by the end of the financial year, an adequate provision is made for such outsanding claims. At the end of each financial year, as required by IRDA the actuarial valuation of the claims liability of an insurer is made by the appointed actuary, and the shortfall, if any is provided as IBNR/IBNER.

Expenses of Management : For managing insurance business certain administrative expenses are incurred such as Employees' remuneration and welfare benefit, managerial remuneration, travel conveyance etc., rent, rate and taxes, repairs, printing and stationery, communication, legal and professional charges, medical fees, auditors fees and expenses, advertisement and publicity, interest and bank charges, depreciation, and others.

These expenses are first aggregated and then apportioned to each class of business *viz.,* Fire, Marine and Miscellaneous revenue account on a reasonable and equiptable basis. Any major expenses (Rs. 5 lacs or in excess of 1% of net premium, whichever is higher) are required to be shown separately.

Section 40C of the Insurance Act, 1938 prohibits an insurer ot spend as expenses of management in excess of the limits prescribed in the Act.

An adequate provision for outstanding expenses is made in the accounts at the end of the financial year. A provision for leave encashment, gratuity etc. at the end of each financial year is made on actuarial basis.

Co-Insurance : As seen earlier, the lead insurer has to collet the full premium alongwith service tax and pay the same to the respective excise authorites. The lead insurer accounts it's own share as premium and balance is shown as payable to other co-insurers. Similarly in case of claim, the entire claim amount is paid by the lead insurer to the policy holder, but only his own share is accounted as claims expense and the balance is shown as amount due from the co-insurer. Lead insurere also recovers certain percentage of the co-insurer's share for managing co-insurance arrangement as a leader. Co-insurance accounts are settled as per the agreement between the co-insurers. Usually, there is a provision for charging of interest for delayed settlment of accounts. At the end of each financial year, provision for outstanding claims, if any is communicated by the lead insurer and balance confirmation certificates are exchanged by all co-insurers.

Investment Accounting : Investments are assets held by an insurer for earning income by way of dividends, rent and interest or for capital appreciation or for other benefits to the insurer. An insurance company makes investment, apart from earning income, to comply with the statutory requirements and also for meeting any unforessen contingences and claims. There are two main sources of investible funds *viz.,* surplus funds arising out of the business and income from interest and dividents on existing investments.

Section 27B, 27C and 27D of the Insurance Act, 1938 lays down certain norms for investment of the funds by an insurance company. Earlier we have seen the procedure to determine the value of investments as laid down in the IRD'S Regulations for preparation of financial statements. Further IRDA has also issued detailed guidelines under IRDA (investment) (amendment) Regulations, 2001 for making investments by the insurer. IRDA prohibits any investment abroad out of policyholders' funds. Accounting entries for investments are involved for buying/ selling investments receipts/accrued and outstanding of interest, dividends, rent, and recording impairment, write off and write down of certain investments.

Foreign Operations : Foreign branch accounts are merged with the Indian operations of an insurer to present global financial position. In addition to the Indian requirements, these offices have to comply with the local laws for preparation of financial statements and get the accounts audited by the local qualified auditores or the Indian firms of auditors, as the case may be. These accounts hwich are prepared in local currencies are converted in Indian currency as per AS11 and merged with Indian accounts.

Consolidation

The accounts of a large insurance company having number of offices in India and abroad, are consolidated at the head office of the company. The accounts prepared by the operating offices in India are audited by the branch auditors. These are consolidated at various regional/zonal offices and the consolidated accounts for the whole region are submitted to head office. At head office, separate accounts are prepared for the re-insurance and investment operations. If the company has foreign branches, their accounts audited by the local statutory auditors or the central statutory auditors are converted in Indian currency and merged with the Indian accounts. Further, following special provisions/reserves are made only at head office while preparing final accounts :

(*a*) ***Unexpired Risk Reserved :*** Most of the general insurance policies are annual policies, which are issued through out the year. Thus at the financial year end, there is unexpired liability under various policies which may occur during the remaining term of the policy beyond the year end and for which the entire premium is accounted as income. Section 64V(1)(*ii*)(*b*) of the Insurance Act, 1938 has provided certain percentage of net premium as Reserve for unexpired risks, as seen earlier, which is the compulsory minimum requirement. In addition to this, if unearned premium exceeds such reserve for unexpired risks, calculated as per the provisions of the Act, the difference is to be accounted as unearned premium.

(*b*) *Provision for terminal benefits of th employees :* Every year provision for leave encashment, gratuity etc. payable to the employees on superannuation is made on actuarial basis at the head office.

(c) *Reserve for Bad and Doubtful Debts :* After doing age-wise analysis of the debtors, a suitable provision is made at head office of an insurer.

(*d*) *Provision for taxation :* Tax liability of an insurance company is governed by the special provisions contained in section 44 of the Income Tax Act. Adequate provision for tax liability (including weath tax) is made at head office.

(*e*) *Provision for Proposed Dividend :* An adequate provision is made for proposed dividend as per the board resolution at head office.

(*f*) IBNR/IBNER provision is made as suggested by the appointed actuary by increasing the outstanding claims reserve.

Thus the central accounts department at head office is responsible for the consolidation of all regional office accounts (where the accounts of various operating offices are consolidated), reinsurance accounts, investment accounts and foreign operation accounts. The consolidation is done with the help of a suitable consolidation software. Fire revenue account, Marine revenue account, Miscellaneous revenue account, Profit and Loss account and Balance Sheed along with 15 schedules is prepared as per formats given in the Part V of the IRDA Regulations for the financial statements.

The final accounts are audited by the statutory auditors appointed by the shareholders' (by C&AG in case of a Govt. company) and presented in the Annual General Meeting for approval.

13.3 ACCOUNTING FOR LIFE INSURANCE COMPANIES

The Accounting function of the life insurance companies is quite different from that of other companies. The major reasons for this are due to :

- Ascertainment of liability in respect of insurance policies issued by the company.
- The concept of Policyholders' Fund and Shareholders' Fund.
- The unit linked business and the related investment valuations involved in the same end.
- Segmental reporting in respect of all the funds maintained by the company.

With the given scenario, the finalisation of accounts of an insurance company involves a log of complexities, which are unique in nature.

The Financial Statements of Insurance Company consists of :

- Revenue Account (Policyholders Account)
- Profit and Loss Account (Shareholders Account)
- Balance Sheet
- Receipts and Payments account (Cash Flow Statement)
- The segmental reports relating to the funds (Revenue accounts and Balance Sheet).

The above statements are to be in conformity with the Accounting Standards issued by ICAI, to the extent applicable to the life insurance business except that :

- Cash Flow Statement needs to be prepared under Direct Method and
- Segmental Reporting shall apply to all insurers irrespective of listing and turnover mentioned in AS 17.

Insurance Regulatory and Development Authority (IRDA) has prescribed specified formats for the preparation of Financial Statements. These formats are in Part V of Schedule A of IRDA (Preparation of Financial Statements and Auditors Report of Insurance Companies) Regulations, 2002.

1. Revenue Account (Policyholders' Account – Technical Account)

The Revenue Account sets out all income and expenses relating to the insurance business.

Income

The income of the technical account comprises of :

- Premium after adjusting reinsurance ceded and reinsurance accepted.
- Income from investments which needs to be shown under different heads like :
  - Interest, Dividend and Rents.
  - Profit on sale redemption of investments.
  - Loss on sale redemption of investments.
  - Transfer gain on revaluation of change in fir value and
  - Amortisation charge

Under the Income head, there will also be Other Income, Foreign Exchange Gain/Loss and other items.

The transfer of funds from Shareholders' Fund to Policy-holders' Accounts is shown separately in the Revenue Account.

Expenses

- Expenses include :

1. Commission
2. Operating Expenses
3. Benefits paid
4. Interim bonus paid and
5. Change in valuation of liability against life policies in force.

Accounting Principles to be followed :

The regulator has also issued instructions as to the Accounting Principles to be followed in the preparation of Financial Statements.

The Premium income is recognised as and when due. For linked business, it is the date when associated units are created. Acquisition cots are expensed out in the period in which they are incurred. Claim costs include the policy benefit amount and the specific claims settlement cots.

Policyholders Fund

The Policyholders Funds need to maintain adequate level of solvency at all times. Separate Funds are maintained for different types of policies like participating Fund, Pension Fund etc. The solvency level is also to be maintained for declaration of bonuses to Participating Fund and Pension Fund.

As we all know, during the initial period, company starts with Shareholders Fund. In order to meet with the above requirements of the Policyholders' Fund, the company needs to transfer funds from Shareholders' Fund. This transfer has been allowed by IRDA during the first five years. The IRDA also specifies that no bonus can be declared by an insurance company if the company is in deficit. To tackle the situation, the transfer from Shareholder's Fund is necessary.

Such transfers from Shareholders' Fund to Policyholders' A/c is irreversible in nature and at no point of time, such amount can be recouped to the Shareholders' Fund. Transfer of such funds is shown in Revenue Account and it adds to the revenue of the Technical Account.

The same amount is treated as expenditure in Profit & Loss account (Shareholders' Account–Non Technical Account).

Actuarial Valuation

The estimation of liability against life policies shall be determined by the appointed actuary of the insurer based on his annual investigation of the life insurance business. The actuarial assumptions are disclosed in the Financial Statements. The valuation process plays a significant role in the determination of the surplus/deficit of the insurance company. The change in valuation of liability against life policies in force is taken to revenue as expenditure, while finding surplus or deficit.

The taxatioon of such surplus is being dealt with by the Income Tax Act in Section 44, Schedule I and Section 115B.

2. Profit and Loss Account (Shareholders' Account – Non-Technical Account) : This Account represents all income and expenses relating to Shareholders' Account (Those not relating to insurance business).

Income

The income comprises mainly of investment or other income created out of Shareholders' Fund.

Expenses

The major components of expenses are :

- Depreciation relating to assets held by shareholders' fund, investment expenses, Directors Fees etc.

- Transfer of funds to Policy-holders' Fund and
- Preliminary Expenses written off

The profit or loss as per the Account is carried to the Balance Sheet as usual.

3. Balance Sheet

The items in the Balance Sheet of a Life Insurance Company includes, other than the normal items–

1. Shareholders' Fund
2. Policy Holders Fund
3. Investments related to Policyholders' Fund, Shareholders' Fund and Assets held to cover linked liabilities Shareholders' Fund includes share capital less preliminary expenses, reserves and surplus and fair value change account.

Policyholders' Fund consists of Policy liabilities, Fair value change relating to policy fund investments, insurance reserves, provision for linked liabilities, Funds for future appropriatios, Surplus allocated to shareholders etc.

The balance in the Funds for future appropriations represents funds, the allocation of which, either to participating policyholders or to shareholders has not been determined at the balance sheet date. Transfers to and from the fund reflect the excess or deficiency of income over expenses and appropriations in each accounting period arising in the Company's policy-holder fund.

Investments of a Life Insurance Company

The Insurance Company has to follow the provisions set out in Section 27 of the Insurance Act, 1938, read with Rule 3 of the IRDA (Investment) Regulations, 2000.

Accordingly, the contorlled fund of the company has to be invested in the specified securites. The assets relating to Pension business, Annuity business and Linked Life Insurance business shall not form part of Controlled Fund.

Separate norms are formulated for investing funds of Pension business and Annuity business.

The funds relating to Unit Linked Insurance business are to be invested as per the pattern of investment offered to and approved by the policyholders. However, the total investment in other than approved category of investments shall at no time exceed 25% of the Fund.

Valuatioon of Investments

Real Estate – Investment Property

The investment property shall be valued at historical cost subject to revaluation at least once in every three years. The change in the carrying amount of the investment property shall be taken to Revaluation Reserve.

Debt Securities

Debt securities, including government securities and redeemable preference shares shall be considered as "held to maturity" securities and shall be measured at historical cost, subject to amortisatioon.

Equity Securities and Derivative Instruments

Listed equity securities ans derivative instruments that are traded in active markets shall be measured at fair value on the balance sheet date. For the purpose of calculation of fair value, the lowest of the last quoted closing price at National Stock Exchange or Bombay Stock Exchange shall be taken.

Unrealised gains and losses arising due to changes in the fair value of listed equity shares and derivative instruments shall be taken to equity under the head "Fair Value Change Account".

Unlisted and other than actively traded equity securities and Derivative Instruments are measured at historical cost.

Loans

Loans are measured at historical cost subject to impairment provisions.

Linked Business

The accounting principles used for valuation of investment are to be consistent with the above mentioned principles. A separate set of financial statement for each segregated fund of the linked business shall be annexed.

Investment Transfer

From Shareholders' Fund to Policyholders' Fund

The IRDA circular details the transfer of investments from Shareholders' Fund to Policyholders' Fund. Such transfers made with the objective of meeting hte defict in Policyholders' Account should be at the cost or market value, whichever is less. In case of debt securities, it shall be at the net amortised cost.

Transfer Between Policyholders' Funds

The Regulator does not allow transfers between different policy-holders' funds.

Purchase/Sale Transactions Between Unit linked Funds

These transactions are likely as part of investment management strategy to limit transactions cost and also arising out of options exercised by policyholders to shift between different unit linked funds. The sale/purchase under such circumstances would be based on the market price of the investments, which are being shifted between unit linked schemes.

During the initial years, security sale at market price shall be permitted from shareholders' assets in the approved category to meet the investment needs to policyholders' funds. Such transactions are allowed where policyholders' fund size is small i.e., upto Rs. 50 crores.

Receipts and Payments Account (Cash Flow Statement)

The cash flow statement of the insurance company needs to be worked out as per Direct method as per the IRDA requirement. The statement depicts the receipts and payments from various business activities. The major items are :

Operating

* Receipts and Payments from policyholders
* Payments to Reinsurers
* Payments to Agents, Employee expenses, Investment income

Investing Activities

* Purchase and sale of investments
* Purchase of fixed assets

Financing Activities

This refers to the issue of share capital or raising of funds from other sources.

5. Segmental Reporting

As per the regulations, every insurance company has to prepare segment wise Revenue Account and Balance Sheet of the business it has done. Accordingly, the company is required to report segment results separately for

Participating, Non-Participicing, Pension, Annuity business and Unit Linked business (Group, Individual–Life and Individual Pension). For the purpose of working out results of such segments, company will decide on the bases on which revenue, expenses, assets and liabilities are to be allocated. The accounting policies used in the segmental reporting are to be disclosed in the Financial Disclosures.

Disclosure Requirements

The IRDA Rules also specify the disclosure requirements, general instructions for preparation of financial statements, and also the contents of the Management Report.

Financial Summary and Ratios

IRDA has also specified the format for Financial Statement summary for the previous financial years and the relevant ratios to be worked out. The summary and the ratios form part of the Financial Disclosures.

13.4 IFRS ON INSURANCE CONTRACTS

IFRS 4 is the first guidance issued by the IASB on accounting for insurance contracts. Under accrual taxation principles, which apply to the calculation of income from most businesses, revenues and expenes are accounted for as they are earned or incurred. In its purest form, this would imply that all assets and liabilities would need to be valued each year to recognise any gain or loss which had occurred during that year. This would impose a significant compliance burden and would require a subjective estimation of value in cases where no direct market price exists for a particular asset. Therefore in most cases the **realisation principle** is applied. In general, an event where the asset or liability becomes fixed and determinable, such as a sale, must occur to trigger the recognition of the amount as revenue or an expense.

However, in some instances, deviations from a pure accrual principle are necessary either to achieve certain policy goals or to facilitate compliance with the tax. In these situations circumsances could arise where the revenues and their associated costs are accounted for with different timing. To avoid this, the **matching principle** is also often applied. In this case an attempt is made to have the expenses associated with revenues recognised at the same time.

Matching Revenues and Expenses

If expenses can be recognised before the associated income is taxed, a deferral tax occurs. If on the other hand, income is recognised without making adequate allowance for related expenses, too much tax will be paid, or it will be paid too soon.

Issues in Accrual Accounting

1. Accrual of Interest
2. Problems with Realisation Taxation
   (*i*) Deferred Recognition of Income
   (*ii*) Acceleration of Loss
   (*iii*) Asset Versus Liability Adverse Selection
   (*iv*) Assets Versus Asset Adverse Selection
3. Mark to Market or Fair Value

Bad and Doubtful Debts

Insurance companies like other financial institutions make loans and purchase bonds issued by governments and corporations. Some portion of these instruments will suffer from a full or partial default, that is they give rise to a bad debt.

For most taxpayers, bad debts may only be recognised to the extent that an amount has previously been included in income. This is a necessary consequence of accrual taxation, which recognises income as it accrues, before payment is made. If it is eventually determined that payment will not be received that it is appropriate that the previous income inclusion be reversed. Losses on other loans, on the other hand would be treated as capital in nature. However for financial institutions, *i.e.*, those companies which are in the business of lending money, it is appropriate to relax this restriction and allow bad debts on the lending assets of the institution to be deducted from income even if they represent the principal of a loan, rather than the reversal of an amount that has previously been accrued into income.

1. Doubtful Debts (Specific Provisions)

A doubtful debt or specific provision is taken when the financial institution determines that the value of the loan is impaired due to doubtful repayment. This may occur before the loan is determined to be bad and removed from company's books.

A specific provisoin is computed on a loan by loan basis based on the probability of recovery net of salvage value (partial write off). In general it requires a precise estimation of the likely value of recovery.

Reserves

Under ordinary tax accounting in many countries, expenses may not be recognised until they become fixed and determinable. Future expenses cannot therefore be recognised while there is still an element of contingency in their determination.

1. Accounting for Reserves

Reserves for future costs must be re-evaluated each year.

2. Discounting

In principle, future payments should not be reflected at face value. The cost to be deducted should reflect the time value of money. Accordingly, the reserve should be the discounted present value of the payment. Thus in the example above, the amounts to be deducted.

3. Transition

The issue of transition cna arise when there are legislated changes in the methods of calculating reserves.

- **no transition,** where the new methods are applied to all policies beginning with the end of year calculation in the year the new mechanism comes into effect.
- **grandfathering,** where the new methods or reserving are only applied to newly issued policies;
- **a fresh start,** (where the policy induced change in base level of reserves is in effect ignored), by recalculating the beginning of the year reserves using the new methods without an income inclusion; and
- **a prorating of** the reserve inclusion arising from the recalculation over a number of years.

The argument for **no transition** would recognise that the amounts accumulated in reserves have already been deducted from income and represent a substantial and continuing deferral of tax.

Under **grandfathering,** the new reserving mechanism is not applied to any previously issued policies.

Under a **fresh start,** the opening balance of reseves would be calculated under the new rules, and the calculation of income for the year would use this new amount as the inclusion from prior year reserves.

13.5 Taxation Aspects of Insurance[2]

13.5.1 Income Tax for Life Insurance Policyholders

Rebate under Sec. 80C

The following are the important income tax provisions applicable to Life Insurance policyholders:

- An LIC policy can be taken in the name of an individual or any member of a Hindu Undivided Family (HUF).
- An individual can claim rebate on LIC premium paid on his/her life, his/her spouse, his/ her children including adult children.

Under Sec. 80C of the Income Tax Act, 1961, a rebate of 20% is allowed on the life insurance premium paid by the assessee under the said act. This rebate is deductible from the total tax payable by the individual/HUF. This total amount of investment in the form of the LIC premium and other specified investment like PPF, NSC, etc. is restricted to Rs. 1,00,000/- per annum. (Assessment year 2008-09)

The aforesaid sums qualify, for the purpose of this section, on the "payment": basis. Even in the case of an assessee, following mercantile system of accounting, payments, which have become due during the previous year but are outstanding on the last day of the previous year, are not eligible for deductions.

Termination of the Unit-linked Insurance Plan before Five Years

Where a member participating in the unit linked plan terminates his participation before making contribution for a period of 5 years. No tax deductions will be allowed in respect of contributions made in such year. Moreover, an amount equal to an aggregate of tax deductions allowed in respect of the contributions to the plan in the past years shall be deemed as tax payable by the assessee of the previous year in which he terminates his participation in the plan.

Discontinuation of the Insurance Plan before Two Years

Where a taxpayer discontinues a policy of the life insurance, before the premium for 2 years have been paid, no tax deductions will be allowed in respect of any premium paid on that policy in the year in which the policy is terminated. Further, the amount of tax deduction allowed in respect of the premium paid in respect of the policy in the year preceding that year will be deemed to be the tax payable by the assess of the year in which the policy is terminated.

In case of the single premium policy, if such policy is surrendered with two years of the date of the commencement of insurance, the amount of deduction of income tax allowed earlier shall be deemed to be the tax payable in the year of surrender.

Deduction in respect of Pension Fund-when available (Sec. 80CCC) (Jeevan Suraksha Policy)

- Provision of the Sec. 80CCC of the Act are applicable to all taxpayers being individuals (may be resident, or non-resident, Indian citizen or foreign citizen.)
- During the previous year, the assessee has paid/deposited a sum under an annuity of the Life Insurance Corporation of India for receiving pension from the fund set up by the said corporation as approved by the controller of Insurance.
- The aforesaid amount is paid out of the income chargeable to tax.
- Amount of the Deduction: If the aforesaid conditions are satisfied, the amount deposited or Rs. 10,000, whichever is lower, is deductible.

- The amount received by the assessee or his nominee, as pension will be taxable in the hands of the assessee or the nominee, as the case may be, in the year of the receipt.
- Rebate (with reference to the amount paid under Sec. 80CCC) will not be available under Sec. 88 to persons to whom deduction under this section has been allowed.
- Under Sec. 80 DDA a deduction up to Rs. 20,000 per annum is allowed from the gross total income, when the contributions or deposits is made with LIC for the maintenance of a handicapped dependent.

Key Man Insurance — Sec. 37(1)

The premium paid by the company is allowed as a 100% deductible business expenditure u/s 37(1) of the Income Tax Act.

The proceeds received by the company at the time of the maturity or death of the key man is treated as income of the company and will be subjected to the tax.

When the company assigns policy to key man for "No consideration" as a retirement benefit, the surrender value proceeds received by the key man is treated as additional salary and hence tax has to be paid by the key man.

Partnership Insurance

The insurance premium under partnership insurance on the lives of the partners is allowed as 100% business expenditure u/s 37 (1) of the Act.

However, the policy proceeds on the death claims will be treated as an income of the firm and is subjected to tax.

Sum Received from Life Insurance Policy – Sec. 10 (10D)

- According to Sec. 10 (10D), any sum received under a life insurance policy, including a sum allocated by the way of bonus on such policy, shall not be included in the total income of the person.
- The exemption is, however, not available in respect of such policy which is specified under Sec. 80 DDA (3)or under a key man insurance policy.

13.5.2 Non Life Insurance

Medical Insurance Premium – Sec. 80 D

- The taxpayer is an individual (may be resident, or non-resident, Indian citizen or foreign citizen) or a Hindu Undivided Family (may be resident, or non-resident).
- Insurance premium is paid by the taxpayer in accordance with the scheme framed in this behalf by the GIC of India and approved by the Central Government. The scheme is known as "Mediclaim" insurance policy.
- The aforesaid premium is paid by cheque.
- It is paid out of income chargeable to tax.
- Mediclaim policy is taken on the health of the following persons:

Taxpayer	*Insured person*
Individual	On the health of the taxpayer, on the health of the spouse dependent parents or dependent children of the tax payer.
Hindu Undivided Family	On the health of any member of the family.

- If the aforesaid conditions are satisfied, then the insurance premium paid or Rs. 15,000. whichever is lower is deductible.

Insurance Claim Received for Damage or Destruction of a Capital Asset – [Sec. 45 (1A)]

- The insurance claim received on account of destruction of asset is not chargeable to tax, as "destruction" does not amount to transfer. The newly inserted sub-section (1A) provides that where any person receives any money or other assets under any insurance from an insurer on account of damage to or destruction of any capital asset, as a result of flood, typhoon, hurricane, cyclone, earthquake or other convulsion of nature, riot or civil disturbance, accidental fire or explosion or because of actions by the enemy or actions taken in combating the enemy, then any profits or gains arising from receipts of such money or other assets shall be chargeable to income tax under the head "Capital Gains" and shall be deemed to be the income of such person in the previous year in which such money or other asset is received.

Insurance Premium [Sec. 36 (1)(i)]

- The amount of any premium paid in respect of insurance against risk of damage or destruction of stocks or stores, used for purposes of business or profession, is allowed as deduction.

Insurance Premium paid by a Federal Milk Co-operative Society [Sec. 36 (i) (ia)]

- Insurance premium paid by the federal milk co-operative society on the lives of cattle, owned by the members of a primary milk co-operative society affiliated to it, is allowable as deduction.

Premia for Insurance on Health of Employees [Sec. 36 [1(ib)]

- An employer can claim deduction in respect of premia paid by him by cheque for insurance on the health of his employees in accordance with the scheme framed by the General Insurance Corporation and approved by the Central Government.
- In the last budget there was a proposal to charge service tax to the insurance premium paid by the insured. The service tax for the insurance premium was proposed to be levied at a rate of 5%. This could act as a serious impediment to the growing insurance business. However it was later on agreed not to charge any service tax on insurance premia.

Income Tax for LIC Agents

The LIC agents can earn commission by procuring business. The commission, generally, is in nature of first year commission, renewal commission and bonus commission. The commission earned is an income, which may be taxable depending on the total income.

- If the income from all sources including LIC commission does not exceed Rs. 50,000 per annum, then one is not liable to pay income tax as it is below taxable limit.
- If the commission earned from LIC is below Rs. 60,000 per annum and if no separate books of accounts is maintained, then the entitlement for deduction is as follows:
  (a) First year Commission – 50%
  (b) Renewal Commission – 15%
- However, if separate bifurcation could be made then LIC agent is entitled to a flat deduction of $33^1/3$% of total commission.
- The LIC commission after claiming deduction as mentioned above will be included with other source of income for tax purposes.
- In case gross commission earned by an agent from LIC exceeds Rs. 60,000 per annum then he cannot claim deduction referred above.

Income from other Sources – Sec. 56(2)

As per the provisions of Sec. 56(2) of the Act, income received in the form of insurance commission is chargeable to tax under the head of "Income from other sources." Income, chargeable under this head is computed in accordance with the method of accounting regularly employed by the assessee. This head of income can be evoked only if all the following conditions are met:

- There is an income;
- That income is not exempt from tax under Sec. 10 to 13A;
- That income is neither salary income, nor rental income from house property, nor income from business/ profession, nor capital gains.

Tax is to be Deducted at Source from Insurance Commission. [Sec. 194 (D)]

- A person responsible for paying to a resident any income by the way of remuneration or reward, whether by the way of commission or otherwise, for soliciting or procuring insurance business including business relating to the continuance, renewal or revival of policies of insurance, is required to deduct income tax thereon at the rates in force (10% for the A.Y. 2002-03).
- Tax shall be deducted a the time of credit of such income to the account of the payee or the payment thereof (by whatever mode), whichever is earlier.
- No tax is required to be deducted at source if the insurance commission credited or paid during the financial year does not exceed Rs. 5,000/-.
- The person receiving insurance commission can make an application in Form No. 13 to the concerned Assessing Officer and obtain a certificate authorizing the person responsible for making payments, by the way of insurance commission, to deduct tax at a lower rate or to deduct no tax, as may be appropriate.

13.5.3 Taxation of Insurance Companies

Section 44 of the Income Tax Act 1961, read with first schedule of the Act deals with taxation of life Insurance business. Till 1976, Life Insurance business was taxed on the higher of Profit on investment income less expenses or Valuation surplus (excluding prior year's surplus or deficit) less 80% of bonuses declared or amounts reserved for policyholders. In the Budget of 1976 government abandoned 'higher of the two' system and adopted the annual average of the surplus disclosed by the actuarial valuation under the Insurance Act, 1938, after excluding from it any surplus or deficit included therein relating to any earlier inter-valuation period. The taxable income so determined is taxed at a flat rate of 12.5% prescribed under the first Schedule of the IT Act. This rate is not affected by the Annual Finance Acts and has remained unchanged since 1977.

Taxation of Life Insurance Companies

The Life Insurance Corporation made a formal representation in February 1974 to the government that the basis of assessment of life insurance should be simplified and in this regard the representation was referred to the Central Board of Direct Taxes (CBDT). One of the important points that emerged in the meeting of the Consultative Committee of the Ministry of Finance, held in December 1974, was that the gross valuation surplus should be the only basis for taxation and the tax should be equal to a specified percentage of a gross surplus. This change came into effect from April 1, 1977. Sec. 115B of the Income-tax Act states that:

- Where the total income of an assessee includes any profits and gains from life insurance business, the income-tax payable shall be the aggregate of the amount generated.
- The amount of income-tax calculated on the amount of profits and gains of the life insurance business included in the total income, at the rate of twelve and one-half percent, and

- The amount of income tax with which the assessee would have been chargeable had the total income of the assessee been reduced by the amount of profits and gains of the life insurance business.

"With this change in the method of taxation, two rates of tax have been introduced. A rate of 12.5 per cent on the computed profits and gains of life insurance business. The normal corporate rate on the net income in the shareholders' fund after excluding the profits from life insurance business."

13.5.4 Problems of Taxation with Emergence of New Players[3]

"Current system of Taxation was workable when there was only one life insurance company and was of the view that it would not work in the new environment where many insurance companies are going to enter the Indian market. For new Insurance companies, the shareholder's profit is a different proportion of the emerging *Valuation surplus.*"

"Currently the Life Insurance industry is taxed on the Valuation Surplus that emerges during the most recent inter-valuation period, and the investment profit on shareholder's funds. All other types of companies are taxed on shareholders' profits. The emerging valuation surplus is distributed as bonuses to policyholders and profits to shareholders. Taxing this way (Valuation surplus) imposes a tax on both shareholders and policyholders. Now with the opening up of the insurance sector to private sector participation, a fresh approach is needed to be adopted to tax the life insurance segment."

The problems of tax treatment of premiums and contribution can be segregated into the following categories:

(i) taxation of policyholder funds;

(ii) taxation of benefits received and latter category includes taxation of transfers between policyholder's funds and

(iii) Shareholder's funds and taxation of shareholders' funds.

- In the case of new companies, the valuation surplus will be negative during the first few years. However, since the rate of tax applicable to the profit and gain from life insurance business is different from that applicable to the balance net income in the shareholders' fund, a loss in the former cannot be set off against the net positive income in the latter.
- During the first three or four years after commencement of operations, till sufficient business volumes build up, the policyholders' fund of a company will be in deficit or may be negative. This however, is a normal occurrence and not a matter for concern. But, in their anxiety to project a healthy image, new companies generally try to wipe out this deficit by appropriate transfers from the shareholder's to policyholders' fund. "Can these transfers be treated as valid business expenses and allowed to be set off against the investment income in the shareholders' fund?"

However, since it is not stipulated either in the Insurance Act or Regulations, that the deficit in the policyholder' fund has to be made good by transfer from the shareholders' fund, the revenue authorities can and may take a view that such transfers cannot be treated as valid business expenses. Any such decision is certain to result in protracted legal battles. Before the introduction of the "dual system of taxation" in 1977, such a problem could not have arisen and so no precedents too may be available."

"There is no singular system of Taxation world-wide – it varies over country to country. Some countries like Japan, Philippines, Hong Kong, Macau have premium-based taxation of Life Insurance business. Whereas in some countries like Malaysia, Insurers are taxed on 'Investment income and capital gains either in lieu of or in addition to a premium based tax. In some countries like Great Britain have adopted a system where insurers have to pay tax on Investment income less expense."

"It is proposed that instead of taxing the emerging surplus at one rate of tax, it be taxed according to the recipient of the surplus. The surplus transferred to the shareholder's fund represents shareholder's profits and therefore they should be taxed at the full corporate tax rate of 38.5% including surcharge. These can be achieved by not directly taxing that part of the surplus transferred to the shareholder's fund. Instead the transfer would go through the shareholder's profit and loss account, where it would directly contribute to the shareholder's profits along with the profits on the shareholder's investment."

Nonlife insurance Companies

Countries are less reluctant to impose premium taxation in nonlife insurance than in life insurance.

Moreover, tax rates with nonlife insurance are generally higher.

Some governments levy other premium-based taxes that can greatly increase the effective tax in nonlife insurance.

13.6 INTERNATIONAL ASPECTS OF TAXATION IN INSURANCE

Taxation of insurance premiums is similar across countries.

The inside interest build-up of annuities during their accumulation period usually receives the same tax treatment as that of other life insurance products. Most countries seem to tax annuity payouts to some degree. Most countries exempt death proceeds paid under qualifying life insurance policies from income taxation.

Governments commonly levy estate duties (taxes).

Tax Relief on Life Insurance Premium

Some tax relief on premiums paid for qualifying, individually issued life insurance products

Austria	Ireland	Portugal
Belgium	Italy	Spain
Denmark	Japan	Sweden
France	Luxembourg	Switzerland
Germany	The Netherlands	Turkey
Greece	Norway	

No tax relief on premiums paid for individually issued life insurance products.

Australia	Iceland	United States
Canada	New Zealand	
Finland	United Kingdom	

Tax Relief on Nonlife Insurance Premium

1. Premiums paid by individuals for personal nonlife insurance policies are not deductible from income for tax purposes.
   - Exceptions exists.
2. Premiums payments by businesses to purchase compulsory insurance and other business-related insurance are commonly tax deductible.
3. Benefits received under personal nonlife insurance policies are tax free.
   - Exceptions exists.
4. For benefits received by a business, such benefits are tax free in many countries.

1. Countries are less reluctant to impose premium taxation in nonlife insurance than in life insurance.
   - Moreover, tax rates with nonlife insurance are generally higher.

2.Some governments levy other premium-based taxes that can greatly increase the effective tax in nonlife insurance.

Other Premium-based Taxes on Nonlife

Category	*Country*	*Charges*
Fire Brigade taxes	Australia	8% in fire insurance.
(leived on fire	Germany	Up to 8% in fire and business interruption insurance.
insurance premiums)		insurance for nuclear installations, property all risks and householders' insurance.
	Portugal	Up to 13% in fire insurance, householders' insurance, motor insurance, and insurance for goods in transit
	Spain	Up to 5% in nonlife insurance
	United Kingdom	£35 per £1 million of gross value of goods insured by fire insurance.
	United States	1–2% in selected states.
Other indirect taxes	Belgium	Up to 17.5% in motor insurance; 6.5% in fire insurance
(levied on certain		
nonlife lines)	France	15% of special contribution of moor liability insured (as a social security budgetary resources)
	Hungary	1% in most nonlife insurance
	Italy	Up to 15% in motor insurance for various parafiscal taxes; 1% in fire and theft insurance.
	Spain	5% in compulsory travel insurance for fund for the insurance of extraordinary risks.
	United States	Up to 2% in selected states.

Nonlife Insurance Companies

1. Premium-based taxation is to be paid irrespective of insurer profitability.
2. Governments usually tax nonlife insurance companies as other corporations.
3. The great majority of countries seem to allow deductions for claims reported but unpaid and certain other reserves.
4. The tax rates in most countries are the same as those applicable to other corporations and as for life insurers.

THE GAZETTE OF INDIA

EXTRAORDINARY

PART III – SECTION 4

INSURANCE REGULATORY AND DEVELOPMENT AUTHORITY, NEW DELHI

THE INSURANCE REGULATORY AND DEVELOPMENT AUTHORITY (PREPARATION OF FINANCIAL STATEMENTS AND AUDITOR'S REPORT OF INSURANCE COMPANIES) REGULATIONS, 2002

NOTIFICATION

New Delhi, the 30th March, 2002.

In exercise of the powers conferred by Section 114A of the Insurance Act, 1938, (4 of 1938),and in suppression of the Insurance Regulatory And Development Authority (Preparation Of Financial Statements And Auditor's Report Of Insurance Companies) Regulations, 2000, Authority, in consultation with the Insurance Advisory Committee, hereby makes the following regulations, namely:

1. Short title and commencement – (1) These regulations may be called the Insurance Regulatory and Development Authority (Preparation of Financial Statements and Auditor's Report of Insurance Companies) Regulations, 2002.

(2) They shall come into force from the date of their publication in the *Official Gazette*.

(3) On and from the commencement of these regulations, The Insurance Regulatory And Development Authority (Preparation of Financial Statements and Auditor's Report of Insurance Companies) Regulations, 2000 shall stand superceded, except as respect to things done or omitted to be done thereunder.

2. Definitions – (1) In these regulations, unless the context otherwise requires –

(a) "*Act*" means the Insurance Act, 1938 (4 of 1938);

(b) "*Authority*" means the Insurance Regulatory and Development Authority established under sub-section (1) of Section 3 of the Insurance Regulatory and Development Authority Act, 1999 (41 of 1999);

(c) All words and expressions used herein and not defined but defined in the Insurance Act, 1938 (4 of 1938), or Insurance Regulatory and Development Authority Act, 1999 (41 of 1999), or Companies Act, 1956 (1 of 1956), shall have the meanings respectively assigned to them in those Acts.

3. Preparation of financial statements, management report and auditor's report –

(1) An insurer carrying on life insurance business, after the commencement of these Regulations, shall comply with the requirements of Schedule A.

(2) An insurer carrying on general insurance business, after the commencement of these Regulations, shall comply with the requirements of Schedule B:

Provided that this sub-regulation shall apply, *mutatis mutandis,* to reinsurers, until separate regulations are made.

(3) The report of the auditors on the financial statements of every insurer and reinsurer shall be in conformity with the requirements of Schedule C, or as near thereto as the circumstances permit.

(4) The Authority may, from time to time, issue separate directions/ guidelines in the matter of appointment, continuance or removal of auditors of an insurer or reinsurer, as the case may be, and such directions/ guidelines may include prescriptions regarding qualifications and experience of auditors, their rotation, period of appointment, etc. as may be deemed necessary by the Authority.

SCHEDULE A

(See Regulation 3)

PART I

Accounting Principles for Preparation of Financial Statements

1. Applicability of Accounting Standards – Every Balance Sheet, Revenue Account [Policyholders' Account], Receipts and Payments Account [Cash Flow statement] and Profit and Loss Account [Shareholders' Account] of an insurer shall be in conformity with the Accounting Standards (AS) issued by the ICAI, to the extent applicable to insurers carrying on life insurance business, except that:

(i) Accounting Standard 3 (AS 3) – Cash Flow Statements – Cash Flow Statement shall be prepared only under the Direct Method.

(ii) Accounting Standard 17 (AS 17) – Segment Reporting – shall apply to all insurers irrespective of the requirememts regarding listing and turnover mentioned therein.

2. Premium – Premium shall be recognised as income when due. For linked business the due date for payment may be taken as the date when the associated units are created.

3. Acquisition Costs – Acquisition costs, if any, shall be expensed in the period in which they are incurred.

Acquisition costs are those costs that vary with and are primarily related to the acquisition of new and renewal insurance contracts. The most essential test is the obligatory relationship between costs and the execution of insurance contracts (i.e., commencement of risk).

4. Claims Cost – The ultimate cost of claims shall comprise the policy benefit amount and specific claims settlement costs, wherever applicable.

5. Actuarial Valuation – Liability for Life Policies – The estimation of liability against life policies shall be determined by the appointed actuary of the insurer pursuant to his annual investigation of the life insurance business. Actuarial assumptions are to be disclosed by way of notes to the account.

The liability shall be so calculated that together with future premium payments and investment income, the insurer can meet all future claims (including bonus entitlements to policyholders) and expenses.

6. Procedure to determine value of investments – An insurer shall determine the values of investments in the following manner:

(a) Real Estate – Investment Property – The value of investment property shall be determined at historical cost, subject to revaluation at least once in every three years. The change in the carrying amount of the investment property shall be taken to Revaluation Reserve.

The insurer shall assess at each balance sheet date whether any impairment of the investment property has occurred.

Gains/ losses arising due to changes in the carrying amount of real estate shall be taken to equity under 'Revaluation Reserve'. The 'Profit on sale of investments' or 'Loss on sale of investments', as the case may be, shall include accumulated changes in the carrying amount previously recognised in equity under the heading 'Revaluation Reserve' in respect of a particular property and being recycled to the relevant Revenue Account or Profit and Loss Account on sale of that property.

The bases for revaluation shall be disclosed in the notes to accounts. The Authority may issue directions specifying the amount to be released from the revaluation reserve for declaring bonus to the policyholders. For the removal of doubt, it is clarified that except for the amount that is released to policyholders as per the Authority's direction, no other amount shall be distributed to shareholders out of Revaluation Reserve Account.

An impairment loss shall be recognised as an expense in the Revenue/Profit and Loss Account immediately, unless the asset is carried at re-valued amount. Any impairment loss of a re-valued asset shall be treated as a revaluation decrease of that asset and if the impairment loss exceeds the corresponding revaluation reserve, such excess shall be recognised as an expense in the Revenue/Profit and Loss Account.

(b) Debt Securities – Debt securities, including government securities and redeemable preference shares, shall be considered as "held to maturity" securities and shall be measured at historical cost subject to amortisation.

(c) Equity Securities and Derivative Instruments that are traded in active markets – Listed equity securities and derivative instruments that are traded in active markets shall be measured at fair value on the balance sheet date. For the purpose of calculation of fair value, the lowest of the last quoted closing price at the stock exchanges where the securities are listed shall be taken.

The insurer shall assess on each balance sheet date whether any impairment of listed equity security(ies)/derivative(s) instruments has occurred.

An active market shall mean a market, where the securities traded are homogenous, availability of willing buyers and willing sellers is normal and the prices are publicly available.

Unrealised gains/ losses arising due to changes in the fair value of listed equity shares and derivative instruments shall be taken to equity under the head 'Fair Value Change Account. The 'Profit on sale of investments' or 'Loss on sale of investments', as the case may be, shall include accumulated changes in the fair value previously recognised in equity under the heading 'Fair Value Change Account' in respect of a particular security and being recycled to the relevant Revenue Account or Profit and Loss Account on actual sale of that listed security.

The Authority may issue directions specifying the amount to be released from the Fair Value Change Account for declaring bonus to the policyholders. For the removal of doubt, it is clarified that except for the amount that is released to policyholders as per the Authority's prescription, no other amount shall be distributed to shareholders out of Fair Value Change Account. Also, any debit balance in Fair Value Change Account shall be reduced from profit free reserves while declaring dividends.

The insurer shall assess, on each balance sheet date, whether any impairment has occurred. An impairment loss shall be recognised as an expense in Revenue/Profit and Loss Account to the extent of the difference between the re-measured fair value of the security/investment and its acquisition cost as reduced by any previous impairment loss recognised as expense in Revenue/ Profit and Loss Account. Any reversal of impairment loss, earlier recognised in Revenue/Profit and Loss Account shall be recognised in Revenue/Profit and Loss Account.

(d) Unlisted and other than actively traded Equity Securities and Derivative Instruments — Unlisted equity securities and derivative instruments and listed equity securities and derivative instruments that are not regularly traded in active markets shall be measured at historical cost. Provision shall be made for diminution in value of such investments. The provision so made shall be reversed in subsequent periods if estimates based on external evidence show an increase in the value of the investment over its carrying amount. The increased carrying amount of the investment due to the reversal of the provision shall not exceed the historical cost.

For the purposes of this regulation, a security shall be considered as being not actively traded, if as per guidelines governing mutual funds laid down from time to time by SEBI, such a security is classified as "thinly traded."

7. Loans — Loans shall be measured at historical cost subject to impairment provisions.

The insurer shall assess the quality of its loan assets and shall provide for impairment. The impairment provision shall not be lower than the amounts derived on the basis of guidelines prescribed from time to time by the Reserve Bank of India, that apply to companies and financial institutions.

8. Linked Business — The accounting principles used for valuation of investments are to be consistent with principles enumerated above. A separate set of financial statements, for each segregated fund of the linked businesses, shall be annexed.

Segregated funds represent funds maintained in accounts to meet specific investment objectives of policyholders who bear the investment risk. Investment income/ gains and losses generally accrue directly to the policyholders. The assets of each account are segregated and are not subject to claims that arise out of any other business of the insurer.

9. Funds for Future Appropriation — The funds for future appropriation shall be presented separately.

The funds for future appropriation represent all funds, the allocation of which, either to the policyholders or to the shareholders, has not been determined by the end of the financial year.

PART II

Disclosures Forming Part of Financial Statements

A. The following shall be disclosed by way of notes to the Balance Sheet:

1. Contingent Liabilities:
   (a) Partly-paid up investments
   (b) Underwriting commitments outstanding
   (c) Claims, other than those under policies, not acknowledged as debts
   (d) Guarantees given by or on behalf of the company
   (e) Statutory demands/liabilities in dispute, not provided for
   (f) Reinsurance Obligations to the extent not provided for in accounts
   (g) Others (to be specified).
2. Actuarial assumptions for valuation of liabilities for life policies in force.
3. Encumbrances to assets of the company in and outside India.
4. Commitments made and outstanding for Loans, Investments and Fixed Assets.
5. Basis of amortisation of debt securities.
6. Claims settled and remaining unpaid for a period of more than six months as on the balance sheet date.
7. Value of contracts in relation to investments for:
   (a) Purchases where deliveries are pending;
   (b) Sales where payments are overdue.
8. Operating expenses relating to insurance business: basis of allocation of expenditure to various segments of business.

9. Computation of managerial remuneration.
10. Historical costs of those investments valued on fair value basis.
11. Basis of revaluation of investment property.

B. The following accounting policies shall form an integral part of the financial statements:

1. All significant accounting policies in terms of the accounting standards issued by the ICAI, and significant principles and policies given in Part I of Accounting Principles. Any other accounting policies, followed by the insurer, shall be stated in the manner required under Accounting Standard AS 1 issued by the ICAI.
2. Any departure from the accounting policies shall be separately disclosed with reasons for such departure.

C. The following information shall also be disclosed:

1. Investments made in accordance with any statutory requirement should be disclosed separately together with its amount, nature, security and any special rights in and outside India;
2. Segregation into performing/ non-performing investments for purpose of income recognition as per the directions, if any, issued by the Authority;
3. Assets to the extent required to be deposited under local laws or otherwise encumbered in or outside India;
4. Percentage of business sector-wise;
5. A summary of financial statements for the last five years, in the manner as may be prescribed by the Authority;
6. Bases of allocation of investments and income thereon between Policyholders' Account and Shareholders' Account;
7. Accounting Ratios as may be prescribed by the Authority.

PART III

General Instructions for Preparation of Financial Statements

1. The corresponding amounts for the immediately preceding financial year for all items shown in the Balance Sheet, Revenue Account, Profit and Loss Account and Receipts and Payments Account shall be given.
2. The figures in the financial statements may be rounded off to the nearest thousands.
3. Interest, dividends and rentals receivable in connection with an investment should be stated at gross amount, the amount of income tax deducted at source should be included under 'advance taxes paid' and taxes deducted at source.
4. (I) For the purposes of financial statements, unless the context otherwise requires —
   (a) the expression 'provision' shall, subject to (II) below mean any amount written off or retained by way of providing for depreciation, renewals or diminution in value of assets, or retained by way of providing for any known liability or loss of which the amount cannot be determined with substantial accuracy;
   (b) the expression 'reserve' shall not, subject to as aforesaid, include any amount written off or retained by way of providing for depreciation, renewals or diminution in value of assets or retained by way of providing for any known liability or loss;
   (c) the expression 'capital reserve' shall not include any amount regarded as free for distribution through the profit and loss account; and the expression 'revenue reserve' shall mean any reserve other than a capital reserve;
   (d) The expression "liability" shall include all liabilities in respect of expenditure contracted for and all disputed or contingent liabilities.

   (II) Where:
   (a) any amount written off or retained by way of providing for depreciation, renewals or diminution in value of assets, or
   (b) any amount retained by way of providing for any known liability or loss,

   is in excess of the amount which in the opinion of the directors is reasonably necessary for the purpose, the excess shall be treated as a reserve and not provision.
5. The company shall make provisions for damages under lawsuits where the management is of the opinion that the award may go against the insurer.
6. Extent of risk retained and re-insured shall be separately disclosed.
7. Any debit balance of the Profit and Loss Account shall be shown as deduction from uncommitted reserves and the balance, if any, shall be shown separately.

PART IV

Contents of Management Report

There shall be attached to the financial statements, a management report containing, *inter alia*, the following duly authenticated by the management:

1. Confirmation regarding the continued validity of the registration granted by the Authority;
2. Certification that all the dues payable to the statutory authorities have been duly paid;
3. Confirmation to the effect that the shareholding pattern and any transfer of shares during the year are in accordance with the statutory or regulatory requirements;
4. Declaration that the management has not directly or indirectly invested outside India the funds of the holders of policies issued in India;
5. Confirmation that the required solvency margins have been maintained;
6. Certification to the effect that the values of all the assets have been reviewed on the date of the Balance Sheet and that in his (insurer's) belief the assets set forth in the Balance-sheets are shown in the aggregate as amounts not exceeding their realisable or market value under the several headings – " Loans", " Investments", "Agents balances", "Outstanding Premiums", "Interest, Dividends and Rents outstanding", "Interest, Dividends and Rents accruing but not due", "Amounts due from other persons or Bodies carrying on insurance business", " Sundry Debtors", " Bills Receivable", " Cash" and the several items specified under "Other Accounts";
7. Certification to the effect that no part of the life insurance fund has been directly or indirectly applied in contravention of the provisions of the Insurance Act, 1938 (4 of 1938) relating to the application and investment of the life insurance funds;
8. Disclosure with regard to the overall risk exposure and strategy adopted to mitigate the same;
9. Operations in other countries, if any, with a separate statement giving the management's estimate of country risk and exposure risk and the hedging strategy adopted;
10. Ageing of claims indicating the trends in average claim settlement time during the preceding five years;
11. Certification to the effect as to how the values, as shown in the balance sheet, of the investments and stocks and shares have been arrived at, and how the market value thereof has been ascertained for the purpose of comparison with the values so shown;
12. Review of asset quality and performance of investment in terms of portfolios, i.e., separately in terms of real estate, loans, investments, etc.
13. A responsibility statement indicating therein that:
    (a) in the preparation of financial statements, the applicable accounting standards, principles and policies have been followed along with proper explanations relating to material departures, if any;
    (b) the management has adopted accounting policies and applied them consistently and made judgements and estimates that are reasonable and prudent so as to give a true and fair view of the state of affairs of the company at the end of the financial year and of the operating profit or loss and of the profit or loss of the company for the year;
    (c) the management has taken proper and sufficient care for the maintenance of adequate accounting records in accordance with the applicable provisions of the Insurance Act 1938 (4 of 1938)/ Companies Act, 1956 (1 of 1956), for safeguarding the assets of the company and for preventing and detecting fraud and other irregularities;
    (d) the management has prepared the financial statements on a going concern basis;
    (e) the management has ensured that an internal audit system commensurate with the size and nature of the business exists and is operating effectively.
14. A schedule of payments, which have been made to individuals, firms, companies and organisations in which Directors of the insurer are interested.

PART V

Preparation of Financial Statements

(1) An insurer shall prepare the Revenue Account [Policyholders' Account], Profit and Loss Account [Shareholders' Account] and the Balance Sheet in Form A-RA, Form A-PL and Form A-BS, as prescribed in this Part, or as near thereto as the circumstances permit.

Provided that an insurer shall prepare Revenue Account and Balance Sheet for the under mentioned businesses separately and to that extent the application of AS 17 shall stand modified:-

(a) Participating policies and Non-participating policies;

(b) (i) Linked business [As defined in regulation 2 (i) of the IRDA (Registration of Indian Insurance Companies) Regulations, 2000]

(ii) Non-Linked business separately for Ordinary Life, General Annuity, Pensions and Health Insurance;

(c) Business within India and business outside India.

(2) An insurer shall prepare separate Receipts and Payments Account in accordance with the Direct Method prescribed in AS 3 – "Cash Flow Statement" issued by the ICAI.

FORM A-RA

Name of the Insurer:

Registration No. and Date of Registration with the IRDA

REVENUE ACCOUNT FOR THE YEAR ENDED 31ST MARCH, 20____.

Policyholders' Account (Technical Account)

Particulars	**Schedule**	**Current Year** (Rs.'000)	**Previous Year** (Rs.'000)
Premiums earned – net			
(a) Premium (b) Reinsurance ceded (c) Reinsurance accepted	1		
Income from Investments			
(a) Interest, Dividends & Rent – Gross (b) Profit on sale/redemption of investments (c) (Loss on sale/ redemption of investments) (d) Transfer/Gain on revaluation/change in fair value*			
Other Income (to be specified)			
TOTAL (A)			
Commission	2		
Operating Expenses related to Insurance Business	3		
Provision for doubtful debts			
Bad debts written off			
Provision for Tax			
Provisions (other than taxation) (a) For diminution in the value of investments (Net) (b) Others (to be specified)			
TOTAL (B)			
Benefits Paid (Net)	4		
Interim Bonuses Paid			
Change in valuation of liability in respect of life policies (a) Gross** (b) Amount ceded in Reinsurance (c) Amount accepted in Reinsurance			
TOTAL (C)			
SURPLUS/ (DEFICIT) (D) = (A) – (B) – (C)			
APPROPRIATIONS			
Transfer to Shareholders' Account			
Transfer to Other Reserves (to be specified)			
Balance being Funds for Future Appropriations			
TOTAL (D)			

Notes:

* Represents the deemed realised gain as per norms specified by the Authority.

** Represents Mathematical Reserves after allocation of bonus.

The total surplus shall be disclosed separately with the following details:

(a) Interim Bonuses Paid:

(b) Allocation of Bonus to policyholders:

(c) Surplus shown in the Revenue Account:

(d) Total Surplus: [(a)+(b)+(c)].

See Notes appended at the end of Form A-PL.

FORM A-PL

Name of the Insurer:
Registration No. and Date of Registration with the IRDA

PROFIT & LOSS ACCOUNT FOR THE YEAR ENDED 31ST MARCH, 20___.

Shareholders' Account (Non-technical Account)

Particulars	Schedule	Current Year (Rs.'000)	Previous Year (Rs.'000)
Amounts transferred from/to the Policyholders Account (Technical Account)			
Income From Investments			
(a) Interest, Dividends & Rent – Gross			
(b) Profit on sale/redemption of investments			
(c) (Loss on sale/ redemption of investments)			
Other Income (To be specified)			
TOTAL (A)			
Expense other than those directly related to the insurance business			
Bad debts written off			
Provisions (Other than taxation) (a) For diminution in the value of investments (Net) (b) Provision for doubtful debts (c) Others (to be specified)			
TOTAL (B)			
Profit/(Loss) before tax			
Provision for Taxation			
Profit/(Loss) after tax			
APPROPRIATIONS			
(a) Balance at the beginning of the year. (b) Interim dividends paid during the year (c) Proposed final dividend (d) Dividend distribution on tax (e) Transfer to reserves/ other accounts (to be specified)			
Profit carried .... to the Balance Sheet			

Notes to Form A-RA and A-PL.

(a) Premium income received from business concluded in and outside India shall be separately disclosed.

(b) Reinsurance premiums whether on business ceded or accepted are to be brought into account gross (i.e. before deducting commissions) under the head reinsurance premiums.

(c) Claims incurred shall comprise claims paid, specific claims settlement costs wherever applicable and change in the outstanding provision for claims at the year-end,.
(d) Items of expenses and income in excess of one percent of the total premiums (less reinsurance) or Rs.5,00,000 whichever is higher, shall be shown as a separate line item.
(e) Fees and expenses connected with claims shall be included in claims.
(f) Under the sub-head "Others" shall be included items like foreign exchange gains or losses and other items.
(g) Interest, dividends and rentals receivable in connection with an investment should be stated as gross amount, the amount of income tax deducted at source being included under 'advance taxes paid and taxes deducted at source".
(h) Income from rent shall include only the realised rent. It shall not include any notional rent.

FORM A-BS

Name of the Insurer:
Registration No. and Date of Registration with the IRDA

BALANCE SHEET AS AT 31ST MARCH, 20____.

	Schedule	Current Year (Rs.'000)	Previous Year (Rs.'000)
SOURCES OF FUNDS			
SHAREHOLDERS' FUNDS:			
SHARE CAPITAL	5		
RESERVES AND SURPLUS	6		
CREDIT/[DEBIT] FAIR VALUE			
CHANGE ACCOUNT			
Sub-Total			
BORROWINGS	7		
POLICYHOLDERS' FUNDS:			
CREDIT/[DEBIT] FAIR VALUE CHANGE			
ACCOUNT POLICY LIABILITIES			
INSURANCE RESERVES			
PROVISION FOR LINKED LIABILITIES			
Sub-Total			
FUNDS FOR FUTURE APPROPRIATIONS			
TOTAL			
APPLICATION OF FUNDS			
INVESTMENTS			
Shareholders'	8		
Policyholders'	8A		
ASSETS HELD TO COVER LINKED LIABILITIES	8B		
LOANS	9		
FIXED ASSETS	10		
CURRENT ASSETS			
Cash and Bank Balances	11		
Advances and Other Assets	12		
Sub-Total (A)			

CURRENT LIABILITIES	13		
PROVISIONS	14		
Sub-Total (B)			
NET CURRENT ASSETS (C) = (A – B)			
MISCELLANEOUS EXPENDITURE (to the extent not written off or adjusted)	15		
DEBIT BALANCE IN PROFIT & LOSS ACCOUNT (Shareholders' Account)			
TOTAL			

CONTINGENT LIABILITIES

Particulars	Current Year (Rs.'000)	Previous Year (Rs.'000)
1. Partly paid-up investments		
2. Claims, other than against policies, not acknowledged as debts by the company		
3. Underwriting commitments outstanding (in respect of shares and securities)		
4. Guarantees given by or on behalf of the Company		
5. Statutory demands/ liabilities in dispute, not provided for		
6. Reinsurance obligations to the extent not provided for in accounts		
7. Others (to be specified)		
TOTAL		

SCHEDULES FORMING PART OF FINANCIAL STATEMENTS

SCHEDULE – 1

PREMIUM

Particulars	Current Year (Rs.'000)	Previous Year (Rs.'000)
1. First year premiums		
2. Renewal Premiums		
3. Single Premiums		
TOTAL PREMIUM		

SCHEDULE – 2

COMMISSION EXPENSES

Particulars	Current Year (Rs.'000)	Previous Year (Rs.'000)
Direct – First year premiums – Renewal premiums – Single premiums		
Add: Commission on Re-insurance Accepted Less: Commission on Re-insurance Ceded		
Net Commission		

Note:

The profit/commission, if any, are to be combined with the Re-insurance accepted or Re-insurance ceded figures.

SCHEDULE – 3

OPERATING EXPENSES RELATED TO INSURANCE BUSINESS

	Particulars	Current Year (Rs.'000)	Previous Year (Rs.'000)
1.	Employees' remuneration & welfare benefits		
2.	Travel, conveyance and vehicle running expenses		
3.	Training expenses		
4.	Rents, rates & taxes		
5.	Repairs		
6.	Printing & stationery		
7.	Communication expenses		
8.	Legal & professional charges		
9.	Medical fees		
10.	Auditors' fees, expenses etc.		
	(a) as auditor (b) as adviser or in any other capacity, in respect of (i) Taxation matters (ii) Insurance matters (iii) Management services; and (c) in any other capacity		
11.	Advertisement and publicity		
12.	Interest & Bank Charges		
13.	Others (to be specified)		
14.	Depreciation		
	TOTAL		

Note: **Items of expenses and income in excess of one percent of the total premiums (less reinsurance) or Rs.5,00,000 whichever is higher, shall be shown as a separate line item.**

SCHEDULE – 4

BENEFITS PAID [NET]

	Particulars	Current Year (Rs.'000)	Previous Year (Rs.'000)
1.	Insurance Claims (a) Claims by Death, (b) Claims by Maturity, (c) Annuities/Pension payment, (d) Other benefits, specify		
2.	(Amount ceded in reinsurance): (a) Claims by Death, (b) Claims by Maturity, (c) Annuities/Pension payment, (d) Other benefits, specify		
3.	Amount accepted in reinsurance: (a) Claims by Death, (b) Claims by Maturity, (c) Annuities/Pension payment, (d) Other benefits, specify		
	TOTAL		

Notes: (a) Claims include specific claims settlement costs, wherever applicable.
(b) Legal and other fees and expenses shall also form part of the claims cost, wherever applicable.

SCHEDULE – 5

SHARE CAPITAL

	Particulars	Current Year (Rs.'000)	Previous Year (Rs.'000)
1.	Authorised Capital Equity Shares of Rs..... each		
2.	Issued Capital Equity Shares of Rs. .....each		
3.	Subscribed Capital Equity Shares of Rs.......each		
4.	Called-up Capital Equity Shares of Rs. .....each		
	Less: Calls unpaid		
	Add: Shares forfeited (Amount originally paid up)		
	Less: Par value of Equity Shares bought back		
	Less: Preliminary Expenses Expenses including commission or brokerage on Underwriting or subscription of shares		
	TOTAL		

Notes:

(a) Particulars of the different classes of capital should be separately stated.
(b) The amount capitalised on account of issue of bonus shares should be disclosed.
(c) In case any part of the capital is held by a holding company, the same should be separately disclosed.

SCHEDULE – 5A

PATTERN OF SHAREHOLDING

[As certified by the Management]

Shareholder	Current Year		Previous Year	
	Number of Shares	% of Holding	Number of Shares	% of Holding
Promoters • Indian • Foreign				
Others				
TOTAL				

SCHEDULE – 6

RESERVES AND SURPLUS

	Particulars	Current Year (Rs.'000)	Previous Year (Rs.'000)
1.	Capital Reserve		
2.	Capital Redemption Reserve		
3.	Share Premium		
4.	Revaluation Reserve		
5.	General Reserves *Less:* Debit balance in Profit and Loss Account, if any *Less:* Amount utilized for Buy-back		
6.	Catastrophe Reserve		
7.	Other Reserves (to be specified)		
8.	Balance of profit in Profit and Loss Account		
	TOTAL		

Note: Additions to and deductions from the reserves shall be disclosed under each of the specified heads.

SCHEDULE – 7

BORROWINGS

	Particulars	Current Year (Rs.'000)	Previous Year (Rs.'000)
1.	Debentures/ Bonds		
2.	Banks		
3.	Financial Institutions		
4.	Others (to be specified)		
	TOTAL		

Notes:

(a) The extent to which the borrowings are secured shall be separately disclosed stating the nature of the security under each sub-head.

(b) Amounts due within 12 months from the date of Balance Sheet should be shown separately.

SCHEDULE – 8

INVESTMENTS-SHAREHOLDERS

	Particulars	Current Year (Rs.'000)	Previous Year (Rs.'000)
	LONG TERM INVESTMENTS		
1.	Government securities and Government guaranted bonds including Treasury Bills		
2.	Other Approved Securities		
3.	Other Investments		
	(a) Shares (aa) Equity (bb) Preference (b) Mutual Funds (c) Derivative Instruments (d) Debentures/ Bonds (e) Other Securities (to be specified) (f) Subsidiaries Investment Properties-Real Estate		
4.	Investments in Infrastructure and Social Sector		
5.	Other than Approved Investments		
	SHORT TERM INVESTMENTS		
1.	Government securities and Government guaranted bonds including Treasury Bills		
2. 3.	Other Approved Securities Other Investments (a) Shares (aa) Equity (bb) Preference (b) Mutual Funds (c) Derivative Instruments (d) Debentures/ Bonds (e) Other Securities (to be specified) (f) Subsidiaries Investment Properties-Real Estate		
4.	Investments in Infrastructure and Social Sector		
5.	Other than Approved Investments		
	TOTAL		

Note: See Notes appended at the end of Schedule-8B.

SCHEDULE – 8A

INVESTMENTS-POLICYHOLDERS

Particulars	Current Year (Rs.'000)	Previous Year (Rs.'000)
LONG TERM INVESTMENTS		
1. Government securities and Government guaranteed bonds including Treasury Bills		
2. Other Approved Securities		
3. (a) Shares (aa) Equity (bb) Preference (b) Mutual Funds (c) Derivative Instruments (d) Debentures/ Bonds (e) Other Securities (to be specified) (f) Subsidiaries (g) Investment Properties-Real Estate		
4. Investments in Infrastructure and Social Sector		
5. Other than Approved Investments		
SHORT TERM INVESTMENTS		
1. Government securities and Government guaranteed bonds including Treasury Bills		
2. Other Approved Securities		
3. (a) Shares (aa) Equity (bb) Preference (b) Mutual Funds (c) Derivative Instruments (d) Debentures/ Bonds (e) Other Securities (to be specified) (f) Subsidiaries (g) Investment Properties-Real Estate		
4. Investments in Infrastructure and Social Sector		
5. Other than Approved Investments		
TOTAL		

Note: See Notes appended at the end of Schedule- 8B.

SCHEDULE – 8B

ASSETS HELD TO COVER LINKED LIABILITIES

Particulars	Current Year (Rs.'000)	Previous Year (Rs.'000)
LONG TERM INVESTMENTS		
1. Government securities and Government guaranteed bonds including Treasury Bills		
2. Other Approved Securities		
3. (a) Shares		

(aa) Equity (bb) Preference (b) Mutual Funds (c) Derivative Instruments (d) Debentures/ Bonds (e) Other Securities (to be specified) (f) Subsidiaries (g) Investment Properties-Real Estate		
4. Investments in Infrastructure and Social Sector		
5. Other than Approved Investments		
SHORT TERM INVESTMENTS		
1. Government securities and Government guaranteed bonds including Treasury Bills		
2. Other Approved Securities		
3. (a) Shares (aa) Equity (bb) Preference (b) Mutual Funds (c) Derivative Instruments (d) Debentures/ Bonds (e) Other Securities (to be specified) (f) Subsidiaries (g) Investment Properties-Real Estate		
4. Investments in Infrastructure and Social Sector		
5. Other than Approved Investments		
TOTAL		

Notes (applicable to Schedules 8 and 8A & 8B):

(a) Investments in subsidiary/holding companies, joint ventures and associates shall be separately disclosed, at cost.

(i) Holding company and subsidiary shall be construed as defined in the Companies Act, 1956:

(ii) Joint Venture is a contractual arrangement whereby two or more parties undertake an economic activity, which is subject to joint control.

(iii) Joint control — is the contractually agreed sharing of power to govern the financial and operating policies of an economic activity to obtain benefits from it.

(iv) Associate — is an enterprise in which the company has significant influence and which is neither a subsidiary nor a joint venture of the company.

(v) Significant influence (for the purpose of this schedule) — means participation in the financial and operating policy decisions of a company, but not control of those policies. Significant influence may be exercised in several ways, for example, by representation on the board of directors, participation in the policymaking process, material inter-company transactions, interchange of managerial personnel or dependence on technical information. Significant influence may be gained by share ownership, statute or agreement. As regards share ownership, if an investor holds, directly or indirectly through subsidiaries, 20 percent or more of the voting power of the investee, it is presumed that the investor does have significant influence, unless it can be clearly demonstrated that this is not the case. Conversely, if the investor holds, directly or indirectly through subsidiaries, less than 20 percent of the voting power of the investee, it is presumed that the investor does not have significant influence, unless such influence is clearly demonstrated. A substantial or majority ownership by another investor does not necessarily preclude an investor from having significant influence.

(b) Aggregate amount of company's investments other than listed equity securities and derivative instruments and also the market value thereof shall be disclosed.

(c) Investment made out of Catastrophe reserve should be shown separately.

(d) Debt securities will be considered as "held to maturity" securities and will be measured at historical costs subject to amortisation.

(e) Investment Property means a property [land or building or part of a building or both] held to earn rental income or for capital appreciation or for both, rather than for use in services or for administrative purposes.

(f) Investments maturing within twelve months from balance sheet date and investments made with the specific intention to dispose of within twelve months from balance sheet date shall be classified as short-term investments.

SCHEDULE – 9

LOANS

Particulars	Current Year (Rs.'000)	Previous Year (Rs.'000)
1. SECURITY-WISE CLASSIFICATION		
Secured		
(a) On mortgage of property (aa) In India (bb) Outside India (b) On Shares, Bonds, Govt. Securities, etc. (c) Loans against policies (d) Others (to be specified)		
Unsecured		
TOTAL		
2. BORROWER-WISE CLASSIFICATION		
(a) Central and State Governments		
(b) Banks and Financial Institutions		
(c) Subsidiaries		
(d) Companies		
(e) Loans against policies		
(f) Others (to be specified)		
TOTAL		
3. PERFORMANCE-WISE CLASSIFICATION (a) Loans classified as standard (aa) In India (bb) Outside India (b) Non-standard loans less provisions (aa) In India (bb) Outside India		
TOTAL		
4. MATURITY-WISE CLASSIFICATION		
(a) Short Term		
(b) Long Term		
TOTAL		

Notes:

(a) Short-term loans shall include those, which are repayable within 12 months from the date of balance sheet. Long term loans shall be the loans other than short-term loans.

(b) Provisions against non-performing loans shall be shown separately.

(c) The nature of the security in case of all long term secured loans shall be specified in each case. Secured loans for the purposes of this schedule, means loans secured wholly or partly against an asset of the company.

(d) Loans considered doubtful and the amount of provision created against such loans shall be disclosed.

SCHEDULE – 10
FIXED ASSETS

(Rs.'000)

Particulars	Cost/ Gross Block				Depreciation				Net Block	
	Opening	Additions	Deductions	Closing	Up to Last Year	For the Year	On Sales/ Adjustments	To Date	As at year end	Previous year
Goodwill										
Intangibles (specify)										
Land-Freehold										
Leasehold Property										
Buildings										
Furniture & Fittings										
Information Technology Equipment										
Vehicles										
Office Equipment										
Others (Specify nature)										
TOTAL										
Work in progress										
Grand Total										
PREVIOUS YEAR										

Note: *Assets included in land, property and building above exclude Investment Properties as defined in note (e) to Schedule 8.*

SCHEDULE – 11
CASH AND BANK BALANCES

Particulars	Current Year (Rs.'000)	Previous Year (Rs.'000)
1. Cash (including cheques, drafts and stamps)		
2. Bank Balances		
(a) Deposit Accounts (aa) Short-term (due within 12 months of the date of Balance Sheet) (bb) Others (b) Current Accounts (c) Others (to be specified)		
3. Money at Call and Short Notice (a) With Banks (b) With other Institutions		
4. Others (to be specified)		
TOTAL		
Balances with non-scheduled banks included in 2 and 3 above		
CASH & BANK BALANCES		
1 In India		
2 Outside India		
TOTAL		

Note: Bank balance may include remittances in transit. If so, the nature and amount shall be separately stated.

SCHEDULE – 12

ADVANCES AND OTHER ASSETS

Particulars	Current Year (Rs.'000)	Previous Year (Rs.'000)
ADVANCES		
1. Reserve deposits with ceding companies		
2. Application money for investments		
3. Prepayments		
4. Advances to Directors/Officers		
5. Advance tax paid and taxes deducted at source (Net of provision for taxation)		
6. Others (to be specified)		
TOTAL (A)		
OTHER ASSETS		
1. Income accrued on investments		
2. Outstanding Premiums		
3. Agents' Balances		
4. Foreign Agencies Balances		
5 Due from other entities carrying on insurance business (including reinsures)		
6. Due from subsidiaries/ holding company		
7. Deposit with Reserve Bank of India [Pursuant to Section 7 of Insurance Act, 1938]		
8. Others (to be specified)		
TOTAL (B)		
TOTAL (A+B)		

Notes:

(a) The items under the above heads shall not be shown net of provisions for doubtful amounts. The amount of provision against each head should be shown separately.

(b) The term 'officer' should conform to the definition of that term as given under the Companies Act, 1956.

(c) Sundry debtors will be shown under item 8 (Others).

SCHEDULE – 13

CURRENT LIABILITIES

Particulars	Current Year (Rs.'000)	Previous Year (Rs.'000)
1. Agents' Balances		
2. Balances due to other insurance companies		
3. Deposits held on re-insurance ceded		
4. Premiums received in advance		
5. Unallocated premium		
6. Sundry creditors		
7. Due to subsidiaries/ holding company		

8. Claims Outstanding		
9. Annuities Due		
10. Due to Officers/ Directors		
11. Others (to be specified)		
TOTAL		

SCHEDULE – 14

PROVISIONS

Particulars	Current Year (Rs.'000)	Previous Year (Rs.'000)
1. For taxation (less payments and taxes deducted at source)		
2. For proposed dividends		
3. For dividend distribution tax		
4. Others (to be specified)		
TOTAL		

SCHEDULE – 15

MISCELLANEOUS EXPENDITURE
(To the extent not written off or adjusted)

Particulars	Current Year (Rs.'000)	Previous Year (Rs.'000)
1. Discount Allowed in issue of shares/ debentures		
2. Others (to be specified)		
TOTAL		

Notes:

(a) No item shall be included under the head "Miscellaneous Expenditure" and carried forward unless:
   1. some benefit from the expenditure can reasonably be expected to be received in future, and
   2. the amount of such benefit is reasonably determinable.

(b) The amount to be carried forward in respect of any item included under the head "Miscellaneous Expenditure" shall not exceed the expected future revenue/other benefits related to the expenditure.

SCHEDULE B

(See Regulation 3)

PART I

Accounting principles for preparation of financial statements

1. Applicability of Accounting Standards — Every Balance Sheet, Receipts and Payments Account [Cash Flow statement] and Profit and Loss Account [Shareholders' Account] of the insurer shall be in conformity with the Accounting Standards (AS) issued by the ICAI, to the extent applicable to the insurers carrying on general insurance business, except that:

(i) Accounting Standard 3 (AS 3) — Cash Flow Statements – Cash Flow Statement shall be prepared only under the Direct Method.

(ii) Accounting Standard 13 (AS 13) — Accounting for Investments, shall not be applicable.

(iii) Accounting Standard 17 (AS 17) — Segment Reporting – shall apply to all insurers irrespective of the requirements regarding listing and turnover mentioned therein.

2. Premium — Premium shall be recognised as income over the contract period or the period of risk, whichever is appropriate. Premium received in advance, which represents premium income not relating to the current accounting period, shall be disclosed separately in the financial statements.

A reserve for unexpired risks shall be created as the amount representing that part of the premium written which is attributable to, and to be allocated to the succeeding accounting periods and shall not be less than as required under Section 64 V(1) (ii) (b) of the Act.

Premium Received in Advance, which represents premium received prior to the commencement of the risk, shall be shown separately under the head '*Current Liabilities*' in the financial statements.

3. Premium Deficiency — Premium deficiency shall be recognised if the sum of expected claim costs, related expenses and maintenance costs exceeds related reserve for unexpired risks.

4. Acquisition Costs — Acquisition costs, if any, shall be expensed in the period in which they are incurred.

Acquisition costs are those costs that vary with, and are primarily related to, the acquisition of new and renewal insurance contracts. The most essential test is the obligatory relationship between costs and the execution of insurance contracts (i.e. commencement of risk).

5. Claims — The components of the ultimate cost of claims to an insurer comprise the claims under policies and specific claims settlement costs. Claims under policies comprise the claims made for losses incurred, and those estimated or anticipated under the policies following a loss occurrence.

A liability for outstanding claims shall be brought to account in respect of both direct business and inward reinsurance business. The liability shall include:

(a) Future payments in relation to unpaid reported claims;

(b) Claims Incurred But Not Reported (IBNR) including inadequate reserves [sometimes referred to as Claims Incurred But Not Enough Reported (IBNER)],

which will result in future cash/asset outgo for settling liabilities against those claims. Change in estimated liability represents the difference between the estimated liability for outstanding claims at the beginning and at the end of the financial period.

The accounting estimate shall also include claims cost adjusted for estimated salvage value if there is sufficient degree of certainty of its realisation.

Actuarial Valuation of claim liability – in some cases

Claims made in respect of contracts where the claims payment period exceeds four years shall be recognised on an actuarial basis, subject to regulations that may be prescribed by the Authority. In such cases, certificate from a recognised actuary as to the fairness of liability assessment must be obtained. Actuarial assumptions shall be suitably disclosed by way of notes to the account.

6. Procedure to determine the value of investments — An insurer shall determine the values of investments in the following manner:-

(a) Real Estate – Investment Property — Investment Property shall be measured at historical cost less accumulated depreciation and impairment loss, residual value being considered zero and no revaluation being permissible.

The Insurer shall assess at each balance sheet date whether any impairment of the investment property has occurred.

An impairment loss shall be recognised as an expense in the Revenue/Profit and Loss Account immediately.

Fair value as at the balance sheet date and the basis of its determination shall be disclosed in the financial statements as additional information.

(b) Debt Securities — Debt securities including government securities and redeemable preference shares shall be considered as "held to maturity" securities and shall be measured at historical cost subject to amortisation.

(c) Equity Securities and Derivative Instruments that are traded in active markets — Listed equity securities and derivative instruments that are traded in active markets shall be measured at fair value as at the balance sheet date. For the purpose of calculation of fair value, the lowest of the last quoted closing price of the stock exchanges where the securities are listed shall be taken.

The insurer shall assess on each balance sheet date whether any impairment of listed equity security(ies)/ derivative(s) instruments has occurred.

An active market shall mean a market, where the securities traded are homogenous, availability of willing buyers and willing sellers is normal and the prices are publicly available.

Unrealised gains/losses arising due to changes in the fair value of listed equity shares and derivative instruments shall be taken to equity under the head 'Fair Value Change Account'. The 'Profit on sale of investments' or 'Loss on sale of investments', as the case may be, shall include accumulated changes in the fair value previously recognised in equity under the heading Fair Value Change Account in respect of a particular security and being recycled to Profit and Loss Account on actual sale of that listed security.

For the removal of doubt, it is clarified that balance or any part thereof shall not be available for distribution as dividends. Also, any debit balance in the said Fair Value Change Account shall be reduced from the profits/free reserves while declaring dividends.

The insurer shall assess, at each balance sheet date, whether any impairment has occurred. An impairment loss shall be recognised as an expense in Revenue/Profit and Loss Account to the extent of the difference between the remeasured fair value of the security/ investment and its acquisition cost as reduced by any previous impairment loss recognised as expense in Revenue/ Profit and Loss Account. Any reversal of impairment loss, earlier recognised in Revenue/Profit and Loss Account shall be recognised in Revenue/Profit and Loss Account.

(d) Unlisted and other than actively traded Equity Securities and Derivative Instruments – Unlisted equity securities and derivative instruments and listed equity securities and derivative instruments that are not regularly traded in active market will be measured at historical costs. Provision shall be made for diminution in value of such investments. The provision so made shall be reversed in subsequent periods if estimates based on external evidence show an increase in the value of the investment over its carrying amount. The increased carrying amount of the investment due to the reversal of the provision shall not exceed the historical cost.

For the purposes of this regulation, a security shall be considered as being not actively traded, if as per guidelines governing mutual funds laid down from time to time by SEBI, such a security is classified as "thinly traded".

7. Loans — Loans shall be measured at historical cost subject to impairment provisions.

The insurer shall assess the quality of its loan assets and shall provide for impairment. The impairment provision shall not be lower than the amounts derived on the basis of guidelines prescribed from time to time by the Reserve Bank of India, that apply to companies and financial institutions.

8. Catastrophe Reserve — Catastrophe reserve shall be created in accordance with norms, if any, prescribed by the Authority. Investment of funds out of catastrophe reserve shall be made in accordance with prescription of the Authority.

PART II

Disclosures forming part of Financial Statements

A. The following shall be disclosed by way of notes to the Balance Sheet:

1. Contingent Liabilities:
   (a) Partly-paid up investments
   (b) Underwriting commitments outstanding
   (c) Claims, other than those under policies, not acknowledged as debts
   (d) Guarantees given by or on behalf of the company
   (e) Statutory demands/liabilities in dispute, not provided for
   (f) Reinsurance obligations to the extent not provided for in accounts
   (g) Others (to be specified)
2. Encumbrances to assets of the company in and outside India.
3. Commitments made and outstanding for Loans, Investments and Fixed Assets.
4. Claims, less reinsurance, paid to claimants in/outside India.
5. Actuarial assumptions for determination of claim liabilities in the case of claims where the claims payment period exceed four years.
6. Ageing of claims – distinguishing between claims outstanding for more than six months and other claims.
7. Premiums, less reinsurance, written from business in/outside India.
8. Extent of premium income recognised, based on varying risk pattern, category wise, with basis and justification therefor, including whether reliance has been placed on external evidence.
9. Value of contracts in relation to investments, for:
   (h) Purchases where deliveries are pending;
   (i) Sales where payments are overdue.

10. Operating expenses relating to insurance business: basis of allocation of expenditure to various classes of business.
11. Historical costs of those investments valued on fair value basis.
12. Computation of managerial remuneration.
13. Basis of amortisation of debt securities.
14. (a) Unrealised gain/losses arising due to changes in the fair value of listed equity shares and derivative instruments are to be taken to equity under the head 'Fair Value Change Account' and on realisation reported in profit and loss Account.
    (b) Pending realisation, the credit balance in the 'Fair Value Change Account' is not available for distribution.
15. Fair value of investment property and the basis therefor.
16. Claims settled and remaining unpaid for a period of more than six months as on the balance sheet date.

B. The following accounting policies shall form an integral part of the financial statements:

1. All significant accounting policies in terms of the accounting standards issued by the ICAI, and significant principles and policies given in Part I of Accounting Principles. Any other accounting policies followed by the insurer shall be stated in the manner required under Accounting Standard AS 1 issued by the ICAI.
2. Any departure from the accounting policies as aforesaid shall be separately disclosed with reasons for such departure.

C. The following information shall also be disclosed:

1. Investments made in accordance with any statutory requirement should be disclosed separately together with its amount, nature, security and any special rights in and outside India.
2. Segregation into performing/ non-performing investments for purpose of income recognition as per the directions, if any, issued by the Authority.
3. Percentage of business sector-wise.
4. A summary of financial statements for the last five years, in the manner as may be prescribed by the Authority.
5. Accounting Ratios as may be prescribed by the Authority.
6. Basis of allocation of Interest, Dividends and Rent between Revenue Account and Profit and Loss Account.

PART III

General Instructions for Preparation of Financial Statements

1. The corresponding amounts for the immediately preceding financial year for all items shown in the Balance Sheet, Revenue Account and Profit and Loss Account should be given.
2. The figures in the financial statements may be rounded off to the nearest thousands.
3. Interest, dividends and rentals receivable in connection with an investment should be stated as gross value, the amount of income tax deducted at source being included under 'advance taxes paid'.
4. Income from rent shall not include any notional rent.
5. (I) For the purposes of financial statements, unless the context otherwise requires —
   (a) the expression 'provision' shall, subject to note II below mean any amount written off or retained by way of providing for depreciation, renewals or diminution in value of assets, or retained by way of providing for any known liability or loss of which the amount cannot be determined with substantial accuracy;
   (b) the expression "reserve" shall not, subject to as aforesaid, include any amount written off or retained by way of providing for depreciation, renewals or diminution in value of assets or retained by way of providing for any known liability;
   (c) the expression capital reserve shall not include any amount regarded as free for distribution through the profit and loss account; and the expression "revenue reserve" shall mean any reserve other than a capital reserve;
   (d) the expression "liability" shall include all liabilities in respect of expenditure contracted for and all disputed or contingent liabilities.

   (II) Where:
   (a) any amount written off or retained by way of providing for depreciation, renewals or diminution in value of assets, or
   (b) any amount retained by way of providing for any known liability

   is in excess of the amount which in the opinion of the directors is reasonably necessary for the purpose, the excess shall be treated for the purposes of these accounts as a reserve and not as a provision.

6. The company should make provisions for damages under lawsuits where the management is of the opinion that the award may go against the insurer.
7. Extent of risk retained and reinsured shall be separately disclosed.
8. Any debit balance of Profit and Loss Account shall be shown as deduction from uncommitted reserves and the balance if any, shall be shown separately.

PART IV

Contents of Management Report

There shall be attached to the financial statements, a management report containing, *inter alia*, the following duly authenticated by the management:

1. Confirmation regarding the continued validity of the registration granted by the Authority;
2. Certification that all the dues payable to the statutory authorities have been duly paid;
3. Confirmation to the effect that the shareholding pattern and any transfer of shares during the year are in accordance with the statutory or regulatory requirements;
4. Declaration that the management has not directly or indirectly invested outside India the funds of the holders of policies issued in India;
5. Confirmation that the required solvency margins have been maintained;
6. Certification to the effect that the values of all the assets have been reviewed on the date of the Balance Sheet and that in his (insurer's) belief the assets set forth in the Balance-sheets are shown in the aggregate at amounts not exceeding their realisable or market value under the several headings – "Loans", "Investments", "Agents balances", "Outstanding Premiums", "Interest, Dividends and Rents outstanding", "Interest, Dividends and Rents accruing but not due", "Amounts due from other persons or Bodies carrying on insurance business", "Sundry Debtors", "Bills Receivable", "Cash" and the several items specified under "Other Accounts";
7. Disclosure with regard to the overall risk exposure and strategy adopted to mitigate the same;
8. Operations in other countries, if any, with a separate statement giving the management's estimate of country risk and exposure risk and the hedging strategy adopted;
9. Ageing of claims indicating the trends in average claim settlement time during the preceding five years;
10. Certification to the effect as to how the values, as shown in the balance sheet, of the investments and stocks and shares have been arrived at, and how the market value thereof has been ascertained for the purpose of comparison with the values so shown;
11. Review of asset quality and performance of investment in terms of portfolios, i.e., separately in terms of real estate, loans, investments, etc.
12. A responsibility statement indicating therein that:
    (i) in the preparation of financial statements, the applicable accounting standards, principles and policies have been followed along with proper explanations relating to material departures, if any;
    (ii) the management has adopted accounting policies and applied them consistently and made judgements and estimates that are reasonable and prudent so as to give a true and fair view of the state of affairs of the company at the end of the financial year and of the operating profit or loss and of the profit or loss of the company for the year;
    (iii) the management has taken proper and sufficient care for the maintenance of adequate accounting records in accordance with the applicable provisions of the Insurance Act 1938 (4 of 1938) / Companies Act, 1956 (1 of 1956), for safeguarding the assets of the company and for preventing and detecting fraud and other irregularities;
    (iv) the management has prepared the financial statements on a going concern basis;
    (v) the management has ensured that an internal audit system commensurate with the size and nature of the business exists and is operating effectively.
13. A schedule of payments, which have been made to individuals, firms, companies and organisations in which Directors of the insurer are interested.

PART V

Preparation of Financial Statements

1. An insurer shall prepare the Revenue Account, Profit and Loss Account [Shareholders' Account] and the Balance Sheet in Form B-RA, Form B-PL, and Form B-BS, or as near thereto as the circumstances permit.

   Provided that an insurer shall prepare Revenue Accounts separately for fire, marine, and miscellaneous insurance business and separate schedules shall be prepared for Marine Cargo, Marine – Other than Marine Cargo and the following classes of miscellaneous insurance business under miscellaneous insurance and accordingly application of AS 17 – Segment Reporting – shall stand modified.

(1) Motor(2) Workmen's Compensation/Employers' Liability (3) Public/Product Liability (4) Engineering (5) Aviation (6) Personal Accident (7) Health Insurance (8) Others

2. An insurer shall prepare separate Receipts and Payments Account in accordance with the Direct Method prescribed in AS 3 – "Cash Flow Statement" issued by the ICAI.

FORM B-RA

Name of the Insurer:

Registration No. and Date of Registration with the IRDA

REVENUE ACCOUNT FOR THE YEAR ENDED 31ST MARCH, 20___.

Particulars	Schedule	Current Year (Rs.'000)	Previous Year (Rs.'000)
1. Premiums earned (Net)	1		
2. Profit/ Loss on sale/redemption of Investments			
3. Others (to be specified)			
4. Interest, Dividend & Rent – Gross			
TOTAL (A)			
1. Claims Incurred (Net)	2		
2. Commission	3		
3. Operating Expenses related to Insurance Business	4		
TOTAL (B)			
Operating Profit/(Loss) from Fire/Marine/ Miscellaneous Business C= (A – B)			
APPROPRIATIONS			
Transfer to Shareholders' Account			
Transfer to Catastrophe Reserve			
Transfer to Other Reserves (to be specified)			
TOTAL (C)			

Note: See Notes appended at the end of Form B-PL.

FORM B-PL

Name of the Insurer:

Registration No. and Date of Registration with the IRDA

PROFIT AND LOSS ACCOUNT FOR THE YEAR ENDED 31ST MARCH, 20___.

Particulars	Schedule	Current Year (Rs.'000)	Previous Year (Rs.'000)
1. OPERATING PROFIT/(LOSS)			
(a) Fire Insurance (b) Marine Insurance (c) Miscellaneous Insurance			
2. INCOME FROM INVESTMENTS			

(a) Interest, Dividend & Rent – Gross (b) Profit on sale of investments Less: Loss on sale of investments			
3. OTHER INCOME (To be specified)			
TOTAL (A)			
4. PROVISIONS (Other than taxation)			
(a) For diminution in the value of investments (b) For doubtful debts (c) Others (to be specified)			
5. OTHER EXPENSES			
(a) Expenses other than those related to Insurance Business (b) Bad debts written off (c) Others (To be specified)			
TOTAL (B)			
Profit Before Tax			
Provision for Taxation			
APPROPRIATIONS (a) Interim dividends paid during the year (b) Proposed final dividend (c) Dividend distribution tax (d) Transfer to any Reserves or Other Accounts (to be specified)			
Balance of profit/ loss brought forward from last year			
Balance carried forward to Balance Sheet			

Notes: to Form B-RA and B- PL

(a) Premium income received from business concluded in and outside India shall be separately disclosed.
(b) Reinsurance premiums whether on business ceded or accepted are to be brought into account gross (i.e. before deducting commissions) under the head reinsurance premiums.
(c) Claims incurred shall comprise claims paid, specific claims settlement costs wherever applicable and change in the outstanding provision for claims at the year-end,.
(d) Items of expenses and income in excess of one percent of the total premiums (less reinsurance) or Rs.5,00,000 whichever is higher, shall be shown as a separate line item.
(e) Fees and expenses connected with claims shall be included in claims.
(f) Under the sub-head "Others" shall be included items like foreign exchange gains or losses and other items.
(g) Interest, dividends and rentals receivable in connection with an investment should be stated as gross amount, the amount of income tax deducted at source being included under 'advance taxes paid and taxes deducted at source"..
(h) Income from rent shall include only the realised rent. It shall not include any notional rent.

FORM B-BS

Name of the Insurer:

Registration No. and Date of Registration with the IRDA

BALANCE SHEET AS AT 31ST MARCH, 20____.

	Schedule	Current Year (Rs.'000)	Previous Year (Rs.'000)
SOURCES OF FUNDS			
SHARE CAPITAL	5		
RESERVES AND SURPLUS	6		
FAIR VALUE CHANGE ACCOUNT			

BORROWINGS	7		
TOTAL			
APPLICATION OF FUNDS			
INVESTMENTS	8		
LOANS	9		
FIXED ASSETS	10		
CURRENT ASSETS			
Cash and Bank Balances	11		
Advances and Other Assets	12		
Sub-Total (A)			
CURRENT LIABILITIES	13		
PROVISIONS	14		
Sub-Total (B)			
NET CURRENT ASSETS (C) = (A - B)			
MISCELLANEOUS EXPENDITURE (to the extent not written off or adjusted)	15		
DEBIT BALANCE IN PROFIT AND LOSS ACCOUNT			
TOTAL			

CONTINGENT LIABILITIES

Particulars	Current Year (Rs.'000)	Previous Year (Rs.'000)
1. Partly paid-up investments		
2. Claims, other than against policies, not acknowledged as debts by the company		
3. Underwriting commitments outstanding (in respect of shares and securities)		
4. Guarantees given by or on behalf of the Company		
5. Statutory demands/ liabilities in dispute, not provided for		
6. Reinsurance obligations to the extent not provided for in accounts		
7. Others (to be specified)		
TOTAL		

SCHEDULES FORMING PART OF FINANCIAL STATEMENTS

SCHEDULE – 1

PREMIUM EARNED [NET]

Particulars	Current Year (Rs.'000)	Previous Year (Rs.'000)
Premium from direct business written Add: Premium on reinsurance accepted Less: Premium on reinsurance ceded		
Net Premium		
Adjustment for change in reserve for unexpired risks		
Total Premium Earned (Net)		

Note: Reinsurance premiums whether on business ceded or accepted are to be brought into account, before deducting commission, under the head of reinsurance premiums.

SCHEDULE – 2

CLAIMS INCURRED [NET]

Particulars	Current Year (Rs.'000)	Previous Year (Rs.'000)
Claims paid		
Direct Add: Re-insurance accepted Less: Re-insurance Ceded Net Claims paid		
Add Claims Outstanding at the end of the year		
Less Claims Outstanding at the beginning		
Total Claims Incurred		

Notes:

(a) Incurred But Not Reported (IBNR), Incurred but not enough reported [IBNER] claims should be included in the amount for outstanding claims.

(b) Claims includes specific claims settlement cost but not expenses of management

(c) The surveyor fees, legal and other expenses shall also form part of claims cost.

(d) Claims cost should be adjusted for estimated salvage value if there is a sufficient certainty of its realisation.

SCHEDULE – 3

COMMISSION

Particulars	Current Year (Rs.'000)	Previous Year (Rs.'000)
Commission paid		
Direct Add: Re-insurance Accepted Less: Commission on Re-insurance Ceded		
Net Commission		

Note: The profit/ commission, if any, are to be combined with the Re-insurance accepted or Re-insurance ceded figures.

SCHEDULE – 4

OPERATING EXPENSES RELATED TO INSURANCE BUSINESS

Particulars	Current Year (Rs.'000)	Previous Year (Rs.'000)
1. Employees' remuneration & welfare benefits		
2. Travel, conveyance and vehicle running expenses		
3. Training expenses		
4. Rents, rates & taxes		
5. Repairs		
6. Printing & stationery		
7. Communication		
8. Legal & professional charges		
9. Auditors' fees, expenses etc		
(a) as auditor (b) as adviser or in any other capacity, in respect of (i) Taxation matters		

(ii) Insurance matters (iii) Management services; and (c) in any other capacity		
10. Advertisement and publicity		
11. Interest & Bank Charges		
12. Others (to be specified)		
13. Depreciation		
TOTAL		

Note: Items of expenses and income in excess of one percent of the total premiums (less reinsurance) or Rs.5,00,000 whichever is higher, shall be shown as a separate line item.

SCHEDULE – 5

SHARE CAPITAL

Particulars	Current Year (Rs.'000)	Previous Year (Rs.'000)
1. Authorised Capital		
Equity Shares of Rs..... each		
2. Issued Capital		
Equity Shares of Rs. .....each		
3. Subscribed Capital		
Equity Shares of Rs.......each		
4. Called-up Capital		
Equity Shares of Rs. .....each		
Less: Calls unpaid		
Add: Equity Shares forfeited (Amount originally paid up) Less: Par Value of Equity Shares bought back Less: Preliminary Expenses Expenses including commission or brokerage on Underwriting or subscription of shares		
TOTAL		

Notes:

(a) Particulars of the different classes of capital should be separately stated.

(b) The amount capitalised on account of issue of bonus shares should be disclosed.

(c) In case any part of the capital is held by a holding company, the same should be separately disclosed.

SCHEDULE – 5A

SHARE CAPITAL

PATTERN OF SHAREHOLDING

[As certified by the Management]

Shareholder	Current Year		Previous Year	
	Number of Shares	% of Holding	Number of Shares	% of Holding
Promoters • Indian • Foreign				
Others				
TOTAL				

SCHEDULE – 6
RESERVES AND SURPLUS

Particulars	Current Year (Rs.'000)	Previous Year (Rs.'000)
1. Capital Reserve		
2. Capital Redemption Reserve		
3. Share Premium		
4. General Reserves Less: Debit balance in Profit and Loss Account Less: Amount utilized for Buy-back		
5. Catastrophe Reserve		
6. Other Reserves (to be specified)		
7. Balance of Profit in Profit & Loss Account		
TOTAL		

Note: Additions to and deductions from the reserves should be disclosed under each of the specified heads.

SCHEDULE – 7
BORROWINGS

Particulars	Current Year (Rs.'000)	Previous Year (Rs.'000)
1. Debentures/ Bonds		
2. Banks		
3. Financial Institutions		
4. Others (to be specified)		
TOTAL		

Notes:

(a) The extent to which the borrowings are secured shall be separately disclosed stating the nature of the security under each sub-head.

(b) Amounts due within 12 months from the date of Balance Sheet should be shown separately.

SCHEDULE – 8
Investments

Particulars	Current Year (Rs.'000)	Previous Year (Rs.'000)
LONG TERM INVESTMENTS		
1. Government securities and Government guaranteed bonds including Treasury Bills		
2. Other Approved Securities		
3. Other Investments		
(a) Shares (aa) Equity (bb) Preference (b) Mutual Funds (c) Derivative Instruments (d) Debentures/ Bonds (e) Other Securities (to be specified)		

(f) Subsidiaries (g) Investment Properties-Real Estate		
4. Investments in Infrastructure and Social Sector		
5. Other than Approved Investments		
SHORT TERM INVESTMENTS		
1. Government securities and Government guaranteed bonds including Treasury Bills		
2. Other Approved Securities		
3. Other Investments		
(a) Shares (aa) Equity (bb) Preference (b) Mutual Funds (c) Derivative Instruments (d) Debentures/ Bonds (e) Other Securities (to be specified) (f) Subsidiaries (g) Investment Properties-Real Estate		
4. Investments in Infrastructure and Social Sector		
5. Other than Approved Investments		
TOTAL		

Notes:

(a) Investments in subsidiary/holding companies, joint ventures and associates shall be separately disclosed, at cost.

(i) Holding company and subsidiary shall be construed as defined in the Companies Act, 1956:

(ii) Joint Venture is a contractual arrangement whereby two or more parties undertake an economic activity, which is subject to joint control.

(iii) Joint control — is the contractually agreed sharing of power to govern the financial and operating policies of an economic activity to obtain benefits from it.

(iv) Associate — is an enterprise in which the company has significant influence and which is neither a subsidiary nor a joint venture of the company.

(v) Significant influence (for the purpose of this schedule) — means participation in the financial and operating policy decisions of a company, but not control of those policies. Significant influence may be exercised in several ways, for example, by representation on the board of directors, participation in the policymaking process, material inter-company transactions, interchange of managerial personnel or dependence on technical information. Significant influence may be gained by share ownership, statute or agreement. As regards share ownership, if an investor holds, directly or indirectly through subsidiaries, 20 percent or more of the voting power of the investee, it is presumed that the investor does have significant influence, unless it can be clearly demonstrated that this is not the case. Conversely, if the investor holds, directly or indirectly through subsidiaries, less than 20 percent of the voting power of the investee, it is presumed that the investor does not have significant influence, unless such influence is clearly demonstrated. A substantial or majority ownership by another investor does not necessarily preclude an investor from having significant influence.

(b) Aggregate amount of company's investments other than listed equity securities and derivative instruments and also the market value thereof shall be disclosed.

(c) Investments made out of Catastrophe reserve should be shown separately.

(d) Debt securities will be considered as "held to maturity" securities and will be measured at historical cost subject to amortisation.

(e) Investment Property means a property [land or building or part of a building or both] held to earn rental income or for capital appreciation or for both, rather than for use in services or for administrative purposes.

(f) Investments maturing within twelve months from balance sheet date and investments made with the specific intention to dispose of within twelve months from balance sheet date shall be classified as short-term investments.

SCHEDULE – 9
LOANS

Particulars	Current Year (Rs.'000)	Previous Year (Rs.'000)
1. SECURITY-WISE CLASSIFICATION		
Secured		
(a) On mortgage of property (aa) In India (bb) Outside India		
(b) On Shares, Bonds, Govt. Securities		
(c) Others (to be specified)		
Unsecured		
TOTAL		
2. BORROWER-WISE CLASSIFICATION		
(a) Central and State Governments		
(b) Banks and Financial Institutions		
(c) Subsidiaries		
(d) Industrial Undertakings		
(e) Others (to be specified)		
TOTAL		
3. PERFORMANCE-WISE CLASSIFICATION		
(a) Loans classified as standard (aa) In India (bb) Outside India (b) Non-performing loans less provisions (aa) In India (bb) Outside India		
TOTAL		
4. MATURITY-WISE CLASSIFICATION		
(a) Short Term		
(b) Long Term		
TOTAL		

Notes:

(a) Short-term loans shall include those, which are repayable within 12 months from the date of balance sheet. Long term loans shall be the loans other than short-term loans.

(b) Provisions against non-performing loans shall be shown separately.

(c) The nature of the security in case of all long term secured loans shall be specified in each case. Secured loans for the purposes of this schedule, means loans secured wholly or partly against an asset of the company.

(d) Loans considered doubtful and the amount of provision created against such loans shall be disclosed.

SCHEDULE – 10
FIXED ASSETS

(Rs.'000)

Particulars	Cost/ Gross Block				Depreciation				Net Block	
	Opening	Additions	Deductions	Closing	Up to Last Year	For the Year	On Sales/ Adjustments	To Date	As at year end	Previous year
Goodwill										
Intangibles (specify)										
Land-Freehold										
Leasehold Property										
Buildings										
Furniture & Fittings										
Information Technology Equipment										
Vehicles										
Office Equipment										
Others (Specify nature)										
TOTAL										
Work in progress										
Grand Total										
PREVIOUS YEAR										

Note: Assets included in land, property and building above exclude Investment Properties as defined in note (e) to Schedule 8.

SCHEDULE – 11

CASH AND BANK BALANCES

Particulars	Current Year (Rs.'000)	Previous Year (Rs.'000)
1. Cash (including cheques, drafts and stamps)		
2. Bank Balances		
(a) Deposit Accounts (aa) Short-term (due within 12 months of the date of Balance Sheet) (bb) Others (b) Current Accounts (c) Others (to be specified)		
3. Money at Call and Short Notice (a) With Banks (b) With other Institutions		
4. Others (to be specified)		
TOTAL		
Balances with non-scheduled banks included in 2 and 3 above		

Note: Bank balance may include remittances in transit. If so, the nature and amount shall be separately stated.

SCHEDULE – 12

ADVANCES AND OTHER ASSETS

Particulars	Current Year (Rs.'000)	Previous Year (Rs.'000)
1. Reserve deposits with ceding companies		
2. Application money for investments		
3. Prepayments		
4. Advances to Directors/Officers		
5. Advance tax paid and taxes deducted at source (Net of provision for taxation)		
6. Others (to be specified)		
TOTAL (A)		
OTHER ASSETS		
1. Income accrued on investments		
2. Outstanding Premiums		
3. Agents' Balances		
4. Foreign Agencies Balances		
5 Due from other entities carrying on insurance business (including reinsures)		
6. Due from subsidiaries/ holding		
7. Deposit with Reserve Bank of India [Pursuant to Section 7 of Insurance Act, 1938]		
8. Others (to be specified)		
TOTAL (B)		
TOTAL (A+B)		

Notes:

(a) The items under the above heads shall not be shown net of provisions for doubtful amounts. The amount of provision against each head should be shown separately.

(b) The term 'officer' should conform to the definition of that term as given under the Companies Act, 1956.

(c) Sundry debtors will be shown under item 8 (Others).

SCHEDULE – 13

CURRENT LIABILITIES

Particulars	Current Year (Rs.'000)	Previous Year (Rs.'000)
1. Agents' Balances		
2. Balances due to other insurance companies		
3. Deposits held on re-insurance ceded		
4. Premiums received in advance		
5. Unallocated premium		
6. Sundry creditors		
7. Due to subsidiaries/ holding company		
8. Claims Outstanding		
9. Due to Officers/ Directors		
11. Others (to be specified)		
TOTAL		

SCHEDULE – 14

PROVISIONS

	Particulars	Current Year (Rs.'000)	Previous Year (Rs.'000)
1.	Reserve for Unexpired Risk		
2.	For taxation (less advance tax paid and taxes deducted at source)		
3.	For proposed dividends		
4.	For dividend distribution tax		
5.	Others (to be specified)		
	TOTAL		

SCHEDULE – 15

MISCELLANEOUS EXPENDITURE
(To the extent not written off or adjusted)

	Particulars	Current Year (Rs.'000)	Previous Year (Rs.'000)
1.	Discount Allowed in issue of shares/ debentures		
2.	Others (to be specified)		
	TOTAL		

Notes:

(a) No item shall be included under the head "Miscellaneous Expenditure" and carried forward unless:
   1. some benefit from the expenditure can reasonably be expected to be received in future, and
   2. the amount of such benefit is reasonably determinable.

(b) The amount to be carried forward in respect of any item included under the head "Miscellaneous Expenditure" shall not exceed the expected future revenue/other benefits related to the expenditure.

SCHEDULE C

(See Regulation 3)

AUDITOR'S REPORT

The report of the auditors on the financial statements of every insurer shall deal with the matters specified herein:

1. (a) That they have obtained all the information and explanations which, to the best of their knowledge and belief were necessary for the purposes of their audit and whether they have found them satisfactory;

   (b) Whether proper books of account have been maintained by the insurer so far as appears from an examination of those books;

   (c) Whether proper returns, audited or unaudited, from branches and other offices have been received and whether they were adequate for the purpose of audit;

   (d) Whether the Balance sheet, Revenue account , Profit and Loss account and the Receipts and Payments Account dealt with by the report are in agreement with the books of account and returns;

   (e) Whether the actuarial valuation of liabilities is duly certified by the appointed actuary including to the effect that the assumptions for such valuation are in accordance with the guidelines and norms, if any, issued by the Authority, and/ or the Actuarial Society of India in concurrence with the Authority.

(ii) Whether the revenue account gives a true and fair view of the surplus or the deficit for the financial year/period;

(iii) Whether the profit and loss account gives a true and fair view of the profit or loss for the financial year/period;

(iv) Whether the receipts and payments account gives a true and fair view of the receipts and payments for the financial year/period;

(b) The financial statements stated at (a) above are prepared in accordance with the requirements of the Insurance Act, 1938 (4 of 1938), the Insurance Regulatory and Development Authority Act, 1999 (41 of 1999) and the Companies Act, 1956 (1 of 1956), to the extent applicable and in the manner so required.

(c) Investments have been valued in accordance with the provisions of the Act and these Regulations.

(d) The accounting policies selected by the insurer are appropriate and are in compliance with the applicable accounting standards and with the accounting principles, as prescribed in these Regulations or any order or direction issued by the Authority in this behalf.

3. The auditors shall further certify that:

(a) they have reviewed the management report and there is no apparent mistake or material inconsistencies with the financial statements;

(b) the insurer has complied with the terms and conditions of the registration stipulated by the Authority.

4. A certificate signed by the auditors [which shall be in addition to any other certificate or report which is required by law to be given with respect to the balance sheet] certifying that:–

(a) they have verified the cash balances and the securities relating to the insurer's loans, reversions and life interests (in the case of life insurers) and investments;

(b) to what extent, if any, they have verified the investments and transactions relating to any trusts undertaken by the insurer as trustee; and

(c) no part of the assets of the policyholders' funds has been directly or indirectly applied in contravention of the provisions of the Insurance Act, 1938 (4 of 1938) relating to the application and investments of the policyholders' funds.

[F.No. IRDA/Reg/03/2002]

N.RANGACHARY, Chairman

Key Terms

- ❒ Shareholder's Account
- ❒ Technical Account
- ❒ Mathematical Reserves
- ❒ Medical Insurance
- ❒ Claims
- ❒ Reserves
- ❒ Catastrope

Questions for Review

1. Write short notes on:
   (a) Catastrophe reserve
   (b) Unrealised gains
   (c) Technical Account
   (d) Claims incurred but not reported
2. List the various tax implications of insurance transactions in India.

Suggested Readings

1. V.K. Singhania, *Direct Taxes*, Taxmann 2010.
2. Joseph C. Nokace, *Life Insurance Accounting*, R.D. Irwin, 1969.
3. Andrew L. McGrindell, *Guide to Insurance Accounting*, Witherby and Company, 1981.
4. Shukla and Grewal, *Advanced Accountancy*, S. Chand & Co., New Delhi, 2007.

Web Resources

- www.indiainfoline.com
- www.irdaindia.com
- www.binaonline.com
- www.insurance-finance.com

Insurance in Global Perspective

Chapter 14

CHAPTER OBJECTIVES

After reading this chapter you will be able to understand :

- *Need for Globalisation*
- *Global Picture of Insurance*
- *Globalisation and its Impact on India*

The global insurance industry has undergone a major change after 11th September attack on the World Trade Center in United States. An estimated loss of $ 70 billion of this event has posed serious questions before the players all around the world to rethink and devise their strategies accordingly. A few insurers have disappeared from the global picture. Also, the cover for terrorism has disappeared from the international markets. Insures have become cautious while underwriting risk on a global basis. They are also increasing the premium and freezing the insurance boundaries. According to Mr. G.V. Rao — "The call for globalisation was a bright signal for the global insurance industry. However, the industry had experienced the worst, untoward incidents also. It was one of the worst affected during the World Trade Center tragedy. This was followed by a series of other events that had an adverse impact on the insurers. Capital market crashes in countries, like UK and Germany, have further debilitated the insurance industry."[1] The wave of liberalisation is on full swing in India and so is the insurance sector.

14.1 GLOBALISATION & LIBERALISATION

Globalisation, according to Penguin Dictionary of Economics, "Stresses the geographical dispersion of industrial and service activities (for example research and development, sourcing of inputs, production, distribution) and the cross boarder networking of companies (for example through joint ventures and the sharing of assets". According to Herman E Daly, Globalisation serves the vision of a single, cosmopolitan, integrated global economy. This definition focuses on the cross border movement of goods, services and resources (financial and human) impacting on the domestic and global assets and employment. Globalisation, thus focuses on an integrated economic world in which the economy is a single market characterised by trade and investment flows, cross border economic activities in production, investment financing, movement of capital, technology, labour, internationalisation of consumption, capital, and services. Economic *liberalisation* is the gateway of globalisation and financial liberation plays the most crucial role in integratión of one country's economy on the global economic network. However, very often the term liberalisation and globalisation are used simultaneously. Important instruments of liberalisation are regulation of financial market to allow foreign capital, foreign investment, to and fro flow of capital etc. reduction of tariff and non-tariff barriers of trade, simplifications of customs measures etc. For successful global integration a country must move to economic liberalization by dismantling entry barriers and Licensing system, reduction in physical restrictions on imports, reduction in control on capital and current account, reforming financial system and opening up financial market to private (domestic and foreign) players, removing controls on foreign capital (FD and portfolio) flow to the country etc.

Globalisation however, is not a new phenomena of the current world activities. Economic historians have traced two strong waves of globalization. The first wave of globalization spread over 1870 – 1914 while the second wave of globalization began roughly in 1960 and continuing. The current wave of globalization is much faster and deeper. Globalization today is fundamentally a new economic phenomenon, and a process to set up a new economic order globally increased integration and interdependence of production, consumption and services. The present wave of globalisation has significantly influenced improved specialisation in resource allocation, productivity enhancement and specialisation and greater innovation, adaptability and utilisation of technology which has necessitated the need for cross border economic activity for all the countries. Resource mobility has not only reduced the cost of production and distribution but also boosted competition across the border.

Drivers of Globalisation : The present wave of globalisation has been significantly influenced by advances in information and computer technology, increased flow of trade and capital. improved specialisation in resource allocation, productivity enhancement and specialisation and greater innovation, adaptability and utilisation of technology which has necessitated the need for cross border economic activity for all the countries. These have not only reduced the cost of production and distribution but also boosted competition across the border.

Therefore important drivers of globalisation are expansion of International Trade, Internationalisation of Financial Market and Migration.

Financial Globalisation : Advancement in information technology, innovation in financial products, and increase in trade and services provided boost to the cross border flow of capital. The process of Globalisation is strongly supported by Financial Globalisation. Financial Liberalisation has forced many countries to open up financial markets and relaxed the rules of intermediation allowing financial services institutions like investment banks, asset management companies, Mutual Funds, Pension Funds etc., to operate in newly liberalised markets. The forces of change unleashed by financial globalization.

14.2 GLOBALISATION OF INSURANCE MARKET

Globalisation of Insurance market, as a part of the overall process of liberalization in emerging and other countries enabled the foreign insurance companies to enter in those countries and benefited both. The driving forces of insurance market globalization has been identified by Swiss Re (Sigma No.4/2000) as the 'push factors' and 'Pull Factors'. The Push factors are the motives behind the movement of foreign insurance companies while the pull factors are the motives behind allowing the foreign companies to operate in local market,

(i) **Push Factors :** Insurance Companies move out to emerging markets due to Increasing Global Trade, Growing Direct Investment, Potential Future Growth in Emerging Markets, Saturation in industrialized countries and Strong growth in emerging countries and expected Efficiency Gains through Diversification, Economics of scale etc.

(ii) **Pull Factors : The important pull factors in emerging markets** - Emerging Markets have Strong Economic growth and Trade, and there are substantial requirements of capital in Emerging Markets to cover major risks.

There are several benefits to the countries allowing foreign insurance companies to operate in their countries which can be broadly classified into Economy related, and Insurance marked related.

Economy Related Benefits to the Local Country : Foreign insurance companies along with local companies add further momentum to mobilization of savings. Institutional net work in the savings market increases, which also influence the savings behaviour of household and corporate savings. Resources and capital allocation in the Domestic Market increases with the increased sophistication brought by the foreign insurance companies It also improves the financial stability in the host country, as well as facilitates improvement in production and Trade.

Insurance Market Related Benefits : Capital structure of entire insurance industry improves because foreign companies brings fresh capital with them. Market efficiency improves due to information dissemination, global operating knowledge and increased competition. Management efficiency increases because foreign companies bring with them global experience and management innovation. Range of available products increases because foreign companies bring with them a wide range of products and product development expertise. Customers' service improves. Increased competition, technology led service, and cost competition finally benefits the consumers. Globalisation also improves Regulatory and Governance system. It also improves market conduct and Ethical Business Standard.

With the removal of entry barriers in emerging and less developed countries there has been an increased flow of funds from developed countries to the emerging and less developed countries.

14.3 NEED FOR GLOBALISATION

Insurers promote financial system efficiency through their role of, both life and non-life, financial intermediary in the following three ways:

1. **Reduction in Transaction Costs:** Because it collects the premium from a very large number of policyholders from different regions of the country and thereby commands huge funds at their disposal.
2. **Creating Liquidity:** Since there is no time lag between occurrence of loss on the one hand and receiving the claim amount by the policyholders. Moreover the funds raised are used for long term projects, which are not required to be paid immediately. Thus liquidity is created in the capital market.
3. **Facilitating Economies of Scale in Investment:** Investment in large projects such as national road projects, railways, ports, power projects facilitate innovations and specialisation's and thereby promote economic efficiency and productivity in the economy.

Benefits and Challenges of Market Access Liberalisation

The opening up of the insurance markets in emerging markets to foreign competition has long been a contentious issue. Numerous arguments, including the unfavourable balance-of-payment effect and the need to protect infant industries, have been advanced to justify measures to confine foreign inroads in the market. It is often the case of striking a fine balance between the stability of the insurance market on the one hand and ensuring efficiency and good value for consumers on the other hand.

Liberalisation enhances efficiency of local insurance market

Benefits of liberalisation for emerging market economies

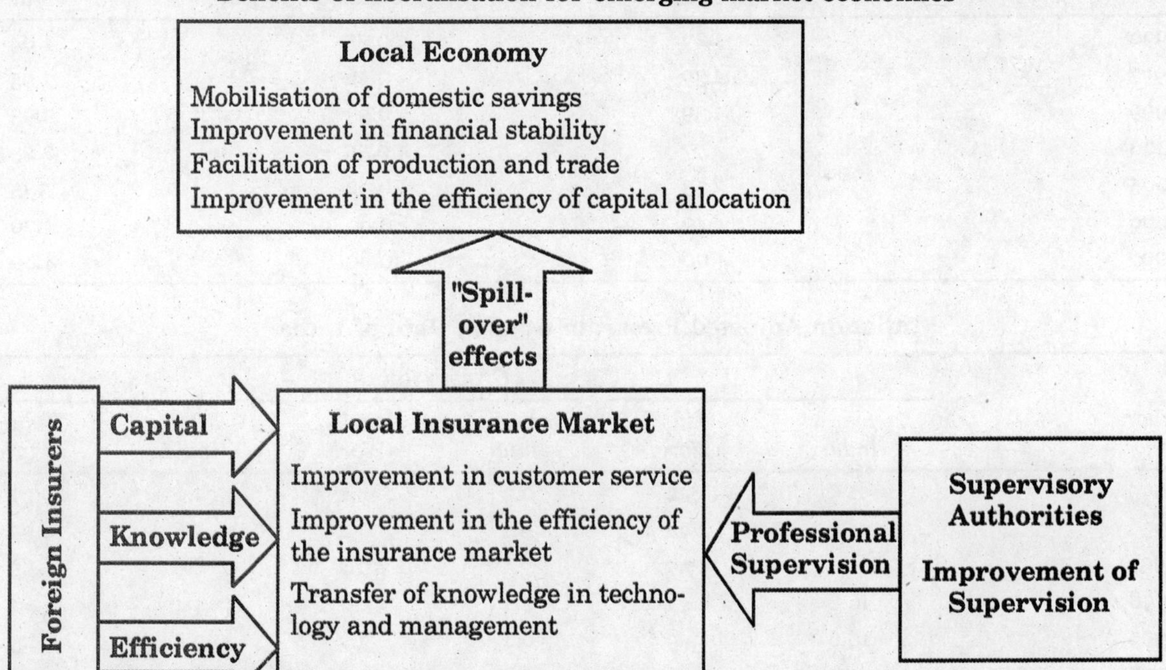

Source : Swiss Re signa N°, 4/2000

14.4 GLOBAL PICTURE OF INSURANCE

World insurance premiums (life and nonlife) totaled $4.1 trillion in 2007, according to Swiss Re. There were 747 mergers and acquisitions in the global insurance industry in 2007, with a reported value of $138 billion, accofding to Conning Research and Consulting. In terms of demand, Japan and the U.S.A. are still the largest insurance markets, accounting for over 70 percent of global premiums. Insurance penetration (premium volume as a percent of GDP) for life insurance is highest in Japan, South Africa, and the Republic of Korea where it averages over 10 percent. For non-life, penetration world-wide averages 3.3 percent of GDP and is highest in the U.S.A. (almost 5 percent) due to the importance of private health and liability insurance.

The strongest companies in terms of global reach include Assicurazioni Generali (with over 70 percent of its business from outside of Italy) and Winterthur Group (with over 60 percent of business from outside of Switzerland).

With continued deregulation and market liberalisation in insurance, economies are moving away from direct controls on premiums, products, and investments towards solvency monitoring through more effective supervision and clear prudential controls. State monopolies used to dominate the insurance market in many economies, but privatisation is increasing and the "non-operational" advantages of domestic insurers are disappearing. Due to regulatory restrictions, expansion abroad used to occur primarily through foreign investment and/or acquisitions; however, new opportunities for export competition are emerging, supported by the spread of electronic commerce.

14.4.1 Global Statistics

Exhibit 14-A

Facts and Figures on Global Insurance[2]

Insurance Penetration

Years	*Premium as percentage of GDP*		
	Life	*Non- Life*	*Total*
1996	1.29	0.55	1.84
1997	1.39	0.56	1.95
1999	1.39	0.53	1.93
2000	1.77	0.55	2.23
2005	2.53	0.62	3.15
2006	4.10	0.60	4.70
2007	4.00	0.60	4.60

Inflation Adjusted Premium Growth Rate of India

Years	*Growth Rate*					
	Life/ India	*Life/ World*	*Non-Life/ India*	*Non-Life/ World*	*Total/ India*	*Total/ World*
1995	11.9	5.2	10.9	2.2	11.6	3.7
1996	5.4	1.27	6.1	0.54	5.6	0.97
1997	11.0	7.7	3.1	0.2	8.6	4.5
1998	16.8	4.1	8.4	0.1	14.4	2.3
1999	10.6	6.9	6.4	1.2	9.4	4.5
2000	21.3	9.1	3.8	2.7	16.6	6.6

The real growth rate of premium in life and non-life for the world accounted for 5.4% and 0.7% in 2007 making a total growth rate of 3.3% till 2007.

Premium Per Capita in US$

Years	*Life/ India*	*Life/ World*	*Non-Life/ India*	*Non-Life/ World*	*Total/ India*	*Total/ World*
1995	4.5	277.2	1.9	197.9	6.4	475.1
1996	5.0	246.7	2.0	184.5	7.0	431.1
1997	5.4	246.4	2.2	176.8	7.6	423.3
1998	6.2	145.3	2.3	125.7	8.6	271.0
1999	6.2	235.4	2.4	151.9	8.5	373.3
2000	7.6	239.9	2.3	145.5	9.9	385.4

The premium per capital of the whole world in 2007 is 607.7 US$ as per the swiss re estimates.

Global premium growth 1980 - 2007
Real Premium Growth Rates

	Non-Life	*Life*	*Total*
1980	-3.3%	2.5%	-1.0%
1981	-0.6%	4.1%	1.3%
982	1.4%	5.3%	3.0%
1983	3.7%	3.4%	3.6%
1984	0.4%	12.0%	7.7%
1985	10.5%	13.5%	11.8%
1986	13.7%	21.5%	17.3%
1987	3.9%	12.6%	8.5%
1988	5.6%	13.0%	9.4%
1989	2.4%	5.0%	3.8%
1990	1.8%	1.4%	1.6%
1991	1.4%	2.7%	2.1%
1992	3.0%	5.7%	4.5%
1993	4.2%	6.4%	5.4%
1994	1.8%	4.1%	3.1%
1995	2.2%	4.9%	3.7%
1996	1.3%	3.3%	2.5%
1997	1.0%	7.9%	4.9%
1998	-0.2%	4.5%	2.5%
1999	1.7%	7.8%	5.3%
2000	3.8%	10.2%	7.7%
2001	5.5%	-1.9%	0.9%
2002	9.3%	3.1%	5.6%
2003	6.4%	-0.6%	2.3%
2004	2.3%	3.5%	3.0%
2005	-0.1%	4.6%	2.6%
2006	3.9%	4.1%	4.0%
2007	0.7%	5.3%	3.3%

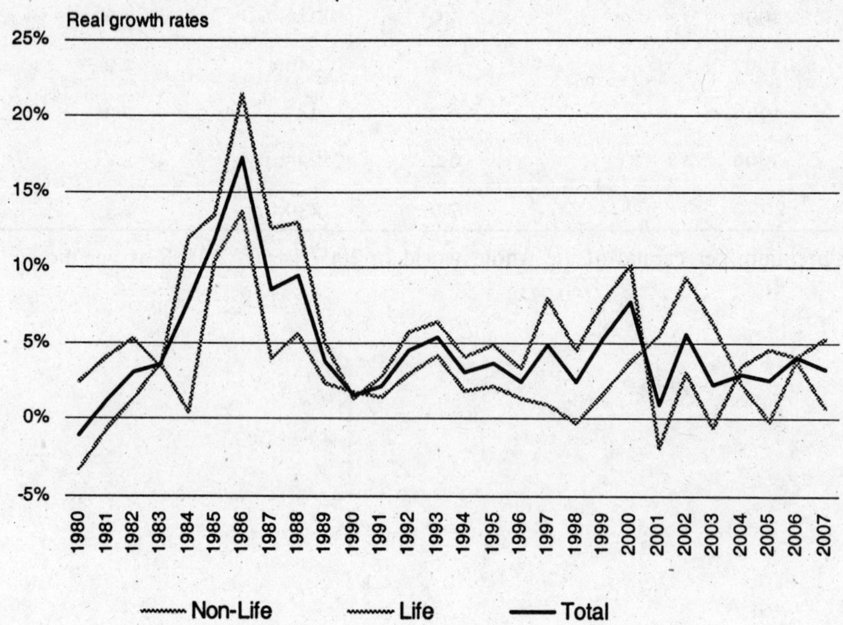

Premium growth since 1980

	Industrialised Countries	*Emerging markets*	*Total*
1980	-1.3%	6.6%	-1.0%
1981	1.1%	8.7%	1.4%
1982	3.0%	5.4%	3.1%
1983	3.3%	9.0%	3.6%
1984	7.9%	5.1%	7.7%
1985	12.2%	3.4%	11.8%
1986	17.7%	9.6%	17.4%
1987	8.2%	11.3%	8.3%
1988	9.5%	7.0%	9.4%
1989	3.3%	13.6%	3.6%
1990	1.4%	7.1%	1.6%
1991	2.1%	6.1%	2.3%
1992	4.2%	11.3%	4.5%
1993	5.2%	11.7%	5.4%
1994	2.8%	12.1%	3.2%
1995	3.5%	9.7%	3.7%
1996	1.7%	3.6%	1.8%
1997	4.6%	11.2%	4.9%
1998	2.9%	6.2%	3.1%
1999	5.2%	7.8%	5.3%
2000	7.1%	12.7%	7.4%
2001	0.5%	14.6%	1.3%
2002	5.0%	13.4%	5.5%
2003	2.0%	10.6%	2.5%
2004	2.5%	9.2%	2.9%
2005	2.2%	7.0%	2.5%
2006	3.1%	15.5%	4.1%
2007	2.8%	12.8%	3.7%
2008	-5.3%	11.0%	-3.6%
2009	-1.8%	3.5%	-1.1%

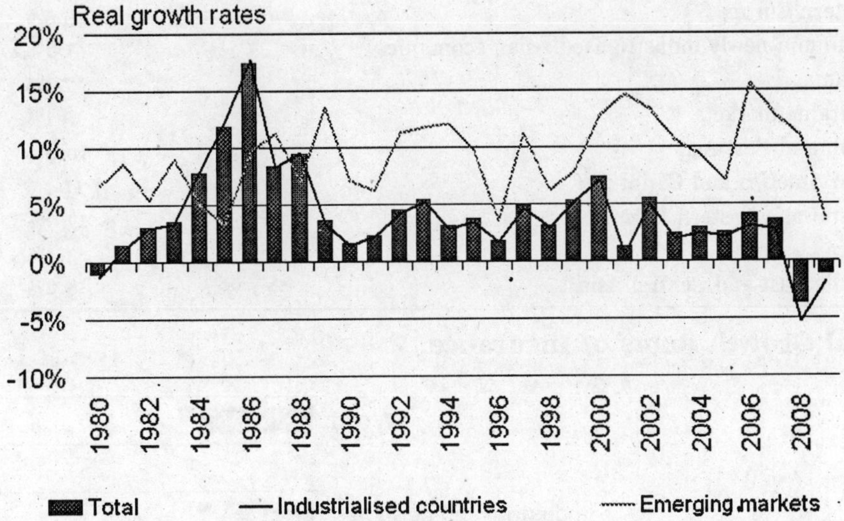

Source: Swiss Re, Economic Research & Consulting, sigma No. 2/2009

Life Business Development by Region

Real Growth Rates Region	*Growth rate 2007*	*Annual average growth rate 1997-2006*
World	5.3%	4.3%
Industrialised countries	4.6%	3.8%
North America	5.3%	3.8%
Western Europe	5.5%	6.9%
Japan and newly industrialised Asian economies	1.8%	0.3%
Oceania	7.9%	1.6%
Emerging markets	13.1%	13.5%
South and East Asia	16.8%	19.3%
Latin America and Caribbean	11.4%	10.4%
Central and Eastern Europe	17.0%	7.6%
Africa	3.4%	7.5%
Middle East and Central Asia	8.7%	5.8%

Real Growth Rates of Insurance

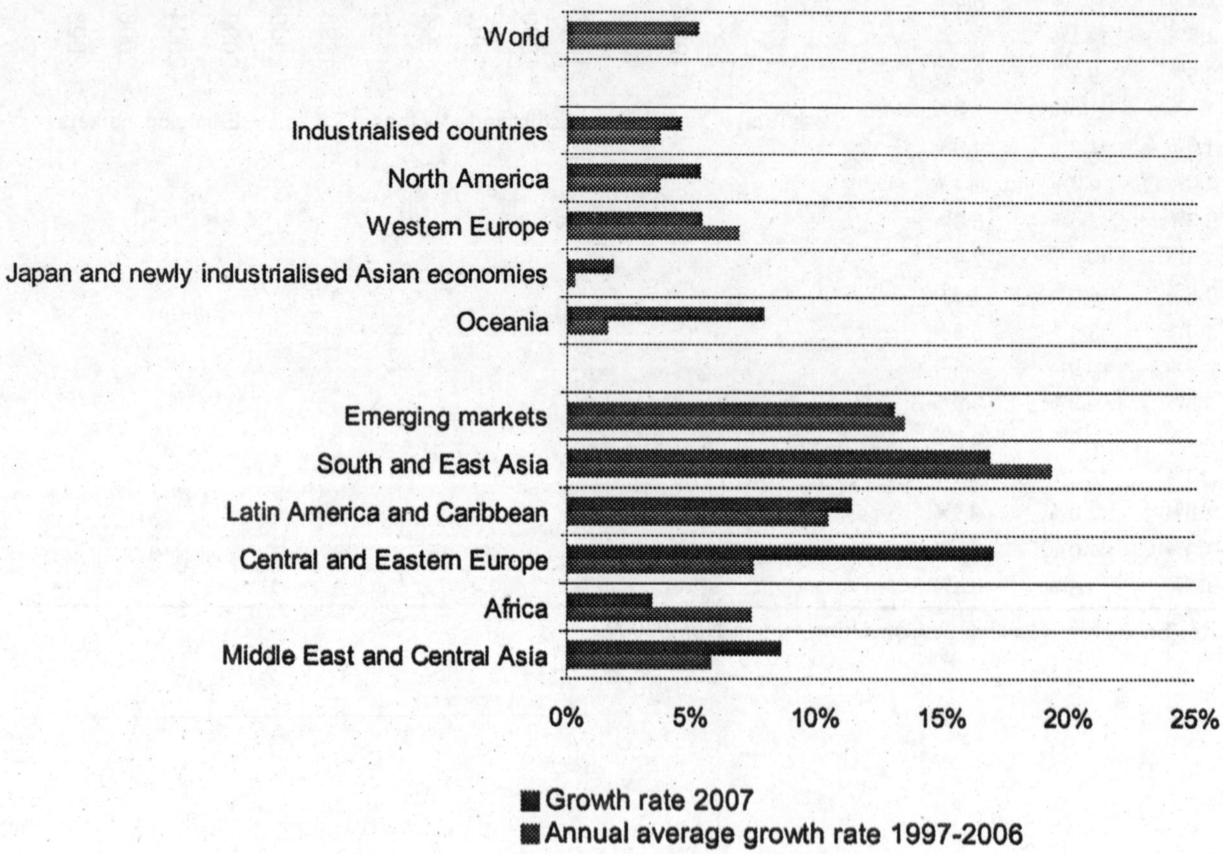

Non-life business development by region

Real Growth Rates Region	*Growth rate 2007*	*Annual average growth rate 1997-2006*
World	0.7%	3.3%
Industrialised countries	-0.4%	2.9%
North America	-1.0%	3.0%
Western Europe	-0.2%	3.7%
Japan and newly industrialised Asian economies	2.1%	0.3%
Oceania	-0.2%	2.9%
Emerging markets	10.2%	8.3%
South and East Asia	13.9%	9.7%
Latin America and Caribbean	8.3%	5.7%
Central and Eastern Europe	11.7%	10.6%
Africa	0.6%	5.0%
Middle East and Central Asia	9.6%	10.7%

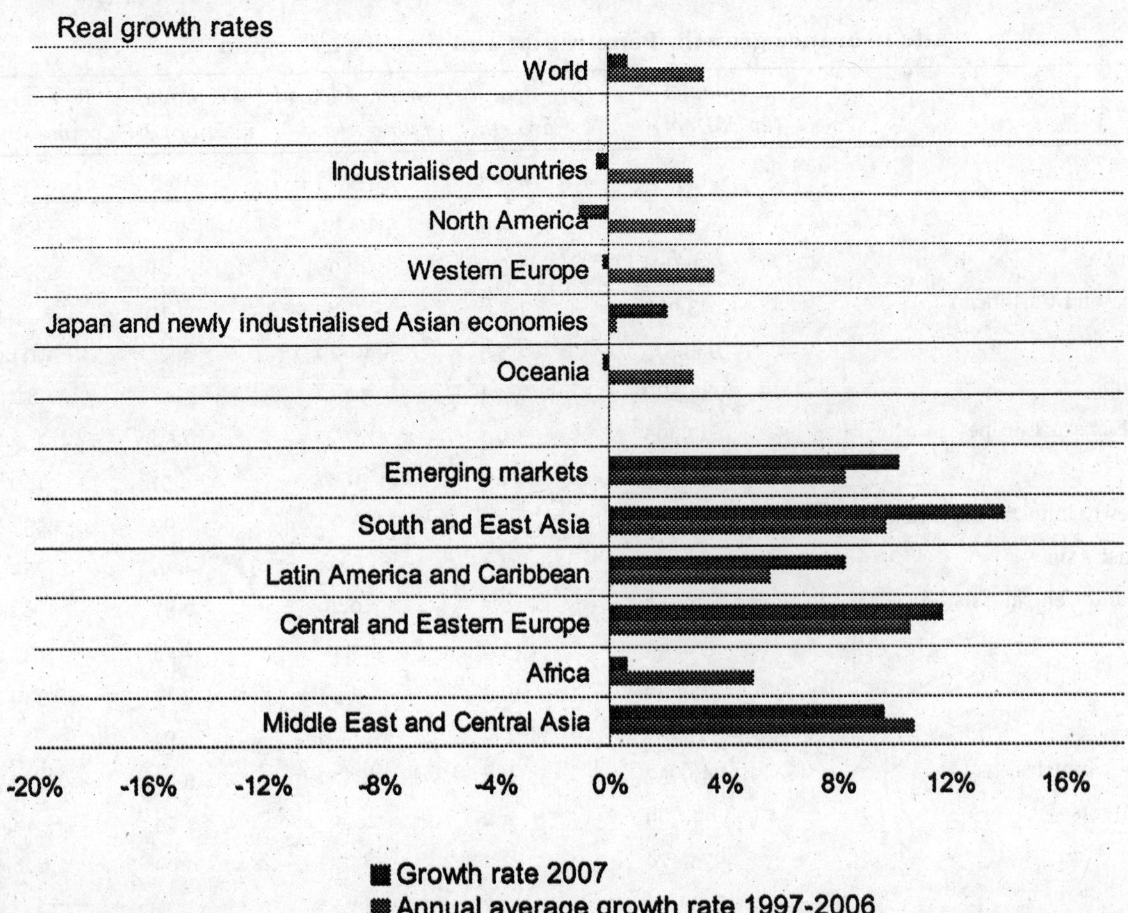

Top ten countries in life and non-life insurance

Life insurance	*2007 premium volume (in USD milllion)*	*Share of emerging markets*	*Non-life insurance*	*2007 premium volume (in USD milllion)*	*Share of emerging markets*
China	58,673	26.4%	China	33,810	17.0%
India	51,322	23.0%	Russia	28,973	14.6%
South Africa	34,430	15.5%	Brazil	20,501	10.3%
Brazil	18,533	8.3%	Mexico	9,763	4.9%
Poland	7,950	3.6%	South Africa	8,345	4.2%
Mexico	7,653	3.4%	Poland	7,677	3.9%
Malaysia	5,573	2.5%	India	7,402	3.7%
Indonesia	4,728	2.1%	Turkey	7,201	3.6%
Thailand	4,521	2.0%	Venezuela	6,977	3.5%
Chile	3,792	1.7%	Argentina	4,471	2.2%
Top 10	197,177	88.6%	Top 10	129,619	68.0%

Source: National insurance authorities, Swiss Re Economic Research & Consulting.

Life nsurance growth, Penetration and density by region

	Premiums (in USDmn)	*Real growth*	*Share of world market (in %)*	*Premiums in % of GDP*	*Premiums per capita (in USD)*
	2009	2009	2009	2009	2009
America	579,626	-12.2	24.86	2.97	631.5
North America	536,001	-13.5	22.99	3.44	1,572.8
Latin America and Caribbean	43,625	7.8	1.87	1.11	75.6
Europe	953,515	3.5	40.90	4.52	1,111.0
Western Europe	935,520	4.1	40.12	5.24	1,811.1
Central and Eastern Europe	17,995	-20.1	0.77	0.58	55.8
Asia	732,267	1.8	31.41	4.51	180.3
Japan and newly industrialised Asian economies	538,067	-1.2	23.08	7.97	2,553.8
South and East Asia	187,355	11.4	8.04	2.45	52.9
Middle East and Central Asia	6,845	0.5	0.29	0.37	22.1
Africa	32,564	-15.0	1.40	2.15	32.3
Oceania	33,592	-19.4	1.44	3.12	930.7
World	2,331,566	-2.0	100.00	4.01	341.2
Industrialised countries	2,046,957	-2.8	87.79	5.01	1,979.9
Emerging markets	284,609	4.2	12.21	1.54	48.8
OECD	1,975,474	-3.2	84.73	4.69	1,606.6
G7	1,573,924	-3.2	67.51	5.06	2,131.8
Euroland	628,772	11.5	26.97	4.64	1,765.1
EU, 27 countries	906,784	3.5	38.89	5.22	1,720.1
NAFTA	543,690	-13.3	23.32	3.30	1,207.1
ASEAN	28,252	2.0	1.21	1.97	55.4

Source: Swiss Re, Economic Research & Consulting, sigma No. 2/2009

Non-life insurance growth, penetration and density by region

	Premiums (in USDmn)	*Real growth*	*Share of world market (in %)*	*Premiums in % of GDP*	*Premiums per capita (in USD)*
	2009	2009	2009	2009	2009
America	769,869	-1.0	44.38	3.94	838.8
North America	702,584	-1.5	40.51	4.50	2,061.7
Latin America and Caribbean	67,285	4.3	3.88	1.71	116.6
Europe	657,105	-1.2	37.88	3.05	750.6
Western Europe	590,433	-0.5	34.04	3.22	1,111.3
Central and Eastern Europe	66,672	-7.5	3.84	2.16	206.9
Asia	257,184	5.6	14.83	1.57	62.8
Japan and newly industrialised Asian economies	160,946	2.2	9.28	2.35	753.8
South and East Asia	74,532	13.9	4.30	0.98	21.1
Middle East and Central Asia	21,706	4.7	1.25	1.17	70.0
Africa	16,723	0.4	0.96	1.10	16.6
Oceania	33,649	2.9	1.94	3.12	932.2
World	1,734,529	-0.1	100.00	2.98	253.9
Industrialised countries	1,485,759	-0.6	85.66	3.60	1,424.9
Emerging markets	248,770	2.9	14.34	1.35	42.7
OECD	1,491,240	-0.7	85.97	3.51	1,201.8
G7	1,170,656	-1.3	67.49	3.65	1,539.0
Euroland	446,144	0.4	25.72	3.40	1,293.5
EU, 27 countries	575,050	-0.7	33.15	3.20	1,054.5
NAFTA	712,249	-1.3	41.06	4.33	1,581.4
ASEAN	16,417	5.3	0.95	1.00	28.0

Source: Swiss Re, Economic Research & Consulting, sigma No. 2/2009

Total insurance growth, penetration and density by region

	Premiums (in USDmn)	*Real growth*	*Share of world market (in %)*	*Premiums in % of GDP*	*Premiums per capita (in USD)*
	2009	2009	2009	2009	2009
America	1,349,495	-6.1	33.19	6.91	1,470.2
North America	1,238,586	-7.1	30.46	7.94	3,634.5
Latin America and Caribbean	110,910	5.7	2.73	2.82	192.2
Europe	1,610,620	1.8	39.61	7.58	1,861.5
Western Europe	1,525,953	2.6	37.53	8.46	2,922.4
Central and Eastern Europe	84,667	-10.9	2.08	2.75	262.7
Asia	989,451	2.8	24.33	6.08	243.1
Japan and newly industrialised Asian economies	699,012	-0.4	17.19	10.33	3,307.6
South and East Asia	261,887	12.1	6.44	3.43	74.0
Middle East and Central Asia	28,552	3.4	0.70	1.54	92.0
Africa	49,287	-11.1	1.21	3.26	48.8
Oceania	67,241	-9.6	1.65	6.24	1,862.9
World	4,066,095	-1.1	100.00	6.98	595.1
Industrialised countries	3,532,716	-1.8	86.88	8.61	3,404.9
Emerging markets	533,379	3.5	13.12	2.89	91.5
OECD	3,466,714	-2.0	85.26	8.20	2,808.4
G7	2,744,580	-2.4	67.50	8.71	3,670.8
Euroland	1,074,916	7.3	26.44	8.04	3,058.5
EU, 27 countries	1,481,834	2.2	36.44	8.42	2,774.6
NAFTA	1,255,938	-6.9	30.89	7.63	2,788.5
ASEAN	44,669	3.2	1.10	2.97	83.4

Source: Swiss Re, Economic Research & Consulting, sigma No. 2/2009

	Emerging Markets	*China*	*India*	*Brazil*	*Russia*	*Po-land*	*S. Africa*	*Vene-zuela*	*Mexico*	*Mala-ysia*	*Indo-nesia*	*Others*
Premium volume 2002	165	165	203	227	232	237	241	245	248	251	253	255
Additional premium volume 2002-2007	111	38	24	5.8	5.0	4.0	3.4	3.3	3.1	2.0	2.0	21

Contribution to emerging market premium growth 2003–2007 (at 2002 prices)

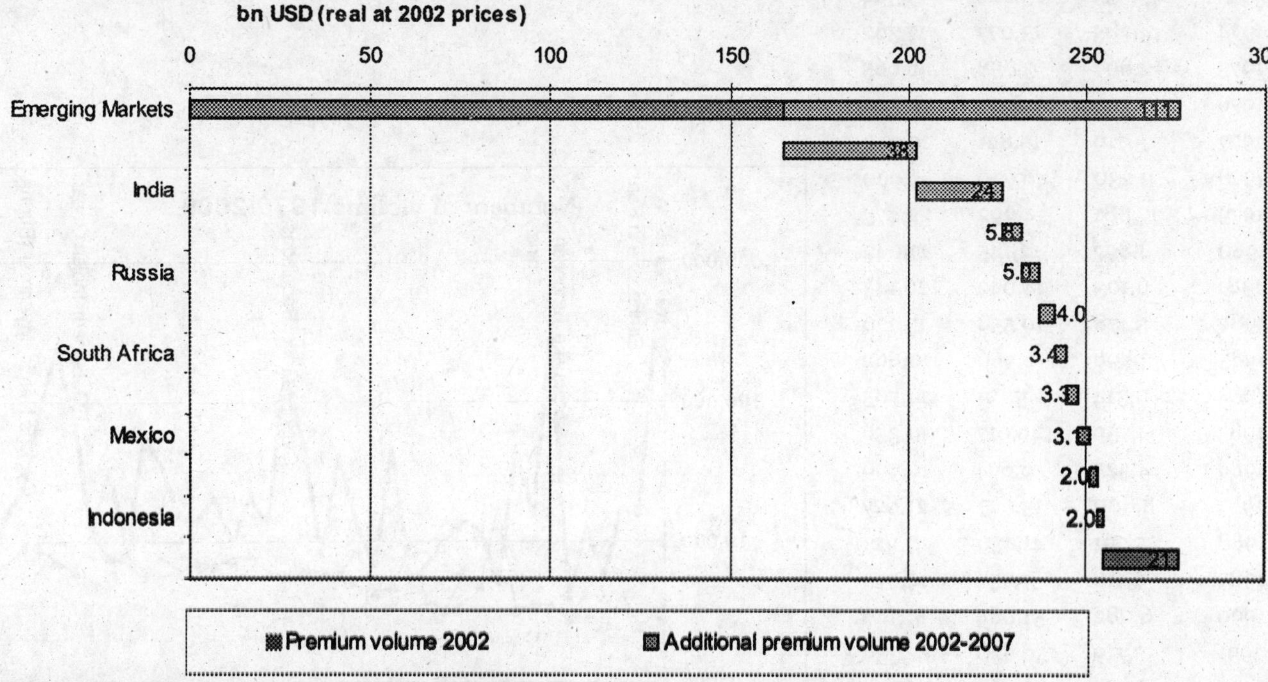

Source: National insurance authorities, Swiss Re Economic Research & Consulting.

In 2013, the global insurance market is forecast to have from written premium of 4.665.10 billion (Date Monitor Research).

Numbers of Victims 1970-2009

Year	*Man-mad disasters*	*Natural catastrophes*	*Grand Total*
1970	2,979	371,063	374,042
1971	2,493	15,388	17,881
1972	4,556	17,385	21,941
1973	3,955	5,629	9,584
1974	4,285	13,077	17,362
1975	2,807	3,858	6,665
1976	3,566	307,950	311,516
1977	3,719	15,821	19,540
1978	3,230	46,730	49,960
1979	17,881	4,992	22,873
1980	4,897	12,145	17,042
1981	6,103	14,042	20,145
1982	3,178	10,558	13,736
1983	3,896	6,966	10,862
1984	9,314	5,191	14,505
1985	4,739	46,617	51,356
1986	4,325	6,674	10,999
1987	8,800	13,027	21,827
1988	5,791	41,430	47,221
1989	6,118	7,954	14,072
1990	6,082	51,064	57,146
1991	5,719	156,620	162,339
1992	6,189	13,468	19,657
1993	8,252	20,797	29,049
1994	7,467	9,868	17,335
1995	6,826	20,787	27,613
1996	7,340	14,001	21,341
1997	6,057	14,480	20,537
1998	7,958	35,014	42,972
1999	5,530	58,276	63,806
2000	7,010	7,931	14,941
2001	7,821	32,951	40,772
2002	10,992	11,453	22,445
2003	6,119	71,962	78,081
2004	7,338	235,168	242,506
2005	8,949	88,608	97,557
2006	8,686	22,520	31,206
2007	6,951	14,785	21,736
2008	5,646	234,729	240,375
2009	5,939	8,977	14,916

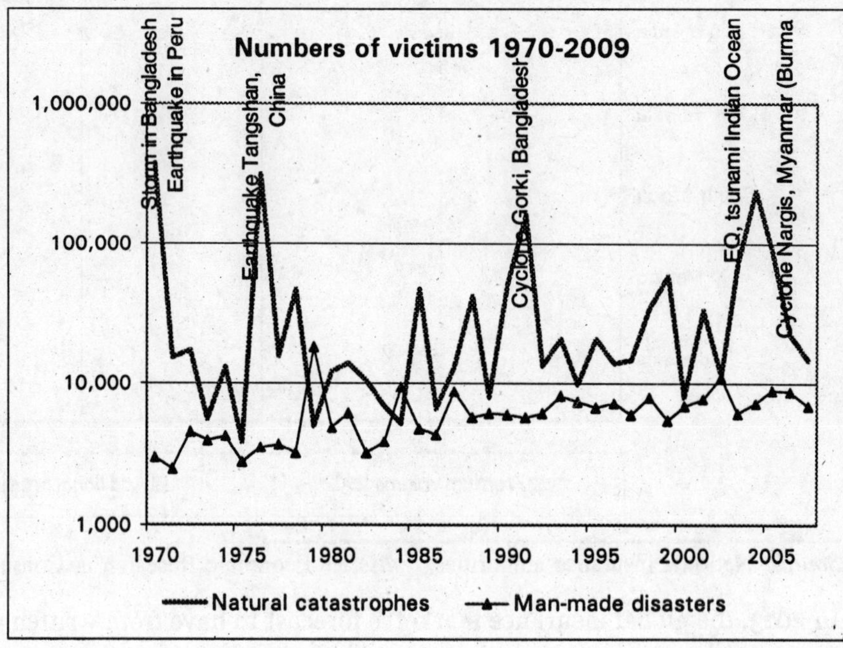

Sigma No 1/2010: Natural catastrophes and man-made disasters in 2009

14.4.2 Global Insurance Markets – Current Scenario

- Insurance companies are developing primarily from industry consolidation rather than the growth of new companies or increased overseas branching. Mergers and acquisitions are especially prevalent in markets where there have been a large number of undifferentiated players, none of which have controlled more than five percent of the market.
- Vertical integration is occurring, with a merging of the roles of agents, underwriters, and risk assessors. At the same time, there is a growth in horizontal integration between insurance firms and other competitors such as financial investment firms, banks, credit card companies, and retailers. But, while consolidation may bring economies of scale, it doesn't solve basic distribution problems.

Top ten Global Insurance Companies by Market Value

Since the recent financial meltdown which began in September 2008, a reshuffling of the market value of the world's largest insurance companies has occured. Below is a list of the top ten insurance companies:

Rank	*Company*	*Market Value ($ billions)*	*Country*
1.	American Intl. Group	$172.24	United States
2.	AXA Group	$66.12	France
3.	Allianz Worldwide	$65.55	Germany
4.	Manulife Financial	$50.52	Japan
5.	Generali Group	$45.45	Italy
6.	Prudential Financial	$39.70	United States
7.	MetLite	$37.94	United States
8.	Aviva	$33.10	United Kingdom
9.	Munich Re Group	$30.99	Germant
10.	Aegon	$26.40	Netherlands

- In order to remain competitive, insurance companies are increasingly "unbundling" the value-added chain, contracting out non-core support services, and specialising in specific market segments. As the business community becomes more sophisticated in understanding risk exposures and risk management, it is increasingly unwilling to incur the high costs of insurance from inefficient, multi-line firms.
- Banks are helping corporate clients set up captives and risk retention groups to bypass the traditional insurance market and acquire more effective exposure coverage at lower administrative costs.
- Alternatives such as captives, risk retention groups, or self-insurance now control 40-45 percent of the total commercial market. Even mid-size companies are moving in this direction by going to "rent-a-captive" where they can rent "space" in a captive as risk takers.
- Internet is the growing as a global distribution channel world-wide, which is increasingly being used for marketing of insurance products and services. This is leading to a sharp rise in use of commercial on-line services, which allow policyholders to view, query, and update policy information. Insurance companies have revised their marketing strategies to accommodate the interactive marketing style of the electronic media.

14.5 Globalisation and its Impact on India

The last millennium ended with a flourish of insurance mergers and acquisitions across the globe. 1999 saw over 630 insurance-related deals world-wide, a 15 percent increase over 1998 figures. Over 33 percent of these deals happened during the last quarter preceding Y2K. And the Asian marketplace has contributed significantly to this activity.

India's developing markets afford huge opportunities for growth, surpassing anything available in the West. Also, in the coming future, large mergers and acquisition activities are expected. Companies with the size to influence the market will obviously gain the best benefits of globalisation. To acquire that influence, a focussed merger and acquisition strategy must be implemented since the current competitive environment may make it impossible to achieve growth through internal developments. Alternative approaches will only slow down the process. Since the stock markets are unrelenting and insatiable in their expectations, insurers will have to turn to mergers and acquisitions to meet these demands.

Other insurers will find it increasingly difficult to retain their markets. And it will become even less viable for them to maintain even partially functional networks or competitive standards and service. If they wish to survive, they will have to either merge or become niche specialists.

India and Korea are the two last countries in Asia to deregulate their financial sectors. Although different markets fundamentally, they both have strong privatisation programmes in place. This renewed focus on privatisation has a twin-pronged impact since it presents greater business opportunities and strengthens to strong link that privatisation shares with deregulation.

Liberalisation of the insurance sectors has allowed foreign insurers to enter the market. Most of the foreign insurers have started rushing to find local partners within the local market. India offers immense possibilities to foreign insurers since it is the world's most populous country, having over a billion people still uninsured. The insurance industry is undergoing major restructuring as firms are moving from being national to global in scope, as economies of scale become increasingly important in commodity product lines. The main insurance areas that have already become globalised include marine, aviation, alternative risk financing, and reinsurance.

For a developing country like India, growth in per capita GNP and education levels brings an increase in demand for *life insurance* products. Most of the economists fell that demand for insurance products will be strongest in the country when –

- individuals are increasingly responsible for their own retirement savings and estate planning due to the removal of government safety nets,
- fewer children to care for aging parents, and
- a movement away from extended family structures to nuclear families.

As the threat of retirees outliving their assets increases, alternate support and wealth conservation mechanisms need to be found. Given their large population bases, India will continue to be high demand market. With the liberalisation and deregulation of the Indian financial sector, the following opportunities will be open for the private insurance companies:

(1) As government's struggle with budget deficits and the threat of an aging population outliving its assets, new opportunities in private insurance financing are opening up in *worker's compensation* and *old age pension schemes*. This is because the government is facing acute shortage of funds to repay the pension to the government employees and is thinking of phasing out such schemes.

(2) The growth of private health care networks brings with it an increased demand for *health insurance*, either through individual contracts or group employee benefit programs.

(3) Other high demand growth areas include *professional and product liability* and *political risk*, especially as developing economies become more attractive to investors.

The world-wide-web (i.e. WWW) has grown rapidly, ushering in widespread usage of e-commerce that has impacted business world-wide changing the methods under which they have traditionally operated. Within India, the relatively immature insurance companies are structured in a way where they are split by:

- product — commercial, personal or life, or
- the distribution method — broker, agency or direct.

The Indian insurance industry cannot remain the exception to the rule any more. Some of them have tried to implement e-business in some form or the other to make their businesses more efficient and effective but no one has taken a gigantic step towards complete commitment for e-business as the way of conducting business. New technology will give customers better, wider and faster access to products and services than the options offered earlier. This freedom of choice will place demands on business and this can be achieved only when insurance companies have revamped and improved their product and delivery service just to stay afloat.

Opportunities and Challenges for India

Globalisation has mixed blessings for India. It has entailed new opportunities for players but also, simultaneously brought threats against the national interests.

Opportunities

1. Opening up of the sector will ensure a larger flow of funds in two ways. More investment will take place in the sector. Further, through competition, a larger portion of savings will find its way into infrastructure through insurance companies. This will change the image of India being a highly under-insured nation.
2. After the nuclear tests, the government needs to hold out a hand of friendship to the West to achieve aims related to national security. Insurance will be a visible gesture.
3. From the view point of the capital markets, opening up of the insurance will have a bullish impact. In the near term, insurance is a highly visible industry and the fact that inspite of motivated opposition, the government is prepared to go ahead sends a positive signal to foreign investors, even if they are not in insurance. In the medium term, insurance companies are traditionally major players in stock markets. LIC and GIC make substantial investment in stocks. Once half-a-dozen companies come and start operating, the size of the pie would become larger and huge investible funds would come in. Insurance companies tend to be value pickers. They invest in stocks with relatively steady earnings and a strong asset base. So when insurers enter the market they will invest in SAIL or SBI, even if they seem sluggish in the short-term.
4. The biggest benefit will be to the stock market because of the actual investment flowing into infrastructure development. When more long-term insurance money flows into these areas, there would be a stupendous impetus to growth. When GDP grows, the stock markets will grow in tandem.
5. The opening up of the insurance sector by the Government of India to private and global players, will lead to phenomenal growth in terms of number of new players, and new products and services.

However, it is critical that when we open the doors for insurance we protect our own national long-term interests.

Threats

1. There is a fear that there will be flight of capital from India; to ensure against this we should stipulate that capital and dividend repatriation should start only after some years. It is also necessary to ensure that domestic capital raised through premium is not repatriated.
2. The other fear is that the foreign insurers will cream the market. A level playing field between LIC and GIC and other foreign companies should be ensured.
3. The biggest fear is ownership, that is the foreign insurers do not control the management of the insurance company through backdoor. To prevent this we should ensure that the day-to-day management is with the Indian partner and foreign holdings do not exceed the ceiling laid down by law.

Globalisation and Regulation Issues in Indian Market

Globalization in the financial services sector has led to strong international linkages. The process of linkages and convergence across sectors and borders creates risks by which financial markets, financial institutions and consumers in one jurisdiction can be adversely affected by a disturbance in another market. The resulting contagion effect has wide ramifications across jurisdictions. This has made the need for international cooperation and co-ordination amongst regulators an imperative.

Regulation of Conglomerates

Corporates seeking global reach and economies of scale through investments; mergers and acquisitions etc. has led to the emergence of large financial congiomerates operating across sectors and across jurisdictions, hastening the need for instituting necessary regulatory approaches to supervise such organizations in a comprehensive manner; and at the same time regorously look at their sectoral integrity through the respective prudential sectoral standards.

Products and the Regulator

Very often, insurers follow the practice of "deal now, detail later". The coverage dispute between insurers, brokers and reinsurers in the World Trade Center disaster has brought the need to ensure contract certainty to the front burner. The regulator has to ensure the policy terms are clear and unambiguous. This could mean lightening the product filing requirements.

E-Commerce and the Regulator

The internet is having an increasingly larger impact on the financial services markets. It seeks to make financial transactions a borderless business. This exposes the business to many potentially unknown risks.

Regulator and Consumer Confidence

Regulator has to play an increasing role in guiding insurers to meet heightened expectations of the consuemrs and the society. Enforcement of adherence to regulatory requirements is a key factor in consumer confidence. The consumer has become aware that the regulator is expected to keep vigil against various risks.

The idea of regulation as a risk management tool operates at three different levels – (1) Off and on-site supervision by the regulator to enforce regulations (2) Self-regulatory approaches including setting industry level standards and benchmarking by industry associations and (3) Effective implementation of corporate governance norms by individual insurers.

Consumer Protection and Market Conduct

Consumer protection is a dominant theme in insurance market in view of the intangibility of the product and prospective nature of claims. Therefore, market conduct regulation involving best sales and marketing practices, guidelines on unfair practices, policyholder protection methods–including product disclosure and transparency guidelines–are to be in place.

Corporate Governance

Enforcement of corporate governance has become a necessary requirement in most jurisdictionms so as to meet stakeholder expectations more appropriately and effectively. Companies are required to implement of transparency, integrity and professionalism.

Key Terms

- ❒ GDP
- ❒ Opportunities
- ❒ Globalisation
- ❒ Penetration
- ❒ Self-insurance
- ❒ Threats

Questions for Review

1. Evaluate the performance of the Indian Insurance sector in terms of Global Insurance Market penetration and growth. Does it indicate vast potential for India? Give reasons for your answer.
2. Briefly list the major fators which accentuated the need for globalisation and privatisation of the Indian Insurance Industry.
3. Discuss the role of insurance in national and international economy.
4. Outline the trends in the evolution of international insurance markets in terms of liberalisation.

Suggested Readings

- Emmett Vaughan and Therese Vaughan, *Essentials of Risk Management and Insurance,* John Wiley and Sons Inc., 2002.
- G.E. Rejda, *Principles of Risk Management and Insurance,* Pearson Education Inc., 2002.
- Harold D. Skipper, *International Risk and Insurance: An Environmental Managerial Approach,* IRWIN, 1998.
- P. Periasamy, *Principles and Practice of Insurance,* Himalaya Publishing House, Delhi, 2003.
- T.S. Balasubramaniam and S.P. Gupta, *Insurance Business Environment,* IC-12, Insurance Institute of India, Mumbai, 2000.

Web Resources

- www.swissre.com
- www.indiainfoline.com
- www.bimaonline.com
- www.irdaindia.org.

Introduction to Life Insurance

Chapter 15

CHAPTER OBJECTIVES

After reading this chapter you will be able to understand :

- *Life Insurance Basics*
- *Life Insurance in India : The Backdrop*
- *Life Insurance Demand and Outlook*
- *Performance of the Life Insurance Sector in India*

15.1 LIFE INSURANCE : MEANING AND DEFINITION

Life Insurance, usually referred to as 'life assurance' insures the insured against the happening of certain event *i.e.* death through the time when it may happen is uncertain. The life insurance contract can be described as 'contingent contracts' because the loss of life cannot be compensated and only a specified sum of money is paid if the insured dies. In addition to this, life insurance is considered a better way of making investment alongwith the benefits of protection against the risks of death.

Section 2 of the Indian Insurance Act, 1938 has defined life insurance as: "Life Insurance business is the business of effecting contracts upon human life."

A life insurance contract may be defined as 'a contract whereby the insurer, in consideration of a premium paid either in lump sum or in periodic instalments, undertakes to pay an annuity or a certain sum of money, either on the death of the insured or on the expiry of a certain number of years.'

In simple words, it may be defined as 'a contract whereby the insurance company, in consideration of periodical premium, agrees to pay a certain amount either on the death or on the maturity of the policy, whichever is earlier.

J. H. Maggee has defined life insurance in the following words: The life insurance contract embodies an agreement, in which, broadly stated, the insurer undertakes to pay a stipulated sum upon the death of the insured, or at some designated time to a designated beneficiary.

As such, under life insurance, the sum assured under policy is paid to the insured if policy matures during his life time and to his nominees in case of death. The premium may be paid in lump sum or in monthly, quarterly, half-yearly or yearly instalments.

15.2 FEATURES OF LIFE INSURANCE

1. Like other contracts of insurance, the life insurance contract is also the outcome of an offer made by the insured and its acceptance by the insurer. Usually, contract of life insurance is made in writing.
2. The insurance company agrees to pay a certain sum of money either on the death of the insured or on the maturity of the policy, whichever is earlier.
3. The insured is under obligation to pay periodically the amount of payment till the death of insured or expiry of the period of policy, whichever is earlier.
4. The contract of life insurance is not a contract of indemnity because the loss caused by the death cannot be calculated in money terms, nor is money any compensation for loss of one's life.

5. Insurable interest must be present in the person insured at the time when the policy is taken in case of life insurance, which may or may not be present at the time of insured's death.
6. Life insurance extends the hand of protection to those who are left support less and helps financially in case of death of the insured. It is also considered to be the best alternative for making savings.
7. Life insurance covers under scope certain other risks which are connected with the human life in addition to the risk of death. For example, in case of total and permanent disability or the living death, temporary disability and medical expenses, compulsory retirement or the economic death risks, etc., have also been covered under the purview of life insurance these days.
8. It relieves the insured from the sword of Damocles *i.e.* various risks and uncertainties which may occur before and after the death of the insured.

15.3 NATURE OF INSURANCE

On the basis of present day economic environment, there are few basic needs for which life insurance is needed. The life insurance is concerned with the hazards that stand across the life of every person that is dying prematurely leaving dependent and that of living to old age without visible means of support.

(a) **Family Protection.** To protect the families from the economic hardships after the death of the bread-winner member of the family.

(b) **Investment of Savings.** Savings provide the new source of income when permanent earning stops and Life Assurance provide an immediate source of income for one's family on the death of an insured person prematurely.

(c) **Additional Way of Earnings.** It provides an insured additional earning by way of bonus and interest credited by the Life Insurance Corporation.

(d) **Helpful at the Time of Cessation of Earnings.** Life Assurance is needed because when one ceases to earn money, insurer provides certain sum of money to the insured as per various terms of policies.

So the fundamental principle of life insurance is to save a person from uncertainties like premature death, old age, etc.

15.4 BENEFITS OF LIFE INSURANCE

The following are the advantages of Life Insurance:

1. Superior Saving Plan : Unlike any other savings plan, a life insurance policy affords full protection against risk of death. In the event of death of a policyholder, the insurance company makes available the full sum assured to the policyholders' near and dear ones In comparison, any other savings plan would amount to the total savings accumulated till date. If the death occurs prematurely, such savings can be much lesser than the sum assured. Evidently, the potential financial loss to the family of the policyholder is sizable.

2. Encourage Saving Habits : Life Insurance encourages saving habits. Long-term savings can be made in a painless manner because of the easy instalment facility built into the scheme. The insured person can pay premiums through monthly, quarterly, half-yearly or yearly instalments. The salary saving scheme, popularly known as SSS; provides a convenient method of paying premium each month through deduction from one's salary. The employer is authorized by the employee to deduct the insurance premium monthly and remit to the life insurance corporation. The Salary Saving Scheme (SSS) can be introduced in any institution or organisation subject to specified terms and conditions laid down by insurer.

3. Suitable for Raising Loans : Life Insurance policy can be given as security to raise a loan even for commercial purposes also. The loan can be raised without any delay on safe security of the policy. Even after an initial period payments if the policy holder finds it difficult to continue with the payment of premium, he can surrender the policy for a surrender value amount with the Life Insurance Corporation

4. Easy Settlement Protection Against Creditors : The maturity value of Life Insurance policy can be protected against the claims of the creditors of the life assured by valid assignment of a policy. The policy holder can nominate a person to whom the policy money would be payable in event of his death.

5. Tax Relief : The Income Tax relief is available for amounts paid by way of premium for life insurance subject to the income tax rates in force. Assesses can avail themselves of provisions in the law for tax relief. In this manner, the assured is required to pay lower premium for his insurance than he would have to pay otherwise. Under Section 80C of the Income Tax Act, 1956, the premium paid is allowed as a deduction from Gross Total Income (GTI). Contribution to pension plans qualifies for deduction under section 80CCC. Also 100% of the premium paid is deductible as expenditure from business income. When these benefits are factored in, it is found that most policies offer returns that are comparable/or even better than other saving modes such as PPF, NSC *etc.* Moreover, the cost of insurance is a very negligible.

6. Estate Duty : Life Insurance ensures the definite sum of money after the death of the insured without resorting to sale of assets at a loss on realization. So it is the best way of making provision for payment of Estate Duty.

7. Economic Protection : Life Insurance provides economic protection to the family members of the insured in case of his untimely death who might be the sole bread-earner of the family. It reduces the sufferings of the families on happening of a contingent event. It is considered to be the most effective devise for providing family security.

8. Investment Element : In Life Insurance, the insured is required to pay the premium. The premium is a kind of investment. The premium is returned to the insured along with additional bonus amount after the expiry of the period of contract.

9. Helpful to the Government : Life Insurance provides long-term funds to the government for different development schemes. This helps the government to develop infrastructure to develop infrastructure and serve the society.

10. Money when Needed : A suitable insurance plan or a combination of different plans can be taken out as life insurance to meet the specific needs that are likely to arise in future, such as children's education, start-in-life or marriage provision, etc. Alternatively, policy money can be so arranged to be made available at the time of one's retirement from service to be used for any specific purpose, such as for the purchase of plot, house or for other investments. Loans are also granted to the policy holders, subject to certain conditions, for house building or for purchase of flats, etc.

11. Ready Marketability and Suitability for Quick Borrowing : A life insurance policy can, after a certain time period (generally three years), be surrendered for a cash value. The policy is also acceptable as a security for a commercial loan, for example, a student loan. It is particularly advisable for housing loans when an acceptable LIC policy may also cause the lending institution to give loan at lower interest rates.

12. Disability and Accidental Death Benefits : Death is not the only hazard that is insured; many policies also include disability benefits. Typically, these provide for waiver of future premiums and payment of monthly installments spread over certain time period. Many policies can also provide for an extra sum to be paid (typically equal to the sum assured) if death occurs as a result of accident.

Life Insurance Players in India

The year 2000 was a defining movement in the history of Indian Insurance Industry. For the first time, the sector was opened up to private companies. Now we find a number of private insurance companies entered into the Indian insurance market. If the FDI is raised from 26% to 49%, the number will be multiplied. Following are the private insurance players in the life insurance sector of insure.

1. Bajaj Allianz Life Insurance Company Limited
2. Birla Sun Life Insurance Co. Ltd.
3. HDFC Standard Life Insurance Co. Ltd.
4. ICICI Prudential Life Insurance Co. Ltd.
5. ING Vysya Life Insurance Co. Ltd.
6. Max New York Life Insurance Co. Ltd.
7. Met Life Insurance Co. Ltd. Pvt. Ltd.
8. Kotak Mahindra Old Mutual Life Insurance Limited
9. SBI Mutual Life Insurance Limited
10. Tata AIG Life Insurance Co. Ltd.
11. Reliance Life Insurance Co. Ltd.
12. Aviva Life Insurance Co. Ltd. Pvt. Ltd.
13. Sahara Life Insurance Co. Ltd.
14. Shriram Life Insurance Co. Ltd.
15. Bharti Life Insurance Co. Ltd.
16. Future Generali Life Insurance Co. Ltd.
17. IDBI Fortis Life Insurance Company Ltd.
18. Canara HSBC Oriental Bank of Commerce Life Insurance Company Ltd.
19. Aegon Religare Life Insurance Company Ltd.
20. DLF Pramerica Life Insurance Company Ltd.

15.5 LIFE INSURANCE DEMAND AND OUTLOOK

Life insurance sector has started acquiring new shapes with newer innovations in the post liberalisation era. Big brands like Birla, Tata, ICICI, HDFC etc. have tied up with foreign partners. The life insurance has been the baby of LIC of India, primarily because of its monopoly till privatisation. Even though the growth has been impressive over years, yet the penetration is pretty low. Let us have a look at the life insurance average index. The number of policies sold is very low *viz.*, 13.2 per 100 persons compared to the Asian counterparts like Malaysia and Japan where it is 37.0 and 201.4 respectively.

The life insurance premium as a percentage of GDP is very low and which is expected in improve in coming years indicating a vast potential for the players.

The expected demand as per research studies show a vast potential to the extent of 650 million estimated for 2005. The key reasons for the optimistic outlook can be described on two accounts:

From the View Point of Investment

1. The life insurance sector has demonstrated in the past, its commitment to provide a steady and secured return compared to other forms of investments.
2. The life insurance premiums offer tax incentives, which have been continuing since long. However, Kelkar Committee recommendations have posed a threat. Yet these have not been implemented.
3. The life investments have proved least risk options compared to stock markets where investors in one form or other have burned hands including the UTI fiasco.

From Social Angle

1. The change in lifestyle and attitudes, shift to nuclear family system have urged the need for insurance.
2. The increasing literacy rate has resulted in channeling of financial resource from savings to financial assets.
3. The life insurance covers can be used as collateral security for obtaining loans, which positively affected the demand for life products.
4. The young population ratio is the highest in India, which is likely to drive the demand for insurance.

From Macro-economic Angle

1. The average annual percentage growth of GDP is approximately 5% (Exhibit 1C).
2. The infant mortality rate is improving *viz.*, 61.467 deaths/1000 live births compared to past (Exhibit 1C)
3. The middle class is expanding and its per capita income is growing.
4. The percentage of financial assets in household savings is growing *viz.*, in 2000-01 it was 11% of the total household savings of 20.9%.

In addition to above, the private players and, also, LIC are coming out with new and innovative products which are likely to attract the potential customers.

Life business development by region

Real growth rates	*Growth rate 2007*	*Annual average growth rate 1997-2006*
Region		
World	5.3%	4.3%
Industrialised countries	4.6%	3.8%
North America	5.3%	3.8%
Western Europe	5.5%	6.9%
Japan and newly industrialised Asian economies	1.8%	0.3%
Oceania	7.9%	1.6%
Emerging markets	13.1%	13.5%
South and East Asia	16.8%	19.3%
Latin America and Caribbean	11.4%	10.4%
Central and Eastern Europe	17.0%	7.6%
Africa	3.4%	7.5%
Middle East and Central Asia	8.7%	5.8%

Life insurance growth, penetration and density by region

	Premiums (in USDmn) 2007	*Real growth 2007*	*Share of world market (in %) 2007*	*Premiums in % of GDP 2007*	*Premiums per capita (in USD) 2007*
America	659,759	6.1	27.57	3.53	732.3
North America	623,950	5.8	26.07	4.09	1,869.3
Latin America and Caribbean	35,809	11.4	1.50	1.04	63.1
Europe	1,035,942	5.6	43.29	5.00	1,222.6
Western Europe	1,017,881	5.5	42.53	5.68	2,014.0
Central and Eastern Europe	18,062	17.0	0.75	0.68	55.5
Asia	623,469	4.3	26.05	4.61	156.7
Japan and newly industrialised Asian economies	493,567	1.8	20.62	8.02	2,331.6
South and East Asia	124,136	16.8	5.19	2.15	35.9
Middle East and Central Asia	5,766	8.7	0.24	0.36	18.7
Oceania	35,807	7.9	1.50	3.42	1,071.4
Africa	38,111	3.4	1.59	3.08	39.6
World	2,393,089	5.4	100.00	4.41	358.1
Industrialised countries	2,174,313	4.7	90.86	5.42	2,142.6
Emerging markets	218,776	13.1	9.14	1.45	38.4
OECD	2,105,446	4.2	87.98	5.10	1,738.7
G7	1,681,968	3.7	70.28	5.51	2,304.5
EU, 15 countries	975,158	5.6	40.75	5.94	2,376.1
NAFTA	631,603	5.8	26.39	3.91	1,434.4
ASEAN	26,988	16.7	1.13	2.16	53.8

Source: Swiss Re, Economic Research & Consulting, sigma No. 4/2007

Life insurance growth, penetration and density by region

	Premiums (in USDmn)	*Real growth*	*Share of world market (in %)*	*Premiums in % of GDP*	*Premiums per capita (in USD)*
	2006	*2006*	*2006*	*2006*	*2006*
America	601,784	4.2	27.24	3.44	672.6
North America	572,860	3.8	25.93	3.95	1,731.8
Latin America and Caribbean	28,923	14.1	1.31	0.98	51.3
Europe	940,586	12.4	42.57	5.30	1,119.6
Western Europe	927,431	12.3	41.98	5.95	1,862.9
Central and Eastern Europe	13,154	19.2	0.60	0.64	40.3
Asia	602,266	3.6	27.26	5.00	154.6
Japan and newly industrialised Asian economies	500,871	0.6	22.67	8.38	2,368.4
South and East Asia	96,627	23.6	4.37	2.06	28.6
Middle East and Central Asia	4,769	5.3	0.22	0.34	15.8
Africa	35,468	21.6	1.61	3.40	38.3
Oceania	29,214	6.1	1.32	3.36	896.3
World	2,209,317	7.7	100.00	4.48	330.6
Industrialised countries	2,033,051	6.6	92.02	5.53	2,026.0
Emerging markets	176,266	21.1	7.98	1.42	31.6
OECD	1,976,063	6.6	89.44	5.24	1,645.0
G7	1,609,706	6.8	72.86	5.66	2,225.7
EU, 15 countries	887,928	12.8	40.19	6.20	2,197.8
NAFTA	579,674	4.0	26.24	3.78	1,320.1
ASEAN	20,299	2.5	0.92	1.96	41.4

Key Terms

- Insurance Coverage Index
- Life Fund
- Technical Account
- Sum Assured
- Revenue Account
- Shareholder's Account

Questions for Review

1. Enumerate the advantage of life insurance to individuals.
2. Evaluate the performance of life insurance sector in the pre and post-liberalisation period.

Suggested Readings

- G.R. Desai, *Life Insurance in India — Its History and Dimensions of Growth,* Macmillan India Ltd., 1973.
- *Insurance Business Environment,* Insurance Institute of India, Mumbai.
- IRDA Annual Report 2001-02.
- R.M. Ray, *Life Insurance in India,* Indian Institute of Public Administration, New Delhi, 1982.
- S.R. Chawla, *Attitude Towards Life Insurance Cover,* NCAER, New Delhi, 1979.
- *Tryst with Trust — A History of Life Insurance,* Life Insurance Corporation of India, 1991.

Web Resources

- www.licindia.com
- www.best-life-insurance-online.com
- www.myiris.com
- www.irdaindia.org

Life Insurance Contracts & Policy Provisions

Chapter 16

Chapter Objectives

After reading this chapter you will be able to understand :

- *Components of a Life Insurance Contract*
- *Procedure for Issuing a Life Insurance Policy*
- *Contractual Provisions Of Life Insurance*
- *Major Policy Alterations*
- *Nomination and Assignment*
- *Revival of Lapsed Policies*
- *Provision of Loan against Policy*
- *Foreclosure of a Policy*

16.1 Basic Components of a Life Insurance Contract

A life insurance policy expresses the terms of contract between the insurer and the insured. The policy document should reveal (*i*) the definition of the risk covered, (*ii*) the duration of the risk, (*iii*) the premium, and (*iv*) the amount of insurance (Ref. Law of Insurance Macgillvary). The policy, however, states rights and privileges of the insured person and his obligations as well. The policy documents will have standardised and printed conditions. Any variation will be provided by suitable endorsements placed on the policy. The life policy contains the following details:

(*a*) **'Heading'** contains the name and address of the Insurer. This also indicate the jurisdiction in cases of legal disputes and also the address where any notices can be served by the Insured against the company.

(*b*) **'Preamble'** states the intention of the parties to the contract in brief and general terms. It introduces both the parties. The receipt of the proposal and declaration as well as the first premium from the proposer are acknowledged. The statement and declarations contained in the proposal and personal statement are stated to be the basis of the agreement.

(c) **'Operative Clause'** mentions the mutual responsibilities and obligations of both the parties as follows :

(*a*) In consideration of payment of the first premium and subsequent premiums as an when they fall due (the payment of premiums is made a condition precedent for performance of the contract by the insurer).

(*b*) The insurer agrees to pay the benefits secured under the policy including bonus in respect of participating policies.

(*c*) On receipt of proof satisfactory to the company.

(*i*) The happening of event on which the benefits are payable,

(*ii*) The title of the person claiming payment.

(*iii*) Age of the life assured, if not already admitted.

(*d*) **'Proviso'** contains two stipulations : (*a*) the conditions and privileges printed on the back of the policy shall be deemed to be a part of the Policy and (*b*) every endorsement placed evidencing alterations etc., shall be deemed to be part of the policy.

(e) **'Schedule'** contains details of the particular contract. The details can be classified as follows:

(a) *Identifying the policyholder :* policy number, date of commencement, date of proposal, name and address of the proposer and life assured.

(b) *Scope of Cover :* plan and term of insurance, sum assured, date of maturity, events on the happening of which the benefits become payable, any additional benefits like accident benefit.

(c) *To whom the sum assured is payable :* specific information and also Name of nominee.

(d) *Premium :* the installment premium, due dates, mode of payment of premium, period during which premiums are payable, dates on last premium.

(e) *Age :* age of the life assured and whether the same has been admitted.

(f) Space for any special provisions.

(f) **'Attestation'** the policy should be stamped and then signed by an authorized official of the company.

(g) **'Conditions and Privileges'** these are usually printed on the back of the Policy Document and can be classified into following groups :

(a) *Conditions :* These explain the nature of the contract : like proof of age here mention is made that premium is calculated on the basis of age and if age has already not been admitted and subsequently proved to be higher than stated, the company reserves to modify any terms of the contract.

- *Forteiture in certain events :* Three events under which the benefits secured under the policy can be forfeited *viz.*, (1) non-payment or premiums subject to non-forfeiture privilege (2) in the event of any condition being contravened and (3) in case there has been untrue or incorrect statements regarding material facts subject to section 45 of insurance contract.
- *Suicide :* This condition stipulates that in the event of death due to suicide within one year from the commencement of risk, the policy shall be void.
- *Other restrictive clauses :* Certain clauses like extra premiums charged for temporary periods, Lien clause, excluding certain risks like accident and disability benefits to physically handicapped persons, pregnancy clauses, etc.,
- *Assignment and Nomination :* This condition merely stipulates that notice of assignment or nomination should be submitted for registration with the insurance company and in registering the notice, the company does not accept any responsibility or express any opinion as to its validity or legal effect.

(b) *Privileges :* Certain privileges are allowed under the policy. For example in payment of Premiums–days of grace allowed, (both in the event of death and when the policy is in force during the days of grace,) full sum assured will be paid subject to deduction of overdue premiums. This privilege also stipulates that in the event of death when the policy is in full force for the full sum assured, the unpaid premium, if any, due before the next policy anniversary will be deducted from the claim amount.

Revival of discontinued policies : A policy lapses if the premium due is not paid before the expiry of the days of grace. Subsequently, the policy can be revived subject to certain conditions, which may vary from company to company. These conditions for revival of a lapsed policy are stated in this privilege.

Non-forfeiture regulations : As per Insurance Act, 1938 a life insurance policy whereunder premiums have been paid for a continuous period of three years cannot wholly lapse by will have to acquire some value. This privilege is referred to as 'Non-forfeiture' regulation. The method of calculation of such value will have to be incorporated in the policy.

16.2 Basic Procedure for Issuing a Life Insurance Policy

Insurance is a contract as discussed earlier. Therefore, the process of life insurance starts with the proposal made by the prospective insured (called as the proposer) in a standard application form issued by insurance companies generally made available by agents. Once the policy has been selected, the proposer has to provide information about income, age and health. If there is a need for medical examination, the report of the medical examiner is sent to the insurance company confidentially. The agent or the development officer generally does a first level underwriting and a report thereon is sent to the company. This report provides information about the financial position and need and adequacy of insurance for the proposer. It also contains the information gathered by the agent/development officer from his personal sources or inquiries made on the basis of the information furnished by the proposer. Thereafter, the documents are scrutinised from various angles particularly age, financial condition and health status.

Age Proof

Scrutiny of age is an important concern for the life insurer because old age people have high probability of dying than the younger ones and premium is calculated on the basis of age groups. Accuracy in age computation resolves hardship both to the insurer and the potential insured in the sense that that correct age avoids the company being affected by lesser premiums or undesired risk bought or risk not bought because of fear. From the insured's perspective, it helps in charging of fair premiums and insurance availability. The proofs of age, which are generally considered are as under:

- Certified extract from municipal or other records made at the time of birth.
- Certificate of Baptism or certified extract from family Bible if it contains age or date of birth.
- Certified extract from School or College if age or date of birth is stated therein.
- Certified extract from Service Register in case of Govt. employees and employees of Quasi-Govt. institutions including Public Limited Companies and
- Passport issued by the Passport Authorities in India.

Alternative Age Proofs, which are also accepted in the industry, are:

- Marriage certificate in the case of Roman Catholics issued by Roman Catholic Church.
- Certified extracts from the Service Registers of Commercial Institutions or Industrial Undertakings provided it is specifically mentioned in such extracts that conclusive evidence of age was produced at the time of recruitment of the employee.
- Certificate of Birth granted by Syedna v. Molana Badruddin Sahib of Baroda.
- Identity Cards issued by Defence Department.
- A true copy of the University Certificate or of Matriculation/Higher Secondary Education, S.S.L. Certificate issued by a Board set up by a State/Central Government.
- Non-standard age proofs like Horoscope, Service Record where age is not verified at the time of entry, E.S.I.S. Card, Marriage Certificate in case of Muslim Proposer, Elder's Declaration, Self-declaration and Certificate by Village Panchayats are accepted subject to certain rules.

Medical Examination

Generally, at some levels and in case of endowment policies, whole life policies, the medical examination is not asked for. However, if the amount of insurance is very high or the age is high or the first level examination has some adverse remarks, then the insurance company may refer the proposal for a thorough examination. Cases of pregnant women, or women with history of miscarriages or abortion are declined. Some times the medical examination may be waived, like in rural areas, where the facilities are not available.

After the above examinations and obtaining special reports, if required, the underwriter may accept or reject the case. Else, he is empowered to modify the sum assured, premium to be charged and manner thereof, impose conditions or provide exclusions in the policy.

In case of untrue or incorrect statement contained in the proposal, personal statement, declaration and connected documents or any material information withheld, subject to the provision of Section 45 of the Insurance Act 1938, wherever applicable, the policy shall be declared void and all claims to any benefits in virtue thereof shall cease.

After the policy is issued, the policyholder in a number of cases finds the terms not suitable to him and desires to change them. LIC allows certain types of alterations during the lifetime of the policy. However, no alteration is permitted within one year of the commencement of the policy with some exceptions. The following alterations are allowed –

- Alteration in class or term
- Reduction in the sum assured
- Alteration in the mode of payment of premiums
- Alteration in the date of commencement of the policy
- Splitting up of a single policy into two or more policies
- Removal of an extra premium
- Alteration from without profit plan to with profit plan
- Alternation in name
- Correction in policies
- Settlement option of payment of sum assured by instalments
- Grant of accident benefit
- Grant of premium waiver benefit under CDA policies
- Alteration in currency and place of payment of policy monies.

A fee for the change or alteration in the policy is charged by the company called as the quotation fee and no additional fee is charged for giving effect to the alteration.

16.3 CONTRACTUAL PROVISIONS OF LIFE INSURANCE

Life Insurance policies contain numerous contractual provisions. The following are the major contractual provisions that the insurance consumers should understand.

(i) Ownership Clause
(ii) Entire–Contract Clause
(iii) In Contestable Clause
(iv) Suicide Clause
(v) Grace Period
(vi) Reinstatement Clause
(vii) Beneficiary Designation

(viii) Change of plan Provision
(ix) Exclusions and Restrictions
(x) Payment of Premium
(xi) Assignment Clause
(xii) Policy Loan Provision

(i) Ownership Clause: The owner of a life insurance policy can be the insured, the beneficiary, a trust or another party. In most cases, the applicant, insured, and owner is the same person. Under the ownership clause, the policy owner possesses all contractual rights in the policy while the insured is living. The policy also provides for a change of ownership. The policyholder can designate a new owner by filling an appropriate form with the company.

(ii) Entire–Contract Clause: The entire–contract clause states that the life insurance policy constitutes the entire contract between the parties. All statements in application (proposal) are considered to be representations rather than warranties. No statement can be used by the insurer to void the policy unless it is a material misrepresentation. In addition, no insurer can change the policy terms without the consent of the policy holder. There are two basic purpose of the clause. First, it presents the insurer from amending the policy without the knowledge or consent of the insured. Second, it protects the beneficiary because any statement made in the contract can not be used by the insurer to deny the claim unless the statement is a material misrepresentation.

(iii) Incondensable Clause: The incontestable clause states that the insurer can not contest the policy after it has been in force (generally) two years during the insured's life time. After the policy has been issued the insurer has two years to discover any irregularities in the contract. After this certain period, the insurer can not contest a death claim on the basis of a material misrepresentation, concealment, or fraud. For example, Mr. x aged 30 purchased a life insurance policy concealing the fact that he had high blood pressure and died after two years, i.e., after the expiry of the contestable period. Then the insurer must pay the claim. The purpose of the incontestable clause is to protect the beneficiary, if the insurer tries to deny payment of the claim years after the policy was issued. It is also useful to the insurer to detect the fraud. If the insured makes a fraudulent misstatement to obtain the insurance, the company has two years to detect the fraud.

(iv) Suicide Clause: The suicide clause states that if the insured commits suicide within a certain period (generally two years) after the policy is issued, the face amount of the insurance will not be paid, there may be only a refund of the premium paid. It the insured commits suicide after the period expires, the policy proceeds are paid just like any other claim. The time period may differ from policy to policy. In case of suicide, to deny the payment of the claim, the insurer must prove conclusively that the insured has committed suicide. By having a suicide clause, the insurer has some protection against the individual who wishes to purchase life insurance with the intention of committing suicide.

(v) Grace Period: A life insurance policy also contains a grace period during which the policy holder has a certain period of days/months to pay an overdue premium. The insurance remains in force during the grace period. If the insured dies within the grace period, the overdue premium is deducted from the policy proceeds. The policy holder may be temporarily short of funds or may have forgotten to pay the premium. In such cases, the grace period provides considerable financial flexibility and presents the policy from lapsing by giving the policy holder addition time to pay the overdue premium.

(vi) Reinstatement Clause: A policy may lapse, of the premium has not been paid by the end of the grace period. The reinstatement (revival) permits the owner to reinstate a lapsed policy. Revival is a fresh contract where in the insurer can impose fresh terms and conditions. To reinstate a lapsed policy, all overdue premium plus interest must be paid from their respective due dates; the policy must have not been surrendered for its cash values; The policy must be reinstated within a certain period (2 or 3 years). Since a substantial amount of money is required to reinstate a policy if the policy lapsed several years earlier, most lapse policies are not generally reinstated.

(vii) Beneficiary Designation: The beneficiary is a person who is designated to receive the proceeds of a life insurance policy. The beneficiary need not have an insurable interest in the insured's life. In many families, husband will name his wife and children as beneficiaries. The owner, however, may also be the beneficiary of the policy. The policy owner can change the beneficiary whenever it is desired. Life insurance policies provide that the interest of a beneficiary terminates, it the beneficiary dies before the insured. In such cases, the policy holder can name a new beneficiary.

(viii) Change of Plan Provision: Life insurance policies may contain a change – of – plan provision that allows policy holders to exchange their present policies for different contracts. Sometimes the original policy may no longer be appropriate, if the family needs and financial objective change. The purpose of this provision in to provide flexibility to the policy holder. If the change is from the original (existing) policy to a higher – premium policy, the policy holder must pay the difference between the policy reserve under the new policy and the policy reserve under the original policy. If the change from original policy to a lower – premium policy, the insurer refunds the difference in cash values under the two policies to policy holder.

(ix) Exclusions and Restrictions: Life insurance policies contain certain exclusion and restrictions. Suicide may be excluded only for the first two years. During war period, same insurer may insert a war clause in the policies, which excludes payment if the insured dies as a direct result of war. Military aviation may also be excluded or be covered only by paying an extra premium. Certain undesirable activities or hobbies of the insured such as auto racing, sky diving may, etc may also be excluded or covered only by payment of extra premium.

(x) Payment of Premium: Life insurance premium can be paid annually, semi – annually, quarterly or monthly. In term assurance, the premium is paid only once in a lump sum. Premium for a some policy will be different if one pays annually and another pays half yearly. For example, if the annual premium for a certain policy is Rs.1000, it does not mean that the quarterly remium will be Rs.250. It will be more than that. Because if the payment is paid other than annually, the policyholder must pay a carrying charge which may be relatively expensive when the true rate of interest is calculated.

(xi) Assignment Clause: The term 'Assignment' describes the situation in which one party transfers its rights and duties under a contract to another party. In many contractual situations, assignment of a contract is allowed. All ownership rights in the policy are transferred to a new owner. The insurer should be notified of the assignment with the written consent of the insured. A life insurance policy is freely assignable to another party, if the insurer is notified properly. A valid assignment of a life insurance policy does not change the life covered by the insurance, but it does change the party who may exercise the benefits of ownership such as naming a beneficiary

(xii) Policy Loan Provision: Life insurance policies contain policy loan provision that allows the policy holder to borrow the cash value. The interest rate may be stated in the policy. Interest on a policy loan must either be paid annually or added to the outstanding loan if not paid. If the loan is not repaid by the time the policy matures as death claim or expiry of term, the face amount of the policy is reduced by the amount of indebt ness. If the total indebt ness exceeds the available cash value of the policy, the policy could lapse. The major advantage of a policy loan is the relatively low rate of interest. However some policies are exempted from loan provision. (e.g.: term assurance ULIPS, etc).

16.4 ALTERATIONS

The policy document embodies the terms of the contract. These terms continue to operate throughout the currency of the policy unless modified by mutual consent of the parties to the contract, *viz.*, the policyholder and the insurer. Situations may arise where the policyholder may desire alterations in the terms of the contract to suit changed circumstances. For example, the policyholder may find it difficult to continue the payment of premiums for the original SA and may like to reduce the SA. Or he may ask for change of mode of payment of premium.

The types of alterations for which requests are normally made are :

(*a*) Alteration in plan or term
(*b*) Reduction in SA
(*c*) Change in mode of payment of premium
(*d*) Alteration in name
(*e*) Change of the nominee
(*f*) Removal of an extra premium.
(*g*) Splitting up of policy into two or more policies
(*h*) Alteration from without profit to with profit plan or vice versa
(*i*) Grant of accident benefit
(*j*) Settlement option of payment of SA by instalments
(*k*) Grant of premium waiver benefit
(*l*) Correction in policies (generally soon after commencement)

Alterations are considered if the policy is in force for the full SA. Alterations are not normally allowed in the first year of the policy, unless they be by way of correction or changes which do not affect the basic insurance contract, like change in addresses, change in nominations, etc.

While considering the request for alterations, the insurer tries to ensure that there is no "adverse selection" against the insurer. That is, the risk should not increase after alteration. Increased SA, increasing the term, change form endowment to anticipated endowment plan, are alterations that increase risk. For this reason, alterations are generally not allowed if they involve change.

(*a*) to a longer term
(*b*) extended the premium paying period
(*c*) from one plan of insurance to another that represents increased risk

Some alterations are made by suitable endorsements on the policy itself. A fresh policy document may be issued if the alterations are of a substantial nature. This will happen, for example, if the policy has to be split into two or more policies incorporating the desired alterations.

A fee is usually charged to effect alterations except in certain cases such as correction of mistakes. No fee is charged for alteration of frequency of mode of payment from quarterly to yearly or half yearly mode because such an alteration reduces the administrative work in servicing the policy. The fee is partly meant to cover expenses and partly to discourage frequency in alterations.

16.5 Issue of Duplicate Policy

A duplicate policy confers on its owner the same rights and privileges as the original policy. The following are the requirements for issuing a duplicate policy :

1. Insertion of an advertisement at the policyholder's cost in one English daily newspaper having wide circulation in the State where the loss is reported to have occurred. A copy of the Newspaper in which the advertisement appeared should be sent to the servicing office one month after its appearance. If no objection

has been lodged with LIC regarding the policy in question, a duplicate policy will be issued after complying further requirements, *i.e.*, Indemnity Bond and payment of charges for preparing duplicate policy and stamp fee.

2. However, the requirement of advertisement and Indemnity Bond may be dispensed with or modified in certain circumstances as given below :
   - loss of policy by theft
   - destruction of policy by fire
   - loss of policy while in custody of an office of government
   - mutilated or damaged policy
   - policy in torn and a part of it is missing
   - policy partially destroyed by white ants.

The need to have a duplicate policy also arises at the time of receiving Maturity Amount or Death Claim, to obtain Surrender Value/Loan and to obtain a Duplicate Policy in other cases.

16.6 NOMINATION

Nomination is the process of identifying a person to receive the policy money in the event of the depth of the Policyholder. Nomination can be done at the inception of the Policy by providing details of nominee in the proposal form. However, if the nomination is not given at the beginning, the policyholder can give it at a later date. This nomination has to be effected by giving notice in a prescribed form to the insurer and getting it endorsed on Policy Bond. Change of Nomination can be done by the Policyholder any time during the term of the Policy and any number of times. For this, the policyholder has to give a notice in a prescribed form to the insurer and get it endorsed at the back of the Policy.

Further, Nomination can be removed any time by the Policyholder without giving prior notice to the Nominee. Nomination can be done only by a policyholder, who is a major, and on a policy on his own life. Under Nomination, the Nominee gets only the right to receive the policy money in the event of the death of the Policyholder. Nomination does not pass on the property in the Policy. If Nominee dies when the Policyholder is still surviving then the nomination would be ineffective. Nomination has no effect if the Policyholder is surviving. If Nominee dies after the death of the policyholder but before receiving policy money, then also Nomination becomes ineffective and only the Legal Heirs of the Policyholder can claim money. In the case of Children's Policies, Nomination is not done until the Child becomes a major. Nomination is governed by Section 39 of Insurance Act 1938.

The nominee is statutorily recognised as a payee who can give a valid discharge to the Corporation for the payment of policy monies. Nomination will be incorporated in the text of the policy at the time of its issue. After the policy is prepared and issued and if no Nomination has been incorporated the assured can ordinarily affect the nomination only by an endorsement on the policy itself. A nomination made in this manner is required to be notified to the Corporation and registered by it in its records. A nomination is not required to be stamped. Any change or cancellation of nomination should be given in writing only by the Life Assured. Nomination under Joint Life Policy can only be a joint nomination. Nomination in favour of a stranger cannot be made as there is no insurable interest and moral hazard may be involved.

Nomination in favour of wife and children as a class is not valid. Specific names of the existing wife and children should be mentioned. Where nomination is made in favour of successive nominees, *i.e.*, nominee "A" failing him to nominee "B" failing whom nominee "C", the nomination in favour of one individual in the order mentioned will be considered. Where the nominee is a minor, an appointee has to be appointed to receive the monies in the event of the assured's death during the minority of the nominee. No nomination can be made under a policy financed from HUF funds. In the case of first endorsement of nomination the date of registration of nomination will be the date of receipt of the policy by the servicing office and in case of any other nomination or cancellation or change thereof, the date of receipt of the policy and/or of notice whichever is later, will be the date of registration.

16.7 ASSIGNMENT

Assignment is a means whereby the beneficial interest, right and title under a Policy gets transferred from Assignor to Assignee. 'Assignor' is the Policyholder who transfers the title, and 'Assignee' is the person who derives the title from the Assignor. Assignment can be made only after acquiring the Policy. Assignment can be done only for consideration–for money or money's worth or goods, moral and meritorious consideration, like Love and Affection. Assignment can be made by mere endorsement on the Policy or by a separate duly stamped Deed. Assignment can be done by the Proposer, Policyholder or the Absolute Assignee. Assignor must be a major, and must have an absolute right over the Policy. Assignment must be in writing and the Assignor's signature along with a Witness is a must. Notice of Assignment should be submitted to the insurer. There are two types of assignments:

1. *Conditional Assignment* whereby the assignor and the assignee may agree that on the happening of a specified event which does not depend on the will of the assignor, the assignment will be suspended or revoked wholly or in part. Conditional Assignment is usually effected for consideration of natural Love and Affection.
2. *Absolute Assignment* whereby all the rights, title and interest which the assignor has in the policy passes on to the assignee without reversion to the assignor or his estate in any event. Absolute Assignment is usually effected for valuable consideration.

On Assigning the Policy, the Assignor loses his right over the Policy and the Assignee gets the right and becomes the owner of the Policy. The Assignee can further re-assign the Policy and he also has a right to sue under the Policy. A valid assignment once made cannot be cancelled. It can be done only by another valid assignment. In all the cases, Assignment automatically cancels an earlier Nomination. However, when the Policy is assigned to the insurer say for loan, Nomination gets affected and it does not get cancelled. Under Conditional Assignment, if the conditional Assignee dies, the benefit under the Policy goes back to the Life Assured if surviving. Otherwise, the benefit goes to Policyholder's Nominee. Under Absolute Assignment, if the Absolute Assignee dies, the benefits under the Policy go to the Legal Heirs of the Assignee. Assignment is governed by Section 38 of Insurance Act, 1938.

An assignment has an effect of directly transferring the rights of the transferor in respect of the property transferred. Immediately on execution of an assignment of the Policy of life assurance the assignor forgoes all his rights, title and interest in the Policy to the assignee. The premium/loan interest notices etc. in such cases will be sent to the assignee. In case the assignment is made in favour of public bodies, institutions, trust etc., premium notices/receipt will be addressed to the official who has been designated by the institutions as a person to receive such notice.

An assignment of a life insurance policy once validly executed, cannot be cancelled or rendered in effectual by the assignor. Scoring of such assignments or super scribing words like 'cancelled' on such assignment does not annul the assignment. And the only way to cancel such assignment would be to get it re-assigned by the assignee in favour of the assignor.

Re-assignment

An assignee may during the currency of the policy re-assign the interest in the policy to the previous assignor, such reassignment will have the effect of cancelling the assignment and the interest title of the policy revert to the previous assignor.

16.8 LAPSE AND REVIVALS

Where the premium is not paid on the due date or within the days of grace, the policy lapses but it can be revived at any time during the remaining period of the policy, subject to medical evidence and arrears of premium along with interest thereon at the applicable rate. If the policy has lapsed within 3 years of the date of commencement it is not entitled to any claims' concession, except days of grace, usually 30 days. As per IRDA guidelines details all those policies who have lapsed is required to be submitted within stipulated time to IRDA.

Revivals

If the premium under a policy is not paid within the days of grace, the policy lapses. Revival is a fresh contract wherein the insurer can impose fresh terms and conditions. In case of LIC, a lapsed policy can be revived within 5 years from the date of first unpaid premium. A policy can be revived under the following types of revival:

1. Ordinary Revival

If a revival of the policy is effected within 6 months from the due of first unpaid premium, no personal statement regarding health is required and the policy is revived on collection of delayed premium plus interest. The rate of interest to be charged for such delayed premium will depend on the date of commencement of the policy.

2. Revival on Non-medical Basis

For revival of the policy on non-medical basis, the amount to be revived should not exceed the prescribed limit for non-medical assurance taken by the life assured.

3. Revival on Medical Basis

If a policy cannot be revived under ordinary revival or revival on non-medical basis it can be revived with medical requirements. The medical requirements will depend upon the amount to be revived.

4. The Other Schemes for Revival are :

- Special Revival Scheme
- Revival by instalment
- Loan-cum-revival
- Survival Benefit-cum-revival

Special Revival Scheme : If the policy was in force for at least 6 months and has not acquired surrender value, the policy may be revived where the original date of the policy is shifted by the period for which the policy was in force. A fresh policy was will have to be issued for the age as on that date. The arrears of premiums will be a nominal amount. The cost of the preparation of the policy will have to be borne by the policyholder.

Special Revival Scheme : If the policy was in force for at least 6 months and has not acquired surrender value, the policy may be revived where the original date of the policy is shifted by the period for which the policy was in force. A fresh policy will have to be issued for the age as on that date. The arrears of premiums will be a nominal amount. The cost of the preparation of the policy will have to be borne by the policyholder.

Revival by Instalment : The policyholder, in that case, can pay arrears of premium by suitable instalments, which should be paid alongwith regular premiums. *The unpaid instalments of premiums are treated as a debt/ charge against the policy.*

Loan cum Revival : If the lapsation period is long, the arrears of premiums could be a very substantial amount, the insurer offers a Loan-cum-Revival scheme, provided the policy has acquired surrender value, notionally on the date of revival.

16.9 POLICY LOANS

Most of the insurance companies give privilege to the policyholder to obtain loans on certain policies subject to certain rules. The policyholder has to apply for a loan in a prescribed form and submit the Policy Bond along with the form duly completed. The loan amount is calculated depending on the Surrender Value (SV) that the policy would have acquired, and approximately 85% of the Surrender Value are given as loan. Loans can also be perceived as riders offered by some private insurance companies. Rate of interest charged on loans taken on insurance policies varies from company to company and from time to time. A policyholder can repay the loan amount either in part of in full, any time during the term of the Policy. For LIC, the minimum repayment should be Rs. 50 and thereafter in multiples of Rs. 10. If the loan amount is not repaid during the term of the Policy or early claim, the amount of loan plus interest, if any, will be deducted from the claim money payable and the balance amount will be paid to the claimant. In case of LIC, if the interest is not paid regularly every half year, then the interest is calculated on compound interest basis. If the premiums are not paid regularly, that is, if the policy is not kept in force, there is a possibility that the loan amount along with accrued interest exceeds the surrender value. At that stage, foreclosure action is taken on the policy.

Generally, plans for Children or special plans like Jeevan Griha and Deferred Annuity/Pension Plans as well as Money Back Plans etc. are not eligible for loans. The requirement for granting a loan are as under :

(*a*) Application for loan with an endorsement of terms and conditions of the loan is being placed on the policy.

(*b*) Policy to be assigned absolutely in favour of the Corporation.

(*c*) A receipt for the loan amount.

In case of LIC, the maximum loan amount available under the policy is 90% of the Surrender Value of the policy (85% in case of paid up policies) including cash value of bonus. The minimum period for which a loan can be granted is six months from the date of its payment. If repayment of loan is desired within this period the interest for the minimum period of six months will have to be paid. In case the policy becomes a claim either by maturity or death within six months from the date of loan, interest will be charged only upto the date of maturity/death.

16.10 FORECLOSURE

Foreclosure means the writing off the policy before its actual maturity. If the balance in the Individual Policyholders' Account falls below minimum stipulated amount, the Company may at any time foreclose and terminate the Policy. When a loan is granted under a policy, the life assured has an option to pay the interest or allow it to accumulate to be adjusted from the policy moneys payable when end the claim arises. This is possible only if the premiums are paid regularly and the policy remains in full force. If the insured defaults in the payment of premium and the surrender values are in adequate to meet the arrears of loan and interest, to service the principal loan and accumulated interest foreclosure may be adopted by the insurer.

1. Before taking a foreclosure action, the policyholder is requested to pay the arrears of loan interest. If he continues default, the policy is foreclosed, policy and surrendered to loan. The balance surrender value after adjusting the principal loan and outstanding loan interest paid to the policyholder. However a foreclosed policy may be reinstated.

2. It is possible to reinstate a foreclosed policy, if desired by the party, provided
    - if the outstanding loan interest with accumulated interest thereon is paid unto date, and
    - a satisfactory evidence of continued good health is provided.
3. The reinstatement of a foreclosed policy is not allowed if the balance surrender value has been paid to the policyholder because it is presumed that policyholder had accepted the foreclosure action.
4. Nomination ceases if there is foreclosure. If life assured dies before payment of the balance surrender value, the amount is not payable to the nominee, but only to the legal heirs of the decreased assured.

16.11 Married Women's Property (MWP) Act Policies

A Married Women's Property Act policy constitutes a trust in favour of the wife and for children and no separate assignment is necessary. The beneficiaries are fully protected from creditors except to the extent of any interest in the policy retained by the assured.

Section 5 : Married Woman May Effect Policy of Insurance

Any married woman may effect a policy of insurance on her own behalf and independently of her husband; and the same and all benefit thereof, if expressed on the face of it to be so effected, shall ensure as her separate property, and the contract evidenced by such policy shall be as valid as if made with an unmarried woman.

Section 6 : Insurance by Husband for Benefit of Wife

(1) A policy of insurance effected by any married man on his own life, and expressed on the face of it to be for the benefit of his wife, or of his wife and children, or any of them, shall ensure and be deemed to be a trust for the benefit of his wife, or of his wife and children, or any of them, according to the interest so expressed, and shall not, so long as any object of the trust remains, be subject to the control of the husband., or to his creditors, or form part of his estate.

When the sum secured by the policy becomes payable, it shall, unless special trustees are duly appointed to receive and hold the same, be paid to the Official Trustee of the [State] in which the office at which the insurance was effected is situate, and shall be received and held by him upon the trusts expressed in the policy, or such of them as are then existing.

And in reference to such sum he shall stand in the same position in all respects as if he had been duly appointed trustee thereof by a High Court, under Act No. XVII of 1864 to constitute an office of Official Trustee.

Nothing herein contained shall operate to destroy or impede the right of any creditor to be paid out of the proceeds of any policy of assurance which may have been effected with intent to defraud creditors.

(2) Notwithstanding anything contained in section 2, the provisions of sub-section (1) shall apply in the case of any policy of insurance such as is referred to therein which is effected-

(*a*) by any Hindu, Muhammadan, Sikh or Jain-

  (*i*) in Madras, after the thirty-first day of December, 1913, or

  (*ii*) in any other territory to which this Act extended immediately before the commencement of the Married Women's Property (Extension) Act 1959, after the first day of April, 1923, or

  (*iii*) in any territory to which this Act extends on and from the commencement of the Married Women's Property (Extension) Act, 1959, on or after such commencement;

(*b*) by a Buddhist in any territory to which this Act extends, on or after the commencement of the Married Women's Property (Extension) Act, 1959:

Provided that nothing herein contained shall affect any right or liability which has accrued or been incurred under any decree of a competent court passed :

(i) before the first day of April, 1923, in any case to which sub-clause (i) or sub-clause (ii) of clause (a) applies; or

(ii) before the commencement of the Married Women's Property (Extension) Act, 1959 (61 of 1959), in any case to which sub-clause (iii) of clause (a) or clause (b) applies.]

When taking a policy, the proposal form filled in by married women in slightly different from the normal proposal forms. A policy can be taken under the married women's property act. The act provides that married women may take a policy on her life or on the life of her husband exclusively for her owns benefit. In the case of single women proponent, sometimes a question is asked enquiring the status of the women—married or to be married, in order to determine the special risk incidental to childbirth. The proposal ends with the declaration to be signed by the proponent and the life proposed. While filling the form, if the beneficiary is absolute, signature of beneficiary is required in all cases. If life to be assured has not attained 18 years of age, a parent's or guardian's signature is required. Following documents are generally required:

- Age proof certificate
- Full medical report.
- Duly completed and signed proposal form.
- Family history record.
- If non-standard age proof, policyholders have to submit extra annexures signed by the proposer.
- Duly filled in agent's confidential report.
- Moral hazard report for sum proposed over Rs 0.1 mn. In all non-medical (general), cases, MHR is necessary irrespective of the sum assured.
- In case of married women, if the age proof contains the maiden name, a declaration giving her maiden name by way of a separate letter duly signed is a must.

A supplementary statement has to be made when the applicant is a Woman which includes the following particulars :

- *Name* : If married, state full maiden name.
- Husband's name and occupation
- How much assurance does he carry and in whose favour
- Document pertaining to property owned by the person
- Statement pertaining to annual income of the individual
- Statement stating dependents supported by the policyholder

The policy issued under this act must be on the life of a married man, and taken out by himself which therefore precludes the joint life policies or Children's Deferred Assurance policies under the act.

The proposer who appoints the trustee may reserve the power to revoke the appointment of trustee and appoint another. Also, no loan can be granted under this policy unless the proposer had while appointing the trustees, specifically authorised the trustees to obtain loan on the policy. The trustees also cannot surrender the policy.

Key Terms

- ❐ Preamble
- ❐ Operative Clause
- ❐ Proviso
- ❐ Schedule

- ❒ Attestation
- ❒ Forteiture
- ❒ Privileges
- ❒ Alterations
- ❒ Exclusions
- ❒ Assignment
- ❒ Foreclosure
- ❒ Conditions
- ❒ Suicide
- ❒ Warranties
- ❒ Grace Period
- ❒ Restrictions
- ❒ Nomination
- ❒ Policy Loan

Questions for Review

1. Write short notes on :
   (a) Conditions and Priviledges in Life Contract (b) Issue of Duplicate Policy
   (c) Married Women Property Act Policies
2. Can a life insurance policy once issued be altered? If yes, how and on what basis?
3. Distinguish between :
   (a) Nomination and Assignment (b) Surrender and Forecloser
4. Distinguish between 'Lapsed Policy' and 'Policy in Force'. What is the name of the process that alters a policy status from 'lapse' into 'in force'? Explain this process in detail.
5. What are the major contractual provisions in a life insurance contract?
6. What are the basic Components of a life insurance contract?
7. Explain the procedure of issuing a life insurance policy.
8. Why proof of age is an important concern for all life insurers? How an insurance company can verify the age proof?
9. Describe the provisions of a suicide clause in a life insurance policy. What protections does it provide to the insurer?
10. What do you mean by policy loan provision? When can a loan be given under a policy? How is loan amount determined?

Suggested Readings

- S.L. Kane, *Principles of Life Insurance,* Himalaya Publishing House, Mumbai, 2003.
- *Practice of Life Assurance,* IC02, Insurance Institute of India, Mumbai, 2003.
- *Practice of Life Assurance,* IC02, Insurance Institute of India, Mumbai.
- Robert I, Mehr, *Life Insurance — Theory and Practice,* Business Publications Inc. 1977.
- T.S. Mann, *Law and Practice of Life Insurance in India,* Deep and Deep, 1987.
- S.S. Huebner, Kenneth Block Jr. and Robert S. Clive, *Life and Health Insurance,* Pearson Edu. 2002.

Life Insurance Products

Chapter **17**

CHAPTER OBJECTIVES

After reading this chapter you will be able to understand :

- *Approaches to Valuation of Human Life*
- *Whole Life Policies*
- *Term Assurance*
- *Endowment Policies*
- *Other Policies Classified*

Life Insurance cover is needed by individuals for various purposes. The choice for a life insurance plan depends upon the need level of the individuals. These needs include the family protection, old age survival for self and dependents, needs for consequences of disability/mishappenings, diminution in the value of assets due to depreciation, inflation and other macro-economic factors. The amount that would be sufficient to satisfy the needs as mentioned and support any dependants for as long as they are in need of support can be estimated by some approaches discussed in following paragraphs.

17.1 APPROACHES TO VALUATION

Human Life Value Approach

The concept of Human life Value (HLV) helps us to arrive at a fairly estimated insurance needs for an earning individual who has to manage day to day maintenance, well being of all his dependants and also has to provide for financial, security in future to these dependents in case of his premature death, through a life insurance cover. The life cover purchased by the income earner is a substitute for the income stream, which may be discontinued on account of disability or an early death. Disability is presumed to be a total and permanent disability making the individual incapable of earning an income.

Economic Value

In terms of physical composition, the worth of a human body is nothing but from a earning capacity perspective, it may be millions of rupees. This earning power does not create any economic value unless its benefits are derived by a person or organization. Therefore a human life has an economic value when monetary value is derived during its existence.

In general the family of an earning individual is completely dependent on him for subsistence, for other comforts and amenities. Family's economic security is protected till the family head is able to continue the flow of income stream as a result of his productive efforts. Out of his present earnings, he also saves for creation of an estate in future to arrange for economic security to his dependants. This potential estate has also to be added to the present economic gain the family is getting. Thus, HLV of an individual is the economic value to his family.

$$H = (E - M) \times an$$

where H = Human Life Value

E = Earnings per annum

M = Charge for Maintenance + Tax Liability + Life Insurance Premium

an = Annuity Factor at a given rate of discount

N = The working period (Retirement age – Present age).

Multiple Approach

This method is a simpler approach leading to a rough estimate. According to this approach, the HLV is equal to a given multiple of current income. The resulting sum, when invested, is designed to produce an income similar to that earned at present. For example, if it were expected that the available interest rate would be 5.5 percent, then a multiple of around 10 times current salary would be invested (that is 5.5% × 10 = 55% of current salary). This approach is based on the assumption that every human being's efforts are directed towards fulfillment of basic physiological needs. The popular need hierarchy theory of Maslow suggests that physiological needs, safety needs and belongingness and love needs get the priority over esteem needs, self–actualizing needs and aesthetic needs. An earning individual has to provide for livelihood and well being of the family members dependent on him. The requirement for an individual in terms of various funds are: Adjustment fund, Clean up fund, Education fund, Marriage fund, Spouse fund, Mortgage Redemption fund, Retirement fund etc.

Capital Retention Approach

This method is similar to the need analysis approach. A minimum capital is assumed to be preserved for distribution to the legal heirs after the death of the individuals for their (heirs') survival.

17.2 Types of Policies

The two basic elements in a life insurance cover are (*a*) death cover and (*b*) risk cover. The insurance plans that provide only the death covers *i.e.* the benefits are paid on the death of the insured person are called as *Term Assurance Plans,* else, the plans under which the benefits are paid on the survival of the insured within a specified period are called as *Pure Endowment Plans.* All types of insurance covers are a mix of these basic elementary plans.

Classification based on time

(*a*) *Whole life :* Whole term, Limited term, Convertible

(*b*) *Term plans :* Limited, Convertible, Renewable

(c) *Endowment plans :* Pure, Joint, Double, Anticipated

Classification based on Premium Payment

1. Single premium policies
2. Level premium policies

Classification based on Claim Payment

(*a*) Fixed sum policies

(*b*) Annuity policies

Classification based on number of persons assured

(*a*) Single life

(*b*) Multiple life

Classification based on Participation in Profit

(*a*) With Profit Policies

(*b*) Without Profit Policies

In addition to above, there may be various categories of policies depends upon the riders attached or a specific purpose of the cover *e.g.* children education policy, marriage policy *etc.*

17.3 TERM LIFE POLICIES

This is simplest and the cheapest form of life insurance policy sold in the market today. The term insurance provides for life insurance protection for the selected term (period of years) only. In case the person (whose life is insured) dies during the term, the benefits are payable under the policy and in case of his survival till the end of the selected term the policy normally expires without any benefit becoming payable. Term insurance may be regarded as temporary insurance and is more nearly comparable with 'Property & casualty insurance' contract than the other forms of life insurance contracts.

For example, if a person insures his life under a 5 years term insurance contract, the insurer does not have any obligation to pay anything unless the person dies before the expiry of the 5-year term. All the premiums paid by the insured are considered to be fully earned by the insurer at the end of the term and the policy has no further value. Because of its nature, the premium for term insurance contracts is relatively low. Term insurance policies are also sold with convertibility, renewability or re-entry guarantees/options.

Convertibility is an option by which the policyholder can get his term insurance contract converted to some other type of life insurance contract before the expiry of the selected term without the need for additional medical examination.

Renewability is an option by which the policyholder can renew the contract for a further period of years without the need for fresh medical examination.

Re-entry option is one whereby a policyholder can continue the policy at the end of the selected term for a further period at a low rate of premium if he establishes his insurability to the satisfaction of the insurer, which commonly is affected by way of fresh medical examinations. If the potential insured cannot prove his insurability, he may get the cover at loaded prices *i.e.* by payment of extra premium.

Terminal Illness Benefit

Terminal illness is a condition where the medical practitioner attending to the life of the assured and a medical examiner duly authorized by the insurance company are of the opinion that the assured is likely to die as a result of the illness within a period of 6 months. Some insurers include an additional benefit under term insurance plans and provide for along with the basic benefits. Another type of covers may be where the insurer provide for a part of the sum assured upon the life assured getting afflicted by a terminal illness. The practice this terminal benefits is not very common. Based on the level of coverage the term insurance policies can be classified into the following types :

1. Level benefit term insurance
   (*a*) Level premium
   (*b*) Increasing (stepped) premium
2. Decreasing benefit term insurance
   (*a*) Mortgage redemption
   (*b*) Payer benefit rider

3. Increasing benefit term insurance
   (*a*) Constant growth
   (*b*) Index linked

Level benefit term insurance policies are those, where the coverage remains constant throughout the term of the insurance policy. The premium payable under the policy may be constant throughout the term or increasing every year with the increase in the insured's age.

Increasing benefit term insurance contracts are those where under the insurance coverage under the contract keeps on increasing periodically over the term. It can either increase at a pre-determined rate or may be index linked.

For example, a term insurance policy for a face value of Rs. 100,000 can start with a coverage for the face value for the first 5 years, can increased by 50% every five years, *viz.*, to Rs. 150,000 during the period from 6th to the 10th years, to Rs. 200,000 from the 11th to 15th years and so on. On the other hand, the insurance coverage under the policy can be linked to an external index like consumer price index or industrial production index and can increase alongwith the index.

Decreasing benefit term insurance policies are those under which the insurance coverage keeps decreasing with the passage of time and the most common among this type of policies is the Mortgage redemption insurance contracts. Here, the insurance policy is linked to a debt availed with the insurance coverage being equal to the outstanding loan at any point of time. As and when the loan is rapid in installments, the insurance coverage is reduced and becomes nil on liquidation of the loan. The payer benefit term insurance is mostly sold as rider (added benefit) to the insurance policies on the lives of minors or dependants. It provides for waiver of payment of premium under the insurance policy on the life of a dependant, upon the death of the parent or guardian on whose life the rider is issued. Hence the coverage is equal to the total balance of premium installments due under the policy of the dependent, which decreases, with the payment of each installment of premium.

17.4 Whole Life Insurance Policies

Whole life insurance policies are intended to provide life insurance protection over the lifetime of the assured. The essence of whole life insurance is that it provides for payment of the assured amount upon the insured's death regardless of when it occurs. Under whole life policies, the payment of the assured sum is a certainty in contrast to the term insurance contracts and obviously, the time of payment of the assured sum is an uncertainty.

Whole life policies can be either participating type or non-participating type. *Participating type policies* are those which are entitled to a share in the distributable surplus (profits) of the life insurance company, whereby the cash value of the policy can goes up, with the announcement of bonus/dividends. *Non-participating policies* have the benefit remaining the same throughout the life of the policy.

There can be the following types of whole life policies:

1. Ordinary whole life insurance
2. Limited payment whole life insurance
3. Convertible whole life insurance
4. Increasing whole life insurance

Ordinary Whole Life

These are plain vanilla type whole life policies, where the insured keeps paying the premium throughout his life and the benefits assured under the policy are payable to the beneficiaries upon the death of the life insured. Here again, based on the mortality assumptions used by the insurers, a certain maximum age is fixed, on survival of the life insured to that age, the policy will be treated as matured and the benefits assured under the policy will be paid to the policyholder in cancellation of the policy.

Limited Payment Life Policies

Here, though the benefits assured under the policy are payable only on the death of the life insured, the premium payment liability can be fixed at the option of the policyholder. He can choose at the outset the number of years he would like to pay the premium and based on that the quantum of premium payable under the policy is determined. Thereafter the premium has to be paid for the chosen term or till death of the insured, whichever is earlier. On completion of the chosen premium payment term, no further premium needs to be paid and the benefits assured under the policy will (including bonus/dividend declared after the premium paying term, if any) will be paid upon the death of the insure.

Convertible Whole Life Insurance

As the name suggests, these are whole life insurance policies with an option to the policyholder to convert them into endowment insurance policy at the expiry of a certain number of years, say 5 years. These are helpful to those people who have a need for a higher sum of insurance but temporarily cannot afford the premium for such a sum under endowment plan.

Increasing Whole Life Insurance Policy

As we have seen in case of term insurance policies, the cover under the whole life policies can also be subjected to a regular increase at a pre-determined level or linked to an external index. Thus the life insured can be provided with an insurance protection commensurate with the inflation level or increased needs.

Special Provision : Most of the insurers provide for payment of the benefits to the life insured himself on his reaching an advanced age, say 85 or 90. Also under plain vanilla Whole Life Policies, even though the conditions stipulate that the premium should be paid for life, insurers normally stop requiring payment of premium on the life insured reaching a selected advanced age, say 75 or 80.

The savings component that builds up in these policies arises because of the level premium system. In assessing the premium for the cover, the actuary has to estimate the expected investment return that will be achieved on the unused premium that builds up in the early years. This figure is always a conservative one to ensure that the premium charged generates sufficient funds to meet the losses when they arise. In practice, the actual return is usually higher and the surplus that accumulates is passes back to the policyholders by way of bonuses. The accumulated bonuses are paid, in addition to the sum insured, when the policy death benefit is paid.

It is possible for the full cost of insurance to be met by one single premium, instead of annual (or more frequent) premiums.

The benefits of whole of life policies include the capacity to terminate and cash in the policy; that is, they have a surrender value, and the capacity to borrow up to 90 percent of that cash value at very competitive interest rates. Many insurers also allow the facility of advancing premium payable from the cash value of the policy described above. Hence, as the cash value accumulates, it is possible to 'skip' a premium payment; the policy will only lapse once the unpaid premiums (plus interest) exceed the cash value.

One variant of whole life assurance contracts is that which provides for payment of a fixed sum of money on the life insured surviving periodic intervals of time from commencement of the policy. One such policy can typically provide for payment of say 10% of the original any time, the policy provides for payment of full sum insured without deduction of the survival benefit instalments. This kind of policy is called an anticipated whole life insurance policy.

This takes care of two different needs that a client may face, *viz.*, providing for the dependants of the insured in case of death and at the same time taking care of the intermittent financial needs of the client himself. This provides for family protection as well as liquidity for the breadwinner.

17.5 Endowment Insurance Policies

Unlike whole life, an endowment life insurance policy is designed primarily to provide a living benefit and only secondarily to provide life insurance. Therefore, it is more of an investment than a whole life policy. Endowment life insurance pays the face value of the policy either at the insured certain age or after a number of years of premium payment.

Endowment life insurance is a method of accumulating capital for a specific purpose and protecting the savings program. Many investors use endowment life insurance to fund anticipated financial needs, such as college education or retirement.

Premium for an endowment life policy is much higher than those for a whole life policy. Endowment policies are of various types of which a few are described as follows:

(*a*) *Pure Endowment :* Where the sum assured is payable to policyholders either on survival or death within the endowment period.

(*b*) *Joint Endowment :* Where the policy covers the risk on two or more lives under the single policy.

(c) *Marriage Endowment :* Where the policy is designed to meet the marriage financing needs of the family member of the policyholder.

Similarly, we have covers like education, children deferred endowment, double cover, triple cover, anticipated endowment policies *etc.*

(*i*) *Endowment Assurance Policy (with or without profits) :* The face value of the policy will be paid either on death of the insured during the period of insurance or on maturity if the insured survives up to the end of the term.

(*ii*) *Bhavishya Jeevan Policy (with profits) :* This is an Endowment Assurance under which premiums during the first five years will be very high and from the sixth year it will be scaled down to almost 1/3rd of the original premium. This is suitable to professionals with a limited going to the Gulf for employment.

(*iii*) *Jeevan Mitra (Double Cover or Triple Cover)* : This is a *with–profit* Endow-ment Assurance with risk coverage to the extent of twice or thrice the face value of the policy. On maturity, the face value of the policy is paid.

(*iv*) *Jeevan Griha (Double Cover or Triple Cover) :* This is a low cost, *without profit* Endowment Assurance. Risk coverage will be twice or thrice the face value of the policy. The face value of the policy is paid in maturity. This plan is most suitable as collateral security for housing loans.

(*v*) *New Jana Raksha (with profits) :* This is an Endowment Plan suitable for people in Rural Areas. After payment of at least two years' premiums, risk is covered for the next 3 years *even if premiums are not paid.* Agriculaturists who depend on the vagaries of nature find this policy very attractive.

(*vi*) *Jeeven Shree (without profits but with guaranteed addition) :* This is an Endowment Assurance, with limited premium paying period, suitable to the *Top End* of the society. The minimum sum assured under this policy is Rs. 5 lakh. The LIC of India allows Key Man Insurance under this plan only.

(*vii*) *Asha Deep II (with profits)* : This is basically an Endowment Assurance plan with a rider to cover four serious illnesses *viz.*, cancer, paralytic stroke leading to permanent disability, kidney failure (both kidneys) and cardiac bye–pass surgery. In case the insured is affected by any one of the above conditions in any year except the first year of the policy, LIC of India (a) pays 50% of the sum assured immediately (b) waives payment of all further premiums (c) pays an annuity of 10% of sum assured till date of maturity and (d) pays the balance of 50% of Sum Assured on death or on maturity with bonus.

Marriage Endowment or Education Annuity (with–profits) : This is an Endowment Assurance, *no immediate payment is made.* Payment in lump sum (in case of Marriage Endowment) and payment in half-yearly installments spread over a period of 5 years (in case of Education Annuity) are arranged on/from date of maturity only. Several benefits are available on maturity.

Money Back Plans : These are all basically Endowment Assurance Policies. But the face value of the policy is paid in installments on survival of the insured at the end of fixed terms during the period of insurance, the balance of the face value of the policy being made available on maturity. In case of death during the period of insurance, the total sum assured (without deducting any survival benefits already paid) will be made available to the beneficiaries. For example, under a 20 year Money Back Policy, on survival of the insured at the end of the 5th year, 10th years and 15th years of the Policy, 20% of sum assured is paid on each occasion. These are called Survival Benefits. The balance of 60% of sum assured along with bonus is paid on maturity. In case of death of the insured any time during the 20 year period, full sum assured along wit accrued bonus is paid without deducting any survival benefits already paid.

Money Back (20 years, 25 years), Jeevan Surabi, Jeevan Sanchay are all different types of Money Back Plan. Jeevan Sneha is a special type of Money Back Plan designed for females. For children also, LIC of India offers a separate Money Back Policy.

Special Plans

(*i*) *For children :* LIC of India has designed several products for children. Children Deferred Assurance Plans, New Children Deferred Assurance Plan, Jeevan Balya, Jeevan Kishore, Children's Money Back Plan, etc. For girls specially, Jeevan Sukanya is offered.

(*ii*) *For the benefit of disabled children :* Parents can take either Jeevan Aadhar or Jeevan Vishwas Policies. In respect of both the policies, exemption from Income Tax is available up to an annual premium of Rs. 20,000 subject to certain conditions.

(*iii*) Jeevan Aadhar is limited payment whole life policy on the life of the parent. On the death of the Parent, 20% of the face value of the policy is immediately paid and the balance of 80% will be converted into annuity payable monthly to the disabled child.

Jeevan Vishwas is an Endowment Policy. Wither on the death of the parent or on maturity of the policy, benefits similar to the Jeevan Aadhar Policy are available to the disable child.

Medical Benefits

LIC has designed a policy by the name *Jeevan Asha* II.

This is an Endowment Assurance with a medical benefit rider. 2% of the face value of the policy is paid every two years (at the option of the insured) to enable the policy owner to have regular medical check–ups. The first such payment is made after three years. Twice during the period of insurance, LIC reimburses expenses up to for 20% to 50% of face value of the policy minor or major surgeries. On death the full sum assured. On maturity of the policy, sum assured less any payments made during the period of insurance is paid.

Joint Life Policies

These are also a kind of Endowment Insurance Products :

(*a*) Jeevan Saathi is a Joint Life Assurance for husband and wife. During the period of insurance, on death of one life, the insurer pays the face value of the policy but subsequently risk coverage continues on the second life till the date of maturity. Premiums payable from the date of death of first life are waived. On maturity or on death of second life, if earlier, face value of the policy is paid.

(*b*) Jeevan Saritha is also a Joint Life Assurance for husband and wife but provides benefit of joint life and last survivorship annuity also apart from lump sum payment on death or maturity.

17.6 ANNUITIES

Annuity Policies

Annuity is a contract that provides an income for a specified period of time.

Annuity schemes are those wherein policyholders regular contributions over a period of time (or a one-time contribution) accumulate to form a corpus with the insurer. The corpus is used to yield a regular income that is paid to policyholders until death starting from the desired retirement age. Some annuity schemes have the option to pay the survivors a lump sum amount upon the death of insured in addition to the regular income while the insured is alive.

For example : Jeevan Dhara and Jeevan Akshay plans currently offer a guaranteed return of 12.5% and 10% respectively in addition to life cover.

Life insurance contracts in simple form are different from the annuity contracts in the sense that the insurer pays in the even of the death of insured in a life insurance contract, while in an annuity contract the insurer stops paying upon the death of the insured.

Annuities are of the following types :

- **Immediate :** An immediate annuity provides income for a guaranteed period of time. Payments begin within one year of purchase. Income payments can either be for life, for a specified number of years or a combination of both.
- **Deferred :** In the case of a deferred annuity, the payments to the annuitant start after a certain deferment period. A deferred annuity is made with either a single purchase payment (Single Premium Deferred Annuity) or several purchase payments over time (Flexible Premium Deferred Annuity). A deferred annuity can be converted into a stream of income at any time after 12 months.
- **Fixed :** A fixed annuity assures minimum rate of return.
- **Variable :** A variable annuity offers a variety of investment fund account portfolios, including growth-oriented portfolios that can help you keep up with inflation. Variable annuity values and income payments may vary based on the underlying performance of the selected portfolio.

Benefits of Annuities

- Helps accumulate long term savings.
- Helps maximize income in retirement
- Provides lifetime of regular income source
- Tax benefits u/s 88 of the Income Tax Act, 1961
- Benefits the beneficiary on the death of the annuitant.

However there is a cost involved if the insured wants to get out of the annuity before a certain specified time.

Options in Annuity

Single life annuity : The annuitant receives income payments for the rest of his/her life.

Single life with period certain : The annuitant receives income for the rest of his or her life. If the annuitant dies before receiving a specific number of payment (period certain), the beneficiary will receive income for the remainder of the period; thus, a minimum number of payments are guaranteed.

Joint and Survivor : The annuitant and the designated joint annuitant will receive income for the rest of their lives. Upon the death of the annuitant, payments would continue to the joint annuitant at a percentage of the original level as selected by the annuitant at the time the income option was chosen.

Joint and survivor with period certain : The annuitant and the designated joint annuitant will receive income for the rest of their lives. If the annuitant and his or her joint annuitant die before a specific number of payments, the beneficiary will receive income for the remainder of the period certain.

17.7 Policies Based on Other Classifications

17.7.1 Premium Payment

The following important policies are issued by the Corporation on the basis of premium payment.

(i) Single Premium Policy: Single Premium Policy is useful to those who desire to provide the whole premium in one installment at the time of taking the policy. Single Premium Policy becomes matured on the assured's death or on his attainment of selected term whichever occurs earlier.

(ii) Level Premium Policy: Unlike single premium policy, under this policy premiums are payable on a regular basis for a selected term or till prior death. It is useful to those persons having regular earnings. Premium is lesser as compared to a single premium policy. The sum assured becomes payable if the assured reaches a particular age or on the assured's death whichever is earlier.

17.7.2 Number of Persons Assured

Policies on the basis of Number of Persons assured are -

(i) Single life Policies: This policy is designed on the basis of number of persons assured. Single Life Policy covers the risk on one individual. It may be issued on one's own life or on another's life. The policy amount is payable to the insured on attaining a selected term or on the death of the life assured whichever is earlier..

(ii) Multiple Life Policies: Multiple Life Policies is a policy issued on the basis of the number of persons assured. The Multiple Life Policies may be joint Life Policies or last Survivorship Policies. Unlike Single Life Policy, Joint Life Policy covers the risks of more than two individuals. The sum assured is payable at the time of maturity or on the event of the death of the first assured whichever is earlier. This policy is useful to partners of a firm or on the lives of husband and wife of a family. Under Last Survivorship Policy, the sum assured shall be payable at the death of last survivor or on the attaining a selected term if earlier.

17.7.3 Participation in Profits

Participating policies refers to the policies, which are entitled for getting the benefit of bonus. Bonus is the share of the profit of the insurance company earned during a particular financial year. Policies issued on the basis of participation in profits are discussed below:

(i) With Profit Policies (or) Participating Policies: With Profit policies are also termed as Participating Policies. Unlike Non- participating Policies, Participating policyholders are entitled to get the share of profits or bonus or benefits or paid up facilities as per the terms and conditions of the Corporation. The sum assured with profits shall become payable to the insured at the end of the maturity or in the event of death if earlier.

(ii) Without Profit Policies (or) Non-Participating Policies: Under this policy, Sum assured will become payable without any paid up facilities to the insured at the end of the selected term or on the death of life assured if earlier.

Key Terms

- Economic Value
- Whole Life Policies
- Term Assurance
- Money Back Policies
- Life Annuity
- Participating Policies
- Single Premium Policy
- Last Survivorship Policy
- Accident and Disability
- Endowment Policies
- Annuities
- Single Life Policies
- Multiple Life Policies
- Non-participating Policies
- Level Premium Policy

Questions for Review

1. Explain the various approaches to valuation of human life for deciding the appropriate risk cover.
2. Discuss the various types of annuity plans.
3. Write short notes on :
   (a) Whole Life Plans
   (b) Money Back Policies
   (c) Marriage Endowment policy
4. Classify life insurance policies based on the mode of payment of premium.
5. Define Endowment Policy. How does it differ from a Whole Life Policy? Is it possible to convert a whole life policy into an endowment policy? If yes, explain how.
6. What are the various kinds of endowment policies?

Suggested Readings

1. S.L. Kane, *Principles of Life Insurance,* Himalaya Publishing House, Mumbai, 2003.
2. *Practice of Life Assurance,* IC02, Insurance Institute of India, 2003.

Web Resources

- *www.licindia.com*
- *www.insurance.yahoo.com*

Life Insurance Underwriting and Rating

Chapter **18**

CHAPTER OBJECTIVES

After reading this chapter you will be able to understand :

- *Principles of Underwriting*
- *Meaning and Definition of Underwriting*
- *Underwriting Considerations*
- *Process of Underwriting*
- *Various Kinds of Rating*
- *Methods of Risk Classification*
- *Factors Affecting the Pricing*
- *Methods of Treating Sub-standard Risks*
- *Documents required for underwriting*

18.1 UNDERWRITING IN LIFE INSURANCE

Life insurance underwriting is mainly concerned with mortality. Mortality risk for an insurer is that the insured will die prior to the stipulated life. An impairment in any respect of a proposed insured's personal health, medical history, health habits, family history, occupation, or other activities that could increase that person's expected mortality risk.3

While underwriting risk of an individual in life insurance, following factors are generally considered by life insurance companies:

(*a*) Age,

(*b*) Sex,

(*c*) Height and weight,

(*d*) Health history (and often family health history – parents and siblings),

(*e*) The purpose of the insurance (such as for estate planning, or business or for family protection),

(*f*) Marital status and number of children,

(*g*) The amount of insurance the applicant already has, and any additional insurance she proposes to buy,

(*h*) Occupation (some are hazardous, and increase the rise of death),

(*i*) Income (to help determine suitability),

(*j*) Smoking or tobacco use this is an important factor, as smokers have shorter lives),

(*k*) Alcohol (excessive drinking seriously hurts life expectancy),

(*l*) Certain hobbies (*e.g.*, race car driving, hang-gliding, piloting non-commercial aircraft), and

(*m*) Foreign travel (certain foreign travel is risky).

Similarly in case of group insurance the following factors are considered:

(*a*) Proposed Coverage – which includes assessment of eligibility, level of benefits which can be offered, administration of the group and the mode of payment to intermediaries.

(*b*) Cause of existence of the relevant group – classified on the basis of the nature of job, specific agendas etc.

(*c*) Size of the group – large groups are always better than small groups for obvious reasons.

(*d*) Nature of Group's business-based on nature of industry, cement plants and coal mines workers are more prone to respiratory/kidney problems.

(*e*) Geographical location of the group.

(*f*) Stability of the group.

(*g*) Attributes of group members – sex, age and work profile.

(*h*) Level of participation – contribution by members or else, no contribution by members.

(*i*) Persistency and prior experiences.

In case of renewals, the most important factor is the claims experience

Underwriters place the potential insureds in the appropriate risk class (based on various criterion) generally classified as follows:

(*a*) *Preferred Class:* where the happening of an adverse event or the possibility of claims is the least, *i.e.*, the inherent risk is lesser than average risk.

(*b*) *Standard Class* : where the risk exposed is at par with the average risk. Most of the insured belong to this class.

(*c*) *Sub-standard Class* : where the anticipated risk is higher than the average risk. Insurance companies typically establish this risk class for proposed insureds who have permanent medical impairments or conditions, are recovering from serious illnesses or accidents, or have occupations or avocations that significantly increase their degree of risk.

The Underwriting Process

The underwriting of life assurance is in quite a different category from other forms of personal insurances. This is because the underwriter assesses the risk at inception only. The company is then guaranteeing cover for sometimes, up to 30 years, or even throughout life. Life assurance underwriting involves looking at medical, occupational and avocation factors as well as the individual's lifestyle. In particular, the extra risk posed by AIDS has led to an increased number of questions on proposal forms, or on a separate questionnaire, about lifestyle, which are designed to identify if the proposer is likely to be in a high risk group for AIDS or HIV.

The underwriting process for life assurance involves – (1) performing field underwriting, (2) reviewing the application in the office, (3) gathering additional information, if required and (4) taking and underwriting decision. Additional information is often required by the underwriter in order to reach a decision. This can be in the form of detailed questionnaires, a report from the proposer's own doctor (Medical Attendant's Report), an examination by an independent doctor (Medical Examiner's Report) and/or specific tests.

Following steps are generally followed by underwriters:

1. Receiving Proposals/Applications

The application for insurance is the source of insurability information that the life insurance company's underwriter will evaluate first. These are generally collected by the field personnel, the agents. There are two basic parts to a typical life insurance application: (1) General Information, and (2) Medical Information.

The General Information section of an application asks general questions, including name, age, address, birth date, sex, income, marital status and occupation. In addition, details about the requested insurance coverage such as type of policy, amount of insurance, name and relationship of the beneficiary, other insurance that the client owns, and additional insurance applications pending as on date.

The Medical Information section of an application focuses on insured's health and asks a number of questions about health history, history of his/her family's as well. The medical section of the application is fairly extensive and must be fully completed. In addition to this, information may also gathered through a medical examination, depending on age and the face amount of coverage.

2. The Medical Report

The average medical examination (which is generally at no cost to the applicant except in case of revivals) may be conducted. Depending on the medical questions are answered, an insurance company may ask the medical doctor(s) of the client for more detail on any conditions in question. This gathering of information is practically a standardized method used with all domestic insurance companies. Life Insurance Companies generally have several sources of information about medical and financial history to assist them in the underwriting process. These include personal medical records and doctor, the Medical Information Bureau, Special Questionnaires, Inspection Reports and even Credit Records.

3. Underwriting Review

Once all of the information has been gathered, an individual from the insurance company (called an underwriter) evaluates the data. At this evaluation, the underwriter is seeking to classify the risk presented to the company. In addition, the underwriter will determine the premium for the policy based on the primary and secondary factors influencing the premium, and the premium rates the company's actuaries have set for your risk profile. As a consumer, here is the hard part to understand in getting a policy: insurance companies have different underwriting guidelines. This is why the least expensive policies are the most stringent on their guidelines. Throughout every step of the underwriting process, the life insurance agent normally provides with details, keeps abreast of where the insured stand in the process and guide and answer to the questions. Ultimately, making the underwriting process less intimidating and more manageable.

If the proposed insured presents a risk more than the risk which the insurance company is willing to cover, the application will be declined by the underwriter.

4. Policy Writing

In life insurance the policy is usually written in a special department whose main task is to issue written contracts in accordance with instructions from the underwriting department and, because most policies are long term in nature, to keep a register of them for future reference. Insurance companies generally use automated systems which generate the computerised client record, records of payment of premium and they do verify that all the requirements of underwriting have been met.Underwriters place the potential insureds in the appropriate risk class (based on various criterion) generally classified as follows:

(a) *Preferred Class:* where the happening of an adverse event or the possibility of claims is the least, *i.e.*, the inherent risk is lesser than average risk.

(b) *Standard Class* : where the risk exposed is at par with the average risk. Most of the insured belong to this class.

(c) *Sub-standard Class* : where the anticipated risk is higher than the average risk. Insurance companies typically establish this risk class for proposed insureds who have permanent medical impairments or conditions, are recovering from serious illnesses or accidents, or have occupations or avocations that significantly increase their degree of risk.

The Underwriting Process

The underwriting of life assurance is in quite a different category from other forms of personal insurances. This is because the underwriter assesses the risk at inception only. The company is then guaranteeing cover for sometimes, up to 30 years, or even throughout life. Life assurance underwriting involves looking at medical, occupational and avocation factors as well as the individual's lifestyle. In particular, the extra risk posed by AIDS has led to an increased number of questions on proposal forms, or on a separate questionnaire, about lifestyle, which are designed to identify if the proposer is likely to be in a high risk group for AIDS or HIV.

The underwriting process for life assurance involves – (1) performing field underwriting, (2) reviewing the application in the office, (3) gathering additional information, if required and (4) taking and underwriting decision. Additional information is often required by the underwriter in order to reach a decision. This can be in the form of detailed questionnaires, a report from the proposer's own doctor (Medical Attendant's Report), an examination by an independent doctor (Medical Examiner's Report) and/or specific tests.

Following steps are generally followed by underwriters:

1. Receiving Proposals/Applications

The application for insurance is the source of insurability information that the life insurance company's underwriter will evaluate first. These are generally collected by the field personnel, the agents. There are two basic parts to a typical life insurance application: (1) General Information, and (2) Medical Information.

The General Information section of an application asks general questions, including name, age, address, birth date, sex, income, marital status and occupation. In addition, details about the requested insurance coverage such as type of policy, amount of insurance, name and relationship of the beneficiary, other insurance that the client owns, and additional insurance applications pending as on date.

The Medical Information section of an application focuses on insured's health and asks a number of questions about health history, history of his/her family's as well. The medical section of the application is fairly extensive and must be fully completed. In addition to this, information may also gathered through a medical examination, depending on age and the face amount of coverage.

2. The Medical Report

The average medical examination (which is generally at no cost to the applicant except in case of revivals) may be conducted. Depending on the medical questions are answered, an insurance company may ask the medical doctor(s) of the client for more detail on any conditions in question. This gathering of information is practically a standardized method used with all domestic insurance companies. Life Insurance Companies generally have several sources of information about medical and financial history to assist them in the underwriting process. These include personal medical records and doctor, the Medical Information Bureau, Special Questionnaires, Inspection Reports and even Credit Records.

3. Underwriting Review

Once all of the information has been gathered, an individual from the insurance company (called an underwriter) evaluates the data. At this evaluation, the underwriter is seeking to classify the risk presented to the company. In addition, the underwriter will determine the premium for the policy based on the primary and secondary factors influencing the premium, and the premium rates the company's actuaries have set for your risk profile. As a consumer, here is the hard part to understand in getting a policy: insurance companies have different underwriting guidelines. This is why the least expensive policies are the most stringent on their guidelines. Throughout every step of the underwriting process, the life insurance agent normally provides with details, keeps abreast of where the insured stand in the process and guide and answer to the questions. Ultimately, making the underwriting process less intimidating and more manageable.

If the proposed insured presents a risk more than the risk which the insurance company is willing to cover, the application will be declined by the underwriter.

4. Policy Writing

In life insurance the policy is usually written in a special department whose main task is to issue written contracts in accordance with instructions from the underwriting department and, because most policies are long term in nature, to keep a register of them for future reference. Insurance companies generally use automated systems which generate the computerised client record, records of payment of premium and they do verify that all the requirements of underwriting have been met.

18.2 METHOD OF RISK CLASSIFICATION IN LIFE INSURANCE

The two methods commonly employed in the classification of risks are :

(*a*) ***Judgement Method :*** The underwriter studies all the features of the life to be insured and on the basis of analysis of various factors takes a decision. Under this method the company depend upon the combined judgement of those in the medical, actuarial, and other areas who are qualified for this work to make underwriting decisions. The judgement method of rating functions effectively when there is only one unfavorable factor to consider whether the decisions to be made is simply whether to accept the proposed insured at standard rates or to reject him or her entirely. However, situations where multiple factors are involved or a proper substandard classification is needed, then this method can not be efficiently applied.

(*b*) ***Numerical Rating :*** In this method, a large number of factors, which influence mortality, are taken in account. For various factors, debits (additions) or credits (subtractions) are made to the scores. The numerical ratings vary from company to company–75 to 500. Illustratively, as rating increases, the quality of risk diminishes. A rating in the range of 75-125 is generally considered as standard and *over and above 125 as sub standard.* An underwriter has to take into account the nature and combined effects of extra risks *e.g.* impairments jointly causing additional extra risks. In these cases some additions are made to the arrived rates calculated independently.

18.3 FACTORS AFFECTING THE PRICING OF LIFE INSURANCE PRODUCTS

Life insurance is an institution which convert uncertainty into certainty. It is not humanly possible to prevent the occurrence of an event (peril) insured against. But the uncertainty of financial loss suffered by a few, because of the happening of the events, can be eliminated and/or reduced to a great extent, by the distribution of a large number of people. Thus, instead of being borne by one, the loss can be distributed equally among all persons facing the risk. Every one of the group of people makes a contribution to a common fund. The measure of this common contribution is called premium.

The premium to be charged under a life insurance policy depends on three factors:

(a) Rate of mortality

(b) Rate of interest

(c) Operational expenses

(a) **Mortality Rate and Premium:** The establishment of any plan of insuring against death requires some means of giving mathematical values to the probabilities of death. This can be accomplished thorough the mortality statistics, i.e., mortality rate. Mortality tables are presentations of such data organised in a form to be usable in estimating the course of future death. The cost of insurance coverage (i.e., premium) is calculated simply by multiplying the sum assured and the value of mortality at a particular age. This is called natural premium.

For example, if at the age of 30, mortality rate is 0.00117, it means that out of a group of 1, 00,000 persons all aged 30 years, 11% are expected to die before they reach age 31. If all these persons wish to take a policy of Rs. 1 lakh for a term of one year, then the premium will be Rs. 117.

(b) **Rate of Interest and Premium :** The second factor which affects premium is interest. In the simplest insurance contracts, the premium is paid in a lump sum when the policy is issued. But the claim payments are made over time, (say after a certain number of years). Insurers invest the premium amount collected in different investment areas and earn interest. This interest is reflected in the calculation of premium. In other words, the premium reflects the time value of money.

The insurance company assumes a certain rate of interest based on its experience, while computing the rates of premium. The premium calculated based on the combination of both mortality rates and interest factor is called **Net Premium.**

Consider the previous example, at the end of the year, 117 persons will claim the sum assured, i.e., insurance company need 117 lakhs at the end of the year. In case of natural premium, i.e., if the insurance company only consider the mortality rate, the y collect 117 lakhs rupees from all 1 lakh people. If the insurance company earns 6% interest, then they have to collect only 110.38 lakhs (117/1.06) from 1 lakh people. This, the premium charged per person will be Rs. 110.38.

(c) **Expenses and Premium:** The third factor which goes into the computation of premiums is the expense factor. There are two types of expenses: (i) Premium related expenses such as agent's commission, renewal expenses (ii) Policy related expenses are added to the net premium to calculate the final premium. This is called **Gross Premium** or **Office Premium.** Process of adding these expenses to the net premium is called loading.

18.4 TREATMENT OF SUB-STANDARD LIFE INSURANCE RISKS

The three broad classifications of sub standard risks are :

(*a*) ***Increasing Extra Risk :*** This category reflects the extra mortality risks caused due to impairments with the increase in age. Persons with extra weight are likely to have blood pressure or heart problems, as they grow older.

(*b*) ***Constant Extra Risk :*** This group reflects the lives with hazard that remain constant through life. These hazards do not create variations in mortality as such *e.g.* permanent total disablement-lost of limbs.

(c) ***Decreasing Extra Risk :*** These lives represent cases where the extra risk decreases with passage of risk since the consideration of proposal. A person who has just been operated for a problem becomes normal over a time period. At the time of proposal the risk was substandard, but with passage of time, it has become a simple risk.

The popular methods of treating sub standard risk are :

(*a*) ***Increase in Premium :*** Increase in normal premium (multiple table extra) is the most common method adopted by the insurance companies for treatment of sub-standard risks. Under its method premiums can be treated as follows:

(*i*) the proposer's age is increased by a few years (*e.g.* 3-5 years) which results in increase in premium or

(*ii*) a special mortality table is developed for each sub-standard classification that reflects the experience of each and a set of gross premium is computed for the classification.

(*b*) ***Flat Extra Premium :*** In situation where the extra risk is expected be constant, a flat extra premium may be changed. The policy remains a standard one for all purposes including dividends and non-forfeiture values.

(c) ***Other Methods :*** The other methods of refund an

(i) Limited death benefit equal to refund of premium if death occurs in the earlier years.

(ii) A lien (contingent debt) may be created an the policy such that upon the assured dies in the lien period, the lien amount shall be deducted from sum payable under the policy.

(iii) A proposal may be declined by the insurer if there is increasing extra risk.

(iv) Restrictive clauses may be imposed as exclusions under the policy.

(v) The insurance cover may be reduced by amount and/or time or the plan may be changed.

(vi) Another option from insurance company is to defer the cover till the extra risk is over.

Mortality Tables are prepared on the basis of study of assured lives for a period of time, usually 3 to 5 years. At every age deaths take place. These are tabulated showing rate of dying and rate of surviving (complementary probability) for every year.

A typical mortality table would appear like this :

1961-64 OM Table

Age at the beginning of the year	*No. of living at the beginning of the year*	*No. of death during the year*	*Yearly probability of death*	*Yearly probability of surviving*
1	2	3	4	5
35	9,78,217	1410	.00144	.99856
36	9,77,807	1535	.00157	.998943
37	9,76,272	1679	.00172	.99828
38	9.74,593	1842	.00189	.99811
39	9,72,751	2033	.00209	.99791
40	9,70718	2242	.00231	.99769
41	9,68,476	2479	.00256	.99744
42	9,65,997	2743	.00284	.99716
43	9,63,254	3044	.00316	.99684
44	9,60,210	3370	.00351	.99633
45	9,56,840	3732	.00390	.99610

This table shows that the chance of dying the at age of 35 is .00144, it increases to .00390 at the age of 45. The last column shows the probability of survival. These probabilities of death and survival are made use of in arriving at *the mathematical value of the risk* for lives belonging to a group whose experience may be expected to more or less compare favourably with the mortality table. If it happens, one can say that the premiums charged are adequate to meet the risk involved. In other words mortality experience is satisfactory.

18.5 CALCULATION OF PREMIUM

In calculating premium the following variable are considered :

(i) Term and Plan

(ii) Riders

(iii) Extras

(iv) Sum Assured

(v) Mode of payment

The rates of premium are quoted per thousand for various age groups. The table rates are then multiplied by the sum assured to arrive at a base premium. Then to the base premium, the addition or dedications are made. Consider the following example :

Sum proposed		Rs. 50,0000
Cover		Money Back Policy
Age (near birthday)		30
Term		35 years
Table Rates		Rs. 27.00 per thousand
Adjustment Rate for high SI		+ Rs. 1.60 per thousand
Double Accident Benefit (DAB)		1%
Mode of payment		Semi-Annual
Calculation		
Tabular Premium (Rs. 5,00,000 × 27/1000)		13,500
Adjussult Benefit for large SI (Rs. 5,00,000 × 1.60/1000)		800
Annual Premium		14,300
DAB Extra (1%)		1430
Total Price		15,730
Semi Annual Premium (15730/2)		**Rs. 7865**
Example 2		
Plan		Whole life
Sum Assured		Rs. 1,00,000
Riders		DAB
Health Extra		5%
Age		31
Premium Payments		35 years
Tabular Premium (Whole life, Premium Payments 35)	Rs.	29.40
Adjustment for large sum assured Rs. 1.50	Rs.	1.60
Adjustment for quarterly mode		Nil
Total		31.00
Annual Premium (31.00 × 100)	Rs.	3,100
Health Extra (5%)	Rs.	155.00
Total annual premium (including extra)	Rs.	3255.00
Quarterly instalment premium	Rs.	813.75

18.6 DOCUMENTS REQUIRED

Age Proof

Scrutiny of age is an important concern for the life insurer because old age people have high probability of dying than the younger ones and premium is calculated on the basis of age groups. Accuracy in age computation resolves hardship both to the insurer and the potential insured in the sense that the correct age avoids the company being affected by lesser premiums or undesired risk bought or risk not bought because of fear. From the insured's perspective, it helps in charging of fair premiums and insurance availability. The proofs of age, which are generally considered are as under :

- Certified extract from municipal or other records made at the time of birth.
- Certificate of Baptism or certified extract from family Bible if it contains age or date of birth.

- Certified extract from School or College if age or date of birth is stated therein.
- Certified extract from Service Register in case of Govt. employees and employees of Quasi Govt. institutions including Public Limited Companies and
- Passport issued by the Passport Authorities in India.

Alternative Age Proofs, which are also accepted in the industry, are :

- Marriage certificate in the case of Roman Catholics issued by Roman Catholic Church.
- Certified extracts from the Service Registers of commercial Institutions or Industrial Undertakings provided it is specifically mentioned in such extracts that conclusive evidence of age was produced at the time of recruitment of the employee.
- Certificate of Birth granted by Syedna v. Molana Badruddin Sahib of Baroda.
- Identity Cards issued by Defence Department.
- A true copy of the University Certificate or of Matriculation/Higher Secondary Education, S.S.L. Certificate issued by a Board set up by a State/Central Government.
- Non-standard age proofs like Horoscope, Service Record where age is not verified at the time of entry, E.S.I.S. Card, Marriage Certificate in case of Muslim Proposer, Elder's Declaration, Selfdeclaration and Certificate by Village Panchayats are accepted subject to certain rules.

Medical Examination

Generally, at some levels and in case of endowment policies, whole life policies, the medical examination is not asked for. However, if the amount of insurance is very high or the age is high or the first level examination has some adverse remarks, then the insurance company may refer the proposal for a thorough examination. Cases of pregnant women, or women with history of miscarriages or abortion are declined. Some times the medical examination may be waived, like in rural areas, where the facilities are not available.

After the above examinations and obtaining special reports, if required, the underwriter may accept or reject the case. Else, he is empowered to modify the sum assured, premium to be charged and manner thereof, impose conditions or provide exclusions in the policy.

In case of untrue or incorrect statement contained in the proposal, personal statement, declaration and connected documents or any material information withheld, subject to the provision of Section 45 of the Insurance Act 1938, wherever applicable, the policy shall be declared void and all claims to any benefits in virtue thereof shall cease.

After the policy is issued, the policyholder in a number of cases finds the terms not suitable to him and desires to change them. LIC allows certain types of alterations during the lifetime of the policy. However, no alteration is permitted within one year of the commencement of the policy with some exceptions. The following alterations are allowed :

- Alteration in class or term
- Reduction in the sum assured
- Alteration in the mode of payment of premiums
- Alteration in the date of commencement of the policy
- Splitting up of a single policy into two or more policies
- Removal of an extra premium
- Alteration from without profit plan to with profit plan
- Alternation in name

- Correction in policies
- Settlement option of payment of sum assured by instalments
- Grant of accident benefit
- Grant of premium waiver benefit under CDA policies
- Alteration in currency and place of payment of policy monies.

A fee for the change or alteration in the policy is charged by the company called as the quotation fee and no additional fee is charged for giving effect to the alteration.

Special Reports

Besides the proposal form, personal statement, agent's report, medical examiner's report and age–proof, special medical reports may be called for, it

(*a*) The SA is very high, say Rs. 5 lakhs or more

(*b*) The age at entry is very high, say, 60 years or more

(*c*) The proposer wants insurance cover under a high-risk plan.

(*d*) The normal medical examination discloses some adverse feature.

The underwriter has the right and discretion to ask for additional information through special reports, if he considers such reports necessary for a fair assessment of risk. These special reports may relate to medical condition or they may relate to income, habits, life styles, etc. He may ask for medical reports, even if the proposal is for non–medical insurance. In the case of key man insurance, the reports may be to establish that the life assured is indeed a key person and that the SA proposed represents fairly the value of that person and that the SA proposed represents fairly the value of that person to the enterprise.

The underwriter arrives at a decision about the acceptance of the proposal, after scrutinising the particulars available in the proposal form, personal statement, the reports of the officials and the medical reports. He may take the expert opinion of a medical referee, who is a senior doctor familiar with implications of medical history in life insurance.

The underwriter may decide to accept the proposal as a proposed at O.R. (Ordinary Rates) or on modified terms. O.R. means that the premium chargeable would be as per the standard premium tables. The modifications would be of the following kind.

(*a*) accepting for a lesser SA than proposed

(*b*) accepting for a shorter term than proposed

(*c*) accepting for a different plan than proposed

(*d*) charging a higher premia than the standard rate

(*e*) imposing a lien which reduces the insurer's liability under the policy for some time, or under some conditions

(*f*) excluding certain specified risks under the policy.

The terms under which the proposal is accepted by the underwriter, will be conveyed to the proposer. If the acceptance is as proposed and at O.R., the deposit paid along with the proposal, if adequate will be adjusted as First Premium and the risk will commence from that time. If the acceptance is on modified terms, the proposer has to agree to those modified terms. The balance of premium if any, will have to be paid. If all the requirements are fulfilled by the proposer, the First Premium is adjusted and the risk commences. The First Premium is adjusted and the risk commences. The First Premium Receipt is the evidence of Commencement of risk, till the policy document is issued.

The specimens of forms included as Annexures to this course are only specimens. They may change from time to time. Each insurer will have its own forms. They will also differ according to the plan of insurance proposed for. But, by and large, the contents would be the same.

Key Terms

- ❒ Underwriting
- ❒ Standard Risk
- ❒ Sub – Standard Risk'
- ❒ Judgment Rating
- ❒ Merit Rating
- ❒ Class Rating
- ❒ Schedule rating
- ❒ Experience rating
- ❒ Retrospective rating
- ❒ Mortality Rate
- ❒ Interest Rate
- ❒ Expenses Loading
- ❒ Medical Examination

Questions for Review

1. How risks are classified in life insurance? What are the various methods of treatment of sub-standard risks?
2. Define Underwriting. What are the objectives of underwriting?
3. What are the major principles of underwriting of a life insurance policy?
4. Explain the various steps of underwriting.
5. How and why sex is considerably an important factor while underwriting a life insurance policy?
6. What are the different methods of rating?
7. Explain the factors affecting the pricing of life insurance products.
8. Write short notes on :
   (a) Mortality Rate
   (b) Medical Examination
9. Assuming that you are an underwriter, explain how will you treat the different classes of Sun-standard risks?
10. Distinguish between :
    (*a*) Standard Life and Sub – standard Life.
    (*b*) Judgment Rating and Class Rating .
11. What are the various document required for underwriting?

    Define surrender Value. Calculate the paid up value and surrender value of a policy on 01/03/2003 as per details below :

SA	Rs. 5,00,000
Plan and term	14-20
Mode of reminpayment	Annual
D.O.C.	10.08.90
F.U.P.	8/03

6. Calculate the amount payable from the following information :

Sum Assured	Rs. 5,00,000
Plan	75-20

Rider	Double Accident Benefit
Death of Assured due to accident	28/07/98
Date of commencement	01/08/86
Survival benefits paid	Rs. 1,00,000 (5th year)
	Rs. 1,00,000 (10th year)

7. **Compute the premium for the following cases.**

(*a*)	SA	Rs. 1,00,000
	Type	Endowment Policy with Profits
	Mode of Premium payment	Half yearly
	Adjustment factor for large SI and half yearly mode	Rs. 1.5 per thousand
	Tabular premium rate	Rs. 36.70 per thousand
	Accident Extra	1%
	Health Extra	0.5%
(*b*)	Type of cover	Whole Life
	SA	Rs. 60,000
	Proposer Age	45 years
	Period of cover	25 years
	DAB and EPDB	1%
	Table rate	Rs. 49.00 per thousand
	Adjustment factor for large SI	Rs. 1.50 per thousand
	Mode of Premium	Quarterly

Suggested Readings

- Gene Stone, Insurance Company Operations, LOMA, 2000.
- Willis Park Rokes, *Human Relations in Handling insurance Claims,* Richard R. Irwin, 1967.
- *"Settling Third Party Insurance Claims Through TPAs."* Daleep Pandita, Insurance Times, Kolkata, Feb. 2003.
- *Claims Management,* Volume I and II ICFAI Press, 2002.
- *Practice of Life Assurance,* IC02, insurance Institute of India, Mumbai.
- Robert I., Mehr, *Life Insurance–Theory and Practice,* Business Publications Inc. 1977.
- T.S. Mann, *Law and Practice of Life Insurance in India,* Deep and Deep, 1987.
- S.S. Huebner, Kenneth Block Jr. and Robert S. Clive, *Life and Health Insurance, Pearson* Education, 2002.

Life Insurance Claims Management

Chapter 19

CHAPTER OBJECTIVES

After reading this chapter you will be able to understand :

- *Various Types of Claims*
- *Documents required to Claim*
- *Major Additional Benefits*
- *Procedure of Claim*
- *Surrender Value*
- *Paid-up Value*
- *Claim Concession*

19.1 TYPES OF CLAIMS

The life insurance claims can be classified in two categories (*a*) Death claims (*b*) Maturity claims. Settlement procedure of each of these is discussed below :

19.1.1 Death Claims

If the insured dies before the expiry of the term of the policy, it is called as death claim. The death of the life assured has to be intimated in writing to the insurer. It may be done by the nominee, assignee, a relative of the life assured, the employer, agent or development officer. Particulars like policy number, name of the life assured, the date of death, the cause of death and the relationship of the informant to the decreased are to be mentioned. The intimation must satisfy two conditions : (*a*) It must be from a concerned person and (*b*) must establish beyond doubt, the identity of the deceased person as the life assured under the policy.

Sometimes, the office need not wait till the intimation of the claim is received. Obituary columns, the concerned agent or newspaper reports in case of accidents or air crashes may give information and the claim action can be initiated. However, care has to be taken to ensure that identity of the deceased is established.

The facts required to the submitted by the claimant are : (*a*) Date of death (*b*) Reason and Place of Death and (*c*) Full details of policies held by the Life assured should also be submitted. Death claims are categorised as Non-Early Death claims and Early Claims. The procedure for processing these claims is different :

***Non-early Death Claims* refer to death of the Life assured occurring after 3 years from the date of commencement of policy or Date of last revival/reinstatement. If the policy is in force till death by regular payment of premiums, full sum assured is payable along with bonus (if it is with a profit policy). The requirements for the settlement of the death claim are :**

- Policy Document
- Death Certificate from the appropriate authority
- Legal evidence of Title, if the claimant is not an assignee/nominee
- Abridged Claim Form
- Discharge Form duly signed

- Assignment/Reassignment deed, if any
- Age proof, if age is not already admitted

Once these documents are received and if they are found in order, claim is settled and payment is made to the person entitled to.

Early claims refer to the death of life assured occurring within 3 years from commencement of policy. The following forms are to be submitted duly completed:

- Statement from the medical attendants who last treated the deceased Life assured.
- Certificate of treatment issued by the hospital authorities where the deceased was treated last.
- Certificate by the employer if the deceased was an employee.
- Certificate of burial/cremation signed by a person who attended the funeral of the deceased.

Where death takes place due to accident, the death has to be reported to the police and a FIR (First Information Report), police inquest report, and post-mortem report (if conducted only) are to be submitted. Wherever death takes place within 2 years from Date of commencement an enquiry is conducted to determine the genuineness of claim. On the basis of these, the decisions to settle accidental benefits are taken. Under MWPA policy the proceeds of the policy will be paid to the trustees. If there is no trustee, the official trustee will step in. But if the beneficiaries are major and competent to contract, payment can be made directly to them without the intervention of trustees. The assured need not sign the discharge voucher.

- In case of absolute assignment, the payment will be made to the assignee. If the assignment is conditional, payment can be made to the assured himself, after satisfying repayment of loan that may be the reason for assignments.
- If the policy is irretrievable lost, advertisement of the loss of the policy is a necessary precaution. Payment can be made on the basis of an indemnity executed by the policyholder together with a surety of means. It is not necessary to issue a duplicate policy.
- The death claim amount is payable to the nominee or the assignee as the case may be. If the life assured has died without making an assignment or nomination, legal evidence of title (proof of ownership) such as succession certificate or letters of administration or probate of a will where a will exists, would be required.
- The insurer may waive strict evidence of title, if the amount involved is small, there is no other estate left by the deceased and there is no dispute among he survivors about the policy moneys.
- If the intimation claim is received after 3 years from the death, the same is time barred. The claimant has to be informed accordingly. However, if the death had occurred with 3 years of the policy's commencement of revival, simultaneous investigation should be conducted to find out the bonafides of the claim, without the knowledge of the claimant. However, if more than three years have elapsed, since the date of risk, the claimant has to be informed that the claim is barred by limitation. But simultaneously claim forms can be issued without prejudice to see if any ex-gratia payment can be made.
- If the death has occurred within 2 years of the date of the policy (that is the date of FPR) the possibility of suppression of evidence cannot be ruled out. Hence, it is necessary to investigate such cases. The reasons for intimating a claim late may be deliberate attempt to tamper with evidence.
- Death can take place suddenly *e.g.* due to cardiac arrest, downing, burns, air crash, suicide, and murder or at the hand of justice. In case of an air crash, a certificate from airline authorities would be necessary certifying that the assured was a passenger on the plane. In case of ship-accident, a certified extract from the logbook of the ship would be needed. In case of sudden heart failures, doctor's certificate will not be forthcoming.

- In case of defence personnel, a certificate from the commanding officer of the Unit is to be obtained. If a court of enquiry is ordered its findings should be obtained.

19.1.2 Maturity Claims

Maturity claims are payable as per the terms of the policy. These policies are generally endowment polices including money back policies. The amount payable at the time of maturity includes sum assured and bonuses/ incentives. The insurer normally sends advance intimations to the insured. The insurer has to satisfy that:

- The life assured is the holder of the policy and his identity is proved.
- The age stands admitted.
- The premiums are all paid.
- The original policy is handed in together with a completed discharge voucher before making payment.

The insurance company is expected to make payment on the maturity date. Post-dated cheques are normally set in advance.

Documents Required

In the case of maturity claims, the insurer will call for the following documents, well before the date of maturity.

- Policy document, if it is not available, it may have been deposited elsewhere as a security for a loan. If policyholder loses the policy, the claim can be settled on the strength of an indemnity bond from the policyholder and a reliable surety of sound financial means. For small amounts, a letter of indeminity may suffice. In case of very small amounts, say Rs. 1,000/- or less, even this can be dispensed with.
- Age proof, if the age is not already admitted.
- Deed of assignment if any.
- Discharge form issued by the office.

If the claim does not determine the policy finally, as in the case of periodical survival payments, the policy document will be returned to the policy holder after due endorsements.

Settlement

Settlement procedure in a maturity claim is simple. After receipt of the completed and stamped discharge voucher from the person entitled to the policy money, along with the policy documents, claim amount will be paid by account payee or crossed and order cheque. In case of survival benefit claims, that is whose sum assured is retuned by instalments, suitable endorsements will be made on the policy document and in policy records, before returning the policy document to the policy holders. If the discharge from is lost in transit, a duplicate discharge form can be issued.

- Where the assured or the person to sign the discharge is known to be mentally deranged, a certificate from a court of law under the Indian Lunacy Act appointing a persons to act as a guardian to manage the properties of the lunatic should be called. If the person has recovered from the mental disorder, a certificate form the Psychiatic Hospital to that effect would be necessary.
- If the assured has been adjudged insolvent by court of law before the policy has matured for payment and if a notice is received from the official assignee of the court along with a certified copy of the court's order declaring assured as insolvent and also on order appointing official assignee as the assignee of the insolvent's estate, the official assignee should be informed about the date of maturity and other details. If the assignee claims the money, the payment has to be made to him under advice to the life assured. If the judicial authority has sold the policy in a court action, the purchaser, who produces certificate of sale, will be entitled to the policy moneys.

- If a prohibitory order of a court of law or a notice from income-tax officer under Section 226 (3) of the Income Tax Act is subsisting, the assured should be asked to have a proper withdrawal order served on the insurer. Otherwise, the insurer will act according to the notice.
- If the life assured is reported to have died before the maturity date, the claim has to be treated as death claim and processed accordingly. But if the assured is reported to have died after the date of maturity but before the receipt is discharged, the claim is to be treated as a maturity claim and paid to the legal heirs. Death certificate and evidence of title would be necessary.
- Under the Evidence Act, a person who has disappeared is presumed to be dead only if he has not been heard of for seven years. In such cases a decree of presumption of death from a court of law would be needed. The premiums must be paid until presumption of death is made, otherwise, the payment would be made after the court decree is obtained, as per the status of the policy as on the date when the premiums stopped.
- Payments of claim amount to claimants who are non-residents of India are governed by the Foreign Exchange Control Regulations.
- If a policy is financed through HUF funds, the policy belongs to HUF and as such the policy moneys would be payable to the Karta of HUF only.

  However, the insurer sometimes provides certain relaxation in settlements of the claims. Legally no claim is acceptable in respect of a lapsed policy or death of the Life assured occurring within 3 years from the date of commencement of the policy. However, some concessions are available and payment of claims are made :

  - If the Life assured had paid at least 3 years' premiums and thereafter if premiums have not been paid, the nominees get proportionate paid up value.
  - In the event of the death of the Life assured within 3 years and the policy is under the lapsed position, nothing is payable.

If minimum 2 years premiums are paid and if death of Life assured occurs within 3 months from the date of first unpaid premium, then full sum assured along with bonus is payable subject to recovery of the premium already fallen due and the premium that falls during the policy anniversary.

Between 3 to 6 months from fully unpaid premium, only 59% of basic sum assured is payable. No bonus is paid and no arrears of premium are received. If death occurs between 6 months to 1 year, from fully unpaid premium only notional paid up value is given.

Double Accident Benefit is provided as an inject to the life insurance cover. For this purpose an extra premium of Rs. 1/- per Rs. 1000/- S.A. is charged. For claiming the benefits under the Accident Benefit the claimant has to produce the proof to the satisfaction of the corporation that the accident is defined as per the policy conditions. Normally for claiming this benefit documents like FIR, Post-morten Report are insisted upon.

Disability Benefit Claims consist of waiver of future premiums under the policy and extended disability benefit consisting in addition of a monthly benefit payment as per policy conditions. The essential condition for claiming this benefit is that the disability is total and permanent so as to preclude him from earning any wage/compensation or profit as a result of the accident.

The LIC has also set-up Ciaims' Review Committees which in cases of repudiation, give opportunity to the claimant to make representation for consideration by the Review committees at the Zonal Office and the Central Office. As a result of such reviews, depending on the merits of each case appropriate sanctions are made.

The Grievance Redressal Machinery has been further expanded with the appointment of Insurance Ombudsman at different centres. At present there are 12 centres operating all over the country. Complaints regarding claims, any dispute regarding premiums, legal construction of the policy in relation to claim and non-issue of insurance document comes under the purview of Ombudsman's consideration.

19.2 Additional Benefits

Riders are the additional benefits that may be added to the policy basic features upon payment of additional premium. These benefits allow the insured to enhance the insurance cover, qualitatively and quantitatively. Riders can customise the insurance product best suited to a given insured's needs. Following are the major additional benefits attached to a life insurance policy.

Accident Benefit and Disability Benefit

Accident and Disability benefit is an additional benefit that can be attached to the basic life cover. In this type benefit, typically, an additional amount equal to the Accident Benefit Rider Sum Assured on death is paid arising as a result of accident and for total and permanent disability arising due to accident (within 180 days from the date of accident) an amount equal to the Accident Benefit Rider Sum Assured will be paid over a period of 10 years in monthly instalments. The disability due to accident should be total and such that the Life assured is unable to carry out any work to earn the living. Following disabilities due to accidents are generally covered by the policies:

(*a*) irrevocable loss of the entire sight of both eyes, or

(*b*) amputation of both hands at or above the wrists, or

(*c*) amputation of both feet at or above ankles, or

(*d*) amputation of one hand at or above the wrist and one foot at or above the ankle.

When the claim for disability is paid, the future payment of premiums is waived and the remaining disability instalments have to be paid by the insured.

No benefit will be paid if accidental death or disability arises due to accident in case of:

(*a*) intentional self-injury, attempted suicide insanity or immorality or the Life Assured is under the influence of intoxicating liquor, drug or narcotic

(*b*) engagement in aviation or aeronautics other than that of a passenger in any air craft

(*c*) injuries resulting from riots, civil commotion, rebellion, war, invasion, hunting, mountaineering, steeple chasing or racing of any kind

(*d*) accident resulting from committing any breach of law

(*e*) accident arising from employment in armed forces or military services or police organisation.

The claimant has to provide a proof that–(*a*) the death or injury was outward, violent and visible means (*b*) the death was caused solely and directly and independently of all other causes, from the accident and (*c*) the death occurred within 120 days or such other period as may have been stipulated in the policy.

The maximum limit of sum assured varies among insurers. For, LIC it is Rs. 5 lakhs combined on all policies on a single life.

Free Look Period

In Unit Linked Insurance Plans, the policyholder has the option of cancelling the policy by writing to the Company stating the reasons for cancellation and by returning the original policy document to the Company, within 15 days of the date of receipt of the policy. If the policy is cancelled, the premium have paid is refunded by repurchasing the units at the unit price applicable on the date of cancellation and deducting the proportionate risk premium for the period on cover and the expenses incurred by the Company on medical examination and stamp duty charges.

Major Surgical Assistance Benefit

This rider provides financial support in the event of medical emergencies that require surgery in addition to the basic policy cover. When this rider is claimed for, a part of the sum assured is paid to the policyholder. Most insurers exclude claims arising from pre-existing injuries or illnesses and other predefined specific events and also, expenses on hospitalisation for ailments that do not require surgery are not covered. The premium paid for this rider qualifies for tax deduction under section 80D of the Income Tax Act, 1961. The premium varies in a large range because only some insurers allow the base policy to continue once a claim is made on the rider.

Waiver of Premium Rider

This rider is invoked when the insured person becomes *totally disabled* or loses his source of revenue because of unemployment owing to an injury or sickness. Thereby, the premiums due on the base policy (and other riders, if any) are waived till the person is able-bodied and employed again. Effectively, this rider acts as"disability insurance" in the life insurance policy. If the premium payment is of a high amount, this rider is of a great benefit. The premium for this rider depends on the premium on the base policy and on other riders. The higher the premium on the basic policy cover and the other riders added, the higher is the premium payable on this rider. The premium paid for this rider qualifies for tax deduction under section 80D of the Income Taxt Act, 1961.

Guaranteed Insurability Option Rider

This rider gives the right to the insured to purchase additional insurance (similar to the basic insurance cover) at different stages, without further medical examination. This rider is useful if there is a need to buy additional insurance to keep pace with changing life circumstances. The insured is not required to give any medical evidence of insurability, even though the health condition deteriorates with age.

19.3 Claims Procedure In Respect Of A Life Insurance Policy

(1) A life insurance policy shall -state the primary documents which are normally required to be submitted by a claimant in support of a claim.

(2) A life insurance company, upon receiving a claim, shall process the claim without delay. Any queries or requirement of additional documents, to the extent possible, shall be raised all at once and not in a piece-meal manner, within a period of 15 days of the receipt of the claim.

(3) A claim under a life policy shall be paid or be disputed giving all the relevant reasons, within 30 days from the date of receipt of all relevant papers and clarifications required. However, where the circumstances of a claim warrant an investigation in the opinion of the insurance company, it shall initiate and complete such investigation at the earliest. Where in the opinion of the insurance company the circumstances of a claim warrant an investigation, it shall initiate and complete such investigation at the earliest, in any case not later than 6 months from the time of lodging the claim.

(4) Subject to the provisions of section 47 of the Act, where a claim is ready for payment but the payment cannot be made due to any reasons of a proper identification of the payee, the life insurer shall hold the amount for the benefit of the payee and such an amount shall earn interest at the rate applicable to a savings bank account with a scheduled bank (effective from 30 days following the submission of all papers and information).

(5) Where there is a delay on the part of the insurer in processing a claim for a reason other than the one covered by sub-regulation (4), the life insurance company shall pay interest on the claim amount at a rate which is 2% above the bank rate prevalent at the beginning of the financial year in which the claim is reviewed by it.

19.4 POLICY OR CLAIM AMOUNT

Generally, the amount of claim will be any one of the following:

(1) Sum Assured

(2) Surrender Value

(3) Paid-up Value

Surrender Value

The term surrender value refers to the amount of money which the insurer agrees to pay in case the life assured decides to surrender his policy before its maturity. It is said that the policyholder wishes to surrender his policy to the insurer and gives up his claim on it. Surrender of policy indicates termination of the contract of insurance.

The amount of surrender value is determined on the basis of actual premium paid and the number of years the policy has been in force. Surrender value increases with each payment of premium. Payment is to be made against the full and final discharge of insurer's liability under the contract.

The calculation of surrender value involves the following steps :

(*a*) Calculate duration elapsed under the policy. This duration will be equal to data of calculation of surrender value less date of commencement to be rounded off to the nearer half year. In otherwords, The elapsed duration is calculated by deducting date of commencement of policy (DOC) from the date of First Unpaid Premium (FUP) i.e., Paid-up Duration = Date of FUP – DOC

(*b*) Calculate the paid up value, inclusive of vested bonus under with profit plans.

(*c*) Ascertain from the tables the appropriate surrender value factor per Rs. 100/- paid-up value, corresponding to plan, duration elapsed and original term.

(*d*) Surrender Value = Paid-up × Surrender value Factor/100.

According to Life Insurance Corporation of India, a policy acquires surrender value only after payment of two or three years premium. Thus, the policy is required to have run for three years before it acquires surrender value. In this regard, some Insurance companies guarantee a minimum surrender value of 40 per cent of the total premium paid.

Paid-up Value

If a policyholder discontinues the payment of premium after atleast two years premiums have been paid and subsequent premium is not paid, the policy does not become void, but continues as a paid-up policy. According to Insurance Act, it is defined as the policy paid up for an amount bearing the same proportion to the amount of original sum assured which the number of premiums paid bears to the total number of premiums payable under the policy as a whole

$$\textit{i.e,.}\ \text{Paid-up Value} = \frac{\text{No. of Premium Paid}}{\text{No. of Premium Payable}} \times \text{Sum Assured}$$

The amount (claim) would be available to the life on maturity or on death whichever is earlier. In case of participating policy, it is assured that bonus or profits will be added to the paid-up value, but future gains or profits are not entitled to such policy.

Note : If this figure is less than the guaranteed surrender value, latter is payable.

Example

Sum Assured	= Rs. 1,00,000
Plans and Term-Endowment (with profits)	= 20 years

Mode of payment	= Semi-annual
Date of commencement	= 01.01.85
Due date of last premium paid	= 01.03.97
Date of calculation of surrender value	= 1.3.1997
Number of years premium paid	= 01.01.97–01.01.85 = 12 years.
Term of the policy	= 20 years
Paid up value	= 12/20 × 1,00,000 = Rs. 60,000 (A)
Vested bonus	= Rs. 77,000 (B)
Paid-up value including vested Bonus	= A + B = Rs. 1,37,000

Following are the major differences between Surrender Value and Paid-up Value

(1)(2)(3)(4)(5) Surrender value is the amount which the insurer is prepared to pay before the date of maturity.If a policyholder wishes to surrender his policy, it means that the assured does not want to continue the policy. Surrender value represents the present cash value (at the time of surrender) of the policy.Surrender value is calculated on the basis of policy and the number of years it has been in force.Surrender value increases with each payment of premium.

(1)(2)(3)(4)(5) Paid-up value is paid to the policyholder at maturity or on death.If a policyholder discontinues the payment of premium, the policy does not become void, but continues as a paid-up policy.Paid-up value represents the value payable on assured's death or at the maturity of the policy.Paid-up value is calculated on the basis of number of years premium paid, number of years premium payable and sum assured with accrued.Paid-up value is always higher than the surrender value, since it is not required to be paid immediately after the last premium.

19.5 Claim Concession

A policy lapses if the premium is not paid. Sometimes, the insurers take a liberal view of the situation and give same treatment as to non-forfeiture and revivals. The practice of LIC is as follows :

(*a*) After at least three full years premiums are paid, the claim will be considered for the full SA, as if the policy had remained in full force, if the death of the life assured occurred within six months from the date of the first unpaid premium.

(*b*) After at least full five years' premiums have been paid, the claim will be considered for the full SA, as if the policy had remained in full force, if the death of the life assured occurred within 12 months from the date of the first unpaid premium.

(c) In both cases, the policy monies will be paid after deducting the outstanding premiums with interest and the premiums, falling due in the current year till the next anniversary of the policy.

19.6 Presumption of Death

Under Section 108 of the Indian Evidence Act, 1872, if it is proved that the person has not been heard of for seven years by those who would have naturally heard by him had he been alive, the presumption of law is that he is dead. In case of death by accident while travelling by aeroplane or rail or natural calamities, the body may not be found. Insurers rely on information-supplied carriers, or other organisations in possession of relevant information. If the policyholder is missing for seven years, his heirs can apply to the appropriate civil court and get a court order declaring that the life assured might be presumed to be dead. A claim is payable if the policy is in force or in a paid-up condition, as on the date of the court's order. The exact date and time of death is not a matter of presumption but of active proof. Therefore, in the absence of any such proof, the date of the court's order could be taken as the Date of Death.

The insurer may also sometimes settle the claim on getting an indemnity bond to protect its interest, in case the presumption of death is later found to be wrong. When the insurer takes the responsibility for such action on its own, without the decree from a court, there is a risk that some other claimant to the estate may raise a challenge later. The insurer will not be able to avoid getting involved in the dispute and having to defend its action.

Key Terms

- Death Claim
- Maturity Claim
- Surgical Assistance Benefit
- Paid – up Value
- Presumption of Death
- Claim Concession
- Accident and Disability Benefit
- Surrender Value
- Waiver of Premium Rider

Questions for Review

1. Write short notes on :
   (*a*) Claim Concessions
   (*b*) Presumption of Death
2. Briefly explain the procedure of settlement of death and maturity (survival) claims.
3. List the documents required for consideration of a claim.
4. What do you mean by paid – up value. Explain how paid – up amount is calculated wit the help of suitable illustration
5. Distinguish between Surrender value and Paid – up value.
6. What is the claim procedure in respect of a life insurance policy?
7. What are the major additional benefits attached to a life insurance policy?

Suggested Readings

1. S.L. Karve, *Principles of Life Insurance,* Himalaya Publishing House, Mumbai, 2005.
2. *Practice of Life Assurance,* ICO2, Insurance Institute of India, Mumbai, 2003.

Group Insurance

Chapter

20

CHAPTER OBJECTIVES

After reading this chapter you will be able to understand :

- *The Characteristics of Group Insurance*
- *Growth of Group Insurance*
- *Importance of Group Insurance*
- *Underwriting Considerations*
- *Eligibility to form Groups*
- *Types of Group Insurance Schemes*
- *Various Social Security Schemes*

20.1 GROUP INSURANCE

In Group Insurance is an extention of individual insurance into class insurance. In group insurance a large number of persons belonging to an identifiable group, like employees in an organization, members of a club or an association are covered under one contract. In a single master policy, called *'master policy'* the employees/ workers members of one group are insured for one year's Term Assurance (OYTA) renewable every year. The contract is between the insurer and the employer, though risk is covered on employees' lives.

The first group insurance policy was issued in 1911 by the Equitable Life Assurance Society of New York. The development of group insurance was insignificant till the early 1960s in India. However by the year end of 2002, the number of persons covered under Group insurance by the LIC was nearly 70% of the individual lives covered. The new entrants are focussing on group insurance for an early market penetration.

Apart from issuing a single master policy to employees of the same organization, the group insurance is being provided to groups which are identifiable and homogeneous like trade–unions, professional organizations, co-operative societies, trade associations, Debtor-Creditor Groups, etc. Group insurance is also useful for Government because it helps in implementing various social welfare schemes providing benefits to poorer sections of the society.

Group insurance possesses several distinguishing features *vis-a-vis* individual life insurance:

1. Group Underwriting replaced for individual underwriting.
2. Master Contract Policy.
3. Lower Cost of Administration
4. Flexibility in design of contract
5. Extensive use of experience rating technique.

Group underwriting is different from individual underwriting. It requires an aggre-gation, which should be homogenous in nature, so that the rate of mortality and mordibility is predictable. Group is the unit of underwriting. An important requirement is that a group already exist for some purpose and it has requested for insurance rather than group being formed for obtaining insurance. Therefore group insurance is provided only to groups, which have been formed for reasons other than obtaining the insurance coverage. Also, the flow of members must be steady in the group and all members should be covered.

A Master Contract Policy is a detailed document setting forth the contractual relationship between the group contract owner and the insurance company. The insureds *viz.*, group members or their beneficiaries are not actually parties to the contract.

When a group insurance scheme is being introduced for employees for the first time, generally an option to enter or exit is allowed. Providing such option is a must because, the opportunity cost may be high *e.g.* loss of some benefits C.S.P.F. in lieu of Group Insurance. For subsequent entrants, group insurance is generally compulsory.

Group insurance do offer insurance protection to persons who are otherwise uninsurable. It is tax effective and cost effective. Group insurance are deeply supported and significantly funded by employees.

However, group insurance suffers from limitations. An important one is the need for individual insurance (which may be expensive) arising out of termination of group or separation from the employment.

Coverage

- Group insurance cover is generally provided to a group of not less than 25 persons.
- Soon upon the cover becomes effective, it lasts for the period till which the insured remains with the employer or the group.
- The eligibility requirement is that an employee must be actively at work and must work no fewer than the normal number of hours in a work week at his or her job on the date when he or she becomes eligible for coverage. The requirement assures a reasonable minimum of health and physical well-being and protects the insurer against serious adverse selection.

  After the completion of the probationary period, under a noncontributory plan, the employee automatically is covered. Under a contributory plan, the employee is given a period of time, known as the **eligibility period,** during which the insured is entitled to apply for insurance without submitting evidence of insurability.

Rating

Group insurance rating involves of two steps :

1. the determination of unit price, referred to as a rate or premium rate for each unit of benefit (*e.g.* Rs. 1,000 of life insurance, Rs. 1 of daily hospital benefit, or Rs. 1 of monthly income disability benefit).
2. the determination of the total price or premium that will be paid by the contract-holder for all of the coverage purchased.

The approach to group insurance pricing differs depending on whether manual rating or experience rating is used. In the manual-rating process, premium rates are established for broad classes of group insurance business. Manual rating is used with small groups for which no credible/reliable individual loss experience is available. This problem exists because the size of the group is such that it is impossible to determine whether the experience is due to random chance or is truly reflective of the risk exposure. Manual rating is also used to establish the initial premiums for larger groups that are subject to experience rating, particularly when a group is being written for the first time. In all but the largest groups, experience rating is used to combine manual rates and the actual experience of a given group to determine the final premium. The relative weights depend on the credibility of the group's own experience.

Manual premium rates (also called tabular rates) are quoted in a company's rate manual. As pointed out earlier, these manual rates are applied to a specific group insurance case in order to determine the average premium rate for the case that will then be multiplied by the number of benefit units to obtain a premium for the group.

Insurance companies that write a large volume of any given type of group insurance rely on their own experience in determining the frequency and severity of future claims.

Experience rating is the process whereby a contractholder is given the financial benefit or held financially accountable for its past claims experience in insurance-rating calculations. Probably the major reason for using experience rating is competition. Charging identical rates for all groups regardless of their experience would lead to adverse selection with employers with good experience seeking out insurance companies that offered lower rates, or they would turn to self-funding as a way to reduce costs. The insurance company that did not consider claims experience would, therefore, be left with only the poor risks.

In evaluating the amount of incurred claims, provision is usually made for catastrophic claim pooling. Both *individual and aggregate stop-loss limits* are established in which exceptionally large claims (above these limits) are not charged to the group's experience. The "excess" portions of claims are pooled for all groups and an average charge is accounted for in the pricing process. The approach is to give weight to the individual group's own experience to the extent that it is credible. In determining the claims charge, a credibility factor, usually based on the size of the group (determined by the number of lives insured) and the type of coverage involved, is used. This factor can vary from zero to one depending on the actuarial estimates of experience credibility and other considerations such as the adequacy of the contingency reserve developed by the group. In effect, the claims charge is a *weighted average* of (1) the incurred claims subject to experience rating and (2) the expected claims, with the incurred claims being assigned a weight equal to the credibility factor and the expected claims being assigned a weight equal to one minus the credibility factor.

20.2 Factors Led to Growth in Group Insurance

Combinations of various factors have resulted in the substantial growth of group insurance in the western world, particularly the USA. A few of these important factors are discussed hereunder.

(1) Industrialisation: The transition from agrarian to industrial economy in the Europe has magnified the economic consequences of death, sickness, accidents and old age. As a result, some employers tried to provide retirement, death and medical benefits in a systematic way through group insurance. In fact companies started offering various kinds of benefit plans to attract and retain talented employees through group insurance.

(2) Organised labour: Though unionism has pressurised employers to broaden the employee benefits offered from time to time, it is in fact the employer's approach to wean away the employees from unionism that made them to offer a variety of benefits. This need for providing variety of benefits on a cost effective scale has ultimately given a boost to group insurance.

(3) Wage Control: During the periods of wage control, immediately after the Second World War, companies started offering benefit plans to attract an retain talented employees through group insurance mechanism. Group health insurance coverage grew rapidly when employers learned it could be treated as a fringe benefit, exempt from wage and salary control.

(4) Cost Advantages: Because of the economics associated with the group underwriting and administration benefits, it became feasible to obtain insurance at lower cost through group mechanism. Besides the employers can deduct group insurance contributions as business expenses and thus save on taxes. Similarly, employees may have no taxable income as a result of employer contributing on their behalf to group insurance.

(5) Inflation: Inflation has also affected the cost of group insurance. Increase in the level of inflation results in increased wages/salaries. As the benefits are linked to wages, the cost of providing benefits to the employees also increases under an inflationary economy. The benefits given in the form of fixed amounts are likely to exert pressure on employees during inflationary period. During such times, companies have resorted to group insurance as a means of cutting cost.

(6) Legislation: In every country, the government has made the inclusion of certain benefits like those for maternity compulsory. Offering such benefits through group insurance mechanism turned out to be a cheaper tool for the employers. Thus, group insurance has picked up momentum. Cumulatively all these factors have led to a substantial growth in group insurance.

20.3 IMPORTANCE OF GROUP INSURANCE

Group insurance has changed the picture of the whole insurance industry. Because of different insurance products, it has been a blessing for both the employers and employees. It offers an element of certainty to employees by comforting the people affected by ill health, disability, unemployment and even premature death, etc., at an affordable price. Following are the benefits of group insurance to both employees and employers.

20.3.1 Benefits to Employees

Employees have been the major gainers of group insurance, which has increased the scope of employee benefit manifold.

(a) Low Cost: The major benefit derived by the employees under the group insurance is the low cost of policy as compared to the individual insurance policy. This is feasible due to large number of employees under the same insurance policy that ultimately reduced the administrative costs.

(b) Employee Benefit Plan: Group insurance is the most popular employee benefit plan. A large section of the working class is found to be unable to obtain an individual insurance policy for oneself/ one's spouse/ family because of its high cost. Thus, it depends solely on the employer to fund its insurance policy.

(c) Flexibility: The concept of group insurance is applicable to all sectors of society and industry. This aspect of group insurance has made it popular among different groups like trade associations and etc.

(d) Tax Deductions: As the benefits are received in the form of group insurance policy, the employee under the group can avail the benefits of tax deductions by contributing to the group insurance policy.

20.3.2 Benefits to The Employers

Group insurance has become an essential employee benefit, and has helped employers in not only improving the productivity of employees but also employee morale in the organisation.

(a) Retention: Many organisations provide group insurance to its employees in the form of an additional benefit to retain them for a longer period. Group insurance benefit not only increases the retention ratio among the employees, but also their productivity and morale.

(b) Public Image: An organisation can always promote its public image through group insurance schemes and thus attract the major productive cream of the market.

(c) Tax Benefits: By providing the group insurance benefit plan, whether contributory or non-contributory to the employees, the employer can avail tax deductions under the taxation rules.

(d) Size of the Organisation: Group insurance is beneficial to all types of organisations, irrespective of size and number of employees.

20.4 ELIGIBILITY OR UNDERWRITING CONSIDERATIONS

Group insurance specifies certain eligibility standards for employees, which would ultimately help both the employer and the employee. There are certain underwriting considerations, which are applicable to all types of group insurance. Following are the major eligibility considerations.

(1) Stability: There must be a steady flow of people through the group, only then expenses like the administration can be controlled. To avoid a large turnover, which can increase the cost of group insurance, the newly hired employees can be asked to go through a probationary period before joining group insurance.

(2) Determination: The insurance company has to decide the method of determining the benefits in a way that individual selection both by the employer and the employee does not generate conflicts. Thus, the employer needs to determine a formula or a specific level of salary or position that forms the basis for determination of benefits.

(3) Purpose of Existence: The most fundamental principle of group insurance is that it should not be solely for the purpose of obtaining the benefits of group insurance. Ex, a group formed by cancer patients. An "employer-employee" relationship should be in existence so as to obtain the benefits of group insurance.

(4) Administration: In case of underwriting the insurance company requires co-operation from the employer for carrying out certain administrative activities and also sharing the cost of such expenses. It is, therefore, essential that the employer is willing to play his part in the success of the group insurance schemes.

(5) Determination of Eligibility: There are certain eligibility conditions, like going through a probationary period that need to be fulfilled. Apart from this, certain group insurance schemes may also limit the eligibility to full time employees or permanent employees only.

(6) Premium: The most important thing to be determined in group insurance scheme is whether the plan would be contributory or non- contributory. If contributory, then what would be the proportion of both the employer and the employee? Certain insurance companies may limit the contribution level of the employees so as not to burden them financially.

(7) Composition: This is another important factor to be considered in underwriting. The age, sex and income of the employee also play an important role in determining the premium and the claims. Like, if a large number of employees are in their old age, then it would result in increased mortality rates.

(8) Industry: In underwriting, the nature of the industry to which the group belongs is also very important for it influences the very health of the employees like in the case of cement industry, the employees are being highly vulnerable to respiratory problems. Hence, the life and health insurance rates are based on the occupational hazards and the turnover rate in the industry.

(9) Geographical Location: Geographical location would influence medical claims to a great extent. For example, medical claims may be less in western India while it could be more in eastern India. Similarly, geographically scattered employees pose more administrative problems and in turn increase the administrative expenses. It is also necessary to check if the employer has proper facilities to service the policy owners.

(10) Persistency: It is not possible for any insurance company to recover the initial administrative expenses like initial high commissions, etc. Therefore, the policy must be in force for a minimum period of 4-5 years so that the insurance company can recover its initial expenses. It is, therefore, important to know the time period for which the group insurance would be functioning as an "employer benefit" in the organisation or how frequently the employer is known to change the insurance companies.

20.5 ELIGIBLE GROUPS FOR GROUP INSURANCE

Group insurance has widened its approach across all sections of the industry and society. This concept of eligibility for availing the benefits of group insurance has stabilized over a period of time. Some of the well-established group eligibility norms are discussed hereunder.

(1) Single Employer: Single employer is the most popular form of group insurance. The employer may be of any kind: a partnership firm, sole proprietorship firm or other form of organisation. Under this form, the employee undertakes to ensure the employee. Here, the employees include even the proprietors, partners of a firm, employees working in an associated company or subsidiary and retained employees. The employer needs to enter into a contract on behalf of the employees. The policy may be contributory or non-contributory. In order to reduce the administrative expenses it is essential that there is high participation from the employees.

(2) Trade Associations: Group insurance specifies certain number of people which is generally more than 10 for obtaining the benefit of insurance coverage. But every organisation may not have the requisite number. Therefore, such organisations form associations and can obtain insurance coverage to their employees. For example, there may be trade association of doctors, lawyers, engineers and etc. The members of the association should belong to the same profession or industry to maintain homogeneity in the group. In such associations, high participation from the employees is needed to reduce the cost of the policy.

(3) Labour Union: At times, Labour Unions provide group coverage for their union members. Under such coverage, policies remain with the union. Usually, union-sponsored policies are contributory in nature.

(4) Negotiated Trusteeship: These Trusteeships are formed through collective bargaining between a union and the employers of the union members. Such employees usually hail from activities like trucking, construction, etc. Employers of such union members make payments to the trusteeship to provide group insurance benefits. The group insurance contract is issued favouring the trustees of the fund. The employers regularly contributes fund to the trustees to meet premium costs and other administrative expenses related to the insurance coverage

(5) Self-insurance: Some big employers at times prefer self-insurance against certain risks. However, from a practical point of view, this may not be always be feasible as very few companies can afford to meet the claims arising out due to death, catastrophic medical expenses or disability from their current revenues. Except for very large employers, it is generally very difficult to make accurate prediction of frequency of claims and allocate the payment of benefits. Even if an employer believes that claims can be met from the current cash flows, it can not wish away the administrative problems associated with the management of claims and other administrative function. So, self-insurance is not advisable in case of group insurance.

(6) Debtor-Creditor Group: The banks, financial institutions, small finance companies and retailers providing loans may form a group and seek coverage under life / health insurance for their debtors. The purpose of such coverage is to ensure that the lenders purpose of such coverage is to ensure that the lenders don't suffer financial losses due to debtor's ill health / disability / premature death. Accordingly, the benefit under the policy is paid directly to the creditors, Even though the debtor is the beneficiary of the policy.

(7) Multiple Employer Trust: In this type of group insurance as the number of employees is few, they urge the employers to enter into multiple employer trusts to provide them with group benefits. The employers who participate should, of course, belong to same category of industry. They need not, of course, form into an association. Each such trust must have a trustee and an administrator. Such trusts get fully insured with an insurer using him or a third-party administrator to act as an administrator.

20.6 TYPES OF GROUP INSURANCE SCHEMES

Group insurance policies offer life insurance protection to all types of groups such as

- Employer-employee groups
- Professionals
- Co-operatives
- Weaker sections of society, etc.

Insurance coverage is provided for people as long their occupations are approved and the rated of payable premium are fairly subsidized under social security group schemes.

Besides providing insurance coverage, insurance corporations design group insurance policies in a manner that employee specific liabilities such as funding of gratuities and payment of pensons are also minimised.

A few of the key features why group insurance schemes are more advantageous are :

- Low rates of payable premium that are based upon the ages, combinations of members, occupations and working conditions.
- Simple insurability conditions such as employees not being absent from duty owing to ill-health at the commitment of the policy period.
- Easy administration since a single master policy is issued to cover all the employee members.

The only conditions for granting a group insurance policy that matter to the insurance corporation are a requisite minimum group size and a minimum particular number. The standard schemes offered by the Life Insurance Corporation are :

- Group Term Insurance Schemes
- Group Insurance Schemes in lieu of EDLI
- Group Gratuity Schemes
- Group Superannuation Schemes
- Group Savings Linked Insurance Schemes (GSLI)
- Voluntary Retirement Schemes (VRS)
- Group Leave Encashment Schemes and
- Group Mortgage Redemption Assurance Scheme
- Social Security Schemes

Group Term Insurance Scheme

It is a term insurance scheme introduced by LIC to provide life insurance protection to all the members of a group subject to some simple insurability conditions without insisting upon any medical evidence. Administration of the scheme is on group basis and cost is low. Group (Term) Insurance Scheme, offers covers only on death and there is no maturity value at the end of the term. Group (Term) Insurance Scheme is at present offered under One-Year Renewable Group term assurance plan (OYRGTA). Every year on Annual Renewal date LIC charges the premium depending upon the changes in size and age distribution of the age group.

Group (term) Insurance Scheme has a number of varieties. The Scheme may provide for a uniform cover to all members of the group or graded covers for different categories of members, cover for all amounts of outstanding housing loans or vehicle advances, or some other benefits (*e.g.*, life cover to supplement pension or PF benefits in case of death). The schemes may have add-ons like Double Accident Benefit, Critical Illness Benefit, Disability benefit etc.

The premium under such scheme may be wholly paid by the employer or the Nodal Agency. However, the scheme may be contributory *i.e.* the members may also contribute. Double Accident Benefit, *i.e.* payment of double the sum assured on death due to accident (without permanent disability benefit), may be allowed under Group Insurance Schemes for an extra premium or Group Insurance Scheme in lieu of EDLIS the insurability condition is that should be a member of the Provident Fund Scheme of the employer. For other GI Schemes of employer-employee groups the insurability condition is that the member should not be absent on ground of sickness on the entry date. For all non-employer-employee Group Schemes the basic insurability condition is that the member should be in good health on the date of entry.

At the commencement and thereafter on each Annual Renewal Date, the Group Policyholder will have to send all the member's data (and particulars of the new entrants from time to time) to the P & GS unit of LIC. Detailed

OYRGTA premium calculation will be made on each Annual Renewal Date. When a claim arises, the particulars of the respective member are to be intimated together with the claim form and death certificate. Group term insurance, being a low–cost insurance providing only risk cover, is suitable for providing social security schemes to the economically weaker sections particularly in developing countries.

Group Gratuity Scheme

Under the Payment of Gratuity Act, 1972, it is employers statutory liability to pay 15 days salary (15/26 of a month's wages) for every completed years service to each of his employees on their exit, for any reason after five years of continuous service, subject to maximum limit of 3.5 lacs. Higher benefits can be paid if the employer so desires. Gratuity payable to the employees can be paid as and when liability arises and can be claimed as deductable expense under P & L A/c of the relevant financial years. However, the sound system of financial management envisages providing for Gratuity liability every year and claiming the tax benefits as it is mandatory as per Accounting Standards 15 (AS15) to account for the liability on Actual basis. This can be done by creating a Trust, managed privately or by LIC and paying the amount to the Trust every year.

Once the employer's liability is established, the employer can provide for such expense ion the following ways:

Pay as you go method – when the payment is made to the employee when he leaves the organisation out of the funds available at that moment of time.

Provisions Method : an estimated amount of gratuity is provide for in the books in every accounting year.

Gratuity Fund Method : Setting up of a Gratuity Fund as an irrevocable trust which would manage the investments of the fund comprising of the contributions, and make payments of gratuity out of the fund. In case of Privately Managed Trust, investment of funds will have to be done as per Income-Tax Act, by the trustees and entire administration of the Trust including Actuarial Valuation will be the responsibility of the Trustees. In case of an insurer management trust *e.g.* LIC managed trust, the job of investment and actuarial valuation is taken over by the corporation free of charge and in addition, the Corporation on the accumulated funds pays interest. Group Gratuity Schemes with the insurer therefore serve the following advantages:

(*a*) Insurer may have better expertise in managing investments than trustees.

(*b*) The insurer generally posses big portfolios, which result in better risk-return management, compared to an individual trust with its relatively small portfolio.

(*c*) The benefit of the group term insurance would logically ensure that that families of employees dying early get the same gratuity as if the employee had completed the full term of service.

(*d*) The insurer has actuarial skills to evaluate the adequacy of the fund from time to time.

Group Gratuity (Cash Accumulation) Scheme of LIC allows employer's initial contribution to be paid on the date of setting up of fund in full or in 5 yearly equated instalments from such date. There is no limit to the amount and deduction to be allowed shall not exceed 8 1/3% of the past salaries. Multi-Employer group is not allowed as per CBDT directions.

Group Superannuation

A pension is a regular payment received after one has retire from active life. In order to retain competent and trained personnel, provision of pension is an important tools and also with continuous improvement in longevity a regular income even after retirement, pension has become a necessity. To provide the pension benefits to employees, an employer has two alternatives under the provisions of Rule 89 of Income Tax Rules 1962.

1. Create a privately managed trust fund and as and when a member retires, purchase annuity from LIC to provide pension for such retiring member.
2. Entrust the Management of the Pension Fund to an Insurer by purchasing its Group Superannuation Scheme.

Pension can be managed and funded in many ways. However, the insurer managed pension offer several advantages including high liquidity, actuarial, legal and taxation assistance to the trustees. In such schemes, the employer contributes a certain fixed percentage of salary of each member. Insurer accumulates such contributions and the accumulated amount is utilized to provide various benefits.

The popular schemes include the following benefits :

1. On the retirement of a member, the corpus (contributions plus interest) is utilised to provide the pension as per the directions of the member.
2. On death of the member, the Pension is payable on the life of the beneficiary. Corpus is utilised towards the payment of pension of the type the beneficiary may opt and the benefit so received is tax free. A lump sum payable by way of death besides the pension, if the employer has taken Group Insurance Scheme in conjunction with the Group Superannuation Scheme.
3. On withdrawl the insured can get the equitable interest transferred to the Superannuation Scheme of the new employer or opt for immediate or deferred pension.

Following pensions schemes are approved by LIC :

1. Life Pension ceasing at death.
2. Life Pension with Return of Capital and Group Pension Terminal Bonus on death.
3. Life Pension guaranteed for 5.10.15 or 20 years and life thereafter.
4. Joint Life Pension payable on the last survivor of the employee and spouse.
5. Joint Life Pension payable to the last survivor of the employee and spouse with return of capital on the death of the last survivor. If desired, 1/3rd of the pension can be commuted at vesting.

Pension Fund Scheme

The maximum annual contribution that an employer can make to the Pension Fund and Provident Fund is restricted by the Income Tax Provisions to 27% of the annual salary (basic plus D.A.) Mostly the employer contributes, but is so desired, both the employer and the employees may contribute, in which case the scheme is called a Contributory Pension Fund Scheme. The provisions relating to the approved Superannuation Scheme are set out in Part 'B' of the Fourth Scheme of the Income-Tax Act, 1961 and Part XIII of the Income Tax Rules, 1962. The income tax concession will be available only if the scheme is approved by the CIT. The annual contribution is treated as a deductible business expense in term of Section 36(1) (iv) of the I.T. Act. In terms of a Notification issued by the Central Board of Direct Taxes.80% of the contribution (s) towards the past service liability are treated as deductible business expenses spread over in the subsequent years of payment. The employee's contribution, in the case of the Contributions scheme qualifies for exemption under Section 80C of the Income-Tax Act.

LIC has also launched a group insurance scheme in conjunction with superannuation scheme. In this scheme, the members of the Group Superannuation scheme can be covered under Group Insurance in conjunction with superannuation scheme so as to provide death risk cover while in service subject to certain conditions.

Group Savings Linked Insurance Scheme

Group Savings Linked Insurance scheme is a low cost cover, which provides insurance without evidence of health. Employers provided certain percentage of employees is willing to join the Scheme can introduce the scheme. For the new entrants to the employer, the membership of the Scheme is compulsory. It is decided on the basis of Group size and the occupation of the group. Premium has two components *i.e.* Risk Premium and Savings Premium. Risk Premium is utilised to offer life cover and the Savings Premium is accumulated in members account. Double accident benefit can be allowed to the extent of the Sum Assured for an extra Premium.

The present rate of interest allowed on saving portion of premium is 8% compounding yearly. Any employee irrespective of his present state of health is eligible to join the scheme subject to certain conditions. The only insurability condition is that the employee should not be absent on medical ground on the date of commencement of the scheme. All employees who have not crossed the retirement age are eligible to join the scheme. All future employees have to join the scheme compulsorily.

Employees' total contribution, savings as well as risk premium is entitled for deduction in income-tax rebate under Sec. 88 of the Income Tax Act. The entire claim amount including interest earned payable on retirement or leaving service or on death is free from income tax. The premium paid by the employer towards insurance cover is treated as business expenses. Employees' total contribution, savings as well as risk premium is entitled for income-tax deduction under Sec. 80C of the Income Tax Act. The entire claim amount including interest earned payable on retirement or leaving service or on death is free from income tax.

Group Mortgage Redemption Assurance Scheme

Group Mortgage Redemption Assurance Scheme, is a Group Insurance Scheme for the borrowers of Housing/ Vehicle Loans from Financial Institutions where Loan is recovered under EMI. Under the Scheme, the premium is payable in a single instalment covering a decreasing life cover. Insurance cover every year will be almost equal to the loan outstanding at the anniversary date of each borrower. The premium under the scheme is dependent upon the age (nearer Birthday) at entry of the member into the Scheme, outstanding loan amount at entry date, term of loan, schedule of repayment and the rate of interest with which the loan was availed.

Any borrower may become member of this scheme. The minimum term of assurance is 3 years and the existing borrowers can join the scheme with certain conditions within 6 months of the commencement of scheme. In case of death of the member during the coverage period, life cover on the anniversary date preceding the date of death is payable. The claim proceeds are used to square off the outstanding loan.

Group Leave Encashment Scheme

Many employers provide Leave Encashment benefit in addition to other retirement benefits to their employees which is a lumpsum amount payable to the employees or their dependants on retirement, death, disablement, voluntary retirement etc. The leave encashment facility available to employees, can be a huge liability to the employers. An option available to the employers is the Group Leave Encashment Scheme where the amount depends upon the leave to the credit of the employee and his/ her salary at the time of exit. Liability is of increasing nature as it is linked with salary as well as leaves position. As per the amended section 209 (3) of the Company's Act 1956 and Accounting Standard (AS-15) dated January, 1995, the employers have to account for the liability in respect of leave encashment facility, if any, available to the employees and to provide for the same in their Annual Accounts. It is, therefore, necessary for the companies to ascertain liability in respect of Leave Encashment facilities, if any, available to the employees and provide for the same in the books of accounts every year. It helps the employers in ascertaining the true cost of their products and services.

Group Leave Encashment Schemes (GLES) of helps the employers in funding of their leave encashment liability. In this scheme the employers submits the employees' data and rules for Leave Encashment to the insurer who makes the actuarial valuation and estimates the funding requirements which shall be quoted to the company. A uniform life cover per employee or graded cover is provided under One Year Renewable Group Term Assurance Plan of LIC. A small term insurance premium will be charged in addition to contributions for funding. A Running Account is maintained under the scheme and the contributions (excluding term assurance premium) will be credited to this account and all claims except term assurance cover will be settled out of the Running Account. Interest at the rate declared by LIC from time to time will be credited to the Running Account at the end of the financial year.

On the exit of an employee or encashment of leaves during the service the Leave Encashment amount will be paid from the Fund of the scheme maintained with LIC.

On the death of an employee, in addition to his/her leave encashment benefit, his/her family will be entitled to the amount of Insurance Cover, which will be tax-free. The insurer does the Actuarial Valuation and provides the certificate as per requirements of the accounting standard AS-15. The amount of Term Insurance Premium paid for Life Insurance Cover is treated as business expenses.

Group Insurance Scheme in Lieu of EDLI

All employees to whom the Employee's Provident Fund and Miscellaneous Provision Act, 1952 applies, have a Statutory liability to subscribe to Employee's Deposit Linked Insurance Scheme, 1976 to provide for the benefit of Life insurance to all their employees. Under the scheme as amended with effect from 24th June, 2000 the insurance benefit is equal to the average balance to the credit of the deceased employee in the Provident Fund during the last 12 months, provided that where such balance exceeds Rs. 35,000, insurance cover would be equal to Rs. 35,000 plus 25% of the amount in excess of Rs. 35,000 subject to a maximum of Rs. 60,000. Thus if the length of service is not adequate and/or the salary is low the average balance may be substantially less and such the benefit to the employee's family is either inadequate or non-existent. The contribution @ 0.50% of each employee's salary is payable by the Employer to the Provident Fund Authorities. However, under Sec. 17(2A) of the act, the employer may be exempted from contributing to this scheme, if he/she has provided for better insurance benefits through alternative scheme.

Group Insurance Scheme in lieu of EDLI offered by LIC has the following features:

3. The premium payable by the employer is usually less than the total contribution being paid by the employer to R.P.F.C; particularly when the salary level is high and average age of the group is low.
4. Settlement of claim is quicker, LIC requires only the death certificate and the Claim Form from the employer. Premium paid by the employer is treated as normal business expenses for Income-Tax purpose.
5. Each employee is covered for a sum assured ranging between 5,000 to 2,00,000 depending upon the current salary and service put in from day one irrespective of the actual balance in the Provident Fund. Alternatively every employee/worker can be covered for a uniform sum assured which will be decided depending upon the group size.
6. Double accident benefit can be allowed to the extent of the Sum Assured for an extra Premium.

20.7 Social Insurance Covers

The Insurance Regulatory and Development Authority Act, 1999 (para 19; First schedule) has amended the Sections 32B and 32C of the Insurance Act, 1938 as under:

Section 32B

Every insurer shall, after the commencement of Insurance Regulatory and Development Authority Act, 1999, undertake such percentages of life insurance business and general insurance business in the rural and social sector, as may be specified, in the Official Gazette by the authority, in this behalf.

Section 32C

Every insurer shall, after the commencement of Insurance Regulatory and Development Authority Act, 1999, discharge the obligations specified under Section 32B to provide life insurance or general insurance policies to those residing in the rural sector, workers in the unorganised sector or informal sector or economically vulnerable or backward classes of the society and other categories of persons as may be specified by the regulations made by the authority and such insurance policies shall include insurance for crops.

The IRDA Regulations 2000 makes it compulsory for the insurers, existing and new to promote the social insurance. Similar to the requirement for the rural sector, the regulations also prescribe for undertaking benchmark percentages for insurances in the social insurance sector for the players.

The *social sector* is defined as including the unorganised sector, the informal sector, the economically vulnerable or backward classes and other categories of persons, both in rural and urban areas.

In case of social sector the requirement is compulsory underwriting of 5000 lives in the first financial year, 7,500 in the second year and so on. Also, the authority may revise the obligation once in 5 years.

Social insurance is the baby of the social security systems prevailing in that country. Social security is the security cover which society furnishes through appropriate organisation against risks to which its members are exposed. The basic idea is to use social means to prevent deprivation and vulnerability to deprivation.

In the literature on development issues, it has often been assumed explicitly or implicitly that developing countries are too poor to be able to *afford* social security systems. Public participation in social security systems can take wide variety of forms and it is very much possible even for poor countries to achieve considerable success on this front. This is not to say that economic growth and social security are not linked. However at the same time, simple economic growth alone cannot ensure improvements in living standards of people. Social intervention is necessary for improving quality of life at the micro level.

Studies carried out by UNICEF and World Bank also provide considerable evidence that it has been the direct public support rather than the average income of the population that has been the driving force behind the success of social security schemes world-wide. In fact, the countries with good primary social security systems are those which have adopted the path of support-led security (as against growth-led security) and have *not waited* to grow rich before resorting to large scale public support to guarantee certain basic capabilities. Notable examples include China, Chile, Cuba, Jamaica and Kuwait.

Need for a Social Security System in India

A large chunk of Indian population lives under abject poverty. They barely manage to earn enough to eat. It is our social obligation to provide our underprivileged brethren with an adequate safety cover.

Only a very small percentage of the working population is employed by the organised sector, which provides benefits like the state pension. A vast majority is either self employed or employed in the rural and unorganised sector. As a result, they are deprived of social benefits such as retirement benefits and disability or death compen-sation. Similarly, health-care although subsidised is thinly and haphazardly spread. State support for the unemployed and disabled is negligible.

Social changes taking place in the country are also resulting into increased need for a social security system. The Joint Family System, which prevailed in India for long is losing its flavour. This system provided a natural safety cover to the members of a family. However, its break-up into nuclear families means that the death or disability of the bread-earner leaves his dependants completely exposed.

A comprehensive social security system includes social insurance, health insurance, disability compensation, unemployment compensation, old-age pension schemes, etc. In India, social security systems are an emerging concept and there is no strong base to start with. Given the constraints on funds and infrastructure availability, social insurance is the only scheme that can be launched at present. Further, opening up of the insurance sector has created increased awareness about insurance and also provides a sustainable revenue model to carry out the task of social insurance.

India — A Special Case

India is a special case compared to many other countries for the implementation of social insurance schemes. A support-led social security system is one that requires active state intervention. The main source of funds provided by the state comes from the taxes it collects. Unfortunately, India has a tiny tax-paying base. Further, social insurance is not a constitutional right of the citizens in India. The cause can again be traced to the fragile economic situation of the country that does not permit any kind of comprehensive social insurance schemes.

Salary Savings Scheme

Under this scheme the premium is deducted from the salary of the employee at source and net is paid to him. The Employer to the insurer remits to the amount so collected. The Salary Savings Scheme can be introduced in an institution or establishment subject to specified terms and conditions.

The scheme is of great benefit to the insurer because the payments of the premium is assured, as long as the employee is in service and the procedures of accounting become simple because there is only one transaction for all the employees under one employer. The minimum number of members is 15 and there is no maximum limit. Since the payment of premium is consistent and guaranteed, the loading on monthly premiums is not charged in SSS policies. The SSS policies can be issued only after the employer has agreed to make deductions regularly from the salaries of the employees and remit the premiums to the insurer. The employee has to authorise the employer to deduct the premium from his salary and such authorisation letters are collected along with the proposal for insurance and are sent to the employer by the insurer.

Logically, there may be a gap between the time the policy is completed and the notice for premium sent to the employer. Therefore, first two premiums are collected in advance.

Shiksha Sahayog Yojana

It is a scholarship scheme launched by LIC on 31.12.2001 for the benefit of children of members of Janashree Bima Yojana. It is for the students studying in ix to xii standards, whose parents are covered under Janashree Bima Yojana. If a student fails and is detained in the same standard, he will not be eligible for scholarship for the next year in the same standard.

Under this scheme, the scholarship of Rs 300/- per quarter per child will be paid for maximum period of 4 years. The benefit is restricted to two children per member (family) only. No premium is charged for the scholarship. A Nodal Agency specified for the purpose, identifies the students. The member of Janashree Bima Yojana whose child is eligible for scholarship has to fill up an application form (available with Nodal Agency) and submit to the Nodal Agency. The applications duly filled up and certified will be sent alongwith the list of the beneficiary students by the Nodal Agency to the concerned LIC,.P&GS Unit for disbursement of scholar-ship/s. The scholarship/s is disbursed to the beneficiary students through the concerned Nodal Agency. As only a limited number of beneficiaries will be provided scholarship under the scheme, the selection for eligible students will be made on the basis of poorest of the poor.

The scheme is administered through Pension and Group Schemes Department of LIC of India.

Janashree Bima Yojana

It was launched by LIC to provide life insurance protection to the rural and urban poor persons below poverty line and marginally above the poverty line in the age group of 18 to 58 years belonging to a member of any of the approved vocation/occupation groups *e.g.* a government department which is concerned with the welfare of any such vocation/occupation group, a Welfare Fund/ Society, Village Panchayat, NGO, Self-Help Group, etc. The minimum number of members is 25.

Key Terms

- Master Policy
- Labour Unions
- Debtor – Creditor Group
- Multiple Employer Trust

- ❒ Group Term Insurance Schemes
- ❒ Group Superannuation Schemes
- ❒ Group Leave Encashment Schemes
- ❒ Pension Fund Scheme
- ❒ Group Gratuity Schemes
- ❒ Group Mortgage Redemption Assurance
- ❒ Group Savings Linked Insurance Schemes
- ❒ Social Security Schemes

Questions for Review

1. What is group insurance? How it is different from individual insurance? Discuss the various group insurance plans available in India.
2. "Each and every life insured is a competent party in a group insurance contract". Do you agree? Justify your answer.
3. Give at least two group insurance schemes in which the employees contribute towards the premium.
4. What are the importance of group insurance to both employer and employees?
5. What are different eligibility groups for group insurance?
6. Mr. Ram owns a garment export unit. Assuming that 15 employees of different age group are working in the unit, suggest him possible ways of getting a group insurance policy for his employees?
7. What are the underwriting considerations, which are applicable to all types of group insurance schemes?
8. What are the standard group insurance schemes offered by the Life Insurance Corporation of India?
9. How does the Government play major role in providing group insurance benefits to rural sector?
10. Write short note on the following:
    (*a*) Shiksha Sahayog Yojana
    (*b*) Group Leave Encashment Scheme
    (*c*) Debtor-Creditor Group
    (*d*) Group Superannuation Scheme

Suggested Readings

1. S.L. Kane, *Principles of Life Insurance,* Himalaya Publishing House, Mumbai, 2003.
2. *Practice of Life Assurance,* IC02, Insurance Institute of India, 2003.
3. *Group and Health Insurance*, ICFAI University press, Hyderabad, 2002

Web Resources

- *www.licindia.com*
- www.insurance.yahoo.com

Life Assurance Management

Chapter **21**

Chapter Objectives

After reading this chapter you will be able to understand :

- *Maintenance of Book by Life Insurance Companies*
- *Rides and Settle option*
- *Valuation of Surplus and distribution*

21.1 Maintanence Of Books

A life insurance company maintains two types of books. One, to comply with the legal requirements and another, to facilitate its operation.

Statutory Books : The following books are to be maintained by all insurance offices :

(*i*) *Register of Policies :* This register will contain the particulars in respect of each policy issued by the insurer such as the name and address of the policy holder, the date when the policy was effected and record of the assignment of the policy (if any).

(*ii*) *Register of Claims :* It contains the particulars of each claims such as the date of claim, the name and address of claimants, the date on which the claim was discharged, date and ground for rejection, in case the claim is rejected.

(*iii*) *The Register of Licensed Insurance Agents :* It contains the particulars of various insurance agents, their names, addresses, particulars of business done and commission due to them.

Subsidiary Books : For proper maintenance of accounts important subsidiary books are maintained according to the convenience of the concern. These are register of proposals and proposal advance cash book, first year's premium cash book, renewal premium cash book, agency and branch cash book, petty cash book, claims cash book, general cash book containing the summary of all previous books, bank cash book, commission register, lapsed and cancelled policies book, journal, agency ledger, policy loan ledger, general loan ledger, investment ledger etc.

Section 24 of the LIC Act states that the Corporation shall have its own fund and all receipts of the Corporation shall be credited thereto and all payments shall be made therefrom.

Section 10(1) of the Insurance Act states that where the insurer carries on life, fire, marine and miscellaneous business, he shall keep a separate account of all receipts and payments in respect of each such class of insurance business.

Section 10(2) states that where the insurer carries on the business of life insurance, all receipts due in respect of such business, shall be carried to and shall form a separate fund to be called the life insurance fund the assets of which shall be kept distinct and separate from all other assets of the insurer and the deposit made by the insurer in respect of life insurance business shall be deemed to be part of the assets of such fund and every insurer shall, within the time limited in sub-section (1) of Section 15 furnish to the Authority a statement showing in detail such assets as at the close of every financial year duly certified by an auditor.

The life insurance fund shall be absolutely for the security of the life policyholders, *i.e.*, claims for other classes of business carried on by the Company cannot be enforced against Life Fund.

Accounts and Balance Sheet

1. Section 11(1) of the Insurance Act states that every insurer in respect of all insurance business transacted by him in India shall after the close of the financial year prepare with reference to that year (*a*) in accordance with the regulations contained in Part I of the First Schedule, a Balance Sheet in the Form set forth in Part II of the schedule; (*b*) in accordance with the regulations contained in Part I of the second schedule, a profit and loss account in the forms set forth in Part II of that schedule.
2. Further, sub-sections (1A) and (1B) of Section 11 of the Insurance Act, 1938 [inserted by IRDA Act, 1999] provide as under :

   (1A) Notwithstanding anything contained in sub-section (1), every insurer, on or after the commencement of the IRDA Act 1999, in respect of insurance business transacted by him and in respect of his shareholders funds, shall, at the expiration of each financial year, prepare with reference to that year, a balance-sheet, a profit and loss account, a separate account of receipts and payments, a revenue account in accordance with the regulations made by the Authority.

   (1B) Every insurer shall keep separate account relating to funds of shareholders and policy-holders.

Every insurance company is required to prepare the financial statements and make disclosures from 30th March 2002 onwards in accordance with the guidelines of IRDA titled The Insurance Regulatory And Development Authority (Preparation Of Financial Statements And Auditors Report Of Insurance Companies) Regulations, 2002.1

The formats of the financial statements applicable as per the said guidelines are:

1. For Life Insurance Business {Schedule A Part V}

(*a*) Revenue Account [Policyholder's Account]	Form No. A-RA
(*b*) Profit and Loss Account [Shareholders' Account]	Form No. A-PL
(*c*) Balance Sheet	Form No. A-BS

2. For General Insurance Business {Schedule B Part V}

(*a*) Revenue Account	Form No. B-RA
(*b*) Profit and Loss Account [Shareholders' Account]	Form No. B-PL
(*c*) Balance Sheet	Form No. B-BS

21.2 VALUATION, SURPLUS AND DISTRIBUTION

The conventional form of life policies is "participating policy" with margins of safety built into the valuation elements to allow for protection for adverse events. Premiums are estimated by calculated on the basis of future expectations (probability) and modelling of mortality, interest and administrative expenses.

These estimations are based on assumptions, which may not hold out to be true. If the expected probability confirms to the actual outcome, the premiums are adequate to service claims else the company would be *ruined* or is in the state of financial problems. For a life insurance company, if every thing goes right, surplus or profits maybe be expected to emerge over the life of a portfolio of business. A large proportion of these surpluses is usually distributed to the policyholders as *bonuses or dividends*. These are addition to the guaranteed return allotted annually by a life insurer to holders of with profit (participating) policies. The size of the bonus depends on the insurer's performance. This bonus ensures that the value of the policyholder's insurance cover remains adequate.

However, before deciding about the distribution of surplus, it is logical to first estimate the amount of surplus, which is popularly called as *actuarial valuation*. Insurance Act, 1938 in India requires that actuarial valuations be done every year. Section 13 of the Act deals with Actuarial Reports & Abstract.

Section 13 : (1) Every insurer carrying on life insurance business shall, in respect of the life insurance business transacted by him in India, and also in the case of an insurer specified in sub clause (a) (ii) or sub clause (b) of clause (9) of section 2 in respect of all life insurance business transacted by him, every year cause an investigation to be made by an actuary into the financial condition of the life insurance business carried on by him, including a valuation of his liabilities in respect thereto and shall cause an abstract of the report of such actuary to be made in accordance with the regulations contained in Part I of the Fourth Schedule and in conformity with the requirements of Part II of that Schedule...

Section 49 : (1) No insurer, being an insurer specified in sub clause (a) (ii) or sub-clause (b) of clause (9) of section 2, who I carries on the business of life insurance or any other class or subclass of insurance business to which Section 13 applies, shall, for the purpose of declaring or paying any dividend to shareholders or any bonus to policy holders or of making any payment in services of any debentures, utilise directly or indirectly any portion of the life insurance fund or of the fund of such other class or sub--class of insurance business, as the case may be, except a surplus shown in the valuation balance sheet in such form as may be specified by the regulations made by the Authority submitted to the Authority as part of the abstract referred to in Section 15 as a result of an actuarial valuation assets and liabilities of the insurer; nor shall he increase such surplus by contributions out of any reserve fund or otherwise unless such contributions have been brought in as revenue account applicable to that class or sub class of insurance business on or before the date of the valuation aforesaid, except when the reserve fund is made up solely of transfers from similar surpluses disclosed by valuations in respect of which returns have been submitted to the Authority under Section 15 of this Act or to the Central Government under Section 11 of the Indian Life Assurance Companies Act, 1912 (6 of 1912):

Provided that payments made out of any such surplus in service of any debentures shall not exceed 50% of such surplus including any payment by way of interest on the debentures, and interest paid on the debentures shall not exceed ten per cent of any such surplus except where the interest paid on the debentures is offset against the interest credited to the fund or funds concerned in deciding the interest basis adopted in the valuation disclosing the aforesaid surplus:

Provided further that the share of any such surplus allocated to or reserved for the shareholders (including any amount for the payment of dividends guaranteed to them, whether by way of first charge or otherwise) shall not exceed such sums as may be specified by the Authority and such share shall in no case exceed 10% of such surplus in case of participating policies and in other cases the whole thereof.

(2) For the purposes of sub section (1) the actual amount of income tax deducted at source during the period following the date as at which the last preceding valuation was made and preceding the date as at which the valuation in question is made may be added to such surplus after deducting an estimated amount for income tax on such surplus, such addition and deduction being shown in an abstract of the report of the actuary referred to in sub-section (1) of section 13.

It therefore follows that any portion of the life insurance fund or of the fund of such other class or sub-class of insurance business cannot be utilised for the payment of bonus to the shareholders/policyholders. Also, the surplus utilisation for servicing debentures cannot exceed 50% and surplus allocation to/reservation for shareholders can, in no case exceed 10% of such surplus in case of participating policies and in other cases the whole thereof.

Section 52 of the act deals with prohibition of business on dividing principle and exempts the life insurers from distributing surpluses based actuarial valuation.

Section 52 : (l) No insurer shall after the commencement of this Act begin, or after 3 years from that date continue to carry on, any business upon the dividing principle, that is to say, on the principle that the benefit secured by a policy is not fixed but depends either wholly or party on the results of a distribution of certain sums amongst policies becoming claims within certain time limits, or on the principle that the premiums payable by a policy holder depend wholly or partly on the number of policies becoming claims within certain time limits:

Provided that nothing in this section shall be deemed to prevent an insurer from allocating bonuses to holders of policies of life insurance as a result of a periodical actuarial valuation either as reversionary additions to the sums insured or as immediate cash bonuses or otherwise:

Provided further that an insurer who continues to carry on insurance business on the dividing principle after the commencement of this Act shall withhold from distribution a sum of not less than 40% of the premiums received during each year after the commencement of this Act in which such business is continued so as to make up the amount required for investment under Section 27.

In a actuarial valuation process following are estimated:

(*a*) liabilities which may exist in future - claim and others

(*b*) stream of premiums expected in future

(*c*) the differential of funds available and liability is compared with the actual existing life fund (Life Assurance Fund).

A solvency situation is implied when the funds are greater than liabilities. Accordingly, the surplus is said to have been generated by the insurer, which may be distributed in various styles as discussed above.

If a surplus situation is established for an insurer based on actuarial valuation, the basis of distribution of the surplus has to be decided. This distribution of surplus may be carried out in various ways :

(*a*) One method is to provide for cash payments or reduction of premiums as the surplus arises, or the accumulated value of the cash bonuses may be paid when the policy becomes a claim or expires. By this method, a separate savings account is attached to the policy and the surplus is credited to the account as it emerges.

(*b*) Another way of distributing surplus is through terminal bonuses paid only when the policy expires. By this method, only survivors get a share of the accumulated surplus.

(*c*) The third method, and perhaps the most widely used, is one in which the profit is distributed to the policyholders by means of increasing the insurance benefits. This method provides a gradual increase in the benefits granted under the policy.

LIC method of distribution of surplus to the policyholders is in the form of *bonus additions*. As a logical principle, the method of bonus distribution must be equitable, simple and capable of being understood by the policyholders. Principle of equity implies that policyholders would receive bonuses equivalent to the contribution made by them to the surplus. The bonus may be declared as per thousand *e.g.* Rs. 5.00 per thousand. Therefore, if the Sum assured is Rs. 10,000 the bonus amount is Rs. 50.

There are many complex considerations that influence that decisions on equity in these matters. As an illustration, the variations in the rates of interest over a period of time can be looked at. The actuary takes a conservative view of the future trends in interest rates. This leads to a reserve larger than what is actually required. The policies at that time had been allowed lower rates of bonuses. The additional reserve earns a higher level of interest than what was assumed benefiting the newer policyholders at a time when the interest rates are falling. At higher rates of interest, longer term policies contribute more, including the interest earned on their additional contribution, than the shorter term policies. The contributions between different types of policies, needs careful analysis. The popular bonus systems are:

(a) *Simple Reversionary Bonus System* : in this system, the bonus is computed as uniform percentage addition to the basic sum assured and is payable on maturity (death/survival). At the time of payment, only the basic SA is reduced in proportion to the premiums paid and the vested bonus remains intact. Alternatively, the cash value of the bonus additions maybe redeemed to the policyholder or future premiums may be adjusted for bonus payments. If the basic sum assured is Rs. 50,000 and the bonus is Rs. 6.00 per thousand, the benefit would increase by Rs. 3,000.

(b) *Compound Reversionary Bonus System* : in this system, the percentage addition is made to the basic sum assured and the vested bonus additions earlier made. If the basic sum assured is Rs. 50,000 and the bonus is Rs. 6.00 per thousand, and the earlier vested bonus is Rs. 5,000, the benefit would increase by Rs. 3,300.

(c) *Tontine Bonus system* : under this system, surplus is distributed only for those policyholders who survive a stipulated period.

Based on equity principle, the amount of bonus paid on all policies of same type is uniform. However, it may vary among the different type of policies. Sometimes, the bonus is declared at a uniform rate but made to vest only after a certain period. It is logical to consider only those policies eligible for bonus, which are in force on the valuation date. Where the claims arise in a policy in a given policy year, the bonus is not paid for that year. However, an interim bonus may be paid along with the claims. This ensures the easy claims settlement and the smoothening of the valuation process. As matter of practice, the LIC pays the final additional bonus on policies where the term is equal to or greater than 15 years and which are and which are in full force at the time when claim arises. Some insurers do not pay bonus on money back policies because a proportionate share of sum assured is returned to the policyholders at regular intervals.

The term of the policy is an important consideration for the calculation of bonus The payment of bonus may also differ among the same type of policies, but different terms. The insurers for various plans and terms generally prepare the bonus charts. The reversionary bonus rates of LIC have been increasing steadily in the last 25 years. Following is an illustration of bonus table of HDFC Standard Life for the year ended 31st March 2006.

Reversionary Bonus

Policy Type	*Reversionary Bonus p.a.*
HDFC Endowment Assurance Plan HDFC Money Back Plan HDFC Children's Plan HDFC Savings Assurance Plan	Rs 22.50 per thousand Sum Assured
HDFC Assurance Plan	Rs 32.50 per thousand Sum Assured
HDFC Regular Premium Pension Plan	Rs 22.50 per thousand Sum Assured
HDFC Single Premium Pension Plan	Rs 50.00 per thousand Sum Assured
HDFC Single Premium Whole of Life Plan	Rs 50.00 per thousand Sum Assured and attaching bonuses

Interim Bonus

Policy Type	*Interim Bonus p.a.*
HDFC Endowment Assurance Plan HDFC Money Back Plan HDFC Children's' Plan	Rs 22.50 Per thousand Sum Assured
HDFC Savings Assurance Plan HDFC Assurance Plan	Rs 32.50 Per thousand Sum Assured

HDFC Regular Premium Pension Plan	Rs 22.50 Per thousand Sum Assured
HDFC Single Premium Pension Plan	Rs 50.00 Per thousand Sum Assured
HDFC Single Premium Whole of Life Plan	Rs 50.00 Per thousand Sum Assured and attaching bonuses

Key Terms

- ❒ Riders
- ❒ Free Look Period
- ❒ Waiver of Premium Rider
- ❒ Settlement Options
- ❒ Life Annuity
- ❒ Surpluses
- ❒ Bonus Additions
- ❒ Tontine Bonus
- ❒ Accident and Disability
- ❒ Major Surgical Assistance Benefit
- ❒ Guaranteed Insurability Option Rider
- ❒ Beneficiary
- ❒ Distribution
- ❒ Actuarial Valuations
- ❒ Reversionary Bonus

Questions for Review

1. What are riders? Briefly explain the various types of riders in life insurance.
2. Enumerate the provisions of the Insurance Act, 1938 dealing with valuation and distribution of surplus.
3. Write short notes on :
   (*a*) Bonus Systems
   (*b*) Settlement Options

Suggested Readings

1. P.K. Gupta, *Insurance and Risk Management,* Himalaya Publishing House, Mumbai, 2004.
2. S.L. Kane, *Principles of Life Insurance,* Himalaya Publishing House, Mumbai, 2003.
3. *Practice of Life Assurance,* IC02, Insurance Institute of India, Mumbai, 2003.

Introduction to General Insurance

Chapter
22

CHAPTER OBJECTIVES

After reading this chapter you will be able to understand :

- *History Framework of General Insurance in India*
- *Industry Structure*
- *GIC – Organisation and Working*

22.1 HISTORICAL FRAMEWORK OF GENERAL INSURANCE IN INDIA

The introduction of general insurance in India is attributable to the Industrial Revolution in the West and the consequent growth of sea-faring trade and commerce in the 17th century. It came to India as a legacy of British occupation. British and other foreign insurance companies through their agencies in India transacted this business.

General Insurance sector in India dates back to 1850, when Tritron Insurance Company, for general insurance was incorporated in 1907, The Indian Mercantile Insurance Co. Ltd. was set up to transact all classes of general insurance business. Insurance Act was passed in 1928 but it was subsequently reviewed and comphrensive legislation was enacted in 1938. In 1957, General Insurance Council, a wing of the Insurance Association of India, framed a code of conduct for ensuring fair conduct and sound business practices. In 1968, the Insurance Act, 1938 was amended to regulate investments and set minimum solvency margin and the Tariff Advisory Committee set up.

Management of Non-Life insurers was taken over by the Central Government in 1971 as a prelude to nationalisation. General Insurance business was nationalised with effect from 1.1.1973 by the General Insurance Business (Nationalisation) Act, 1972.

Prior to 1973 General Insurance was urban-centric, catering mainly to the needs of organized trade and Industry. 107 insurers including branches of foreign companies operating the country were amalgamated. GIC was incorporated as a company in 1972 and it commenced business on January 1st 1973. The Government of India subscribed to the capital of GIC. GIC, in turn subscribed to the capital of four companies. All the four companies are government companies registered under the Companies Act. These are:

- National Insurance Co. Ltd.
- New India Assurance Co. Ltd.
- Oriental Fire and General Insurance Co. Ltd.
- United India Insurance Co. Ltd.

"The main objectives of nationalisation were to ensure the development of the general insurance business in sympathy with the best of interest and advantage to the community. Further, these companies were required to promote competition in the economy and to prevent the concentration of wealth and growth of monopoly. They were supposed to spread their activities over geographical area, innovate new products as per the requirements of different segments of population and also meet social objectives through formulating policies for weaker sections of society."[1]

These subsidiaries carry out the entire major portion of the general insurance business in the country and surrender 20% of it to GIC through the obligatory reinsurance premium on a quota share basis. However, certain new players have also ventured into the general insurance business.

- Tata AIG General Insurance Co. Ltd.
- Bajaj Allianz General Insurance Co. Ltd.
- Reliance General Insurance Co. Ltd.
- Royal Sundraram General Insurance Co. Ltd.
- IFFCO TOKIO General Insurance Co. Ltd.
- ICICI Lombard General Insurance Co. Ltd.

22.2 Industry Structure

Presently GIC is the leader in General Insurance business and is under the Ministry of Finance. Of course, it has to and is accountable to IRDA. As per the IRDA guidelines, every insurance company has to report on specific matters to IRDA within a time schedule. The current and emerging structure of the industry is given is Exhibit 22.1 and 22.2.

Exhibit 22.1

CURRENT STRUCTURE OF THE INDUSTRY

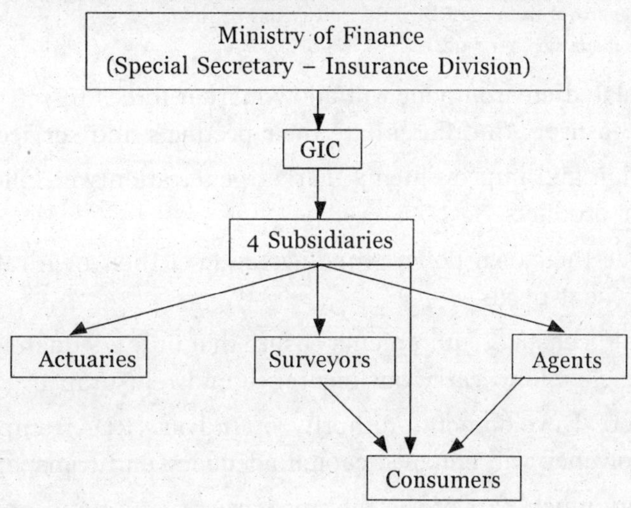

Source: The ET Knowledge Series ~ Insurance 2001-02.

In addition to IRDA, GIC along with its subsidiaries will be required to report to Ministry of Finance also. The professionalism will be strengthened both in the public and private sector, viz., Actuaries who were and present consultants to the insurance companies are expected to be employed with the respective organisation. With an increase in competition in the industry, merges and acquisitions will become common phenomenon. Also, newer distribution channels are likely to bring a sweeping change in the product efficiency and customer-oriented strategies of insurance companies.

22.2.1 Issues in General Insurance Business

Strengths/Opportunities

- The intense competition brought about by deregulation has encouraged the industry to innovate in all areas; from underwriting, marketing, policy holder servicing to record keeping
- Aggressive marketing strategies by private sector insurers will buoy consumer awareness of risk and expand the markets for products

Exhibit 22.2

Emerging Structure of the industry

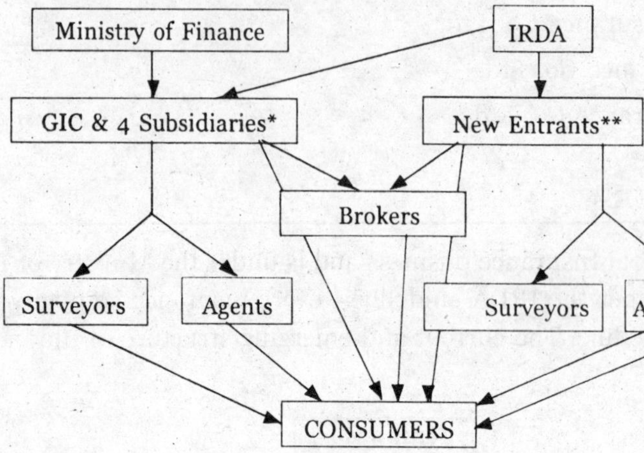

* Depending on recommendations made to the government, the four subsidiaries could be merged or made independent bodies.

** New entrants would require an approval from the RBI if they are banks or finance cos.

Sources: The ET Knowledge Series ~ Insurance 2001-02.

- Competition in a deregulated environment will allow market forces to set premiums that are appropriate for exposures and push insurers to differentiate their products and services
- Innovations in distribution and improvements market penetration will follow public and private insurers compete to market their products
- Allowing insurers to issue their own policy wondings and set their own rates will enable underwriters to tallor products to meet client needs
- The existence of stringent licensing requirements ensure that only adequately capitalized and professionally managed companies are eligible to carry out insurance and reinsurance
- The insurance Regulatory Development Authority of India's (RDA) emphasis on quarterly reporting/ monitoring of insurer solvency will enhance capital adequacy and transparency
- Licensed brokers are very much part of the intermediary structure and only those with adequate capital, professional experience and expertise will be licensed by IRDA

Weaknesses/Challenges

- Premiums rates will remain under pressure due to intense competition on the more profitable lines
- Falling premium income-without a corresponding reduction in clams-is likely to drive down profits
- Reinsurance is likely to cost more as treaty reinsurers reduce ceding commissions to compensate for the lower rates following deregulation
- Public and private sector insurers greater reliance on their investment portfolios to generate sufficient income and gains for net profits would subject them to the volatility of the financial markets
- Private insurers need to raise more capital, otherwise growth could be constrained since reliance on reinsurance for capital relief is not always viable or available
- Traditional distribution channels, especially tied agents, need to be improved to match the new product offerings
- There is general lack of transparency as financial and operational data for insurers are not readily available as none of India's insurers are directly listed on stock exchanges

- Like all developing economies on a fast track, the shortage of trained insurance professionals and technicians at all levels cannot be recommended in the short term
- Natural catastrophes will always be present the Indian sub-continent is vulnerable to cyclones, floods, hurricanes and earthquakes, and until there is a national capacity (similar to the terrorism pool) to manage losses, dependence on overseas reinsurers will continue.

22.2.2 De-Tariffing

India's general insurance industry has undergone de-tariffing in three phases:

= 1994-marine cargo, personal accident, health, banker liability and aviation

= 2005-06-marine hull segment

= 2007-fire, engineering and motor own damage (OD). However, the de-tariffing did not immediately allow for free pricing. Instead, insurers were required to follow the "file and use" method, whereby they were expected to file a charter of proposed rates, which was than approved by IRDA.

The restrictions on price discounts during the initial periods were intended to ensure orderly price adjustments. They were removed in January 2008. The only segment that remains under a tariff regime is the third party motor business, although there has been a large upward revision in this area's premium rates by regulators in recent times. Moreover, commercial third party motor business, which has traditionally contributed to adverse claims ratios, has been moved to a common pool, resulting in loss sharing.

22.3 GIC — Organisation and Working

General Insurance Corporation of India came into picture with the nationalisation of the general insurance sector by promulgating the General Insurance Business (Nationalisation) Act, 1972 and four subsidiaries were formed. As per Section 18 the said Act, the GIC has to perform the following functions.

The functions of the Corporation are stated in Section 18 to be

(a) the carrying on of any part of the general insurance business if it thinks it desirable to do so;

(b) aiding, assisting and advising the companies in the matter of setting up standards of conduct and sound practice in general insurance business and in rendering efficient service to policy holders;

(c) advising the companies in the matter of controlling their expenses and investment of funds; and

(d) issuing directions to companies in relation to the conduct of general insurance business.

22.3.1 Organisation

Table 22.1

Current Structure of GIC Ministry of Finance Insurance Division GIC

Subsidiaries	*Subsidiaries*	*Foreign Joint*	*In India*	*Abroad*	*Ventures*
National Insurance Co. Ltd. (Kolkata)	New India Assurance Co. Ltd. (Mumbai)	Oriental Insurance Co. Ltd. (Delhi)	United India Insurance Co. Ltd. (Chennai)	Kenindia Assurance Co. Ltd. (Nairobi)	Others
India International Pte. Ltd. (Singapore)		New India International Ltd. (UK)			Other

Source: The ET Knowledge Series Insurance 2001-02.

The current structure of GIC is given in Exhibit 13.3. There is a likely possibility that the four subsidiaries of GIC be made independent Government entities and GIC would come under the joint preview of Ministry of Finance and the IRDA. (Exhibit 13.4) This may be a better step in light of competition in the industry.

22.2 The performance of GIC and its subsidiaries for the financial years 1998-99 to 2000-01 are given in Table 22.1.

22.4 PERFORMANCE STATISTICS (1992-93 TO 2000-01)

As said earlier, the General Insurance business was nationalised in 1972. After this period the sector grew gradually with many new developments. Till 1992-93, the growth was overall good. Net premium income registering 14.57%.

However the claim ratio rose sharply from 50.8% to 68.7% during 1972-73 to 1992-93 primarily due to motor insurance losses.

Higher yields has also resulted in a sharp increase in investment income.

Let us have a look at statistics of the recent past viz. period from 1996-97 to 1999-2000.

Table 22.2

Industry Performance: Post Nationalisation Period Up To 1993

	1972-73	*1979-80*	*1984-85*	*1990-91*	*1991-92*	*1992-93*
Net Premium Income	222	481	1,191	2,742	3,450	3,868
Net Claims Payable	113	296	795	1,898	2,303	2,839
Net Commission, Expenses of Management & Other Charges	68	121	287	652	802	908
Unexpired Risk Reserve	23	49	97	311	422	240
Underwriting Profit/Loss	18	15	12	– 118	– 77	– 119
Interest, Dividend & Rents	21	87	245	603	808	915
Other Income (Net)	– 0.7	– 7	6	– 3	– 62	17
Profit Before Tax	38	92	264	482	669	779
Profit Before Tax (excluding dividend from subsidiary cos.)	38	78	235	445	613	723
Tax Provision	21	49	107	148	241	276
Net Profit	14	43	157	334	428	503
Net Profit (excluding dividend from subsidiary cos.)	14	29	129	298	372	447
Capital & Reserve (including Reserve for Unexpired Risk and Investment Reserve)	239	620	1,427	3,403	4,275	4,965
Capital & Free Reserves	99	315	695	1791	2,242	2,602

Source: The Malhotra Committee Report 1993.

The performance of the general insurance sector in the said period has been impressive. The statistics shows that capital and funds have grown from Rs. 8,501 crores in 1996-97 to Rs. 133,694 crores implying a growth rate of almost double.

Table 22.3

(Figure in Millions of Rs.)

Particulars	*1990-91*	*1996/97*	*1997/98*	*1998/99*	*1999/00*
Capital & Funds	34024	85,011	100,492	118,819	133,694
To Assets	66808	187576	215,720	245,572	279,202
Gross Direct Premium	29130	73,479	80,856	91,575	99,822
Net Premium Income	27424	67,331	73,571	84,025	93,634
Investment Income & Profit Less Outgo	5,998	17,203	20,077	21,536	24,917
Profit Before Tax	4815	10,919	16,236	14,670	11,526

Source: www.interlinkre.Com

The net premium income has also registered a CAGR of 27% (approx.) during the period 1990-91 to 1999-200. Investment in the industry have also increased by 16.52 times (during the period 1996-97 to 2000-01) viz., Rs. 1,447 crores to Rs. 23,849 crores.

Also, the ratio of Net Premium income to Gross Premium has gone up from 91.67% in 1996-97 to 95.36% (1999-2000). The figures are likely to improve further because of growing competition and enhanced focus on cost optimisation.

Distribution of Gross Direct Premium

Table 22.4

Gross Direct Premium Income

(Rs. in Crores)

		Fire		*Misc.*		*Marine*		*Total*	
No.	*Company*	*2001-02*	*2000-01*	*2001-02*	*2000-01*	*2001-02*	*2000-01*	*2001-02*	*2000-01*
1.	National	496.16	408.09	1732.04	1505.99	211.2	203.80	2439.4	2117,88
2.	New India	1106.70	654.24	2728.64	2073.09	362.73	313.84	4198.07	3041.17
3.	Oriental	531.03	471.28	1753.00	1540.49	214.60	187.90	2498.63	2199.67
4.	United India	636.99	526.11	1889.28	1635.42	255.21	279.56	2781.48	2441.09
	Sub-Total	2770.88	2059.72	8102.96	6754.99	1043.74	985.10	11917.58	9799.81
5.	Royal Sundaram	17.9	0.0006	50.44	0.235	2.78		71.12	0.2356
6.	Reliance	45.84	0.9356	29.07	0.1317	1.74		76.65	1.0673
7.	Iffco-Tokio	36.15	3.7013	31.02	2.086	3.34	0.0451	70.51	5.8324
8.	Tata AIG	19.36		49.91		9.18		78.45	
9.	ICICI Lombard	10.98		16.12				27.1	
10.	Bajaj Allianz	27.88		112.71		1.35		141.94	
	Sub-Total	158.11	4.6375	289.27	2.4527	18.39	0.045	465.77	7.1353
	Grand Total	2928.99	2064.36	8392.23	6757.44	1062.13	985.15	12383.35	9806.95

Exhibit 22.5
Claim Distribution and players

Table 22.5

Equity Share Capital of Non-Life Insurance Companies
(As on 31st March)

(*RS. CRORE*)

Insurer	*2007-08*	*2006-07*	*2005-06*	*2004-05*	*2003-04*	*2002-03*	*2001-02*
Non life insurers							
Bajaj Allianz	110.23	110.13	110.05	110.00	110.00	110.00	110.00
Cholamandalam	141.96	141.96	141.96	141.96	141.96	105.00	49.50
Future Generlai	150.00						
HDFC Ergo	150.00	125.00	125.00	120.00	120.00	101.00	
ICICI Lombard	377.36	335.71	245.00	220.00	220.00	110.00	110.00
IFFCO-TOKIO	220.00	220.00	220.00	100.00	100.00	100.00	100.00
Reliance	107.15	103.07	102.00	102.00	102.00	102.00	102.00
Royal Sundaram	170.00	140.00	140.00	130.00	130.00	130.00	130.00
Tata AIG	225.00	225.00	195.00	125.00	125.00	125.00	125.00
Universal Sompo	150.00						
Sub-Total (Private Sector)	*1801.70*	*1400.87*	*1279.01*	*1048.96*	*1048.96*	*883.00*	*726.50*
National	100.00	100.00	100.00	100.00	100.00	100.00	100.00
New India	200.00	200.00	200.00	150.00	100.00	100.00	100.00
The Oriental	100.00	100.00	100.00	100.00	100.00	100.00	100.00
United India	150.00	150.00	100.00	100.00	100.00	100.00	100.00
Sub-Total (Public Sector)	550.00	550.00	500.00	450.00	400.00	400.00	400.00
Total (Non-Life)	2351.70	1950.87	1779.01	1498.96	1448.96	1283.00	1126.50]
Specialised insurers							
AIC	200.00	200.00	200.00	200.00	200.00		
ECGC	900.00	800.00	700.00	600.00	500.00	440.00	390.00
Stand-alone Health insurance companies							
Apollo DKV *	100.55						
Star Health & Allied	108.60	105.00	105.00				
Re-insurer GIC	430.00	430.00	430.00	215.00	215.00	215.00	215.00

Key Terms

- ❒ Claim Ratio
- ❒ Technical Reserves
- ❒ Sectoral Investments
- ❒ Reserve for unexpired risks
- ❒ Gross Direct Premium
- ❒ Miscellaneous Insurance
- ❒ Revenue Account

Questions for Review

1. Briefly trace the performance of General Insurance Industry from Nationalisation to Privatisation.
2. Compare the performance of various subsidiaries of GIC for the financial year 2000-01 to 2001-02.

Suggested Readings

1. *Practice of General Insurance*, Insurance Institute of India, Mumbai, 1997.
2. P. Periasamy, *Principles and Practice of Insurance,* Himalaya Publishing House, 2003.
3. IRDA Annual Report, 2001-02.

Web Resources

- www.bimaguru.com
- www.irdaindia.org
- www.insure.com

Practice of Non-Life Insurance

Chapter 23

Chapter Objectives

After reading this chapter you will be able to understand :

- *Issue of Insurance Policies*
- *Rating Procedures*
- *Types of Non-life Insurance*
- *Claim Settlements*

23.1 Issue of Insurance Policies

Insurance being a contract, requires the offer and acceptance as its main essentials. In case of general insurance, the proposal form (printed and standardised) for respective class of insurance is to be submitted by the insurer to the insurance company. However, in case of marine cargo insurance, it is not customary to use a proposal form, rather sometimes a questionnaire is used. In some cases of large industrial fire risks the proposal form is not used because of the inspection carried out earlier before the acceptance of risk. The proposal form generally contains *inter-alia* information about the profile of the proposer, the past and previous insurance, loss experiences etc. In some cases of insurance, special questions are also asked to further explore the attributes of the risk proposed to be bought.

What is General Insurance?

Insurance other than 'Life Insurance' falls under the category of General Insurance. General Insurance comprises of insurance of property against fire, burglary etc, personal insurance such as Accident and Health Insurance, and liability insurance which covers legal liabilities. There are also other covers such as Errors and Omissions insurance for professionals, credit insurance etc.

Non-life insurance companies have products that cover property against Fire and allied perils, flood storm and inundation, earthquake and so on. There are products that cover property against burglary, theft etc. The non-life companies also offer policies covering machinery against breakdown, there are policies that cover the hull of ships and so on. A Marine Cargo policy covers goods in transit including by sea, air and road. Further, insurance of motor vehicles against damages and theft forms a major chunk of non-life insurance business.

In respect of insurance of property, it is important that the cover is taken for the actual value of the property to avoid being imposed a penalty should there be a claim. Where a property is undervalued for the purposes of insurance, the insured will have to bear a rateable proportion of the loss. For instance if the value of a property is Rs.100 and it is insured for Rs.50/-, in the event of a loss to the extent of say Rs. 50/-, the maximum claim amount payable would be Rs.25/- (50% of the loss being borne by the insured for underinsuring the property by 50%). This concept is quite often not understood by most insureds.

Personal insurance covers include policies for Accident, Health etc. Products offering Personal Accident cover are benefit policies. Health insurance covers offered by non-life insurers are mainly hospitalization covers either on reimbursement or cashless basis. The cashless service is offered through Third Party Administrators who have arrangements with various service providers, i.e., hospitals. The Third Party Administrators also provide service for reimbursement claims. Sometimes the insurers themselves process reimbursement claims.

Accident and health insurance policies are available for individuals as well as groups. A group could be a group of employees of an organization or holders of credit cards or deposit holders in a bank etc. Normally when a group is covered, insurers offer group discounts.

Liability insurance covers such as Motor Third Party Liability Insurance, Workmen's Compensation Policy etc offer cover against legal liabilities that may arise under the respective statutes—Motor Vehicles Act, The Workmen's Compensation Act etc. Some of the covers such as the foregoing (Motor Third Party and Workmen's Compensation policy) are compulsory by statute. Liability Insurance not compulsory by statute is also gaining popularity these days. Many industries insure against Public liability. There are liability covers available for Products as well.

There are general insurance products that are in the nature of package policies offering a combination of the covers mentioned above. For instance, there are package policies available for householders, shop keepers and also for professionals such as doctors, chartered accountants etc. Apart from offering standard covers, insurers also offer customized or tailor-made ones.

Suitable general Insurance covers are necessary for every family. It is important to protect one's property, which one might have acquired from one's hard earned income. A loss or damage to one's property can leave one shattered. Losses created by catastrophes such as the tsunami, earthquakes, cyclones etc have left many homeless and penniless. Such losses can be devastating but insurance could help mitigate them. Property can be covered, so also the people against Personal Accident. A Health Insurance policy can provide financial relief to a person undergoing medical treatment whether due to a disease or an injury.

Most general insurance covers are annual contracts. However, there are few products that are long-term. It is important for proposers to read and understand the terms and conditions of a policy before they enter into an insurance contract. The proposal form needs to be filled in completely and correctly by a proposer to ensure that the cover is adequate and the right one.

Underwriting has been discussed in detail in Chapter 24. So, once it is decided that the risk shall be bought and the consideration is received, the *cover notes* are generally issued in advance of policy. A cover note is a sufficient evidence of an insurance cover. Cover notes are sometimes issued pending negotiations or rate fixation. In case of motor insurance, *certificate of insurance* is issued.

The policy document is a formal one, evidencing the contract of insurance. When the contract is in the preview of TAC, the wordings should be exactly on the same pattern as prescribed. The main parts of a standard insurance policy are – heading, recital clause, insuring clause, schedule, authentication, conditions and warranties etc. The special clauses in an insurance policy can be inserted by attachments known as endorsements. Whenever the insurance polices are interpreted, these are to be in whole and in their usual sense. Insurance policies generally expire at the end of one year and must be renewed immediately. It is not obligatory on part of the insurer to send notice to the insured, but as a business practice they do inform him.

General insurance or non-life insurance policies, including automobile and homeowners policies, provide payments depending on the loss from a particular financial event. General insurance typically comprises any insurance that is not determined to be *life insurance*. It is called property and casualty insurance in the U.S. and Non-Life Insurance in Continental Europe. In the UK, General insurance is broadly divided into three areas; *personal lines, commercial lines* and *London market*. In India, general; insurance is classfied as Fire, Marine and miscellaneous insurances.

Some examples of Non-Life Insurance Policies are :

Commercial

Fire Policies

- Fire Consequential Loss

- Fire Insurance
- Consequential Loss (Fire) Insurance Policy (Bajaj Allianz)

Liabilities

- Medical Establishment
- Public Liability - Act
- Product Liability
- Public Liability - Industrial Risks

Travel

- Globetrotter Overseas Corporate Travel Insurance(ICICI Lombard)

Engineering

- Advance Loss of Profits
- Civil Engineering Completed Risk
- Contractor's Plant & Machinery
- Erection All Risks
- Machinery Insurance Policy
- Boiler & Pressure Plant
- Contractor's All Risks
- Deterioration of Stocks
- Industrial All Risks
- Machinery Loss of Profit

Guarantee Insurance

- Fidelity Guarantee Insurance
- Guarantee-Missing Documents Indemnity
- Fidelity Guarantee Policy (Bajaj Allianz)
- Business Credit Shield (New India Assurance)

Motor

- Commercial Vehicles

Miscellaneous

- Banker's Indemnity
- Electronic Equipment Policy
- LPG Dealers
- Office Umbrella
- Special Contingency
- Business Guard Jyothi (Tata-AIG)
- Merchant's Cover(ICICI Lombard)
- Burglary Insurance
- Jewellers' Block
- Money Insurance
- Shopkeepers' Policy
- Business Guard Sanjeevini (Tata-AIG)
- Trade Protector(IFFCO Tokio)

Marine

- Marine Insurance

Generic

Personal Accident

- Bhagyasree Child Welfare
- Personal Accident
- NRI Accident Insurance Policy
- Executive Guard (Tata-AIG)
- Janata Personal Accident
- Traffic Accident Policy
- Rajarajeswari Mahila Kalyan
- Family Guard (Tata-AIG)

- Personal Accident (Bajaj Allianz)
- Personal Accident (IFFCO Tokio)
- Personal Accident (Cholamandalam)
- Accident Shield (Royal Sundaram)
- Personal Accident (ICICI Lombard)

Health

- Mediclaim
- For Retired Persons
- Hospital Cash Daily Allowance Policy (Bajaj Allianz)
- Critical Illness (Bajaj Allianz)
- Health Guard (Bajaj Allianz)
- Health shield (Royal Sundaram)

Motor

- Motor Car Insurance
- Two Wheeler Insurance

Property

- All Risks Insurance
- Burglary Insurance
- Sampoorna Suraksha Bima
- Burglary Insurance (Bajaj-Allianz)
- Domestic Appliances Policy
- Electronic Equipment Insurance
- Fire Policy-Home
- Householder's Package Policy
- Pedal Cycle Policy
- Plate Glass Insurance
- Transit Insurance
- TV Policy
- Householder's Insurance (Bajaj Allianz)
- Home Secure (Tata-AIG)
- Office Package Insurance (Bajaj Allianz)
- Money Insurance (Bajaj Allianz)
- Plate Glass Insurance (Bajaj Allianz)
- Home & Family Protector (IFFCO Tokio)
- Standard Fire & Special Perils (IFFCO Tokio)
- Burglary & House Breaking (IFFCO Tokio)
- Home Shield (Royal Sundaram)
- Home Insurance (ICICI Lombard)

Liabilities' Insurance

- Directors' & Officer's Liability
- Employers' Liability
- Golfers' & Sportsmen
- Pets (Dog Insurance)
- Professional Indemnity
- Public Liability
- Public Liability (Bajaj Allianz)
- Professional Indemnity (ICICI Lombard)

Gun Insurance

- Gun Insurance

Travel

- Baggage Insurance Policy
- Standard Overseas Mediclaim Policy (withdrawn)
- Overseas Mediclaim Policy
- Suhana Safar
- Travel Companion (Bajaj-Allianz)
- Travel Guard (Tata-AIG)
- Travel Shield (Royal Sundaram)
- Travel protector (IFFCO Tokio)
- Globetrotter Overseas Individual Travel Insurance (ICICI Lombard)

23.2 Rating Procedures

The rates for various classes of general insurance are based on the risk classes and associated hazards. The rates for various insurance products are prescribed on the basis of experiences and attributes of the subject matter of insurance. In case of fire insurance, the parameters for classification of risks are occupancy of the premises (residential places, commercial places, industrial/manufacturing premises, exposure to heating, lighting, ignition manufacturing processes), types and ingredients of construction etc. In case of motor vehicles, the classification is done on the basis of manufacturing design, use and value. The prices of various subject matter of insurance are subject to discrimination based on the risk and loss exposures.

The Tariff Advisory Committee (TAC) has prescribed the rates for various products relating to Fire, Marine (Hull), Motor, Engineering and Workmen Compensation Insurance. TAC prescribes the minimum rates, loading for various hazards and incentives for risk improvements for various classes of insurance. Other than these classes, the rates are market determined. However, the rate which a company charges for insurance products, as a general rule should not be less than the base minimum actuarial calculation and cover for expenses.

Hazards

In case of fire insurance the main physical hazards are – construction, occupancy, nature of flooring (applicable to buildings), process of manufacture, situation etc. In case of marine insurance these are – the life of the vessel, voyage route, loading/unloading conditions, the warehousing facilities, nature and value of stocks, packing methodology etc. In case of motor vehicles, age, nature, type of the vehicle, the concession of the vehicle and use of the vehicle are important hazards. Similarly, in case of fidelity insurance, the accounting and control systems, the method of check and supervision etc. are important. In case of burglary insurance, the value of the article, the circumstances, the location etc. are important physical hazards.

The moral hazards may be dishonesty, carelessness (no worry insurance company will pay), deliberately inflated losses, economic conditions etc.

All hazards associated with a given proposal are assessed and rates are fixed accordingly. In case the risk is high, the proposal is declined or *warranties may be imposed*. A survey of the insurable property is generally carried out by the agent or the I^{st}/IInd level underwriter. The limits on the claims may be *excess* or *franchisee*. The motto behind fixing these limits is to restrict the small claims and the total amount of claims. When the loss exceeds the excess limit, full amount is paid under the franchisee clause and the Blanca is paid under the excess clause.

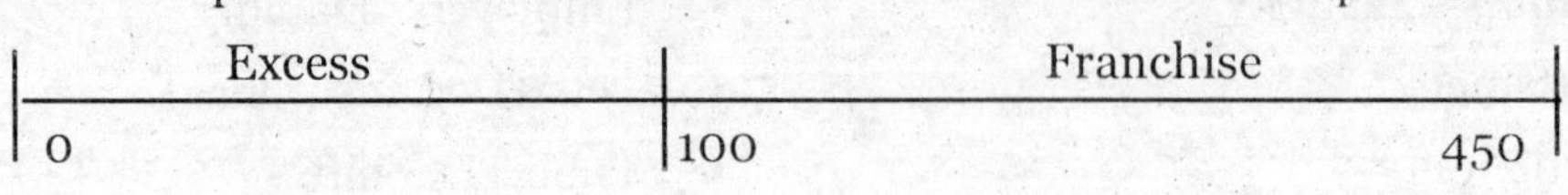

If the claim made is 90, nothing shall be paid. If the claim is 300, then 200 will be paid.

Premiums

The premiums in case of non-life insurance are generally on an annual basis. If the insurance cover is for less than 12 months, special scales *short scales* may be used as prescribed for various products. If the consideration for the premium totally or partially fails without fraud or otherwise on part of the assured or his agents then, the premiums shall be accordingly returned (Sec. 84 of the Insurance Act, 1938). Premium is refunded only when the policy provides for it. The premium conventionally has to be received in advance with the proposal. The policy comes into force only when the premium is actually received.

22.3 Claim Settlements

All insurance contracts are based on the information provided by the insured in the proposal form. The proper settlement of claim essentially requires a thorough knowledge of the various legal aspects, practices and procedures etc. The insurance company is known by its efficiency in claims settlement. The correctness of the information furnished in the proposal form is verified at the time of a claim, when physical inspection of the property is done. In case of any misrepresentation, it would be the prerogative of the Insurance Company to avoid a claim, or avoid the policy itself, or pay a claim for a reduced amount. Therefore the proposal form initiated at the time of buying insurance plays an important role as it affects the consequential claims under the policy contract. The claim settlement generally involves the following procedure:

1. *Notice of Loss:* The loss or damage should be reported to the insurer immediately within the time frame of the policy conditions. Immediate notice of loss allows the insurer to investigate the loss early and protect its interests.
2. *Claim Form:* On receipt of claim intimation, the insurer will forward a claim form. Claim forms vary with classes of insurance. Claim forms usually contain information such as time of loss, cause of loss, place and extent of loss, circumstances when loss took place etc. apart from the general information about the claimant. The claimant has to submit the completed claim form along with an estimate of the loss to the insurer. It is preferable to submit an itemised estimate with separate values.
3. *Scrutinisation:* The claim made by the insured shall be scrutinised for (a) policy in force at the time of loss, (b) coverage of the policy, (c) subject matter of the insurance, (d) adequacy of the notice of loss etc.
4. *Investigation and Assessment:* The insurer will arrange for inspection of the damaged items to assess the loss. In case of major losses, specialist-licensed surveyor/loss assessors are deputed. The insured has to provide the required documents to substantiate the extent of loss. In case the cause of loss is not established, it is for the insured to prove that the loss or damage has occurred due to an insured peril.
5. *Settlement and Arbitration:* On agreement of claim amount between the insured and the insurer, the claim is settled. Otherwise, in case of dispute, the matter is generally referred to the arbitrators under the Arbitration Act, 1960.

The claim settlement procedure for various classes of insurance is discussed in detail in Chapter 38.

Key Terms

- Cover Note
- Settlement
- TAC
- Franchizee
- Arbitration
- Certificate of Insurance
- Excess

Questions for Review

1. List the insurance products regulated by tariff Advisory Committee.
2. Briefly explain the claim settlement process in case of general insurances.

Suggested Readings

1. *Practice of General Insurance,* ICII, Insurance Institute of India, Mumbai, 1999.
2. S.S. Heubner *et. al., Property and Liability Insurance,* Prentice-Hall, 1982.
3. Irving Pfeffer and Others, *Perspectives on Insurance,* Prentice-Hall, 1974.

Web Resources

- www.bimaguru.com
- www.bimaonline.com
- www.indutr-magic.com

Fire Insurance

Chapter **24**

CHAPTER OBJECTIVES

After reading this chapter you will be able to understand :

- *Nature of Fire Insurance Contracts*
- *Standard and Special Fire Covers*

24.1 FIRE INSURANCE CONTRACTS

Section 2(6A) of Insurance Act, 1938 defines "Fire insurance business" as "the business of effecting, otherwise than incidentally, to some other class of insurance business, contracts of insurance against loss by incidental to fire or other occurrence customarily included among the risks insured against in fire insurance policies."

The contract of fire insurance is similar to other contracts and comes into being when a person seeking insurance protection enters into a contract with the insurer to indemnify him against the loss of property by or incidental to fire and or lighting, explosion etc. There is no statutory enactment for regulation of fire business in India akin to Marine insurance which is governed by the Indian Marine Insurance Act, 1963.

24.1.1 Features of a Fire Insurance Contract

(a) *It is personal in nature* : It does not ensure the safety of the insured property. Its purpose is to see that the insured does not suffer loss by reason of his interest in the insured property. So it is personal in nature in the sense that it involves the payment of money if the loss occurs.

(b) *Cause of fire is immaterial :* The insurer irrespective of the cause of fire will reimburse the loss due to fire. The doctrine of cause proxima applied unless there is a suspicion of fraud or wilful act or otherwise falling outside the scope of the contract.

(c) *Indivisibility :* The fire insurance contract covers the fire losses in whole and generally indivisible unless specifically provided by the contract.

24.1.2 Application of Insurance Principles to Fire Insurance

Insurable Interest

Ownership is a conclusive evidence of an insurable interest. Where the property is charged or mortgaged to a financier as security, the financier acquires insurable interest. The insurable interest in fire insurance must exist at the time of cover, continue throughout its currency and should exist at the time of loss. In case the subject matter of insurance is transferred, the policy does not transfer automatically, it must be agreed by the insurer and endorsed on the policy document.

Indemnity

The indemnity for loss or damage suffered is the reinstatement or the market value. In case of property, market value or the reinstatement value is used. However, stocks are valued on the basis of market value. The sum insured should always represent the true value of the property.

Utmost Good Faith

The insured is bound to disclose all material facts to the insurer, which have a bearing on the contract. If the subject matter of insurance is materially altered, the insured should give notice the insurer immediately. The guiding principle states that the insured should assume as if uninsured all times and accordingly is bound to take care of the insured property always.

Subrogation and Contribution

The insurers are entitled to subrogation rights when they have indemnified the losses to the insured and can proceed to recover the losses from third parties. In case the property has been insured from more than one insurer, the rateable proportion shall apply in the event of claims.

24.2 FIRE INSURANCE PROPOSALS

Acceptance of fire insurance proposals is governed by regulations of Tariff Advisory Committee All India Fire Tariff. A fire insurance proposal generally requires the following information.

Proposer's Details

- Name and address including phone, fax no. and e-mail address.
- Business and its nature of the proposer.
- Paid-up capital of the proposer's enterprise.
- Names of various parties having insurable interest.
- Location of risk to be covered and insurance period.
- Whether the fire insurance was declined by other insurers or accepted subject to special conditions in respect of given proposal.
- Claims experience.

Coverage

- Inclusion of Flood, Cyclone, type of perils and inclusion/deletion of Riot, Strike, Malicious damage, Terrorism.
- Coverage of Plinth and foundation to be covered along with the building.
- Whether Add-on covers required.

Details of Property

- Type of property–commercial/residential.
- If shop whether hazardous goods (as per list) are stored; if so, whether the stock value exceeds 5% of the total stock value.
- If warehouse/godown (not located in a manufacturing unit), details of the goods stored.
- If industrial/manufacturing unit details of goods manufactured and capacity utilisation.
- Utilities
- Height of building.
- Age of building
- Fire Protection devices
- Construction material details.

Declaration is normally required as to the authentication of information furnished.

Risk Inspection Report

Risk Inspection Report is generally prepared to arrive at a correct risk assessment and rate the proposal. The risk inspection generaly covers the following :

- Generic Information
- Process of Manufacturing/Provision
- Fire Protection Mechanism
- Moral Hazards
- Claims Experience
- Conclusion and Comments.
- Lighting, Heating and Power
- Exposure Details
- Management and Supervision of proposed risk
- Sum Insured and PML–Adequacy and Efficiency.
- Risk Improvement Measures

Section 64 VB of the Insurance Act requires that no risk can be assumed unless and until the full premium is received in advance.

24.2.1 Warranties

Class of Construction

"Warranted that the buildings are not of Kachcha construction consisting of walls and/or roofs of wooden planks/thatched leaves and/or grass/hay of any kind/bamboo/plastic cloth/asphalt cloth/canvas/tarpaulin and the like."

Fea Warranty

"Warranted that Fire Extinguishing Appliances in respect of which discount is given shall conform to the Tariff Advisory Committee regulations and shall be maintained in efficient working condition at all times and an annual maintenance contract with an external agency shall be in force at all times throughout the currency of this policy."

Apart from warranties which are not in printed form the other ones are types in policy. Special clauses, extensions, etc. (if applicable) are also attached and referred to in the Schedule.

24.3 FIRE INSURANCE COVERAGES

24.3.1 Standard Fire Policy

The fire insurance policy has been nomenclatured Section II of the All India Fire Tariff as Standard Fire and Special Perils Policy. The standard risks covered, add-on covers, exclusions, conditions as prescribed by the tariff are described as follows2 :

Standard Risks

Fire

Destruction or damage to the property insured by its own fermentation, natural heating or spontaneous combustion or its undergoing any heating or drying process cannot be treated as damage due to fire. For *e.g.*, paints or chemicals in a factory undergoing heat treatment and consequently damaged by fire is not covered. Further, bring of property insured by order of any Public Authority is excluded from the scope of cover.

Lightning

Lightning may result in fire damage or other types of damage, such as a roof broken by a falling chimney struck by lightning or cracks in a building due to a lightning strike. Both fire and other types of damages caused by lightning are covered by the policy.

Explosion/Implosion

Explosion is defined as a sudden, violent burst with a loud report. An explosion is caused inside a vessel when the pressure within the vessel exceeds the atmospheric pressure acting externally on its surface. An explosion may cause fire damage or concussion damage. An implosion means bursting inward or collapses. This takes place when the external pressure exceeds the internal pressure. This policy, however, does not cover destruction or damage caused to the boilers (other than domestic boilers), economisers or other vessels in which steam is generated and machinery or apparatus subject to centrifugal force by its own explosion/implosion. These risks can be covered in a Boiler and Pressure Plant Insurance Policy, which is specially designed to handle these risks.

Aircraft Damage

The loss or damage to the property (by fire or otherwise) directly caused by aircraft and other aerial devices and/or articles dropped there from is covered. However, destruction or damage resulting from pressure waves caused by aircraft travelling at supersonic speed is excluded from the scope of the policy.

Riot, Strike, Malicious and Terrorism Damage

The act of any person taking part along with others in any disturbance of public peace (other than war, invasion, mutiny, civil commotion etc.) is construed to be a riot, strike or a terrorist activity. Any loss or physical damage to the property insured directly caused by such activity or by the action of any lawful authorities in suppressing such disturbance or minimising its consequences is covered. Further the wilful act of any striker or locked out worker, in connection with a strike or a lock out, or the action of any lawful authority in suppressing such act, resulting in visible physical damage by external means, is also covered. Malicious act would mean an act with malicious intent but excluding omission of any kind by any person, resulting in visible physical damage to the insured property, whether or not the act is committed in the course of disturbance of public peace or not. Burglary, housebreaking, theft or larceny does not constitute a malicious act for the purpose of this cover. Total or partial cessation of work or the retarding or interruption or cessation of any process or operations; or, permanent dispossession resulting from confiscation, commandeering, requisition or destruction by order of the Government or any lawfully constituted authority; or permanent or temporary dispossession of any building or plant or unit or machinery resulting from the unlawful occupation by any person of the same or prevention of access to the same, are not covered.

Storm, Cyclone, Typhoon, Tempest, Hurricane, Tornado, Flood and Inundation

Storm, Cyclone, Typhoon, Tempest, Tornado and Hurricane are all various types of violent natural disturbances that are accompanied by thunder or strong winds or heavy rainfall. Flood or Inundation occurs when the water rises to an abnormal level. Flood or inundation should not only be understood in the common sense of the terms, *i.e.,* flood in river or lakes, but also accumulation of water due to choked drains would be deemed to be flood.

Impact Damage

Impact by any Rail/Road vehicle or animal by direct contact with the insured property is covered. However, such vehicles or animals should not belong to or owned by the insured or any occupier of the premises or their employees while acting in the course of their employment.

Subsidence and Landslide Including Rockslide

Destruction or damage caused by Subsidence of part of the site on which the property stands or Landslide/Rockslide is covered. While Subsidence means sinking of land or building to a lower level, Landslide means sliding down of land usually on a hill. However, normal cracking, settlement or bedding down of new structures; settlement or movement of made up ground; coastal or river erosion; defective design or workmanship or use of defective materials; and demolition, construction, structural alterations or repair of any property or groundworks or excavations, are not covered.

Bursting and/or Overflowing of Water Tanks, Apparatus and Pipes

Loss or damage to property by water or otherwise on account of bursting or accidental overflowing of water tanks, apparatus and pipes is covered.

Missile Testing Operations

Destruction or damage due to impact or otherwise from trajectory/projectiles in connection with missile testing operations by the Insured or anyone else, is covered.

Leakage from Automatic Sprinkler Installations

Damage caused by water accidentally discharged or leaked out from automatic sprinkler installations in the insured's premises is covered. However, such destruction or damage caused by repairs or alterations to the buildings or premises; repairs removal or extension of the sprinkler installation; and defects in construction known to the insured, are not covered.

Bush Fire

This covers damage caused by burning, whether accidental or otherwise, of bush and jungles and the clearing of lands by fire, but excluding destruction or damage caused by Forest Fire.

The policy may be extended to cover earth quake, fire and shock; deterioration of stock in the cold storages following power failure as a result of insured peril, additional expenditure involved in removal of debris, architect, consulting engineers' fee over and above the amount covered by the policy, forest fire, spontaneous combustion and impact damage due to own vehicles. In case of a partial loss, Insurance Company shall effect payment for repairs and replacement. In case of policy with reinstatement value clause, cost of reinstatement will be paid on completion of reinstatement subject to overall limit of the sum insured. Insurance company may at its option, also repair or replace the affected property instead of paying for the cost of restoration.

Exclusions

This policy does not cover :

1. 5 per cent of each and every claim resulting from lighting/ storm/tempest/flood/inundation/subsidence and landslide including rockslide covered under the policy.
2. Loss destruction or damage caused by war, invasion, act of foreign enemy hostilities or war-like operations (whether war is declared or not), civil war, mutiny, civil commotion assuming the proportions of or amounting to a popular rising, military rising, rebellion, revolution, insurrection or military or usurped power.
3. Loss, destruction or damage directly or indirectly caused to the property insured by :
   - Ionising radiations or contamination by radioactivity from any nuclear fuel or from any nuclear waste from the combustion of nuclear fuel.
   - The radioactive toxic, explosives or other hazardous properties of any explosive nuclear assembly or nuclear component thereof.
4. Loss, destruction or damage caused to the insured property by pollution or contamination excluding :
   - Pollution or contamination which itself results from a peril hereby insured against.
   - Any peril hereby insured against which itself results from pollution or contamination.

5. Loss, destruction or damage directly to solution or unset precious stones curios, works of art for an amount exceeding Rs. 10,000, manuscripts plans, drawings, securities, obligations or documents of any kind stamps, coins or paper money, cheques, books of accounts or other business books, computer systems, records, explosives unless otherwise expressly stated in the policy.
6. Loss, destruction or damage to the stocks in cold storage premises caused by change of temperature.
7. Loss, destruction or damage to any electrical and/or electronic machine, apparatus, fixture or fitting (excluding fans and electrical wiring in dwellings) arising from or occasioned by over-running, excessive pressure, short circuiting, arcing, self-heating, or leakage of electricity, from whatever cause (lightning included).
8. Expenses necessarily incurred on : (*i*) Architect's surveyor's and consulting engineer's fees and (*ii*) Debris removal by the insured following a loss, destruction or damage to the property insured by an insured peril in excess of 3 per cent and 1 per cent of the claim amount, respectively.
9. Loss of earnings, loss by delay, loss of market or other consequential or indirect loss or damage or any kind or description whatsoever.

The clauses covered above are subject to the normal general conditions of the insurance company.

Add-on Covers

The insurers can issue the standard fire policy as per the New Fire Tariff along with added benefits at the option of the policyholders by charging additional premium. These added benefits or add-on covers are as follows :

- Architect's, surveyor's and consulting engineer's fees (in excess of 3 per cent claim amount).
- Debris removal (in excess of 1 per cent of claim amount).
- Deterioration of stocks in cold storage premises due to power failure following damage due to an insured peril.
- Forest fire.
- Impact damage due to insured's own vehicles, forklifts and the like and articles dropped therefrom.
- Spontaneous combustion.
- Omission to insure additions, alterations or extensions.
- Earthquake (fire and shock) as per minimum rates and excess applicable as specified in the Tariff.

In respect of the above add-on covers. The insurance company will compulsorily deduct 5 per cent of each claim before paying the claim proceeds to the insured.

The standard policies exclude certain perils from the scope of cover. The main reasons for the exclusions are :

(*i*) To restrict the cover to normal coverage required by the typical or average insured. Personal Accident Policy which provides for the agreed benefits to be paid under certain specified Contingencies, does not cover medical expenses, which can be included on payment of an additional premium. Similarly, Workmen Compensation Policy indemnifies the insured against his liability at law to his direct employees, and provides for the Insureds legal liability to employees of sub-contractor to be included by payment of premium at a tariff rate on the wages payable to workmen of sub-contractor. Similarly, policy can be extended to cover medical expenses, and the diseases specified in Part III of the Schedule C on payment of an additional premium.

(*ii*) To exclude loss which are of an extra-ordinary or catastrophic nature, *e.g.*, the earthquake peril for locations involving storage of materials, and industrial/manufacturing risks. In view of concentration of material, property involving huge sum insured, perils of earthquake, and/or flood etc. Could cause losses which might assume proportion of a catastrophe. While for residences, offices, shops and for Tiny Sector, etc., these perils (of earthquake and flood, etc.) are offered as in-built perils, as for these risks, perils of earthquake and flood may not cause catastrophic losses.

(*iii*) To precisely define and clarify the scope of cover. For example, to prevent disputes in the event of a loss which is akin to fire but is not within the meaning of the policy, spontaneous combustion is excluded under fire policy.

(*iv*) To exclude risks which may be accepted after obtaining more underwriting information or arranging inspection, *e.g.*, flood risk in fire insurance, pollution cover under public liability policy, and cover for exports under Products Liability Policy.

(*v*) To exclude losses which are convertible under other policies. This eliminates duplication of coverage. For example, the general public liability policy excludes liability arising out of the use of Motor Vehicle, because a Motor Third Party Policy is available. Similarly, Plate Glass Policy does not cover loss of or damage by fire, which can be covered separately under a Fire Insurance Policy.

(*vi*) To exclude risks which cause losses of high degree of frequency, *e.g.* the risks of larceny under Burglary (Business Premises) Policy, and shortages, which are discovered at periodic stock taking.

(*vii*) To exclude loss which are caused intentionally, *e.g.*, suicide under personal accident policies.

(*viii*) To exclude losses, which are inevitable, *e.g.* wear and tear and depreciation under motor policies and 'inherent vice' under marine cargo policies.

(*ix*) To exclude losses which are commercially uninsurable *e.g.* war and nuclear risks.

(*x*) The standard policies may also exclude certain classes of property from the coverage. For example, the fire policy excludes certain classes of property, *e.g.* documents, coins, paper money, books of account, unless expressly stated in the policy. The intention is to ascertain the existence of such property and, if necessary to include certain classes of property in the coverage subject to special terms and conditions. Similarly curios, works of art, paintings can be covered after obtaining valuation report, from the Director of Museum and stamps collection can be covered on production of valuation certificate from Philatelic Society.

24.3.2 Standard Policy Coverages

The tariff Advisory Committee has prescribed three types of fire coverages *viz.*, Policy A, Policy B and Policy C.

Policy A

Fire Policy A covers the following perils–(*i*) fire, (*ii*) lightning, (*iii*) explosion/implosion, (*iv*) impact damage, (*v*) aircraft damage, (*vi*) riot, strike and malicious and terrorist damage, (*vii*) storm, cyclone, tempest, hurricane, tornado, flood and inundation, (*viii*) earthquake, (*ix*) sub-sidence and landslide (including rockslide).

Only Policy A can be issued to cover artisans workshops, bio-gas plants, village and cottage industries, tiny sector or small scale industries.

Policy B

Fire Policy B covers the perils–(*i*) fire, (*ii*) lightning, (*iii*) explosion/implosion, (*iv*) impact damage (*v*) aircraft damage, (*vi*) riot, strike and malicious and terrorist damage. (The cover is similar to Policy C).

The tariff permits exclusion of riot, strike and malicious and terrorist damage perils, with specified reduction in the premium rate under the policy.

Policy C

Fire Policy (Policy 'C') is issued to cover industrial/manufacturing risks and storage risk and covers–(*i*) fire, (*ii*) lightning (*iii*) explosion/implosion, (*iv*) impact damage, (*v*) riot, strike and malicious and terrorist damage. The riot, strike and malicious and terrorist damage perils can be excluded on specific request with an agreed reduction in the premium rate.

The fire policy C may be extended to cover special perils on payment of extra premium. These special perils are:

(*a*) Spontaneous combustion
(*b*) Earthquake (shock and fire)
(*c*) Storm tempest, flood and inundation
(*d*) Subsidence and landslide
(*e*) Accident Leakage or contamination of oil
(*f*) Spoilage of stock/machinery due to interruption of process of manufacture by insured perils
(*g*) Deterioration of stocks due to power failure following damage to premises of Public Power Stations
(*h*) Bursting/overflowing of water tanks, apparatus and pipes
(*i*) Sprinkler leakage
(*j*) Bush or forest fire
(*k*) Subterranean fire
(*l*) Missile testing operations cover.

Fire Policy A and B (Simple Risks) : Fire Policy A and B are issued in respect of dwellings, offices, hotels and shops, educational institutions, etc.

24.4 SPECIAL COVERAGES

Apart from standard coverages, fire, policy may also be issued to meet the specific requirements of clients. Some of these are :

(*a*) Reinstatement Value Polices
(*b*) Stock Policies
(*c*) Consequential Loss Policies.

24.4.1 Reinstatement Value Policies

In this policy, attaching the Reinstatement Value Clause of the fire policy modifies the basis of settlement of claims. Under the latter policy, losses are settled on the basis of market value of the property on the date of fire. This value, which takes into account depreciation, wear and tear, etc. will not be found adequate by the insured who desires to replace the property by a new one of the same kind, type of capacity. *This policy is issued in respect of building, plant, machinery, furniture & fixtures, fittings etc.*

Under the policy, the insurers pay, not the depreciated value (*i.e.* market value) but *the cost of replacement of the damaged property by new property of the same kind*. The advantages are obvious–during inflationary periods the new reinstatement value is far higher than the depreciated value. The sum insured is required to reflect the new replacement value and not the market value as under the normal fire policy. The reinstatement value clause of the policy places liability on the insured to complete the reinstatement work within 12 months of the loss/damage. Else, the claim will be settled on the basis of normal indemnity (market value). Also of the cost of reinstatement > Sum Insured, the rateable proportion applies.

24.4.2 Policies for Stocks

There are three types of policies for stocks.

Floater Policies

Stocks at various locations can be covered under one sum insured by floater policies, since these policies take care of frequent changes in sum insured at various locations.

These policies may be issued to cover stocks in one amount situated in a more than one specified building situated (1) within the limits of one city/town/village, (2) more than one city/village/town but upto 50 locations, (3) for more than 50 locations in various cities/towns/villages. **The Floating policies are not issued in respect** of immovable property nor are they issued to Transport Contractors and Cleaning and Forwarding Agents.

Floating policies for risks situated within the limits of one city/town/village may be issued by charging 25% loading over and above the highest rate applicable to any one risk. 50% loading over and above the highest rate applicable to any one risk is charged under Policies covering upto 50 locations in more than one city town/ village.

The maximum sum insured at any one location should not be more than 10% of the total sum insured. It is essential that the insured should have a good internal audit and accounting procedure under which total amount of risk and locations can, if required, be established. The condition of average is applied to the limit of sum insured at each location, and also to the total sum insured under the policy.

A policy issued to cover in one amount, more than 50 locations in various cities/towns/villages is subject to the undernoted regulations :

Total sum insured in respect of all locations should not be less than Rs. 3 crores.

The maximum sum insured at any one location should not be more than 10% of the total sum insured.

The address of the locations should be declared to the company, at the inception, and changes advised as and when they occur. However, when locations cannot be identified or change is very frequent, the requirement of specifying address of locations is relaxed, but the number of unspecified locations should not exceed 10% the total number of locations, or 20 locations whichever is lower.

The insured should have a good internal audit and accounting procedure to establish total amount at risk and locations at a particular time.

The pro-rata conditions of average is applied to the limit of sum insured at each location and also to the total sum insured under the policy.

Declaration Policies

Declaration policies are useful to businesses, which face frequent fluctuations in stock quantity or value. Insurance companies can issue these policies subject to the following conditions.

- The minimum sum insured is Rs. 1 crore.
- Monthly declarations based on the average of the highest value at risk on each day or highest value on any day of the month are to be submitted by the insured to the insurer.
- Reduction in sum insured is not allowed under the policy.
- The insured cannot claim refund of premium on adjustment based on the declarations in excess of 50 per cent of the total premiums.
- The basis of value for declaration shall be the market value prior to the loss or as otherwise agreed to between the insurance company and the insured.

Exclusions

Declaration policies cannot be issued in respect of insurance required for a short period stocks undergoing process and stocks at railway sidings. Also, these policies are not sanctioned to (a) Transport contractors and Forwarding and clearing agents (b) in respect of stock-in-process (c) insurances for short period.

Advantages

(1) The premium is limited to the actual amount of risk irrespective of the sum insured.

(2) The liability of the insurer is concurrent under the policy.

(3) Provision for adjustment of premium is an incentive to the insured to effect cover for the maximum amount.

Example

Assume that the sum insured is Rs. 1,00,00,000 and the rate per mille is Re. 1.20. The insured is liable to pay a provisional premium of Rs. 12,000. Now, if the aggregate of monthly declarations comes out to be Rs. 13,20,00,000. The average monthly declaration value will be Rs. 1,10,00,000 (Rs. 13,20,00,000/12). Accordingly, the premium on the policy will be Rs. 13,200 (Rs. 1,10,00,000 × 1.20). The additional premium to be borne by the insured will be Rs. 1,200.

Floater Declaration Policies

These policies combine the features of the floater and declaration policies. All rules relating to Floater Policies and Declaration Policies shall apply here except :

- The minimum premium retention of the insurance company shall be 80 per cent of the annual premium.
- Minimum sum insured is Rs. 2 crore.

24.4.3 Consequential Loss Policies

Coverage and Suitability

This policy is suitable for business establishments and corporate for whom business interruption would mean heavy monetary loss in view of huge fixed costs. Fire consequential loss policy provides cover for expenses and increased cost of working as a result of business interruption following a loss covered by the fire policy. Insurance cover can be taken for the maximum period of the anticipated interruption in the event of loss. In addition, the supplier's and the customer's premises on which the business is dependent, cost of auditors fee (required to submit the monetary claim) can also be insured.

Because of the business interruption following a loss, there may be a reduction in turnover and this may affect the anticipated gross profit. Fixed costs are to be incurred immaterial of the production activity. Consequential loss policy covers reduction in gross profit due to business interruption. The additional expenditure necessarily incurred for avoiding or reducing the fall in turnover during the interruption period is covered under this policy. Also, there are overhead expenses of running the business such as salaries, wages, taxes, interest etc. which continue to be incurred inspite of the interruption of the production.

Premium

Premium chargeable depends on the type of industry/business, the anticipated gross profit, indemnity period chosen and additional covers required. Refund of premium (not exceeding 50%) can be claimed based on the actual gross profit figures as per the audited balance sheet after the expiry of the policy.

Basic fire policy to cover the assets at the business premises is a prerequisite. For claiming benefits under this policy the *loss* should first be admitted under the fire policy. Amount of gross profit required to be insured, the indemnity period, details of the business premises to be covered and additional covers required shall be provided in the proposal form.

Advantage

In case of major fire loss, the business operations get interrupted resulting in reduced turnover and eventually in loss of profits. It is a well known fact that fixed or standing charges have to be incurred immaterial whether there has been any production or not. All these are not covered by the normal fire policy. It is here that the consequential loss policy comes into force. Thus, for overall protection to the business and its profitability, consequential policy is necessary in addition to the fire insurance policy.

24.5 FIRE UNDERWRITING & RATING

24.5.1 Rate Fixation in Fire Insurance

The rate of fire insurance is prescribed by All India Fire Tariff. Insurers may charge rate higher than the tariff rates. The computation of rate is done in the following manner :

(*a*) Base rates are arrived for the class of property

(*b*) Reduction in rates is allowed for deletion of STF1 and/or RSMTD perils, if opted not to be included

(*c*) Extra tariff is added for Hazardous Assets

(*d*) Discount is allowed for claims experience

(*e*) Further discount is allowed for betterment of risks

The rates of insurance generally depend upon the nature of physical hazards, classification of risks, loss experience and nature of risks. Following considerations are taken into account while fixing premiums :

- Premium rating depends on the type of occupancy-whether industrial or otherwise.
- All property located in an industrial complex will be charged on rate depending on the product(s) made.
- Facilities outside industrial complexes will be rated depending on the nature of occupancy at individual location.
- Storage areas will be rated based on the hazardous nature of goods held.
- Additional premium is charged to include "Add on" covers.
- Discount in premium is given based on past claims history and fire protection facilities provided at the premises.
- The insured can also opt out riot, strike, malicious and terrorism damage covers and flood group and perils for reduction in premium.

The risks are classified as simple risks, Industrial/Manufacturing risks, Utilities, Storage risks, Tank farms/ Gasholders Risks (Section III–VII of the tariff).

24.5.2 Fire Insurance Documents

Proposal Form

The proposal form contains the following information :

- ❑ Details of the proposer–location details, nature and location of risk, nature of business, financial performance, claims history, existing insurances etc.

- ❑ Type of coverage–inclusions and exclusions opted for
- ❑ Details of subject matter of insurance
- ❑ Sum Insured–computation basis and basis of indemnity.
- ❑ Insured Declaration/Authentication
- ❑ Risk inspection report
- ❑ *Cover note*
- ❑ A cover note is issued pending issue of policy. It contains the following information :
  - ❖ Proposer details
  - ❖ Sum Insured
  - ❖ Details of risk covered
  - ❖ Details of premium
  - ❖ Date of issue and validity
  - ❖ Date of commencement and expiry of cover
  - ❖ Authentication
  - ❖ Warranties and clauses

Policy Document

The fire policy must follow the format prescribed by the tariff. It contains the all the information as contained in the cover note as mentioned above. In addition, it contains the endorsement and alterations made to the policy.

24.5.3 Cancellation of Policies

If insurance is cancelled at the option of insured, the retention of premium shall be at short period scale. Else if the insurance is cancelled by the Insurer, the insurer refunds the premium on pro-rata basis.

If the policy is cancelled on account of :

- ❑ an order by a local authority/state/central govt.
- ❑ a building is completed when it was in course of construction
- ❑ demolition
- ❑ the premium is refunded pro-rata basis.

24.5.4 Mid-Term Cover

Mid-term cover are not granted for STFI and/or RSMTD perils. Whenever they are granted, the following conditions apply :

- ❑ Insurers must receive a specific advice from the insured accompanied by payment of additional premium.
- ❑ Cover shall commence 15 days after the receipt of premium.
- ❑ Premium rates prescribed in the Tariff are charged on short period scale basis on full sum insured for the balance period *i.e.,* upto the expiry of the policy.

Mid-term increase in sum insured is also allowed on pro-rata basis.

24.5.5 Claims Experience Discount

Claims experience discount is the discount offered on the basis of favourable claims experience. This discount may be offered on all policies covering the Insured's interest on the principle of one risk–one rate or of the preceding three policy periods.

This discount is applicable to risks rateable under Sections IV, V, VI & VII of the All India Fire Tariff.

Discounts (%)	Incurred Claims Ratio
15	Upto 5%
10	Above 5% and upto 10%
5	Above 10% and upto 15%

24.5.6 FEA Discount

Fire Extinguishing Appliances discount is offered for risk improvement as per the following conditions :

- Fire Extinguishing system shall be erected and tested as per the regulations of the TAC.
- Certificate from Professionals/Professional Agencies confirming the efficiency of the system and its compliance with the Rules shall be submitted by the Insured to insurer at stipulated times.
- The installation of the system shall be maintained in efficient working order at all times and annual maintenance contract with an approved external agency shall be in force.

	Type of Installation	Discount %
(a)	Hand Appliances & Trailer Pumps/Fire Engines	2.5
(b)	Hand Appliances & Hydrant System	5
(c)	Hand Appliances & Sprinkler/Fixed Water Spray System	7.5
(d)	Hand Appliances + Hydrant System & Sprinkler/Fixed Water Spray System	10

(*Source* : Fire and Conequential Loss Insurance, IC57, Insurance Institute of India, Mumbai).

The above discounts are non cumulative and are unaffected by the presence of hand appliances.

24.6 Fire Insurance Claims

24.6.1 Fire Claims Procedure

Fire insurance claims settlement is a comprehensive procedure requires the scrutiny of fire policy, its extensions and schedule attached. The onus of proof in a fire claim is that of insured and the insurer has to verify whether the causa proxima was a covered peril or not. Following procedure is generally followed after receipt of a claim notice from the insured :

Basic Verification

On receipt of intimation of a claim, the first step is to verify that :

- Whether the policy is in force (affective).
- The perils covered under the policy include cause of loss.
- The property affected and location involved are both covered as per the policy schedule.
- The interest involved is the same as referred to in the policy.

Allotment of Claim Number

If the above conditions are satisfied then the claim is registered by the insurer and a claim number (unique) is allotted, which is to be used as reference for any future correspondence regarding the claim.

Issue of Claim Form

After the registration of the claim, a claim form is issued to the insured for completion and return. The following information is required by a claim form :

- Name of the insured, policy number and address.
- Date, time, cause and circumstances of fire or occurrence of insured peril.
- Details of damage property.
- Sound value of the property at the time of fire. Where the insurance consists of several items, a declaration is required for the value of each item under which the claim is made.
- Amount claimed after deduction of salvage value.
- Situation and occupancy of premises in which the fire occurred.
- Capacity in which the insured claims, whether as owner or mortgagee or the like.
- Any other person(s) interested in the damage property.
- If any other insurance on such property was in force.

A claim settlement procedures is devoted to :

- Determine the amount of loss.
- Determine the method of settlement applicable.
- Explain the decision on claim to relevant parties.
- Notify the claimant in accordance with policy guidelines and code of Practice.
- Complete the claim documentation.
- Payment and related formalities.

Appointment of Surveyor

In case the amount of claim made is small, the claim is simple and straight forward and is usually investigated by the official of the insuring company and processed and settled on the basis of investigation report and claim form. But if the loss is expected to be large, then independent loss surveyors and loss assessors are appointed to carry out a detailed investigation of the loss. These surveyors should have a license, to act as loss surveyors, issued by the Controller of Insurance. The surveyor is furnished with all the information and documents which help him determining the amount of loss and subsequently the liability of the insurance company.

Investigation Report and Discharge Voucher

The report of the loss surveyor and a discharge voucher is sent to the assured for his consent and signature and return. The receipt of such voucher duly signed by the assured initiates the insurers to send the cheque with an amount of the claim. The discharge voucher is to be signed by all the persons whose name appears in the policy document, and the cheque is drawn in favor of all the parties as mentioned in the policy. When the insurance is on co-insurance basis, the surveyor is appointed by the leading insurer. Where the losses involved are large and reinsurance arrangement provide for the 'cash loss settlements'. If the loss amount exceeds the pre agreed figure, the insurers are entitled to recover the reinsurers' share immediately on payment of loss to the insured.

Where a difference arises regarding the quantum of compensation, the condition 11 of the Fire Policies 'A' and 'B' and condition 13 of Standard Fire Policies 'C' are invoked and the case is then referred to arbitrators appointed by the parties.

Disputes arises when the insurer repudiates the liability by stating that the loss is not covered under the terms and conditions of the policy or there has been a misrepresentation or fraud on the part of the insured or there has been a breach of warranty. The disputes may also concern the amount of indemnification as assessed by the insurer *vis-a-vis* as required by the insured. The insured in such cases can go to consumer redressal forums or the parties by mutual agreement can appoint an arbitrator or the insured can move the Court of law, directly or if not satisfied with the decision of the arbitrator or the consumer forum, as the case may be.

On the happening of any loss or damage to any of the property insured by this policy, the insurer may :

- Take the possession of the building or the premises where the loss of damage has taken place;
- Take possession or required to be delivered to it any property of the insured in the building or on the premises at the time of the loss or damage as per policy condition;
- Keep in possession of any such property and examine, sort, arrange, remove or otherwise deal with the same and
- Sell any such property or dispose off the same for the account of the concerned.

In case of assignment, the insurer may be required to make payments to other than the insured, who claims to be entitled to the payment under the policy, after producing necessary documents which may include :

- Probate of the deceased's will
- Letter of administration
- Certificate of appointment in case of appointment of a trustee in bankruptcy.

24.6.2 Extent of Indemnity

Indemnity is determined by the following :

- The value of the subject matter of the insurance affected which depends upon the following parameters :
  - The value at the time of loss
  - The value at the place of loss
  - The real or intrinsic value excluding any sentimental value
  - Prospective profit or other consequential and indirect losses are excluded
- The sum insured under the policy for the affected property.
- The extent of insurable interest of the assured in the property on which the insurance policy is affected.
- Value of salvage.
- Application of *pro rata* average.
- Deduction for any excess, if any.
- The contribution condition in cases where more than one insurance policy covers the same property.
- All rights and remedies arising out of the loss passes to insurers by subrogation.
- In case of successive losses, the sum insured under the policy will be reduced by the amount of the loss paid and the reduced sum insured is the sum insured for subsequent losses.

24.6.3 Valuation Under Valued Policies

In the case of valued policies, the valuation is placed on the subject-matter of the policy, except in case of fraud or mistake, conclusively establishes the sum required for the purpose of full indemnity in case of total loss. In such cases the insured does not need to prove the amount of loss that has taken place and on his proving of total loss he is entitled to recover the full amount even though the practical result may be to give more than true indemnity. In the cases of partial loss, where the subject matter is not destroyed but only damaged, the insured being entitled to indemnity only, cannot recover more then the amount of damage sustained by him. In such cases it is immaterial whether the policy is valued, because what is actually valued is the subject matter of insurance and not the amount of loss.

24.6.4 Valuation Under Unvalued Policies

In case of unvalued policies, the amount of insurance specified in the policy does not necessarily represent the true measure of indemnity. In such cases, it is generally determined according to the intrinsic value or the market value on the date the fire occurred.

Where the insured has limited insurable interest, he is precluded from recovering more than the value of his interest in the subject matter of insurance. Otherwise principle of indemnity and good faith would be violated.

- The form of the policy enables the assured to recover the full amount.
- The insured, at the time of insuring, intends to insure the whole value of the subject matter for the purpose of covering not merely his own limited interest but also the interest of all other persons who are interested in the subject-matter.
- There is no law which prohibits the insured from recovering the full amount.

24.7 Progress of Fire Insurance

Fire insurance is its present form has evolved after the incident of "Great Fire" which destroyed various buildings and inherent assets in the year 1066 and it lasted for many days. The first fire policy came in 1667. The fire insurance also developed during the industrial revolution.

The fire insurance was in nascent stage in India till liberalisation even though, the fire insurance commercially developed in British times. Some of the early companies included Sun Insurance, Royal Ex?? Assurance, Phoenix Assurance during 17-9-1790 period. GIC was nationalised in 1972 and since then its four subsidiaries were having monopoly till 1999.

The share of business of GIC and its subsidiaries in 1972 was more than 75% of the total premium collected. It rose to around Rs. 180 crores with monopoly of GIC and its subsidiaries in 1981. The fire insurance business has recorded a substantial rise thereafter *viz.*, the group direct premium in 1987 was around Rs. 425 crore which went up to Rs. 1219.38 crores in 1993-94 and Rs. 2390 crores in 1999-2000 (Exhibit 24A).

FIRE INSURANCE STATISTICS

Exhibit 24A : Business Generated (Gross Direct Premium - Rs. in crores)

Companies	*1993-94*	*1994-95*	*1995-96*	*1996-97*	*1997-98*	*1998-99*	*1999-2000*
GIC	160.39	180.35	204.60	226.56	246.99	263.03	295.00
NIC	221.82	224.63	292.71	319.56	339.37	374.49	418.41
OIC	210.85	234.80	287.39	316.74	354.64	362.69	421.43
NIAC	361.14	416.03	500.65	482.33	567.28	581.89	726.77
UII	265.19	294.66	347.79	397.72	425.85	464.47	529.27
Total	**1219.39**	**1350.47**	**1633.14**	**1742.91**	**1934.13**	**2046.57**	**2390.88**

Profits (Rs. in crores)

Companies	*1993-94*	*1994-95*	*1995-96*	*1996-97*	*1997-98*	*1998-99*	*1999-2000*
GIC	39.12	28.02	14.43	57.32	86.43	89.48	91.62
NIC	39.39	12.35	15.43	46.30	89.09	61.16	90.42
OIC	44.25	45.26	-2.47	34.14	101.63	88.36	52.13
NIAC	57.49	52.74	65.89	98.08	153.17	165.68	134.29
UII	67.79	79.13	38.18	91.71	113.28	134.60	172.65
Total	**248.04**	**217.50**	**131.46**	**327.55**	**543.60**	**539.28**	**541.11**

24.7.1 Profitability Before Privatisation

Fire insurance has been a profitable business for the India insurers. The profit (operating) earned by GIC in the year 1999-2000 was 31.00% of Gross Direct Premium Income and that of UTI was 32.62%. Both the companies have been outperformers. During the period 1993-94 to 1999-2000, there were no instances of losses except one in 1995-96 when OIC incurred a marginal loss. (Exhibit 24B)

Exhibit 24B : Profit %age

Companies	*1993-94*	*1994-95*	*1995-96*	*1996-97*	*1997-98*	*1998-99*	*1999-2000*
GIC	24.39%	15.54%	7.05%	25.30%	34.99%	34.02%	31.06%
NIC	17.76%	5.50%	5.27%	14.49%	26.25%	16.33%	21.61%
OIC	20.99%	9.28%	-0.86%	10.78%	28.66%	24.36%	12.37%
NIAC	15.92%	12.68%	13.16%	20.33%	27.00%	28.47%	18.48%
UII	25.56%	26.85%	10.98%	23.06%	26.60%	28.98%	32.62%

24.7.2 Post Liberalisation Progress

Premium Income

After privatisation, especially in the year 2000-01, the fire premium dipped slightly and afterward started growing at a fast rate. During this time many private companies ventured into the fire insurance business significant among them are Reliance General Insurance, IFFco-Tokio and Bajajk Allianz, Royalk Sundaram took a quantum leap in the year 2002-03 and declined afterwards. As per the figures of 2004-05, the prominent among the private players was ICICI Lombard (Exhibit 24C).

The income of the public sector companies also witnessed a growth immediately after privatisation till 2002-03 and it declined afterwards. This is attributable to the aggressive marketing strategies and new product offerrings by the private players.

Exhibit 24C : Fire Insurance (Gross Direct Premium Income)

Fire Insurance Statistics

Business Generated(Gross Direct Premium - Rs. in crores)

Companies	*1993-94*	*1994-95*	*1995-96*	*1996-97*	*1997-98*	*1998-99*	*1999-2000*
GIC	160.39	180.35	204.60	226.56	246.99	263.03	295.00
NIC	221.82	224.63	292.71	319.56	339.37	374.49	418.41
OIC	210.85	234.80	287.39	316.74	354.64	362.69	421.43
NIAC	361.14	416.03	500.65	482.33	567.28	581.89	726.77
UII	265.19	294.66	347.79	397.72	425.85	464.47	529.27
Total	**1219.39**	**1350.47**	**1633.14**	**1742.91**	**1934.13**	**2046.57**	**2390.88**

Profits(Rs. in Crores)

Companies	*1993-94*	*1994-95*	*1995-96*	*1996-97*	*1997-98*	*1998-99*	*1999-2000*
GIC	39.12	28.02	14.43	57.32	86.43	89.48	91.62
NIC	39.39	12.35	15.43	46.30	89.09	61.16	90.42
OIC	44.25	45.26	-2.47	34.14	101.63	88.36	52.13
NIAC	57.49	52.74	65.89	98.08	153.17	165.68	134.29
UII	67.79	79.13	38.18	91.71	113.28	134.60	172.65
Total	**248.04**	**217.50**	**131.46**	**327.55**	**543.60**	**539.28**	**541.11**

Profit %age

GIC	24.39%	15.54%	7.05%	25.30%	34.99%	34.02%	31.06%
NIC	17.76%	5.50%	5.27%	14.49%	26.25%	16.33%	21.61%
OIC	20.99%	19.28%	-0.86%	10.78%	28.66%	24.36%	12.37%
NIAC	15.92%	12.68%	13.16%	20.33%	27.00%	28.47%	18.48%
UII	25.56%	26.85%	10.98%	23.06%	26.60%	28.98%	32.62%

Fire Insurance (Gross Direct Premium Income)

Company	*2000-01*	*2001-02*	*2002-03*	*2003-04*	*2004-05*	*2005-06*	*2006-07*	*2007-08*	*2008-09*
National	460.87	491.83	507.85	515.77	537.64	483.94	492.52	380.72	393.59
New India	760.29	859.89	867.46	775.2	788.88	839.63	909.98	743.43	773.33
Oriental	485.03	521.67	532.64	524	493.95	546.89	540.07	478.2	440.65
United India	606.03	635.89	604.18	631.32	590.91	645.48	664.34	524.3	570.8
ECGC*	-	-	39.16	-	-	-	-	-	-
GIC*/Others**	-	-	55.42	-	-	-	-	3.51	29.85
Royal Sundaram	-	17.9	103.52	50.53	63.01	91.74	98.39	68.87	48.84
Reliance	-	45.84	49.91	46.36	53.58	47.76	145.88	143.27	136.84
Iffco-Tokio	-	36.15	123.75	142.88	172.78	236.29	291.02	215.17	195.28
TATA AIG	-	19.36	60.64	78.44	83.71	116.27	136.95	129.77	144.76
ICICI Lombard	-	10.98	5.32	239.46	277.45	308.47	393.83	471.35	283.02
Bajaj Allianz	-	27.88	-	120.29	219.42	351.4	370.31	273.49	253.06
Cholamandalam	-	-	-	25.44	47.78	72.83	77.98	68.3	53.84
HDFC-Chubb	-	-	-	0.36	1.81	6.81	11.1	12.83	58.79
Total	2312.22	2667.39	2949.85	3150.05	3330.92	3747.51	4132.37	3513.21	3382.65

***Others include Future Gereali and Universal Sompo*

Market Shares

The monopoly of the public players was seriously hit after privitisation. It is evident from Table 6.5 that the shares of public sector companies is declining and that of private players is picking up. In 2004-05 the share of private players was 27.60% which is remarkable. (Exhibit 24D)

Exhibit 24D : Market Share

Public Co. Share	100.00%	94.07%	85.16%	77.66%	72.39%	67.14%	63.09%	60.53%
Private Co. Share	0.00%	5.93%	14.84%	22.34%	27.61%	32.86%	36.91%	39.47%

Growth Rates

Fire insurance business has been growing but at an erratic rate. The year 2001-02 saw a negative growth rate when the insurance sector was opened for pubic players. The Compounded Average Growth rate for the eleven year period from 1993-94 to 2008-09 is around 7.04% which is satisfactory when compared to other counterparts in the developing countries of the world.

Exhibit 24E : Fire Insurance

Years	*1993-94*	*1994-95*	*1995-96*	*1996-97*	*1997-98*	*1998-99*	*1999-2000*	*2000-01*
Gross Direct Premium	1219.39	1350.47	1633.14	1742.91	1934.13	2046.57	2390.88	2312.22
Annual Growth Rate		10.75%	20.93%	6.72%	10.97%	5.81%	16.82%	-3.29%
Years	2001-02	2002-03	2003-04	2004-05	2005-06	2006-07	2007-08	2008-09
Gross Direct Premium	2667.39	2949.85	3150.05	3330.92	3747.51	4132.37	3513.21	3382.65
Annual Growth Rate	15.36%	10.59%	6.79%	5.74%	12.51%	10.27%	-14.98%	-3.72%
Compounded Average Growth Rate			*7.04%*					

Exhibit 24F : Fire Insurance

(Opearting Profits-Rs. Crores)

Company	*2003-04*	*2004-05*	*2005-06*	*2006-07*	*2007-08*
National	197.43	138.69	27.22	123.32	21.28
New India	294.77	230.83	19.57	233.02	283.36
Oriental	161.63	138.69	51.61	144.98	-16.77
United India	233.46	184.77	115.74	2.83	97.13
ECGC*	-	-	-	-	-
GIC*/Others**					-12.10
Royal Sundaram	9.23	7.24	11.53	18.81	6.38
Reliance	6.00	7.34	7.93	35.77	24.44
Iffco-Tokio	15.66	28.15	36.97	46.00	14.99
TATA AIG	19.63	17.93	22.49	28.08	24.93
ICICI Lombard	38.31	52.35	48.13	73.85	18.05
Bajaj Allianz	22.52	47.24	46.91	79.21	71.92
Cholamandalam	0.40	1.79	-0.70	17.90	19.50
HDFC-Chubb	-0.54	-0.27	-0.66	1.64	2.24
Total	**998.5**	**854.75**	**386.74**	**805.41**	**555.35**

24.8 Fire Reinsurance – An Illustration

Reinsurance of fire business in India is primarily headed by GIC in accordance with the IRDA guidelines. The obligatory session (20% quota share) is compulsorily needed to GIC and rest is dealt by treaties. The quota cession is retained in India itself to protect drainage of foreign exchange. The treaties take into account the sum insured and probable maximum loss. This requires classification of risk as illustrated below :

Non-risk Booked Risks : Smaller risks having sum insured less than Rs. 5 crores, which are not normally entered into the risk register maintained for the purpose-retention is 100% in India and reinsurance is affected using excess of loss cover.

Booked Risks : Medium Risks – Sum insured > Rs. 5 crores and PML < Rs. 26 crores.

The risks are entered in the register and are termed as Risk Booked. The underwriting of medium sized risks is as under :

Obligatory	20.00%
Net Account	45.00%
Market fire pool	30.00%
Cos. Fire surplus treaty	0.5.00%
Total	**100.00%**

The Indian market retention for Medium Size Risks is 95%.

Listed Risks : All risks having a PML greater than Rs. 26 crores are classified as listed risks.

Key Terms

- ❒ Reinsurance
- ❒ Facultatives
- ❒ Surplus
- ❒ Risk Register
- ❒ Treaty
- ❒ Obligatory Cessions
- ❒ Reinsurance Arrangements
- ❒ FEA Discount
- ❒ TAC
- ❒ Pro-rata basis
- ❒ AIFT
- ❒ Shot-period Scale
- ❒ Gross Direct Premium
- ❒ Underwriting Experience
- ❒ Operating Profit
- ❒ CAGR
- ❒ Valued Policy
- ❒ Discharge Voucher
- ❒ Inspection Report
- ❒ Unvalued Policy
- ❒ Adjustment
- ❒ Claim Register
- ❒ Surveyor
- ❒ Add-on-cover
- ❒ Consequential Loss
- ❒ Declaration Policies
- ❒ Floater Policies
- ❒ Reinstatement Value Policies

Suggested Readings

- Irving Pfeffer and David, R., Klock, *Perspectives on Insurance,* Prentice Hall, Englewood Ciffs, 1974.
- *Fire and Consequential Loss Insurance,* Insurance Institute of India, Mumbai, 2004.
- www.globalreinsurance.com
- www.reinsurance.org
- www.re-world.com
- *Fire and Consequential Loss Insurance,* IC 57, Insurance Institute of India, Mumbai 2001.
- *IRDA Annual Report 2001-02.*
- *Insurance Law Manual,* Taxmann, 2001.
- *All India Fire Tariff prescribed by Tariff Advisory Committee.*
- IRDA Reports.
- Articles on Insurance.
- CAG Reports.
- *Fire and Consequential Loss Insurance,* IC 57, Insurance Institute of India, Mumbai 2001.
- *IRDA Annual Report 2001-02.*
- *Insurance Law Manual,* Taxmann, 2001.
- *All India Fire Tariff prescribed by Tariff Advisory Committee.*
- Fire and consequential Loss Insurance, IC57 Insurance Institute of India, Mumbai, 2004.

- Gupta, P.K., Insurance and Risk Management, Himalaya Publishing House, Mumbai, 2004.
- All India Fire Tariff prescribed by Tariff Advisory Committee.

Questions for Review

1. Give an example of how fire exposure worth Rs. 5000 crores would be reinsurance using various arrangement.
2. Briefly explain the steps in filing and settlement of fire claims.
3. What are the rights of the insurer, once a claim is admitted under the fire policy?
4. Write short notes on :
   (*a*) Arbitration
   (*b*) Limited Insurable Interest.
5. Briefly comment on the progress of Fire Insurance in India.
6. What major changes have took place in the fire insurance business segment after privatisation?
7. Briefly explain the various underwriting considerations in fire insurance business.
8. Discuss the importance of "depreciation factor" in fire insurance loss assessment.
8. Explain how basis rate are arrived at under the Consequential Loss (Fire) cover?
10. Define fire insurance. Explain the important features of a standard fire policy.
11. Write short notes on :
   (*a*) Fire Extinguishing Appliance Discount
   (*b*) Dual Basis of Wages Insurance
   (c) Debris Removal Clause.
12. Distinguish between :
   (*a*) Standard Fire Policy and Reinstatement Value Policy
   (*b*) Floater and Declaration Policies
   (*c*) Originating Factors vs. Contributory Factors

Marine Insurance

Chapter 25

CHAPTER OBJECTIVES

After reading this chapter you will be able to understand :

- *Evolution of Marine Insurance and Marine Covers*
- *Marine Ratings*
- *Maritime Clauses*
- *Marine Claim Settlement Procedure*
- *Marine Losses and Frauds*

Marine insurance is the oldest branch of insurance industry. In 1769, Lloyds of London was formed in 1779, the underwater at Lloyds adopted a uniform marine insurance policy which is widely adopted now through out the world.

25.1 INTRODUCTION

Insurance on the risks of transportation of goods is one of the oldest and most vital forms of insurance. The value of goods shipped by business firms each year cost millions of rupees. These goods are exposed to damage or loss from numerous transportation perils. The goods can be protected by ocean marine and inland marine contracts. Ocean marine insurance provides protection for goods transported over water. All types of ocean going vessels and their cargo can be insured by ocean marine contracts, the legal liability of ship owners and cargo owners can also be insured. Inland marine insurance provides protection for goods shipped on land. It includes insurance on imports and exports, domestic shipments, and means of transportation such as bridges and tunnels. In addition, inland marine insurance can be used to insure fine art, jewellery, fur and other properties.

25.2 HISTORY OF MARINE INSURANCE

Ocean marine insurance is one of the earliest forms of insurance. Commerce by ship was well-established in the Mediterranean Sea, 2000 years before the birth of Christ. The Babylonians, Phoenicians, Greeks and Romans were great sea traders. Coincident with the development of this trade, insurance transactions emerged as distinct commercial agreements. *Bottomary* was a transaction protecting an owner from financial loss if his ship was destroyed. The bottomary loan was an early forerunner of ocean marine insurance. On the other hand, some elements of the modern insurance transaction were missing. Actuarial science was not practiced, although the Phoenicians were noted mathematicians, so premiums were probably not based on mathematical estimates but on intuition. Today, judgmental estimates remain the basis of marine underwriting. The early sea traders and moneylenders also lacked a highly developed body of law like that providing the environment for the modern insurance transaction.

Respondentia loans were comparable to bottomary loans, the difference being the subject of the loan. Otherwise, the transaction was comparable. A merchant, placing cargo on a ship, would take out a loan using the cargo as collateral. The moneylender, for a premium in addition to the regular interest charged, agreed to forgive the loan if the cargo were lost. Again, modern ocean marine cargo insurance is very similar to the respondentia loan. Evidences of marine insurance contrait are found in Mediterranean voyages the literature of 1400 also indicates the charging of prime for marine insurance policies. The law of Wishky (1300), the Ordinance of Barcelona (1435) and the Guidon de la Mar (1600) provide evidence of marine insurance development in Europe. In 1779, the underinites at Lloyds adopted a uniform marine insurance contract which is a common form of policy in use today.

During the period 1720-1820, the companies like London Association and Royal Exchange Association enjoyed major marine insurance market share.

In 1909, the Marine Insurance (Gambling Policies) Act was adopted and the modest pattern of British regulation was set as it is in substance today.

Major international markets for marine includes U.K., U.S., Europe, Japan, etc. The most dominated UK Marine Insurance market includes players like Lloyds, mutual association and affiliates of non UK based insurance companies.

25.3 Marine Insurance – Definition and Types

A contract of marine insurance is an agreement whereby the insurer undertakes to indemnify the assured in a manner and to the extent thereby agreed, against marine losses, that is, the losses incidental to marine adventure. Marine insurance cover gives financial protection from total loss or partial damage of sea going ships and cargoes. In return for the payment of a premium, the underwriter of a marine risk or 'line' insures the ship owner, ship–charterer or merchant, for part or the whole value of a ship or cargo. Freight charges paid in advance may be insured by the ship-owner. Each type of marine insurance requires an assessment of the nature, size are value of the risk and the underwriter calculate his premium according to the quality of the ship or cargo and the destination and route of the voyage at risk. Marine insurance contracts are amongst the least charging and most familiar of all types of risk business. *There is a marine adventure when any insurable property is exposed to marine perils*. Marine perils also known as perils of the seas, means the perils consequent on, or incidental to, the navigation of the sea or the perils of the seas, such as fire, war perils, pirates, rovers, thieves, captures, Jettisons, barratry and any other perils which are either of the like, kind or may be designed by the policy. Marine Insurance business means the business of effecting contracts of insurance upon vessels of any description, including cargoes, freights and other interests which may be legally insured minor in relation to such vessels, cargoes and freights, goods, wares, merchandise and property of whatever description insured for any transit by land or water or both, and whether or not including warehome risks or similar risks in addition or as incidental to such transit and includes any other risks customarily included among the risks insured against in marine insurance policies. The two broad categories of marine insurance are – ocean marine insurance and inland marine insurance.

25.3.1 Ocean Marine Insurance

Ocean marine insurance is one of the forms of transportation insurance. The ocean marine contracts are incredibly complex, reflecting basic marine law, trade customs, and court interpretations of the various policy provisions. Ocean marine insurance can be divided into four basic classes to reflect the various insurable interests :

Hull Insurance covers physical damage to the ship or vessel. It is similar to collision insurance that covers physical damage to a automobile caused by collision. Hull insurance is always written with a deductible. In addition, it contains a collision liability clause that covers the owner's legal liability if the ship collides with another vessel or damages its cargo. However, the running down clause does not cover legal liability on that vessel arising out of injury or death to other persons, damage to piers and docks, and personal injury and death of crew members.

Cargo Insurance covers the shipper of the goods if the goods are damaged or lost. The policy can be written to cover a single shipment. If regular shipments are made, an open-cargo policy can be used that insures the goods automatically when a shipment is made. The shipper is required to report periodically the number of shipments that are made. The open-cargo policy has no expiration date and remains in force until it is cancelled.

Protection and Indemnity (P&I) Insurance is usually written as a separate contract that provides comprehensive liability insurance for property damage or bodily injury to third parties. P&I insurance protects the ship owner for damage caused by the ship to piers, docks and harbour installations, damage to the ship's cargo, illness or injury to the passengers or crew, and fines and penalties.

Freight Insurance indemnifies the ship owner for the loss of earnings if the goods are damaged or lost and are not delivered.

Ocean marine insurance has certain fundamental concepts :

Covered Perils : an ocean marine policy provides broad coverage for certain specified perils, including perils of the sea, such as damage or loss from bad weather, high waves, collision, sinking, and stranding. Other covered perils include loss from fire, enemies, pirates, thieves, jettison (throwing goods overboard to save the ship), barratry (fraud by the master or crew at the expense of the ship or cargo owners), and similar perils. Ocean marine insurance can also be written on an "all-risks" basis. All unexpected and fortuitous losses are covered except those losses specifically excluded. Common exclusions are losses due to delay, war, inherent vice (tendency of certain types of property to decompose), and strikes, riots, or civil commotion.

Particular Average : in marine insurance the word average refers to a partial loss. A particular average is a loss that falls entirely on a particular interest, as contrasted with a general average, a loss that falls on all parties to the voyage. Under the free of particular average clause (FPA), partial losses are not covered unless the loss is caused by certain perils, such as stranding, sinking, burning or collision of the vessel. The FPA clause can be written with franchise deductible, where the franchise amount is stated as a percentage of the insured property. Thus, an FPA clause of 3% means that a covered loss under 3% falls entirely on the insured; if the loss is 3% or more, the insurer pays the loss in full.

General Average : a general average is a loss incurred for the common good and consequently is shared by all parties to the venture. Each party must pay its share of the loss based on the proportion that its interest bears to the total value in the venture. Four conditions must be satisfied to have a general average loss :

- *Necessary :* the sacrifice is necessary to protect all interests in the venture–ship, cargo, and freight.
- *Voluntary :* the sacrifice must be voluntary.
- *Successful :* the effort must be successful. At least part of the value must be saved.
- *Free from Fault :* any party that claims a general average contribution from other interests in the voyage must be free from fault with respect to the risk that threatens the venture.

Sue and Labour : under this the insured is required to do everything possible to save and preserve the goods in case of loss. The insured who fails to do this has violated a policy condition, hence loses the rights of recovery.

Abandonment : in ocean marine insurance, two types of total losses are recognized: actual and constructive. Actual total loss occurs when the property is completely destroyed. Constructive total loss occurs when, even though the ship or other subject matter of insurance is not totally destroyed, it would cost more to restore it than it is worth. The ship may be abandoned to the insurer and the insured collects the full amount of the policy. The salvage then belongs to the insurer, who is usually in a better position to dispose of it than the insured because the insurer deals with salvage companies all over the world and is experienced in such matters.

Warehouse to Warehouse : under the terms of the warehouse to warehouse clause, such protection as is afforded under the insuring agreement extends from the time the goods leave the warehouse of the shipper, even if it is located far inland, until they reach the warehouse of the consignee.

Coinsurance : although an ocean marine policy does not contain a specific coinsurance clause, losses are settled as if there is a 100 percent coinsurance clause. An ocean marine policy is a valued contract, by which the face amount is paid if a total loss occurs. If the insurance carried does not equal the full value of the goods at the time of loss, the insured must share in the loss.

Warranties : there are two types of warranties in marine insurance : express and implied. Express warranties are written into the contract and become a condition of the coverage relating to potential causes of an insured event. And can be of the type free of capture and seizure warranty (FC&S), strike, riot and civil commotion (SR&CC), delay warranty and trading warranty. Implied warranties are not written into the policy but become a part of it by custom. Breach of warranty in marine insurance voids the coverage, even if the breach is immaterial to the risk. It can be of types of seaworthiness, deviation and legality.

25.3.2 Inland Marine Insurance

Inland marine insurance grew out of ocean marine insurance. Ocean marine insurance first covered property from the point of embarkation to the place where the goods landed. As commerce and trade developed, the goods had to be shipped over land as well. Inland marine insurance developed in the 1920s to cover property being transported over land, means of transportation such as bridges and tunnels, and property of a mobile nature.

Commercial property that can be insured by inland marine contracts can be conveniently classified into five categories :

- Domestic Goods in Transit.
- *Property Held by Bailees :* bailees are legally liable for damage to customer's property only if they or their employees are negligent.
- *Mobile Equipment and Property :* inland marine property floaters can be used to cover property that is frequently moved from one location to another.
- *Property of Certain Dealers :* certain "block" policies are used to insure dealers. Most policies provide coverage on an "all-risks" basis.
- *Means of Transportation and Communication :* this refers to property at a fixed location that is used in transportation or communication.

For purposes of regulation, inland marine contracts are classified into two categories; *filed forms* and *nonfiled forms.* With filed forms, the policy forms and rates are filed with the state insurance department. Filed forms are typically used in situations where there are a large number of potential insurers and the loss exposures are reasonably homogenous. In contrast, non-filed forms refer to policy forms and rates that are not filed with the state insurance department. Nonfiled forms are used in situations where the insured has specialized or unique needs, the number of potential insureds is relatively small, and the loss exposures are diverse.

25.4 Nature of Marine Insurance Contract

Marine insurance contract being a contract should first satisfy the essential elements of a valid contract. In addition it should satisfy the insurance principles as applicable to marine insurance. Further, there are specific provisions given in the Marine Insurance Act, 1973.

The essential elements of a marine insurance contract from the perspective of Indian Contract Act *inter alia* includes :

(*a*) *Offer* – in the form of proposal.

(*b*) *Acceptance* – issue of a covernote/policy.

(*c*) *Consideration* – premium payable on the policy

Insurance Principles Applied to Marine Business

Utmost Good Faith

The insured to bound to disclose all material facts to the insurer before the contract is entered into.

Example

If an equipment is transported and insurance cover was obtained as such implying as is a new one and actually the equipment is one which has been renovated, the insurer may cancel the contract as it was a concealment of fact.

However, if there is certain information, which reduces the exposure, to the insurer or which the insurer is bound to have known or waived *suo moto*, the contract is valid.

If the insurance is affected through a proper or agent, it is the duty of agent/broker to disclose all material facts. These facts not only include the communicated facts but also (by principal) facts in his knowledge. He must also know every circumstance in ordinary course of business and as communicated by his principal. All representations (material fact/fact/expectations or belief) must be communicated to the insular before obtaining the cover.

Insurable Interest

The insured may not have insurable interest at the time of contract, but he must have a reasonable expectation of acquiring it and it must exist at the time of loss. As per the provisions of the Marine Insurance Act, 1963, every person has an insurable interest who is interested in a maritime adventure". The insurable interest may be :

(*a*) *Defeasible :* which is brought to an end by during the tenure of the voyage by occurrence of an event other than maritime perils. For example–cessation of insurable interest of the seller upon the transfer of title to the buyer.

(*b*) *Contingent :* which attaches during the tenure of the voyage on the happening of the contingent event. For example when the goods are sold on FOB terms to the buyer, when the goods are loaded on the vessel, the seller interest terminates, but if the goods are returned by the buyer, the interest again attaches for the seller.

It is essentially required that something must exist feasible which may be exposed to marine perils and there must be some legal or justified relationship which imply a benefit to the holder by its preservation and the insured is affected by its damage/less/detention or occurrence of a liability in connection thereof.

Marine Insurance Act provides that in the event of "lost or not lost" clauses in marine insurance contract, the assured may recover the loss even though at that moment he has not acquired any interest because of ignorance. However, if the insured was aware of loss and the insurer was not informed, the claim may be denied on the grounds of violation of utmost good faith.

Now-a-days cargo and hull policy forms have disformed with "lost or not lost" clauses. But some ICC clauses provide that if the insured property suffers loss/damage before assured acquires interest, he is protected by the policy condition if any only if risk is transferred to him. In case of PPI (Policy Proof of Interest) policies, the underwriter may dispene with evidence of insurable interest. However, no action is tonable against them if claim is denied. Insurer has insurable interest in respect of risk underwritten which entitles him to get it reinsured.

In case of freight, the cargo owner has insurable interest in freight advanced.

Indemnity

Section 3 of the Act says that indemnity is "in the manner and to the extent thereby agreed". The indemnity depends on the contact. In case of valued policies, the measure of indemnity is the agreed value. However, in case of unvalued policies, unless provided, the indemnity has to be calculated as per the provisions of the Section 18 of the Marine Insurance Act, 1963. Indemnity valuation is difficult because values of cargo keeps on changing and its value increase the more and more it gets closer to destination. Another method of indemnity valuation is :

CIF Value of Goods

\+ Allowance (%) for overheads

\+ Allowance (%) for profit.

Subrogation

The insurer on the payment of claims for losses which may be partial or total, is subrogated to all the rights and remedies of the assured in respect of the subject matter insured. In case of total loss, insurer is entitled to take over the interest of assured in toto. In case of partial loss, the insurer has not such rights. His rights are limited to the idemnity made. A letter of subrogation is generally taken from the insureds when claims are paid, in situations where the recovery is possible from third parties. If under recovery from third parties, a value greater than insured value is recovered, assured is entitled to proceeds, subject to reimbursement of claim amount due to insurers.

Contribution

When for the same subject matter of marine insurance, there are more than one policy such that sums insured exceed the indemnity allowed by the act, the assured shall be deemed to be cover insured and rateable proportion shall apply to such cases. If the insured has recovered more that indemnity value, the excess amount shall be held in trust by him.

Warranties

Warranties, common to marine insurance contracts are the promises by the insured that something shall be done or shall be done or a certain state of affairs exist or do not exist. The logical reason for imposing warranties by the insurers is to safeguard their interest from hazards and they can avoid liability in case of breach. Warranties may be :

Expressed : appearing in the policy *e.g.* warranties relating to packing, shipping time period, survey/inspection etc. In case of hull insurance express warranties include :

1. *Trading Warranty* : area of operation.
2. *Disbursement Warranty :* employment or use of the vessel for specific trade or traders.
3. *Registration/licencing Warranty* : for the vessels engaged in fishing or sailing activities.

Proximate Cause : The liability of insurers in limited to insured perils. If it is established that insured perils was the remote cause that resulted in damage/loss, the claim may be denied by the insurer.

25·5 MARINE INSURANCE POLICIES[1]

Marine insurance policies cover risks associated with transhipments of goods like :

1. Transit of heavy goods such as rail engines by shipping vessels or
2. Consignment of diamonds sent by post or

3. Movement of household goods by rail/road/air.
4. Risks vary with the type of business transacted whether it is by importers, exporters or trading house.
5. Some form of life and transit risks is still undertaken by Indian Posts & Telegraphs Dept.

Salient Features

- The striking features of Marine Insurance policies is that they are issued on 'agreed value basis'.
- The values agreed may include all expenses incurred or to be incurred and some amount of profit margins as well. As such the valuation of the consignment is important and it should be based on supporting evidence.

A marine insurance policy :

(*a*) Must be signed by or on behalf of insurer.

(*b*) May be executed and issued to insured after the conclusion of the contract.

(*c*) Must *interalia* include–the description of insured, subject matter of insurance, sum insured, insurer description, period of enforcement, covered perils, exclusion etc.

(*d*) If the subject matter of the insurance is in general terms, the policy relates to insurable interest.

(*e*) If the insurers are more than one, the joint policy represents separate contract with the respective insurers.

(*f*) A marine insurance policy must be authenticated by the issuer (insurer).

The contracts can be supply of goods on :

1. Ex-factory/godown/warehouse basis.
2. F.O.B. basis (free on board-values arrived at, may include sale price, packing and incidentals, insurance and freight for local transit until goods are placed on the ocean going vessel).
3. F.O.R. (values until placed on railway wagon as in the case of FOB).
4. C & F (cost and freight values as in CIF, except the insurance costs).

C.I.F. (cost insurance and freight would be sale price and incidental charges, insurance charges from warehouse to warehouse basis or any other point of delivery and all freight charges).

25.5.1 Types of Policies

There are different types of marine policies known by different names according to the manner of their execution or the risk they cover.

The major classification of marine insurance policies is :

(*a*) Policies covering damage/loss to ship/vessel/carrier hull, risk during repairs/construction, transfer risk, fleet cover.

(*b*) Policies providing cover against loss/damage to cargo particular average, general average.

(*c*) Policies protecting against third party liabilities–collision, protection against damage/loss, pollution cover, etc.

(*d*) Policies covering loss of freight etc.

Accordingly the following popular covers are discussed here :

Voyage Policy

The voyage policy is issued to cover up a specific transit from a particular point to another. The cover ceases upon the carrier reaching the town of destination. In all the policies, the scope of cover can be :

(i) *Basic cover* : Basic cover is described in ICC-C clause.

(ii) *Wider cover* : Wider cover is described by ICC-B.

(iii) *All Risks cover* : All risks cover by ICC-A.

(iv) All risks cover does not pay all losses.

(v) All risks cover can be extended against "Delay start up" or 'Consequential Loss due to Marine delays' or 'Advance loss of profits' risks.

(vi) While the basic policy document contains general conditions, the scope of cover and exceptions and special exclusions are attached by separate clauses known as Institute Cargo Clauses (ICC).

Extensions of Voyage Policy

(i) *FOB risks cover* : The road/rail transit risks can be extended until the goods are placed on board of the ocean going vessel, which may involve country craft/lighter risks also.

(ii) *Sellers' contingency risks* : FOB cover can further be extended against 'Sellers contingency risks'.

(iii) *Warehouse to warehouse basis* : the policy covers all risks right from the moment the goods are dispatched from the supplier's warehouse till they reach the buyers' warehouse.

Annual Policy

If a business involves regular dispatch of goods throughout the year, and the quantity can be reasonably estimated in advance, an annual policy can be obtained on the basis of estimated annual dispatches. Premiums collected in advance will be adjusted at the end of the year. In case of annual policies, the previous year's turn over and the estimated increase during the current year is the basis for fixing sum insured for annual policy.

Declaration Policy

An alternative to annual policy is declaration policy. A policy can be obtained for any specific amount so that every dispatch to be insured for transit risks can be declared as agreed to and accounted until the sum insured is exhausted. The policy can be extended for a further sum. In case of declaration policies, one has to take a policy equivalent to 3 months estimated dispatches, which can be extended any number of times. All the dispatches should be declared without exception as per terms agreed to.

Special Declaration

If sum insured selected is more than Rs. 2 crores, a special declaration policy can be obtained for which volume discount in premium is allowed. The annual dispatches should be reasonably estimated and the policy taken. However, the sum can be extended for a couple of times in extraordinary cases of genuine reasons. In case of special declaration policies, the minimum sum insured should be Rs.2 crores and the policies should be for sums equivalent to estimated annual dispatches. The declarations can be made at an agreed period (even after a loss). As the entire premium has to be paid in advance, volume discounts are offered.

Open Cover

It is a memorandum of agreement by which the insured will set out the terms of cover and rates of premium for one-year transaction of Marine dispatches. The open cover is not a Policy and it is not negotiable. A Certificate of insurance is issued for each declaration duly stamped for appropriate value and the Certificate will be negotiable.

Duty Policy

A deviation in Marine Insurance is to issue custom duty payable for imports by the same Marine Policy though there may not be any transit risks involved. In case of CIF contracts, the exporter to the extent of CIF values would have arranged the Insurance only. Custom Duty payable, if any, would be the responsibility of the importers and they can separately obtain Custom Duty policy on 'stand alone basis'.

Another special feature of custom duty policy is that it is a pure indemnity policy and the insured is paid the exact amount of loss of custom duty as a result of loss or damage to the consignment. The policy should be obtained before the vessel reaches the port of destination. Duty policy can be obtained much after dispatch of goods but before the vessel reaches the port of discharge.

Increased Value Policy

Increased value if goods imported are damaged in transit and such goods can be procured locally at prices higher than the CIF + custom duty, the increased value policy covers such difference in value. This is purely an indemnity policy and for the benefit of the insured only and cannot be assigned to others. The policy should be obtained before the overseas vessel reaches the port of destination.

Marine Delays (Marine LOP)

In case of new project where equipment has to be procured indigenously or by imports, any loss or damage to the equipment during transit may involve ordering of fresh equipment which leads to delay in completion of the project, commencement of production and thereby loss of profits. The Financial institutions who are interested in timely completion of the project for their debt servicing, would like this risk covered by an Insurance contract and the Marine (cargo) insurance policy can be extended against what are known as 'consequential loss due to Marine delays' or simply–Delay start up.

Marine Policy as a Part of Builders Risk (Marine cum Erection)

In case of Marine cum Erection Insurance policy, Marine risks are followed by storage risks, erection and testing. In the standard Marine (cargo) policy, the cover ceases after the goods are delivered at the site of erection. In a project site, it is not possible to examine any internal damage to the consignment and such losses don't surface till the time of erection. If any damage were found at the time of erection attributable to Transit risks, the marine policy and erection policy bear 50% each of the cost of damage. This is possible only if both Marine policy and erection policy is taken from the same insurers.

25.5.2 Nature of Marine Policies

- Marine policies, except increased policies, are freely assignable. Marine policy document is a fundamental requirement for discounting invoices with local bankers without waiting for the importer to receive the overseas shipments and pay the invoices.
- Even for sale contract on FOB basis when the insurable interest ceases (the goods are placed overboard by the seller) by a notional extension of principle of insurable interest, the risk can be covered by 'Sellers Contingency Policy'.
- Consignments sold without the support of a 'letter of credit' can also be insured for importer default to pay by "Export Credit Guarantee Corporation of India".

But for the Marine insurance policies, the trade, industry and commerce would not have developed to the present levels of turnovers anywhere in the world. A manufacturer can export their produce with confidence as their dispatches have the support of Marine insurance policies, and they can also discount their bills with local Bankers without waiting for the bills being paid by the overseas importers after they receive the goods which may take months by ocean transit. Marine Insurance Policy is one of the important documents besides Invoice and Bill of Lading.

While there is no Tariff rate of premium and the insurers can charge any rate depending upon the nature of goods, the mode of trans-shipment, type of package, the voyage route and the past claims experience. However extended covers like SRCC and War risks (for overseas cargo) risks are governed by special regulations and the premiums collected will be credited to the Central Government.

Shipping vessels are listed according to their age, drought weight and their classification by G.I.C. for approval. Full details of every shipping vessel built anywhere in the world would be available in 'Lloyds Register' (issued by Lloyds of London). Minimum standards are fixed. Any vessel falling short of these standards will attract loading of premium. Service Tax and Stamp duty is always collected from the insured separately along with premiums.

Except in the case of increased value policies, no formál proposal form eliciting insurance history, claims history or matters relating to physical or moral hazards, which are common in all other policies, is called for. However simple details of the property in transit, type of packing, mode of transport and values are to be provided in Marine Questionnaire form. The reason being that all Marine Insurance policies (cargo) are easily assignable to any one and one should have insurable interest at the time of a claim and not necessarily at the time of insurance. The policy is assigned by simply endorsing the policy on its reverse.

Open cover is a memorandum of agreement between the two parties and it is not negotiable. Increased value policy is obtained to take care of market fluctuation of prices and it can be obtained much after dispatch of goods but before the vessel reaches the port of discharge. A completed proposal form is required in this case.

25.6 MARINE INSURANCE POLICY CONDITIONS

The standard form of marine insurance cover includes standard policy conditions known as clauses which are attached to the policy document. These clauses define the time period, scope and coverage of the marine policy. In case of international trade and transit, the clauses drafted by the technical and clauses committee of the Institute of London underwriters are adopted globally to maintain uniformity. Therefore, these are popularly nomenclatured as "INSTITUTE..... CLAUSES". In case of exclusive inland transit, the clauses drafted by Tariff Advisory Committee (TAC) are used by the insurers. These are called as Inland Transit Risk Clauses.

26.6.1 Insurance Cargo Clauses (ICC)

ICC has three set of clauses A, B and C which have grouped the various elements risks covered, exclusions, claims settlement procedure, loss minimisation, etc.

ICC (C)

It covers loss of or damage to the subject matter insured, "reasonably attributable to" :

(*i*) Fire or explosion.

(*ii*) Vessel of craft being stranded, grounded, sunk or capsized.

(*iii*) Overturning or derailment of land conveyance.

(*iv*) Collision or contact of vessel, craft or conveyance with any external object other than water.

(*v*) Discharge of **cargo** at a port of distress.

It also covers loss or of damage to the subject matter insured caused by :

(*i*) General average sacrifice.

(*ii*) Jettison.

"C" clauses provide major casualty coverage during the land, air or sea transit.

Liability under both to blame collection clause of the contract of affreighment

ICC (B)

It provide all the cover that is available under the "C" clauses, but in addition cover is given for loss or of damage to the subject matter insured "reasonably attributable to" :

(i) Earthquake, volcanic eruption or lightening.

The insurance also covers loss of or damage to the subject matter caused by :

(i) Washing overboard.

(ii) Entry of sea, lake or river water into the vessel, craft, hold, conveyance, container, liftvan or place of storage.

(iii) Total loss of any package lost overboard or dripped while loading on to or unloading from vessel or craft.

The "B" clauses provide significant additional coverage; wet damage from sea, lake or river water and accidents in loading and discharging, but there is no coverage for theft, shortage and non-delivery.

ICC (A)

Provide coverage for all risks of loss or damage to the subject matter insured. The words "all risks" should be understood in the context of the "A" clause to cover "fortuitous loss", but not "loss that occurs inevitably."

Principle Exclusions

(i) *Wilful Misconduct of the Assured* : Even if the loss I proximately caused by an insured peril it is excluded if it is attributable to the willful misconduct (deliberate damage) of the Assured.

(ii) Ordinary leakage, ordinary loss in weight or volume or ordinary wear and tear. Examples of losses excluded within this category would include evaporation, natural shrinkage.

(iii) Inadequate sufficiency or unsuitability of packing or preparation of packing of the subject matter insured it is the duly of the insured if act as if uninsured. Clearly if goods are sent insufficiently packed to withstand the normal handling anticipated during transit, then any loss that arises therefrom should not be for insurers to pay.

(iv) Inherent vice or nature of the subject matter insured examples of excluded loss would include blowing of the tins containing foodstuffs or spontaneous combustion of a cargo liable to self heating.

(v) *Delay :* The insurer is not responsible for any loss, damage or expense proximately caused by delay although the delay can be caused by a peril insured against. Losses through delay could include loss of market or deterioration in respect of perishable goods which would not be recoverable even if the cause of the delay was peril insured such as a collision.

(vi) *Insolvency or Financial Default of Carriers :* This exclusion clause was introduced to discourage Assureds from shipping their goods on vessels whose owners, managers, charterers or operators might be infinancial distress. In practice the clause would exclude all types of claims for recovery and forwarding of goods arising from the abandonment of an insured voyage where the proximate cause was the financial distress of one of the aforementioned parties.

(vii) *Unseaworthiness and Unfitness Exclusion :* This only applies where the assured or their agents are privy to this information prior to loading.

(viii) *War and Strikes, Riots and Civil Commotions :* These risks are excluded under A, B and C clauses but can be written back into the policy.

Duration of Cover

Duration of risk starts from the moment the good, leave the warehouse or other place of storage at the place named in the policy to commence transit.

Termination of Contract of Carriage Clause

If the contrast of carriage is terminated at a post or place other than the policy destination, or the transit in otherwise terminated before the delivery of goods, then the insurance terminates automatically.

25.6.2 Institute War Clauses (Air Cargo) *(excluding sendings by Post)*

Risks Covered

1. This insurance covers, except as provided in Clause 2 below, loss of or damage to the subject-matter insured caused by :
   - war civil war revolution rebellion insurrection, or civil strife arising therefrom, or any hostile act by or against a belligerent power.
   - capture seizure arrest restraint or detainment, arising from risks covered under 1.1 above, and the consequences thereof or any attempt thereat.
   - derelict mines torpedoes bombs or other derelict weapons of war.

Exclusions

2. In no case shall this insurance cover
   - loss damage or expense attributable to wilful misconduct of the Assured.
   - ordinary leakage, ordinary loss in weight or volume, or ordinary and tear of the subject-matter insured
   - loss damage or expense caused by insufficiency or unsuitability of packing or preparation of the subject-matter insured (for the purpose of this Clause 2.3 "packing" shall be deemed to include stowage in a container or liftvan but only when such stowage is carried out prior to attachment of this insurance or by the Assured or their servants)
   - loss damage or expense caused by inherent vice or nature of the subject-matter insured
   - loss damage or expense arising from unfitness or aircraft conveyance container or liftvan for the safe carriage of the subject-matter insured, where the Assured or their servants are privy to such unfitness at the time the subject-matter insured is loaded therein
   - loss damage or expense proximately caused by delay, even though the delay be caused by a risk insured against
   - loss damage or expense arising from insolvency or financial default of the owners managers charterers or operators of the aircraft
   - any claim based upon loss of or frustration of the voyage or adventure
   - loss damage or expense arising from any hostile use of any weapon of war employing atomic or nuclear fission and/or fusion or other like reaction or radioactive force or matter.

Duration of cover is similar to that in ICC (A), (B) and (C) but it is more restricted.

25.6.3 Institute Strikes Clauses (Cargo)

Risks Covered

1. This insurance covers, except as provided in Clauses 3 and 4 below, loss of or damage to the subject-matter insured caused by
   - strikers, locked-out workmen, or persons taking part in labour disturbances, riots or civil commotions.
   - any terrorist or any person acting from a political motive.

2. This insurance covers general average and salvage charges, adjusted or determined according to the contract of affreightment and/or the governing law and practice, incurred to avoid or in connection with the avoidance of loss from a risk covered under these clauses.

Exclusions

3. In no case shall this insurance cover
   - loss damage or expense attributable to wilful misconduct of the Assured
   - ordinary leakage, ordinary loss in weight or volume, or ordinary wear and tear of the subject-matter insured
   - loss damage or expense caused by insufficiency or unsuitability of packing or preparation of the subject-matter insured (for the purpose of this Clause 3.3. "packing" shall be deemed to include stowage in a container or liftvan but only when such stowage is carried out prior to attachment of this insurance or by the Assured or their servants).
   - loss damage or expense caused by inherent vice or nature of the subject-matter insured
   - loss damage or expense proximately caused by delay, even though the delay be caused by a risk insured against (except expenses payable under Clause 2 above)
   - loss damage or expense arising from insolvency or financial default of the owners managers charterers or operators of the vessel
   - loss damage or expense arising from the absence shortage or withholding or labour of any description whatsoever resulting from any strike, lockout, labour disturbance, riot or civil commotion
   - any claim based upon loss of or frustration of the voyage or adventure
   - loss damage or expense arising from the use of any weapon of war employing atomic or nuclear fission and/or fusion or other like reaction or radioactive force of matter
   - loss damage or expense caused by war civil war revolution rebellion insurrection, or civil strife arising therefrom, or any hostile act by or against a belligerent power.
4. In no case shall this insurance cover loss damage or expense arising from
   - unseaworthiness of vessel or craft,
   - unfitness of vessel craft conveyance container or liftvan for the safe carriage of the subject-matter insured.

   where the Assured or their servants are privy to such unseaworthiness or unfitness, at the time the subject-matter insured is loaded wherein.

Duration

5. This insurance attaches from the time the goods leave the warehouse or place of storage at the place named herein for the commencement of the transit, continues during the ordinary course of transit and terminates either
   - on delivery to the Consignees' or other final warehouse or place of storage at the destination named herein,
   - on delivery to any other warehouse or place of storage, whether prior to or at the destination named herein, which the Assured elect to use either
   - for storage other than in the ordinary course of transit or
   - for allocation or distribution, *or*

- on the expiry of 60 days after completion of discharge overside of the goods hereby insured from the oversea vessel at the final port of discharge, whichever shall first occur.

25.6.4 Other Incidental Clauses and Warranties

Pair or Set Clause

A provision in many property and inland marine policies that the insurer is not liable for the total value of a set of items if only one item has been lost, damaged or destroyed. The loss settlement is based on the proportion that the lost or damaged part beares to the total value of the set.

Cutting Clause

A provision that damage portion should be out off and the balance utilised.

Label Clause

That the goods are properly labelled. It generally limits the liability of insurer to the cort of repacking and re-labelling the affected good.

Garbling Clause

It provides that the insurer will pay the cost of garbling which reduces further loss.

25.6.5 Inland Transit Clauses

Clause A

Covers all risks except the general exclusions as in case of ICC.

Clause B

It is a basic cover which insures for physical loss/damage to subject matter insured caused by :

(*a*) fire, lighting, breakage of bridges

(*b*) collision, everturning of carrying vehicle

(*c*) derailment or accidents of like nature to the carrying railway wagon/vehicle.

Clause C

It covers physical loss/damage to the subject matter insured caused by :

(*i*) fire (*ii*) lightening.

Duration of Cover

Starts with loading of goods into wagon/carrier for commencement of transit and continues during transit including customary shipments and ends with the goods are unloaded at destination railway station or destination point (is transit is by road).

25.6.6 Institute Time Clauses – Hull

The various hull clauses are classified into 26 broad categories as given below :

Category	**A**	–	**Risks Covered and Risks Excluded**
Clause No.	6	–	Perils
Clause No.	7	–	Pollution Hazard

Clause No.	11	–	General Average and Salvage
Clause No.	14	–	New for Old
Clause No.	15	–	Bottom Treatment
Clause No.	16	–	Wages and Maintenance
Clause No.	17	–	Agency Commission
Clause No.	23	–	War Exclusion
Clause No.	24	–	Strikes Exclusion
Clause No.	25	–	Malicious Acts Exclusion
Clause No.	26	–	Nuclear Exclusion
Category	**B**	–	**Amount Payable**
Clause No.	12	–	Deductible
Clause No.	18	–	Unrepaired Damage
Clause No.	19	–	Constructive Total Loss
Clause No.	13	–	Duty of Assured (Sue & Labour)
Category	**C**	–	**Collision Liability**
Clause No.	8	–	3/4th Collision Liability
Clause No.	9	–	Sistership
Category	**D**	–	**Claims Procedure**
Clause No.	10	–	Notice of Claim and Tenders
Category	**E**	–	**Warranties**
Clause No.	1	–	Navigation
Clause No.	3	–	Breach of Warranty
Clause No.	21	–	Disbursements Warranty
Category	**F**	–	**Miscellaneous**
Clause No.	2	–	Continuation
Clause No.	4	–	Termination
Clause No.	5	–	Assignment
Clause No.	20	–	Freight Waiver
Clause No.	22	–	Returns for lay up and cancellation.

The provision in the aforesaid clauses is similar to the various institute clauses discussed earlier.

25.7 Special Marine Covers

Special Declaration Policy

This is basically an open policy of 12 months duration and such policies are issued to concerns having estimated annual turnover of Rs. 2 crores or above. All transits upto the sum insured are covered without any exception and total value of goods in **transit** are required to be declared at least once in a quarter in the form of a certified statement. Final premium is adjusted (downward only) on the basis of actual annual turnover of goods covered. Mid-term increase in sum insured is also permissible twice during a year. Since the insurer get a sizable premium at the inception, they grant cash discount (called turnover discount) ranging from 20% to 50% on the premium.

Multi-transit/Stock Throughout Policies

A Marine Policy terminates if during the **transit** the goods come into the control of the assured for storage other than in ordinary course of **transit,** allocation or re-distribution. Subsequent transits are considered separate. Multi-**transit** policies ensure continuous cover even in case of such exigencies. Irrespective of the number of **transit** the cover stays operative. Storage periods which may or may not include some processing can also be covered.

Package Policy for Plantation Owners (Tea, Coffee, Rubber, Cardamon)

Cover commences from the collection point of green/raw/plucked plantation, continues during storage and various stages of processing in the factory, subsequent **transit** to anywhere in the world including further storage at intermediate and final destination godowns and terminates on delivery to the final customer.

Package Policy for Exporters

Exporters having DEEC certificates under DES can have this package policy which covers import of raw materials from overseas, storage, processing and export to overseas customers.

Duly Insurance Policy

Importers may take out insurance policy to cover the additional value of goods resulting due to payment of customs duty.

Sellers Contingency Policy

In almost all exports where credit is allowed by the seller to the buyer and the goods are not exported on CIF basis, responsibility for the goods passes to the buyer when the goods are loaded on to the overseas vessel but ownership does not change until the buyer accepts the goods and relative documents. Thus, if the seller is allowing credit to the buyer and has shipped goods on FOB terms.

25.8 Cargo Underwriting

Cargo underwriting needs a careful assessment of the various factors which are considered in arriving at a decision to accept/reject risk, acceptance of risk subject to conditions and premium to be charged.

No standardized proposal form and procedure for cargo underwriting exists. The onus is on the proposer to disclose all factors material to the risk and correspondingly the underwriter has to make all inquiries in detail relating to a risk. These are :

(*a*) Name and address of the proposer and his business or trade.

(*b*) Name and address of the bankers involved and Letter of Credit number if the transaction is under documentary credit,

(*c*) Subject matter to be insured.

(*d*) Type of packing and its authentication.

(*e*) Value of the interest to be insured and the sum to be insured.

(*f*) An analysis or break-up of the sum insured components of the sum insured individually ascertained and summed up.

(*g*) Whether the proposer has declared the entire transit for insurance or is the insurance proposed in respect of a part of the whole transit.

(*h*) Description of the "voyage" including transhipments, if any, and details of interior or land transits.

(*i*) Name of the carrying vessel or shipping line for transit.

(*j*) Other term and conditions of insurance

Underwriting Factors – Cargo Risks

1. The Vessel

One of the important consideration in cargo risk rating is the carrying vessel. As per ICC clauses, the carrying vessel must comply with the classification standards by recognised bodies.

The clauses stipulate that the rates agreed for insurance apply to cargoes carried on mechanically self-propelled vessels, or those constructed by steel, or classified by one of the recognized societies. This helps to restrict agreed rates on an Open Cover to apply only to goods carried on vessels complying with the standard requirements of the Institute Classification Clause. Cargoes not complying with Classification Clause are subject to additional premium.

GIC has a special scheme of approving vessels for vessels engaged in exports business. Under the scheme, the vessel is approved for a particular voyage only as long as the ship remains in the same ownership and is not given out to any charter. Similar system is applicable to vessels engaged in import cargos to Indian ports. Normal rates of premium are charged on such approved vessels.

2. The Voyage of Transit

ICC cover is from "Warehouse to Warehouse" which includes land transit by rail or road form the time the goods leave the warehouse to the port of shipment. It also includes air carriage in some areas as specified in the cover. Under the Transit Clause of the ICC no cover is provided during any period before transit actually commences.

If cargo is by inland transit by rail/road from destination port to consignee's warehouse or to an alternative place for storage or for allocation of for distribution, the underwriters must consider the nature of such interior transits in terms of distances from ports and methods of conveyance employed.

3. The Nature of Cargo to be Insured

The nature of the product or commodity insured from the point of view of susceptibility to damage through various causes is a vital consideration for an underwriter to be taken into account. ICC(A) covers all risks of loss or damage to the subject matter of insurance. Underwriting must ascertain what is accidental, fortuitous, and unexpected and also natural, ordinary and usual in its nature (normal/obvious), with regard to particular circumstances. Nature of goods must be ascertained with respect to various perils.

Losses arising from careless handling, improper stowage, theft, pilferage, non-delivery etc., (extraneous perils) are provided in the ICC(B) and ICC(C) must be able to visualise such extraneous risks.

4. Packing

Packing ensures that the goods reach destination in the same perfect condition in which they were when they left the shipper's premises. Packing is an important factor in risk improvement as it helps in preventing cargo losses. Insufficient, adequate, improper unsuitable and defective packing increases physical hazards and severity of losses.

As per ICC clauses, "In no case shall this insurance cover loss, damage or expense caused by insufficiency or unsuitability, of packing or preparation of the subject matter insured ("packing" shall be deemed to include stowage in a container or liftvan, but only when such stowage is carried out prior to attachment of this insurance by the assured).

Following factors are usually considered in packing :

- Strength of the packing material
- Weight of the package unit
- Package unit mobility–handling and costs
- Nature of goods packed
- Hazards and perils of transit.

5. *Type of Cover*

Underwriting involves determination of appropriate cover based on various factors including characteristic of a given vessel or voyage or the nature of cargo and packing. A common set of risk factors are specified by ICC(A), CBI and (C).

ICC(C) risks provide the base rate and additions are made for risk added by ICC(B) & ICC(A) and further additional covers.

25.9 Hull Underwriting

A proposal form is submitted by the shipowner which starts the process of underwriting. On the basis of proposal form, the various perils and hazards associated with the hull are ascertained.

A. Technical details of the vessel :

(*a*) Type of the vessel

(*b*) Construction of the vessel (wood, fibreglass, steel etc.)

(*c*) Name of the builders and place where builts.

(*d*) Age of the vessel (year of manufacture)

(*e*) Tonnage (GRT and DWT)

(*f*) Dimensions

(*g*) Whether the vessel is equipped with (*i*) twin screws (*ii*) double bottom (*iii*) collision bulkhead

(*h*) Method of propulsion and particulars of engine/machinery

(*i*) Particulars of fire extinguishing equipment.

(*j*) Value of the vessel, cargo usually carried, records of ownership and management.

(*k*) Claims experience.

If the physical hazards are detected the insurer may insist on a pre-insurance survey, imposition of warranties, limiting the scope of the cover, imposing adequate excess to be born by the assured and loading of premium and putting additional terms and conditions. Else, the proposal will be rejected for moral hazards.

In India, all ocean-going vessels beyond a certain value are rated by the Tariff Advisory Committee (T.A.C). A Technical Assistance Group (Hull) consisting of experienced persons dealing in hull insurance is appointed by T.A.C. For vessels falling under the category of oceangoing vessels, the insurers have to approach T.A.C. for rating. The rating as well as the terms and conditions of insurance will depend on the experience of the underwriter. T.A.C. has laid down Tariffs in respect of following risks :

- Fishing vessels
- Sailing vessels
- Inland vessels
- Dredgers

Hull Rating

Various factors are considered by the underwriters to calculate a rate for the hull risk. In calculating the rate of premium to be charged the hull risk is divided into two parts: (*i*) the total loss element of risk and (*ii*) average loss element (termed as "ex T.L."). Accordingly, it is customary to agree a separate rate for each part of the risk and to combine these to arrive at the overall rate that will appear in the policy and called the "Slip Rate". The total loss rate is taken as the current market rate for total loss. It is a rate percent applied to the insured value of the vessel and is thus conditioned by the value factor of the ship. The ex. T.L. is determined by the size of the ship. It is a fixed amount say Rs. 35 multiplied by the Dead Weight tonnage (DWT) of the vessel or the Gross Register Tonnage (GRT).

The Total Loss Rate for the vessel is fixed after considering various factors like the age of the vessel, type, value, claims history, world total loss experience of that type of ship, ownership and management factors, special nature of trade etc. The "ex T.L. premium takes into account factors like the size of the vessel and the degree of its sophistication, trading limits, fleet record etc.

All the premiums are clubbed and the resultant premium divided by the insured value (IV) which is translated into a single rate called as slip rate.

Example

Line	–	SAFE SHIPPING LINE
Vessel	–	M.V. "OCEAN MASTER"
Year built	–	2004
G.R.T.	–	10,000
Insured Value	–	Rs. 15,00,00,000
Type	–	General cargo carrier
Trading	–	Worldwide, subject to Institute Warranties
Total Loss Rate	–	0.75%
Rate for "other than Total loss" (ex. T.L.)	–	Rs. 50/- per GRT
Deductible	–	Rs. 6,00,000

Calculation of Premium

(A) Total Loss Premium @ Rs. 0.75% on Rs. 15,00,00,000 = Rs. 11,25,000

(B) Ex T.L. Premium @ Rs. 50 per GRT *i.e.* 50 × 10,000 = Rs. 5,00,000

(A) + (B) = Total Premium = Rs. 15,25,000

"Slip Rate" is expressed as : $\frac{16,25,000 \times 100}{15,00,00,000} = 1.083$

Base Premium is calculated by applying the slip rate to the IV of the vessel.

Hull Rating (Renewals)

The Joint Hull Committee in London is responsible for the structure of the Joint Hull formula, which is a basis recommended for rating renewal insurances in respect of ships insured in the London market. In India, the rating of ocean-going vessels in a fleet on renewal is done by T.A.C based on the "Indian Hull Understanding". The application forms should be submitted to the T.A.C. within 60 days of the renewal date of the fleet with the full claims statistics available of both paid and outstanding claims. The committee determines the renewal rates on the basis of :

(*a*) The category of the fleet based on the total sum insured under Hull and Machinery interests.

(*b*) Fleet experience, *i.e.*, net premiums and losses paid and outstanding for a stated period.

Normally claims experience of past four years and current year are considered.

25.10 MARINE LOSSES

Marine losses under the marine policy are defined in the Marine Insurance Act, 1963. These may be of following types :

1. Total Loss	–		Actual or Constructive
2. Partial Loss	–	(*a*)	Particular Average
		(*b*)	General Average
3. Expenses	–	(*a*)	Sue and Labour Charges
		(*b*)	Particular Charges
		(*c*)	Salvage Charges

4. Extra charges which include fees of surveys, sale of property etc.

Actual Total Loss

Section 57(1) of the Marine Insurance Act, 1963 defines actual total loss as the loss where the subject-matter insured is destroyed, or so damaged as to cease to be a thing of the kind insured, or where the assured is irretrievably deprived thereof.

Section 58 of the Act provides that if no news has been received after the lapse of a reasonable period, it is presumed to be an actual total loss on account of a marine peril.

Constructive Total Loss

Section 60 (1) defines a constructive total loss as the loss when the subject-matter is reasonably abandoned because either :

(*a*) actual total loss appears unavoidable, or

(*b*) to prevent actual total loss requires expenditure exceeding the saved value.

Section 60(2) in addition, provides that there is a constructive total loss when the insured is deprived of the subject-matter and,

(*a*) it is unlikely that he can recover it, or

(*b*) the cost of recovery would exceed its value when recovered.

Therefore, a constructive total loss would occur if the cost of repairing the damage would exceed the value of the ship when repaired.

The cost of repairs is ascertained on the basis of estimates prepared by the insurers' surveyors and those representing the shipowners.

Section 60(2) (iii) provides that there is constructive total loss of goods where the cost of repairing the damage and forwarding the goods to their destination would exceed their value on arrival. The latter cost would include such charges as landing, drying, and warehousing, reshipping and onward carriage to the port of destination.

Section 61 of the Act states "where there is a constructive total loss the assured may either treat the loss as a partial loss, or abandon the subject-matter insured to the insurer and treat the loss as if it were an actual total loss."

Section 56 of the Act provides that any loss other than a total loss is a partial loss.

Section 64(1) defines a particular average loss as the partial loss of the subject matter insured, caused by a peril insured against, and which is not a general average loss.

Particular average, therefore implies a fortuitous partial loss caused by a an insured peril. Examples of particular average include damage to the ship by stranding, running a ground, collision or damage to the cargo by fire, seawater etc.

General average loss defined in Section 66(1) of the Act as "a loss caused by or directly consequential on a general average act. It includes a general average expenditure as well as a general average sacrifice".

Section 66(2) provides that "There is a general average act where any extraordinary sacrifice or expenditure is voluntarily and reasonably made or incurred in time of peril for the purpose of preserving the property imperilled in the common adventure."

Particular Charges

Section 64(2) of Marine Insurance Act, 1963 defines particular charges as expenses incurred by or on behalf of the assured for the safety or preservation of the subject-matter insured. They are expenses other than general average and salvage charges.

Sue and Labour Clause

This clauses enforces common law duty of the assured and his agents to act at all times, though uninsured, and to take such measures as may be reasonable for the purpose of averting or minimising loss or damage which is covered by the insurance.

Examples of the sue and labour charges are :

(*i*) Hides damaged by sea-water; reconditioning expenses at an intermediate port to prevent aggravation of damage are sue and labour charges.

(*ii*) Due to a maritime casualty a ship puts into a port of refuge for repairs which would take some weeks. The cost of extra fodder fed to the live cattle insured against 'All Risks' during the period of repairs is sue and labour charge.

(*iii*) The additional cost of forwarding cargo from a port of refuge to earn the freight payable on delivery at destination is recoverable, if, in the absence of such cost, a claim could result for a total loss on freight.

Extra Charge

Survey fees are payable only if the loss is payable under the policy.

Salvage Charges

Section 65 of Marine Insurance Act defines salvage charges as the charges that are recoverable under maritime law by a salvor independently of marine contract.

Average Adjusters

Average adjuster adjust the general average losses. He has specialised knowledge and the/also the parties reputation for strict impartiality which ensure that his findings are acceptable to all concerned. The adjuster's fees are allowed in general average calculation.

25.11 Settlement of Claims

Marine insurance claims are of two broad types–marine hull and marine cargo. Both are dealt separately in the following sections.

25.11.1 Marine Hull

Types of Marine Hull Claims

Marine Hulls are divided into three groups *viz.* :

(*a*) Oceangoing vessels and other vessels rated exclusively by the Tariff Advisory Committee.

(*b*) Vessels insured under Builder's Risk Policies, Ship Repairer's Liability Policies, Ship Breaking Policies and the Charterer's Liability Policies.

(c) All the vessels and/or operations of which rates have been provided in Marine Hull Manual under specific Tariffs or otherwise and all other vessels/operations not covered by (*a*) and (*b*) above.

The types of hull claims are :

- Total Loss/Constructive Total Loss;
- Particular Average/Particular Charges *i.e.,* Partial Losses/Expenses;
- Salvage and Salvage Charges–either Salvage Awards or Salvage under contract;
- General Average;
- Collision Liability;
- Liability and Non-liability Claims (such as wreck removal) falling under the P & l section for the policy where such cover is granted;
- Sue & Labour charges;
- Personal Accident Claims for crew covered under Sailing/Fishing vessels Tariffs.

Following claims are generally considered for reference to professional Average Adjusters :

(1) All claims falling under Category 1.1 "A" unless the claim involved is straightforward and also for a nominal amount.

(2) (*a*) GA or GA/PA claims on vessels under Category 1.1 "C".

(*b*) Collision Liability claims requiring cross Liability adjustment in respect of risk falling under Category 1.1 "B" and "C".

5.2.1.2 Procedures of Claims Settlement

Following considerations are important while deciding on *Ocean going vessels* :

(*a*) nature and quantum of claims likely to arise under this category;

(*b*) likelihood of occurrence of loss in distant foreign waters;

(c) involvement of laws and practices of foreign jurisdictions, and

(*d*) involvement of foreign professional and/or firms like surveyors, repair yards, adjusters, solicitors, arbitrator, courts, etc.

The current system of processing these claims in accordance with the international practices and these practices are likely to continue except in so far as the provisions of the Indian Statutes are concerned.

Sundry Hulls (including Sailing vessels, Fishing vessels, Inland vessels etc.).

Following procedure is generally adopted for claim settlement :

- A Licensed Surveyor is appointed in all cases of Partial Losses/Expenses. Also licensed Surveyor are appointed in case of TL/CTL only where the vessel or its wreck, of reasonable value is available for inspection or making reasonable attempt to salvage.

- On receipt of loss intimation a letter is written "on *without prejudice basis* to the insured advising about the appointment of Surveyor and/or investigator requesting the insured to render full co-operation to the Surveyor/Investigator appointed and to return the claim form duly completed and signed.
- Notice of Abandonment of the vessel/wreck in writing is a prerequisite for a constructive Total Loss Claim. Practically speaking, insurers decline *prima facie* acceptance of the Notice of Abandonment. However, insurer's refusal to accept abandonment does not legally prejudice the insured's claim for a CTL once the Notice of Abandonment has been issued by the insured and received by the insurer. Notwithstanding this the insurer generally refuse acceptance of abandonment of the wreck till the probable liabilities attaching to the wreck (Port and other dues, statutory requirement of wreck removal in case of vessel sunk in navigate channel; etc.) are reasonably estimated as considered.
- Total loss claim is settled on the basis of the statements and documents, as also the investigator/s Surveyor's report as the case may be if the circumstances are found to be reasonably acceptable. As per the Marine Insurance Act, following acceptance of a claim for total loss of a vessel, the insurers become entitled to the wreck or the proceeds thereof, if any. However, before enforcing such entitlement, the insurers ascertain whether or not any liability, statutory or otherwise, is reasonably likely to attach to such wreck or proceeds thereof.
- Since Marine Hull Policy is issued for a composite sum insured, representing the aggregate values of Hull and Machinery and showing Hull or Machinery values separately in the policy being prohibited, no claim for total or Constructive Total Loss is considered for settlement on the basis of and on account of either Hull or Machinery value alone.
- In case of partial loss, surveyors are duty bound to achieve assessment net of salvage, if any because it is difficult and very often not economical for the underwriters to get involved in salvage take-over and disposal. However, where this is not possible, arrangements are made to take over the salvage from the insured before the settlement of the claim and disposed accordingly.
- Claims occurring in foreign waters are generally dealt with in the same manner as in the case of Ocean-going vessels.

Documents Required

The documents required for the settlement of Sundry Hull claims are :

(1) A final survey Report *inter-alia* incorporating the following :

(*a*) Name of the registered owner of the vessel.

(*b*) Identity of the vessel including registration details. License particulars including validity thereof wherever applicable.

(*c*) The details of loss suffered.

(*d*) The Surveyor's observation on the alleged circumstances of the loss.

(*e*) The reasonable probability of the alleged circumstances giving rise to the losses noticed and/or claimed.

(*f*) Quantification of repairs/replacement cost, Salvage, Sue and labour etc. Where applicable.

(*g*) Cause of loss as per the Perils Clause of the Policy and the deposit to be collected by the steamer.

In lieu of cash deposit, steamer companies often accept unlimited guarantee of the Insurance Company covering the goods.

Documents for General Average Claims

1. Original Policy or certificate of insurance duly endorsed.
2. Bill of Lading (signed copy)

3. Invoice (original or signed copy)
4. A copy of Notice declaring General Average by the Shipowner/Agent.
5. General Average Deposit Receipt (GADR) on the original Lloyds form duly endorsed.

(GADR indicates the name of the steamer, details of the casualty, the Bill of Lading no., the provisional net arrived value of the goods, description of the goods, the name of the GA Adjusters, the amount of the deposit by the consignees etc.)

General Average Guarantee and Counter Guarantee

As an alternative to cash deposit ship owners are willing to accept a Guarantee from a bank or if the goods are insured from the insurers. Insurers grant this Guarantee on the behalf of the insured in terms of which they agree to pay the General Average Contribution. In such cases, a Counter Guarantee is obtained from the insured. The Counter Guarantee is required because the General Average adjustment may be based on a contributory value of the cargo which may be higher than its insured value.

Letter of Transfer

This letter is signed by the consignees whereby they :

(*i*) surrender their rights in respect of the deposit paid to ship owners by the insurers;

(*ii*) agree to transfer the deposit amount to the credit of the insurers;

(*iii*) authorize the insurers to receive from the ship owners the difference between the amount of general average as adjusted and the amount of the deposit;

(*iv*) undertake to refund to the insurers any sum deducted by the ship owners from the deposit which may not be recoverable under the insurance policy; and

(*v*) undertake to repay to the insurers, if the contributory value exceeds the insured value the proportion of general average applying to such value.

If it is reported that the General Average Act has included sacrifice of cargo, then the consignee clear the damaged cargo only after the General Average Survey is conducted by the ship's Surveyors.

Consignments by Rail/Road

In the case of sea/air/multi-modal transport/postal claims, the insured has to furnish evidence of : (1) insurance, (2) transit, (3) value and (4) loss. The following documents are required to be submitted to insurers in support of claims under rail/road transit policies :

General Documents

1. Original policy or certificate of insurance duly endorsed.
2. Invoice (original or copy)/packing list/weight specification.
3. Independent Surveyor's Report, if any.
4. Letter of Subrogation (if recovery is possible).

Other Documents Depending on the Nature of Claim

1. Original Railway Receipt (Non-delivery cases)
2. Copy of the Railway Receipt (damage claim)
3. Original Consignment Note (Non-delivery cases–Road transit claims)
4. A copy of the Consignment Note (Damage claim–Road transit claims)

5. 'Non-delivery' or 'Partial delivery' certificate from the Railways/Road Transport Operators.
6. Open Delivery/Assessment Delivery Certificate (Rail/Road)
7. Certified copy of the Remarks in the Railway Delivery Book (Damage claims).
8. Certified copy of the remarks in the delivery Challan (Road Transit Claims).
9. Copy of (*a*) Notice of claim lodged on the carriers (Rail/Road) (*b*) Acknowledgement (*c*) Subsequent correspondence with the carriers.
10. Special Power of Attorney (Rail Transit Claims).
11. Letter of Authority (Rail Transit Claims).

Marine Cargo

Documents generally required for settlement of various types of cargo claims are as under :

General

(*a*) Original insurance policy/declaration under the open policy duly endorsed by the insured. A letter of indemnity may be furnished if the original is lost.

(*b*) Original or a signed copy of sale invoice along with packing list wherever is available.

(*c*) Signed copy of Bill of Lading (in case of sea voyage)/Air Consignment Note (for air cargo/MTD/CTD (For multi-modal transport)/postal receipt for sending by post.

(*d*) Triplicate or exchange control copy of Bill of entry (to facilitate verification of the date of filing to ascertain whether there has been any delay and also to check duty payment details).

(*e*) In case of General Average. G.A. Guarantee and Counter Guarantee of original Cash Deposit Receipt with the Letter of Transfer as the case may be. Reference be made to the separate para on G.A.

(*f*) Letter of Subrogation duly stamped and executed (only where recovery from carriers/other third parties is possible).

(*g*) Special Power of Attorney (wherever recovery from Railway/other carriers is involved. In other cases as required).

25.12 MARINE CARGO LOSSES AND FRAUDS

Cost of Maritime frauds worldwide runs into millions of dollars.

Incidence of frauds in shipping business is not something new. The earliest incident on record goes back to 360 BC in syracuse when a ship owner tried to cheat a buyer who had advanced money to him for bringing a cargo of corn, by scutting the vessel after sailing for a few days without loading the cargo at all. In earlier times, trade between merchants of different countries was totally based on mutual trust. The transaction was invariably in cash; and as it happened sometimes unscrupulous agents or shipowners simply disappeared with the money, whilst others returned with false reports of robbery or piracy on high seas. Over the years, as trading activities increased manifold between the maritime nations, the simple process of dependence on mutual trust alone gave way to a written undertaking or pledge. It is reported that the Ventians first thought of and developed the system of trade between merchants through the mechanism not the Letter of Credit, which has, over the years undergone several changes and modifications to suit the requirements and complexities of modern trade.

Sometimes economic sanctions against some countries by other nations of the world encourage frausters to take advantage of such situations of scarcity of essential commodities and follow the path of deception to make profits from fraudulent deals.

Marine Fraud can be described as a criminal act in international trade concerning the shipping industry. The term Maritime Fraud includes a host of wrongful acts. Expert involved in the investigation of such frauds feel that such acts have increased over the years with the growth of international trade. However, only a small proportion of fraudulent acts are at all reported. In fact, a large number of cases are never reported by the affected parties for fear of delays due to protracted investigation, increase in insurance premiums, bad publicity and staffing red tape.

Criminal acts on high seas exist in a variety of ways as mentioned below :

1. *Maritime Piracy :* These are illegal acts of violence or detention of a vessel on high seas by the crew of another vessel, generally outside the jurisdiction of any state. Sometimes, acts of piracy may lead to hijacking of a vessel.
2. *Maritime Insurance Fraud :* Deliberate scuttling of over-insured vessel by the owners.
3. *Deviation Fraud :* This arises when the ship owner directs the cargo to another destination with the intention of selling the same for gain. Obviously, this involves changes of name of the importer and non-arrival of the cargo at the appointed destination.
4. *Bill of Lading Fraud :* It involves forgery of Bills of Lading in respect of non-existing goods or differences in the quantity or quality of the goods. This can be described as a fraud by the seller or buyer against ship owners or the carriers.
5. *Charters Party Fraud :* It is generally committed by the charterers against the ship owners.
6. *Agency Fraud :* It involves impersonation of agents and concealing of identities.
7. *Other Documentary Frauds :* It involves fraud in various other documents used in Maritime trade transactions.

In any international trade deal relating to export/import business, a number of parties are involved–Buyer, Seller, Ship owner, Charterer, Ship's master and crew, insurer, Banker, Broker or Agent etc. Documents form the basis of such transactions and thus, numerous possible combinations and permutations can arise for fraudulent activities. From the record of various documentary fraud cases studied and investigated during the last couple of decades, the types of fraud can be broadly categorized as under :

- Fraud committed by a trader against another trader, ship owner, banker or insurer.
- Fraud committed by a charterer against a ship owner;
- Fraud committed by a ship owner or trader against an insurer;
- Fraud committed by a charterer or ship owner against a trader.

25.13 Marine Stock Throughout Policy

STP is popularly known as 'Cradle to Grave' Coverage. This policy was introduced in mid 1970 mainly for the following reasons : to have a single policy as against multiple marine and property policies; to avoid property tariff; to expand marine premium during soft marine market; and to obtain broader coverage for static risks under marine portfolio.

Marine STP is the process of insuring both stock and transit/inventory exposures under a 'Single Policy' to ensure seamless protection to the assured on a worldwide basis.

Stock Throughput Policy is suitable for organizations that source raw materials or semi finished goods for further value addition. These organizations then store and distribute finished goods across the world.

Inputs & Output : Raw materials, Work in Progress and Finished Goods that are in transit on World to World basis. All locations are covered such as assured's factory (ies)/Job Workers/Sub-Contractors/Warehouses (3rd

Party taken on lease or on rent) when cargoes are not in course of transit within the meaning of Marine Insurance. Movements of other items related to operations as for example :

- Import of plant and machinery on C&F/FOB or similar terms
- Import of plant and machinery on CIF terms with DIC extension.
- Purchase of plant and machinery from local/domestic market
- To & Fro journey when plant or machinery sent to repairer's workshop for repairing and overhauling etc.

Stock Risk is different from Transit risks (in course of transit) is a static risk, always exposed to fire, AOG and social perils. Total exposure of inventory/stock at any point of time in a particular area/region is always greater than the single carrying limit.

Stocks are usually kept at various 3rd party locations where different cargoes can be stored/kept (including hazardous and non-hazardous material) and warehouse keepers tend to offer less care in terms of handling and storage etc.

Severity Analysis

Line	*Claims Frequency*	*Size of the loss*
Static	Low	High
Marine	Low to Medium	Low to Medium

Risk Covered

There are two ways of underwriting a Marine Stock Throughput policy.

1. *All Risks :* All Risks of physical loss or damage from any external cause.
2. Transit Risk on All Risks basis and Static Risk other than in course of transit on named perils basis (with add on covers).

Major Exclusions

Goods at retail outlets, insured property (ies) in the open or outbuilding, any property other than the subject matter insured, policy deductible, consequential loss/legal liability, loss resulting from unexplained or mysterious disappearance or shortage discovered on taking inventory, misplacing or misfiling of information or clerical or accounting errors, loss or damage to goods and merchandise caused by or resulting from misappropriation, conversion, infidelity or any dishonest act on the part of the assured or other party of interest, his or their employees or agents, processing risk, theft unless following forcible and/or violent entry into or exit from the premises and act of terrorism are some of the major exclusions.

Benefits of STP from Assured's Point of View

- *Seamless Protection :* A single policy provides comprehensive protection against both, Transit (inland and Ocean Marine) and Inventory/Stock exposures.
- *Coverage :* STP offers broader coverage under static risk as against Standalone Property policy.
- *Premium Payment :* Premium can be paid in installments in order to assist cash flow of the company.
- *Policy Administration :* This policy is very simple to administer since there is no need for declaring individual shipments. It is adjusted against final sales value/turnover achieved by the company.
- It helps in elimination of duplicity of coverage – no need for multiple policies for both transit and inventory/stock risks.
- It also eliminates dispute on concealed damage claims between Marine and Property Underwriters.

Marine STP - Challenges for Insurers

Marine Stock Throughput Policy has the following challenging features :

- Need for co-ordination between Marine Underwriter and Property Underwriter for pricing and terms for static risks.
- Continuous review of static risk in order to control accumulation for AOG/Social perils.
- Requirement of loss control effort through COPE (Construction, Occupation, Protection and Exposure) Survey where the value of stock is high in named locations.
- There is no standard policy form for Marine STP since each risk is unique and each policy needs to be tailor-made in terms of deductible, basis of valuation, price, scope of cover, exclusions, warranties etc.
- Soft market conditions force Marine Underwriters to accept undesired extensions.
- A single static risk loss can have negative impact on marine book.

The Indian insurance market needs more expertise to underwrite this specialized class of business in terms of coverage, pricing and deductible. The following are certain concerns when underwriting a STP Policy :

- *Quality Issues :* Construction/Occupancy/Protection of the Warehouse/Storage Premises.
- Nat Cat Exposures
- Social Perils
- Accumulation Control
- RI Support/Capacity

The various causes of marine losses are : (*a*) Theft Pilferage and non-delivery, (*b*) Handling and Stowage damage, (*c*) Loss from water damage and (*d*) Marine perils. Maritime frauds can be categorised as follows:

(*a*) Scuttling of ships–deliberate sinking of ships.

(*b*) Documentary Frauds–the manipulation of shipping frauds, use of forge documents.

(*c*) Chartering of vessels–fraudulent chartering companies.

(*d*) Cargo thefts–deviation of ships from standard routes, "paper shipping companies".

Apart from various measures taken by the concerned parties, following should be taken into care to reduce the frequency of frauds :

(*a*) Vessels approved by GIC (entered in IRS) should be used.

(*b*) Exercise of reasonable care and diligence wile dealing with unknown parties or parties new in the business.

(*c*) Payments should be affected by confirmed IRLC.

(*d*) The agents involved in the whole process should be reliable.

(*e*) Reputed charterer should be hired.

Marine Insurance Statistics

Business Generated(Gross Direct Premium - Rs. in crores)

Companies	*1993-94*	*1994-95*	*1995-96*	*1996-97*	*1997-98*	*1998-99*	*1999-2000*
GIC	141.01	154.32	175.69	176.23	181.75	189.92	193.51
NIC	136.05	128.02	154.55	140.26	151.75	155.69	148.70
OIC	122.19	125.27	152.25	141.94	142.17	149.60	146.33
NIAC	195.39	189.86	222.93	219.88	212.64	227.40	216.44
UII	155.72	150.95	182.84	163.98	173.88	169.73	176.94
Total	**750.36**	**748.42**	**888.26**	**842.29**	**862.19**	**892.34**	**881.92**

Profits(Rs. in Crores)

Companies	1993-94	1994-95	1995-96	1996-97	1997-98	1998-99	1999-2000
GIC	45.42	39.50	38.71	58.38	70.82	72.97	57.20
NIC	6.04	-11.62	11.52	-3.88	4.19	-17.82	2.65
OIC	15.54	14.39	-13.06	42.77	10.67	15.74	4.11
NIAC	9.23	-1.13	51.74	7.98	72.71	77.39	34.69
UII	19.65	15.53	-13.24	40.04	8.15	32.51	30.21
Total	**95.88**	**56.67**	**75.67**	**145.29**	**166.54**	**180.79**	**128.86**

Profit %age

GIC	32.21%	25.60%	22.03%	33.13%	38.97%	38.42%	29.56%
NIC	4.44%	-9.08%	7.45%	-2.77%	2.76%	-11.45%	1.78%
OIC	12.72%	11.49%	-8.58%	30.13%	7.51%	10.52%	2.81%
NIAC	4.72%	-0.60%	23.21%	3.63%	34.19%	34.03%	16.03%
UII	12.62%	10.29%	-7.24%	24.42%	4.69%	19.15%	17.07%

Marine Insurance (Gross Direct Premium Income)

Company	*2000-01*	*2001-02*	*2002-03*	*2003-04*	*2004-05*	*2005-06*	*2006-07*	*2007-08*	*2008-09*
National	203.80	207.16	219.06	187.18	251.29	173.43	204.89	174.98	200.78
New India	313.84	339.30	344.40	259.21	252.49	299.78	321.02	437.28	446.10
Oriental	187.90	205.65	228.07	218.93	235.41	325.11	347.83	339.06	332.59
United India	279.56	255.21	339.14	300.14	243.80	203.97	263.95	300.83	338.02
ECGC*	-	-	-	-	-	-	-	-	-
GIC*	-	-	-	-	-	-	-	-	-
Royal Sundaram	-	2.78	13.02	13.38	16.80	18.29	18.44	19.55	19.97
Reliance	-	1.74	8.91	13.19	12.70	10.74	17.85	34.24	37.00
Iffco-Tokio	0.05	31.02	18.41	24.49	30.87	46.13	128.26	66.43	113.70
TATA AIG	-	9.18	27.33	30.89	40.85	47.88	70.15	97.86	111.82
ICICI Lombard	-	-	8.91	43.59	82.53	85.71	155.24	216.72	216.47
Bajaj Allianz	-	1.36	7.41	20.72	44.96	54.33	71.25	75.18	88.17
Cholamandalam	-	-	0.16	5.82	15.90	17.00	26.56	32.66	36.56
HDFC-Chubb	-	-	-	-	0.50	1.72	2.41	3.29	8.29
Future Generali	-	-	-	-	-	-	-	0.72	6.63
Universal Sompo	-	-	-	-	-	-	-	-	0.54
Shriram	-	-	-	-	-	-	-	-	-
Bharti AXA	-	-	-	-	-	-	-	-	0.61
Total	**985.15**	**1053.40**	**1214.82**	**1117.54**	**1228.10**	**1284.09**	**1627.85**	**1798.80**	**1957.25**

Market Share

Private Co. Share	99.995%	95.626%	93.073%	86.392%	80.042%	78.054%	69.889%	69.610%	67.313%
Public Co. Share	0.005%	4.374%	6.927%	13.608%	19.958%	21.946%	30.111%	30.390%	32.687%

Key Terms

- General Average
- Particular Average
- Sue and Labour Charges
- Maritime Frauds
- Extraneous Risk
- ExT.L.
- Hull Insurance
- Cargo Insurance
- Annual Policy
- Institute Clauses
- Voyage Policy
- Extra Charges
- Constructive Total Loss
- Partial Loss
- Slip Rate
- Base Premium
- GRT
- Average
- ICC Clauses
- Declaration Policy
- Package Policy
- Open Cover

Questions for Review

1. Distinguish between :
   (*a*) Open Cover and Open Policy
   (*b*) General Average and Particular Average
   (*c*) Total Loss and Constructive Total Loss.
2. Briefly explain the various types of marine losses and maritime frauds and methods to prevent them.
3. List the documents required for settlement of :
   (*a*) Cargo claims
   (*b*) Hull claims
4. Trace the history of marine insurance. Is marine insurance a profitable business in India? If so, why?
5. Briefly explain the various types of marine insurance covers available in India.
6. Briefly discuss the various insurance principles as applied to insurance business in India.
7. Briefly discuss the various factors considered for underwriting of cargo insurances.
8. List the various items of information in Hull Insurance proposal form.

Suggested Readings

1. Marine Insurance Claims, IC66, Insurance Institute of India, Mumbai, 2005.
2. IRDA Annual Reports.
3. *IRDA Annual Report 2001-02.*
4. *Marine Insurance,* IC67, Insurance Institute of India, Mumbai.
5. Barry Supple, *A History of British Insurance,* Cambridge University Press, 1970.
6. *The ET Knowledge Series,* Insurance, 2001-02.

Automobile Insurance

Chapter
26

Chapter Objectives

After reading this chapter you will be able to understand :

- *Automobile Insurance Losses*
- *Automobile Insurance Covers*
- *Claim Settle in Motor Insurance*

Motor Insurance originated in U.K. where the first motor insurance policy was introduced into England in 1894 to cover third party liabilities. And in 1899 the policy was extended to cover the accidental damage similar to what is known as comprehensive policy. In India the Motor Vehicles Act was passed in 1939 and in 1946 the third party insurance was introduced compulsorily.

The need for compulsory motor insurance is obvious. There has been a phenomenal rise in the motor accidents in the last 4-5 years. Much of these are attributable to a sudden spurt in the number of vehicles. Every vehicle before being driven on roads has to be compulsorily insured. The automobile insurance policy represents a combined coverage of the vehicles including accessories, loss or damage to his property or life and the third party coverage.

26.1 Overview of The Losses Due to Automobile Ownership and Usage

The major sources of loss exposure arising from the automobile accidents are[1] :

- Legal liability for harm caused to others as a result of negligence
- Bodily injury
- Property damages and or theft of vehicles

Risk managers realise that insurance should be considered within the context of all available risk management tools. There are several ways to lower losses from automobile accidents[2] :

(1) reduce the frequency and severity of accidents,

(2) restrict payments, and

(3) redistribute expenses and losses.

Loss Control and Prevention

The loss to the automobile insurance service providers is mainly in the form of claims arising from accidents. Accidents can be minimised by providing better infrastructure in terms of roads, limit on speed and other sophisticated traffic control measures. Also, automobile manufacturers must be encouraged to continuously pursue enhancement of the safety measures in the vehicles.

Globally speaking, there has been a demand for smaller, light-weight vehicles, which has resulted in increased severity of accidents and consequential losses.

1. Harrington & Neihaus, *Risk Management and Insurance,* McGraw Hill, 1999, p. 533.
2. J.S. Triechmann, S.G. Gistavson and R. E. Hoyt, *Risk Management and Insurance,* South-Western College Publishing, 2001, pp. 270-272.

Restriction on Claims

Putting restrictions on the insured's claims in the sense the fraudulent claims can be easily detected and effectively reduce the cost to the insurers. Another way is to incentivise the good clients by way of attractive rates and discounts.

Redistribution of Losses and Expenses

The auto liability claims, which frequently arise from driver's negligence, can be tackled through redistributions. In such a mechanism, first the guilty party is to be determined and then the guilty party pays to the suffered party the amount of loss. Such processes are generally channelled through the judicial system.

Automobile Coverages[3]

The coverage for automobiles differs in countries. However, in most of the developed countries following types of coverage are available :

Automobile Liability Insurance

Automobile Liability Insurance protects the insured against the loss arising from legal liability when his or her automobile injures someone or damages another's property.

Medical Payments Coverage

Automobile Medical Payments coverage reimburses the insured and members of the insider's family for medical expenses that result from automobile accidents. The protection also applies to other occupants of the insured's automobile.

Physical Damages Insurance

Automobile Physical Damage Coverage insures against the loss of the policyholder's own automobile. The coverage is written under the two insuring agreements (also called as Comprehensive coverage) and Collusion–which indemnifies for collusion losses. Physical damage coverage applies to the insured auto regardless of the default. If the other driver is at fault, the insured that carry collusion coverage has the option of proceeding against the other driver or collecting under his or under policy coverage. In India, the GIC offers two types of policy coverage. Form A policy cover is legally compulsory under the Motor Vehicles Act, while Form B policy is optional, known as comprehensive cover. Both of these are discussed in section 14.3 of this chapter.

26.2 NEED FOR AUTOMOBILE INSURANCE[4]

In Indian conditions, the vehicles are subject to many hazards like potholes, open manholes, puddles, untarred roads, traffic management system, poor pedestrian management, absence of footpaths for pedestrians, jaywalkers, increasing number of accidents etc. which accentuate the need for automobile insurance. Some of these hazards are discussed below :

Footpaths

As footpaths are encroached by hawkers, pedestrians have a tough time dodging between vehicles to reach the other end of the road. Large potholes and manholes are a common sight and during the monsoon the situation can get only worse causing untold damage to your vehicle.

---

3. Vaughan and Vaughan, *Essentials of Risk and Insurance Management and Insurance,* John Wiley and Sons. Inc., 2001, pp. 435-436.
4. www. Insuremagic.com/Auto Insurancebasics — Need for Automobile Insurance.htm

Drunken Driving

Drunken driving is another very common feature. Be it a car, a two-wheeler, or even a truck, drunken driving is one of the major reasons for increase in accidents. Though drunken driving is a punishable offence the penalty has hardly proved to be a deterrent.

Reckless Driving

Besides, rash driving by youngsters is another of the dangerous realities that you should consider. Majority of the youngsters drive recklessly caring little for the law, causing serious accidents resulting in loss of life or limb.

Theft

Cases of stolen cars are on the rise. Experts in stealing cars are well aware of the loopholes that can be exploited and accordingly have also been successful in manipulating with the chasis number of vehicles in order that they are not traced.

Fire

Other than these there is also a danger of fire or theft of vehicle. Therefore, vehicle insurance under such unsafe conditions is a must not only to cover risks towards the owner and the vehicle but also to cover the financial liability that may arise from an accident in which the other party is injured. The cost of repairs that you would have to pay to the other party in case of an accident may be exorbitant. Besides if the accident involves hospitalisation too, the expenses can go through the roof. It would be a great burden if all these costs are borne by the individual. The insurance company can indemnify against such losses and the financial liability arising thereof.

Should Auto Insurance be made Compulsory?

If the auto insurance is not made compulsory, there is a strong possibility that some may not buy these voluntarily. This is because most of them think that the cost of accidents or losses will fall on others or they underestimate the risk of loss. "Economic arguments for compulsory insurance laws in these people to consider more of the costs of their actions when deciding whether to drive, what kind of car to buy, how safely to drive, and so on."[5]

The economic rationale for insurance may be that it affects people's decision to drive. Some people are likely to forgive driving if the insurance is made compulsory since it acts as a financial disincentive. Another could be that it encourages people to drive safely, which may reduce cost of risk. Those who criticise compulsory auto insurance plead that it results in lowering the disposable income or it results in a shift of income from lower group to the higher group. Also, the success of the compulsory law depends on its enforcement and way it is perceived by the insureds. In India, most of the insurance companies are facing huge losses due to false/heavy claims, the insurance being used for dubious advantages.

26.3 TYPES OF MOTOR INSURANCE POLICIES

The All India Motor Tariff governs motor insurance business in India. According to the Tariff, all classes of vehicles use two types of Policy Forms. They are Form A and Form B. Form A, or what is commonly known as Act Policy, covers Act Liability, which is a compulsory requirement of the Motor Vehicles Act. No vehicle can be used without this minimum insurance cover. Use without such insurance is a penal offence. The following liabilities can be covered in this policy :

- Unlimited liability towards Third Party bodily injury;
- Liability towards Third Party Property Damage to the extent of Rs. 6000/- only;

5. Harrington & Neihaus, *op. cit.* pp. 553-554.

- Unlimited liability towards bodily injury of passengers of the vehicle;
- Liability towards employees of the owner of the vehicle while travelling in or using it, against bodily injury, to the extent required under the Workmen's Compensation Act.

Form B, or what is commonly known as Comprehensive Policy, is an optional cover, which takes care of the following additional losses and liabilities :

- Loss or damage to the vehicle and its accessories and extra fittings, protection and removal costs, and towing disabled vehicles (only for commercial vehicles).
- Liability towards Third Party Property Damage, in excess of Rs. 6000/-.
- Liability towards employees under Common Law and Fatal Accidents Act, over and above the liability under Workmen's Compensation Act.
- Personal Accident Benefits for the owner, passengers and employees.

The above losses or liabilities can be separately covered in conjunction with the liabilities covered under the Act Policy, by taking a Comprehensive Policy paying an additional premium.

26.3.1 Form A Policy

As per the provisions of Motor Vehicles Act, all the vehicles plying in the Territorial Limits of India must possess an ACT POLICY at all times. The violation is punishable with fine etc., as per Motor Vehicle Act (as prevalent at the time of detection). As described earlier, this policy covers:

(1) Third Party Property Damage/Bodily Injury (Fatal or Non-fatal) when Insured vehicle is used in a public place,

(2) Insured's legal liability, as per Motor Vehicle Act, arising out of accident caused by or arising out of the use of the vehicle anywhere in India, and

(3) Such liability as above in respect of injury (fatal or non-fatal) to any third party and damage to any third parties' property.

The owners of the vehicle having insurable interest in it undertake this policy. The period of the cover is generally a period of 12 months from the date of inception. However, Short period covers are also available at higher rates. Subject to limit of liability laid down in the Motor Vehicle Act, the policy pays the insured's legal liability for death/disability for third party, loss or damage to third party property. Also, the liability for claimant's cost is also met (Maximum Rs. 6,000/-) unless additional premium for opting unlimited cover is paid. In addition, all costs and expenses incurred with insurer's written consent are paid.

In case of death of the Insured/Person entitled to compensation for a liability incurred under this policy, his legal heirs will be indemnified as in the case of the Insured, subject to the limitations of use of the vehicle provided that the Driver was holding a valid and effective driving license.

Third Party (A person other than Insured and the Insurer) who is injured/dies due to an accident with the Insured Vehicle, the amount of compensation adjudged by the Motor Accident Claims Tribunal is made good by the insurers and is payable to the legal heir of the deceased or the injured. The amount of compensation is unlimited/has no preset limit.

All costs and expenses are incurred by the insured with Insurer's written consent. The compensation payable to Third Party for damage to its property (movable or fixed) is restricted to Rs. 6000/- {Rupees Six Thousand Only}, irrespective of the amount adjudged by the Motor Accident Claims Tribunal/Court. This compensation limit can be increased to Unlimited by paying of an additional Premium at the time of taking insurance. All costs and expenses incurred by Insured with Insurer's written consent.

Claims arising out of and in the course of employment of a person in the employment of the Insured are compensated to the extent of Rs. 20,000 when an Employee (other than paid driver) is in the driving seat.

When vehicle is used outside the geographical area, when used contrary to limitation as to use, driven by a person other than the driver as stated in the clauses mentioned in the policy of insurance.

26.3.2 Form B Policy[6]

Form B is an optional cover, which offers some specific advantages. Although the Act Policy Form A is identical for different classes of vehicles, the comprehensive policy cover differs for various classes of vehicles. For private cars and motorcycles, there are two Sections in the Comprehensive Policy. Additionally, Section III is provided for commercial vehicles.

SECTION I

It concerns loss or damage to the vehicle and covers the risks like :

- Fire, Explosion, Self-ignition and Lightning
- Burglary, Housebreaking and Theft
- Riot, Strike, Malicious and Terrorism Damage
- Earthquake
- Flood, Typhoon, Hurricane, Storm, Tempest, Inundation, Cyclone, Hailstorm
- Accidental External Means
- Transit by road, rail, inland waterway, lift, elevator or air.

For motorcycles and commercial vehicles, the risk of frost damage is also covered. From the above coverage, for all classes of vehicles, the risks of riot, strike, malicious and terrorism damage, earthquake and flood and storm; can be opted out of with a consequent discount in premium. In addition to these, cover is also available for 'Protection and Removal Costs' and 'Authorisation of Repairs'. If a motor vehicle is disabled as a result of loss or damage due to the perils mentioned above, the insurance company bears the reasonable cost of protection and removal to the nearest repairer and the cost of redelivery to the owner/insured subject to a maximum limit, in respect of any one accident. The limits for various class of vehicles are as follows:

Motor Cycles/Scooters :	Rs.	300
Private Car & Taxis	Rs.	1,500
Other Commercial Vehicles	Rs.	2,500

The owner/insured is also allowed to authorise repair expenses upto Rs. 500/- per accident.

SECTION II

It covers the liabilities towards third parties, *i.e.,* liabilities of bodily injuries and property damage.

SECTION III

It is applicable to commercial vehicles. It covers the vehicle while it is being used for the purpose of [Towing Disabled Vehicles.' This section covers Third Party Liabilities that the insured vehicle or the one being towed for reward/remuneration. Further, the insurance company is also not liable for damages to the towed vehicle or any property being conveyed thereby.

Benefits of Comprehensive Policy Cover – An Illustration

Mr. Tom has an Act Only policy covering his private car. He employs a paid driver. While driving the vehicle, after dropping Mr. Tom at his office, the vehicle collides with a truck and the driver dies on the spot. Being an

6. www. Insuremagic.com/Auto Insurancebasics — Risk covered by a Comprehensive Policy.htm

old car, Mr. Tom had nothing much to lose and that is why he had not taken a Comprehensive Policy. However, the family of the driver lost their breadwinner.

As an employer, Mr. Tom is liable to compensate for the driver, since he was driving the vehicle in course of employment. The Motor Vehicles Act, 1988 makes it compulsory to insure liabilities under Workmen's Compensation Act.

Accordingly, the legal heir of the deceased driver filed an application to the Labour Commissioner and an Award of Rs. 1,50,000 was passed against the employer. Mr. Tom, equipped with an Act Policy, approached the insurance company, who in turn satisfied the Award. The legal heir of the driver received the compensation from the Labour Court soon after and everyone was happy.

The liability for compensation as per the Workmen's Compensation Act, depends on the wages of the employee and his age, and represents mainly the loss of earnings. However, other losses representing mental pain and agony for the family, loss of consortium, future expenses on dependents and loss of prospective earnings are not accommodated in this compensation.

The legal heir of the driver, in the instant case then approached the Motor Accident Claims Tribunal, demanding a compensation of Rs. 1,00,000 towards these losses. The Tribunal passed an award of Rs. 50,000, found reasonable as per provisions of Common Law and Fatal Accidents Act. Mr. Tom had an Act Policy, which did not cover this liability, and he was saddled with the responsibility of satisfying the Court Order. You can imagine the financial burden he had to bear. Had he taken a Comprehensive Policy, covering his driver by payment of a small premium, he would not have to face this difficulty. The insurance company would have paid this additional amount of compensation too. It is, therefore, always beneficial and advisable to take a comprehensive policy covering these liabilities.

Exclusions to the Comprehensive Insurance Cover

This insurance does not cover loss or damage caused due to :

(*a*) Driver being under intoxication

(*b*) Vehicle being driven by a person not holding an effective, valid licence.

It also does not cover :

(*a*) Damage to tyres (unless the vehicle is also damaged).

(*b*) Wear and tear, mechanical breakdown.

Calculation of Premiums

In the case of Comprehensive Insurance Cover, for the purpose of premium, vehicles are categorized as follows:

Private Car

This is used for personal purposes. The premium is computed on the following basis:

- Geographical area of use and cubic capacity
- Value of the vehicle.

Accessories are to be specified separately under electrical and non-electrical items.

Two-wheeler

It is used for personal purposes only. Premium is calculated on cubic capacity and value of vehicle. Accessories are to be specified. Theft of accessories is not covered, unless the vehicle is stolen at the same time.

Commercial Vehicle

This is a vehicle used for hire and is classified as follows :

Goods-carrying commercial vehicle : In this case premium is calculated on carrying capacity–gross vehicle weight and value of the vehicle. Accessories extra, as specified.

Passenger-carrying commercial vehicle : In this case premium is calculated on carrying capacity of the vehicle–number of passengers and value of the vehicle. Accessories extra, as specified.

26.3.3 Auto Policy in United States

The personal auto policy, famous in the U.S. includes four main types of coverage:[7]

(*a*) "third party" liability coverage for liability to third parties harmed by negligence of an insured person;

(*b*) "first party" medical payments coverage for the insured, or in states with no-fault or related laws, personal injury protection coverage for the insured's medical expenses and loss of income;

(*c*) uninsured and under insured motorists coverage for losses caused to an insured by drivers without liability insurance and drivers with comparatively low liability insurance limits; and

(*d*) coverage for physical damage to or theft of insured autos.

The auto liability coverage in the personal auto policy provides broad coverage for liability for bodily injury and property damage to other parties arising out of the use of an automobile by an insured person. As is customary with the liability insurance, the insurer also agrees to defend the insured and bear the defence costs and is responsible for negotiating and setting the claims. Personal auto liability coverage may be sold with a "single limit" that specifies the maximum amount that the insurer will pay for all damages from a single accident.

Under the first-party auto medical payments coverage, the auto owner can receive payment for medical expenses arising out of an accident. Coverage is for the medical expenses for the named insured and family members hurt in any auto and other persons that are hurt while occupying a covered auto. Coverage limits under such policies are comparatively low.

In U.S. with no-fault or related laws, the personal auto policy includes personal injury protection coverage for the named insured, family members, and parties hurt while occupying a covered auto instead of medical payment coverage.

26.4 Factors Considered for Premium Rating

Automobile insurance pricing has always been a matter of controversies to the consumers, service providers and the regulators. Auto claims have increased significantly in India since last 10 years. Auto insurance rates charged to different customers reflect differences in the discounted expected costs of providing coverage. In order to classify different persons into homogeneous groups with respect to expected claim costs, insurers generally use rate classification system that include (1) driver classes that reflect the characteristics of individual insureds, and (2) territorial rating to reflect expected differences in claim costs for people that live in different geographical areas (holding individual characteristics constant). Of course, physical damage rates also depend upon the value and type of vehicle. Liability insurance rates sometimes also depend on the type of vehicle, given evidence that certain vehicles are more likely to be involved in at-fault accidents. The major factors considered in establishing driver classes and the use of territorial rating factors are:9

Driver Classes

The parameters are Age, Gender, and Marital Status, Use of automobile, driving education and driving record. The insureds in younger age group, the males, the married ones and new and inexperienced drivers have on

7. Harrington & Neihaus, *Risk Management and Insurance,* McGraw-Hill, 1999. p. 534.

average high accidental claims. The loading on the premium increases by the numbers and amount of accident claims.

Territorial Rating

Large cities have higher average claim costs followed by suburban areas, smaller cities, and small towns or rural areas. In India, the geographical areas have been classified into Group A and Group B.

Motor/Automobile Insurance business in India is governed by the All India Motor Tariff, which lays down the premium rates, terms and conditions. The main factors taken into consideration for rating in India are vehicle classifications on several parameters, the geographical area of operations and experiences.

Vehicle Classification

Vehicles are generally classified on the basis of its technical specifications, its value or use.

Technical Specifications ("The Type")

The typology of a vehicle is more or less based on its cubic capacity or gross vehicle weight and its carrying capacity. Heavier vehicles are more exposed to accidents since the resultant damages they incur are more. Similarly, vehicles with higher carrying capacity expose more passengers to risk. Therefore heavier vehicles attract higher premium rate. In private cars, taxis and motorcycles, the factor is the cubic capacity. The more the cubic capacity, the higher the premium rate. Whereas in goods-carrying commercial vehicles and passenger-carrying commercial vehicles, the criteria are gross vehicle weight and passenger carrying capacity respectively.

The Value of the Vehicle

The premium rate is applied on the value of the vehicle to arrive at the premium payable. It is the owner/insured who has to select a correct value of the vehicle and declare the same for insurance. This value is known as the Insured's Estimated Value (IEV) in motor insurance and represents the sum insured.

Normally, this value is arrived at by considering the age of the vehicle and its present purchase price. A Maruti 800 was purchased in 1998 for Rs. 1,80,000/- Considering the conventional 10% depreciation each year and the present purchase price of a similar vehicle at Rs. 2,00,000/- the IEV for year 2000 is Rs. 1,80,000 less 20% of Rs. 2,00,000 = Rs. 40,000.00

IEV = Rs. 1,40,000.00

However, this is not sufficient for deriving the correct IEV of the vehicle in terms of motor insurance. In motor insurance, the basis for payment of claims is the market value of the vehicle at the place and time of loss. This market value may be understood as, the price that the vehicle would fetch in the second-hand market. For certain vehicles, there is a good demand in the second-hand market. Maruti is one of them. The 1998 model mentioned above may fetch a price of say, Rs. 1,50,000. In such situations, the correct IEV for the Maruti of 1998 model should be Rs. 1,50,000.

Now take the case of a Premier Padmini car of 1998 model. The purchase price in 1998 was say, Rs. 1,80,000/-. The depreciated value in year 2000 works out to Rs. 1,40,000. But, the second-hand value would be at most Rs. 30,000, since it has virtually no demand in the market.

In this case, the correct IEV should be Rs. 30,000/- only. It is not worthwhile to insure your vehicle at a higher value since that will increase the premium payable but, in case of total loss, only the market value would be payable.

In motor insurance, the IEV is the limit of liability per accident and not for the entire period of insurance. In cases of partial loss or losses, which may be made good by repairs, there is no limit to the number of accidents in any period of insurance. Suppose the Premier Padmini car, as described above, claims for two accidents in the year 2000, the first for an amount of Rs. 20,000/- and the second for Rs. 15,000/- under its insurance policy with IEV of Rs. 30,000/-. Both these claims can be recovered from the insurance company, since their respective values are within the limit of IEV, irrespective of the fact that the insured in this process recovers more amount during the period of insurance than he was insured for.

However, if the vehicle is totally lost or damaged and cannot be repaired, the insured would be paid the market value or IEV, whichever is less. It is very important to select a correct IEV for insurance. There is a tendency of motor vehicle owners to declare a lower value for insurance to reduce the premium expenditure. Although, insurance companies check the IEV for its sufficiency before accepting the insurance, this is not a correct practice as the insured is exposed to a greater loss in case the vehicle is totally lost or damaged.

The Use of the Vehicle

Risk exposure varies in relation to the use the vehicle is put to. Private cars are lesser exposed than taxis, as the latter is used extensively for maximum revenue. Taxi's therefore attract a higher premium rate. Similarly, goods carrying vehicles, which are used as private carriers and transport, only their owners' goods attract a lower premium, than those used as public carriers for transporting goods for hire.

The Geographical Area of Operation

The area of operation of a vehicle also has a direct bearing on the premium rate. This is so because, certain areas of operation are more congested with high densities of population and road traffic than others and poses higher exposure to accidents. For this purpose, the tariff differentiates two zones in India, i.e., Zone A and Zone B, for private cars and taxis. Zone A represents the Chennai region and Mumbai region (excluding Mumbai city) and Zone B represents the Kolkata region, Delhi region and Mumbai city. In Zone B, the densities of population and road traffic are more and hence attract a higher premium rate.

Such differential rating does not apply to commercial vehicles such as trucks and buses, as these vehicles normally travel throughout India for their operation. However, a discount is allowed on the premium for commercial vehicles used as contract carriage, school buses, public and private buses used for carrying passengers/workers and operate within a radius of 50 kilometres from the city limits.

Details of States under Zone A & Zone B

	Zone A	*Zone B*
Andhra Pradesh	Andaman & Nicobar Islands	Mumbai City
Goa, Daman, Diu	Arunachal Pradesh	Nagaland
Gujarat	Assam	Orissa
Karnataka	Bihar	Punjab
Kerala	Delhi	Rajasthan
Madhya Pradesh	Haryana	Sikkim
Maharashtra	Himachal Pradesh	Tripura
(Excluding Mumbai City)	Lakshadweep Islands	Uttar Pradesh
Pondicherry	Manipur	West Bengal
Tamil Nadu	Mizoram	

The Claims Experience

Unfavourable claims experience is obviously a bad risk. The tariff has adopted a system called the "No Claim discount", to give discounts for good claims experience and a loading for bad experience. The claim experience of expiring year's policy is the basis for allowing discount or charging a loading.

26.5 MOTOR INSURANCE CLAIMS

25.5.1 Own Damage Claims

Documents

Following Documents generally required for settlement of motor claims. However depending on the merits of the case, a particular document may not be necessary or an alternate document could be used to serve the purpose of the Insurer.

(a) *Claim form* required to be completed.

(b) *Registration Certificate* : the details usually verified from the RC can instead be obtained from purchase details of the vehicle if the circumstances so warrant.

(c) *Driving License* : as per policy condition the driver is required to hold an effective driving license both in terms of the period validity and the class of vehicle that is being driven at the time of the accident. The MV Act provides for a grace period of 30 days after expiry of a license during which period the license may be accepted as effective, provided the holder has not been qualified from holding a license. For loss sustained by parked vehicles, driving license may not be relevant.

(d) *Load Challan/Trip Sheet* : to verify that the load carried was within the permissible limits and the trip sheet giving details of number of passengers carried in the vehicle.

(e) *Fitness Certificate* : the fitness certificate indicates the roadworthiness of a commercial vehicle.

(f) *Report to Police* : a copy of the FIR and Panchanama is required wherever third parties are involved in an accident.

(g) *Survey Report* : surveyor ascertains the damage, assess the quantum of payable claim, verify vehicular documents and confirm that the loss/damage being claimed for is in conformity with the narration of the accident. Wherever replacement of parts is allowed surveyors physically verify serial numbers as appearing on major parts, which carry such numbers.

Procedure

- In order to proceed for claim, the insured immediately informs the insurer.
- The policy documents are verified to ensure that the policy is force and the loss is entered in the claims register and the claim form is issue to the insured to be completed and returned.
- The insurer, immediately on receipt of intimation of loss, either in writing or over telephone, a surveyor is appointed based on the estimate of repairs. The surveyors are supplied with the copy of the claim form, copy of policy and the repairer's estimate.
- In case of major accidents, the insured would be asked to arrange for photographs of the vehicle at the spot of the accident, showing all the external damages and the number plate of the vehicle. The photo expenses are to be reimbursed upto Rs. 500. Alternatively, the insured may inform the nearest office of the insurer to arrange for such photographs.
- The survey report is examined and settlement is done based on surveyor's recommendations.
- If reinspection after repair is considered necessary it may be conducted by the same surveyor who has assessed the loss.
- Conventionally, the payment is made to the repairer directly.

- If for any reason, to be specified, the driving license cannot be produced, the claim may be considered only on non-standard basis. However for settlement of such claims the authority should be vested only with the Managers and above in the RO. Where the driving license is not endorsed for tourist taxis, since, different practices prevail in different states, it is necessary to check the local practice. The claim is to be treated as standard or non-standard on the basis of the practice prevailing in the state where the accident occurs and this will be decided by a Manager and above in the RO.
- The repairers are bound to keep aside the value of salvage and if the salvage is desired to be retained, the value is deducted from the claim bill.

Partial Loss Claims

A. Submission of bills/cash can be dispensed with for claims upto Rs. 50,000 in respect of private cars and two wheelers only, subject to

(*a*) The survey report correctly indicating the cost of parts allowed for replacement

(*b*) Claims being settled on the basis of a report of reinspection after repairs by the surveyor certifying that the repairs and replacements have been carried out as per assessment. For other classes of vehicles bills/cash memos have to be obtained and verified.

B. If surveyor confirms replacement of the engine and chassis if allowed for replacement and indicates the new numbers, claims may be settled whilst simultaneously advising the insured that

(*a*) As per the provision of the Motor Vehicles Act, the new numbers have to be incorporated in the RC book.

(*b*) Insurance company be informed about the incorporation of the new numbers in the RC book for endorsing on the policy document to facilitate settlement of future claims.

(*c*) Where the vehicle is totally damaged or when the net cost of repairs is almost close to the market value of the IEV the claim could be considered to be a total loss. Such total loss claims should be encouraged on net of salvage basis i.e., salvage being retained by the insured and an appropriate amount towards salvage value as determined by the surveyor in consultation with the company be deducted from the total loss amount.

(*d*) However, if the insured to retain the salvage, arrangements should be made for the safe custody of the damaged vehicle to prevent further loss or damage. The RTO should be informed by Registered AD post. An inventory on the major parts should be taken before taking possession of the vehicle. Immediate steps thereafter should also be taken for its disposal as per company's guidelines for disposal of salvage.

26.5.2 Theft Claims

1. *Partial Loss due to Theft* : Theft of parts/accessories from a vehicle should be reported to the police immediately by the insured. If parts are found missing or changed after recovery of stolen vehicle this be recorded in panchanama/recovery memo. Final police investigation report will also be required. However, if the competent authority is satisfied about the genuineness of the loss, final investigation report may be waived provided the insured sends a registered AD letter to the SP/ACP requesting that the insurer should be informed of any recovery.
2. *Total Loss due to Theft* : Unless claims settling authority is fully satisfied, investigation of the theft to be arranged by an investigator who may be appointed with specific terms of reference.

3. The following documents should be collected from the insured in addition to a certified copy of the FIR, for considering "on account" payment of the admissible claim after expiry of 90 days from the date of loss.
   (*a*) Surrender of the Registration Book and the Tax Book to the insurer duly transferred in the name of the insurers. The RTO is to be informed about the theft of the vehicle and this should be entered in Tax Book so that further tax will not accrue.
   (*b*) Letter of indemnity and subrogation.
   (*c*) Ignition keys of the vehicle.
   (*d*) Certificate of insurance and the original insurance policy, if not stolen with the vehicle.
   (*e*) Specially worded discharge voucher.
4. The balance payment may be released on receipt of the Final Police Investigation Report or on expiry of a suitable waiting period from the date of the "on account" payment, after obtaining the discharge voucher in full and final settlement of the claim.
5. The Police and the Registration authorities and the NCRB should be notified in writing about disposal of the claim on "total loss" basis following theft of the vehicle. They should be requested to advise the company if the vehicle is recovered subsequently. Immediately after receipt of advise from the Police regarding recovery of the vehicle, necessary steps for taking possession of the vehicle from the Police custody should be taken and, if necessary, an advocate should be appointed for filing recovery application in the court.
6. Municipal Authorities, where applicable and the RTO should be advised by registered Letter with Acknowledgement. Due to record 'non use' of the vehicle on account of theft and about the cancellation of the Insurance Certificate.
7. If the vehicle is recovered subsequently, the insured will have the option to repay the claim amount already paid and retain the recovered vehicle. If the vehicle is found damaged, the insured will be indemnified against loss of damage. The insured should be advised to obtain recovery memo from the Police and to get the vehicle surveyed at the Police Station before taking delivery, as mentioned under partial loss theft claims.
8. In cases of criminal breach of trust each case should be dealt with an individual basis depending upon facts of each case and subject to legal opinion.

26.5.3 Third Party Bodily Injury Claims : Fatal and Non-fatal

1. *Intimation of Claim* : Intimation about an accident resulting into third party claim is received through various sources :
   (*a*) Insured directly or by mention in passing whilst lodging own damage claim
   (*b*) Claimant
   (*c*) MACT/Courts by notice
   (*d*) Through accident report from police in Form 54 prescribed under Central Motor Vehicles Rules, 1989.
2. *Investigation* : Investigation about the accident to collect the relevant data to quantify reasonable and just compensation as per the specified formats in respect of all third party claims is mandatory. The companies should ensure that this investigation helps the insurance company in finalizing out of court settlement at the earliest.
3. *Appointment of Advocate :* On receipt of notice from the MACT a competent advocate from the panel may be appointed if necessary. The following relevant documents and information should be given to him/her

immediately to enable him/her to draft written statement (w/s) on behalf of the Company and ensure that the proper defense is taken where necessary and no frivolous statements are made.

4. *Policy Copy* : Duly certified true copy of the complete policy with the relevant clauses and endorsements as actually attached with the original issued covering the vehicle at the material time of accident.
5. *Driving Licence :* In case it has been observed that driver was not duly licensed the necessary information should be given to the advocate. Though under Section 149(2) of the MV Act, 1988, Insurance Company has no liability if the driver is not duly licensed, the onus to prove that the driver was not holding a license rests on insurance company and this obligation is required to be discharged fully to the satisfaction of the court.
6. *Compliance Policy Conditions* : If a breach of a specific policy condition has been observed it should be brought to the notice of the Advocate to enable proper defense if possible.
7. (*a*) Written statement on behalf of the insurance company incorporating all defenses available as enumerated under Section 149 of MV Act should be promptly filed.
   (*b*) Wherever necessary when there is collusion between the insured and the claimants or when the insured fails to defend the claim, the company's advocate must be instructed to obtain the MACT's permission under Section 170 of the MV Act to Defend the claim on merits.
8. *Payment of No Fault Liability Claims* : If liability under affected policy is established after taking into consideration the foregoing defenses, company should take immediate steps to deposit No Faulty Liability amount as per Section 140 of the MV Act, 1988.
9. *Payment of Fault Liability Claims* : Companies may initiate action to settle such claims either through
   (*a*) Jald Rahat Yojna
   (*b*) Lok Adalats
   (*c*) Direct negotiation with the claimant through DICC & RICC.
10. *Jald Rahat Yojna :* Section 152 of MV Act, 1988 authorizes insurance company to settle motor third party non-fatal bodily injury claims where claimant is an adult without claimants taking recourse to MACTs. Industry has already launched the Scheme since 1991.

Guidelines for Placing Claims in Lok Adalats

- Maximum participation and disposal of large number of claims in Lok Adalats sessions should be ensured.
- Companies should place the claims normally falling within the following parameters before lok adalat :
  (*a*) where occurrence of the accident is within the policy period.
  (*b*) where estimated liability is not expected to be exceeding Rs. 5,00,000 per application for compensation.
  (*c*) where no substantial point of law is involved.
  (*d*) where no defences are available under Section 149 of the MV Act, 1988, such as driver not holding effective driving license and breach of policy condition relating to limitations as to use.
  (*e*) where policy record shows that the driver was holding effective driving license.
  (*f*) where despite concerted efforts on the part of the insurance companies. They are not in a position to prove conclusively to the satisfaction of the court that a person drove the vehicle not duly licensed.
  (*g*) since there is a provision of automatic transfer of insurance in pursuance of Section 157 of MV Act, 1988 the companies cannot take defense of non-transfer of insurance of the vehicle on their books.
  (*h*) where more than one vehicle insured with different insurance companies is involved in an accident resulting into a third party claim, companies should agree for settlement on 50-50 basis to apportion the liability between them.

- Companies should not accept conditional settlement such as subject to verification of certain documents, production of documents etc.
- On having reached the agreement for compromise settlement concerned MACT issues a Consent Order specifying *inter alia* the period during which the agreed amount should be deposited. On receipt of such order, companies must deposit the amount as agreed to with the MACT within 30 days from the date of award as per schedule.
- In the event of lok adalat for pending appeals before High Courts is organized, such claims where quantum of compensation is in dispute may be considered.
- Appeals which are filed to decide a point of law should not be considered for placing before lok adalat.
- Applications for compensation filed by the paid employees may also be placed before lok adalat, whether wider legal liability is covered or not.

26.5.4 Motor Accident Claims Tribunals

Motor Vehicles Act, 1939 provides that a State Government may, by notification in the Official Gazette, constitute one or more Motor Accidents Claims Tribunals(MACT) for such area as may be specified in the notification for the purpose of adjudicating upon claims for compensation in respect of accidents involving the death of, or bodily injury to, persons arising out of the use of motor vehicles, or damages to any property of a third party so arising, or both

Provided that where such claim includes a claim for compensation in respect of damage to property exceeding rupees two thousand, the claimant may, at his option. refer the claim to a civil court for adjudication, and where a reference is so made, the Claims Tribunal shall have no jurisdiction to entertain any question relating to such claim.

A Claims Tribunal shall consist of such number of members as the State Government may think fit to appoint and where it consists of two or more members, one of them shall be appointed as the Chairman thereof.

110A. Application for compensation may be made to the tribunal (a) by the person who has sustained the injury or by the owner of the property or where death has resulted from the accident, 1[by all or any of the legal representatives of the deceased; or by any agent duly authorised by the person injured or all or any of the legal representatives of the deceased, as the case may be.

Every application under sub- section (1) shall be made to the Claims Tribunal having jurisdiction over the area in which the accident occurred, and shall be in such form and shall contain such particular as may be prescribed.

26.5.5 Hit and Run Accidents and Solatium Fund

Motor Vehicles Act, 1939 contains special provisions as to compensation in cases of hit and run motor accidents. Section 109B and section 109C define " hit and run motor accident" means an accident arising out of the use of a motor vehicle or motor vehicles the identity whereof cannot be ascertained in spite of reasonable efforts for the purpose. The Central Government may, by notification in the Official Gazette, establish a Fund to be known as the Solatium Fund. The amount of compensation is Rs.25,000/- in the event of death and Rs.12,500/- for grievous injuries. The prescribed forms are available with the Mandal Revenue Officer of the respective Mandal. The applicant shall submit the application seeking the compensation in the prescribed form to the Claims Enquiry Officer of the Sub-division/Taluk or Mandal where the accident takes place.

Aggrieved party has to submit an application within 6 months from the date of accident.

An application made after 6 months but not after 12 months from the date of accident may be accepted by the Claims Enquiry Officer, if he is satisfied that there are reasonable grounds to condone the delay.

On receipt of the claim application, the Claims Enquiry Officer shall

- Obtain a copy of the inquest report, FIR, post mortem or certificate of injury as the case may be from the concerned authorities and hold an enquiry in respect of claims arising out of hit and run accidents.
- Decide the rightful claimants.
- Submit the report to the Claims Settlement Commissioner.

On receipt of the report of the Claims Enquiry Officer, the Claims Settlement Commissioner will sanction the claim. Claims Settlement Commissioner means the District Magistrate, the Deputy Commissioner, the Collector, or other Officer in-charge of a Revenue District in a State appointed by the State Government.

The Claims Enquiry Officer has to submit his report to Claims Settlement Commissioner within a month's time from the date of receipt of the claim application.

The Claims Settlement Commissioner shall sanction the claim within a period of 15 days from the date of receipt of the report and communicate the sanction order along with the duly discharged receipt and the undertaking in the prescribed form to the Nominated Office of the Insurance Company.

Where the Claims Settlement Commissioner has any doubt in respect of the report submitted by the Claims Enquiry Officer, he shall return the report for further enquiry indicating the specific points on which the enquiry is to be made.

Claims arising out of death payment shall be made to the legal representatives of the deceased as decided by the Claims Enquiry Officer and in respect of grievous hurt the payment shall be made to the person injured.

Once the sanction order together with the discharge receipt and the undertaking in the prescribed form is received from Claims Settlement Commissioner, the Insurance Company will effect payment within 15 days from the date of receipt of the sanction order. The payment is made by cheque or demand draft through registered post with an acknowledgement due directly to the claimant.

Appendix 26 : Motor Insurance Statistics

Business Generated(Gross Direct Premium - Rs. in crores)

Companies	*1993-94*	*1994-95*	*1995-96*	*1996-97*	*1997-98*	*1998-99*	*1999-2000*
GIC	-	-	-	-	-	-	-
NIC	231.25	267.81	345.67	444.14	511.17	612.48	699.08
OIC	-	-	-	-	-	-	-
NIAC	451.29	532.38	629.68	-	806.76	936.68	1031.06
UII	278.46	340.69	408.94	487.64	543.78	661.03	712.11
Total	**961.00**	**1140.88**	**1384.29**	**931.78**	**1861.71**	**2210.19**	**2442.25**

Profits(Rs. in Crores)

Companies	*1993-94*	*1994-95*	*1995-96*	*1996-97*	*1997-98*	*1998-99*	*1999-2000*
GIC	-	-	-	-	-	-	-
NIC	-60.69	-124.88	-83.71	-192.75	-213.19	-298.67	-309.01
OIC	-	-	-	-	-	-	-
NIAC	-70.42	-284.48	-210.04	-	-284.83	-221.48	-369.92
UII	-110.81	-209.87	-249.73	-298.08	-301.79	-334.54	-419.56
Total	**-241.92**	**-619.23**	**-543.48**	**-490.83**	**-799.81**	**-854.69**	**-1098.49**

Profit %age

GIC	-	-	-	-	-	-	-
NIC	-26.24%	-46.63%	-24.22%	-43.40%	-41.71%	-48.76%	-44.20%
OIC	-	-	-	-	-	-	-
NIAC	-15.60%	-53.44%	-33.36%	-	-35.31%	-23.65%	-35.88%
UII	-39.79%	-61.60%	-61.07%	-61.13%	-55.50%	-50.61%	-58.92%

Motor Insurance (Gross Direct Premium Income)

Company	2005-06	2006-07	2007-08	2008-09
National	1846.41	1986.58	2146.30	2146.29
New India	2174.50	2034.73	2034.30	2000.29
Oriental	1495.36	1739.79	1608.38	1491.30
United India	1138.16	1233.18	1434.90	1563.49
ECGC*	-	-	-	
GIC*	-	-	-	
Royal Sundaram	233.09	303.39	409.56	529.91
Reliance	26.52	455.51	1267.37	1164.82
Iffco-Tokio	378.08	448.90	499.19	683.24
TATA AIG	239.82	273.09	253.25	224.79
ICICI Lombard	454.44	1142.55	1279.07	1321.29
Bajaj Allianz	536.61	843.87	1386.37	1503.39
Cholamandalam	52.35	97.16	1224.41	319.53
HDFC-ergo	158.03	138.32	140.38	158.78
Future Generali	-	-	-	94.88
Universal Sompo	-	-	-	3.92
Shriram	-	-	-	112.72
Bharti AXA	-	-	-	17.39
Total	**8733.37**	**10697.07**	**13683.48**	**13336.03**

Market Share

Private Co. Share	76.195%	65.385%	52.793%	53.999%
Public Co. Share	23.805%	34.615%	47.207%	46.001%

Key Terms

- ❐ Bodily Injury
- ❐ Legal Liability
- ❐ Act only Policy
- ❐ Comprehensive Policy
- ❐ Maturity Claim
- ❐ Premium Rating

Questions for Review

1. Is automobile insurance compulsory in India? What types of insurance covers are available for automobiles?
2. Write short notes on :

   (*a*) No claim discount.

(*b*) Factors considered for premium rating.

(*c*) Insured Declared Value.

3. Briefly explain the various documents required for settlement of own damage and third party documents.
4. Explain the major point of differences between the procedure for settlement of third party claims and own damage claims.

Suggested Readings

- Harrington & Niehaus, *Risk Management and Insurance,* McGraw-Hill, 1999.
- J.C. Trieschmann, S.G. Gistavson and R.E. Hoyt, *Risk Management and Insurance,* South-Western College Publishing, 2001.
- Vaughan and Vaughan, *Essentials of Risk Management and Insurance,* John Wiley and Sons Inc., 2001.
- *Insurance Law Manual,* Taxmann, 2001.
- *Motor Insurance,* IC 72, Insurance Institute of India, Mumbai, 2003.

Health Insurance

Chapter 27

Chapter Objectives

After reading this chapter you will be able to understand :

- *Health Insurance Basics*
- *Health Insurance Scheme*
- *Imperative for Health Insurance in India*

27.1 Health Insurance Basics

Health insurance is a safeguard against rising medical costs. A health insurance policy is a contract between an insurer and an individual or group, in which the insurer agrees to provide specified health insurance at an agreed-upon price (the premium). Depending upon the policy, premium may be payable either in a lumpsum or in installments. Health insurance usually provides either direct payment or reimbursement for expenses associated with illnesses and injuries. The cost and range of protection provided by health insurance depends on the insurance provider and the policy purchased. There are many health concerns including the following which accentuate the demand for health insurance:

(a) Environmental pollution is causing serious health problems to humans.

(b) The fast spreading AIDS, poisonous gases, various wastes including nuclear waste generated by the people are seriously endangering the life on earth.

(c) A person may face serious monetary problems for the medical treatment and hospitalisations during life.

Now-a-days, most companies give the benefit of health insurance to its employees.

27.2 Current Scenario

Healthcare, with global revenue of over Rs. 2.75 trillion is the largest industry in the world. The nation of India with a population of 1000 million experiences a vast inequity that exists in the healthcare industry with barely 3 per cent of the population covered by some form of health insurance, either social or private. During the last 50 years, India has made considerable progress in improving its health status. Death rate has reduced from 40 to 9 per thousand, infant mortality rate reduced from 161 to 71 per thousand live births and life expectancy increased from 31 to 63 years. However, many challenges remain and these are: life expectancy 4 years below world average, high incidence of communicable diseases, increasing incidence of non-communicable diseases, neglect of women's health, considerable regional variation and threat from environment degradation. At any given point of time 40 to 50 million of population are on medication for major sickness. About 200 million days are lost annually. The annual rate (range) of out-patient: rural 30-152/1000, urban 9-81/1000 and for hospitalisation: rural 16-76/1000, urban 5-38/1000.

In India, presently the health insurance exists primarily in the form of Mediclaim policy offered to the individual or to any group, association or corporate bodies. Although, total expenditure on health in India is nearly 6 per cent of the entire GDP, the government spending is less than 25 per cent against the average spending of 30-40 per cent in other developing countries. Penetration of Mediclaim is currently done by state-owned insurance companies, covering only about 2.5 million people i.e. less than 0.50 per cent of the country's population.

The primary health care system in India is managed mainly by the shallow structure of government health-care facilities and other public-health care systems in a traditional model of health funding and provision. But, it is unable to justify the demand for health security for 200 million Indian health insurable population mainly due to service costs being out of the reach of many people, absence of good and effective number of physicians, low rate of education programs, less number of hospitals, poor medical equipment and over all, the poor budget of government towards the health program.

27.3 HEALTH INSURANCE SCHEMES

Based on ownership the existing health insurance schemes can be broadly divided into the following categories:-

(a) Government or State-based Systems (including CGHS and ESIS)

(b) Market-based Systems (Private and Voluntary)

(c) Employer provided Insurance Systems

(d) Member Organization (NGO or Cooperative)-based Systems

27.3.1 Government/State Based Systems

The best documented and largest system of health care delivery in India is the diverse network of hospitals, primary health Centres, community health centres, dispensaries and speciality facilities financed and managed by the Central and State local Governments. These facilities are officially available to the entire population either free or for nominal charges. Along with some other networks of village health workers, maternal and child health programmes and speciality disease prevention programmes these public facilities carry out a central role in India's primary health care system. Studies have shown that these facilities are mostly underfunded, understaffed and short of drugs and essential supplies and that they sometimes suffer from low morale and inadequate motivation.

The health facilities made available to the public are managed and operated under the authority of central and state agencies. The state governments mostly own and manage the public sector delivery system and have to bear the costs of operation. But the Central Government plays a major role in the planning, financing and transfer of resources that determine new investment in health facilities and specialised programmes. Much of the funding for health facilities originates from the Union Ministry of Health and Family Welfare and is channelled to the state governments, which retain considerable authority for the spending decisions. Virtually all decisions are made by the central and state governments – including the staffing and supply decisions, with little autonomy for the providers of health care at the lower levels. Over the years, the Central Government has been the main source of funds for the primary health care facilities, whereas the states bear the major responsibility of recurrent costs, especially the costs of running hospitals. This system has added to the overall inefficiency of public health facilities.

27.3.1.1 Central Government Health Scheme

The Central Government Health Scheme (CGHS) was introduced in 1954 as a contributory health scheme to provide comprehensive medical care to the central government employees and their families. It was basically designed to replace the cumbersome and expensive system of reimbursements (Ministry of Health and Family Welfare, *Annual Report 1993-94*). Separate dispensaries are maintained for the exclusive use of the central government employees covered by the scheme. Over the years, the coverage has grown substantially with provision for the non-allopathic system of medicines as well as for allopathic. In addition, the CGHS reimburses patients for part of their out of pocket costs on treatment at the government hospitals and some other facilities.

The list of beneficiaries includes all categories of current as well as former government employees, members of parliament and so on. Since the large central bureaucracy in India definitely belongs to the middle-income and high-income categories, they are likely to make above-average use of health services. The CGHS has been in the recent past, widely criticised from the point of view of quality and accessibility.

27.3.1.2 Employees State Insurance Scheme

Established in 1948, the Employees State Insurance Scheme (ESIS) is an insurance system which provides both the cash and the medical benefits. It is managed by the Employees State Insurance Corporation (ESIC), a wholly government-owned enterprise. It was conceived as a compulsory social security benefit for workers in the formal sector. The original legislation creating the scheme allowed it to cover only factories which have been 'using power' and employing 10 or more workers.

However, since 1989 the scheme has been expanded, and it now includes all such factories which are 'not using power' and employing 20 or more persons. Mines and plantations are explicitly excluded from coverage under the ESIS Act.

27.3.2 Market Based Systems

GIC Mediclaim Coverages

The GIC holds a major share in the market-based health insurance segment. It introduced the standard " Mediclaim" health insurance scheme in 1986, and became operational in 1987. This product was later on modified in 1997 to allow for premium differentials for various age groups meant for both individuals and groups. As on date, the GIC and its subsidiaries offer the following products:

Mediclaim or Hospitalization Benefit Insurance Policy

Suitability

Anyone in the age group of 5 to 80 years can take the policy. Children in the age group below the age of 5 years can also be covered from the age of 3 months onwards provided one or both of the parents are covered concurrently. Higher limits are permitted if the policy is in renewal for the preceding three years. Suitable for persons of any nationality but treatment should be availed of within the country and the claim is paid in Indian currency.

Salient Features

- Provides cover, which takes care of medical expenses following hospitalization from sudden illness or accident.
- Cover extends to pre-hospitalisation and post-hospitalisation for periods of 30 days and 60 days respectively.
- Domiciliary hospitalisation is also covered.

Benefits

- Reimbursement of medical expenses.
- Discount in insurance premium is allowed on family package, cumulative bonus and health check. In case of family package cover, a single member can avail of the entire policy limits.
- Pre-existing diseases not covered.
- The premium paid by a cheque upto a maximum of Rs. 10,000 is totally exempt from income tax.

Domiciliary Hospitalisation

The term means that a patient can be treated at home when he is not in a fit condition to be moved to the hospital or where there is no accommodation in the specialist hospital provided,

1. The treatment was for a period not less than 3 days.
2. The sub-limits of sum insured towards domiciliary hospitalisation are furnished in the sum insured and premium schedules.

Exclusions

- The facility is not available if any illness is contracted within 30 days from the commencement of risk except in case of an accident.
- Any pre-existing diseases.
- Treatment for cataracts, benign prostatic hypertrophy, hydrocele, congenital internal diseases, fistula in anus, piles, sinusitis and related disorders for 1st year of policy.
- All the expenses incurred in respect of any treatment relating to pregnancy or childbirth.
- AIDS or conditions of similar kind.
- Directly or indirectly connected with war or nuclear waste.

Requirements

A completed proposal form. If the prosper is a 'Diabetic', a separate questionnaire completed by the family physician.

Bhavishya Arogya Insurance Policy

Suitability

Bhavishya Arogya is a life term policy where medical benefits are made available after retirement of the insured. Therefore, by paying premiums during the earning period, one can make a provision for medical benefits after retirement. Persons in the age group of 25 to 55 years are eligible for this policy.

Salient Features

- The policy provides hospitalization benefits for lifetime after retirement age of the insured.
- Premiums can be paid in equated annual installments up to the age of retirement.
- Premiums can also be remitted in lumpsum on one time basis. Discount is offered for one time payment.

Benefits

The policy comes into force after retirement and provides for hospitalization and domiciliary hospitalization benefits, following an accident or sickness.

A sub-limit of Rs. 20,000 for any one accident or illness is fixed.

Other Conditions

- The minimum sum to be insured is Rs. 50,000 and can be increased in multiples of Rs. 10,000 as a unit, thereafter.
- For every Rs. 10,000 increase of sum insured, the premium is loaded by 20%.
- Maximum sum insured is Rs. 2 lakh.
- After commencement of the risk (i.e after retirement) cumulative bonus @ 5% for every successive claim free year is added upto a maximum of 50%.

- In case of death of insured before retirement, refund of premium will be at a pre-determined scale and is payable to the nominee/assignee.
- In the event of voluntary cancellation of the policy, the refunds will be 75% of the set scales applicable for death claims, provided there is no claim under the policy.

Requirements

- A completed proposal form.
- Proof of age is necessary as the payments of premiums depends on the age.

LIC Coverages

The Life Insurance Corporation of India introduced a special insurance programme in 1993 which covered medical expenses for only four dreaded diseases. It was withdrawn and introduced subsequently in 1995. At present the modified versions are available in the form of two products viz. Jeevan Asha and Asha Deep. A brief of these plans is as follows:

Jeevan Asha

Features

- Open ended scheme.
- Covers many surgical procedures.
- Fixed benefit for surgical treatment can be availed twice (subject to conditions).
- Exclusive Double/Triple accident benefit.
- Option to switch over from existing Jeevan Asha plan.

Suitable for

The Jeevan Asha II plan is apt for people who whose family history tends to show a hereditary lineage of maladies and afflictions that have required major or minor surgery from time to time.

Special Features

Under the Jeevan Asha plan, the major surgical procedures covered for are:

- Nervous system (non-malignant causes).
- Respiratory system.
- Cardiovascular system.
- Haemic and lymphatic system.
- Endocrine system.
- Ocular system.
- Muskoskeletal system.

Benefits

Survival Benefits

- 2% of the sum assured paid every second year. Option to get lumpsum benefit for any health emergency at a later date.
- Payment of full Sum assured + Guaranteed addition @ Rs.70/- per thousand sum Assured + Loyalty addition. (Subject to deduction of Survival & Surgical benefits paid earlier).

Plan Parameters

	Minimum	Maximum
Entry Age (years)	18	50
Sum Assured (Rs.)	50000	500000
Term (years)	15	25
Mode of Payment: Maximum Maturity Age		
Policy loan available: Monthly, Quarterly, Half-Yearly, Yearly	65 years	No

Salary Saving Scheme.

Asha Deep

Features

Cover the risk of four major ailments namely, Cancer (malignant), Paralytic stroke resulting in permanent disability, Renal failure of both kidneys or Coronary artery diseases where by-pass surgery has been done.

Suitable for

The Asha Deep II (with profits) policy is best suited for people if they anticipate or have a family history of serious diseases like Cancer, Paralysis, Renal failure and Coronary disease.

Special Feature

During the term of the policy, if the life assured is afflicted by any of the major ailments listed above and the same is established as per rules (in case of Coronary artery disease, the life assured must have undergone the by-pass surgery), the policyholder will be eligible for the following benefits, provided, the policy is in force for the full sum assured.

Immediate payment of 50% of the sum assured.

Waiver of premiums falling due from the policy anniversary immediately following the date on which the conditions for the eligibility to the benefits are established.

Payment of an amount equal to 10% of the sum assured, every year commencing from the policy anniversary falling on or after the date of affliction and ending with the policy anniversary preceding the date of maturity or the date of death of the life assured, whichever is earlier.

Payment of balance 50% of the sum assured and vested bonuses on the date of maturity or on death of life assured, whichever is earlier. The bonuses will be calculated on the full sum assured even though 50% of the sum assured would have been paid earlier.

A lien for a period of one year will be imposed on all policies under this plan. That is, if the life assured is afflicted by any of the four ailments mentioned above and its onset falls within a period of one year from the date of issue of first premium receipt, then the policyholder will not be eligible for additional benefits mentioned under sub-section (a) above.

If the life assured does not get afflicted by any of the diseases mentioned above, the full sum assured and vested bonuses will be paid on the date of maturity or on death of the life assured, whichever is earlier.

Diseases Covered

Brief description of major ailments covered under this plan with relevant definition (medical terms referred herein will bear meaning as given in the Butterworth's Medical Dictionary).

Cancer (malignant)

It is the presence of uncontrolled growth and spread of malignant cells. The definition 'cancer' includes leukaemia, lymphomas and Hodgkin's disease.

Exclusions

This excludes non-invasive carcinoma(s) in-situ, localised non-invasive tumour(s) revealing early malignant changes and tumour(s) in presence of HIV infection or AIDS; any skin cancer excepting malignant melanoma(s) are also to be included.

Paralytic Stroke

(Cerebro-vascular accidents): Death of a portion of the brain due to vascular causes such as Haemorrhage (cerebral), Thrombosis (cerebral), Embolism (cerebral) causing total permanent disability of two or more limbs persisting for 3 months after the illness.

Exclusions

Transient/Ischaemic attacks.

Stroke-like syndromes resulting from Head injury.

Intracranial space occupying lesions like abscess, traumatic haemorrhage and tumour.

Tuberculous meningitis, pyogen meningitis and meningococcal meningitis.

Renal Failure

It is the renal failure stage due to chronic irreversible failure of both the kidneys. It must be well documented. The life assured must produce evidence of undergoing regular haemodialysis and other relevant laboratory investigations and doctor's certification.

Coronary artery disease where the by-pass surgery has been actually done:

The use of surgery on the advice of a consultant cardiologist to correct narrowing or blockage of one or more coronary arteries.

Exclusions

Non-surgical techniques such as the use of either balloon or laser via a catheter introducer through the arterial system are excluded.

Nature of evidence required to establish eligibility for benefits under this plan will be as stipulated by the corporation.

Benefits

Survival Benefits

Sum Assured and vested Bonus on maturity.

Death Benefits

Natural: If the life assured is not afflicted by any of the specified ailments, the legal heirs get the full Sum assured + Accrued bonus.

Accidental: Accidental benefits available to the life assured whether afflicted or not afflicted by any of the specified ailments —

Plan Parameters

	Minimum	*Maximum*
Entry Age (years)	18	50
Sum Assured (Rs.)	50,000	5,00,000
Term (years)	15	25
Mode of Payment: Maximum Maturity Age		
Policy Loan Available: Monthly, Quarterly, Half-Yearly, Yearly		
	65 years	yes

Salary Saving Scheme: Health Polices offered by private players.

Bajaj Allianz and Royal Sundaram have also ventured into the health insurance business last year. Bajaj Allianz is presently offering three products titled (a) Health Guard, (b) Critical Illness and (c) Hospital Cash Daily Allowance Policy. Royal Sundaram is offering Health Shield. The details of these policies are given below:

Hospital Cash Daily Allowance Policy – Bajaj Allianz

Suitability

- Policy provides for the cash benefits in the event of insured person(s) being hospitalised due to sickness or accident. It provides cash for each and every completed day of hospitalisation. It can be taken by anyone in the age group of 3 months to 60 years.

Salient Features

- The Company pays a daily allowance for every day of hospitalisation. The daily allowance can to be Rs. 500/- Rs. 1000/- or Rs. 2000/- per day, at the option of the insured.
- The policy pays for a maximum of 30/60 days of hospitalisation per policy period, irrespective of number of confinements to hospital/nursing home per policy period. Number of days of hospitalisation shall be selected by the insured.
- A day for this purpose may be a period of 12 hours reckoned from the time of hospitalisation but must include 0300 hours.
- Dependant spouse and children can also be covered under the policy. The benefits payable to the dependants shall be linked to that of insured as above regardless of the fact whether they are employed or not. Further discounts are given if spouse and children are insured.
- There is no limit on the number of children to be covered. The minimum age for the children is 3 months with maximum being 21 years.
- Premium paid upto Rs. 15,000 per annum is eligible for tax benefit under Section 80 D of IT Act.
- In case of ICU admission double the scheduled amount will be paid (maximum of 7 days).
- There is no need to submit medical bills. Only a discharge certificate is sufficient for admitting the claim.

Annual premium table (Indicative):

Coverage per day	*Proposer Age*	*Premium (Rs.) for 30 day cover*	*Premium (Rs.) for 60 day cover*
	Upto 25 years	200	240
	Above 25 upto 40 years	220	270
	Above 40 upto 50 years	350	480
Rs. 500	Above 50 upto 55 years	390	520
	Above 55 upto 60 years	470	620
	Upto 25 years	280	450
	Above 25 upto 40 years	320	520
Rs. 1,000	Above 40 upto 50 years	550	1,020
	Above 50 upto 55 years	600	1,120
	Above 55 upto 60 years	740	1,320
	Upto 25 years	520	880
	Above 25 upto 40 years	600	1,020
	Above 40 upto 50 years	1,160	2,020
Rs. 2,000	Above 50 upto 55 years	1,260	2,200
	Above 55 upto 60 years	1,560	2,600

Service tax 5%; Family discount 5%.

Benefits

The policy pays a daily allowance for every day of hospitalisation. The daily allowance depends on the amount selected by the insured. Number of days of hospitalisation is limited to 30/60 days per policy period, as selected by the insured.

Exclusions

1. Pre-existing disease.
2. Treatment not carried out by a qualified Medical Practitioner.
3. Cosmetic and plastic surgery, unless resulting from an accident.
4. Officially recognised epidemics.
5. Suture of skin.
6. Any expense of hospitalisation incurred during the first 30 days of insurance.
7. Dental treatment or surgery of any kind unless due to accident requiring hospitalisation.
8. Procedures concerned with sterilisation or infertility.
9. Treatment arising from or traceable to pregnancy, childbirth including caesarian section.
10. Voluntary medical termination of pregnancy during first 12 weeks from the date of conception.
11. Drunken driving.
12. Sexual diseases.
13. AIDS and related problems.
14. War and nuclear perils.

15. Naval or military or Airforce operations requiring the use of arms.
16. Natural perils like avalanche, earthquake, volcanic eruption or any kind of natural hazard.
17. Epilepsy, fits of any kind.
18. Any sanatoriums, spa or rest cures or long term care or hospitalisation undertaken as a preventive measure.
19. Racing of any kind.
20. Sexual dysfunction, trans-sexual surgery and related services.
21. Physiotherapy.
22. Weight reduction, improvement/enhancement therapy.
23. Connected with aircraft or watercraft or similar craft other than as a fare paying passenger.
24. Consequential loss or legal liability or any kind.

Health Guard – Bajaj Allianz

Suitability

Policy provides for the cash benefits in the event of insured person(s) being hospitalised due to sickness or accident. It also offers you cashless benefit and medical reimbursement for hospitalisation expenses.

Salient Features

- Policy provides for the cash benefits in the event of insured person(s) being hospitalised due to sickness or accident.
- Cashless facility: With Health Guard, the member has access to the cashless facility at various hospitals across India (*Subject to exclusions and conditions*).
- The member can opt for hospitals besides the empanelled ones, in which case the expenses incurred by him shall be reimbursed within 14 working days from submission of all the documents.
- Pre and post-hospitalisation expenses: Covers relevant medical expenses incurred 60 days prior to and 90 days after hospitalisation.
- Cumulative bonus of 5% to your sum assured for every claim free year.
- Family discount of 5% is available.
- Waiver of pre-existing diseases: Pre-existing diseases are normally excluded at the time of taking the policy, however, from 5th year onwards it is covered if the policy is continuously renewed for 4 years with the company and the insured has declared such ailment while taking the policy for the first time.

Benefits

- Policy provides financial assistance in case of hospitalisation following an accident or sickness.
- Policy holder can avail cashless hospitalisation facility in the Networked Hospitals.
- Premiums paid under the policy are eligible for tax rebate under Section 80-D of the Income Tax Act 1961.
- Health check up for maximum amount of Rs. 1,000 at the end of continuous four claims free year.
- Covers ambulance charges in an emergency subject to limit to Rs. 1,000.

Premium Table

Indicative Premium Table: All the premiums are per annum

Age (Yrs.) Sum insured (Rs.)	3m-25yrs.	26-40	41-50	51-55	56-60	61-65	66-70	71-75
1,00,000	1,023	1,481	2,176	2,436	3,216	3,298	3,373	3,451
2,00,000	1,554	2,587	3,978	4,479	5,964	6,110	6,255	6,585
3,00,000	2,095	3,492	5,552	6,342	8,490	8,697	8,904	9,571
4,00,000	4,544	4,938	7,542	8,951	9,174	10,665	10,919	
5,00,000	5,355	5,820	9,161	10,911	11,184	13,040	13,350	

Other Conditions

- Age from 5-75 years.
- Age at entry: not more than 55 years.
- Children below 5 years can be insured if the parents are concurrently insured with Bajaj Allianz.

Exclusions

The policy is not paid in case of:

- All diseases/injuries existing at the time of proposing this insurance.
- Any disease contracted during the first 30 days of commencement of the policy.
- Certain disease such as hernia, cataract, piles, sinusitis shall be covered after a waiting period of 2 years.
- Non allopathic medicine.
- Congenital diseases.
- All expenses arising from AIDS and related diseases.
- Cosmetic, aesthetic or related treatment.
- Use of intoxicating drugs, alcohol.
- Network Hospitals.

Critical Illness — Bajaj Allianz

Suitability

The policy can be availed by any one in the age group of 6 to 59 for a sum assured between Rs. 50,000 and Rs. 50,00,000.

Salient Features

- Policy provides financial assistance in the event of life insured contracting to any of the covered critical illness.
- The policy covers first heart attack, by-pass surgery (coronary artery), stroke, cancer, kidney failure, major organ transplantation, multiple sclerosis, aorta graft surgery, primary pulmonary arterial hypertension, and paralysis.
- Unlike in most medical insurance polices where settlement is on reimbursement basis, benefits under this plan are paid in advance.
- Expenses like donor expenses in a transplant surgery can be paid out of the amount received under this cover both in India and abroad.

- Claims procedure is simple and all the insured needs to do is submit the claim form along with certificate from the specialist confirming occurrence of the critical illness.
- Premiums paid are exempt under Section 80D of Income Tax Act.

Benefits

The benefit amount is payable as soon as the life insured contracts to any of the covered illness and survives 30 days after the diagnosis.

Premium Table

Indicative Premium Table – All the premiums are per annum.

Insured	*35 years*	*45 years*
1,00,000	300	800
2,00,000	600	1,600
5,00,000	1,500	4,000

Recommendations

Statistics have shown a rise in the incidence of life threatening diseases. Advancement of technology and rapid progress made in medical sciences has helped us cure such life threatening diseases. However, financial strain to both the affected person and his/her family is extremely painful. Hence, this policy which provides financial support in such event is recommended.

Exclusions

- Any critical illness for which care, treatment or advice was recommended or which was first manifested or contracted before the start of the policy period, or for which a claim has or could have been made under any earlier policy.
- Any critical illness diagnosed within the first 90 days.
- Death within 30 days following the diagnosis of the critical illness.
- Presence of HIV/AIDS infection.
- Treatment arising from or traceable to pregnancy or childbirth, including caesarian section. Birth defects.
- Occupational diseases.
- War, invasion, act of foreign enemy, terrorism, hostilities (whether war be declared or not), civil war, rebellion and/or revolution.
- Naval or military operations of the armed forces or air force and participation in operations requiring the use of arms or which are ordered by military authorities for combating terrorists, rebels and the like. Any natural peril.
- Consequential losses of any kind, be they by way of loss of profit, loss of opportunity, loss of gain, business interruption.

Health Shield – Royal Sundaram

Suitability

The policy covers hospitalisation expenses following sickness or accident and can be availed by any one in the age group of 90 days to 75 years.

Salient Features

- This is a medical insurance policy providing financial assistance in case of hospitalisation following any sickness or accident.
- Single policy can be issued to cover spouse, dependent children and dependent parents. Family discount of 10% can be availed of, if three persons or more are insured.
- Cumulative bonus: Sum insured is increased by 5% for every claim free year without any increase in premium. However, cumulative bonus is subject to a maximum of 50%.
- Premium paid under the policy, subject to a maximum of Rs. 10,000, is eligible for income tax exemption under Section 80 D of IT Act 1961.
- Policyholder can avail cashless hospitalisation facilities in certain networked hospitals provided pre-admission authorisation has been obtained from the insure/insurer's TPA.
- Policyholder can have online access to family's medical history, illnesses and information on hospitals using unique user id and password on www.royalsundaram.com.

Benefits

- The policy pays for all in-patient hospitalization expenses in case of accidents/illnesses covered under the policy up to the amount of the sum insured, provided hospitalisation is for a minimum period of 48 hours.
- Certain cases which does not require 48 hours hospitalization are also covered such as kidney stone removal, tonsillectomy, eye surgery, D&C and cataract. Cataract is covered only from the second year of insurance.
- Pre-hospitalisation and post hospitalisation expenses for 30 days and 60 days respectively are payable.
- Expenses on maternity are covered after 9 months of inception of cover.

Requirements

- Completed proposal form.

Recommendations

With the corporatisation of hospitals, cost of medical treatment is on the rise, at times making the treatment inaccessible to a common man. This policy enables the policyholder to avail of the best of the treatment without any financial constraints (Subject to sum assured limit).

27.3.3 Employee-Managed Systems

"Employer-managed health facilities", and the "reimbursement of health expenses by employers" are the other means of health insurance in India. Generally, the public sector undertakings and big industrial houses have their own dispensary and hospitals and provide medicines, etc, across the counter, usually within the company premises/township. These include defence services also. Also, educational institutions, particularly universities also provide medical services to their employees.

In addition, there are various medical reimbursement plans offered by employers for private medical expenses in the private sector including commercial banks and autonomous institutions. Also, in some organisations we may find a self-insurance system known as medical benefit or medical allowance scheme. Under this scheme, employees incurring medical expenses are required to submit their claims to their employers for reimbursement, and reimbursements are not linked to their individual contribution. Such coverages generally vary according to the employee's salary or designation. Overall, the performance of these systems in India have been satisfactory.

27.3.4 NGO Systems

Health facilities are also provided by voluntary and charitable or Non-government organisations(NGOs). Some of the important NGOs are Child In Need Institute (CINI), Self-employed Women's Association (SEWA), Streehitkarni and Parivar Seva Sanstha. The health care facilities offered by these organisations are a part of their main objectives. Though, these are not exactly health insurance programmes, yet they have potential to generate awareness and associate themselves with the major health insurers.

27.4 Imperatives for Health Insurance in India

Health insurance in India need an immediate attention in the following areas:

- Focus on public spending on primary and health care services
- Reformation of ESIS and CGHS
- Withdrawal of public services on "ability to pay basis"
- Restructuring of premiums
- Increase in visibility and awareness
- Discourage specific exclusions for disease in health care policies
- Encouragement of health insurance for those specially vulnerable.

27.5 Micro Health Insurance In India

Micro-insurance refers to protection of assets and lives against insurable risks of target populations."

Microinsurance – A Bit of History

Microinsurance is not a new invention. The "Industrial insurance" sold at factory gates in American cities in the early 1900s made the Metropolitan Life insurance Company the largest company - not just insurance company- in the world at that time. Their industrial insurance was the forerunner of today's commercial microinsurance. It was simply a response to a market demand managed in a manner that made the products appropriate for the market. The delivery channels - agents at the factory gates - were specific to this market. The premiums reflected the particular risks of the factory worker market. Coverage responded to the workers' specific needs. Premium collection - on payday as the workers exited the factories - was efficient. In short, industrial insurance was a response to a market niche that provided access to quality insurance products for low income workers, and access to a huge market for the insurers.

From industrial workers making premium payments at the factory gates, to increased efficiency of factory management collecting premiums, or even covering their employees directly, this historical microinsurance moved into the mainstream. From here, many developed countries were able to generate substantial pools of investment funds that helped drive ever-growing economies.

The Salient Features of the IRDA regulations on micro insurance are :

- Health insurance sold under the "general micro-insurance product" or the "life micro-insurance product" definition must cover ("cap") no less than Rs. 5,000 (per individual) or Rs. 10,000 (per household). Although not specifically stated in the Regulations, it is assumed that this cap applies for the entire period of the contract (rather than to a single episode of illness).
- The minimal period of coverage is one year. The Regulations do not specify the terms for renewal, and this implies that insurers could decide to renew or not to renew any policy at the end of the affiliation period.

Incidentally, insurers could also change the terms of the policy and the premium it commands, which *de facto* means that insurers could cherry pick. And insurers can decide whether to accept an offer of insurance in the first place or refuse it.

- Minimum and maximum age of the insured is left to insures' discretion. The Regulations do not require the insurer to justify such exclusions, or to maintain the same age limitations for all insured.

Research suggests that the poor in Indian are willing to pay more than Rs. 600 per family per year for health insurance (10), we have found that most of the poor in India are able to pay in the range of Rs. 150 to Rs. 250 for a family per annum (11). Premiums are usually collected during a specific period and this coincides with period of high economic activity in the community. This is community rated premium and is applicable irrespective of the risk status of the individual.

For this premium, the insured usually get protected against hospitalisation expenses, similar to the 'mediclaim' policies. While many NGOs also provide primary and ambulstory care, this is usually from other sources and not the insurance fund. This naturally makes the entire package more attractive and acceptable to the individual (12). Many of the MHI schemes have realised the need to minimise exclusions, *e.g.* at Karuna trust, Student's Health Home and ASHWINI, all conditions (including pre-existing ones and deliveries) are covered. In some cases, where the MHI scheme has linked up with an insurance company; there are exclusions, *e.g.* SEWA, deliveries are not covered. These schemes usually have an upper limit to the sum assured, and this ranges from Rs. 1250 (at RAHA) to Rs. 200,000 (at Yeshasvini). Most upper limits of sum assured ranged between Rs. 5,000 to Rs. 10,000 during the period of our study and covered most of the hospitalization expenses. However, this low sum assured also implies that the insured patient is not fully protected (13) and needs to make some supplementary out of pocket payment.

Claims and reimbursements are usually managed by the NCO staff. Wherever possible, cashless systems have been introduced, though the reimbursement mechanism also exists especially in the "agent" model. In the SEWA model, the insurance company has delegated this responsibility to the 'Insurance committee' of SEWA. This committee meets monthly and processes the submitted claims. These claims are either accepted or rejected and the decision is forwarded to the insurance company who reimburses accordingly. This form of social audit has been very effective in controlling fraud and has balanced the information asymmetry that is the bane with insurance products.

Micro-insurance refers to the protection of assets and lives against insurable risks of target populations such as micro-entrepreneurs, small farmers and the landless, women and low income people through formal, institutions. Such products are often bounded with micro-savings and micro-credit, thereby allocating scarce resources to micro-investments with the highest marginal rates of return. Microinsurance is the most underdeveloped part of microfinance. Yet various schemes exist that are viable, benefiting both the institutions and their clients. Such schemes have generally served two major purposes: (*i*) they have contributed to loan security; and (*ii*) they have served as instruments of resource mobilization. The greatest challenge for microinsurance lies in the combination of viability and sustainability with outreach.

Micro Insurance Delivery Channels

- Partnerships between insurers and distribution agents like cooperatives and MFis (*e.g.* Zurich Botivla and Banco Sol).
- Self-insuring MFis that assume the risk of offering insurance to their clients (*e.g.* Spandana, India).
- Informal mutual assistance schemes (*e.g.* burial societies, South Africa).
- Healthcare providers offering health care schemes (*e.g.* Nkoranza Community Health Insurance Plan, Chana).

- Regulated insurance companies that serve the low income market directly (*e.g.* Delta Life, Bangladesh).
- Insurance companies that target the low. Income market through retailers (*e.g.* Seguros Aztecan and Electra, Mexico).
- Community-based schemes that pool funds, carry risk and manage a relationship with a healthcare provider (L'Union Technique *de la* Mutualite Malience, Mali).

Most Common Types of Microinsurance Products

- Credit life
- Term life / Personal accident
- Savings life
- Property insurance
- Endowment life
- Health insurance
- Agriculture

Key Stakeholders in the Development of Microinsurance

- Potential and current policyholders
- Actual and potential delivery channels
- Risk carriers
- Industry associations, networks
- Insurance infrastructure: training, technical assistance, research, data warehousing.
- Policymakers, regulators and supervisors
- Bonous and development agencies.

Gross Direct Premium Health Business

Rs. in lakhs

Insurers	*2008-09*	*2007-08*
National	89722	69036
New India	135567	120942
Oriental	70986	53263
United	90072	69496
Public-total	386347	312736
Royal Sundaram	11431	10378
Reliance	31082	27562
Iffco-tokio	14099	11402
Tata aig	7389	6830
ICICI Lombard	97380	8159
Bajaj allianz	33343	24340
Cholamandalam	16589	10938
Hdfcergo	5601	2823
Future generali	5081	343
Universal sompo	308	
Shriram #		
Bharti Axa #	151	
PRIVATE-TOTAL	222453	176705
GRAND TOTAL	608600	489442

Key Terms

- Heath insurance
- Mediclaim
- CGHS
- NGO sponsored systems
- Medical Reimbursement
- Health insurance systems
- CSIS

Questions for Review

1. Define Health Insurance. Briefly trace the history of health insurance in India.
2. List the various health insurance systems in India. What is the opinion as to the performance of these systems?
3. Evaluate the medicare plans of LIC and GIC. Do you think that life insurance products can provide an umbrella cover which includes health insurance?
4. Write short notes on :
   (a) Mediclaim policy of GIC
   (b) Health Care issues in India
   (c) Micro insurance.

Rural Insurance

Chapter
28

Chapter Objectives

After reading this chapter you will be able to understand :

- *Need and Potential of Rural Insurance*
- *Legal Framework for Rural Insurance*
- *Various Rural Insurance Policies*

28.1 Need and Potential of Rural Insurance

The insurance sector has been mostly confined to cities. However, in the rural areas where human life and income-generating rural assets need more protection, there is tremendous scope for developing insurance business. The rural sector so far has been grossly neglected since last 50 years from the privileges of insurance cover, though a silent economic revolution can be seen now in the villages.

With the opening of the insurance sector to the private sector and foreign companies, the time has come when the government should pay serious attention to covering the rural areas. While it is true that access to insurance cover depends on the literacy/awareness levels and assured income, well-planned and organised efforts by committed private sector companies can yield rich dividends from the rural areas. This is because:

(1) A large number of rural districts have witnessed significant growth and prosperity;

(2) Access to reliable and authentic data and information has improved considerably, which can enable quick and correct decision-making;

(3) There are specific functionaries and agencies in the rural areas, which can help, explore and exploit insurance business in the untapped rural market.

Rural Banking as Catalyst

"With a decline in the public investment in agriculture, the rural banking system has been encouraging the farm development through provision of credit facilities for production of crops including horticulture, plantation, forestry; purchase of farm equipment; livestock and fish farming; irrigation facilities and installation of diesel engines etc. Bank credit is also provided for establishing village/cottage industries, stocking/supplying farm inputs and cattle-feed, and business and trade purposes. From 1969-70 to 1999-2000, up to Rs 3.1 crore has been provided to the farm sector."[1]

"With enhanced incomes, and further supplemented by bank credit, the rural population is acquiring consumer durables, constructing houses, purchasing vehicles, computers, and so on.

All these assets need to be protected from damage/loss, natural or man-made. Thus, the rural areas offer enormous opportunities for committed private insurance companies in both life and non-life insurance schemes."

The efforts by the private insurance players, of course, backed by business, can have direct positive impact on rural development and the economic growth. Insurance in the farm sector can supplement the advances of science and technology.

1. Mr. A.R. Patel web article on Rural Insurance.

Both the conventional players, LIC and GIC have been providing some insurance cover in rural areas. But, they are insufficient to meet the exact requirements of the rurals. There is an immense need of creating awareness among people. The rural customers often contend that the claim lodgement and settlement procedure is time-consuming and cumbersome. "Cattle insurance under the government-sponsored Integrated Rural Development Programme and crop insurance have not met with the expected results."

"Besides, the village profile available with each of the branches of nationalised/public sector banks contain exhaustive data on the population, cultivating households, categories of farmers, classification of workers, livestock, cropping pattern, farm equipment and machinery and so on.

There are more than 1,75,000 rural credit outlets in addition to the offices of the District Rural Development Agency, the District Industries Centre, and the District Development Manager of nationalised banks and Lead District Manager of the Lead Bank. All these institutions and agencies can offer considerable information to insurance companies."

Modus Operandi

Those willing to enter into rural insurance or improvise must do the following:

- Design tailored products.
  Establish efficient methods of premium collection and claims settlements.
- Create awareness for the need of insurance products.
- Educated unemployed youths of the villages can be trained and become valuable assets for the companies. While insurance companies are eager to build their business in the urban areas, there is a hitherto untapped potential for business in the rural areas, which can be exploited.
- The Centre and the State governments must encourage private and foreign insurance companies to enter the rural areas, and provide protection to rural assets from damage and loss due to natural and man-made calamities. For this purpose, reasonable and need-based concessions/relief in taxation and subsidies, required infrastructural facilities and administrative support must be extended, at least for ten years. The government may consider appointing an Expert Committee on Rural Insurance to work out the modalities for private and foreign companies interested in entering the rural areas.

(The paragraphs in quotes mentioned in this section are the views of Mr. A.R. Patel — a Mumbai-based rural credit specialist.)

28.2 Legal Framework

The Insurance Regulatory and Development Authority Act, 1999 (para 19; First schedule) has amended the Section 32B and 32C of the Insurance Act, 1938 as under:

Section 32B

Every insurer shall, after the commencement of Insurance Regulatory and Development Authority Act, 1999, undertake such percentages of life insurance business and general insurance business in the rural and social sector, as may be specified, in the *Official Gazette* by the authority, in this behalf.

Section 32C

Every insurer shall, after the commencement of Insurance Regulatory and Development Authority Act, 1999, discharge the obligations specified under Section 32B to provide life insurance or general insurance policies to those residing in the rural sector, workers in the unorganised sector or informal sector or economically vulnerable or backward classes of the society and other categories of persons as may be specified by the regulations made by the authority and such insurance policies shall include insurance for crops.

The IRDA Regulations 2000 makes it compulsory for the insurers, existing and new to promote the rural insurance.[2] The regulations prescribe for undertaking benchmark percentages for insurances in the rural insurance sector for the players.

The *rural sector* has been defined as a place which, as per the latest census, the population is not more than 5,000, the density of population is not more than 400 per sq. km. and at least 75% of the male working population is engaged in agriculture.

The regulations provide that those who are proposing to carry on the life insurance business in the year 2000 or later, are required by these regulations to write in the rural sector, at least 5% of the total policies written directly in the first financial year, 7% in the second financial year and so on. In case of non-life insurance, 2% of the total gross premium income written direct in that year, 3% in the second year and so on. Also, the authority may revise the obligation once in 5 years.

28.3 VARIOUS RURAL INSURANCE POLICIES

Aqua Culture Insurance

Suitability: This policy is suitable for licensed farms or farms provided in accordance with the Government Notification for growing brackish water shrimp/fresh water prawns by adopting extensive/modified extensive/ semi-intensive systems.

Salient Features: The Policy grants cover under two sections:

Section I: Basic cover, which covers only losses due to natural calamities.

Section II: Comprehensive cover granting cover for disease also. Policy is usually given for a period of 4½ months.

The basic cover provides compensation for total loss of shrimp/prawns due to:

Summer kill, pollution from external source, poisoning, riot, strike and malicious acts of third parties, terrorism, explosion/implosion, air craft and aerial devices or articles dropped therefrom, impact damage, earthquake, storm, tempest, cyclone, flood and inundation, volcanic eruption and other convulsions of nature. Comprehensive cover in addition to basic cover encompasses death due to diseases except those caused by bad management and nutritional deficiencies.

Benefits: In the event of a fortuitous event resulting in a loss, the basis of loss settlement will be the sum insured, which is fixed as follows:

Sum Insured = Number of seeds released X expected survival rate (%) X expected average body weight in grams X input cost per Kg.

For losses upto 4th fortnight stage, maximum liability shall be restricted to 80% of the input cost only. From 5th fortnight onwards claims are admitted as a percentage of biomass.

Deductions towards salvage are made.

Where the percentage of loss at any stage equals or exceeds 80 % of the total shrimps/prawns insured, it will be treated as total loss.

Premium: Premium rates have been fixed as follows:

	Zones	*Section-I (Basic)*	*Section-II (Comprehensive)*
(a)	For highly cyclone prone zones	3%	7½%
(b)	Others	2%	6%

2. Annexure 22-A.

Requirements: The farm should obtain statutory licence for setting up and conducting aqua-culture operations in the area as per Government legislation.

The ponds should be prepared as per prescribed, recommended and established standards. The seed should be healthy, of good quality, selected as per prescribed norms and obtained from well-known source. The seed should be of high quality and procured from reputed firms. Holiday period as recommended by MPEDA or such Government agency should be observed.

All matters concerning farming practices, norms, stipulations; guidelines recommended by competent Government agency, fisheries department research institutes, fisheries college etc. should be complied with.

Cattle Insurance

Suitability: This policy is suitable for the farmer - who owns the cattle and the banks/financial institutions which have financed the purchase of cattle under IDP /DRDA /DPAP schemes.

Salient Features: "Cattle" refers to Cows and Buffaloes, Stud Bulls, Bullocks, He Buffaloes, Calves and Heifers. The Policy is usually given for a period of 12 months or for a long term of 3 to 5 years as per term of loan. The policy covers loss due to death, accident, illness or disease of the animal.

A qualified veterinary officer's certificate is necessary for accepting the proposal and also for fixing the value of the cattle which forms the basis for loss settlement. The policy also covers transit of cattle from the place of purchase to stable located within 80 Km. For transit above the stipulated distance, additional premium @ 1 % is charged.

Benefits: The policy pays for the market value of the animal prior to the accident or the sum insured whichever is less. A veterinary surgeon's certificate will be necessary to claim the amount in the case of death of the cattle.

Premium

Premium is charged on the market value of the cattle at the following rates.

S.No.	*Type of Animal*	*Rate of Premium*	
		For Death Cover	*Additional Rate for permanent total disability and from yielding milk*
1.	Animals financed under Government Scheme	2.25 %	0.85 %
2.	Non scheme Animals	4.00 %	1.00 %
3.	Exotic Animals	6.00 %	1.00 %

Minimum Premium of Rs. 50/- per policy is chargeable. Discounts are allowed in the case where full advance premium is paid under long-term policies and group policies. However premium is loaded in case of adverse claim ratio.

Requirements: Veterinary examination and tagging of the animals is necessary for granting insurance cover. Natural identification marks and colour should be clearly noted in the proposal form along with the veterinarian's report.

Indian economy is based on agriculture and about 75% of the population still depend on agriculture, dairy farming and agro-based small-scale industry. Sound agricultural base can only lead to economic stability. Hence, farmers have to be adequately protected against the various hazards. It is for this reason GIC has introduced various rural insurance schemes not only to offer financial protection to rural masses but also to fulfil the social objective of their upliftment. Chief among such schemes is the cattle insurance policy whereby the livelihood of the farmer is protected against accidental causes. Thus, this cover attains utmost importance amongst rural insurance policies.

Failed Well Insurance

Suitability: Wells financed by Co-operative societies, financial institutions, banks, Government sponsored schemes can be covered under this policy against the risk of low or no yield provided the selection of site is made on scientific principles and methods.

Salient Features: The well sites located in areas mapped by state geological departments having potential for borewells for yields upto 1000 gallons per hour are covered by this policy. Yield will be tested by pumping intermittently for 6 hours by a 2HP/3HP submersible pump.

If the yield is below 500 gallons, the well shall be deemed to be a total failure.

If the yield is between 500 to 1000 GPH, policy pays for the proportion the actual yield bears to assured yield.

Following types of wells are covered under this policy:

- Shallow tube wells
- Filter point wells
- Dry wells
- Bore wells
- Dug cum bore wells

Benefits : Drilling cost at Rs.160 per metre upto a depth of 80-90 metres is payable subject to a limit of Rs.15,000 per borewell. The following costs are included.

Transportation of equipment upto Rs.350/-; Yield testing charges upto Rs.500/-; Spot investigation charges upto Rs. 250; Labour charges for fixing casing pipe; cleaning and dewatering charges.

However, the following are excluded:

- Expenses incurred but not specifically covered.
- Natural calamities, riot and strike, quality of water, structural failure cessation of work, wilful act and negligence, defective design and material, bad workman-ship, war and allied perils. Policy is subject to an excess of 17.5% of claim amount.

Premium: Rate of premium is 17.5% of sum insured.

Requirements: The proposal shall be accompanied by site selection report obtained from qualified geo-hydrologist approved by the insurers. The test is to be based on geophysical methods only, such as electrical relativity logging, vertical sounding etc., taking into account at least 250 m between two wells. The permission from local Municipal authority for digging the well and signature of bank wherever applicable shall be obtained. Open wells shall have a minimum diameter of 10 ft and depth of 30 ft. Borewells shall have a diameter of 6 inches and installed upto hard rock zone and properly sealed. Wells should be rested for 24 hours before testing.

It is not rare that despite the scientific exploration, yield in the wells may not match the guaranteed yield. It is in such a situation, this insurance comes to the rescue of the well owner. Thus, this cover is recommended.

Farmers' Package Insurance

Suitability: This policy is suitable for the farmers who wish to cover all their property and assets under a single package policy. The Policy can be issued either to individual farmers or a group.

Salient Features: Personal effects, household goods, village/cottage industrial units belonging to the farmer are covered under this insurance.

This Policy has 14 Sections offering coverage as follows:

Section 1: Covers the residential building of the farmer including contents and farm produce kept in the building from fire and allied perils.

Section 2: Covers the loss or damage to stock of farm produce from fire and allied perils. Stocks in godown and in open are covered.

Section 3: Covers all the contents in the premises against burglary, house-breaking and terrorist acts.

Section 4: Covers loss or damage to TV /VCP /VCR of the insured due to fire/burglary/theft, electrical or mechanical breakdown of accidental external means.

Section 5: The policy covers loss or damage to pedal cycle by accident, burglary, house-breaking, or fire.

Section 6: Covers the insured and his family against personal accident and death due to accidental reasons.

Section 7: Provides fire cover to artisans, tiny sector units, village and cottage industries.

Section 8: Cover death of animals due to diseases or accident including fire/lightning/famine.

Section 9: Covers agricultural pumpset upto 10 HP capacity from the risks of fire/theft/burglary and breakdown risks.

Section 10: Covers over 500 poultry birds in the farm located within the insured premises due to any accident.

Section 11: Covers fraud committed by any salaried employee of the insured in the premises.

Section 12: Covers accompanied baggage lost or damaged during travel anywhere in India.

Section 13: Covers animal drawn vehicle from risks of damage to the vehicle, personal accident, third party liability from accidental causes. The policy also covers the life of the driver.

Section 14: Covers loss or damage to agricultural tractors and its accessories due to accidental reasons. Unnamed passengers (upto 6) travelling on such tractors are covered.

Benefits: Policy offers compensation as per limits of liability / as per sum insured set against each section.

Premium: Rates of premium are fixed for individual sections. If more than 4 sections are covered, upto 15% discount is available. When more than 6 sections are covered, upto 20% discount is allowed.

This policy has been introduced keeping the needs of the rural farmer in view. As this policy provides a comprehensive cover against all the risks which can be envisaged and also eliminates the need to take various policies to cover different risks, the policy is extremely beneficial, economical and thus recommended.

Fish Insurance

Suitability: This policy is devised for fresh water fish rearers to cover stock of fry/fingerlings/fish/breeders of breeds like Rohu, Katla, Mrigal, Common Carp, Silver Carp or any other recognised breeds.

Salient Features: The policy covers total loss to the fish due to accident or disease during the period of insurance. The cover includes loss due to pollution, poisoning, malicious act by third parties, riot and strike. Partial loss of any kind is not covered.

Flood and allied risks are covered as an extension on payment of extra premium.

The policy can also be extended to cover the fish rearing pond, bunds, sluices etc. against fire and natural calamities on payment of additional premium.

Policy is issued for the rearing period subject to a maximum period of 12 months from the date of stocking.

Benefits: Since the value of fish increases due to growth and inputs, settlement of any loss will be effected as per the scheduled valuation fixed on fortnightly basis (the table of valuation will be attached to the policy). The value depends on the cost of fry/fingerlings, cost of input and other incidental expenses.

Premium: Insurance has to be effected on the sum insured of final stage of rearing period (Peak value). Premium will be charged @ 2.4% on the peak value. Flood perils are covered by charging 1% extra in non-flood prone areas and 2% in case of flood prone areas. Fish rearing ponds can be covered @ 0.5% of the value of ponds in non-flood prone area and 1 % in flood prone areas.

Requirements: The proposal form should be duly completed and certified by the Government fishery official. If the pond is subsidised by Bank/FFDA, a copy of the techno-economic feasibility report is to be provided for deciding the sum insured/peak value/input cost for the items stated in the declaration sheet. Specimen copies of daily fish culture records are to be submitted. For flood cover to bunds, a certificate from Government fishery extension officer regarding construction and viability of bunds is to be provided.

Even though the fish farming is lucrative, offers high yields and profits, the experience during the recent years has been especially bad both for the farmers as well as the insurance companies. Insurance companies therefore adopt strict underwriting practices and compliance of warranties to minimise losses and also extend their technical assistance, which explains why it makes good sense in taking this insurance.

Floriculture Insurance

Suitability: Growers of commercial flowering plants such as rose, crysanthemum and jasmine having adequate agricultural expertise in the subject may take out this policy.

Salient Features: This policy covers only plants whilst growing in the farm/green house/poly-house against total loss or damage due to

- Fire including forest fire and bush fire
- Lightning
- Acts of terrorism, riot and strike
- Storm, hailstorm, cyclone, flood and inundation
- Earthquake
- Impact damage by rail/road/air vehicles and animals.

Additional Covers: Policy may be extended to cover risks of loss due to drought, pests, and diseases specific to flowering plants.

Benefits: The Policy covers the input costs incurred till the time of loss. These are the recurring expenses incurred to raise/maintain the plants such as soil preparation, fertiliser, manure, cost of plants/seeds/saplings, cost of planting/sowing and Pruning, pesticides, insecticides, irrigation, labour charges and other costs specifically covered. Claims exceeding 50% of the total sum insured per hectare or Rs. 1,000/- whichever is less only shall be admitted. Each and every claim is subject to an excess of 20%.

Premium: Premium is charged on the sum insured opted as follows:

Risk Cover	*Rate*
Basic cover	1.25%- 2.5%
Under glass house/Green House in open field	
Additional Cover (Pests/diseases & drought)	
Under glass house/Green house in open field	0.75%-1.5%

Requirements: At the time of taking out insurance, the plants should be at least one month old after plantation/transplantation i.e., the plants should be well established in the soil. Insurance cover will be granted subject to pre-acceptance inspection by insurers and feasibility report from State Agricultural Directorate/Expert's opinion being received.

Floriculture requires constant supervision and maintenance. Despite all the precautions, the plants are exposed to risks from pests and unknown diseases or action of natural calamities. It is for this reason, coverage of the plantation under this policy is strongly recommended.

Lift Irrigation/Sprinkler Insurance

Suitability: This policy is suitable for the agriculturist using the lift irrigation or sprinkler installation for cultivation.

Salient Features: This policy covers loss or damage to intake well, delivery chambers, jackwell, pump-house, water storage tank, pipe lines, cables, starters and motors of the lift irrigation system or sprinkler installation arising out of

- Fire and allied perils
- Flood, earthquake and land slide
- Accidental damage to machinery and pipe line
- Bursting of pipe lines
- Theft

Benefits: On the occurrence of a loss, claims will be paid for the cost of restoration to the extent of sum insured set against each item.

An excess of 1 % the machinery value subject to a minimum of Rs.1000/- per claim is applicable. Theft claims are paid on receipt of non-traceable certificate from the police.

Premium: A rate of 1% on the cost of the entire system is applicable for insurance under this policy. The sum insured shall be the new replacement cost including freight, customs duty and erection costs. Terrorist risk can be included in the cover at an extra premium.

Requirements: Duly filled in proposal giving the details of the machinery and their individual replacement costs should be submitted.

Loss due to breakdown, theft or accidental reasons to the machinery not only is a loss in itself, but also has consequential effect that the crop is affected. It is necessary that the system is repaired/reinstated to mitigate the losses. This policy comes to aid in such situations and is therefore recommended.

Plantation/Horticulture Insurance

Suitability: This policy is suitable for individual farmer-owner or tenant engaged in cultivation of horticultural trees or plantations or an association/organised and registered body of farmers engaged in cultivation of specified crops. Also bodies procuring inputs, processing/marketing of the produce can take this policy.

Salient Features: Horticultural trees/orchards such as citrus fruits (Orange, Lime, Sweet Lime), Grapes, Chikoo, Pomegranate, Banana and Plantations such as Rubber, Eucalyptus, Poplar, Sugarcane, Betelvine, Cardamom, Sweet Chilli, Oil Palm, Teakwood, Strawberry, Tea, Apple and Coconut can be covered by this policy. The Policy covers loss or damage due to fire (including forest and bush fire), lightning, storm, hail storm, cyclone and other such natural calamities/acts of terrorist to fruits in respect of horticultural crops

Tree in Case of Plantations

Additional Covers: Unseasonal rains and frost in case of grape vines and tea, loss or damage by wild animals in case of sugarcane, banana; drought and disease in case of banana, flood and inundation in case of teak plantations; disease and pests in case of tea plantations and betelvine are the additional covers available.

Benefits: Claims are paid to the extent of 80% of the assessed loss subject to the overall limit of the sum insured. Sum insured shall be based on the cost of cultivation i.e. input cost or cost of raising/development of trees. Only such claims exceeding 10% of sum insured per acre or minimum of Rs.1000/- shall be admitted. Input costs on account of loss or damage to the horticultural crop/plantations are covered. Loss of yield is not covered.

Premium: Premium shall be charged for different crops as follows:

	Type of Crop	*Rate*
1.	Horticultural Crops	5.0%
	*Citrus fruits, Chikoo, Pomegranate, Banana, Grapes	
2.	Plantations	1.25%
	* Rubber, Eucalyptus, Poplar, Teak wood, Tea, Mango	
3.	Sugarcane	1.25%
4.	Betelvine	6.0%
5.	Sweet Chilli (Capsicum)	4.4%
6.	Coconut	
	3 months to 3 years	0.60
	4 years to 7 years	0.50
	8 years and upto 50 years	1.50%

Requirements: Inter cropping may be done only if it does not interfere with normal growth and health of the trees. No smoking or cooking shall be allowed in the open fields and within 30 m of the property insured. Dry vegetation & leaves should be removed periodically.

Recommendations: Plantations are exposed to a variety of perils ranging from pests to forest fires. It becomes very difficult for the farmer to come out of the effects of loss in the absence of comprehensive insurance cover. It is for this reason, this insurance policy is devised which is very popular and hence recommended.

Poultry Insurance

Suitability: This policy is suitable for the poultry farmers, the beneficiaries of schemes sponsored by DRDA, DPAP, IRDP and financial institutions providing assistance to poultry units.

Salient Features: This comprehensive policy is issued to cover poultry consisting of Broiler chicks/Layer chickens/ Cocks & hens in the poultry farms. A minimum number of 100 broilers/500 layers or 200 birds per batch in the hatchery can be covered under the policy.

The policy provides compensation for loss to birds dead due to accident (including fire, lightning, flood, cyclone, earthquake, riot, strike, and terrorist act); diseases contacted or occurring during the period of insurance.

Benefits: Policy provides compensation when the mortality rate of the birds exceeds the following limits.

Bird	*Age*	*Mortality Rate*
Broilers	1 day to 6 Weeks	More than 5 % of the batch size
Layers	1 day to 8 weeks	More than 5 % of the batch size
	9th week to 20th week	More than 3 % of numbers at beginning of 9th week
	21st week to 72nd week	More than 1 % of numbers at the beginning of 21st week.

In the event of death of birds 80% of the bird value or as decided by the veterinary surgeon whichever is less is paid. There is an additional deductible of 20% in case of Gumbore disease.

Requirements: A Certificate from a qualified veterinarian is required. In case of layer farms having more than 5000 birds, insurance company 's veterinary officer or panel doctor shall carry out inspection. All the birds in the farm should be insured. Standard practices of poultry rearing, record keeping shall have to be practised.

Out break of epidemics/natural calamities such as cyclone result in widespread loss to the poultry affecting the financial position of the poultry owner. The policy comes handy in such a situation and benefits the farmer.

National Agricultural Insurance Scheme (NAIS)

Premium: Premium rates depend on the age of the bird; whether or not they are financed under IRDP scheme as follows:

Bird	*Age*	*Premium* For IRDP scheme	*Rate* Non IRDP scheme
Broilers	1 day to 8 weeks	0.25 % per bird/batch	1.5% (6.0% p.a.)
	1 day to 6 weeks	1.00 % per bird p.a.	1.2% (4.8% p.a.)
Layers	1 day to 20 weeks	–	3.2 %
	21 weeks to 72 weeks	–	3.5 %
	1 day to 72 weeks	0.8 % per bird	5.5 %
Parent stock (hatchery)	–	–	5.0%

(Rashtriya Krishi Bima Yojana - RKBY) – Coverage and Claims Settlement

The objectives of the NAIS are :

1. To provide insurance coverage and financial support to the farmers in the event of failure of any of the notified crop as a result of natural calamities, pests & diseases.
2. To encourage the farmers to adopt progressive farming practices, high value inputs and higher technology in Agriculture.
3. To help stabilise farm incomes, particularly in disaster years.

NAIS covers all farmers including sharecroppers, tenant farmers growing the notified crops in the notified areas are eligible for coverage. The Scheme covers following groups of farmers:

a. ***On a compulsory basis*** :All farmers growing notified crops and availing Seasonal Agricultural Operations (SAO) loans from Financial Institutions i.e. Loanee Farmers.

b. ***On a voluntary basis***: All other farmers growing notified crops (i.e., Non-Loanee farmers) who opt for the Scheme.

The cover extend to yield losses due to non preventable risks, viz.:

a. Natural Fire and Lightning

b. Storm, Hailstorm, Cyclone, Typhoon, Tempest, Hurricane, Tornado etc.

c. Flood, Inundation and Landslide

d. Drought, Dry spells

e. Pests/Diseases etc.

Losses arising out of war & nuclear risks, malicious damage & other preventable risks are excluded. There are three levels of Indemnity, viz., 90%, 80% & 60% corresponding to Low Risk, Medium Risk & High Risk areas available for all crops (cereals, millets, pulses & oilseeds and annual commercial / annual horticultural crops) based on Coefficient of Variation (C.V.) in yield of past 10 years' data. However, the insured farmers of unit area may opt for higher level of indemnity on payment of additional premium based on actuarial rates. The Threshold yield (TY) or Guaranteed yield for a crop in an Insurance Unit is the moving average based on past three years Average Yield in case of Rice & Wheat and five years Average Yield in case of other crops, multiplied by the level of indemnity.

Calculation of Coverage and Indemnity

If the 'Actual Yield' (AY) per hectare of the insured crop for the defined area [on the basis of requisite number of Crop Cutting Experiments (CCEs)] in the insured season, falls short of the specified 'Threshold Yield' (TY), all the insured farmers growing that crop in the defined area are deemed to have suffered shortfall in their yield. The Scheme seeks to provide coverage against such contingency. 'Indemnity' is calculated as per the following formula :

$$\frac{\text{Shortfall in Yield}}{\text{Threshold yield}} \text{ X Sum Insured for the farmer}$$

{Shortfall in Yield = 'Threshold Yield – Actual Yield' for the Defined Area}.

GIC is the implementing agency (IA) of the scheme. Loss assessment and modified indemnity procedures in case of occurrence of localized perils, such as hailstorm, landslide, cyclone and flood where settlement of claims is on individual basis, shall be formulated by IA in coordination with State / UT Govt. The loss assessment of localized risks on individual basis will be experimented in limited areas initially and shall be extended in the light of operational experience gained. The District Revenue administration will assist IA in assessing the extent of loss. The A&O expenses are shared equally by the Central Government & respective State Government on sunset basis [100% in 1st year, 80% in 2nd year, 60% in 3rd year, 40% in 4th year, 20% in 5th year and 'zero' thereafter].

Procedure for Approval & Settlement of Claims

The claims are dependent upon the yield data supplied by the states. Once the Yield Data is received from the State/UT Govt. as per the prescribed cut-off dates, claims are estimated and settled by the insurers. The claim cheques along with claim particulars are released to the individual Nodal Banks. The Banks at the grass-root level, in turn, credit the accounts of the individual farmers and display the particulars of beneficiaries on their notice board. In the context of localised Phenomenon viz. Hailstorm, landslide, cyclone and flood, the IA prescribes the procedure to estimate such losses at individual farmer level in consultation with DAC/State/UT. Settlement of such claims is on individual basis between IA and insured.

To meet Catastrophic losses, a Corpus Fund has been created with contributions from the Government of India and State / UT on 50:50 basis. A portion of Calamity Relief Fund (CRF) shall be used for contribution to the Corpus Fund. The Corpus Fund is managed by Implementing Agency (IA).

Selection of the Banks for claims payment has been made on the basis of Service Area Approach (SAA) of RBI or at the option of the Banks (where Co-operative Banks have good network). The Department of Agriculture, Agricultural Statistics, Directorate of Economics and Statistics, Department of Co-operation, Revenue Department of the State Government will be actively involved in smooth implementation of the Scheme.

Cattle Insurance

Cattle insurance covers indigenous cross-bred and exotic cattle owned by private owners and financial institutions i.e. Bank financed, Military diary farms, Co-opt. Dairies, Corporate dairies. The cover extends to death of cattle due to accident inclusive of flood, cyclone, famine or any other fortuitous circumstances, diseases, surgical operations, riot & strike, terrorism, earthquake. In case of transit beyond specified distance by Road or Rail by additional premium has to be paid by the insured. The cover excludes losses due to malicious act, accident/ diseases contracted prior to commencement of risk, transit by air or sea, intentional slaughter, theft or clandestine sales, missing of insured animals, war and allied perils, nuclear exclusion clause.

This policy covers the animals like Cows, buffaloes, bullocks, camels, sheep, goats, horses, ponies, mules etc. Identification of animals and valuation is as per the veterinary certificate and or declaration of the purchase committee. Claims for cattle insurance are generally settled for the sum insured or market value prior to illness, whichever is less. In case of PTD of animals, the claim will be restricted to 75% of the sum insured. In order to claim, notice must be given to the insurance company with prescribed time.

Documents to be submitted at the time of the claim:

(1) Identity proof of the cattle exposed to adverse events

(2) Veterinary Doctor Certificate

(3) Claim form duly filled

Ordinarily the claims must be settled within 15 days from the lodgement and completion of formalities. Recently, the companies are using RFID tags to prevent fraudulent claims.

Livestock Insurance Scheme

The Livestock Insurance Scheme has been formulated with the twin objective of providing protection mechanism to the farmers and cattle rearers against any eventual loss of their animals due to death and to demonstrate the benefit of the insurance of livestock to the people and popularize it with the ultimate goal of attaining qualitative improvement in livestock and their products.

Guidelines for Implementation of Livestock Insurance Scheme

1. Livestock Sector is an important sector of national, especially rural economy. The supplemental income derived from rearing of livestock is a great source of support to the farmers facing uncertainties of crop production, apart from providing sustenance to poor and landless farmers.
2. For promotion of the livestock sector, it has been felt that along with providing more effective for disease control and improvement of genetic quality of animals, a mechanism of assured protection to the farmers and cattle rearers needs to be devised against eventual losses of such animals. In this direction, the Government has approved a new centrally sponsored scheme on Livestock Insurance on pilot basis to be implemented during the 10th Plan. The continuance of the scheme beyond that will be based on a critical assessment of its performance during this period. The broad guidelines, subject to the plausible discretion of the Chief Executive Officers, to be followed by the States for implementing the scheme are detailed below:

Implementing Agency

3. Department of Animal Husbandry, Dairying & Fisheries is implementing the Centrally Sponsored Scheme of 'National Project for Cattle and Buffalo Breeding (NPCBB) with the objective of bringing about genetic up-gradation of cattle and buffaloes by artificial insemination as well as acquisition of proven indigenous animals. NPCBB is implemented through State Implementing Agencies (SIAs) like State Livestock Development Boards. In order to bring about synergy between NPCBB and Livestock Insurance, the latter scheme will also be implemented through the SIAs. Almost all the states have opted for NPCBB. In states which are not implementing NPCBB or where there are no SIAs, the livestock insurance scheme will be implemented through the State Animal Husbandry Departments.

Executive Authority

4. The Chief Executive Officer of the State Livestock Development Board will also be the executive authority for this scheme. In those states where no such Boards are in place, the Director, Department of Animal Husbandry will be the Executive Authority of the scheme. The CEO will have to get the scheme implemented in various districts through the senior most officer of the Animal Husbandry Department in the district; the necessary instructions for this purpose will have to be issued by the State Government. The Central funds for premium subsidy, payment of honorarium to the Veterinary Practitioners, awareness creation through Panchayats etc. will be placed with the S.I.A. As Executive Authority of the scheme, the Chief Executive Officers will be responsible for execution, and monitoring of the scheme. The main functions of the CEO will be:

(*i*) Managing the Central funds carefully and in accordance with instructions issued by the Department of Animal Husbandry, Dairying and Fisheries, Government of India.

(*ii*) Calling quotations from the insurance companies for implementing the scheme, carrying out negotiations with them and selecting suitable company (companies).

(*iii*) Signing the contract with the selected insurance company/companies.

(*iv*) Payment of subsidy premium to the Insurance Company (including advance, if any and its subsequent adjustment).

(*v*) Preparing district wise list of veterinary practitioners (Government /Private) and providing the same to the insurance company and also to concerned Panchayati Raj bodies.

(*vi*) Creating awareness among the general public as well as the officials whose services may be required for implementation of the scheme;

(*vii*) Carrying out field inspections and also facilitating field inspections by Central teams;

(*viii*) Release of funds to the District Officers in charge of the Department of Animal Husbandry for payment of honorarium to the Veterinary Practitioners.

(*ix*) Regular monitoring and preparation of reports for submission to the Central/State Governments.

(*x*) Such other functions necessarily required for efficient implementation of the scheme.

The Principal Secretary/Secretary in-charge Animal Husbandry of the State Governments/Director of State Animal Husbandry Department will ensure availability of sufficient infrastructure in terms of manpower and other logistic support to the CEO/District level officer, needed for effective implementation of the scheme. (The exact name, designation, address of CEO/District Officer in-charge for Insurance work will be made available to Central Government and same will be prominently displayed on important places within the district and especially in the rural areas of the district. Any change in the name and designation of CEO will also be properly communicated to all concerned.) For effective implementation and monitoring of the scheme, if states feel necessity, a district committee could be formed suitably involving the officers/organizations having interest in the field of Animal Husbandry. The Dairy Cooperative Societies, if interested, could also be involved and given responsibility of implementing the scheme wherever possible.

Districts in which the scheme will be implemented

5. The scheme is to be implemented during 2005-06 and 2006-07 on pilot basis in 100 selected districts. During its pilot stage, the scheme will be restricted to crossbred and high yielding cattle and buffaloes only. The list of districts selected for this purpose based on the population of female cross-bred and high yielding cattle and of buffaloes as per 17th livestock census as the main criterion is given in Annexure-I. The scheme is to be implemented in these districts only.

Selection of Insurance Companies

6. In order to get the maximum benefit in terms of competitive premium rates, easier procedures of issue of policy and settlement of claims, Chief Executive Officer will be empowered to decide upon the Insurance company(s) and the terms and conditions. While selecting Insurance Company, besides premium rates offered, their capacity to provide services, terms and conditions and service efficiency should also be taken in to account. The CEO will invite quotations in writing from those public and private general insurance companies having a fairly wide network in the state or a considerable part of the state. The CEO should select the Insurance Company/Companies after negotiating with the insurance companies for successful and efficient implementation of the scheme and popularizing the scheme amongst the livestock owners. If any Insurance Company is offering cover for any type of disability in addition to death of the insured

animal, such offer could be considered, however, no subsidy in the premium for such additional risk coverage will be provided. The entire cost of premium on account of the risk coverage other than death of the animal has to be borne by the beneficiaries. However, if any additional risk covers is offered as a package along with death cover and the premium rate is not exceeding the maximum limit of 4.5% for annual policies and 12% for three year policies, such offer could be accepted and subsidy could be provided. As mentioned above, the CEO has to ensure that the premium rate agreed to is competitive. Under no circumstances, the rate of premium should exceed 4.5% for annual policies and 12% for three year policies. Normally, a single insurance company should be entrusted for insurance with the work in a district. However, for the purposes of encouraging competition and popularizing the scheme more than one insurance company may be allowed to operate in a district, if other terms and conditions are remaining same. Default in settlement of claim or any types of deficiency in services on part of Insurance Companies could be brought to the notice of the Insurance Regulatory and Development Authority which is a nodal authority in the country in this regard.

Involvement of Veterinary Practitioners

7. The active involvement of the veterinary practitioners at the village level is required for the successful implementation of the scheme. They are to be associated with the work of identification and examination of the animals to be covered under the scheme, determination of their market price, tagging of the insured animals and finally issuing veterinary certificates as and when a claim is made. Besides, being in touch with the farmers and cattle-rearers, they may also help in promoting and popularizing the scheme. As far as possible, only the veterinary practitioners working with the state government may be involved. Private veterinary practitioners may be involved only if Government veterinary practitioners are not available. A list of such veterinary practitioners will be prepared for every district by the district officer of the Department of Animal Husbandry. The list of veterinary practitioners will be made available with the insurance company selected for the district as well as to the concerned Panchayati Raj bodies.

Commencement of Insurance Policy Cover and Adjustment of Premium Subsidy

8. In order to generate confidence among the cattle owners about the efficacy of the scheme, it is important that the policy cover should take effect once the basic formalities like identification of animal, its examination by the veterinary practitioner, assessment of its value and its tagging along with payment of 50% of the premium to the insurance company or its agent by the cattle owner. The selected insurance company will have to agree to this. However, it is possible that the insurance company may point out a provision in the Insurance Act that insurance cover can take effect only after the whole premium is paid in advance. In order to take care of this problem, there could be an arrangement by which certain amount is paid in advance to the insurance company directly by the CEO. This amount should not exceed 50% of the premium of the number of animals expected to be insured in a period of 3 months. The insurance company, on its part, should issue instructions to their branches that as and when 50% of the premium is paid by the cattle owner, they should issue the policy by suitably adjusting the balance 50% from this advance. The insurance company should prepare monthly statements of the policies issued indicating the assessed value of each animal and the Government share for each district duly countersigned by the district officer of the Animal Husbandry Department and submit to the CEO so that, that much amount can be recouped to the insurance company by the CEO. Target of getting the number of animals insured in a three months period for payment of advance to the Insurance Company should be on realistic basis and recouping of the advance fund should be on the basis of subsequent progress made by the concerned insurance Company. As the scheme in its present form will not continue beyond 31st March, 2007, the CEO should, as far as possible, ensure that no advance is outstanding with the insurance company beyond that period.

In any case, if any such amount remains outstanding, the insurance company should be asked to pay the same forthwith in the first week of April, 2007. This should be suitably incorporated in the agreement to be executed with the insurance company.

Animals to be covered under the scheme and selection of beneficiaries

9. All those female cattle/buffalo yielding at least 1500 litre of milk per lactation are to be considered high yielding and hence can be insured under the scheme for maximum of their current market value. Animals covered under any other insurance scheme/plan scheme will not be covered under this scheme. Benefit of subsidy is to be restricted to two animals per beneficiary and is to be given for one time insurance of an animal up to a maximum period of three years. The farmers will have to be encouraged to go for a three-year policy which is likely to be more economical and useful for getting the real benefit of insurance on occurrence of natural calamities like flood and drought etc. However, if a livestock owner prefers to have an insurance policy for less than three years period for valid reasons, benefit of the subsidy under the scheme would be available to them also, with the restriction that no subsidy would be available for further extension of the policy. Field performance recording of the NPCBB could also be involved for identification of beneficiaries. The Gram Panchayats will assist the Insurance Companies in identifying the beneficiaries.

Determination of Market Price of the Animal

10. An animal will be insured for the maximum of its current market price. The market price of the animal to be insured will be assessed jointly by the beneficiary, authorized veterinary practitioner and the insurance agent.

Identification of insured animal

11. The animal insured will have to be properly and uniquely identified at the time of insurance claim. The ear tagging should, therefore, be fool proof as far as possible. The traditional method of ear tagging or the recent technology of fixing microchips could be used at the time of taking the policy. The cost of fixing the identification mark will be borne by the Insurance companies and responsibility of its maintenance will lie on the concerned beneficiaries. The nature and quality of tagging materials will be mutually agreed by the beneficiaries and the Insurance Company. The Veterinary Practitioners may guide the beneficiaries about the need and importance of the tags fixed for settlement of their claim so that they take proper care for maintenance of the tags.

Change of owner during the validity period of insurance

12. In case of sale of the animal or otherwise transfer of animal from one owner to other, before expiry of the Insurance Policy, the authority of beneficiary for the remaining period of policy will have to be transferred to the new owner. The modalities for transfer of livestock policy and fees and sale deed etc required for transfer, should be decided while entering into contract with the insurance company.

Settlement of Claims

13. The method of settlement of claim should be very simple and expeditious to avoid unnecessary hardship to the insured. While entering into contract with the insurance company, the procedure to be adopted/ documents needed for settlement of claim should be clearly spelt out. In case of claim becoming due, the payment of insured amount should be made within 15 days positively after submission of requisite documents. While insuring the animal, CEOs must ensure that clear cut procedures are put in place for settlement of claims and the required documents are listed and the same is made available to concerned beneficiaries along with the policy documents.

Effective Monitoring of the Scheme

14. The present scheme is a pilot scheme only. The continuance of the scheme during XI plan will be considered after critical review of the scheme during pilot stage. In view of this, there is need of strict monitoring at different stages. The monitoring should be in terms of financial releases, number of animals insured and type of insurance. Monitoring at the Central and State levels is extremely important. CEO will be required to make special efforts for effective monitoring. Secretary in-charge Animal Husbandry in State Government/ Director of state animal Husbandry will take periodic review of the implementation of the scheme.

Payment of Honorarium to the Veterinary Practitioners

15. The involvement of veterinary officer in the scheme is from beginning to end. His active interest and support is essential for success of the scheme. In view of this it is essential to provide some incentive to the veterinary practitioners to motivate them to carry out these activities wholeheartedly. It has been decided to pay an honorarium of Rs.50/- per animal at the stage of insuring the animal and Rs. 100/- per animal at the stage of issuing veterinary certificate (including conducting post-mortem, if any) in case of any insurance claim. Central Government will provide the amount needed for payment of honorarium to the S.I.As. The CEOs should ensure that Boards will pay to Veterinary Practitioners at end of each quarter depending on number of animals insured and veterinary certificates issued by them in that quarter.

Publicity

16. The scheme is new and people inclusive of the concerned officials are not much aware of the scheme. Therefore, public as well as the machinery involved in this have to be made aware of the scheme and benefits thereof. Pamphlets, posters, wall paintings, radio talks, TV clippings etc. will help in creating awareness among the farmers about the benefits of insuring their high yielding animals under the scheme. Publicity campaigns on special occasions like animal fairs etc. will also be taken up for wide publicity. The Panchayati Raj institutions will be involved in publicity in a big way. The task of disseminating information on the scheme and inviting farmers to offer their animals for identification for insurance will be entrusted to the Intermediate Panchayats. For this purpose the CEOs are empowered to provide assistance not exceeding Rs. 5000/- for each intermediate Panchayat (in both cash and in the form of publicity material).

Commission to Insurance Agents

The active and dedicated involvement of insurance agent is most essential for efficient implementation of the scheme. The insurance company should be persuaded to pay at least 15% of the premium amount to the agent out of their premium income. While entering into contract with the Insurance Company, this has to be ensured by the implementing agency.

Annexure 28-A

INSURANCE REGULATORY AND DEVELOPMENT AUTHORITY

New Delhi, the 14th July, 2000

(Obligations of Insurers to Rural and Social Sectors) Regulations, 2000

In exercise of the powers conferred by Section 32C read with Section 32B of the Insurance Act, 1938, (4 of 1938), the Authority, in consultation with the Insurance Advisory Committee, hereby makes the following regulations, namely:-

1. Short Title and Commencement

(1) These regulations may be called the Insurance Regulatory and Development Authority (Obligations of Insurers to Rural or Social Sectors) Regulations, 2000.

(2) They shall come into force from the date of their publication in the *Official Gazette*.

2. Definitions

1. In these regulations, unless the context otherwise requires —

   (a) *"Act"* means the Insurance Act, 1938 (4 of 1938);

   (b) *"Authority"* means the Insurance Regulatory and Development Authority established under the provisions of Section 3 of the Insurance Regulatory and Development Authority Act, 1999 (41 of 1999);

   (c) *"Rural sector"* shall mean any place as per the latest census which has — (*i*) a population of not more than five thousand; (*ii*) a density of population of not more than four hundred per square kilometre; and (*iii*) at least seventy five per cent of the male working population is engaged in agriculture;

   (d) *"Social sector"* includes unorganised sector, informal sector, economically vulnerable or backward classes and other categories of persons, both in rural and urban areas;

   (e) *"Unorganised sector"* includes self-employed workers such as agricultural labourers, bidi workers, brick kiln workers, carpenters, cobblers, construction workers, fishermen, hamals, handicraft artisans, handloom and khadi workers, lady tailors, leather and tannery workers, papad makers, powerloom workers, physically handicapped self-employed persons, primary milk producers, rickshaw pullers, safai karmacharis, salt growers, seri culture workers, sugarcane cutters, tendu leaf collectors, toddy tappers, vegetable vendors, washerwomen, working women in hills, or such other categories of persons.,

   (f) *"Economically vulnerable or backward classes"* means persons who live below the poverty line;

   (g) *"Other categories of persons"* includes persons with disability as defined in the Persons with Disabilities (Equal Opportunities, Protection of Rights, and Full Participation) Act, 1995 and who may not be gainfully employed; and also includes guardians who need insurance to protect spastic persons or persons with disability;

   (h) All words and expressions used herein and not defined herein but defined in the Insurance Act, 1938 (4 of 1938), or in the Insurance Regulatory and Development Authority Act, 1999 (41 of 1999), shall have the meanings respectively assigned to them in those Acts.

3. Obligations

Every insurer, who begins to carry on insurance business after the commencement of the Insurance Regulatory and Development Authority Act, 1999 (41 of 1999), shall, for the purposes of Sections 32B and 32C of the Act, ensure that he undertakes the following obligations, during the first five financial years, pertaining to the persons in —

(a) Rural sector, (*i*) in respect of *a life insurer* — (I) five per cent in the first financial year; (II) seven per cent in the second financial year; (III) ten per cent in the third financial year; (IV) twelve per cent in the fourth financial year; (V) fifteen per cent in the fifth year; of total policies written direct in that year; (*ii*) in respect of *a general insurer*, — (I) two per cent in the first financial year; (II) three per cent in the second financial year; (III) five per cent thereafter, of total gross premium income written direct in that year.

(b) Social sector, in respect of all insurers, — (I) five thousand lives in the first financial year; (II) seven thousand five hundred lives in the second financial year; (III) ten thousand lives in the third financial year; (IV) fifteen thousand lives in the fourth financial year; (V) twenty thousand lives in the fifth year;

Provided that in the first financial year, where the period of operation is less than twelve months, proportionate percentage or number of lives, as the case may be, shall be undertaken. Provided further that, in case of a general insurer, the obligations specified shall include insurance for crops. Provided further that the Authority may normally, once in every five years, prescribe or revise the obligations as specified in Regulation 3.

4. Obligations of Existing Insurers

(1) The obligations of existing insurers as on the date of commencement of IRDA Act shall be decided by the Authority after consultation with them and the quantum of insurance business to be done shall not be less than what has been recorded by them for the accounting year ended 31st March, 2000.

(2) The Authority shall review such quantum of insurance business periodically and give directions to the insurers for achieving the specified targets.

Key Terms

- ❒ Rural Banking
- ❒ Acqua Culture Insurance
- ❒ Failed Well Insurance
- ❒ Floriculture Insurance
- ❒ Horticulture Insurance
- ❒ Rural insurance covers
- ❒ Cattle Insurance
- ❒ Farmer's Package Insurance
- ❒ Lift Insurance
- ❒ Poultry Insurance

Questions for Review

1. Briefly explain the various rural insurance covers available in India.
2. List the IRDA provisions on obligations of insurers to rural sectors.

Suggested Readings

1. N.K. Rustagi, *Crop Insurance in India — An Analysis,* B.R. Publishing Corporation, 1988.
2. K.N. Rao, *Crop Insurance: Past, Present and Future, An Article Published in Vision,* Journal published by MDI, Gurgaon, July-Dec. 2002.
3. Syed M. Ahsan, *Agricultural Insurance: A New Policy for Developing Countries,* Gower Publishing Co. Ltd., 1985.
4. Strategies for Rural Markets, Anabil Bhattacharya, *Insurance Time,* Kolkata, October 2002.

Web Resources

- www.bimaguru.com
- www.irdaindia.org
- www.bimaonline.com

Social Insurance

Chapter 29

CHAPTER OBJECTIVES

After reading this chapter you will be able to understand :

- *What is Social Insurance?*
- *Characteristics and Need for Social Insurance*
- *Legal Framework for the Social Insurance*
- *Social Insurance in India*
- *Unemployment Insurance*

Social Insurance through various programs provides a safety net against the financial insecurity that can result from premature death, unemployment, poor health, job related disabilities and old age. These programs are especially vulnerable to individuals and families with limited incomes. However in India Social Insurance concept is in its premature stage, due to vast cultural, economic, social diversities.

29.1 WHAT IS SOCIAL INSURANCE?

The government on a compulsory basis generally provides social insurance. It is not easy to precisely define because the government can use the power and resources to apply the insurance method or modification of it in a variety of ways. In the developed countries like U.S. there has been a tendency to look first to the private insurance industry for the coverage of risk that society deem important. When such risks have not been handled adequately by private insurance, social insurance programme comes into picture.

29.2 CHARACTERISTICS AND NEED FOR SOCIAL INSURANCE

The main characteristics of social insurance are:

- Social insurance is based on the law, rather than on contract. Cost and benefit are established by and can be changed by government.
- Hence coverage is compulsory for all persons to whom the law applies. They cannot choose to decline to participate, nor can they select the coverage or the amount of the benefits.
- The objective is to provide some minimum level of economic security for the large portion of the population. The basic ideology is to provide an economic system that stresses free enterprise and individual initiative, people should not rely entirely upon government programs.
- The focus of social insurance is to provide maximum benefits to the lower income groups. Unless lower income groups are subsidised to high income groups, the payments of the former will not be large enough to furnish the minimum level of protection that are desired.
- Social insurance usually covers only those who are or who have been employed. Most social insurance plans are concerned for interruption of income (by death, unemployment or retirement) earned through employment.

29.3 Legal Framework for Social Insurance

The Insurance Regulatory and Development Authority Act, 1999 (para 19; First schedule) has amended the Sections 32B and 32C of the Insurance Act, 1938 as under:

Section 32B

Every insurer shall, after the commencement of Insurance Regulatory and Development Authority Act, 1999, undertake such percentages of life insurance business and general insurance business in the rural and social sector, as may be specified, in the Official Gazette by the authority, in this behalf.

Section 32C

Every insurer shall, after the commencement of Insurance Regulatory and Development Authority Act, 1999, discharge the obligations specified under Section 32B to provide life insurance or general insurance policies to those residing in the rural sector, workers in the unorganised sector or informal sector or economically vulnerable or backward classes of the society and other categories of persons as may be specified by the regulations made by the authority and such insurance policies shall include insurance for crops.

The IRDA Regulations 2000 makes it compulsory for the insurers, existing and new to promote the social insurance.[1] Similar to the requirement for the rural sector, the regulations also prescribe for undertaking benchmark percentages for insurances in the social insurance sector for the players.

The *social sector* is defined as including the unorganised sector, the informal sector, the economically vulnerable or backward classes and other categories of persons, both in rural and urban areas.

In case of social sector the requirement is compulsory underwriting of 5000 lives in the first financial year, 7,500 in the second year and so on. Also, the authority may revise the obligation once in 5 years.

29.4 Social Insurance in India

Social insurance is the baby of the social security systems prevailing in that country. Social security is the security cover which society furnishes through appropriate organisation against risks to which its members are exposed. The basic idea is to use social means to prevent deprivation and vulnerability to deprivation.

In the literature on development issues, it has often been assumed explicitly or implicitly that developing countries are too poor to be able to *afford* social security systems. Public participation in social security systems can take wide variety of forms and it is very much possible even for poor countries to achieve considerable success on this front. This is not to say that economic growth and social security are not linked. However at the same time, simple economic growth alone cannot ensure improvements in living standards of people. Social intervention is necessary for improving quality of life at the micro level.

Studies carried out by UNICEF and World Bank also provide considerable evidence that it has been the direct public support rather than the average income of the population that has been the driving force behind the success of social security schemes world-wide. In fact, the countries with good primary social security systems are those which have adopted the path of support-led security (as against growth-led security) and have *not waited* to grow rich before resorting to large scale public support to guarantee certain basic capabilities. Notable examples include China, Chile, Cuba, Jamaica and Kuwait.

Need for a Social Security System in India

A large chunk of Indian population lives under abject poverty. They barely manage to earn enough to eat. It is our social obligation to provide our underprivileged brethren with an adequate safety cover.

Only a very small percentage of the working population is employed by the organised sector, which provides benefits like the state pension. A vast majority is either self employed or employed in the rural and unorganised sector. As a result, they are deprived of social benefits such as retirement benefits and disability or death compensation. Similarly, health-care although subsidised is thinly and haphazardly spread. State support for the unemployed and disabled is negligible.

Social changes taking place in the country are also resulting into increased need for a social security system. The Joint Family System, which prevailed in India for long is losing its flavour. This system provided a natural safety cover to the members of a family. However, its break-up into nuclear families means that the death or disability of the bread-earner leaves his dependants completely exposed.

A comprehensive social security system includes social insurance, health insurance, disability compensation, unemployment compensation, old-age pension schemes, etc. In India, social security systems are an emerging concept and there is no strong base to start with. Given the constraints on funds and infrastructure availability, social insurance is the only scheme that can be launched at present. Further, opening up of the insurance sector has created increased awareness about insurance and also provides a sustainable revenue model to carry out the task of social insurance.

India — A Special Case

India is a special case compared to many other countries for the implementation of social insurance schemes. A support-led social security system is one that requires active state intervention. The main source of funds provided by the state comes from the taxes it collects. Unfortunately, India has a tiny tax-paying base. Further, social insurance is not a constitutional right of the citizens in India. The cause can again be traced to the fragile economic situation of the country that does not permit any kind of comprehensive social insurance schemes.

Social Insurance Schemes of GIC

GIC has launched certain social insurance covers like Krishi Bima Yojana, Personal Accident social security scheme, hut insurance scheme. However, the experience has been that most of these are failure in the sense these schemes failed to achieve the objectives for which these were floated. Similar is the case of LIC.

Social Insurance Schemes of LIC

Life Insurance Corporation of India (LIC) has taken the initiative and launched several social insurance schemes. Some of the schemes launched by LIC in the past are: Landless Agricultural Labourers Scheme, Group Insurance Scheme for beneficiaries of the Integrated Rural Development Program, Rural Group Life Insurance Schemes and the Krishi Shramik Samajik Suraksha Yojana (2001). Most of the social insurance schemes launched could not achieve their desired objective as a large chunk of the population covered under these schemes were not even aware of them. In August 2000, LIC launched the Janashree Bima Yojana as a single scheme to replace the older social insurance schemes. The objective of this scheme is to provide life insurance protection to the rural and urban poor living below the poverty line and marginally above the poverty line. This is a group insurance scheme and the minimum size of the group is 25. The annual premium is Rs. 200 per member per annum. The member/nodal agency/state government pays half the premium and the remaining half is borne out of the Social Security Fund. There are 40 occupational groups, which can be covered under Janashree Bima Yojana. They range from beedi workers and handloom tailors to construction workers and safai karmacharis.

Creation of a Separate Body for Social Insurance

The Central Government of India created the Social Security Fund in 1988. LIC was given the responsibility for managing the Fund. However, performance data for the past five years on the social insurance front is not encouraging.

Exhibit 29-A

Description	*1996-97*	*1997-98*	*1998-99*	*1999-00*	*2000-01*
Existing lives renewed	44,86,884	47,57,476	47,72,082	46,23,797	46,62,281
New Lives	4,48,143	2,62,456	1,28,158	3,26,190	74,610
Total	49,35,027	50,19,941	49,00,240	49,49,987	47,36,891

The number of new lives covered in the last one year is less than the number of people born in India in one day. Providing social insurance to all is a mammoth task and requires a set-up fully dedicated to this task. On the front of social insurance, various recommendations have been made by researchers extracts of which are follows:

- Cost minimisation is a basic requirement on which any social security system is built. Instead of all the insurance companies complying with the social requirement (as imposed by IRDA) individually, it has been proposed that a common pool of funds be generated and channelled towards the same objective. This will prevent duplication of work and thereby reduce administrative and implementation costs.
- At the same time, with the entry of private insurance players in the country, it is all the more difficult for LIC to do justice to both — its commercial insurance business and meeting social obligations. The need for a separate body dedicated to social insurance is therefore obvious.
- The biggest concerns in implementation of social schemes are being able to reach the target population and cost effectiveness. Therefore only group insurance can be introduced in such schemes. It is a time-tested fact that Government bodies have not been able to make inroads among the masses in a cost-effective manner. Further, given that India has a very narrow tax base and low tax revenue, work-based and community-based social insurance systems should be encouraged.
- Decentralisation i.e. participation of local people in administration and implementation of such schemes is essential. Therefore, it is necessary to have a nodal agency that can interact with people on behalf of the insurer and with the insurer on behalf of the group. The *introduction of a nodal agency* would also reduce the administrative overheads of the insurer thereby reducing overall cost. There are several advantages of the use of a nodal agency for implementation of social life insurance schemes.
  (a) Local level participation and ownership ensures that implementation would suit local requirements and hence there are higher chances of success.
  (b) This structure combines advantages of centralised policy making with localised implementation.
  (c) It effectively bypasses poor functioning of the public sector hierarchy.

However these recommendations pertain only to the delegated authority and not devolved authority. The insurer will collect the premium directly from the nodal agency and the nodal agency will do the collection in parts or at one time from the group members.

Registered bodies like co-operatives, unions (such as taxi unions etc.), associations (such as fishermen associations), self help groups and registered NGOs etc. are ideally suited to act as nodal agencies.

Co-operatives

As per statistics of the National Co-operative Union of India, there are 1.4 lakh primary agricultural co-operatives and 3.6 lakh primary non-credit co-operatives. The agricultural co-operatives cover 13.7 crore people whereas the non-credit co-operatives cover 6.4 crore people. In the present scenario, co-operatives fit very well to act as the nodal agency and offer immense potential for reaching out to the masses of India.

Associations

Associations are widely spread across the country in different occupational groups and hence provide a platform to tap the people associated with such associations.

Self Help Groups

Self Help Group is a concept utilised by NABARD to develop the habit of thrift saving among very poor people who are devoid of any sort of financial system. At present, their main function is to collect money in small instalments from members at regular intervals and form a common pool. It also provides credit to its members, when required. These groups are linked to the local bank either directly or through NGOs. Through NGOs, government bodies and banks, vast number of self-help Groups have been established in the recent years. Fuelled by enthusiasm at all stakeholder levels, it has expanded rapidly throughout India, including marginal and tribal areas. In light of the above facts, Self Help Groups can also be used as nodal agencies.

Critical Success Factors in Selection of Nodal Agencies

- *High level of mutual trust*

  People should have faith in the nodal agency, especially when targeted people are less educated and are from the low-income group.

- *Monetary transactions*

  The existence of a monetary transaction is the single most critical operational factor for success. In the case where existing interactions between the individuals and the nodal agency involves monetary transactions, it becomes much easier to collect money efficiently and on time.

- *Frequency of interaction of nodal agency with the group*

  High frequency of interaction adds to mutual understanding between the individuals and the nodal agency.

- *Organisational structure of the nodal agency*

  The organisation structure of the nodal agency should be conducive to the implementation of social insurance schemes. The structure should ensure simplicity of the process for the individuals covered. The nodal agency's structure should also ensure the transparency of its operations. This would help in inspiring trust among the people.

- *Interests of the nodal agency*

  From the nodal agency's perspective, the implementation of any such scheme should be in line with its objectives. It has been observed that in case of most co-operatives, the primary intention was to help its members. However, some NGOs were looking for monetary incentives to cover their costs.

29.5 Unemployment Insurance

Unemployment Insurance is designed to provide short term protection for regularly employed persons who lose their jobs and who are willing and able to work. Unemployment insurance has several basic objectives:

- Provide cash income during involuntary unemployment.
- Help unemployed workers find jobs
- Encourage employers to stabilize employment
- Help stabilize economy.

Unemployment insurance is a popular concept in developed countries like U.S. where they have well defined laws and regulations. However, in India it will take a long time to come.

29.6 Salary Savings Scheme

Under this scheme the premium is deducted from the salary of the employee at source and net is paid to him.

The Employer to the insurer remits to the amount so collected. The Salary Savings Scheme can be introduced in an institution or establishment subject to specified terms and conditions.

The scheme is of great benefit to the insurer because the payments of the premium is assured, as long as the employee is in service and the procedures of accounting become simple because there is only one transaction for all the employees under one employer. The minimum number of members is 15 and there is no maximum limit. Since the payment of premium is consistent and guarrateed, the loading on monthly prtemiums is not charged in SSS policies. The SSS policies can be issued only after the employer has agreed to make deductions regularly from the salaries of the employees and remit the premiums to the insurer. The employee has to authorise the employer to deduct the premium from his salary and such authorisation letters are collected along with the proposal for insurance and are sent to the employer by the insurer.

Logically, there may be a gap between the time the policy is completed and the notice for pemium sent to the employer. Therefore, first two premiums are collected in advance.

Shiksha Sahayog Yojana

It is a scholarship scheme launched by LIC on 31.12.2001 for the benefit of children of members of Janashree Bima Yojana. It is for the students studying in ix to xii standards, whose parents are covered under Janashree Bima Yojana. If a student fails and is detained in the same standard, he will not be eligible for scholarship for the next year in the same standard.

Under this scheme, the scholarship of Rs 300/- per quarter per child will be paid for maximum period of 4 years. The benefit is restricted to two children per member(family) only. No premium is charged for the scholarship. A Nodal Agency specified for trhe purpose, identifies the students. The member of Janashree Bima Yojana whose child is eligible for scholarship has to fill up an application form (available with Nodal Agency) and submit to the Nodal Agency. The applications duly filled up and certified will be sent alongwith the list of the beneficiary students by the Nodal Agency to the concerned LIC, P&GS Unit for disbursement of scholarship/s. The scholarship/s is disbursed to the beneficiary students through the concerned Nodal Agency. As only a limited number of beneficiaries will be provided scholarship under the scheme, the selection for eligible students will be made on the basis of poorest of the poor.

The scheme is administered through Pension and Group Schemes Department of LIC of India.

Janashree Bima Yojana

It was launched by LIC to provide life insurance protection to the rural and urban poor persons below poverty line and marginally above the poverty line in the age group of 18 to 58 years belonging to a member of any of, the approved vocation/occupation groups e.g. a government department which is concerned with the welfare of any such vocation/occupation group, a Welfare Fund/ Society, Village Panchayat, NGO, Self-Help Group, etc. The minimum number of members is 25.

Key Terms

- ❒ Social Insurance Schemes
- ❒ Unemployment Insurance
- ❒ Self-help Groups
- ❒ Nodal Agency

Questions for Review

1. Define social insurance and state its main features. List the various provisions of IRDA Regulation on social insurance.

2. Critically evaluate the state of social insurance scheme in India what steps can be taken to make them more effective?

Suggested Readings

1. Irving Pfeffer and David R. Klock, *Perspectives on Insurance,* Prentice-Hall, Englewood Cliffs, 1974.
2. IRDA Annual Reports.
3. Mark D. Dorfman, *Fundamentals of Insurance,* Prentice-Hall, 2002.

Web Resources

- www.irdaindia.org
- www.bimaonline.com
- www.bimaguru.com

Project and Engineering Insurance

Chapter 30

CHAPTER OBJECTIVES

After reading this chapter you will be able to understand :

- *Need for Project and Engineering Insurance*
- *Various types of Standard and customized covers*

Every project leader within the corporate sector knows that nothing but an unqualified success of a project can ensure the repayment of costs involved or loans availed. In case of any delays or failure of a project, liquid funds will have to be made available to replace the costs incurred as well as repay the loans taken. Ever since India has been ushered into the era of liberalization, privatization and globalization, Project insurance has emerged as the need of the hour. The demand for Project insurance is increasing with major emphasis placed on infrastructure projects, besides other large projects.

At times, tried and tested risk management tactics have proved themselves effective in stemming the risks. But now, every Risk Manager would rather look for a new technique that could reflect the changing times. Everyone is looking for a modern and up-to-the mark risk management strategy. Since the industrial scenario is changing so quickly, Risk Managers in India have been forced to steel themselves for a challenging albeit an interesting assignment that should ensue within this new millennium by

- Adapting to the 'Global Scenario' and 'Modern Technology'
- Providing the latest Risk Management tactics as well as sustained Risk
- Management support for the development of industry within the Indian sub-continent.

Although new technology results in optimization of productivity and production, it also creates new and unheard-of risks. Introducing new technology is similar to developing a new sub-culture in engineering, erection, construction, commissioning and innovation in handling and transport of materials. Since automation also intensifies the chances of risks occurring due to human error, the repercussions are bound to be costly. Since Risk Management means efficiently managing the risks, it should be oriented towards the prevention rather than the cure, itself.

30.1 RISKS ASSOCIATED WITH NEW PROJECTS

Risks, which might have a significant impact on the construction or operation of a project, can be grouped as—

1. *Commercial Risks:* Related to potential problems during construction resulting in delays and escalation of costs.
2. *Operational Risks:* Poor performance that translates in failure in generating adequate cash to pay the lending financial institutions.
3. *Risks of Disparity:* Difference between supply and markets resulting in the inability to produce assured capacity.
4. *General Risks:* Vendor's inability to utilize power generated.
5. *Political Risks:* Most likely to affect non-Indian investors as they are mere spectators to the ongoing bureaucratic scenario.

Basically, Risk Management is aimed at analyzing risks, controlling and financing them. Ideally, the Risk Manager must review the efficiency of the risk management decisions taken and also make appropriate changes that ensure proper handling of risks.

30.2 THE HISTORY OF ENGINEERING INSURANCE

The development of engineering insurance began in England around the middle of the 19th century in the wake of the Industrial Revolution.

The Industrial Revolution had been triggered by the inventions of steam boilers by Papin in 1690 and by Newcomen in 1725, and the double-acting industrial steam engine by James Watt in 1781. The increasing use of steam boilers and steam engines permitted the switch from manual labour in workshops to machine-based production in factories, thus changing the face of technology and society.

The factory worker joined the craftsman and gradually replaced him. The explosion of steam boilers and the rupture of the large flywheels of steam engines were new and unfamiliar types of property damage that also led to personal injuries in the factories and their surroundings.

As a result, the British boiler operators founded the Manchester Steam Users Association in 1854 with the aim of regularly inspecting its members' steam boilers for deficiencies and instructing the operating personnel on how to use them properly.

This established the institution of technical inspection and, at the same time, the profession of an inspection and later of an insurance engineer. The number of boiler explosions declined considerably, and design methods and materials were improved. Manufacturers' production operations were supervised by independent experts, as were erection and commissioning.

In 1859, a number of engineers had the idea not only of preventing damage by way of inspections but also of offering insurance protection for property damage and personal injuries, and founded – likewise in Manchester– the Steam Boiler Assurance Company.

Just seven years later, in 1866, the Hartford Steam Boiler Inspection & Insurance Company came into being in the USA, originally with the intention of offering inspections and insurance protection for the locomotives of the private railway companies. This company has since become the largest insurance and inspection company for engineering risks in the USA.

A host of inventions in the 19th century accelerated the process of industrialization and the demand for adequate insurance protection. Electric motors, generators, transformers, water and steam turbines, gas engines, petrol and diesel engines resulted in the flourishing of power engineering and the energy industry.

The supply of electricity in Germany began with the decentralized generation of electricity in industrial companies to drive the machines and in the municipalities for lighting the streets. The year 1900 witnessed the first steam turbine installation with an output of 1 MW at the power station in Elberfeld. From these origins, the electricity supply system based on the pioneering ideas and successful trials of Oskar v. Miller in the second half of the 19th century developed into a central and now trans-European grid with ratings of up to 1,300 to 1,500 MW in nuclear power stations in Germany and France.

As a result of the progress made in compressor and pump construction, together with hygienic sewage disposal in conurbation areas, the gas and water industries led to the establishment of modern gas, water and sewage systems for the rapidly growing cities. The new machinery being used needed adequate insurance protection. In the UK and the USA, the steam boiler insurers started providing this cover under the name of "engine insurance".

30.2.1 Machinery Insurance

In Germany, this boom in economic development began, somewhat later, in the second half of the 19th century. Rapid growth and confidence in the ability to realize new business ideas led to a wave of new businesses being set up in what came to be known as the "founder era" ("Gründerzeit").

One of these successful founders was the 36-year-old Karl Thieme, who, in cooperation with respected industrialists and bankers from Munich, founded the Münchener Rückversicherungs-Gesellschaft in Munich in 1880 and Allianz Versicherungs-AG in Berlin in 1890. In 1898, one of his employees, Chief Engineer Fritz Böhrer, who had gathered extensive experience with losses in his time as technical director of a printing company, suggested something that had not been available in Germany up to that time – an innovative "insurance for machines and mechanical devices for all industrial companies, electricity, gas and water works, etc.".

In 1898/99 Böhrer carried out a written survey among various commercial and industrial companies in Bavaria. Following an analysis of this survey, which confirmed the need for machinery insurance, the new product was introduced in conjunction with other participating insurance companies and marketed as "accident insurance" for machinery supplementary to an existing public liability insurance policy.

All risks cover with named exclusions

Thieme, who was always open to new ideas and greatly interested in innovative insurance schemes for his young company and its clients, backed Böhrer's idea entirely. From the very outset, this machinery insurance was designed as all risks cover with named exclusions – quite the opposite of the policies for steam boilers, which only offered insurance protection for property damage caused by named perils, e.g. explosion.

On 1st January 1900, what was then the Munich Branch of Allianz Versicherungs-AG was granted a licence to sell this machinery insurance – initially for the Kingdom of Bavaria. The Imperial Supervisory Office in Berlin later extended this licence to several primary insurers all over Germany in 1903 and 1904.

With this product, the then still young Munich Re wanted to offer its cedants an insurance cover designed to meet the needs of the flourishing commercial and industrial business. With the help of specially selected agents, business with the new product was rapidly expanded and offered for machinery in virtually every sector. More and more insurers became active in the new class.

30.2.2 Global Ventures

Munich Re also marketed machinery insurance outside Germany – in Austria, Hungary, Italy, Switzerland, Norway, Denmark, the Netherlands and, ultimately, also overseas. Thieme continued to support Böhrer's idea of machinery insurance through various difficulties of the pioneering years. In this way, the fortuitous meeting of Thieme, the courageous entrepreneur, and Böhrer, the visionary engineer, helped machinery insurance become a success. To put the new class of insurance on a broader footing, insurance for financial losses resulting from insured machinery losses – known at that time as operating loss insurance – was introduced on 15th August 1910 as an early forerunner of machinery loss of profits insurance.

30.2.3 Project Insurance

All Risk Project Insurance Policy: Project Insurance is an all-inclusive insurance cover for any damage to project material whilst in transit, risks of damage on site and while being erected or commissioned under an "All Risks Project Insurance Policy." This policy has been designed after bearing in mind the various risks associated with erection of a factory right from the shipment of the first consignment, the subsequent storage, civil construction, erection of plant and machinery, commissioning and trials until the end of the trial period when commercial production commences. Any damages or injury to the third party is covered under this policy. This policy is more commonly known as *Marine-cum-Erection* policy.

Marine-cum-Erection Insurance: Although people tend to think that there are major differences between Project insurance and Marine-cum-Erection insurance, they are essentially the one and the same since the scope of cover is strikingly similar in both. This is also an "All Risks Insurance" which provides cover against the *loss* or damage to the consignments during transit or damage during storage, handling, erection, testing and commissioning stages. This policy also covers Third Party Liability due to indemnifiable accidents at project site. The cover commences right from the moment goods leave the manufacturer's/supplier's premises (warehouse) in a foreign country and remains in force during voyage to any Indian port and thereafter during inland transit to the site of erection; during storage at site; during shifting of goods for the purpose of erection and continues to be in force until completion of erection, testing and commissioning.

While availing this cover, the proposer (insured) must ensure the following :

• While availing the policy, insured should take care of the insurance obligations under the contract. The provision and contents in the relevant portion of the Tender have to be taken.	• Document are to be examined and appropriate policy will have to be taken.
• The sum insured will have to be properly arrived at, since the Prime Cost of the Plant and Equipment will not be a subject matter for adjustment.	• Any extension of Policy Period or Testing Period will be costlier as compared to such period being included in the anticipated period, while selecting the policy period at inception.
• In respect of imported equipment's invoice value in Foreign Currency and Exchange Rates are to be furnished, based on which the value of the equipment's in Indian Rupees will be arrived at.	• Even if the extension of the policy is required to be taken at a later date, it would be more economical to opt for a longer extension period than several extensions of small periods.
• The Project period selected for insurance purpose will have to take into account possible delays during execution and accordingly it is advisable to have buffer period to take care of shippage.	• The possibility of having higher excess under the policy has to be considered, which will have the facility of discount in the premium rate.
• The testing period selected will also have to take into	

Escalation

In order to take care of increase in value due to escalation in the basic project cost, duties appreciation in Foreign Currency and fluctuation in the Exchange Rate, the escalation provision may be availed at the inception of the policy. The maximum permissible limit is 50 per cent escalation and premium is charged on half the escalation amount.

Basic Insurance Cover

This insurance cover under Project Insurance Policy comprises of two parts.

1. The first is coverage for transit to take care of the interest during the transit from the various suppliers' warehouses to the site of erection.
2. The second is the storage-cum-erection coverage to take care of the interest during storage, erection, testing and commissioning.

The transit risks covered are "All Risks" plus war, strike, riot and civil commotion for imports and strike, riot and civil commotion for inland transit.

For the erection portion, the risks covered are any accident, fire, riot and strike, lightning, malicious damage, storm, tempest, flood and inundation, earthquake, act of God perils, tearing apart due to centrifugal forces, short-circuiting, faults in erection, lack of skill and carelessness, and theft and burglary of property stored at the site of erection. It also covers damages to equipment during the commissioning and testing, till handed over to the principals.

Additional Covers

The risks of one project differ from another. In order to meet the particular requirements of the project concerned, care should be taken to check on which additional coverage/s out of those listed below is/are required and action taken thereon.

- Dismantling Cover
- Third Party Liability Cover
- Deletion of 60 days Clause in Ocean Policy
- Maintenance Period
- Additional Transits
- Additional Customs Duty.
- Express Delivery
- Testing of Second-hand Machinery
- Cross Liability Cover
- Terrorism Cover
- Clearance and Removal of Debris

Storage Risks at Fabricators' Premises/Workshop

In short, the cover is against all risks of physical loss or damage arising out of operation of any one or more of the following perils:

- *Location Risks:* Fire, Lightning, Theft and Burglary.
- *Handling Risks:* Impact from falling objects, Collision, failure of Cranes or Tackles.
- *Operational Risks:* Failure of safety devices, Leakage of Electricity, Insulation failures, Short-circuit, Tearing apart on Account of centrifugal forces. Explosion.
- *Human Risks:* Carelessness, Negligence, Faults in erections, Malicious Element, Damage, Strikes and Riots, Terrorism
- *Acts of God:* Earthquake, Storm, Tempest, Hurricane, Flood.
- Subsidience: Landslide, Rockslide.

Insurance policies that are required after completion of project are:

- Fire insurance
- Machinery Breakdown Insurance
- Advance loss of Profit
- Public Liability Insurance

30.3 ENGINEERING INSURANCE

Shortly after World War I – and mainly because of the instability of the currency resulting from the hyperinflation in the fateful crisis year of 1923 – the capital goods industry began to look for the most comprehensive insurance protection possible against risks to the calculated earnings of the contracting companies and their suppliers during the construction of technical facilities.

This demand was met by erection all risks insurance (EAR), which was launched on the market by Atlantic-Versicherung and Allianz in 1924 with the support of Munich Re. Erection all risks insurance offered the contractor the benefit of having simple, complete cover based on the all risks model, encompassing inter alia the risks of fire, explosion and natural hazards.

The advantages of the new product were so convincing that erection all risks insurance rapidly asserted itself in continental Europe, but also in the UK and the USA, either under the name construction insurance or as builders' risk insurance. In recent years this property insurance has been supplemented by the corresponding financial loss insurance, named advance loss of profits insurance (ALoP) or delay in start-up (DSU) insurance. The worldwide spread of risks by way of reinsurance helped this difficult class of business become a success, even though erection all risks insurance is exposed to major losses to a far greater extent than machinery insurance. As erection all risks insurance was designed to protect contractors during the erection and test testing of facilities, there was still a need for insurance to cover the risks to be borne by the contractor under his guarantee obligation after handing over the machinery to the operator.

The machinery guarantee insurance required for this purpose was introduced in 1927. This insurance covers the costs of repairing consequential damage to insured property caused by faulty design, materials, erection, etc. Machinery guarantee insurance offers a further supplement to the comprehensive range of engineering insurance products, but antiselection makes it very difficult for the insurance industry to operate profitably in this class.

Apart from various covers available for projects before and after implementation, specific covers are also available for various items of plant and machinery and equipments. Some of these are discussed as below.

(a) Boiler Insurance

(b) Erection Insurance

(c) Storage-cum-Erection

(d) Marine-cum-Erection

(e) Loss of Profits (Machinery) Insurance

(f) Contractors all risk policy

(g) Machinery Breakdown insurance.

Civil Engineering Completed Risks Insurance Policy

This cover is provided to owners and operators of civil engineering structures can have comprehensive insurance protection against loss or damage after the construction work has been completed and the facilities are taken over. This policy is suitable for completed works such as runways, railway lines, bridges, flyovers, jetties, tunnels, dams, canals, harbours, dry docks, water pipe lines, irrigation systems, reservoirs, etc. The policy offers cover against loss or damage due to :

1. Fire
2. Lightning
3. Explosion/implosion
4. Riot, strike & malicious damage
5. Impact by any rail, road or water borne vehicle or animal
6. Storm, cyclone, typhoon, tempest, hurricane, tornado, flood & inundation, wave action
7. Subsidence, landslide and rockslide
8. Earthquake, fire and shock, tsunami
9. Frost, avalanche, ice

Extra Covers

Further hazards depending on the location and type of risk can be included like bush fire, volcanic action, blasting operations, cover for removal of debris following a loss at additional premium.

In case of damages which can be repaired, the policy provides for payment of costs necessary to restore the items to their condition immediately before the occurrence of the damage. In case of total loss, the actual value of the items immediately before the occurrence of the loss is payable to the extent the costs are included in the sums insured. Since the policy is on indemnity basis, only incurred costs are payable. Loss assessment is subject to adjustments for under insurance, salvage and policy excess. Premium is charged for the type of civil works covered, the earthquake zone in which the property is located, the additional covers required and the past claims experience. The insured has to file a proposal form giving full description of the civil works proposed to be insured, the geographical conditions, exposure to the risks, maintenance details and the values for which insurance is required need to be submitted. The documents generally required for processing engineering claims are as under:

(a) Copy of the policy complete with terms, conditions and warranties.
(b) Claim form duly completed by the insured.
(c) Survey report should include –
  (i) Clear indication of the cause of loss
  (ii) Extent of damage and loss
  (iii) Establishment of liability
  (iv) Assessment of loss occurrence of riot is in the public knowledge, production
  (v) Confirmation of compliance of policy terms, conditions and warranties.
  (vi) Admissibility of the claim.
(d) Photographs (if necessary)
(e) Police report, and (if necessary)
(f) Fire Brigade report (if necessary)

The steps involved in the loss adjustment are as under:

Gross loss assessed

(a) Less: depreciation, if any,
(b) Less: Salvage
(c) Less: Under Insurance
(d) Less: Excess
(e) Net Claim Payable

Note: Items (e) and (f) may be waived if the survey report is clear and does not cause any doubt on the occurrence as well as the extent of loss. Where occurrence of riot is in the public knowledge, production of Final Police Investigation Report and Fire Brigade report may be waived.

In case of the theft losses it is necessary to collect a copy of the first information report or proof of complaint lodged by the insured with the police, such as Registered A/D letter. Final Investigation Report may be waived depending upon the merits of the case.

30.4 ENGINEERING ALL RISKS INSURANCE

The first record of insurance specifically for building structures, contractors' all risks insurance (CAR), dates back to 1929 and the construction of Lambeth Bridge over the Thames in London. In Germany, this type of insurance was introduced in 1934 under the name of "Bauleistungsversicherung", when severe restrictions were imposed on the possibilities for creating reserves for outstanding losses to the detriment of the building contractors.

The insurance terms and conditions were derived from erection all risks insurance, with which the companies had already acquired ten years of experience. Nowadays, contractors' all risks insurance cover is increasingly extended by a corresponding loss of profits cover, which provides compensation for the financial losses suffered by principals as a result of delays in completion caused by property damage.

EAR policy is designed to protect the interest of civil contractors and Firms involved in construction activity against the damage or destruction of various civil engineering projects undertaken by them. The policy is suitable for all types of civil engineering construction works ranging from small buildings to massive dams as they are susceptible to damage by a variety of external and internal causes during the course of construction. This is a comprehensive policy designed to cover all risks associated with civil works right from the time of commencement of works at site till the contract works are taken over or put into use. The policy covers:

1. Fire / lightning.
2. Accidental damage during construction like dropping or falling, defective workmanship and material, lack of skill, negligence, malicious act and human error.
3. Act of God perils such as flood and inundation, earthquake.
4. Collapse, collusion, impact.
5. Theft and burglary, malicious and terrorist damage.

Policy may be extended to cover air freight, additional customs duty, express freight, over time wages, expenses for clearance an removal of debris, damage to surrounding property, third party liability, escalation in costs, contractor's plant and machinery at the construction site, defects in construction which surface during maintenance period for which the contractor is liable under the terms of agreement with the principal. Claims are payable at the prevailing market rates for restoration of affected property to the condition immediately before the occurrence of damage. Cost of any improvement and modifications will not be admitted. The amount of loss payable is subject to under insurance if any, and the policy excess. Premium chargeable depends on the nature of the project, the project cost, the project period, geographic location and the period of testing. Discount in premium is allowed for large projects with sum insured more than 100 crores, the higher deductibles opted and for the fire protection available at the site. Premium may be paid in installments where the project period exceeds 1 year. In case of early completion of the project also, refund of premium may be claimed for the balance period of insurance.

30.5 Contractor's Plant and Machinery Insurance Policy

This policy is suitable for contractors involved in construction business for covering all kinds of construction equipment like compressors, heavy duty cranes, boring machines, bulldozers, pipe jacking, and hauling equipment, pavers, excavators, loaders, road rollers, tunnel boring machines etc. can be covered under this policy. The policy offers cover against loss or damage due to sudden unforeseen eventualities such as:

1. Fire, lightning, explosion/implosion/aircraft damage, riot strike, malicious and terrorist damage, earthquake, subsidence, landslide, rockslide, storm, tempest, hurricane, typhoon, tornado, flood and inundation as are covered by the fire policy.
2. Burglary & theft
3. Damages while at work due to faulty handling, dropping or falling, collision and impact.

The policy can be extended to cover the additional risks of third party property damage and injuries; loss or damage to surrounding property, expenses incurred on overtime, express freight, air freight, additional customs duty, clearance of debris following a loss for additional premium. In the event of a loss, costs necessarily incurred for restoration or repairs of the damaged equipment including transportation costs to and fro repair shop, customs duties, taxes etc to the extent included in the sum insured are paid. Policy also covers transit risk of the equipment within the project site. However, damages to exchangeable parts, electrical or mechanical breakdown, and accidents resulting from over load or similar tests are excluded. The policy is subject to excess as stated in the policy. Rate of premium depends on the type of equipment and the location at which it operates. Premium is charged on the reinstatement cost of the equipment. The potential insured has to submit a proposal form giving details of contractor's plant and machinery item wise, the individual values proposed for insurance and the geographical location of the project site where the equipment shall be used. In case additional covers are required they should be specifically mentioned.

At the time of claim settlement the validity of the policy at the time of occurrence and identification of damaged equipment/item is verified. The surveyor generally confirms the accidental damage to the equipment. For items fabricated by the contractor and replacement values not available, the surveyor assesses the loss on the basis of actual costs incurred by the insured.

30.6 Deterioration of Stock Insurance

Breakdown and cold storage machinery may cause rise in temperature of cold storage chambers leading to Deterioration of stock. This policy covers such losses to the stocks in cold storage. The policy is suitable for the owner of the cold storage (individual or a cooperative society) or those who take the cold storage on lease or hire for storage of perishable commodities.This policy covers loss or damage to the stocks in cold storage following breakdown of the cold storage plant. The deterioration of the stocks can be due to:

1. Rise in temperature
2. Sudden and unforeseen escape of refrigerants into the cold storage rooms.

However, the following causes are not covered:

1. Shrinkage, inherent defects or diseases, natural putrefaction, etc.
2. Improper storage, damage to packing material, insufficient air circulation
3. Any willful act or gross negligence of insured or his representatives
4. Loss due to overloading of plant
5. Fire perils including riot, strike, malicious and terrorism damages, war perils
6. Loss arising out of failure of any part requiring periodical renewal; wear and tear parts
7. Operation of fuses and similar devices

Policy can be extended to cover damage to stocks resulting from failure of public electric supply. In the event of a loss, the market value of the commodities lost and reasonable expenses incurred to avoid or minimize such loss or damage, say for transferring the goods from one cold storage to the other are paid. In case of a total loss, claim is paid subject to the overall limit of sum insured under the policy. The sum insured should represent the maximum value of stocks in the cold storage at any given time. Certificates issued by Government authorities that the stocks are unfit for consumption should be provided in support of the claim made. Premium depends on the nature and value of goods stored, the age and condition of the refrigeration plant, stand by/ repair and/ or replacement facilities, nature of refrigerant, alternative storage facilities available, past claims experience and similar other factors. Proposal form should be submitted duly filled giving the nature of commodities stored, details of the refrigeration plant, stand by /maintenance and repair facilities available. The refrigeration plant should be covered under machinery breakdown insurance policy. Following loss minimization measures are insisted by the surveyors while settlement claims:

(i) No fresh stock should be loaded in the cold storage chambers.

(ii) Cold storage doors should be sealed to maintain temperature and avoid temperature rise.

(iii) If possible, the insured should be requested of shift stocks to some other running cold storage premises preferably in cool evening/night period or by refrigerated vans.

(iv) The insured should be requested to carry out repairs to the refrigerator plant most expeditiously.

(v) If there is no possibility of completing the repairs immediately, the insured should be advised to unload stocks from cold chamber for disposal in the local market as quickly as possible, and at the best available price in association with the surveyor/local authorities.

30.6.1 Erection All Risks Insurance

This policy is suitable for the principal or contractors of a project being erected as the project is exposed to various external risks during the construction period and damage to plant and machinery and the supporting structures due to accidents cause financial loss apart from delay in implementation of the project. Interest of all the sub-contractors may be covered by one policy for operational flexibility. This is a comprehensive insurance policy designed to cover any sort of contingency right from the moment the materials are unloaded at the project site and continues during the entire project period until the project is tested, commissioned and handed over. The policy covers the following perils:

1. Location risks: Fire, lightning, theft and burglary.
2. Handling risks: Impact from falling objects, collision, failure of chains or tackles.
3. Operational risks: Failure of safety devices, leakage of electricity, failure of insulation, short circuit, explosion, etc.
4. Risks of human element: Negligence, carelessness, faults in erection, malicious damage, riots and strikes.
5. Act of God: Storm, tempest, hurricane, flood, inundation, landslide, rockslide, and earthquake.
6. Extra covers: Cover for contractors plant and equipment, third party liability, surrounding property, removal of debris, escalation, express freight, overtime charges, additional customs duty are provided at suitable additional premium.

Claims are payable at the prevailing market rates for restoration of affected property to the condition immediately before the occurrence of damage. Cost of any improvement and modifications will not be admitted. The amount of loss payable is subject to under insurance if any, and the policy excess. Premium chargeable depends on the nature of the project, the project cost, the project period, geographic location, the period of testing. Discount in premium is allowed for large projects with S.I more than 100 crore, the higher deductibles opted and for the fire protection available at the site. Premium may be paid in installments where the project period exceeds 1 year.

30.6.2 Industrial All Risks Insurance

This coverage is provided to all major industrial units (other than petrochemical risks) having over all sum insured of Rs. 100 crores and above in one or more locations in India are eligible to take Industrial All Risks Insurance Policy. The policy offers cover against damage due to all perils covered by:

A. Fire and special perils policy.

B. Burglary insurance policy.

C. Machinery Breakdown/ Boiler explosion/ Electronic equipment Insurance.

D. Business Interruption due to fire and special perils policy.

Losses due to the following are excluded:

1. Faulty material/ workmanship/ defective design and material.
2. Inherent vice, defects, deteriorations, and normal wear and tear.
3. Collapse or cracking of buildings.
4. Pollution, contamination, shrinkage, rust, corrosion, scratching, & temperature changes
5. Larceny, fraud, dishonesty, inventory losses, shortage on delivery
6. Willful act, negligence; wars and nuclear risks.

Machinery loss of profit cover is optional. Debris removal, escalation and other covers available as extensions to fire policy can be covered for additional premium. The policy offers widest range of cover compared to that provided by individual operational policies. Under insurance to the extent of 15% is ignored. Sine the insurance is on reinstatement value basis; all expenses for restoration of the damaged property will be covered to the full extent. The policy is however, subject to an excess of 5% of claim amount with a lower limit of 5 lakhs and upper limit of Rs. 50 lakhs. Premium rates for the policy are based on :

1. The cover opted
2. Claims experience
3. Deductibles opted
4. Risk assessment report of the engineer (for MLOP)

30.6.3 Machinery Insurance Policy

This policy is suitable for every industry which operates on machines and for whom breakdown of plant and machinery is of serious consequence. Monetary costs involved for restoration of machine to its original state are covered by the machinery (breakdown) insurance policy. The policy offers cover against loss or damage to the plant and machinery due to sudden and unforeseen reasons whilst the machinery is at work or at rest caused by:

1. Faulty material, design, construction or erection.
2. Vibration, mal-adjustment, mal-alignment
3. Defective lubrication, loosening of parts, stress, molecular fatigue, heating, centrifugal force, explosion/ implosion.
4. Electrical faults and failures.
5. Failure of connected machinery or protective devices.
6. Lack of skill/carelessness of the operators
7. Falling, impact, collision and the like
8. Obstruction or entry of foreign bodies into the machine

Additional expenses required to repair & restore the damaged machinery like overtime, express freight, surrounding property, third party liability, additional customs duty, air freight can be covered on payment of necessary additional premium.

In case of partial loss, all expenses necessary for restoration of the affected machinery will be paid to the extent insured in the policy. Claims will be paid in full provided the machine is adequately insured. Depreciation is not applied except for parts with limited life or which are subject to wear and tear. Excess at 1% of sum insured shall be deducted from all claims. Where the repair cost exceeds the cost of the machine, loss will be dealt on 'total loss basis ' i.e claim will be settled for the depreciated cost of the machine as on the date of loss. Premium is charged on the reinstatement value of individual machinery. The machine as a whole should be insured. Premium rates depend on the type of machine; the industry in which it is used and its value. Discounts are offered based on factors such as stand-by facilities, spares available and claims experience provided the value of all machinery at a particular location exceeds Rs.10 crores. While sett,ling claims, the test reports of the damaged parts if deemed necessary by the surveyor and/or suggested by the insurers is to be submitted to the insurer/surveyor. The claim payable may include costs of dismantling transportation to the repairer's shop, repairs and re-transportation and re-erection and other incidental expenses. If damaged equipment being sent out is covered under a Marine Transit Policy, the cost of such insurance may also be reimbursed. If repeated losses are reported on the same equipment, the underwriting office can take the help of an outside expert to ascertain the precise cause of repeated losses and suggest measures for avoidance/minimization of re-occurrence of breakdown/ loss. The exclusion of damage to Belts, Ropes, Chains, Rubber Tyres, Dyes, Moulds, etc. is to be considered. As to the oil and other operation media in the transformer and equipment, these may be reimbursed when specifically covered under the policy.

The losses under the other extensions like additional custom duty, air freight, express freight, etc., are to be assessed separately and the underwriting office should confirm the availability of additional sum insured specifically for such items of expenditure while recommending the claim for settlement. If the assessment involves additional expenses for repair/ replacement, the surveyor should confirm that the expenses are reasonable.

30.6.4 Loss of Profits Policy

This policy is suitable for industries where interruptions or delays as a result of machinery breakdown or boiler explosion result in huge consequential losses. Where the time lag between the breakdown or loss and the restoration is large, this policy compensates for the loss of profits during the intervening period.

The policy offers cover against consequential losses following loss or damage to the property insured under machinery breakdown and/or boiler and pressure plant insurance. This policy covers actual financial losses suffered by the insured due to business interruption arising from:

1. Reduction in turnover and
2. Increase in cost of working

The standard policy thus insures the loss of gross profits in the business following accident to the machinery, boiler and pressure plant, as a result of material damage loss covered under the corresponding machinery breakdown and boiler explosion policies. The losses as a result of reduced turnover because of the machinery damaged and the additional expenditure necessarily incurred for avoiding or reducing the fall in turnover for the interruption period are compensated under this policy. However, the policy is subject to a time excess of 7 days (14 days in case of petrochemical risks) which means that interruptions for periods less than or equal to these periods are not covered. Premium rates depend on the critical nature of the machinery covered by the breakdown or explosion policies; their relative importance and contribution to final output; the repairs, maintenance and stand by facilities available and the indemnity period opted.

Key Terms

- ❒ Engineering Insurance
- ❒ EAR Insurance
- ❒ Stock Insurance

Questions for Review

1. Briefly explain the need for engineering insurance and the various covers available in India.
2. Write short notes on:
   (a) Engineering All Risk Policy
   (b) Loss of Profits Policy

Suggested Readings

1. Engineering Insurance, IC 77, Insurance Institute of India, Mumbai, 1999.
2. Miscelleneous Insurance, IC 78, Insurance Institute of India, Mumbai, 1991.

Web Resources

- www.cpg.org
- www.insureitech.com
- www.insure.com
- www.pepeinsurance.com

Liability Insurance

Chapter
31

CHAPTER OBJECTIVES

After reading this chapter you will be able to understand :

- *Various types of Tort Liabilities*
- *Specific Statutory Liabilities Covers*

Liability insurance covers provide indemnity to the insured in respect of financial consequences arising out of liability under the civil law. The civil liability arises either due to the operation of :

(a) Law of torts

(b) Specific Statutory Enactments

31.1 TORT LIABILITIES

A legal wrong is a voilation of a person's legal rights, or a failure to perform a legal duty owed to a certain person or to the socitey as a whole. These wrongs may either be crimes(againsty the society), breach of contracts or torts. A tort is a civil wrong for which the law allows a remedy in the form of pecuniary damages. Tort may be of following types:-

(a) Intentional Torts – frauds, infringment of rights, assault, trespas etc.

(b) Strict Liability- absolute liabilty in respect of loss or injury due to use of hazardous subtances, occupational injury to employees etc.

(c) Negligence – failure to perform duties

Some of the specific tort liability covers are discussed in following sections.

31.1.1 Product Liability

This insurance is intended to provide an indemnity to the insured (upto the limit of liability) in the event of a claim being brought against him. This may be caused by anything harmful or defective in the products sold or supplied by the insured in connection with the business specified. The insurer in addition reimburses all costs and expenses incurred with its written consent defending such a claim for compensation. The insurance does not cover the cost of removing, replacing or repairing defective products or loss of use thereof.

Liability for injury or damage caused by a defective product may arise due to the operation of Sale of Goods Act or Consumer Protection Act. The product liability policy seeks to indemnify the insured against his legal liability to pay compensation (including claimants costs, fees and expenses) in respect of injury damage or pollution for third parties for claims arising out of accidents due to any defects in the products specified in the policy during the period of the insurance and first made against the insured during the policy period. For the purpose of determining the indemnity granted:

1. Injury shall mean death, bodily injury, illness or disease of or to any person
2. Damage shall mean actual and / or physical damage to the atmosphere or of any water, land or other tangible property

3. Pollution shall mean pollution or contamination of the atmosphere or of any water, land or other tangible property
4. Product shall mean any tangible property after it has left the custody or control of the Insured which has been designed, specified, formulated, manufactured, constructed, installed, sold, supplied, distributed, treated, serviced, altered or repaired by on behalf of the Insured
5. Accident shall mean a fortuitous event or circumstance which is sudden, unexpected and unintentional including resultant continuous, intermittent or repeated exposures arising out of the same fortuitous event or circumstances

The product policy is on 'Claims made' basis. This means that the accident giving rise to the claim shall occur during the period of insurance and further that the claim shall be first made against the insured during the policy period. The retroactive date is the date of commencement of the first 'Claims made' product liability policy. This date remains unaltered as long as the policy has been renewed without break and there has been no substantial material change in the risk. The policy does not cover :

Special Exclusions

1. The policy excludes liability for costs in the repair, reconditioning, modification or replacement of any part of any product which is or is alleged to be defective.
2. For cost arising out of the recall of any product or part thereof.
3. Arising out of any product which is intended for incorporation into the structure, machinery or control of any aircraft.
4. Arising out of deliberate, willful or intentional non-compliance of any statutory provision.
5. Arising out of pure financial loss such as loss of goodwill, loss of market, etc.
6. Arising out of fines, penalties, punitive and exemplary damages.
7. For injury and/or damage occurring prior to the Retroactive date shown in the schedule.
8. Arising out of deliberate, conscious or intentional disregard of the insured's technical or administrative management of the need to take all reasonable steps to prevent claims.
9. For injury to any person under a contract of employment or apprenticeship with insured where such injury arises out of the execution of such contract.
10. Arising out of contractual liability which would not have existed in the absence of the specific contract.
11. Arising out of any product guarantee.
12. Arising out of claims for failure of the goods or products to fulfill the purpose for which they were intended

In addition, War and Nuclear Perils are specifically excluded. The policy does pays for **loss or damage due to**

- War and war like perils
- Wear and tear, depreciation, consequential loss
- Nuclear group of perils
- Gross and wilful negligence of Insured
- Violation of policy conditions
- Loss/damage/liability where Insured's family or Insured's employee are involved as principal/accessory
- Intentional act/self injury/ influence of drug/intoxicant.

Additional Covers

- Vendors' Liability extension
- Technical collaborators liability
- Products manufactured by sub-contractors/licensed manufacturers on their own brand name can also be covered under the same policy.

Claims arising out of accidents during the policy period due to defects in the products covered by the policy are payable. The policy also covers injury to third party and pollution liability on account of products covered. Indemnity is extended to officials of the insured in their business capacity. Officers, committees and members of insured's welfare associations personal representatives of the estate. All costs, fees and expenses incurred in investigation, defense and settlement of claim made against the insured, cost of representation at any inquiry or other proceedings in respect of matters having direct relevance to the claim made against the insured are covered by the policy subject to the overall limits stated in the policy.

31.1.2 Directors' and Officers' Liability Insurance

In a recent spate of litigation, a number of adverse court verdicts regarding the liability of directors and officers of companies to a third party were passed where the directors and officers were held personally liable for payment of compensation to the third party. Ordinarily, the directors and officers are bound by duty towards the company itself, shareholders, employees, creditors, customers, competitors, members of the public, government and other regulatory bodies. Any breach or non-performance in the duties can result in claims against the companies and/or its directors of the company by reason of any wrongful act in their respective capacity. The Directors' and Officers' Liability Insurance policy has been designed specifically to meet any financial liabilities imposed upon them.

This policy provides cover for directors and officers of a company to reduce the impact of potential litigation owing to

- Failure of supervision.
- Inaccuracy in statements of financial accounts.
- Lack of judgement and good faith.
- Mismanagement of funds.
- Mis-statements in prospectuses.
- Allotment of shares.
- Unauthorised loans or investments.
- Failure to obtain competitive bids.
- Imprudent expansion resulting in a loss.
- Using inside information.
- Unwarranted dividend payment, salaries or compensation.
- Misleading statements filed with the stock exchange.
- Misrepresentation in acquisition agreement for the purchase of another company.
- Wrongful dismissal of an employee.

Risks covered

This policy covers all claims made in event of

- Mergers, takeovers and divestment.
- Changes in control of shareholding.
- Shareholder claims.
- Trustee accountability and responsibility.
- Administrative liabilities.
- Disposal of old firm/ entry of new owners.
- Liquidation.
- Share issues.
- Misdeeds of co-directors.
- Customs and excise allegations.
- Termination of employment.
- Miscellaneous litigation.

Compensation Offered

The extent of indemnity being severely restricted by the Companies' Act will reimburse the extent of legal costs expended only if the Director/ Officer successfully defends the act taken against him. Also, coverage is available on a 'claims made' basis and applies only to claims made against the Board of Directors during the policy period, irrespective of when the wrongful act occurred.

The cover applies to

- Liabilities arising from any claim made against Directors and/ or Officers of the company by reason of any wrongful act in their respective capacity.
- Liabilities against the company where it is required to indemnify the Directors/ Officers pursuant to common or statutory law provisions or Memorandum and Articles of Association.
- The company and its subsidiaries that are under the common control of the Directors/ Officers.

Exclusions

- The policy does not pay for the losses arising from any claim.
- Prior and pending litigation and claims submitted under previous policies.

Bodily injury, sickness, disease, emotional distress, death, damage or destruction of tangible property including loss.

- Insured v/s Insured. viz. Directors suing each other.
- Illegal personal profit and remuneration.
- Deliberate, dishonest or fraudulent acts.
- Pollution and/ or contamination.
- Insider trading.
- Outside directorship (can be covered with specific information).

31.1.3 Employer's Liability

Workmen Compensation Act, 1923 and the common law impose liability of an employer for employment injury (including death) of any of his employees who is a 'workman' as defined under the Act. Section 3 of the Act provides that the employer is liable for compensation if personal injury is caused to workmen by accident arising out of and in the course of employment. Also if the workman contacts any disease, specified in the Act as an occupational disease, the illness is deemed to be injury by accident arising out of and in the course of employment.

Coverage of the Policy under the WC Act,1923

- Indemnity to insured against his liability as an 'employer' to accidental injuries (including fatal) sustained by the 'workman' whilst at work.
- On extra premium-medical, surgical, and hospital expenses including the cost of transport to hospital for accidental employment injuries

- Liability in respect of diseases mentioned in Part C / schedule III of WC Act, on additional premium; which arise out of and in the course of employment

The rates of insurance are prescribed by the tariff which is in two forms:-

Table A – Indemnity against the legal liability for accident to employees under :

(a) Workmen Compensation Act, 1923

(b) Fatal Accident Act, 1855

(c) Common Law

Table B – indemnity cover for legal liability arising under :-

(a) Fatal Accident Act, 1855

(b) Common Law

Compensation

Subject to the provisions of WC Act the amount of compensation / reimbursable is as follows:-

- Where employment injury results in death, then 40%-50% of the monthly wages of the deceased multiplied by the relevant factor or Rs. 20,000/- which ever is more.
- Permanent Total Disablement 50%-60% of the monthly wages of the injured disabled (PTD) workman multiplied by relevant factor or Rs. 24,000/- which ever is more.
- *Permanent Partial Disablement* - (a) For an injury specified in Part II of disablement (PPD) schedule. The percentage of loss of earning capacity caused applied to the compensation payable for permanent total disablement (b) For an injury not specified in schedule - the percentage of permanent loss of earning capacity as assessed by qualified Medical Practitioners applied to the compensation payable for permanent total disablement.
- Where more than one injury caused by same accident it shall be aggregate but in any case not to exceed the amount payable for permanent total disablement
- Temporary disablement - A half monthly payment equivalent to 25 % (total or partial) of monthly wages of the workman to be paid in accordance with the provisions of Sub section (2) of the WC Act.
- Actual medical expenses incurred in connection with on-duty accident ranging from Rs.80/- to 2400/- per case as per the option given at the inception of the policy by the insured and extra premium paid.
- Legal costs and expenses incurred with the Company's consent.

Exclusions

- Any injury which does not result in fatality or partial disablement for period exceeding 3 days
- First 3 days of disablement where the total disablement is less than 28 days
- For any non-fatal injury caused by any accident which is directly attributable to
  - (a) Influence of drinks or drugs
  - (b) Willful disobedience of an order for securing safety of the workman
  - (c) Willful removal or disregard of safety guard device.
- War group and nuclear group of perils
- Liability to employees of contractors of the insured (unless specifically declared)
- Employee who is not a "workman" as per WC act.
- Liability of insured assumed under an agreement

- For occupational diseases mentioned in part "C" of schedule III of WC Act , unless cover is extended on extra premium.
- Increase due to any change in statute provisions after policy had incepted under more than one statute / one forum for the same injury

31.1.4 Professional Indemnity policies

The Professional Indemnity Insurance Policy is available for all doctors, medical establishments, contractors, engineers, architects, interior decorators, chartered accountants, financial accountants, management consultants, lawyers, advocates, solicitors and counsel

Jurisdiction applicable under the Professional Indemnity policy will be within Indian Courts.

Under this cover, the policyholder will be covered for any professional act or omission occurring during the period of insurance provided the policy is renewed without interruption and is in force at the time of claim. Any claims arising out of act or omission of policyholder have to be made in writing during the policy period. The retroactive date of the policy is the period commencing from the date and hour mentioned in the policy and expiring at midnight on the expiry date mentioned in the policy. If the policyholder notifies any event or circumstance as a claim during the period of policy and if insurance company accepts it, then the insurer will deal with the claim. The **"Extended Claim Reporting Clause"** allows the policyholder a time limit up to 90 days from cancellation or non-renewal of policy to notify claims which had taken place during the period of insurance. And the only condition is that another policy does not exist.

31.2 Specific Statutory Liabilities

Public Liability Insurance

The Public Liability Insurance Act, 1991 imposes "no fault" liability in respect of use of hazardous substances as specified by the Act. The object of this Act is to provide through insurance immediate relief to persons affected due to "accident" while "handling" "hazardous substance" by the owners on "no fault liability basis". This has also been brought under Tariff. The definition of "Owner" is so comprehensive as to cover any person who owns or has control over any hazardous substance at the time of accident. This includes any Firm or its partners. Association or its members, Company or its Directors and all other persons associated and responsible to that Company in the conduct of their business. The various terms like "Accident", "Hazardous substances" as defined in Section 2 of the Act are given below.

"Accident" means an accident involving a fortuitous, sudden or unintentional occurrence while handling any hazardous substance resulting in continuous, intermittent or repeated exposure to death of, or injury to any person or damage to any property but does not include an accident by reason only of war or radioactivity.

"Handling" in relation to any hazardous substance, means the manufacture, processing, treatment, package, storage, transportation by vehicle, use, collection, destruction, conversion, offering for sale, transfer or the like of such hazardous substance.

"Hazardous Substance" means any substance or preparation which is defined as hazardous substance under the Environment (Protection) Act, 1986 and exceeding such quantity as may be specified by notification by the Central Government.

"Hazardous Substance" means any substance or preparation which, by reason of its chemical properties or handling is liable to cause harm to human beings, other living creatures, plants, micro-organism, property or the environment (as per the Environment (Protection) Act, 1986).

31.3 LABILITY INSURANCE

Public Liability All Risks Cover

Policy covers all amounts one is legally liable to pay third party during the policy period including legal costs and expenses subject to the limit of indemnity terms and conditions of the policy. This policy indemnifies against amounts one is legally liable to pay as damages to the third party victims of an accident. This includes compensation for accidental death-bodily injury or disease to third parties, damage to or loss of property belonging to third parties arising out of an accident including legal costs incurred with the prior consent of the insurer, legal and civil liabilities of the directors and officers of the company.

Additional Covers

Additional (optional) covers are available for additional premium:

1. *Pollution risks* – caused by a sudden, unintended and unexpected cause which takes place at a specific time and place during the policy period.
2. *Transportation risks* – Outside the premises arising out of an accident directly caused by dangerous materials or hazardous substances while being transported by rail, road or pipeline.
3. *Cover for multiple units* – Non-manufacturing premises of the insured such as offices, depots, godowns etc. located at different places incidental to insured's business activities can be covered.
4. *Technical collaborators, Liability* – This can be included in the main policy subject to reinsurer's approval.

Maximum Liability

Any one accident : Minimum equal to Paid up Capital upto a maximum of Rs.5 crores.

Any one year : Three times of 'Any one accident' limit subject to a maximum of Rs.15 crores.

In case of claim/s exceeding the above statutory limit/s, it is to be met by the Environmental Relief Fund to be set up under Section 7A of the Act and managed by the Authority appointed by the Central Government.

The liability beyond the total of the insurance and the Relief / Fund is to be borne by the "Owner". Every owner , in addition to premium, has to pay to the insurer and equivalent amount to be credited to the said fund. Howver, the central government has powers to exempt any establihment from compulsory insurance, if a fund has been established and maintained for an amount not less than Rs. 5.0 crores or equal to the paid up caital of the establishment, in any nationalized bank for meeting liability under the act.

Schedule of Compensation

1. Reimbursement of medical expenses incurred upto a maximum of Rs. 12,500/- in each case.
2. For a fatal accident the relief will be Rs. 25,000/- per person in addition to reimbursement of medical expenses, if any incurred on the victim upto a maximum of Rs. 12,500/-.
3. For permanent total or permanent partial disability or other injury or sickness, the relief will be :
    a. Reimbursement of medical expenses incurred, if any, upto a maximum of Rs.12,500/- in each case and,
    b. Cash relief on the basis of percentage of disablement as certified by an authorized physician. The relief for total permanent disability will be Rs.25,000/-.
4. For loss of wages due to temporary partial disability which reduce the earning capacity of the victim, there will be a fixed monthly relief not exceeding Rs.1,000/- per month upto a maximum of 3 months provided the victim has been hospitalized for a period exceeding 3 days and above 16 years of age.
5. In respect of damage to private property, upto Rs.6,000/- per claim.

6. Apart from Public liability insurance Act policy, policies are also available to cover the legal liability of the insured against third parties for claims arising due to industrial accidents. Two different types of policies are available to cover accidents in industries like factories etc and non industries like hotels, schools, exhibitions and storage tanks etc.

Claim Procedure

- The Insured has to give written notice to the company as soon as possible of any claim made against him (or any specific event or circumstance that may give rise to a claim being made against the Insured) which forms the subject of indemnity under the policy and shall give all such additional information as the company may require.
- Every claim, writ, summons or process and all documents relating to the event shall be forwarded to the Company immediately after they are received by the Insured, alongwith the claim form duly filled up.
- No admission, offer, promise or payment shall be made or given by or on behalf of the insured without the written consent of the company.
- The insured will have the right to take over and conduct in the name of the Insured in defense of any claim in case of voluntary public liability policies.
- In the event of liability rising under the policy or payment of a claim under the policy, the limit of indemnity per anyone year under the policy shall get reduced to the extent of quantum of liability to be paid or actual payment of such claim.
- No claim is payable under the policy unless the cause of action arises in India and the liability to pay claim is established against the Insured in an Indian Court. It is also to be understood that only Indian Law shall be applicable in such action.

31.3.1 Other Laws

85. The other statues which have a bearing on Public Liability insurance are as follows :

Water (Prevention and Control of Pollution) Act, 1974

The Central and State Pollution Control Boards are established under the Act. The fnctions of the Board, *inter alia,* are to control sewage and industrial effluent discharge. The consent of the Board is required to establish any industry which is likely to discharge sewage or trade effluent.

Air (Prevention and Control of Pollution) Act, 1981

dThis Act is structured along the lines of Water Act but in relation to air pollution.

The Environment (Protection) Act, 1986

Is a comprehensive legislation for enforcement of measures for protection of the environment and for co-ordination of the activities of Pollution Control Boards constituted under the Water and Air Act.

The Factories Act, 1948

The 1987 amendment–V Act has introduced special provisions relating to hazardous activities.

The Central Motor Vehicles, 1989 and 1993, have fixed certain responsibilities on the consignor, the transporter and also the driver for the safe carriage of hazardous goods.

Key Terms

- ❒ Liability Insurance
- ❒ Tort
- ❒ Public Liability
- ❒ Product Indemnity

Questions for Review

1. Briefly explain the need for project insurance and the various covers available in India.
2. Write short notes on:
   (a) Banker's Indemnity Policy
   (b) Fidelity Guarantee Insurance
   (c) Legal Liability Insurance.
3. Briefly explain the provisions of Public Liability insurance Act, 1991 with respect to compulsory insurance and the schedule of compensation.
4. Outline the cover available in the policy under the Workmen Compensation Act, 1923.

Suggested Readings

1. Engineering Insurance, IC 77, Insurance Institute of India, Mumbai, 1999.
2. Miscelleneous Insurance, IC 78, Insurance Institute of India, Mumbai, 1991.
3. Barry D. Smith *et. al.*, Property and Liability Insurance Principles, Insurance Institute of America, 1994.
4. G.E. Rejda, Principles of Insurance and Risk Management, Pearson Education, 2002.
5. Liability and Engineering Insurance, Insurance Institute of India, Mumbai, 2000.

Web Resources

- www.cpg.org
- www.insureitech.com
- www.insure.com
- www.pepeinsurance.com

Miscellaneous Insurance

Chapter 32

Chapter Objectives

After reading this chapter you will be able to understand :

- *Aviation Insurance*
- *Other Insurances*

This chapter illustrates some special classes of insurance.

32.1 Aviation Insurance

Aircraft Comprehensive Insurance Policy

The Policy covers (a) Loss or damage to the aircraft, (b) legal liability to the third party and passengers (c) Legal liability for freight, mail etc. carried (d) Personal accident risk to the pilots, crew and ground staff (e) Loss of professional licence of pilots and other crew members.

Air Line Insurance (Hull and Liability)

The hull policy covers loss and accidental damage (including emergency landings) to air and ground risks; the liability policy covers the airline against legal action from third parties or customers in respect of death, injury or physical damage to property. Most airlines have 'manuscript' wordings devised by the brokers, insurers and purchasers to reflect individual needs, circumstances and preferences. Hull claims are quickly determined and settled. Liability losses are usually complex, as accidents often result from a combination of factors. Often liability will be split with other parties, such as airports and particularly, manufacturers.

Airline Insurance (Hull War)

These policies provide cover to airlines for loss of or damage to their property (aircraft and spares). The risks covered are excluded from hull all risks policies and arise from war or war related activities including:

- War invasion, hostilities, civil war, rebellion, attempted coups etc.
- Strikes, riots, civil commotion or labour disturbances.
- Sabotage.
- Hijacking (attempted or actual) or seizure of control (including pilot suicide).
- Acts for political or terrorist purposes.
- Confiscation, naturalisation, detention etc. for the use of any government or public authority.

Product Liability

Product liability covers an insured's legal liability to third parties for injury and loss or damage arising out of the defective design or manufacture of an aircraft product. It encompasses all types of aircraft products, for example, airframes, engines, seats and minor components.

General Aviation

General aviation is the insurance of "all aircraft other than commercial and military aircraft, and commercial aircraft capable of carrying less than 40 passengers." Different insurers use different definitions. Often planes that can carry between 40 and 60 passengers may be included in either this book or the airline book, depending on the insurer's reinsurance program.

Miscellaneous Covers

There are a number of other types of aviation cover available. Long term policies (of up to 3 years) are common for each of these types of covers.

Aviation Insurance can be purchased in two ways: (1) from a "direct writing" company where the insured contacts the company direct; or *(2)* through an independent insurance agent who represents several companies. The Indian aviation insurance business is worth around $20 million. In India, the major chunk of this business is owned by GIC. However hardly 2 per cent of the same is retained by it since the premium is large, various complexities are involved and as the risk is huge and it will have to be reinsured. On a global basis, the loss ratio in general aviation insurance has exceeded 1.1 to as much as 1.25 or more for the last several years. The key reasons that the insurance companies have been losing money, in aviation business are:

1. The cost of repairs is increasing fast.
2. The number of insured accidents is up.
3. The value of the aircraft is soaring.

To keep insurance costs under control in the current difficult environment, aircraft and aviation business owners have to think on the following aspects:

- Self-insurance
- Matching equipment to needs
- Optimise maintenance costs
- Promote revenues
- Promote personal aviation
- Focus on safety.

Additional Covers

The risks of one project differ from another. In order to meet the particular requirements of the project concerned, care should be taken to check on which additional coverage/s out of those listed below is/are required and action taken thereon.

- Dismantling Cover
- Express Delivery
- Third Party Liability Cover
- Testing of Second-hand Machinery
- Deletion of 60 days Clause in Ocean Policy
- Cross Liability Cover
- Maintenance Period
- Terrorism Cover
- Additional Transits
- Clearance and Removal of Debris
- Additional Customs Duty.

Storage Risks at Fabricators' Premises/Workshop

In short, the cover is against all risks of physical loss or damage arising out of operation of any one or more of the following perils:

- *Location Risks:* Fire, Lightning, Theft and Burglary.
- *Handling Risks:* Impact from falling objects, Collision, failure of Cranes or Tackles.
- *Operational Risks:* Failure of safety devices, Leakage of Electricity, Insulation failures, Short-circuit, Tearing apart on Account of centrifugal forces. Explosion.
- *Human Risks:* Carelessness, Negligence, Faults in erections, Malicious Element, Damage, Strikes and Riots, Terrorism
- *Acts of God:* Earthquake, Storm, Tempest, Hurricane, Flood.
- Subsidience: Landslide, Rockslide.

Other Insurance Policies that are required are:

- Empoyer's Liability/Workmen's Compensation
- Employee's Sickness and Accident/Travel Insurance
- Office/Documents/Cash/Computers, etc.
- Motor damage and Third Party
- Public and Product liability.

32.2 OTHER INSURANCES

The various other classes of insurance are:

A. Burglary Insurance

The various covers available in this category are:

- Burglary (Business Premises) Policy
- Burglary (Private Residences) Policy
- Burglary All Risks Policy
- Money-in-transit Insurance
- Baggage Insurance Policy

B. Jewellers' Block

The policy is specially designed to take care of all risks of a jeweller whose business involve sale of articles of high value in small bulk like jewelry gold and silver articles, diamonds and precious stones, wrist watches etc. This is a package policy covering risks like fire, lightning, explosion, strike, riot, malicious damage, burglary, housebreaking, theft, robbery and hold ups. For risks up to a sum insured of Rs.25 lakhs the stocks are to be kept in Standard Safes after business hours and in the case where sum insured is up to Rs. 10 crores, stocks should be kept in Burglar Proof safe after business hours and in case of values insured being above Rs 10 crores, the stocks should be kept in a number of Burglar Proof Safes, after business hours.

C. Banker's Indemnity

This policy is suitable for Banks, NBFC's and other institutions who deal with operations involving money. The policy provides contingency against the following contingencies:

1. Loss in premises due to fire, riot and strike, burglary or house breaking or hold up resulting in loss to money/securities at the premises.
2. Lost, stolen, mislaid, misappropriated or made away either due to negligence or fraud of employees of the insured whilst in transit.
3. Direct financial loss by bogus, fictitious or forged or raised cheque/drafts/FDRs or forged endorsements.
4. Loss to money and/or operations by dishonesty.
5. Loss due to fraud and/or dishonesty or criminal act of the insured's employees.
6. Loss by robbery, theft or by other courses to the parcels insured with the post office.
7. Infidelity or criminal acts by appraisers on the approved list.
8. Infidelity or criminal acts by Janata Agents/Chhoti Bachat Yojana Agents/Pygmy Collectors.

The indemnity provided under this policy in respect of direct losses shall not exceed the sums insured set against each cover. Excess is applicable except for fire and burglary claims. By charging appropriate premium, the sum insured under the policy is maintained constant so as to have full cover even after a claim. The insured is required to lodge a complaint with the police and take all practical steps to recover the property lost/apprehend the guilty person/take departmental action in the event of a loss.

D. Fidelity Guarantee Insurance

Fidelity guarantee covers are provided to indemnify the pecuniary loss suffered by the acts of dishonesty, fraud, forgery, larany, default etc. by employees occupying the positions of trust. These policies can be taken by individuals for self (Individual policy guaranteeing one name) or by employees, for the specific employees' as group, (collective policy) or for employees unnamed, for group as a whole (floater policy). The policy can be taken for specific positions rather than names e.g., accountant, cashier etc. (Positions policy). Blanket covers are also available for entire staff or group of employees. Guarantee policy-missing documents indemnity are also available in respect of people who may be in possession of voluminous documents like shares and bond certificates, bank deposits, real estate and there is a high degree of risk in possession of those documents.

E. Business Insurances

Business Guard Sanjeevani: Suitable for Business establishments with needs for sum insured in excess of Rs. 10 lakhs and up to Rs. 1 crore. It is a comprehensive and specially designed policy, offering different limits of coverage permitting insured to select a cover as per his specific requirement. It covers fire, public liability, burglary, money in safe and personal accidents.

Business Guard Jyothi: It is a comprehensive package which covers losses arising out of a variety of perils including fire, public liability, burglary and money-in-safe. Additionally, it offers the business owner a personal accident insurance.

Trade Protector: This Policy is suitable for shops, retail agencies, dealers, restaurants, hair dressers, boutiques, beauty parlours, laundries, video game parlours, hotels, guest houses or any other business establishments who want to take comprehensive insurance protection under one package policy.

F. Personal Accident Insurance

These covers are non-tariff. These policies provide for accidental injury to body which results in death or disablement. The scope of these covers can be extended to medical expenses. The popular ones are:

(a) Bhagyashree Child Welfare – to cover the cost of education of one girl child if one or both the parents die, during an accident.

(b) Janata personal accident policy — a low cost policy covering death or loss of limbs due to accident for sum assured upto Rs. 25,000.

(c) Personal accident — covers death or bodily injury due to an accident.

Other than these covers, specific covers are available for road or rail accidents (Traffic Accident Policy), NRI's and their family (NRI accident insurance policy), womens (Rajrajeshwari Mahila Kalyan), accident cover and cash compensation for leave (Executive Guard etc.)

G. Other Policies

- Horse Insurance
- Cycle Risk Shaw Insurance
- Pedal Cycles Insurance
- Plate Glass Insurance
- Household Appliances Insurance
- Shopkeepers' Policy (Composite)
- Carriers Legal Liability
- LPG Dealers
- Office Umbrella
- Special Contingency
- Electronic Equipment Policy
- Gun Insurance
- Baggage Insurance

Other Miscellaneous Insurance Statistics

Business Generated (Gross Direct Premium - Rs. in crores)

Companies	*1993-94*	*1994-95*	*1995-96*	*1996-97*	*1997-98*	*1998-99*	*1999-2000*
GIC	353.05	424.50	517.55	622.11	691.69	816.79	911.38
NIC	172.18	188.42	254.06	299.65	321.43	393.46	425.13
OIC	472.21	532.34	645.78	755.63	856.39	1045.95	1174.43
NIAC	303.37	335.09	384.59	1231.12	516.42	619.63	681.18
UII	243.32	236.85	291.59	352.80	397.87	481.69	496.23
Total	**1544.13**	**1717.20**	**2093.57**	**3261.31**	**2783.80**	**3357.52**	**3688.35**

Profits (*Rs. in Crores*)

Companies	*1993-94*	*1994-95*	*1995-96*	*1996-97*	*1997-98*	*1998-99*	*1999-2000*
GIC	-72.44	-198.95	-147.01	-197.37	-220.78	-264.08	-378.35
NIC	20.37	-30.68	21.18	2.01	17.62	30.30	-23.88
OIC	-47.95	-190.43	-252.40	-242.17	-224.99	-361.36	-354.74
NIAC	41.00	55.45	42.88	-185.01	75.66	-26.84	1.68
UII	38.99	4.29	3.31	2.41	8.03	39.40	-59.63
Total	**-20.03**	**-360.32**	**-332.04**	**-620.13**	**-344.46**	**-582.58**	**-814.92**

Profit %age

GIC	-20.52%	-46.87%	-28.40%	-31.73%	-31.92%	-32.33%	-41.51%
NIC	11.83%	-16.28%	8.34%	0.67%	5.48%	7.70%	-5.62%
OIC	-10.15%	-35.77%	-39.08%	-32.05%	-26.27%	-34.55%	-30.21%
NIAC	13.51%	16.55%	11.15%	-15.03%	14.65%	-4.33%	0.25%
UII	16.02%	1.81%	1.14%	0.68%	2.02%	8.18%	-12.02%

Miscellaneous Insurance (Gross Direct Premium Income)

Company	*2000-01*	*2001-02*	*2002-03*	*2003-04*	*2004-05*
National	1505.99	1666.47	2136.67	2688.15	3010.98
New India	2073.09	2313.14	2709.38	3011.27	3169.44
Oriental	1540.49	1719.16	2042.7	2089.18	2288.42
United India	1635.42	1763.86	2024.74	2136.73	2109.75
ECGC*	-	338.52	374.78		
GIC*	280.08				
Royal Sundaram	0.24	50.44	132.26	193.85	250.89
Reliance	0.13	29.87	121.34	101.49	95.41
Iffco-Tokio	2.09	3.34	91.39	154.86	292.99
TATA AIG	-	49.91	156.69	234.17	323.68
ICICI Lombard	-	16.13	70.82	203.68	513.89
Bajaj Allianz	-	112.71	228.43	335.5	587.24
Cholamandalam	-	9.31	65.77	105.57	
HDFC-Chubb	-	9.49	112.57	173.32	
Total	**7037.53**	**8063.55**	**10108.00**	**11327.22**	**12921.58**

Market Share

Private Co. Share	99.965%	92.548%	88.183%	87.624%	81.868%
Public Co. Share	0.035%	7.452%	11.817%	12.376%	18.132%

Miscellaneous Insurance - Underwriting Experience

Company	*2000-01*	*2001-02*	*2002-03*	*2003-04*	*2004-05*
National	393.71	-319.32		76.29	-164.35
New India	496.33	-632.59		-295.92	-53.05
Oriental	-312.66	-476.32		61.85	76.29
United India	-488.69	-248.1		-114.14	-181.75
ECGC*	**	**			
GIC*	-487.36	-501.37		-323.52	56.7
Royal Sundaram	**	**		-9.96	-7.1
Reliance	**	**		-6.05	-6.37
Iffco-Tokio	**	**		-5.6	-6.49
TATA AIG	**	**		-16.15	3.07
ICICI Lombard	**	**		-4.3	-10.42
Bajaj Allianz	**	**		3.13	24.96
Cholamandalam	**	**		-16.8	-10.42
HDFC-Chubb	**	**		-29.58	-11.6
				-680.75	-290.53

** Details Not Provided/Available

Key Terms

- ❐ Project Insurance
- ❐ Aviation Insurance
- ❐ Fidelity Insurance
- ❐ Business Insurance

Questions for Review

1. Write short notes on:
   (a) Aviation Insurance
   (b) Banker's Indemnity Policy
   (c) Fidelity Guarantee Insurance

Suggested Readings

1. Miscelleneous Insurance, IC 78, Insurance Institute of India, Mumbai, 1991.
2. Barry D. Smith *et. al.*, Property and Liability Insurance Principles, Insurance Institute of America, 1994.

Web Resources

- www.cpg.org
- www.insure.com
- www.insureitech.com
- www.pepeinsurance.com

Functions and Organization of Insurers

Chapter 33

Chapter Objectives

After reading this chapter you will be able to understand :

- Type of Insurance Organisations
- Organisational Structure of Insurance Companies
- Functions of Insurers

33.1 Type of Insurance Organisations

Insurance organisations can be classified in various ways. They can be classified on the basis of their risk coverage *viz.*, life, property, health etc. or on the basis of their agency system *e.g.* exclusive agency, independent agency or direct selling. Insurance companies can also be classified on the basis of registration :

1. *Domestic :* This type of insurance company is incorporated and formed under the laws of the state in which it is domiciled. For example, a company incorporated in India– under the Companies Act, 1956 is domestic to India and is foreign to the other states.
2. *Foreign :* This type of insurance company is also domestic company as it is domiciled in one state but it is licensed to do business in another state. For example, a California domiciled company doing business in Nevada because it met the licensure requirements. In India, foreign companies can have joint ventures only.
3. *Alien :* This type of insurance company is often confused with a Foreign insurance company. The Alien company is the one that is formed under the laws of a country other than the operating countries. For example, a company organized under the laws of Canada and doing business in the United Staes would be an Alien company in this country. However, if it is properly licensed, it can do business in the United States.
4. *Authorized (Admitted) and Unauthorized (Unadmitted) :* Upon applying for approval to do business in a state, the insurance company receives a certification of authority from the state Insurance Department (Divison). Once they receive this certificate they become known as an admitted, or authorized, company. Companies without a certificate of authority are known as unadmitted, or unauthorized, companies.

Another way to categorize insurance companies is by the type of service offered. For example, a *monoline* company provides ony one type of insurance coverage, while a *multiple line* company provides more than one kind of insurance. A *financial services company* provides not only insurance but also financial services to customers. Also, the insurers can be classified on the basis of their formation from legal point of view e.g., stock companies or mutual companies.

33.1.1 Stock Companies

A stock insurance company is owned and controlled by its common stockholders. Most of the insurance companies in India are stockholders type. The stockholders i.e., the shareholders appoint a board of directors who in turn appoint officers for running the operations of the company. The profit from operations is distributed to the shareholders in the form of dividends.

The policy covers issued by these companies, by definition, are non-participating implying that none except the benefit contracted shall be paid to the policyholders and no dividends accordingly shall be paid. However, sometimes, these companies do sell participating policies. In those cases, the policyholders not only get the policy dividends, but also the stock dividends.

33.1.2 Mutual Companies

Mutual Insurance organisations, popularly known as mutuals, are generally non-profit organisations owned by the policyholders. The initial surplus for a mutual insurance company is contributed by either the policyholders or a financial intermediary who must be repaid with interest or surplus accumulates. Any earnings in excess are redistributed to the policyholders. Either distributing as dividends or reduction in the renewal premiums can accomplish this. Policyholders in a mutual company are just like shareholders entitled to attend the board meetings, cast votes on resolutions etc.

Mutuals may be of the following types:

(a) *Assessment Mutuals:* With an assessment mutual, the policy owner may or may not pay a premium when the policy begins, but they are responsible for a premium based upon their fair share of the losses and expenses at the end of the period. Therefore, policy owners in assessment mutuals pay their fair share. Assessment mutuals generally insure exposures that are not stable. For example, if an exposure is based on product sales or payroll, they may not know what the exact exposure will be at the beginning of the period. Therefore, at the end of the period, an audit determines the actual exposure and the policy owner then pays a premium based on the final figure.

(b) *Advance Premium Mutuals:* Advanced premium mutuals have policy owners pay their premiums when their insurance begins and they become eligible for a dividend when the policy period ends. They generally insure stable exposures – that is ones that do not change significantly over the policy period. Increased dividends come from better than expected expenses, investment earnings and losses.

(c) *Factory Mutuals:* Factory mutuals provide substantial loss prevention services including regular inspections of the insured premises. Only those meeting strict safety and construction qualifications can qualify for coverage (highly protected risks). Large up-front and multi-year deposits are made which generally tie up funds. However, if companies qualify, costs to insure can be significantly less.

(d) *Farm Mutuals:* Farm mutuals are community based and owned by the policyholders. They are run by a board of directors who are policyholders. These companies serve the insurance needs of local home owners, farm and other business operators.

(e) *Perpetual Mutuals:* Perpetual mutuals charge a single large advance premium which earns enough investment income to cover all future losses and expenses.

(f) *Fraternal Mutuals:* These are primarily social organisations, most of which are organised to serve particular religious, nationality, or labour groups. In U.S., most of the fraternal issuers issue non-assessable policies.

33.1.3 Reciprocal or Inter-insurance Exchanges

Reciprocal exchanges are sometimes called as inter-insurance exchanges. A reciprocal is an association, the members of which exchange insurance. Reciprocal exchanges are not-for-profit, unincorporated, associations of individuals. So and therefore, someone (an individual or a corporation) is granted the legal ability to transact business for the group. This person is identified as the attorney-in-fact and is responsible (and paid) for providing all the administrative services needed including sales and underwriting. Initial capital is obtained from either:

(1) prepayment of excessive premiums by members, which are contributions to surplus, or (2) contributions in the form of sub-ordinated loans made by attorney-in-fact. Surplus is also accumulated by retention of earnings. The attorney-in-fact receives percentage of premiums.

33.1.4 Lloyd's of London

Lloyd's is the world's best known insurance brand with 46 managing agents and 75 syndicates. This is because Lloyd's is not an insurance company but a society of members, both corporate and individual, who underwrite in syndicates on whose behalf professional underwriters accept risk. Supporting capital is provided by investment institutions, specialist investors, international insurance companies and individuals (Exhibit 33A).

(a) It's underwriters sometimes insure "unusual" loss exposures, and thereby Lloyd's receives a good deal of publicity.

(b) It's worldwide reputation for prompt and fair claims settlements, on even the largest losses.

(c) It's financial capacity to handle large exposures.

(d) It's reputation for innovation and expertise in many technical areas.

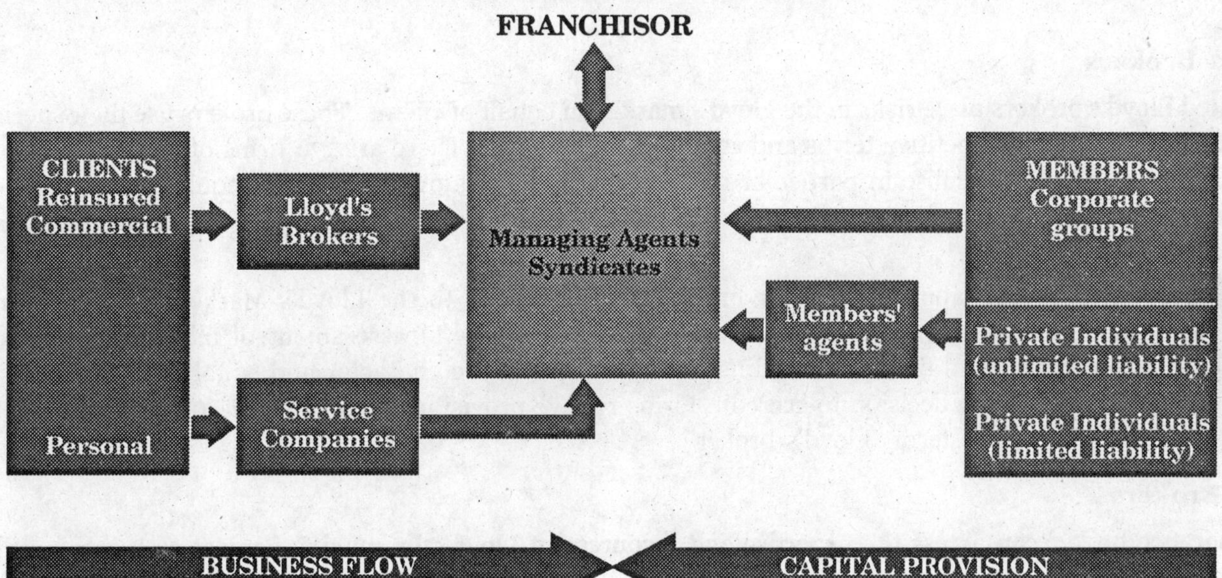

Lloyd's brokers bring business to the market. The risks placed with underwriters originate from clients and other brokers and intermediaries all over the world. Together, the syndicates underwriting at Lloyd's form one of the world's largest commercial insurers and a leading reinsurer.

Exhibit 33A is a basic representation of the structure of the market and its participants. A detailed description of the participants is enumerated in following paragraphs.

Members of Lloyd's

Members of Lloyd's, or 'capital providers' as they are often known, accept insurance business through syndicates on a separate basis for their own profit and loss (in other words, members of Lloyd's are not jointly responsible for each other's losses). The membership of Lloyd's is currently made up of companies, individuals and Scottish Limited Partnerships. Individual members, or 'Names' as they are often known, tend to support a number of syndicates, whereas some corporate members only underwrite through a single syndicate.

Syndicates

Lloyd's members conduct their insurance business in syndicates, each of which is run by a managing agent. The syndicates operating within the market cover many speciality areas including:

- Marine
- Aviation
- Catastrophe
- Professional indemnity
- Motor

Syndicates tailor solutions to respond to the specific risks of the client base.

Syndicates compete for business, thus offering choice, flexibility and continuing innovation. Syndicates cover either all or a portion of the risk and are staffed by underwriters, the insurance professionals on whose expertise and judgement the market depends.

Managing Agents

It is the responsibility of the managing agent to employ the underwriting staff and manage the syndicate on the members' behalf. The managing agent must be a company specifically established for the purpose of managing a syndicate, and it may not carry out any other function. A managing agent may be responsible for more than one syndicate.

Lloyd's Brokers

Accredited Lloyd's brokers place risks in the Lloyd's market on behalf of clients. These brokers use their specialist knowledge to negotiate competitive terms and conditions for clients. There are 176 firms of brokers working at Lloyd's, many of whom specialise in particular risk categories. Each Lloyd's broker is required to demonstrate an understanding of the Lloyd's market, as part of Lloyd's assessment of its suitability to be accredited as a Lloyd's Broker.

Lloyd's operates an accreditation process for brokers seeking access to the Lloyd's Market. All brokers must satisfy all relevant regulatory requirements. Lloyd's performs a careful assessment of all applicant brokers, affirming their reputation and financial standing and investigating the character and suitability of officers and employees before making the decision to accredit. Firms receive provisional accreditation for three years before becoming entitled to use the term "Lloyd's broker".

Local Brokers

Any insurance broker can access the expertise and resources of Lloyd's by making contact with an accredited Lloyd's broker.

Lloyd's of London has had much financial difficulty over the past two decades. The organization has experienced losses more than 12.6 billion dollars from 1987 to 1992. About $5 billion in assessments from losses in 1993 were unmet by names in 1995. Many participants were declared bankrupt. A major source of the losses occurred from liability coverage and reinsurance written on exposures in the United States. Lloyd's is in the process of re-organising its operations and financial arrangements to overcome reported problems.

33.1.5 Selecting the Form of Organisation

The laws of the region generally govern selecting the form of insurance organisation. In India, to carry on the business of insurance, the insurer has to register himself as a company under the Companies Act, 1956 and obtain a license from IRDA.[1] Various arguments are put in favour of both stocks and mutuals. Arguments often made favouring stock insurers include.[2]

1. www.irda.org Insurance Regulatory and Development Authority (Registration of Indian Insurance Companies) Regulations, 2000.
2. www.instruct.nmu.edu/business/Sgraci/355% 20Answers/chap5.html.

(a) the capital contribution by owners is an additional source of funds (beyond the mutual insurer's surplus accounts) to absorb the results of unfavourable operations.

(b) since stock insurers are profit oriented, they tend to be efficient.

(c) stock insurers generally operate through independent agents who may represent their clients' interests better than companies using "captive" agents.

(d) stock companies generally have lower initial premiums (at least in their non-participating policies).

Arguments favouring mutual companies include:

(a) they are non-profit organisations, and in the long run they may provide insurance more economically, since the insureds share in the results of favourable operations.

(b) because no dividends are paid to "outside" owners, mutuals are able to provide insurance more cheaply.

33.1.6 Demutalization

When a mutual insurance company coverts itself to a stock insurance company, the conversion process is called as Demutalization. The rationale for a mutual to demutualize may be:

(1) Tax advantages

(2) The stock form allows companies to raise capital in the financial markets and thus helps strengthen and stabilises financial operations.

(3) Stock insurers have more flexibility in designing capital structure.

(4) Down stream holding companies may be set up under the stock form.

The various obstacles to Demutualization include the legal, cost, regulatory, tax and accounting problems of the conversion. Though, demutualization of insurance companies is not visible, yet demutualization of stock exchanges can be seen in India.

33.2 Organisational Structure of Insurance Companies

The organisational structure of insurance company must coincide with the business model of the insurance organisation. The structure of insurers may differ on various parameters including the nature of coverages, location, form of organisation, level of authority, legal restrictions etc. The two specimen of organisation structure based on Personnel and Geographical Location are given in Exhibit 33-B.

There is no uniformity of practice as to organisational structure and titles vary from one company to another so that the terminology and the structure of an individual company may not coinside but all of the functions will be performed under some title or another. In most of the insurance companies, the authority for company's management stems from its stockholders or policyholders as the case may be. These groups elect the composition of board of directors.

Board of Directors

The board of directors performs a trusteeship function and is concerned with such matters as long-range planning, finances, and evaluation of results. The function of the board of directors is to formulate the overall plan of action for the company in the best interests of the owners taking into account the interests of policyholder's, staff, the public and the effect of market competition. The board is responsible for the overall direction of the company and for selecting officers to manage it (Exhibit 33C).

Boards comprise both executive and non-executive members. The former are involved in the day-to-day operations of the company and are members of the senior management. Non-executive directors come from many other areas and could give the benefit o their experience in other business pursuits.

Exhibit 33-B

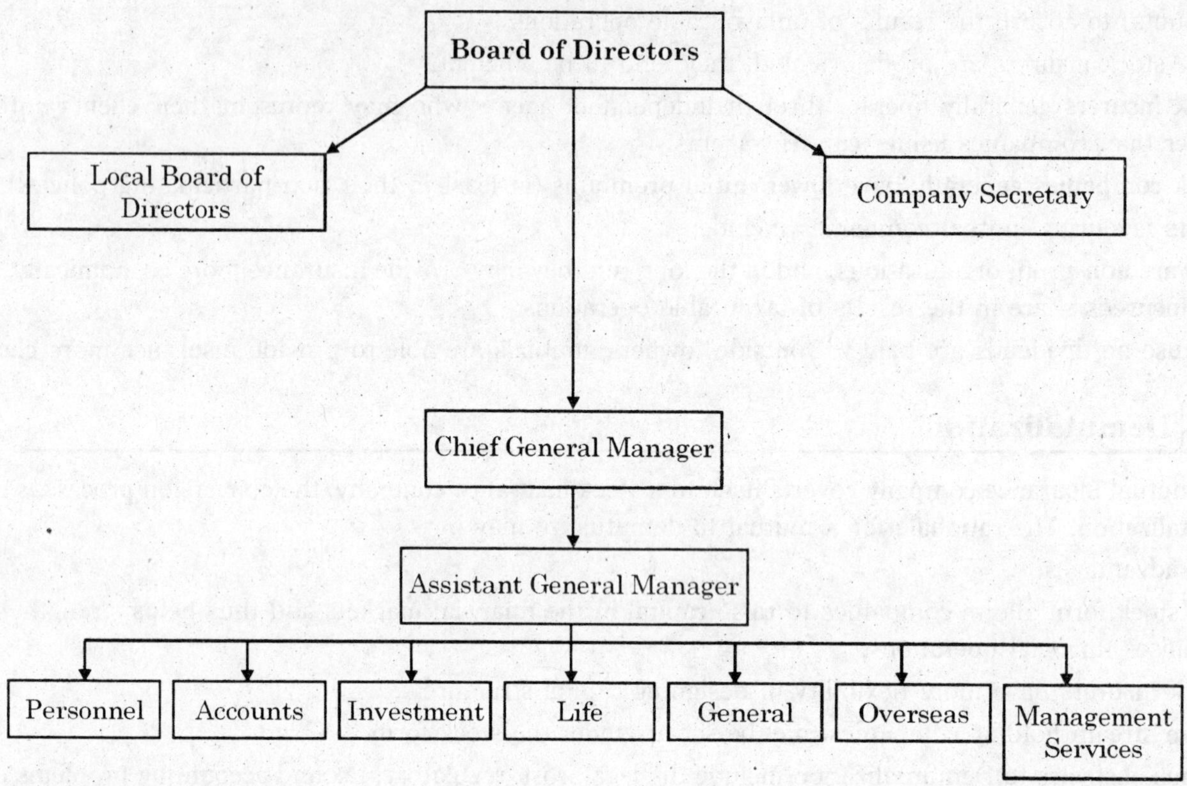

Local Board of Directors

Some companies have board of director's attached to local offices, they are non-executive and are appointed to promote the interests of the company locally and to give advice on local affairs to the branch manager.

General Manager

The chief general manager is the chief executive of the company and is assisted by a deputy and several assistants depending upon the size of the company. The Chief General Manager is charged with the responsibility of implementing the policy laid down by the board. Each assistant general manager has a given area of responsibility.

Company Secretary

The responsibilities are those of administration of the organization and ensuring the company complies with company and insurance laws.

Management Services

The activities and costs of a large insurance company are so vast that separate departments have been set department of specialists to advice on any change in plan which may be necessary in the future. In this way it is hoped that the company can cope with change and progress smoothly in a rapidly changing world.

Personnel

It is essential that any large organization be well staffed with the right kind of people, which is primarily the job of the personnel department.

Investments

The large funds of the insurance company have to be effectively managed, the long term and short-term investments of a company are looked into by the investment manager for security and income.

Head Office

It is the main controlling office of the insurance company. The main burden of management and underwriting work is carried out in the head office.

Regional Offices

Some companies operate on partly decentralized system where certain zonal or regional offices have underwriting authority for branches within their region.

Exhibit 33-C

ORGANISATION CHART OF AN ALL LINES INSURANCE COMPANY

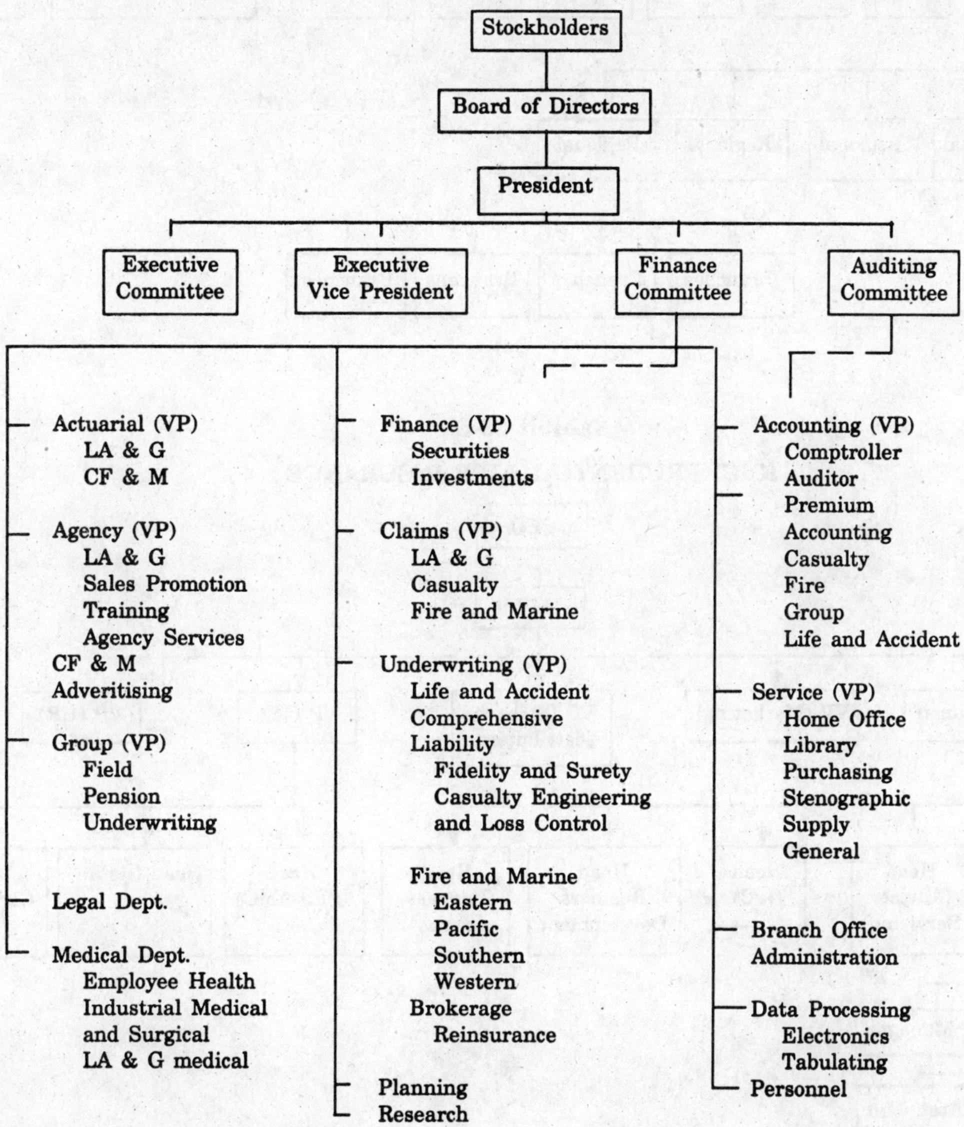

LA & G Life, Accident and Group CF & M Casualty, Fire and Marine
LA & H Life, Accident and Health

Exhibit 33-D

ORGANIZATION STRUCTURE OF LIC

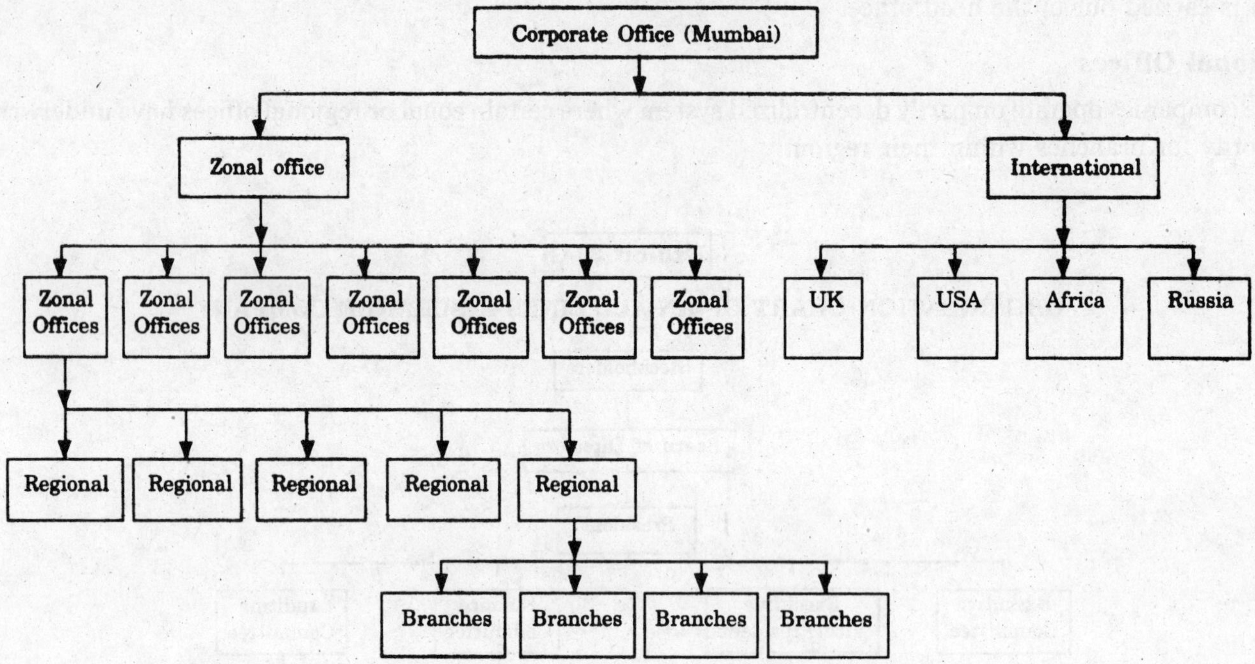

Exhibit 33-E

ICICI PRUDENTIAL LIFE INSURANCE

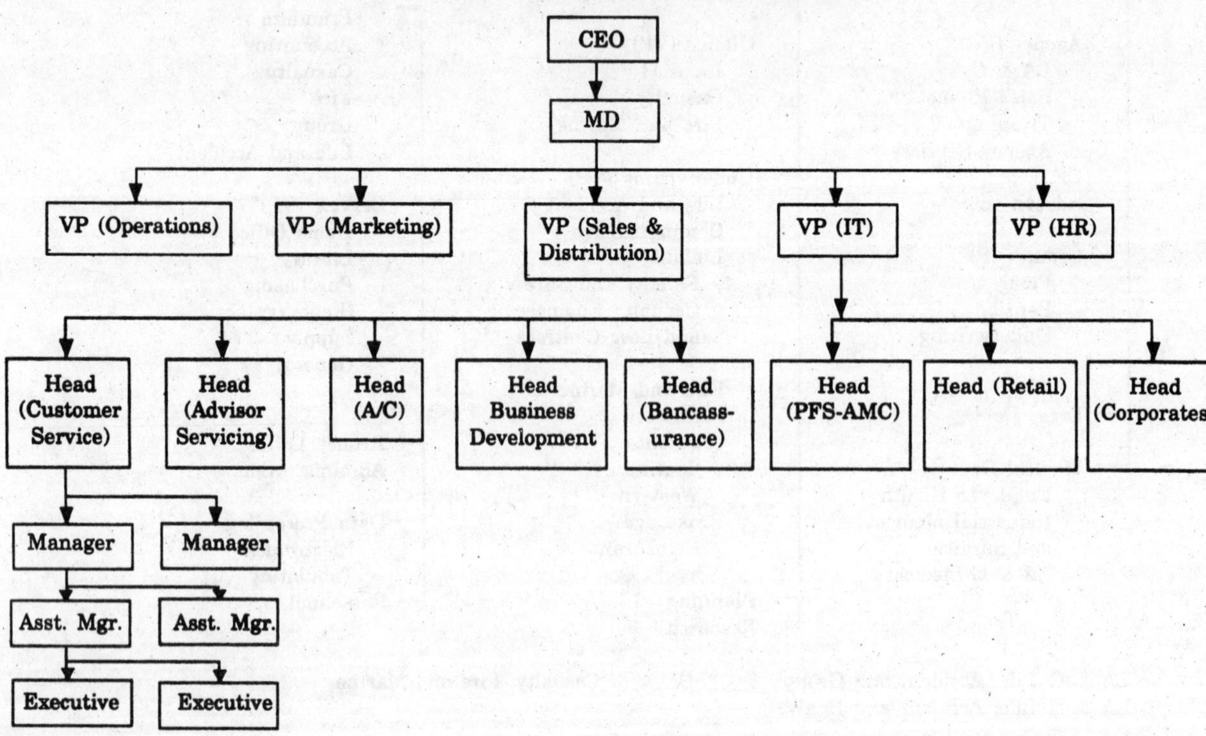

Note: **The above structures have been taken on the basis of personal discussions with the officials of respective companies.**

Main Branches

They are responsible, for underwriting within their area and that of their sub-branches. They control the operations of sub-branches and report to the regional offices.

Sub-Branches

Sub-branches are the first level offices for an insurance company. The prime purpose of a sub-branch is to promote sales promotion in their respective areas.

Regional System

Under this system the country was divided into regions and the principal branch became the regional office, it took over the underwriting policy drafting and claims work from the head office. In this way an attempt was made to remove the disadvantages of the two systems while retaining the advantages.

33.2.1 Organisational Structure of few Insurance Players

The organisation structures of LIC and ICICI Prudential Life Insurance are give in Ehibit 24(d) and 24(e) respectively.

33.2.2 Centralisation vs. Decentralisation

Centralisation and Decentralisation of organisation structure offer distinctive advantages and disadvantages.

Centralisation

Advantages

- Uniformity of policy
- Most economic use of mechanized methods
- Branches relieved of routine duties and can concentrate on selling.

Disadvantages

- Higher costs
- Poor service as administration is away from company.

Decentralization

Advantages

- Local officials best understand local conditions
- Good local service is possible
- Branch staff become more knowledgeable.

Disadvantages

- Many experts required and hence high costs
- Branches inundated with lot of routine work instead of concentrating on selling.

33.3 Functions of Insurers

The various tasks in an insurance organisation may be classified on various basis including the following:

(1) function, including sales, underwriting, administration, claims etc.

(2) product, including life, property and liability, marine insurance etc.

(3) territory, including local, regional, national and international.

(4) customer type, including individual consumers, commercial enterprises, private institutions or government, and

(5) executive interest:

insurance, many an industry of specialists, striving for achieving the model of large numbers, involves numerous functions which can be grouped as follows:[3]

(a) those necessary to perpetuate the identity and health of the corporate entity, including the president, secretary-treasurer, controller and investments; (2) those necessary for the offering of insurance protection, including sales, underwriting and claims adjustment, and (3) (6) those that complement and allow the other functions to operate, including general counsel, actuarial, statistics, engineering personnel administration, and so on.

Following departments are generally found in an insurance company.

1. **Actuarial:** This is the most important department concerned with all the financial functions (calculation of premiums) policy reserves, non-forfeiture values and dividends) of a life or health insurance company and with rate making in property and liability insurance. It conducts the various mathematical studies, determines rates and reserves for management on various facets of insurance business. They also play a key role in the development of new insurance products and their calculation can make or mar insurance business. The head office of insurance organisations generally have a full-fledged actuarial department headed by actuaries.

2. **Underwriting:** It is responsible for selecting, classifying and rating risks. The major tasks of underwriting department are to select a portfolio of risks which will contribute to the profits and surplus of the insurer at an optimum level, to achieve equity among the policyholders, to avoid adverse selection against the insurance company, and to protect the company from the danger of catastrophic losses. This department is concerned with policy forms, policy-writing, determination of prohibited risks, reinsurance and experience review. The underwriter in an insurance company formulates and enforces rules that specify the characteristics, rates and reinsurance requirement of risks that he is willing to accept. Credit agencies, statistical agencies, appraisal services and investigation bureaus are extensively used in insurance.

3. **Sales and Marketing:** Sales department of an insurance company plays a vital role in the achievement of corporate goals. Insurance business is a business of law of large numbers. The law requires the insurer to attract a sufficient number of exposures to allow credible ratio prediction.

   The sales department must generate sufficient exposure subject to actuaries prediction that actual losses will not be more than predicted losses. Insurance being a service business, requires marketing department to play a key role in delivery.

   The marketing department conducts research for identification of target customers, helps in maintaining and promoting the distribution system and also plays an active role in development of new products. It is the most vibrant department in an insurance organisation since it has to necessary deal with all the other departments of the organisation.

4. **Accounting:** Insurance accounting is a complex issue regulated by laws of respective countries. A typical problem in accounting for insurance companies pertains to creation of "reserves for contingencies" which are probabilistic and therefore difficult to predict. In India, IRDA has prescribed the formats in which the financial statements are to be prepared by the life and non-life insurance companies and report to various concerned parties.

5. **Investing and Financing:** Insurance companies are often referred to as "closed end investment trusts engaged in the underwriting of risks as a means of obtaining funds for investment." Investment activity is crucial although not the dominant function. Funds are held for long periods of time, interest rates are

guaranteed to the policyholder, and the insurer is obliged to seek the best possible rates of return. The investment problem is complicated by the large size of insurance company investment portfolios.

The investment department is responsible for managing the insurer's portfolio of investments, which may include: government securities, corporate bonus, direct placement loans, mortgages, preferred stock, common stock, real estate, and other business interests. Within the constraints of regulation and prudent financial management, the investment department attempts to optimize income and capital gains. If the investment department is successful, there will be an increase in surplus which will raise the insuring capacity of the company.

Communication between the investment and underwriting departments is imperative. Both functions place the assets of the insurer at risk. Both deal with risk portfolios. When combined, the two portfolios represent the total risk to which the insurer's assets are exposed. The two departments must be aware of each other's activities and goals in order that the potential variation in earnings created by the total portfolio or risks does not exceed some predetermined level.

The investment department is also required to assist the insurance company in complying with the guidelines of IRDA on assets, liabilities and solvency margin of insurance and the investment norms.

6. **Legal:** Insurance, being a contract essentially requires legal department in every assurance organisation to maintain order in the multitude of conflicting statutes and court rulings. In addition to the design and interpretation of insurance contracts, the legal department has responsibility for: counselling the claims department, determining the validity of security covenants, foreclosing on unpaid mortgage debts, reviewing agency contracts for the sales department, and providing advice on insurance statutes and regulatory promulgations. In addition, the legal department is also responsible for compliance of various laws including on matters required as per IRDA rules and regulation.

7. **Claims:** Claims department is entrusted with the responsibility of handling claims, which is also the social purpose of an insurance company. The claims department perform the key function of verifying and settling claims presented. This requires an awareness of respective coverages, ability to quantify losses and capacity to settle claims on a fair basis. Litigation and subrogation matters are dealt by this department in addition to the assistance in the establishment and revision of loss reserves. These functions are more extensive in property liability insurance than life insurance because of the higher frequency of losses, the predominance of partial losses and the uncertainty of the amount of loss in individual cases.

   In life insurance losses are settled relatively quickly with little need for extensive claims investigation. The only expectations are deaths that may have been caused by excluded perils, such as suicides, or death claims arising from mysterious disappearance. In most other lines of insurance the investigation required by the adjuster can be extensive. A claim for disability income insurance benefits requires the determination of the extent and nature of the alleged disability. A claim for property damage insurance benefits requires an examination of the damaged property to determine if the damage was caused by a covered peril and, if so, the value of the loss. Liability insurance claims probably require the most extensive investigations by the claims department. Liability claims have a higher loss potential, and they also involve many human and subjective factors that are not easily communicated on a claim form.

8. Other Departments

(*a*) *Engineering:* The insurance engineer deals primarily with loss control or loss prevention and is used most frequently in property and liability insurance. The evaluation of the effectiveness of safety guards around machinery, of boiler and other pressure vessel capacities, and of elevator conditions is the responsibility of the engineer. Furthermore, he contributes data for the underwriter whereby the latter may determine the rate structure appropriate for a given technical risk.

(*b*) *Administrative/Personnel:* The administrative department performs a wide range of services ranging from personnel to purchasing, mailrooms to storage, stenographic to inventory maintenance. All of the housekeeping arrangements including the maintenance of properties usually fall within the purview of this department.

(*c*) *Statistical:* The statistician is an important technician within the company, particularly in property and liability insurance where the accumulation of intercompany experience is required to provide an adequate statistical base for rate making. Rarely is this a large department, but the coding and statistical output are very important to both the actuary and the underwriter. In India, this department furnishes information to various government authorities. Statistical department may be a sub-department of the actuarial department and generally exists in corporate office.

The personnel function includes recruitment, training, selection, maintenance of employee records, employee remuneration and incentives and other similar functions.

Key Terms

- ❒ Assessment Mutuals
- ❒ Advance Premium Mutuals
- ❒ Perpetual Mutuals
- ❒ Reciprocal Exchanges
- ❒ Organisation Structure
- ❒ Farm Mutuals
- ❒ Factory Mutuals
- ❒ Fraternal Mutual
- ❒ Lloyd's of London
- ❒ Insurer Functions

Questions for Review

1. **Distinguish between Stock companies and mutual companies. Briefly explain the various types of mutual companies.**
2. **Explain the vaious function performed in an insurance organisation.**

Suggested Readings

1. Mack S. Dorfman, *Fundamentals of Insurance*, Prentice-Hall, 2002.
2. Irving Pfeffer and David R. Klock, *Perspectives on Insurance,* Prentice-Hall, Englewood Cliffs, 1974.
3. P.A. Bawcutt, *Captive Insurance Companies — Establishment, Operational Management,* Woodhead Falkner Ltd. 1982.

Product Design & Development

Chapter **34**

Chapter Objectives

After reading this chapter you will be able to understand :

- *Product Development Process*
- *Product Design/Development — Major Concerns in Indian Development in Insurance Industry*
- *Product Design in Emerging Scenario*

34.1 Product Development Process

A business firm faces many threats from the environment, such as, changes in social, economic, political conditions; technology and supply conditions; change in comforts and conditions; change in social customs and habits; change in expectations and requirements etc. People always seek better things — better products and services, more convenience in products and more value for money. In addition, there is the ever-present competition acting as another source of threats. Firms need new product development for combating the threats and also to stay closer to the consumer. The new products offer new avenues of growth and thus secure the viability and sustainability of the firm.

New products become necessary from the profit angle too. Products that are already established often have their limitations in enhancing the profit level of the firm. It thus becomes essential for business firms to bring in new products to replace old, declining and losing products. New products become part and parcel of the growth requirements of the firm and in many cases, new profits come only through new products.

Thus, new product development is a major component of the firm's product policy. It is not enough if existing product lines are appraised properly, products are positioned effectively and brand decisions taken wisely. For higher levels of growth, a firm has to look beyond its existing products.

34.1.1 Classification of New Products

New products can be broadly classified into two groups –

(i) New products arising out of technological innovations i.e., products having a new functional utility.

(ii) New products arising out of marketing-oriented modifications i.e., new version of existing products. The newness may be due to some changes in design, the addition of a new feature, repositioning of the existing product, offering the existing product with new sales appeal to a new market segment.

34.1.2 Stages in New Product Development

The companies best able to execute New Product Development (NDPL) and Launch efficiently have an advantage over their competitors. The challenges involved are reducing the time to market the product and effective usage of scarce internal resources.

NPDL can be defined as a process that starts with the identification of an opportunity in the market pertaining to the necessity of a product and ends will the successful lunch of the product in between are many activities to define the requirements, develop and test a product concept fully define and structure the product; source for suppliers involved; plan the manufacturing and supply chain; and prepare marketing programs. On top of that, it is about defining the product strategy, managing the overall product program, and monitoring all the projects and activities needed to drive the NPDL process. NPDL is in itself a huge study process where in depth analyses are done at each and every stage.[1]

Stages of product development differ from company to company. Product development is generally carried out at top levels of management, yet all the parties associated are involved. Following stages are generally involved:

(i) *Generating New Product Ideas:* New ideas emanate from customers, dealers, in-company sources including the market research group and external research organizations. Consumer problems are the most fertile ground for the generation of new product ideas.

Various Sources of Information are:

(a) Customers
(b) Intermediaries
(c) Product development executives
(d) Employees
(e) Consultants
(f) Consumer Groups
(g) Insurance Journals and Magazines
(h) Legal pronouncement.

(ii) *Idea Screening:* Ideas are rigorously screened by evaluation committees. Answers are sought to questions like:

(a) Is there a felt need for the new product?
(b) Is it an improvement over the existing product?
(c) Is it close to our current lines of business? Or does it take us to a totally new line of business?
(d) Can the existing production and marketing organizations handle the product? Or does it need extra expertise in production and marketing front?

(iii) *Concept Testing:* What is tested at this stage is the 'product concept' itself – whether the prospective consumers understand the product idea, whether they are receptive towards the idea, whether they actually need such a product and whether they will try out such a product if it is made available to them. This exercise helps the company bring the product concept into clearer focus and thrash out the vagueness associated with the new product idea.

(iv) *Business/Market Analysis:* This stage decided whether from the financial and marketing point of view, the project is worth proceeding with. The project's overall impact on the corporation's financial position with and without the new product are estimated and compared.

The responsibilities of various departments are:

(a) Marketing – Market Analysis to assess customer needs and make a sales forecast.
(b) Actuarial – Develops product specifications and resulting impact on product portfolios.
(c) Underwriting – Preparation of manuals.
(d) Claim Administration – Formulation of claim administration systems for the product in question.
(e) Legal/Compliance – Compliance with legal formalities and various modalities.

---

1. J. Roy & A. Agarwal, New Product Development & Launch, IRDA Journal August, 2006.

(f) Information Systems – Assess whether the insurer has adequate operating systems to accommodate the new product.

(g) Client Services – Assesses the procedural requirements of the new product.

(h) Marketing – Development of plan of action and guidelines for setting the products.

(i) Investment – Determines alongwith the actuarial department, the investment needs of the new product.

(j) Accounting – The financial reporting requirements of the new product.

(v) *Actual Development of the New Product:* The firm develops the product as such. A pilot production facility is set up. By this time, the firm is by-and-large committed to the new product. In the actual development of the product, production and marketing departments are actively involved, besides R & D.

(vi) *Commercialisation* — is the implementation phase of product development. It includes:

(a) Policy filing, which is the process of obtaining all required regulatory approvals for the product from all applicable jurisdiction.

(b) Designing promotional and training materials for the product.

(c) Educating and training staff and sales agents in administrative procedures and forms required to sell, administer and service the product.

(d) Launching all information systems necessary to market and administer product.

In insurance sense, it is called as technical design stage which include drafting of the policy documents, forms and procedures, commission structures, underwriting and issue specification.

New Product Development is highly expensive, time-consuming and risk-laden affair. This is because new products suffer from a high attrition rate:

(a) Many new product ideas do not reach the market at all. Considerable time, money and effort are thus wasted in new product venture.

(b) Even those new products, which manage to reach the market after years of preparation and work, often fail.

(c) Even with successful new products, in many cases, the success is short-lived; they die out after the initial boom.

Hence, the critical factors in new product success are:

(1) A unique and superior product idea that yields a real benefit to the consumer.

(2) Strong technical/production expertise.

(3) A strong market orientation on part of the company.

34.1.3 Pricing Strategy for New Products

As there are no precedents for new products, there are no trends to indicate how the market will react to different levels of pricing, and sketchy information for demand is available. So *Demand-Based Pricing* is out of question. Similarly, *Competition-Based Pricing* cannot be used because competition will be a later phenomenon. *(Cost + Pricing)* is difficult to use since the R & D expenditure would have been shared by several new product ideas and apportioning it to a particular product may become difficult. Such impoderals have prompted marketing experts to comment that new product pricing has to be done in a vacuum.

Pricing of new insurance products generally involves four steps:

(1) Drafting a Pricing Strategy

(2) Vetting by Actuaries

(3) Rate Setting and Testing

(4) Managing of Pricing Outcomes.

Product Development and implementation covers the entire gamut of assessing the need for a product, designing, testing and launching of a new of an adapted product.

The journey starts from answering the basic question of whether the customer wants needs the specific product or not. In the first place a lot of research is done on the need of the customer, his preferences, positioning of the product *vis-a-vis* the competitors, the cost of the entire launch and whether the product would add to the profits of the company.

Once a decision is taken to go ahead with the introduction, the product is properly designed as per the existing business practices and also taking into account the regulatory aspects, especially in case of financial products. The product is tested in a small portion of the market and some fine tuning is done. After putting in place the mechanism of selling and servicing the product the Agents. Brokers *etc.* and segmenting the market into Wholesale, Retail, of any other segment depending upon the product the enters the market.[2]

34.2 PRODUCT DESIGN/DEVELOPMENT — MAJOR CONCERNS IN INDIAN INSURANCE INDUSTRY

One of the major issues in the overall liberalized scenario in the insurance sector is distinctly to be in the area of development of new products. Continuous activity in this area is very crucial to determine the overall profitability and growth of any insurer. The major reason for opening up of the insurance sector is that the sector has not been pro-active, in terms of development of products suited to consumer needs and wants.

Pre Nationalization[3]

Prior to the Nationalization of General Insurance companies, the companies followed the practice of the London or US Market. This was basically due to the fact that most of the companies were units of either British or American companies and it was logical that they follow the practice of their principles. The Indian companies, which were few in number, emulated the foreign companies and very marginal amount of innovation happened.

Past Liberalization[4]

The rest scope of product development and innovation came in this are. The two important happenings which gave a boost to product development were Globalization and the entry of private insurance companies.

In order to compete globally and due to the fact that private companies brought the fact that private companies brought fresh ideas to the industry, a lot of product development has taken place. Both the public and private insurance companies, in order to remain competitive have introduced a lot of new products. There does not appear a sea charge in the offerings but the products are better packaged.

The development of any enterprise draws its inspiration from the overall environment in which it has to function, which includes economic and social factors and more importantly the legal framework (Acts and Regulations), which the insurance industry is supposed to be working under.

2. A.R. Belsare, Product Development in General Insurance, IRDA Journal August, 2006.

3. *Ibid.*

4. *Ibid.*

Any activity of product development should be carried out in the best interests of the community. From this point of view, the product development since 1973 has been directed towards meeting this goal by the Indian Insurance Sector. The GIC along with its 4 subsidiaries in the last 3 decades of operation have developed 150 new products and met the aspirations of the customers. Integrated Rural Development Programme (IRDP) was developed for the rural base, to eliminate poverty and provide employment opportunities to the rural people.

In addition, the industry tried to work out a solution for developing out a solution for healthcare products – Mediclaim, Overseas Mediclaim, and Travel related products were introduced. Other segments, more industrial in nature were covered by products like an industrial All Risk Policy.

Project insurance, particularly in the construction phase, was introduced to take care of the delayed start-up/ advance loss of profits need of the clients. This was made possible in early 1990s with the liberalization of the Indian economy, with the financing going more and more in the hands of the private sector. Opening up of the financial services sector saw developing of covers for various stock exchanges, brokers, custodial services and depositories to cover financial risk. In addition, products were developed for segment on women.

Changing Scenario : With the IRDA Act in place and the sector having been opened to private participation including foreign multinationals the responsibility to develop new products is not limited to the nationalized companies. Various regulations required for the new players to function have also been defined thereby making overall environment conducive to developing new products and competition. In a way, product development now and in times to come will be on the market forces and it will be on these forces that the success or failure of reforms will depend.

Policyholder Expectations : Identification of the consumer need, which acts as a stimulant for product innovation itself flows from the process of analyzing consumer megatrend. These involve analyzing major economic and social shifts in an economy that effect business environment, directly or indirectly. These changes are themselves created by shifts in demographic profile, changes in consumer behaviour and preferences, qualitative changes in environment and future trends that these expectations are likely to take at the micro level. Identifying the expectations of policyholders or the aspirations of a customer of an insurance service would involve the following steps:

- Provide knowledge for initiating development of products.
- Convert knowledge into products which offer value to customers.
- Envisaging goals simultaneously at 3 horizons —
  (a) growth of current business
  (b) expanding for future growth
  (c) options for future growth

When the new products are developed, existing products themselves undergo a change, but in base of insurance the old ones do not phase out because the fundamental needs are not disregarded. Market is abound with such examples where products continue to cater to their target market segments while at the same time new products continue to get developed for niche markets. It all depends on the overall marketing philosophy of an organization.

Role of Technology: Product development has to be supplemented by a series of knowledge trends along with the environmental factors that make the entire process of product development a continuous one. Technology is a crucial element in competitive scenario, particularly when e-commerce is likely to be the order of the day. Technology as a distribution tool is at present in nascent stage but has a great potential for providing a platform to develop cost effective supply chain. In the long-run, technology will be used for creating new products as well as delivering value for money insurance products. Also servicing of the product will be done with the help of state-of-art technology. The advantage of being technologically efficient leads to minimizing distribution costs and increases greatly the speed of providing efficient service.

The Product Itself: Insurance product promises a service in the event of specified perils operating on a risk. There have been products, which have been developed for niche consumer markets but they have been few. Developing a standardised product is inexpensive, faster and achieves economies of scale in mass selling. With the decline in the product life-cycle of an insurance product-either the product life-cycle has to be extended by innovating on the existing product or devise new and customized product after taking into account market requirements.

Product Development: Role of Tariffs and After: The Indian regulator at different forums have categorically stated that insurers will be free to develop products on their own without having any regulatory interference. The only condition is that life insurer will develop products in the life portfolio and a non-life insurer will concentrate only in non-life sector. The policyholders expectations are, therefore, possible to be identified and met in devising appropriate covers. As far as pricing for developing products is concerned, the market has till now been used to tariffs, governed by the Tariff Advisory Committee (TAC). The tariff prices are rigid, and are nor responsive in terms and conditions as per requirements of the market.

The emerging market trends indicate that tariffs may have to make way for non-tariff regime over a period of time. The non-tariff products will have the following broad features:

- simplicity
- quality: first for use
- customization
- easy accessiblity
- speed
- customer friendly documentation
- relevance to risk

Intermediaries: Market is going to experience the emergence of intermediaries in developing business and servicing clients. At present, an agent represents the insurance company in front of a customer. It is expected that in due course of time insurance brokers will emerge.

In international market, a product a never static, it evolves constantly. Change in the product is driven by consumer needs. A lot of research is happening constantly on the effectiveness of a product, consumer need being paramount. Super specialization is the hallmark of the US and UK markets. There are insurers and reinsurers who specialize in a particular product to such an extent, that they are the best in the that field. This helps them in giving the best available product for a particular need.

34.3 Product Design in Emerging Scenario

A Common axiom holds that 80% of a product's cost is determined during the first 20% of development. So if insurers make a few wrong turns at early stage, the product development costs would skyrocket. To achieve maximum benefit for the design process, the cross-cultural research team should be included in development discussions and in each step of the way. This allows the research team to find enhancements that may add little or nothing to the cost, but contribute significantly to the perceived value and profit margin.

Following steps must be taken to design an effective insurance product to current environment :

(1) Define the Procedures: The following steps should be taken:

- Begin research planning with line managers by early identifying the overall research objective. Confirm the consistency of the objective in each of the national market.

Define all aspects of the procedural operations to ensure reliability in the data collection process. The same instructions should be followed during each questionnaire, interview, and observation.

Incorporate Study Control: A thorough investigation of external factors should be done to minimize their impact on results.

Cultural Similarities: Alongwith the differences in culture should be looked for, the similarities should not be ignored. Differentiating a product for a certain group may create more problems that solve it. Main purpose of the insurer is to come to global decision on a new product design.

Counting the Costs: The depth and breadth of the actuarial research, the competitive analysis, and the market analysis determine the costs. One way to hold down the costs is to use internal resources to the fullest extent.

Premium Rating and Product Design: With the deregulation, new foreign entrants and increasing consumer awareness – innovative products design, new marketing techniques and timely product launches is essential to stay ahead of the competition. Sophisticated premium rating and the flexibility to respond quickly to changing market trends are increasingly recognized as the key to meet this challenge.

(2) Analysis of the Market: Determine the exact nature of the market and the requirements of the customer base. This will include:

(a) estimating the size of the current and potential market.

(b) analyzing market trends and profitability

(c) determining the products and rating methods used by the competition

(d) evaluating competing products in terms of price and cover

(e) investigating who actually makes the decision to buy a particular type of product

(f) identifying the principal reasons for buying the product

(g) comparing the benefits of different distribution methods and advising on the most effective methods for remunerating sales distribution channels.

(3) Analysis of DATA: Accurate premium rating depends critically on collecting relevant data in an appropriate format, and then analyzing this data using the right statistical techniques. The insurers can address these central issues by:

(a) advising on the design of databases and the collation of statistical information.

(b) analyzing claims experience to determine the effect that rating factors have upon the risk

(c) comparing these theoretical results with the relativity's implicit in the existing rating structure, and interpreting the results.

(d) considering the possible effect upon the portfolio of introducing particular rating changes.

(e) Providing financial projections of future results, based on the calculated premium rates

(f) Undertaking sensitivity analysis

Hence, new product design and development must identify the similarities and differences of various cultures and must allow companies to capitalize on commonalties or respond to differences appropriately. A well-designed product would answer most consumer needs.

Key Terms

- ❒ Product Design
- ❒ Product Development
- ❒ Market Analysis
- ❒ Intermediaries
- ❒ Competition based pricing
- ❒ Demand Based Pricing
- ❒ Idea Generation
- ❒ Classification of Products
- ❒ Concept testing

Questions for Review

1. Briefly explain the new product development process. Do you think that pricing is an integral part of product development?
2. List the major areas of concern for insurers in India with reference to product development and customisation.

Suggested Readings

- D.C. Srivastava, *et. al. Indian Insurance Industry — Transition and Prospects,* New Century Publications, 2002.
- IRDA.

Underwriting

Chapter **35**

CHAPTER OBJECTIVES

After reading this chapter you will be able to understand :

- *Philosophy of Underwriting*
- *Principles of Inderwriting*
- *Underwriting in Life Insurance*
- *Underwriting Non-life Insurance*

35.1 PHILOSOPHY OF UNDERWRITING

35.1.1 History of Underwriting

Underwriting as an art began in the United Kingdom since Victorian times. Where upon a group of sailors/ traders began the practice to insure against the perils involved in a sea voyage, it included the insuring of the goods in transit against known perils such as piracy, weather perils and goods getting destroyed in the voyage against the payment of a pre-agreed sum by the trader(s). The practice evolved with the times and the insurance model took shape. In the early days of marine insurance, the details of a ship or cargo to be insured were described on a slip. This slip was taken to Lloyd's and the person, who was to carry the risk read the details, then signed the slip under the details of the risk. In this way, the person carrying the risk became known as the *underwriter*. The genesis of the insurance business also evolved from the United Kingdom and the first insurers were the Lloyd's industries.

35.1.2 Underwriting Defined

Underwriting is the prices of selecting and classifying exposures. It is directly related to rate-making or the pricing function of an insurer, because computed rates contemplate some composition of loss-producing characteristics to which they will be applied.

Underwriting is the insurance function that is responsible for assessing and classifying the degree of risk a proposed insured or group represents and making a decision concerning coverage of that risk.[1]

Underwriting includes all the activities necessary to select risks offered to the insurer in such a manner that general company objectives are fulfilled.

The person responsible for evaluation and acceptance/rejection of risks and computation of premium is called as the *underwriter*. Accordingly, the decision made by the underwriter concerning risk classification and rating is called as the *underwriting* decision. Underwriting decisions are crucial for insurers since they can make or mar an insurance company. Good underwriting helps the insurance companies in many ways. It make them financially stronger and helps secure competitive advantage. This is obvious in the sense that if risks are assessed properly, pricing will be effective and therefore the company can well compete and build up reputation.

1. Gene Stone, *Insurance Company Operations,* LOMA 2000, p. 234.

In life insurance business, underwriting is performed by home or regional office personnel, who scrutinize applications for coverage and make decisions as to whether they will be accepted, and by agents, who produce the applications initially in the field, but these decisions may be subject to post underwriting at a higher level because the contracts are cancellable on due notice to the insured. In life insurance, agents seldom have authority to make binding underwriting decisions. In all fields of insurance, however, agency personnel usually do considerable screening of risks before submitting them to home office underwriters.

35.1.3 The Trade-off

The underwriting exercise is a trade-off between the business and survival. If the insurance company sets high standards for risk which can be undertaken, the company may loose market and consequentially, the potential premium income which can be threat to survival. If the insurance company charges too much of premium in a fashion that is become excessive, the company will loose competitive advantage. Also, if the company undertakes risk with a loose assessment in a zeal to get business, it may be dangerous because the possibility of claims may increase substantially. Hence and therefore, a proper balance is to be maintained between business and good business.

35.1.4 The Conflict

The conflict between production and underwriting are common to insurance companies. The underwriting department may have turned down business that has been previously sold by an agent, an apparent conflict of interest arises between these two areas. The problem is similar to that which exists between credit and sales in other firms, with a good sale ruined because credit is not approved. Neither the agent nor the underwriter will profit long by underwriting that is too strict or too loose. The former will choke off acceptable business and may create unnecessary expenses in cancelling business already bound by the agent, whereas the latter invites such substantial losses that the company may be forced to withdraw entirely from a given line, to the detriment of the agent.

35.1.5 Twin Guiding Principles

The two main principles of underwriting are *Adverse Selection* and *Persistency*. The underwriter must always guard himself against the adverse selection of risks. There is tendency on part of the potential insureds, those who are more likely to be affected by the happening of the adverse event, to go for insurance cover compared to ones who are well off. For example – *Ceteris Paribus*, a healthy person is less likely to go for an insurance cover than the one who becomes frequently ill. Accordingly, the potential business for the insurers would represent these class. Therefore, the underwriter should carefully appraise the inherent risk in such cases and fix the premium so as to avoid likely significant losses.

In addition, the underwriter must not offer products which the consumers cannot afford. Also the premium fixed for the insureds must be consistent enough to support the cash flow model of the insurers. The continuous renewal of policies is must to business retention. The underwriter should carefully examine the paying capacity of the potential customer before offering a product, if large number of policies are surrendered or lapsed, the company will be ruined.

35.2 The Objectives and Principles of Underwriting

The primary objective of underwriting is to see that the applicant accepted will not have a loss experience that is very different from that assumed when the rates were formulated. To this end, certain standards of selection relating to physical and moral hazards are set up when rates are calculated, and the underwriter must see that these standards are observed when a risk is accepted. For *e.g.*, a company may decide that it will accept no fire exposures situated in areas where there is no fire department protection or will accept no one for life insurance who has had cancer within the previous five years.

When reviewing an application for property insurance for a piece of property, such as a farm, that is located where there is no fire department protection or when reviewing an application for life insurance in which the individual had cancer four and half years ago, the underwriter asks the question, "Can I make an exception for this application, or must I reject it because it does not come within the technical limitations of my instructions?" In answering this question, the underwriter visualizes what would happen to the company's loss experience if a very large number of identical risks were accepted. If the aggregate experience would be very unfavourable, the underwriter will probably reject the application.

The objectives of underwriting can be therefore expressed as follows:

1. *Product Equitable to Customer* – The underwriter should fairly assess the risk in a proposal and fix the premium justifiable to the consumer.
2. *Deliverable to the Customer* – Consumers are the final authority for buying the products. If the marketers are not able to sell so that the product becomes undeliverable, the onus is on the underwriters to carry an introspection of the various factors that caused differences between the consumers and company's expectations.
3. *Financially Feasible to the Insurance Company* — The insurers are not in the business of charity. The underwriting benefit must be reflected by the financial statements. Although, the underwriters are not directly involved in the pricing of insurance products, yet their contribution is as vital as that of actuaries, because they operationalise the business of risk.

Most of the insurance companies formulate underwriting policy which provides the framework for underwriting decisions. It is also called as the *underwriting philosophy*. The underwriting policy specifies the line of insurance that will be written as well as prohibited exposures, the amount of coverage to be permitted on various types of exposure, the area of the country in which each line will be written, and similar restrictions. Generally, the individual who applies the underwriting rules and guidelines, called the desk underwriter, do not involve in forming the company underwriting.

The underwriting philosophy also describes in general terms how the underwriter will use reinsurance for its risk management.[2] The underwriting philosophy can be translated into *underwriting guidelines* which specify the general standards that specify which applicants are to be assigned to the risk established for each insurance product.

In life insurance, the underwriter is assisted by medical reports from the physicians that examined the applicant, by information from the agent, by an independent report (called inspection report) on the applicant prepared by an outside agency created for that purpose, and by advice from the company's own medical advisor. In property-liability insurance (as well as life insurance), the underwriter has the services of reinsurance facilities and credit departments to report on the financial standing of applicants and also can review loss histories of applicant.

Requisites of Good Underwriting

- The guiding philosophy of good underwriting is to know the risk features and factors of every risk offered for acceptance. Underwriter must determine the serious physical hazards inherent in the particular risk and the steps taken by an insured to minimize them. He should be able to visualize the risk even if he did not visit it, from the reports given and from the detailed proposal form furnished. The above pre-supposes that the insurer provides him with the expense needed in respect of each industry that he is asked to underwrite.

- An Underwriter should be aware of the minimum risk management steps to impose by insurers in respect of each risk. He should evaluate the risk management steps a proposer on his own has implemented such as safety audit measures; staff drills to fight fires and breakdowns; investigations and remedial steps taken to prevent recurrence of fires and breakdowns *etc.*
- The moral hazard of the proposer in respect of house keeping, staff relations, compliance with legal enactments, the effectiveness of corporate governance and past claims experience; and steps taken to avoid recurrence of accidents.
- The environmental issues of a proposal such as his competition, peculiarities of his particular trade or business and its vagaries must also be evaluated.
- The Underwriter should be exposed to the claim occurrences of the risks that he usually accepts.
- Familiarity with IT to extract data and information, and analytical skills to reduce problems to their bare bones is another skill that is essential in underwriting.

35·3 UNDERWRITING IN LIFE INSURANCE

Life insurance underwriting is mainly concerned with mortality. Mortality risk for an insurer is that the insured will die prior to the stipulated life. An impairment in any respect of a proposed insured's personal health, medical history, health habits, family history, occupation, or other activities that could increase that person's expected mortality risk.[3]

While underwriting risk of an individual in life insurance, following factors are generally considered by life insurance companies:

(a) Age,

(b) Sex,

(c) Height and weight,

(d) Health history (and often family health history – parents and siblings),

(e) The purpose of the insurance (such as for estate planning, or business or for family protection),

(f) Marital status and number of children,

(g) The amount of insurance the applicant already has, and any additional insurance s/he proposes to buy,

(h) Occupation (some are hâzardous, and increase the rise of death),

(i) Income (to help determine suitability),

(j) Smoking or tobacco use this is an important factor, as smokers have shorter lives),

(k) Alcohol (excessive drinking seriously hurts life expectancy),

(l) Certain hobbies (e.g., race car driving, hang-gliding, piloting non-commercial aircraft), and

(m) Foreign travel (certain foreign travel is risky).

Similarly in case of group insurance the following factors are considered:

(a) Proposed Coverage – which includes assessment of eligibility, level of benefits which can be offered, administration of the group and the mode of payment to intermediaries.

2. Gene Stone, *op. cit.,* p. 243.
3. *Ibid.*

(b) Cause of existence of the relevant group – classified on the basis of the nature of job, specific agendas etc.

(c) Size of the group – large groups are always better than small groups for obvious reasons.

(d) Nature of Group's business-based on nature of industry, cement plants and coal mines workers are more prone to respiratory/kidney problems.

(e) Geographical location of the group.

(f) Stability of the group.

(g) Attributes of group members – sex, age and work profile.

(h) Level of participation – contribution by members or else, no contribution by members.

(i) Persistency and prior experiences.

In case of renewals, the most important factor is the claims experience

Underwriters place the potential insureds in the appropriate risk class (based on various criterion) generally classified as follows:

(a) *Preferred Class:* where the happening of an adverse event or the possibility of claims is the least, i.e., the inherent risk is lesser than average risk.

(b) *Standard Class* – where the risk exposed is at par with the average risk. Most of the insured belong to this class.

(c) *Sub-standard Class* – where the anticipated risk is higher than the average risk. Insurance companies typically establish this risk class for proposed insureds who have permanent medical impairments or conditions, are recovering from serious illnesses or accidents, or have occupations or avocations that significantly increase their degree of risk.[4]

35.3.1 The Underwriting Process

The underwriting of life assurance is in quite a different category from other forms of personal insurances. This is because the underwriter assesses the risk at inception only. The company is then guaranteeing cover for sometimes, up to 30 years, or even throughout life. Life assurance underwriting involves looking at medical, occupational and avocation factors as well as the individual's lifestyle. In particular, the extra risk posed by AIDS has led to an increased number of questions on proposal forms, or on a separate questionnaire, about lifestyle, which are designed to identify if the proposer is likely to be in a high risk group for AIDS or HIV.

The underwriting process for life assurance involves – (1) performing field underwriting, (2) reviewing the application in the office, (3) gathering additional information, if required and (4) taking and underwriting decision. Additional information is often required by the underwriter in order to reach a decision. This can be in the form of detailed questionnaires, a report from the proposer's own doctor (Medical Attendant's Report), an examination by an independent doctor (Medical Examiner's Report) and/or specific tests.

Following steps are generally followed by underwriters:

1. Receiving Proposals/Applications

The application for insurance is the source of insurability information that the life insurance company's underwriter will evaluate first. These are generally collected by the field personnel, the agents. There are two basic parts to a typical life insurance application: (1) General Information, and (2) Medical Information.

The General Information section of an application asks general questions, including name, age, address, birth date, sex, income, marital status and occupation. In addition, details about the requested insurance coverage

4. *Ibid.*, p. 244.

such as type of policy, amount of insurance, name and relationship of the beneficiary, other insurance that the client owns, and additional insurance applications pending as on date.

The Medical Information section of an application focuses on insured's health and asks a number of questions about health history, history of his/her family's as well. The medical section of the application is fairly extensive and must be fully completed. In addition to this, information may also gathered through a medical examination, depending on age and the face amount of coverage.

2. The Medical Report

The average medical examination (which is generally at no cost to the applicant except in case of revivals) may be conducted. Depending on the medical questions are answered, an insurance company may ask the medical doctor(s) of the client for more detail on any conditions in question. This gathering of information is practically a standardized method used with all domestic insurance companies. Life Insurance Companies generally have several sources of information about medical and financial history to assist them in the underwriting process. These include personal medical records and doctor, the Medical Information Bureau, Special Questionnaires, Inspection Reports and even Credit Records.

3. Underwriting Review

Once all of the information has been gathered, an individual from the insurance company (called an underwriter) evaluates the data. At this evaluation, the underwriter is seeking to classify the risk presented to the company. In addition, the underwriter will determine the premium for the policy based on the primary and secondary factors influencing the premium, and the premium rates the company's actuaries have set for your risk profile. As a consumer, here is the hard part to understand in getting a policy: insurance companies have different underwriting guidelines. This is why the least expensive policies are the most stringent on their guidelines. Throughout every step of the underwriting process, the life insurance agent normally provides with details, keeps abreast of where the insured stand in the process and guide and answer to the questions. Ultimately, making the underwriting process less intimidating and more manageable.

If the proposed insured presents a risk more than the risk which the insurance company is willing to cover, the application will be declined by the underwriter.

4. Policy Writing

In life insurance the policy is usually written in a special department whose main task is to issue written contracts in accordance with instructions from the underwriting department and, because most policies are long term in nature, to keep a register of them for future reference. Insurance companies generally use automated systems which generate the computerised client record, records of payment of premium and they do verify that all the requirements of underwriting have been met.

Documents Required at the Time of Underwriting

Age Proof

Scrutiny of age is an important concern for the life insurer because old age people have high probability of dying than the younger ones and premium is calculated on the basis of age groups. Accuracy in age computation resolves hardship both to the insurer and the potential insured in the sense that the correct age avoids the company bring affected by lesser premiums or undesired risk bought or risk not bought because of fear. From the insured's perspective, it helps in charging of fair premiums and insurance availability. The proofs of age, which are generally considered are as under:

- Certified extract from municipal or other records made at the time of birth.

- Certificate of Baptism or certified extract from family Bible if it contains age or date of birth.
- Certified extract from School or College if age or date of birth is stated therein.
- Certified extract from Service Register in case of Govt. employees and employees of Quasi Govt. institutions including Public Limited Companies and
- Passport issued by the Passport Authorities in India.

Alternative Age Proofs, which are also accepted in the industry, are:

- Marriage certificate in the case of Roman Catholics issued by Roman Catholic Church.
- Certified extracts from the Service Registers of commercial Institutions or Industrial Undertakings provided it is specifically mentioned in such extracts that conclusive evidence of age was produced at the time of recruitment of the employee.
- Certificate of Birth granted by Syedna v. Molana Badruddin Sahib of Baroda.
- Identity Cards issued by Defence Department.
- A true copy of the University Certificate or of Matriculation/Higher Secondary Education, S.S.L. Certificate issued by a Board set up by a State/Central Government.
- Non-standard age proofs like Horoscope, Service Record where age is not verified at the time of entry. E.S.I.S. Card. Marriage Certificate in case of Muslim Proposer, Elder's Declaration, Self declaration and Certificate by Village Panchayats are accepted subject to certain rules.

Medical Examination

Generally, at some levels and in case of endowment policies, whole life policies, the medical examination is not added for. However, if the amount of insurance is very high or the age is high or the first level examination has some adverse remarks, then the insurance company may refer the proposal for a thorough examination. Cases of pregnant women, or women with history of miscarriages or abortion are declined. Some times the medical examination may be waived, like in rural areas, where the facilities are not available.

After the above examinations and obtaining special reports, if required, the underwriter may accept or reject the case. Else, he is empowered to modify the sum assured, premium to be charged and manner thereof, impose conditions or provide exclusions in the policy.

In case of untrue or incorrect statement contained in the proposal, personal statement, declaration and connected documents or any material information withheld, subject to the provision of Section 45 of the Insurance Act 1938 wherever applicable, the policy shall be declared void and all claims to any benefits in virtue thereof shall cease.

After the policy is issued, the policyholder in a number of cases finds the terms not terms not suitable to him and desires to charge them. LIC allows certain types of alterations during the lifetime of the policy. However, no alteration is permitted within one year of the commencement of the policy with some exceptions. The following alterations are allowed:

- Alteration in class or term
- Reduction in the assured
- Alteration in the mode of payment of premiums
- Alteration in the date of commencement of the policy
- Splitting up of a single policy into two or more policies
- Removal of an extra premium
- Alteration from without profit plan to with profit plan

- Alteration in name
- Correction in policies
- Settlement option of payment of assured by installments
- Grant of accident benefit
- Grant of premium waiver benefit under CDA polices
- Alteration in currency and place of payment of policy monies.

A fee for the change or alteration in the policy is charged by the company called as the quotation fee and no additional fee is charged for giving effect to the alteration.

Special Reports

Besides the proposal form, personal statement agent's report, medical examiner's report and age-proof, special medical reports may be called for, it

(*a*) The SA is very high, say Rs. 5 lakhs or more

(*b*) The age at entry is very high, say, 60 years or more

(*c*) The proposer wants insurance cover under a high-risk plan.

(*d*) The normal medical examination discloses some adverse feature.

The underwriter has the right and discretion to ask for additional information through special reports, if he considers such reports necessary for a fair assessment of risk These special reports may relate to medical condition of they may relate in income, habits, life styles *etc.* He may ask for medical reports, even if the proposal is for non-medical insurance. In the case of key man insurance, the reports may be to establish that the life assured is indeed a key person and that the SA proposal represents fairly the value of that person and that the SA proposed represents fairly the value of that person to the enterprise.

The underwriter arrives at a decision about the acceptance of the proposal, after scrutinising the particulars available in the proposal form, personal statement, the reports of the officials and the medical reports. He may take the expert opinion of a medical referee, who is a senior doctor familiar with implications of medical history in life insurance.

The underwriter may decide to accept the proposal as a proposed at O.R. (Ordinary Rates) or on modified terms. O.R. means that the premium chargeable would be as per the standard premium tables. The modifications would be of the following kind.

(*a*) accepting for a lesser SA than proposed

(*b*) accepting for a shorter term than proposed

(*c*) accepting for a different plan than proposed

(*d*) charging a higher premia than the standard rate

(*e*) Imposing a lien which reduces the insurer's liability under the policy for some time, or under some conditions.

(*f*) excluding certain specified risks the policy.

The terms under which the proposal is accepted by the underwriter, will be conveyed to the proposer. If the acceptance is as proposed and at O.R. the deposit paid along with the proposal, if adequate will be adjusted as First Premium and the risk will commence from that time. If the acceptance is on modified terms, the proposer has to agree to those modified terms. The balance of premium if any will have to be paid. If all the requirements are fulfilled by the proposer, the First Premium is adjusted and the risk commences. The First Premium is adjusted and the risk commences. The First Premium Receipt is the evidence of Commencement of risk, till the policy document is issued.

35·4 UNDERWRITING IN NON-LIFE INSURANCE

The underwriting of commercial, business insurances is a much more complicated and involved task. Commercial insurances range from small shops and factories to large multinational corporations, with operations in many countries throughout the world. The degree of complexity of the underwriting required would obviously vary with the sheer size of the risk, but certain basic principles are still recognizable.

The essence of the task is that the underwriter has to evaluate the hazard associated with the risk, which is being proposed. In small cases he may be able to do this from reading a proposal form and corresponding with the sponsor. It may be that a local inspector is asked to call and see the shop or factory for himself. In large cases this is simply impossible. Detail of the risk could not be confined to a proposal form since there is just too much information to condense, no matter how large the form may be. The insurance companies may take the help of brokers in these cases. The broker in these cases will be in a position to prepare the case for the underwriter. This may mean site inspections by the broker and the preparation of plans and reports on the relevant aspects of the risk. This documentation, which may be extremely extensive, is then passed to the underwriter and negotiation can commence on the terms, conditions, cover and price.

Several sources of information are available to the underwriter regarding the hazards of a commercial applicant for property and liability insurance:

(*a*) *Application Containing the Insurers Statements:* The basic source of underwriting information is the application, which varies for each line of insurance and for each type of coverage. The broader and more liberal the contract, usually more detailed information is required. The questions on the application are designed to give the underwriter the information needed to decide whether to accept the exposure, reject it or ask for additional information.

(*b*) *Information from the Agent or Broker:* In some line of non-life insurance, the agent may exercise his underwriting authority. For commercial insurances, the profit-sharing contracts are also entered with the agents, whereby the agent derives a special incentive if the business brought by him has resulted in a profit to the company.

(*c*) *Prior Experiences:* The past history of claims is also a source of information. In case of existing clients where the claims experience has been unfavourable, the insurance company penalises i.e. loads premium for new businesses or renewals of the existing ones.

(*d*) *Inspection:* Surveys are also conducted by the company's specialists/consultants to find out the accuracy of information as contained in the proposal form.

Underwriting Practices

Underwriting of non-life insurance in India is generally carried out by a department called as "new-business department." Most of the underwriting work is performed at Branch and Divisional office level, of course, in accordance with the underwriting policy and rules framed by the head office of the insurance company. The underwriting guidelines cover the following:[5]

(a) acceptance of normal risks irrespective of sum issued

(b) acceptance of normal risks upto specified sum insured

(c) acceptance of normal classes of business with prior approval of the controlling office (the controlling office may be head office/regional office).

(d) acceptance of risks with prior approval for the controlling office

(e) acceptance of risks subject to underwriting safeguards

(f) procedural matters.

5. Practice of General Insurance, Insurance Institute of India, p. 156.

The risks in fire, marine and motor insurance have generally high levels of limits of acceptance. However, in some classes of insurances, the limits are fairly low. Some of these are:[6]

(i) All risk insurance on jewellery etc.

(ii) Baggage insurance

(iii) Personal Accident Insurance

(iv) Special Contingency Insurance

For higher limits in these cases, the approval of controlling office is essential.

In case of fire insurance, only standard fire and special-perils policy with the permitted "Add-on" covers if any, can be issued premiums and specified by Tariff Advisory Committee.

- Unless otherwise specifically provided for Policy (ies) covering Buildings and/or contents shall show blockwise separate amount on (i) Building (ii) Machinery and Accessories (iii) Stock and Stock-in-process (iv) Furniture and other contents.
- It is permissible to exclude Storm, Tempest, Flood and Inundation group of perils and or Riot, Strike, Malicious and Terrorism Damage perils at inception of the Policy by deleting the relevant perils from the Policy. The deletion should apply for the entire policy in one complex/compound/location covering the entire interest of the insured under one or more policy (ies) without any option for the selection. Reduction in premium rates for such deletion (s) may be allowed as shown under the relevant sections of the Tariff. When these perils are deleted from the scope of the policy, the general exclusions shall include these perils.

Any risk, which has not been provided for by TAC is referred to the Committee for rating. Provisional rate of Rs. 2.50 per mile is charged in such cases for covering the risks under Standard Fire and Special Perils Policy. No discounts and/or agency commission is be allowed on this rate. For add-on covers, additional rates provided in Section VIII is to be charged.

Rates shown under the tariffs are minimum rates. Insurers may charge rates higher than those given under the tariff.

The risks above the normal kind of risks are normally declined by the insurance companies. Otherwise, they are accepted by changing a higher premium and imposing restrictive conditions, clauses and warranties. For example, risks in ammunition, explosive, fireworks, celluloid, match factories etc. In a fire policy, special perils can be accepted subject to the inspection of risk. Similarly, for consequential loss policy, the audit of accounts is a must.

In case of marine insurance, the declined risks may be billion, currency over specified limits, quit in secondhand drums against leakage's, second hand machinery against breakage etc. The age of the cargo carrying vessel is an important factor in marine insurance underwriting.

In motor insurance, acceptance of comprehensive risk is subject to the specified year of the manufacture/ assembly of the vehicle. An underwriter before acceptance of risk may conduct an inspection of the vehicle. Similarly, military disposal vehicles can be covered by Act only, risks comprehensive insurance on imported cars is allowed subject to incorporation of an excess clause.[7]

Underwriting experience of various insurance players is given in Annexure 35A and 35B.

---

6. Practice of General Insurance, *op. cit.*, p. 156-157.
7. Practice of General Insurance, *op. cit.*, p. 159.

Annexure 35A

UNDERWRITING EXPERIENCE AND PROFITS OF PUBLIC SECTOR COMPANIES

(Rs. Lakh)

	New India		Oriental		National		United		Total	
	2007-08	2006-07	2007-08	2006-07	2007-08	2006-07	2007-08	2006-07	2007-08	2006-07
Net Premium	491428	475177	287868	287973	318798	285536	288066	252953	1386159	1301640
Incurred claims (Net)	417748	364361	260222	235886	283884	239422	250628	214206	1212481	1053875
	85.01%	76.68%	90.40%	81.91%	89.05%	83.85%	87.00%	84.68%	87.47%	80.97%
Commission, Expenses of Management	147834	154348	95496	85385	110159	91952	104916	96222	458406	427906
	30.08%	32.48%	33.17%	29.65%	34.55%	32.20%	36.42%	38.04%	33.07%	32.87%
Increase in Reserve for Unexpired Risk	10285	21666	244	18897	16945	8780	17857	15629	45331	64971
	2.09%	4.56%	0.08%	6.56%	5.32%	3.07%	6.20%	6.18%	3.27%	4.99%
Underwriting Profit/Loss	(84439)	(65198)	(68095)	(52194)	(92190)	(54617)	(85335)	(73104)	(330059)	(254112)
	−17.55%	−14.38%	−23.67%	−19.40%	−30.54%	−19.73%	−31.58%	−30.80%	−24.62%	−19.82%
Gross Investment Income	234619	225507	114315	116010	118092	105480	157725	131426	624751	578423
Other Income Less Other Outgo	1966	1084	(1986_	(853)	(8696)	(5280)	(6576)	(6288)	(15292)	(11337)
Profit Before Tax	152146	161393	44235	62964	17206	45583	65814	52034	279400	321974
Income Tax Deducted at Source and Provision for Tax	12033	15398	43305	13237	863	3455	2651	(852)	58851	31238
Net Profit After Tax	**140113**	**145995**	**930**	**49727**	**16343**	**42128**	**63162**	**52886**	**220548**	**290763**

Figure in bracket negative amounts.

Source : IDRA Reports

Statement 35B

UNDERWRITING EXPERIENCE AND PROFITS OF PUBLIC SECTOR COMPANIES

(Rs. Lakh)

Particulars	Royal Sundaram		Bajaj Allianz		Tata AIG		Reliance		IFFCO Tokio		ICICI-Lombard		Cholamandalam		HDFC CHUBB		Future total Generali	Universal Sompo	Total	
	2007-08	2006-07	2007-08	2006-07	2007-08	2006-07	2007-08	2006-07	2007-08	2006-07	2007-08	2006-07	2007-08	2006-07	2007-08	2006-07	2007-08	2006-07	2007-08	2006-07
Net Premium	53306	38995	175255	103976	52801	41582	133745	50431	73775	58057	177977	145077	32113	15926	16758	13311	184	(43)	715871	467316
Claims Incurred (NET)	29815	20374	94570	55563	24695	20711	75068	17318	50474	39589	122832	81384	15565	7077	11477	8003	58	0	424555	250289
	55.93%	52.30%	53.96%	53.44%	46.77%	49.81%	56.13%	34.34%	68.42%	68.66%	69.02%	56.10%	48.47%	44.43%	68.49%	60.12%	31.41%	-0.26%	59.31%	53.56%
Commission, Expenses of Management	19060	13543	50072	26676	23047	18122	48341	10169	1971	16287	42460	30826	10946	58344	6958	6879	1934	726	223254	128337
	35.75%	34.77%	28.57%	25.66%	43.65%	43.58%	36.14%	20.16%	26.72%	28.05%	23.86%	21.25%	34.09%	36.63%	41.52%	51.68%	1052.68%	-1705.14%	31.19%	27.46%
Increase in Reserve for Unexpired Risk	8723	5597	33711	20123	7417	3418	37741	26006	9808	3297	21258	38412	7227	3198	1753	(718)	312	1	127951	99333
	16.36%	14.37%	19.24%	19.35%	14.05%	8.22%	28.22%	51.57%	13.29%	5.68%	11.94%	26.48%	22.51%	20.08%	10.46%	-5.39%	170.04%	-1.74%	17.87%	21.26%
Underwriting Profit/Loss	(4291)	(559)	(3098)	1615	(2357)	(669)	(27406)	(3062)	(6219)	(1387)	(8573)	(5545)	(1626)	(182)	(3430)	(853)	(2121)	(769)	(59890)	(10642)
	-9.62%	-1.67%	-2.19%	1.93%	-5.19%	-1.75%	-28.55%	-12.53%	-9.72%	-2.43%	-5.47%	-5.20%	-6.53%	-1.43%	-18.53%	-6.77%	1647.72%	1776.26%	-10.19%	-2.89%
Gross Investment Income	4802	3287	18648	8890	5035	3797	10411	3195	7354	5708	22448	13590	2643	1574	1440	1463	542	881	74205	41504
Other Income Less Other Outgo-34		(11)	1240	1198	14	177	711	91	50	(76)	(852)	(33)	37	(12)	313	(359)	(123)	(151)	1204	975
Profit Before Tax	477	2718	16790	11703	2692	3305	(16284)	224	1186	4246	13022	8012	1054	1379	(1677)	250	(1701)	(39)	15519	31837
Income Tax Deducted at Source and Provision for Tax	6	600	6228	4166	1075	1148	271	61	470	1533	2735	1176	330	130	23	50	8	(9)	11136	8863
Net Profit After Tax	471	2119	10562	7537	1617	2157	(16555)	163	716	2713	10287	6836	724	1249	(1700)	200	(1709)	(30)	4383	22974

Note : Figure in brackets indicate negative amounts

Source : IDRA Reports

Key Terms

- ❒ Adverse Selection
- ❒ Underwriting Philosophy
- ❒ Comprehensive Risks
- ❒ Persistency
- ❒ Claims experience

Questions for Review

1. Define underwriting. Briefly explain the trade-off and conflict in underwriting business.
2. Explain the process of underwriting in life and non-life insurance business.
3. Comment on the various underwriting practices in India.

Suggested Readings

1. *Practice of General Insurance,* IC 11, Insurance Institute of India, Mumbai, 1999.
2. Genes store, Insurer Company, Operations, LOMA 2000.
3. Vaughan & Vaughan, *Essentials of Risk Management and Insurance,* John Wiley & Sons, 2002.

Web Resources

- www.life-insurance-underwriting.org
- www.insuranceinform.org
- www.insuremagic.com

Insurance Pricing

Chapter 36

CHAPTER OBJECTIVES

After reading this chapter you will be able to understand :

- *Fundamentals of Insurance Pricing*
- *Pricing Objectives*
- *Types of Rating*
- *Life Insurance vs. Non-life Insurance Pricing*
- *Rate Making Entities*

Pricing of Insurance products is mysterious to most of the people. It is different from the pricing of tangible where you can figure out the cost of inputs. Also, in other services, the cost of providing them can be estimated with some judgement. Insurance is the business of buying risk. Therefore, most people think in terms of what they paid for buying a risk cover and what they paid for the cover. When an insurers sells a policy, it has no way of knowing what will be the realised cost of the policy because it depends upon whether or not the policy buyer has losses and, if so, how many and how large they are. Of course, this is the reason that different people are charged different prices for policies providing the same kinds and amounts of insurance.

36.1 FUNDAMENTALS OF INSURANCE PRICING

Pricing of insurance products is typical in the sense that in insurance transactions, the sales price (i.e. the premium) is collected before stipulated services, namely claim payments, are duly provided. "Two collary are usually drawn: (a) insurance pricing is rather a delicate actuarial exercise; and thus (b) technical reserves must be built up to represent the liabilities towards policyholders to ensure that the inherent promises to them do not become failed promises. These reserves are then invested on financial markets and placed under the supervision of the relevant regulatory authority. This is precisely why insurance firms are usually viewed as fulfilling an important financial intermediary function."[1]

"A fundamental principle of insurance pricing is that if insurers are to sell coverage willingly, they must receive premiums that

(1) are sufficient to fund their expected claim costs and administrative costs and

(2) provide an expected profit to compensate for the cost of obtaining the capital necessary to support the sale of coverage."[2]

The premium level that is just sufficient to fund the insurer's expected cost and provide insurance company owners with a fair return on their invested capital is known as the fair premium.

Actuaries generally calculate the base premium on the basis of expected claims distribution using principle of equivalence (P = ps) such that

$$P = E(S) + k + R$$

1. Briyo and Varenne, *Insurance From Underwriting to Derivatives,* John Wiley & Sons Ltd., 2001, p. 6.
2. Harrington and Niehaus, *Insurance & Risk Management,* Mc Graw-Hill, p. 115.

Where E(S) represents the mathematical expectation of claims, k denotes ongoing company running costs, while R is a risk premium which allows for coverage of unforeseen deviations in the claims amount to be paid, but still provides the company with "normal" profits i.e. this standard pricing mechanism relies upon the so-called "law of large numbers. Within a large, diversified and homogeneous underwriting portfolio, the claims burden should converge towards its expected value.

Exhibit 36-A

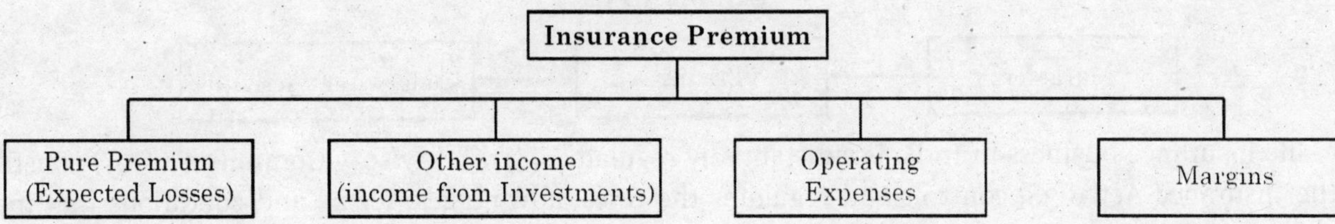

Pure Premium

It is the most important component of the insurance premiums. Based on actuarial calculations, it includes the amount needed to cover expected losses and loss adjustment expenses.

Operating Expenses

Operating Expenses include the sales commission and other marketing costs, taxes, and the cost of handling claims. The size of this component of premium varies from one line to another, largely dependent upon the extent and variety of policyholder services that the insurer provides.

Margin and Other Incomes

It includes an allowance for (a) contingencies, and (b) underwriting gain or profit. Contingency funds are needed to meet unexpected increase in the number or size of benefit payments and underwriting gains are needed to provide funds for financing growth and expansion.

Rating Terminology

- Insurance prices are called as *Premiums*. Premiums are based on rates and rates are based on per unit of exposure.
- The term *rate* is used synonymous with premium in the insurance business. It is the price per unit of insurance.
- *Exposure unit* are quantitative units used in insurance pricing.
- *Loading* refers to the amount that must be added to the pure premium for other expenses, profit and margin for contingencies.

Exhibit 36-B

Kind of Insurance	*Exposure Unit*
Automobile	Automobile insured (IEV)
Fire	Rs. per 100
Liability (Products)	Rs. per 1,000
Worker's Compensation	Rs. per 100
Life	Rs. per 1,000

36.2 Pricing Objectives

Pricing of insurance products is a critical issue. The underwriting/actuarial department in the insurance company is highly conservative and tries to fix the prices *all-inclusive.* On the contrary, in a competitive environment, it becomes a problem to sell the product at mathematical prices and they are forced to offer incentives thereby reducing realised prices. [Exhibit 36(c)]

Exhibit 36-C

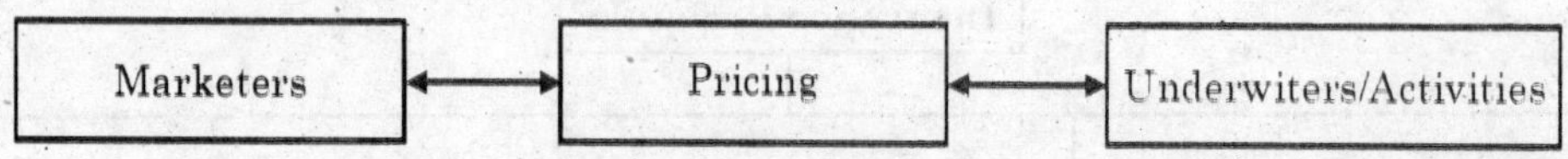

The non-life insurance business in India is substantially regulated. Tariff Advisory Committee (TAC) constituted under the Insurance Act 1938, controls and regulates the rates, advantages, terms and conditions that may be offered by insurers in respect of General Insurance Business relating to Fire, Marine (Hull), Motor, Engineering and Workmen Compensation. All other products are non-tariff. These rates are also called as statutory standards. In addition to these regulations the pricing of insurance products must achieve the following general objectives:

(a) *Adequacy*: The rate must be adequate to generate the premium income the insurer needs to pay its claims and expenses. In addition, the insurers' income must be adequate to assure fair rate of return to the investors of funds. Also, they are sufficient to finance continuing growth and expansion.

Rating is matter of regulation by IRDA whose objective is to protect the interests of the policyholders and the shareholders. This means that the rates must be adequate enough to meet all future losses and expenses in the time and to pay a fair return on the capital employed by the shareholders for this risk taking business. If the rates are not adequate, an insurer may become insolvent causing total loss to the policyholders' fund as well as the shareholders' fund; and cause total loss of public faith and confidence in insurance industry.

However, in insurance business, rate adequacy measurement is really complicated because of the simple reason that insurer does not know the actual costs at the time of selling the policy. Price is estimated on loss forecasting process based on statistical methods. The premium is collected in advance in view of law of large numbers (projected); and expected claim costs and other expenses. If the insurer fails to achieve the targeted number or volume of business and if the actual claim costs, especially catastrophic losses, are more than the statistically projected or forecasted loss, price collected may not be sufficient to pay all claims and expenses during the policy period. As a result, policyholders, shareholders, third-party claimants and other beneficiaries may be financially harmed. This is the major concern for the regulatory authority all over the globe.[3]

(b) *Reasonableness:* The rates must not be so excessive that allows insurance companies to earn abnormal gains. There is no recipe for reasonableness, but what the insurance company can justify to the potential buyers in a free market condition is considered as reasonable.

(c) *Fairness:* The rates must not be "unfairly discriminatory". The insurance rates must be fair and must discriminate among the buyers fairly. Since the rates must vary with classifications as principle, they must not create unrest among the group of buyers. In other words, the rates must not be same for hetro-groups and must not be different for homo-groups.

(d) *Simplicity, Consistency and Flexibility:* The rating system must be simple to understand and inexpensive to use. The rate must not change frequently under circumstances warrant (responsiveness to changes in the

3. R.C. Guria, Rating the Risks Right, IRDA Journal, September, 2006.

number of expected claims and losses). There should not be any rate-cutting at the cost of shareholders' fund or other policyholders' fund. For example, if inflation causes increase in medical expenses reimbursement or payment in more automobile repair claims, the corresponding Mediclaim insurance premium or Motor OD premium need to be enhanced.

(e) *Encouragement of loss control measures :* The insurer's rating policy should encourage loss-control activities that may reduce both loss-frequency and severity. With proper risk inspection and risk analysis, the insurer may find out the weakness of loss prevention measures and guide the insured accordingly to improve the arrangements so that frequency and severity can be reduced; and accordingly fire rates can be also reduced. In this regard Hazop Study, Fault Tree Analysis or Dow Index Analysis; and regular risk identification analysis deserve special mention. Also, the pricing mechanism should encourage the reduction of losses.

(f) *Availability of Insurance to the larger section of the society :* Because of the unreasonable prices, certain sections of the society find it difficult to obtain coverage easily at a reasonable price. So, to ensure availability of insurance products for larger section of the society as per their affordability, the insurers must have ability for proper loss forecasting; and stable, simple and transparent pricing system. Insurance business cannot be run in today's global market only with business objectives regardless of social objectives and regulatory objectives.

36.3 TYPES OF RATING

Insurance rating assesses the cost of the insurance product. Depending upon the type of rating, the price to the buyer may be – (a) entirely different from the one paid by another, (b) same as that paid by other customers or (c) similar to that paid by others, but more or less than the amount for one reason or another. There are basically three recognised rate-making methods:

- Judgement rating
- Class rating
- Merit rating
  - Schedule rating
  - Experience rating
  - Retrospective rating

36.3.1 Judgement Rating

It is used when the risk proposed to be bought is so unusual that little or no statistical information about similar risk is available. Each exposure is individually evaluated, and the rate is determined largely by the underwriter's judgement. Such cases are not unusual to the insurers when the loss exposures are so diverse that a class rate cannot be calculated, or when credible loss statistics are not available. When the judgement rating is used, each premium is unique and is based on the opinion of the person making it. It is widely used in ocean marine insurance and in some lines of inland marine insurance.

36.3.2 Class Rating

Class rates are the most common rate in insurance business. Insured risks are classified on the basis of one or several important features and all that belong to the same class are subject to the same rate per unit of exposure. The rate charged reflects the claims experience for the class as a whole. It is based on the assumption that future losses to insured will be determined largely by the same set of factors. This type of rating is also termed as manual rating because the various classifications and the respective rates are in the form of printing manuals.

Life insurance is one of the line where class rates are used viz. rates based on age, gender, healthiness, smoking and drinking habits etc. Class rating is also used for homeowners insurance, automobile insurance, workers compensation and health insurance. The twin considerations in class rating are:

How many different classifications and rates should there be?

How many characteristics of the covered risks should class rating take into account?

These two go together because the number of classifications depend upon the number of rating factors that are considered; the more the factors, the more the classifications. Following aspects are taken into considerations for Class Rating :

- ❑ Risk grouping/classification
- ❑ Homogeneous Group in respect of the following aspects
    - Nature of occupancy (Trading/Manufacturing)
    - Properties of materials (flammability, reactivity, toxicity, flash point etc.)
    - Properties of products
    - Nature and height of constructions
    - Process hazard (reaction operation, boiling point, flash point, ignition point etc.)
    - Plant/Process. (types, maintenance etc.)
    - Protection Systems and Appliances
- ❑ Credible Data Bank for proper Statistical Analysis and technical justification
- ❑ Probability Distribution of Loss for the particular class of risk
- ❑ Law of large numbers
- ❑ Reinsurance rate

The class rate may be determined by dividing the amount of incurred losses and loss adjustment expenses by the number of exposure units. Incurred losses include all losses paid during the accounting period, plus amounts held as reserves for the future payment of losses that have already occurred during the same period. Loss adjustment expenses are the expenses incurred by the company in adjusting losses during the same accounting period.

Another technique could be to compare the actual loss ratio with the expected loss ratio, and the rate is adjusted accordingly. The actual loss ratio is the ratio of incurred losses and loss adjustment expenses to earned premiums. The expected loss ratio is the percentage of the premiums that is expected to be used to pay losses.

When rates are based on just a few factors, many other characteristics of each exposure are ignored. Number of rating classes is dilemma for the rate-maker. The greater the number of classes, the more the factors that can be taken into account and therefore the more similar risks in any given class will be. On the other hand, increasing the number of classes reduces the number of insured in each one. Law of large number tell that the greater the number of exposures in each class, the more reliable the prediction of future losses will be. Hence, there are reasons for having so many classes and also for having a few. Increasing the number of classes causes the risks in each class to be more nearly alike, but reducing the number of classes causes the rates to be based on a larger body of data and to be more reliable.

Some Essential Considerations of Class Rating

(*a*) **Homogeneity of Group :** The homogeneity of the class must be established with respect to nature of property, frequency and severity of loss faced by the homogeneous group.

(*b*) **Statistical Analysis for Estimated Claim Costs :** To arrive at fair premium depends on Statistical Analysis consisting of Measure of Central Tendency, Dispersion, Analysis of Probability Distribution and Variance Analysis.

36.3.3 Merit Rating

Merit rating is a modification of the class rating. It modifies the class rate of a particular class insured based on individual loss experience. It is based on the assumption that the loss experience of a particular insured will differ substantially from the loss experience of the other insured. In doing so, it reflects the extent to which a specific risk differs from the others in the same class. The various types of merit-rating plans are:

36.3.3.1 Schedule Rating

Under this plan, each exposure is individually rated. In calculation of schedule rates the first step is to examine the risk (the person or object insured) in order to identify the features that are likely to cause losses or to prevent them. Then the risk is compared with the average or standard risk of its type. Finally deductions are made from the standard rate, for this risk's desirable features and additions are made for its undesirable features, the resultant rate is rate that is tailored made to reflect the characteristics of risk for which it is used. The scheduled rating system (for a building) takes into account the following major factors:

- Occupancy
- Construction
- Location
- Protection
- Maintenance
- Exposures
- House Keeping and Maintenance
- Loss Prevention or Control Measures
- Management outlook and attitude for loss prevention/control measures

The various additions to and subtractions from the basic rate are based upon the judgement of the person who develop the overall scheduled rating system and important feature of this system is that it identifies the factors entering into an insured's rate.

36.3.3.2 Experience Rating

This type of rating modifies the class rate on the basis of claim experience of a particular exposure. The actual losses for a period generally of two or three years is compared with the average risks in the same class. The rate is reduced if the risk has a better record than the average, it is increased if the record is worst than average. Experience rating is used only for large risks viz. large enough to have many losses each year reflecting a trend. Experience Rating is general restricted to large customers paying large amount of premium for different classes of business' for reasonable long period. Hence, this type of rating is generally limited to larger firms that generate a sufficiently high volume of premiums and more credible experience. This type of rating may be applied to Workmen's Compensation Insurance, Liability Insurance or Group Mediclaim Insurance safely as it is being followed in other countries, which have been in deregulation for a pretty long time.

36.3.2.3 Retrospective Rating

Contrary to experience rating retrospective rating modifies the insurance cost on the basis of current experience. This is generally done by making a provision in the policy contract that final rates will be determined *retrospectively*. Generally a range indication maximum and minimum is specified and the final premium is determined after the policy expires and depends upon the amount of losses incurred during the year. If the losses are very small the insured will pay the minimum premium otherwise if they are very large the insured will be charged the maximum premium. Usually the premium lies between maximum and minimum premium. Retrospective rating increases the insured's incentive to control losses, because the pay-off in premium savings can be substantial. It is generally applied to large liability and workers compensation policies. Retrospective Rating is widely use din USA for W.C. Policy, General Liability Policy, Auto Liability Policy, Property damage and Burglary policy for large firms.

Principally, rating will be made on risk process and cost of particular risk but not on subsidy from other funds. If proper rating method is followed by Indian insurers, fire insurance premium will get reduced substantially effecting greater market penetration, and higher productivity and efficiency.

The root of the success and survival of insurance industry lies in its skill and capability to rate the risks right. Freedom to fix price for the risk gives the real strength of the foundation and autonomy of the industry. In the tariff free regime, Indian insurance companies will be put to real test of their ability and capacity for autonomy.

36.4 OTHER RATING CONSIDERATION

Apart from the above rating philosophy there may be special conditions and rates applied to certain cases.

36.4.1 Pricing and Deductible

A deductible is voluntarily accepted by an insured to bear the first part of the amount of any claim at a figure higher than the standard excess impacts the rating of the product sold to the particular client. In a package or mega policy, deductibles are arranged separately for material damage insurance or at a combined figure with the associated business interruption insurance in each case with or without an aggregate limit. The use of deductible is on the rise nowadays because of mainly two factors – (*i*) capacity of the insured to bear loss (self insurance), and (*ii*) Saving of insurance cost. So if the price of product is not competitive and commensurate with the nature of risk, insurer may opt for higher deductible and increase his capacity of self-insurance. While deciding discount on deductible, the insurer takes into consideration the size of the deductible and the insured's past loss experience apart from the basis selected by the application of the insured.

36.4.2 Pricing and Warranties

As price of a product depends on its quality and specification, the price of a promise in an insurance contract depends on the nature and number of conditions/warranties and exclusions. But there are certain limitation *e.g.* in the Fire policy, there are thirteen exclusions and fifteen conditions. If any of these conditions or exclusions is removed, price can be reduced accordingly, provided the insurer has got some past loss experience and fair idea of loss forecasting for such type of product. Now a question arises as to whether an insurer can charge premium nine times the normal premium for cover for a particular class of risk without any of the nine standard exclusions applicable for standard product for that class of risk. It is neither prudent nor permissible under regulatory norms, as such pricing of a specially customized product for a particular client on his offer may not be supported by technical analysis of appropriate statistical data of past loss; and loss forecasting of the specially designed product different from the standard product based on past experience and filed with IRDA under the requirement of "File and Use".

36.4.3 Pricing and IRDA Requirements

- Design and rating of products must be on sound and prudent underwriting basis.
- All literature relating to the product should be in simple language for easy understanding by the public.
- The insurance product should comply with the requirements of the IRDA (Protection of Policyholders' Interests) Regulations 2002.
- Insurers should use similar wordings for describing the same cover.
- The pricing of products should be based on support of appropriate data and technical justification.
- Margins built into rates shall be consistent with the experience of the insurer in respect of commission, expenses of management, contingencies and profit; and
- Insurer should confirm that it has taken necessary steps to ensure that competition will not lead to unprincipled rate cutting and other improper methods.

Risk Inspection and Risk Identification by Line Underwriters : This has to be ensured while applying internal guide rates for the small and simple risks as they are doing now while applying tariff. In this regard the underwriters may look into the following aspects especially over and above the guidelines prescribed in the underwriting policy of the company for arriving at merit rating or experienced rating as mentioned above.

1. Risk Inspection Report
2. Risk Analysis and Loss Control Measures
3. Risk Classification
4. FEA Arrangements Review
5. Security Measures Review
6. Class of Construction (1, 11, Open, Other)
7. Statement of House Keeping and Hazards
8. Class of Construction (1, 11, Open, Other)
9. Process Control (manual, electric, electronic)
10. Market Trend and Expected Claim Costs
11. Special Characteristics of particular risks
12. Loss Experienced as per Data bank of the client
13. Reference to Guide Rates
14. Provisions for good features Discount or loading for bad risks as inspection report

In addition, the underwriting policy must specify the guidelines as to how the risks are to be identified, analyzed and evaluated for application of proper guide rates by the line underwriters for the small and simple risks to be underwritten by them to maintain uniformity and standard in implantation of underwriting policy and its control all over the country. The said policy must also prescribe the basis, ways and means of scheduled rating or merit rating as the case may be.

36.5 Rating in Life Insurance

The process of rate making in life insurance involve the logical steps of risk classification, pricing using mortality tables and adjustments.

Method of Risk Classification in Life Insurance

The two methods commonly employed in the classification of risks are:

(*a*) ***Judgement Method :*** The underwriter studies all the features of the life to be insured and on the basis of analysis of various factors takes a decision. Under this method the company depend upon the combined judgement of those in the medical actuarial and other areas who are qualified for the work to make underwriting decisions. The judgement method of rating functions effectively when is only one unfavorable factor to consider whether the decisions to be made is simply whether to accept the proposed insured at standard rates or to reject him or her entirely. However situations where multiple factors are involved or a proper substandard classification is needed, then this method can not be efficiently applied.

(*b*) ***Numerical Rating :*** In this method a large number of factors, which influence mortality, are taken in account. For various factors, debits (additions) or credits (subtractions) are made to the scores. The numerical ratings very from company to company-75 to 500 Illustratively, as rating increases, the quality of risk diminishes. A rating in the range of 75-125 is generally considered as standard and *over and above 125 sub standard.* An underwriter has to take into account the nature and combined effects of extra risks *e.g.* impairments jointly causing additional extra risks. In these cases some additions are made to the arrived rates calculated independently.

In pricing of life insurance products, the main factors used in rating are (*a*) mortality, (*b*) expenses, and (*c*) interest. The first step to rate is to identify the risk class.

Mortality Tables are prepared on the basis of study of assured lives for a period of time, usually a to 5 years. At every age deaths take place. These are tabulated showing rate of dying and rate of surviving (complementary probability) for every year.

A typical mortality table would appear like this:

1961-64 OM Table

Age at the beginning of the year	*No. of living at the beginning of the year*	*No. of death during during the year*	*Yearly probability of death*	*Yearly probability of surviving*
1	2	3	4	5
35	9,78,217	1410	00144	99856
36	9,77,807	1535	00157	99894
37	9,76,272	1679	00172	99828
38	9,74,593	1842	00189	99811
39	9,72,751	2633	00209	99791
40	9,70718	2242	00231	99769
41	9,68,476	2479	00256	99744
42	9,65,997	2743	00284	99716
43	9,63,254	3044	00316	99384
44	9,60,210	3370	00351	99633
45	9,56,840	3732	00390	99610

This table shows that the chance of dying the at age of 35 is .00144, it increases to .00390 at the age of 45. The last column shows the probability of survival. These probabilities of death and survival are made use of arriving at the *mathematical value* of the risk for lives belonging to a group whose experience may be expected to more or less compare favourably with the mortality table. If it happens, one can say that the premiums charged are adequate to meet the risk involved. In other words mortality experience is satisfactory.

Treatment of Sub-Standard Life Insurance Risks

The three broad classifications of sub standard risks are:

(*a*) ***Increasing Extra Risk :*** This category reflects the extra mortality risks caused due to impairments with the increase in age. Persons with extra weight are likely to have blood pressure or heart problems, as they grow older.

(*b*) ***Constant Extra Risk :*** This group reflects the lives with hazard that remain constant through life. These hazards do not create variations in mortality as such *e.g.* permanent total disablement-lost of limbs.

(*c*) ***Decreasing Extra Risk :*** These lives represent cases where the extra risk decreases with passage of risk since the consideration of proposal. A person who has just been operated for a problem becomes normal over a time period. At the time of proposal the risk was substandard, but with passage of time, it has become a simple risk.

The popular methods of treating sub standard risk are:

(*a*) ***Increase in Premium :*** Increase in normal premium (multiple table extra) is the most common method adopted by the insurance companies for treatment of sub-standard risks. Under its method premiums can be treated as follows:

(*i*) the proposer's age is increased by a few years (*e.g.* 3-5 years) which results in increases in premium or

(*ii*) a special mortality table is developed for each sub-standard classification that reflects the experience of each and asset of gross premium is computed for the classification.

(*b*) ***Flat Extra Premium :*** In situation where the extra risk is expected is constant, a flat extra premium may be changed. The policy remains standard one for all purposes including dividends and non-forfeiture values.

(*c*) ***Other Method :*** The other methods of refund an

(*i*) Limited death benefit equal to refund of premium if death occurs in the earlier years.

(*ii*) A lien (contingent debt) may be created an the policy such that upon the assured dies in the lien period, the lien amount shall be deducted from sum payable under the policy.

(*iii*) A proposal may be declined by the insurer if there is increasing extra risk.

(*iv*) Restrictive clauses may be imposed as exclusions under the policy.

(*v*) The insurance cover may be reduced by amount and/or time or the plan may be changed.

(*vi*) Another option from insurance company is to defer the cover till the extra risk is over.

Calculation of Premium

In calculating premium the following variable are considered:

(*i*) Term and Plan

(*ii*) Riders

(*iii*) Extras

(*iv*) Sum Assured

(*v*) Mode of payment

The rates of premium are quoted per thousand for various age groups. The table rates are then multiplied by the sum assured to arrive at a base premium. Then to the base premium, the addition or dedications are made. Consider the following example :

Sum proposed	Rs. 50,0000
Cover	Money Back Policy
Term	35 years
Table Rates	Rs. 27,00 per thousand
Adjustment Rate for high SI	+ Rs. 1.60 per thousand
Double Accident Benefit (DAB)	1%
Mode of percent	Semi-Annual

Calculation

Tabular Premium (Rs. 5,00,000 × 27/1000)	13,500
Adjustment Benefit for large SI (Rs. 5,00,000 × 1.60/1000)	800
Annual Premium	14,300
DAB Extra (1%)	1430
Total Price	15,730
Semi Annual Premium (15730/2)	Rs. 7865

Example 2

Plan	Whole life
Sum-Assured	Rs. 1,00,000
Riders	DAB
Health Extra	5%
Age	31
Premium Payments	35 years

Tabular Premium (Whole life, Premium Payments 35)	Rs. 29.40
Adjustment for large sum assured Rs. 1.50	Rs. 1.60
Adjustment for quarterly mode	Nil
Total	31.00
Annual Premium (31.00 × 100)	Rs. 3,100
Health Extra (5%)	Rs. 155.00
Total annual premium (including extra)	Rs. 3255.00
Quarterly instalment premium	Rs. 813.75

36.6 LIFE INSURANCE VS. NON-LIFE INSURANCE PRICING

Pricing of life Insurance products is simpler and life insurance rates are more stable and precise. In life insurance, the main factors used for determining the premium rates are (a) Mortality, (b) expenses and (c) interest. The insurers from time to time including the IRDA Annual Reports also publish the mortality statistics. In non-life insurance the insurers make estimates of the claims cost based on past experience, which are subject to review from time to time. The factors considered when pricing general insurance products are (a) Claims cost, (b) business acquisition cost, (c) management expenses, (d) margin for fluctuations in claims experience and (e) a reasonable profit. Accordingly, the life insurance and non-life insurance pricing can be distinguished as follows:

36.7 RATE MAKING ENTITIES

The individual insurers or professional rate making organisations may determine insurance rates. However, actuaries are generally involved in the rate-making process.

Basis	*Life Insurance*	*Non-life Insurance*
Simplicity	Relatively simple-class rating system based on insured's age and sex is logical and easy to understand – except in group insurance, neither experience nor retrospective rating is used.	Complicated-several rating systems are used for variety of exposures- for commercial risks, schedule, experience and retrospective rating is used.
Stability	Do not change frequently – average mortality rates scarcely change from year to year- also, overheads costs do not change substantially year to year.	Wide fluctuations accountable to operating environment, claims experiences.
Precision	Exact calculations because mortality expenses, investment income are stable-pool is significantly large – adverse event is certain – claims known in advance – no 'ifs' and 'buts'.	Rating is less precise-losses and their amounts are uncertain – losses subject to circumstances– maximum amount is specified – but not the loss payment amount.

Professional Rate-making Organisations

Professional rate making organisations are the specialists that perform the rating work for the insurance companies. The reason for existence of such organisations is that many companies do not have the sufficient data of their own. By working together and pooling their premium and loss data, they can develop a more reliable rating information. Co-operative rate-making is also suitable for smaller companies.

Actuaries

Actuaries are the specialists in the mathematics of insurance, who carry out the prime responsibility of the rate-making process either working in companies or otherwise. They make financial sense of the future by applying mathematical models to problems of insurance and finance. Actuaries are experts who perform actuarial analysis of insurance rates, rating procedures, rating plans, and schedules of insurance companies. These are professionals who are experienced in reviewing and analysing insurance operations, reserves and underwriting procedures and provide technical assistance regarding actuarial matters to policy examiners and other technical staff. They perform the following functions:

(*a*) Developing new forms of insurance to meet the changing needs of consumers.

(*b*) Determining the reserves needed to meet the future obligations.

(*c*) Analysing the expenses and earnings and providing database for distribution of surpluses.

(*d*) Conducting research studies on claims experiences, projecting future claims and earnings.

(*e*) Communicating with the company officials, agents, policyholders, and regulatory authorities about company policies and practices.

Qualified actuaries are in great demand in India with few qualified ones available. It is considered to be one of the best career options. One must have a professional qualification from the Actuarial Society of India or such institutions abroad. The actuarial profession in the world is about 150 years old. In 1848 the Institute of Actuaries was established in London. The Actuarial Society of India was established in Bombay in 1944. In exercise of the powers conferred by clause (zd) of sub section (2) of Section 114A of the Insurance Act, 1938 (4 of 1938), the Insurance Regulatory and Development Authority, in consultation with the Insurance Advisory committee has made certain regulations regarding Actuaries. According to the guidelines, an insurer registered to carry on insurance business in India shall, subject to sub-regulation (2), appoint an actuary who shall be known as the

Appointed Actuary for the purpose of the Act. A person shall be eligible to be appointed as an appointed actuary for an insurer if he or she shall be –

(*a*) Ordinary resident in India.

(*b*) A fellow member of the Actuarial Society of India.

(*c*) An Employee of the life insurer, in case of life insurance business.

(*d*) An Employee of the insurer or a consulting actuary, in case of general insurance business.

(*e*) A person who has not committed any breach of professional misconduct.

(*f*) A person against whom no disciplinary action by the Actuarial Society of India or any other actuarial body is pending.

(*g*) Not an appointed actuary of another insurer.

(*h*) A person who possesses a Certificate of Practice issued by the Actuarial Society of India; and

(*i*) Not over the age of seventy years.

Every insurer shall seek the approval of the Authority for the appointment of appointed actuary, submitting the application in form IRDA-AA-1. The text of the IRDA guidelines concerning actuaries are given in Annexure 36A.

36.8 Rate Making in General Insurance

In general insurance, apart from the normal rating procedures, the rates may be regulated for certain classes of products. Tariff Advisory Committee, to certain extent, controls the prices on some specific classes of insurances. 'Tariff' is defined as *fixed rate* on which a product or service is offered to customer. In tariff or regulated market condition either price or features of an offering or both are fixed and monitored by some regulator in market.

36.8.1 Tariff Advisory Committee

In 1896, Bombay Association of fire was established, under the close supervision of fire office committee in UK. In 1905, this association was replaced by *Fire insurance association* with offices at Bombay, Culcutta, Delhi and Madras. Bombay association of Fire initiated the regulation of rates, term and conditions and they were adopted by the Fire insurance association. The insurance association of India with membership of all insurers adopted the structure pertaining to rates, terms and conditions determined by Tariff committee under the control of the *Tariff advisory council.*

Later, *Tarif Advisory Committee* (TAC) was formed by another amendment to the insurance Act replacing the Tariff committee. TAC is a statutory body under the insurance Act, 1938. The IRDA Act, 1999, along with the resultant modifications to the insurance Act have reconfirmed the regulatory role of TAC.

Section 64V of Insurance Act, 1938 defines TAC as a body that controls and regulates the rates, terms and advantages of general Insurance business in India.

36.8.2 What is a Tariff Rate?

Tac fixes the tariffs regarding the general insurance product. "A tariff is merely a schedule of premium rates and policy terms and conditions applicable to risks in a class of business". A tariff rate in the Indian context is the minimum rates to be charged for a tariff cover with a prescribed wording : a reduced rate charged amounts to a breach of tariff provision. When all the insurance companies operating in a market follow tariff system of pricing, the market is said to be tariffed market *viz.*, the Indian General Insurance Market. Under such a system, Insurers have no choice of product and price differentiation. Tariff system leaves very little scope for competition among the insurance companies. Product differentiation is absent. The insurance companies. Product differentiation is absent. The insurers can compete on the basis of customer services instead of competing on price and product differentiation. *Tariff rate is the price of a general insurance product.* In Life Insurance, premium is the price. Tariff rates prescribed by IRDA should be followed by all General Insurance Companies

36.8.3 Basic General Insurance Product Pricing Structure

- Claims cost
- Management cost
- Business acquisition cost
- Margins and reasonable profits.

36.8.4 Objectives of Maintaining System of Tariffs

- Ensuring the long-term financial stability of Insurance enterprises
- Facilitating classification of risks according to their special characteristics.
- To provide rates for various insurance products.
- To prevent uneconomic competition by containing predatory rate war which could lead to chaos bankruptcy and loss of credibility of the market.
- Maintaining Market Stability
- To ensure that rates and terms are equitable and nondiscriminatory.
- To ensure a moderate competition.
- Making rate setting more scientific and base it on systematic analysis.

36.8.5 Why Detariffing?

Initially tariffs were introduced to protect the customer's interest. But for insurance companies, tariff system leaves very little scope for competition. Since the liberalisation of insurance sector, many companies (General Insurance) have entered in the market. It is also a known fact that when sellers are more, the customer will usually end up with a fair deal.

Moreover all the companies that are in general insurance business have big plan for future. It can be expected that they will always play safe. Finally we have a watchdog (IRDA) which can award a red card to the erring plays. In the present scenario, market should move towards a free rate regime according to transparent plan. Marketing every one subject to tariff is not a desirable long -term solution. Privatisation and tariff cannot go hand in hand and hence the shift from tariff to detariff regime. In due course of shifting from tariffing to detariffing regime, the rates would fall in line with international trends. This process should be encouraged.

36.9 Detariffing and its Impact on India

The final phase of the detariff process is likely to provide opportunities for the following :

- ❑ expanded and enhanced cover;
- ❑ customized cover for a specific exposure or peril;
- ❑ cover on a first-loss basis; and
- ❑ CAT perils-only cover.

Annexure 36 A

THE GAZETTE OF INDIA : EXTRAORDINARY

[PART III —SEC. 4]

INSURANCE REGULATORY AND DEVELOPMENT AUTHORITY,
NEW DELHI

NOTIFICATION

New Delhi, the 14th July, 2000

Insurance Regulatory and Development Authority (Appointed Actuary) Regulations, 2000

F.No.IRDA/Reg./7/2000 –

In exercise of the powers conferred by clause (zd) of sub-section (2) of section 114A of the Insurance Act, 1938 (4 of 1938), the Insurance Regulatory and Development Authority, in consultation with the Insurance Advisory Committee, hereby makes the following regulations, namely:

1. Short title and commencement : (1) These regulations may be called the Insurance Regulatory and Development Authority (Appointed Actuary) Regulations, 2000.

(2) They shall come into force from the date of their publication in the *Official Gazette*.

2. Definitions : (1) In these regulations, unless the context otherwise requires —

(a) "Act" means the Insurance Act, 1938 (4 of 1938);

(b) "Actuarial Society of India" means Actuarial Society of India registered under Societies Registration Act 1860; (21 of 1860);

(c) "Appointed Actuary" means an actuary mentioned in Regulation 3 below;

(d) "Authority" means the Insurance Regulatory and Development Authority established under sub-section (1) of Section 3 of the Insurance Regulatory and Development Authority Act, 1999 (41 of 1999);

(e) "Professional Standard" means the standard of practice specified, with the concurrence of the Authority, by the Actuarial Society of India by issue of guidance notes to its members.

(2) All words and expressions used herein and not defined herein but defined in the Insurance Act, 1938 (4 of 1938), or in the Insurance Regulatory and Development Authority Act, 1999 (41 of 1999), shall have the meanings respectively assigned to them in those Acts.

3. Procedure for Appointment of an Appointed Actuary: (1) An insurer registered to carry on insurance business in India shall, subject to sub-regulation (2), appoint an actuary, who shall be known as the 'Appointed Actuary' for the purposes of the Act.

(2) A person shall be eligible to be appointed as an appointed actuary for an insurer, if he or she shall be –

(i) ordinarily resident in India;

(ii) a Fellow Member of the Actuarial Society of India;

(iii) an employee of the life insurer, in case of life insurance business;

(iv) an employee of the insurer or a consulting actuary, in case of general insurance business;

(iv) a person who has not committed any breach of professional conduct;

(v) a person against whom no disciplinary action by the Actuarial Society of India or any other actuarial professional body is pending;

(vi) not an appointed actuary of another insurer;

(vii) a person who possesses a Certificate of Practice issued by the Actuarial Society of India; and

(viii) not over the age of seventy years.

(3) An insurer shall seek the approval of the Authority for the appointment of appointed actuary, submitting the application in Form IRDA-AA-1.

(4) The Authority shall, within thirty days from the date of receipt of application, either accept or reject the same:

Provided that before rejecting the application, the Authority shall give an opportunity of being heard to the insurer.

(5) If an insurer does not receive approval within thirty days of the receipt of such application by the Authority, the insurer shall deem that the approval has been granted by the Authority.

(6) An insurer, who is unable to appoint an appointed actuary in accordance with sub-regulation (2), shall make an application to the Authority in writing for relaxation of one or more conditions mentioned in sub-regulation 2.

(7) The Authority shall, on receipt of the application referred to in sub-regulation (6), communicate its decision to the insurer within thirty days of receipt of such application.

(8) The appointment of an appointed actuary shall take effect from the date of approval by the Authority.

4. Effect of rejection of the application: The insurer shall, within four weeks of rejection of the application referred to under regulation 3, apply to the Authority for the appointment of a person other than the one rejected by it under regulation 3 as an appointed actuary, for the purposes of these regulations.

5. Life Insurer not to carry on business of insurance without an appointed actuary: A life insurer shall not carry on business of insurance without an appointed actuary.

6. Cessation of Appointment of Appointed Actuary: (1) An appointed actuary shall cease to be so, if he or she has been given notice of withdrawal of approval by the Authority on the following grounds:

(a) that he or she ceases to be eligible in accordance with sub-regulation (2) of regulation (3), or;

(b) that he or she has, in the opinion of the Authority, failed to perform adequately and properly the duties and obligations of an appointed actuary under these regulations.

(2) The Authority shall give an appointed actuary a reasonable opportunity of being heard, if he or she has been given a notice of withdrawal of approval by it.

(3) If a person ceases to be an appointed actuary of an insurer otherwise than on the grounds mentioned in sub-regulation (1), the insurer and the appointed actuary shall intimate the Authority the reasons therefor within fifteen days of such a cessation.

7. Powers of Appointed Actuary: (1) An appointed actuary shall have access to all information or documents in possession, or under control, of the insurer if such access is necessary for the proper and effective performance of the functions and duties of the appointed actuary.

(2) The appointed actuary may seek any information for the purpose of sub-regulation (1) of this regulation from any officer or employee of the insurer.

(3) The appointed actuary shall be entitled —

(a) to attend all meetings of the management including the directors of the insurer;

(b) to speak and discuss on any matter, at such meeting,—

(i) that relates to the actuarial advice given to the directors;

(ii) that may affect the solvency of the insurer;

(iii) that may affect the ability of the insurer to meet the reasonable expectations of policyholders; or

(iv) on which actuarial advice is necessary;

(c) to attend, –

(i) any meeting of the shareholders or the policyholders of the insurer; or

(ii) any other meeting of members of the insurer at which the insurer's annual accounts or financial statements are to be considered or at which any matter in connection with the appointed actuary's duties is discussed.

8. Duties and obligations: In particular and without prejudice to the generality of the foregoing matters, and in the interests of the insurance industry and the policyholders, the duties and obligations of an appointed actuary of an insurer shall include:

(a) rendering actuarial advice to the management of the insurer, in particular in the areas of product design and pricing, insurance contract wording, investments and reinsurance;

(b) ensuring the solvency of the insurer at all times;

(c) complying with the provisions of the Section 64 V of the Act in regard to certification of the assets and liabilities that have been valued in the manner required under the said section;

(d) complying with the provisions of the Section 64 VA of the Act in regard to maintenance of required solvency margin in the manner required under the said section;

(e) drawing the attention of management of the insurer, to any matter on which he or she thinks that action is required to be taken by the insurer to avoid –

(i) any contravention of the Act; or

(ii) prejudice to the interests of policyholders;

(f) complying with the Authority's directions from time to time;

(g) in the case of the insurer carrying on life insurance business,–

(i) to certify the actuarial report and abstract and other returns as required under section 13 of the Act;

(ii) to comply with the provisions of Section 21 of the Act in regard to further information required by the Authority;

(iii) to comply with the provisions of Section 40-B of the Act in regard to the bases of premium;

(iv) to comply with the provisions of the Section 112 of the Act in regard to recommendation of interim bonus or bonuses payable by life insurer to policyholders whose policies mature for payment by reason of death or otherwise during the inter-valuation period;\

(v) to ensure that all the requisite records have been made available to him or her for the purpose of conducting actuarial valuation of liabilities and assets of the insurer;

(vi) to ensure that the premium rates of the insurance products are fair;

(vii) to certify that the mathematical reserves have been determined taking into account the guidance notes issued by the Actuarial Society of India and any directions given by the Authority;

(viii) to ensure that the policyholders' reasonable expectations have been considered in the matter of valuation of liabilities and distribution of surplus to the participating policyholders who are entitled for a share of surplus;

(ix) to submit the actuarial advice in the interests of the insurance industry and the policyholders;

(h) in the case of the insurer carrying on general insurance business to ensure, –

(i) that the rates are fair in respect of those contracts that are governed by the insurer's in-house tariff;

(ii) that the actuarial principles, in the determination of liabilities, have been used in the calculation of reserves for incurred but not reported claims (IBNR) and other reserves where actuarial advice is sought by the Authority;

(iii) informing the Authority in writing of his or her opinion, within a reasonable time, whether,—

(i) the insurer has contravened the Act or any other Acts;

(ii) the contravention is of such a nature that it may affect significantly the interests of the owners or beneficiaries of policies issued by the insurer;

(iii) the directors of the insurer have failed to take such action as is reasonably necessary to enable him to exercise his or her duties and obligations under this regulation; or

(iv) an officer or employee of the insurer has engaged in conduct calculated to prevent him or her from exercising his or her duties and obligations under this regulation.

9. Absolute Privilege of Appointed Actuary: (1) An appointed actuary shall enjoy absolute privilege to make any statement, oral or written, for the purpose of the performance of his functions as appointed actuary. This is in addition to any other privilege conferred upon an appointed actuary under any other Regulations.

(2) Any provision of the letter of appointment of the appointed actuary, which restricts or prevents his duties, obligations and privileges under these regulations, shall be of no effect.

10. Applicability to reinsurance business: These regulations shall apply to reinsurers carrying on reinsurance business in India.

Form IRDA-AA-1

Particulars of Appointed Actuary

1. Name of Insurer:
2. Name of Actuary:
3. Residential Address with telephone number:[Residential addresses during the last five years have to be furnished].
4. Official Address with telephone number:
5. Date of Appointment:
6. Date & Place of Birth.
7. Annual Remuneration & Fringe Benefits.
8. Shareholding (in per cent of share holding) in the Indian Insurance Company (for which the applicant is the Appointed Actuary) and also in the promoter's companies, if any.
9. Professional Qualifications:
10. Working Experience (give also particulars of previous experience as Appointed Actuary in India or elsewhere).
11. Achievements and special positions held presently or previously.
12. Names, countries of incorporation, addresses and principal activities of any other firms or companies in which the applicant was a director, partner, proprietor or an employee.
13. Particulars of any criminal conviction for offences in India or elsewhere:
14. Has the applicant been adjudicated bankrupt during the last ten years? If so, give details:
15. Has the applicant been disciplined by any professional bodies or any insurance regulator? If so give details:

Certification:

I hereby certify that the information given in this form is complete, true and correct, and also enclose the Certificate of Practice issued by the Actuarial Society of India.

Place:

Date:

Signature of Actuary

Countersigned by the principal officer of the Insurer:

N. RANGACHARY, Chairperson

[No. Advt.-3/4/Exty/161/2000]

Key Terms

- Pure Premium
- Margin
- Judgement Rating
- Experience Rating
- Actuaries
- Operating Expenses
- Exposure Unit
- Class Rating
- Retrospective Rating
- Rate-making Organisations

Questions for Review

1. Briefly explain the major determinants of insurance pricing. Do you think that their respective weightages vary from organisation to organisation?
2. What is rating? Briefly explain the various classes of rating.
3. "In order for insurance rates to be fair, they must discriminate fairly among the various policyholders." Explain.
4. What general comparisons can be made between life insurance pricing and non-life insurance pricing?

Suggested Readings

1. J.S. Trieschmann *et al., Risk Management and Insurance*, South-Western College Publishig, 2001.
2. Harrington and Michaus, *Insurance and Risk Management*, McGraw-Hill, 1999.
3. Briyo *et al., Insurance From Underwriting to Derivatives*, John Wiley & Sons Ltd., 2001.

Marketing of Insurance Products

Chapter 37

CHAPTER OBJECTIVES

After reading this chapter you will be able to understand :

- *The Marketing Concept*
- *Marketing of Insurance Products*
- *Critical Success Factors for Insurance Players*
- *Distribution Channels*
- *Marketing Strategies of Insurance Players in India*

The new millennium has exposed the insurance sector to new challenges of competition and struggle for survival. The era of privatization, liberalization, deregulation and globalization has let loose a sense of urgency and neo-activism. Indian politico-economic think tank realised the obsolescence of remaining insular and monopolistic in the insurance sector. The insurance services industry nationally and internationally is huge, growing, and of critical significance to the health of economy as well as of individual businesses, investors, consumers and employees. The progress of Insurance business in any developing country like ours is generally linked with the rapid industrialisation and overall progress of the Country. In the emerging scenario, the insurance sector must pay attention to product innovation, appropriate pricing and speedy settlement of claims.

The marketing function of insurance is of unique importance because the insurance company can succeed only if it sells a large number of policies and spreads its risk among the insureds. To accomplish this, it must rely on its marketing organisation. No matter how efficiently an insurer manages all of its functions, its sales force is the key to the company's success.

37.1 THE MARKETING CONCEPT

Over the years, marketing has undergone substantial changes both in nature, role and functions. Modern concept of marketing is different from the traditional concepts. Under the former, marketing is conducted the philosophy, that products made are matched with markets, i.e., the firm takes the responsibility on itself to design, develop and sell its products to suit the needs of its customer-the basic principle followed is ""Caveat Vendor", i.e., *let the seller beware.* The main objective behind this thinking is to satisfy customer through constant study of their changing needs and wants. While, under the later, the firm does not take any responsibility for its goods- the philosophy that works is of "Caveat Emptor", i.e., *let the buyer beware.* The goods are produced as per the decision of the marketing manager and are put on the market, and the purpose of marketing ends.

Modern Views on Marketing

'Marketing' has a special significance in modern management of business and industry and is one of the important managerial concepts. Unless it is properly understood and put into practice in the right use, many of the business or industrial enterprise will collapse or prove a failure in their achievements. This will be clear when it is realised that marketing is a total system of interacting business activities (*viz.,* marketing and production) designed to plan, price, promote and distribute want-satisfying products and services to the present and potential customers. It means in other words, that (i) business decisions should be "market or customer oriented" rather than product oriented gearing their operations primarily to the effective satisfaction of customer wants and needs; (ii) marketing is a dynamic business process – a total, integrated process (of matching products in the markets), rather than a fragmented assortment of institutions and functions. Marketing is not only one activity, nor it is exactly the sum of several; rather it is the result of the interaction of many activities involving movement of goods and services from producers to ultimate consumers or industrial users; and also those activities which are involved in "evaluating these markets and adjusting product characteristics to market needs". (*iii*) the marketing programme starts with the germination of the product idea and continues till the customers' wants are completely satisfied, which may be sometime after the sale is made; (*iv*) marketing programme is done with a maximum of effectiveness and a minimum of costs, and (*v*) marketing must increase profitable sales over the long run.

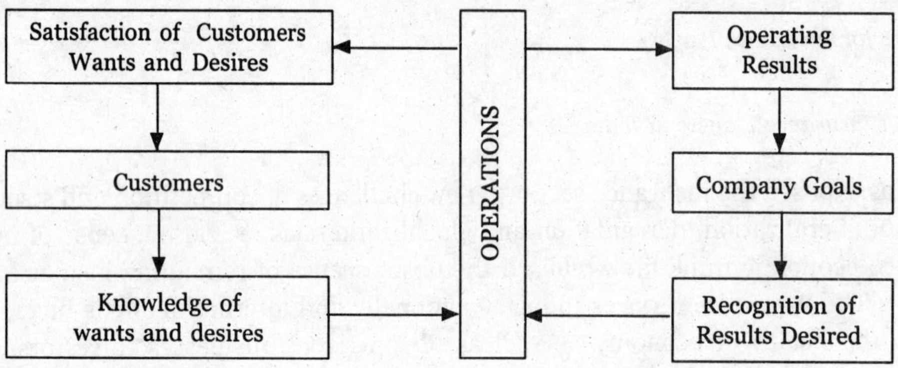

According to Theodore Levitt

"Management must think itself not as producing products but as providing customer creating value satisfactions. It must put this idea into every nook and cranny of the organisation. It has to do this continuously and with the kind of flair that excites and stimulates the people in it. Otherwise, the company will be merely a series of pigeon-holed parts, with no consolidation sense of purpose or direction. In short, the organisation must learn to think of itself not as producing goods or services but as buying customers, as doing the things that will make people want to do business with it".[1]

Mr. J.B. Kitterick, the former president of the General Electric Company states that:[2]

"Marketing Concept introduces the marketing men at the beginning rather than at the end of the production cycle and would integrate marketing into each phase of business. Thus, marketing through its studies and research will establish for engineers, the designers and the manufacturing men *what the customer wants in a given product, what price he is willing to pay and where and when it will be wanted.* Marketing would have authority in product planning, production scheduling and inventory control as well as in sales, distribution and serving the product."

Marketing concept is "a way of thinking", or "a management philosophy" about an organisation's total marketing activities. When the philosophy is adopted, it affects not only marketing activities but also all the organisation's activities – including planning of action, control, objectives, follow-through etc.; finance and other activities which are geared toward satisfying customers' needs, wants and desires.

Marketing concept means" developing a strategy to get the product in front of customers so they have the opportunity to buy it..... determining scientifically what products or services to make and how best to market them to meet consumer needs."[3] Planning, developing strategy systematically and scientifically selecting among

1. Levitt, Theodore, "Marketing Myopia", *Harward Business Review,* July-August, 1960, p. 56.
2. General Electric Company, *Annual Report for 1952.*
3. Bell Martin, L., *Marketing Concepts and Strategy,* 1979, p. 8.

available alternatives and controlling the operation in order to provide customer satisfaction are relatively new implications in the marketing concept.

Ingredients or Components of Marketing Concept

The marketing concept has the following main basic features:

(i) Adoption of a predominantly *market or customer* orientation.

(ii) A coordinated set of activities that allows the organisation to achieve the goals.

(iii) Result oriented marketing:

37.2 MARKETING OF INSURANCE PRODUCTS

The Indian Insurance Industry is poised for interesting and demanding time. Though the industry has been serving customers since 19th century, the nationalisation of the industry in 1956 titled the scales in favour of the provider, the Life Insurance Corporation (LIC). While the LIC did expand aggressively to cover various part of the country, the customer has no choice when it came to selection the life insurance provider. The transition of the industry from public monopoly to a competitive environment now present very interesting opportunities, both to the new players and to the customers. It is apparent that the new players have an opportunity to test out their various hypothesis but also to apply learning's from overseas markets, the customers will have a greater choice when it comes to choosing a provider or a solution for his needs. For the customers, the most important functions of an insurance company include produce design distribution services, delivery and investment performance. The common link between the provider and the customer. *The distribution chain* in now assuming focus with new players exploring various possibilities to reach out to customers and to service them effectively. The future of Insurance market and accordingly the marketing strategy is likely to be influenced by three new developments: (a) the convergence of financial services, (b) rise of E-commerce and (c) the emergence of new distribution channels. In fact, the marketing strategies for the players would be significantly influenced by the value propositions of time and cost reduction, effective CRM and profitability.

Issues in Insurance Marketing

The peculiar nature of the insurance industry creates implementation of marketing strategy a difficult task in the following ways:

- Insurance is unpatented, subjective, requires prior experience and physical evidence is difficult to establish.
- There is a involvement of customers in production of services, mass production is impossible.
- The services cannot be inventoried and standardised.

37.3 CRITICAL SUCCESS FACTORS FOR INSURANCE PLAYERS

In the current industry scenario, the following factors must be carefully examined for the success of the any insurance company in particular and the industry in general:

• Change in the Attitude of the Population

Insurance has always been used as a tax saving tool. But, in light of the Kelkar Committee recommendations, the lusture would wipeout once they are implemented. Therefore only those will survive who can educate the people to secure/insure their future against any unknown calamity and make a shield around their families and businesses.

• Open and Transparent Environment Created Under the IRDA

It has been seen that any sector open up in India there are always gray areas and unsure policies. These are not exactly what any players, be it Indian or foreign, looks for. It creates an air of uncertainty in all the decision making process. Insurance as a sector requires players who are strong financially and are willing to wait for returns. There confidence can be bolstered only if there are open and a transparent policy guidelines. This will also help the consumers feel safe that the regulatory is an active one and cares to do everything possible to keep things under control and help the insurance environment grow maturely.

- **Well-established Distribution Network**

Distribution is going to be key area for the success of an insurance company in Indian market. Public Sector banks like SBI, PNB etc. can be one of the leaders in distribution because of their huge network and long existence.

- **Trained Professionals to Build and Sell the Product**

Conventionally, insurance agents are considered to be the only and best salesman for insurance products. In wake of the growing competition, the players will require an excellent sales team to sell their products. There will be mass shifts in the industry, which is evident from the fact the new players are poaching a lot of LIC personnel.

- **Rationale Approach to the Investment Criteria**

This is a very critical area as far as the government and the players are concerned. IRDA has framed guidelines, which provide for the investment pattern for the players to meet its social obligations. The players feel that the compulsion is unjust and will affect their return on investments. This factors has been elucidated as a success factor as it is in the larger interests of the society. The more the people insured, the better the revenues, followed by better security, followed by better morale and productivity.

- **Stringent Accounting Practice to Prevent Failures Amongst the Insurers**

Every insurer has the hard-earned money of the masses. Any failure of the insurer on account of unwarranted profligacy will cost the nation in general and the insured in particular. To prevent any underhand working of the insurer and to prevent them from going bust, a stringent accounting practice is imperative.

- **Level Playing Field at all Stages of Development in the Sector for all the Players**

It is the responsibility of the government to provide an unbiased environment in order to have level playing field for the players.

37·4 DISTRIBUTION CHANNELS

Traditionally, the life insurers have been solely depended on the agency distribution force. On the contrary, the general insurance business has depended totally on the development officers. The scenario has been different for the general insurers a no agency commission was payable for writing business more than 10 lakh, thus prohibiting brokers. The new private insurer coming in with the liberalisation of the sector will add more channel of distribution in the Indian market parallel to that existent. Innovation and diversification will become the buzzards in the business. Emerging scenario is evolving as a generic model in markets around the globe. Even in markets, which are consolidating like Europe, re-strategising distribution has been deciding the success for the insurers. The situation has become more complex with the development in systems and software technology and changing social patterns. All these have conspired to cause an upheaval in the traditional distribution methods. The new evolving system will now have to integrate the three players in the insurance market:

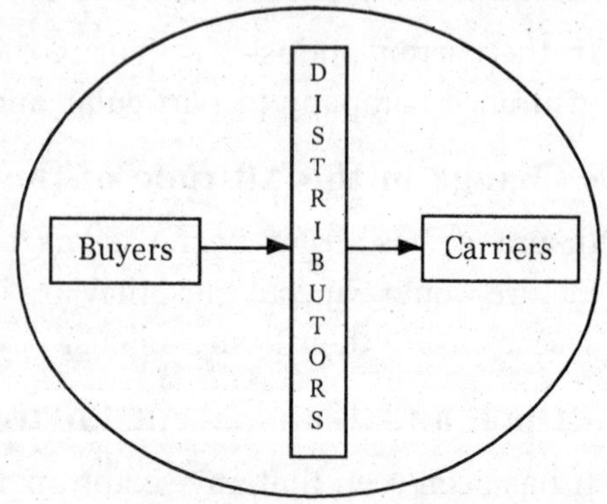

The *buyers* will consist of consumers, employees, and employers. The *carriers* or the policy issuers will focus mainly on life and annuities, property and casualties, health and ancillaries. The critical link in the system will be the *distributor*. Those who will provide value-added and low-cost services will be the survivors.

37.4.1 Traditional Channel of Distribution

Agents

Most of the life insurance companies in India follow the traditional route of marketing through agents. In case of private players they are nomenclature as Insurance Advisors /Planners. The companies emphasis on building a good field force, trained to get people thinking about their family's financial security and recommend appropriate policies for their needs. The agents are trained to be sensitive to the dominant issues in any family's life like education and marriage of children. Most life insurance agents are trying to sell the broad concept of pre-planning your life. The success of LIC with its direct field force, rather, army of 6,51,000 agents is exemplary. In case of non-life also much of the distribution work is done by the agents or development officers.

Brokers

Insurance brokers are professionals who assess risk on behalf of a client, advise on the mitigation of that risk, identify the optimal insurance policy structure, bring together the insured and insurers, carry out work preparatory to insurance contracts and where necessary, assist in the administration and performance of such contracts, in particular when claims arise.

Unlike insurance agents who are retained by Insurance Companies, Brokers are retained by the insured and therefore their primary responsibility is towards the insured. Some of the benefits of introducing brokers in the Indian market are:

- *Improvement in Customer Service:* with increased competition, insurance brokers have a greater motivation to introduce new and innovative products, to be more responsive to consumer needs and to deliver higher terms quality services. Indian corporate and consumers benefit directly in terms of service as well as product and policy innovation, and are consequently able to secure appropriate insurance cover more cost effectively.
- *Transfer of Technology and Managerial Know-how:* Insurance brokers introduce international best practice in technical skills and products, training programmes systems and technology, and managerial techniques. Currently the availability of trained manpower is a major constraint in the development of the insurance broking business in India and international players can contribute heavily in bridging this gap.
- *Benefits to Insurance Companies:* Most major global insurance companies spend the majority of their time handling commercial and industrial risk. They find dealing with brokers to be easier and speedier because only the intricate points or special requirements need detailed discussion. Brokers also assist in creating insurance awareness, increasing market penetration and act as a catalyst to increase competition and improve customer service.
- *Foreign Exchange Considerations:* Brokers enable Indian insurers to increase their retention capacities by applying their international reinsurance skills in optimising their reinsurance programmes, thereby effecting further saving in foreign exchange outflow. In addition, they can assist the local insurers to develop new products and accordingly increase the premium base.

37.4.2 New Distribution Channels

The new channels of distribution for the Indian insurance industry are:

- *Direct Marketing* : Company owned sales team concept is now employed by a majority of the new players and has proved effective sin customer creation and retention.
- *Brokers/Corporate Agents* : Authorised by IRDA to sell and customised products on behalf of insurance companies.
- *Independent Financial Advisors* : Authorised agents of insurance companies having tie ups may be with more than one company.
- *Telemarketing* : Marketing through telephonic devices, generating leads through cold calls and forwarding the leads to the main sales team of the company
- *Work site Marketing* : Under this strategy, the seller sends his team to the target group and explains the products and services suitable to them. Organisations such as the groups: HDFC, ICICI, Kotak Mahindra are using this kind of distribution strategy effectively.
- *Retail Chains* : Cross selling of products at retail outlets
- *Internet Marketing* : Internet based product offerings.
- *Bancassurance :* Distribution of insurance products by banks (this is elaborated in detail in next section)

37.4.3 Bancassurance

Bancassurance denotes a partnership between a life insurance company and a banking institution. The need (for the insurance company) to access a large base of customers and a desire (on the part of the bank) to offer arrange of financial products leads to these partnership in different forms. A trusting relationship with customers, branch name recognition, customer profitability measurement systems in banks, cash management relationship with corporations and the fact that Bancassurance distribution is more cost effective than traditional distribution are some of the key attractions of this channel. 27 public sector banks and 196 regional rural banks account for 92% of the branch network in India.

With over 60,000 branches of commercial banks and an average population served per branch of 15,000, Bancassurance is expected to be a critical distribution strategy for the insurance companies. In fact, the network includes 33,000 rural branches and 14,000 semi-urban branches, about 60% of the total number of branches. Key issues to be addressed to make Bancassurance successful are:

- Both the bank and insurance company need *to improve effectiveness of the sales* channels by identifying and gaining access to target customers, adding push to market pull, training of sales staff, differentiating performance from competition and controlling selling cost per unit sold.
- *Product needs to be tailored* to meet the need of the customer base and for new distribution channels.
- *Communication* needs to be streamlined to address any cultural issues between the bank staff and the insurance staff. Similarly, differences in compensation structures need to be handled sensitively before these start affecting the moral of the branch staff.
- *Traditional processes need to be redesigned* not only to take advantage of the new technology, but also to effect a streamlined system between bank and the insurance company. Technology can be used to put effective use in sales support function, staff training. Smoother processing, and online integrated information system.
- *Information system needs to be reviewed* and performance measurement parameters need to be specially adapted to Banacassurance.

- Skills need to be developed an reallocation of assets and resources — financial and human may also be required between the bank and Insurance Company.

Bank writing the risk themselves is not perminable in India since RBI has restricted this to a few bank like Vysya Bank and SBI.

Bancassurance Types

Leveraged Life Distribution: Under this model, the life insurance company takes the lead in partnership, while several banks act as corporate agents to provide access to middle market leads.

Leveraged Bank Distribution: Under leveraged bank distribution, it is the bank that takes the lead as in the partnership, while the life insurance companies supply products for it's Bancassurance efforts. This model calls for a large bank with a range of effective distribution channels (branches, ATMs, mail, phones).

Bank/Life Joint Venture: The third and final type of partnership brings a bank with a well developed customer database together with a large life insurer with strong product and channel experience to develop a powerful new distribution model. In this type of venture the bank provides the lead and its reputation and brand name, while the insurer brings products and underwriting and servicing expertise. The partners combine their individual expertise to forge a best practice Bancassurance operation with tailored products, tailored distribution and lead generation mechanism.

This model may be applied to SBI Life Insurance. It has access to some 117 million holders of term deposits through 14,000 branches of the State Bank of India (SBI), which serve as a ready platform, a ready distribution channel.

Other players such as ING Vysya are also looking at this option. They seek to set-up branches in many main cities, moving gradually into the semi-urban and rural areas. Bancassurance reaffirms the fact that people like to see the insurer remains within sight, over the years.

37·5 MARKETING STRATEGIES OF INSURANCE PLAYERS IN INDIA

Insurance companies the marketing strategy involve in mobilising and utilising its intangible or invisible assets which will enable the company to:

- Develop customer relationship that retains the loyalty of existing customers and enable new customer segment and market areas to be served effectively and efficiently.
- Introduce new innovative products and services desired by targeted customer segment.
- Produce customised high quality products and service at low cost and with short lead times.
- Mobilise employee skills and motivation for continuous improvements in process capabilities, quality and response times.
- Deploy information technology, databases and systems in an optimum manner.

The marketing strategy cannot be taken up in isolation. Major elements of the organisation, viz., structure, systems, processes, employees, organisational cultures and above all the shared values should be appropriately integrated in implementation of the strategy. The basic tool for diagnosing competitive advantages and finding ways to enhance is to enhance it is the value chain, which divides a company into discrete activities it perform in designing, producing, marketing and distributing its products.

A business value design is the totality of how a company selects its customers, defines the tasks it will perform itself and those it will out source, configure its resources, goes to the market, creates utility to the customer and earning profits from the activities.

A strategy worth the name must take into account both the disaggregative as well as aggregative aspects of the business value design of the company. Competitive advantage for a company stems from many discrete activities in the value chain. Each of these activities can contribute to the companies' relative cost position or create a basis for a differentiation. Thus, the disaggregative aspects are important contributors to the strategy formulation process.

Coming to aggregative aspects, each generic strategy implies different skills and requirements for success, which commonly translates into difference in organisational structure and culture. Hence marketing strategies in the insurance sector would revolve around products and companies and their thrust areas would be a function of environmental, competitive, and technological factors in a dynamic environment.

37.5.1 Punchline of Some Players

Life Insurance Corporation of India	"Life is Beautiful",
	"Jindgi ke sath bhi jindgi ke baad bhi"
Birla Sun Life Insurance	"Your Dreams, Our Commitment"
ICICI Prudential Life Insurance	"We cover you at every step in life"
HDFC Standard Life Insurance	Making Life Easier for you"
OM Kotak Mahindra Life Insurance	"Jeene ki Azaadi"
ING Vysya Life Insurance	"Adding life to insurance"
TATA AIG Life Insurance	"With you always"
Max New York Life Insurance Company	"Your partner for life"
Bajaj Allianz	"We cover almost everything"
AMP Sanmar	"Creating better futures"

37.5.2 Market Strategies of Some Insurance Policies

Life Insurance Corporation of India

LIC is the leader in the insurance sector with majority of the market share. LIC has recently tied up Corporation Bank and Vijay Bank for distribution of its products. It has linked all its 2048 branches through computer network. LIC strategy is to launch customised and focussed insurance products for various sections of the society. As a matter of customer retention, it has launched a highly optimistic compaign of revival of lapsed policies. LIC has first introduced online premium payment facilities LIC is planning to go deep in the rural markets because of its established brand name. LIC is one of biggest advertiser of its products utility a wide large of products viz. print and electronic media, sponsoring events, roadshows etc., the company is following both mass marketing and segmentation strategy to promote its products. However, the focus of its promotional activities is on tax benefit and returns from insurance. The company has realised competition from private sector and it is thinking aggressively for effective CRM.

ICICI Prulife

The strategy of ICICI prulife is to achieve scale in premium income and distribution force in shortest time. It is the major competitor to LIC in India. The company is using tools like workstation marketing, corporate marketing, road shows, stall in trade fair, loading etc. Research statistics shows that the awareness level of ICICI prulife has grown substantially in the last one year. The strategies of ICICI prulife are mostly pro-active in nature. The focus is more on direct selling apart from communication and building personal relations.

HDFC Standard Life

HDFC is the leader in housing finance in India and Standard life is the UK market leader. The company is using direct marketing tactics to build HDFC brand and convincing the customers, insurance as a protection tool. The company strives to build strong foundation for distribution in the initial years and focus on shareholders' value. The company is marketing at worksite and to corporate customers through its customised product offerings HFDC standard life has adopted a multichannel distribution model to popularize and market its products. The company also simultaneously attempts to sell its products as long term investment plans.

Max New York Life (MNYL) is operating with 2500 agents spread in 9 cities in India. It is using individual agents as its primary sources of distribution. It offers a suite of flexible products with many options and riders that can be customised to over 250 different combination. The company is using various methods like media advertising, event sponsorship etc. and tools like direct marketing relationship building to generate awareness and build customer base. The core of MNYL lies in offering more of protection policies and whole life policies. The company places emphasis on the quality of its first sales personnel i.e. agents.

Metfile is a global leader in the financial services and in India, as a part of the company's strategy, it has tied up with Geojet Infofin Technologies for marketing and distribution of insurance products across the country. The company has followed a strategy of phase-wise introduction of products in the market. The company is following the "Bundlemethod" of product offering which includes investment options ranging from insurance, equities, derivatives, mutual funds, bonds, TPOs to enable meticulous investment planning by analysing the needs, requirements risk profile of the customers.

The company has a focus on south-Indian and J&K market and has plane to expand distribution network in a phased manner. The company is also focussing on selling of group policies.

Tata-AIG

The company claims to have expertise in assessing the appropriateness of risk covered, as well as uniqueness of the risks faced by them. The company follows the mass marketing strategy to cover as many as lives as possible in the initial years of its operation. The company is also trying to build its brand by stressing on the creditworthiness of the company and its partners.

Bajaj Allianz

It is one of the important competitor to government general insurance companies. The company's focus is on "Cashless" insurance products (automobile). The company is advertising in local newspapers, television and hoardings for generating awareness. In the two-wheeler segment, a major chunk of the customers are assured. But, over and above, the company is highly cautious in underwriting of risks.

Others

Birla sun life is distinguishing itself in two ways:

(a) In terms of products – only unit linked products

(b) In terms of target products — largely high net worth individuals, with a high average sum insured AVIVA, ING Vysya are targeting the customer base of respective banking partners.

SBI standard life wants to utilise the huge network of SBI with three major concerns:

(a) Simple Products

(b) Branch-wise segmentation and product offerings

(c) Smaller Average size of policies

OM Katak Mahindra is pursuing the middle income affluent segment compared to man marketing strategy of others. The focus is on high network individuals. The company plans to widen its network to top 20 cities of the country, the concentration being on western region.

Key Terms

- ❒ Marketing
- ❒ Marketing Strategy
- ❒ Critical Success Factors
- ❒ Distribution Channels
- ❒ Bancassurance

Questions for Review

1. Define marketing. Explain the important factors to be considered while marketing of insurance products.
2. Write short notes on:
   (a) Bancassurance
   (b) Marketing strategies of insurance players
   (c) Distribution of insurance products.

Suggested Readings

1. D.I. Hawkins. *et al., Consumer Behaviour — Building Marketing Strategy,* Irwin, McGraw-Hill, 2001.
2. G.N. Bajpai and Jyoti Mavare, *The Marketing of Insurance — Strategies for Success,* Abhinav Publishing Industries Pvt. Ltd., 1994.
3. D.C. Srivastava and Shashank Srivastava, *Indian Insurance Industry — Transition and Prospects,* New Century Publications, 2001.
4. Christopher Lovelock, *Services Marketing — People, Technology, Strategy,* Prentice-Hall, 2001.

Web Resources

- www.insurancemarketingtips.com
- www.imcgroup.com
- www.banknetindia.com
- www.mjans.com
- www.consumerindia.com

Claims Management

Chapter 38

CHAPTER OBJECTIVES

After reading this chapter you will be able to understand :

- *Introduction to Claims Management*
- *Claim Settlement in General Insurance*
- *Claims Management in Life Insurance*

38.1 INTRODUCTION TO CLAIMS MANAGEMENT

The prompt settlement of a valid claim is an important function of an insurance organisation. In fact, the efficiency of the organization is tested whenever a claim arises, by the time that is taken by the insurers to finalize it. The speed, courtesy and fairness with which an insurer administers claims reflect the level of services the company provides to its customers and significantly affect customer satisfaction. The goodwill of the organisation depends primarily on the claims satisfaction levels among its customers.

The insured and insurer are the parties to the contract of insurances, wherein the insured is under an obligation to declare and disclose all the information related to the subject insured and pay the agreed insurance premium. The insured has every right to claim for the loss suffered on happening of the event. The insurer has the right to receive the premium of insurance and is under an obligation to pay the insurance claim when the risk results in loss to the insured.

The insured has every right to transfer the interest or assign it to the nominees or the third parties to the contract. The insurance agents play an important role and act as intermediaries between the insured and the insurer and also help the insurer settle the claims. The surveyors and assessors undertake investigation or assessment of the loss and help the insurer in the speedy payment of claims.

The claims system passes through two stages, the *claims management* and the *claims handling*. Claims handling is an integral part of claims management and executes the decisions made by the claims management machinery of an insurance company. Every insurance company has to design a proper claims system that should be in tune with its organizational structure and its philosophy. It should be efficient to enable the insurance company settle the claims in an effective and speedy manner and enhance its image as a better insurance provider.

The claimants are required to follow certain claims procedures as per their contractual obligations with the insurance company. The claimant or the insured has to first give the notice of happening of the event either orally or in written. If the terms of the contract expressly state that the notice should be given in writing, it has to be followed. The notice should be given at the earliest possible time upon happening of the insured event. Like for *e.g.*, claimants have to give a timely notice upon happening of the insured event in case of marine and fire insurance.

The claim has to be made by the parties who are the eligible claimants to the contract. Even the legal heirs can also claim the insurance amount only when the insured expires and the insurable interest or the interest on the property along with other property is devolved due to operation of the law. The onus of proving the loss lies on the insured and he should submit a proof of the event, proof of loss and compliance of terms of the contract and it will help in speedy settlement of claims by the insurance company.

The insured will be at a disadvantageous position if they take their policies either by under-representing or overstating their interest or assets in the insurance contract. Generally insurance companies dissuade insurance company from pursuing such tactics as it will create mistrust and defeat the very purpose of taking insurance. Moreover, it will act as a deterrent for the healthy growth of insurance business.

In an insurance contract, equal responsibility lies on the insurer to undertake proper follow up of the claims raised by the insured. After receiving the notice of the incident or happening of the event either formally or informally, the insurer has to mobilize the resources at his disposal for the speedy settlement of claims. Insurer has to direct the various intermediaries like agents, loss assessors and surveyors, etc., to access the veracity of the claims information provided by the insured.

The insurer has to undertake his own departmental enquiries like, checking whether the policy cover was available at the time of the accident or happening of event, or whether the policy is in force or all the premiums are paid, etc. Upon being satisfied that the policy is in force, insurer is bound to honor the commitment raised by the claimant. Apart from the internal enquiries, the reports filed by the intermediaries like agents, loss assessors, surveyors, etc., will lend concrete evidence and support for the insurer in settling the claims filed by the claimant.

The insurer, after verifying the facts, takes a decision either to accept or reject the claim. If the insurer decides to pay the claimant, the claims are paid after duly verifying his identity and eligibility to receive the same. If however the insurer rejects the claims, a proper attention has to be paid by the insurer in informing the same to the insured and explain the reasons thereof. The insurance laws however provide that if the insured is not satisfied with the reply or the reasons for rejecting the claims, he has every right to approach the suitable claims settlement machinery and get the justice. If the insurer is willing to settle the claims through negotiations, the parties should settle the disputes amicably.

An effective claims settlement process has numerous benefits for the insurance company. The claims settlement process of an insurance company includes various claims settlement procedures laid out and implementation of its claims decisions taken. Claims settlement has much wider implications and extends to the managerial, legal and accounting functions. It presents a complex subject matter to be handled with utmost care and diligence by the insurance companies. The stakes involved in maintaining a healthy claims settlement practice are high. If poor practices are followed, the repercussions will extend to other branches of the insurance company and adversely affect the financial performance of the insurance company.

Insurance contracts lay upon the insured to follow certain warranties and conditions, either before or after the commencement of the policy depending upon the subject matter involved. When claims are filed, the insured has to observe the settled rules and procedures and the insurer has also to reciprocate in a similar manner by undertaking appropriate steps for speedy disposal of claims. The failure to comply with by either of the parties and even when the parties involved in the contract intend to benefit from the contract, will only lead to delays and disputes in the settlement of claims.

In every insurance company effective claim administration is of paramount importance since it results in cash outflows. Though, the insurers are legally and morally liable to service the contracted claims, yet it becomes extremely important to correctly assume the claims filed in order to decline (a) claims with fraudulent intentions (b) claims filed due to incorrect interpretations of clauses contained in the policy document.

In India, motor insurance claims have become a major threat to the survival of insurance companies because of high fraudulent claim proportions.

Most of the insurance companies have a well-defined claims department which undertakes the various activities of claim administration. Experienced professionals are generally employed by the insurance companies known as claim analysts. They evaluate, assess and maintain the records of various claims made in the claim department.

The hierarchical structure of the department may vary with the levels of authority for passing of claims usually specified in terms of monetary limits. The claims department executive are in constant touch with the other departments of the insurance company, especially the underwriters so as to facilitate the process of buying risk and balancing adverse exposures. The companies also provide the guidelines to facilitate the decision-making process of the claim analysts and carrying on the claim administration.

38.2 Claim Settlement in General Insurance

All insurance contracts are based on the information provided by the insured in the proposal form. The correctness of the information furnished in the proposal form is verified at the time of a claim, when physical inspection of the property is done. In case of any misrepresentation, it would be the prerogative of the Insurance Company to avoid a claim, or avoid the policy itself, or pay a claim for a reduced amount. It should therefore be understood that the completed proposal form plays an important role as it effects the claims under the policy. For a claim to be admissible under the policy of following requirements are paramount[1] :

- The insured should have paid the appropriate premium
- The subject matter affected by the peril should have been covered for insurance
- The loss to the insured should have been caused by one of the perils insured
- The peril should have taken place within the period of insurance
- The loss claimed by the insured should not fall under any of the exclusions of the policy.

A repudiation of the claim by the insurer, on the other hand, would arise only when the policy holder fails to comply with any of the following :

- Conditions precedent to the contract
- Conditions subsequent to the contract and
- Conditions precedent to liability.

Conditions precedent to the contract relate to non-disclosure or mis-representation of material facts by the proposer which would affect the judgment of the insurer in accepting the proposal and fixing the appropriate rates, terms and conditions for the coverage sought for.

Conditions subsequent to the contract broadly relate to the Dos and Don'ts by the policyholder during the period of insurance.

Conditions precedent to liability relate to requirements to be complied with by the policyholder if and when a loss is sustained by him arising out of an insured peril.

Following are some important points that are of relevance in a claim settlement procedure:

- The loss or damage should be reported to the insurer immediately. On receipt of claim intimation, the insurer will forward a claim form.
- The completed claim form along with an estimate of the loss has to be submitted to the insurer. It is preferable to submit an itemized estimate with separate values. The insurer will arrange for inspection to the damaged items to assess the loss.
- In case of major losses, a specialist-licensed surveyor is deputed.
- The insured has to provide the required documents to substantiate the extent of loss.
- In case the cause of loss is not established, it is for the insured to prove that the loss or damage has occurred due to an insured peril.

On agreement of claim amount between the insured and the insurer, the claim is settled.

1. Arun Agarwal, Repudiation – The Last Resort, IRDA Journal, September, 2008.

38.2.1 Broad Pattern of Claim Settlement

- **Preliminary:** Insurers insist on an early notification of a loss and the policy provides for the time limit within which notice of loss shall be given by the insured. On receiving of notice of loss, the relevant policy particulars are checked to see if the insurance is in force. The claim form is thereafter issued to the insured. The claim is allotted a number and necessary entries are made in the claims register. Preliminary intimation of loss is sent to the co-insurers and facultative reinsurers, if applicable.
- **Survey:** As per the Section 64 UM of Insurance Act, all losses more than Rs. 20,000 must be surveyed by independent licensed surveyors and assessors who are appointed by the insurance companies. A typical loss survey report deals with, among other things the cause and extent of loss as also the observance of warranties and other terms and conditions.
- **Settlement:** The claim is processed on the basis of the survey report, the claim form and other supporting documents. Settlement is made by cross cheque and payment details are entered in claims register as also in the relevant policy records.

38.2.2 General Guidelines for Settlement of Claims

Introduction: The guidelines described are more of a general nature, and it is many a times there that some of the guidelines laid down cannot in practice be complied with due to particular circumstances of the case. Such non-compliance need not, therefore, render the claim as invalid. The Claim Settling Authority uses discretion by recording the reasons.

Appointment of Surveyor

The Insurance Act stipulates that all claims of Rs. 20,000 and above are to be surveyed by surveyor. Therefore for the claim less than Rs. 20,000/- survey by licensed surveyor is not mandatory. Such losses may not be surveyed by the Company's officials (in house survey) if survey is required.

Ministry of Finance vides Gazette notification no. Part II Section 3(ii) dated 30/5/70 have exempted certain clauses of claims from the operations of Section 64 UM sub-section (10) irrespective of the claim amount and hence such claims can be processed without insisting on a report from a licensed surveyor.

The following must be kept in view before a surveyor is appointed for any claim:

(a) The surveyor should be holding a valid license.

(b) The surveyor should be selected depending upon the type of loss and the nature of the subject matter involved.

(c) For assessment of some losses specific technical expertise may be required and consultants having such technical expertise may be associated with surveyors. The consultant's remuneration should be negotiated in advance bearing the expertise in mind. This will be in addition to the survey fee payable.

(d) Wherever business interruption losses are involved, the surveyors for the material damage and the business interruption losses, if several, should be competent to complement one another. One surveyor can be utilized for both the losses if the company is satisfied about the surveyor's competence for both the jobs.

(e) Appointment of the joint surveyors may be done on the merits of the case.

Guidelines for authority for appointment of surveyor will be as per circulars issued from time to time.

Where a servicing DO is approached for appointment of surveyor even though they are not the policy issuing office, surveyor must be appointed by the servicing DO immediately, with intimation to the policy issuing office.

Appointment of Investigator

Depending upon the circumstances it may be necessary to appoint an investigator to verify the claimed version of loss. A separate surveyor appointment may be considered if any actual physical survey/assessment is possible and called for.

The letter appointing the investigator should mention the terms of reference and make it clear that the report should contain no inferences or doubts unless these are well documented and substantiated and can stand the scrutiny of a court if so required.

In the absence of laid down schedule of fees for investigators, it is advisable to negotiate and decide the fees to be paid in addition to expenses actually incurred before actually appointing the investigator and the determined/decided fee recorded in the letter of appointment.

Processing of Claims

Documents generally required for processing of claims are specified on the respective sections and as far as possible all documents must be called for from the insured in one go and not in the piecemeal.

"ON Account" Payment: Pending final assessment of the claim an "on account" payment may be considered subject to confirmation of the following:

- Loss due to occurrence of a peril covered by the policy
- Establishment of the policy
- The minimum liability that might arise under the policy.

After approval of the claim by the competent authority, the insured/claimant should be advised of the final amount of claim approved, with details thereof.

Remaining formalities of obtaining full and final discharge and bank/financial institution's discharge (where required) should be completed before release of the amount of claim.

If the loss or any part thereof is recoverable from a Third Party, a letter of subrogation and/or assignment and special power of Attorney, to suit special cases, is to be sent to the insured for completion on the requisite stamp paper and return before settlement.

Co-insurance: The leader will process the claim on the behalf of all co-insurers. A decision by the leader regarding claim settlement, taken at the appropriate level according to the existing tenets of delegation of financial authority, shall be final and binding on the co-insurers. Claims decided at the appropriate level by the leader will not be processed again by co-insurer(s), regardless of the amount. The leader will intimate to the co-insurer details of a claim settled by him with copies of all relevant reports and documents. The co-insurer will settle his share of claim within 15 days from the receipt of such intimation from the leader without any delay.

In case of a claim requiring board decision, the decision taken by the Board of the leader shall be binding on the other co-insurers. There shall be no separate need for the co-insurers to approach their respective Boards for decision in respect of such claims. A suitable note may, however, be placed by the co-insurers before their respective Boards for information in such cases.

Close Proximity Cases: Detailed investigation should be immediately instituted when a loss occurs in a close proximity, i.e., within 5 days for all classes of insurance (except marine voyage policies), of the date of inception of risk. The close proximity mentioned here is in reference to new insurance or where there has been a break in insurance. Close proximity investigation should also be carried out in cases where it is found that insurance has been taken out significantly later than it ought to have been taken, i.e., the risk has remained un-insured or inadequately insured prior to the insurance cover under reference.

Rectification of Policy after a Loss

Rectification of a policy after a loss is reported for reasons other than breach of condition/warranty should be carried out as under:

(a) Where rectification involves collection of additional premium, the additional premium may be charged only on the affected policy in which the claim has arisen.

(b) Rectification can be done by the Authority Competent for settlement of the claim.

Repudiation of Claims

If a claim warrants repudiation, the competent authority would be the authority competent to settle the claim. Letter of repudiation may state the reasons and/or the policy condition under which it is repudiated.

Re-opening of Claim Files

Reopening of claim file can be done by the authority one step higher than the appropriate claim settlement authority.

38.2.3 Fire Insurance Claims

Under Fire insurance variety of buildings, machineries, equipments, and stocks are involved. In addition to the competent surveyor it becomes essential that the company officials should visit the site of losses reported as far as possible.

If the estimate of loss is within Rs. 20,000/- and loss of profits claim is not involved, the office shall have the discretion to waive an independent survey and settle the claim on the bases of the claim form and other supporting documents and after being satisfied that it is admissible under the policy and that the amount claimed is reasonable and consistent with the extent of damage. Where necessary, an authorized official in the DO may inspect the damage, if necessary.

Processing of Claims: The documents generally required for processing fire claims are:

(i) Copies of the policy complete with terms, conditions and warranties.

(ii) Claim form duly completed by the insured.

(iii) Survey report should include –

  (a) Indication of the cause of loss

  (b) Establishment of liability

  (c) Assessment of loss

  (d) Confirmation of compliance of policy terms, conditions and warranties

  (e) Admissibility of the claim.

(iv) Photographs (if necessary)

(v) Police report and (if necessary)

(vi) Fire Brigade report (if necessary)

Note: Items (v) and (vi) may be waived if the survey report is clear and does not cause any doubt on the occurrence as well as the extent of loss.

Claims arising out of Act of God Perils: In addition to the documents specified under 2.1 above, other documents like newspaper cuttings, photographs and meteorological reports are helpful in substantiating such losses. Where the incident is localized, not reported in the media or not recorded by the Meteorological

Department, the surveyor should enquire about the incident from local government/statutory authorities and support the description of the occurrence and the loss by taking photographs of the damage. Where the surveyor confirms the incident clearly and unambiguously, the documents detailed above may be waived.

While processing the claims, attention is to be paid to concurrent policy(ies) and financial Institute clauses.

Losses Reported under the RSMTD Peril: In case of isolated losses under the above endorsement, copy of the First Information report lodged with police and their Final Investigation report should be furnished.

The surveyor should give a detailed report on the occurrence and confirm that the loss/damage is admissible under the policy. Loss/damage if any, arising out of omission or commission not involving should be segregated.

Disposal at Salvage: Salvage from fire and allied peril losses tend to deteriorate faster. Therefore, disposal of the salvage should be undertaken on priority basis for and on behalf of the concerned parties without waiting for the liability to be established. However, the provision of the disposal of salvage guidelines is to be followed.

Disposal of Claims where all Records Required for the Assessment of Claims is Destroyed in the Fire and/or Allied Peril Risks like Flood etc. : Settlement in these circumstances is generally negotiated because of non-availability of accounting records and other evidences. Therefore, the surveyor should be advised to assess such losses on a realistic and reasonable basis after discussions with the insured, Bank/Financial institution (if involved), and if required with suppliers/customers/statutory bodies like tax authorities, excise authorities etc. and the concerned Insurance Company.

General: Where the loss estimate is more than Rs. 50 lakhs intimation is to be sent to LPA requesting for inspection. Where the loss estimate is more than Rs. 1 crore intimation is to be sent to TAC also.

Loss of Profits/Consequential Loss/Business Interruption Losses: Claims under these policies have to be monitored regularly by the office to ensure that the insured is doing the needful to minimize the period of indemnity as much as possible.

In case the surveyor for MD loss is different from the consequential loss, co-ordination between the two has to be ensured. Control is to be maintained by the Insurer.

38.2.4 Motor Insurance Claims

Guidelines for Settlement of Claims-Own Damage

1. The Documents Generally required for settlement of motor claims are given below. However depending on the merits of the case, a particular document may not be necessary or an alternate document could be used to serve the purpose of the company. However, if the competent authority is satisfied that the loss is genuine all efforts should be made to expedite settlement of the claim.

(a) Claim form required to be completed.

(b) *Registration Certificate:* the details usually verified from the RC can instead be obtained from purchase details of the vehicle if the circumstances so warrant.

(c) *Driving License:* as per policy condition the driver is required to hold an effective driving license both in terms of the period validity and the class of vehicle that is being driven at the time of the accident. The MV Act provides for a grace period of 30 days after expiry of a license during which period the license may be accepted as effective, provided the holder has not been qualified from holding a license. For loss sustained by parked vehicles, driving license may not be relevant.

(d) *Load Challan/Trip Sheet:* to verify that the load carried was within the permissible limits and the trip sheet giving details of number of passengers carried in the vehicle.

(e) *Fitness Certificate:* the fitness certificate indicates the roadworthiness of a commercial vehicle.

(f) *Report to Police:* a copy of the FIR and Panchanama is required wherever third parties are involved in an accident.

(g) *Survey Report:* surveyor should ascertain the damage, assess the quantum of payable claim, verify vehicular documents and confirm that the loss/damage being claimed for is in conformity with the narration of the accident. Wherever replacement of parts is allowed surveyors must physically verify serial numbers as appearing on major parts, which carry such numbers.

2. Damage Claims

1. Immediately on receipt of intimation of loss, either in writing or over telephone, a surveyor should be appointed based on the estimate of repairs.

In case of major accidents, the insured would be asked to arrange for photographs of the vehicle at the spot of the accident, showing all the external damages and the numberplate of the vehicle. The photo expenses are to be reimbursed upto Rs. 500. Alternatively, the insured may inform the nearest office of the insurer to arrange for such photographs.

2. *Driving Licence:* if for any reason, to be specified, the driving license cannot be produced, the claim may be considered only on non-standard basis. However for settlement of such claims the authority should be vested only with the Managers and above in the RO. Where the driving license is not endorsed for tourist taxis, since, different practices prevail in different states, it is necessary to check the local practice. The claim is to be treated as standard or non-standard on the basis of the practice prevailing in the state where the accident occurs and this will be decided by a Manager and above in the RO.

1. *Reinspection:* if reinspection after repair is considered necessary it may be conducted by the same surveyor who has assessed the loss.
2. *Partial Loss Claims:*

A. Submission of bills/cash can be dispensed with for claims upto Rs. 50,000 in respect of private cars and two wheelers only, subject to

   (a) The survey report correctly indicating the cost of parts allowed for replacement

   (b) Claims being settled on the basis of a report of reinspection after repairs by the surveyor certifying that the repairs and replacements have been carried out as per assessment. For other classes of vehicles bills/cash memos have to be obtained and verified.

B. If surveyor confirms replacement of the engine and chassis if allowed for replacement and indicates the new numbers, claims may be settled whilst simultaneously advising the insured that

   (a) As per the provision of the Motor Vehicles Act, the new numbers have to be incorporated in the RC book.

   (b) Insurance company be informed about the incorporation of the new numbers in the RC book for endorsing on the policy document to facilitate settlement of future claims.

      (a) Where the vehicle is totally damaged or when the net cost of repairs is almost close to the market value of the IEV the claim could be considered to be a total loss. Such total loss claims should be encouraged on net of salvage basis i.e., salvage being retained by the insured and an appropriate amount towards salvage value as determined by the surveyor in consultation with the company be deducted from the total loss amount.

      (b) However, if the insured to retain the salvage, arrangements should be made for the safe custody of the damaged vehicle to prevent further loss or damage. The RTO should be informed by Registered AD post. An inventory on the major parts should be taken before taking possession of the vehicle. Immediate steps thereafter should also be taken for its disposal as per company's guidelines for disposal of salvage.

Theft Claims

1. *Partial Loss due to Theft:* Theft of parts/accessories from a vehicle should be reported to the police immediately by the insured. If parts are found missing or changed after recovery of stolen vehicle this be recorded in panchanama/recovery memo. Final police investigation report will also be required. However, if the competent authority is satisfied about the genuineness of the loss, final investigation report may be waived provided the insured sends a registered AD letter to the SP/ACP requesting that the insurer should be informed of any recovery.

2. *Total Loss due to Theft:* Unless claims settling authority is fully satisfied, investigation of the theft to be arranged by an investigator who may be appointed with specific terms of reference.

3. The following documents should be collected from the insured in addition to a certified copy of the FIR, for considering "on account" payment of the admissible claim after expiry of 90 days from the date of loss.

(a) Surrender of the Registration Book and the Tax Book to the insurer duly transferred in the name of the insurers. The RTO is to be informed about the theft of the vehicle and this should be entered in Tax Book so that further tax will not accrue.

(b) Letter of indemnity and subrogation.

(c) Ignition keys of the vehicle.

(d) Certificate of insurance and the original insurance policy, if not stolen with the vehicle.

(e) Specially worded discharge voucher.

4. The balance payment may be released on receipt of the Final Police Investigation Report or on expiry of a suitable waiting period from the date of the "on account" payment, after obtaining the discharge voucher in full and final settlement of the claim.

5. The Police and the Registration authorities and the NCRB should be notified in writing about disposal of the claim on "total loss" basis following theft of the vehicle. They should be requested to advise the company if the vehicle is recovered subsequently. Immediately after receipt of advise from the Police regarding recovery of the vehicle, necessary steps for taking possession of the vehicle from the Police custody should be taken and, if necessary, an advocate should be appointed for filing recovery application in the court.

6. Municipal Authorities, where applicable and the RTO should be advised by registered Letter with Acknowledgement. Due to record 'non use' of the vehicle on account of theft and about the cancellation of the Insurance Certificate.

7. If the vehicle is recovered subsequently, the insured will have the option to repay the claim amount already paid and retain the recovered vehicle. If the vehicle is found damaged, the insured will be indemnified against loss of damage. The insured should be advised to obtain recovery memo from the Police and to get the vehicle surveyed at the Police Station before taking delivery, as mentioned under partial loss theft claims.

8. In cases of criminal breach of trust each case should be dealt with an individual basis depending upon facts of each case and subject to legal opinion.

Guidelines for Settlement of Motor Third Party Claims

Third Party Bodily Injury Claims: Fatal and Non-fatal

1. *Intimation of Claim:* Intimation about an accident resulting into third party claim is received through various sources:

(a) Insured directly or by mention in passing whilst lodging own damage claim

(b) Claimant

(c) MACT/Courts by notice

(d) Through accident report from police in Form 54 prescribed under Central Motor Vehicles Rules, 1989.

2. *Investigation:* Investigation about the accident to collect the relevant data to quantify reasonable and just compensation as per the formats enclosed in respect of all third party claims is mandatory. The companies should ensure that this investigation helps the insurance company in finalizing out of court settlement at the earliest.

3. *Appointment of Advocate:* On receipt of notice from the MACT a competent advocate from the panel may be appointed if necessary. The following relevant documents and information should be given to him/her immediately to enable him/her to draft written statement (w/s) on behalf of the Company and ensure that the proper defense is taken where necessary and no frivolous statements are made.

4. *Policy Copy:* Duly certified true copy of the complete policy with the relevant clauses and endorsements as actually attached with the original issued covering the vehicle at the material time of accident.

5. *Driving Licence:* In case it has been observed that driver was not duly licensed the necessary information should be given to the advocate. Though under Section 149(2) of the MV Act, 1988, Insurance Company has no liability if the driver is not duly licensed, the onus to prove that the driver was not holding a license rests on insurance company and this obligation is required to be discharged fully to the satisfaction of the court.

6. *Compliance Policy Conditions:* If a breach of a specific policy condition has been observed it should be brought to the notice of the Advocate to enable proper defense if possible.

7. (a) Written statement on behalf of the insurance company incorporating all defenses available as enumerated under Section 149 of MV Act should be promptly filed.

(b) Wherever necessary when there is collusion between the insured and the claimants or when the insured fails to defend the claim, the company's advocate must be instructed to obtain the MACT's permission under Section 170 of the MV Act to Defend the claim on merits.

8. *Payment of No Fault Liability Claims:* If liability under affected policy is established after taking into consideration the foregoing defenses, company should take immediate steps to deposit No Faulty Liability amount as per Section 140 of the MV Act, 1988.

9. *Payment of Fault Liability Claims:* Companies must initiate action to settle such claims either through

(a) Jald Rahat Yojna

(b) Lok Adalats

(c) Direct negotiation with the claimant through DICC & RICC.

10. Jald Rahat Yojna: Section 152 of MV Act, 1988 authorizes insurance company to settle motor third party non-fatal bodily injury claims where claimant is an adult without claimants taking recourse to MACTs. Industry has already launched the Scheme since 1991.

11. Guidelines for Placing Claims in Lok Adalats: Maximum participation and disposal of large number of claims in Lok Adalats sessions should be ensured.

(A) Companies should place the claims normally falling within the following parameters before lok adalat:

(a) where occurrence of the accident is within the policy period.

(b) where estimated liability is not expected to be exceeding Rs. 5,00,000 per application for compensation.

(c) where no substantial point of law is involved.

(d) where no defences are available under Section 149 of the MV Act, 1988, such as driver not holding effective driving license and breach of policy condition relating to limitations as to use.

(e) where policy record shows that the driver was holding effective driving license.

(f) where despite concerted efforts on the part of the insurance companies. They are not in a position to prove conclusively to the satisfaction of the court that a person drove the vehicle not duly licensed.

(g) since there is a provision of automatic transfer of insurance in pursuance of Section 157 of MV Act, 1988 the companies cannot take defense of non-transfer of insurance of the vehicle on their books.

(h) where more than one vehicle insured with different insurance companies is involved in an accident resulting into a third party claim, companies should agree for settlement on 50-50 basis to apportion the liability between them.

(B) Companies should not accept conditional settlement such as subject to verification of certain documents, production of documents etc.

(C) On having reached the agreement for compromise settlement concerned MACT issues a Consent Order specifying *inter alia* the period during which the agreed amount should be deposited. On receipt of such order, companies must deposit the amount as agreed to with the MACT within 30 days from the date of award as per schedule.

(D) In the event of lok adalat for pending appeals before High Courts is organized, such claims where quantum of compensation is in dispute may be considered.

(E) Appeals which are filed to decide a point of law should not be considered for placing before lok adalat.

(F) Applications for compensation filed by the paid employees may also be placed before lok adalat, whether wider legal liability is covered or not.

In case of shortage/damage, 3 booking months from booking in case of non-delivery.

38.2.5 Marine Insurance Claims

Marine Hull

1. Introduction : (A) For the sake of convenience and also in view of the different nature of deployment, operations and hazards encountered, for the purpose of these guidelines Marine Hulls are divided into three groups viz.:

(a) Oceangoing vessels and other vessels rated exclusively by the Tariff Advisory Committee.

(b) Vessels insured under Builder's Risk Policies, Ship Repairer's Liability Policies, Ship Breaking Policies and the Charterer's Liability Policies.

(c) All the vessels and/or operations of which rates have been provided in Marine Hull Manual under specific Tariffs or otherwise and all other vessels/operations not covered by (A) and (B) above.

(B) The types of claims which occur in connection with Hull Insurance are:

(i) Total Loss/Constructive Total Loss;

(ii) Particular Average/Particular charges i.e., Partial Losses/Expenses;

(iii) Salvage and Salvage Charges – either Salvage Awards or Salvage under contract;

(iv) General Average;

(v) Collision liability;

(vi) Liability and Non-liability Claims (such as wreck removal) falling under the P & l section for the policy where such cover is granted;

(vii) Sue & Labour charges;

(viii) Personal Accident Claims for crew covered under Sailing/Fishing vessels Tariffs.

(C) Notwithstanding the expertise available in Company, the following claims should generally be considered for reference to professional Average Adjusters:

(1) All claims falling under Category 1.1 "A" unless the claim involved is straightforward and also for a nominal amount.

(2) (A) GA or GA/PA claims on vessels under Category 1.1 "C".

(B) Collision Liability claims requiring cross Liability adjustment in respect of risk falling under Category 1.1 "B" and "C".

Though selection of Average Adjusters is prerogative of the Hull Owners they should be advised to engage adjusters who have established offices in India as far as possible.

2. Procedure : (A) Oceangoing vessels

In view of:

(a) nature and quantum of claims likely to arise under this category;

(b) likelihood of occurrence of loss in distant foreign waters;

(c) involvement of laws and practices of foreign jurisdictions, and

(d) involvement of foreign professional and/or firms like surveyors, repair yards, adjusters, solicitors, arbitrator, courts, etc.

The current system of processing these claims in accordance with the international practices and traditions will continue except in so far as the provisions of the Indian Statutes are concerned.

(B) Sundry Hulls (Refer. 1.1 including Sailing vessels, Fishing vessels, Inland vessels etc.)

(1) While a Licensed Surveyor should be appointed in all cases of Partial Losses/Expenses, such licensed Surveyor is to be appointed in case of TL/CTL only where the vessel or its wreck, of reasonable value is available for inspection or making reasonable attempt to salvage. Refer 2.2 of General Guidelines.

(2) On receipt of loss intimation a letter may be written "on *without prejudice basis* to the insured advising about the appointment of Surveyor and/or investigator requesting the insured to render full co-operation to the Surveyor/Investigator appointed and also to return the claim form duly completed and signed.

(3) Notice Abandonment of the vessel/wreck in writing is a prerequisite for a constructive Total Loss Claim. As a matter of practice, insurers must decline *prima facie* acceptance of the Notice of Abandonment. However, insurer's refusal to accept abandonment does not legally prejudice the insured's claim for a CTL once the Notice of Abandonment has been issued by him and received by the insurer. Notwithstanding this the insurer must still refuse acceptance of abandonment of the wreck till the probable liabilities attaching to the wreck (Port and other dues, statutory requirement of wreck removal in case of vessel sunk in navigate channel; etc.) are reasonably estimated as considered.

(4) Total loss claim can be settled on the basis of the statements and documents, as also the investigator/s Surveyor's report as the case may be if the circumstances are found to be reasonably acceptable. As per the Marine Insurance Act, following acceptance of a claim for total loss of a vessel, the insurers become entitled to the wreck or the proceeds thereof, if any. However, before enforcing such entitlement, it is advisable to ascertain whether or not any liability, statutory or otherwise, is reasonably likely to attach to such wreck or proceeds thereof.

(5) Since Marine Hull Policy is issued for a composite sum insured, representing the aggregate values of Hull and Machinery and showing Hull or Machinery values separately in the policy being prohibited, no claim for total or Constructive Total Loss can be considered for settlement on the basis of and on account of either Hull or Machinery value alone.

(6) In case of partial loss, as far as possible, efforts should be made by the Surveyors to achieve assessment net of salvage, if any because it is difficult and very often not economical for the underwriters to get involved in salvage take-over and disposal. However, where this is not possible, arrangements should be made to take over the salvage from the insured before the settlement of the claim and it should be disposed of as early as possible as per the guidelines for the disposal of salvage.

(7) Claims occurring in foreign waters should be dealt with in the same manner as in the case of Ocean-going vessels.

3. Processing of Claim and Documentation : The documents required for the settlement of Sundry Hull claims are:

(1) A final survey Report *inter-alia* incorporating the following:

(a) Name of the registered owner of the vessel.

(b) Identity of the vessel including registration details. License particulars including validity thereof wherever applicable.

(c) The details of loss suffered.

(d) The Surveyor's observation on the alleged circumstances of the loss.

(e) The reasonable probability of the alleged circumstances giving rise to the losses noticed and/or claimed.

(f) Quantification of repairs/replacement cost, Salvage, Sue and labour etc. Where applicable.

(g) Cause of loss as per the Perils Clause of the Policy and the deposit to be collected by the steamer. Company would be credited into a properly constituted Trust Account jointly with the average adjusters.

In lieu of cash deposit, steamer companies often accept unlimited guarantee of the Insurance Company covering the goods. As far as possible the dealing office should arrange for the General Average Guarantee to be given as per prevailing financial order.

As soon as any intimation is received regarding GA and any request from the insured for issuance of GA Guarantee is received. H.O. Marine Dept. should be intimated with full details.

Documents for General Average Claims

1. Original Policy or certificate of insurance duly endorsed.
2. Bill of Lading (signed copy)
3. Invoice (original or signed copy)
4. A copy of Notice declaring General Average by the Shipowner/Agent.
5. General Average Deposit Receipt (GADR) on the original Lloyds form duly endorsed.

(GADR indicates the name of the steamer, details of the casualty, the Bill of Lading no., the provisional net arrived value of the goods, description of the goods, the name of the GA Adjusters, the amount of the deposit by the consignees etc.)

4. General Average Guarantee and Counter Guarantee : As an alternative to cash deposit ship owners are willing to accept a Guarantee from a bank or if the goods are insured from the insurers. Insurers grant this Guarantee on the behalf of the insured in terms of which they agree to pay the General Average Contribution. In such cases, a Counter Guarantee is obtained from the insured. The Counter Guarantee is required because the General Average adjustment may be based on a contributory value of the cargo which may be higher than its insured value.

Letter of Transfer

This letter is signed by the consignees whereby they

(i) surrender their rights in respect of the deposit paid to ship owners by the insurers;

(ii) agree to transfer the deposit amount to the credit of the insurers;

(iii) authorize the insurers to receive from the ship owners the difference between the amount of general average as adjusted and the amount of the deposit;

(iv) undertake to refund to the insurers any sum deducted by the ship owners from the deposit which may not be recoverable under the insurance policy; and

(v) undertake to repay to the insurers, if the contributory value exceeds the insured value the proportion of general average applying to such value.

If it is reported that the General Average Act has included sacrifice of cargo, then the consignee should clear the damaged cargo only after the General Average Survey is conducted by the ship's Surveyors.

38.2.6 Claims on Consignments by Rail/Road

Claims Documents (Rail/Road)

As in the case of sea/air/multi-modal transport/postal claims, the insured has to furnish evidence of (1) insurance, (2) transit, (3) value and (4) loss.

The following documents are required to be submitted to insurers in support of claims under rail/road transit policies:

General Documents

1. Original policy or certificate of insurance duly endorsed.
2. Invoice (original or copy)/packing list/weight specification.
3. Independent Surveyor's Report, if any.
4. Letter of Subrogation (if recovery is possible).

Other Documents Depending on the Nature of Claim

1. Original Railway Receipt (Non-delivery cases)
2. Copy of the Railway Receipt (damage claim)
3. Original Consignment Note (Non-delivery cases – Road transit claims)
4. A copy of the Consignment Note (Damage claim – Road transit claims)
5. 'Non-delivery' or 'Partial delivery' certificate from the Railways/Road Transport Operators.
6. Open Delivery/Assessment Delivery Certificate (Rail/Road)
7. Certified copy of the Remarks in the Railway Delivery Book (Damage claims).
8. Certified copy of the remarks in the delivery Chilean (Road Transit Claims).
9. Copy of (a) Notice of claim lodged on the carriers (Rail/Road)
   (b) Acknowledgement
   (c) Subsequent correspondence with the carriers.
10. Special Power of Attorney (Rail Transit Claims).
11. Letter of Authority (Rail Transit Claims).

Statutory Time Limits for Lodging Claim and for Filing Suits

The following list is indicative which are liable to change from time to time as per law and companies should act on the actual positions at law at the material time in each case.

Time Limit *Negligent Party*	*For Filing Claims*	*Filing Suit*
Major ports	7 days from the date of discharge	6 months from the date of discharge
Steamer Company	Application for steamer Survey of Goods should be within 3 days of Date of discharge. Notice of claim to be served as quickly as possible but definitely within 1 year from the date of discharge	1 year from the date of discharge
"Where CTD is issued"	—	9 months from the Date of discharge or is applicable at the material time
Customs Authority	Refund of Duty should be claimed within 6 months from the date of payment of duty	—
Air Carriers	7 days from the date of (Domestic delivery in the case of damage/ shortage, 14 days from the date of booking In case of non-delivery	2 years from the date of booking or the date of arrival of aircraft (applicable)
Air Carriers (International)	14 days and 21 days respectively for above circumstances	- do -
Railways	6 months from the date of booking	3 years from the date of delivery of damaged goods or the date when delivery ought to have been given (as applicable)
Road Carriers	6 months from the knowledge of loss/Date of transport receipt (as applicable)	- do -
Postal Authorities	1 month from date of delivery	3 years from date of delivery

38.2.7 Marine Cargo

Documentation to Support Claims

Ex: Ship, Air port, Multi-modal Transport.

1. Documents Generally Required for Settlement of Various Types of Claims are as Under:

General

(a) Original insurance policy/declaration under the open policy duly endorsed by the insured. A letter of indemnity may be furnished if the original is lost.

(b) Original or a signed copy of sale invoice along with packing list wherever is available.

(c) Signed copy of Bill of Lading (in case of sea voyage)/Air Consignment Note (for air cargo/MTD/CTD (For multi-modal transport)/postal receipt for sending by post.

(d) Triplicate or exchange control copy of Bill of entry (to facilitate verification of the date of filing to ascertain whether there has been any delay and also to check duty payment details).

(e) In case of General Average. G.A. Guarantee and Counter Guarantee of original Cash Deposit Receipt with the Letter of Transfer as the case may be. Reference be made to the separate para on G.A.

(f) Letter of Subrogation duly stamped and executed (only where recovery from carriers/other third parties is possible).

(g) Special Power of Attorney (wherever recovery from Railway/other carriers is involved. In other cases as required).

In case of short landing/non-delivery of complete consignment

Full set of original Bill of Lading/Air Consignment Note/Postal Receipt, etc. as applicable endorsed in favour of insurers. The original contract of affreightment should be endorsed by the carrier confirming shortlanding/non-delivery of the entire consignment by them or with a separate shortlanding/non-delivery certificate. An undertaking to be obtained from the claimant that he would take delivery of the cargo, it traced, under an insurance survey.

In Case of Partial Non-delivery/Short Landing

Non-delivery and/or landed but missing certificate from the sea-air/CTO/carrier/postal authority/Port Trust, as applicable.

In Case of Partial Loss or Damage

(a) Assessment report by sea/air/CTO carrier/postal authority

(b) Survey Report of independent surveyor (if survey has not been waived)

(c) Claim form/claim bill.

In case of a consignee's claim to be settled in India for export shipment, Banker's Certificate confirming non-receipt of export proceeds in India in an appointed manner.

Non-delivery (short landing or landed but missing)

Specific Documentation: The claimant should be requested to apply for Either shortlanding certificate or landed but missing certificate from the port authorities or the Steamer Company within the period allowed under statute/Port rules. When the short landing or landed but missing certificate is obtained, the claimant should be asked to send notice to the carrier or the Port Authorities, as the same may be for the value of lost cargo (CIF value and/or duty and/or profit) and obtain their acknowledgement claim on the carrier or the port authorities should be accompanied by:

(i) Original of shortlanding or landed but missing certificate

(ii) Copy of bill of lading

(iii) Copy of Invoice.

Individuals or agencies specialized in the work of tracing missing cargo should be engaged to trace the missing cargo of high values. Where such certificates are not forthcoming in time, notice to carries and port authorities etc., must be served by the claimant within the statutory time limits for the value of cargo not received.

Total and/or Constructive Total Loss

Where total and/or constructive total loss of the cargo has been caused whilst in the custody of the steamer company or port authorities:

(i) Copy of valued claim on the carrier/port authorities (as the case may be)and acknowledgement thereof.

(ii) Notice of abandonment in case of C.T.L. to customs authorities.

(iii) Open assessment/delivery certificate/ship survey report.

Particular Average — Partial Loss i.e., Theft, Pilferage, Shortage and Other Damages (in cases where loss or damage is reported before clearance from the dock)

(i) Steamer/port survey report.

(ii) Customs examination certificate before clearance of consignment from docks.

(iii) Independent survey report.

As regards claim for the shortage from externally sound cases, it is essential to ask claimants to refer the matter to their suppliers about the policy of short packaging at their end. Only on receipt of confirmation from the suppliers about correct packing as per invoice further processing of claims on merits should be done. Surveyors should be asked to examine whether there was sufficient empty space in the case to hold the missing items or whether the missing items were replaced by some foreign materials by comparing the weight of consignment stated in the invoice/packing list with the package received at the destination in order to determine skilful pilferage in transit. It may also be checked as to whether the missing items had been extracted by Customs for examination or other purposes.

Claim under Duty and Increased Value Insurance Policy

In the case of certified shortlanding no duty is payable. Claims other than shortlanding have to be scrutinized with due regard to the basis of duty insurance and may be authorized for payment for the actual value of the loss including the actual customs duty paid but to exceeding the proportionate insured value on duty.

As regards Increased Value Insurance, the claim would be payable for proportionate increased value insured under the policy as per the Increased Value Insurance Clause.

As provided in the duty insurance clause a claim under "duty"/"increased value" policy is admissible only if the loss is admissible in terms of the cover granted under the same policy covering the same consignment. This provision however need not apply to cases where the CIF is insured overseas, due to contractual obligation. Further, if a marine claim is within the ambit of the policy conditions but declined by the insurers for other reasons like non-compliance of Section 64 VB of the Insurance Act this will not affect the admissibility of the duty claim. Therefore the claimant is required to furnish to the company proof of the liability for loss under the Marine Policy as per terms and conditions of the policy.

The other documents required are:

(i) Original Duty Insurance Policy duly endorsed

(ii) Copy of Bill of Lading

(iii) Bill of Entry

(iv) Survey Report

(v) Copies of correspondence exchanged with customs/carriers relating to the claim lodged with them.

General Average

In the event of the Steamer Company declaring General Average, the steamer Agents to make cash will call upon the consignees Deposit before delivery of the consignment at destination. The consignees should be asked not to comply with this, without prior written concurrence of the dealing office. The concurrence can be given after ensuring that Lloyd's form of bond or similarly worded form is used.

(i) Copy of Certificate of Registration and License, if any, issued by the concerned authorities;

(ii) Original of the Certificate/Letter of the Cancellation of registration of vessel in respect to Total Loss claims.

(iii) Weather Report for the relevant place, date and time from the competent authority in case adverse Weather Warranty is involved:

(iv) Affidavits and/or statements by the owner, Tindal and all members of the crew separately of the insured vessel and/or rescuing vessel, if any made to any authority such as Police, Magistrate, Notary Public, Port Office, Indian Consulate etc.

(v) Marine Casualty Form issued by Mercantile Marine Department where applicable.

N.B.: Marine Casualty form is available only if any member of the crew including Tindal has survived the casualty. If all the crew members including the Tindal employed in the particular adventure die due to the casualty or are missing beyond trace, the Marine Casualty Form is not issued by Mercantile Marine Department as no statement from any of the crew regarding the casualty can be recorded by the Department. However, in such cases, the Mercantile Marine Department issues a certificate confirming that the casualty has been reported to them.

(vi) Police Report for claims within the territorial waters and for SRCC claims.

(vii) The loss should be reported to the Port Authorities if occurring within the port area.

(viii) In view of the localized and small scale operation, 'Salvage Charges covered under the Fishing Vessels Policy is to be seen differently from that under Ocean-going vessels Policy inasmuch as neither the Lloyd's Open Form for salvage agreement nor any international professional salvor is ever likely to be involved in salving such vessels. Therefore, in most of the cases the salvage services rendered to fishing vessels will be contracted salvage and for the purpose of eliminating unnecessary complications, it is advisable to treat such salvage charges as Sue and Labour costs for all practical purposes. It is however, to be ascertained that the amounts claimed for such costs are both actually incurred judiciously and reasonably incurred as also incurred to avoid or minimize a loss that would otherwise be admissible under the policy.

(ix) In the event of a Total and/or constructive Total Loss claim being considered for admission, the original insurance policy duly discharged by the insured is to be collected. However, where the original policy is reported to be lost an appropriate Letter of indemnity in lieu thereof should be obtained from the insured.

(x) In the event of a claim for partial Loss/Expenses, Salvage, Salvage Charges or Sue and Labour Charges, original repair bills, cash memos and similar documents duly verified and certified by the Surveyor as also Salver's/diver's Report where applicable, are to be furnished. Claims for Sue and Labour charges may have to be considered for settlement over and above the TL/CTL claim settlement. For these also original bills/cash memos in support of expenses incurred are required.

(xi) For the claims other than TL/CTL, the applicable deductible should be first deducted from the total claim amount as provided for in the clauses attached to and forming part of the policy.

In addition to the above, the following documents have to be collected for sailing vessel claims.

(i) Certificate of Inspection

(ii) Free Board Certificate before commencement of the voyager,

(iii) Cargo Manifest

(iv) Load Line Certificate

(v) Port Clearance Certificate.

In case of Fishing Vessels, wherever the provisions of the Merchant Shipping (Amendment) Act 1983 Part XVA, Section 435A to X are applicable, the Surveyors should be directed to report on the compliance thereof.

Fixed Jetties and Pontoons

Since these are fixed structures and are included in the Hull Department more as an extension of the principles of Hull Insurance than for any other reason, in the event of losses it is advisable to process such claims as 'Engineering claims and proceed accordingly.

However, since some losses may be found to be appropriate to be dealt with in accordance with the practices of Hull Department like in the event of fixed Pontoon getting un-moorred accidentally going adrift and ultimately sustaining damage or getting standard/grounded, such claims should be processes in line with practices of the Hull Department.

Situations which are not explicitly provided for here, should be handled in consultation with the competent authority/Head office.

38.2.8 Engineering Insurance Claims

1. The documents generally required for processing engineering claims are as under:

(a) Copy of the policy complete with terms, conditions and warranties.

(b) Claim form duly completed by the insured.

(c) Survey report should include —

(i) Clear indication of the cause of loss

(ii) Extent of damage and loss

(iii) Establishment of liability

(iv) Assessment of loss occurrence of riot is in the public knowledge, production

(v) Confirmation of compliance of policy terms, conditions and warranties.

(vi) Admissibility of the claim.

(d) Photographs (if necessary)

(e) Police report, and (if necessary)

(f) Fire Brigade report (if necessary)

Note: Items (e) and (f) may be waived if the survey report is clear and does not cause any doubt on the occurrence as well as the extent of loss. Where occurrence of riot is in the public knowledge, production of Final Police Investigation Report and Fire Brigade report may be waived.

In case of the theft losses it is necessary to collect a copy of the first information report or proof of complaint lodged by the insured with the police, such as Registered A/D letter. Final Investigation Report may be waived depending upon the merits of the case.

The steps involved in the loss adjustment should be as under:

Gross Loss Assessed

(a) Less: depreciation, if any,

(b) Less: Salvage

(c) Less: Under Insurance

(d) Less: Excess

(e) Net Claim Payable

Policy type wise additional requirements are as follows:

2. MCE Policies

Marine practice to be followed for settlement of Marine claims under MCE policies.

In case of mega projects, the services of an on-site representative/outside project monitoring agency could be retained to:

(a) Monitor the progress of the project activity.

(b) Receive report, on general condition prevailing at site, from loss minimization point of view;

(c) Co-ordinate with different authorities at site;

(d) Collect required documents for claims already lodged to expedite disposal;

(e) Conduct survey of losses falling within the self-survey limit;

(f) Preliminary survey of losses.

Incident expenses like supervision charges, storage charges may be considered to the extent they are included in the sum insured and actually incurred. When the replacement value is not ascertainable the assessment can be based on the original invoice value plus escalation if provided in the policy. However, it may be left to the surveyor to arrive at the value.

The loss under various extensions like additional custom duty, air-freight, express freight, overtime wages, etc. are to be assessed separately. The expense under these extensions will be available only when incurred by the insured. The liability under these extensions will be over and above the ones allowed under the standard policy provided the limit is not exhausted by earlier settled claims and /or claims reported but pending settlement.

If the claim is assessed both under the main policy and extensions like additional custom duty, express freight, over-time wages etc. the specified excess will be applied for each of these sections separately.

3. Contractors' All Risk Insurance

The surveyor shall confirm that the damage is not due to faulty design as the policy completely excludes loss due to faulty design unlike the erection policy where only a particular portion is excluded and resultant damage is paid.

Excess as specified is to be applied.

4. Contractor's Plant and Machinery Insurance

Being an annual policy, the validity of the policy at the time of occurrence should be verified.

Identification of the damaged equipment/item should be asked for a confirm Coverage under the policy. This is necessary since selection of equipment for Insurance is allowed.

The surveyor should confirm the accidental damage to the equipment.

For items fabricated by the contractor and replacement values not available, the surveyor should assess the loss on the basis of actual costs incurred by the insured.

5. Machinery Insurance

(i) Test reports of the damaged parts if deemed necessary by the surveyor and/or suggested by the insurers is to be submitted to the insurer/surveyor.

(ii) The surveyor should confirm repairs/replacement.

The claim payable may include costs of dismantling transportation to the repairer's shop, repairs and re-transportation and re-erection and other incidental expenses. If damaged equipment being sent out is covered under a Marine Transit Policy, the cost of such insurance may also be reimbursed.

If repeated losses are reported on the same equipment, the underwriting office can take the help of an outside expert to ascertain the precise cause of repeated losses and suggest measures for avoidance/minimization of re-occurrence of breakdown/loss.

The exclusion of damage to Belts, Ropes, Chains, Rubber Tyres, Dyes, Moulds, etc. is to be considered. As to the oil and other operation media in the transformer and equipment, these may be reimbursed when specifically covered under the policy.

The losses under the other extensions like additional custom duty, air freight, express freight, etc., are to be assessed separately and the underwriting office should confirm the availability of additional sum insured specifically for such items of expenditure while recommending the claim for settlement. If the assessment involves additional expenses for repair/ replacement, the surveyor should confirm that the expenses are reasonable.

6. Boiler Explosion Insurance

(a) Copy of the certificate issued by inspectorate of boilers (wherever applicable) for operation.
(b) Boiler inspection report on the occurrence.

7. Loss of Profits Insurance

A loss of profit claim is admissible only if loss or damage to machinery or boiler covered under corresponding policy is admissible.

As selection of equipment under the MLOP is allowed, the underwriting office should re-confirm the coverage of the equipment involved. (Attention is drawn to the applicable time excess and surveyor is to be appointed in consultation with Regional Office/Head Office only in those cases where interruption period is likely to exceed the time excess.) As the selection of the indemnity period is made depending upon the type of machinery, the underwriting office should make a policy copy available to the LOP surveyor and draw his attention to the indemnity period against the affected item.

The material damage surveyor and the loss of profit surveyor should report on the step initiated by them in helping the insured to reduce the period of indemnity by expediting repair/ replacements or adopting temporary measures. As a principle, the company engineer should be associated as far as possible along with the surveyor to minimize the loss under the Machinery Loss of Profit policy.

8. Electronic Equipment Insurance

Since the selection of equipment is allowed, the underwriting office should confirm the existence of cover for the damaged item.

Various exclusions under the basis policy.

It should be ensured that claim does not fall under any of the exclusion.

9. Deterioration of Stocks

The surveyor should ensure that the insured takes following loss minimization measures:

(i) No fresh stock should be loaded in the cold storage chambers.
(ii) Cold storage doors should be sealed to maintain temperature and avoid temperature rise.
(iii) If possible, the insured should be requested of shift stocks to some other running cold storage premises preferably in cool evening/night period or by refrigerated vans.
(iv) The insured should be requested to carry out repairs to the refrigerator plant most expeditiously.
(v) If there is no possibility of completing the repairs immediately, the insured should be advised to unload stocks from cold chamber for disposal in the local market as quickly as possible, and at the best available price in association with the surveyor/local authorities.

10. ALOP

Following action is to be taken:

(a) For a material damage reported under a Marine Cargo policy or a Project policy, the HO should immediately take steps to monitor the facts of delay in repairs/ replacement that may trigger a claim under the ALOP/marine ALOP section.
(b) Deputation of surveyors for ALOP claim should be only with the authorization of the HO (Tech.).

11. CECR

All the general regulation as mentioned in the manual should be followed and surveyors with good knowledge of civil engineering should be utilized.

38.2.9 Miscellaneous Insurance

Miscellaneous Accident Insurance includes a number of covers, which are in the nature of package policies. In this situation specific guidelines applicable to the respective sections are to be followed. Further, in Personal Insurance sentiment and emotions play a major role. These policies are designed as user-friendly covers and a high degree of tact and skill of persuasion is vital in handling such claims.

In addition to some general considerations, certain especial features to be considered claims under different types of covers are as under:

38.2.10 Workmen's Compensation Insurance

In addition to the claims form, the scrutiny of all the following documents are required:

(a) Medical Certificate

(b) Wages Statement

(c) Proof of age as recorded by the employer.

Temporary disablement claims requires payment of fortnightly compensation to the employee directly against proper receipt.

For the permanent total disablement claims, the memorandum of agreement is required to be submitted to the W/C Commissioner while depositing compensation as per Workmen Compensation Act.

For fatal claims, the perusal of death certificate and post mortem report is important before depositing the amount with W/C Commissioner.

38.2.11 Personal Accident Insurance

The scrutiny of the following documents is important while processing the personal accident claims:

(a) Duly completed claim form.

(b) Report of attending doctor.

(c) Investigation reports like lab tests, x-rays and reports essential for confirmation of the injury.

(d) Police reports, wherever necessary.

(e) Certificate of proof of age of dependent child in case the claim is under education grant provision.

(f) Medical bill corresponding to doctors prescription where medical extension is granted.

In case of fatal accident cases the following documents need to be scrutinized:

(a) Death Certificate

(b) Post mortem export (wherever applicable)

(c) Coroner's report (wherever applicable)

(d) Inquest report (wherever applicable).

In respect of fatal claims the payment is to be made to the assignee named under the policy. If there is no assignee the payment is made to the legal representative as identified by the Will/Probate/Letter of Administration/Succession Certificate. Where the above documents are not available and the amount of claim is upto Rs. 5,00,000/- the following procedure is followed:

(i) An affidavit from the claimant that he/she is the legal heir of the decreased.

(ii) An affidavit from other near relatives of the decreased that they have no objection if the claim amount is paid to the claimant.

(iii) Surety bonds executed by persons of reasonable standing.

In case of group policy the payment is to be made to the individual beneficiary only. However claim payment to the employer in respect of the employee is acceptable. Where provision is made for writing the name of the beneficiary and if Insured organization wants payment to be made directly to such beneficiary, joint discharge should be obtained.

The policy is to be obtained for cancellation in case of claim involving death, permanent total disablement, loss of two limbs, one limb and one eye i.e. whenever the capital sum insured becomes payable.

In case of permanent partial disability claim the policy should be obtained for endorsement for reducing the capital sum insured. The weekly benefit is however based on original C.S.I.

Weekly compensation is not paid unless the total claim amount is ascertained and agreed.

For claims of exaggerated amount or for claims of doubtful nature the finding of panel physician or surgeon is obtained.

38.2.12 Mediclaim

The following documents are required:

(a) Hospitalization claim form

(i) Duly completed claim form

(ii) Bills, receipts and discharge card from the hospital

(iii) Cash memos from the hospital

(iv) Bills from chemists supported by proper prescription

(v) Receipt and pathological test reports from a pathologist supported by the note from attending medical practitioner/ surgeon prescribing such pathological tests.

(vi) Nature of operations performed and surgeon's bill and receipt.

In case of mediclaim claims the receipts and bills need to be original but copies of treatment papers, diagnostic reports etc. have to be retained after verification with the originals if the Insured wishes to keep the originals.

(b) The following issues are taken special care of:

(i) In case previous medical history is not shown and discharge card, admission papers of the hospital are called for

(ii) That the admission to the hospital is not for routine checkup

(iii) That figures and/or dates of purchase in the cash memos are not altered by way of erasure superimposition of writing or added writing with a different ink

(iv) That treatment taken is in line with the disease.

- In the case of death of insured after having incurred medical expenses the amount of admissible claim is reimbursed to legal representative of the deceased or any other insured family member submitting original bills etc. after proper declaration that the person did actually incur those expenses.

- In exceptional circumstances where the treatment involves high expenses, on account payment might be considered if dealing office is satisfied about the admissibility of the claim.

38.2.13 Theft Claim

In case of personal effects the invoice/bill is not insisted upon but market value is the basis of claim settlement. While final police report is called for, where it is not forthcoming within a period of 6 months of the loss, the claim is settled on the basis of the First Information Report lodged provided the other documents are in order. Indemnity bond is obtained before settlement.

38.2.14 Burglary Insurance

The following documents are important while processing such claims:

(i) Duly completed claim form.

(ii) Final investigation report from the police.

(iii) Survey report.

(iv) Photographs.

In case of small losses the dealing office arranges for settlement of claim on the basis of completed claim form, First Information Report registered with the police provided the office is satisfied about the genuineness of the claim.

It is considered preferable to appoint an investigator with surveyor's license and knowledge of accounts as assessment of losses involves checking books of accounts.

Waiver of Final Investigation Report of the police is sometimes considered at the discretion of the Competent Authority so long as the investigator cum surveyor's report does not raise any doubt regarding the cause and quantum of loss. Subrogation/indemnity letter from the Insured is a must.

38.2.15 Money Policy

The following documents are considered important while processing claims:

(1) Duly completed claim form

(2) Final Investigation Report from the police

(3) Survey report.

In case of losses reported from the premises, the procedure followed for settlement of Claims is on similar lines as that of burglary policy.

However, if infidelity of the employee is involved, departmental proceedings and/or criminal action is initiated against the erring employee wherever applicable and such reports are obtained.

The limit per sending declared will be maximum indemnity and the average will not apply if the cash carried is more than the limit intimated.

Since the policy is on adjustment basis, the annual estimate of carrying does not have any bearing on the claim.

38.2.16 Banker's Indemnity Insurance

The following documents are considered important:

(i) Duty Completed claim form

(ii) First Information Report to the police

(iii) Survey Report.

The Banker's Indemnity Cover being wide in nature, sometimes-legal opinion is sought before settlement of any major and/or doubtful claim in nature.

Reinstatement of the sum insured: additional premium is either collected or deducted from the claim account. The policy is subject to single reinstatement clause by which the company's liability under the policy is restricted to double in the sum insured in the policy schedule. Care has to be taken if there are number of claims under the same policy. Although forgery of documents is covered under the policy, it is to be noted that this relates to the specified documents only issued by the bank and none-other. Policy does not cover claim involving losses prior to retroactive date. In case of change in Insurer, fresh retroactive date is applied or effected.

38.3 CLAIMS MANAGEMENT IN LIFE INSURANCE

The delivery of the promise from the insurer's side is by payment of a claim. Delivering the promise is indeed that moment of truth, a culmination of the cycle which completes the obligations placed upon the insurer in the insurance.[2]

In life insurance the purpose of claim activity is served by fairly assessing the economic value of man to his family, trade or occupation. At the first level the person who buys insurance gets the comfort that his family will indeed by taken care of in the event of his death. He is thus enabled to participate in economic activity without worries. Admittedly productivity without worries. Admittedly productivity without worries would be much higher.

Thereafter, at the subsequent level, when a claim is paid to the family, this puts the family out of economic distress and on to normal human productive activity. These family members in turn, become wealth generators for the economy.

The fact that the claim monies being paid usually belong to the spouse and children of the person insured/ deceased makes the purpose of life insurance claims that much more altruistic, immediate and relevant.

Critical aspects in claims handling in Life Insurance

1. Trusteeship element in the Claims Function

Documentation should be principally intended to establish the fact, cause of the event along with surrounding circumstances. IT should not be covered into a ritual which would have a significant effect of slowing down claim payment.

Claims Department, as trustees of the policyholders, are representatives of the faith which has been reposed in the Insurers by the customers at the time of paying the premiums and it is a responsibility cast upon them to be fair, just and honorable at the time of opening the sluice gates of this pool.

Documentation : It must be recognized that the document always follows a fact. For instance, death occurs first and the death certificate follows. As much as the focus has to be on proving the legitimacy of the claim, in the current scenario, exhaustive documentation mandated for claims processing is *passe*. Documentation should be principally intended to establish the fact, cause of the event along with surrounding circumstances. It should not be covered into a ritual which would have a significant effect of slowing down claim payment. Whilst completing documentation we should not lose sight of the fundamental purpose mentioned above.

Interpretation of the Contract : It is important that the text of the contract has to be interpreted in spirit along with the word. It should not to be used as an offensive weapon against the customer. However, any waiver of the stringent checks and conditions in the contract at the time of a claim to facilitate interpretation of the

2. S. Belavadi, Empathizing with the Claimant, IRDA Journal, May 2006.

spirit of the contract in favour of the customer has to be controlled and monitored because of the risk of inconsistency in interpretation and implementation.

Investigation : Professional investigation of life insurance claims is at an embryonic stage. The investigators are largely drawn from the pool of investigators who were working for the general insurance industry.

The tone of investigations has to border on sensitivity as the entire process revolves around a deceased person and a bereaved family.

Fraud – An Exception : *All Insurers are in the business of paying claims to serve the purpose of insurance.* Section 45 of the Insurance Act, rulings of ombudsmen and consumer courts all over are pointers to the fact that the room for 'forcing decisions on gullible insureds' is progressively a thing of the past.

Through the entire insurance life cycle from prospecting through policy issuance and servicing a claim, the golden key is the deliverance of the promise. No moment of truth can be greater than a claim handled well.

Life insurance companies depending upon the types of polices sold by them receive a variety of claims. However the claims can be simply categorised as (a) Maturity claims (b) Death claims. Certain features are common to all life insurance claims. These are:

- Policy must be in force at the time of claims.
- Insured must be covered by the policy.
- Nothing was outstanding to the insurer at the time of claim.
- The claim is covered by the policy.
- Whether the claim requires a scrutiny from legal angle.

Let us study the procedure for settlement of death and maturity claims.

38.3.1 Maturity Claims

Maturity claims are payable as per the terms of the policy. These policies are generally endowment polices including money back policies. The amount payable at the time of maturity includes sum assured and bonuses/ incentives. The insurer normally sends advance intimations to the insured. The insurer has to satisfy that–

- The life assured is the holder of the policy and his identity is proved.
- The age stands admitted.
- The premiums are all paid.
- The original policy is handed in together with a completed discharge voucher before making payment.

The insurance company is expected to make payment on the maturity date. Post-dated cheques are normally set in advance.

Documents Required

In the case of maturity claims, the insurer will call for the following documents, well before the date of maturity.

- Policy document, if it is not available, it may have been deposited elsewhere as a security for a loan. If policyholder loses the policy, the claim can be settled on the strength of an indemnity bond from the policyholder and a reliable surety of sound financial means. For small amounts, a letter of indemnity may suffice. In case of very small amounts, say Rs. 1,000/- or less, even this can be dispensed with.
- Age proof, if the age is not already admitted.
- Deed of assignment if any.
- Discharge form issued by the office.

If the claim does not determine the policy finally, as in the case of periodical survival payments, the policy document will be returned to the policy holder after due endorsements.

Settlement

Settlement procedure in a maturity claim is simple. After receipt of the completed and stamped discharge voucher from the person entitled to the policy money, along with the policy documents, claim amount will be paid by account payee or crossed & order cheque. In case of survival benefit claims, that is whose sum assured is retuned by instalments, suitable endorsements will be made on the policy document and in policy records, before returning the policy document to the policy holders. If the discharge form is lost in transit, a duplicate discharge form can be issued.

- Where the assured or the person to sign the discharge is known to be mentally deranged, a certificate from a court of law under the Indian Lunacy Act appointing a persons to act as a guardian to manage the properties of the lunatic should be called. If the person has recovered from the mental disorder, a certificate form the Psychiatric Hospital to that effect would be necessary.
- If the assured has been adjudged insolvent by court of law before the policy has matured for payment and if a notice is received from the official assignee of the court along with a certified copy of the court's order declaring assured as insolvent and also on order appointing official assignee as the assignee of the insolvent's estate, the official assignee should be informed about the date of maturity and other details. If the assignee claims the money, the payment has to be made to him under advice to the life assured. If the judicial authority has sold the policy in a court action, the purchaser, who produces certificate of sale, will be entitled to the policy moneys.
- If a prohibitory order of a court of law or a notice from income-tax officer under Section 226 (3) of the Income Tax Act is subsisting, the assured should be asked to have a proper withdrawal order served on the insurer. Otherwise, the insurer will act according to the notice.
- If the life assured is reported to have died before the maturity date, the claim has to be treated as death claim and processed accordingly. But if the assured is reported to have died after the date of maturity but before the receipt is discharged, the claim is to be treated as a maturity claim and paid to the legal heirs. Death certificate and evidence of title would be necessary.
- Under the Evidence Act, a person who has disappeared is presumed to be dead only if he has not been heard of for seven years. In such cases a decree of presumption of death from a court of law would be needed. The premiums must be paid until presumption of death is made, otherwise, the payment would be made after the court decree is obtained, as per the status of the policy as on the date when the premiums stopped.
- Payments of claim amount to claimants who are non-residents of India are governed by the Foreign Exchange Control Regulations.
- If a policy is financed through HUF funds, the policy belongs to HUF and as such the policy moneys would be payable to the Karta of HUF only.

When Insurance Act, 1938 itself is a time-tested legislation, Section 45 of the Act that enables life insurers to repudiate life insurance claims stood the test of time, withstanding the rancour of legal pronouncements. The section protects the claimants of a claim by shifting the onus of proving the reasons for repudiation on to the life insurer in the event of a policy resulting into a death claim, two years after the commencement of the policy while safeguarding the interests of insurer and its other policy holders to call in questions the bona fides of the claim that resulted within two years of commencement of the policy. This section also attracted the attention of various committees that examined the provisions of insurance law.

38.3.2 Death Claims

If the insured dies before the expiry of the term of the policy, it is called as death claim. The death of the life assured has to be intimated in writing to the insurer. It may be done by the nominee, assignee, a relative of the life assured, the employer, agent or development officer. Particulars like policy number, name of the life assured, the date of death, the cause of death and the relationship of the informant to the decreased are to be mentioned. The intimation must satisfy two conditions (a) It must be from a concerned person and (b) must establish beyond doubt, the identity of the decreased person as the life assured under the policy.

Sometimes, the office need not wait till the intimation of the claim is received. Obituary columns, the concerned agent or newspaper reports in case of accidents or air crashes may give information and the claim action can be initiated. However, care has to be taken to ensure that identity of the deceased is established.

In the case of claims by death, after receipt of intimation of death, the following documents are generally required:

- Policy document.
- Deeds of assignments/reassignments.
- Proof of age, if age is not already admitted.
- Certificate of death.
- Legal evidence of title, if the policy is not assigned or nominated.
- Form of discharge executed and property witnessed.

If the claim has accrued with 3 years from the commencement of policy, following additional requirements may be called for in order to remove any suspicion of suppression of material facts at the time of proposal.

- Statement from the last medical attendant giving details of last illness and treatment.
- Statement from the hospital if the deceased had been admitted to a hospital.
- Statement from the person, who had attended last funeral rites and had seen the dead body.
- Statement from the employer, if the deceased was an employee, showing details of the leave.

❑ If the life assured had an unnatural death, such as accident, suicide or unknown cause, police inquest report, panchanama, chemical analyser's report, post-mortem report, Coroner's report, etc. would also be looked into. Depending on preliminary data, a special inquiry may also be ordered.

❑ The holder of the policy is entitled for payment if the policy has not been assigned in favour of anyone else or dealt with it in any other manner like depositing it with a bank for getting overdraft. Under MWPA policy the proceeds of the policy will be paid to the trustees. If there is no trustee, the official trustee will step in. But if the beneficiaries are major and competent to contract, payment can be made directly to them without the intervention of trustees. The assured need not sign the discharge voucher.

❑ In case of absolute assignment, the payment will be made to the assignee. If the assignment is conditional, payment can be made to the assured himself, after satisfying repayment of loan that may be the reason for assignment.

❑ If the policy is irretrievable lost, advertisement of the loss of the policy is a necessary precaution. Payment can be made on the basis of an indemnity executed by the policyholder together with a surety of means. It is not necessary to issue a duplicate policy.

❑ The death claim amount is payable to the nominee or the assignee as the case may be. If the life assured has died without making an assignment or nomination, legal evidence of title (proof of ownership) such as succession certificate or letters of administration or probate of a will where a will exists, would be required.

❑ The insurer may waive strict evidence of title, if the amount involved is small, there is no other estate left by the deceased and there is no dispute among he survivors about the policy moneys.

❑ If the intimation claim is received after 3 years from the death, the same is time barred. The claimant has to be informed accordingly. However, if the death had occurred with 3 years of the policy's commencement of revival, simultaneous investigation should be conducted to find out the bonafides of the claim, without the knowledge of the claimant. However, if more than three years have elapsed, since the date of risk, the claimant has to be informed that the claim is barred by limitation. But simultaneously claim forms can be issued without prejudice to see if any ex-gratia payment can be made.

- If the death has occurred within 2 years of the date of the policy (that is the date of FPR) the possibility of suppression of evidence cannot be ruled out. Hence, it is necessary to investigate such cases. The reasons for intimating a claim late may be deliberate attempt to tamper with evidence.
- Death can take place suddenly e.g. due to cardiac arrest, downing, burns, air crash, suicide, and murder or at the hand of justice. In case of an air crash, a certificate from airline authorities would be necessary certifying that the assured was a passenger on the plane. In case of ship-accident, a certified extract from the logbook of the ship would be needed. In case of sudden heart failures, doctor's certificate will not be forthcoming.
- In case of defence personnel, a certificate from the commanding officer of the Unit is to be obtained. If a court of enquiry is ordered its findings should be obtained.

38.4 Repudiation of Claims

Insurance is a contract between two parties wherein the insurer on receipt of a consideration (premium) contracts to indemnify the insured (proposer) for the losses sustained by the insured following the operation of the perils against which the designated subject matter was insured.[3]

It is a general principle of any contract that a valid contract may be avoided (or rescinded) by one of the parties to it on the ground of a misrepresentation, either by a positive act or by an omission, made during pre-contractual negotiations.

What is misrepresentation or non-disclosure does, where it is established to be material and induced the contract to the prejudice of the other party, is that the party who has been induced to enter the contract may rescind the contract from its inception. This is the ordinary remedy available to the person who as concluded a contract on the basis of a misrepresentation. The contract is not void, but is voidable from inception.

Repudiation of a contract means a refusal to perform the duty or obligation owed to the other party to refuse to accept something or someone as true, good or reasonable.

The better terms are *"rejection of a claim"* and *"denial or liability"*.

Insurers may refuse to pay claims for a variety of reasons. As all insurance is an agreement (contract) between the insured and the insurer, the insurer will always rely on the insurance agreement, which is contained in :

(*i*) The Schedule of insurance, read together with (*ii*) The Policy

Some reasons that insurer may offer when rejecting (refusing payment) a claim are :

- False statements made when applying for insurance;
- Failure to disclose relevant facts when applying for insurance;
- Claim does not fall within the items insured under the policy;
- Failure of the insured to comply with the terms of the agreement;
- Fraud;
- Inordinate and unreasonable delay for the reporting of the incident which may lead to a claim;
- Failure to pay the premium on time/at all;
- No consequential losses covered under policies.

3. Sanjay Seth, Repudiation of Claims – What triggers them?, IRDA Journal, September, 2008.

STATEMENT 34

Incurred Claims Ratio-Private Sector

Particulars	Net Earned Premium							Claims Incurred (Net)							Incurred Claims Ratio						
	Fire	Marine	Motor	Health	Others	2007-08	2006-07	Fire	Marine	Motor	Health	Others	2007-08	2006-07	Fire	Marine	Motor	Health	Others	2007-08	2006-07
	(Rs. Lakh)							(Rs. Lakh)							(Rs. Lakh)						
Royal Sundaram	2144	453	29749	8305	3933	44583	33358	929	367	22856	3719	1944	29815	20374	43.35	80.95	76.83	44.78	49.44	66.87	61.08
Bajaj Allianz	12256	3897	92566	17808	15017	141544	83853	4976	3166	61817	15171	9439	94570	55563	40.60	81.25	66.78	85.19	62.86	66.81	66.26
Tata Aig	1662	4426	24809	3708	10779	45385	38165	657	3612	15305	2778	2344	24695	20711	39.50	81.60	61.69	74.93	21.74	54.41	54.27
Reliance	3845	1094	71660	13617	5788	96003	24426	2674	1288	53013	15269	2824	75068	17318	69.54	117.76	73.98	112.14	48.79	78.19	70.90
IFFCO Tokio	6364	4207	37945	723	8228	63967	54760	4226	4301	28976	8750	4221	50474	39859	66.40	102.24	76.36	121.14	51.30	78.91	72.79
ICICI Lombard	*10865*	*1830*	*87333*	*40662*	*16028*	*156718*	*106665*	*5794*	*3220*	*66505*	*40170*	*7143*	*122832*	*81384*	*53.33*	*175.93*	*76.15*	*98.79*	*44.57*	*78.38*	*76.30*
Cholamandalam	*3266*	*981*	*14073*	*2967*	*3599*	*24886*	*12728*	*1172*	*978*	*9353*	*2761*	*1302*	*15565*	*7077*	*35.88*	*99.73*	*66.46*	*93.03*	*36.16*	*62.55*	*55.60*
HDFC CHUBB	*161*	*142*	*12017*	*1692*	*993*	*15005*	*14029*	*34*	*132*	*8491*	*2411*	*409*	*11477*	*8003*	*20.80*	*93.35*	*70.66*	*142.46*	*41.25*	*76.49*	*57.05*
Future Generali	*(148)*	*(15)*	*2*	*25*	*8*	*(129)*		*3*	*4*			*50*	*50*		*-2.36*	*-24.58*	*0.00*	*0.00*	*650.71*	*-44.84*	
Universal Sompo	*(43)*					*(43)*									*0.00*					*0.00*	
Total	**40371**	**17015**	**370154**	**960087**	**64371**	**587920**	**367983**	**20464**	**17069**	**266316**	**91030**	**29677**	**424555**	**250289**	**50.69**	**100.32**	**71.95**	**94.81**	**46.10**	**72.21**	**68.02**

STATEMENT 58

INDIVIDUAL DEATH CLAIMS — 2007-08

(Benefit Amount in Rs crore)

Life Insurer	*Claims pending at start of year*		*Claims intimated / booked*		*Total Claims*		*Claims paid*		*Claims repudiated*		*Claims written back*		*Claims pending at end of year*		*Break up of claims pending — duration wise (Policies)*				
	No. of Policies	*Benefit Amount*	*No. of Policies*	*Benefit Amount*	*No. of Policies*	*Benefit Amount*	*No. of Policies*	*Benefit Amount*	*No. of Policies*	*Benefit Amount*	*No. of Policies*	*Benefit Amount*	*No. of Policies*	*Benefit Amount*	*<3 mths*	*3-<6 mths*	*6-<1yr*	*>1yr*	*Total*
Aviva	106	2.11	841	13.75	**947**	**15.86**	654	6.99	121	3.80	-	-	172	5.07	118	20	16	18	172
							(69.06)	(44.07)	(12.78)	(23.96)	-	-	(18.16)	(31.97)	(68.60)	(11.63)	(9.30)	(10.47)	
Bajaj Allianz	267	4.50	6262	104.41	**6529**	**108.92**	5065	79.46	689	14.18	-	-	775	15.27	634	77	37	27	775
							(77.58)	(72.96)	(10.55)	(13.02)	-	-	(11.87)	(14.02)	(81.81)	(9.94)	(4.77)	(3.48)	
Bharti Axa	0	0.00	26	0.74	**26**	**0.74**	9	0.17	10	0.20	-	-	7	0.36	6	1	-	-	7
							(34.62)	(22.61)	(38.46)	(27.80)	-	-	(26.92)	(49.60)	(85.71)	(14.29)	-	-	
Birla Sunlife	10	2.25	1450	35.88	**1460**	**38.13**	1334	31.06	109	4.28	-	-	17	2.79	4	3	4	6	17
							(91.37)	(81.46)	(7.47)	(11.22)	-	-	(1.16)	(7.32)	(23.53)	(17.65)	(23.53)	(35.29)	
Future Generali	-	-	-	-	-	-	-	-	-	-	-	-	-	-	-	-	-	-	-
							-	-	-	-	-	-	-	-	-	-	-	-	
HDFC Std	242	5.55	1820	28.30	**2062**	**33.86**	1665	23.27	87 2.	76	-	-	310	7.83	194 66	37	13	310	
							(80.75)	(68.72)	(4.22)	(8.15)	-	-	(15.03)	(23.13)	(62.58)	(21.29)	(11.94)	(4.19)	
ICICI Pru	151	4.02	6481	56.37	**6632**	**60.39**	5831	44.37	436	9.11	-	-	365	6.91	280	40	18	27	365
							(87.92)	(73.47)	(6.57)	(15.09)	-	-	(5.50)	(11.44)	(76.71)	(10.96)	(4.93)	(7.40)	
IDBI Fortis	-	-	-	-	-	-	-	-	-	-	-	-	-	-	-	-	-	-	-
							-	-	-	-	-	-	-	-	-	-	-	-	
ING Vysya	171	2.83	771	10.79	**942**	**13.62**	526	7.42	132	2.26	3	0.03	281	3.92	169	75	28	9	281
							(55.84)	(54.49)	(14.01)	(16.56)	(0.32)	(0.19)	(29.83)	(28.76)	(60.14)	(26.69)	(9.96)	(3.20)	
IDBI																			
Kotak Mahindra	145	2.55	558	22.48	**703**	**25.03**	414	19.76	178	3.65	-	-	111	1.62	74	27	5	5	111
							(58.89)	(78.95)	(25.32)	(14.58)	-	-	(15.79)	(6.47)	(66.67)	(24.32)	(4.50)	(4.50)	
Max NewYork	358	9.13	1989	38.55	**2347**	**47.69**	2121	41.51	221	5.75	-	-	5	0.43	4	-	1	-	5
							(90.37)	(87.04)	(9.42)	(12.06)	-	-	(0.21)	(0.90)	(80.00)	-	(20.00)	-	
MetLife	70	3.19	271	11.26	**341**	**14.45**	162	5.44	73	3.50	-	-	106	5.50	67	22	4	13	106
							(47.51)	(37.67)	(21.41)	(24.23)	-	-	(31.09)	(38.10)	(63.21)	(20.75)	(3.77)	(12.26)	
Reliance Life	14	0.35	1001	14.78	**1015**	**15.13**	925	13.00	86	1.99	-	-	4	0.14	4	-	-	-	4
							(91.13)	(85.88)	(8.47)	(13.18)	-	-	(0.39)	(0.94)	(100.00)	-	-	-	
Sahara	21	0.16	165	1.68	**186**	**1.84**	82	0.66	9	0.12	-	-	95	1.06	47	35	9	4	95
							(44.09)	(36.03)	(4.84)	(6.52)	-	-	(51.08)	(57.45)	(49.47)	(36.84)	(9.47)	(4.21)	
SBI Life	187	3.25	2124	30.50	**2311**	**33.75**	1883	25.96	164	2.42	1	0.01	263	5.36	152	58	25	28	263
							(81.48)	(76.92)	(7.10)	(7.17)	(0.04)	(0.03)	(11.38)	(15.88)	(57.79)	(22.05)	(9.51)	(10.65)	
Shriram	68	1.14	328	4.90	**396**	**6.04**	155	1.95	76	1.43	-	-	165	2.67	108	39	15	3	165
							(39.14)	(32.24)	(19.19)	(23.61)	-	-	(41.67)	(44.14)	(65.45)	(23.64)	(9.09)	(1.82)	
Tata AIG	193	3.59	1471	24.68	**1664**	**28.28**	929	15.27	413	6.66	-	-	322	6.35	83	38	69	132	322
							(55.83)	(53.99)	(24.82)	(23.55)	-	-	(19.35)	(22.46)	(25.78)	(11.80)	(21.43)	(40.99)	
Private Total	2003	44.64	25558	399.08	27561	443.72	21755	316.28	2804	62.12	4	0.04	2998	65.29	1944	501	268	285	2998
							(78.93)	(71.28)	(10.17)	(14.00)	(0.01)	(0.01)	(10.88)	(14.71)	(64.84)	(16.71)	(8.94)	(9.51)	
LIC *	9982	205.43	539779	3976.80	**549761**	**4182.23**	531653	3918.72	6223	90.54	335	31.60	11550	141.37	5054	2911	2186	1399	11550
							(96.71)	(93.70)	(1.13)	(2.16)	(0.06)	(0.76)	(2.10)	(3.38)	(43.76)	(25.20)	(18.93)	(12.11)	
Industry Total	11985	250.07	565337	4375.88	577322	4625.95	553408	4235.00	9027	152.66	339	31.64	14548	206.66	6998	3412	2454	1684	14548
							(95.86)	(91.55)	(1.56)	(3.30)	(0.06)	(0.68)	(2.52)	(4.47)	(48.10)	(23.45)	(16.87)	(11.58)	

Note: Figures in brackets show percentage of the respective total claims. * In the Annual Report for FY 2006-07, total individual death claim figures of LIC erroneously included group as well as foreign office business claims also. In the current FY, the figures pertain to individual death claims arising in the Indian operations of LIC.

Key Terms

- Tindal
- Cargo
- Surveyor
- Investigator
- Hull
- Voyage
- Close Proximity Clause
- Repudiation
- Rectification
- God Perils
- Third Party Claims
- No fault claims
- General Average
- Particular Average

Questions for Review

1. Briefly describe the documents of claims relating to Marine Insurance covers.
2. List the various points of differences between life insurance and non-life insurance claims.
3. "Claims Management is crucial effective to the success and growth of an insurance company." Discuss.

Suggested Readings

1. Gene Stone, Insurance Company Operations, LOMA, 2000.
2. Willis Park Rokes, *Human Relations in Handling Insurance Claims,* Richard R. Irwin, 1967.
3. *"Settling Third Party Insurance Claims Through TPAs."* Daleep Pandita, Insurance Times, Kolkata, Feb. 2003.
4. *Claims Management,* Volume I & II, ICFAI Press, 2002.

Insurance Intermediaries

Chapter

39

Chapter Objectives

After reading this chapter you will be able to understand :

- *Distribution of Insurance Products*
- *Insurance Intermediaries and their Functioning*
- *Surveyors and Loss Assessors*
- *Third Party Administrators*
- *Agents*
- *Brokers*
- *Corporate Agents*
- *Bancassurance*
- *Statistics on Intermediaries*

The new private insurers coming in with the liberalisation of the sector have added more channel of distribution in the Indian market parallel to that existent. Innovation and diversification will become the buzzwords in the business. Emerging scenario is evolving as a generic model in markets around the globe. Even in markets, which are consolidating like Europe, re-strategising distribution has been deciding the success for the insurers. The situation has become more complex with the development in systems and software technology and changing social patterns. All these have conspired to cause an upheaval in the traditional distribution methods. The new evolving system will now have to integrate the three players in the insurance market – the buyers, the carriers and the distributors.

39.1 Distribution of Insurance Products

Traditionally, the life insurers have been solely depended on the agency distribution force. On the contrary, the general insurance business has depended totally on the development officers. The scenario has been different for the general insurers, a no agency commission was payable for writing businesses more than 10 lakh, thus prohibiting brokers.

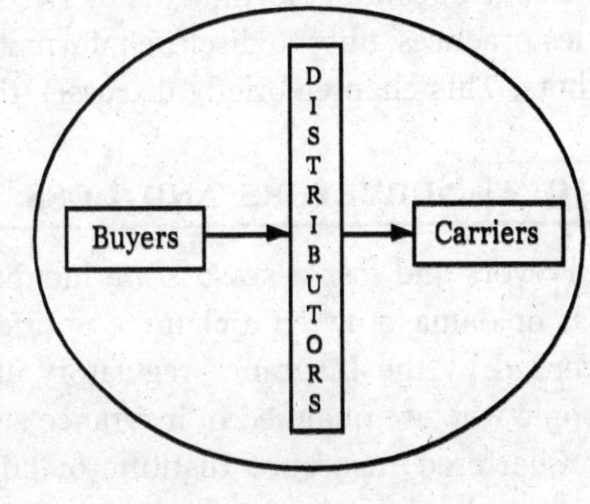

In the emerging scenario, there will be three players – the *buyers* will consist of consumers, employees, and employers and the *carriers* or the policy issuers will focus mainly on life and annuities, property and casualties, health and ancillaries and, the critical link in the system will be the *distributor*. Those who will provide value-added and low-cost services will be the survivors.

Traditional Channel of Distribution

- Agents
- Brokers

New Distribution Channels

- Direct Marketing
- Corporate Agents
- Independent Financial Advisors
- Telemarketing
- Website Marketing
- Retail Chains
- Internet Marketing
- Bancassurance
- Microfinance Companies
- NGOs

39.2 Insurance Intermediaries and their Functioning

Insurance industry in India has seen lot of changes since the opening of the sector for private participation. Industry has witnessed entry of a plethora of companies and is to witness many more to foray. There has been a lot of innovation both on the products front and also on service front. Innovation on the service front include providing call centre facilities, providing personalized financial planning tools, e-servicing of products and the recent one is the introduction of third party administrators. The various insurance intermediaries from the consumer's and marketer's perspective are:

(a) Agents
(b) Brokers
(c) Surveyors and Loss Assessors
(d) Third Party Administrators
(e) Corporate Agents

The Insurance Regulatory and Development Authority (IRDA) has formulated a code of conduct for Insurance Brokers and agents and prescribed strict penalties including cancellation of licences for default and manipulation. The code of conduct formulated by IRDA covers the entire gamut of activities including relationship with clients, sales practices, duty to disclose information to clients, claims, advertising, sub-brokers and remuneration among others. This chapter briefly discusses these intermediaries in the following sections.

39.3 Surveyors and Loss Assessors

Surveyors and loss assessors are independent professionals appointed by an insurance company to assess the loss or damage, when a claim is notified under a policy issued by them. An insurance surveyor must be duly licensed by the Insurance regulatory and development authority. Licenses are issued to technically qualified people who are qualified in insurance subjects and are Fellows or Associates of the Insurance Institutes of India or Chartered Insurance Institute of London or any other technically qualified like Engineering graduates or diploma holders in any discipline, Chartered Accountants, Graduates in Medical Sciences. A surveyor after obtaining the license, may be empanelled by any or all of the insurance companies in India. The insurance company selects a surveyor who is qualified to undertake the assessment of loss or damage in relation to the policy issued and also depending upon the estimated loss involved.

His duties include:

- Investigate and confirm the cause of loss.
- Advise the insured to take good care of salvage to mitigate the loss.
- To ensure that insured has taken all necessary steps to contain the loss.
- Assess the quantum of loss.
- Determine the liability of the insurers within the framework of the policy conditions.
- To act on behalf of the insurance company in disposal of salvage to realize maximum value.

Though the surveyor is appointed by the insurance companies, he is required to be impartial and objective in his assessment, favouring neither the insurers nor the insured, who are the two parties to the contract under a policy. This necessitates a high degree of professionalism.

Since long time, the general insurance industry was suffering on account of dissatisfaction with the surveyor's loss assessment report and delay in the settlement of claims. Therefore, IRDA has issued regulations pertaining to surveyors and loss assessors which categorises on the basis of their qualification, practical experience and past experiences. The code of conduct regarding the professional and ethical requirements for conduct of their professional work is also specified in Chapter VI of the IRDA Regulations for Surveyors and Loss Assessors, 2000. Surveyors must strive for objectivity in professional and business judgment while behaving ethically and with integrity in their professional pursuit acting impartially and complying with due diligence, care and skill with regard to technical and professional standards expected of them.

Exhibit 39-A

Financial limits of Categorized Surveyors and Loss Assessors

Department	*Category A*	*Category B*	*Category C*
LOP	Above Rs. 50 lakhs	Upto Rs. 50 lakhs	Nil
Fir (Flood, Cyclone, Earthquake)	Above Rs. 25 lakhs	Upto Rs. 25 lakhs	Upto Rs. 10 lakhs
Engineering	above Rs 10 lakhs	Upto Rs. 10 lakhs	Upto Rs 5 lakhs
Motor (Public, Private)	Above Rs. 1.5 lakhs	Upto Rs 1.5 lakhs	Upto Rs.75,000
Miscellaneous (inclusive of non-tariff)	Above Rs. 3 lakhs	Upto Rs. 3 lakhs	Upto Rs. 1 lakh
Marine Cargo	Above Rs. 3 lakhs	Upto Rs. 3 lakhs	Upto Rs. 1 lakh
Marine hull	Above Rs. 10 lakhs	Upto Rs. 10 lakhs	Upto Rs. 50,000

The Government of India and the Authority, have established Indian Institute of Insurance Surveyors and Loss Assessors (IIISLA) in order to promote self-regulation and professionalism amongst the surveyors as a part of further reforms in the insurance sector. Annexure 39-A contains the text of the said regulations. The financial limits of categorised surveyors and loss assessors are given above.

Exhibit 39-B

Category	*Total number of Surveyors (individual) categorized as on 31st March, 2002*						
	Fire	*Marine Cargo*	*Marine Hull*	*Engg.*	*Motor*	*Misc.*	*LOP*
A	379	179	24	225	916	310	58
B	1213	1035	63	1954	3231	2055	138
C	1586	2264	80	2090	2521	2688	60
Total	3178	3478	167	4269	6668	5053	256

Category	Total number of Surveyors (individual) categorized as on 31st March, 2002						
	Fire	Marine Cargo	Marine Hull	Engg.	Motor	Misc.	LOP
A	379	179	24	225	916	310	58
A	69	28	8	41	19	40	17
B	89	88	20	83	54	121	32
C	102	133	4	73	31	82	3
Total	260	249	32	197	104	243	52

Source: IRDA Annual Report 2001-02.

39.4 THIRD PARTY ADMINISTRATORS

Third party administrators are the new breed of intermediaries in the health insurance sector which facilitate the access of the policyholders to a network of hospitals/nursing homes. The introduction of whom will benefit both the insured and the insurer. TPA's maintain the databases of policyholders and issue them identity cards with unique identification numbers and handle all the post policy issues including claim settlements. They run a 24-hour toll-free number, which can be accessed from anywhere in the country. They have full-time medical practitioners under their employment who spontaneously take decision on whether the ailment is covered under the policy.

TPA's benefit both the insurer and insured. For insured, better services are obtained and for insurers, they substantially reduce the administrative costs. TPA license is granted to companies registered under the Companies Act 1956 having a minimum paid up capital of Rs. 1.00 crores with foreign participation not exceeding 26%. License is usually granted for a period of 3 years. Earlier, the insured was reimbursed all the hospitalisation expenses, but with introduction of TPA's all the hospitalisation services operate on *cashless* basis since the payment is directly made to them.

TPAs are entitled to commission by insurers on a mutually agreeable terms but, as per the IRDA guidelines it can not exceed 15% of premium amount. TPAs have to tie-up with hospitals, which offer hospitalisation services. Each TPA may tie-up with any number of insurers and like wise each insurer can empanel any number of TPAs.

Procedure

- All the records of medical insurance policies of an insurer are transferred to the TPA who generally issue identity cards to all the policyholders, which they have to show to the hospital authorities before availing any hospitalisation services. In case of a claim, policyholder has to inform TPA on 24 hour toll free line provided by the TPA.
- On informing the TPA, policyholder will be directed to a hospital where the TPA has a tied up arrangement. However, policyholder will have the option to join any other hospital of his choice, but in such case payment shall be on reimbursement basis.
- TPA issues an authorisation letter to the hospital, for the treatment wherein the TPA will pay for the treatment. TPA will be tracking the case of the insured at the hospital and at the point of discharge, all the bills will be sent to TPA.
- TPA makes the payment to the hospital and sends all the documents necessary for consideration of claims, along with bills to the insurer.
- Insurer reimburses the TPA.

Presently, the role of TPA is confined to medical/health services. However their job can be extended to:

- Documentation and policy issuing.
- Legal services and claims recovery services under subrogation rights.
- Record verification under adjustment policies.
- Medical examination services for life insurance policies and overseas Mediclaim policies.
- Co-insurance recovery services for both premiums and claims.
- Follow up of recoveries from reinsurance companies.
- Servicing of motor policies.
- Inspection and assessment of risk prior to issuance of policy.
- Arbitration services.

TPA are also matter of concern to Insurance Companies and Regulator. The TPA claims are on the rise and complaints against TPA with a further faster rate. TPA claims data is given in Exhibit 28C on next page.

39.5 AGENTS

Most of the life insurance companies in India follow the traditional route of marketing through agents. In case of private players they are nomenclatured as Insurance Advisors/ Planners. The companies generally emphasise on building a good field force, trained to get people thinking about their family's financial security and recommend appropriate policies for their needs. Agents have traditionally proved to be highly successful means of distribution of insurance products. The professional agent has been the strongest link between the life insurer and the customer. The professional agent has the onerous role of explaining the concepts, terms and conditions, benefits and privileges of the insurance contract. He has to analyze the financial requirements and risks faced by the customers and market insurance plans suited to the needs and means of the customers. All insurance companies, and life insurance companies in particular, have recognized the paramount importance of this channel. The number of agents has grown at a spectacular rate. Every insurance agent has to obtain a licence from IRDA before conduct of insurance business and follow a code of conduct prescribed thereunder. A text of the guidelines dealing with licensing of insurance agents is given in Annexure 39-A. The success of LIC with its direct field force, rather, army of 6,51,000 agents, is exemplary. In case of non-life also much of the distribution work is done by the agents or development officers. Training institutes have developed all over the country inculcating professional skills and teaching the intricacies of plans, the concepts, terms and conditions, benefits and privileges of insurance contracts to the ever increasing number of agents. Of course there has turnover of agents.

In general insurance the retail agent markets mainly the personal lines of Fire, Motor, Burglary, Household Insurance, Travel Insurance and Health Insurance. Due to the low ticket size, the number of agents has not increased astronomically as in life insurance. There is a feeling amongst general insurers that there is a necessity to liberalise the present rules to attract more agents by allowing agents to sell products of more than one non-life insurer.

Corporate agent is a concept introduced with a view to taking advantage of the presence of a large number of entities with a sizeable client base, contacts and goodwill already operating in the market. With multi locations and a network of people assisting them, these entities have a different structure and purpose. Hence their existing network could be utilized to market insurance. The corporate agent could thus be defined as a person meaning a firm or company formed under the Companies Act, 1956 or a banking company or a Bank/RBB or a co-operative society registered under the Co-operative Societies Act, 1912 or a panchayat or a NGO/MFI covered under the Co-op Societies Act or a NBFC registered with RBI or any other Institute. They assist greatly in the spread of insurance through the greater reach of the institutions.

THIRD PARTY ADMINISTRATORS - CLAIMS DATA : 2007-08

Sl.No.	*Name of TPA*	*No.of*	*No. of Claims Settled*			
		Claims Received	*Within 1 month*	*Within 1-3 months*	*Within 3-6 months*	*More than 6 months*
1	Parekh Health Management	14305	9490 (66.34)	3592 (25.11)	160 (1.12)	13 (0.09)
2	Medi Assist India Private Ltd.	210089	117984 (56.16)	57024 (27.14)	8141 (3.88)	2358 (1.12)
3	MD India Healthcare Services (P) Ltd.	108730	93026 (85.56)	2356 (2.17)	410 (0.38)	Nil
4	Paramount Health Services Pvt. Ltd.	325176	319173 (98.15)	8376 (2.58)	593 (0.18)	88 (0.03)
5	E Meditek Solutions Ltd.	217799	189659 (87.08)	16220 (7.45)	4969 (2.28)	Nil 0
6	Heritage Health Services	36684	21329 (58.14)	11697 (31.89)	2144 (5.84)	279 (0.76)
7	Universal Mediaid Services Ltd.	1232	855 (69.40)	295 (23.94)	117 (9.50)	Nil
8	Medicare TPA Services (I) Pvt. Ltd	64238	43039 (67.00)	7332 (11.41)	156 (0.24)	58 (0.09)
9	Family Health Plan Ltd.	215396	147064 (68.28)	6129 (28.38)	Nil	Nil
10	Raksha TPA Pvt. Ltd.	95451	76745 (80.40)	10806 (11.32)	2512 (2.63)	Nil
11	TTK Healthcare Services Ltd.	289709	246766 (85.18)	22607 (7.80)	3840 (1.33)	2987 (1.03)
12	East West Assist Pvt. Ltd.	2894	1693 (58.50)	527 (18.21)	86 (2.97)	11 (0.38)
13	Med Save Health Care Ltd.	81740	41777 (51.11)	25488 (31.18)	2916 (3.57)	258 (0.32)
14	Genins India Ltd.	106543	72316 (67.87)	24145 (22.66)	9828 (9.22)	1889 (1.77)
15	Alankit Healthcare	17961	11559 (64.36)	5813 (32.36)	2397 (13.35)	1460 (8.13)
16	$ Health India TPA Services Pvt. Ltd.	80464	60393 (75.06)	14710 (18.28)	2370 (2.95)	Nil
17	Good Health Plan Ltd.	14017	12584 (89.78)	6 (0.04)	1 (0.01)	Nil
18	Vipul Medcrop Pvt. Ltd.	57784	17181 (29.73)	22785 (39.43)	7130 (12.34)	3156 (5.46)
19	Park Mediclaim Consultants Pvt. Ltd	17064	9595 (56.23)	5397 (31.63)	500 (2.93)	98 (0.57)
20	Safeway Mediclaim Services	209	125 (59.81)	23 (11.00)	2 (0.96)	Nil
21	Anmol Medicare Ltd.	18	4 (22.22)	4 (22.22)	Nil	Nil
22	Dedicated Healthcare Services (India) Private Limited	29356	21018 (71.60)	2498 (8.51)	636 (2.17)	Nil
23	Grand Healthcare India Pvt. Ltd.	Nil	-	-	-	-
24	Rothshield Healthcare Nill	-	-	-	-	-
25	Sri Gokulam	Nil	-	-	-	-
26	Focus Healthcare Pvt. Ltd	Nil	-	-	-	-
27	Anyuta Medinet Healthcare Pvt. Ltd.	Nil	-	-	-	-
	TOTAL	**1986859**	**1513375 (76.17)**	**302830 (15.24)**	**48908 (2.46)**	**12660 (0.64)**

Note: Figure in brackets indicate the ratio (in per cent) of claims to the total claims received.

$ Formarly known as Bhaichand Amoluk Ins. Services Pvt. Ltd.

39.6 BROKERS

Insurance brokers are professionals who assess the specific insurance needs of the client, evaluate the risk and suggest a suitable insurance cover for the clients. IRDA's Annual Report 2001-02 describes brokers as "Insurance brokers, as professionals, are expected to fill the void in terms of providing for specific insurance needs of the client, by assessing the risk on behalf of the client, advise on the mitigation of the specified risk, identifying the optimal insurance policy structure, bring together the insured and insurers, carry out work preparatory to insurance contracts and, where necessary, assist in the administration and performance of such contracts, in particular when claims arise." As per the said report, "The advent of brokers on the scene is likely to result in improvement in customer service, transfer of technology and managerial know-how, benefits to insurance companies through increased market penetration and facilitate increased retention capacities by optimising reinsurance programmes."

IRDA has issued guidelines for issue of licence and regulation of affairs to insurance brokers and insurance consultants in 2002. Text of these guidelines is given in Annexure 39-B.

As per the said guidelines, the brokers are divided into following categories:

Category I	—	Direct General Insurance broker
Category II	—	Direct Life Insurance broker
Category III	—	Reinsurance broker
Category IV	—	Composite broker
Category V	—	Insurance Consultant

Some of the important provisions as contained therein are:

- The guidelines specifically provide the qualification norms and their functions for various classes of brokers.
- The net worth requirement for composite insurance brokers is Rs. 2.50 crores (with a cap of 26% on foreign equity participation). For direct brokers and reinsurance brokers it is Rs. 50 lakhs and Rs. 2.00 crores respectively. In case of insurance consultants, a bank guarantee of Rs. 5.00 lakhs has to be furnished to IRDA.
- The brokerage is determined by the IRDA in accordance with market practices but it cannot exceed 30% of the premium. This commission shall be paid by the brokers to the insurers.
- Every broker has to maintain a solvency margin – Rs. 25 lakhs or 10% of the gross brokerage and fees received in the previous year, whichever is higher. A statement of solvency margin from the auditors shall be furnished by the broker to the authority.
- The brokers are to maintain the books of accounts as prescribed and have to submit the audited financial statements and report thereon within 60 days from the end of the accounting year. The records are to be preserved for at least 5 years.

Exhibit 38D gives an overview of a typical insurance brokerage firm.

Exhibit - 38D

Typical Structure of an Insurance Brokerage Firm

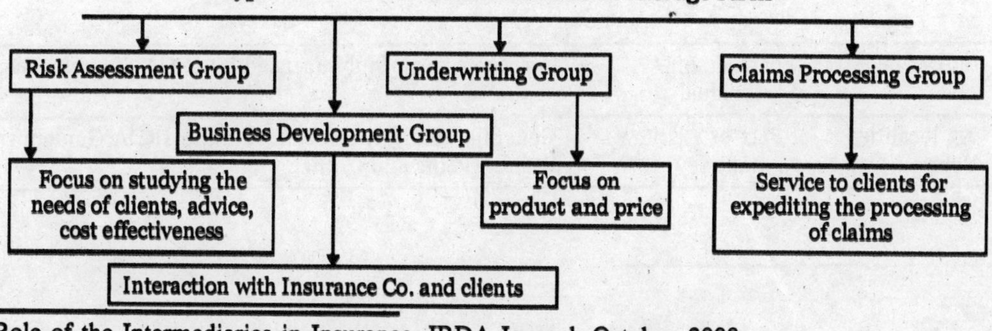

1. S.K. Sethi, Role of the Intermediaries in Insurance, IRDA Journal, October, 2008.

- The brokers have to disclose information on various matters as and when it is required by the authority. The brokers are also required to facilitate inspection when it is ordered.

Unlike insurance agents who are retained by Insurance Companies, Brokers are retained by the insured and therefore their primary responsibility is towards the insured. Some of the benefits of introducing brokers in the Indian market are:

- ***Improvement in Customer Service:*** With increased competition, insurance brokers have a greater motivation to introduce new and innovative products, to be more responsive to consumer needs, and to deliver higher terms quality services. Indian corporates and consumers benefit directly in terms of service as well as product and policy innovation, and are consequently able to secure appropriate insurance cover more cost effectively.
- ***Transfer of Technology and Managerial Know-how:*** Insurance brokers introduce international best practice in technical skills and products, training programmes, systems and technology, and managerial techniques. Currently the availability of trained manpower is a major constraint in the development of the insurance broking business in India and international players can contribute heavily in bridging this gap.
- ***Benefits to Insurance Companies:*** Most major global insurance companies spend the majority of their time handling commercial and industrial risks. They find dealing with brokers to be easier and speedier because only the intricate points or special requirements need detailed discussion. Brokers also assist in creating insurance awareness, increasing market penetration and act as a catalyst to increase competition and improve customer service.
- ***Foreign Exchange Considerations:*** Brokers enable Indian insurers to increase their retention capacities by applying their international reinsurance skills in optimising their reinsurance programmes, thereby effecting further saving in foreign exchange outflow. In addition, they can assist the local insurers to develop new products and accordingly increase the premium base.

39.7 CORPORATE AGENTS

Corporate agents is a new concept recently introduced by IRDA to facilitate the ditribution of insurance products by the corporates. The main agenda to promote corporate agents is to facilitate "bancassurance" in India. IRDA report of 2001-02 expresses concerns on this issue and states that in India, the public sector banks and regional rural banks and microcredit institutions have wide reach and can help fulfil the basic objective of deeper insurance penetration in the country. IRDA has also issued guidelines for Licensing of corporate agents which provide for minimum educational qualifications for specified persons, and practical training requirements and code of conduct.

Comparison of various insurance intermediaries[2]

Type of Intermediaries/ Parameter	*Agent*	*Corporate Agent*	*Insurance Brokerage Firm*
Set up	Individual	Partnership/ Individual	Corporate setup duly licensed by IRDA after thorough analysis
Area Coverage Investment	2-3 localities None	Part of a city Small, Say	Generally many cities. According to IRDA Guidelines, Up to Rs. 100 lakhs shop/office

(Contd...)

2. *Ibid.*

Type of Intermediaries/ Parameter	*Agent*	*Corporate Agent*	*Insurance Brokerage Firm*
Representing	1Co.Only	1 Co. Only	Non Life – 18 Life – 21 Health – 2
Strategy toward client	Selling only	Selling only	Assist the client in buying the right product at right price from right insurance comlpany.
Product Range Competency	Cannot be 100%	Cannot be 100% say Motor only	100%
Service Offered	Partial catering to	Partial calering to clients	Complete from Risk Assessement to Claim Lodging/Settlements individual clients say motor only
Professional Liability Insurance	Does not have this policy	Does not have this policy	As per IRDA rules have professional liability policy issued by insurance co in its favor. This is very favorable for clients

Product coverage by various Insurance Intermediaries – Examples

Agent	Scooter, Motor, Household, Mediclaim
Corporate Agent	Motor Vehicle – May be corporate agent is DSA of a Bank for Auto loan or is an automobile dealer, Overseas Mediclaim (Travel Agents), Very few corporate agents offer comprehensive service
IBF's	Some offer Non-Life Insurance only. Most offer Life + Non-Life + Health – all products, all companies.

The general opinion is that it is better to deal with IBFs focusing on corporate clients and handling all products as they can handle all aspects of your organizational needs *e.g.* group insurance, gratuity, superannuation, key man also.

39.8 BANCASSURANCE

Bancassurance is a concept that has rewritten the way in which insurance products are distributed in many parts of the world and has the potential to do the same in many other markets. By offering a holistic financial services package, encompassing banking, insurance, lending and investment products, banks can maximise distribution of products to a captive customer base. In markets where it is firmly established bancassurance channels can take an impressive market share of new life business – around 55% in France and between 20% and 30% in many other European countries.

***Bancassurance** (a french term) is a partnership between a life insurance company and a banking institution.* The need (for the insurance company) to access a large base of customers and a desire (on the part of the bank) to offer a wide range of financial products leads to these partnership in different forms. The main tenats of bancassurance's trusting relationship with customers, branch name recognition, customer profitability measurement systems in banks, cash management relationship with corporations and the fact that bancassurance distribution is more cost effective than traditional distribution are some of the key attractions of this channel. 27 public sector banks and 196 regional rural banks account for 92% of the branch network in India.

With over 60,000 branches of commercial banks and an average population served per branch of 15,000, bancassurance is expected to be a critical distribution strategy for the insurance companies. In fact, the network includes 33,000 rural branches and 14,000 semi-urban branches, about 60% of the total number of branches.

Need for Bancassurance

The traditional channels of insurance are becoming costlier and obsolete by the day in India. The commission paid to the agents ranges from 5%-10% of annual premium throughout the length of the underlying policy. In contrast, the banking channels will cost just around 20% for one time, reducing the burden for the insurance companies. Declining productivity of the insurance agents and heating competition, where the insurers are finding it increasingly difficult to maintain their market share, has also made a strong case for Bancassurance. The availability of huge customer database at the banks have enabled insurers to design products that fit the choice range of the customers, increasing its popularity, thus essentuate the need for bancassurance.

Also from banker's perspective, there are several reasons why banks should seriously consider Bancassurance, the most important of which is increased return on assets (ROA). One of the best ways to increase ROA, assuming a constant asset base, is through fee income. Banks that build fee income can cover more of their operating expenses, and one way to build fee income is through the sale of insurance products. Banks that effectively cross-sell financial products can leverage their distribution and processing capabilities for profitable operating expense ratios.

By leveraging their strengths and finding ways to overcome their weaknesses, banks could change the face of insurance distribution. Sale of personal line insurance products through banks meets an important set of consumer needs. Most large retail banks engender a great deal of trust in broad segments of consumers, which they can leverage in selling them personal line insurance products. In addition, a bank's branch network allows the face to face contact that is so important in the sale of personal insurance.

Another advantage banks have over traditional insurance distributors is the lower cost per sales lead made possible by their sizable, loyal customer base. Banks also enjoy significant brand awareness within their geographic regions, again providing for a lower per-lead cost when advertising through print, radio and/or television. Banks that make the most of these advantages are able to penetrate their customer base and markets for above-average market share.

Other bank strengths are their marketing and processing capabilities. Banks have extensive experience in marketing to both existing customers (for retention and cross selling) and non-customers (for acquisition and awareness). They also have access to multiple communication channels, such as statement inserts, direct mail, ATMs, telemarketing, etc. Banks' proficiency in using technology has resulted in improvements in transaction processing and customer service.

By successfully mining their customer databases, leveraging their reputation and 'distribution systems' (branch, phone, and mail) to make appointments, and utilizing 'sales techniques' and products tailored to the middle market, European banks have more than doubled the conversion rates of insurance leads into sales and have increased sales productivity to a ratio which is more than enough to make bancassurance a highly profitable proposition.

Bancassurance Models

- *Distribution Alliance* : In this model, the insurance company ties up with the bank for distribution of insurance products.
- *Joint Venture between Insurer and Bank* : This type of partnership brings a bank with a well developed customer database together with a large life insurer with strong product and channel experience to develop a powerful new distribution model. In this type of venture the bank provides the lead and its reputation and brand name, while the insurer brings products and underwriting and servicing expertise. The partners combine their individual expertise to forge a best practice bancassurance operation with tailored products, tailored distribution and lead generation mechanism. This model may be applied to SBI Life Insurance. It has access to some 117 million holders of term deposits through 14,000 branches of the State Bank of India (SBI), which serve as a ready platform and a ready distribution channel. Other players such as ING Vysya are also looking at this option. They seek to set-up branches in many main cities, moving gradually into the semi-urban and rural areas.

- *Leveraged Life Distribution* : Under this model, the life insurance company takes the lead in partnership, while several banks act as corporate agents to provide access to middle-market leads.
- *Leveraged Bank Distribution* : Under leveraged bank distribution, it is the bank that takes the lead as in the partnership, while the life insurance companies supply products for it's bancassurance efforts. This model calls for a large bank with a range of effective distribution channels (branches, ATMs, mail, phones).

Each model has its own particular advantages, however they all share common features which can create competitive advantage:

- Enhanced customer service — providing convenience, simplicity and value in a "one stop" environment.
- Leverage of existing assets — such as valuable, often vast, customer databases.
- More income — generated from an increase in overall product sales and better customer retention.
- Greater productivity — a bancassurance sales person's productivity has been measured to be 55% higher than the agency equivalent.
- Quality sales culture — that is customer driven.
- Improved staff retention — higher levels of satisfaction among sales staff through good training and remuneration schemes.
- Cross-selling opportunities — strengthening customer relationship management.

Advantages and Disadvantages of Bancassurance Models

Model	*Advantages*	*Disadvantages*
Pure distributor. The bank acts as an intermediary offering products of more than one insurance company.	The bank, acting as intermediary, is able to offer new lines of products to its customer base without having to make significant upfront investment.	Both the bank and the insurance company have a 'fragmented' view of the relationship with the customer.
	This model works well in markets where customers value advisor independence	
Strategic alliance: The bank sells the products of only one insurance company	The bank is able to select the best insurance provider in terms of the quality of products offered, brand image, the quality of after-sales service etc.	There are low levels of integration between the bank and the insurance company as both companies operate as separate entities.
	This model offers the bank an easy way of increasing the portfolio of products without investing large amounts of money.	Bank staff may be reluctant to sell insurance due to low product knowledge.
	This model offers low risk in terms of required investment. The insurance company gains access to the bank's customer base without having to make a major financial investment.	Administration issues may arise from the fact that the customer does not have a clear understanding of who is responsible for which product or who should be contacted in the case of claim.
Joint Venture : The bank and the insurer establish a jointly owned insurance company or distributor, thus creating a new entity	There are equal partnerships and joint decision making Partners can leverage each others' strengths in the new venture as each one will be focusing on its line of business	Insurers may feel that they lose control of the distribution side of the operation as the bank acts as the distributor Bank staff may be reluctant to sell insurance products

(Contd...)

Model	*Advantages*	*Disadvantages*
	Products are designed specially for banking customers	
Financial holding company : A holding company owns both an insurer and a bank	Operations and systems can be fully integrated There is high capability to leverage on bank's existing customer and other service provisions. One-stop shopping for financial services is possible for customers There is potential for fully integrated products.	

Key issues to be addressed to make bancassurance successful are :

- Both the bank and insurance company need **to improve effectiveness of the sales channels** by identifying and gaining access to target customers, adding push to market pull, training of sales staff, differentiating performance from competition and controlling selling cost per unit sold.
- **Product needs to be Tailored** to meet the need of the customer base and for new distribution channels.
- **Communication** needs to be streamlined to address any cultural issues between the bank staff and the insurance staff. Similarly, differences in compensation structures need to be handled sensitively before these start affecting the moral of the branch staff.
- Traditional **processes need to be redesigned** not only to take advantage of the new technology, but also to effect a streamlined system between bank and the insurance company. Technology can be used to put effective use in sales support function, staff training, smoother processing, and online integrated information system.

Choosing the Right Partner in Bancassurance

Important or critical factor for a successful Bancassurance partnership is :

- Full commitment from both the partners in a deal
- Brand/Franchise
- Large Customer Base
- Capital Strength
- Complementary products and services and new economy distribution system
- Regional Technology Platform
- **Information system needs to be reviewed** and performance measurement parameters need to be specially adopted to bancassurance.
- **Skills need to be developed** and reallocation of assets and resources — financial and human may also be required between the bank and Insurance Company.

Referrals : this is a new concept very similar to getting a prospecting list and leads to effect sales with customers. It is evident that in addition to banks, there could be various other entities which could act as a referral provider due to the large database of members/clients, like credit cardholders association members, society members etc. In short, such institutions could share or market their database to provide leads to the intermediaries to sell insurance products. The referral provider is not a licensed intermediary, but can be regulated by the insurance Regulator, through approval of the terms of the agreement, between the insurer and the referral provider. The U.K. model of introducer envisages introduction of customers to insurance products and insurers. The regulatory provisions inter alia envisages access to database, voluntary participation of the customers, contract only between insurers and insured, no principal-agent relationship between referral/introducer and insurer.

Referral providers enhance the penetration of insurance through provision of good prospecting lists and the vast databases. Hence this model could be encouraged and regulated with tight guidelines to prevent any abuses especially in compensation levels, which should be in relation to the services rendered.

Details of Individual Agents of Life Insurers – 2007-08

Insurer	*As on April 1, 2007*	*Additions*	*Deletions*	*As on March 31, 2008*
Private	890152	772910	336314	1326748
LIC	1103047	234852	144155	1193744
Total	1993199	1007762	2520492	

One major concern that emerges from the data is the high percentage of turnover of agents. In 2007-08, while the total number of agents appointed is 10.07 lakhs, the number of agents terminated is as high as 4.80 lakhs. The high turnover is a huge drain on the financials of the insurers who spend lot of money and time on prospecting, appointing and training of these agents. The policies procured by these agents are rendered orphan or their termination and thereafter result often into lapsation due to lack of servicing support.

Insurer	*As on April 1, 2007*	*Additions*	*Deletions*	*As on March 31, 2008*
Private	1906	442	278	2070
LIC	409	55	119	345
Total	**2315**	**497**	**397**	**2415**

39.9 Statistics on Intermediaries

AGENTS LICENSED BY THE AUTHORITY (2005-2006)
(Individual and Corporate)

LIFE INSURERS

	Individual Agents		*Corporate Agents*		*Total*		
Name	***New***	***Renewal***	***New***	***Renewal***	***New***	***Renewal***	***Total***
ALLIANZ BAJAJ LIFE INSURANCE CO. LTD.	78,826	1365	18	8	78,844	1373	80,217
TATA AIG LIFE INSURANCE CO. LTD.	18,051	1277	10	10	18,061	1287	19,348
AMP SANMAR INSURANCE CO.LTD.	14,034	255	4	0	14,038	255	14,293
BIRLA SUN LIFE	11,101	778	15	19	11,116	797	11,913
AVIVA LIFE INSURANCE CO INDIA PVT. LTD.	9,178	23	2	1	9,180	24	9,204
HDFC STANDARD LIFE INSURANCE CO LTD.	14,762	1940	6	9	14,768	1949	16,717
ICICI PRUDENTIAL LIFE INSURANCE	41,552	2930	1	6	41,553	2,936	44,489
ING VYSYA LIFE INSURANCE CO. PVT. LTD.	13,689	354	0	0	13,689	354	14,043
LIFE INSURANCE CORPORATION OF INDIA	155,250	316752	15	59	155,265	316,811	472,076
MAX NEW YORK LIFE INSURANCE CO.LTD.	11,941	596	10	2	11,951	598	12,549
METLIFE INDIA INSURANCE CO. PVT. LTD.	8,217	124	1	1	8,218	125	8,343
OM KOTAK MAHINDRA LIFE INSURANCE CO.LTD.	6,920	443	5	6	6,925	449	7,374
SAHARA INDIA LIFE INSURANCE CO. LTD .	80	1	0	0	80	1	81
SHRIRAM LIFE INSURANCE CO. LTD.	5,935	2	0	0	5,935	2	5,937
SBI LIFE INSURANCE CO. LTD.	4,794	310	3	5	4,797	315	5,112
SUB TOTAL	**394,330**	**327,150**	**90**	**126**	**394,420**	**327276**	**721,696**

GENERAL INSURERS

TATA AIG GENERAL INSURANCE CO. LTD.	248	89	1	9	249	98	347
BAJAJ ALLIANZ GENERAL INSURANCE CO. LTD.	1,484	234	2	5	1,486	239	1,725
CHOLAMANDALAM MS GEN. INSURANCE CO. LTD.	102	33	0	1	102	34	136
EXPORT CREDIT GUARANTEE CORPORATION OF INDIA LTD.	0	0	1	0	1	0	1
HDFC CHUBB GENERAL INSURANCE CO. LTD.	40	2	0	0	40	2	42
ICICI LOMBARD GENERAL INSURANCE CO. LTD.	1,099	71	4	1	1,103	72	1,175
IFFCO-TOKIO GENERAL INSURANCE CO. LTD.	1,060	80	2	2	1,062	82	1,144
THE NEW INDIA ASSURANCE CO. LTD.	2,308	7038	5	11	2,313	7,049	9,362
NATIONAL INSURANCE CO. LTD.	2,331	6534	0	13	2,331	6,547	8,878
THE ORIENTAL INSURANCE CO. LTD.	5,017	5198	1	7	5,018	5,205	10,223
RELIANCE GENERAL INSURANCE CO. LTD.	122	46	0	1	122	47	169
ROYAL SUNDARAM ALLIANCE INSURANCE CO LTD.	74	64	2	6	76	70	146
UNITED INDIA INSURANCE CO. LTD.	1,426	5739	8	30	1,434	5,769	7,203
SUB TOTAL	**15,311**	**25,128**	**26**	**86**	**15,337**	**25,214**	**40,551**
GRAND TOTAL	**409,641**	**352,278**	**116**	**212**	**409,757**	**352,490**	**762,247**

AGENTS LICENSED BY THE AUTHORITY (2005-2006)
(Urban and Rural)

LIFE INSURERS

Name	*Urban*	*Rural*	*Total*
ALLIANZ BAJAJ LIFE INSURANCE CO. LTD.	65651	14566	80217
TATA AIG LIFE INSURANCE CO. LTD.	18920	428	19348
AMP SANMAR INSURANCE CO.LTD.	11805	2488	14293
BIRLA SUN LIFE	11811	102	11913
AVIVA LIFE INSURANCE CO INDIA PVT. LTD.	8985	219	9204
HDFC STANDARD LIFE INSURANCE CO. LTD.	14582	2135	16717
ICICI PRUDENTIAL LIFE INSURANCE	43962	527	44489
ING VYSYA LIFE INSURANCE CO. PVT. LTD.	13238	805	14043
LIFE INSURANCE CORPORATION OF INDIA	186919	285157	472076
MAX NEW YORK LIFE INSURANCE CO.LTD.	12251	298	12549
METLIFE INDIA INSURANCE CO. PVT. LTD.	7895	448	8343
OM KOTAK MAHINDRA LIFE INSURANCE CO.LTD.	6761	613	7374
SAHARA INDIA LIFE INSURANCE CO. LTD.	71	10	81
SHRIRAM LIFE INSURANCE CO. LTD.	2163	3774	5937
SBI LIFE INSURANCE CO. LTD.	4413	699	5112
SUB TOTAL	**409,427**	**312,269**	**721,696**

GENERAL INSURERS

Name	*Urban*	*Rural*	*Total*
TATA AIG GENERAL INSURANCE CO. LTD.	336	11	347
BAJAJ ALLIANZ GENERAL INSURANCE CO. LTD.	1512	213	1725
CHOLAMANDALAM GENERAL INSURANCE CO. LTD.	111	25	136
EXPORT CREDIT GUARANTEE CORPORATION OF INDIA LTD.	1	0	1
HDFC CHUBB GENERAL INSURANCE CO. LTD.	42	0	42
ICICI LOMBARD GENERAL INSURANCE CO. LTD.	1107	68	1175
IFFCO-TOKIO GENERAL INSURANCE CO. LTD.	1103	41	1144
THE NEW INDIA ASSURANCE CO. LTD.	5837	3525	9362
NATIONAL INSURANCE CO. LTD.	5633	3245	8878
THE ORIENTAL INSURANCE CO. LTD.	6879	3344	10223
RELIANCE GENERAL INSURANCE CO. LTD.	161	8	169
ROYAL SUNDARAM ALLIANCE INSURANCE CO. LTD	114	32	146
UNITED INDIA INSURANCE CO. LTD.	4344	2859	7203
Sub Total	27,180	13,371	40,551
GRAND TOTAL	**436,607**	**325,640**	**762,247**

STATEMENT 54

INDIVIDUAL NEW BUSINESS PERFORMANCE OF LIFE INSURERS FOR 2007-08 — CHANNEL WISE

(Premium in Rs Crore) (Policies in nos.)

Life Insurer	*Individual Agents*		*Corporate Agents*				*Brokers*		*Direct Selling*		*Total Individual New Business*		*Referrals*	
			Banks		*Others**									
	Policies	Premium	Policies	Premium	Policies	Premium	Policies	Premium	Policies	Premium	Policies	Premium	Policies	Premium
1	2	3	4	5	6	7	8	9	10	11	12	13	14	15
Aviva**	204183	307.80	24208	87.89	1094	1.62	15097	42.02	143760	571.36	388342	1010.69	143640	562.82
	(52.58)	(30.45)	(6.23)	(8.70)	(0.28)	(0.16)	(3.89)	(4.16)	(37.02)	(56.53)			(36.99)	(55.69)
Bajaj Allianz	2029281	4155.80	84802	216.09	1452756	1727.38	23423	39.43	154084	347.90	3744346	6486.60	107114	269.63
	(54.20)	(64.07)	(2.26)	(3.33)	(38.80)	(26.63)	(0.63)	(0.61)	(4.12)	(5.36)			(2.86)	(4.16)
Bharti Axa	40419	61.35	669	0.94	-	-	3695	7.83	29291	39.87	74074	109.98	-	-
	(54.57)	(55.78)	(0.90)	(0.86)	-	-	(4.99)	(7.12)	(39.54)	(36.25)			-	-
Birla Sunlife	588797	1127.35	44040	485.61	19090	48.35	36302	73.99	82	0.23	688311	1735.53	4551	8.67
	(85.54)	(64.96)	(6.40)	(27.98)	(2.77)	(2.79)	(5.27)	(4.26)	(0.01)	(0.01)			(0.66)	(0.50)
Future Generali	468	0.18	-	-	-	-	48	0.01	284	0.22	800	0.41	-	-
	(58.50)	(42.69)	-	-	-	-	(6.00)	(2.63)	(35.50)	(54.68)			-	-
HDFC Std	666932	1289.01	204948	951.97	12542	25.14	3891	7.25	60299	75.19	948612	2348.57	8713	15.90
	(70.31)	(54.89)	(21.61)	(40.53)	(1.32)	(1.07)	(0.41)	(0.31)	(6.36)	(3.20)			(0.92)	(0.68)
ICICI Pru	1700548	4528.93	256027	1253.01	271196	657.55	26645	81.99	658694	522.82	2913110	7044.30	580672	283.18
	(58.38)	(64.29)	(8.79)	(17.79)	(9.31)	(9.33)	(0.91)	(1.16)	(22.61)	(7.42)			(19.93)	(4.02)
IDBI Fortis	1200	2.55	1954	9.34	-	-	4	0.01	-	-	3158	11.90	-	-
	(38.00)	(21.42)	(61.87)	(78.47)	-	-	(0.13)	(0.11)	-	-			-	-
ING Vysya	268486	518.85	39694	68.24	16002	31.21	589	1.73	35298	74.93	360069	694.97	35298	74.96
	(74.57)	(74.66)	(11.02)	(9.82)	(4.44)	(4.49)	(0.16)	(0.25)	(9.80)	(10.78)			(9.80)	(10.79)
Kotak Mahindra	139566	475.68	32069	206.70	107103	193.05	19116	58.06	15636	41.55	313490	975.04	1190	2.91
	(44.52)	(48.79)	(10.23)	(21.20)	(34.16)	(19.80)	(6.10)	(5.95)	(4.99)	(4.26)			(0.38)	(0.30)
Max NewYork	508319	988.02	35879	95.10	299469	416.02	5074	15.15	24590	41.86	873331	1556.16	3810	8.13
	(58.20)	(63.49)	(4.11)	(6.11)	(34.29)	(26.73)	(0.58)	(0.97)	(2.82)	(2.69)			(0.44)	(0.52)
MetLife	117313	310.52	100416	453.20	12607	6.68	4816	14.70	-	-	235152	785.10	55521	261.91
	(49.89)	(39.55)	(42.70)	(57.73)	(5.36)	(0.85)	(2.05)	(1.87)	-	-			(23.61)	(33.36)
Reliance Life	567657	1305.73	1766	3.73	71517	135.10	27563	59.98	405212	834.53	1073715	2339.06	378285	775.96
	(52.87)	(55.82)	(0.16)	(0.16)	(6.66)	(5.78)	(2.57)	(2.56)	(37.74)	(35.68)			(35.23)	(33.17)
Sahara	108972	121.47	-	-	112	0.64	-	-	-	-	109084	122.11	-	-
	(99.90)	(99.48)	-	-	(0.10)	(0.52)	-	-	-	-			-	-
SBI Life	559789	2145.29	351292	1570.38	12177	19.78	2137	6.26	134	0.87	925529	3742.58	-	-
	(60.48)	(57.32)	(37.96)	(41.96)	(1.32)	(0.53)	(0.23)	(0.17)	(0.01)	(0.02)			-	-
Shriram	74948	219.10	-	-	3272	8.36	305	0.83	30604	81.57	109129	309.85	30604	81.57
	(68.68)	(70.71)	-	-	(3.00)	(2.70)	(0.28)	(0.27)	(28.04)	(26.32)			(28.04)	(26.32)

1	2	3	4	5	6	7	8	9	10	11	12	13	14	15
Tata AIG	341189	447.59	43399	286.16	74996	48.42	21484	41.51	15881	9.81	496949	833.50	-	-
	(68.66)	(53.70)	(8.73)	(34.33)	(15.09)	(5.81)	(4.32)	(4.98)	(3.20)	(1.18)			-	-
Private Total	7918067	18005.22	1221163	5688.36	2353933	3319.31	190189	450.76	1573849	2642.71	13257201	30106.35	1349398	2345.63
	(59.73)	(59.81)	(9.21)	(18.89)	(17.76)	(11.03)	(1.43)	(1.50)	(11.87)	(8.78)			(10.18)	(7.79)
LIC #	36834544	48510.21	472447	640.86	245790	142.58	37214	22.97	-	-	37589995	49316.62	-	-
	(97.99)	(98.36)	(1.26)	(1.30)	(0.65)	(0.29)	(0.10)	(0.05)		-			-	-
Industry Total	44752611	66515.43	1693610	6329.22	2599723	3461.89	227403	473.73	1573849	2642.71	50847196	79422.97	1349398	2345.63
	(88.01)	(83.75)	(3.33)	(7.97)	(5.11)	(4.36)	(0.45)	(0.60)	(3.10)	(3.33)			(2.65)	(2.95)

Note: (1) Figures in brackets show percentage to total individual new business of each insurer procured through the respective channel

(2) New business premium includes first year premium and single premium. *Any entity other than banks but licensed as a corporate agent.

(3) The leads obtained through referral arrangements have been included in the respective channels. # Does not include its overseas new business premium

** It has been confirmed by the insurer that the no. of policies have been taken net of all cancellations including freelooks during the financial year.

STATEMENT 55

GROUP NEW BUSINESS PERFORMANCE OF LIFE INSURERS FOR 2007-08 — CHANNEL WISE

(Premium in Rs Crore) (Schemes and lives in nos.)

Business Insurer	Individual Agents			Corporate Agents						Brokers			Direct Selling			Total Group New			Referrals		
				Banks			Others*														
	Schemes	Lives covered	Premium	Schemes	Lives covered	Premium	Schemes	Lives covered	Premium	Schemes	Lives covered	Premium	Schemes	Lives covered	Premium	Schemes	Lives covered	Premium	Schemes	Lives covered	Premium
1	2	3	4	5	6	7	8	9	10	11	12	13	14	15	16	17	18	19	20	21	22
Aviva	28	5036	5.62	1	14263	0.57	9	350885	2.08	6	10383	0.72	72	288693	34.28	116	669260	43.27	-	-	-
	(24.14)	(0.75)	(12.99)	(0.86)	(2.13)	(1.32)	(7.76)	(52.43)	(4.81)	(5.17)	(1.55)	(1.66)	(62.07)	(43.14)	(79.22)				-	-	-
Bajaj Allianz	-	-	-	-	1402	0.64	-	1238	3.81	-	-	-	396	1996685	183.43	396	1999325	187.89	-	-	-
	-	-	-	-	(0.07)	(0.34)	-	(0.06)	(2.03)	-	-	-	(100.00)	(99.87)	(97.63)				-	-	-
Bharti Axa	-	-	-	1	1462	3.24	3	7550	0.02	-	-	-	-	-	-	4	9012	3.25	-	-	-
	-	-	-	(25.00)	(16.22)	(99.41)	(75.00)	(83.78)	(0.59)	-	-	-	-	-	-				-	-	-
Birla Sunlife	-	-	-	-	-	-	-	-	-	-	-	-	148	160755	223.34	148	160755	223.34	-	-	-
	-	-	-	-	-	-	-	-	-	-	-	-	(100.00)	(100.00)	(100.00)				-	-	-
Future Generali	-	-	-	-	-	-	-	-	-	8	45745	0.97	1	25871	1.11	9	71616	2.08	-	-	-
	-	-	-	-	-	-	-	-	-	(88.89)	(63.88)	(46.41)	(11.11)	(36.12)	(53.59)				-	-	-
HDFC Std	-	-	-	-	-	-	-	-	-	-	-	-	246	293614	336.80	246	293614	336.80	-	-	-
	-	-	-	-	-	-	-	-	-	-	-	-	(100.00)	(100.00)	(100.00)				-	-	-
ICICI Pru	5	9383	3.08	2	149317	95.38	-	13229	0.20	10	3415	48.57	101	451506	843.22	118	626850	990.45	1	2052	1.63
	(4.24)	(1.50)	(0.31)	(1.69)	(23.82)	(9.63)	-	(2.11)	(0.02)	(8.47)	(0.54)	(4.90)	(85.59)	(72.03)	(85.13)				(0.85)	(0.33)	(0.16)
IDBI Fortis	-	-	-	-	-	-	-	-	-	-	-	-	-	-	-				-	-	-
	-	-	-	-	-	-	-	-	-	-	-	-	-	-	-				-	-	-
ING Vysya	-	-	-	-	-	-	-	-	-	8	1611	0.16	18	123169	9.31	26	124780	9.48	1	131	0.01
	-	-	-	-	-	-	-	-	-	(30.77)	(1.29)	(1.72)	(69.23)	(98.71)	(98.28)				(3.85)	(0.10)	(0.07)
Kotak Mahindra	-	-	-	-	-	-	-	-	-	149	251277	24.99	132	398860	106.59	281	650137	131.58	-	-	-
	-	-	-	-	-	-	-	-	-	(53.02)	(38.65)	(18.99)	(46.98)	(61.35)	(81.01)				-	-	-
Max NewYork	267	216447	7.77	1	166058	27.05	-	-	-	-	-	-	14	106997	6.85	282	489502	41.67	-	-	-
	(94.68)	(44.22)	(18.64)	(0.35)	(33.92)	(64.91)	-	-	-	-	-	-	(4.96)	(21.86)	(16.45)				-	-	-
MetLife	9	19446	0.68	-	-	-	2	2488	0.22	4	60859	4.50	63	148165	34.85	78	230958	40.26	-	-	-
	(11.54)	(8.42)	(1.70)	-	-	-	(2.56)	(1.08)	(0.55)	(5.13)	(26.35)	(11.18)	(80.77)	(64.15)	(86.57)				-	-	-
Reliance Life	-	-	-	-	-	-	-	-	-	99	287046	8.95	263	462236	403.04	362	749282	411.99	-	-	-
	-	-	-	-	-	-	-	-	-	(27.35)	(38.31)	(2.17)	(72.65)	(61.69)	(97.83)				-	-	-
Sahara	-	-	-	-	-	-	8	371	0.004	-	-	-	-	-	-	8	371	0.004	-	-	-
	-	-	-	-	-	-	(100.00)	(100.00)	(100.00)	-	-	-	-	-	-				-	-	-
SBI Life	-	-	-	-	965023	318.69	2	109366	16.92	-	-	-	91	62182	714.64	93	1136571	1050.24	-	-	-
	-	-	-	-	(84.91)	(30.34)	(2.15)	(9.62)	(1.61)	-	-	-	(97.85)	(5.47)	(68.05)				-	-	-
Shriram	-	-	-	-	-	-	-	-	-	-	-	-	6	15429	0.14	6	15429	0.14	-	-	-
	-	-	-	-	-	-	-	-	-	-	-	-	(100.00)	(100.00)	(100.00)				-	-	-

1	2	3	4	5	6	7	8	9	10	11	12	13	14	15	16	17	18	19	20	21	22
Tata AIG	7	1575	0.31	-	-	-	-	-	-	10	46262	4.33	64	535176	126.37	81	583013	131.01	-	-	-
	(8.64)	(0.27)	(0.23)	-	-	-	-	-	-	(12.35)	(7.93)	(3.31)	(79.01)	(91.79)	(96.46)				-	-	-
Private Total	316	251887	17.46	5	1297525	445.56	24	485127	23.25	294	706598	93.18	1615	5069338	3023.99	2254	7810475	3603.45	2	2183	1.64
	(14.02)	(3.22)	(0.48)	(0.22)	(16.61)	(12.36)	(1.06)	(6.21)	(0.65)	(13.04)	(9.05)	(2.59)	(71.65)	(64.90)	(83.92)				(0.09)	(0.03)	(0.05)
LIC	3766	4984410	1077.82	760	470428	47.13	254	189085	17.58	168	14218	6.37	17656	2108000	9507.48	22604	26738141	10656.38	-	-	-
	(16.66)	(18.64)	(10.11)	(3.36)	(1.76)	(0.44)	(1.12)	(0.71)	(0.16)	(0.74)	(0.05)	(0.06)	(78.11)	(78.84)	(89.22)				-	-	-
Industry Total	4082	5236297	1095.28	765	1767953	492.69	278	674212	40.83	462	720816	99.55	19271	26149338	12531.47	24858	34548616	14259.83	2	2183	1.64
	(16.42)	(15.16)	(7.68)	(3.08)	(5.12)	(3.46)	(1.12)	(1.95)	(0.29)	(1.86)	(2.09)	(0.70)	(77.52)	(75.69)	(87.88)				(0.01)	(0.01)	(0.01)

Note: (1) Figures in brackets show percentage to total group new business of each insurer procured through the respective channel.

(2) New business premium includes first year premium and single premium.

(3) The leads obtained through referral arrangements have been included in the respective channels.

* Any entity other than banks but licensed as a corporate agent.

FEE STRUCTURE FOR INSURERS AND VARIOUS INTERMEDIARIES

Sl. No.	*Processing Fee*	*Registration Fee*	*Renewal Fee*	*Periodicity of Renewal*	
1.	Insurers (Life/Non life/ Reinsurance)		Rs. 50,000	1/10th of 1 per cent of Gross Direct Premium written in India subject to minimum of Rs. 50,000 and maximum of Rs. 5 crore	Every year (by 31st December)
2.	Third Party Administrators	Rs. 20,000	Rs. 30,000	Rs. 30,000	3 years
3.	Brokers Direct Broker		Application Fee: Rs. 20,000 Renewal Fee: Rs. 1,000	A sum calculated at the rate of 0.50 per cent of remuneration earned in the preceding financial year subject to minimum of Rs. 25,000 and maximum of Rs. 1,00,000	3 years
	Reinsurance Broker		Application Fee: Rs. 25,000 Renewal Fee: Rs. 1,000	A sum calculated at the rate of 0.50 per cent of remuneration earned in the preceding financial year subject to minimum of Rs. 75,000 and maximum of Rs. 3,00,000	3 years
	Composite Broker		Application Fee: Rs.40,000 Renewal Fee: Rs. 1,000	A sum calculated at the rate of 0.50 per cent of remuneration earned in the preceding financial year subject to minimum of Rs. 1,25,000 and maximum of Rs. 5,00,000	3 years
4.	Surveyors and Loss Assessors				
	Individual Category	A	Rs.10,000	Rs. 200 for every category	5 years
		B	Rs. 7,500		
		C	Rs. 5,000		
	Corporate Category	A	Rs. 25,000	Rs. 200 for every category	5 years
		B	Rs. 20,000		
		C	Rs. 15,000		
5.	Corporate Agents		Rs. 250 for corporate insurance executive Rs.500 for specified person	Rs. 200	3 years

INSURANCE OMBUDSMEN

Sl.No.	Centre	Ombudsman	Postal Address	Contact Details
1.	Ahmedabad	Mr. Amitabh	2nd Floor, Ambica House, Near C.U. Shah College, 5 Navyug Colony, Ashram Road, Ahmedabad – 380 014	Tel: 079-27546150, 27546139 Fax:079-27546142 E-mail: insombahd@rediffmail.com
2.	Bhopal	Mr. N.A. Khan	Janak Vihar Complex, 2nd Floor, Malviya Nagar, Bhopal – 462 011	Tel: 0755-2769201, 2769202, Fax:0755-2769203 E-mail:bimalokpalbhopal@airtelbroadband.in
3.	Bhubaneswar	Mr. S.K. Dhal	62, Forest Park, Bhubaneswar–751009	Tel: 0674- 2596461 (direct) Fax:0674-2596429 Email : ioobbsr@dataone.in
4.	Chandigarh	Mr. K.M. Chadha	S.C.O. No.101-103, 2nd Floor, Batra Building,Section 17-D, Chandigarh – 160 017	Tel: 0172 - 2706196 Fax: 0172-2708274 E-mail : ombchd@yahoo.co.in
5.	Chennai	Mr. K. Sridhar	Fatima Akhtar Court, 4th Floor, 453 (old 312)Anna Salai, Teynampet, Chennai – 600 018	Tel: 044 - 24333678 Fax: 044-24333664 E-mail : insombud@md4.vsnl.net.in
6.	Delhi	Mr. R. Beri	2/2 A, 1st Floor, Universal Insurance Bldg. Asaf Ali RoadNew Delhi – 110 002	Tel: 011-23239611 Fax: 011-23230858 E-mail : iobdelraj@rediffmail.com
7.	Guwahati	Mr. Sarat Chandra Sarma	Jeevan Nivesh, 5th Floor, Nr. Panbazar Overbridge S.R. RoadGuwahati – 781 001	Tel: 0361-2131307 Fax: 0361-2732937 E-mail : omb_ghy@sify.com
8.	Hyderabad	Mr. P.A. Chowdary	6-2-46, 1st Floor, 'Moin Court' Lane Opp. Saleem Function Palace, A.C. Guards, Lakdi-ka-pul, Hyderabad – 500 004	Tel: 040-23325325 Fax:040-23376599 E-mail : hyd2_insombud@sancharnet.in
9.	Ernakulam	Mr. James Muricken	2nd Flr., CC 27/ 2603, Pulinat Building, Opp. Cochin Shipyard, M.G. Road, ERNAKULAM - 682 015	Tel: 0484-2358734 Fax:0484-2359336 E-mail: iokochi@asianetglobal.com
10.	Kolkata	Mr. K. Rangabha-shyam	North British Building, 29, N.S.Road,3rd Floor, Kolkata – 700 001	Tel: 033-22134869 Fax: 033-22134868 E-mail : iombkol@vsnl.net
11.	Lucknow	Mr. M.S. Pratap	Jeevan Bhawan Phase-2, 6th FloorNawal Kishore Road, HazratganjLucknow – 226 001	Tel: 0522-2201188 Fax:0522-2231310 E-mail: ioblko@sancharnet.in
12.	Mumbai	Mr. R.K. Vashishtha	3rd Floor, Jeevan Seva Annexe, Above MTNL,S.V. Road, Santacruz (W), Mumbai-400054	Tel: 022-226106928 Fax: 022-26106052 Email: ombudsman@vsnl.net

39.10 OMBUDSMAN

Ombudsman traces its history to Sweden way back in 19th century and it literally means an authority that is empowered to investigate individual complaints against public authorities, departments etc. Later it has been adopted in many countries including UK, Australia etc.

In India the idea of insurance ombudsman was first mooted in the year 1998. Central government by the powers conferred on it by sub section (1) section 114 of insurance act 1938 has set up an ombudsman specifically for Insurance sector. Main objective of insurance ombudsman is redressal and settlement of disputes arising between insured and insurer. Insurance ombudsman is a quasi-judicial body established for speedy settlement of disputes in fair, impartial and judicial manner.

Any individual policyholder (including a sole proprietor but not partnerships or companies) or his legal heir can approach the Insurance Ombudsman for complaints in respect of policies on personal lines of business.

Personal lines of business include coverage under Personal Accident policies, Mediclaim, insurance of property of the individual such as motor vehicles, household articles etc. There is no fee or charge required to be paid and there is no requirement to approach the Ombudsman through a lawyer. However, before approaching Ombudsman, a representation should be made to the insurance Company. If no reply is received within one month or the reply is not satisfactory, the Ombudsman can be approached. The maximum limit for the amount under dispute for which the Ombudsman can entertain is Rs.20 lakhs and Complaints can be made to Ombudsman within one year of the rejection by insurer of the representation of the complainant or the insurer's final reply to the Complainant's representation.

Types of Complaints

The insurance ombudsman may consider or receives the complaints regarding :

- Partial or total repudiation of claims
- Delay in settlement of claims
- Legal construction of policy(policy wordings)
- Premium paid or payable
- Non-issue of insurance documents to customers after receipt of premium.

An insurance ombudsman cannot act on :

- Any complaint which falls outside the territorial limits of the ombudsman
- Any complaint where the claims amount is more than 20 lakhs.
- Any dispute/issue/complaint which is under trial in any other judicial or quasi-judicial body.
- Where the complaint is not regarding personal lines of business.
- Where the complaint is filed by any artificial judicial person
- Any complaint which is lodged after one year from the date of issue of first reply by the insurer.

Procedure for Redressel

1. The insured has to apply in writing to the IO under whose jurisdiction the insurer falls. A complaint may be filed either by the insured or his legal heirs and should clearly state the name and address of the insurer against whom the complaint is made, nature and circumstances giving rise to dispute, nature of loss sustained by the complainant and relief sought from IO.
2. The complainant has to substantiate his claim with all the documentary evidences.

3. The IO would first act as a mediator to settle the grievance on a mutually agreeable basis. This mediation process would be for a maximum of one month. After hearing both the parties IO may pass an award, which if acceptable to the complainant, is sent to insurer for final execution. Insurer has to comply with the award within 15 days and it has to be informed to the IO.
4. If the grievance is not settled on a mutually agreeable basis, IO gives a speaking award within a period not exceeding three months. If the complainant is not satisfied with the award, he can appeal in any other forum or court, however such facility is not available to the insurer.
5. An award passed by the IO has to be complied with, by the insurer within the 15 days. However, no action lies if the insurer opts for non-compliance of the award because he no judicial powers for the execution of award compared to other judicial systems like consumer forums, civil courts etc.

No advocates are allowed to represent insurer/complainant to argue their respective cases. Further IO being a non-judicial authority, does not have the powers of summoning particular persons/witness and examining them on oath. Another specific feature of IO is that it can pass award for ex-gratia settlement of disputes, while such powers of exgratia settlement are not vested with other redressal mechanisms such as consumer courts etc.

39.11 LOK ADALATS

The enactments or legal aid boards of state governments establish Lok Adalat (Lok Nyayalaya). It settles dispute through conciliation and compromise. Lok Adalat accepts the cases which could be settled by conciliation and compromise, and pending in the regular courts within their jurisdiction. As per Chapter XI of the Lok Nyayalaya Rules, 1986, special provisions are made to settle amicably the cases pending before MACT.

Since April 1985, Lok Adalats have been exclusively organised for settlement of motor third party claims. Although the concept of Lok Adalat was very much vogue since early years. This form was made available for settlement of Motor Third Party claims under the initiative of former Chief Justice of India, Shri. P. N. Bhagwati.

The First Lok Adalat was held in Chennai in 1986.The Lok Adalat is presided over by a sitting or retired judicial officer as the chairman, with two other members, usually a lawyer and a social worker. There is no court fee. If the case is already filed in the regular court, the fee paid will be refunded if the dispute is settled at the Lok Adalat. The procedural laws, and the Evidence Act are not strictly followed while assessing the merits of the claim by the Lok Adalat.

The primary requisite for seeking relief in Lok Adalat is that both parties in dispute should agree for settlement and its decision is binding on the parties to the dispute and its order is capable of execution through legal process. No appeal lies against the order of the Lok Adalat.

Lok Adalats have been successful in settling huge number of Third Party claims referred by Motor Accident Claim Tribunal (MACT). Except matters relating to offences, which are not compoundable, a Lok Adalat has jurisdiction to deal with all matters. Matters pending or at pre-trial stage, provided a reference is made to it by a court or by the concerned authority or committee, when the dispute is at a pre-trial stage and not before a Court of Law it can be referred to Lok Adalat.

Legal Services Authorities Act was promulgated in 1987, which aimed to organise Lok Adalat to secure that the operation of legal system promotes justice on the basis of an equal opportunity. The Act gives statutory recognition to the resolution of disputes by compromise and settlement by the Lok Adalats.

According to Legal Services Authorities (Amendment) Act 1994, Lok Adalat settlement is no longer a voluntary concept. By this Act, Lok Adalat has got statutory character and has been legally recognised.

Constitution of Lok Adalats

Section 18 – Organisation of Lok Adalats

(1) Every State Authority or District Authority or the Supreme Court Legal Services Committee or every High Court Legal Services Committee or, as the case may be, Taluk Legal Services Committee may organise Lok Adalats at such intervals and places and for exercising such jurisdiction and for such areas as it thinks fit.

(2) Every Lok Adalat organised for an area shall consist of such number of -

(a) serving or retired judicial officers; and

(b) other persons,

of the area as may be specified by the State Authority or the District Authority or the Supreme Court Legal Services Committee or the High Court Legal Services Committee, or as the case may be, the Taluk Legal Services Committee, organising such Lok Adalats.

(3) The experience and qualifications of other persons referred to in clause (b) of sub-section (2) for Lok Adalats organised by the Supreme Court Legal Services Committee shall be such as may be prescribed by the Central Government in consultation with the Chief Justice of India.

(4) The experience and qualifications of other persons referred to in clause (b) of sub-section (2) for Lok Adalats other than referred to in sub-section (3) shall be such as may be prescribed by the State Government in consultation with the Chief Justice of the High Court.

(5) A Lok Adalat shall have jurisdiction to determine and to arrive at a compromise or settlement between the parties to a dispute in respect of -

(i) any case pending before; or

(ii) any matter which is falling within the jurisdiction of, and is not brought before, any court for which the Lok Adalat is organised.

Provided that the Lok Adalat shall have no jurisdiction in respect of any case or matter relating to an offence not compoundable under any law.

Section 19

1. Central, State, District and Taluk Legal Services Authority has been created who are responsible for organising Lok Adalats at such intervals and place.
2. Conciliators for Lok Adalat comprise the following:

A. A sitting or retired judicial officer.

B. other persons of repute as may be prescribed by the State Government in consultation with the Chief Justice of High Court.

Reference of Cases

Section 20 : Cases can be referred for consideration of Lok Adalat as under:-

1. By consent of both the parties to the disputes.
2. One of the parties makes an application for reference.
3. Where the Court is satisfied that the matter is an appropriate one to be taken cognisance of by the Lok Adalat.
4. The principles of justice, equity, fair play and other legal principles shall guide compromise settlement.
5. Where no compromise has been arrived at through conciliation, the matter shall be returned to the concerned court for disposal in accordance with Law.

Effect of the Orders

Section 21 - After the agreement is arrived by the consent of the parties, award is passed by the conciliators. The matter need not be referred to the concerned Court for consent decree.

1. Award of Lok Adalat : (1) Every award of the Lok Adalat shall be deemed to be a decree of a civil court or, as the case may be, an order of any other court and where a compromise or settlement has been arrived at, by a Lok Adalat in a case referred to it under sub-section (1) of Section 20, the court-fee paid in such case shall be refunded in the manner provided under the Court Fees Act, 1870 (7 of 1870).

(2) Every award made by a Lok Adalat shall be final and binding on all the parties to the dispute, and no appeal shall lie to any court against the award.

Proceedings to be Recognised as Judicial

Every proceedings of the Lok Adalat shall be deemed to be judicial proceedings for the purpose of summoning of witnesses, discovery of documents, reception of evidences, requisitioning of Public record etc.

Section 22 - **Powers of Lok Adalats :** (1) The Lok Adalat shall, for the purposes of holding any determination under this Act, have the same powers as are vested in a civil court under the Code of Civil Procedure, 1908 (5 of 1908), while trying a suit in respect of the following matters, namely :

(a) the summoning and enforcing the attendance of any witness and examining him on oath;

(b) the discovery and production of any document;

(c) the reception of evidence on affidavits;

(d) the requisitioning of any public record or document or copy of such record or document from any court or office; and

(e) such other matters as may be prescribed.

(2) Without prejudice to the generality of the powers contained in sub-section(1), every Lok Adalat shall have the requisite powers to specify its own procedure for the determination of any dispute coming before it.

(3) All proceedings before a Lok Adalat shall be deemed to be judicial proceedings within the meaning of Sections 193, 219 and 228 of the Indian Penal Code (45 of 1860) and every Lok Adalat shall be deemed to be a civil court for the purpose of Section 195 and Chapter XXVI of the Code of Criminal Procedure, 1973(2 of 1974).

ANNEXURE 39-A

THE GAZETTE OF INDIA : EXTRAORDINARY

[PART III – SEC. 4]

INSURANCE REGULATORY AND DEVELOPMENT AUTHORITY,
NEW DELHI

NOTIFICATION

New Delhi, the 14th July, 2000

Insurance Regulatory and Development Authority (Licensing of Insurance Agents) Regulations, 2000

F.No.IRDA/Reg./7/2000.–

In exercise of the powers conferred by sub-section (6) of Section 42 and clauses (k), (l), (m), (n), (o) and (p) of sub-section (2) of Section 114A of the Insurance Act, 1938 (4 of 1938), the Authority, in consultation with the Insurance Advisory Committee, hereby makes the following regulations, namely:

1. Short Title and Commencement: (1) These regulations may be called Insurance Regulatory and Development Authority (Licensing of Insurance Agents) Regulations, 2000.

(2) They shall come into force on the date of their publication in the *Official Gazette*.

2. Definitions: In these regulations, unless the context otherwise requires, –

(a) *"Act"* means the Insurance Act, 1938 (4 of 1938);

(b) *"Approved Institution"* means an Institution engaged in education and/or training particularly in the area of insurance sales, service and marketing, approved and notified by the Authority;

(c) *"Authority"* means the Insurance Regulatory and Development Authority established under the provisions of Section 3 of the Insurance Regulatory and Development Authority Act, 1999 (41 of 1999);

(d) *"Composite insurance agent"* means an insurance agent who holds a licence to act as an insurance agent for a life insurer and a general insurer;

(e) *"Corporate Agent"* means a person other than an individual as specified in clause (i);

(f) *"Designated person"* means an officer normally in charge of marketing operations, as specified by an insurer, and authorised by the Authority to issue or renew licences under these regulations;

(g) *"Examination Body"* means an Institution, which conducts pre-recruitment tests for insurance agents and which is duly recognised by the Authority;

(h) *"Licence"* means a certificate of licence to act as an insurance agent issued under these regulations;

(i) *"Person"* means ---

(i) an individual;

(ii) a firm; or

(iii) a company formed under the Companies Act, 1956 (1 of 1956), and includes a banking company as defined in clause (4A) of section 2 of the Act;

(j) *"Practical Training"* includes orientation, particularly in the area of insurance sales, service and marketing, through training modules as approved by the Authority;

(k) *"Proposal form"* means an application for purchase of an insurance product which shall be the basis of insurance contract;

(*l*) *"Prospect"* means a potential purchaser of an insurance product;

(*m*) *"Recognised Board or Institution"* means such board or institution as may be recognised by any State Government or the Central Government.

All words and expressions used herein and not defined but defined in the Insurance Act, 1938(4 of 1938), or in the Insurance Regulatory and Development Authority Act, 1999 (41 of 1999), shall have the meanings respectively assigned to them in those Acts.

3. Issue or Renewal of Licence: (1) A person desiring to obtain or renew a licence (hereinafter referred to as "the applicant") to act as an insurance agent or a composite insurance agent shall proceed as follows:-

(a) the applicant shall make an application to a designated person —

(i) in Form IRDA-Agents-VA, if the applicant is an individual;

(ii) in Form IRDA-Agents-VC, if the applicant is a firm or a company:

Provided that the applicant, who desires to be a composite insurance agent, shall make two separate applications.

(b) The fees payable by the applicant to the Authority shall be as specified in Regulation 7.

(2) The designated person may, on receipt of the application along with the evidence of payment of fees to the Authority, and on being satisfied that the applicant, —

(i) possesses the qualifications as specified under Regulation 4;

(ii) possesses the practical training as specified under Regulation 5;

(iii) has passed the examination as specified under Regulation 6;

(iv) has furnished the application complete in all respects;

(v) has the requisite knowledge to solicit and procure insurance business; and

(vi) is capable of providing the necessary service to the policyholders;

grant or renew, as the case may be, a licence in Form IRDA-Agents-VB, along with identity card in Form IRDA-Agents-VZ:

Provided that in the case of a corporate agent, the identity card shall be in Form IRDA-Agent-VY.

Provided further that such identity card from one life insurer and such identity card from one general insurer shall be provided to the applicant seeking licence to act as a composite insurance agent.

Provided further that in the case of a firm or a company, all of its partners or directors, as the case may be, shall fulfil the requirements of sub-clauses (i) to (iii).

Provided further a licence issued in accordance with this regulation shall entitle the applicant to act as insurance agent for one life insurer or one general insurer or both, as the case may be.

(3) If the designated person refuses to grant or renew a licence under this regulation, he shall give the reasons therefor to the applicant.

4. Qualifications of the Applicant: The applicant shall possess the minimum qualification of a pass in 12th Standard or equivalent examination conducted by any recognised Board/Institution, where the applicant resides in a place with a population of five thousand or more as per the last census, and a pass in 10th Standard or equivalent examination from a recognised Board/ Institution if the applicant resides in any other place.

5. Practical Training: (1) The applicant shall have completed from an approved institution, at least, one hundred hours' practical training in life or general insurance business, as the case may be, which may be spread over three to four weeks, where such applicant is seeking licence for the first time to act as insurance agent.

Provided that the applicant shall have completed from an approved institution, at least, one hundred fifty hours' practical training in life and general insurance business, which may be spread over six to eight weeks, where such applicant is seeking licence for the first time to act as a composite insurance agent.

(2) Where the applicant, referred to under sub-regulation (1), is —

(i) an Associate/Fellow of the Insurance Institute of India, Mumbai;

(ii) an Associate/Fellow of the Institute of Chartered Accountants of India, New Delhi;

(iii) an Associate/Fellow of the Institute of Costs and Works Accountants of India, Calcutta;

(iv) an Associate/Fellow of the Institute of Company Secretaries of India, New Delhi;

(v) an Associate/Fellow of the Actuarial Society of India, Mumbai;

(vi) a Master of Business Administration of any Institution / University recognised by any State Government or the Central Government; or

(vii) possessing any professional qualification in marketing from any Institution / University recognised by any State Government or the Central Government—

he shall have completed, at least, fifty hours' practical training from an approved institution.

Provided that such applicant shall have completed from an approved institution, at least, seventy hours' practical training in life and general insurance business, where such applicant is seeking licence for the first time to act as a composite insurance agent.

(3) An applicant, who has been granted a licence after the commencement of these regulations, before seeking renewal of licence to act as an insurance agent, shall have completed, at least twenty-five hours' practical training in life or general insurance business, as the case may be, from an approved institution.

Provided that such applicant before seeking renewal of licence to act as a composite insurance agent shall have completed from an approved institution, at least, fifty hours' practical training in life and general insurance business.

6. Examination: The Applicant shall have passed the pre-recruitment examination in life or general insurance business, or both, as the case may be, conducted by the Insurance Institute of India, Mumbai, or any other examination body.

7. Fees Payable: (1) The fees payable to the Authority for issue or renewal of licence to act as insurance agent or a composite insurance agent shall be rupees two hundred and fifty.

(2) The additional fees payable to the Authority, under the circumstances mentioned in sub-section (3) of Section 42 of the Act, shall be rupees one hundred.

8. Code of Conduct: (1) Every person holding a licence, shall adhere to the code of conduct specified below:

(i) Every insurance agent shall, —

(a) identify himself and the insurance company of whom he is an insurance agent;

(b) disclose his licence to the prospect on demand;

(c) disseminate the requisite information in respect of insurance products offered for sale by his insurer and take into account the needs of the prospect while recommending a specific insurance plan;

(d) disclose the scales of commission in respect of the insurance product offered for sale, if asked by the prospect;

(e) indicate the premium to be charged by the insurer for the insurance product offered for sale;

(f) explain to the prospect the nature of information required in the proposal form by the insurer, and also the importance of disclosure of material information in the purchase of an insurance contract;

(g) bring to the notice of the insurer any adverse habits or income inconsistency of the prospect, in the form of a report (called "Insurance Agent's Confidential Report") along with every proposal submitted to the insurer, and any material fact that may adversely affect the underwriting decision of the insurer as regards acceptance of the proposal, by making all reasonable enquiries about the prospect;

(h) inform promptly the prospect about the acceptance or rejection of the proposal by the insurer;

(i) obtain the requisite documents at the time of filing the proposal form with the insurer; and other documents subsequently asked for by the insurer for completion of the proposal;

(j) render necessary assistance to the policyholders or claimants or beneficiaries in complying with the requirements for settlement of claims by the insurer;

(k) advise every individual policyholder to effect nomination or assignment or change of address or exercise of options, as the case may be, and offer necessary assistance in this behalf, wherever necessary;

(ii) No insurance agent shall,——

(a) solicit or procure insurance business without holding a valid licence;

(b) induce the prospect to omit any material information in the proposal form;

(c) induce the prospect to submit wrong information in the proposal form or documents submitted to the insurer for acceptance of the proposal;

(d) behave in a discourteous manner with the prospect;

(e) interfere with any proposal introduced by any other insurance agent;

(f) offer different rates, advantages, terms and conditions other than those offered by his insurer;

(g) demand or receive a share of proceeds from the beneficiary under an insurance contract;

(h) force a policyholder to terminate the existing policy and to effect a new proposal from him within three years from the date of such termination;

(i) have, in case of a corporate agent, a portfolio of insurance business under which the premium is in excess of fifty percent of total premium procured, in any year, from one person (who is not an individual) or one organisation or one group of organisations;

(j) apply for fresh licence to act as an insurance agent, if his licence was earlier cancelled by the designated person, and a period of five years has not elapsed from the date of such cancellation;

(k) become or remain a director of any insurance company;

(iii) Every insurance agent shall, with a view to conserve the insurance business already procured through him, make every attempt to ensure remittance of the premiums by the policyholders within the stipulated time, by giving notice to the policyholder orally and in writing.

9. Cancellation of licence: The designated person may cancel a licence of an insurance agent, if the insurance agent suffers, at any time during the currency of the licence, from any of the disqualifications mentioned in sub-section (4) of Section 42 of the Act, and recover from him the licence and the identity card issued earlier.

10. Issue of duplicate licence: The Authority may issue a duplicate licence, replace a licence lost, destroyed, or mutilated on payment of a fee of rupees fifty.

11. Non-application to existing insurance agents: Nothing contained in Regulations 4 to 6 of these Regulations shall apply to the existing agents before the commencement of these Regulations.

Forms Annexed:

FORM IRDA-AGENTS-VA: As per Regulation 3: APPLICATION FOR A LICENCE/ RENEWAL OF LICENCE TO ACT AS AN INSURANCE AGENT

FORM IRDA-AGENTS-VB: As per Regulation 3: APPLICATION FOR A LICENCE/ RENEWAL OF LICENCE TO ACT AS AN INSURANCE AGENT

FORM IRDA-AGENTS-VC: As per Regulation 3: APPLICATION FROM A FIRM OR COMPANY FOR A LICENCE/ RENEWAL OF LICENCE TO ACT AS AN INSURANCE AGENT

FORM IRDA-AGENTS-VZ: As per Regulation 3: Agent's Identity Card

FORM IRDA-AGENTS-VY: As per Regulation 3: Corporate Agent's Identity Card.

ANNEXURE 39-B

To be published in the Gazette of India Extraordinary,

[Part III, Section 4]

INSURANCE REGULATORY AND DEVELOPMENT AUTHORITY,
NEW DELHI

NOTIFICATION

New Delhi, the 16th October, 2002

INSURANCE REGULATORY AND DEVELOPMENT AUTHORITY (INSURANCE BROKERS) REGULATIONS, 2002

F. No, IRDA/Reg/10/ 2002 — In exercise of the powers conferred by Section 114A of the Insurance Act, 1938 (4 of 1938) read with Sections 14 and 26 of the Insurance Regulatory and Development Authority Act, 1999 (41 of 1999) the Authority in consultation with the Insurance Advisory Committee, hereby makes the following regulations, namely:

(1) **Short Title and Commencement** — (1) These regulations may be called the Insurance Regulatory and Development Authority (Insurance Brokers) Regulations, 2002.

(2) They shall come into force on the date of their publication in the *Official Gazette*.

Definitions — (1) Unless the context otherwise requires, —

(a) *"Act"* means the Insurance Act, 1938 (4 of 1938);

(b) *"Advisory Committee"* means the Advisory Committee constituted under Section 25 of the Insurance Regulatory and Development Authority Act (41 of 1999);

(c) *"Authority"* means the Insurance Regulatory and Development Authority established under sub-section (1) of Section 3 of Insurance Regulatory and Development Authority Act, 1999 (41 of 1999);

(d) *"composite broker"* means an insurance broker who for the time-being licensed by the Authority to act as such, for a remuneration, arranges insurance for his clients with insurance companies and/or reinsurance for his client/s;

(e) *"direct broker"* means an insurance broker who for the time-being licensed by the Authority to act as such, for a remuneration carries out the functions as specified under regulation 3 either in the field of life insurance or general insurance or both on behalf of his clients;

(f) *"enquiry officer"* means an officer of the Authority, or any other person having experience in insurance business, who is appointed by the Authority under regulation 37, to hold an enquiry against an insurance broker;

(g) *"form"* means the forms specified under these regulations;

(h) *"inspecting authority"* means one or more of its officers appointed by the Authority to discharge the functions stated in regulation 29;

(i) *"insurance broker"* means a person for the time-being licensed by the Authority under regulation 11, who for a remuneration arranges insurance contracts with insurance companies and/ or reinsurance companies on behalf of his clients.

Explanation: *The term "insurance broker" wherever it appears in these regulations shall be deemed to mean a direct broker, a reinsurance broker or a composite broker, as the case may be, unless expressly stated to the contrary;*

(j) *"person"* means —

(i) an individual; or

(ii) a firm; or

(iii) a company formed under the Companies Act, 1956 (1 of 1956); or

(iv) a co-operative society registered under the Co-operative Societies Act, 1912 or under any law for the registration of co-operative societies; or

(v) any other person recognized by the Authority to act as an insurance broker;

(k) *"principal officer"* means –

(i) proprietor, in the case of a proprietary concern; or

(ii) a partner, in the case of a partnership firm; or

(iii) a director, who is responsible for the activities of the insurance broking in the case of a body corporate;

(iv) or the chief executive officer appointed exclusively to carry out the functions of an insurance broker;

(l) *"regulations"* means Insurance Regulatory and Development Authority (Insurance Brokers) Regulations, 2002;

(m) *"reinsurance broker"* means an insurance broker who, for a remuneration, arranges reinsurance for direct insurers with insurance and reinsurance companies.

Words and expressions used and not defined in these regulations but defined in the Insurance Act, 1938 (4 of 1938), or the Life Insurance Corporation Act, 1956 (31 of 1956) or the General Insurance Business (Nationalisation) Act, 1972 (57 of 1972), or Insurance Regulatory and Development Authority Act, 1999 (41 of 1999) shall have the meanings respectively assigned to them in those Acts or the rules and regulations made thereunder, as the case may be.

3. Functions of a Direct Broker: The functions of a direct broker shall include any one or more of the following:

(a) obtaining detailed information of the client's business and risk management philosophy;

(b) familiarising himself with the client's business and underwriting information so that this can be explained to an insurer and others;

(c) rendering advice on appropriate insurance cover and terms;

(d) maintaining detailed knowledge of available insurance markets, as may be applicable;

(e) submitting quotation received from insurer/s for consideration of a client;

(f) providing requisite underwriting information as required by an insurer in assessing the risk to decide pricing terms and conditions for cover;

(g) acting promptly on instructions from a client and providing him written acknowledgements and progress reports;

(h) assisting clients in paying premium under Section 64 VB of Insurance Act, 1938 (4 of 1938);

(i) providing services related to insurance consultancy and risk management;

(j) assisting in the negotiation of the claims; and

(k) maintaining proper records of claims;

4. Functions of a Re-insurance Broker: The functions of a re-insurance broker shall include any one or more of the following:

(a) familiarising himself with the client's business and risk retention philosophy;

(b) maintaining clear records of the insurer's business to assist the reinsurer(s) or others;

(c) rendering advice based on technical data on the reinsurance covers available in the international insurance and the reinsurance markets;

(d) maintaining a database of available reinsurance markets, including solvency ratings of individual reinsurers;

(e) rendering consultancy and risk management services for reinsurance;

(f) selecting and recommending a reinsurer or a group of reinsurers;

(g) negotiating with a reinsurer on the client's behalf;

(h) assisting in case of commutation of reinsurance contracts placed with them;

(i) acting promptly on instructions from a client and providing it written acknowledgements and progress reports;

(j) collecting and remitting premiums and claims within such time as agreed upon;

(k) assisting in the negotiation and settlement of claims;

(l) maintaining proper records of claims; and

(m) exercising due care and diligence at the time of selection of reinsurers and international insurance brokers having regard to their respective security rating and establishing respective responsibilities at the time of engaging their services.

5. Functions of Composite Broker: A composite broker shall carry out any one or more of the functions mentioned in regulations 3 and 4.

6. Application for Grant of Licence: (1) An application by a person for grant of a licence as an insurance broker shall be made in Form A to the Authority.

(2) The application under sub-regulation (1) shall be made for any one or more of the following categories, namely:

(a) direct broker;

(b) reinsurance broker;

(c) composite broker;

alongwith the requisite fees as specified in regulation 18.

7. Application to Conform to the Requirements: An application, not complete in all respects and not conforming to the instructions specified in the Form A and these regulations, shall be rejected.

Provided that, before rejecting any such application, the applicant shall be given a reasonable opportunity to complete the application in all respects and rectify the errors, if any.

8. Furnishing of Information, Clarification and Personal Representation: (1) The Authority may require an applicant to furnish any further information or clarification for the purpose of disposal of the application, and, thereafter, in regard to any other matter as may be deemed necessary by the Authority.

(2) The applicant or its principal officer shall, if so required, appear before the Authority for a personal representation in connection with an application.

9. Consideration of Application: (1) The Authority while considering an application for grant of a licence shall take into account, all matters relevant to the carrying out of the functions by the insurance broker.

(2) Without prejudice to the above, the Authority in particular, shall take into account the following, namely:-

(A) whether the applicant is not suffering from any of the disqualifications specified under sub-section (5) of Section 42 D of the Act;

(B) whether the applicant has the necessary infrastructure, such as, adequate office space, equipment and trained manpower to effectively discharge his activities;

(C) whether the applicant has in his employment a minimum of two persons who have the necessary qualifications specified in clause (F) below and experience to conduct the business of insurance broker;

(D) whether any person, directly or indirectly connected with the applicant, has been refused in the past the grant of a licence by the Authority.

Explanation: For the purposes of this sub-clause, the expression *"directly or indirectly connected"* means a relative in the case of an individual, and in the case of a firm or a company or a body corporate, an associate, a subsidiary, an interconnected undertaking or a group company of the applicant. It is hereby clarified that these terms shall have the same meanings as ascribed to them in the Companies Act, 1956 (1 of 1956) or MRTP Act, 1969 (54 of 1969), as the case may be.

(E) whether the applicant fulfils the capital requirements as specified in regulation 10 and deposit requirements as specified in regulation 22;

(F) whether the principal officer of the applicant -

(i) possesses the minimum qualification of :

(a) Bachelors/Masters degree in Arts, Science, or Social Sciences or Commerce or its equivalent from any institution/ university recognized by any State Government or the Central Government; or

(b) Bachelor's degree in engineering or its equivalent from any institution/ university recognized by any State government or the Central Government; or

(c) Bachelor's degree in law or its equivalent from any institution/ University recognized by any State Government or the Central Government; or

(d) Masters in Business Administration or its equivalent from any institution/ university recognized by any State Government or the Central Government; or

(e) Associate/ Fellow of the Insurance Institute of India, Mumbai; or

(f) Associate/Fellow of the Institute of Risk Management, Mumbai; or

(g) Any post graduate qualification of the Institute of Insurance and Risk Management, Hyderabad; or

(h) Associate/Fellow of the Institute of Chartered Accountants of India , New Delhi; or

(i) Associate/Fellow of the Institute of Cost and Works Accountants of India, Kolkata; or

(j) Associate/Fellow of the Institute of Company Secretaries of India, New Delhi; or

(k) Associate/Fellow of the Actuarial Society of India; or

(l) Certified Associateship of the Indian Institute of Bankers, Mumbai; or

(m) Any other qualification specified from time to time by the Authority under these regulations; and

(ii) the principal officer of the applicant has received at least one hundred hours of theoretical and practical training from an institution recognised by the Authority from time to time.

Provided that where the principal officer of the applicant:

(a) has been carrying on reinsurance related activity or insurance consultancy for a continuous period of seven years, preceding the year in which such an application is made; or

(b) has for a period of, not less than seven years prior to the application made to the Authority has been a principal underwriter or has held the position of a Manager in any one of the nationalised insurance companies in India; or

(c) is an Associate/ Fellow of the Insurance Institute of India, Mumbai; or Associate/ Fellow of the Institute of Risk Management, Mumbai; or Associate/ Fellow of the Actuarial Society of India; or any post graduate qualification of the Institute of Insurance and Risk Management, Hyderabad;

(d) the theoretical and practical training from an institution recognised by the Authority from time to time according to a syllabus approved by the Authority shall be fifty hours.

(iii) has passed an examination, at the end of the period of training mentioned in the proviso above, conducted by the National Insurance Academy, Pune or any other examining body recognised by the Authority.

(G) whether the principal officer has not violated the code of conduct as specified in Schedule III to these regulations;

(H) that the applicant is not engaged in any other business other than the main objects of the applicant; and

(I) the Authority is of the opinion that the grant of licence will be in the interest of policyholders.

Exception: In the case of applications made to the Authority immediately following the notification of these regulations, the requirements under sub-regulation (2)(C) shall stand modified to the extent that instead of two qualified persons mentioned in the requirement be scaled down to one person, who should have qualified himself at the latest by the time of the grant of a licence under these regulations. This exception may be available only to applications made to the authority upto 31st March, 2003.

(3) Any employee responsible for soliciting and procuring insurance business on behalf on an insurance broker shall also have to fulfill the requirements mentioned in sub-regulations (1) and (2) above and a list of such employees need to be provided to the Authority and acknowledged by it.

10. Requirements of Capital: (1) Any applicant seeking to become an insurance broker under these regulations should satisfy the following conditions:

(i) it shall have a minimum amount of capital as mentioned below:

Category	*Minimum Amount (Rupees)*
(a) Direct broker	fifty lakhs
(b) Reinsurance broker	two hundred lakhs
(c) Composite broker	two hundred and fifty lakhs

(ii) the capital in the case of a company limited by shares and a cooperative society shall be in the form of equity shares;

(iii) the capital in the case of other applicants shall be brought in cash;

(iv) the applicant shall exclusively carry on the business of an insurance broker as licensed under these regulations.

(2) No part of the capital of an applicant shall be held by a non-Indian interest beyond 26% at any time. For the purposes of these regulations, the calculations of non-Indian interest shall be made in the same manner as specified in Insurance Regulatory And Development Authority (Registration of Indian Insurance Companies) Regulations, 2000 for an insurer.

11. Procedure for Licensing: The Authority on being satisfied that the applicant fulfills all the conditions specified for the grant of licence, shall grant a licence in Form B and send an intimation thereof to the applicant mentioning the category for which the Authority has granted the licence. The licence shall be issued subject to the insurance broker adhering to the conditions and the code of conduct as specified by the Authority from time to time.

12. Validity of Licence: A licence once issued shall be valid for a period of three years from the date of its issue, unless the same is suspended or cancelled pursuant to these regulations.

13. Renewal of Licence: (1) An insurance broker may, within thirty days before the expiry of the licence, make an application in Form A to the Authority for renewal of licence.

Provided however that if the application reaches the Authority later than that period but before the actual expiry of the current licence, an additional fee of rupees one hundred only shall be payable by the applicant to the Authority.

Provided further that the Authority may for sufficient reasons offered in writing by the applicant for a delay not covered by the previous proviso, accept an application for renewal after the date of the expiry of the licence on a payment of an additional fee of seven hundred and fifty rupees only by the applicant.

(2) An insurance broker before seeking a renewal of licence, shall have completed, atleast twenty five hours of theoretical and practical training, imparted by an institution recognized by the Authority from time to time.

(3) The application for a renewal, under sub-regulation (1) shall be dealt with in the same manner as is specified under regulation 9.

(4) The Authority, on being satisfied that the applicant fulfills all the conditions specified for a renewal of the licence, shall renew the licence in Form B for a period of three years and send an intimation to that effect to the applicant.

(5) An insurance broker licensed under these regulations for a specified category may also apply for the grant of a licence by the Authority for any other category by fulfilling the requirements of these regulations. However, such application shall be made only after a lapse of one year from the grant of a licence in the first instance.

14. Procedure Where a Licence is not Granted — (1)Where an application for grant of a licence under regulation 6 or of a renewal thereof under regulation 13, does not satisfy the conditions set out in regulation 9, the Authority may refuse to grant the licence.

Provided that no application shall be rejected unless the applicant has been given a reasonable opportunity of being heard.

(2) The refusal to grant a licence shall be communicated by the Authority within thirty days of such refusal to the applicant stating therein the grounds on which the application has been rejected.

(3) Any applicant, if aggrieved by the decision of the Authority, may apply within a period of thirty days from the date of receipt of such intimation, to the Chairman of the Authority for a reconsideration of its decision.

(4) The Chairman of the Authority shall consider such an application and communicate his decision thereon to the applicant in writing within six weeks of the receipt thereof.

15. Effect of Refusal to Grant Licence: Any applicant, whose application for grant of a licence under regulation 6 or of a renewal thereof under regulation 13 has been refused by the Authority, shall, on and from the date of the receipt of the communication under regulation 13(2) cease to act as an insurance broker. He, however, shall continue to be liable to provide services in respect of contracts already entered into through him. Such a service shall continue only upto the period of expiry of those current contracts, details of which shall be disclosed to the Authority on receipt of the communication under regulation 13.

16. Issue of a Duplicate Licence — (1) In the event of a licence being lost or destroyed or mutilated, an insurance broker shall submit to the Authority an application alongwith a fee of rupees one thousand requesting for the issue of a duplicate licence and with a declaration giving full details regarding the issue of the licence and its loss or destruction or mutilation.

(2) The Authority, after satisfying itself that the original licence has been lost, destroyed or mutilated, shall issue a duplicate licence in Form B with an endorsement thereon that it is a duplicate one.

17. Action Against a Person Acting as an Insurance Broker without a Valid Licence—

(1) Notwithstanding and without prejudice to initiation of any criminal proceedings against any person, who acts as an insurance broker without holding a valid licence issued under these regulations, the Authority may invoke against such a person penal action under the Act.

(2) Where the person falling under sub-regulation (1), is a company or firm or body corporate, without prejudice to any other proceedings which may be taken by the Authority against the company or firm or body corporate, every director, manager, secretary or other officer of the company or body corporate, and every partner of the firm, who is knowingly a party to such a contravention shall also be liable to be proceeded against.

18. Payment of Fees and the Consequences of Failure to Pay Fees — (1) Every applicant eligible for the grant of a licence shall pay such fees in such a manner and within such a period as specified in Schedule II.

(2) Where an insurance broker fails to pay the annual fees payable under sub-regulation (1), the Authority may suspend the licence, whereupon the insurance broker shall cease to carry on business for the period during which the suspension subsists.

19. Remuneration — (1) No insurance broker shall be paid or contract to be paid by way of remuneration (including royalty or licence fees or administration charges or such other compensation), an amount exceeding:

(A) on direct general insurance business —

(i) on tariff products:

(a) 10 percent of the premium on that part of the business which is compulsory under any statute or any law in force;

(b) 12½ percent of the premium on others.

(ii) on non-tariff products:

17½ percent of the premium on direct business.

(B) on direct life insurance business —

(i) individual insurance

(a) 30 percent of first year's premium

(b) 5 per cent of each renewal premium

(ii) annuity

(m) An

(a) immediate annuity or a deferred annuity in consideration of a single premium, or where only one premium is payable on the policy:

2 percent of premium

(b) deferred annuity in consideration of more than one premium:

(i) 7½ percent of first year's premium

(ii) 2 percent of each renewal premium group insurance and pension schemes:

(a) one year renewable group term insurance, gratuity, superannuation, group savings linked insurance — 7½ percent of risk premium

Note: Under group insurance schemes there will be no remuneration for the savings component.

(b) single premium —

2 percent of risk premium

(c) annual contributions, at new business procurement stage - 5 percent of non risk premium with a ceiling of Rupees three lakhs per scheme.

(d) single premium new business procurement stage -

0.5 percent with a ceiling of Rupees five lakhs per scheme.

(e) remuneration for subsequent servicing -

(i) one year renewable group term assurance -

2 percent of risk premium with a ceiling of rupees 50, 000/- per scheme.

(C) on reinsurance business :

(i) as per market practices prevalent from time to time.

Explanation: For purposes of the procurement of business, an insurer shall not pay an agency commission, allow a special discount, and pay a remuneration to brokers for the same insurance contract.

The settlement of accounts by insurers in respect of remuneration of brokers shall be done on a monthly basis and it must be ensured that there is no cross settlement of outstanding balances.

20. Ceiling on Business from Single Client : (1) The business of the insurance broker shall be carried in such a manner that, not more than 50 percent of the premium (quantum, receipts, etc. as the case may be) in the first year of business, 40 percent of the premium in the second year of business, and 30 percent of the premium from the third year of business onwards shall emanate from any one client.

Note: For the purposes of this regulation, the term "client" shall include, in the case of a firm or a company, an associate or a subsidiary or a group concern under the same management.

(2) The decision of the Authority as to whether a company, a business or an organisation is under the same management shall be final.

21. Code of Conduct : Every insurance broker shall abide by the Code of Conduct as specified in Schedule III.

22. Deposit Requirements : (1) Every insurance broker shall before the commencement of his business, deposit and keep deposited with any scheduled bank a sum equivalent to 20% of the initial capital in fixed deposit, which shall not be released to him unless the prior permission of the Authority is obtained.

Provided that the Authority may impose a separate limit of deposit, in any case not exceeding Rupees one hundred lakhs, for a person covered by regulation 2(1)(j)(v).

(2) Every insurance broker shall furnish to the Authority as and when called upon to do so a statement certified by the Bank in which such fixed deposit is kept.

23. Segregation of Insurance Money : (1) The provisions of Section 64 VB of the Act shall continue to determine the question of assumption of risk by an insurer.

(2) In the case of reinsurance contracts, it may be agreed between the parties specifically or as part of international market practices that the licensed reinsurance broker or composite broker can collect the premium and remit to the reinsurer and/ or collect the claims due from the reinsurer to be passed on to the insured. In these circumstances the money collected by the licensed insurance broker shall be dealt with in the following manner:

(a) he shall act as the trustee of the insurance money that he is required to handle in order to discharge his function as a reinsurance broker and for the purposes of this regulation it shall be deemed that a payment made to the reinsurance broker shall be considered as payment made to the reinsurer;

(b) ensure that 'insurance money' is held in an 'Insurance Bank Account' with one or more of the Scheduled Banks or with such other institutions as may be approved by the Authority;

(c) give written notice to, and receive written confirmation from, a bank, or other institution that he is not entitled to combine the account with any other account, or to exercise any right of set-off, charge or lien against money in that account;

(d) ensure that all monies received from or on behalf of an insured is paid into the 'Insurance Bank Account' which remains in the `Insurance Bank Account' to remain in deposit until it is transferred on to the reinsurer or to the direct insurer.

(e) ensure that any refund of premium which may become due to a direct insurer on account of the cancellation of a policy or alteration in its terms and conditions or otherwise shall be paid by the reinsurer directly to the direct insurer.

(f) Interest on recovery/payment received shall be for the benefit of the direct insurer or reinsurer;

(g) only remove from the 'Insurance Bank Account' charges, fees or commission earned and interest received from any funds comprising the account;

(h) take immediate steps to restore the required position if at any time he becomes aware of any deficiency in the required "segregated amount."

24. Professional Indemnity Insurance : (1) Every insurance broker shall take out and maintain and continue to maintain a professional indemnity insurance cover throughout the validity of the period of the licence granted to him by the Authority.

Provided that the Authority shall in suitable cases allow a newly licensed insurance broker to produce such a guarantee within fifteen months from the date of issue of original licence.

(2) The insurance cover must indemnify an insurance broker against—

(a) any error or omission or negligence on his part or on the part of his employees and directors;

(b) any loss of money or other property for which the broker is legally liable in consequence of any financial or fraudulent act or omission;

(c) any loss of documents and costs and expenses incurred in replacing or restoring such documents;

(d) dishonest or fraudulent acts or omissions by brokers' employees or former employees.

(3) The indemnity cover –

(a) shall be on a yearly basis for the entire period of licence;

(b) shall not contain any terms to the effect that payments of claims depend upon the insurance broker having first met the liability;

(c) shall indemnify in respect of all claims made during the period of the insurance regardless of the time at which the event giving rise to the claim may have occurred.

Provided that an indemnity insurance cover not fully conforming to the above requirements shall be permitted by the Authority in special cases for reasons to be recorded by it in writing.

(4) Limit of indemnity for any one claim and in the aggregate for the year in the case of insurance brokers shall be as follows:

Category of Insurance Broker	*Limit of Indemnity*
(a) Direct broker	three times remuneration received at the end of every financial year subject to a minimum limit of rupees fifty lakhs.
(b) Reinsurance broker	three times remuneration received at the end of every financial year subject to a minimum limit of rupees two crores and fifty lakhs.
(c) Composite broker	three times remuneration received at the end of every financial year subject to a minimum limit of rupees five crores.

(5) The un-insured excess in respect of each claim shall not exceed five percent of the capital employed by the insurance broker in the business.

(6) The insurance policy shall be obtained from any registered insurer in India who has agreed to –

(a) provide the insurance broker with an annual certificate containing the name and address, including the licence number of the insurance broker, the policy number, the limit of indemnity, the excess and the name of the insurer as evidence that the cover meets the requirements of the Authority;

(b) send a duplicate certificate to the Authority at the time the certificate is issued to the insurance broker; and

(c) inform the insurer immediately of any case of voidance, non-renewal or cancellation of cover mid-term.

(7) Every insurance broker shall –

(a) inform immediately the Authority should any cover be cancelled or voided or if any policy is not renewed;

(b) inform immediately the insurer in writing of any claim made by or against it;

(c) advise immediately the insurer of all circumstances or occurrences that may give rise to a claim under the policy; and

(d) advise the Authority as soon as an insurer has notified that it intends to decline indemnity in respect of a claim under the policy.

25. Maintenance of Books of Account, Records, etc. – (1) Every insurance broker shall prepare for every accounting year –

(i) a balance sheet or a statement of affairs as at the end of each accounting period;

(ii) a profit and loss account for that period;

(iii) a statement of cash/fund flow;

(iv) additional statements on insurance broking business as may be required by the Authority.

Note: For purposes of this regulation, the accounting year shall be a period of 12 months (or less where a business is started after 1st April) commencing on the first day of the April of an year and ending on the 31st day of March of the year following, and the accounts shall be maintained on accrual basis.

(2) Every insurance broker shall submit to the Authority, a copy of the audited financial statements as stated in sub-regulation (1) alongwith the auditor's report thereon within ninety days from the close of the accounting year alongwith the remarks or observations of the auditors, if any, on the conduct of the business, state of accounts, etc., and a suitable explanation on such observations shall be appended to such accounts filed with the Authority.

(3) Every insurance broker shall, within ninety days from the date of the Auditor's report take steps to rectify any deficiencies, made out in the auditor's report and inform the Authority accordingly.

(4) All the books of account, statements, document, etc., shall be maintained at the head office of the insurance broker or such other branch office as may be designated by him and notified to the Authority, and shall be available on all working days to such officers of the Authority, authorised in this behalf by it for an inspection.

(5) All the books and documents, statements, contract notes etc., referred to in this regulation and maintained by the insurance broker shall be retained for a period of atleast ten years from the end of the year to which they relate.

26. Submission of Half-yearly Results : (1) Every insurance broker shall before 31st October and 30th April each year furnish to the Authority a half-yearly un-audited financial statement containing details of performance, financial position, etc., alongwith a declaration confirming the fulfillment of requirements of capital in accordance with the provisions of regulation 10 and deposit requirements in accordance with the provisions of regulation 22.

(2) Failure to comply with the regulation of sub-regulation (1) will lead to an action, in accordance with the provisions of regulation 34 being taken against the insurance broker.

27. Internal Control and Systems : Every insurance broker shall ensure that a proper system of internal audit is practised in business and that his internal controls and systems are adequate for the size, nature and complexity of his business.

28. Disclosures to the Authority : (1) An insurance broker shall disclose to the Authority, as and when required by it, in any event not later than thirty days of a requisition, the following information, namely —

(i) his responsibilities with regard to the placement of an insurance contract;

(ii) any change in the information or particulars previously furnished, which have a bearing on the licence granted to it;

(iii) the names of the clients whose insurance portfolio he manages or has managed;

(iv) any other requirement specified by the Authority from time to time.

Provided that in case of a person specified in regulation 2(1)(j)(v) the Authority may call for and obtain such information as it deems fit.

29. Authority's Right to Inspect — (1) The Authority may appoint one or more of its officers as an "inspecting authority" to undertake inspection of the premises of the insurance broker to ascertain and see how the business is carried on , and also to inspect the books of accounts, records and documents of the insurance broker for any of the purposes specified in sub-regulation (2).

(2) The purposes referred to in sub-regulation (1) may be as follows, namely: —

(i) to ensure that the books of account are being maintained in the manner required

(ii) to ensure that the provisions of the Act, rules, regulations are being complied with;

(iii) to investigate the complaints received from any insured, any insurer, other insurance brokers or any other person on any matter having a bearing on the activities of the insurance broker; and

(iv) to investigate the affairs of the insurance broker *suo motu* in the, interest of proper development of insurance business or in policy holders' interest.

30. Notice Before Inspection — (1) Before undertaking an inspection under regulation 29, the Authority shall give a notice of ten days to an insurance broker for that purpose.

(2) Notwithstanding anything contained in sub-regulation (1), where the Authority is satisfied that in the interests of the policyholders no such notice shall be given, it may, for reasons recorded in writing, direct that the inspection of the affairs of the insurance broker be taken up without such notice.

(3) The insurance broker shall allow the inspecting authority to have full access to the premises occupied by such insurance broker or by any other person on his behalf and also extend all facilities for examining books, records, documents and computer data in the possession of the insurance broker.

(4) The inspecting authority, in the course of inspection, shall be entitled to examine or record statements of any principal officer or employee of the insurance broker and have the powers to seize or make copies of documents/ records.

(5) It shall be the duty of every such person to give to the inspecting authority all assistance in connection with the inspection which the insurance broker may reasonably be expected to give.

(6) Failure to comply with the requirements of the Authority in this regard or failure to cooperate with the inspecting officers shall result in suspension of licence.

31. Submission of Report to the Authority — The inspecting authority shall submit an inspection report to the Authority within 90 days of the completion of the inspection.

32. Communication of Findings, etc. — (1) The Authority shall, after consideration of the inspection report, communicate its findings to the insurance broker and give him a reasonable opportunity of being heard before any action is taken by the Authority on the findings of the inspecting authority.

(2) On receipt of the explanation, if any, from the insurance broker, the Authority may direct the insurance broker to take such measures as the Authority may deem fit.

33. Appointment of Investigator — (1) The Authority may appoint a chartered accountant or an actuary or any qualified and experienced individual in the field of insurance to investigate the books of accounts or the affairs of the insurance broker.

Provided that the person so appointed shall have the same powers of the inspecting authority as are mentioned in regulation 29 and the obligations of the insurance broker in regulation 29 shall be applicable to the investigation under this regulation.

Explanation: For the purposes of this regulation the expression "chartered accountant" shall have the same meaning as given in Section 226 of the Companies Act, 1956 (1 of 1956), and the expression 'actuary' shall mean a member of the Actuarial Society of India.

(2) The expenses and costs of such an investigation shall be recovered by the Authority from the insurance broker whose affairs had been caused to be investigated.

34. Cancellation or Suspension of Licence with Notice — (1) The licence of an insurance broker may be cancelled or suspended after due notice and after giving him a reasonable opportunity of being heard if he —

(a) violates the provisions of the Insurance Act,1938 (4 of 1938), Insurance Regulatory And Development Authority Act, 1999 (41 of 1999) or rules or regulations, made thereunder;

(b) fails to furnish any information relating to his activities as an insurance broker as required by the Authority;

(c) furnishes wrong or false information; or conceals or fails to disclose material facts in the application submitted for obtaining a licence;

(d) does not submit periodical returns as required by the Authority;

(e) does not co-operate with any inspection or enquiry conducted by the Authority;

(f) fails to resolve the complaints of the policyholders or fails to give a satisfactory reply to the Authority in this behalf;

(g) indulges in rebates or inducements in cash or kind to a client or any of the client's directors or other employees or any person acting as an introducer;

(h) is found guilty of misconduct or his conduct is not in accordance with the Code of Conduct specified in Schedule III;

(i) fails to maintain the capital requirements in accordance with the provisions of regulation 10;

(j) fails to pay the fees or the reimbursement of expenses under these regulations;

(k) violates the conditions of licence;

(l) does not carry out his obligations as specified in the regulations;

(m) if the principal officer does not acquire practical training and pass the examination within the stipulated period as specified in regulation 9.

(2) In the circumstances where the Authority feels that the establishment of an insurance broker is only to divert funds within a group of companies or their associates, it can after due enquiries made by it cancel the licence granted to the insurance broker.

35. Cancellation or Suspension of Licence without Notice — The licence of an insurance broker may be cancelled or suspended without notice, if he —

(a) violates any one or more of the requirements under the code of conduct specified in Schedule III;

(b) is found guilty of fraud, or is convicted of a criminal offence;

(c) commits such defaults, which require immediate action in the opinion of the Authority, provided that the Authority has communicated the reasons for the cancellation in writing;

(d) the insurance broker has not commenced the business within six months of being granted a licence.

36. Manner of Making Order of Cancellation/Suspension with Notice — The licence of an insurance broker shall not be cancelled unless an enquiry has been held in accordance with the procedure specified in regulation 37.

37. Manner of Holding Enquiry Before Suspension or Cancellation — (1) For the purpose of holding an enquiry under regulation 36, the Authority may appoint an enquiry officer;

(2) the enquiry officer shall issue to the insurance broker a notice at the registered office or the principal place of business of the insurance broker, as the case may be, calling for such information as he considers necessary for the conduct of an enquiry;

(3) the insurance broker may, within fifteen days from the date of receipt of such a notice, furnish to the enquiry officer a reply together with copies of documentary or other evidence relied on by him or sought by the enquiry officer;

(4) the enquiry officer shall, give a reasonable opportunity of hearing to the insurance broker to enable him to make submissions in support of his reply made under sub-regulation(3);

(5) the insurance broker may either appear in person or through any person duly authorised by him to present its case;

(6) if it is considered necessary, the enquiry officer may require the Authority to present its case through one of its officers; and

(7) the enquiry officer shall, after taking into account all relevant facts and submissions made by the insurance broker, submit a report to the Authority within 90 days of the completion of the enquiry proceedings.

38. Show-cause Notice and Order — (1) On receipt of the report from the enquiry officer, the Authority shall consider it and issue a show-cause notice to the insurance broker if the contents of the report warrant a suspension or cancellation of the licence granted to him.

Provided that no such notice is required, in case the provisions of regulation 35 are attracted.

(2) The insurance broker shall within twenty-one days of the date of receipt of the show cause notice send a reply to the Authority.

(3) The Authority after considering the reply to the show cause notice shall, as soon as possible, but not later than thirty days from the receipt of the reply, pass such an order as it deems fit.

Provided, however, where the insurance broker on serving of the notice under this regulation fails to furnish any reply within the stated period, the Authority may after the expiry of such time proceed to decide the case *ex parte*.

(4) The Authority shall send a copy of the order made under clause (3) to the insurance broker.

39. Publication of Order of Suspension or Cancellation — The order of cancellation or suspension of the licence made under sub-regulation (3) of regulation 38, shall be published in one of the daily newspapers in the English language and one newspaper in the regional language as the Authority may consider fit.

40. Effect of Cancellation or Suspension of Licence — (1) On and from the date of suspension or cancellation of the licence, the insurance broker, shall cease to act as an insurance broker.

(2) An insurance broker however shall continue to service the contracts already concluded through him for a period of six months within which suitable arrangements shall be made by him for having the contracts attended to by another licensed insurance broker.

(3) The Authority in such an event may pass such an order as it thinks fit for the disposal of the deposit of the insurance broker made under regulation 22.

41. General — (1) From the date of commencement of these regulations no person can function as a broker or an insurance intermediary unless a licence has been granted to him by the Authority under these regulations.

(2) Any disputes arising between an insurance broker and an insurer or any other person either in the course of his engagement as an insurance broker or otherwise may be referred to the Authority by the person so affected; and on receipt of the complaint or representation, the Authority may examine the complaint and if found necessary proceed to conduct an enquiry or an inspection or an investigation in terms of these regulations.

SCHEDULE I

FORM A: As per regulations 6 and 13: APPLICATION FOR GRANT OF LICENCE/RENEWAL OF LICENCE

FORM B: As per regulations 11 and 16: LICENCE

SCHEDULE II

As per regulation 18: FEES

SCHEDULE III

CODE OF CONDUCT

[see regulation 21]

1. Every insurance broker shall follow recognised standards of professional conduct and discharge his functions in the interest of the policyholders.

2. Conduct in Matters Relating to Clients Relationship : Every insurance broker shall:

(a) conduct its dealings with clients with utmost good faith and integrity at all times;

(b) act with care and diligence;

(c) ensure that the client understands his relationship with the broker and on whose behalf the broker is acting;

(d) treat all information supplied by the prospective clients as completely confidential to themselves and to the insurer(s) to which the business is being offered;

(e) take appropriate steps to maintain the security of confidential documents in their possession;

(f) hold specific authority of client to develop terms;

(g) understand the type of client it is dealing with and the extent of the client's awareness of risk and insurance;

(h) obtain written mandate from client to represent the client to the insurer and communicate the grant of a cover to the client after effecting insurance;

(i) obtain written mandate from client to represent the client to the insurer/ reinsurer; and confirm cover to the insurer after effecting re-insurance, and submit relevant reinsurance acceptance and placement slips;

(j) avoid conflict of interest.

3. Conduct in Matters Relating to Sales Practices : Every insurance broker shall:

(a) confirm that it is a member of the Insurance Brokers' Association of India or such a body of brokers as approved by the Authority which has a memorandum of understanding with the Authority;

(b) confirm that he does not employ agents or canvassers to bring in business;

(c) identify itself and explain as soon as possible the degree of choice in the products that are on offer;

(d) ensure that the client understands the type of service it can offer;

(e) ensure that the policy proposed is suitable to the needs of the prospective client;

(f) give advice only on those matters in which it is knowledgeable and seek or recommend other specialist for advice when necessary;

(g) not make inaccurate or unfair criticisms of any insurer or any member of the Insurance Brokers Association of India or member of such body of brokers as approved by the Authority;

(h) explain why a policy or policies are proposed and provide comparisons in terms of price, cover or service where there is a choice of products;

(i) state the period of cover for which the quotation remains valid if the proposed cover is not effected immediately;

(j) explain when and how the premium is payable and how such premium is to be collected, where another party is financing all or part of the premium, full details shall be given to the client including any obligations that the client may owe to that party; and

(k) explain the procedures to follow in the event of a loss.

4. Conduct in Relation to Furnishing of Information : Every insurance broker shall:

(a) ensure that the consequences of non-disclosure and inaccuracies are pointed out to the prospective client;

(b) avoid influencing the prospective client and make it clear that all the answers or statements given are the latter's own responsibility. Ask the client to carefully check details of information given in the documents and request the client to make true, fair and complete disclosure where it believes that the client has not done so and in case further disclosure is not forthcoming it should consider declining to act further;

(c) explain to the client the importance of disclosing all subsequent changes that might affect the insurance throughout the duration of the policy; and

(d) disclose on behalf of its client all material facts within its knowledge and give a fair presentation of the risk.

5. Conduct in Relation to Explanation of Insurance Contract : Every insurance broker shall:

(a) provide the list of insurer(s) participating under the insurance contract and advise any subsequent changes thereafter;

(b) explain all the essential provisions of the cover afforded by the policy recommended by him so that, as far as possible, the prospective client understands what is being purchased;

(c) quote terms exactly as provided by insurer;

(d) draw attention to any warranty imposed under the policy, major or unusual restrictions, exclusions under the policy and explain how the contract may be cancelled;

(e) provide the client with prompt written confirmation that insurance has been effected. If the final policy wording is not included with this confirmation, the same shall be forwarded as soon as possible;

(f) notify changes to the terms and conditions of any insurance contract and give reasonable notice before any changes take effect;

(g) advise its clients of any insurance proposed on their behalf which will be effected with an insurer outside India, where permitted, and, if appropriate, of the possible risks involved; and

6. Conduct in Relation to Renewal of Policies : Every insurance broker shall:

(a) ensure that its client is aware of the expiry date of the insurance even if it chooses not to offer further cover to the client;

(b) ensure that renewal notices contain a warning about the duty of disclosure including the necessity to advise changes affecting the policy, which have occurred since the policy inception or the last renewal date;

(c) ensure that renewal notices contain a requirement for keeping a record (including copies of letters) of all information supplied to the insurer for the purpose of renewal of the contract;

(d) ensure that the client receives the insurer's renewal invitation well in time before the expiry date.

7. Conduct in Relation to Claim by Client : Every insurance broker shall:

(a) explain to its clients their obligation to notify claims promptly and to disclose all material facts and advise subsequent developments as soon as possible;

(b) request the client to make true, fair and complete disclosure where it believes that the client has not done so. If further disclosure is not forthcoming it shall consider declining to act further for the client;

(c) give prompt advice to the client of any requirements concerning the claim;

(d) forward any information received from the client regarding a claim or an incident that may give rise to a claim without delay, and in any event within three working days;

(e) advise the client without delay of the insurer's decision or otherwise of a claim; and give all reasonable assistance to the client in pursuing his claim.

Provided that the insurance broker shall not take up recovery assignment on a policy contract which has not been serviced through him or should not work as a claim's consultant for a policy which has not been serviced through him.

8. Conduct in Relation to Receipt of Complaints : Every insurance broker shall:

(a) ensure that letters of instruction, policies and renewal documents contain details of complaints handling procedures;

(b) accept complaints either by phone or in writing;

(c) acknowledge a complaint within fourteen days from the receipt of correspondence, advise the member of staff who will be dealing with the complaint and the time table for dealing with it;

(d) ensure that response letters are sent and inform the complainant of what he may do if he is unhappy with the response;

(e) ensure that complaints are dealt with at a suitably senior level;

(f) have in place a system for recording and monitoring complaints.

9. Conduct in Relation to Documentation : Every insurance broker shall:

(a) ensure that any documents issued comply with all statutory or regulatory requirements from time to time in force;

(b) send policy documentation without avoidable delay;

(c) make available, with policy documentation, advice that the documentation shall be read carefully and retained by the client;

(d) not withhold documentation from its clients without their consent, unless adequate and justifiable reasons are disclosed in writing and without delay to the client. Where documentation is withheld, the client must still receive full details of the insurance contract;

(e) acknowledge receipt of all monies received in connection with an insurance policy;

(f) ensure that the reply is sent promptly or use its best endeavours to obtain a prompt reply to all correspondence;

(g) ensure that all written terms and conditions are fair in substance and set out, clearly and in plain language, client's rights and responsibilities; and

(h) subject to the payment of any monies owed to it, make available to any new insurance broker instructed by the client all documentation to which the client is entitled and which is necessary for the new insurance broker to act on behalf of the client.

10. Conduct in Matters Relating to Advertising : Every insurance broker shall conform to the relevant provisions of the Insurance Regulatory and Development Authority (Insurance Advertisements and Disclosure) Regulations, 2000, and:

(a) ensure that statements made are not misleading or extravagant;

(b) where appropriate, distinguish between contractual benefits which the insurance policy is bound to provide and non-contractual benefits which may be provided;

(c) ensure that advertisements shall not be restricted to the policies of one insurer, except where the reasons for such restriction are fully explained with the prior approval of that insurer;

(d) ensure that advertisements contain nothing which is in breach of the law nor omit anything which the law requires;

(e) ensure that advertisement does not encourage or condone defiance or breach of the law;

(f) ensure that advertisements contain nothing which is likely, in the light of generally prevailing standards of decency and propriety, to cause grave or widespread offence or to cause disharmony;

(g) ensure that advertisements are not so framed as to abuse the trust of clients or exploit their lack of experience or knowledge;

(h) ensure that all descriptions, claims and comparisons, which relate to matters of objectively ascertainable fact shall be capable of substantiation.

11. Conduct in Matters Relating to Receipt of Remuneration : Every insurance broker shall:

(a) disclose whether in addition to the remuneration prescribed under these regulations, he proposes to charge the client, and if so in what manner;

(b) advise the client in writing of the insurance premium and any fees or charges separately and the purpose of any related services;

(c) if requested by a client, disclose the amount of remuneration or other remuneration it receives as a result of effecting insurance for that client. This will include any payment received as a result of securing on behalf of the client any service additional to the arrangement of the contract of insurance; and

(d) advise its clients, prior to effecting the insurance, of their intention to make any deductions from the amount of claim collected for a client, where this is a recognised practice for the type of insurance concerned.

12. Conduct in Relation to Matters Relating to Training : Evefy insurance broker shall:

(a) that its staff are aware of and adhere to the standards expected of them by this code;

(b) ensure that staff are competent, suitable and have been given adequate training;

(c) ensure that there is a system in place to monitor the quality of advice given by its staff;

(d) ensure that members of staff are aware of legal requirements including the law of agency affecting their activities; and only handle classes of business in which they are competent;

(e) draw the attention of the client to Section 41 of the Act, which prohibits rebating and sharing of commission.

13. Every insurance broker shall display in every office where it is carrying on business and to which the public have access a notice to the effect that a copy of the code of conduct is available upon request and that if a member of the public wishes to make a complaint or requires the assistance of the Authority in resolving a dispute, he may write to the Authority.

14. An insurance broker as defined in these regulations shall not act as an insurance agent of any insurer under Section 42 of the Act.

15. Every insurance broker shall abide by the provisions of the Insurance Act, 1938 (4 of 1938), Insurance Regulatory And Development Authority Act 1999 (41 of 1999), rules and regulations made thereunder which may be applicable and relevant to the activities carried on by them as insurance brokers.

ANNEXURE 39 C

To be Published in the Gazette of India Extraordinary

[Part III Section 4]

INSURANCE REGULATORY AND DEVELOPMENT AUTHORITY,
NEW DELHI

Insurance Surveyors and Loss Assessors (Licencing, Professional Requirements and Code of Conduct) Regulations, 2000

NOTIFICATION

New Delhi, the ————————, 2000

F.No. IRDA/Reg./11/2000.–

In exercise of the powers conferred by Sections 42D, 64UM and 114A of the Insurance Act, 1938 (4 of 1938) and Section 26 of the Insurance Regulatory and Development Authority Act, 1999 (41 of 1999), the Authority, in consultation with the Insurance Advisory Committee, hereby makes the following regulations, namely:

Chapter I : PRELIMINARY

1. Short Title, Commencement and Application

(1) These regulations may be called the Insurance Surveyors and Loss Assessors (Licencing, Professional Requirements and Code of Conduct) Regulations, 2000.

(2) They shall come into force on the date of their publication in the *Official Gazette* and shall apply to all licensed insurance surveyors and loss assessors.

2. Definitions: In these regulations, unless the context otherwise requires, –

(a) *"Act"* means the Insurance Act, 1938 (4 of 1938);

(b) *"Applicant"* means any person who applies for the grant of a surveyor's and loss assessor's licence or renewal thereof;

(c) *"Authority"* means the Insurance Regulatory and Development Authority established under sub-section (1) of Section 3 of the Insurance Regulatory and Development Authority Act, 1999 (41 of 1999);

(d) *"Designated Person"* means an officer of the Authority detailed by the Authority to discharge the functions assigned to him under all or any of these regulations;

(e) *"Inspecting Authority"* means the person(s) appointed by the Authority to inspect and investigate the affairs of any surveyor and loss assessor;

(f) *"IRDA Act"* means the Insurance Regulatory and Development Authority Act, 1999 (41 of 1999);

(g) Words and expressions used and not defined in these regulations but defined in the Insurance Act, 1938 (4 of 1938) or Insurance Regulatory and Development Authority Act, 1999 (41 of 1999) or the General Insurance Business (Nationalisation) Act, 1972 (57 of 1972), or in any rules or regulations made under those Acts, shall have the meanings respectively assigned to them in those Acts or rules or regulations, as the case may be.

Chapter II : LICENSING PROCEDURE

3. Application for, and Matters Relating to, Grant of Licence

(1) Every person who is an individual and intending to act as a surveyor and loss assessor in respect of general insurance business shall apply to the Authority for grant of licence in FORM–IRDA-1-AF as given in the Schedule to these regulations.

(2) The Authority shall, before granting licence, take into consideration all matters relating to the duties, responsibilities and functions of surveyor and loss assessor and satisfy itself that the applicant is a fit and proper person to be granted a licence. In particular and without prejudice to the foregoing, the Authority shall satisfy itself that the applicant, in addition to submitting the application complete in all respects:-

- (a) satisfies all the applicable requirements of section 64UM read with Section 42D of the Act and rule 56A of the Insurance Rules, 1939;
- (b) possesses such additional technical qualifications as may be specified by the Authority from time to time;
- (c) has furnished evidence of payment of fees for grant of licence, depending upon the categorisation;
- (d) has undergone a period of practical training, not exceeding 12 months, as contained in Chapter VII of these regulations; and
- (e) furnishes such additional information as may be required by the Authority from time to time.

(3) The Authority on being satisfied that the applicant is eligible for grant of licence, shall grant the same in FORM-IRDA-2-LF as given in the Schedule to these regulations and send an intimation to the applicant together with an identity card mentioning the particular class or category of general insurance business namely, fire, marine cargo, marine hull, engineering, motor, miscellaneous and loss of profit for which the Authority has granted licence and the licence shall remain valid for a period of five years from the date of issue thereof, unless cancelled earlier.

(4) A surveyor and loss assessor, whose licence has been cancelled or suspended for any reason, may submit an application for issuance of licence, after the expiry of three years from the date of such cancellation or suspension, and, such an application shall be treated as a fresh case, and, accordingly, the applicant shall satisfy all the requirements of sub-regulation (2).

(5) A surveyor and loss assessor shall be subject to categorisation as specified in Chapter V of these regulations.

(6) A licence issued, before the commencement of these regulations, by the Controller of Insurance or his authorised representative shall be deemed to have been issued in accordance with these regulations.

4. Corporate Surveyors and Loss Assessors

(1) Where the applicant is a company or firm, the Authority shall be satisfied that all the directors or partners, as the case may be, possess one or more of the qualifications specified in Section 64UM(1)D(i) of the Act and none of such directors or partners, as the case may be, suffers from any of the disqualifications mentioned in Section 42 D of the Act read with Section 42(4) of the Act.

(2) The applicant referred to in (1) shall apply in FORM-IRDA-3-AF as given in the Schedule to these regulations.

(3) The Authority on being satisfied that the applicant is eligible for grant of licence, shall grant the same in FORM-IRDA-4-LF as given in the Schedule to these regulations, and, all the provisions of regulation 3 above, shall apply *mutatis mutandis* to corporate surveyors.

5. Fee Structure

On and from May 1, 2001, the fee payable to the Authority by fresh applicants for grant of licence to act as surveyors and loss assessors, category wise, shall be as stated in the following table:

S. No.	Category of Surveyor	Amount payable by individuals Surveyor and Loss Assessor Rs.	Amount payable by Corporate and Loss Assessor Rs.
1.	A	Ten thousand	Twenty five thousand
2.	B	Seven thousand five hundred	Twenty thousand
3.	C	Five thousand	Fifteen thousand

6. Application to Conform to the Requirements

Any incomplete application not conforming to the requirements of these regulations shall be rejected.

Provided that before rejecting any such application, the applicant shall be given a reasonable opportunity to make good the application.

7. Renewal of Licence

(1) An insurance surveyor and loss assessor, desiring to renew the licence granted earlier, either under these regulations or prior to the commencement of these regulations, shall apply to the Authority atleast thirty days before the expiry of the period of validity thereof, in FORM-IRDA-5-AF (for individuals)/ FORM-IRDA-6-AF (for corporate surveyors) as given in the Schedule to these regulations, alongwith a renewal fee of two hundred rupees.

Provided that the Authority may, if it is satisfied that undue hardship would be caused otherwise, accept any application, within six months of its expiry on payment by the applicant of a penalty of seven hundred and fifty rupees.
Provided further that a licence not so renewed can be revalidated only as a fresh case.

(2) A licence so renewed shall be valid for five years from the date of renewal, unless cancelled earlier. The renewed licence shall be in FORM-IRDA-7-LF or FORM-IRDA-8-LF, as the case may be.

(3) Every applicant, be it an individual or a company or a firm, while applying for renewal of the licence shall certify to the Authority that he or any of its directors or any of its partners, as the case may be, has:

(i) not contravened any of the provisions of the Act or the IRDA Act, or any rules or regulations made under those Acts or any order or direction issued by the Authority;

(ii) not made a statement which is false in material particulars with regard to his eligibility for the licence or renewal thereof or in any of the activities transacted by him or them or the matters connected therewith as a Surveyor and Loss Assessor;

(iii) neither had his licence cancelled or suspended under the Act, nor had violated the Code of Conduct prescribed under these regulations;

(iv) discharged the duties and responsibilities as a professional;

(v) not been negligent in the discharge of his obligations;

(vi) not been sentenced to a term of imprisonment by any Court of law.

8. Procedure where licence is not be granted or renewed, or where licence is to be suspended or cancelled —

(1) Where an applicant does not satisfy the provisions of the Act and these regulations, the Authority may reject the application for grant of licence or renewal thereof and refund to the applicant not more than 60 per cent of the fee received:

Provided that no application shall be rejected unless the applicant has been given a reasonable opportunity to make good the application within a time frame as may be deemed appropriate by the Authority, according to the facts and circumstances of each case.

(2) The refusal shall be communicated to the applicant within thirty days of such refusal, stating the grounds of rejection.

(3) Where it is found that a surveyor and loss assessor suffers from any of the disqualifications or has knowingly contravened any provisions of the Act or the IRDA Act, or the rules or regulations made under those Acts or any order or direction or instruction issued by the Authority, the Authority may, after giving such surveyor and loss assessor an opportunity of being heard, cancel his licence, with effect from such date as may be specified by it and the Authority shall notify such cancellation in the *Official Gazette*.

(4) The Authority may refuse to grant or renew licence, or suspend or cancel a licence already granted, to a surveyor and loss assessor, if he/it:

(i) fails to discharge the duties and responsibilities in a satisfactory and professional manner; or

(ii) violates the code of conduct prescribed under these regulations; or

(iii) makes a statement which is false in material particulars with regard to the eligibility for obtaining licence or has, after the issue or renewal of such licence, acquired any of the disqualifications provided under sub-section (4) of Section 42 of the Act, read with clause D of sub-section (1) of Section 64UM of the Act.

Provided that the Authority shall give a reasonable opportunity, to the person concerned, of being heard, before such refusal or suspension or cancellation. The Authority shall notify only cancellations in the *Official Gazette.*

Provided further that the powers conferred on the Authority in this sub-regulation are without prejudice to the powers conferred on it by sub-section (7) of Section 64UM of the Act.

(5) The refusal or suspension or cancellation of licence referred to in sub-regulation (4) shall take effect from the date of such refusal, suspension or cancellation, as the case may be, and, no such surveyor and loss assessor shall carry out any survey and loss assessment work thereafter, including the jobs on hand. All such pending jobs shall be returned by him/ it to the insurer or the insured, as the case may be.

9. Suspension of the Licence

(1) A licensed surveyor and loss assessor whose licence is proposed to be suspended by the Authority may be granted an opportunity before suspending the licence.

Provided, however, that the Authority may not follow this procedure if the continued employment of the licensed surveyor and loss assessor is considered to be detrimental to the cause of insurance underwriting.

(2) The period of suspension will be indicated in the order of the Authority.

(3) On receipt of the order of suspension, the licensed surveyor and loss assessor may file an appeal with the Authority asking for revocation of suspension. The Authority may designate an officer who will hear the representation of the licensed surveyor and loss assessor and make such orders as are deemed fit. The order made in this regard shall be communicated to the suspended surveyor and loss assessor.

(4) If, on the basis of the order of the designated person, the Authority restores the licence of the surveyor and loss assessor, it will indicate the date from which the restoration will take place.

(5) During the period of suspension, the surveyor and loss assessor shall be prohibited from carrying out any surveys and all work that was handled prior to suspension and has remained incomplete shall be returned to an insurer or the insured as the case may be.

(6) The licence granted by the Authority may be cancelled by the Authority where the surveyor and loss assessor does not represent within a period of 45 days from the date of order of suspension.

(7) Any order of suspension or revocation of the order thereof shall be intimated to the insurers.

10. Issue of Duplicate Licence/Identity Card

(1) A person to whom a licence has been issued or renewed, shall, if such licence and/or Identity Card is/are lost, destroyed or mutilated, make an application in FORM-IRDA-9 given in the Schedule to these regulations to the Authority requesting for issuance of duplicate thereof, along with a fee of five rupees.

(2) The application referred to in sub-regulation (1) shall contain full particulars of licence/identity card and as to how the loss/destruction or mutilation has occurred, and the application shall be accompanied by mutilated pieces, if any, in possession of the person making the application.

(3) The Authority, on being satisfied, may issue a duplicate licence and/or identity card in FORM-IRDA-10-LF as given in the Schedule to these regulations.

(4) The duplicate so issued shall remain in force for the remainder of the period of validity of the licence and/or identity card, unless cancelled earlier, and the duplicate shall bear an endorsement thereon that it is a duplicate.

Chapter III : CONSTITUTION AND FUNCTIONS OF SURVEYORS AND LOSS ASSESSORS COMMITTEE

11. Constitution

(1) The Authority shall constitute a Committee to be called "Surveyors and Loss Assessors Committee" (herein after referred to as "the Committee"), for assisting the Authority on the matters and affairs relating to Insurance Surveyors and Loss Assessors.

(2) The Committee may consist of the following persons:-

(i) an Officer of the Authority;

(ii) two representatives of the Surveyors and Loss Assessors;

(iii) a representative of Insurers;

(iv) a representative of the policyholders;

(3) The Committee will be for a period of three years and will be presided over by the officer of the Authority.

12. Functions of the Committee

(1) The Committee shall perform the following functions:-

(i) recommending the syllabus for examination and practical training requirements for persons to qualify as surveyors and loss assessors;

(ii) recommending to the Authority for its consideration to recognise foreign qualifications and training for the purposes of grant of licence to act as surveyors and loss assessors;

(iii) improving and developing the status and standard of the profession of surveyors and loss assessors;

(iv) co-ordinating with educational or other institutions, having as their objects, wholly or partly, similar to those of the profession of surveyors and loss assessors, in such manner as may be conducive for the attainment of common objectives;

(v) looking into the matters of professional misconduct, indiscipline, non-adherence to code of conduct by surveyors and loss assessors; and dealing with complaints of insured/insurer in respect of survey work done by surveyors and loss assessors;

(vi) discharging any other function, which may be entrusted by the Authority, from time to time.

(2) The Committee may meet as frequently as necessary to conduct its affairs.

(3) The members of the Committee, other than the officer of Authority will be entitled to such allowances as may be determined by the Authority from time to time.

Chapter IV : DUTIES AND RESPONSIBILITIES OF A SURVEYOR AND LOSS ASSESSOR

13. (1) A surveyor and loss assessor shall, for a major part of the working time, investigate, manage, quantify, validate and deal with losses (whether insured or not) arising from any contingency, and report thereon, and carry out the work with competence, objectivity and professional integrity by strictly adhering to the code of conduct expected of such surveyor and loss assessor.

(2) The following, shall, *inter alia,* be the duties and responsibilities of a surveyor and loss assessor:-

- (i) declaring whether he has any interest in the subject-matter in question or whether it pertains to any of his relatives, business partners or through material shareholding;

  Explanation: For the purpose of this clause 'relatives' shall mean any of the relatives as mentioned in Schedule IA to the Companies Act, 1956;
- (ii) maintaining confidentiality and neutrality without jeopardising the liability of the insurer and claim of the insured;
- (iii) conducting inspection and re-inspection of the property in question suffering a loss;
- (iv) examining, inquiring, investigating, verifying and checking upon the causes and the circumstances of the loss in question including extent of loss, nature of ownership and insurable interest;
- (v) conducting spot and final surveys, as and when necessary and comment upon franchise, excess/under insurance and any other related matter;
- (vi) estimating, measuring and determining the quantum and description of the subject under loss;
- (vii) advising the insurer and the insured about loss minimisation, loss control, security and safety measures, wherever appropriate, to avoid further losses;
- (viii) commenting on the admissibility of the loss as also observance of warranty conditions under the policy contract;
- (ix) surveying and assessing the loss on behalf of insurer or insured;
- (x) assessing liability under the contract of insurance;
- (xi) pointing out discrepancy, if any, in the policy wordings;
- (xii) satisfying queries of the insured/insurer and of persons connected thereto in respect of the claim/loss;
- (xiii) recommending applicability of depreciation and the percentage and quantum of depreciation;\
- (xiv) giving reasons for repudiation of claim, in case the claim is not covered by policy terms and conditions;
- (xv) taking expert opinion, wherever required;
- (xvi) commenting on salvage and its disposal wherever necessary.

(3) A surveyor or loss assessor shall submit his report to the insurer as expeditiously as possible, but not later than 30 days of his appointment.

Provided that in exceptional cases, the afore-mentioned period can be extended with the consent of the insured and the insurer.

Chapter V : CATEGORISATION OF SURVEYORS

14. (1) A surveyor and loss assessor shall be categorised, as mentioned in sub-regulation (3), based on the following criteria:

- (i) professional qualifications;
- (ii) training undergone;
- (iii) experience as a surveyor and loss assessor and any other relevant professional experience;
- (iv) any other criteria, as may be specified by the Authority from time to time.

(2) The categorisation shall be done and reviewed from time to time on the basis of a point system evolved by the Authority in consultation with the Committee referred to in Chapter III of these regulations.

(3) The categorisation shall consist of allocation of one or more specified departments of insurance business, based on the factors mentioned above and shall include categorisation of the surveyors and loss assessors into three categories, viz., Category A, Category B and Category C.

(4) Every surveyor and loss assessor, whether a company or firm or an individual, shall be eligible to carry on the work as a surveyor or loss assessor, as per the categorisation specified in the licence.

Chapter VI : CODE OF CONDUCT

15. Every surveyor and loss assessor shall –

(1) behave ethically and with integrity in the professional pursuits. Integrity implies not merely honesty but fair dealings and truthfulness;

(2) strive for objectivity in professional and business judgment;

(3) act impartially, when acting on instructions from an insurer in relation to a policy holder's claim under a policy issued by that insurer;

(4) conduct himself with courtesy and consideration to all people with whom he comes into contact during the course of his work;

(5) not accept or perform survey works in areas for which he does not hold a licence;

(6) not accept or perform work which he is not competent to undertake, unless he obtains some advice and assistance, as will enable him to carry out the work competently;

(7) carry out his professional work with due diligence, care and skill and with proper regard to technical and professional standards expected of him;

(8) keep himself updated with all developments relevant to his professional practice;

(9) at all times maintain proper record for work done by him and comply with all relevant laws;

(10) assist and encourage his colleagues to obtain professional qualifications, and, in this behalf, provide free articleship and/or practical training for a period of twelve months;

(11) maintain a register of survey work, containing the relevant information, in FORM-IRDA-11 as given in the Schedule to these regulations, and shall keep important records of the survey reports, photographs and other important documents for a period of three years and furnish the same and such other specified returns, as and when called for by the Authority or by any investigating authority or the insurer;

(12) disclose to all parties concerned his appointment, where the acceptance or continuance of such an engagement may materially prejudice, or could be seen to materially affect the interests of any interested party. As soon as a conflict of interest is foreseen, every surveyor and loss assessor shall notify all interested parties immediately and seek instructions for his continuance;

(13) not disclose any information, pertaining to a client or employer or policyholder acquired in the course of his professional work, to any third party, except, where consent has been obtained from the interested party, or where there is a legal right or duty enjoined upon him to disclose;

(14) neither use nor appear to use, any confidential information acquired or received by him in the course of his professional work, to his personal advantage or for the advantage of a third party.

Chapter VII : PRACTICAL TRAINING

16. (1) An applicant seeking a licence to act as a surveyor and loss assessor shall undergo a period of practical training of not less than twelve months with a surveyor and loss assessor as specified below:

(2) The surveyor under whom an applicant will be trained shall belong to category A or category B as classified by the Authority while granting a licence;

(3) The trainee shall maintain a record of training received during the period and shall get it certified by the surveyor and loss assessor under whom he has trained and the certificate shall be attached to the application for seeking grant of a licence under regulation 3;

(4) The licence to be granted to an applicant to act as a surveyor and loss assessor shall be in that particular area for which he has been trained;

(5) If a surveyor and loss assessor already licensed by the Authority seeks to obtain a similar licence for acting as a surveyor in a category other than for which he is licensed, he shall undergo a period of training not less than six months under a surveyor and loss assessor holding either Category A or Category B licence issued by the Authority to act in that particular area.

17. The Authority may also prescribe the passing by an applicant of an examination on the successful completion of the training prescribed above for the grant of a licence under Regulation 3. The examination may be conducted either by the Authority itself or by an institution authorised by it in this behalf.

Chapter VIII : MISCELLANEOUS

18. Register of Licensed Insurance Surveyors and Loss Assessors

(1) The Authority shall maintain a register of all licensed insurance surveyors and loss assessors containing the following particulars:-

(i) full name, date of birth, domicile, residential and professional address;
(ii) the date on which name is entered in the Register;
(iii) licence number and period of validity;
(iv) professional and other qualifications;
(v) areas of survey work licensed to be undertaken;
(vi) categorisation of the surveyor and loss assessor;
(vii) any other particulars as may be prescribed by the Authority from time to time.

Provided that in the case of corporate surveyors, the particulars to be entered in the register, shall be with reference to every director or partner, as the case may be.

(2) The Authority shall, delete the particulars of surveyors and loss assessors, who are no longer alive, or whose licence has been cancelled or suspended.

(3) The Authority shall cause the publication of the relevant particulars entered in the register, as may be considered appropriate by it, at such intervals and in such manner, as may be deemed fit.

19. Submission of returns: Every licensed surveyor and loss assessor shall:

(a) furnish such of the document, statement, account, return or report, as and when required by the Authority, and comply with such directions, as may be issued by the Authority in this behalf, from time to time; and

(b) submit an annual statement in FORM-IRDA-12 given in the Schedule to these regulations.

20. Inspection

(1) The Authority, may appoint one or more persons as inspecting authority to undertake inspection of survey work, books, records and documents, or to investigate any *bona fide* complaint received against a surveyor and loss assessor.

(2) The inspecting authority shall, as soon as possible, submit an inspection report to the Authority.

(3) The inspecting authority shall be given all information demanded by it for the purpose of carrying out inspection/ investigation work, and shall be extended all possible co-operation, to facilitate the conduct of its work.

(4) The Authority shall, after consideration of the inspection report, communicate the findings of the inspecting authority to the surveyor and loss assessor, and shall also give him a reasonable opportunity of being heard before any action is taken by the Authority on the findings of the inspection report.

21. Power to Clarify

In case of any doubt or ambiguity in regard to any of these regulations, the same shall be clarified by the Chairperson of the Authority.

Key Terms

- ❐ Financial Risk
- ❐ Agents
- ❐ Licensing
- ❐ Surveyors and Loss Assesors
- ❐ Buyers
- ❐ Distributors
- ❐ Credit Risk
- ❐ Corporate Agents
- ❐ Third Part Administrators
- ❐ Bancassurance
- ❐ Carriers

Questions for Review

1. Define Bancassurance. Briefly explain the various models of bancassurance.
2. Briefly explain the IRDA guidelines for regulation of various insurance intermediaries.
3. Distinguish between:
   (a) Agents and Brokers
   (b) Agents and corporate agents.

Suggested Readings

1. Roderick Claws, *A Textbook of Insurance Broking,* Woodhead Faulomers Ltd., 1980.
2. D.C. Srivastava and Shashank Srivastava, *Indian Insurance Industry, Transition and Prospects,* New Century Publication 2001.
3. Y. Chandrashekhar: and KBS Kumar Article — "Bancassurance: Big forces together" in *"Banking in the New Millennium",* ICFAI Press, 2001.

Financial Aspects in Insurance Companies

Chapter **40**

CHAPTER OBJECTIVES

After reading this chapter you will be able to understand :

- *Financial Objectives of an Insurance Company*
- *Responsibilities of Financial Managers*
- *Planning Financial Goals and Strategies*
- *Measuring the performance of an Insurance Company*
- *Asset Liability Management (ALM) in Insurance Companies*

The crux of the insurance game is that the insurance companies are in the business of collecting money from a group of insureds and redistributing the same to a few of them on the occurrence of an event as contracted. Apart from event based distribution, money is sometimes paid if the event does not occur(survival benefit) as in the case of life insurance. Therefore, financial management in insurance companies is of paramount importance since sufficient funds are required to be kept as reserves and also to be invested so that returns arising thereon can be distributed among the policyholders as committed. The financial manager of the insurance company has to play an important role in the sense that he has to optimise the considerations of various categories of decision makers viz. underwriters, agents and the marketers, shareholders etc. and none the less – the regulators.

40.1 FINANCIAL OBJECTIVES OF AN INSURANCE COMPANY

The twin financial objectives of an insurance company are:

(a) *Solvency:* the ability to meet financial obligations.

(b) *Profitability:* to maximize the returns to its stakeholders.

Solvency

Every insurance company is required to maintain the minimum standard of capital and surplus as required by law. The legal minimum standard of capital *varies,* based on the degree of risk associated with an insurer's investments and the specific lines of businesses the insurer sells. IRDA has prescribed the solvency margin requirements both for life and the non-life business. (Annexure 40A).

In normal course of conducting its business, an insurance company faces potentially serious risk that can threaten its statutory solvency. These may be classified as :

- *Asset risk* : The risk of loss of an investment for a reason other than a change in market interest rates.
- *Pricing risk* : The possibility that the insurer's experience on claims/expenses will be different from the one expected.
- *Interest rate risk* : Arising out of fluctuations in the market interest rates. The examples are :
  - Loss on sale of a bond when market interest rates rise
  - The inability of an insurer to earn a rate of return on its assets that equals or exceeds the interest rates guaranteed in its insurance contracts

— Disintermediation when the customers remove money from one financial intermediary and place the money in other financial intermediary to earn a higher rate of return.

General business risk : The risk of losses resulting from ineffective general business practices or environmental factors beyond the insurer's control

A common measure of solvency is capital ratio described as >> Capital Ratio = Capital & Surplus/Assets.

Profitability

An insurer must, by nature of business plan and organise the business to ensure the long-term profitability which enables the insurer to:

- Provide funds for investments
- Ensuring payment of dividends to stake holders
- Obtain high quality ratings from insurance rating agencies
- Provide funds to develop products, product lines and distribution channels
- Provide funds for expansion and acquisition

A common measure of profitability is return on capital ratio described as >> Return on Capital = Earnings/ Capital & Surplus.

40.2 Responsibilities of Financial Managers

Financial managers in an insurance company are generally assigned the following functions:

- *Planning the Company's Financial Strategy* : The financial managers have to decide on the solvency and profitability goals and strategies and also how they have to met.
- *Managing Capital and Surplus* : Analyse the capital and surplus needs for internal risk management, regulatory requirements and rating agency requirements. The estimation of capital requirements may be for funds needed to finance desired level of business growth, the amount of funds needed for strategic uses such as acquisition, development of systems etc.
- *Managing Cash Flows* : Cash flow management is important so that adequate funds are available to manage the operations, service claims and liabilities and are also available for investment to meet expected return targets.
- *Managing Investments* : The investment managers trade in various short-term and long-term securities and assets to implement various stipulated investment strategies in line with the regulator's guidelines.
- *Financial Reporting* : Reporting on company's performance to various parties including the regulating agencies.
- *Measuring Financial Performance* : Analysis of the financial statements and interpretation for future decision making and control.
- *Auditing and Internal Control* : Establishment of various processes and control measures to ensure the achievement of the desired objectives. It also includes the compliance with the various statutory requirements.

40.3 Planning Financial Goals and Strategy

General financial goals of all the insurers are to maximise profits and maintain high level of solvency. The insurer has to maintain a trade-off between the two since pursuing profitability involves risk-taking, whereas, protecting solvency involves risk avoidance. Finding the correct balance between the two is crucial to the *financial success* of an insurance company. The financial strategy for an insurance company is polarised towards the investment of stakeholders funds. Financial strategy is akin to the investment strategy of course, after accounting for solvency margins. An investment strategy helps to determine where to invest how to invest and when to invest to get a proper return within expected period. It would be extremely difficult to survive without an investment strategy. It starts with identifying the investment objective, selecting the sector and company to invest on and them to invest and monitor the investment. To determine investment strategy the following points should be kept in mind:

- *Financial Goals* : How much money will is needed after particular period of time?
- *Time Horizon* : How much time-period in hand until the money is required?
- *Risk* : What is the financial risk bearing capacity?
- *Return* : How much is expected after a period of time?

Once the financial goals of an insurance company are established and risk-return relationships are known, the strategy has to be formulated. The financial strategies can assume any of the following forms:

- *Aggressive* : The insurance company places strong emphasis on profitability but potentially threatens its solvency. For example – investing in relatively high-risk assets, developing many new and unusual products, expanding into new lines of business, instituting new distribution systems etc.
- *Conservative* : The insurance company avoids strategies that can endanger solvency and enhances its rate of return gradually. For example – investing in relatively low risk assets, developing traditional products for existing markets, using existing distribution systems etc.

Investment Criteria for the Indian Insurance Companies

All insurers are governed by the investment criteria laid down by the IRDA. (Annexure 40B)

For Non-life Insurer

- The total investment in gifts, state government and other guaranteed securities should be at least 30%.
- An additional 10% will have to be invested in the infrastructure sector and social sector, while another 5% minimum will be allocated for housing sector.
- Balance 55% is to be invested in the markets as per guidelines stipulated.
- The criteria for investment in the rural sector for a general Insurance company is the following percentage of the total policies written in the corresponding year.
- 2% in the 1st financial year, 3% in the 2nd the financial year, 5% in the 3rd financial year.

For Life Insurer

- Life insurance companies will have to invest 25% in the government and another 25% in other approved securities.
- 15% of investment will have to be invested in the infrastructure sector and social sector.
- The balance 35% will be available to the companies to invest in the capital markets were the return on investment are significantly higher.
- The criteria for investment in the rural sector for Life Insurance companies is the following % of the total policies written in the corresponding year.

  5% in the 1st financial year, 7% in the 2nd financial year, 10% in the 3rd financial year, 12% in the 4th financial year, 15% in the 5th financial year.

The investment norms as laid down by IRDA leaves little room for insurance companies. This has both types of effects. On the positive side, it saves combines from indulging into risky and fraudulent investments, fuelling the priority sectors and thus poses public faith and interest. Contrarily, it prevents companies from investing into investment with high/ attractive returns and returns, obviously being lower on gifts and other government securities, leaves less than optimal returns to the stockholders.

Prudential Norms

- The insurers, both Life and Non-life, should not invest than 15% of the total capital employed in equity shares and debentures.
- Loans are not to form more than 10% of the estimated annual accretion of funds.
- On accounting norms for the sector separate statements would be required for any activity which yields 10 per cent or more revenue.
- To ensure that there is never a lack of audit in the insurance company, there will be two auditors, one with tenure of four years and the second with a five-year tenure.

40.4 Measuring the Performance of an Insurance Company

The measures of performance for an insurance company are different from other industries in the sense that most of the factors of performance are rough estimates. However, the performance measurement essential involves the following steps:

- Ensuring suitable measurements of performance
- Use for standardized procedures
- Constant review of measures and procedures

Criteria of performance differ from company to company and country to country. Still, the following are generally recognised as most common measures:

A. External
B. Operational
C. Ratio-based

The external measures of performance includes parameters of:

(a) Service: Service to the policyholders is measured in terms of speed and fairness of claims settlement, the extent of coverages and reasonableness of underwriting practices. "Service entails a ready response to policy holders inquiries, the recognition and implementation of all rights under a contact and flexibility in ammeding contracts to meet the financial needs of in succeeds. Liberty with respect to cancellation features and stability of practices are other criteria."[1] The service quality may be measured by the number and type of complaints from policyholder on various aspects like policy servicing, claims handling, premius payments etc.

(b) Cost: The insurance companies may be compared on the basis of prices of insurance products. The cost of services as included in the prices may effectively evaluation insurance since actuarial calculations don of differ significantly among insucceds.

(c) Equity among Policyholders: It means that insured pays a premium reflecting the hazards presented. When there is perfect equity, law of averages does not work and there is no credibility. Insurance are bond to generate credibility. So, the rate stretcher should efficiently reflect the risk expose.

(d) Financial Strength: It is the earliest, quantifiable criteria. The financial strength can be measured in terms of adjusted net worth, policyholder surplus, rescues or financial ratios. Though the financial data is derived from published (and prescribed) financial sentiment, yet care must be taken since financial statements are often affected by varying accounting policies interpretations and presentation.

The appraisal of an insurance company's effectiveness requires its evaluation in functional areas. These include the following:

(a) *Organisation and Management:* Design of the organisation structure, quality of management, specialised training etc.

(b) *Product research and development:* response to dynamic market conditions, attempting new market approach and exhibiting a fresh enthusiasm about a product line affects insurer's performance.

(c) *Underwriting and Re-insurance:* codification of rating criteria, supervision of procedures, review of reinsurance programs for maximising opportunities.

(d) Proving flexibility offered to the extent not regulated by the authority

(e) *Claims Control:* speedy follow-up on claim and procedures, systematic and frequent review of files. Ideally the delays between occurrence and reporting of claims, between reporting of claims and investigation and between investigation and settlement should be minimised.

(f) *Marketing:* average selling cost free unit combined with loss experience is an ideal measure. "Effective marketing requires an agency force that is vital a minimum policy size is maintained at an adequate or economical level, and an average size of written premiums that is profitable.

(g) *Investments:* return and quality of the portfolio

(h) *Financial Planing:* range of plans

(i) *Adaptability to Environment:* adaptation to local needs and awareness of the special characteristics of different markets.

40.5 ASSET LIABILITY MANAGEMENT (ALM)

ALM is the most important activity for the financial managers in an insurance company in the sense that cash flows arising out of assets and liabilities must match together to support the insurer's strategic objective of solvency and profitability. "ALM is a cash flow management program for co-ordinating the financial effects of the insurer's product liabilities and with the financial effects of the business investment though ALM, financial managers identify the patterns of company's cash out flows and them construct a portfolio of assets that will produce patterns of cash inflows which when combined with the cash inflows from operations are sufficient to meet the company's obligations on time. In applying ALM principles, an insures estimates the timing and amount of claims that a product will generate in a specified period".

Insurance companies provide services which expose them to certain kinds of risks such as credit risk, interest risk and liquidity risk. Also, the assets and liability items have their respective characteristic in regard to rates/ price and tenure. The cash flow and cash requirements arising out of anticipated or unusual liability in claims also pose additional challenge. Asset-Liability Management (ALM) helps to measure and monitor these characteristics and identify mismatches which need to be managed.

In Indian insurance industry the liquidity and interest rate risk have gone up. Risks are now compounded by the increased complexity of product design, more stringent scrutiny from regulators and a greater availability of various investing options for the public, at large. The management of assets is increasingly becoming a challenge compared to liability as the money and investment markets are becoming more volatile and choppy.

The non-life insurance sector is characterized with a yearly tenure contracts. The asset-liability management problem is largely limited to each flow management and liquidity management so as to service the claims efficiency. The same is being achieved through the reserving methods applied to each line of business. The penetration of typically long tail liability insurance and long term managed health insurance products in India is low. These products, especially liability products, bring in additional amount of risk for the insurers as a huge claim can arise even after many years of the coverage period.

In life insurance, the importance of the asset-liability management increases manifold. Life insurance contracts are normally longer term contracts of more than 10 years. Life insurers have to manage both their assets in terms of risk/return profiles of the investments and liabilities which emerge from the design and pricing of the product by the insurer and the business mix in terms of premium mode, maturity profile etc.

ALM helps avoid a situation where asset values fall short of the liabilities arising out of the insurance contracts which can in extreme cases lead to bankruptcy or insolvency of the insurer. Traditionally, the scope of ALM was mostly limited to the 'asset' side and hence ALM process is about choosing the investment portfolio to match the liabilities *i.e.,* hedging of liabilities.

Methods of ALM Generic Methods of ALM[1]

Over time, three basic methods of ALM have been developed. Each of these methods tends to focus on different aspects of the risks.

- **Cash Flow Matching :** Cash Flow Matching involves term wise matching of positive and negative cash flows to identify any potential points of a liquidity crisis. The positive cash flows originating from the assets at the end of each term, say quarter, are calculated and the same is done for the liabilities. In order to ensure a perfectly hedged position, the net cash flows should be zero in each term.

  The method is simple to implement, though it comes with its drawbacks. The method is unable to factor in interest rate risk as the cash flows are assumed as deterministic. Uncertainties of cash flows due to exogenous factors such as a catastrophe are difficult to factor, especially for non-life insurers. And finally, the method imposes restrictions on the exposure of the firm. For example, if a firm strongly believes in a rising yield cure, for the next few years, it might want to position its portfolio in order to gain from riding the yield curve.

- **Duration/convexity analysis or Immunization :** A more simple, but effective way to address interest rate risk is using duration and convexity matching. The process involves structuring the company's portfolio so that impact of a change in interest rates on the value of liabilities offsets the corresponding impact on the asset values. The duration of a portfolio is the weighted average of the time periods of the portfolio's cash flows. Once the company has computed the duration of its assets and liabilities, it should make sure that the two are equal. If, for example, the durations of assets and liabilities are both 10 years, a 0.1% increase in the interest rates will decrease the value of assets and liabilities 1%, thus providing a perfect offset. Convexity analysis, done along with duration analysis, provides a more accurate method of immunization, by taking care of changes in the value of duration due to interest rate movements.

  Immunization comes with its own drawbacks. The duration of many assets and liabilities is difficult to estimate, especially in non-life insurance. Also, the method is unable to deal with liquidity risk in a sufficient manner. While the market value of the firm's assets and liabilities might remain constant with changes in interest rates, the firm might get into a liquidity trap. Finally, duration/convexity analysis only works in the scenario that the yield curve movements are parallel. In a non-parallel movement of yield curve, the analysis breaks down.

- **Scenario Analysis :** Scenario analysis was adopted by the National Association of Insurance Commissioners in the US in 1993, to verify that they hold sufficient reserves.

1. Ashwin Parekh, Asset–Liability Management by Insurers, IRDA Journal, May, 2008.

A simple analysis might consider five scenarios, say reflecting assumptions that over the next 2 years, interest rates will rise 200 basis points, or rise 100 basis points, or are flat, or decline 100 basis points, or decline 200 basis points. The next step is to project what will happen under each one in terms of the value of assets and liabilities. An elaborate analysis might project, under each scenario, a bank's cash-flow statement and balance sheet at each time step.

While scenario analysis does address most of the concerns raised in the earlier two methods, it has its own drawbacks, it only addresses risk due to the specific scenarios considered. Also, scenario analysis is highly dependent on assumptions and output of the analysis is only as good as these assumptions.

Dynamic Financial Analysis (DFA)

While all the methods focus on different aspects or asset-liability risk, no single method is capable of comprehensively dealing with all the aspects of ALM. DFA is one of the forms of ALM that has gained acceptance in the insurance industry as it is more effective in dealing with a broader range of ALM issues. The DFA consists of five main components :

- *Initial Conditions :* Initial conditions summarize the past performance of the company being analyzed and the economy at large.
- *Scenario Generator :* The scenario generator constructs a set of plausible scenarios for general economic conditions, the firm's assets and its liabilities. The outputs of these simulations are often summarized as distributions.
- *Financial Calculator :* The financial calculator translates scenarios into financial results. The level of detail under which the calculator operates will depend on the subject under discussion.
- *Optimiser :* An optimizer uses a single summary statistic, or a pair of summary statistics in order to evaluate and select among different strategic alternatives. The single summary statistic can be a utility measure or a return on capital measure such as risk adjusted return on capital. The bivariate approach often involves creating a map called the efficient frontier which depicts a set of strategies that maximizes the financial reward for a given level of risk.
- *Result :* Finally, the model provides a set of results summarizing the lessons learned from the simulation. These include distributions of key measures and some indication of which choice variables most critically affect the results.

Some ground rules for the grouping are :

- Consider segregated funds separately (when no cross subsidy is possible)
- Consider each asset class separately
- Group bonds and derivatives by maturity
- Group equities and property into a single index.

ALM in Insurance Companies follows the typical procedures :

- Identifying key objectives
- Selecting an appropriate methodology
- Assembling reliable data
- Implementation of the model
- Producing relevant output
- Developing additional stress testing requirements for the ALM model

Factors Impacting Asset Liability Management[2]

Category of Plans : There are primarily three categories of plans currently being sold in the Indian market *viz.*

- Nonparticipating non linked endowment contracts
- Participating non linked endowment contracts
- Unit Linked Insurance Plans ("ULIPs")

Nature of contracts (or the liabilities) being sold is one of the most important defining criteria for the extent of asset liability management required. Non-participating non-linked contracts have significant investment guarantees and an insurer can have an upside/downside if the assets perform differently from the guaranteed rates. Participating contracts, as the name suggests, have an element of discretion and sharing of experience between the policyholders and insurer, and hence the investment risk is reduced but only to a limited extent. ULIPs are a class of contracts where the entire investment risk under a standard contract is passed on to the policyholders and hence the investments are made in accordance with the policyholder's chosen assets. Hence, asset liability management assumes prime importance in case of nonparticipating and participating non-linked contracts.

Issues in ALM

- Duration Mismatch
- Inconsistency of Financial Measures
- Reinvestment Risk
- Impact of Lapsation and Mortality

Evolution of ALM

Both regulatory factors and economic factors have given rise to different ALM practices. The regulatory factors are :

- Investment regulation
- Tax regulations

The economic environment factors are :

- Financial market depth/liquidity
- Economic stability
- Economic booms

IAIS's Work on ALM

The IAIS *Insurance core principles* (ICPs) that relate directly to ALM are :

ICP 18 : Risk assessment and management : The supervisory authority requires insurers to recognise the range of risks that they face and to assess and manage them effectively.

Essential Criteria a : The supervisory authority requires and checks that insurers have in place comprehensive risk management policies and systems capable of promptly identifying, measuring, assessing, reporting and controlling their risks.

Essential Criteria b : The risk management policies and risk control systems are appropriate to the complexity, size and nature of the insurer's business. The insurer establishes an appropriate tolerance level or risk limit for material sources of risk.

2. Sunil Kakkar, ALM in Insurance Companies, IRDA Journal, May 2008.

ICP 21 : Investments : The supervisory authority requires to comply with standards on investment activities. These standards include requirements on investment policy, asset mix, valuation diversification, asset-liability matching, and risk management.

Essential Criteria i : The supervisory authority requires that insurers have in place effective procedures for monitoring and managing their asset-liability positions to ensure that their investment activities and asset positions are appropriate to their liability and risk profiles.

The need for an appropriate application of ALM is also addressed in two other IAIS papers :

(i) *Standard on asset management by insurance companies (1999), paragraph 4 :* A key driver of the asset strategy adopted by an insurer will be its liabilities profile, and the need to ensure that it holds sufficient assets of appropriate nature, term and liquidity to enable it to meet those liabilities as they become due. Detailed analysis and management of this asset-liability relationship will therefore be a pre-requisite to the development and review of investment policies and procedures which seek to ensure that the insurer adequately manages the investment-related risks to its solvency. The analysis will involve, inter alia, the testing of the resilience of the asset portfolio to a range of market scenarios and investment conditions, and the impact on the insurer's solvency position.

(ii) *Guidance paper on investment risk management (2004), paragraph 8 :* This paper should be considered in conjunction with other principles, standards or guidance papers developed by the IAIS, in particular the *Principles on capital adequacy and solvency (2002),* the *solvency control levels guidance paper (2003)* and the *Stress testing by insurers guidance paper (2003).* Given the particular importance of the liability structure in determining the investment policies, and the key role of asset-liability management for insurers, this paper should be considered together with any IAIS work thereon.

The IAIS Standard on asset-liability management (2006) paper describes best practices for asset-liability management (ALM) that a well managed insurer would be expected to follow and identifies 11 minimum requirements.

Supervisors should ensure that insurers in their jurisdiction meet these requirements. The requirements set out in this standard apply to both life and non-life business. Insurers should understand the risks they are exposed to and develop ALM policies to manage them effectively. They should apply techniques appropriate for the nature of their business, the risks they undertake and local market conditions. Every insurer should have an ALM policy, but not all ALM risks need to be assessed using complex techniques. For example, simple or short term business may call for less complex ALM techniques.

The IAIS has also developed an accompanying *issues paper on asset-liability management* (2006). It provides additional information on asset-liability measurement, and management techniques; and contains an appendix with definitions of ALM related terms.

SRI and Relevance of ALM

Socially responsible investing (SRI) consists in the inclusion of non-financial criteria, such as environmental, social and governance considerations, into the process of investment decision-making. It aims at achieving non-financial results as well as a financial return.

Three main SRI strategies are available for responsible investors: screening, shareholder activism and community investing. The practice of screening, the first SRI strategy, consists in choosing securities based on social or environmental criteria; the choice process may be negative, positive, or a combination of both.

The second option open to socially responsible investors is shareholder activism. The ownership of company shares provides investors with rights and responsibilities, and they should use their rights as corporate owners to advocate whatever cause they deem appropriate ranging from animal protection to access for the disabled, for instance.

Lastly, the third identified SRI strategy resides in community investing. For instance, financial institutions choosing this path can propose low interest rate loans to people who earn a low or moderate income, and who would otherwise be at a loss to finance affordable housing; they can develop such programs either in poor areas of the cities of rich countries, or in villages in developing countries.

The choice of insurance companies to adopt SRI policies is a matter of consistency between risk management and financial management.

40.6 Ratio Analysis in Insurance Companies

The obvious purpose of ratio analyes is to gauge the financial position and performance of a business organisations from the reported financial statements so as to felicitate decision-making. Financial statements of insurer generally suffers from following limitation:

(1) The statement, by nature, are interim since the actual status of an insurance company cannot be known with certainty, unless the business is sold or liquidated.

(2) The loss reserves, Created in books are rough estimates provisional in nature and cannot be accurate and precise

(3) Transactions summarised in the statements occur at different times are subject to balancing, inflation and other factors and can therefore be misleading without adjustments.

(4) Insurers reputation number and quality of personnel are generally not reflected.

The analyst needs performance criteria, which are susceptible to easy comparison, and bench mark of performance that reveal important relationships between the elements of insurance company financial statements.

Ratios are commonly used to express, measure, analyse and interpret these financial relationships.

Though every financial ratio serves a useful purpose in evaluation of an insurer, safe conclusion cannot be drawn from a review of a single ratio. Therefore, all ratios are to be examined and inferences be drawn. Familiarity with the insurer in question is an important complement to ratio analysis following insurance ratios are generally calculated:

(1) $$\text{Loss Ratio} = \frac{\text{Loss incurred}}{\text{Premium earned}}$$

or $$\frac{\text{Loss incurred + Loss Adjustment Expenses}}{\text{Premium earned}}$$

The second ratio mentioned above is commonly used by financial analysts. Since there is considerable time lag between calendar and policy years the following ratio is also calculated:

$$\frac{\text{Losses + Loss Adjustment Expenses + Reserve for losses incurred but not reported}}{\text{Net premium written}}$$

Since different premium are charged for similar risk among companies the analyst must carefully analyse the rate structure of various companies.

(2) $$\text{Expense Ratio} = \frac{\text{Expenses Incurred}}{\text{Premium written}}$$

This ratio is commonly used to determine the cost of acquisition. However, it may be distorted by special marketing practices or by the particular commission structure of a given company.

(3) Combined Ratio (Trade Ratio)

= Loss Ratio + Expense Ratio

Though, it is crude, but still is a powerful tool of analysis

(4) Kenney Rule: Roger Kenney is a famous author of various popular insurance ratios for measuring capacity of an insurance company some of these are:

Net premiums $\leq 3 \times$ Policyholders Surplus

(For property – liability insurance)policyholders surplus $3\frac{1}{2} \times$ Total Reserves

Though, there is no scientific justification, these ratios are frequently adopted by regulatory authorities in developed countries.

(5) Cover Ratio = $\dfrac{\text{Net Premium Written}}{\text{Loss Reserves + Policyholder's Surplus}}$

In countries like UK, this ratio is used as a measure of financial strength.

(6) Actual excepted mortality: This ratio very common in life insurance, measures the relationship between tabular mortality and actual mortality and is useful in testing the adequacy of rates and reserves. However, it lacks universal applicability because of difference in underwriting classification rates, tables etc.

(7) Interest realisation ratio = $\dfrac{\text{Interest earned}}{\text{Interest projected}}$

Ideally it should be $\geq 100\%$

(8) Lapse Ratio = $\dfrac{\text{Policies lapsed during the year}}{\text{Policies in force at the beginning}}$

or $\dfrac{\text{Policies lapsed}}{\text{Policies at the beginning + Policies made}}$

(9) Attrition ratio =

$$\frac{\text{Insurance in force at the begining of the year + Insurance} - \text{insurance written during the year} - \text{insurance-in-force at the end of the year}}{\text{Insurance written during the year}}$$

This ratio measures how much new production is required to overcome the force of attrition of business already existing in books.

40.7 Risk-Return Trade off

The income (result) of the insurance companies can be divided into two:

(a) *Technical result* (under writing income) – which represents the balance between products sold (principally insurance premiums) and expenses directly associated with insurance per se (principally claims and administrative expenses).

(b) *Financial results* – which represents the income generated by the investment of the collected premiums. The time leg between the collection of premiums and payment of claims give rise to investment opportunities.

"Ideally, a financially viable insurance firm requires not only that overall profits be positive enough to allow for a face risk-adjusted return on invested capital, but also, by implication that both segments (the underwriting and the financial result) should be receptacle profitable on a stand alone basis

Technical reserves measure the pending liabilities to the various policyholders and usually comprise the so-called loss reserves and the premium reserves. A company's loss reserve, computed by actuaries is the amount set aside to provide for outstanding claims, both reported and not reported (IBNR). As such, it is the insurance company's primary source of long-term debt. This type of debts, by definition is far riskier than traditional debt since neither the magnitude, nor the timing is known in advance. Also claims are affected by extraneous factors, such as Judicial decisions. The premium reserve also called as unearned premium reserve, corresponds to the balance of risks that are still to run after the balance sheet date.

The expected return on an insurance companies equity (g_R) and the expected return on its portfolio of invested assets (g_a) are expressed as:

$$\gamma_R = \gamma_f + \beta_R (\gamma_m - \gamma_f)$$

$$\gamma_a = \gamma_f + \beta_a (\gamma_m - \gamma_f)$$

Where γ_f is risk free return

γ_m – return or market portfolio

β_R and β_a – are measures of sensitivity to market.

Also $$\gamma_R = \frac{mP + \gamma_a(k + T)}{K}$$

Where m - underwriting margin

P - underwritten premium

K - equity reserves

T - technical reserves

Funds generating co-efficient (T/P) is the ratio of technical reserves over underwritten premiums.

Premium-to-surplus ratio (P/K) indicates the degree of insurance leverage taken by the insurance company. Since, issuance of policies is tantamount to borrowing money to leverage asset investments the insurance activity has resemblance with hedge funds the expected return on the insurance company's surplus

Is therefore

$$\gamma_R = mS + \gamma a\ (gs + 1)$$

where stands for premium to surplus ratio and g for the funds generating co-efficiency the profitability of an insurance company is dependent on the following:

(a) the level of underwriting profit or loss, reflecting the pricing level of risk and the level of claims.

(b) the level of investment yield, reflecting yield available in the market.

(c) the level of investment pool relative to the under writing return.

According to buffet the return on equity of an insurance company can be stated as:

$$\gamma_R = P_L\ ((\text{asset return 1} - \text{cost of float})\ \text{leverage}) + \text{asset return 2})$$

Where asset return 1 is defined as the financial return generated by the investment of technical reserves on the capital market and asset return 2 in defined as the financial return generated by the investment of shareholder's paid inequity on the capital market. The cost of float is defined as the technical reserves divided by shareholder's paid in capital.

40.8 Valuation of Assets, Liabilities and Technical Provisions

Valuation of assets and liabilities is crucial for asset liability management, cash flow, investment management and profitability of the insurance companies, as any mismatch and incorrect valuation would impact the balance sheet, profit and loss; and in turn would lead to excess or inadequate capital.

The market, income, and cost approaches are generally accepted under fair value measurement method of valuation. Under the market approach, prices for market transactions for identical or comparable assets or liabilities are used. The income approach uses valuation techniques to discount future cash flows to a present value amount. The cost approach is based on the current replacement cost such as the cost to buy or build a substitute comparable asset after adjusting for obsolescence. Availability and reliability of data related to the asset or liability is a major factor in selection of method for valuation. The purpose of valuation which may be financial reporting, consolidation, Mergers and Acquisition, initial Public Offer, Reorganization, Leverage buy out or sale may also impact the choice of the valuation method.

Generally, a single or multiple valuation technique may be needed based on the situation and a multiple valuation method would be used to value assets, liabilities and provisions.

40.8.1 QIS4 on Assets and Liabilities Valuation

The purpose of QIS4 is to specify the frameworks for valuating of assets, liabilities and technical provisions of insurance companies such that the required capital for maintaining solvency can be assessed. QIS4 proposes principle based valuation method for Assets and Liabilities.

The principles specified in QIS are :

- The assessment should be made using an economic, market-consistent valuation of all assets and liabilities.
- Mark to market, mark to model, proxies and national accounting figure would be the valuation techniques to be used in that order. Where marking to model valuation technique is used it has to be benchmarks, extrapolated or otherwise calculated from a market input, in which case characteristics of model and inputs used should be specified.
- In the case of ring-fenced funds in place which separated part of the resources from the rest of the business, the calculation of the liabilities and assets for each ring-fenced fund should include all cash-flows in and out of that fund.
- For solvency purposes, the economic value of most intangible assets is considered to be nil or negligible, since they very rarely have a cashable value. Accordingly Goodwill, brand value and similar intangible assets are not valued in calculating solvency capital.
- Valuations can be based on accounting figures when the difference between economic value and accounting value is insignificant; and/or the cost of calculating economic value is uneconomical.

Assumptions

The QIS4 guidelines for any underlying assumption are as follows :

- Where no credible information is available, the assumption used should be realistic.
- Cash-flow projections should reflect expected demographic, legal, medical technological, social or economic developments.
- Appropriate assumptions for future inflation should be built into the cash-flow projections. Care should be taken to identify the type of inflation to which particular cash-flows are exposed. For some cash-flows, the link may be to consumer prices, but there are other links such as salary inflation, which tends to exceed consumer price inflation.
- The inflation used in the calculations should be the market consistent base underlying inflation plus the necessary amount to reflect the specific features of the cost or cash-flows.

IFRS and Solvency II

International Financial Reporting Standard (IFRS) is the common accounting standard in Europe. If is expected that India will adopt IFRS as accounting standard by 2011. Solvency II framework accepts IFRS standard as proxy for valuing many of the balance sheet items. CEIOPS has identified items where IFRS valuation rules might be considered consistent with economic valuation, and where necessary, adjustments to IFRS are proposed which are intended to bring the IFRS treatment closer to an economic valuation approach.

In all cases where IAS valuation is accepted for solvency purposes but the insurers use internal valuation model which is different, a suitable explanation is to be provided by the insurers.

Balance Sheet Item	*Recommended Valuation and Solvency Adjustment for QIS4*
Intangible Assets	
Goodwill on Acquisitions; and Intangible Assets	Valued at nil for solvency purposes.
Tangible Assets	
Property, Plant and Equipment	IAS 16 revaluation model as given below is accepted if valuation is recent. *Initial Valuation* - At cost *Subsequent Valuation* – cost model : cost less any depreciation and impairment loss; – revaluation model : fair value at date of revaluation less any depreciation or impairment In other cases using fair value at balance sheet date using economic value should be considered.
Inventories	IAS valuation of – at the lower of cost and net realisable value is acceptable.
Finance Leases	The treatment under IAS 17, to the extent that fair value and not the present value of the minimum lease payment is used, is considered an acceptable proxy for valuation on an economic value basis.
Investments	
Investment Property	IAS valuation basis of initially at cost; then either fair value model or cost model is an acceptable proxy.
Participants in subsidiaries, associates and joing ventures	Fair value treatment as in IAS 39.
Held to maturity investments	Amortised cost.
Loans and Receivables	
Available for sale financial assets	Fair value with valuation through equity.
Financial assets at fair value through profit or loss	Fair value with valuation adjustment through profit and loss account.
Other Assets	
Non-current assets held for sale or discontinued operations	The treatment under IFRS 5, to the extent that fair value and not the carrying amount is used, is considered an acceptable proxy for valuation on an economic value basis.

(Contd...)

Balance Sheet Item	*Recommended Valuation and Solvency Adjustment for QIS4*
Deferred tax assets	The treatment under IAS 12 is an acceptable proxy for valuation on an economic value basis. Participants are not required to include in their solvency balance-sheet a deferred tax item specifically related to the change in value of technical provisions arising from the move from Solvency I to Solvency II. However, in line with the economic approach underpinning Solvency II, all expected future cash-out and inflows related to taxes applicable under the fiscal regime currently in force in each country should be recognized in the solvency balance-sheet. In particular, to the extent that a deferred tax item currently appears on the accounting balance-sheet in relation to technical provisions, this should be included in the QIS4 balance sheet.
Current Tax Assets	As under IAS 12–Current tax assets are measured at the amount expected to be recovered.
Cash and Cash equivalents	Current tax assets are measured at the amount expected to be recovered.
Impairment	IAS 36 and IAS 39 to be applied where relevant.
Provisions	Similar to IAS 37 where in the amount recognized is the best estimate of the expenditure required to settle the present obligation at the balance sheet date.
Financial Liabilities	
Financial Liabilities at fair value though profit or loss	Fair value with valuation adjustments through profit and loss account.
Other Financial liabilities and amounts payable	All financial liabilities should be valued at fair value in accordance with the guidance provided in IAS 39 with no adjustment, where applicable, for own credit standing. If a different valuation basis is used, full explanation must be provided.
Other Liabilities	
Deferred Tax Liabilities	As in IAS 12, Deferred tax liabilities cannot be discounted and are measured at the tax rates expected to apply when the liability is settled and must be reviewed at each Balance Sheet date. Participants are not required to include in their solvency balance-sheet a deferred tax item specifically related to the change in value of technical provisions arising from the move from Solvency I to Solvency II. However, in line with the economic approach underpinning Solvency II, all expected future cash-out and in flows related to taxes applicable under the fiscal regime currently in force in each country should be recognized in the solvency balance-sheet. In particular, to the extent that a deferred tax item currently appears on the accounting balance-sheet in relation to technical provisions, this should be included in the QIS4 balance sheet.
Current Tax Liabilities	Unpaid tax for current and prior periods is recognised as a liability. Current tax liabilities are measured at the amount expected to be paid.
Employee Benefits	
Short term employee benefits	As in IAS 19, Recognise undiscounted amount expected to be paid as a liability (accrued expense), after deducting any amount already paid.
Post employment benefits including pensions, Other Long Term employee benefits and Termination Benefits.	As in IAS 19

40.8.2 Valuation of Technical Provisions

Technical provisions consist of premium and claims provisions; and are likely to be the biggest amount in balance sheet of insurers apart from investment. Fair Value of technical provision is imperative for arriving at the capital requirement and solvency of the insurer.

The technical provisions are established with respect to all obligations towards policyholders and beneficiaries of insurance contracts. The calculation of technical provision should be based on current exist value and should reflect the amount for which they could be transferred or settled.

The technical provision is equal to the sum of a best estimate and a risk margin where both are valued separately, with the exception of hedgeable (re)insuance obligations. Stress is on using current and credible information for calculation purposes.

For non-life direct insurance, the amounts of technical provisions should be indicated for each of the insurance categories :

- ❑ Accident and health – workers' compensation
- ❑ Accident and health – health insurance
- ❑ Accident and health – others not included under first two items
- ❑ Motor, third-party, liabitity
- ❑ marine, Aviation and Transport
- ❑ Fire and other property damage
- ❑ Third-party Liability.
- ❑ Credit and Suretyship
- ❑ Legal expenses
- ❑ Assistance
- ❑ Miscellaneous non-life insurance

Proportional non-life reinsurance should be treated as direct insurance. *i.e.,* It should be allocated to one of the 12 lines of business (LOBs) listed in the previous paragraph.

Non-proportional reinsurance shall be split into propriety, casualty and Marine, Aviation and Transport (MAT) business.

For those Non-life LOBs which have contracts similar to life insurance, participants should disclose separately the best estimate of liabilities similar in nature to 'standard' applicable non life principles and the best estimate of liabilities where life principles need to used.

40.8.3 Techniques of Valuation

There are three techniques specified for technical provisions valuation :

- ❑ Best Estimate
- ❑ Simplified and
- ❑ Proxies.

Best Estimate

The best estimate method use' the time value of money, using the relevant risk-free interest rate term structure and is equal to the probability-weighted average of future cash-flows.

The principles behind Best Estimate Valuation of technical provisions are:

- The calculation of technical provisions is based on their current exit value.
- The calculation of technical provisions shall make use of and be consistent with the information provided by the financial markets and generally available data on insurance technical risk.
- The technical provisions are established with respect to all obligations towards policyholders and beneficiaries of insurance contracts.
- The value of the technical provisions is equal to the sum of best estimate and a risk margin.
- The calculation of best estimate should be based upon current and credible information and realistic assumptions and be performed using adequate actuarial method and statistical techniques.
- The cash-flow projection used in the calculation of the best estimate should take into account all the cash in-and out-flows required to settle the obligations over their lifetime.
- The best estimate should be calculated gross, without deduction of the amounts recoverable from reinsurance contracts and special purpose vehicles.
- The valuation of the best estimate for claims outstanding provisions and for premium provisions should generally be carried out separately. However, if such a separate treatment is not practical, valuation could be done together.
- Insurers should use statistical method compatible with current actuarial 'best practice' and should take into account all factors that might have a material impact on the expected future claims experience. Typically, this will require the use of claims data on an occurrence/accident year basis or an underwriting year basis for the run-off triangles.
- "Goodness-of-fit" tests should be applied to all statistical methods considered. The results from this analysis should be taken into account together with the estimate of future trends, the relevance of past data (particularly the inclusion of exceptional events) and other elements of actuarial judgment in determining the best estimate provisions.

Premiums Provisions

Premium provisions substitute current unearned premium provisions and unexpired risk provisions. Premium provisions relate to the coverage period when the insurer provides the service of accepting and managing the risk to its policyholders. The calculation of the best estimate of the premium provision relates to all future claim payments arising from future events post the valuation date that will be insured under the insurer' existing policies that have not yet expired, administrative expenses and to all expected future premiums.

Premium provision is determined on a prospective basis taking into-account the expected cash-in and cash-out flows and time value of money. The expected cash flows should be determined by applying appropriate methodologies and underlying models and using assumptions that are deemed to be realistic for the line of business of homogenous groups of risk.

Post-claims Technical Provisions

Post-claims technical provisions relate to the settlement period between claims being incurred and claims being settled. During the settlement period, the insurer is at risk due to uncertainties regarding the number of claims not yet reported. (IBNR claims), the stochastic nature of claim sizes and the timing of claim payments as well as uncertainties related to changes in the legal environment.

For short-tail claims, either the result of their individual valuation (case by case) or the result of sound statistical method may be assumed as reasonable proxies of their best estimate, provided it is proved to be a consistent method by back testing.

For claims with significant uncertainty, in either timing or amount, generally long tail claims; the best estimate should in principle be valued using relevant actuarial methods based on run-off triangles. To guarantee that the insurer controls both model and parameter errors, some general principles are suggested.

The best estimate should be assessed using at least two different method that could be considered reliable and relevant. Judgment should then be used to choose the most appropriate method. A most appropriate method is a technique which is part of best practice and which captures the nature of the liability most adequately. If the available data do not offer a robust behavior to be integrated directly into run-off triangles and treated through generally accepted actuarial method, the participant will try to adjust the historical date using objective and verifiable criteria, maintaining in any case homogeneity of different series used. If this adjustment were not possible or reliable, case by case assessment is preferable to the application of too heterogeneous method or to inconsistent sets of data. However, if it is considered that the claims handlers consistently under or over estimate claims, this should be reflected in the overall best estimate provision.

40.8.4 Risk Margin, Reinsurance and Hedging

The risk margin is to ensure that the value of technical provisions is equivalent to the amount that (re) insurance undertaking would be expected to require to take over and meet the (re)insurance obligation. It is to be calculated by determining the cost of providing an amount of eligible own founds equal to the Solvency Capital Requirements necessary to support the insurance (re)obligation over their lifetime.

The (re)insurance obligations are split into "hedgeable" and "non-hedgeable". The valuation of the technical provisions should cover both hedgeable and non-hedgeable (re)insurance obligation. Where there is an unsure distinction between hedgeable and non-hedgeable cash-flows, or where market-consistent values cannot be derived; the non-hedgeable approach should be followed.

A cost-of-capital methodology should be used in the determination of the risk margin.

Under the cost-of-capital approach, the risk margin is calculated by determining the cost of providing an amount of eligible own funds equal to the SCR necessary to support the insurance and/or reinsurance obligations over their lifetime. In order to do so, participants should produce a projection of their insurance and/or reinsurance obligations until their extinction and then, for each year, participants should determine the amount of the SCR to be me by undertaking facing such obligations.

For the purpose of QIS4, participants are requested to perform their SCR calculation on the basis of the standard formula, when calculating the risk margin, even if it should be possible to use the output of an approved internal model to perform the SCR calculation under the future Solvency II framework.

Where the risk margin calculation is based on the standard formula, it should be calculated net of reinsurance. Where participants calculate the risk margin using an internal model, they can either perform one single net calculation or two separate calculations.

The risk muddles that need to be taken into account in the cost-of-capital calculations are operational risk, underwriting risk with respect to existing business and counterparty default risk with respect to ceded reinsurance. The QIS4 framework provides detail for arriving at this risk and however is not discussed here as this beyond the purview of this article.

40.8.5 Other Considerations

Insurance company's valuation differs due to inherent uncertainty is estimating its labilities and assets. Discounting of cash flows, expenses, reinsurance recovery and default risk needs special attention.

Discounting

Cash-flow should be discounted at the risk-free discount rate applicable for the relevant maturity at the valuation date. These should be derived from the risk-free interest rate term structure at the valuation date. Where the financial market provides no data for a maturity, the interest rate should be interpolated or extrapolated fashion.

To determine that alternative risk free interest rate term structure, a model which is close to the model used by the European Central Bank could be used. In Indian scenario this could be model used by RBI.

Expenses

Expenses that will have to be incurred in the future to service in insurance contract are cash flows for which a technical provision should be calculated. For the valuation, firms should make assumptions with respect to future expenses arising from commitments made on or prior to, the valuation date.

All future administrative costs, including investment management, commissions, claims expenses and an appropriate amount of overheads should be considered. Expense assumptions should include an allowance for future cost increases. These should take into account the types of cost involved. The allowance for inflation should be consistent with the economic assumptions made. For disability income and other similar types of business, claims expenses may be a significant factor.

To the extent that future deposits or renewal premiums are considered in the evaluation of best estimate, expenses relating to those future deposits and renewal premiums should usually be taken into consideration as well. Expenses related to the cash flows due to future premiums are excluded if the latter are excluded from the evaluation of the best estimate.

Firms should consider their own analysis of expense, future business plans and any relevant market data. As an alternative to using the analysis of their own expenses and future business plans, a new company (with anticipated cost-overruns for an initial period) may consider the likely level of costs that would be incurred if the administration of existing policies were outsourced to a third party.

Whenever the present value of expected future contract loadings is taken as a starting point, any shortfall relative to future expenses that will have to be incurred in the future to service an insurance contract should be recognised as an additional liability (and the opposite).

Reinsurance Liabilities and Special Purpose Vehicle (SPV)

The best estimate of the insurance liabilities of the insurers should be calculated gross of reinsurance contracts and SPV arrangements. The value of reinsurance recoverables should be adjusted in order to take account of expected tosses due to counterparty default, whether this arises from insolvency, dispute or another reason.

In certain types of reinsurance, the timing of recoveries and that of direct payments might markedly diverge, and this should be taken into account when valuing reinsurance and SPV recoverables. Recoverables should also fully take into account cedents' deposits. In particular, if the deposit exceeds the best estimate claim on the recoverable is negative.

Risk of Counterparty Default and Margin Assessment

As there is a possibility of default by counter party, the associated risk or default has to be calculated and appropriated/provided for.

The counter part default assessment should has to be calculated and appropriated/provided for.

The counter part default assessment should be based on an assessment of the probability of default of the counterparty and average loss, resulting from such a default (loss-given-default). The assessment should also take the duration of the reinsured liabilities into account. Credit spreads, rating judgements, information relating to the supervisory solvency assessment, and the financial reporting of the counterparty are some of the sources of information that could be used for assessing the risk. The assessment of the probability of default should take into account the fact that the probability increases with the time horizon of the assessment and the average probability should be assessed.

If no reliable estimate of the loss-given-default is available, 50% of the value of the amounts recoverable should be used. If no reliable estimate of the probability of default is available, the probability of default of the counterparty according to the default risk sub-module of the SCR standard formula should be used for a time horizon of one year.

As far as recoverables are covered by a collateral or a letter of credit, the probability of default of the collateral or the letter of credit occurring at the same time as the default of the counterparty, along with its loss-given-default may replace the probability of default and the loss-given-default of the counterparty.

The adjustment for expected loss should be calculated separately for each counterparty. However if the estimates of the probability of default and the loss-given-default of several counter parties coincide, no separate calculation is necessary under the simplified approach.

Future Premiums from Existing Contracts

The cash flows included in the best estimate of the (re)insurance liability should only include cash flows associated with the current insurance contracts and any existing ongoing obligation to service policyholders. This should not include expected future renewals that are not included within the current insurance contracts.

Recurring premiums should be included in the determination of future cash flows, with an assessment of the future persistency based on actual experience and anticipated future experience.

Where a contract includes options and guarantees that provide rights under which the policyholder can obtain a further contract on favourable terms (for example, renewal with restrictions on re-pricing or further underwriting) then these options or guarantees should be included in the valuation of the insurance liability arising under the existing contract. Where no such restrictions on re-pricing or underwriting exist, there is no ongoing obligation to service policyholders.

In particular, future premiums should be included in the determination of future cash flows when the payment of future premiums by the policyholder is legally enforceable or guaranteed amounts at settlement are fixed at subscription date.

Simplified Method

A simplified method uses actuarial methods and statistical techniques to calculate insurance liabilities and is appropriate in case the risk underwritten by insurance companies is not complex in risk and scope. Simplified method is advised in the case of following scenarios:

- Homogenous group of risk that is not complex
- The insured risks underwritten are stable and claims pay out could be predicted with great certainty or future claims related cash flow could be projected with greater accuracy.
- Liability valued is not material in absolute terms or relative to the overall amount of total best estimate.
- This guidance on materiality is applicable with respect to all simplifications to determine the value of the best estimate and/or risk margin.

Proxy Method

Proxy method can be used where there is insufficient company-specific data of appropriate quality to apply a reliable statistical actuarial method for the determination of the best estimate or when the calculation of an economic value is unjustifiable and impractical in terms of cost incurred and benefits derived.

The following table specifies applicable actuarial and other proxy method for calculating various provisions :

It is possible that an insurance company may use any of the above methods to value its assets, liabilities and technical provision subject to the fact that consistency is maintained and wherever a deviation takes place, it should be ensured that the method is appropriate and explanation be provided.

To conclude, the global nature of insurance business and insurance companies has creater a need, wherein the regulators across the globe are looking at convergence in accounting and reporting standards. With the emergence of IFRS as a possible global standard, it is expected that EU's initiative towards Solvency II could become accepted as a standard for valuation for Solvency Capital Requirements and Mandatory Capital Requirements calculation by regulators outside Europe also.

QIS4 framework provides guidance for valuing the Assets Liabilities and Technical Provisions of the Insurance Companies, considering the complexities involved in organization, funding model, lines of business, complexity of the products sold, portfolio strength, and reinsurance arrangements. It provides for co-existence of standard and internal models for valuation. The fact it is still evolving would mean that it might undergo some changes but it is hoped that the underlying principle would not change much. Insurance being a highly regulated business it is expected that testing capital adequacy for solvency purpose would be a prime method of valuation in addition to valuation conducted for any other purpose.

ANNEXURE 40-A

THE GAZETTE OF INDIA : EXTRAORDINARY
[PART III – SEC. 4]

INSURANCE REGULATORY AND DEVELOPMENT AUTHORITY, NEW DELHI

NOTIFICATION

New Delhi, the 14th July, 2000

Insurance Regulatory and Development Authority (Assets, Liabilities, and Solvency Margin of Insurers) Regulations, 2000

F.No. IRDA/Reg./7/2000

In exercise of the powers conferred by clauses (y), (z) and (za) of sub-section (2) of section 114A of the Insurance Act, 1938, (4 of 1938), read with section 26 of the Insurance Regulatory and Development Authority Act, 1999 (41 of 1999), the Authority, in consultation with the Insurance Advisory Committee, hereby makes the following regulations, namely:–

Short Title and Commencement – (1) These regulations may be called the Insurance Regulatory and Development Authority (Assets, Liabilities, and Solvency Margin of Insurers) Regulations, 2000.

(2) They shall come into force from the date of their publication in the *Official Gazette.*

2. Definitions – (1) In these regulations, unless the context otherwise requires ––

(a) "*Act*" means the Insurance Act, 1938 (4 of 1938);

(b) "*Authority*" means the Insurance Regulatory and Development Authority established under sub-section (1) of section 3 of the Insurance Regulatory and Development Authority Act, 1999 (41 of 1999);

(2) All words and expressions used herein and not defined but defined in the Insurance Act, 1938 (4 of 1938), or in the Insurance Regulatory and Development Authority Act, 1999 (41 of 1999), or in any Rules or Regulations made thereunder, shall have the meanings respectively assigned to them in those Acts or Rules or Regulations.

3. Valuation of Assets – Every insurer shall prepare a statement of the value of assets in Form IRDA- Assets- AA in accordance with Schedule I.

4. Determination of Amount of Liabilities – Every insurer shall prepare a statement of the amount of liabilities in accordance with Schedule II-A, in respect of life insurance business, and in Form HG in accordance with Schedule II-B, in respect of general insurance business, as the case may be.

5. Determination of Solvency Margin – Every insurer shall prepare a statement of solvency margin in accordance with Schedule III-A, in respect of life insurance business, and in Form KG in accordance with Schedule III-B, in respect of general insurance business, as the case may be.

6. Health Insurance Business – Where the insurer transacts health insurance business, providing health covers, the amount of liabilities shall be determined in accordance with the principles specified under these Regulations.

7. Business outside India – Where the insurer transacts insurance business in a country outside India, and submits statements or returns or any such particulars to a public authority of that country, he shall enclose the same along with the Forms specified in accordance with these Regulations and the Insurance Regulatory and Development Authority (Actuarial Report and Abstract) Regulations, 2000.

Provided that if the appointed actuary is of the opinion that it is necessary to set additional reserves over and above the reserves shown in the statements or returns or any such particulars submitted to the public authority of a country outside India, he may set such additional reserves.

8. Furnishing of Forms – The Forms, namely, Form IRDA- Assets- AA , Form HG, and Form KG, shall be furnished separately for Business within India and Total Business transacted by the insurer.

9. Personal Visit of Appointed Actuary to the Authority – The Authority may, if considered necessary and expedient, ask the appointed actuary to make a personal visit to the office of the Authority to elicit from him any further information.

Schedule I

VALUATION OF ASSETS

(see Regulation 3)

1. Interpretation : In this Schedule, unless the context otherwise requires, 'non-mandated investments' means those investments that are neither approved securities nor approved investments.

2. Values of Assets : (1) The following assets should be placed with value zero –

(a) Agent's balances and outstanding premiums in India, to the extent they are not realised within a period of thirty days;

(b) Agents' balances and outstanding premiums outside India, to the extent they are not realisable;

(c) Sundry debts, to the extent they are not realisable;

(d) Advances of an unrealisable character;

(e) Furniture, fixtures, dead stock and stationery;

(f) Deferred expenses;

(g) Profit and loss appropriation account balance and any fictitious assets other than pre-paid expenses;

(h) Reinsurer's balances outstanding for more than three months;

(i) Preliminary expenses in the formation of the company;

(2) The value of computer equipment including software shall be computed as under:–

(*i*) seventy five per cent of its cost in the year of purchase;

(*ii*) fifty per cen of its cost in the second year;

(*iii*) twenty-five per cent of its cost in the third year; and

(*iv*) zero per cent thereafter.

(3) All other assets of an insurer have to be valued in accordance with the Insurance Regulatory and Development Authority (Preparation of Financial Statements and Auditor's Report of Insurance Companies) Regulations, 2000.

3. Statement of Assets : Every insurer shall prepare a statement of assets in Form IRDA-Assets-AA.

Form IRDA-Assets - AA

(See Regulation 3)

INSURANCE REGULATORY AND DEVELOPMENT AUTHORITY
(ASSETS, LIABILITIES, AND SOLVENCY MARGIN OF INSURERS) REGULATIONS, 2000.

Statement of Assets as at 31st March, 20____.

Form Code: [ ][ ][ ][ ][ ][ ][ ][ ][ ]

Name of Insurer: Registration Number: Date of registration: ________

Classification: Business Within India/ Total Business

Item No.	*Category of Asset*	*Policyholders' funds: Amount (in rupees lakhs) as per (a) below*	*Shareholders' funds: Amount (in rupees lakhs) as per (a) below*
(1)	*(2)*	*(3)*	*(4)*
01	Approved Securities		
02	Approved Investments		
03	Deposits		
04	Non-Mandated Investments		
05	Other Assets, specify		
06	Total		
07	Fair Value Change Account		
08	Adjusted Value of Assets: (6) – (7)		

I certify that the statement has been prepared in accordance with Schedule I.

Place — Name and Signature of Appointed Actuary. (in case of a life insurer)

Date — Name and Signature of Auditor (in case of a general insurer)

Notes: The statement shall show the value of the above-mentioned categories of assets in accordance with Regulation 2 in Schedule I.

Schedule II-A

Valuation of Liabilities — Life Insurance

(See Regulation 4)

1. Interpretation — In this Schedule, —

(*a*) "valuation date", in relation to an actuarial investigation, means the date to which the investigation relates.

(*b*) "universal life contracts" means those contracts that are presented in an unbundled form. The contracts where policyholders have an option to invest in units of insurer's segregated fund(s) shall be treated as "linked business"; and others shall be treated as "non-linked business".

(*c*) "segregated funds" means funds earmarked in respect of linked business.

2. Method of Determination of Mathematical Reserves

(1) Mathematical Reserves shall be determined separately for each contract by a prospective method of valuation in accordance with sub-paras (2) to (4)..

(2) The valuation method shall take into account all prospective contingencies under which any premiums (by the policyholder) or benefits (to the policyholder/beneficiary) may be payable under the policy, as determined by the policy conditions. The level of benefits shall take into account the reasonable expectations of policyholders (with regard to bonuses, including terminal bonuses, if any) and any established practices of an insurer for payment of benefits.

(3) The valuation method shall take into account the cost of any options that may be available to the policyholder under the terms of the contract.

(4) The determination of the amount of liability under each policy shall be based on prudent assumptions of all relevant parameters. The value of each such parameter shall be based on the insurer's expected experience and shall include an appropriate margin for adverse deviations (hereinafter referred to as MAD) that may result in an increase in the amount of mathematical reserves.

(5)

(i) The amount of mathematical reserve in respect of a policy, determined in accordance with sub-para (4), may be negative (called "negative reserves") or less than the guaranteed surrender value available (called "guaranteed surrender value deficiency reserves") at the valuation date.

(ii) The appointed actuary shall, for the purpose of section 35 of the Act, use the amount of such mathematical reserves without any modification;

(iii) The appointed actuary shall, for the purpose of sections 13, 49, 64V and 64VA of the Act, set the amount of such mathematical reserve to zero, in case of such negative reserve, or to the guaranteed surrender value, in case of such guaranteed surrender value deficiency reserves, as the case may be.

(6) The valuation method shall be called "Gross Premium Method'.

(7) If in the opinion of the appointed actuary, a method of valuation other than the Gross Premium Method of valuation is to be adopted, then, other approximations (e.g. retrospective method) may be used.

Provided that the amount of calculated reserve is expected to be atleast equal to the amount that shall be produced by the application of Gross Premium Method.

(8) The method of calculation of the amount of liabilities and the assumptions for the valuation parameters shall not be subject to arbitrary discontinuities from one year to the next.

(9) The determination of the amount of mathematical reserves shall take into account the nature and term of the assets representing those liabilities and the value placed upon them and shall include prudent provision against the effects of possible future changes in the value of assets on the ability of the insurer to meet its obligations arising under policies as they arise.

3. Policy Cash Flows : The gross premium method of valuation shall discount the following future policy cash flows at an appropriate rate of interest —

(a) premiums payable, if any, benefits payable, if any, on death; benefits payable, if any, on survival; benefits payable, if any, on voluntary termination of contract, and the following, if any:-

(i) basic benefits,

(ii) rider benefits,

(iii) bonuses that have already been vested as at the valuation date,

(iv) bonuses as a result of the valuation at the valuation date, and

(v) future bonuses (one year after valuation date) including terminal bonuses (consistent with the valuation rate of interest);

(b) commission and remuneration payable, if any, in respect of a policy (This shall be based on the current practice of the insurer). No allowance shall be made for non-payment of commissions in respect of the orphaned policies;

(c) policy maintenance expenses, if any, in respect of a policy, as provided under sub-para (4) of para 5;

(d) allocation of profit to shareholders, if any, where there is a specified relationship between profits attributable to shareholders and the bonus rates declared for policyholders.

Provided that allowance must be made for tax, if any.

4. Policy Options : Where a policy provides built-in options, that may be exercised by the policyholder, such as conversion or addition of coverage at future date(s) without any evidence of good health, annuity rate guarantees at maturity of contract, etc., the costs of such options shall be estimated and treated as special cash flows in calculating the mathematical reserves.

5. Valuation Parameters : **(1) The valuation parameters** shall constitute the bases on which the future policy cash flows shall be computed and discounted. Each parameter shall have to be appropriate to the block of business to be valued. An appointed actuary shall take into consideration the following :

(a) The value(s) of the parameter shall be based on the insurer's experience study, where available. If reliable experience study is not available, the value(s) can be based on the industry study, if available and appropriate. If neither is available, the values may be based on the bases used for pricing the product. In establishing the expected level of any parameter, any likely deterioration in the experience shall be taken into account;

(b) The expected level, as determined in clause (a) of this sub-para, shall be adjusted by an appropriate Margin for Adverse Deviations (MAD), the level of MAD being dependent on the degree of confidence in the expected level, and such MAD in each parameter shall be based on the Guidance Notes issued by the Actuarial Society of India, with the concurrence of the Authority

(c) The values used for the various valuation parameters should be consistent among themselves.

(2) **Mortality rates** to be used shall be by reference to a published table, unless the insurer has constructed a separate table based on his own experience:

Provided that such published table shall be made available to the insurance industry by the Actuarial Society of India, with the concurrence of the Authority.

Provided further that such rates determined by reference to a published table shall not be less than hundred per cent. of that published table.

Provided further that such rates determined by reference to a published table may be less than hundred per cent. of that published table if the appointed actuary can justify a lower per cent.

(3) Morbidity rates to be used shall be by reference to a published table, unless the insurer has constructed a separate table based on his own experience:

Provided that such published table shall be made available to the insurance industry by the Actuarial Society of India, with the concurrence of the Authority:

Provided further that such rates determined by reference to a published table shall not be less than hundred per cent of that published table.

Provided further that such rates determined by reference to a published table may be less than hundred per cent of that published table if the appointed actuary can justify a lower per cent.

(4) Policy Maintenance Expenses shall depend on the manner, in which they are analysed by the insurer, *viz.*, fixed expenses and variable expenses. The variable expenses shall be related to sum assured or premiums or benefits. The fixed expenses may be related to sum assured or premiums or benefits or per policy expenses. All expenses shall be increased in future years for inflation, the rate of inflation assumed should be consistent with the valuation rate of interest.

(5) Valuation Rates of Interest, to be used by appointed actuary-

(a) shall be not higher than the rates of interest, for the calculation of the present value of policy cash flows referred to in para 4, determined from prudent assessment of the yields from existing assets attributable to blocks of life insurance business, and the yields which the insurer is expected to obtain from the sums invested in the future, and such assessment shall take into account —

(i) the composition of assets supporting the liabilities, expected cash flows from the investments on hand, the cash flows from the block of policies to be valued, the likely future investment conditions and the reinvestment and disinvestment strategy to be employed in dealing with the future net cash flows;

(ii) the risks associated with investment in regard to receipt of income on such investment or repayment of principal;

(iii) the expenses associated with the investment functions of the insurer;

(b) shall not be higher than, for the calculation of present value of policy cash flows in respect of a particular category of contracts, the yields on assets maintained for the purpose of such category of contacts;

(c) in respect of non-participating business, shall recognise the risk of decline in the future interest rates;

(d) in respect of participating business, shall be based on the assumption (with regard to future investment conditions), that the scale of future bonuses used in the valuation is consistent with the valuation rate of interest, and

(e) in respect of single premium business, shall take into account the effect of changes in the risk-free interest rates.

(6) Other Parameters, may be taken into account, depending on the type of policy. In establishing the values of such parameters, the considerations set out in this Schedule shall be taken into account.

6. Applicability to Reinsurance : (1) This Schedule shall also apply to the valuation of business in the books of reinsurers.

(2)As regards the business ceded by insurers, this Schedule shall be applicable to the net sums at risk retained by the insurer.

(3)Reinsurance arrangement with an element of borrowing in the form of deposit or credit of any kind from insurer's reinsurers without the prior approval of the Authority shall not be treated as credit for reinsurance for the purpose of determination of required solvency margin.

7. Additional Requirements for Linked Business : (1) Reserves in respect of linked business shall consist of two components, namely, unit reserves and general fund reserves.

(2) Unit reserves shall be calculated in respect of the units allocated to the policies in force at the valuation date using unit values at the valuation date.

(3) General fund reserves (non-unit reserves) shall be determined using a prospective valuation method set out in this Schedule, which shall take into account of the following, namely:-

(a) premiums, if any, payable in future;

(b) death benefits, if any, provided by the general fund (over and above the value of units);

(c) management charges paid to the general fund;

(d) guarantees, if any, relating to surrender values or minimum death and maturity benefits;

(e) fund growth rates and management charges. (The values of these parameters, along with others, shall be determined in accordance with para 5);

(f) negative reserves, if any, shall be dealt with in accordance with sub-para (5) of para 2

8. Additional Requirements for Provisions : The appointed actuary shall make aggregate provisions in respect of the following, where it is not possible to calculate mathematical reserves for each policy, in the determination of mathematical reserves:

(a) Policies in respect of which extra premiums have been charged on account of underwriting of under-average lives that are subject to extra risks such as occupation hazard, over-weight, under-weight, smoking history, health, climatic or geographical conditions;

(b) Lapses policies not included in the valuation but under which a liability exists or may arise;

(c) Options available under individual and group insurance policies;

(d) Guarantees available to individual and group insurance policies;

(e) The rates of exchange at which benefits in respect of policies issued in foreign currencies have been converted into Indian Rupees and what provision has been made for possible increase of mathematical reserves arising from future variations in rates of exchange;

(f) Other, if any.

9. Statement of Liabilities : An insurer shall furnish a statement of liabilities in accordance with the Insurance Regulatory and Development Authority (Actuarial Report and Abstract) Regulations, 2000.

Schedule II-B

Valuation of Liabilities (General Insurance)

(See Regulation 4)

1. Interpretation : In this schedule, –

(*a*) *"Reserve for claims incurred but not reported (IBNR")* means the reserve for claims incurred but not reported on the balance sheet date, and includes reserve for claims which may be inadequately reserved;

(*b*) *"Reserve for outstanding claims"* means the reserve for outstanding claims as mentioned in para 2(1)(b)(iii) of this Schedule.

2. Determination of Liabilities : An insurer shall –

(i) Place a proper value in respect of the following items, namely:

  (I) provision for bad and doubtful debts,

  (II) reserve for dividends declared or recommended, and outstanding dividends in full,

  (III) amount due to insurance companies carrying on insurance business, in full,

  (IV) amount due to sundry creditors, in full,

  (V) provision for taxation, in full, and

  (VI) foreign exchange reserve.

(ii) Determine the amount of following reserves, in the manner specified herein below for each reserve:-

(a) reserve for unexpired risks, shall be, in respect of, –

  (I) Fire business, 50 per cent,

  (II) Miscellaneous business, 50 per cent,

  (III) Marine business other than marine hull business, 50 per cent; and

  (IV) Marine hull business, 100 per cent,

of the premium, net of re-insurances, received or receivable during the preceding twelve months;

(b) reserve for outstanding claims shall be determined in the following manner:-

(I) where the amounts of outstanding claims of the insurers are known, the amount is to be provided in full;

(II) where the amounts of outstanding claims can be reasonably estimated according to the insurer, he may follow the 'case by case method' after taking into account the explicit allowance for changes in the settlement pattern or average claim amounts, expenses and inflation;

(c) reserve for claims incurred but not reported (IBNR) shall be determined using actuarial principles. In such determination, the appointed actuary shall follow the Guidance Notes issued by the Actuarial Society of India, with the concurrence of the Authority, and any directions issued by the Authority, in this behalf.

3. Statement of Liability : Every general insurer shall prepare a statement of liabilities in Form HG, certified by an auditor approved by the Authority in accordance with Section 64V of the Act, and also certified by its appointed actuary in respect of IBNR reserves. The statement shall be furnished to the Authority alongwith the returns mentioned in section 15 of the Act.

Form HG

(See Regulation 4)

Insurance Regulatory and Development Authority
(Assets, Liabilities and Solvency Margin) Regulation, 2000.

TABLE I : STATEMENT OF LIABILITIES as at 31st March, 20 __

Form Code: [ ][ ][ ][ ][ ][ ][ ][ ]

Name of Insurer: Registration Number: Date of registration: ______

Classification: Business Within India/Total Business

Item No.	*Description*	*Reserves for unexpired risks*	*Reserve for Outstanding Claims*	*IBNR Reserves*	*Total Reserves*
(1)	*(2)*	*(3)*	*(4)*	*(5)*	*(6)*
01	**Fire**				
02	**Marine**				
	Sub class:				
	Marine Cargo				
	Marine Hull				
03	**Miscellaneous**				
	Sub class:				
	Motor				
	Engineering				
	Aviation				
	Liabilities				
	Rural insurance				
	Others				
04	**Health Insurance**				
05	**Total Liabilities**				

Certification from Auditor (approved by the Authority)

I certify that the above statement represents the liabilities of the insurer which have been determined in the manner prescribed in the Insurance Regulatory and Development Authority (Assets, Liabilities and Solvency Margin of Insurers) Regulations, 2000 and the amounts of such liabilities are fair and reasonable. I also further certify that the above statement includes the IBNR reserves which have been determined by the appointed actuary and his certificate is furnished herein below.

Qualifications, if any (in regard to the determination of liabilities):

Place:

Date:

Name and Signature of the Auditor

Certification from the Appointed Actuary

I certify that the IBNR reserves in the statement above represent, in my opinion, true and fair amount.

Qualifications, if any (in regard to the determination of IBNR reserves):

Place:

Date:

Name and Signature of the Appointed Actuary

Schedule III-A

(See Regulation 5)

DETERMINATION OF SOLVENCY MARGINS — LIFE INSURERS

1. Interpretation — In this Schedule –

(a) 'Available Solvency Margin' means the excess of value of assets (furnished in IRDA- Form- AA) over the value of life insurance liabilities (furnished in Form H as specified in Regulation 4 of Insurance Regulatory and Development Authority (Actuarial Report and Abstract) Regulations, 2000) and other liabilities of policyholders' fund and shareholders' funds;

(b) "Solvency Ratio" means the ratio of the amount of Available Solvency Margin to the amount of Required Solvency Margin.

2. Determination of Solvency Margin — Every insurer shall determine the required solvency margin, the available solvency margin, and the solvency ratio in Form K as specified under Insurance Regulatory and Development Authority (Actuarial Report and Abstract), Regulations, 2000.

Schedule III-B

(See Section 5)

DETERMINATION OF SOLVENCY MARGINS — GENERAL INSURERS

1. Interpretation — In this Schedule –

(a) "Available Solvency Margin" means the excess of value of assets (furnished in Form IRDA-Assets- AA) over the value of liabilities (furnished in Form HG), with further adjustments as shown in Table III of Form KG.

(b) "Solvency Ratio" means the ratio of the amount of Available Solvency Margin to the amount of Required Solvency Margin.

2. Determination of Solvency Margin — Every insurer shall determine the required solvency margin, the available solvency margin, and the solvency ratio in Form KG.

Form KG

(See Regulation 5)

Insurance Regulatory and Development Authority
(Assets, Liabilities and Solvency Margin) Regulation, 2000.

TABLE I - STATEMENT OF SOLVENCY MARGIN:
(General Insurers) as at 31st March, 20____.

		Form Code: [ ][ ][ ][ ][ ][ ][ ][ ]
Name of Insurer:	Registration Number:	Date of registration: ______
Classification: Business	Within India/ Total Business	Classification Code:[ ]

TABLE I : REQUIRED SOLVENCY MARGIN BASED ON NET PREMIUM AND NET INCURRED CLAIMS (IN RS. LAKHS)

Item No.(Class of business)	*Description*	*Gross Premiums*	*Net Premiums*	*Gross Incurred claims*	*Net Incurred Claims*	*RSM-1*	*RSM-2*	*RSM*
(1)	*(2)*	*(3)*	*(4)*	*(5)*	*(6)*	*(7)*	*(8)*	*(9)*
01	**Fire**							
	Marine:							
02	Marine Cargo							
03	Marine Hull:							
	Miscellaneous:							
04	Motor							
05	Engineering							
06	Aviation							
07	Liability							
08	Rural Insurance							
09	Others							
10	Health Insurance:							
12	**TOTAL**							

Notes: (1) RSM-1 in the above table means Required Solvency Margin based on net premiums, and shall be determined as twenty per cent of the amount which is the higher of the Gross Premiums multiplied by a Factor A as specified below and the Net Premiums.

(2) RSM-2 in the above table means Required Solvency Margin based on net incurred claims, and shall be determined as thirty per cent. of the amount which is the higher of the Gross Net Incurred Claims multiplied by a Factor B as specified below and the Net Incurred Claims.

Item No.	*Description (Class of business)*	*A*	*B*
(1)	*(2)*	*(3)*	*(4)*
01	**Fire**	**0.5**	**0.5**
02	**Marine:** Marine Cargo	0.7	**0.7**
03	Marine Hull:	**0.5**	**0.5**
04	**Miscellaneous:** Motor	0.85	**0.85**
05	Engineering	0.5	**0.5**
06	Aviation	**0.9**	**0.9**
07	Liability	**0.85**	**0.85**
08	Rural Insurance	**0.5**	**0.5**
09	Others	**0.7**	**0.7**
10	Health	**0.85**	**0.85**

(3) RSM means Required Solvency Margin and shall be the higher of the amounts of RSM-1 and RSM-2.

TABLE II - AVAILABLE SOLVENCY MARGIN AND SOLVENCY RATIO

Item	*Description*	*Notes No... Amount*	*(1)*	*(2)*	*(3)*	*(4)*
01	Available Assets in Policyholders' Funds:					
	Deduct:					
02	Liabilities					
03	Other Liabilities					
04	**Excess in Policyholders' Funds** (01 - 02 - 03)					
05	Available Assets in Shareholders Funds:					
	Deduct:					
06	Other Liabilities					
07	**Excess in Shareholders' Funds:** (05 -06)					
08	Total ASM (04)+(07)					
09	**Total RSM**					
10	**Solvency Ratio (Total ASM/Total RSM)**					

Certification

I, , the Auditor, certify that the above statements have been prepared in accordance with the Section 64VA of the Insurance Act, 1938, and the amounts mentioned therein are true to the best of my knowledge.

Place: Name and Signature of the Auditor

Date:

Countersignature: Principal Officer

Notes:

1. Item No. 1 shall be the amount of the Adjusted Value of Assets in respect of policyholders' funds as mentioned in Form IRDA-Assets-AA.
2. Item No. 2 shall be the amount of Total Liabilities as mentioned in Form HG.
3. Item No. 3 shall be the amount of other liabilities arising in respect of policyholders' funds and as mentioned in the Balance Sheet
4. Items No. 5 shall be the amount of the Total Assets in respect of shareholders' funds as mentioned in Form IRDA-Assets-AA.
5. Item Nos. 6 shall be the amount of other liabilities arising in respect of shareholders' funds and as mentioned in the Balance Sheet.

N. RANGACHARY, Chairperson

[No. Advt.-3/4/Exty/161/2000]

Annexure 40-B

TO BE PUBLISHED IN THE GAZETTE OF INDIA EXTRAORDINARY [PART III – SEC. 4]

Insurance Regulatory and Development Authority (Investment) Regulations, 2000

NOTIFICATION

New Delhi, the 14th August, 2000

F.No. IRDA/ Reg./ 8/ 2000

In exercise of the powers conferred by Sections 27A, 27B, 27D and 114A of the Insurance Act, 1938 (4 of 1938), the Authority in consultation with the Insurance Advisory Committee, hereby makes the following regulations, namely:

1. Short Title and Commencement

(1) These regulations may be called the Insurance Regulatory and Development Authority (Investment) Regulations, 2000.

(2) They shall come into force on the date of their publication in the *Official Gazette.*

2. Definitions

In these regulations, unless the context otherwise requires –

(a) 'Act' means the Insurance Act, 1938 (4 of 1938).

(b) 'Accretion of funds' means investment income, gains on sale/ redemption of existing investment and operating surplus.

(c) 'Authority' means the Insurance Regulatory and Development Authority established under sub-section (1) of Section 3 of the Insurance Regulatory and Development Authority Act, 1999 (41 of 1999).

(d) 'Principal Officer' means any person connected with the management of an insurer or any other person upon whom the Authority has served notice of its intention of treating him as the principal officer thereof.

(e) All words and expressions used herein and not defined but defined in the Insurance Act, 1938 (4 of 1938), or in the Insurance Regulatory and Development Act, 1999 (41 of 1999), or in any Rules or Regulations made thereunder, shall have the meanings respectively assigned to them in those Acts or Rules or Regulations.

3. Regulation of Investments

(1) Life Business: Without prejudice to Section 27 or Section 27A of the Act – Every insurer carrying on the business of life-insurance shall invest and at all times keep invested his controlled fund in the following manner:

S. No.	*Type of Investment*	*Percentage*
(i)	Government Securities	25%,
(ii)	Government Securities or other approved securities (including (I) above)	Not less than 50%,
(iii)	Approved Investments as specified in **Schedule I**	
(a)	Infrastructure and Social Sector *Explanation:* For the purpose of this requirement, Infras-tructure and Social Sector shall have the meaning as given in regulation 2(h) of Insurance Regulatory and Development Authority (Registration	Not less than 15%

	of Indian Insurance Companies) Regulations, 2000 and as defined in the Insurance Regulatory and Development Authority (Obligations of Insurers to Rural and Social Sector) Regulations, 2000 respectively.	
(b)	Others to be governed by Exposure/Prudential Norms specified in Regulation 5	Not exceeding 20%
(iv)	Other than in Approved Investments to be governed by Exposure/Prudential Norms specified in Regulation 5	Not exceeding 15%

(2) Pension and General Annuity Business: Every insurer shall invest and at all times keep invested assets of Pension Business, General Annuity Business and Group Business in the following manner:-

S. No.	*Type of Investment*	*Percentage*
(i)	Government securities, being not less than	20%
(ii)	Government Securities or other approved securities inclusive of (i) above, being not less than	40%
(iii)	Balance to be invested in Approved Investments as specified in **Schedule I** and to be governed by Exposure/Prudential Norms specified in Regulation 5	Not exceeding 60%

Note: For the purposes of this sub-regulation:

(a) No unapproved investments shall be made.

(b) All investments shall be made in graded securities and the grading shall not be less than of 'very strong' rating by a reputed and independent rating agency (e.g. AA of Standard and Poor).

(c) Every insurer shall invest assets in securities which are actively traded in any Stock Exchange in India and which are attributable to segregated funds, in respect of linked business.

4. Regulation of Investments

(1) General Business: Without prejudice to Section 27 or Section 27B of the Act, - Every insurer carrying on the business of general insurance shall invest and at all times keep invested his total assets in the manner set out below:

S. No.	*Type of Investment*	*Percentage*
(i)	Central Government Securities **being not less than**	20%
(ii)	State Government securities and other Guaranteed securities including (i) above **being not less than**	30%
(iii)	Housing and Loans to State Government for Housing and Fire Fighting equipment, **being not less than**	5%
(iv)	Investments in Approved Investments as specified in **Schedule II**	
(a)	Infrastructure and Social Sector **Explanation:** For the purpose of this requirement, Infrastructure and Social Sector shall have the meaning as given in regulation 2(h) of Insurance Regulatory and Development Authority (Registration of Indian Insurance Companies) Regulations, 2000 and as defined in the Insurance Regulatory and Development Authority (Obligations of Insurers to Rural and Social Sector) Regulations, 2000 respectively	Not less than 10%

(b) Others to be governed by Exposure/Prudential Norms specified in Regulation 5 — Not exceeding 30%

(v) Other than in Approved Investments to be governed by Exposure/Prudential Norms specified in Regulation 5 — Not exceeding 25%

Note: All investments shall be made in graded securities and the grading shall not be less than of 'very strong' rating by a reputed and independent rating agency (e.g. AA of Standard and Poor)

(2) Reinsurance Business: Every reinsurer carrying on reinsurance business in India shall invest and at all times keep invested his total assets in the same manner as set out in sub-regulation (1), until such time separate regulations in this behalf are made by the Authority.

5. Exposure/Prudential Norms

Without prejudice to anything contained in Sections 27A and 27B of the Act, every insurer shall limit his investments based on the following exposure norms:

(A) Exposure Norms

Type of Investment	*Limit for Investee Company*	*Limit for the entire group to which the investee company belongs*	*Limit for the industry sector to which the investee company belongs*
(a) Equity/ Preference Shares/ Convertible portion of Debentures at face value. (b) Debentures - (face value) including private placed NCD and Non convertible portion of Convertible Debentures. (c) Short/ Medium/ Long Term Loans and any other direct financial assistance.	(i) **As on any date** Not exceeding 20% of the total capital employed*. (ii) During the year Not exceeding 5% of estimated annual accretion of funds	(i) **As on any date** Not exceeding 15% of the total capital employed* of the group companies. (ii) During the year Not exceeding 10% of estimated annual accretion of funds.	Not exceeding 15% of the total capital employed* in all such companies.

(B) Exposure Norms for Investment in Public Financial Institutions

Equity Share and Preference Shares (at their face value).	Not exceeding 15% in general of the paid up equity/preference capital of the institution or the existing holding % level, if higher.
Investment in Equity Capital, Bonds, Debentures, Term Loans.	Not exceeding 10% of the capital employed by an institution as per the last audited Balance Sheet.
Total Investment vis-à-vis Net Worth of the Company.	Not exceeding 60% of Net Worth of the institution.
Total Investment in a Financial Year.	7.5% of annual accretions.
Total Investments in all the Financial Institutions.	Annual aggregate financial assistance to all Develop-ment Financial Institutions put together in a single year shall not exceed 20% of the estimated annual accretions for the year.

* Total capital employed means total of equity shares, preference shares, debentures, long/ medium/ short term loans (excluding public deposits), free reserves but excluding revaluation reserves, of the investee company as shown in its last audited balance sheet.

(C) Prudential Norms

The prudential norms for various instruments shall be as under:

(i) Debentures

Norms for Fully Convertible Debentures and Partly Convertible Debentures:

Investment decisions are related to attractiveness of equity shares to be received as a result of conversion. Due consideration is also given to the factors, viz

(a) rate of interest at the time of subscription to said debentures,

(b) appreciation and

(c) dividend income likely to be received from the equity shares.

Similar considerations also apply for Non-Convertible (NC) Debentures with detachable warrants attached to it.

Norms for Non-Convertible Debentures and Non-Convertible Debentures with warrants attached:

1. *Eligibility Amount*		
(a)	Working Capital Debentures	20% of the current assets, loans and advance minus outstanding amount of existing working capital NC Debentures.
(b)	Project Finance	As appraised by the Investment Committee
(c)	Normal Capital Expenditure	As assessed by the Investment Committee

Asset Cover (as specified in Schedule III)

First *pari passu* charge on fixed assets of the company offered as security with a minimum of **1.25 times** including proposed borrowings (excluding revaluation of assets).

Debt Equity Ratio (as specified in Schedule III)

Not to exceed 2:1 including the proposed NC Debenture issue. However, in case of capital intensive project debentures, higher ratio upto 4:1 may be considered.

Interest Cover (as specified in Schedule III)

Not less than 2 times for the latest year or on the basis of the average of the immediately preceding three years after including the interest on the proposed debentures at the applicable rate.

Dividend Pay-out

Minimum dividend of 10% in each of the two years out of the immediately preceding three years including the latest year.

(ii) Term Deposits and Loans with Non-Banking Companies

The insurer need to place the deposits with a view to cater to working capital needs of the corporate sector. The placement of the deposit are to be decided after evaluating financial and non-financial aspects of the performance parameters of the companies. The analysis need to include study of financial position, track record and other features such as quality of management, future prospects and market potential for the company's products. Credit rating of borrower should be uniformly maintained at a position which is indicative of a very strong financial position being not less than AA of Standard and Poor or equivalent rating of any other reputed and independent rating agency.

The maximum amount of Short Term Deposit that may be placed with any company is restricted to Rs 2 crores or 10% of net worth whichever is less.

The various norms/parameters for the placement of term loans are as under:

Particulars	*Limits*
Unsecured borrowing as a % of net worth.	Not to exceed 25% of net worth including the proposed loan, subject to networth of the borrowing company being not less than Rs. 15 crores.
Interest Cover.	Atleast 2.5 times including interest on proposed loans.
Debt/ Equity Ratio.	Not to exceed 2:1.
Current Ratio.	Not less than 1.33:1.
Dividend Record.	Atleast 10% for the last 5 years or 15% and above for 3 out of 5 years.
Listing	Equity shares of the Company shall be listed on any recognised stock exchange and the price should continuously been quoting above par atleast for 12 months prior to the date of sanction of loan.
Collateral Security	Cheques shall be obtained for principal and interest amount. Personal guarantee of promoters and pledge of shares may be taken.

(iii) Infrastructure and Social Sector

In the case of projects/ works in the infrastructure and social sector undertaken by a person other than a company, the norms indicated in the table above shall have to be met to the extent applicable.

(iv) Guidelines on Subscription to Preference Shares

(a) Companies whose preference shares are selected for investment should have sound financial position and steady income earning capacity.

(b) The dividend payable on the preference shares should be cumulative.

(c) The preference shares shall be redeemable.

(d) Preference capital after proposed issue shall not exceed 100% of equity capital.

(e) Dividend should have been paid on equity shares for two years out of immediately preceding three years.

(f) Preference dividend should have been paid for 3 years or 3 out of 4 or 5 years including latest 2 years if the preference shares are issued earlier.

(g) Non-dividend paying preference shares should not be considered for investment.

(h) Dividend cover on the basis of average profit of last 3 to5 years should be 3 times.

6. Returns to be Submitted by the Insurer

Every insurer shall submit to the Authority the following returns within such time, at such intervals and verified/certified in such manner as indicated there against. These returns shall be in addition to those prescribed in Insurance Rules, 1939. The Authority may, by any general or special order, modify or relax any requirement relating to the above.

7. Power to Call for Additional Information

The Authority may, by general or special order, require from the insurers such other information in such manner, intervals and time limit as may be specified therein.

8. Duty to Report Extraordinary Events Affecting the Investment Portfolio

Every insurer shall report to the Authority forthwith, the effect or the probable effect of any event coming to his knowledge, which could have an adverse impact on the investment portfolio held by him.

9. Constitution of Investment Committee

Every insurer shall constitute an Investment Committee which shall consist of a minimum of two non-executive directors of the Insurer, the Principal Officer, Chiefs of Finance and Investment divisions, and wherever appointed actuary is present, the Appointed Actuary. The decisions taken by the Investment Committee shall be properly recorded and be open to inspection by the officers of the Authority.

10. Miscellaneous

(1) Valuation of Assets and Accounting of Investments shall be as per the Insurance Regulatory and Development Authority (Preparation of Financial Statements and Auditor's Report of Insurance Companies) Regulations, 2000.

(2) The Authority may, by any general or special order, modify or relax requirement relating to regulation 5.

SCHEDULE I

(See Regulation 3)

LIST OF APPROVED INVESTMENTS FOR LIFE BUSINESS

'Approved Investments' for the purposes of Section 27A of the Act shall be as follows:

(a) All approved investments specified in Section 27A of the Act except

(i) clause (b) of sub-section (1) of section 27A of the Act;

(ii) first mortgages on immovable property situated in other country as stated in clause (m) of subsection (1) of section 27A of the Act

(iii) immovable property situated in other country as stated in clause (n) of subsection (1) of section 27A of the Act

In addition the Authority under powers given vide clause (s) of sub-section(1) section 27A of the Act declares the following investments as approved investments:

(b) All secured loans, deposits, debentures, bonds, other debt instruments, shares and preference shares rated as 'very strong' or more by a reputed and independent rating agency (e.g. AA of Standard and Poor);

(c) Deposits with banks (e.g. in current account, call deposits, notice deposits, term deposits, certificates of deposits, etc) and with Primary Dealers recognised by RBI included for the time being in the Second Schedule to the Reserve Bank of India Act, 1934 (2 of 1934);

(d) Commercial papers issued by a company having a 'very strong' or more rating by a reputed and independent rating agency (*e.g.* AA of Standard and Poor);

(e) Investments in Venture Capital Funds of such companies/ organisations which have a proven track record and have been rated 'very strong' or more by a reputed and independent rating agency (*e.g.* AA of Standard and Poor).

Explanation: For this purpose any investment in the shares or debentures or short or medium or long term loans or deposits with private limited companies shall not be treated as 'approved investments'.

SCHEDULE II

(See Regulation 4)

LIST OF APPROVED INVESTMENTS FOR GENERAL BUSINESS

'Approved Investments' for the purpose of Section 27B of the Act shall be as follows:

(a) All approved investments specified in Section 27B of the Act except

(i) clause (b) of sub-section (1) of section 27A of the Act;

(ii) immovable property situated in other country as stated in clause (n) of subsection (1) of section 27A of the Act

(iii) first mortgages on immovable property situated in other country as stated in clause (i) of subsection (1) of section 27B of the Act

In addition the Authority under powers given vide clause (j) of sub-section(1) section 27B of the Act declares the following investments as approved investments:

(b) All secured loans, deposits, debentures, bonds, other debt instruments, shares and preference shares rated as 'very strong' or more by a reputed and independent rating agency (e.g. AA of Standard and Poor);

(c) Loans to State Government for Housing and Fire Fighting Equipment.

(d) Deposits with banks (e.g. in current account, call deposits, notice deposits, term deposits, certificates of deposits, etc) and with Primary Dealers recognised by RBI included for the time being in the Second Schedule to the Reserve Bank of India Act, 1934 (2 of 1934);

(e) Commercial papers issued by a company having a 'very strong' or more rating by a reputed and independent rating agency;

(f) Treasury Bills issued by RBI, Inter Bank Repo of RBI and Bills Rediscounting.

(g) Investments in Venture Capital Funds of such companies/ organisations which have a proven track record and have been rated 'very strong' or more by a reputed and independent rating agency (e.g. AA of Standard and Poor).

Explanation: For this purpose any investment in the shares or debentures or short or medium or long term loans or deposits with private limited companies shall not be treated as 'approved investments'.

S. No	*Form No as annexed to these regulations*	*Short description*	*Periodicity of returns*	*Time limit for submission*	*Verified/Certified by*
1	Form 1	Statement of investment and income on investment	Yearly	Within 30 days from the date of Board approval of audited accounts.	Principal Officer/ Chief (Investment)
2	Form 2	Statement of down graded investments.	Quarterly	Within 21 days of the end of each quarter.	Principal Officer/ Chief (Investment)
3	Form 3A	Statement of Investment of Controlled Fund (Life) – Compliance Report	Quarterly	Within 21 days of the end of each quarter.	Principal Officer/ Chief (Investment)
4	Form 3B	Statement of Investment of Total Assets (General) – Compliance Report	Quarterly	Within 21 days of the end of each quarter.	Principal Officer/ Chief (Investment)
5	Form 4	Prudential Investment Norms – Compliance Report	Yearly	Within 30 days from the date of Board approval of audited accounts.	Principal Officer/ Chief (Investment)

SCHEDULE III

(See Regulation 5)

Asset Cover:

Asset Cover shows the relationship between Fixed Assets and secured loans. It is to be calculated by dividing Fixed Assets by Secured Loans. Details of working are as under:

FIXED ASSETS

Net Block of the Fixed Assets

Add: Capital Work in Progress

Less: Revaluation Reserves

Less: Goodwill

Less: Assets not available viz. exclusively charged assets. Vehicles, leased assets, etc.

TOTAL (A)

SECURED LOANS

First Charge debentures

Secured Term Loans

Deferred Payment Guarantee (if assets are not exclusively charged)

Proposed Borrowings

TOTAL (B)

Asset Cover (A/B)

Debt Equity Ratio

The relationship describing the lendor's contribution against owner's contribution shall be debt equity ratio. It shall be calculated by dividing long term debt by Networth. Details of working are as under:

First Charge Debentures (Gross Block less Depreciation)

Secured Term Loan

Deferred Payment Guarantee

Second Charge Debentures

Non-convertible Part of Existing convertible debentures

Non-convertible Part of proposed convertible debentures

Unsecured Term Loans

Proposed Borrowings

DEBT (A)
Equity Share Capital
Preference Share Capital
Free Reserves
Convertible part of Existing Convertible Debentures
Convertible part of Proposed Convertible Debentures
Total
Less: Miscellaneous Expenses
NET WORTH (B)
Debt Equity Ratio (A/B)

Interest Cover

Interest Cover shows the number of times the interest charges are covered by funds that are ordinarily available for payment. It shall be calculated by dividing Profit before depreciation, Interest and Tax (PBDIT) by Interest Charges. Details of working are as under:

Profit before Tax
Add: Depreciation
Add: Financial Charges
Add: Non-Recurring Expenses
Less: Non-Recurring Income
PBDIT (A)
Existing Financial Charges
Add: Interest on proposed borrowings
FINANCIAL CHARGES (B)
Interest Cover (A/B)

Insurance Regulatory and Development Authority (Distribution of Surplus) Regulations 2002

These regulations deal with distribution of surplus by insurance companies. The two types of policyholders defined in the regulations are as follows :

"Participating Policyholders" means the holders of 'par policies' and 'policies with deferred participation in profits', which are defined in the INSURANCE REGULATORY AND DEVELOPMENT AUTHORITY (Actuarial Report and Abstract Regulations) REGULATIONS, 2000;

"Non-participating Policyholders" means the holders of 'non par policies' which is defined in the INSURANCE REGULATORY AND DEVELOPMENT AUTHORITY (Actuarial Report and Abstract Regulations) REGULATIONS, 2000;

a life insurer registered under section 3 of the Insurance Act, 1938 shall be required to maintain separately :

(*a*) a life fund for partipating policyholders and

(*b*) a life fund for non participating policyholders.

The life insurer can distribute the valuation surplus arising out of valuation of assets and liabilities in the following manner:

(*a*) one hundred per cent in case of a life fund maintained for non-participating policyholders.

(*b*) one-ninth of the surplus allocated to policyholders in case of a life fund maintained for participating policyholder.

Provided that an insurer shall, however, be required to obtain prior approval of the Authority in cases where the said allocation is not the one-ninth of the surplus.

Provided further that an insurer shall not allocate of reserve exceeding ten per cent of the said actuarial surplus policy shareholders.

Questions for Review

1. "An insurance company has to solve the trade-off between solvency and profitability." Comment.
2. Write short notes on:
   (a) ALM in Insurance Companies.
   (b) Financial ratios for an insurance company.

Suggested Readings

1. Irving Pfeffer and David R. Klock, *Perspectives on Insurance,* Prentice-Hall, 1974.
2. G. Clayton and W.T. Osborn, *Insurance Company Investment — Principles and Policy,* George Allen and Unwinted, London, 1985.
3. Eric Baigs and Francois de Valenne, *Insurance — From Underwriting to Derivatives,* John Wiley & Sons Ltd., 2001.
4. J. David Cummins and Scott A. Harington, *Fair Rate of Return in Property — Liability Insurance,* Kalwer Nighoff Publishing, Boston, 1987.

Web Resources

- www.irdaindia.org
- www.actuaries.org
- www.edhec-risk.com

Reinsurance

Chapter 41

CHAPTER OBJECTIVES

After reading this chapter you will be able to understand :

- *Introduction to Reinsurance*
- *Role of the Reinsurers*
- *Techniques of Reinsurance*
- *Nature of Reinsurance Risks*
- *Reinsurance in Indian Perspective*

Although to many, reinsurance is a relatively unknown aspect of the insurance industry, its roots can be traced as far back as the late 14th century. From that time forward, reinsurance evolved into the business as it operates today. While the early focus of reinsurance was in the marine and fire insurance lines, it has expanded during the last century to encompass virtually every aspect of the modern insurance market. Reinsurance is a device whereby the insurance company may reduce its risk by transferring a portion to one or more insurance companies. Reinsurance is a special, highly technical, competitive industry whose existence makes possible a more effective institution of risk.

41.1 INTRODUCTION TO REINSURANCE

Reinsurance Defined

Reinsurance is a transaction in which one insurer agrees, for a premium, to indemnify another insurer against all or part of the loss that insurer may sustain under its policy or policies of insurance. The company purchasing reinsurance is known as the ceding insurer; the company selling reinsurance is known as the assuming insurer, or, more simply, the reinsurer. Reinsurance can also be described as the "insurance of insurance companies".

Reinsurance provides reimbursement to the ceding insurer for losses covered by the reinsurance agreement. It enhances the fundamental objective of insurance — to spread the risk so that no single entity finds itself saddled with a financial burden beyond its ability to pay. Reinsurance can be acquired either directly from a reinsurer or through a broker or reinsurance intermediary.

Objectives of Reinsurance

Insurers purchase reinsurance for essentially four reasons: (1) to limit liability on specific risks; (2) to stabilise loss experience; (3) to protect against catastrophes; and (4) to increase capacity. Different types of reinsurance contracts are available in the market commensurate with the ceding company's goals.

Limiting Liability

By providing a mechanism in which companies limit loss exposure to levels commensurate with net assets, reinsurance allows insurance companies to offer coverage limits considerably higher than they could otherwise provide. This function of reinsurance is crucial because it allows all companies, large and small, to offer coverage limits to meet their policyholders' needs. In this manner, reinsurance provides an avenue for small-to-medium size companies to compete with industry giants. In calculating an appropriate level of reinsurance, a company takes into account the amount of its available surplus and determines its retention based on the amount of loss it can absorb financially. Surplus, sometimes referred to as policyholders' surplus, is the amount by which the assets of an insurer exceed its liabilities.

A company's retention may range from a few lakh rupees to thousands of crores. The reinsurer indemnifies the loss exposure above the retention, up to the policy limits of the reinsurance contract. Reinsurance helps to stabilise loss experience on individual risks, as well as on accumulated losses under many policies occurring during a specified period.

Stabilisation

Insurers often seek to reduce the wide swings in profit and loss margins inherent to the insurance business. These fluctuations result, in part, from the unique nature of insurance, which involves pricing a product whose actual cost will not be known until sometime in the future. Through reinsurance, insurers can reduce these fluctuations in loss experience, thus stabilising the company's overall operating results.

Catastrophe Protection

Reinsurance provides protection against catastrophic loss in much the same way it helps stabilise an insurer's loss experience. Insurers use reinsurance to protect against catastrophes in two ways. The first is to protect against catastrophic loss resulting from a single event, such as the total fire loss of a large manufacturing plant. However, insurers also seek reinsurance to protect against the aggregation of many smaller claims, which could result from a single event affecting many policyholders simultaneously, such as an earthquake or a major hurricane. Financially, the insurer is able to pay losses individually, but when the losses are aggregated, the total may be more than the insurer wishes to retain.

Through the careful use of reinsurance, the disruptive effects catastrophes have on an insurer's loss experience can be reduced dramatically. The decisions a company makes when purchasing catastrophe coverage (*e.g.*, size of retention and coverage limits) are unique to each individual company and vary widely depending on the type and size of the company purchasing the reinsurance and the risk to be reinsured.

Increased Capacity

Capacity measures the rupee amount of risk an insurer can assume based on its surplus and the nature of the business written. When an insurance company issues a policy, the expenses associated with issuing that policy— taxes, agent commissions, administrative expenses — are charged immediately against the company's income, resulting in a decrease in surplus, while the premium collected must be set aside in an unearned premium reserve to be recognised as income over a period of time. While this accounting procedure allows for strong solvency regulation, it ultimately leads to decreased capacity because the more business an insurance company writes, the more expenses that must be paid from surplus, thus reducing the company's ability to write additional business.

Companies experiencing rapid expansion are particularly susceptible to the timing problem between expenses (which must be debited immediately) and income (which must be credited over time) generated by new business. By reinsuring a portion of the business it writes, an insurance company reduces the problem of decreased surplus. Through reinsurance, the company shares a portion of its underwriting expenses with its reinsurer and reduces the drain on surplus.

Reinsurance also permits the ceding company to expand capacity by permitting the ceding company to take credit for reinsurance on the annual accounting statement it files with state regulators.

If the reinsurer satisfies certain regulatory requirements intended to assure the security of the reinsurance arrangement, the ceding company may count as asset reinsurance payments owed to it on claims it has paid, thus expanding its surplus. The ceding company can also reduce liabilities and loss reserves attributable to the business ceded to the reinsurer.

In addition, the ceding company often receives a ceding commission from the reinsurer as reimbursement for expenses, such as agent commissions and overhead, associated with acquiring the business being reinsured. The ceding commission is added directly to the ceding company's surplus, thus increasing it further.

Another type of reinsurance transaction, which may affect surplus, is known as *loss portfolio transfer*. In such an arrangement, one insurer cedes to another insurer its reserves for incurred but unpaid losses and loss adjustment expenses. Typically, these reserves are associated with a particular class or line of business, such as medical malpractices. The ceding insurer transfers cash to the assuming insurer equal to the assuming insurer's estimate of the present value of these liabilities, plus an amount the reinsurer may require to carry the additional risks involved in the transfer.

In addition, reinsurers often provide insurers with a variety of other services. Some reinsurers provide guidance to insurers in underwriting, claims reserving and handling investments and even general management. These services are particularly important to smaller companies or companies interested in entering new lines of insurance.

In any discussion of reinsurance, limitations of the business must be considered along with the advantages. First and foremost, reinsurance does not change the inherent nature of a risk being insured. Thus, it does not make a bad risk insurable or an exposure more predictable or desirable. While it may limit an insurance company's exposure to a risk, the total risk exposure is not altered through the use of reinsurance.

41.2 ROLE OF THE REINSURERS

Reinsurance is governed by the same principles as for insurance. But instead of covering property or casualty risks directly, the reinsurer insures insurance companies. Reinsurance spans the diversity of situations specific to each type of insurance and is consequently more complex and much broader in range, since it covers the whole world. An insurance company issues contracts called *policies*. The insurance company is the direct or primary insurer of an individual or a business. The policy is written in its name, making it liable for all claims arising under the policy. The insured deals exclusively with the insurance company. But the insurance company spreads its risks arising under the policy by transferring all or part of those risks to one or more reinsurance companies.[1]

In the event of a claim, the insurance company must pay to the insured the full amount of compensation due under the policy. It is then up to the insurance company to recoup the sums corresponding to the risk transferred from its reinsurers. At the beginning of each year, the insurance company takes out contracts with one or more reinsurance companies to cover it for policies issued to its customers for the year in question. Reinsurers in turn usually cede a share of the risk they accept to other reinsurers known as retrocessionnaires; this system is roughly equivalent to bank syndicates. To put it differently as discussed in section 41.1, the reinsurer performs three essential services, together with a number of additional services.

First, reinsurance enables direct writing companies to even out their results when major, exceptional, losses occur: a hurricane or an earthquake for instance can seriously affect the accounts of an insurance company. Reinsurance considerably reduces this type of potential imbalance.

Second, insurance companies use reinsurance to increase the maximum amount they are able to cover as primary insurer for any given potential loss or loss category; in other words, their available capacity is increased. As a result, insurance companies can write more risks, or larger risks, without becoming over-extended.

Third, reinsurance also provides insurers with the large amounts of cash needed in the event of a major loss, enabling them to manage their assets safely and profitably.

1. www.bimaguru.com

In addition to the above services the reinsurance companies also provide the following advisory services to their ceding companies:

Formulating the Reinsurance Program

The types of reinsurance cover selected can considerably influence the profitability and solvency of an insurance company.

Support Services

This range from training of technical and administrative personnel to practical assistance in organisation, accounting and data processing, risk inspection and co-operation in claims settlement.

Specialised Services

In certain highly specialised areas such as major public works' projects or death term life insurance policies written on substandard patients, reinsurers are more familiar with the relevant statistic and rates applicable, and they have the permanent capacity available to cover cedants' exposures.

Capital Base

In most of the developing/ developed countries laws have been enacted on the minimum ratio of capital to retained premiums needed to transact business. This ratio is referred to as the solvency margin. It means that a dynamic but narrow capital base insurance company must rely heavily on reinsurance in order to grow; reinsurance can in some instances play a more direct role in financing insurance companies. In life insurance, for example, considerable outlays are required to build up marketing outlets and other facilities needed when new types of policies are first issued. Reinsurers are often called on as partners to help finance this type of investment; in turn they are entitled to share in the return on the investment.

Reinsurers are often a source of hard currency for ceding companies in weak currency countries. Many developing nations reinsure imported equipment and machinery in order to secure the hard currency needed for repairs or replacements in the event of damage or destruction.

41.3 TECHNIQUES OF REINSURANCE

The two main types of reinsurance agreements are *proportional* and *excess of loss*. A reinsurance contract written on a proportional basis simply prorates all premium, losses and expenses between the insurer and the reinsurer on a pre-arranged basis. The proportional approach is used extensively in property reinsurance. Excess of loss contracts require the primary insurer to keep all losses up to a predetermined retention and the reinsurer to reimburse the company for any losses above that retention, up to the limits of the reinsurance contract. In simplest terms, retention is analogous to the deductible a policyholder may have on a personal insurance policy, such as an automobile or homeowner's policy. These are detailed in section 41.33.

The reinsurance coverages can be broadly classified into two — *treaties* and *facultatives*.

41.3.1 Reinsurance Treaties

Reinsurance treaties are a form of comprehensive coverage bought by ceding companies, either directly or through a reinsurance broker, to protect all or a share of their portfolios for a given class of business. All policies covering risks insured under a treaty are automatically reinsured; in other words the reinsurer cannot decline a risk coming under the treaty. Treaties may be either proportional or non-proportional.[2]

Non-proportional Treaty

In this type of treaty, reinsurance cover begins once the amount of the claim exceeds a predetermined amount. Let us imagine a reinsurance treaty for Rs. 400 crores in excess of Rs. 100 crores; this is what reinsurers call a Rs. 500 crores cover with a deductible of Rs. 100 crores. If a loss occurs and its total cost is less than the Rs. 100 crores, only the primary insurer is concerned. If, however, the cost of the claim is in excess of the Rs. 100 crores, the direct-writing company pays its share equal to Rs. 100 crores and the reinsurance company the remainder, up to Rs. 400 crores. The reinsurance premium for this type of business is computed on the basis of the amounts insured under each individual policy the treaty covers, referred to as *portfolio exposure*, and other factors such as previous loss statistics.

Proportional Treaty

In this type of treaty, the reinsurer and ceding company share the premium and losses proportionally. If an insurance company for example takes out a proportional cover for 40% of its portfolio and if the claims amount to a total of Rs. 100 crores, the insurer pays 60%, or Rs. 60 crores and the reinsurer the remaining 40%, or Rs. 40 crores. The reinsurer will have received 40% of the original premium the ceding company charged its insureds, and will pay a percentage of the premiums representing a fraction of the ceding company's expenses incurred in acquiring and managing the business. This is known as the *commission* or acquisition expense.

In most cases, reinsurance companies only accept a share of a treaty. Each year, insurance companies provide their reinsurers with information on intended policies concerning maximum exposures, estimated premium income, classes of business, marketing strategies etc. Before the start of the year, they finalise treaty conditions with the lead reinsurer exclusions, commissions, and so forth. They then invite other reinsurers to accept a share in their treaties, depending on the program announced and terms negotiated.

41.3.2 Facultatives

Facultative insurance is an optional case by case method that is used when the ceding company receives application for insurance that exceeds its retention limit.[3] Facultative treaties are inter company agreements for optional or voluntary reinsurance transactions. Facultative covers are written on an individual risk basis when a primary company insures risks for amounts in excess of its treaty capacity or risks not covered by its treaties. The lead reinsurer assesses each risk individually and, in consultation with the insurance company, sets the rates and terms of the primary cover. Facultatives serve essentially to cover major industrial and civil engineering risks and, for much smaller amounts, insurers' exposure to liability claims. The reinsurer retains the right to accept or reject any business offered by the insurance company.

41.3.3 Reinsurance Arrangements

Types of Reinsurance

Reinsurance may be written on either a proportional basis or Non-proportional basis. A reinsurance contract written on a proportional basis simply prorates all premiums, losses and expenses between the insurer and the reinsurer on a prearranged basis. This, in proportional reinsurance (which includes quota share and surplus reinsurance), the reinsured obtains coverage for only a portion or percentage of the loss or risk from the reinsurer. The extent of coverage is based on the percentage of premiums paid to the reinsurer.

Non-proportional reinsurance comes to fore if the loss suffered by the insurer exceeds a certain amount, called the retention or priority. This requires the primary insurer to keep all losses up to a predetermined level of retention, and the reinsurer to reimburse the company for any losses above that level of retention, upto the limits of the reinsurance contract.

Quota Share Reinsurance

In this type of arrangement, the reinsurer receives a quota share of both the exposures and the premiums *less* agreed costs incurred by the ceding company in writing the business.

Pro-rata Reinsurance

It states that the reinsurer will assume all risk upto some specific policy and will cede a portion of the risk above the retention limit.

Excess-of-loss Reinsurance

It specifies the extent of reinsurance in terms of losses rather than in terms of liability. Under such a treaty, the ceding company would pay all claims upto a specified amount per event or per period. Any losses over the agreed amount would be paid in full or part as agreed by the reinsurer. This is different from quota and pro-rata arrangements in the sense that agreement does not refer to any specific policy but covers all of the insurer's business. This type of arrangement is in the nature of catastrophe coverage. Excess of Loss reinsurance can be of three forms – 'Per Risk XL'; 'Per Occurrence or Per Event XL' (Catastrophe or Cat XL), and "Aggregate XL"; whereas 'Stop Loss', unlike Excess of Loss does not cover individual claims. It protects a *cedant* against an aggregate amount of claims over a particular time period, in excess of a specified percentage of the earned premium income.

Loss Ratio Reinsurance

It provides for reimbursement by the reinsurer when a specific loss ratio is exceeded. The loss ratio is generally the ratio of losses incurred to premiums earned. The loss ratio is generally fixed in such a fashion that it is over the normal one and, at such a level that the insurer could not bear without sustaining severe damages to its financial condition. Therefore, this arrangement is also a kind of catastrophe coverage.

41.4 NATURE OF REINSURANCE RISKS

As stated previously, the two major types of reinsurance are proportional and excess of loss. Because the ceding insurer and the reinsurer automatically share all premiums and losses covered by the contract on a pre-agreed prorated basis, there are no characteristics uniquely attributable to the risk associated with proportional reinsurance. On the other hand, a great deal of uncertainty characterises the risk associated with excess of loss reinsurance. This uncertainty stems from the fact that the level of risk is dependent on the nature of the reinsurance undertaking. In addition to the actual risk being underwritten, reinsurers must take into account the overall stability of the ceding insurer and the layer of coverage on which the reinsurer is being asked to participate. Reinsurance, particularly excess of loss reinsurance, is characterised by relatively low and unstable claims frequency and very high but also unstable loss severity. Due in part to this unique nature of the reinsurance business, reinsurers may absorb a disproportionate share of total losses. The lines of insurance in which liability is slowest to manifest itself or develop — the "long tail" lines — create the worst problems for reinsurers. By the end of this century, only a small portion of the ultimate liability on reinsurance contracts issued today covering general liability exposures will be known to reinsurers. Into the first decade of the twenty-first century, a significant portion of the ultimate payout on losses will still be unknown to reinsurers. These losses will be adjudicated in the social, legal and economic environments prevailing in the future, but the premiums to pay those losses must be collected now.

Insurance loss costs are determined by a combination of frequency (how many claims per unit), severity (average cost of each claim) and the total number of units insured. Generally, the higher the number of similar units insured, the more reliable the data. This is particularly true in automobile property damage liability insurance. There are many automobiles insured and year to year the frequency of claims is relatively stable.

Evaluating insurance risk depends on the law of large numbers, which is often not applicable to reinsurance. Relevant and credible loss data are often unavailable. Therefore, in contrast to an insurance underwriter, a reinsurance underwriter depends much more on professional judgement and experience to evaluate the nature of an exposure.

General liability insurance contracts traditionally provide coverage for losses occurring during the policy term, regardless of when the loss is reported. This type of contract, called an occurrence policy, leaves the insurer exposed to claims, which may be filed many years after the policy expires. Certain exposures, such an environmental liability, are particularly susceptible to this latency factor commonly referred to as the long tail. Reporting delays create serious problems for all insurers, but marked differences exist in reinsurer loss development patterns. The retention feature of excess of loss reinsurance is the primary basis for these differences. Many claims are not initially valued at ultimate cost. Because the ceding insurer's reserve is within the retention established in the reinsurance contract, the ceding insurer may not report such claims to its reinsurer. However, when the claim is ultimately paid, it may exceed the retention. It is only at this point, usually after considerable time has passed, that the reinsurer is notified. Reinsurers are trying to mitigate this problem by requiring all serious injuries to be reported, regardless of the insurer's reserve, and by conducting on-site visits to examine claims files to better determine the likelihood of losses under the reinsurance contract.

"Reinsurance is used heavily in commercial lines, which have demonstrated considerable instability over the past several years in frequency and severity of losses and often have long tails. All insurers and reinsurers set aside loss reserves for claims, which have been incurred but not, reported (IBNR). As claims are reported to the company, these reserves are reduced."

Companies use a variety of methods to establish IBNR reserves. Because IBNR is such a major component of reinsurers' reserves, much effort is taken in determining and making these calculations. Despite the use of sophisticated professional techniques, these reserves, representing future loss payments, are extremely sensitive to changes in social, legal and economic environments. Thus, they represent a "best guess estimate" of future loss payments.

If IBNR reserves represent only a small portion of a company's total loss reserves, the impact of these unknown claims on total losses reported on past policies is likely to be small. If, however, IBNR reserves represent a large portion of a company's reserves, the impact on total losses reported on past policies may be significant. Reinsurers, particularly those participating in casualty and workers' compensation lines, fit into this latter category.

The impact of inflation on insurers' claims liability typically results from increases in the cost of living, increases in the number of claims paid and increase in large jury verdicts, which raise settlement costs. Insurers and reinsurers have been hit by all three, but the impact has been more pronounced on reinsurers, because their losses develop much more slowly and may not be capped to a retention limit.

If losses are paid within a relatively short period following the issuance of an insurance policy, inflation has little effect on claims payments. However, in many instances the reinsurer may not become aware for years, sometimes decades, of a loss it will ultimately pay. For this reason, inflation's impact on reinsurers may be dramatic. During the last decade, retention levels were reached and exceeded with unexpected frequency in nearly all lines of insurance.

The Reinsurance Contract

Based on its business needs, an insurer negotiates with a reinsurer, directly or through a broker, to determine the terms, conditions and costs of a reinsurance contract. Under a reinsurance contract, an insurer is indemnified for losses occurring on its insurance policies and covered by the reinsurance contract. There are no standard reinsurance contracts although two basic types, treaty and facultative, are used and adapted to meet individual insurers' requirements.

Underwriting treaty reinsurance differs greatly from that of facultative reinsurance. Reinsurance treaties automatically cover all risks written by the insured that fall within their terms unless they specifically exclude exposures. While treaty reinsurance does not require review of individual risks by the reinsurer, it demands a careful review of the underwriting philosophy, practice and historical experience of the ceding insurer, as well as a thoughtful evaluation of the company's attitude toward claims management and engineering control and management's general background, expertise and planned objectives.

Facultative reinsurance contracts cover individual underlying policies and are written on an individual basis. Stated simply, facultative reinsurance covers a specific risk. Both facultative and treaty contracts may be written on a proportional or an excess of loss basis, or a combination of both.

A facultative agreement covers a specific risk of the ceding insurer. A reinsurer and ceding insurer agree on facultative terms and conditions in each individual contract. In contrast, a reinsurance treaty is a broad agreement covering some portion of a particular class or classes of business (e.g., an insurer's entire workers' compensation or property book of business). Historically, treaties remain in force for long periods of time and are renewed on a fairly automatic basis unless either party wishes to negotiate a change in terms.

Facultative reinsurance agreements often cover catastrophic or unusual risk exposures. Prior to the 1950's, U.S. insurers made relatively little use of facultative reinsurance and Lloyd's of London was virtually the sole source of facultative coverages. U.S. reinsurers began to compete with Lloyd's for facultative business in the 1950's and today facultative reinsurance plays a major role in the U.S. reinsurance market.

Facultative reinsurance requires substantial personnel and technical resources for underwriting individual risks. Often, facultative business presents significant potential for loss, thus a reinsurer must have the necessary staff knowledge to underwrite each exposure accurately.

Facultative reinsurance contracts are also used to supplement treaty arrangements when treaties contain specific exclusions, such as exposures involving long haul trucking or munitions manufacturing. Insurers may fill coverage voids created by reinsurance treaty exclusions by negotiating a separate facultative reinsurance contract for a particular policy or group of policies.

Certain classes of risks anticipated to develop significant losses may adversely affect an insurer's treaty experience. Although not excluded from a treaty, these risks may be placed facultatively. For example, a primary insurer that may not ordinarily provide commercial automobile coverage might agree, as a service to its insured, to write such a policy as an accommodation. The company may then seek facultative reinsurance to protect its loss experience under treaty agreements. The reinsurer providing an insurer's treaty coverage may not necessarily provide its facultative reinsurance.

Reinsurers also purchase their own reinsurance protection, called *retrocessions*, in the same forms and for the same reasons as ceding insurers. By protecting reinsurers from catastrophic losses, as well as an accumulation of smaller losses, retrocessions stabilise reinsurer results, thus serving the same risk-spreading objectives as the initial reinsurance transaction.

Reinsurance relationships range from the simple to the complex. An insurer may enter into a single reinsurance treaty to cover certain loss exposures or may purchase numerous treaties until the desired level of reinsurance protection is achieved. This process, known as layering, uses two or more reinsurance agreements to obtain desired level of coverage. At the time a claim comes due, the reinsurers respond in a predetermined sequence, as necessary, to cover the loss. Layering of reinsurance coverage is no different in principle than the layering of excess and umbrella coverage by a policyholder, or the purchase of specific risk coverage through a rider on an insurance policy. It is simply a means of securing the type and amount of insurance or reinsurance protection desired by a purchaser.

Certain fundamental principles underlie all reinsurance contracts, regardless of how simple or complex the reinsurance transaction. First, the only parties to a reinsurance contract are a reinsured company and its reinsurer.

All contractual rights and obligations run only between these two companies. Second, the proceeds collectible under the reinsurance contract are an asset of the ceding company. Finally, as a contract of indemnification, the reinsurance is payable only after the reinsured company has paid losses due under its own insurance or reinsurance agreements, unless there is an insolvency clause, which allows the receiver of an insolvent insurer to collect on reinsurance contracts.

41.5 Reinsurance in Indian Perspective

41.5.1 Reinsurance Exposure of GIC in a Fire Portfolio

After the nationalisation of insurance business, the GIC was made responsible for reinsurance protection. 20% of the small risks and medium risks in a fire portfolio are currently ceded to GIC. 25% of the listed risks are also ceded subject to a maximum of Rs. 50 crores, In market place, 30% of each risk is ceded to pool and retroceded back which is fully retained by the companies, subject to a monetary limit of Rs. 750 crores Probable Maximum Loss (PML). The net retention of GIC is Rs. 125 crores (maximum) and Rs. 15 crores (Absolute).

Fire Reinsurance – An Illustration

Reinsurance of fire business in India is primarily headed by GIC in accordance with the IRDA guidelines. The obligatory session (20% quota share) is compulsorily needed to GIC and rest is dealt by treaties. The quoto cession is retained in India itself to protect drainage of foreign exchange. The treaties taken into account the sum insured and probable maximum loss. This requires classification of risk as illustrated below :

Non-risk Booked Risks : Smaller risks having sum insured less than Rs. 5 crores, which are not normally entered into the risk register maintained for the purpose-retention is 100% in India and reinsurance is affected using excess of loss cover.

Booked Risks : Medium Risks – Sum insured > Rs. 5 crores and PML < Rs. 26 crores.

The risks are entered in the register and are termed as Risk Booked. The underwriting of medium sized risks is as under :

Obligatory	20.00%
Net Account	45.00%
Market Fire Pool	30.00%
Cos. Fire Surplus Treaty	0.5.00%
Total	**100.00%**

The Indian market retention for Medium Size Risks is 95%.

Listed Risks : All risks having a PML greater than Rs. 26 crores are classified as listed risks.

Example :

PML	Rs.	1000 crores
Obligatory Cession (20%)	Rs.	200 crores
Ist Surplus Treaty (10%)	Rs.	100 crores
IInd Surplus Treaty (10%)	Rs.	100 crores
Facultative Insurance	Rs.	100 crores
Total Underwritten Rest	**Rs.1000 crores**	

The schedule of obligatory sessions to GIC is given in Exhibit 41A.

Exhibit 41A

Obligatory Cessions Received by GIC

Class	*Limit of Cession in Sum Insured or PML*	*Reinsurance Commission*	*Profit Commission*
Fire, IAR, CL	Rs. 100 Crores PML per risk	35%	25%
Mega Risks	Rs. 100 Crores PML per risk	Lead Terms	20%
Marine Cargo, War & SRCC	Rs. 10 Crores sum insured per policy	25.0%	10% at the end of 36 months
Marine Hull, War & SRCC	Rs. 16 Crores sum insured per vessel	Net rated risks: 5% Gross rated risks : 17.5%	
Motor	No limit	20%	Nil
Workmen's Compensation	No limit	20%	Nil
General Aviation Hull	No limit	12.5%	Nil
General Aviation Liability	No limit	12.5%	Nil
Aviation (Airlines)	Rs. 120 crores sum insured per risk on hull and corresponding percentage share on other insurances	Average Terms	Nil
Oil and Energy	Rs. 15 crores sum insured per risk	5%	Nil
All Liability Products excluding financial liability	Rs. 5 crores per policy including USA/Rs. 10 crores per policy excluding USA	25%	Nil
Financial, credit & guarantee lines, mortgage insurance, special contingency policies, etc.	Rs. 10 crores sum insured per event	10%	Nil
Other Miscellaneous	No limit*	25%	Nil
Machinary Breakdown, Boiler Explosion and related loss of profits	Rs. 30 crores PML but where PML exceeds 33.3%, Rs. 90 crores sum insured on each risk, material damage and loss of profits combined.	30%	25%
Contractor's all Risks, Erection All Risks, Advanced Loss of Profits, DSU insurances	Rs. 60 crores PML but where PML exceeds 33.3%, Rs. 180 crores sum insured on each risk material damage and loss of profits combined.	30%	25%

41.5.2 Regulation of Reinsurance Business

Reinsurance monitoring encompasses not only submission of reinsurance programme of the companies but also includes examination of reinsurance programme of the companies. The Authority checks whether all classes of business being underwritten by the company are covered in the reinsurance programme. It verifies the retentions proposed by the insurers in their programme. Unduly low retentions will result in greater cessions and high retentions can affect the stability of the company. Therefore every insurer is required to explain the reasons for keeping the retentions being proposed and what the overall retention ratios which the company is striving for with the proposed reinsurance programme will be. The Authority also checks the cost of reinsurance programme and the outgo of foreign exchange.

An important aspect in reinsurance is to ensure that the company is not fronting on behalf of the foreign partner. The Authority verifies this aspect. The submission of treaty slips and excess of loss cover notes by the companies and their subsequent examination is part of the Authority supervision, to ensure that the company complies with what has been proposed in their reinsurance programme. Another important aspect of reinsurance is the security rating of the reinsurer. The reinsurer has to be financially sound in order to support the direct insurer in times of claims. The Authority specifies that all reinsurers must have at least a BBB rating. As part of the monitoring, the Authority checks the rating of the reinsurers. It also gives specific approval to the insurance companies in case the total reinsurance premium being placed with the reinsurer exceeds 10%. The purpose is to ensure the spread of risks and ensure compliance. IRDA has encouraged the Indian insurers to form domestic pools such as the terrorism pool and the Indian Motor Third Party Pool. IT checks on the domestic pool arrangements organized by Indian Reinsurer to ensure that the arrangement is fair to all and that reinsurance protection of the pool is in place and as per the regulations.

The direct insurers submit to the Authority on annual basis reinsurance statistics which include the results of their various proportional and non-proportional treaties as well as the names and percentage of the reinsurers. This analysis of the statistics offers important insights of the functioning of the reinsurance treaties and contracts. It also enables the Authority to evaluate whether these treaties and contracts are working efficiently; and whether the terms and conditions are prejudicial to the insurer and public interests; or not. The results also throw up areas of concern which can be taken up with the direct insurers. The Authority also examines the underwriting policy for underwriting inward reinsurance business and carries out a check to ensure that persons possessing knowledge and experience are responsible for taking decisions in accepting inward reinsurance business as this is a specialized and technical subject. The examination of the policy on inward reinsurance business covers the classes of business underwritten, geographical scope, underwriting limits and profit objectives.

Legal Framework

The mandate to IRDA in respect of reinsurance lies in the provisions of Section 14(1) and 14(2) of the IRDA Act, 1999 as well as Sections 34F, 101A, 101B and 101C of the Insurance Act, 1938. In addition, IRDA has framed reinsurance regulations for general insurers which lay down the ground rules in placement of reinsurance with the reinsurers.

Section 34F of the Insurance Act, 1938 gives powers to IRDA to issue directions regarding reinsurance treaties. In case IRDA is of the view or believes that an insurer is entering or is likely to enter into reinsurance treaties or reinsurance contracts which are not favourable to the insurer or are detrimental to the public interests, it may direct the insurer to modify the terms and conditions or not renew such a treaty or contract. Section 101A of the Insurance Act, 1938 specifies that every insurer shall cede such percentage of premium under every policy written in the country to the "National Reinsurer" or may be specified by IRDA in consultation with the Reinsurance Advisory Committee. While Section 101B deals with the Constitution of the Reinsurance Advisory Committee, Section 101C pertains to the powers of IRDA to examine the reinsurance treaties of insurers.

IRDA also notified the Reinsurance regulations in the year 2000 (Annexure 41A). The reinsurance regulations require every insurer to draw up its reinsurance programme keeping in mind the following objectives : (*a*) maximise retention within the country; (*b*) develop adequate capacity; (*c*) secure the best possible protection for the reinsurance costs incurred; (*d*) simplify the administration of business. It requires every insurer to maintain the maximum possible retention commensurate with its financial strength and volume of business. Under the regulations, every insurer shall file its reinsurance programme with the Authority 45 days prior to commencement of financial year and copy of treaty slips and cover notes within 30 days of beginning of the financial year. The insurers are required to place their reinsurance business outside India with only those reinsurers having a rating of at least BBB (with Standard & Poor) or its equivalent. Surplus over and above the domestic reinsurance arrangements classwise can be placed with the reinsurers subject to a limit of 10% of the total reinsurance premium ceded outside India being placed with any one reinsurer. Lastly, every insurer is required to submit to the Authority statistics relating to its reinsurance transactions.

Features of Reinsurance Supervision

The impetus to the growth of the market can be achieved only by solid reinsurance support, which can be provided by reinsurers alone. Reinsurance help reduce volatility and accordingly the uncertainty in the insurer's pricing of risks. In purchasing reinsurance, the insurers seek to improve their financial performance and security. The regulator's role in all this is to ensure that the reinsurance programme of every insurer is guided by the objectives laid down in the regulations. The responsibility of the Authority does not end here. It extends to other areas which have an important bearing on the conduct of insurance business in the country and includes reinsurance supervision.

The apex insurance regulatory body IRDA has issued two sets of separate regulations for general insurance and life insurance business (Annexure 41A).

41.5.3 Issues and Challenges in Indian Reinsurance

The Indian reinsurance market at this juncture is at the crossroads of becoming an industry on par with the best international standards or turning into a regional market. At the forefront are issues and challenges which would require the combined efforts of all the stakeholders *viz.,* the regulator, the insurers and the reinsurers to take it to higher levels.

Obligatory Cessions : GIC currently gets 15% cessission on obligatory basis.

Under the various WTO rounds of negotiations, it has been the consistent demand of different member countries of WTO on India to remove these compulsory cessions.

Retentions : Reinsurance portfolio has a direct impact on the solvency of an insurer. Net retentions are declining these days.

Facultative Placements : The statistics furnished by the industry reveal that significant reinsurance premium is being ceded outside India by way of facultative placements. It becomes imperative for insurers to have adequate reinsurance support at all times for such natural catastrophe perils.

Alternate Risk Transfer (ART) : Recently many insurers have used new forms of ART. The insurers should be careful while choosing the new forms of reinsurance over the traditional ones.

Foreign Reinsurers : Financial stability of the reinsurer would lend a perception to the Indian consumer and Indian insurer that their second contract of insurance with such an insurance company would protect their interest.

Detariffing : The stage is set for the next phase of detariffing when the terms and conditions of insurance contracts will also be freed.

Retentions : The Authority has observed that the overall retention of the private sector players is less as compared to that of public sector companies.

Security of Reinsurers : Another area of concern is the security rating of the reinsurers.

Recoverables : The outstanding loss recoveries in insurance companies are in the range of hundreds of crores and rising.

Accumulation Exposures : The Indian insurance industry is constrained by lack of data on accumulations.

41.6 GLOBAL REINSURANCE MARKET

Reinsurance market has developed actively since the last century but as in the case of primary business, developed countries provided the main market of this business. The total reinsurance premium globally is on an increase. The reinsurance market can be divided into the following categories:

1. International Professional Reinsurers numbering 10 and increasing.
2. International insurers actively engaged in reinsurance assumed business as well.
3. Miscellaneous group reinsurers/direct insurers in developing countries.
4. Lloyds of London.
5. Market in Bermuda and similar centres

86% of the reinsurers are concentrated in Europe (60%), US (18%) and Bermuda (8%). As regards Asian markets, Singapore is emerging as a major hub. Reinsurance major players are opening offices in Singapore. Even Swiss Re transacts the Asian business through its Singapore office. The proportional market share is expected to decline gradually.

As regards the Indian market, reinsurers were apprehensive about detariffing and subsequent fall in property premium. Many good reinsurers decided to stay away from the Proportional treaties of Indian companies. Most of the insurance companies in India slashed the commission rates ranging from 3% to 7% in order to see that treaties remain attractive for reinsurers. Some companies did away with profit commission and in fact resorted to Sliding Scale commission which was a rational step. The global market is looking at India in a post detariff scenario.

Exhibit 41B

Comparison between the reinsurance retentions in 1999-2000 and 2005-06

	1999-2000			*2005-06*		
	Gross Prem. (Rs. in mn)	*Net Prem. (Rs. in mn)*	*Ret Ratio*	*Gross Prem (Rs. in mn)*	*Net Prem (Rs. in mn)*	*Ret Ratio*
Fire, IAR, CL	23,562	21,920	93.03%	36820.99	24003.86	65.19%
Marine Cargo	7,933	7,141	90.01%	7795.78	6733.77	86.38%
Marine Hull	2,471	1,083	43.83%	5417.98	1182.25	21.82%
Engineering	Included in Other Misc. class			9421.12	6849.54	72.70%
Motor	34,282	34,282	100.00%	84981.73	80647.74	94.90%
Aviation	2,063	156	7.59%	3989.27	531.32	13.32%
Other Misc.	27,245	24,011	88.13%	50250.68	44085.22	87.73%
Total	**97,559**	**88,596**	**90.81%**	**198677.54**	**164033.70**	**82.56%**

41.7 REINSURANCE TRADING

It is known that insurance companies also do reinsurance business and this activity is not restricted to professional reinsurer only. The reasons are as follows :

1. When the ceding companies reach a certain size and financial strength, they are also able to offer capacity to their counterparts elsewhere. This would be particularly suitable where the insurer cannot expand its operation directly.

2. Such extended operation helps the insurer to achieve better spread and balance in his portfolio since the experience at different places at different times of the same business could be different. By inference, the overall exposure offers suitable self-adjustment.
3. The outflow of reinsurance premium can be reduced on a net basis through the inflow of premium from assumed reinsurance.
4. The exercise can help in reducing foreign exchange outgo provided the selection is right.

Trading can be either Reciprocal or Non-Reciprocal. In the case of reciprocal trading, the reinsurance outward is placed with a reinsurer who can provide matching inward business in terms of premium and profit. At one time, reciprocal trading was quite popular but its days are now numbered for various reasons.

Non-recriprocal trading is active inward reinsurance without any obligation to provide matching business in exchange.

The performance of global reinsurance market is given in Annexure 41A and 41B.

ANNEXURE 41A

Top 40 Global Reinsurance Groups Ranked By Net Reinsurance Premiums Written

Ranking	Company	Country	Net Reinsurance Premiums Written (Mil. $) 2007	2006
1.	Munich Reinsurance Co.	Germany	30,292.9	27,425.2
2.	Swiss Reinsurance Co.	Switzerland	27,706.6	23,841.1
3.	Berkshire Hathaway Re1	U.S.	17,398.0	11,576.0
4.	Hannover Rueckversicherung AG	Germany	10,630.0	9,353.5
5.	Lloyd's[2,3]	U.K.	8,362.9	8,445.3
6.	SCOR SE	France	7,871.7	4,885.2
7.	Reinsurance Group of America, Inc.	U.S.	4,906.5	4,343.0
8.	Transatlantic Holdings Inc.	U.S.	3,952.9	3,633.4
9.	Everest Reinsurance Co.	Bermuda	3,919.4	3,875.7
10.	PartnerRe Ltd.	Bermuda	3,757.1	3,689.5
11.	Tokio Marine Group2	Japan	2,936.4	2,783.4
12.	Korean Reinsurance Co.	Korea	2,796.8	2,349.5
13.	XL Re Ltd	Bermuda	2,781.3	2,959.7
14.	Transamerica Re (AEGON)	U.S.	2,173.0	1,957.7
15.	Odyssey Re	U.S.	2,089.4	2,160.9
16.	General Ins. Corp. of India	India	2,085.1	1,489.8
17.	Sompo Japan Insurance Inc.[1]	Japan	1,837.3	1,788.1
18.	Mitsui Sumitomo Insurance Co. Ltd.[1]	Japan	1,805.8	1,724.3
19.	White Mountains Re Group Ltd.	Bermuda	1,752.4	1,737.2
20.	Caisse Centrale de Reassurance	France	1,642.6	1,508.7
21.	Mapfre Re	Spain	1,569.7	1,298.5
22.	AXIS Capital Holdings Ltd.[1]	Bermuda	1,537.1	1,528.8
23.	QBE Insurance Group Ltd.	Australia	1,509.2	1,212.5
24.	ACE Tempest Reinsurance Ltd.	Bermuda	1,484.6	1,796.7
25.	Toa Re Co. Ltd.	Japan	1,385.2	1,286.3
26.	Aioi Insurance Co. Ltd.[1]	Japan	1,208.7	1,131.5
27.	Arch Capital Group Ltd.	U.S.	1,184.4	1,365.4
28.	Platinum Underwriters Holdings, Ltd.	Bermuda	1,119.8	1,176.6
29.	PARIS RE	Switzerland	1,113.5	1,254.0
30.	R+V Versicherung AG[1]	Germany	1,053.5	861.7
31.	Endurance Specialty Holdings Ltd.[1]	Bermuda	1,051.6	1,327.9
32.	Deutsche Rueckversicherung AG	Germany	1,021.0	878.5
33.	RenaissanceRe Holdings Ltd.	Bermuda	1,018.7	1,078.3
34.	Aspen Insurance Holdings Ltd.[1]	Bermuda	1,008.3	1,028.5
35.	IRB-Brasil Resseguros S.A.	Brazil	900.3	910.3
36.	NIPPONKOA Insurance Co. Ltd.[1]	Japan	837.2	790.9
37.	Max Capital Group Ltd	Bermuda	796.6	634.7
38.	Amlin Group[1]	U.K.	782.4	742.5
39.	Catlin Group Ltd.[2]	Bermuda	740.2	N.A.
40.	W.R. Berkley Corp.[1]	U.S.	682.2	892.8
	Total		**162,702.3**	**142,723.6**

Group Notes

1. Adjusted shareholders' funds are for the group as a whole, including both its direct and reinsurance operations.
2. Net premiums written and the combined ratio relate to reinsurance business only; all other items include direct business.
3. The data presented is based on the published pro-forma accounts for the Market, which represent an aggregation of all syndicates participating at Lloyd's. As such, some premium included for Lloyd's may also be included by other groups in this list that consolidate their Lloyd's operations.

ANNEXURE 41B

SWIN RE REPORT

Regional Perspective

Emerging regions		*Performance 2009*	*Outlook 2010*
Asia	Life	Growth moderated across the board in early 2009, but some early signs of recovery were emerging towards year-end.	A strong rebound could materials once interest in investment-linked insurance products recovers.
	Non-life	Growth remained strong in China and India, partly due to government-sponspred infrastructure projects.	Recovery in non-life demand will continue into 2010.
		Trade-related insurance demand was hit hard in most markets. Motor insurance was down, but improved towards year-end on recovering car sales.	Trade-related insurance and motor insurance are expected to recover.
		Profitability was supported by the lack of major insurance losses, though several typhoons have resulted in significant economic losses.	The current strong pipeline in infrastructure construction projects will continue to support the property and engineering business in 2010.
Latin America	Life	The slowdown in life insurance business since 2008 continued into early 2009. Business, however, is stabilising alongside improvements in the real economies.	The recovery will be in line with the improving economic outlook.
			Demand for pension-related insurance will remain strong and will support premium growth in 2010 and onwards.
	Non-life	Non-life business remained weak in Chief but otherwise was fairly resilient in other regional markets.	Growth is expected to accelerate, reflecting the recovery of the regional economies.
		Business in Mexico has been supported by a multi-year, multi-line programme of the state-owned oil company.	The expected recovery in new car sales will be a major driver of non-life premium growth, given the dominance of motor in total non-life business.
		Motor insurance business contracted across the region, with the exception of Brazil, reflecting the lower rate of car sales.	Business lines, including engineering and surety, will start to benefit from investments in infrastructure.
Eastern Europe	Life	Growth remained depressed in early 2009, but showed signs of improvement in the second half.	Business is expected to recover but only slowly. Market consolidation is expected in Russia.
		In Russia, compulsory medical business continue to grow. Otherwise, businesses are sustaning further declines.	In Polanr, economic resilience will support a recovery in insurance demand.
		In Poland, the life business contracted from a hgh base in 2008 (when tax exemption was offered of life saving products).	The absence of insurance growth in Hungry is due to lingering economic problems.
	Non-life	Business is expected to have contracted in most Eastern European markets but probably most heavily in Russia.	A slow recovery in expected in 2010 but growth could remain elusive in some markets still plagued by economic problems.
		Motor hull performance remains weak while MTPL is growing slowly at best.	In Polanr, economic resilience will support a recovery in insurance demand.
Middle East	Life	The life business in the Middle East in generally underdeveloped with a very small business volume. Growth slowed in 2009.	Growth will accelerate modestly in 2010 due to the improving economic outlook.
	Non-life	Stable to lower growth continued to be driven by compulsory lines.	Compulsory health and motor insurance will continue to drive growth.
		The pipeline of government-sponsored construction projects is supporting engineering and property lines.	

ANNEXURE 41C

INSURANCE REGULATORY AND DEVELOPMENT AUTHORITY

(General Insurance — Reinsurance) Regulations, 2000

New Delhi, the 14th July, 2000

In exercise of the powers conferred by Section 114A of the Insurance Act, 1938(4 of 1938), the Authority in consultation with the Insurance Advisory Committee hereby makes the following regulations, namely:

Chapter I : PRELIMINARY

1. Short Title and Commencement

These regulations may be called the Insurance Regulatory and Development Authority (Reinsurance) Regulations, 2000 and are issued in pursuance of Section 114 of the Act.

They shall come into force from the date of its publication in the *Official Gazette*.

These regulations apply to all general insurers transacting direct insurance business.

2. Definitions

'The Act' means the Insurance Act, 1938 (4 of 1938).

'The Authority' means the Insurance Regulatory and Development Authority constituted under sub-section (1) of Section 3 of the Insurance Regulatory and Development Authority Act, 1999.

'Cession' means the unit of insurance passed to a reinsurer by the insurer, which has issued a policy to the original insured. A cession accordingly may be the whole or a portion of a single risk, defined policies or defined sections of business, as agreed in the reinsurance contract.

'Facultative' means the reinsurance of part of or all of a single policy in which cession is negotiated separately. The reinsurer and the insurer has the option of accepting or declining each individual submission.

'Indian re-insurer' means an insurer who carries on exclusively reinsurance business and is approved in this behalf by the Central Government;

'Pool' means any underwriting operation of insurance or reinsurance in which the participants assume a predetermined and fixed interest in all business written subject to agreed scope of business and limits.

'Retrocession' means the transaction whereby a reinsurer cedes to another Insurer all or part of the reinsurance it has previously assumed.

'Retention' means the amount, which an insurer assumes, for its own account. In pro rata contracts, the retention may be a percentage of the policy limit. In excess of loss contracts, the retention is an amount of loss.

'Treaty' means a reinsurance agreement between an insurer and a reinsurer, usually for one year or longer, which specifies the limits of liabilities and terms of reinsurance in respect of a portfolio of business.

Words and expressions used and not defined in these regulations but defined in the Insurance Act, 1938 or the General Insurance Business Nationalisation Act, 1972 or Insurance Regulatory and Development Authority Act, 1999 rules made under this Act shall have the meanings respectively assigned to them in those Acts or the rules as the case may be.

CHAPTER II

3. Procedure to be Followed for Reinsurance Arrangements

The Reinsurance Programme shall continue to be guided by the following objectives to:

(*a*) maximise retention within the country;

(*b*) develop adequate capacity;

(*c*) secure the best possible protection for the reinsurance costs incurred;

(*d*) simplify the administration of business.

Every insurer shall maintain the maximum possible retention commensurate with its financial strength and volume of business. The Authority may require an insurer to justify its retention policy and may give such directions as considered necessary in order to ensure that the Indian insurer is not merely fronting for a foreign insurer.

Every insurer shall cede such percentage of the sum assured on each policy for different classes of insurance written in India to the Indian reinsurer as may be specified by the Authority in accordance with the provisions of Part IVA of the Insurance Act, 1938.

The reinsurance programme of every insurer shall commence from the beginning of every financial year and every insurer shall submit to the Authority, his reinsurance programmes for the forthcoming year, 45 days before the commencement of the financial year;

Within 30 days of the commencement of the financial year, every insurer shall file with the Authority a photocopy of every reinsurance treaty slip and excess of loss covernote in respect of that year together with the list of reinsurers and their shares in the reinsurance arrangement;

The Authority may call for further information or explanations in respect of the reinsurance programme of an insurer and may issue such direction, as it considers necessary;

Insurers shall place their reinsurance business outside India with only those reinsurers who have over a period of the past five years counting from the year preceding for which the business has to be placed, enjoyed a rating of at least BBB (with Standard & Poor) or equivalent rating of any other international rating agency. Placements with other reinsurers shall require the approval of the Authority. Insurers may also place reinsurances with Lloyd's syndicates taking care to limit placements with individual syndicates to such shares as are commensurate with the capacity of the syndicate.

The Indian Reinsurer shall organise domestic pools for reinsurance surpluses in fire, marine hull and other classes in consultation with all insurers on basis, limits and terms which are fair to all insurers and assist in maintaining the retention of business within India as close to the level achieved for the year 1999-2000 as possible. The arrangements so made shall be submitted to the Authority within three months of these regulations coming into force for approval.

Surplus over and above the domestic reinsurance arrangements class-wise can be placed by the insurer independently with any of the reinsurers complying with sub-regulation (7) subject to a limit of 10% of the total reinsurance premium ceded outside India being placed with any one reinsurer. Where it is necessary in respect of specialised insurance to cede a share exceeding such limit to any particular reinsurer, the insurer may seek the specific approval of the Authority giving reasons for such cession.

Every insurer shall offer an opportunity to other Indian insurers including the Indian Reinsurer to participate in its facultative and treaty surpluses before placement of such cessions outside India.

The Indian Reinsurer shall retrocede at least 50% of the obligatory cessions received by it to the ceding insurers after protecting the portfolio by suitable excess of loss covers. Such retrocession shall be at original terms plus an over-riding commission to the Indian Reinsurer not exceeding 2.5%. The retrocession to each ceding insurer shall be in proportion to its cessions to the Indian Reinsurer.

Every insurer shall be required to submit to the Authority statistics relating to its reinsurance transactions in such forms as the Authority may specify, together with its annual accounts.

4. Inward Reinsurance Business

Every insurer wanting to write inward reinsurance business shall have a well-defined underwriting policy for underwriting inward reinsurance business. The insurer shall ensure that decisions on acceptance of reinsurance business are made by persons with necessary knowledge and experience. The insurer shall file with the Authority a note on its underwriting policy stating the classes of business, geographical scope, underwriting limits and profit objective. The insurer shall also file any changes to the note as and when a change in underwriting policy is made.

5. Outstanding Loss Provisioning

Every insurer shall make outstanding claims provisions for every reinsurance arrangement accepted on the basis of loss information advices received from Brokers/ Cedants and where such advices are not received, on an actuarial estimation basis.

In addition, every insurer shall make an appropriate provision for incurred but not reported (IBNR) claims on its reinsurance accepted portfolio on actuarial estimation basis.

INSURANCE REGULATORY AND DEVELOPMENT AUTHORITY

(Life Insurance – Reinsurance) Regulations, 2000

NEW DELHI, THE 22ND DECEMBER, 2000

In exercise of the powers conferred by Section 114A of the Insurance Act, 1938, read with Sections 14 and 26 of the Insurance Regulatory and Development Authority Act, 1999, the Authority, in consultation with the Insurance Advisory Committee hereby makes the following regulations, namely:

1. Short Title and Commencement

(1) These regulations may be called the Insurance Regulatory and Development Authority (Life Insurance - Reinsurance) Regulations, 2000.

(2) They shall come into force on the date of their notification in the *Official Gazette*.

2. Definitions

In these regulations, unless the context otherwise requires:

(a) *'Act'* means the Insurance Act 1938 (4 of 1938);

(b) *'Authority'* means the Insurance Regulatory and Development Authority established under sub-section (1) of Section 3 of the Insurance Regulatory and Development Authority Act 1999 (41 of 1999);

(c) *'Retention'* means the amount of risk which an insurer assumes for his own account.

(d) Words and expressions used and not defined in these regulations but defined in the Insurance Act, 1938 (4 of 1938) or Insurance Regulatory and Development Authority Act, 1999 (41 of 1999), shall have the meanings respectively assigned to them in those Acts as the case may be.

3. Procedure to be Followed for Reinsurance Arrangements

Every life insurer shall draw up a programme of reinsurance in respect of lives covered by him.

The profile of such a programme, duly certified by the Appointed Actuary, which shall include the name(s) of the reinsurer(s) with whom the insurer proposes to place business, shall be filed with the Authority, at least forty five days before the commencement of each financial year, by the insurer.

Provided that the Authority may, if it considers necessary, elicit from the insurer any additional information, from time to time, and the insurer shall furnish the same to the Authority forthwith.

The Authority shall scrutinise such a programme of reinsurance as referred to in sub-regulation (2), and may suggest changes, if it consider necessary, and the insurer shall incorporate such changes forthwith in his programme.

Every insurer shall retain the maximum premium earned in India commensurate with his financial strength and volume of business.

The reinsurer, chosen by the insurer, shall enjoy a credit rating of a minimum of BBB of Standard and Poor or equivalent rating of any international rating agency.

Provided that placement of business by the insurer with any other reinsurer shall be with the prior approval of the Authority.

Provided further that no programme of reinsurance shall be on original premium basis unless the Authority approves such programme.

Provided further that no life insurer shall have reinsurance treaty arrangement with its promoter company or its associate/group company, except on terms which are commercially competitive in the market and with the prior approval of the Authority, which shall be final and binding.

Every insurer shall submit to the Authority statistics relating to its reinsurance transactions in such forms as it may specify, together with its annual accounts.

4. Inward Reinsurance Business

Every insurer who wants to write inward reinsurance business shall adopt a well-defined underwriting policy for underwriting inward reinsurance business.

An insurer shall ensure that decisions on acceptance of reinsurance business are made by persons with adequate knowledge and experience, preferably in consultation with the insurer's appointed actuary.

An insurer shall file with the Authority, at least forty five days before the commencement of each financial year, a note on its underwriting policy indicating the classes of business, geographical scope, underwriting limits and profit objective.

An insurer shall also file any changes to the note referred to in sub-regulation (3) as and when a change in underwriting policy is made.

ANNEXURE 41(d)

GLOSSARY OF REINSURANCE TERMS[4]

Accident Year Experience: Reinsurance experience calculated by matching the total value of all losses occurring during a given twelve-month period (i.e., the dates of loss fall within the period) with the premiums earned for the same period. See also Calendar Year Experience and Policy Year Experience.

Acquisition Costs: All expenses directly related to acquiring insurance or reinsurance accounts, i.e., commissions paid to agents, brokerage fees paid to brokers, and expenses associated with marketing, underwriting, contract insurance and premium collection.

Admitted (Authorised) Reinsurance: Reinsurance for which credit is given in the ceding company's Annual Statement because the reinsurer is licensed or otherwise authorised to transact business in the jurisdiction in question.

Aggregate Excess of Loss Reinsurance: A form of excess of loss reinsurance which indemnifies the ceding company against the amount by which all of the ceding company's losses incurred during a specific period (usually 12 months) exceed either (1) a predetermined amount or (2) a percentage of the company's subject premiums (loss ratio) for the specific period. This type of contract is also commonly referred to as "stop loss" reinsurance or "excess of loss ratio" reinsurance.

Arbitration Clause: A provision found in many reinsurance contracts whereby the parties agree to submit their disputes to an unofficial tribunal of their own choosing rather than a court of law, generally subject to selection criteria and procedures set out in the clause, which produces an opinion ultimately enforceable by a court of law.

Assume: To accept all or part of a ceding company's insurance or reinsurance on a risk or exposure.

Assumption of Liability Endorsement: A statement of coverage by the reinsurer under which payment is guaranteed to a party not in privity with the reinsurance contract.

Automatic Facultative Binder (AFB) or Automatic Facultative Treaty: See Facultative Treaty.

Base Premium: See Subject Premium.

Binder: A record of reinsurance coverage pending replacement by a formal reinsurance contract, usually a facultative certificate.

Bordereau: A report provided periodically by the reinsured detailing the reinsurance premiums and/or reinsurance losses with respect to specific risks ceded under the reinsurance agreement.

Broker: An intermediary who negotiates reinsurance contracts between the ceding company and the reinsurer(s). The broker generally represents the ceding company and receives a commission, almost always from the reinsurer(s), for placing the business and performing other necessary services.

Broker Market: The collective reference to those reinsurance companies, which accept business mainly from reinsurance brokers. See Direct Writing Reinsurer.

Bulk Reinsurance: A transaction sometimes defined by statute as any quota share, surplus aid or portfolio reinsurance agreement through which, of itself or in combination with other similar agreements, an insurer assumes all or a substantial portion of the liability of the reinsured company.

Burning Cost: See Pure Loss Cost.

Calendar Year Experience: Reinsurance experience calculated by matching the total value of all losses incurred during a given twelve-month period (regardless of the dates of loss) with the premiums earned for the same period. As the name implies, Calendar Year Experience is usually calculated for a twelve-month period beginning January 1st. Accident Year Experience and Policy Year Experience are related but not synonymous terms.

Capacity: The largest amount of insurance or reinsurance available from a company or the market in general. Also used to refer to the maximum amount of business (premium volume) which a company or the total market could write based on financial strength.

Catastrophe Reinsurance: A form of excess of loss reinsurance which, subject to a specific limit, indemnifies the ceding company in excess of a specified retention with respect to an accumulation of losses resulting from a catastrophic event or series of events arising from one occurrence. Catastrophe contracts can also be written on an aggregate basis under which protection is afforded for losses over a certain amount for each loss in excess of a second amount in the aggregate for all losses in all catastrophes occurring during a period of time (usually one year).

Cede: To transfer to a reinsurer all or part of the insurance or reinsurance risk written by a ceding company.

Ceding Commission: In calculating a reinsurance premium, an amount allowed by the reinsurer for part or all of a ceding company's acquisition and other overhead costs, including premium taxes. It may also include a profit factor. See Overriding Commission.

Ceding Company: (Also Cedent, Reinsured, Reassured) - The insurer which cedes all or part of the insurance or reinsurance risk it has written to another insurer/reinsurer.

Cession: The amount of insurance risk transferred to the reinsurer by the ceding company.

Claims-Made Coverage: Any form of insurance under which the trigger of coverage is the presentation (or "making") of a claim against the insured rather than the date on which the loss occurred. A claims-made policy can provide for varying limitations as to the length of time prior to the policy period during which the loss event could have occurred (the "retroactive period") and the length of time after the policy has terminated during which the claim must be presented (the "tail" or "extended reporting period").

Clash Cover (or Contingency Cover): An excess of loss reinsurance agreement with a retention level equal to or higher than the maximum limits written for any one reinsured policy or contract. Usually applicable to casualty lines of business, the clash cover is intended to protect the ceding company against accumulations of loss arising from multiple insureds and/ or multiple lines of business for one insured involved in one loss occurrence.

Combination Plan Reinsurance: A reinsurance agreement which combines the excess of loss and the quota share forms of coverage within one contract, with the reinsurance premium established as a fixed percentage of the ceding company's subject premium. After deducting the excess recovery on any one loss for one risk, the reinsurer indemnifies the ceding company based on a fixed quota share percentage. If a loss does not exceed the excess of loss retention level, only the quota share coverage applies.

Commutation Agreement: An agreement between the ceding insurer and the reinsurer that provides for the valuation, payment and complete discharge of all obligations between the parties under particular reinsurance contract(s). Although more common where the ceding insurer or reinsurer has concerns about the other party's financial condition, commutation agreements can be used whenever the parties wish to settle and discharge all future obligations.

Commutation Clause: The clause in a reinsurance agreement which provides for the valuation, payment, and complete discharge of all obligations between the ceding company and the reinsurer, including future obligations for reinsurance losses incurred. The clause is most often found in workers compensation reinsurance contracts where future payments are of a continuous and generally known value.

Contingent Commission: (Also Profit Commission) – A commission feature whereby the cedent is allowed a commission based on the reinsurer's profitability under the reinsurance contract.

Continuous Contract: A form of reinsurance contract for accepting new business which does not terminate automatically but rather is intended to continue from year to year unless one of the parties delivers notice of intent to discontinue or termination is mutually agreed to in accordance with the termination provisions of the contract.

Cover Note: A statement indicating that the coverage has been effected.

Credit for Reinsurance: A statutory accounting procedure permitting a ceding company to treat amounts due from reinsurers as assets or reductions from liability based on the status of the reinsurer.

Cut-Off (Also Clean-cut): The termination provision of a reinsurance contract stipulating that the reinsurer shall not be liable for loss as a result of occurrences taking place after the date of termination.

Cut-Through Endorsement: An endorsement added to an insurance policy to provide that, in the event of the insolvency of the insurance company, the amount of any loss which would have been recovered from the reinsurer by the insurance company will be paid instead directly to the policyholder by the reinsurer. Also referred to as an Assumption of Liability Endorsement (ALE). See Guarantee Endorsement.

Deposit Premium: The amount of premium (usually for an excess of loss reinsurance contract) which the ceding company pays to the reinsurer on a periodic basis during the term of the contract. This amount is generally determined as a percentage of the estimated amount of premium, which the contract will produce, based on the rate and estimated subject premium. It is often the same as the Minimum Premium but may be higher or lower. The deposit premium will be adjusted to the higher of the actual developed premium or the minimum premium after the actual subject premium has been determined.

Direct Writing Reinsurer: A reinsurance company which develops its business by using its own personnel and does not (ordinarily) accept business from a broker or intermediary.

Drop-Down: See Second Event Retention.

Earned Reinsurance Premium: (1) That part of the reinsurance premium applicable to the expired portion of the policies reinsured, or (2) that portion of the reinsurance premium which is deemed earned under the reinsurance contract.

Evergreen Clause: See Letter of Credit.

Excess of Loss Ratio Reinsurance: See Aggregate Excess of Loss Reinsurance.

Excess of Loss Reinsurance: A form of reinsurance which, subject to a specified limit, indemnifies the ceding company against the amount of loss in excess of a specified retention. It includes various types of reinsurance, such as catastrophe reinsurance, per risk reinsurance, per occurrence reinsurance and aggregate excess of loss reinsurance. See also Non-Proportional Reinsurance.

Excess Per Risk Reinsurance: A form of excess of loss reinsurance which, subject to a specified limit, indemnifies the ceding company against the amount of loss in excess of a specified retention for each risk involved in each occurrence.

Experience Rating (Loss Rating, Merit Rating): A method of rating under which the reinsurance rate is based upon the reinsured's own experience, actual or reconstructed, rather than upon the exposure inherent in the business. See also Retrospective Rating and Prospective Rating.

Exposure Rating: A method of rating, usually applied to excess of loss reinsurance, under which the rate is determined, based on an analysis of the exposure inherent in the business to be covered and not on the loss experience the business has demonstrated in the past. Both exposure rating and loss rating can be used by the reinsurance underwriter to determine the price which is quoted.

Extra-Contractual Obligations (ECO) Clause: A clause in a reinsurance treaty which protects the ceding company against all or part of its liability arising from claim settlement activities and falling outside of strict policy provisions.

Facultative Certificate of Reinsurance: A contract formalising a reinsurance cession on a specific risk.

Facultative Obligatory Treaty: (Also Semi-obligatory Treaty) - A reinsurance contact under which the ceding company may cede exposures or risks of a defined class that the reinsurer must accept if ceded.

Facultative Reinsurance: Reinsurance of individual risks by offer and acceptance wherein the reinsurer retains the "faculty" to accept or reject each risk offered by the ceding company.

Facultative Treaty: A reinsurance contract under which the ceding company has the option to cede and the reinsurer has the option to accept or decline classified risks of a specific business line. The contract merely reflects how individual facultative reinsurance shall be handled.

Finite Reinsurance: (Non-traditional Reinsurance, Limited Risk Reinsurance, and Financial Reinsurance) – A term used to describe a broad spectrum of treaty reinsurance arrangements which provide reinsurance coverage at lower margins than traditional reinsurance, in return for a lower probability of loss to the reinsurer. This reinsurance is often multi-year and financially oriented, and can provide a means of financial management beyond that usually provided by traditional reinsurance.

Flat Rate: (1) A fixed rate not subject to any subsequent adjustment; (2) A reinsurance premium rate applicable to the entire premium income derived by the ceding company from the business ceded to the reinsurer as distinguished from a rate applicable to excess limits.

Following Reinsurer: A reinsurer which accepts the business ceded based on the terms of a contract primarily negotiated by another reinsurer, known as the lead reinsurer. (See Lead Reinsurer).

Fronting: Arrangements by which an authorised insurer, for a specified fee or premium, issues its policies to cover certain risks underwritten or otherwise managed by unauthorised insurers and then transfers all, or substantially all of its liability to such unauthorised insurers by means of reinsurance.

Funds Withheld: A provision in a reinsurance treaty under which the premium due the reinsurer, usually an unauthorised reinsurer, is not paid but rather is withheld by the ceding company to enable the ceding company to reduce the provision for unauthorised reinsurance in its statutory statement. The reinsurer's asset, in lieu of cash, is "Funds held by or deposited with reinsured companies".

Gross Line: The total limit of liability accepted by an insurer on an individual risk (net line plus all reinsurance ceded).

Ground Up (From the): A phrase referring to reinsurance losses subject to the contract under consideration before the application of the retention, but after reduction because of any other reinsurance which inures to the benefit of the coverage being considered. Also sometimes used to describe losses before reduction for inuring reinsurance.

Guarantee Endorsement: An endorsement added to an insurance policy covering the policyholder's mortgaged property to provide that, in the event of the insolvency of the insurance company, the reinsurer shall pay directly to the mortgagee and/or the policyholder the amount of loss which would have been recovered from the reinsurer by the insurance company.

Indexing: A procedure sometimes incorporated into an excess of loss reinsurance treaty to adjust the retention and limit according to the value of a specified public economic index (for example: wage, price, or cost-of-living.)

Insolvency Clause: A contractual provision, generally required by statute or regulation as a prerequisite to receiving credit for reinsurance, under which the reinsurer agrees, in the event of the ceding insurer's insolvency, to pay its reinsurance obligations under the contract whether or not the insurer has paid its obligations.

Intermediary Clause: A contractual provision, generally required by statute or regulation as a prerequisite to receiving credit for reinsurance, in which the parties agree to effect all transactions through an intermediary and the credit risk of the intermediary, as distinct from other risks, is imposed on the reinsurer.

Lead Reinsurer: The reinsurer on a contract recognised as having the major role in negotiating the reinsurance coverage terms of that contract.

Letter of Credit (LOC): Within the context of reinsurance, a banking instrument established on a "standby" basis to secure recoverables from non-admitted reinsurers to enable the ceding company to reduce the provision for unauthorised reinsurance in its statutory statement.

Line of Business: The general classification of business as utilised in the insurance industry, i.e., fire, allied lines, homeowners, etc.

Line Sheet (Also Line Guide): A schedule showing the limits of liability to be written by a ceding company for different classes of risk and (usually) also showing the lines which can be ceded to proportional reinsurance treaties.

Loss Adjustment Expense (LAE): The expense incurred by the ceding insurer in the defense and settlement of claims under its policies but not the insurer's overhead expenses. The definition of LAE depends on the terms of the reinsurance contract.

Loss Development: The difference between the estimated amount of loss(es) as initially reported to the reinsurer and the amount of an evaluation of the same loss(es) at a later date or the amount paid in final settlement(s).

Loss Loading or "Multiplier": (Also Loss Conversion Factor) — A factor is applied to the anticipated losses (or loss cost) for an excess of loss reinsurance agreement in order to develop the reinsurance premium (or rate.) This factor provides for the reinsurer's loss adjustment expense, overhead expense, and profit margin.

Loss Rating: A method of rating, usually applying to excess of loss reinsurance, under which the rate is determined based on the ceding insurer's historical loss experience, actual or reconstructed, rather than on the exposure inherent in the business. Both loss rating and exposure rating can be used as different rating approaches by the reinsurance underwriter to calculate the price, which is quoted.

Minimum Premium: An amount of premium which will be charged (usually for an excess of loss reinsurance contract), notwithstanding that the actual premium developed by applying the rate to the subject premium could have produced a lower figure. See Deposit Premium.

Net Retained Liability: The amount of insurance which a ceding company keeps for its own account and does not reinsure in any way (except in some instances for Catastrophe Reinsurance).

Net Loss: The amount of loss sustained by an insurer after deducting all applicable reinsurance, salvage, and subrogation recoveries.

Ninety Day Rule: The Annual Statement requirement which provides that an insurer must establish a provision for certain balances when it has reinsurance recoverables over ninety days past due.

No Claims Bonus: A form of profit commission under which the ceding company receives a stated percentage of the premium ceded in the event no claims are presented under the reinsurance treaty for a stipulated period of time. The no claims bonus differs from an ordinary profit commission in that no distribution occurs if any claims are made even if the treaty may have produced a profit.

Non-Admitted Reinsurance: Reinsurance for which no credit is given in the ceding company's statutory statement because the reinsurer is not licensed or authorised in the jurisdiction in question.

Non-Proportional Reinsurance: See Excess of Loss Reinsurance.

Obligatory Treaty: Reinsurance contract under which business must be ceded in accordance with contract terms and must be accepted by the reinsurer.

Occurrence Coverage: A description of coverage for an event that "occurred" within the time specified in the insurance agreement, regardless of the date the claim is actually submitted.

Offset (Set-Off): The reduction of the amount owed by one party to a second party by crediting the first party with amounts owed to it by the second party. The existence and scope of offset rights may be determined by contract language as well as statutory, regulatory and judicial law.

Over-Line: The amount of insurance or reinsurance exceeding the insurer's or reinsurer's normal capacity inclusive of automatic reinsurance facilities.

Overriding Commission: An allowance paid to the ceding company over and above the acquisition cost to allow for overhead expenses and often including a margin for profit.

Participating Reinsurance: See Pro Rata Reinsurance.

Pay Back: (1) A method of rating under which the underwriter sets the price based upon his view of how frequently the loss event might occur over a period of time. Thus, if the underwriter felt that the loss would occur only once in five years, the price would be set (without regard to expenses and profit margins) to be equal to the limit divided by five and the contract would thus be said to have a "five year pay back." See also Rate on Line. (2) Can also refer to premium charged in addition to the cost of an ongoing program for prior losses and, thus "pay back" reinsurers.

Placement Slip: A temporary record of reinsurance arrangements for which coverage has been effected, pending replacement by a formal reinsurance contract. Also known as a slip. See Binder.

Policy Year Experience: (Also Underwriting Year Experience) — Reinsurance experience calculated with all applicable premiums and losses assigned to the particular period (usually a 12 month period) in which each reinsured policy becomes effective. See also Accident Year Experience and Calendar Year Experience.

Pool (Also Association, Syndicate): An organisation of insurers or reinsurers through which pool members underwrite particular types of risks with premiums, losses, and expenses shared in agreed amounts.

Portfolio: The liability of an insurer for the unexpired portion of the in-force policies or outstanding losses or both for a described segment of the insurer's business.

Portfolio Reinsurance: The transfer of portfolio via a cession of reinsurance. See also Assumption.

Portfolio Return: Resumption by a ceding company of a portfolio.

Portfolio Run-Off: Continuing the reinsurance of a portfolio until all ceded premium is earned or all losses are settled or both.

Premium Base: See Subject Premium.

Primary: In reinsurance this term is applied to the nouns: insurer, insured, policy and insurance and means respectively: (1) the insurance company which initially originates the business, i.e., the ceding company; (2) the policyholder insured by the primary insurer; (3) the initial policy issued by the primary insurer to the primary insured; (4) the insurance covered under the primary policy issued by the primary insurer to the primary insured (sometimes called "underlying insurance").

Priority: The term used in some foreign reinsurance markets meaning retention.

Profit Commission: See Contingent Commission.

Proportional Reinsurance: See Pro Rata Reinsurance

Pro Rata Reinsurance: (Also Quota Share, Proportional and Participating Reinsurance)-A generic term describing all forms of quota share and surplus reinsurance in which the reinsurer shares a pro rata portion of the losses and premiums of the ceding company.

Prospective Rating (Also Self Rating): A type of Experience Rating used in arriving at the reinsurance rate and premium for a specified period, based in whole or in part, on the loss experience of a prior period.

Provisional Rate, Premium, or Commission: Tentative amounts subject to subsequent adjustment.

Pure Loss Cost (Also Burning Cost): The ratio of the reinsurance losses incurred to the ceding company's subject premium.

Quota Share Reinsurance: A form of pro rata reinsurance indemnifying the ceding company for a fixed percent of loss on each risk covered in the contract in consideration of the same percentage of the premium paid to the ceding company.

Rate: The percentage or factor applied to the ceding company's subject premium to produce the reinsurance premium or the percent applied to the reinsurer's premium to produce the commission.

Rate On Line: Same as payback except that the price is quoted as a percentage of the limit. Thus, a 20 percent rate on line would be equivalent to a five-year payback.

Reassured: See Ceding Company.

Reciprocity: A mutual exchange of reinsurance between two or more companies.

Reinstatement: A provision in an excess of loss reinsurance contract, particularly catastrophe and clash covers, that provides for reinstatement of a limit which is reduced by the occurrence of a loss or losses. The number of times that the limit can be reinstated varies, as does the cost of the reinstatement.

Reinsurance: The transaction whereby the assuming insurer, for a consideration, agrees to indemnify the ceding company against all, or a part, of the loss which the latter may sustain under the policy or policies which it has issued.

Reinsurance Premium: The consideration paid by a ceding company to a reinsurer for the coverage provided by the reinsurer.

Reinsured: See Ceding Company.

Reinsurer: The insurer, which assumes all, or a part of the insurance or reinsurance risk written by another insurer.

Reserve: An amount, which is set aside to provide for payment of a future obligation.

Retention: The amount of risk the ceding company keeps for its own account or the account of others.

Retrocession: A reinsurance transaction whereby a reinsurer (the retrocedant) cedes all or part of the reinsurance risk it has assumed to another reinsurer (the retrocessionaire).

Retrospective Rating (Also Self Rating): A type of Experience Rating used in arriving at the reinsurance rate and premium for a specified period based on the loss experience for that period.

Run-Off: A termination provision of a reinsurance contract that stipulates the reinsurer remains liable for loss as a result of occurrences taking place after the date of termination for reinsured policies-in-force at the date of termination until their expiration or for a specified time period.

Schedule F: The Annual Statement schedule that provides information on a company's reinsurance transactions.

Second Event Retention (Drop-Down): An approach to establishing the retention level in excess of loss reinsurance (usually catastrophe) under which the amount of the retention is reduced for the second (or subsequent) loss occurrence.

The theory is that the ceding company can afford to retain a given retention level on one loss, but for additional loss(es) needs protection over the lower retention.

Self-Rating: See Prospective Rating and Retrospective Rating.

Set-Off (Offset): The reduction of the amount owed by one party to a second party by crediting the first party with amounts owed to it by the second party. The existence and scope of offset rights may be determined by contract language as well as statutory, regulatory and judicial law.

Share Reinsurance: See Pro Rata Reinsurance.

Sliding Scale Commission: A commission adjustment on earned premiums whereby the actual commission varies inversely with the loss ratio, subject to a maximum and minimum.

Special Acceptance: The specific agreement by the reinsurer to include under reinsurance contract a risk not included within the terms of the contract.

Special Termination Clause (Also Sudden Death Clause): A clause sometimes found in reinsurance contracts allowing one or both parties to terminate fully the contract and coverage for future occurrences upon the happening of some specified condition or event, such as the insolvency or merger of the other party, by providing shorter notice than is otherwise required to terminate the contract if such condition or event had not happened.

Stop Loss Reinsurance: See Aggregate Excess of Loss Reinsurance.

Subject Premium (Also Base Premium, Premium Base, and Underlying Premium): The ceding company's premiums (written or earned) to which the reinsurance premium rate is applied to produce the reinsurance premium. Sometimes also called GNEPI or GNWPI (Gross net earned, or written, premium income) or SMPI (subject matter premium income).

Surplus Reinsurance (Also Surplus Share Reinsurance): A form of pro rata reinsurance under which the ceding company cedes that portion of its liability on a given risk which is greater than its net line. As consideration, the reinsurer receives that portion of the total premium, which the surplus bears to the total liability.

Target Risk: (1) Certain high valued bridges, tunnels and fine arts collections which are excluded from reinsurance contracts and release the reinsurer of any potential high accumulation of liability on any one risk from various sources; (2) a large hazardous risk on which insurance is difficult to place; or (3) a large attractive risk which is considered a target for competing insurance companies and producers. See also Total Insured Value.

Term Contract: A form of reinsurance contract written for a stipulated term (usually one year). The contract automatically expires at the end of the term and renewal must be negotiated. See also Continuous Contract.

Total Insured Value (TIV): A clause in a reinsurance contract which stipulates that losses relating to risks which have a total insured value in excess of a given amount will not be protected under the contract. In many contracts this clause replaced the Target Risk Clause.

Treaty: A reinsurance contract under which the reinsured company agrees to cede and the reinsurer agrees to assume risks of a particular class or classes of business.

Ultimate Net Loss: The term applied to the reinsurer's loss under a reinsurance contract, generally the gross loss less any recoveries from other insurance which inure to the benefit of the contract in question.

Underlying: The amount of insurance or reinsurance on a risk (or occurrence) which applies to a loss before the next higher excess layer of insurance or reinsurance attaches.

Underlying Premium: See Subject Premium.

Unearned Reinsurance Premium: That part of the reinsurance premium applicable to the unexpired portion of the policies reinsured.

Working Cover: A contract covering an amount of excess reinsurance in which loss frequency is anticipated.

Key Terms

- ❒ Financial Risk
- ❒ Reinsurance
- ❒ Treaty
- ❒ Credit Risk
- ❒ Facultatives
- ❒ Reinsurance Arrangements

Questions for Review

1. Define Reinsurance. Briefly explain the various objectives of reinsurance.
2. "Reinsurance is a well thought well structured expense for insurance company? Explain.
3. Distinguish between Facultatives and Treaties.

Suggested Readings

1. Irving Pfeffer and David, R. Klock, *Perspectives on Insurance*, Prentice-Hall, Englewood Cliffs, 1974.
2. Insurance Chronicle Various Issues, ICFAI Press, Hyderabad.

Web Resources

- www.globalreinsurance.com
- www.reinsurance.org
- www.re-world.com
- www.swissre.com

Information Technology in Insurance

Chapter 42

CHAPTER OBJECTIVES

After reading this chapter you will be able to understand :

- *The Need for Information Technology*
- *Technologies for Insurance*
- *IT Applications in Functional Areas*
- *Insurance and Electronic Commerce — E-insurance*
- *Information Technology and LIC*
- *IT Department in an Insurance Company*

42.1 THE NEED FOR INFORMATION TECHNOLOGY

The rapid innovations in the field of information and communication technology has posed serious challenges for the insurance industry in India. The use and application of information technology in wide variety of insurer's operations has now become strategic in the sense that it has direct impact on the productivity of resources, and a sweepening impact on reducing the cost of various activities.

With the arrival of private insurance players, the competition has become more intense and an important role is being played by the insurance sector. Even though the use of information technology is not new to the insurance sector, yet we may find tight compartmentalisation regarding the use of information technology in various departments of the insurance companies including the major players since last 50 years. The most visible of these departments are accounting, policy issue and servicing, claim processing, sales management etc. The innovations in information technology can be effectively utilised in the following areas:

- Speedy and correct issuance of documents
- Expeditious disposal of claims
- Proper building of accounts and statistics

Quality Assurance & Efficiency

Therefore the imperative for all the insurers, especially LIC and GIC is to build up an efficient interface between the various departments and segments. This would reduce the paper work, improve efficiency of service delivery and provide competitive advantage to the insurance companies.

42.2 Technologies for Insurance[1]

There has never been a time when the effective use of information technology has been more crucial to the success of the insurance industry. The insurance markets are being revolutionised by technology at a high speed pace. IT and software solutions, allowing cross-border trade to become electronic and paperless, are increasingly on offer to importers, exporters, shipping companies and financial institutions.

1. www.insurancetechnologies.com

In a country like India where the risk factors are quite variable depending upon demographic and geographical spread, it is the ability of the insurers in properly administering its business which can ensure their survival. The networking facilities which have become available today enable the insurance industry to have in place systems for providing on the spot service facilities for its customers while keeping its data base at a centralized location. A hybrid combination *i.e.,* a semi-centralized data base for servicing of policies (data bases pertaining to servicing units of a particular area at an intervening place) and its consolidation in real time at central data base can be another useful model. This kind of arrangement provides interesting working model, reduces cost of servicing but at the same time enables different users to access the data base and provide service on anywhere any time basis with M.I.S. generation at all levels.[2]

Dependint upon the movement of data and its access over network/leased lines/V-set, it is necessary arrangement and bandwidth. The threat to the data base can come from the in-house user and/or from a competitor or any other outsider or corruption of the disk/server space due to hardware problems. Therefore, it is not only the establishment of network system but an effective I.T. security policy which must be put in place and be operational.

Following technological advancements can really enhance the performance of insurance companies.

Database Management Systems

The principles of tracking and measuring responses can pay off for the conventional insurance industry. To find more clients, insurer needs to consider many factors, including lapsation, cash value, premium and competition. But the need to record and study the characteristics of persistency- the length of time we retain policies, customers and agents is most important for insurance companies.

In order to find out profitable combinations of households or clients, products and agents, a database with five to ten years' history is of immense importance. Such historical retention was prohibitively expensive in the past. But clear advantages of new PC (Personal computer) and RISC (Reduced Instruction Set Computing) technology gives companies power to keep tens of millions of policies on a device with thousands of bytes of data per policy/client/agent. Analyisng a 10-year database is cost effective. Reviewing the database provides information on how many clients have actually migrated not just how many policies have lapsed or surrendered. Using database technology companies can get a comprehensive, performance, loyalty, and lost opportunity.

Data Warehouse

Data warehousing technology is based on integrating a number of information systems into a 'one stop shopping' database to achieve vision of making company national in scope, but regional in focus. Traditionally, the sale of policies and the claim settlement are two separate areas for the insurance companies. Data warehousing allows managing by profit levels with an integrated approach rather than by limiting losses. Data mining can be used as a means to control costs and increase revenue resulting in enormous earning for effective users.

Decision Support Systems

The path of business applications of computers, computer based information systems (CBIS), encompasses many stages including the very early applications like transactions processing systems (TPS) followed by the management information systems (MIS). The computer applications like decision support systems (DSS), expert systems (ES) and executive information systems (EIS) are still awaited in insurance business. Office automation (OAS) happens to be a continuously ongoing, dynamic process for any business. Companies need to utilise decision support systems by implementing data warehouses that pull information from existing legacy systems into a customer information database. Such decision support systems will equip the insurance managers with ability to allow for customised products and services that are more in line with what customers want.

2. S.K. Kapahi, Technology in Life Insurance, IRDA Journal, April 2006.

Group Linking Software

Group-linking software enables sharing of information and particularly suits document heavy insurance business. Tracking of policy application shows how information that is input and accessed from a number of locations can increase efficiency.

Imaging and Work-flow Technologies

The proposal forms may be scanned into an imaging system, data may be extracted for update to computer and for automated underwriting workflow may be implemented.

Mapping

Insurers to meet different needs, such as identifying loss prone areas or geographic claim analysis, can use Mapping technology. It helps the insurer to analyse the extent of its network i.e. the insurer can determine whether it has too many or too few agency force in a particular area.

Call Centre Technology

Good customer service is a crucial element in gaining, maintaining and retaining profitable customer. Call centre concept based on interactive voice response services (IVRS) is gaining importance in this aspect. Employees based the primitive concept of call centre on an enquiry system providing information services to customers through telephone line answers. The totally automated computerised exchange but lacks in flexibility i.e. only predefined queries are serviced.

Video Linking

A video linking facility between two remote units of an insurance company or between an insurer and a broker allows underwriters at one place and brokers at other unit to discuss risk inherent in a proposal face to face.

Cat Models

Catastrophic models use data from the recent spate of natural disasters that helps develop more predictions of insurers' property exposures in future disasters. Using this data curious "what-if" scenarios of probable maximum loss (PML) using the best estimate available at an insurer's exposures are tested. Finally an underwriting policy that limits the company's exposure to catastrophic losses is implemented.

Intranet, Extranet and Internet

Intranet is the network connecting different offices of the same business to permit the internal data within the business. *Extranet* is a network allowing the business to communicate with business partners like suppliers, vendors, banners, regulations etc. on the electronic channel. *Internet* is a global network of many computer networks. Any user, who would like to exchange some information with other user at a remote location, can log into the computer of Internet provider via modem or an Internet access CPU (IAC). The Internet and online service providers are providing opportunities to create new forums that can be utilised by everyone worldwide. Insurers can browse through many useful sites on the Internet.

42.3 IT Applications in Functional Areas

Even though the information technology has wide application in all the spheres of the insurance business, yet following are the most important ones in respective functional areas:[3]

3. R.K. Agarwal, Role of Information Technology in the Insurance Industry, *The Chartered Secretary*, August 2001, pp. 902-904.

Marketing

The scope for use of Information Technology in marketing function is tremendous. It may start from the consumer accquitance to an insurance product to claims settlement or further selling of new products or developing consumers for the products.

Information technology can be integrated with almost all the P's of marketing. It may help in formulation and implementation of various marketing strategies including pricing, promotion and customisation strategies. Some of these areas are discussed below.

Consumer Awareness

The use of Information Technology may be path breaking for the insurance companies since conventionally the awareness of the insurance products in India is low. With the use of Internet the information about the products and pricing policies can be made available to the public in few seconds and much transparency in operations can be established. There are numerous websites available which can help the prospective customers to compare the insurance products of various issuers and decide the product suited to his needs. Also, the information about the new products changes in the existing ones and of course, the information on various discounts and incentives can be provided at a much faster rate and lower cost.

Customer Services

The insurance being a *service* needs high concerns in terms of services. Customer service requires maximum attention and should span the entire gamut of activities in the purchase of a product i.e. right from the dissemination of information, documentation to policy administration and claim settlement. The service quality standards of the new private insurance players have posed a threat to the-then giants viz. the LIC and GIC. The investments in the personnel and knowledge systems have helped private player's companies build significant domain expertise. The emerging areas of IT applications are:

(1) Market Research
(2) Consumers targeting and segmentation
(3) Customisations of products
(4) Easy procedures like premium payments, claims settlements, tracking of brokers and agents
(5) Complaints management/grievance handling
(6) Intermediary analysis.

Finance

Information technology can be effectively used for internal management viz. Accounting, treasury management, financial performance reporting etc. and as well as in resource mobilisation, portfolio management, investment planning etc.

Human Resource Management

Application of IT in Human Resource Management is obvious. It can be effectively utilised in (1) recruitment and selection, (2) training, (3) performance appraisal, (4) promotions, transfers and dismissals, (5) valuations etc.

Research and Development

R & D has been made an easy task with the increasing use of IT. Surveys and research on market potential, analysis of markets, tracking with international norms and developments are the profound areas of IT applications.

When disaster occurs, the most important factor for the insurer is to provide a sense of confidence to its customers that their interest will be protected. This requires an instant communication and quickly meeting the instantaneous demands of the customers. The demands may be in relation to knowing the system of filing of claims, settlement of claims, or general information alone etc. Technology, therefore, at such a stage comes to the help of the insurer. It may so happen that the technology intervention itself may get affected by the disaster. Therefore, the business continuity plan and minimum recovery time to restore the original system is of paramount importance for the insurers.

Management Information System

The insurance management today needs to take informed business decisions based on correct up-to-date M.I.S. returns; and generation of M.I.S automatically and its escalation from the operating level to the highest level is possible only with the help of technology. An informed, data based decision is always likely to be more helpful in bringing in policy changes, mid term corrections, strategy planning, etc. which are only possible with the usage of information technology and centralized data bases.

Any profit in the insurance sector is based on probability of the event happening, return on investments, reduction in fixed administration cost and variable cost and to provide the returns expected by stakeholder. The principles of actuarial science provide the basic framework for making all these calculations. The speed of making available different models of actuarial calculations, however, depends on the capabilities of the applied technology. A number of different models can be constructed. The fact however, will remain regarding acceptability of the product by the customers.

Regulatory Control

All insurance companies design their products based on their own assumed parameters and making certain assumptions. Also the results of their business activities depend upon reliability of their data and actual results; vs. assumed norms and expected results. The regulator has to ensure that the insurance companies work within permissible, acceptable norms and have sufficient solvency margins. It will be practically impossible to have any kind of guidance and control mechanism if it has to work on a mutual basis. The proper usage of technology can help the regulator to test the veracity of claims of the different insurers against the acceptable norms of parameters which give an idea about health of business operations of the insurers. It can also give lead time to the regulator if any insurance company is heading for any minor/major disaster which will adversely affect its customers and the insurance industry. The usage of I.T. can help regulator having common norms for the industry and test check for all the insurers for particular kind of business against these norms. Here again technology lends a big helping hand to the Regulator.

The various applications of information technology in life and non-life insurance companies broken into identifiable area are given in Annexure 42A.

42.4 Insurance and Electronic Commerce – E-insurance

On a global basis, there is mad rush of companies willing to enable their business. E-insurance *ispo-facto*, not aloof, is one of the growth areas in India. Enormous opportunities are being created by the Internet's new connectivity such as improving customer's service, reducing cycle time, becoming more cost effective, and selling goods, services, or information to an expanded global customer base. As entire industries are being reshaped and rules for competition are changing, enterprises need to rethink the strategic fundamentals of their business in order to be successful. Globally, insurance on the net has lagged behind other financial service products such as banking and brokerage. Of the total online users only 5% used insurance service online.

This lag was due to lack of relevant and adequate content. Traditional insurers, while leveraging on new information technologies, have been slow to utilise the Internet as an alternative distribution channel. Generally the largest insurers have been focused on static marketing presence online, encompassing product information,

FAQ's and quotes. Only a few insurers have added the ability to submit applications online. This lack of participation in the e-business revolution is seen across lines. The insurance companies attribute two factors for the slow take off. First and foremost, insurance is a product that is sold and not bought. The Internet is perceived to be a buyer's medium, with online customers able to search quickly and for the most competitive prices and variety of products. Insurance is one product that cannot be easily commoditized. The more personal the selling process the greater the difficulty in using the net as a medium for selling. Insurance is one product, which involves personalised selling. The process of insurance sales requires a series of face-to-face interactions.

42.4.1 International Trends

The convergence effect of IT is being felt by the insurance industry as well in developed countries. In the US, personal savings are almost evenly distributed between banking, insurance, mutual fund and other financial institutions. The insurance industry is expected to lose market share to banking and other financial institutions. Customers today expect enhance levels of service due to increased competition. This customer demand is likely to result in non-traditional access to specific information. The global online insurance market is expected to achieve an exponential growth in the near future. In the life insurance segment alone, the total online business will grow to $21 billion by 2003. Premium income from the non-life policies will go up to $18 billion in the next three years. The Gartner Group in a study conducted by them says that in a year 25% of all customer contacts and enquiries for enterprises will come via the Internet, e-mail and online forms. Bancassurance customer service, which has been almost exclusively done via the telephone (96% of all transactions), will become increasingly e-mail based in the next four years; decreasing telephone related service by 28%.

In response to these trends in customer preference, insurers are mobilising their online sales and customer account management capabilities. This move towards building Internet based business solutions benefits the insured by providing greater flexibility, greater customisation of information and improved customer service for the insurance company, this drastically reduces the costs involved. Similarly, by essentially outsourcing administrative and cost intensive processes such as policy administration to customers, the cost of administration and servicing the insurance policy also decreases sharply.

42.4.2 E-Insurance in India

The intriguing question before all associated with the insurance industry is that will it be possible for private companies or even public sector monoliths to sell insurance online in India in the near future? Insurance companies will probably have to wait for Internet penetration to increase and the still ambiguous e-commerce rules to take concrete form. However, what is not debatable is that new private entrants will change the rules of the game for the Indian insurance business, both in the life and the non-life segment, unfolding opportunities for software engineers and professional agents.

To peep into the possibilities and opportunities emerging out of the integration of insurance and information technology, various organisations have organised seminars and conferences in the recent past to explore the possibilities of selling insurance on the Net and gauge the opportunities for the growing Indian software industry. According to T. Ramanan of Assocham, life insurers were among the first to go online with informative content and features like actuarial calculators. However, according to him, they have been relatively slow to embrace online commerce, which currently makes up about 1 per cent of the total term life market. Only 12 per cent of insurance companies globally sell policies online. Experts expect the percentage of term life sold over the Internet to increase from 1 per cent to 15 per cent by 2003, which in monetary terms works out to $21 billion. Although traditionally term life insurance has been sold through independent agents, the big shift will become manifest sooner than later. And more importantly Indians cannot watch from the sidelines as this paradigm shift in the insurance sector takes place. In the non-life sector, automobile policies are popular over the Internet. Premium income, points out the paper, is expected to rise to $18 billion from about $1 billion currently. The growth of global online insurance business augurs well for the Indian IT sector. The exponential growth in the online insurance business will unfold significant business opportunities for software companies/consultants. The opportunities that rise out of this will be both global and local, because new entrants will have to either fine tune or prepare customized packages for the Indian market. Online insurance will also help companies reduce costs and keep premiums low, a pre-requisite in a price sensitive market like India. The government, however, will have to address problems relating to bandwidth on an urgent basis to make online insurance a reality in India. Other major challenges to face Indian insurers will be to design and develop strategies for delivering services to well segmented customers. The third challenge lies in developing the right combination of customer segments and applicable distribution channel strategies.

Most Web sites offer contact numbers of their branch officers where one can get further details of the products on offer. The Agent locator feature, available on **maxnewyorklife.com, iciciprulife.com and on bimaonline.com** help one locate an insurance agent most accessible to you based on a search facility. One would expect downloadable proposal forms on insurance web sites, but these are missing in most cases. Only **licindia.com** seems to offer downloadable proposal and claim forms for a few of the schemes.

42.4.3 Benefits of Electronic Insurance

E-insurance provides multiple benefits to the insurer and the existing and prospective insureds:

- Information collected is better and cheaper
- Speed of response — Issuance of policy and settlement of claims is faster
- Provides new ways of doing business in competitive market
- Flexible pricing and customised services
- Global accessibility i.e. lapse of physical boundaries
- Increased sales without additional sales force
- Immediate premium collection and funds transfer
- Reduced cost per transaction
- 24*7 availability i.e. round the clock availability of information
- Real time knowledge base building.

42.4.4 Life Insurers on the Web

Insurers	*Website*
LIC of India	www.licindia.com
Om Kotak Mahindra	www.omkotakmahindra.com
Max New York Life	www.maxnewyorklife.com
Birla Sun Life	www.birlasunlife.com
ING Vysya Life	www.ingvysyalife.com
HDFC Standard Life	www.hdfcinsurance.com
ICICI Prudential Life	www.iciciprulife.com
Portals on life insurance	www.bimaonline.com
	www.bimaguru.com

The features offered by most of the Indian insurers' websites are :

1. Basic details of the various products classified by type — endowment, whole life, money back policies etc.
2. A primer on insurance basics explaining the need for insurance, glossary of insurance terms, FAQ's etc.
3. Downloadable forms (not offered by all), online customers help lines, tax, and premium and bonus calculators.
4. Sections on the various tax benefits of insurance products on offer.
5. A 'contact' mechanism whereby you can get in touch with their nearest branch office or marketing personnel.
6. Customers can also compute the premium for various policies in a matter of seconds, using premium calculators.
7. These sites also serve as a virtual community for insurance professionals with features such as the latest insurance news, career opportunities, insurance education, message board for discussions and events in insurance sector.

42.4.5 Major Factors Affecting E-insurance

- **Growth of net:** it is estimated that India would have about 150 million net users by 2010. These figures represent a huge buying potential.
- **Competition pressures:** insurance companies because of competitive pressures would be driven into Internet rather than a clear ROI justification.
- **Customer:** the availability of net-based services will be a huge factor for customer retention.
- **Cross sells:** when linked with other financial products, a portfolio approach to investment, savings and risk coverage will increase cross sells and customer loyalty and retention.
- **Costs:** in the beginning e-insurance will be a cost factor rather than a profit driver, but in the long run it will be a cost reducing factor.

42.4.6 E-Insurance Business Challenges

Electronic insurance will not only provide many benefits but will also pose business and technological changes.

Business Challenges

- *Disintermediation increases business:* Study has shown that the cost of distribution decreases with the increased value of connection. Products with relatively high fixed costs and low value such as travel, credit or burial insurance are relatively expensive to produce. Customers pay a high price per dollar of coverage for these products. The Internet allows the disintermediation of this relatively high overhead for these low face value products. This means that prices can be lowered and more insurance can be sold by reducing the transaction costs of the exchange.
- *Reorganisation of companies-Virtual Companies:* Many insurers will be prompted by the opportunities presented by E-commerce to restructure the packaging of insurance services. Insurance companies using e-commerce may re-engineer, outsource, and/or streamline their management functions, or marketing and distribution arms. To more efficiently deliver these services, some insurers will be able to reduce their significant investments in physical facilities and certain personnel. E-commerce will enable independent agency insurers to more easily adapt their distribution mechanism to market competition and expedite their transactions with intermediaries.

- *Insurance customers what do they want*: Customers could get better and different service through the Internet. It is possible to obtain quotes from a number of companies. In some cases, the Internet provides rating agencies' evaluation of insurers. The Internet and outsourcing can provide additional cost savings to the consumer. Technology can bring the customer closer to the insurance contract, by removing layers of inefficiencies. Consumers will also obtain price comparisons for relatively generic contracts, such as life insurance and rates for a standard set of auto insurance coverage for given vehicle and driver characteristics. Consumers also could have access to internal records to see where their claims are in terms of payment, when their next annuity payment is due, and how their mutual fund is performing. This can be done without calling a burdensome voicemail system, being put on hold, or finding a person who can give them the desired information efficiently.
- *The Death of Insurance Agent:* One of the reasons why insurers have been slow to use electronic commerce could be the fear of swallowing up the agent's business. The Internet does not necessarily imply the death of the agent. Many insurers are examining their agent's role in the process and are also developing direct contacts with the insured through their web presence. Agents could enhance their advisory role to consumers as their paper and money processing functions diminish.

Technological Challenges

One of the most prominent challenges of e-commerce is security. It is very evident that many users are reluctant to do business on the Internet due to security reasons.

Security

Database Security: The business database security is utmost important. This has to be monitored by security of the web server and web access.

Web Server Security: Security policies should be defined like who is allowed access, nature of the access and who authorises such access? etc.

Password sniffing: Protection against password sniffing is to avoid using plain text user names and reusable passwords.

Network Scanning Programmes: Automated tools should be used to scan your network. These tools check for well-known security related bugs in network programs such as send mail and FTPD.

Physical Security: One can ensure physical security by having an alarm system that calls the police, having a key-lock on the computer power supply.

Web Access Security: Host based restrictions can be implemented using a firewall to block incoming HTTP connections to a particular web server.

Transmission Security: Encryption is a key technology to ensure transaction security.

Privacy: Privacy is likely to be a growing concern as internet-based communications and commerce increase. Designers and operators of web sites who disregard the privacy of users do so at their own peril.

42.5 INFORMATION TECHNOLOGY AND LIC[3]

LIC has been one of the pioneering organisations in India who introduced the leverage of Information Technology in servicing and in their business. Data pertaining to almost 10 crone policies is being held on computers in LIC. The computers were introduced in 1964 in LIC. Unit Record Machines introduced in late 1950's were phased out in 1980's and replaced by Microprocessors based computers in Branch and Divisional Offices for Back Office Computerisation. Standardisation of Hardware and Software commenced in 1990's. Standard Computer Packages were developed and implemented for Ordinary and Salary Savings Scheme (SSS) Policies.

Front End Operations

With a view to enhancing customer responsiveness and services, in July 1995, LIC started a drive of On-line Service to policyholders and agents through computers which enables policyholders to receive immediate policy status report, prompt acceptance of their premium and get Revival Quotation, Loan Quotation on demand. Incorporating change of address can be done on line. Quicker completion of proposals and dispatch of policy documents have become a reality. All 2048 branches across the country have been covered under front-end operations. So LIC claims that all its 100 divisional offices have achieved the distinction of 100% branch computerisation. New payment related Modules pertaining to both ordinary and SSS policies have been added to the Front End Package catering to Loan, Claims and Development Officers' Appraisal to reduce time lag and ensure accuracy.

Metro Area Network

A Metropolitan Area Network, connecting 74 branches in Mumbai was commissioned in November, 1997, enabling policyholders in Mumbai to pay their Premium or get their Status Report, Surrender Value Quotation, Loan Quotation etc. from any branch in the city. The System has been working successfully. More than 10,000 transactions are carried out over this Network on any given working day. Such Networks have been implemented in other cities also.

Wide Area Network

All 7 Zonal Offices and all the MAN centres are connected through a Wide Area Network (WAN). This enables the customer to view his policy data and pay premium from any branch of any MAN city. As at May 2002, there were 91 centres in India with more than 1200 branches networked under WAN.

Interactive Voice Response Systems (IVRS)

IVRS, functional in 58 centres all over the country, enables customers to ring up LIC and receive information (e.g. next premium due, Status, Loan Amount, Maturity payment due, Accumulated Bonus etc.) about their policies on the telephone. This information could also be faxed on demand to the customer.

Website

LIC's website, www.licindia.com, displays information about LIC and its subsidiaries-LIC (International) E.C., LIC (Nepal) Ltd., LIC Mutual Fund, LIC Housing Finance and their products. The addresses/e-mail Ids of its Zonal Offices, Zonal Training Centres, Management Development Centre, Overseas Branches, Divisional Offices and also all Branch Offices are also provided. LIC has given its policyholders a unique facility to pay premiums through Internet absolutely free and view their policy details on Internet premium payments.

Information Kiosks

LIC has set up Interactive Touch screen based Multimedia KIOSKS in prime locations in metros and some major cities for dissemination information to general public on various products and services offered. These KIOSKS enable the users to provide policy details and accept premium payments.

Info Centres

It has also set up call centres to provide information about our Products, Policy Services, Branch addresses and other organisational information.

42.6 IT Department in an Insurance Company

42.6.1 Functions

The IT department in an insurance company performs the following functions:

- Provision of hardware and software resources.
- Adoption of latest technologies for competitive advantage.
- Training of employees – at operating, head and controlling offices on office automation and networks.
- Advise the top management on Business Process Re-engineering (BPR).
- Develop, maintain and implement insurance related application.
- Maintenance of networks.

42.6.2 Set-up

Generally the insurance organisation has three-tier set-up – Operating office (BO/DO), Controlling Offices (RO/DO) and Central Office (HO). The organisation and responsibilities of the IT department and its sub-departments is more or less in the hierarchical order of the various offices. The IT department at HO is responsible to the chairman/CEO of the organisation for implementation of IT plan. The department is responsible for procuring new technologies, conducting training and preparing the broad IT policy framework. The RO and BO are respectively responsible to the CO. The Head of the IT department may have the following functional managers with their respective tasks:

Technology Manager	➢ Evaluation and acquisition of new technologies in hardware, software, networking and packaged solutions ➢ Recruitment and supervision of system and network engineers ➢ Conducting of various training programmes
Systems Manager	➢ Systems analysis and design ➢ Functional specifications ➢ Development of application and user manuals ➢ Assignment of work to project leaders, system analysts and programmers ➢ Evaluation of studies
Network Manager	➢ Network Administration (Including WAN) ➢ User administration, systems security, e-mail etc. ➢ Controlling and supervision of network administrators
Operations Manager	➢ Maintenance of hardware ➢ Job scheduling, backups and file control ➢ Assigning work to operators and DEOs ➢ Training of users ➢ Controlling of data flow

Annexure 42-A

Life Insurance Applications

- Policy Servicing
- New Business
- Claims
- Billing
- Loans
- Statistics & MIS
- Accounts & Audit

General Insurance Applications

- Policy Management & Underwriting
- Co-insurance
- Reinsurance
- Claims
- Accounts & Audit
- Statistics & MIS

Reinsurance System

- Inward insurance
- Outward insurance
- Reinsurance accounts
- MIS

Risk Management System

- Assessment
- Valuation
- Management

Investment System

- Term Loans
- Money market operations
- Investment Accounts

Pesonnel System

- Payroll
- Performance Appraisal
- MIS
- Leave & Attendence
- Employee Benefits

Office Services

- Purchases
- Inventory
- Tours & Travels
- Corporate Accounting

Key Terms

- ❒ Information Technology
- ❒ DBMS
- ❒ LAN
- ❒ E-Insurance
- ❒ Portals
- ❒ WAN

Questions for Review

1. Briefly explain the applications of information technology in various functional areas of insurer operation.
2. Write short notes on :

   (*a*) e-insurance

   (*b*) Insurance websites and portals

Suggested Readings

1. Information Technology, IC21, Insurance Institute of India, Mumbai, 2000.
2. D.C. Srivastava *et. al., Indian Insurance Industry — Transition and Prospects,* New Century Publications, 2001.

Risk Management in Insurance Companies

Chapter **43**

Chapter Objectives

After reading this chapter you will be able to understand :

- *Key elements of risk management in insurance companies*
- *Types of insurance risk and hedging techniques*

Risk is more integral to the insurance business via-a-vis other businesses. This is because of the economic development of the insurance sector in the last decade and its direct linkage with the financial system of the economy. Also, the markets have become more complex with new risks emerging continuously. Insurer are not specialised to handle such type of risks. Also, the differences in the regulations across the financial sector may imply increased use of risk vehicle needing least capital requirements. This chapter provides a background of the risk management practices in insurance companies in light of these developments.

43.1 Introduction

Insurers are in the risk business and in the process of providing insurance and other financial services, they assume various kinds of actuarial and financial risks. Other businesses use insurance services because of their ability to provide actuarial risk pooling through their major product lines of life, property/casualty and health insurance, pension products, annuities, and other financial instruments. At the same time, they are major providers of funds to the capital market particularly to the fixed income sectors. In performing these roles they generally act as a principal in the transaction. As such, they use their own balance sheet to facilitate the transactions and to absorb the risks associated with them. Therefore, risk management and the necessary procedures for risk control is crucial task for insurers. Risks facing all financial institutions including insurance companies can be segmented into three separable types from a management perspectives-

(a) risks that can be eliminated or avoided by standard business practices;

(b) risks that can be transferred to other participants, and

(c) risks that must be actively managed at the firm level.

In the first of these cases, the practice of risk avoidance involves actions to reduce the chances of idiosyncratic losses from standard insurance activity by eliminating risks that are superfluous to the institution's business purpose. Common risk avoidance practices include at least three types of actions. The standardization of process, insurance policies, contracts and procedures to prevent inefficient or incorrect financial decisions is the first of these. Another is the construction of portfolios on both sides of the balance sheet that benefit from diversification and the application of the Law of Large Numbers and Central Limit Theorem, which reduce the effects of any one loss experience. Finally, the implementation of incentive compatible contracts with the institution's management to require that employees be held accountable is the third. In each case, the goal is to rid the firm of risks that are not essential to the financial service provided, or to absorb only an optimal quantity of a particular kind of risk.

Actuarial risk can be transferred to reinsurers. Catastrophe risk can be offset somewhat by undertaking a position in catastrophe futures and perhaps even in catastrophe bonds. Interest rate risk can be hedged or transferred through interest rate products such as swaps, caps, floors, futures, or other derivative products. Insurance policies and lending documents can be altered to effect a change in their duration and convexity. Equity market risk can be reduced with an appropriate futures position in equities. In addition, they can offer products, which absorb some financial risks, while transferring some of these risks to the purchaser. Defined contribution pension plans and variable universal life policies are clear examples of this approach. Finally, the insurer can buy or sell financial claims and reinsurance to diversify or concentrate the risk that results from servicing its client base. To the extent that the market understands the actuarial and financial risks of the insurance policies underwritten by the firm, they can be sold in part or in whole at their fair value. Unless the institution has a comparative advantage in managing the attendant risk and/or a desire for the embedded risk they contain, there is no reason for the insurer to absorb such risks, rather than transfer them[1].

43.2 Risk Management Elements

Risk management in insurance companies revolves around four key elements that is essential to implementing a broad based risk management system.

43.2.1 Standards and Reports

This involves two different conceptual activities, i.e., standard setting and financial reporting. Underwriting standards, risk classification, and standards of review are traditional tools of risk control. Consistent evaluation and rating of exposures of various types are essential for management to understand the risks on both sides of the balance sheet, and the extent to which these risks must be mitigated or absorbed. The standardization of financial reporting by outside audits, regulatory reports, and ratings agency evaluations is essential for investors to gauge asset quality and firm level risk. But the types of information collected and the manner in which it is assembled and presented in statutory accounting reports are inadequate for the purposes of managing an insurance company.

43.2.2 Underwriting Authority and Limits

Another technique for internal control of active management is the use of position limits, and/or minimum standards for participation. In terms of the latter, the domain of risk taking is restricted to only those customers or assets that pass some prespecified quality standard. Limits are imposed to cover exposures to counter parties, credits, and overall position concentrations relative to various types of risks. In general, each person who can commit capital, whether on the asset or liability side of the ledger, will have a well-defined limit. This applies to underwriters, portfolio managers, lenders, and traders. Summary reports show limits, as well as current exposure by business unit on a periodic basis.

Investment Guidelines or Strategies

Investment guidelines and recommended positions for the immediate future is the next key element. Here, strategies are outlined in terms of concentration and commitments to particular areas of the market, the extent of desired asset/liability mismatching or exposure to interest rate risk, and the need to hedge against systematic risks of a particular type. These limits lead to passive risk avoidance and/or diversification, because managers generally operate within position limits and prescribed rules. Beyond this, guidelines offer firm level advice as to the appropriate level of active management, given the state of the market and the willingness of senior management to absorb the risks implied by the aggregate portfolio.

1. Risk Management by Insurers – An Analysis of the Process http://knowledge.wharton.upenn.edu/paper.cfm?paperID=236

Such guidelines extend to firm level hedging and asset/liability matching. In addition, securitization and even derivative activity are rapidly growing techniques of position management open to participants looking to reduce their exposure to be in line with management's guidelines.

Similar guidelines are required on the liability side of the balance sheet. Underwriting standards and strategies are needed to ensure that the risks accepted conform to the parameters that the insurer is capable and willing to accept. They also foster better pricing of products, and prevent any one underwriter from compromising the future solvency of the firm.

Incentive Schemes

To the extent that the firm can enter incentive compatible contracts with senior management, line managers, and sales agents and make compensation related to the risks borne by these individuals, then the need for elaborate and costly controls is lessened. However, such incentive contracts must be consistent with the insurers' financial goals and require proper internal control systems. Such tools, which include underwriting risk and loss analysis, investment risk analysis, the allocation of costs, and the setting of required returns to various parts of the organization is not trivial. Notwithstanding the difficulty, well-designed systems align the goals of managers with other stakeholders in a most desirable way.

43.3 Risks in Providing Insurance Services

Actuarial View of Risks

Globally Society of Actuaries standards are adopted by insurance companies for risk classification. These are of four types. C-1, C-2, C-3 and C-4.

(a) C-1 risks are **asset risks**, which arise from the possibility that borrowers of insurer funds may default on their obligations to the company, or that the market value of an insurer's investment assets may decline. This category include interest rate risk, credit risk, market risk, and currency risk.

C-2 risk is **pricing risk**, which stems from uncertainty about future operating results relating to items such as investment income, mortality and morbidity, frequency and severity of claims and losses, administrative expenses, sales and lapses. If an insurer's pricing is based on assumptions that prove inadequate, it may not be able to meet its obligations to policy owners.

C-3 risk is **asset/liability matching risk**, which springs from the impact of fluctuating interest and inflation rates on the values of assets and liabilities. If the impact of fluctuating rates is different on assets than on liabilities, the values of assets and liabilities will change by different amounts, and could expose the insurer to insolvency.

C-4 risks are **miscellaneous risks**, generally thought to be beyond the ability of insurers to predict and manage, but they nevertheless represent real risk to the company. These risks include tax and regulatory changes, product obsolescence, poor training of employees and sales agents, and malfeasance, malversation, or misconduct of managers or other employees and also the risk that laws or legal interpretations will change in a way that will alter the firm's obligations *ex post*. One new category is **C-5** risk, which is the havoc that arises when a person who has strong political ambitions or is running for higher political office is appointed to be state insurance commissioner.

B. The Financial View of Risks

Standard financial risk framework is an alternative to the actuarial decomposition of risk which is unique to the insurance industry. The financial risks can be broken into six generic types: actuarial, systematic, credit, liquidity, operational and legal risks.

Actuarial risk is the risk that arises from raising funds via the issuance of insurance policies and other liabilities. It is the risk that the firm is paying too much for the funds it receives, or alternatively, the risk that the firm has received too little for the risks it has agreed to absorb. If an insurer invests its funds in efficiently traded securities, it should expect to have, on average, a zero net economic profit. If the insurer pays too much for these funds it cannot expect to earn a satisfactory profit in the long run. Another aspect of actuarial risk is that during any given time period, the underwriting losses will be in excess of those projected. This could happen for two reasons. First, the expectations themselves may be based on an inadequate knowledge of the loss distribution. Second, the losses may exceed their expectations in the normal course of business simply because losses fluctuate around their mean. The degree to which they deviate from the mean will depend, of course, on the characteristics of the loss distribution, which depend on the nature of the risks insured.

Systematic risk is the risk of asset and liability value changes associated with systematic factors. It is sometimes referred to as market risk. This risk can be hedged but cannot be diversified completely away. Insurance sector is greatly affected by changes in the general level of interest rates, basis risk, and inflation in case of non-life insurance business. Because of the insurers' dependence on these systematic factors, most try to estimate the impact of these particular systematic risks on performance, attempt to hedge against them, and thus limit the sensitivity of their financial performance to variation in these undiversifiable factors.

Insurance companies carry out interest rate sensitivity analysis to measure and manage the firm's vulnerability to interest rate variation. At the same time, insurers with large corporate bond, mortgage and common stock holdings closely monitor their *basis risk*. Also, to the extent that the frequency and severity of claims are influenced by *inflation risk*, expected losses will also be affected. This is particularly the case where insurance policies are written on a replacement cost basis. The inflation of concern can be general inflation, affecting repair costs, medical costs, and the like, or specific and localized inflation.

Credit risk is the risk that a borrower will not perform in accordance with its obligations. Credit risk may arise from either an inability or unwillingness on the part of the borrower to perform in the pre-committed contracted manner. This can affect the investor holding the bond or lender of a loan contract, as well as other investors and lenders to the creditor. The real risk from credit is the deviation of portfolio performance from its expected value. Accordingly, credit risk is diversifiable but difficult to eliminate completely, as general default rates themselves exhibit much fluctuation. The idiosyncratic nature of some portion of these losses remains a problem for creditors in spite of the beneficial effect of diversification on total uncertainty particularly for insurers that take on highly illiquid assets. In such cases, the credit risk is not easily transferred, and accurate estimates of loss are difficult to estimate.

Liquidity risk is described as the risk of a funding crisis which for example may be a situation would inevitably be associated with an unexpected event, such as a large claim or a write down of assets, a loss of confidence or a legal crisis. Because insurers operate in markets where they may receive clustered claims due to natural catastrophes, or massive requests for policy withdrawals and surrenders due to changing interest rates, their liabilities can be said to be somewhat liquid. Their assets, however, are sometimes less liquid, particularly where they invest in private placements and real estate. Given this situation, it is important for an insurer to maintain sufficient liquidity to easily handle any demands for cash. Otherwise, an insurer that would be solvent without a sudden demand for cash may have to sell off illiquid assets at concessionary prices, leading to large losses, further demands for cash, and potential insolvency.

Operational risk is associated with the problems of accurately processing claims, and accurately processing, settling, and taking or making delivery on trades in exchange for cash. It also arises in record keeping, processing system failures and compliance with various regulations.

Legal risks are endemic in financial contracting and are separate from the legal ramifications of credit and operational risks. New statutes, court opinions and regulations can put formerly well established transactions into contention even when all parties have previously performed adequately and are fully able to perform in the future. For example, changes in the application of statutes of limitations for filing suits have affected the losses arising from property/liability policies. Similarly, the change to joint and several liability rules has also altered the distribution of risks that may be covered by insurance policies.

Another type of legal risk arises from the activities of an institution's management, employees and agents. Fraud, violations of regulations or laws, and other actions can lead to catastrophic loss. Even a situation where the insurer legally fulfills all of its contract obligations can result in massive litigation if some policy owners had different expectations or understandings about the performance of their policies than what was specified in the contracts.

Every insurer faces a different exposure to each of these risks, depending on its business mix. In all its activities, an insurer must decide how much business to originate, how much to finance, how much to reinsure, and how much to contract to agents. In so doing, it must weigh both the return and the risk embedded in the asset and liability portfolios. Management of the insurance company must measure the expected profit and evaluate the prudence of the various risks enumerated above to be sure that the result achieves the stated goal of maximizing shareholder value, in the case of a stock insurer, or maximizing ownership interests, in the case of a mutual or reciprocal insurer. If the product's expected profit warrants the risk, then the activity is added to the insurer's balance sheet, and the risk must be managed.

43.4 Insurance Risk Management Systems

Management of Actuarial Risk

Insurers are typically have sophisticated models to manage actuarial risk. Life insurance prices are determined using conservative static assumptions regarding loss distributions and interest rates, which is also undergoing change because of the high interest rate volatility. Life insurance policies create complexities because of options—settlement options, policy loan options, over-depositing privileges, and surrender or renewal privileges, on the part of the insured, and discretionary dividend and crediting rate options on the part of the insurer. Insurers use option framework to value and manage these risks.

Non-life insurers use modern valuation software for pricing liabilities especially Option-adjusted arbitrage-free valuation tools that are useful given the imprecision associated with many of the risks that are insured. Few options are also available compared to those available in life policies, and nominal values are often not guaranteed; guarantees are sometimes in terms of covering repair costs, replacement costs, medical costs, and so forth. Even when there are nominal maximum amounts of coverage, the losses below the maximum are subject to additional uncertainty because of inflation.

Reports and standards for underwriting life/health and property/casualty risks is conventional technique. Underwriting limits are established to limit authority to a certain amount. While insurance agents may have temporary binding authority, it is a common practice to have a party who is not involved in the policy sale to review the underwriting and make a determination whether the risk will ultimately be accepted and insured. Insurers are typically better at keeping track of sales commissions than in tracking losses to a particular sales agent or underwriter.

Also based on loss experience, insurers place restrictions on further sales or more severe limitations on underwriting; alternatively, the activities of these sales agents and underwriters could be subject to greater oversight. These days an area of greatest concern in the area of actuarial risk is the misalignment of incentives between owners of the insurance firm and its sales and marketing staff. This has also been highlighted in Chapter 34. Employees and agents whose compensation is tied to sales growth are therefore strong proponents of more "competitively-priced" insurance policies. Senior management often comes from a sales background, and is sympathetic with the notion that what is good for the insurance agents are good for the company. Pricing actuaries, who are supposed to be the watchmen and gatekeepers in this area, are often placed under tremendous pressure to alter their assumptions so that the company's products can be priced more competitively.

43.5 Management of Systematic Risk

Systematic Risk of Liabilities

Insurers use generic or some internally developed software to manage systematic risk. Duration and convexity measures are used to hedge the interest rate risk. Insurers feel need enough reliable data on which to specify the relation of lapses and policy surrenders to interest rate movements. Also inflation affects the liabilities to a significant extent. It is generally thought that interest rate risk accounts for only a small portion of the change in the value of liabilities over time, and that other risks, such as actuarial risk, price regulation, legal risk, underwriting risk, inflation risk, and event or catastrophe risk swamp the influence of interest rate movements on the pricing and valuation of property and casualty insurance liabilities.

Systematic Risk of Assets

Insurers are concerned with interest rate risk more than other systematic risk factors since it affects the value of fixed income assets, which constitute the majority of their assets. Asset values are also to be affected by basis risk, default risk, liquidity risk, call risk, prepayment risk, extension risk, sinking fund options, convertibility, real estate and equity risk.

Many insurers use the actuarial software mentioned earlier to estimate the durations and convexities of their investments. Some develop their own, more sophisticated in-house programs for estimating values of both sides of the balance sheet.

Asset/Liability Management

Asset-liability management is critical for the insurers. Insurers typically use duration and convexity estimates for the liability side of the balance sheet, and Modified Macaulay duration measures for the asset side.

In setting limits on the amount of systematic risk the company desires to retain, a common approach is the one used by a leading multi-line insurer. The company places limits on its desired portfolio structure to reflect the variety of risks to which it is exposed. Limits are set on individual asset holdings, on industry concentration, and on asset type including mortgage backed securities and collateralized mortgage obligations, all in a risk-based capital context.

For the balance sheet as a whole, limits are employed in two different ways. One approach is to impose a limit on the amount of duration mismatch allowed, either for particular product lines or for aggregating across all assets and liabilities. These restrictions may be applied on a product segmentation basis, or on an aggregate portfolio basis.

Some firms simply transfer the assets between portfolio segments and use some sort of internal transfer pricing mechanism. Assets are acquired by the firm and then allocated to each product group according to perceived needs. This is done to foster a better sense of accountability and used in performance evaluation.

The other limit is a restriction on the amount of scenarios that are allowed to reveal losses due to asset/liability mismatches. These limits are typically placed not only on the distribution of final simulated results, but also on the evolution of solvency over time associated with the simulations.

Management of Credit Risk

Insurance firms are generally very focused on credit risk, as are rating agencies and regulatory authorities. They produce weekly and monthly reports that monitor the credit risk of their assets. They rely on outside rating agencies, such as Moody's, Standard and Poor's, Duff and Phelps, and Dunn and Bradstreet. Many insurers have their own due diligence requirements to meet before they will take on an investment that has credit risk. They undertake internal credit risk ratings, in some ways quite similar to those of rating agencies.

Insurers produce "Watch Lists" of firms they feel are in financial jeopardy, likely to be downgraded or become insolvent. They often have a dual track credit risk assessment, one for the asset itself, and another for the underlying collateral. They place limits on the portfolio exposure by industry, by geographic region, by business (e.g., real estate prohibited), and by company. They also have lists of approved counter parties for brokerage, settlement and swaps.

Liquidity Risk

Liquidity is not as big a concern with many insurance firms as it is in other financial institutions since most of their policies are less liquid than their assets. Life insurance companies issue policies that commonly feature high surrender charges. These charges are either explicitly stated, or implicit in the schedule of cash build-up. For example, a single premium deferred annuity, with annual crediting rate reset and a seven year maturity, may feature surrender charges beginning at 7-10% during the first year, and declining in steps toward zero at maturity. Similarly, universal life and whole life products often have very low surrender values during the first year or two of a policy, and begin building up rapidly after that point. Other policies, such as variable universal life, have surrender provisions that act much like a mutual fund, where the amount received depends on the value of the underlying fund. In case of non life businesses, the liquidity risk comes mostly from event risk or catastrophe risk. Most policies do not feature cash values that are easily accessible through surrender, although some policies will allow insured to cancel prior to maturity and receive a portion of their premium. Moreover, the policies are typically very short term, renewable annually.

It is seen that non-life Insurers, in terms of the accounting policies mark-to market a larger portion of their fixed income securities than life companies, and also tend to hold more liquid, shorter term securities on average. Since their liquidity concerns almost always stem from event risk or catastrophe risk, they can avoid some of these risks by reinsuring portions of their books of business, and by broadly diversifying their risk portfolios geographically, by industry, and by type of risk. Alternatively, they can hold large amounts of liquid surplus assets. Insurers typically have a company's asset/liability committee is typically responsible for measuring and managing liquidity risk.

For other risks like operating risk, are a natural outgrowth of their business and insurers employ standard risk avoidance techniques to mitigate them. Standard business judgment is used in this area to measure the costs and benefits of both risk reduction expenditures and system designs, as well as operational redundancy.

43.5.1 IRDA Framework for Risk Management

Every insurer has maintain a solvency margin as per the Insurance Regulatory and Development Authority (Assets, Liabilities, and Solvency Margin of Insurers) Regulations, 2000 given in Appendix 40A. These guidelines limit the quantum of business done in various classes and help to management the credit and liquidity risk.

The limits on various classes of investments that can be made by insurance companies are provided in the Insurance Regulatory and Development Authority (Investment) (amendment) Regulations, 2001(Appendix 40B). This permits better ALM and takes care of systematic and defaults risks.

Actuarial risk is dealt by Insurance Regulatory and Development Authority (Actuarial Report and Abstract) Regulations, 2000 that require the insurer to report on the product details, premium computation etc.

Besides, reinsurance is compulsory in some classes of general insurance business as per GIC guidelines. Also, disclosures in financial statements provide necessary insight to the risk management by the insurance companies.

43.5.2 Catastrophic Risk and its management

Catastrophic risk event affect large number of exposure units. Catastrophic risk is a low-probability event which can lead to major and typically irreversible losses for example global environmental hange, sub-prime crises etc. Catastrophe risk modeling technology has become a vital tool for quantifying, managing, and transferring risk in the insurance industry. For insurance sector, financial stability requires complete portfolio management of natural hazard risks evident from major catastrophes. Hurricane Andrew in Florida, the Kobe Earthquake in Japan, the Northridge Earthquake in California, and Windstorms Lothar and Martin in Europe, Tsunami in India indicate that insurance markets that catastrophe risk should be proactively underwritten and managed. Financial statements of insurance companies as per IRDA guidelines also indicate the reserves and provisions to be made for catastrophic risk.

43.6 CAT Bonds

CAT bonds are popular instruments to model CAT risk. Catastrophe bonds[2] (also known as cat bonds) are risk-linked securities that transfer a specified set of risks from a sponsor to investors. They are often structured as floating rate bonds whose principal is lost if specified trigger conditions are met. If triggered the principal is paid to the sponsor. The triggers are linked to major natural catastrophes. Catastrophe Bonds are typically used by *insurers* as an alternative to traditional catastrophe *reinsurance*.

Investors choose to invest in catastrophe bonds because their return is largely uncorrelated with the return on other investments in fixed income or in equities, so cat bonds help investors achieve diversification. Investors also buy these securities because they generally pay higher interest rates (in terms of spreads over funding rates) than comparably rated corporate instruments, as long as they are not triggered.

Key categories of investors who participate in this market include *hedge funds*, specialized catastrophe-oriented funds, and asset managers. *Life insurers*, reinsurers, banks, *pension funds*, and other investors have also participated in offerings.

Cat bonds are often rated by an global agencies like *Standard & Poor's, Moody's*, or *Fitch Ratings*. A typical corporate bond is rated based on its probability of default due to the issuer going into *bankruptcy*. A catastrophe bond is rated based on its probability of default due to an *earthquake* or *hurricane* triggering loss of principal. This probability is determined with the use of *catastrophe models.* Most catastrophe bonds are rated below *investment grade* (BB and B category ratings), and the various rating agencies have recently moved toward a view that securities must require multiple events before occurrence of a loss in order to be rated investment grade.

Examples of cat bond sponsors include insurers, reinsurers, corporations, and government agencies. Over time, frequent issuers have included *USAA*, Hartford, *Swiss Re*, *Munich Re*, *Liberty Mutual*, *SCOR*, *Hannover Re*, *Allianz*, and Tokio Marine & Fire."

APPENDIX 43A

THE GAZETTE OF INDIA: EXTRAORDINARY **[PART III –SEC. 4]**

INSURANCE REGULATORY AND DEVELOPMENT AUTHORITY, NEW DELHI

NOTIFICATION

New Delhi, the 14th July, 2000

Insurance Regulatory and Development Authority (Actuarial Report and Abstract) Regulations, 2000

F.No.IRDA/Reg./7/2000.–

In exercise of the powers conferred by clause (g) of sub-section (2) of section 114A of the Insurance Act, 1938, (4 of 1938), the Authority, in consultation with the Insurance Advisory Committee, hereby makes the following regulations, namely:-

Short title and commencement : (1) These regulations may be called the Insurance Regulatory and Development Authority (Actuarial Report and Abstract) Regulations, 2000.

(2) They shall come into force from the date of their publication in the Official Gazette.

2. Definitions : In these regulations, unless the context otherwise requires :

"Act" means the Insurance Act, 1938(4 of 1938);

"Authority" means the Insurance Regulatory and Development Authority established under sub-section (1) of section 3 of the Insurance Regulatory and Development Authority Act, 1999 (41 of 1999);

"extra premium' means a charge for any risk not provided for in the minimum contract premium;

"group business" means those insurance contracts which are group policies as mentioned under sub-section (2) of section 4 of the Act;

"guarantees" means the terms in regard to benefits or premiums or charges, which may not be altered during the currency of the policy;

"individual business" means individual insurance contracts issued on single/joint lives;

"inter valuation period" means, as respects any valuation, the period to the valuation date of that valuation from the valuation date of the preceding valuation in connection with which an abstract was prepared under the Act or under the enactments repealed by the Act, or, in a case where no such valuation has been made in respect of the class of business in question, from the date on which the insurer began to carry on that class of business;

"maturity date" means a fixed date on which benefit may become payable either absolutely or contingently;

"non-par policies" or "policies without participation in profits" means policies which are not entitled for any share in surplus (profits) during the term of the policy;

"office yearly premium" means regular premium (excluding extra premiums which are required to be shown separately) payable by the policyholder to secure the basic benefits under the policy in a policy year ;

"options" means the rights available to a policyholder under a policy;

"par policies" or "policies with participation in profits" means polices which are not non-par policies as defined under clause (i);

"policies with deferred participation in profits" means polices entitled for participation in profits after a certain period from the date of commencement of the policy,

"premium term" means the period during which premiums are payable;

"riders" or "rider benefits" means add-on benefits, which are in addition to basic benefits under a policy;

"valuation date" means as respects any valuation the date as at which the valuation is made;

All words and expressions used herein and not defined but defined in the Insurance Act, 1938 (4 of 1938), or in the Insurance Regulatory and Development Authority Act, 1999 (41 of 1999), or in any Rules or Regulations made thereunder shall have the meanings respectively assigned to them in those Acts or Rules or Regulations.

Procedure for Preparation of Actuarial Report and Abstract. — **(1)** The Abstract and Statements must be so arranged that the number and letters of the paragraphs correspond with Regulation 4.

The Abstracts and Statements shall be furnished to the Authority, within nine months from the end of the period to which they refer to, in accordance with sub-section (1) of section 15 of the Act.

Four copies of the Abstracts and Statements shall be furnished to the Authority in accordance with sub-section (1) of section 15 of the Act, and one of the four copies so furnished shall be signed by the persons as mentioned in sub-section (2) section 15 of the Act.

There shall be appended to every such Abstract and Statement -

a certificate signed by the principal officer that full and accurate particulars of every policy under which there is a liability, either actual or contingent, has been furnished to the appointed actuary for the investigation; and

a certificate signed by the appointed actuary with his remarks, if any, to the effect that:-

i) the data furnished by the principal officer has been included in conducting the valuation of liabilities for the purpose of investigation;

reasonable steps have been taken to ensure the accuracy and completeness of the data;

he has complied with provisions of the Act,

he has complied with guidance notes issued by the Actuarial Society of India with the concurrence of the Authority,

in his opinion, the mathematical reserves are adequate to meet the insurer's future commitments under the contracts, and the policyholders' reasonable expectations.

Requirements Applicable to Abstract and Statements.—(1) Abstracts and statements shall be prepared separately in respect of –

Linked Business;

Non-Linked Business; and

Health Insurance Business.

(2) An insure shall prepare the following statements which shall be annexed to the abstract prepared in accordance with these regulations, namely:-

in respect of Linked Business,—

Form LB-1;

Form LB-2;

Form LB-3;

Form LB-4;

Form IA;

(b) in respect of Non-Linked Business,—

Form NLB-1;

Form NLB-2;

Form DD;

Form DDD;

Form DDDD;

Form IA;

(c) in respect of Health Insurance Business,—

Form LB-1;

Form LB-2;

Form LB-3;

Form NLB-1;

Form IA.

Summary statements—

Form K;

Form IRDA-AA as specified under Regulation 4 of Insurance Regulatory and Development Authority (Assets, Liabilities, and Solvency Margin of Insurers) Regulations, 2000;

Form H;

Form I;

Statement of Composition and Distribution of surplus in respect of policyholders' fund as specified under Regulation 8;

(3) Each Abstract shall show—

The **Valuation Date**.—The date on which valuation (investigation) is done;

New Products.—A brief description of new products introduced during the inter-valuation period giving salient features;

Foreign Operations- A brief description of the foreign operations of the insurer, during the inter-valuation period;

Valuation Method.— A brief description of ——

(i) the methods adopted in the determination of mathematical reserves in respect of insurance products;

(ii) the method by which age at entry, premium term, maturity date, valuation age, period from the valuation date to the maturity date, have been treated for the purpose of valuation;

(iii) the method of allowing for-

(I) incidence of premium income: and

(II) premiums payable otherwise than annually;

(e) **Valuation bases.**— (i) Valuation parameters used in the valuation shall be furnished in the manner as specified in the table hereunder:-

Description	*Mortality basis Used*	*Morbidity basis basis used*	*Inflation rate*	*Interest Rate*	*Expenses*	*Future bonuses, if any*	*Others please specify*	*Remarks*
(1)	(2)	(3)	(4)	(5)	(6)	(7)	(8)	(9)
(a) Insurance Product:								
(*i*) Regular Premium								
(*ii*) Single premium and Fully paid up								
(iii) Reduced Paid up								
(b) Insurance Product:								
(i) Regular Premium								
(ii) Single premium and Fully paid up								
(iii) Reduced Paid up								

Expenses related to premiums, sum assured, annuity, etc., and per policy shall be specified separately under Column (5 of the table;

Items such as terminal bonus, in case of with profit contracts, management charges, etc., in respect of linked business, shall be specified under Column (8) of the table;

(f) Other Adjustments (Provisions).– The methods by which provision, if any, has been made for the following matters, including a statement of bases wherever necessary,-

Policies in respect of which extra premiums have been charged on account of underwriting of under-average lives that are subject to extra risks such as occupation hazard, over-weight, under-weight, smoking history, health, climatic or geographical conditions;

Lapsed policies not included in the valuation but under which a liability exists or may arise;

Options available under individual and group insurance policies;

Guarantees available to individual and group insurance policies;

The rates of exchange at which benefits in respect of policies issued in foreign currencies have been converted into Indian Rupees and what provision has been made for possible increase of mathematical reserves arising from future variations in rates of exchange;

(g) Further Information.—The following information shall be appended:-

Returns on Assets as specified under Regulation 5;

Distribution of surplus as specified under Regulation 6;

Principles adopted in distribution of surplus as specified under Regulation 7;

Negative Reserves and Guaranteed Surrender Value Deficiency Reserves as specified under Regulation 9;

Miscellaneous, if any.

5. Returns on assets.– (1) The average gross rates of interest yielded by the assets may be determined expressing the investment income as percentage of the mean fund. [$i = 2 \times I / (A + B - I)$; where i is the gross yield; I = Investment Income; A = the assets at the beginning of the financial year, and B= the assets at the end of the financial year; Investment Income (shown in the Revenue Account) should include the amount of the unrealised gain taken into revenue account, A and B have to be adjusted value of assets shown in the Balance Sheet.].

(2) The average gross rates of interest, referred to under sub-regulation (1), shall be furnished for each fund maintained by an insurer.

6. Distribution of surplus. – The basis adopted in the distribution of surplus as between the shareholders and the policyholders, and whether such distribution was determined by the instruments constituting the company, or by its regulations or by-laws or how otherwise shall be mentioned.

7. Principles adopted in distribution of profits.—- The general principles adopted in distribution of profits among policyholders, including statements on following points, shall be furnished:-

(i) Whether the principles were determined by instruments constituting the insurer, or by its regulations or by-laws or how otherwise;

The number of years premium to be paid, period to elapse and other conditions to be fulfilled before a bonus is allotted;

Whether the bonus is allocated in respect of each year's premium paid, or in respect of each calendar year or year of assurance or how otherwise; and

Whether the bonus vests immediately on allocation, or, if not, conditions of vesting.

8. Statement of composition of surplus and distribution of surplus in respect of policyholders' funds.–(1) A statement, showing total amount of surplus arising during the inter-valuation period, and the allocation of such surplus, shall be furnished separately for participating business and for non-participating business, with the particulars as mentioned below:-

Composition of Surplus:

Surplus shown under Form I:

Interim Bonuses paid during the inter-valuation period:;

Terminal Bonuses paid during the inter-valuation period:

Loyalty Additions or other forms of bonuses, if any, paid during the inter-valuation period;

Sum transferred from shareholders' funds during the inter-valuation period:;

Amount of surplus, from policyholders' funds, brought forward from preceding valuation:

Total Surplus (total of the items (a) to (f)):

Distribution of Surplus:

Policyholders' Fund:

To Interim Bonuses paid;

To Terminal Bonuses

To Loyalty Additions or any other forms of bonuses, if any;

Among policyholders with immediate participation giving the number of polices which participated and the sums assured thereunder (excluding bonuses);

Among policyholders with deferred participation, giving the number of polices which participated and the sums assured thereunder (excluding bonuses);

Among policyholders in the discounted bonus class giving the number of polices which participated and the sums assured thereunder (excluding bonuses);

To every reserve fund or other fund or account (any such sums passed through the accounts during the inter valuation period to be separately stated);

As carried forward un-appropriated.

Shareholders' Fund:

To the shareholders' funds(any such sums passed through the accounts during the inter valuation period to be separately stated);

Totals:

Total Surplus allocated: (total of the items (a) to (i))

(2) Specimen of Bonuses allotted to policies for one thousand rupees together with the amounts apportioned under the various manners in which the bonus is receivable, for each type of participating product, shall be furnished.

9. Negative Reserves and Guaranteed Surrender Value Deficiency Reserves.—- A brief description of treatment adopted for negative reserves and guaranteed surrender value deficiency reserves shall be furnished.

10. Notes applicable to all Forms.—(1) Each Form mentioned under sub-regulation (2) of Regulation 4 shall have the following description:—

Classification;

Category;

Division;

Sub-Class; and

Group:

There shall be two Classifications, namely, Business within India, and Total Business (consisting of Business within India and Business outside India), with **Classification Codes** 1 and 2 respectively.

There shall be three Categories, namely, Linked Business, Non-linked Business and Health Insurance Business, with **Category Codes** 1, 2 and 3 respectively, under each Classification;

There shall be two Divisions, namely, Individual Business and Group Business, with **Division Codes** 1 and 2 respectively under Category Codes 1, 2 and 3;

There shall be three Sub-Classes, namely, Life Business, General Annuity, and Pension, with Sub-Class Codes 1,2 and 3 respectively, under Category Codes 1 and 2, and two Sub-Classes, namely, Linked Business, Non-Linked Business, with Sub-Class Codes 1, and 2 respectively, under Category Code 3.

There shall be four Groups under each Sub-Class, with Group Codes as specified under sub-regulation (7).

The details of Group Codes under each Category shall be as follows:-

Group Code

(a) Category Code 1 —Linked Business,—-**consisting of Insurance Products,—**

in respect of Division Code 1 - Individual Business, and under each Sub-Class Code —

(i) with guarantees -with participation in profits: A;

(ii) with no guarantees- with participation in profits: B;

(iii) with guarantees -without participation in profits: C;

(iv) with no guarantees- without participation in profits: D;

in respect of Division Code 2 - Group Business, and under each Sub-Class Code —

(i) with guarantees -with participation in profits: A;

(ii) with no guarantees- with participation in profits: B;

(iii) with guarantees -without participation in profits: C;

(iv) with no guarantees- without participation in profits: D;

(b) Category Code 2 —Non-Linked Business,— **consisting of Insurance Products,—**

in respect of Division Code 1 - Individual Business, —

(I) Sub-Class Code 1 - Sub-Class—Life Business,—

(i) with participation in profits: A;

(ii) with deferred participation in profits: B;

(iii) under discounted Bonus system: C;

(iv) without participation in profits: D;

(II) Sub-Class Codes 2, 3 - Sub-Class—General Annuity/Pension, as the case may be,—

(i) Immediate Annuities with participation in profits: A;

(ii) Immediate Annuities without participation in profits: B;

(iii) Deferred Annuities with participation in profits: C;

(iv) Deferred Annuities without participation in profits: D;

(2) in respect of Division Code 2 - Group Business, —

(I) Sub-Class Code 1 - Sub- Class- Life Business, where—

(i) **Premiums are guaranteed for not more than one year:-**

(a) with participation in profits: A;

(b) without participation in profits: B;

(ii) Premiums are guaranteed for more than one year:-

(a) with participation in profits: C;

(b) without participation in profits: D;

(II) Sub-Class Codes 2, 3 - Sub-Class—General Annuity/Pension, as the case may be,—

(i) Immediate Annuities with participation in profits: A;

(ii) Immediate Annuities without participation in profits: B;

(iii) Deferred Annuities with participation in profits: C;

(iv) Deferred Annuities without participation in profits: D;

(c) Category Code 3 — Health Insurance Business,— consisting of Insurance Products,

in respect of Division Code 1 – Individual Business——

(I) Sub-Class Code 1 – Linked Business;—

(i) with guarantees -with participation in profits: A;

(ii) with no guarantees- with participation in profits: B;

(iii) with guarantees -without participation in profits: C;

(iv) with no guarantees- without participation in profits: D;

(II) Sub-Class Code 2-Non-Linked Business; -

(i) with participation in profits: A;

(ii) with deferred participation in profits: B;

(iii) under discounted Bonus system: C;

(iv) without participation in profits: D;

in respect of Division Code 2 – Group Business;——

(I) Sub-Class Code 3 – Linked Business;

(i) with guarantees -with participation in profits: A;

(ii) with no guarantees- with participation in profits: B;

(iii) with guarantees -without participation in profits: C;

(iv) with no guarantees- without participation in profits: D;

(II) Sub-Class Code 4-Non-Linked Business -

(i) Premiums are guaranteed for not more than one year:-

(a) with participation in profits: A;

(b) without participation in profits: B;

(ii) Premiums are guaranteed for more than one year:-

(a) with participation in profits: C;

(b) without participation in profits: D;

"Nil" Statements shall be furnished for those Forms where the insurer has no transactions.

Information relating to insurance products shall be given in Forms in the following order of insurance products, wherever required:-

Whole Life Assurances, Endowment Assurances,

Anticipated Endowment Plans (Money Back Plans),

Pure Endowments, Double Endowments,

Term Insurance Contracts, and Others (specifying each).

All figures shall be furnished in thousands and all amounts shall be furnished in Indian rupees.

In respect of Group Business, 'the number of policies' in Forms, wherever applicable, shall be read as 'number of schemes'.

Rider Benefits shall be furnished in Forms, wherever required, in the order of (a) Accident Covers –double, triple, (b) Disability Covers, (c) Dread Disease Covers , and (d) Others (specifying each).

Other Adjustments, shall be furnished in Forms, wherever necessary, for instance, Provision for Deaths due to AIDS.

Key Terms

- Actuarial Risk
- Liquidity Risk
- Credit Risk
- Catastrophic Risk
- CAT Bonds
- Systematic Risk
- Financial Risk
- Options
- Duration
- Convexity

Questions for Review

1. Briefly explain the risk management techniques employed by insurance companies.
2. Write short notes on:

   CAT Bonds

   Elements of risk management for insurers

Suggested Readings

1. Emett Vaughan and Therese Vaughan, *Essentials of Risk Management and Insurance*, John Wiley and Sons Inc., 2002.
2. Kenneth A. Froot, *The Financing of Catastrophic Risk,* The University of Chicago Press, 1999.
3. Risk Management, IC-86, Insurance Institute of India, Mumbai.
4. René Doff, *Risk Management for Insurers -Risk Control, Economic Capital and Solvency II,* Risk Books, 2007.

Web Resources

- www.erisks.com
- www.insure-magic.com
- www.sra.org
- www.rmis.org
- www.aria.org